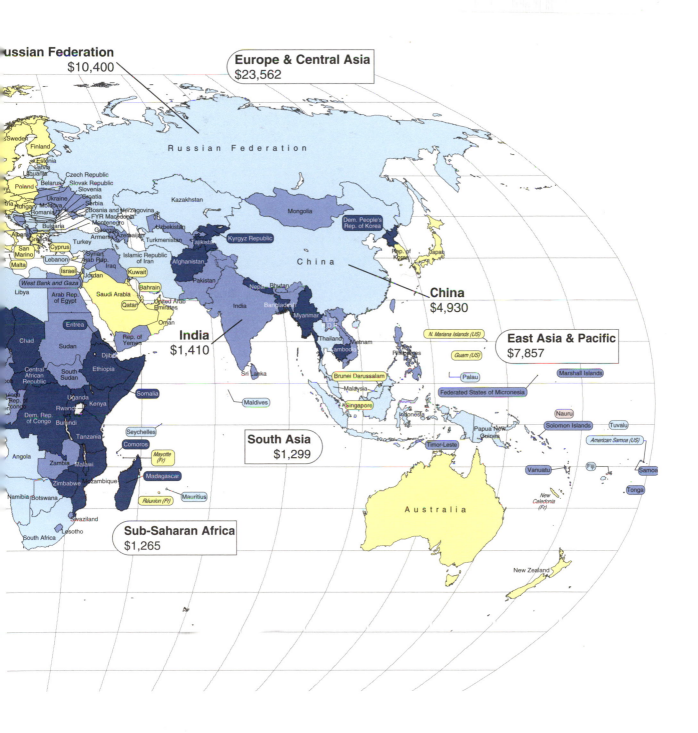

Russian Federation
$10,400

Europe & Central Asia
$23,562

Russian Federation

Sweden
Finland
Estonia
Latvia
Lithuania
Czech Republic
Belarus
Slovak Republic
Slovenia
Poland
Croatia
tria
Hungary Moldova Serbia
Romania
Bosnia and Herzegovina
FYR Macedonia
Montenegro
Bulgaria
Albania
Georgia
Armenia Azerbaijan
Greece
Turkey
San Marino
Cyprus
Malta
Lebanon
Syrian Arab Rep.
Israel
Jordan
Iraq
West Bank and Gaza
Libya
Arab Rep. of Egypt
Saudi Arabia
Kazakhstan

Uzbekistan

Turkmenistan

Kyrgyz Republic
Tajikistan

Islamic Republic of Iran

Afghanistan

Pakistan

Kuwait
Bahrain
Qatar
United Arab Emirates
Oman
Rep. of Yemen

Mongolia

Dem. People's Rep. of Korea

Rep. of Korea

Japan

China

China
$4,930

Nepal Bhutan

India

Bangladesh

Myanmar

Lao PDR

Thailand
Vietnam
Cambodia

India
$1,410

Sri Lanka

Maldives

N. Mariana Islands (US)

Guam (US)

Philippines

Brunei Darussalam

Malaysia

Singapore

Palau

East Asia & Pacific
$7,857

Marshall Islands

Federated States of Micronesia

Indonesia

Nauru

Solomon Islands

Tuvalu

American Samoa (US)

Eritrea
Chad
Sudan
Djibouti
South Sudan
Central African Republic
Ethiopia
Somalia
inea
Rep. of onqo
Uganda
Rwanda
Kenya
Dem. Rep. of Congo
Burundi
Tanzania

Seychelles

Comoros

Mayotte (Fr)

South Asia
$1,299

Papua New Guinea

Timor-Leste

Vanuatu

Fiji

Samoa

Tonga

New Caledonia (Fr)

Angola
Zambia
Malawi
Namibia Botswana
Zimbabwe Mozambique

Madagascar

Réunion (Fr)
Mauritius

South Africa
Swaziland
Lesotho

Sub-Saharan Africa
$1,265

Australia

New Zealand

Economic Development

TWELFTH EDITION

Michael P. Todaro
New York University

Stephen C. Smith
The George Washington University

PEARSON

Boston Columbus Indianapolis New York San Francisco Upper Saddle River
Amsterdam Cape Town Dubai London Madrid Milan Munich Paris Montréal Toronto
Delhi Mexico City São Paulo Sydney Hong Kong Seoul Singapore Taipei Tokyo

For Donna Renée

and

For Renee, Martin, and Helena

Vice President, Editor in Chief: Donna Battista
Executive Editor: David Alexander
Program Manager: Lindsey Sloan
Director of Marketing: Maggie Moylan Leen
Marketing Manager: Lori DeShazo
Team Lead, Project Management: Jeff Holcomb
Senior Production Project Manager:
  Liz Napolitano
Supplements Editor: Andra Skaalrud
Manager, Rights & Permissions: Michael
  Joyce
Rights & Permissions Coordinator: Samantha
  Graham
Senior Procurement Specialist: Carol Melville

Cover Designer: Jonathan Boylan
Cover Art: motif: Elenasz/Shutterstock; top
left: Ranplett/Vetta/Getty Images; top right:
Charles Harker/Shutterstock; bottom right:
Dmitryh Kalinovsky/Shutterstock; bottom
left: Steve Estvanik/Shutterstock.
Project Coordination, Text Design, and
  Electronic Page Makeup: Cenveo®
  Publisher Services
Printer/Binder: Edwards Brothers Malloy
Cover Printer: Lehigh-Phoenix Color/
  Hagerstown
Typeface: 10/12 Palatino

Credits and acknowledgments borrowed from other sources and reproduced, with permission, in this textbook appear on the appropriate page within text.

Library of Congress Cataloging-in-Publication Data

Todaro, Michael P.
  Economic development / Michael P. Todaro, New York University, Stephen C. Smith, The George Washington University. -- Twelfth Edition.
      pages cm
  Includes bibliographical references and index.
  ISBN 978-0-13-340678-8 -- ISBN 0-13-340678-4
  1. Economic development. 2. Developing countries--Economic policy. I. Smith, Stephen C., Date- II. Title.
  HD82.T552 2014
  338.9009172'4--dc23

                                        2014011530

10 9 8 7 6 5 4 3

www.pearsonhighered.com

ISBN 10: 0-13-340678-4
ISBN 13: 978-0-13-340678-8

The Pearson Series in Economics

Abel/Bernanke/Croushore
*Macroeconomics**

Bade/Parkin
*Foundations of Economics**

Berck/Helfand
The Economics of the Environment

Bierman/Fernandez
Game Theory with Economic Applications

Blanchard
*Macroeconomics**

Blau/Ferber/Winkler
The Economics of Women, Men, and Work

Boardman/Greenberg/Vining/Weimer
Cost-Benefit Analysis

Boyer
Principles of Transportation Economics

Branson
Macroeconomic Theory and Policy

Bruce
Public Finance and the American Economy

Carlton/Perloff
Modern Industrial Organization

Case/Fair/Oster
*Principles of Economics**

Chapman
Environmental Economics: Theory, Application, and Policy

Cooter/Ulen
Law & Economics

Daniels/VanHoose
International Monetary & Financial Economics

Downs
An Economic Theory of Democracy

Ehrenberg/Smith
Modern Labor Economics

Farnham
Economics for Managers

Folland/Goodman/Stano
The Economics of Health and Health Care

Fort
Sports Economics

Froyen
Macroeconomics

Fusfeld
The Age of the Economist

Gerber
*International Economics**

González-Rivera
Forecasting for Economics and Business

Gordon
*Macroeconomics**

Greene
Econometric Analysis

Gregory
Essentials of Economics

Gregory/Stuart
Russian and Soviet Economic Performance and Structure

Hartwick/Olewiler
The Economics of Natural Resource Use

Heilbroner/Milberg
The Making of the Economic Society

Heyne/Boettke/Prychitko
The Economic Way of Thinking

Holt
Markets, Games, and Strategic Behavior

Hubbard/O'Brien
*Economics**

*Money, Banking, and the Financial System**

Hubbard/O'Brien/Rafferty
*Macroeconomics**

Hughes/Cain
American Economic History

Husted/Melvin
International Economics

Jehle/Reny
Advanced Microeconomic Theory

Johnson-Lans
A Health Economics Primer

Keat/Young/Erfle
Managerial Economics

Klein
Mathematical Methods for Economics

Krugman/Obstfeld/Melitz
*International Economics: Theory & Policy**

Laidler
The Demand for Money

Leeds/von Allmen
The Economics of Sports

Leeds/von Allmen/Schiming
*Economics**

Lynn
Economic Development: Theory and Practice for a Divided World

Miller
*Economics Today**

Understanding Modern Economics

Miller/Benjamin
The Economics of Macro Issues

Miller/Benjamin/North
The Economics of Public Issues

Mills/Hamilton
Urban Economics

Mishkin
*The Economics of Money, Banking, and Financial Markets**

*The Economics of Money, Banking, and Financial Markets, Business School Edition**

*Macroeconomics: Policy and Practice**

Murray
Econometrics: A Modern Introduction

O'Sullivan/Sheffrin/Perez
*Economics: Principles, Applications and Tools**

Parkin
*Economics**

Perloff
*Microeconomics**

*Microeconomics: Theory and Applications with Calculus**

Perloff/Brander
*Managerial Economics and Strategy**

Phelps
Health Economics

Pindyck/Rubinfeld
*Microeconomics**

Riddell/Shackelford/Stamos/Schneider
Economics: A Tool for Critically Understanding Society

Roberts
The Choice: A Fable of Free Trade and Protection

Rohlf
Introduction to Economic Reasoning

Roland
Development Economics

Scherer
Industry Structure, Strategy, and Public Policy

Schiller
The Economics of Poverty and Discrimination

Sherman
Market Regulation

Stock/Watson
Introduction to Econometrics

Studenmund
Using Econometrics: A Practical Guide

Tietenberg/Lewis
Environmental and Natural Resource Economics

Environmental Economics and Policy

Todaro/Smith
Economic Development

Waldman/Jensen
Industrial Organization: Theory and Practice

Walters/Walters/Appel/Callahan/Centanni/Maex/O'Neill
Econversations: Today's Students Discuss Today's Issues

Weil
Economic Growth

Williamson
Macroeconomics

Brief Contents

v

Contents

Case Studies
and
Boxes

Case Studies

Boxes

Preface

Economic Development, Twelfth Edition, presents the latest thinking in economic development with the clear and comprehensive approach that has been so well received in both the developed and developing worlds.

The pace and scope of economic development continues its rapid, uneven, and sometimes unexpected evolution. This text explains the unprecedented progress that has been made in many parts of the developing world but fully confronts the enormous problems and challenges that remain to be addressed in the years ahead. The text shows the wide diversity across the developing world and the differing positions in the global economy that are held by developing countries. The principles of development economics are key to understanding how we got to where we are, how great progress has been made in recent years, and why many development problems remain so difficult to solve. The principles of development economics are also key to the design of successful economic development policy and programs as we look ahead.

The field of economic development is versatile and has much to contribute regarding these differing scenarios. Thus, the text also underlines common features that are exhibited by a majority of developing nations, using the insights of the study of economic development. The few countries that have essentially completed the transformation to become developed economies, such as South Korea, are also examined as potential models for other developing countries to follow.

Both theory and empirical analysis in development economics have made major strides, and the Twelfth Edition brings these ideas and findings to students. Legitimate controversies are actively debated in development economics, and so the text presents contending theories and interpretations of evidence, with three goals. The first goal is to ensure that students understand real conditions and institutions across the developing world. The second is to help students develop analytic skills while broadening their perspectives of the wide scope of the field. The third is to provide students with the resources to draw independent conclusions as they confront development problems, their sometimes ambiguous evidence, and real-life development policy choices—ultimately, to play an informed role in the struggle for economic development and ending extreme poverty.

New to This Edition

- *Global crisis*. This edition includes a major update and expansion of the new section on the impacts and potential longer-term implications of the recent global financial crisis on economic development, examining conditions that caused the crisis, its aftermath, and possible broader implications and large differences across developing nations and regions.

- *Prologue in Chapter 1.* Chapter 1 is launched with a new introductory section that describes for students how much has changed over the past two decades in a majority of countries in the developing world and in greater autonomy and nascent leadership of some developing countries in international economic and political relationships. The chapter compares conditions today to those prevailing in 1992—a pivotal period in a number of ways, which is also close to the time when many students were born.

- *Violent conflict.* The Eleventh Edition provided an entirely new major section on the causes and consequences of violent conflict, postconflict recovery and development, and prevention of conflict through an improved understanding of its major causes; the Twelfth Edition more fully develops and extends this section, incorporating recent developments.

- *Findings Boxes.* The Eleventh Edition also introduced a new textbook feature of Findings boxes, reporting on empirical research results in the field that are wide-ranging in both methods and topics. New Findings boxes address such topics as long-lasting impacts of colonial institutions (Peru); how coordination and monitoring by villagers leads to better health outcomes (Uganda); how social norms facilitated or constrained changing patterns of fertility (Bangladesh); and comparative impacts of conditional versus unconditional cash transfers to the poor (Malawi). Other boxes examine global findings such as unmet contraceptives demand across countries. The number of Findings boxes has been approximately doubled for the Twelfth Edition. The Findings boxes also illustrate empirical methods for students—in an intuitive introductory manner—such as the use of instruments; randomized control trials; regression discontinuity; and fixed effects; as well as the painstaking design, implementation, and robust analysis of survey data; growth diagnostics; and systematically applied qualitative research. The Findings boxes in this edition are listed on pages xvii-xviii.

- *Policy Boxes.* Other boxes address policy issues. New policy boxes examine such topics as the efforts of Niger—one of the world's poorest countries—to adapt to the climate change already impacting the country and to build resilience against unknown future climate change; and what we learned from the 2011–2012 famine in the Horn of Africa. Other new policy boxes address global findings, such as the extent of contraception use and the extent of still-unmet demand for contraceptives in developing countries; and the UN's new unexpectedly increased population projections through this century. Policy boxes in this edition are listed on pages xvii-xviii.

- *New, full-length, three-way comparative case study of Costa Rica, Guatemala, and Honduras.* The full-length, end-of-chapter comparative case studies have long been one of the most popular features of the text. For this edition, an entirely new three-way comparative case study of Costa Rica, Guatemala, and Honduras is introduced at the end of Chapter 14, which addresses topics of conflict, foreign investment, remittances, and foreign aid; the study also addresses the themes of very long-term comparative development addressed in some of the existing and updated case studies, such as those comparing Ghana and Côte d'Ivoire; Pakistan and Bangladesh; and Haiti and the Dominican Republic. Each of the comparative cases also has a special theme, such as human development, poverty, environment, and structural transformation.

- *New topics.* Other new topics briefly introduced in this edition include short sections on the new firm-level international trade research and the developing countries; the emergence of "Sustainable Development Goals" as successors to the MDGs; corporate social responsibility; and food price trends.

- *New measures.* Measurement is an ever-present issue in the field of economic development. The United Nations Development Program released its Multidimensional Poverty Index in August 2010 and its New Human Development Index in November 2010. The text examines the index formulas, explains how they differ from earlier indexes, reports on findings, and reviews issues surrounding the active debate on these measures. Each has been updated since its initial release, as covered in the Twelfth Edition. Note: From surveys we know many instructors are still using the traditional Human Development Index (HDI), which is reasonable, since it permeates a majority of the literature on the subject. So, we have maintained a very substantial and detailed section on the traditional HDI, which now appears in a new Appendix 2.1 in Chapter 2; it includes a number of country applications and extensions, as in previous editions. You can teach either or both of the indexes, without losing the thread in later chapters.

- *Updated statistics.* Change continues to be very rapid in the developing world. Throughout the text, data and statistics have been updated to reflect the most recent available information at the time of revision, typically 2011 or 2012, and sometimes 2013.

- *Additional updates.* Other updates include a further expansion of the section on microfinance, including new designs, potential benefits, successes to date, and some limitations; further expanded coverage of China; and expanded coverage and analysis of the growing environmental problems facing developing countries.

Audience and Suggested Ways to Use the Text

- *Flexibility.* This book is designed for use in courses in economics and other social sciences that focus on the economies of Africa, Asia, and Latin America, as well as developing Europe and the Middle East. It is written for students who have had some basic training in economics and for those with little formal economics background. Essential concepts of economics that are relevant to understanding development problems are highlighted in boldface and explained at appropriate points throughout the text, with glossary terms defined in the margins as well as collected together at the end of the book in a detailed Glossary. Thus, the book should be of special value in undergraduate development courses that attract students from a variety of disciplines. Yet the material is sufficiently broad in scope and rigorous in coverage to satisfy any undergraduate and some graduate economics requirements in the field of development. This text has been widely used both in courses taking relatively qualitative and more quantitative approaches to the study of economic development and emphasizing a variety of themes, including human development.

- The text features a 15-chapter structure, convenient for use in a comprehensive course and corresponding well to a 15-week semester but with enough breadth to easily form the basis for a two-semester sequence. However, the chapters are now subdivided, making it easier to use the text in targeted ways. To give one example, some instructors have paired the sections on conflict (14.5) and on informal and micro finance (15.4) with Chapter 5 on poverty.

- *Courses with a qualitative focus.* For qualitatively oriented courses, with an institutional focus and using fewer economic models, one or more chapters or subsections may be omitted, while placing primary emphasis on Chapters 1, 2, 5, 6, 8, and 9, plus parts of Chapters 7 and 10, and other selected sections, according to topics covered. The text is structured so that the limited number of graphical models found in those chapters may be omitted without losing the thread, while the intuition behind the models is explained in detail.

- *Courses with a more analytic and methods focus.* These courses would focus more on the growth and development theories in Chapter 3 (including Appendices such as 3.3 on endogenous growth) and Chapter 4, and highlight and develop some of the core models of the text, including poverty and inequality measurement and analysis in Chapter 5, microeconomics of fertility and relationships between population growth and economic growth in Chapter 6, migration models in Chapter 7, human capital theory, including the child labor model and empirics in Chapter 8, sharecropping models in Chapter 9, environmental economics models in Chapter 10, tools such as net present benefit analysis and multisector models along with political economy analysis in Chapter 11, and trade models in Chapter 12. Regarding methods, these courses could also expand on material introduced in some of the Findings boxes and subsections into more detailed treatments of methods topics such as use of instrumental variables, randomization, regression discontinuity, and growth empirics, including origins of comparative development and analysis of convergence (which is examined in Chapter 2). Endnotes and sources suggest possible directions to take. The text emphasizes in-depth institutional background reading accompanying the models that help students to appreciate their importance.

- *Courses emphasizing human development and poverty alleviation.* The Twelfth Edition can be used for a course with a human development focus. This would typically include the sections on Amartya Sen's capability approach and Millennium Development Goals in Chapter 1, the new section on conflict in Chapter 14, the discussion of microfinance institutions in Chapter 15, and a close and in-depth examination of Chapters 2 and 5. Sections on population policy in Chapter 6; diseases of poverty and problems of illiteracy, low schooling, and child labor in Chapter 8; problems facing people in traditional agriculture in Chapter 9; relationships between poverty and environmental degradation in Chapter 10; and roles of nongovernmental organizations (NGOs) in Chapter 11 would be likely highlights of this course.

- *Courses emphasizing macro and international topics.* International and macro aspects of economic development could emphasize sections 2.6 and 2.7 on convergence, and long-run growth and sources of comparative development; Chapter 3 on theories of growth (including the three detailed appendixes to that chapter); Chapter 4 on growth and multiple-equilibrium models; and Chapters 12 through 15 on international trade, international finance, debt and financial crises, direct foreign investment, aid, central banking, and domestic finance. The book also covers other aspects of the international context for development, including the new section on financial crisis (13.6), implications of the rapid pace of globalization and the rise of China (Chapter 12 and such case studies as Brazil in Chapter 1 and China in Chapter 4), the continuing struggle for more progress in sub-Saharan Africa, and controversies over debt relief and foreign aid (Chapter 14).

- *Broad two-semester course using supplemental readings.* Many of the chapters contain enough material for several class sessions, when their topics are covered in an in-depth manner, making the text also suitable for a yearlong course or high-credit option. The endnotes and sources offer many starting points for such extensions.

Guiding Approaches and Organization

The text's guiding approaches are the following:

1. It teaches economic development within the context of a *major set of problems,* such as poverty, inequality, population growth, the impact of very rapid urbanization and expansion of megacities, persistent public health challenges, environmental decay, and regions experiencing rural stagnation, along with the twin challenges of government failure and market failure. Formal models and concepts are used to elucidate real-world development problems rather than being presented in isolation from these problems.

2. It adopts a *problem- and policy-oriented approach*, because a central objective of the development economics course is to foster a student's ability to understand contemporary economic problems of developing countries and to reach independent and informed judgments and policy conclusions about their possible resolution.

3. It simultaneously uses the *best available data* from Africa, Asia, Latin America, and developing Europe and the Middle East, as well as *appropriate theoretical tools* to illuminate common developing-country problems. These problems differ in incidence, scope, magnitude, and emphasis when we deal with such diverse countries as India, Pakistan, Bangladesh, China, the Philippines, Kenya, Botswana, Nigeria, Ghana, Côte d'Ivoire, Argentina, Brazil, Chile, Mexico, Haiti, and the Dominican Republic. Still, a majority face some similar development problems: persistent poverty and large income and asset inequalities, population pressures, low levels of education and health, inadequacies of financial markets, and recurrent challenges in international trade and instability, to name a few.

4. It focuses on a wide range of developing countries, not only as *independent nation-states*, but also in their growing *relationships to one another*, as well as in their *interactions with rich nations in a globalizing economy*.

5. Relatedly, the text views development in both domestic and international contexts, stressing the *increasing interdependence of the world economy* in areas such as food, energy, natural resources, technology, information, and financial flows.

6. It recognizes the necessity of treating the problems of development from an *institutional* and *structural* as well as a market perspective, with appropriate modifications of received general economic principles, theories, and policies. It thus attempts to combine relevant theory with realistic institutional analyses. Enormous strides have been made in the study of these aspects of economic development in recent years, which are reflected in this edition.

7. It considers the economic, social, and institutional problems of underdevelopment as closely interrelated and requiring *coordinated approaches* to their solution at the local, national, and international levels.

8. The book is organized into three parts. Part One focuses on the nature and meaning of development and underdevelopment and its various manifestations in developing nations. After examining the historical growth experience of the developed countries and the long-run experience of the developing countries, we review four classic and contemporary theories of economic development, while introducing basic theories of economic growth. Part Two focuses on major domestic development problems and policies, and Part Three focuses on development problems and policies in international, macro, and financial spheres. Topics of analysis include economic growth, poverty and income distribution, population, migration, urbanization, technology, agricultural and rural development, education, health, the environment, international trade and finance, debt, financial crises, domestic financial markets, direct foreign investment, foreign aid, violent conflict, and the roles of market, state, and nongovernmental organizations in economic development. All three parts of the book raise fundamental questions, including what kind of development is most desirable and how developing nations can best achieve their economic and social objectives.

9. As part of the text's commitment to its comprehensive approach, it covers some topics that are not found in other texts on economic development, including growth diagnostics, industrialization strategy, innovative policies for poverty reduction, the capability approach to well-being, the central role of women, child labor, the crucial role of health, new thinking on the role of cities, the economic character and comparative advantage of nongovernmental organizations in economic development, emerging issues in environment and development, financial crises, violent conflict, and microfinance.

10. A unique feature of this book is the in-depth case studies and comparative case studies appearing at the end of each chapter. Each chapter's case study reflects and illustrates specific issues analyzed in that chapter. In-chapter boxes provide shorter case examples.

Comments on the text are always welcome; these can be sent directly to Stephen Smith at ssmith@gwu.edu.

Supplementary Materials

The Twelfth Edition comes with PowerPoint slides for each chapter, which have been expanded and fully updated for this edition.

    The text is further supplemented with an *Instructor's Manual* by Chris Marme of Augustana College. It has been thoroughly revised and updated to reflect changes to the Twelfth Edition. Both the PowerPoint slides and the *Instructor's Manual* can also be downloaded from the Instructor's Resource Center at www.pearsonhighered.com/irc.

Acknowledgments

Our gratitude to the many individuals who have helped shape this new edition cannot adequately be conveyed in a few sentences. However, we must record our immense indebtedness to the hundreds of former students and contemporary colleagues who took the time and trouble during the past several years to write or speak to us about the ways in which this text could be further improved. We are likewise indebted to a great number of friends (far too many to mention individually) in both the developing world and the developed world who have directly and indirectly helped shape our ideas about development economics and how an economic development text should be structured. The authors would like to thank colleagues and students in both developing and developed countries for their probing and challenging questions.

    We are also very appreciative of the advice, criticisms, and suggestions of the many reviewers, both in the United States and abroad, who provided detailed and insightful comments for the Eighth, Ninth, Tenth, Eleventh, and Twelfth Editions:

U.S. Reviewers

Mohammed Akacem, METROPOLITAN STATE UNIVERSITY OF DENVER
William A. Amponsah, GEORGIA SOUTHERN UNIVERSITY
Erol Balkan, HAMILTON COLLEGE
Karna Basu, HUNTER COLLEGE, CITY UNIVERSITY OF NEW YORK
Valerie R. Bencivenga, UNIVERSITY OF TEXAS, AUSTIN

Sylvain H. Boko, WAKE FOREST UNIVERSITY
Michaël Bonnal, UNIVERSITY OF TENNESSEE AT CHATTANOOGA
Milica Z. Bookman, ST. JOSEPH'S UNIVERSITY
Jim Cobbe, FLORIDA STATE UNIVERSITY
Michael Coon, HOOD COLLEGE
Lisa Daniels, WASHINGTON COLLEGE
Fernando De Paolis, MONTEREY INSTITUTE
Luc D'Haese, UNIVERSITY OF GHENT
Quentin Duroy, DENISON UNIVERSITY
Can Erbil, BRANDEIS UNIVERSITY
Yilma Gebremariam, SOUTHERN CONNECTICUT STATE UNIVERSITY
Abbas P. Grammy, CALIFORNIA STATE UNIVERSITY, BAKERSFIELD
Caren Grown, AMERICAN UNIVERSITY
Kwabena Gyimah-Brempong, UNIVERSITY OF SOUTH FLORIDA
Bradley Hansen, MARY WASHINGTON COLLEGE
John R. Hanson II, TEXAS A&M UNIVERSITY
Seid Hassan, MURRAY STATE UNIVERSITY
Jeffrey James, TILBURG UNIVERSITY
Barbara John, UNIVERSITY OF DAYTON
Pareena G. Lawrence, UNIVERSITY OF MINNESOTA, MORRIS
Tung Liu, BALL STATE UNIVERSITY
John McPeak, SYRACUSE UNIVERSITY
Michael A. McPherson, UNIVERSITY OF NORTH TEXAS
Daniel L. Millimet, SOUTHERN METHODIST UNIVERSITY
Camille Soltau Nelson, TEXAS A&M UNIVERSITY
Thomas Osang, SOUTHERN METHODIST UNIVERSITY
Elliott Parker, UNIVERSITY OF NEVADA, RENO
Julia Paxton, OHIO UNIVERSITY
Meenakshi Rishi, SEATTLE UNIVERSITY
James Robinson, UNIVERSITY OF CALIFORNIA, BERKELEY
Monthien Satimanon, MICHIGAN STATE AND THAMMASAT UNIVERSITY
Andreas Savvides, OKLAHOMA STATE UNIVERSITY
Rodrigo R. Soares, UNIVERSITY OF MARYLAND
Michael Twomey, UNIVERSITY OF MICHIGAN, DEARBORN
Wally Tyner, PURDUE UNIVERSITY
Nora Underwood, UNIVERSITY OF CALIFORNIA, DAVIS
Jogindar Uppal, STATE UNIVERSITY OF NEW YORK
Evert Van Der Heide, CALVIN COLLEGE
Adel Varghese, ST. LOUIS UNIVERSITY
Sharmila Vishwasrao, FLORIDA ATLANTIC UNIVERSITY
Bill Watkins, CALIFORNIA LUTHERAN UNIVERSITY
Janice E. Weaver, DRAKE UNIVERSITY
Jonathan B. Wight, UNIVERSITY OF RICHMOND
Lester A. Zeager, EAST CAROLINA UNIVERSITY

U.K. Reviewers

Arild Angelsen, AGRICULTURAL UNIVERSITY OF NORWAY
David Barlow, NEWCASTLE UNIVERSITY

Sonia Bhalotra, UNIVERSITY OF BRISTOL
Bernard Carolan, UNIVERSITY OF STAFFORDSHIRE
Matthew Cole, UNIVERSITY OF BIRMINGHAM
Alex Cunliffe, UNIVERSITY OF PLYMOUTH
Chris Dent, UNIVERSITY OF HULL
Sanjit Dhami, UNIVERSITY OF NEWCASTLE
Subrata Ghatak, KINGSTON UNIVERSITY
Gregg Huff, UNIVERSITY OF GLASGOW
Diana Hunt, SUSSEX UNIVERSITY
Michael King, TRINITY COLLEGE DUBLIN
Dorothy Manning, UNIVERSITY OF NORTHUMBRIA
Mahmood Meeskoub, UNIVERSITY OF LEEDS
Paul Mosley, UNIVERSITY OF SHEFFIELD
Bibhas Saha, UNIVERSITY OF EAST ANGLIA
Colin Simmons, UNIVERSITY OF SALFORD
Pritam Singh, OXFORD BROOKES UNIVERSITY
Shinder Thandi, UNIVERSITY OF COVENTRY
Paul Vandenberg, UNIVERSITY OF BRISTOL

Their input has strengthened the book in many ways and has been much appreciated.

Our thanks also go to the staff at Pearson in both the United States and the United Kingdom, particularly David Alexander, Lindsey Sloan, Liz Napolitano, and Kate Brewin.

Finally, to his lovely wife, Donna Renée, Michael Todaro wishes to express great thanks for typing the entire First Edition manuscript and for providing the spiritual and intellectual inspiration to persevere under difficult circumstances. He reaffirms here his eternal devotion to her for always being there to help him maintain a proper perspective on life and living and, through her own creative and artistic talents, to inspire him to think in original and sometimes unconventional ways about the global problems of human development.

Stephen Smith would like to thank his wonderful wife, Renee, and his children, Martin and Helena, for putting up with the many working Saturdays that went into the revision of this text.

Michael P. Todaro

Stephen C. Smith

PART ONE

Principles and Concepts

1

Introducing Economic Development: A Global Perspective

Development can be seen . . . as a process of expanding the real freedoms that people enjoy.
—*Amartya Sen, Nobel laureate in economics*

Our vision and our responsibility are to end extreme poverty in all its forms in the context of sustainable development and to have in place the building blocks of sustained prosperity for all.
—*Report of the High-Level Panel of Eminent Persons on the Post-2015 Development Agenda, 2013*

Under necessaries, therefore, I comprehend, not only those things which nature, but those things which the established rules of decency, have rendered necessary to the lowest rank of people.
—*Adam Smith,* The Wealth of Nations

We are at an auspicious moment in history when successes of past decades and an increasingly favorable economic outlook combine to give developing countries a chance—for the first time ever—to end extreme poverty within a generation....to create a world for our children which is defined not by stark inequities but by soaring opportunities. A sustainable world where all households have access to clean energy. A world where everyone has enough to eat. A world where no one dies from preventable diseases. A world free of poverty.
—*Jim Yong Kim, World Bank President, 2013*

Prologue: An Extraordinary Moment

Two pictures of the developing world compete in the media for the public's attention. The first is misery in places like rural Africa or unsanitary and overcrowded urban slums in South Asia. The second is extraordinary dynamism in places like coastal China. Both pictures convey important parts of the great development drama. Living conditions are improving significantly in most, though not all, parts of the globe—if sometimes slowly and unevenly. The cumulative effect is that economic development has been giving rise to unprecedented global transformations.

Consider the world of 1992, a time when the divide between the rich developed nations and the low-income developing nations was apparently widening. Rich countries were growing faster than poor countries; and the dominance of high-income industrialized nations in the global order was clear-cut. The United States had just won the Cold War, with the Soviet Union disintegrating in the last days of 1991. The end of the Cold War also saw the European Union in the ascendency, full of confidence with its high-profile Europe '92 Single Market project. The real estate and stock market bubble in Japan was just beginning to deflate, with almost no one predicting the protracted stagnation that would follow Japan's long period of high economic growth.

Yet in 1992, many developing nations, including Brazil, Russia, India, China, and South Africa (now sometimes grouped by the media as the "BRICS"), found themselves in precarious conditions if not full-scale crisis. Brazil—like most of Latin America—was still struggling to emerge from the 1980s' debt crisis. Russia was descending into depression after the collapse of its Soviet economy. India was trying to rebound from its worst economic crisis since independence. China had launched its period of very rapid growth, but the 1989 massacre in Tiananmen Square was a fresh memory and future prospects for reform and growth in China were uncertain. Meanwhile, the end of apartheid was still being negotiated in South Africa, while the continent as a whole was entering its second consecutive lost decade of slow economic growth, and pessimism prevailed. Despite pressing development needs, there were widespread concerns that with the end of the Cold War, the rich world would lose interest in development assistance. And at the 1992 Earth Summit, while the world was taking its first tentative steps to acknowledge and try to restrain climate change due to global warming, almost no one imagined that 20 years later China and India would be among the top three greenhouse gas emitters.

But since 1992, we have moved from a sharp dualism between a rich Center and a backward Global South periphery to more dynamic and complex relationships. Asia has been growing at an average rate almost triple that of high-income Western countries, and growth has returned to Africa, heralding the promise of an era of global convergence.[1] The scale of transformation is immense.

Health has improved strongly, with dramatic declines in child mortality; and the goal of universal primary education is coming into sight. Poverty has fallen. While about two-fifths of the global population lived in extreme poverty in 1990, the fraction has fallen to about one-fifth today. The number of people living in extreme poverty in China (on less than $1.25 per day) fell from about 743 million in 1992 to 157 million in 2009. India has seen substantial, if less dramatic, reductions in poverty; social programs in Brazil such as Bolsa Familia have helped substantially reduce the country's once intractible poverty problems. The enormous growth of innovations such as mobile phones and of availability of credit for small enterprises have led to benefits and fueled a new optimism.

At the same time, the future of economic development and poverty reduction is far from assured—many people who have come out of poverty remain vulnerable, the natural environment is deteriorating, and national economic growth remains uncertain. Economic development is a process, not of years, but of many decades. After the 2011 media celebration of the "BRICS" economic growth, there were reminders that the process remains uneven and uncertain. In Brazil economic growth fell from a spike of close to 7.5% in 2010 to under 1% in 2012. Growth in India, topping 10% for the first time in 2010, fell to barely a third that level in 2012. Growth in China fell from over 10% in 2010 to below 8% in 2012 with projections of a permanently slower pace of perhaps 7%. In 2012 growth in South Africa was little more than 3%. Growth per person was slower as populations continued to grow. When financial markets were unsettled during the summer of 2013, many investors started withdrawing money from these and other developing countries.

Meanwhile, many in the development community were dismayed by a 2013 report showing the number of people living in poverty in Africa had yet to decline, and the average income of those remaining poor had still not risen above its long-term level of just 70 cents per day. And climate change talks, also launched in 1992, proceeded at a snail's pace, even as greenhouse gas emissions reached record levels and the impacts of climate change had become all too visible in low-income countries, threatening to reverse progress in South Asia as well as Africa.

But while optimism that other countries could soon match China's historically high growth rates dimmed, nonetheless the potential for dramatic catch-up remained as bright as ever. The media pessimism that prevailed in the summer of 2013 was no more warranted than the blind optimism of just two years earlier. Realism is needed—both about the daunting challenges and the exciting opportunities. Gains for the developing world in recent years have been genuine and substantial—in some cases transformative—with many developing countries steadily closing the gap with the developed world, particularly in health and education, and very often in income. Prospects remain strong in coming years, particularly for middle-income countries; yet the high volatility of growth is just one hint at the remaining broader development challenges, as we will examine throughout this text.

This book will explain what lies behind the headline numbers and the sweep of development patterns, presenting the necessary analytic tools and the most recent and reliable data—on challenges ranging from poverty to international finance. To begin, even today many of the world's poorest people have benefited little, if at all, from the new global prosperity.

1.1 How the Other Half Live

As people throughout the world awake each morning to face a new day, they do so under very different circumstances. Some live in comfortable homes with many rooms. They have more than enough to eat, are well clothed and healthy, and have a reasonable degree of financial security. Others—and these constitute a majority of the earth's more than 7 billion people—are much less fortunate. They may have inadequate food and shelter, especially if they are among the poorest third. Their health is often poor, they may not know how to read or write, they may be unemployed, and their prospects for a better life are uncertain at best. About two-fifths of the world's population lives on less than $2 per day, part of a condition of **absolute poverty**. An examination of these global differences in living standards is revealing.

If, for example, we looked first at a family of four in North America, we would probably find an annual income of over $50,000. They would live in a comfortable suburban house with a small yard or garden, and two cars. The dwelling would have many comfortable features, including a separate bedroom for each of the two children. It would be filled with numerous consumer goods, electronics, and electrical appliances, many of which were manufactured outside North America in countries as far away as South Korea and China. Examples might

Absolute poverty A situation of being unable to meet the minimum levels of income, food, clothing, health care, shelter, and other essentials.

include computer hard disks made in Malaysia, DVD players manufactured in Thailand, garments assembled in Bangladesh, and mountain bikes made in China. There would always be three meals a day and plenty of processed snack foods, and many of the food products would also be imported from overseas: coffee from Brazil, Kenya, or Colombia; canned fish and fruit from Peru and Australia; and bananas and other tropical fruits from Central America. Both children would be healthy and attending school. They could expect to complete their secondary education and probably go to a university, choose from a variety of careers to which they might be attracted, and live to an average age of 78 years.

This family, which is typical of families in many rich nations, appears to have a reasonably good life. The parents have the opportunity and the necessary education or training to find regular employment; to shelter, clothe, feed, and educate their children; and to save some money for later life. Against these "economic" benefits, there are always "noneconomic" costs. The competitive pressures to "succeed" financially are very strong, and during inflationary or recessionary times, the mental strain and physical pressure of trying to provide for a family at levels that the community regards as desirable can take its toll on the health of both parents. Their ability to relax, to enjoy the simple pleasures of a country stroll, to breathe clean air and drink pure water, and to see a crimson sunset is constantly at risk with the onslaught of economic progress and environmental decay. But on the whole, theirs is an economic status and lifestyle toward which many millions of less fortunate people throughout the world seem to be aspiring.

Now let us examine a typical "extended" family in a poor rural area of South Asia. The household is likely to consist of eight or more people, including parents, several children, two grandparents, and some aunts and uncles. They have a combined real per capita annual income, in money and in "kind" (meaning that they consume a share of the food they grow), of $300. Together they live in a poorly constructed one- or two-room house as tenant farmers on a large agricultural estate owned by an absentee landlord who lives in the nearby city. The father, mother, uncle, and older children must work all day on the land. The adults cannot read or write; the younger children attend school irregularly and cannot expect to proceed beyond a basic primary education. All too often, when they do get to school, the teacher is absent. They often eat only two (and sometimes just one) meals per day; the food rarely changes, and the meals are rarely sufficient to alleviate the children's persistent hunger pains. The house has no electricity, sanitation, or fresh water supply. Sickness occurs often, but qualified doctors and medical practitioners are far away in the cities, attending to the needs of wealthier families. The work is hard, the sun is hot, and aspirations for a better life are continually being snuffed out. For families such as theirs, the only relief from the daily struggle for physical survival lies in the spiritual traditions of the people.

Shifting to another part of the world, suppose we were to visit a large city situated along the coast of South America. We would immediately be struck by the sharp contrasts in living conditions from one section of this sprawling metropolis to another. There would be a modern stretch of tall buildings and wide, tree-lined boulevards along the edge of a gleaming white beach; just a few hundred meters back and up the side of a steep hill, squalid shanties would be pressed together in precarious balance.

If we were to examine two representative families—one a wealthy and well-connected family and the other of peasant background or born in the slums—we would no doubt also be struck by the wide disparities in their individual living conditions. The wealthy family lives in a multiroom complex on the top floor of a modern building overlooking the sea, while the peasant family is cramped tightly into a small makeshift dwelling in a shantytown, or *favela* (squatters' slum), on the hill behind that seafront building.

For illustrative purposes, let us assume that it is a typical Saturday evening at an hour when the families should be preparing for dinner. In the penthouse apartment of the wealthy family, a servant is setting the table with expensive imported china, high-quality silverware, and fine linen. Russian caviar, French hors d'œuvres, and Italian wine will constitute the first of several courses. The family's eldest son is home from his university in North America, and the other two children are on vacation from their boarding schools in France and Switzerland. The father is a prominent surgeon trained in the United States. His clientele consists of wealthy local and foreign dignitaries and business-people. In addition to his practice, he owns a considerable amount of land in the countryside. Annual vacations abroad, imported luxury automobiles, and the finest food and clothing are commonplace amenities for this fortunate family in the penthouse apartment.

And what about the poor family living in the dirt-floored shack on the side of the hill? They too can view the sea, but somehow it seems neither scenic nor relaxing. The stench of open sewers makes such enjoyment rather remote. There is no dinner table being set; in fact, there is usually too little to eat. Most of the four children spend their time out on the streets begging for money, shining shoes, or occasionally even trying to steal purses from unsuspecting people who stroll along the boulevard. The father migrated to the city from the rural hinterland, and the rest of the family recently followed. He has had part-time jobs over the years, but nothing permanent. Government assistance has recently helped this family keep the children in school longer. But lessons learned on the streets, where violent drug gangs hold sway, seem to be making a deeper impression.

One could easily be disturbed by the sharp contrast between these two ways of life. However, had we looked at almost any other major city in Latin America, Asia, and Africa, we would have seen much the same contrast (although the extent of inequality might have been less pronounced).

Now imagine that you are in a remote rural area in the eastern part of Africa, where many small clusters of tiny huts dot a dry and barren land. Each cluster contains a group of extended families, all participating in and sharing the work. There is little money income here because most food, clothing, shelter, and worldly goods are made and consumed by the people themselves—theirs is a **subsistence economy**. There are few passable roads, few schools, and no hospitals, electric wires, or water supplies. In many respects, it is as stark and difficult an existence as that of the people in that Latin American *favela* across the ocean. Yet perhaps it is not as psychologically troubling because there is no luxurious penthouse by the sea to emphasize the relative deprivation of the very poor. With the exception of population growth and problems of the increasingly fragile environment, life here seems to be almost eternal and unchanging—but not for much longer.

Subsistence economy An economy in which production is mainly for personal consumption and the standard of living yields little more than basic necessities of life—food, shelter, and clothing.

A new road is being built that will pass near this village. No doubt it will bring with it the means for prolonging life through improved medical care. But it will also bring more information about the world outside, along with the gadgets of modern civilization. The possibilities of a "better" life will be promoted, and the opportunities for such a life will become feasible. Aspirations will be raised, but so will frustrations as people understand the depth of some of their deprivations more clearly. In short, the **development** process has been set in motion.

Development The process of improving the quality of all human lives and capabilities by raising people's levels of living, self-esteem, and freedom.

Before long, exportable fruits and vegetables will probably be grown in this region. They may even end up on the dinner table of the rich South American family in the seaside penthouse. Meanwhile, radios made in Southeast Asia and playing music recorded in northern Europe have become prized possessions in this African village. In villages not far away, mobile phone use has been introduced and is growing rapidly. Throughout the world, remote subsistence villages such as this one are being linked up with modern civilization in an increasing number of ways. The process, well under way, will become even more intensified in the coming years.

Finally, imagine you are in booming East Asia; to illustrate, a couple born in obscure zhuangs (rural areas) in populous central Sichuan Province grew up in the 1960s, going to school for six years and becoming rice farmers like their parents. The rice grew well, but memories of famine were still sharp in their commune, where life was also hard during the Cultural Revolution. Their one daughter, let's call her Xiaoling, went to school for ten years. Much of the rice they and their commune grew went to the state at a price that never seemed high enough. After 1980, farmers were given rights to keep and sell more of their rice. Seeing the opportunity, they grew enough to meet government quotas and sold more of it. Many also raised vegetables to sell in a booming city 100 kilometers up the river and other towns. Living standards improved, though then their incomes stagnated for many years. But they heard about peasants moving first to cities in the south and recently to closer cities—making more money becoming factory workers. When their daughter was 17, farmers from the village where the mother grew up were evicted from their land because it was close to lakes created by an immense dam project. Some were resettled, but others went to Shenzhen, Guangzhou, or Chongqing. Xiaoling talked with her family, saying she too wanted to move there for a while to earn more money. She found a city that had already grown to several million people, quickly finding a factory job. She lived in a dormitory, and conditions were often harsh, but she could send some money home and save toward a better life. She watched the city grow at double digits, becoming one of the developing world's new megacities, adding territories and people to reach over 15 million people. After a few years, she opened a humble business, selling cosmetics and costume jewelry to the thousands of women from the countryside arriving every day. She had five proposals of marriage, with parents of single men near where she grew up offering gifts, even an enormous house. She knows many people still live in deep poverty and finds inequality in the city startling. For now she plans to stay, where she sees opportunities for her growing business and a life she never imagined having in her village.

Listening to the poor explain what poverty is like in their own words is more vivid than reading descriptions of it. Listen to some of the voices of the

BOX 1.1 The Experience of Poverty: Voices of the Poor

When one is poor, she has no say in public, she feels inferior. She has no food, so there is famine in her house; no clothing, and no progress in her family.

—A poor woman from Uganda

For a poor person, everything is terrible—illness, humiliation, shame. We are cripples; we are afraid of everything; we depend on everyone. No one needs us. We are like garbage that everyone wants to get rid of.

—A blind woman from Tiraspol, Moldova

Life in the area is so precarious that the youth and every able person have to migrate to the towns or join the army at the war front in order to escape the hazards of hunger escalating over here.

—Participant in a discussion group in rural Ethiopia

When food was in abundance, relatives used to share it. These days of hunger, however, not even relatives would help you by giving you some food.

—Young man in Nichimishi, Zambia

We have to line up for hours before it is our turn to draw water.

—Participant in a discussion group from Mbwadzulu Village (Mangochi), Malawi

[Poverty is] . . . low salaries and lack of jobs. And it's also not having medicine, food, and clothes.

—Participant in a discussion group in Brazil

Don't ask me what poverty is because you have met it outside my house. Look at the house and count the number of holes. Look at the utensils and the clothes I am wearing. Look at everything and write what you see. What you see is poverty.

—Poor man in Kenya

poor about the experience of poverty in Box 1.1.[2] From these, together with the voices of the poor recorded in Box 5.1 and Box 8.1, it is clear that what people living in poverty need and want extend beyond increased income to health, education, and—especially for women—empowerment. These correspond to enhanced capabilities and to the achievement of the Millennium Development Goals (and its emerging successor, the Sustainable Development Goals), introduced later in this chapter.

This first fleeting glimpse at life in different parts of our planet is sufficient to raise various questions. Why does affluence coexist with dire poverty, not only on different continents, but also within the same country or even the same city? Can traditional, low-productivity, subsistence societies be transformed into modern, high-productivity, high-income nations? To what extent are the development aspirations of poor nations helped or hindered by the economic activities of rich nations? By what process and under what conditions do rural subsistence farmers in the remote regions of Nigeria, Brazil, or the Philippines evolve into successful commercial farmers? What are the implications of the surprisingly long stagnation in rich countries following the financial crisis for further progress on development and poverty reduction? These and many other questions concerning international and national differences in standards of living, in areas including health and nutrition, education, employment, environmental sustainability, population growth, and life expectancies, might be posed on the basis of even this very superficial look at life around the world.

This book is designed to help students obtain a better understanding of the major problems and prospects for broad-based economic development, paying special attention to the plight of the half or more of the world's population for whom low levels of living are a fact of life. However, as we shall soon discover, the process in **developing countries** cannot be analyzed realistically without also considering the role of economically developed nations in directly or indirectly promoting or retarding that development. Perhaps even more important to students in the developed nations is that as our earth shrinks with the spread of modern transport and communications, the futures of *all* peoples on this small planet are becoming increasingly interdependent. What happens to the health and economic welfare of poor rural families and many others in the developing regions of Asia, Africa, the Middle East, or Latin America will in one way or another, directly or indirectly, affect the health and economic welfare of families in Europe and North America, and vice versa. The steady loss of tropical forests contributes to global warming; new diseases spread much more rapidly thanks to increased human mobility; economic interdependence steadily grows. It is within this context of a common future for all humankind in the rapidly shrinking world of the twenty-first century that we now commence our study of economic development.

Developing countries Countries of Asia, Africa, the Middle East, Latin America, eastern Europe, and the former Soviet Union that are presently characterized by low levels of living and other development deficits. Used in the development literature as a synonym for *less developed countries*.

1.2 Economics and Development Studies

The study of economic development is one of the newest, most exciting, and most challenging branches of the broader disciplines of economics and political economy. Although one could claim that Adam Smith was the first "development economist" and that his *Wealth of Nations,* published in 1776, was the first treatise on economic development, the systematic study of the problems and processes of economic development in Africa, Asia, and Latin America has emerged only over the past five decades or so. Although development economics often draws on relevant principles and concepts from other branches of economics in either a standard or modified form, for the most part it is a field of study that is rapidly evolving its own distinctive analytical and methodological identity.[3]

The Nature of Development Economics

Traditional economics is concerned primarily with the efficient, least-cost allocation of scarce productive resources and with the optimal growth of these resources over time so as to produce an ever-expanding range of goods and services. Traditional neoclassical economics deals with an advanced capitalist world of perfect markets; consumer sovereignty; automatic price adjustments; decisions made on the basis of marginal, private-profit, and utility calculations; and equilibrium outcomes in all product and resource markets. It assumes economic "rationality" and a purely materialistic, individualistic, self-interested orientation toward economic decision making.

Traditional economics An approach to economics that emphasizes utility, profit maximization, market efficiency, and determination of equilibrium.

    Political economy goes beyond traditional economics to study, among other things, the social and institutional processes through which certain groups of economic and political elites influence the allocation of scarce productive

Political economy The attempt to merge economic analysis with practical politics—to view economic activity in its political context.

resources now and in the future, either for their own benefit exclusively or for that of the larger population as well. Political economy is therefore concerned with the relationship between politics and economics, with a special emphasis on the role of power in economic decision making.

Development economics
The study of how economies are transformed from stagnation to growth and from low-income to high-income status, and overcome problems of absolute poverty.

Development economics has an even greater scope. In addition to being concerned with the efficient allocation of existing scarce (or idle) productive resources and with their sustained growth over time, it must also deal with the *economic, social, political*, and *institutional* mechanisms, both public and private, necessary to bring about *rapid* (at least by historical standards) and *large-scale improvements* in levels of living for the peoples of Africa, Asia, Latin America, and the formerly socialist transition economies. In comparison with the **more developed countries (MDCs)**, in most **less developed countries**, commodity and resource markets are typically highly imperfect, consumers and producers have limited information, major structural changes are taking place in both the society and the economy, the potential for multiple equilibria rather than a single equilibrium is more common, and disequilibrium situations often prevail (prices do not equate supply and demand). In many cases, economic calculations are heavily influenced by political and social priorities such as unifying the nation, replacing foreign advisers with local decision makers, resolving tribal or ethnic conflicts, or preserving religious and cultural traditions. At the individual level, family, clan, religious, or tribal considerations may take precedence over private, self-interested utility or profit-maximizing calculations.

More developed countries (MDCs) The now economically advanced capitalist countries of western Europe, North America, Australia, New Zealand, and Japan.

Less developed countries A synonym for *developing countries*.

Thus, development economics, to a greater extent than traditional neoclassical economics or even political economy, must be concerned with the economic, cultural, and political requirements for effecting rapid structural and institutional transformations of entire societies in a manner that will most efficiently bring the fruits of economic progress to the broadest segments of their populations. It must focus on the mechanisms that keep families, regions, and even entire nations in poverty traps, in which past poverty causes future poverty, and on the most effective strategies for breaking out of these traps. Consequently, a larger government role and some degree of coordinated economic decision making directed toward transforming the economy are usually viewed as essential components of development economics. Yet this must somehow be achieved despite the fact that both governments and markets typically function less well in the developing world. In recent years, activities of nongovernmental organizations, both national and international, have grown rapidly and are also receiving increasing attention (see Chapter 11)

Because of the heterogeneity of the developing world and the complexity of the development process, development economics must be eclectic, attempting to combine relevant concepts and theories from traditional economic analysis with new models and broader multidisciplinary approaches derived from studying the historical and contemporary development experience of Africa, Asia, and Latin America. Development economics is a field on the crest of a breaking wave, with new theories and new data constantly emerging. These theories and statistics sometimes confirm and sometimes challenge traditional ways of viewing the world. The ultimate purpose of development economics, however, remains unchanged: to help us understand developing economies in order to help improve the material lives of the majority of the global population.

Why Study Development Economics? Some Critical Questions

An introductory course in development economics should help students gain a better understanding of a number of critical questions about the economies of developing nations. The following is a sample list of 30 such questions, followed by the chapters (in parentheses) in which they are discussed. They illustrate the kinds of issues faced by almost every developing nation and, indeed, every development economist.

1. What is the real meaning of *development*? Do the Millennium Development Goals fit with these meanings? (Chapter 1)

2. What can be learned from the historical record of economic progress in the now developed world? Are the initial conditions similar or different for contemporary developing countries from what the developed countries faced on the eve of their industrialization or in their earlier phases? (Chapter 2)

3. What are economic institutions, and how do they shape problems of underdevelopment and prospects for successful development? (Chapter 2)

4. How can the extremes between rich and poor be so very great? Figure 1.1 illustrates this disparity. (Chapters 2, 3, 4, and 5)

5. What are the sources of national and international economic growth? Who benefits from such growth and why? (Chapters 3 and 5)

6. Why do some countries make rapid progress toward development while many others remain poor? (Chapters 2, 3, and 4)

7. Which are the most influential theories of development, and are they compatible? Is underdevelopment an internally (domestically) or externally (internationally) induced phenomenon? (Chapters 2, 3, and 4)

8. What constraints most hold back accelerated growth, depending on local conditions? (Chapter 4)

9. How can improvements in the role and status of women have an especially beneficial impact on development prospects? (Chapters 5, 6, 7, 8, 9, and 10)

10. What are the causes of extreme poverty, and what policies have been most effective for improving the lives of the poorest of the poor? (Chapters 5, 6, 7, 8, 9, 10, and 11)

11. With world population superseding 7 billion people, on its way to a projected 9 billion before mid-century, is rapid population growth threatening the economic progress of developing nations? Does having large families make economic sense in an environment of widespread poverty and financial insecurity? (Chapter 6)

12. Why is there so much unemployment and underemployment in the developing world, especially in the cities, and why do people continue to migrate to the cities from rural areas even when their chances of finding a conventional job are slim? (Chapter 7)

FIGURE 1.1   World Income Distribution

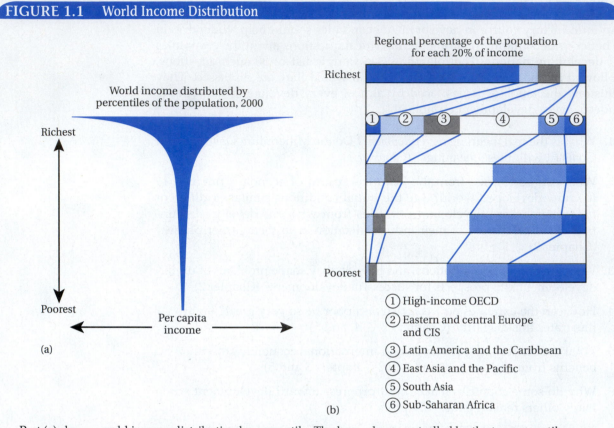

Part (a) shows world income distribution by percentile. The huge share controlled by the top percentiles gives the graph its "champagne glass shape." Part (b) shows the regional shares of global income. For example, a large majority of people in the top 20% of the global income distribution live in the rich countries. Most of those in the bottom 60% live in sub-Saharan Africa and Asia. OECD is the Organization for Economic Cooperation and Development. CIS is the Commonwealth of Independent States.

Source: From *Human Development Report, 2005*, p. 37. Reprinted with permission from the United Nations Development Programme.

13. Under what conditions can cities act as engines of economic transformation? (Chapter 7)

14. Wealthier societies are also healthier ones because they have more resources for improving nutrition and health care. But does better health also help spur successful development? (Chapter 8)

15. What is the impact of poor public health on the prospects for development, and what is needed to address these problems? (Chapter 8)

16. Do educational systems in developing countries really promote economic development, or are they simply a mechanism to enable certain select groups or classes of people to maintain positions of wealth, power, and influence? (Chapter 8)

17. As more than half the people in developing countries still reside in rural areas, how can agricultural and rural development best be promoted? Are higher agricultural prices sufficient to stimulate food production, or are rural institutional changes and infrastructure (land redistribution, local government reform, roads, transport, education, credit, etc.) also needed? (Chapter 9)

18. What do we mean by "environmentally sustainable development"? Are there serious economic costs for pursuing sustainable development as opposed to simple output growth, and who bears the major responsibility for global environmental damage—the developed North or the developing South? (Chapter 10)

19. Are free markets and economic privatization the answer to development problems, or do governments in developing countries still have major roles to play in their economies? (Chapter 11)

20. Why do so many developing countries select such poor development policies, and what can be done to improve these choices? (Chapter 11)

21. Is expanded international trade always desirable from the point of view of the development of poor nations? Who gains from trade, and how are the advantages distributed among nations? (Chapter 12)

22. When and under what conditions, if any, should governments in developing countries adopt a policy of foreign-exchange control, raise tariffs, or set quotas on the importation of certain "nonessential" goods in order to promote their own industrialization or to ameliorate chronic balance of payments problems? (Chapter 12)

23. What has been the impact of International Monetary Fund "stabilization programs" and World Bank "structural adjustment" lending on the balance of payments and growth prospects of heavily indebted less developed countries? (Chapters 12 and 13)

24. What is meant by **globalization**, and how is it affecting the developing countries? (Chapters 12, 13, and 14)

> **Globalization** The increasing integration of national economies into expanding international markets.

25. Should exports of primary products such as agricultural commodities and iron ore be promoted, or should all developing countries attempt to industrialize by developing their own manufacturing industries as rapidly as possible? (Chapter 13)

26. How did so many developing nations get into such serious foreign-debt problems, and what are the implications of debt problems for economic development? How do financial crises affect development? (Chapter 13)

27. What is the impact of foreign economic aid from rich countries? Should developing countries continue to seek such aid, and if so, under what conditions and for what purposes? Should developed countries continue to offer such aid, and if so, under what conditions and for what purposes? (Chapter 14)

28. Should multinational corporations be encouraged to invest in the economies of poor nations, and if so, under what conditions? How have the emergence

of the "global factory" and the globalization of trade and finance influenced international economic relations? (Chapter 14)

29. What is the role of financial and fiscal policy in promoting development? (Chapter 15)

30. What is microfinance, and what are its potential and limitations for reducing poverty and spurring grassroots development? (Chapter 15)

The following chapters analyze and explore these and many related questions. The answers are often more complex than one might think. Remember that the ultimate purpose of any course in economics, including development economics, is to help students think *systematically* about economic problems and issues, and formulate judgments and conclusions on the basis of relevant analytical principles and reliable statistical information. Because the problems of development are in many cases unique in the modern world and not often easily understood through the use of traditional economic theories, we may often need unconventional approaches to what may appear to be conventional economic problems. Traditional economic principles play a useful role in enabling us to improve our understanding of development problems, but they should not blind us to the realities of local conditions in less developed countries.

The Important Role of Values in Development Economics

Economics is a social science. It is concerned with human beings and the social systems by which they organize their activities to satisfy basic material needs (e.g., food, shelter, clothing) and nonmaterial wants (e.g., education, knowledge, spiritual fulfillment). It is necessary to recognize from the outset that ethical or normative *value premises* about what is or is not desirable are central features of the economic discipline in general and of development economics in particular. The very concepts of economic development and modernization represent implicit as well as explicit value premises about desirable goals for achieving what Mahatma Gandhi once called the "realization of the human potential." Concepts or goals such as economic and social equality, the elimination of poverty, universal education, rising levels of living, national independence, modernization of institutions, rule of law and due process, access to opportunity, political and economic participation, grassroots democracy, self-reliance, and personal fulfillment all derive from subjective value judgments about what is good and desirable and what is not. So too, for that matter, do other values—for example, the sanctity of private property, however acquired, and the right of individuals to accumulate unlimited personal wealth; the preservation of traditional hierarchical social institutions and rigid, inegalitarian class structures; the male head of household as the final authority; and the supposed "natural right" of some to lead while others follow.

When we deal in Part Two with such major issues of development as poverty, inequality, population growth, rural stagnation, and environmental decay, the mere identification of these topics as problems conveys the value judgment that their improvement or elimination is desirable and therefore good. That there is widespread agreement among many different groups of people—politicians, academics, and ordinary citizens—that these are desirable goals does not alter the fact that they arise not only out of a reaction to an objective empirical or positive analysis of what is but also ultimately from a subjective or normative value judgment about what should be.

It follows that value premises, however carefully disguised, are an inherent component of both economic analysis and economic policy. Economics cannot be value-free in the same sense as, say, physics or chemistry. Thus, the validity of economic analysis and the correctness of economic prescriptions should always be evaluated in light of the underlying assumptions or value premises. Once these subjective values have been agreed on by a nation or, more specifically, by those who are responsible for national decision making, specific development goals (e.g., greater income equality) and corresponding public policies (e.g., taxing higher incomes at higher rates) based on "objective" theoretical and quantitative analyses can be pursued. However, where serious value conflicts and disagreements exist among decision makers, the possibility of a consensus about desirable goals or appropriate policies is considerably diminished. In either case, it is essential, especially in the field of development economics, that one's value premises always be made clear.[4]

Economies as Social Systems: The Need to Go Beyond Simple Economics

Economics and economic systems, especially in the developing world, must be viewed in a broader perspective than that postulated by traditional economics. They must be analyzed within the context of the overall **social system** of a country and, indeed, within an international, global context as well. By "social system," we mean the interdependent relationships between economic and noneconomic factors. The latter include attitudes toward life, work, and authority; public and private bureaucratic, legal, and administrative structures; patterns of kinship and religion; cultural traditions; systems of land tenure; the authority and integrity of government agencies; the degree of popular participation in development decisions and activities; and the flexibility or rigidity of economic and social classes. Clearly, these factors vary widely from one region of the world to another and from one culture and social setting to another. At the international level, we must also consider the organization and rules of conduct of the global economy—how they were formulated, who controls them, and who benefits most from them. This is especially true today with the spread of market economies and the rapid globalization of trade, finance, corporate boundaries, technology, intellectual property, and labor migration.

Resolving problems to achieve development is a complicated task. Increasing national production, raising levels of living, and promoting widespread employment opportunities are all as much a function of the local history, expectations, values, incentives, attitudes and beliefs, and institutional and power structures of both the domestic and the global society as they are the direct outcomes of the manipulation of strategic economic variables such as

Social system The organizational and institutional structure of a society, including its values, attitudes, power structure, and traditions.

savings, investment, product and factor prices, and foreign-exchange rates. As the Indonesian intellectual Soedjatmoko, former rector of the United Nations University in Tokyo, so aptly put it:

> Looking back over these years, it is now clear that, in their preoccupation with growth and its stages and with the provision of capital and skills, development theorists have paid insufficient attention to institutional and structural problems and to the power of historical, cultural, and religious forces in the development process.[5]

Just as some social scientists occasionally make the mistake of confusing their theories with universal truths, they also sometimes mistakenly dismiss these noneconomic variables as "nonquantifiable" and therefore of dubious importance. Yet these variables often play a critical role in the success or failure of the development effort.

As you will see in Parts Two and Three, many of the failures of development policies have occurred precisely because these noneconomic variables (e.g., the role of traditional property rights in allocating resources and distributing income or the influence of religion on attitudes toward modernization and family planning) were excluded from the analysis. Although the main focus of this text is on development economics and its usefulness in understanding problems of economic and social progress in poor nations, we will try always to be mindful of the crucial roles that **values**, **attitudes**, and **institutions**, both domestic and international, play in the overall development process.

1.3 What Do We Mean by Development?

Because the term *development* may mean different things to different people, it is important that we have some working definition or core perspective on its meaning. Without such a perspective and some agreed measurement criteria, we would be unable to determine which country was actually developing and which was not. This will be our task for the remainder of the chapter and for our first country case study, Brazil, at the end of the chapter.

Traditional Economic Measures

In strictly economic terms, *development* has traditionally meant achieving sustained rates of growth of **income per capita** to enable a nation to expand its output at a rate faster than the growth rate of its population. Levels and rates of growth of "real" per capita **gross national income (GNI)** (monetary growth of GNI per capita minus the rate of inflation) are then used to measure the overall economic well-being of a population—how much of real goods and services is available to the average citizen for consumption and investment.

Economic development in the past has also been typically seen in terms of the planned alteration of the structure of production and employment so that agriculture's share of both declines and that of the manufacturing and service industries increases. Development strategies have therefore usually focused on rapid industrialization, often at the expense of agriculture and rural development.

With few exceptions, such as in development policy circles in the 1970s, development was until recently nearly always seen as an economic phenomenon in

Values Principles, standards, or qualities that a society or groups within it considers worthwhile or desirable.

Attitudes The states of mind or feelings of an individual, group, or society regarding issues such as material gain, hard work, saving for the future, and sharing wealth.

Institutions Norms, rules of conduct, and generally accepted ways of doing things. Economic institutions are humanly devised constraints that shape human interactions, including both informal and formal "rules of the game" of economic life in the widely used framework of Douglass North.

Income per capita Total gross national income of a country divided by its total population.

Gross national income (GNI) The total domestic and foreign output claimed by residents of a country. It comprises gross domestic product (GDP) plus factor incomes accruing to residents from abroad, less the income earned in the domestic economy accruing to persons abroad.

which rapid gains in overall and per capita GNI growth would either "trickle down" to the masses in the form of jobs and other economic opportunities or create the necessary conditions for the wider distribution of the economic and social benefits of growth. Problems of poverty, discrimination, unemployment, and income distribution were of secondary importance to "getting the growth job done." Indeed, the emphasis is often on increased output, measured by **gross domestic product (GDP)**.

The New Economic View of Development

The experience of the first decades of post–World War II and postcolonial development in the 1950s, 1960s, and early 1970s, when many developing nations did reach their economic growth targets but the levels of living of the masses of people remained for the most part unchanged, signaled that something was very wrong with this narrow definition of development. An increasing number of economists and policymakers clamored for more direct attacks on widespread absolute poverty, increasingly inequitable income distributions, and rising unemployment. In short, during the 1970s, economic development came to be redefined in terms of the reduction or elimination of poverty, inequality, and unemployment within the context of a growing economy. "Redistribution from growth" became a common slogan. Dudley Seers posed the basic question about the meaning of development succinctly when he asserted:

> The questions to ask about a country's development are therefore: What has been happening to poverty? What has been happening to unemployment? What has been happening to inequality? If all three of these have declined from high levels, then beyond doubt this has been a period of development for the country concerned. If one or two of these central problems have been growing worse, especially if all three have, it would be strange to call the result "development" even if per capita income doubled.[6]

This assertion was neither idle speculation nor the description of a hypothetical situation. A number of developing countries experienced relatively high rates of growth of per capita income during the 1960s and 1970s but showed little or no improvement or even an actual decline in employment, equality, and the real incomes of the bottom 40% of their populations. By the earlier growth definition, these countries were developing; by the newer poverty, equality, and employment criteria, they were not. The situation in the 1980s and 1990s worsened further as GNI growth rates turned negative for many developing countries, and governments, facing mounting foreign-debt problems, were forced to cut back on their already limited social and economic programs.

But the phenomenon of development or the existence of a chronic state of underdevelopment is not merely a question of economics or even one of quantitative measurement of incomes, employment, and inequality. As Denis Goulet forcefully portrayed it:

> Underdevelopment is shocking: the squalor, disease, unnecessary deaths, and hopelessness of it all!…The most empathetic observer can speak objectively about underdevelopment only after undergoing, personally or vicariously, the "shock of

Gross domestic product (GDP) The total final output of *goods* and *services* produced by the country's economy, within the country's territory, by residents and nonresidents, regardless of its allocation between domestic and foreign claims.

underdevelopment." This unique culture shock comes to one as he is initiated to the emotions which prevail in the "culture of poverty." The reverse shock is felt by those living in destitution when a new self-understanding reveals to them that their life is neither human nor inevitable....The prevalent emotion of underdevelopment is a sense of personal and societal impotence in the face of disease and death, of confusion and ignorance as one gropes to understand change, of servility toward men whose decisions govern the course of events, of hopelessness before hunger and natural catastrophe. Chronic poverty is a cruel kind of hell, and one cannot understand how cruel that hell is merely by gazing upon poverty as an object.[7]

Development must therefore be conceived of as a multidimensional process involving major changes in social structures, popular attitudes, and national institutions, as well as the acceleration of economic growth, the reduction of inequality, and the eradication of poverty. Development, in its essence, must represent the whole gamut of change by which an entire social system, tuned to the diverse basic needs and evolving aspirations of individuals and social groups within that system, moves away from a condition of life widely perceived as unsatisfactory toward a situation or condition of life regarded as materially and spiritually better. No one has identified the human goals of economic development as well as Amartya Sen, perhaps the leading thinker on the meaning of development.

Amartya Sen's "Capability" Approach

The view that income and wealth are not ends in themselves but instruments for other purposes goes back at least as far as Aristotle. Amartya Sen, the 1998 Nobel laureate in economics, argues that the "capability to function" is what really matters for status as a poor or nonpoor person. As Sen puts it, "the expansion of commodity productions...are valued, ultimately, not for their own sake, but as means to human welfare and freedom."[8]

In effect, Sen argues that poverty cannot be properly measured by income or even by utility as conventionally understood; what matters fundamentally is not the things a person has—or the feelings these provide—but what a person *is*, or can be, and does, or *can do*. What matters for well-being is not just the characteristics of commodities consumed, as in the utility approach, but what use the consumer can and does make of commodities. For example, a book is of little value to an illiterate person (except perhaps as cooking fuel or as a status symbol). Or as Sen noted, a person with a parasitic disease will be less able to extract nourishment from a given quantity of food than someone without parasites.

To make any sense of the concept of human well-being in general, and poverty in particular, we need to think beyond the availability of commodities and consider their use: to address what Sen calls **functionings**, that is, what a person does (or can do) with the commodities of given characteristics that they come to possess or control. Freedom of choice, or control of one's own life, is itself a central aspect of most understandings of well-being. A functioning is a valued "being or doing," and in Sen's view, functionings that people have reason to value can range from being healthy, being well-nourished, and well-clothed, to being mobile, having self-esteem, and "taking part in the life of the community."[9]

Functionings What people do or can do with the commodities of given characteristics that they come to possess or control.

Sen identifies five sources of disparity between (measured) real incomes and actual advantages:[10] first, personal heterogeneities, such as those connected with disability, illness, age, or gender; second, environmental diversities, such as heating and clothing requirements in the cold or infectious diseases in the tropics, or the impact of pollution; third, variations in social climate, such as the prevalence of crime and violence, and "social capital"; fourth, distribution within the family—economic statistics measure incomes received in a family because it is the basic unit of shared consumption, but family resources may be distributed unevenly, as when girls get less medical attention or education than boys do; fifth, differences in relational perspectives, meaning that some goods are essential because of local customs and conventions. For example, necessaries for being able, in Adam Smith's phrase, "to appear in public without shame," include higher quality clothing (such as leather shoes) in high-income countries than in low-income countries.

In a richer society, the ability to partake in community life would be extremely difficult without certain commodities, such as a telephone, a television, or an automobile; it is difficult to function socially in Singapore or South Korea without an e-mail address. And minimal housing standards to avoid social disgrace also rise strongly with the average wealth of the society.

Thus, looking at real income levels or even the levels of consumption of specific commodities cannot suffice as a measure of well-being. One may have a lot of commodities, but these are of little value if they are not what consumers desire (as in the former Soviet Union). One may have income, but certain commodities essential for well-being, such as nutritious foods, may be unavailable. Even when providing an equal number of calories, the available staple foods in one country (cassava, bread, rice, cornmeal, potatoes, etc.) will differ in nutritional content from staple foods in other countries. Moreover, even some subvarieties of, for example, rice, are much more nutritious than others. Finally, even when comparing absolutely identical commodities, one has to frame their consumption in a personal and social context. Sen provides an excellent example of bread, the most basic of commodities. It has product "characteristics" such as taste and nutrition such as protein; and it helps to meet conventions of social exchange in the sense of breaking bread together. But many of these benefits depend on the person and her circumstances, such as her activity level, metabolism, weight, whether she is pregnant or lactating, nutrition knowledge, whether she is infected with parasites, and her access to medical services. Sen goes on to note that functioning depends also on (1) "social conventions in force in the society in which the person lives, (2) the position of the person in the family and in the society, (3) the presence or absence of festivities such as marriages, seasonal festivals and other occasions such as funerals, (4) the physical distance from the homes of friends and relatives..."[11]

In part because such factors, even on so basic a matter as nutrition, can vary so widely among individuals, measuring individual well-being by levels of consumption of goods and services obtained confuses the role of commodities by regarding them as ends in themselves rather than as means to an end. In the case of nutrition, the end is health and what one can do with good health, as well as personal enjoyment and social functioning. Indeed, the capacity to maintain valued social relationships and to network leads to what James Foster and Christopher Handy have termed *external capabilities*, which are "abilities to function that are conferred by direct connection or relationship with another person." But measuring well-being using the concept of utility, in any of its standard definitions, does not offer enough of an improvement over measuring consumption to capture the meaning of development.[12]

As Sen stresses, a person's own valuation of what kind of life would be worthwhile is not necessarily the same as what gives pleasure to that person. If we identify utility with happiness in a particular way, then very poor people can have very high utility. Sometimes even malnourished people either have a disposition that keeps them feeling rather blissful or have learned to appreciate greatly any small comforts they can find in life, such as a breeze on a very hot day, and to avoid disappointment by striving only for what seems attainable. (Indeed, it is only too human to tell yourself that you do not want the things you cannot have.) If there is really nothing to be done about a person's deprivation, this attitude of subjective bliss would have undoubted advantages in a spiritual sense, but it does not change the objective reality of deprivation. In particular, such an attitude would not prevent the contented but homeless poor person from greatly valuing an opportunity to become freed of parasites or provided with basic shelter. The functioning of a person is an *achievement*. Sen provides the example of bicycling "[B]icycling has to be distinguished from possessing a bike. It has to be distinguished also from the happiness generated by [bicycling]... A functioning is thus different both from (1) having goods (and the corresponding characteristics), to which it is posterior, and (2) having utility (in the form of happiness resulting from that functioning), to which it is, in an important way, prior."[13]

To clarify this point, in his acclaimed 2009 book, *The Idea of Justice*, Sen suggests that subjective well-being is a kind of psychological state of being—a functioning—that could be pursued alongside other functionings such as health and dignity. In the next section, we return to the meaning of happiness as a development outcome, in a sense that can be distinguished from conventional utility.

Capabilities The freedoms that people have, given their personal features and their command over commodities.

Sen then defines **capabilities** as "the freedom that a person has in terms of the choice of functionings, given his personal features (conversion of characteristics into functionings) and his command over commodities."[14] Sen's perspective helps explain why development economists have placed so much emphasis on health and education, and more recently on social inclusion and empowerment, and have referred to countries with high levels of income but poor health and education standards as cases of "growth without development."[14a] Real income is essential, but to convert the characteristics of commodities into functionings, in most important cases, surely requires health and education as well as income. The role of health and education ranges from something so basic as the nutritional advantages and greater personal energy that are possible when one lives free of parasites to the expanded ability to appreciate the richness of human life that comes with a broad and deep education. People living in poverty are often deprived—at times deliberately—of capabilities to make substantive choices and to take valuable actions, and often the behavior of the poor can be understood in that light.

For Sen, human "well-being" means *being well*, in the basic sense of being healthy, well nourished, well clothed, literate, and long-lived, and more broadly, being able to take part in the life of the community, being mobile, and having freedom of choice in what one can become and can do.

Development and Happiness

Clearly, happiness is part of human well-being, and greater happiness may in itself expand an individual's capability to function. As Amartya Sen has argued, a person may well regard happiness as an important functioning for her well-being.[15] In recent years, economists have explored the empirical relationship across countries and over time between subjectively reported satisfaction and happiness and factors such as income. One of the findings is that the average level of happiness or satisfaction increases with a country's average income. For example, roughly four times the percentage of people report that they are not happy or satisfied in Tanzania, Bangladesh, India, and Azerbaijan as in the United States and Sweden. But the relationship is seen only up to an average income of roughly $10,000 to $20,000 per capita, as shown in Figure 1.2.[16] Once incomes grow to this point, most citizens have usually escaped extreme poverty. At these levels, despite substantial variations across countries, if inequality is not extreme, a majority of citizens are usually relatively well nourished, healthy, and educated. The "happiness science" findings call into question the centrality of economic growth as an objective for high-income countries. But they also reaffirm the importance of economic development in the developing world, whether the objective is solely happiness or, more inclusively and persuasively, expanded human capabilities.

FIGURE 1.2   Income and Happiness: Comparing Countries

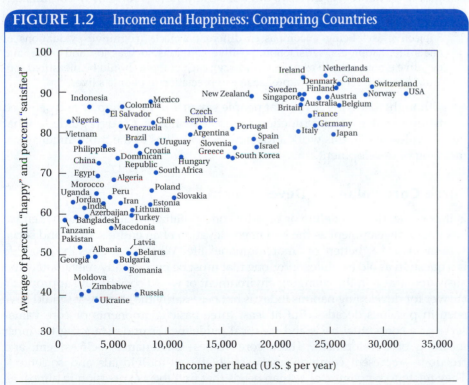

Source: From *Happiness: Lessons from a New Science* by Richard Layard, copyright © 2005 by Richard Layard. Used by permission of The Penguin Press, a division of Penguin Group (USA) Inc. and United Agents Ltd. (www.unitedagents.co.uk) on behalf of the author.

Not surprisingly, studies show that financial security is only one factor affecting happiness. Richard Layard identifies seven factors that surveys show affect average national happiness: family relationships, financial situation, work, community and friends, health, personal freedom, and personal values. In particular, aside from not being poor, the evidence says people are happier when they are not unemployed, not divorced or separated, and have high trust of others in society, as well as enjoy high government quality with democratic freedoms and have religious faith. The importance of these factors may shed light on why the percentage of people reporting that they are not happy or satisfied varies so widely among developing countries with similar incomes. For example, the fraction of people who are *not* happy and satisfied on average is 4½ times as great in Zimbabwe as in Indonesia, despite somewhat higher incomes in Zimbabwe, and over 3 times as great in Turkey as in Colombia, despite somewhat higher incomes in Turkey at the time of the study. Many opinion leaders in developing nations hope that their societies can gain the benefits of development without losing traditional strengths such as moral values and trust in others—sometimes called *social capital*.

The government of Bhutan's attempt to make "gross national happiness" rather than gross national income its measure of development progress has attracted considerable attention.[17] Informed by Sen's work, its indicators extend beyond traditional notions of happiness to include capabilities such as health, education, and freedom. Happiness is not the only dimension of subjective well-being of importance. As the 2010 Stiglitz-Sen-Fitoussi ("Sarkozy") Commission on the Measurement of Economic Performance and Social Progress put it:

> Subjective well-being encompasses different aspects (cognitive evaluations of one's life, happiness, satisfaction, positive emotions such as joy and pride, and negative emotions such as pain and worry): each of them should be measured separately to derive a more comprehensive appreciation of people's lives.[18]

Although, following Sen, what people say makes them happy and satisfied as just one among valued functionings is at best only a rough guide to what people value in life, this work adds new perspectives to the multidimensional meaning of development.

Three Core Values of Development

Is it possible, then, to define or broadly conceptualize what we mean when we talk about development as the sustained elevation of an entire society and social system toward a "better" or "more humane" life? What constitutes the good life is a question as old as philosophy, one that must be periodically reevaluated and answered afresh in the changing environment of world society. The appropriate answer for developing nations today is not necessarily the same as it would have been in previous decades. But at least three basic components or core values serve as a conceptual basis and practical guideline for understanding the inner meaning of development. These core values—**sustenance**, **self-esteem**, and **freedom**—represent common goals sought by all individuals and societies.[19] They relate to fundamental human needs that find their expression in almost all societies and cultures at all times. Let us therefore examine each in turn.

Sustenance: The Ability to Meet Basic Needs   All people have certain basic needs without which life would be impossible. These life-sustaining basic

Sustenance The basic goods and services, such as food, clothing, and shelter, that are necessary to sustain an average human being at the bare minimum level of living.

Self-esteem The feeling of worthiness that a society enjoys when its social, political, and economic systems and institutions promote human values such as respect, dignity, integrity, and self-determination.

Freedom A situation in which a society has at its disposal a variety of alternatives from which to satisfy its wants and individuals enjoy real choices according to their preferences.

human needs include food, shelter, health, and protection.[20] When any of these is absent or in critically short supply, a condition of "absolute underdevelopment" exists. A basic function of all economic activity, therefore, is to provide as many people as possible with the means of overcoming the helplessness and misery arising from a lack of food, shelter, health, and protection. To this extent, we may claim that economic development is a necessary condition for the improvement in the quality of life that is development. Without sustained and continuous economic progress at the individual as well as the societal level, the realization of the human potential would not be possible. One clearly has to "have enough in order to be more."[21] Rising per capita incomes, the elimination of absolute poverty, greater employment opportunities, and lessening income inequalities therefore constitute the *necessary* but not the *sufficient* conditions for development.[22]

Self-Esteem: To Be a Person   A second universal component of the good life is self-esteem—a sense of worth and self-respect, of not being used as a tool by others for their own ends. All peoples and societies seek some basic form of self-esteem, although they may call it authenticity, identity, dignity, respect, honor, or recognition. The nature and form of this self-esteem may vary from society to society and from culture to culture. However, with the proliferation of the "modernizing values" of developed nations, many societies in developing countries that have had a profound sense of their own worth suffer from serious cultural confusion when they come in contact with economically and technologically advanced societies. This is because national prosperity has become an almost universal measure of worth. Due to the significance attached to material values in developed nations, worthiness and esteem are nowadays increasingly conferred only on countries that possess economic wealth and technological power—those that have "developed."

As Denis Goulet put it, "Development is legitimized as a goal because it is an important, perhaps even an indispensable, way of gaining esteem."[23]

Freedom from Servitude: To Be Able to Choose   A third and final universal value that we suggest should constitute the meaning of development is the concept of human freedom. Freedom here is to be understood in the sense of emancipation from alienating material conditions of life and from social servitude to nature, other people, misery, oppressive institutions, and dogmatic beliefs, especially that poverty is predestination. Freedom involves an expanded range of choices for societies and their members together with a minimization of external constraints in the pursuit of some social goal we call development. Amartya Sen writes of "development as freedom." W. Arthur Lewis stressed the relationship between economic growth and freedom from servitude when he concluded that "the advantage of economic growth is not that wealth increases happiness, but that it increases the range of human choice."[24] Wealth can enable people to gain greater control over nature and the physical environment (e.g., through the production of food, clothing, and shelter) than they would have if they remained poor. It also gives them the freedom to choose greater leisure, to have more goods and services, or to deny the importance of these material wants and choose to live a life of spiritual contemplation. The concept of human freedom also encompasses various components of political freedom, including personal security, the rule of law, freedom of expression, political participation, and equality of opportunity.[25]

Although attempts to rank countries with freedom indexes have proved highly controversial,[26] studies do reveal that some countries that have achieved high economic growth rates or high incomes, such as China, Malaysia, Saudi Arabia, and Singapore, have not achieved as much on human freedom criteria.

The Central Role of Women

In light of the information presented so far, it should come as no surprise that development scholars generally view women as playing the central role in the development drama. Globally, women tend to be poorer than men. They are also more deprived in health and education and in freedoms in all its forms. Moreover, women have primary responsibility for child rearing, and the resources that they are able to bring to this task will determine whether the cycle of transmission of poverty from generation to generation will be broken. Children need better health and education, and studies from around the developing world confirm that mothers tend to spend a significantly higher fraction of income under their control for the benefit of their children than fathers do. Women also transmit values to the next generation. To make the biggest impact on development, then, a society must empower and invest in its women. We will return to this topic in more depth in Chapters 5 through 9 and 15.

The Three Objectives of Development

We may conclude that development is both a physical reality and a state of mind in which society has, through some combination of social, economic, and institutional processes, secured the means for obtaining a better life. Whatever the specific components of this better life, development in all societies must have at least the following three objectives:

1. *To increase the availability and widen the distribution of basic life-sustaining goods* such as food, shelter, health, and protection

2. *To raise levels of living*, including, in addition to higher incomes, the provision of more jobs, better education, and greater attention to cultural and human values, all of which will serve not only to enhance material well-being but also to generate greater individual and national self-esteem

3. *To expand the range of economic and social choices* available to individuals and nations by freeing them from servitude and dependence, not only in relation to other people and nation-states, but also to the forces of ignorance and human misery

1.4 The Future of the Millennium Development Goals

In September 2000, the 189 member countries of the United Nations at that time adopted eight **Millennium Development Goals (MDGs)**, committing themselves to making substantial progress toward the eradication of poverty

Millennium Development Goals (MDGs) A set of eight goals adopted by the United Nations in 2000: to eradicate extreme poverty and hunger; achieve universal primary education; promote gender equality and empower women; reduce child mortality; improve maternal health; combat HIV/AIDS, malaria, and other diseases; ensure environmental sustainability; and develop a global partnership for development. The goals are assigned specific targets to be achieved by 2015.

and achieving other human development goals by 2015. The MDGs are the strongest statement yet of the international commitment to ending global poverty. They acknowledge the multidimensional nature of development and poverty alleviation; an end to poverty requires more than just increasing incomes of the poor. The MDGs have provided a unified focus in the development community unlike anything that preceded them.[27]

The eight goals are ambitious: to eradicate extreme poverty and hunger; achieve universal primary education; promote gender equality and empower women; reduce child mortality; improve maternal health; combat HIV/AIDS, malaria, and other diseases; ensure environmental sustainability; and develop a global partnership for development. The goals are then assigned specific targets deemed achievable by 2015 based on the pace of past international development achievements. The goals and targets are found in Table 1.1.

Appropriately, the first MDG addresses the problem of extreme poverty and hunger. The two targets for this goal are more modest: to reduce by half

TABLE 1.1 Millennium Development Goals and Targets for 2015

Goals	Targets
1. Eradicate extreme poverty and hunger	• Reduce by half the proportion of people living on less than $1 a day • Reduce by half the proportion of people who suffer from hunger
2. Achieve universal primary education	• Ensure that all boys and girls complete a full course of primary schooling
3. Promote gender equality and empower women	• Eliminate gender disparity in primary and secondary education, preferably by 2005, and at all levels by 2015
4. Reduce child mortality	• Reduce by two-thirds the mortality rate among children under 5
5. Improve maternal health	• Reduce by three-quarters the maternal mortality ratio
6. Combat HIV/AIDS, malaria, and other diseases	• Halt and begin to reverse the spread of HIV/AIDS • Halt and begin to reverse the incidence of malaria and other major diseases
7. Ensure environmental sustainability	• Integrate the principles of sustainable development into country policies and programs; reverse the loss of environmental resources • Reduce by half the proportion of people without sustainable access to safe drinking water • Achieve significant improvement in the lives of at least 100 million slum dwellers by 2020
8. Develop a global partnership for development	• Develop further an open, rule-based, predictable, nondiscriminatory trading and financial system; includes a commitment to good governance, development, and poverty reduction—both nationally and internationally • Address the special needs of the least developed countries; includes tariff and quota free access for least developed countries' exports; enhanced program of debt relief for heavily indebted poor countries (HIPCs) and cancellation of official bilateral debt; and more generous official development assistance (ODA) for countries committed to poverty reduction • Address the special needs of landlocked countries and small-island developing states • Deal comprehensively with the debt problems of developing countries through national and international measures in order to make debt sustainable in the long term • In cooperation with developing countries, develop and implement strategies for decent and productive work for youth • In cooperation with pharmaceutical companies, provide access to affordable essential drugs in developing countries • In cooperation with the private sector, make available the benefits of new technologies, especially information and communications

Source: From "Millennium Development Goals" (accessed via www.undp.org). Reprinted with permission from the United Nations Development Programme.

the proportion of people living on less than $1 a day and to reduce by half the proportion of people who suffer from hunger. "Halving poverty" has come to serve as a touchstone for the MDGs as a whole. To achieve this target requires that progress be made on the other goals as well.

As reported by the United Nations Development Programme (UNDP), the halving of global poverty was achieved by 2012, but if current trends continue, not all of the other targets will be achieved; and great regional disparity is obscured when global averages are reported, as East Asia has done far better than sub-Saharan Africa.[28] Shockingly, in a world of plenty, the target of cutting the proportion of people who are chronically hungry in half by 2015 is very unlikely to be achieved. Some conditions even worsened after a food price spike in 2008 and thereafter as a result of the global economic crisis. And the UNDP highlights that if global trends continue through 2015, the reduction in under-5 mortality will reach roughly one-quarter, far below the target reduction of two-thirds. This means that the target will be missed by 4.4 million avoidable deaths in 2015. Universal primary enrollment will not be achieved unless faster progress can be made in sub-Saharan Africa. Projecting current trends, there will still be 47 million children out of school in 2015. And the UNDP reports that the gap between the current trends and the target of halving poverty represents an additional 380 million people still living on less than $1 a day in 2015.

The goal of ensuring environmental sustainability is essential for securing an escape from poverty. This is immediately seen by looking at two of the targets: reduce by half the proportion of people without access to safe drinking water and achieve significant improvement in the lives of at least 100 million slum dwellers. But more generally, without protecting the environment of the poor, there is little chance that their escape from poverty can be permanent. Finally, the governments and citizens of the rich countries need to play their part in pursuit of the goal of "global partnership for development."

The MDGs were developed in consultation with the developing countries, to ensure that they addressed their most pressing problems. In addition, key international agencies, including the United Nations, the World Bank, the International Monetary Fund (IMF), the Organization for Economic Cooperation and Development (OECD), and the World Trade Organization (WTO), all helped develop the Millennium Declaration and so have a collective policy commitment to attacking poverty directly. The MDGs assign specific responsibilities to rich countries, including increased aid, removal of trade and investment barriers, and eliminating unsustainable debts of the poorest nations.[29]

However, the MDGs have also come in for some criticism.[30] For example, some observers believe that the MDG targets were not ambitious enough, going little beyond projecting past rates of improvement 15 years into the future. Moreover, the goals were not prioritized; for example, reducing hunger may leverage the achievement of many of the other health and education targets. At the same time, although the interrelatedness of development objectives was implicit in the MDGs' formulation, goals are presented and treated in reports as stand-alone objectives; in reality, the goals are not substitutes for each other but complements, such as the close relationship between health and education. Further, the setting of 2015 as an end date for the targets could discourage rather than encourage further development assistance if it were not met. Moreover, when the MDGs measure poverty as the fraction of the population below the $1-a-day line, this is arbitrary and fails to account for the intensity of poverty—that a given amount of extra income to a family with a per capita income of, say, 70 cents a day makes a bigger impact on poverty than to a family earning 90 cents per day (see Chapter 5). Other critics have complained that $1 a day is too low a poverty line and about the lack of goals on reducing rich-country agricultural subsidies, improving legal and human rights of the poor, slowing global warming (which is projected to harm Africa and South Asia the most), expanding gender equality, and leveraging the contribution of the private sector. While the reasonableness of some of these criticisms may be questioned, it should be acknowledged that the MDGs do have some inherent limitations.

Sector A subset (part) of an economy, with four usages in economic development: technology (modern and traditional sectors); activity (industry or product sectors); trade (export sector); and sphere (private and public sectors)

With the imminent expiration of the MDGs, the UN coordinated global efforts to launch its successor, Sustainable Development Goals (SDGs), with the May 2013 agenda-setting report of the High-Level Panel of Eminent Persons on Development Agenda.[31] This highly diverse panel of political leaders from every part of the world agreed upon a bold approach that is expected to substantially influence the eventual shape of the post-2015 agenda, the SDGs. The panel repeatedly stressed that it is "a universal agenda" for all countries, developed as well as developing and without exceptions, "to be driven by five big, transformative shifts." These universal shifts are:

1. Leave no one behind—to move "from reducing to ending extreme poverty, in all its forms;" in particular, to "design goals that focus on reaching excluded groups."

2. Put sustainable development at the core, "to integrate the social, economic, and environmental dimensions of sustainability."

3. Transform economies for jobs and inclusive growth, while moving to sustainable patterns of work and life.

4. Build peace and effective, open, and accountable institutions for all, which "encourage the rule of law, property rights, freedom of speech and the media, open political choice, access to justice, and accountable government and public institutions."

5. Forge a new global partnership so that each priority should involve governments and also others, including people living in poverty, civil society and indigenous and local communities, multilateral institutions, business, academia, and philanthropy.

The High-Level Panel also agreed on well-recognized and illustrative universal goals and national targets for the SDGs, including an outright end by 2030 of poverty, hunger, child marriage, and preventable under-5 deaths, and specific targets on stunting, social protection coverage, and maternal mortality. The debate will be lively throughout 2014 and 2015.

1.5 Conclusions

Development economics is a distinct yet very important extension of both traditional economics and political economy. While necessarily also concerned with efficient resource allocation and the steady growth of aggregate output over time, development economics focuses primarily on the economic, social, and institutional mechanisms needed to bring about rapid and large-scale improvements in standards of living for the masses of poor people in developing nations. Consequently, development economics must be concerned with the formulation of appropriate public policies designed to effect major economic, institutional, and social transformations of entire societies in a very short time.

As a social science, economics is concerned with people and how best to provide them with the material means to help them realize their full human potential. But what constitutes the good life is a perennial question, and hence economics necessarily involves values and value judgments. Our very concern with promoting development represents an implicit value judgment about good (development) and evil (underdevelopment). But development may mean different things to different people. Therefore, the nature and character of development and the meaning we attach to it must be carefully spelled out. We did this in section 1.3 and will continue to explore these definitions throughout the text.

The central economic problems of all societies include traditional questions such as what, where, how, how much, and for whom goods and services should be produced. But they should also include the fundamental question at the national level about who actually makes or influences economic decisions and for whose principal benefit these decisions are made. Finally, at the international level, it is necessary to consider the question of which nations and which powerful groups within nations exert the most influence with regard to the control, transmission, and use of technology, information, and finance. Moreover, for whom do they exercise this power?

Any realistic analysis of development problems necessitates the supplementation of strictly economic variables such as incomes, prices, and savings rates with equally relevant noneconomic institutional factors, including the nature of land tenure arrangements; the influence of social and class stratifications; the structure of credit, education, and health systems; the organization and motivation of government bureaucracies; the machinery of public administrations; the nature of popular attitudes toward work, leisure, and self-improvement; and the values, roles, and attitudes of political and economic elites. Economic development strategies that seek to raise agricultural output, create employment, and eradicate poverty have often failed in the past because economists and other policy advisers neglected to view the economy as an interdependent social system in which economic and noneconomic forces are continually interacting in ways that are at times self-reinforcing and at other times contradictory. As you will discover, underdevelopment reflects many individual market failures, but these failures often add up to more than the sum of their parts, combining to keep a country in a poverty trap. Government can play a key role in moving the economy to a better equilibrium, and in many countries, notably in East Asia, government has done so; but all too often government itself is part and parcel of the bad equilibrium.

Achieving the Millennium Development Goals will be an important milestone on the long journey to sustainable and just development. Although progress has been substantial, many of the interim targets remain unachieved—nor do the MDGs include all of the critical objectives of development. The emerging Sustainable Development Goals, planned as the MDGs' successor after 2015, will be even more ambitious, including the full eradication of extreme poverty.

Despite the great diversity of developing nations—some large, others small; some resource-rich, others resource-barren; some subsistence economies, others modern manufactured-good exporters; some private-sector oriented, others to a large degree run by the government—most share common problems that define their underdevelopment. We will discuss these diverse structures and common characteristics of developing countries in Chapter 2.

The oil price shocks of the 1970s, the foreign-debt crisis of the 1980s, and the twenty-first-century concerns with economic globalization, economic imbalances and financial crises, global warming, and international terrorism have underlined the growing interdependence of all nations and peoples in the international social system. What happens to life in Caracas, Karachi, Cairo, and Kolkata will in one way or another have important implications for life in New York, London, and Tokyo. It was once said that "when the United States sneezes, the world catches pneumonia." A more fitting expression for the twenty-first century would perhaps be that "the world is like the human body: If one part aches, the rest will feel it; if many parts hurt, the whole will suffer."

Developing nations constitute these "many parts" of the global organism. The nature and character of their future development should therefore be a major concern of *all* nations irrespective of political, ideological, or economic orientation. There can no longer be two futures, one for the few rich and the other for the very many poor. In the words of a poet, "There will be only one future—or none at all."

Progress in the Struggle for More Meaningful Development: Brazil

There are two faces of development in Brazil. World-competitive industry coexists with stagnant, protected sectors. Modern agriculture coexists with low-productivity traditional practices. But Brazil is in the midst of a spurt of economic development that might herald a lasting transformation for a country often considered synonymous with inequality and unmet potential. Economic growth has returned, health and education have improved markedly, the country's democratization has proved durable, and inequality—among the highest in the world—has at long last started to fall. But there is still a long way to go to achieve genuine development in Brazil. Growth remains vulnerable to world commodity prices, and social progress remains tenuous as revealed by the widespread protest demonstrations that erupted in 2013.

Many Brazilians have been frustrated with the uneven pace of development and are known for telling self-deprecating jokes such as "Brazil is the country of the future—and always will be." Brazil has even been cited as an example of a country that has experienced "growth without development." But despite huge inequities, Brazil has made economic and social progress. Extremely high economic inequality and social divisions do pose a serious threat to further progress in Brazil. But there are growing reasons to hope that Brazil may overcome its legacy of inequality so that the country may yet join the ranks of the developed countries.

Brazil is of special interest in part because its growth performance from the 1960s through the early 1980s was the best in Latin America, with at least some parallels with East Asian export policy and performance, although Brazil had a larger role for state-owned enterprises, much lower education

and other social expenditures, and much higher inflation.

Brazil's performance is followed widely in the developing world, as it is the largest and most populous country in Latin America; with close to 200 million people, it is the world's fifth-largest country in both area and population. Brazil is consolidating its role as the lead country in the Latin America and Caribbean region; it is a key member of the G20 leading economies; and one of a group of developing countries pushing for fairer international trade rules. It is one of four influential countries referred to by the media and financial analysts as the "BRICs" (Brazil, Russia, India, and China, often expanded to include South Africa).

Although over two decades of military rule ended in Brazil in 1985, an ongoing debt crisis, years of stagnant incomes, and extremely high inflation followed. It took drastic policies to reduce inflation, and incomes continued to stagnate in the aftermath. The 1980s and the 1990s have been described as "lost decades" for development. So the recent signs of palpable progress, especially since about 2004, have been welcomed with relief and growing enthusiasm among many Brazilians. Although the country remains politically divided between the center-left and the center-right, a striking convergence has been achieved on policies agreed to be necessary for equitable and sustained growth, ranging from active poverty reduction programs to relatively orthodox monetary policies. The economy has been growing more rapidly (if inconsistently), in part due to commodity exports to China, from soybeans to iron ore. One persistent worry is whether the economy could continue to grow rapidly if commodity prices, which have been

much higher in recent years, revert to their very long-term trends for decline (see Chapter 12), or the slowing growth in China curtails demand for Brazil's products—both genuine worries by 2013. High crime remains a problem, especially in the *favelas* (slums).

But despite the nation's early and now resumed growth, other indicators of development in Brazil lagged, eventually undermining growth prospects. Benefiting from much higher incomes than Central American countries and spared the destructiveness of civil war, Brazil, it would seem, should have been in a much better position to fight extreme poverty and improve economic equity and social indicators. Instead, despite recent improvement, the country has continued to see a higher percentage of its population in poverty than would be expected for an upper-middle-income country. Brazil remains one of the countries with the highest levels of inequality in the world. So how should Brazil's development performance be evaluated and future priorities chosen?

Income and Growth

Growth is generally necessary, though not sufficient, for achieving development. In 2011, Brazil's per capita income was close to $11,000, still well under a quarter of that of the United States but more than nine times greater than that of Haiti (World Bank data).

Growth has been erratic, with substantial swings over time. Data for growth of gross domestic product (GDP) per capita are sometimes presented for the periods 1965–1990, when for Brazil it was 1.4%, and for 1990–2000, when it was 1.5%. This appears to suggest a remarkable stability. But the former figures combine the booming years from 1967 to 1980 and Brazil's "lost decade of development" of the 1980s. Nevertheless, performance through this period was still better than most other countries of Latin America. In 2000–2011, average annual per capita growth rose to about 2.8% (World Bank data). But wide swings continue, with a spike close to 7% in 2010 slowing to a near standstill by the end of 2012.

Brazil has had an export policy stressing incentives for manufacturing exports, as well as protections for domestic industry, with numerous parallels with Taiwan and South Korea in their earlier formative stages (see Chapter 12). Its percentage share of manufactured exports in total exports grew dramatically, reaching 57% in 1980, although it dropped dramatically during the lost decade of the 1980s. Although the share of manufactured exports increased again, reaching a new peak of 58% in 2000, it has fallen steadily since, to 45% in 2008, and by 2011, this figure had fallen to just 34% (World Bank data). Although part of this decline reflected an increase in commodity prices, it is still a striking reversal that probably increases the vulnerability of the Brazilian economy (see Chapter 12). Brazil must decide whether to respond to its good fortune of a period of high commodity prices as a spur to action or an excuse for complacency.

Brazil's prolonged status as a highly indebted country (see Chapter 13) was a substantial drag on growth performance, as were continued problems with infrastructure. Recently, however, the Industrial, Technological and Foreign Trade Policy (*PITCE*) program has been actively working to upgrade the quality and competitiveness of Brazilian industry.

High and growing taxes may have also slowed formal-sector employment growth. The overall tax burden increased from about 25% of gross national income to nearly 40% in the decade from 1993 to 2004, before leveling off (it was about 38% in 2012). Payroll taxes are high and as many as half of Brazil's labor force now works in the informal sector, where taxes may be avoided (and labor rights and regulation circumvented).

However, Ricardo Hausmann, Dani Rodrik, and Andrés Velasco argue that Brazil does not lack for productive investment ideas, nor is concern about government behavior the factor holding back investment. Using their decision tree framework to identify the most binding constraints on economic growth (see Chapter 4), Hausmann, Rodrik, and Velasco argue that Brazil has high returns to investment and is most constrained by a lack of savings to finance its productive opportunities at reasonable interest rates. In raising domestic savings, Hausmann has emphasized the importance of "creating a financially viable state that does not over-borrow, over-tax or under-invest."

Technology transfer is critical to more rapid growth, competing internationally, and beginning to catch up with advanced countries. Brazil has

made notable progress. The country is viewed as being at the cutting edge of agricultural research and extension in commercially successful export crops such as citrus and soybeans. After a disastrous attempt to protect the computer industry in the 1980s was abandoned, Brazil has begun to see the expansion of a software industry, as also seen in India. But Brazil has not absorbed technology to the degree that East Asian countries have.

Social Indicators

Brazil's human development statistics compare unfavorably with many other middle-income countries such as Costa Rica and quite a few low-income countries, let alone with the advanced industrialized countries. As of 2007, Brazil ranked just 85th on the United Nations Development Programme's 2013 Human Development Index (explained in Chapter 2), eight positions lower than would be predicted by its income, and below such countries as Peru, Mauritius, and Azerbaijan.

In Brazil, life expectancy at birth in 2011 was 73 years, compared with 81 in South Korea. Brazil's under-5 mortality rate is 16 per 1,000 live births, an impressive improvement from its 2000 rate of 36 per 1,000 but still high compared with 10 in similar-income Costa Rica and just 5 in Korea (World Bank data). But about 7% of all children under the age of 5 still suffer from malnutrition in Brazil (World Bank data).

Brazil suffers from a high incidence of child labor for its income level, as a World Bank study and reports by the International Labor Office have underlined. As many as 7 million children still work in Brazil, despite the country's having officially made the eradication of child labor a priority. (For an analysis of the problems of child labor and appropriate child labor policies, see Chapter 8.) In the education sphere, Brazil's officially reported adult literacy rate has now risen to 90% (independent observers have concluded that Brazil's effective literacy is under 50%), while that of similar-income Costa Rica is 96%. Helping explain this difference, in Costa Rica, six years of school attendance are mandatory, and 99% attendance is reported.

The UNDP concluded that

> the unequal distribution of social spending is no doubt a major factor in maintaining inequality and thus poverty….The bulk of the benefits go to the middle classes and the rich. Close to a third of the poorest fifth of the population does not attend primary school. But the sharpest differences show up in secondary and tertiary education. More than 90% of the poorest four-fifths of the population do not attend secondary school, and practically none make it to universities. Only primary schools end up being relatively targeted to the poor, not because the government succeeds in targeting resources, but because richer households send their children to private schools. Public expenditures on secondary and tertiary education are very badly targeted to the poor. For scholarships—chiefly to graduate students—four-fifths of the money goes to the richest fifth of the population.

In fact, with public universities offering free tuition to mostly high-income undergrads as well as grad students, the distortion is even greater. Moreover, corruption and waste limit the effectiveness of government expenditures. And the quality of primary schools in poor areas remains low.

So while the persistence of poverty in Brazil is undoubtedly due in part to mediocre growth relative to East Asia or to Brazil's potential, the most important explanation is the highly concentrated distribution of income, worsened by inequitable social spending.

Development depends on a healthy, skilled, and secure workforce. Ultimately, a slower improvement in health, education, and community development can feed back to a slower rate of growth, a process that has plagued Brazilian development. A hopeful sign is the role played now in Brazil by a free press, strengthened basic rights, and a very active but peaceful political competition. These elements can be a precursor of expanded capabilities in Amartya Sen's analysis.

Poverty

Perhaps the most important social indicator is the extent of extreme poverty among a country's people. Poverty has been high in Brazil for an upper-middle-income country. There has been progress; a World Bank study found that Brazil's average per capita income grew by 220% in the high-growth years from 1960 to 1980, with a 34% decline in the share of the poor in the population. On the other hand, similarly sized Indonesia grew 108% from 1971 to 1987, with a 42% decline in poverty incidence. And some of the ground gained on poverty

was subsequently lost in Brazil in the 1980s and 1990s. According to World Bank estimates, in 2009, some 10.8% of the population of Brazil lived on less than $2 per day. And according to the most recent data, 6.1% actually lived in extreme poverty, with incomes below $1.25 per day (World Bank, *2013 World Development Indicators*), worse than some low-income countries such as Sri Lanka. But this may actually be an underestimate. According to a Brazilian government research institute cited by the United Nations Development Programme, an even more shocking 15% of Brazilians have incomes of less than $1 a day. However, poverty is now falling, and the recent Bolsa Familia (family stipend) government program has received high marks for addressing poverty through its "conditional cash transfers" of resources to poor families, provided that they keep children vaccinated and in school; it is similar to the Mexican Progresa/Oportunidades program that is the subject of the end-of-chapter case study for Chapter 8. It must also be mentioned that physical security remains a pressing problem in Brazil, with violent gangs having extensive sway. This problem can have the greatest negative impact on people living in poverty.

Inequality

For decades, Brazil's inequality in income (as well as in land and other assets) has ranked among the worst in the world. High inequality not only produces social strains but can also ultimately retard growth, as examined in detail in Chapter 5. The degree of income inequality in Brazil is reflected in the low share of income going to the bottom 60% and the high share to the top 10% of the population, as seen in the following income distribution data for Brazil (2009 survey data, from the *2013 World Development Indicators*):

Fraction of Population	Share Received (%)
Lowest 10%	0.8
Lowest 20%	2.9
Second 20%	7.1
Third 20%	12.4
Fourth 20%	19.0
Highest 20%	58.6
Highest 10%	42.9

As these figures show, the top 10% of income earners receive about 43% of national income, while the bottom 40% receive just 10%. The UNDP concludes that high inequality is the reason for the high level of extreme poverty and the very slow rate of poverty reduction. Inequality in assets is also high. In recent years, inequality in Brazil has moderated somewhat, although it remains among the highest in the world. In addition to Bolsa Familia and other social program innovations, Brazilian analysts generally conclude that a recent increase in (and enforcement of) the minimum wage also has reduced inequality; this has had, wide impact as many local government workers receive the minimum wage.

Land Reform

Land is very unequally distributed in Brazil, and there is both an efficiency and a social equity case for land reform (a subject discussed in Chapter 9). But land reform has been repeatedly blocked in Brazil by the political power of large plantation owners (*fazenderos*). In response, impoverished farmers in the "landless movement," or MST, have increasingly seized land, often arable but unused land within large plantations. Thousands of families have taken part. Farmers have also settled in fragile rain forest areas, finding themselves unable to acquire land in areas that are more agriculturally suitable and less ecologically sensitive. In response, the government has initiated a land reform program, but the results to date have been modest in relation to the scope of the problem.

Sustainability of Development

As described in Chapter 10, growth that relies on running down the natural environment is contrasted with sustainable development, which preserves the ecology on which future income and people's health vitally depend. But Brazilians across the political spectrum appear determined not to acknowledge destruction of forests as a genuine or pressing problem. Deforestation of the Brazilian Amazon rain forest displays conflicts between short- and long-term development goals and the consequences of huge inequality and state intervention on behalf of the rich. Despite their destructiveness, economic activities in the Amazon often benefited in the past from ill-conceived subsidies, now curtailed. Grandiose showcase development projects and schemes, such as subsidized ore mining, charcoal-consuming industries, and cattle ranching, were carried out on a large scale.

The encouragement of rain forest settlement seemed to be a politically inexpensive alternative to land reform. In the end, the best lands became concentrated in the hands of large, powerful farmers. Rights of indigenous peoples were flagrantly violated, with some terrible atrocities committed by settlers. Ecological campaigners and activists among rubber-tappers whose livelihoods were threatened were attacked and sometimes murdered. In the meantime, much of these fragile lands appears to have become irreversibly degraded. Many of the subsidies have now been withdrawn, and at least some protections and "extractive reserves" have been put in place, but rain forest destruction is hard to reverse. Forest management in other tropical rain forests has led to a rapid growth in ecotourism and very high, profitable, and sustainable fruit yields. Products that can be harvested without serious ecological disruption include fibers, latex, resins, gums, medicines, and game. However, it is clear that this cannot protect land on the vast scale at risk. Because the rest of the world benefits from Brazil's rain forests through prevention of global warming, ecological cleansing, and the irreplaceable biodiversity needed for future antibiotics and other medicines and goods, the international community should be prepared to pay something to ensure its continuation, such as paying forest dwellers to preserve and protect natural resources. Financial support for land reform outside sensitive areas is one clear direction.

Problems of Social Inclusion

Few discussions about poverty in Brazil pay much attention to race. But about half of the population of Brazil is of African or mulatto heritage. As a result, it is sometimes noted that Brazil is the world's largest black nation after Nigeria. And most of the poor in Brazil are black or mulatto. Although racial discrimination is a crime in Brazil, no one has ever been sent to jail for it. According to one estimate, the average black worker receives only 41% of the salary of the average white worker. Most of the millions of Brazilians living in the worst *favelas*, or shantytown slums, are black. The endemic extreme poverty of the Northeast, which has lagged development standards of the Southeast for decades, afflicts indigenous and mulatto populations. Although the Northeast has only about 30% of Brazil's population, an estimated 62% of the country's extreme poor live

in the region. Black representation in government is shockingly rare, even in the states where nonwhites make up a majority of the population. University places are overwhelmingly claimed by whites. Some progress has been made, but Brazil may need a stronger movement comparable to the U.S. civil rights struggle of the 1960s. But in the absence of overt Jim Crow laws, it is sometimes hard to identify the appropriate target. Some form of meaningful affirmative action may be the only way to begin to overcome the problem.

Conclusion

It might be most accurate to say that Brazil has experienced some economic growth without as much social development as could be expected from its income level, rather than the more blanketing "growth without development," which applies better to countries such as Pakistan, Gabon, and Equatorial Guinea. But continuing racial disparities, unjust treatment of indigenous peoples, lack of access of the poor to fertile land, extremely high inequality and surprisingly high poverty for its income level, and the danger that growth will prove ecologically unsustainable all mean that Brazil will have to continue its recent efforts to make social inclusion and human development, as well as environmental sustainability, top priorities if it is to resume and maintain rapid economic growth, let alone achieve true multidimensional development.

Part of the explanation for high rates of income poverty and poor social indicators in Brazil is the relatively slower growth that has prevailed since the early 1980s, excepting its recent spurt. But a major explanation is that government social spending on health, education, pensions, unemployment benefits, and other transfers are going to the well-off, frequently to those in the top 20% of income distribution. Government policy has often had the effect of worsening inequality rather than softening it. The Bolsa Familia program is an important recent exception that has made a substantial impact in Brazil. Bolsa Familia transfers income to poor families on the condition that their children stay in school, thus providing current consumption as well as the potential of future higher earnings for families trapped in chronic poverty.

In November 2002, the left-leaning labor leader Luiz Inacio Lula da Silva, known universally as

Lula, was elected president of Brazil on a platform promising greater equity. This generated a lot of excitement in the country, with renewed hopes for greater social inclusion; his first term saw some renewal of growth and a greater public policy focus on poverty, with some improvements in the *favelas* and better rural nutrition, for example, but the rate of progress on social inclusion was disappointingly slow for many Brazilians. Lula was reelected in 2006, and the general view is that the following four years went well, with steadier growth and significant improvements in many social indicators; and Lula's Worker's Party successor, Dilma Rousset—who was imprisoned and tortured during military rule—won the 2010 presidential election to become the first woman to lead Brazil. But substantial unrest emerged in the country in 2013, and many questions remain. Many Brazilians find the contrast between slum neighborhoods and gleaming new sports facilities that can be seen from them a grating reminder of dubious development priorities. Can steady progress be made on the racial divide, physical security, environmental decay, poverty, inequality, high borrowing costs, needed diversification of exports, and high and inefficient government spending? If so, the outlook for Brazil is bright.

Sources

Anderson, Anthony B. "Smokestacks in the rainforest: Industrial development and deforestation in the Amazon basin." *World Development* 18 (1990): 1191–1205.

Anderson, Anthony B., ed. *Alternatives to Deforestation.* New York: Columbia University Press, 1990.

Assunção, Juliano, "Land reform and landholdings in Brazil," UNU-WIDER Research Paper No. 2006/137, November 2006.

Baer, Werner. *The Brazilian Economy: Growth and Development.* Boulder, Colo.: Rienner, 2008.

Bank Information Center. *Funding Ecological and Social Destruction: The World Bank and the IMF.* Washington, D.C.: Bank Information Center, 1990.

Bauman, Renato, and Helson C. Braga. "Export financing in the LDCs: The role of subsidies for export performance in Brazil." *World Development* 16 (1988): 821–833.

Binswanger, Hans P. "Brazilian policies that encourage deforestation in the Amazon." *World Development* 19 (1991): 821–829.

Dinsmoor, James. *Brazil: Responses to the Debt Crisis.* Washington, D.C.: Inter-American Development Bank, 1990.

Downing, Theodore E., Susanna B. Hecht, and Henry A. Pearson, eds. *Development or Destruction? The Conversion of Tropical Forest to Pasture in Latin America.* Boulder, Colo: Westview Press, 1992.

The Economist, Special Report on Brazil (November 14, 2009): http://www.economist.com/specialreports/displayStory.cfm?story_id=E1_TQRNJQRV.

Erber, Fabio Stefano. "The development of the electronics complex and government policies in Brazil." *World Development* 13 (1985): 293–310.

Fields, Gary. *Poverty Inequality and Development.* New York: Cambridge University Press, 1980.

Hausmann, Ricardo, Dani Rodrik, and Andrés Velasco. "Growth diagnostics." In *One Economics, Many Recipes: Globalization, Institutions, and Economic Growth,* by Dani Rodrik. Princeton, N.J.: Princeton University Press, 2007.

Hausmann Ricardo. "In search of the chains that hold Brazil back." October 31, 2008. http://papers.ssrn.com/sol3/papers.cfm?abstract_id=1338262.

INCRA (Brazilian agency for land reform), http://www.incra.gov.br.

Sercovich, Francisco Colman. "Brazil." *World Development* 12 (1984): 575–600.

Siddiqi, Faraaz, and Harry Anthony Patrinos. *Child Labor: Issues, Causes, and Interventions.* World Bank, n.d. http://www.worldbank.org.

United Nations Development Programme. *Human Poverty Report, 2000–2009* (annual). New York: United Nations, 2000–2009.

World Bank. *Eradicating Child Labor in Brazil.* Washington, D.C.: World Bank, 2001.

———. *Global Monitoring Report, 2007.* Washington, D.C.: World Bank, 2007. (See in particular Table A.1, p. 226.)

———. *World Development Indicators, 2010.* Washington, D.C.: World Bank, 2010.

Yusuf, Shahid. *Globalization and the Challenge for Developing Countries.* Washington, D.C.: World Bank, 2001. ■

Notes: The Instituto Brasileiro de Geografia e Estatística (IBGE) provides data on Brazil that supplements that found in the World Development Indicators and other international sources. See www.ibge.gov.br/english. This case study benefits greatly from annual exchanges on evolving policies and conditions with Brazilian civil servants.

Concepts for Review

Absolute Poverty	Gross domestic product	Sector
Attitudes	Gross national income (GNI)	Self-esteem
Capabilities	Income per capita	Social system
Developing countries	Institutions	Subsistence economy
Development	Less developed countries	Sustenance
Development economics	Millennium Development Goals	Traditional economics
Freedom	(MDGs)	Values
Functionings	More developed countries (MDCs)	
Globalization	Political economy	

All boldfaced terms that appear in the text are listed in Concepts for Review at the end of each chapter. A glossary at the back of the book provides quick-reference definitions for these and other, more general economic concepts.

Questions for Discussion

1. Why is economics central to an understanding of the problems of development?

2. Is the concept of the developing world a useful one? Why or why not?

3. What do you hope to gain from this course on development economics?

4. Briefly describe the various definitions of the term *development* encountered in the text. What are the strengths and weaknesses of each approach? Do you think that there are other dimensions of development not mentioned in the text? If so, describe them. If not, explain why you believe that the text description of development is adequate.

5. Why is an understanding of development crucial to policy formulation in developing nations? Do you think it is possible for a nation to agree on a rough definition of *development* and orient its strategies accordingly?

6. Why is a strictly economic definition of *development* inadequate? What do you understand *economic development* to mean? Can you give hypothetical or real examples of situations in which a country may be developing economically but may still be underdeveloped?

7. How does the concept of "capabilities to function" help us gain insight into development goals and achievements? Is money enough? Why or why not?

8. What forces may be at work in giving the Millennium Development Goals such a high profile in international economic relations?

9. What critical issues are raised from the examination of development problems and prospects facing Brazil?

10. It has been said that ending extreme poverty and achieving genuine development are *possible* but not *inevitable* and that this gives the study of economic development its moral and intellectual urgency. What is meant by this? Comment and evaluate.

Notes

1. United Nations Development Programme, "The Rise of the South: Human Progress in a Diverse World," *Human Development Report 2013.* New York: United Nations Development Programme, 2003. Poverty figures are drawn from the World Bank.

2. "Voices of the Poor" boxed quotations throughout the text are for the most part drawn from the World Bank "Voices of the Poor" Web site, http://www.worldbank.org/poverty/voices/overview.htm. The Voices project was undertaken as background for the World Development Report, *Attacking Poverty*. The results were published for the World Bank by Oxford University Press in a three-volume series titled *Can Anyone Hear Us? Crying Out for Change*, and *From Many Lands*, edited by Deepa Narayan.

3. See Paul Krugman, "Toward a counter-counter-revolution in development theory," *Proceedings of the World Bank Annual Conference on Development Economics, 1992* (Washington, D.C.: World Bank, 1993), p. 15. See also Syed Nawab Haider Naqvi, "The significance of development economics," *World Development* 24 (1996): 975–987.

4. For a classic argument on the role of values in development economics, see Gunnar Myrdal, *The Challenge of World Poverty* (New York: Pantheon, 1970), ch. 1. A more general critique of the idea that economics can be "value-free" is to be found in Robert Heilbroner's "Economics as a 'value-free' science," *Social Research* 40 (1973): 129–143, and his *Behind the Veil of Economics* (New York: Norton, 1988). See also Barbara Ingham, "The meaning of development: Interactions between 'new' and 'old' ideas," *World Development* 21 (1993): 1816–1818; Paul P. Streeten, *Strategies for Human Development* (Copenhagen: Handelshøjskolens Forlag, 1994), pt. 1; Selo Soemardjan and Kenneth W. Thompson, eds., *Culture, Development, and Democracy* (New York: United Nations University Press, 1994); and Mozaffar Qizilbash, "Ethical development," *World Development* 24 (1996): 1209–1221.

5. Soedjatmoko and Anne Elizabeth Murase, *The Primacy of Freedom in Development* (Lanham, Md.: University Press of America, 1985), p. 11.

6. Dudley Seers, "The meaning of development," paper presented at the Eleventh World Conference of the Society for International Development, New Delhi (1969), p. 3. See also Richard Brinkman, "Economic growth versus economic development: Toward a conceptual clarification," *Journal of Economic Issues* 29 (1995): 1171–1188; and P. Jegadish Gandhi, "The concept of development: Its dialectics and dynamics," *Indian Journal of Applied Economics* 5 (1996): 283–311.

7. Denis Goulet, *The Cruel Choice: A New Concept in the Theory of Development* (New York: Atheneum, 1971), p. 23. Reprinted with permission from Ana Maria Goulet.

8. Amartya Sen, "Development Thinking at the Beginning of the 21st Century." In *Economic and Social Development in the XXI Century.* Emmerij, Luis (Ed.) Inter-American Development Bank and Johns Hopkins University Press, Washington, D.C. [Also available as LSE working paper, Copyright Amartya Sen, at http://eprints.lse.ac.uk/6711/.] See also Sen, *Commodities and Capabilities* (Amsterdam: Elsevier, 1985). We thank Sabina Alkire and James Foster for their helpful suggestions on updating this section for the Twelfth Edition to reflect Professor Sen's latest thinking on his capability approach, including ideas reflected in his recent book, *The Idea of Justice*.

9. Amartya Sen, *Commodities and Capabilities*, p. 12.

10. Sen, *Commodities and Capabilities*, pp. 25–26; and *Development as Freedom*, pp. 70–71.

11. Sen, *Commodities and Capabilities*, pp. 25–26. From *Commodities and Capabilities* by Amartya Sen. Copyright © 1999 by Amartya Sen. Reprinted with permission.

12. Ibid., p. 21. Sen points out that even if we identify utility with "desire fulfillment," we still suffer from the twin defects of "physical-condition neglect" and "valuation neglect." He notes that "valuing is not the same thing as desiring." Ignoring a person's objectively deprived physical condition just because the person considers this subjectively unimportant yields an obviously defective measure of well-being. The paper by Foster and Handy is "External Capabilities," in *Arguments for a Better World: Essays in Honor of Amartya Sen*, eds. Kaushik Basu and Ravi Kanbur (Oxford: Oxford University Press, 2008).

13. Ibid., pp. 10–11. From *Commodities and Capabilities* by Amartya Sen. Copyright © 1999 by Amartya Sen. Reprinted with permission.

14. Amartya Sen, *Commodities and Capabilities*, p. 13.

14a. See, for example, William Easterly, "The political economy of growth without development: A case study of Pakistan," in *In Search of Prosperity: Analytic Narratives on Economic Growth*, ed. Dani Rodrik (Princeton, N.J.: Princeton University Press, 2003).

15. Sen, *Commodities and Capabilities*, p. 52.

16. See Richard Layard, *Happiness: Lessons from a New Science* (New York: Penguin, 2005), esp. pp. 32–35 and 62–70. The data on happiness and satisfaction are based on an average of the two responses. For more on the underlying data and analysis, see http://cep.lse.ac.uk/layard/annex.pdf. For a critique of some aspects of this research, see Martin Wolf, "Why progressive taxation is not the route to happiness," *Financial Times*, June 6, 2007, p. 12. For an excellent review of the literature through 2010 that puts the data and their interpretation in useful perspective, see Carol Graham, *Happiness around the World: The Paradox of Happy Peasants and Miserable Millionaires* (New York: Oxford University Press, 2010).

17. For the revised happiness index formula being considered in Bhutan, see http://www.grossnationalhappiness.com/gnhIndex/introductionGNH.aspx. The formula is closely related to the Alkire-Foster Multidimensional Poverty Index, introduced in Chapter 5. For earlier background see Andrew C. Revkin, "A new measure of well-being from a happy little kingdom," *New York Times*, October 4, 2005, http://www.nytimes.com/2005/10/04/science/04happ.html.

18. Commission on the Measurement of Economic Performance and Social Progress, p. 16, http://www.stiglitz-sen-fitoussi.fr/documents/rapport_anglais.pdf accessed November 12, 2010.

19. See Goulet, *Cruel Choice*, pp. 87–94.

20. For a description of the "basic needs" approach, see Pradip K. Ghosh, ed., *Third World Development: A Basic Needs Approach* (Westport, Conn.: Greenwood Press, 1984).

21. Goulet, *Cruel Choice*, p. 124.

22. For an early attempt to specify and quantify the concept of basic needs, see International Labor Organization, *Employment, Growth, and Basic Needs* (Geneva: International Labor Organization, 1976). A similar view with a focus on the notion of entitlements and capabilities can be found in Amartya Sen, "Development: Which way now?" *Economic Journal* 93 (1983): 754–757. See also United Nations Development Programme, *Human Development Report, 1994* (New York: Oxford University Press, 1994).

23. Goulet, *Cruel Choice*, p. 90. For an even more provocative discussion of the meaning of individual self-esteem and respect in the context of Latin American development, see Paulo Freire, *Pedagogy of the Oppressed* (New York: Continuum, 1990).

24. W. Arthur Lewis, "Is economic growth desirable?" in *The Theory of Economic Growth* (London: Allen & Unwin, 1963), p. 420. For an outstanding and thoughtful analysis of the importance of freedom in development by a leading Developing World intellectual, see Soedjatmoko, *Primacy of Freedom*. See also Sen, *Development as Freedom*.

25. For a "political freedom index," see United Nations Development Programme, *Human Development Report, 1992* (New York: Oxford University Press, 1992), pp. 20, 26–33. The Heritage Foundation and the *Wall Street Journal* produce an annual "Index of Economic Freedom." For 2014 rankings of 165 countries from "free" to "repressed," see http://www.heritage.org/index/.

26. For a commentary from the UNDP on why its freedom index was discontinued, see United Nations Development Programme, *Human Development Report, 2000*, pp. 90–93, esp. box 5.2, at http://hdr.undp.org/docs/statistics/understanding/resources/HDR2000_5_2_freedom_indices.pdf.

27. United Nations Development Programme, *Human Development Report, 2003—Millennium Development Goals: A Compact among Nations to End Human Poverty* (New York: Oxford University Press, 2003), also available at http://hdr.undp.org/reports/global/2003.

28. The United Nations issues annual reports on progress and challenges toward achieving the MDGs. The 2006 and 2009 reports, on which this section also draws, can be accessed at http://mdgs.un.org. The World Bank also publishes the *Global Monitoring Report* on the MDGs. The 2010 monitoring report found that the global economic crisis slowed progress on poverty reduction, hunger, child and maternal health, access to clean water, and disease control, and is expected to have impacts beyond 2015. See *Global Monitoring Report 2010: The MDGs after the Crisis*, January 1, 2010, at http://web.worldbank.org. See Report of the Secretary-General, *Keeping the Promise: A Forward-Looking Review to*

Promote an Agreed Action Agenda to Achieve the Millennium Development Goals by 2015, February 12, 2010 http://www.un.org/ga/search/view_doc.asp?symbol=A/64/665.

29. Despite some disappointments of slow rates of achievement of several targets in some regions, the September 2010 UN summit to review progress on the MDGs underscored its role as a global rallying point and measure of development success.

30. See Jan Vandemoortele, "Can the MDGs foster a new partnership for pro-poor policies?" in *NGOs and the Millennium Development Goals: Citizen Action to Reduce Poverty*, eds. Jennifer Brinkerhoff, Stephen C. Smith, and Hildy Teegen (New York: Palgrave Macmillan, 2007), and Sabina Alkire with James Foster, "The MDGs: Multidimensionality and Interconnection," at www.ophi.org.uk/wp-content/uploads/OPHI-RP-8a.pdf.

31. High-Level Panel of Eminent Persons on the Post-2015 Development Agenda, *A New Global Partnership: Eradicate Poverty and Transform Economies Through Sustainable Development: The Report of the High-Level Panel of Eminent Persons on the Post-2015 Development Agenda*, May 30, 2013, http://www.post2015hlp.org/featured/high-level-panel-releases-recommendations-for-worlds-next-development-agenda.

Comparative Economic Development

2

Among countries colonized by European powers during the past 500 years, those that were relatively rich in 1500 are now relatively poor....The reversal reflects changes in the institutions resulting from European colonialism.
— *Daron Acemoglu, Simon Johnson, and James A. Robinson, 2002*

Emerging powers in the developing world are already sources of innovative social and economic policies and are major trade, investment, and increasingly development cooperation partners for other developing countries.
— *Helen Clark, Administrator, United Nations Development Programme, 2012*

The developing world has made substantial economic development progress in recent years. But the most striking feature of the global economy remains its extreme contrasts. Output per worker in the United States is about 10 times higher than it is in India and more than 50 times higher than in the Democratic Republic of Congo (DRC).[1] In 2011, real income per capita was $48,820 in the United States, $3,640 in India, and $340 in the DRC.[2] If the world were a single country, its income would be distributed more unequally than every nation except Namibia.[3] There are also enormous gaps in measures of welfare. Life expectancy is 79 in the United States, 65 in India, and just 48 in the DRC. The percent of children who are underweight is less than 3% in the United States but 43% in India and 24% in the DRC. Whereas almost all women are literate in the United States, just 51% are in India and 57% in the DRC.[4] How did such wide disparities come about? In today's world, with so much knowledge and with the movement of people, information, and goods and services so rapid and comparatively inexpensive, how have such large gaps managed to persist and even widen? Why have some developing countries made so much progress in closing these gaps while others have made so little?

In this chapter, we introduce the study of comparative economic development. We begin by defining the developing world and describing how development is measured so as to allow for quantitative comparisons across countries. Average income is one, but only one, of the factors defining a country's level of economic development. This is to be expected, given the discussion of the meaning of development in Chapter 1.

We then consider 10 important features that developing countries tend to have in common, on average, in comparison with the developed world. In each case, we also discover that behind these averages are very substantial differences in all of these dimensions among developing countries that are important to appreciate and take into account in development policy. These areas are the following:

1. Lower levels of living and productivity

2. Lower levels of human capital

3. Higher levels of inequality and absolute poverty

4. Higher population growth rates

5. Greater social fractionalization

6. Larger rural populations but rapid rural-to-urban migration

7. Lower levels of industrialization

8. Adverse geography

9. Underdeveloped financial and other markets

10. Lingering colonial impacts such as poor institutions and often external dependence.

The mix and severity of these challenges largely set the development constraints and policy priorities of a developing nation.

After reviewing these commonalities and differences among developing countries, we further consider key differences between conditions in today's developing countries and those in now developed countries at an early stage of their development, and we examine the controversy over whether developing and developed countries are now converging in their levels of development.

We then draw on recent scholarship on comparative economic development to further clarify how such an unequal world came about and remained so persistently unequal, and we shed some light on the positive factors behind recent rapid progress in a significant portion of the developing world. It becomes quite clear that colonialism played a major role in shaping institutions that set the "rules of the economic game," which can limit or facilitate opportunities for economic development. We examine other factors in comparative development, such as nations' levels of inequality. We will come to appreciate why so many developing countries have such difficulties in achieving economic development but also will begin to see some of the outlines of what can be done to overcome obstacles and encourage faster progress even among today's least developed countries.

The chapter concludes with a comparative case study of Bangladesh and Pakistan.

2.1 Defining the Developing World

The most common way to define the developing world is by per capita income. Several international agencies, including the Organization for Economic Cooperation and Development (OECD) and the United Nations, offer classifications of countries by their economic status, but the best-known system is that of the International Bank for Reconstruction and Development (IBRD), more commonly known as the **World Bank**. (The World Bank is examined in detail in Box 13.2). In the World Bank's classification system, 213 economies with a population of at least 30,000 are ranked by their levels of gross national income (GNI) per capita. These economies are then classified as **low-income countries (LICs)**, lower-middle-income countries (LMCs), upper-middle-income countries (UMCs), high-income OECD countries, and other high-income countries. (Often, LMCs and UMCs are informally grouped as the **middle-income countries**.)

With a number of important exceptions, the developing countries are those with low-, lower-middle, or upper-middle incomes. These countries are grouped by their geographic region in Table 2.1, making them easier to identify on the map in Figure 2.1. The most common cutoff points for these categories are those used by the World Bank: Low-income countries are defined as having a per capita gross national income in 2011 of $1,025 or less; lower-middle-income countries have incomes between $1,026 and $4,035; upper-middle-income countries have incomes between $4,036 and $12,475; and high-income countries have incomes of $12,476 or more. Comparisons of incomes for several countries are shown graphically in Figure 2.2.

Note that a number of the countries grouped as "other high-income economies" in Table 2.1 are sometimes classified as developing countries, such as when this is the official position of their governments. Moreover, high-income countries that have one or two highly developed export sectors but in which significant parts of the population remain relatively uneducated or in poor health, or social development is viewed as low for the country's income level, may be viewed as still developing. Examples may include oil exporters such as Saudi Arabia and the United Arab Emirates. Upper-income economies also include some tourism-dependent islands with lingering development problems, which now face daunting climate change adaptation challenges. Even a few of the high-income OECD member countries, notably Portugal and Greece, have been viewed as developing countries at least until recently—a perception that grew again with the ongoing economic crises (e.g., in October 2013 S&P Dow Jones reclassified Greece from "developed market" to "emerging market."). Nevertheless, the characterization of the developing world as sub-Saharan Africa, North Africa and the Middle East, Asia (except for Japan and, more recently South Korea and perhaps two or three other high-income economies), Latin America and the Caribbean, and the "transition" countries of eastern Europe and Central Asia including the former Soviet Union, remains a useful generalization. In contrast, the developed world constituting the core of the high-income OECD is largely comprised of the countries of western Europe, North America, Japan, Australia, and New Zealand.

Sometimes a special distinction is made among upper-middle-income or newly high-income economies, designating some that have achieved relatively

World Bank An organization known as an "international financial institution" that provides development funds to developing countries in the form of interest-bearing loans, grants, and technical assistance.

Low-income countries (LICs) In the World Bank classification, countries with a GNI per capita of less than $1,025 in 2011.

Middle-income countries In the World Bank classification, countries with a GNI per capita between $1,025 and $12,475 in 2011.

TABLE 2.1   Classification of Economies by Region and Income, 2013

Country	Code	Class	Country	Code	Class	Country	Code	Class
East Asia and the Pacific			**Latin America and the Caribbean**			**Sub-Saharan Africa**		
American Samoa‡	ASM	UMC	Antigua and Barbuda	ATG	UMC	Angola*	AGO	UMC
Cambodia*	KHM	LIC	Argentina	ARG	UMC	Benin*	BEN	LIC
China	CHN	UMC	Belize‡	BLZ	LMC	Botswana†	BWA	UMC
Fiji‡	FJI	LMC	Bolivia†	BOL	LMC	Burkina Faso*†	BFA	LIC
Indonesia	IDN	LMC	Brazil	BRA	UMC	Burundi*†	BDI	LIC
Kiribati*‡	KIR	LMC	Chile	CHL	UMC	Cameroon	CMR	LMC
(North) Korea, Dem. Rep.	PRK	LIC	Colombia	COL	UMC	Cape Verde‡	CPV	LMC
Lao PDR*†	LAO	LMC	Costa Rica	CRI	UMC	Central African Rep.*†	CAF	LIC
Malaysia	MYS	UMC	Cuba‡	CUB	UMC	Chad*†	TCD	LIC
Marshall Islands‡	MHL	LMC	Dominica‡	DMA	UMC	Comoros*‡	COM	LIC
Micronesia, Fed. Sts.‡	FSM	LMC	Dominican Republic‡	DOM	UMC	Congo, Dem. Rep.*	COD	LIC
Mongolia†	MNG	LMC	Ecuador	ECU	UMC	Congo, Rep.	COG	LMC
Myanmar	MMR	LIC	El Salvador	SLV	LMC	Côte d'Ivoire	CIV	LMC
Palau‡	PLW	UMC	Grenada‡	GRD	UMC	Eritrea*	ERI	LIC
Papua New Guinea‡	PNG	LMC	Guatemala	GTM	LMC	Ethiopia*†	ETH	LIC
Philippines	PHL	LMC	Guyana‡	GUY	LMC	Gabon	GAB	UMC
Samoa*‡	WSM	LMC	Haiti*‡	HTI	LIC	Gambia, The*	GMB	LIC
Solomon Islands*‡	SLB	LMC	Honduras	HND	LMC	Ghana	GHA	LIC
Thailand	THA	UMC	Jamaica‡	JAM	UMC	Guinea*	GIN	LIC
Timor-Leste*‡	TLS	LMC	Mexico	MEX	UMC	Guinea-Bissau*‡	GNB	LIC
Tonga‡	TON	LMC	Nicaragua	NIC	LMC	Kenya	KEN	LIC
Tuvalu	TUV	LMC	Panama	PAN	UMC	Lesotho*†	LSO	LMC
Vanuatu*‡	VUT	LMC	Paraguay†	PRY	LMC	Liberia*	LBR	LIC
Vietnam	VNM	LMC	Peru	PER	UMC	Madagascar*	MDG	LIC
Europe and Central Asia			St. Kitts and Nevis‡	KNA	UMC	Malawi*†	MWI	LIC
Albania	ALB	LMC	St. Lucia‡	LCA	UMC	Mali*†	MLI	LIC
Armenia†	ARM	LMC	St. Vincent and the			Mauritania*	MRT	LIC
Azerbaijan†	AZE	LMC	Grenadines‡	VCT	UMC	Mauritius‡	MUS	UMC
Belarus	BLR	UMC	Suriname‡	SUR	UMC	Mayotte	MYT	UMC
Bosnia and Herzegovina	BIH	UMC	Uruguay	URY	UMC	Mozambique*	MOZ	LIC
Bulgaria	BGR	UMC	Venezuela, RB	VEN	UMC	Namibia	NAM	UMC
Georgia	GEO	LMC	**Middle East and North Africa**			Niger*†	NER	LIC
Kazakhstan†	KAZ	UMC	Algeria	DZA	UMC	Nigeria	NGA	LMC
Kosovo	KSV	LMC	Djibouti*	DJI	LMC	Rwanda*†	RWA	LIC
Kyrgyz Republic†	KGZ	LIC	Egypt, Arab Rep.	EGY	LMC	Sao Tome and Principe*‡	STP	LMC
Latvia	LVA	UMC	Iran, Islamic Rep.	IRN	UMC	Senegal*	SEN	LMC
Lithuania	LTU	UMC	Iraq	IRQ	LMC	Seychelles‡	SYC	UMC
Macedonia, FYR†	MKD	UMC	Jordan	JOR	LMC	Sierra Leone*	SLE	LIC
Moldova†	MDA	LMC	Lebanon	LBN	UMC	Somalia*	SOM	LIC
Montenegro	MNE	UMC	Libya	LBY	UMC	South Africa	ZAF	UMC
Romania	ROU	UMC	Morocco	MAR	LMC	South Sudan	SSD	LIC
Russian Federation	RUS	UMC	Syrian Arab Rep.	SYR	LMC	Sudan*	SDN	LMC
Serbia	SRB	UMC	Tunisia	TUN	LMC	Swaziland†	SWZ	LMC
Tajikistan†	TJK	LIC	West Bank and Gaza	WBG	LMC	Tanzania*	TZA	LIC
Turkey	TUR	UMC	Yemen, Rep.*	YEM	LMC	Togo*	TGO	LIC
Turkmenistan†	TKM	UMC	**South Asia**			Uganda*†	UGA	LIC
Ukraine	UKR	LMC	Afghanistan*†	AFG	LIC	Zambia*†	ZMB	LMC
Uzbekistan†	UZB	LMC	Bangladesh*	BGD	LIC	Zimbabwe†	ZWE	LIC
			Bhutan*†	BTN	LMC			
			India	IND	LMC			
			Maldives*‡	MDV	UMC			
			Nepal*†	NPL	LIC			
			Pakistan	PAK	LMC			
			Sri Lanka	LKA	LMC			

(*Continued*)

TABLE 2.1   (Continued)

Country	Code	Class	Country	Code	Class	Country	Code	Class
High-Income OECD Countries			Spain	ESP		Guam‡	GUM	
Australia	AUS		Sweden	SWE		Hong Kong, China	HKG	
Austria	AUT		Switzerland	CHE		Isle of Man	IMN	
Belgium	BEL		United Kingdom	GBR		Israel	ISR	
Canada	CAN		United States	USA		Kuwait	KWT	
Czech Rep.	CZE		**Other High-Income Economies**			Liechtenstein	LIE	
Denmark	DNK		Andorra	AND		Macao, China	MAC	
Finland	FIN		Antigua and Barbuda‡	ATG		Malta	MLT	
France	FRA		Aruba‡	ABW		Monaco	MCO	
Germany	DEU		Bahamas, The‡	BHS		Netherlands Antilles‡	ANT	
Greece	GRC		Bahrain‡	BHR		New Caledonia‡	NCL	
Hungary	HUN		Barbados‡	BRB		Northern Mariana Islands‡	MNP	
Iceland	ISL		Bermuda	BMU		Oman	OMN	
Ireland	IRL		Brunei Darussalam	BRN		Poland	POL	
Italy	ITA		Cayman Islands	CYM		Puerto Rico‡	PRI	
Japan	JPN		Channel Islands	CHI		Qatar	QAT	
Korea, Rep. (South)	KOR		Croatia	HRV		San Marino	SMR	
Luxembourg	LUX		Cyprus	CYP		Saudi Arabia	SAU	
Netherlands	NLD		Estonia	EST		Singapore‡	SGP	
New Zealand	NZL		Equatorial Guinea*	GNQ		Slovenia	SVN	
Norway	NOR		Faeroe Islands	FRO		Taiwan, China	TWN	
Portugal	PRT		French Polynesia‡	PYF		Trinidad and Tobago‡	TTO	
Slovak Republic	SVK		Greenland	GRL		United Arab Emirates	ARE	

* least developed countries
† landlocked developing countries
‡ small island developing states

Source: Data from World Bank, *World Development Indicators*, 2013 (Washington, D.C.: World Bank, 2013) and WDI online; United Nations; and http://www.iso.org.

Newly industrializing countries (NICs) Countries at a relatively advanced level of economic development with a substantial and dynamic industrial sector and with close links to the international trade, finance, and investment system.

Least developed countries
A UN designation of countries with low income, low human capital, and high economic vulnerability.

Human capital Productive investments in people, such as skills, values, and health resulting from expenditures on education, on-the-job training programs, and medical care.

advanced manufacturing sectors as **newly industrializing countries (NICs)**. Yet another way to classify the nations of the developing world is through their degree of international indebtedness; the World Bank has classified countries as severely indebted, moderately indebted, and less indebted. The United Nations Development Programme (UNDP) classifies countries according to their level of human development, including health and education attainments as low, medium, high, and very high. We consider the traditional and new UNDP Human Development Indexes in detail later in the chapter.

Another widely used classification is that of the **least developed countries**, a UN designation that as of 2012 included 49 countries, 34 of them in Africa, 9 in Asia, 5 among Pacific Islands, plus Haiti. For inclusion, a country has to meet each of three criteria: low income, low **human capital**, and high economic vulnerability. Other special UN classifications include landlocked developing countries (of which there are 30, with 15 of them in Africa) and small island developing states (of which there are 38).[5]

Finally, the term *emerging markets* was introduced at the International Finance Corporation to suggest progress (avoiding the then-standard phrase *Third World* that investors seemed to associate with stagnation). While the term is appealing, we do not use it in this text for three reasons. First, *emerging market* is widely used in the financial press to suggest the presence of active stock and bond markets; although financial deepening is important, it is only one aspect of economic development. Second, referring to nations as *markets* may lead to an underemphasis on some non-market priorities in development. Third, usage varies, and there is no established or generally accepted designation of which markets should be labeled as *emerging* and which as yet to emerge (the latter now sometimes dubbed *frontier markets* in the financial press).

The simple division of the world into developed and developing countries is sometimes useful for analytical purposes. Many development models apply across a wide range of developing country income levels. However, the wide income range of the latter serves as an early warning for us not to overgeneralize. Indeed, the economic differences between low-income countries in sub-Saharan Africa and South Asia and upper-middle-income countries in East Asia and Latin America can be even more profound than those between high-income OECD and upper-middle-income developing countries.

2.2 Basic Indicators of Development: Real Income, Health, and Education

In this section, we examine basic indicators of three facets of development: real income per capita adjusted for purchasing power; health as measured by life expectancy, undernourishment, and child mortality; and educational attainments as measured by literacy and schooling.

Purchasing Power Parity

In accordance with the World Bank's income-based country classification scheme, **gross national income (GNI)** per capita, the most common measure of the overall level of economic activity, is often used as a summary index of the relative economic well-being of people in different nations. It is calculated as the total domestic and foreign **value added** claimed by a country's residents without making deductions for **depreciation** (or wearing out) of the domestic **capital stock**. **Gross domestic product (GDP)** measures the total value for final use of output produced by an economy, by both residents and nonresidents. Thus, GNI comprises GDP plus the difference between the income residents receive from abroad for factor services (labor and capital) less payments made to nonresidents who contribute to the domestic economy. Where there is a large nonresident population playing a major role in the domestic economy (such as foreign corporations), these differences can be significant (see Chapter 12). In 2011, the total national income of all the nations of the world was valued at more than U.S. $66 trillion, of which about $47 trillion originated in the economically developed high-income regions and about $19 trillion was generated in the less developed nations, despite their representing about five-sixths of the world's population. In 2011, Norway had 240 times the per capita income of Ethiopia and 63 times that of India.

Per capita GNI comparisons between developed and less developed countries like those shown in Figure 2.2 are, however, exaggerated by the use of official foreign-exchange rates to convert national currency figures into U.S. dollars. This conversion does not measure the relative domestic purchasing

Gross national income (GNI)   The total domestic and foreign output claimed by residents of a country, consisting of gross domestic product (GDP) plus factor incomes earned by foreign residents, minus income earned in the domestic economy by nonresidents.

Value added   The portion of a product's final value that is added at each stage of production.

Depreciation (of the capital stock)   The wearing out of equipment, buildings, infrastructure, and other forms of capital, reflected in write-offs to the value of the capital stock.

Capital stock   The total amount of physical goods existing at a particular time that have been produced for use in the production of other goods and services.

Gross domestic product (GDP)   The total final output of goods and services produced by the country's economy within the country's territory by residents and nonresidents, regardless of its allocation between domestic and foreign claims.

FIGURE 2.1   Nations of the World, Classified by GNI Per Capita

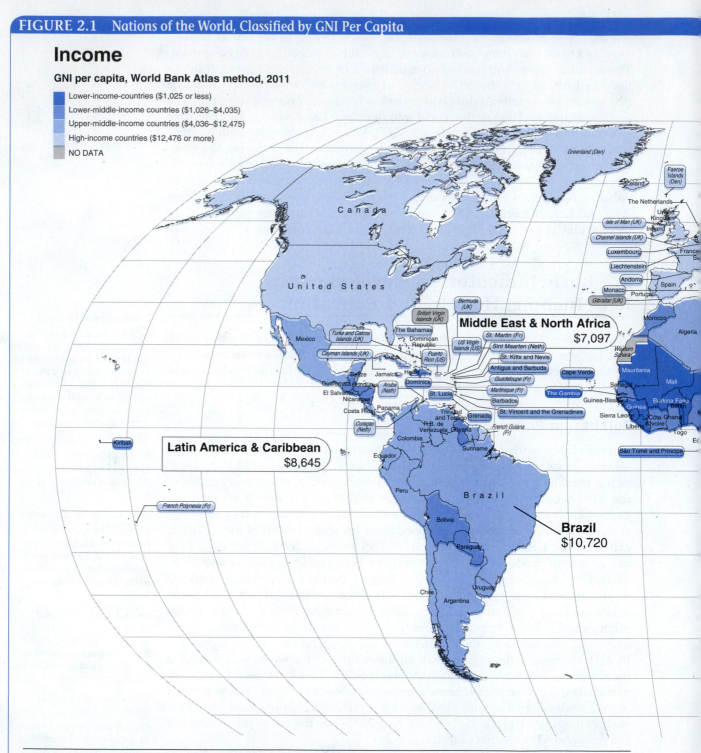

Income

GNI per capita, World Bank Atlas method, 2011

- Lower-income-countries ($1,025 or less)
- Lower-middle-income countries ($1,026–$4,035)
- Upper-middle-income countries ($4,036–$12,475)
- High-income countries ($12,476 or more)
- NO DATA

Middle East & North Africa $7,097

Latin America & Caribbean $8,645

Brazil $10,720

Source: Data from *Atlas of Global Development*, 4th ed., pp. 16-17: World Bank and Collins. 2013. *ATLAS OF GLOBAL DEVELOPMENT: A VISUAL GUIDE TO THE WORLD'S GREATEST CHALLENGES, FOURTH EDITION.* Washington, DC and Glasgow: World Bank and Collins. doi: 10.1596/978-0-8213-9757-2. License: Creative Commons Attribution CC BY 3.0

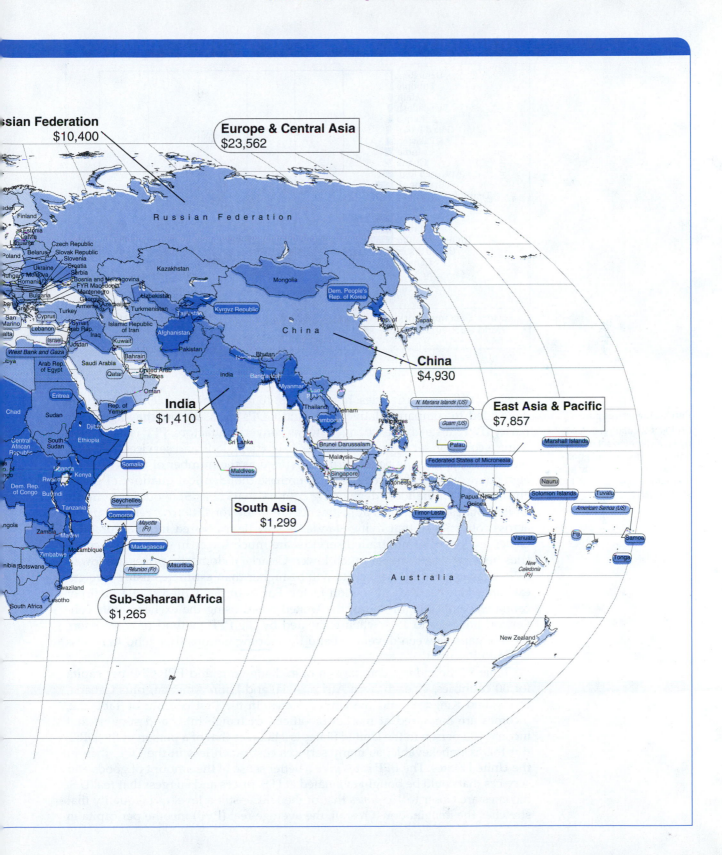

Russian Federation
$10,400

Europe & Central Asia
$23,562

China
$4,930

India
$1,410

East Asia & Pacific
$7,857

South Asia
$1,299

Sub-Saharan Africa
$1,265

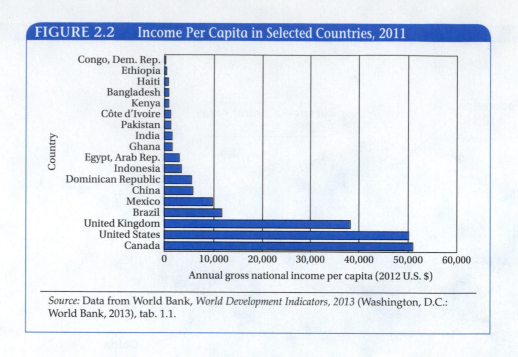

FIGURE 2.2   Income Per Capita in Selected Countries, 2011

Annual gross national income per capita (2012 U.S. $)

Source: Data from World Bank, *World Development Indicators, 2013* (Washington, D.C.: World Bank, 2013), tab. 1.1.

power of different currencies. In an attempt to rectify this problem, researchers have tried to compare relative GNIs and GDPs by using **purchasing power parity (PPP)** instead of exchange rates as conversion factors. PPP is calculated using a common set of international prices for all goods and services. In a simple version, *purchasing power parity* is defined as the number of units of a foreign country's currency required to purchase the identical quantity of goods and services in the local developing country market as $1 would buy in the United States. In practice, adjustments are made for differing relative prices across countries so that living standards may be measured more accurately.[6] Generally, prices of nontraded services are much lower in developing countries because wages are so much lower. Clearly, if domestic prices are lower, PPP measures of GNI per capita will be higher than estimates using foreign-exchange rates as the conversion factor. For example, China's 2011 GNI per capita was only 10% of that of the United States using the exchange-rate conversion but rises to 17% when estimated by the PPP method of conversion. Income gaps between developed and developing nations thus tend to be less when PPP is used.

Table 2.2 provides a comparison of exchange rate and PPP GNI per capita for 30 countries, 10 each from Africa, Asia, and Latin America, plus Canada, the United Kingdom and the United States. In the first column of Table 2.2, incomes are measured at market or official exchange rates and suggest that income of a person in the United States is 242 times that of a person in the DRC. But this is unbelievable, as many services cost much less in the DRC than in the United States. The PPP rates give a better sense of the amount of goods and services that could be bought evaluated at U.S. prices and suggest that real U.S. incomes are closer to 135 *times* that of the DRC—still a level of inequality that stretches the imagination. Overall, the average real (PPP) income per capita in

	GNI Per Capita (U.S. $)	
Country	**Exchange Rate**	**Purchasing Power Parity**
Bangladesh	770	1,910
Bolivia	2,020	4,890
Botswana	7,070	15,550
Brazil	10,700	11,410
Cambodia	800	2,180
Canada	46,730	41,390
Chile	12,270	19,820
China	4,940	8,390
Colombia	6,090	9,600
Congo, Dem. Rep.	200	360
Costa Rica	7,660	11,910
Côte d'Ivoire	1,140	1,780
Dominican Republic	5,190	9,350
Egypt, Arab Rep.	2,760	6,440
Ghana	1,420	1,830
Guatemala	2,870	4,760
Haiti	700	1,190
India	1,450	3,680
Indonesia	2,930	4,480
Kenya	810	1,690
Korea, Rep.	20,870	29,860
Mexico	8,970	15,930
Niger	330	600
Nigeria	1,260	2,270
Pakistan	1,120	2,880
Peru	5,120	9,390
Philippines	2,200	4,120
Senegal	1,070	1,940
Thailand	4,620	8,710
Uganda	470	1,230
United Kingdom	37,840	35,950
United States	48,550	48,820
Vietnam	1,270	3,250
Low income	554	1,310
Middle income	3,923	6,802
High income	36,390	36,472

TABLE 2.2 A Comparison of Per Capita GNI in Selected Developing Countries, the United Kingdom, and the United States, Using Official Exchange-Rate and Purchasing Power Parity Conversions, 2011

Source: Data from World Bank, *World Development Indicators, 2013* (Washington, D.C.: World Bank, 2013), tab. 1.1.

high-income countries is more than 28 times that in low-income countries and more than 5 times higher than in middle-income countries.

Indicators of Health and Education

Besides average incomes, it is necessary to evaluate a nation's average health and educational attainments, which reflect core capabilities. Table 2.3 shows some basic indicators of income, health (the under-5 mortality rate for 1990 and 2011, plus the rate of malnutrition and life expectancy), and education

TABLE 2.3   Commonality and Diversity: Some Basic Indicators

	Prevalence of Malnutrition Underweight % of Children Under Age 5	Primary Completion Rate Total % of Relevant Age Group		Under-5 Mortality Rate Total per 1,000 Live Births		Life Expectancy
	2005-11	1991	2011	1990	2011	
Bangladesh	41.3	46	..	139	46	69
Bolivia	4.5	71	95	120	51	67
Botswana	11.2	89	97	53	26	53
Brazil	2.2	92	..	58	16	73
Cambodia	29	38	90	117	43	63
Central African Republic	28	28	43	169	164	48
Chile	0.5	..	95	19	9	79
China	3.4	109	..	49	15	73
Colombia	3.4	73	112	34	18	74
Congo, Dem. Rep.	28.2	49	61	181	168	48
Costa Rica	1.1	80	99	17	10	79
Côte d'Ivoire	29.4	43	59	151	115	55
Cuba	1.3	94	99	13	6	79
Dominican Republic	3.4	63	92	58	25	73
Egypt, Arab Rep.	6.8	..	98	86	21	73
Ethiopia	29.2	23	58	198	77	59
Ghana	14.3	65	94	121	78	64
Guatemala	13	..	86	78	30	71
India	43.5	63	97	114	61	65
Indonesia	18.6	89	108	82	32	69
Mexico	3.4	88	104	49	16	77
Mozambique	18.3	27	56	226	103	50
Niger	39.9	18	46	314	125	55
Nigeria	26.7	..	74	214	124	52
Pakistan	30.9	..	67	122	72	65
Peru	4.5	..	97	75	18	74
Philippines	20.7	89	92	57	25	69
Senegal	19.2	41	63	136	65	59
Uganda	16.4	..	55	178	90	54
Vietnam	20.2	..	104	50	22	75
Low income	22.6	46	67	164	95	59
Middle income	16	83	94	82	46	69
High income	1.7	97	101	12	6	79
East Asia & Pacific	5.5	84	..	..	21	72
Latin America & Caribbean	3.1	84	102	53	19	74
Middle East & North Africa	6.3	77	91	70	32	72
South Asia	33.2	63	88	119	62	66
Sub-Saharan Africa	21.4	52	69	178	109	55

Note: Some of the specific countries listed in Table 2.3 differ from those listed in Table 2.2 due to differing availability of the most recent comparable data by topic; for example, primary completion rate was not available for Haiti; and income was not available for Cuba.

Source: World Bank, *World Development Indicators 2013*, and World Bank WDI online, accessed 1 August 2013.

(the primary completion rate for 1991 and 2011). (Each country's region and income grouping can be found in Table 2.1). Life expectancy is the average number of years newborn children would live if subjected to the mortality risks prevailing for their cohort at the time of their birth. Undernourishment means consuming too little food to maintain normal levels of activity; it is what is often called the problem of hunger. High fertility can be both a cause and a consequence of underdevelopment, so the birth rate is reported as another basic indicator. Literacy is the fraction of adult males and females reported or estimated to have basic abilities to read and write; functional literacy is generally lower than the reported numbers.

Table 2.3 shows these data for the low-, lower-middle-, upper-middle-, and high-income country groups. The table also shows averages from five developing regions (East Asia and the Pacific, Latin America and the Caribbean, the Middle East and North Africa, South Asia, and sub-Saharan Africa) and from 30 illustrative countries balanced across developing regions similar to those in Table 2.2 (with a few substitutions due to data availability).

Note that in addition to big differences across these income groupings, the low-income countries are themselves a very diverse group with greatly differing development challenges.

For example, even Bangladesh has a real income that is now more than five times greater than the DRC; and India's income is more than 10 times greater. Under-5 malnutrition (underweight) is higher in Bangladesh, at 41.3%, than DRC (a still very high 28.2%). The under-5 mortality rate in Bangladesh is 46, while that of the DRC is nearly quadruple that number at 168. Life expectancy in Congo is just 48, compared with 69 in Bangladesh. But while India and Bangladesh clearly do better overall than countries like the DRC, most low- and lower-middle-income countries still face enormous development challenges as seen by comparing these statistics even to Botswana, Peru, or Thailand

2.3 Holistic Measures of Living Levels and Capabilities

The New Human Development Index

The most widely used measure of the comparative status of socioeconomic development is presented by the United Nations Development Programme (UNDP) in its annual series of *Human Development Reports*. The centerpiece of these reports, which were initiated in 1990, is the construction and refinement of its informative **Human Development Index (HDI)**. This section examines the New HDI, initiated in 2010 (the well-known traditional HDI—the UNDP centerpiece from 1990–2009—is examined in detail in Appendix 2.1). Box 2.2 summarizes "What Is New in the New HDI."

The New HDI, like its predecessor, ranks each country on a scale of 0 (lowest human development) to 1 (highest human development) based on three goals or end products of development: *a long and healthy life* as measured by life expectancy at birth; *knowledge* as measured by a combination of average schooling attained by adults and expected years of schooling for school-age children; and a *decent standard of living* as measured by real per capita gross

Human Development Index (HDI) An index measuring national socioeconomic development, based on combining measures of education, health, and adjusted real income per capita.

Diminishing marginal utility
The concept that the subjective value of additional consumption lessens as total consumption becomes higher.

domestic product adjusted for the differing purchasing power parity of each country's currency to reflect cost of living and for the assumption of **diminishing marginal utility** of income.

There are two steps in calculating the New HDI: first, creating the three "dimension indices"; and second, aggregating the resulting indices to produce the overall New Human Development Index (NHDI).

After defining the relevant minimum and maximum values (or lower and upper "goalposts"), each dimension index is calculated as a ratio that basically is given by the percent of the distance above the minimum to the maximum levels that a country has attained.

$$\text{Dimension index} = \frac{Actual\ Value - Minimum\ Value}{Maximum\ Value - Minimum\ Value} \quad (2.1)$$

The health (or "long and healthy life") dimension of the New HDI is calculated with a life expectancy at birth index, which takes a minimum value of 20 years and a maximum value of 83.57 years (the observed maximum value for any country). For example, for the case of Ghana this is:

$$\text{Life expectancy index} = (64.6 - 20)/(83.6 - 20) = 0.701 \quad (2.2)$$

The education ("knowledge") component of the HDI is calculated with a combination of the average years of schooling for adults aged 25 and older and expected years of schooling for a school-age child now entering school. As explained by the UNDP, these indicators are normalized using a minimum value of 0, and maximum values are set to the actual observed maximum value of mean years of schooling from the countries in the time series, 1980–2012, which is 13.3 years estimated for the United States in 2010. For Ghana, the average years of schooling among adults is 7 years, so the mean years of schooling subindex is calculated as:

$$(7.0 - 0)/(13.3 - 0) = 0.527 \quad (2.3)$$

We can think of this as saying that Ghana is about 53% of the way to the global standard of average education.

In considering expected future education, the highest value (cap, or "goalpost") is given as 18 years (which we may think of as approximately corresponding to a master's degree).

For Ghana, the expected number of years of schooling for a child entering school now is estimated at 11.4 years. The expected years of schooling subindex is then calculated as:

$$(11.4 - 0)/(18.0 - 0) = 0.634 \quad (2.4)$$

The education index is then calculated as a version of the geometric mean of the two subindexes.[7]

The standard of living (income) component is calculated using purchasing-power-adjusted per-capita gross national income (GNI). For Ghana, the income index then is (where ln stands for natural log):

$$\text{Income index} = [\ln(1{,}684) - \ln(100)]/[\ln(87{,}478) - \ln(100)] = 0.417 \quad (2.5)$$

Using these three measures of development and applying the formula to data for all 187 countries for which data is available, the HDI currently ranks countries into four groups: low human development (0.0 to 0.535), medium human development (0.536 to 0.711), high human development (0.712 to 0.799), and very high human development (0.80 to 1.0).

The component indexes of the NHDI are computed by taking the difference between the country's actual achievement and the minimum goalpost value, and then dividing the result by the difference between the overall maximum goalpost and minimum goalpost values. But in calculating the overall index, in place of the arithmetic mean, a geometric mean of the three indexes is used (a geometric mean is also used to build up the overall education index from its two components).

Let's look at why this change is important and how the calculations are done.

Computing the NHDI The use of a geometric mean in computing the New HDI is very important. When using an arithmetic mean (adding up the component indexes and dividing by 3) in the HDI, the effect is to assume perfect substitutability across income, health, and education. For example, a higher value of the education index could compensate, one for one, for a lower value of the health index. In contrast, use of a geometric mean ensures that poor performance in any dimension directly affects the overall index. Thus, allowing for imperfect substitutability is a beneficial change; but there is active debate about whether using the geometric mean is the most appropriate way to accomplish this.[8]

Thus, as the UNDP notes, the new calculation "captures how well rounded a country's performance is across the three dimensions." Moreover, the UNDP argues "that it is hard to compare these different dimensions of well-being and that we should not let changes in any of them go unnoticed."

So in the New HDI, instead of adding up the health, education, and income indexes and dividing by 3, the New HDI is calculated with the geometric mean:

$$NHDI = H^{1/3}E^{1/3}I^{1/3} \qquad (2.6)$$

where H stands for the health index, E stands for the education index, and I stands for the income index. This is equivalent to taking the cube root of the product of these three indexes. The calculations of the NHDI are illustrated for Ghana in Box 2.1.

Table 2.4 shows the 2013 values of the New HDI for a set of 31 countries. South Korea has achieved the status of a fully developed country, ranking below Canada but above the United Kingdom. Countries such as the United Arab Emirates, Turkey, Guatemala, Gabon, Côte d'Ivoire, Pakistan, Papua New Guinea, and South Africa perform more poorly on the New HDI than would be predicted from their income level, while the reverse is true of South Korea, Chile, Bangladesh, Cuba, Madagascar, and Ghana. Countries such as Russia, Mexico, India, and Niger perform on the New HDI just about as predicted by their income levels.

Income predicts rather weakly how countries will perform on education and health, or on the NHDI in particular. For example, Cuba and Egypt have nearly the same real income per person, but Cuba ranks 59th on the New HDI (44 points

BOX 2.1 Computing the New HDI: Ghana

Example: Ghana

Indicator	Value
Life expectancy at birth (years)	64.6
Mean years of schooling	7.0
Expected years of schooling	11.4
GNI per capita (PPP $)	1,684
Indexes	

Note: Values are rounded.

Life expectancy index $= \dfrac{64.6 - 20}{83.6 - 20} = 0.701$

Mean years of schooling index $= \dfrac{7.0 - 0}{13.3 - 0} = 0.527$

Expected years of schooling index $= \dfrac{11.4 - 0}{18.0 - 0} = 0.634$

Education index $= \dfrac{\sqrt{0.527 \times 0.634} - 0}{0.971 - 0} = 0.596$

Income index $= \dfrac{\ln(1,684) - \ln(100)}{\ln(87,478) - \ln(100)} = 0.417$

Human Development Index

$= \sqrt[3]{0.701 \times 0.558 \times 0.417} = 0.596$

UN income estimate will differ somewhat from World Bank estimate.

Source: UNDP, *Human Development Report, 2013*, Technical Notes (online):, http://hdr.undp.org/en/media/HDR%202013%20technical%20notes%20EN.pdf.

above where predicted by its income level) and Egypt ranks 112th (6 below where predicted by income). Mexico and Gabon have a very similar income, but Mexico is 4 places above what would be predicted by its income and Gabon is 40 points below. Bangladesh and Pakistan have an identical New HDI ranking, but Pakistan has a much higher income, and Bangladesh is 9 places higher than expected while Pakistan is 9 places below; see the case study at the end of this chapter for a detailed examination of diverging development in these two countries.

The UNDP now also offers the Inequality-Adjusted Human Development Index (IHDI)—which imposes a penalty on the HDI that increases as inequality across people becomes greater—and the Gender Inequality Index (GII), as well as an important innovation, the Multidimensional Poverty Index (MPI), which is examined in detail in Chapter 5.

Clearly, the Human Development Index, in its Traditional as well as New forms, has made a major contribution to improving our understanding of what constitutes development, which countries are succeeding (as reflected by rises in their NHDI over time), and how different groups and regions within countries are faring. By combining social and economic data, the NHDI allows nations to take a broader measure of their development performance, both relatively and absolutely.

Although there are some valid criticisms, the fact remains that the New HDI and its Traditional version considered in Appendix 2.1, when used in

TABLE 2.4	2013 New Human Development Index and its Components for Selected Countries					
Country	NHDI Rank	Life Expectancy at Birth	Mean Yrs Schooling (of Adults)	Expected Years Schooling (of children)	GNI Per Capita	New HDI value	GNI Per Capita Rank Minus HDI Rank
United States	3	78.7	13.3	16.8	43,480	0.937	6
Canada	11	81.1	12.3	15.1	35,369	0.911	5
South Korea	12	80.7	11.6	17.2	28,231	0.909	15
United Kingdom	26	80.3	9.4	16.4	32,538	0.875	5
Chile	40	79.3	9.7	14.7	14,987	0.819	13
United Arab Emirates	41	76.7	8.9	12	42,716	0.818	−31
Russian Federation	55	69.1	11.7	14.3	14,461	0.788	0
Cuba	59	79.3	10.2	16.2	5,539	0.78	44
Mexico	61	77.1	8.5	13.7	12,947	0.775	4
Costa Rica	62	79.4	8.4	13.7	10,863	0.773	12
Brazil	85	73.8	7.2	14.2	10,152	0.73	−8
Turkey	90	74.2	6.5	12.9	13,710	0.722	−32
Sri Lanka	92	75.1	9.3	12.7	5,170	0.715	18
China	101	73.7	7.5	11.7	7,945	0.699	−11
Gabon	106	63.1	7.5	13	12,521	0.683	−40
Egypt	112	73.5	6.4	12.1	5,401	0.662	−6
Botswana	119	53	8.9	11.8	13,102	0.634	−55
South Africa	121	53.4	6.7	10.6	9,594	0.629	−42
Guatemala	133	71.4	4.1	10.7	4,235	0.581	−14
Ghana	135	64.6	7	11.4	1,684	0.558	22
Equatorial Guinea	136	51.4	5.4	7.9	21,715	0.554	−97
India	136	65.8	4.4	10.7	3,285	0.554	−3
Kenya	145	57.7	7	11.1	1,541	0.519	15
Bangladesh	146	69.2	4.8	8.1	1,785	0.515	9
Pakistan	146	65.7	4.9	7.3	2,566	0.515	−9
Madagascar	151	66.9	5.2	10.4	828	0.483	28
Papua New Guinea	156	63.1	3.9	5.8	2,386	0.466	−15
Côte d'Ivoire	168	56	4.2	6.5	1,593	0.432	−9
Burkina Faso	183	55.9	1.3	6.9	1,202	0.343	−18
Chad	184	49.9	1.5	7.4	1,258	0.34	−20
Niger	186	55.1	1.4	4.9	701	0.304	−4

Source: 2013 Human Development Report 2013, Table 1, pages 144-147 (New York: United Nations Development Programme, 2013)

conjunction with other economic measures of development, greatly increase our understanding of which countries are experiencing development and which are not. And by modifying a country's overall NHDI to reflect income distribution, gender, regional, and ethnic differentials, as presented in recent Human Development Reports, we are now able to identify not only whether a country is developing but also whether various significant groups within that country are participating in that development.[9]

2.4 Characteristics of the Developing World: Diversity within Commonality

As noted earlier, there are important historical and economic commonalities among developing countries that have led to their economic development

BOX 2.2 What Is New in the New Human Development Index

In November 2010, the UNDP introduced its New Human Development Index (NHDI), which has eight notable changes, each with strengths but also a few potential drawbacks.

1. Gross national income (GNI) per capita replaces gross domestic product (GDP) per capita. This should be an unambiguous improvement: GNI reflects what citizens can do with income they receive, whereas that is not true of value added in goods and services produced in a country that go to someone outside it, and income earned abroad still benefits some of the nation's citizens. As trade and remittance flows have been expanding rapidly, and as aid has been better targeted to very low-income countries, this distinction has become increasingly important.

2. The education index has been completely revamped. Two new components have been added: the average actual educational attainment of the whole population and the expected attainment of today's children. Each of these changes to the index has implications. Use of actual attainment—average years of schooling—as an indicator is unambiguously an improvement. Estimates are regularly updated, and the statistic is easily compared quantitatively across countries. And even though it is at best a very rough guide to what is actually learned—on average, a year of schooling in Mali provides students with much less than a year of schooling in Norway—this is the best measure we have at present because more detailed data on quality that are credible and comparable are simply not available.

3. Expected educational attainment, the other new component, is somewhat more ambiguous: It is not an achievement but a UN forecast. History shows that much can go wrong to derail development plans. Nevertheless,

there have also been many development upside surprises, such as rapid improvements in educational attainment in some countries; there is a risk that low expectations will prove discouraging. Note that life expectancy, which remains the indicator for health, is also a projection based on prevailing conditions.

4. The two previous components of the education index, literacy and enrollment, have been correspondingly dropped. In contrast to expected attainment, literacy is clearly an achievement, and even enrollment is at least a modest achievement. However, literacy has always been badly and too infrequently measured and is inevitably defined more modestly in a less developed country. And enrollment is no guarantee that a grade will be completed or for that matter that anything is learned or that students (or teachers) even attend.

5. The upper goalposts (maximum values) in each dimension have been increased to the observed maximum rather than given a predefined cutoff. In some ways, this returns the index to its original design, which was criticized for inadequately recognizing small gains by countries starting at very low levels.

6. The lower goalpost for income has been reduced. This is based on updated estimates for the historic low for recorded income for any country.[10]

7. Another minor difference is that rather than using the common logarithm (log) to reflect diminishing marginal benefit of income, the NHDI now uses the natural log (ln), as used in the fifth equation in Box 2.1. This reflects a more usual construction of indexes.

8. Possibly the most consequential change is that the NHDI is computed with a geometric mean rather than a simple arithmetic mean, as examined previously.

problems being studied within a common analytical framework in development economics. These widely shared problems are examined here in detail on an issue-by-issue basis. At the same time, however, it is important to bear in mind that there is a great deal of diversity throughout the developing world, even within these areas of broad commonality. The wide range of income, health, education, and HDI indicators already reviewed is sometimes called a "ladder of development."[11] Different development problems call for different specific policy responses and general development strategies. This section examines the 10 major areas of "diversity within commonality" in the developing world.

Lower Levels of Living and Productivity

As we noted at the outset of the chapter, there is a vast gulf in productivity between advanced economies such as the United States and developing nations, including India and the DRC, but also a wide range among these and other developing countries. And as we have seen, all countries with averages below what is defined as high income are considered developing in most taxonomies (and some in the high-income range as defined by the World Bank are still considered developing). The lower average levels but wide ranges of income in developing areas are seen in Table 2.3. Even when adjusted for purchasing power parity and despite extraordinary recent growth in China and India, the low- and middle-income developing nations, with more than five-sixths (84%) of the world's people, received only about 46% of the world's income in 2011, as seen in Figure 2.3a. Though resulting from a number of deeper causes, the wide disparity in income largely corresponds to the large gaps in output per worker between developing and developed countries as seen in Figure 2.3b.[12]

At very low income levels, in fact, a vicious circle may set in, whereby low income leads to low investment in education and health as well as plant and equipment and infrastructure, which in turn leads to low productivity and economic stagnation. This is known as a *poverty trap* or what Nobel laureate Gunnar Myrdal called "circular and cumulative causation."[13] However, it is important to stress that there are ways to escape from low income, as you will see throughout this book. Further, the low-income countries are themselves a very diverse group with greatly differing development challenges.[14]

Some star performers among now high-income economies such as South Korea and Taiwan were once among the poorest in the world. Some middle-income countries are also relatively stagnant, but others are growing rapidly—China most spectacularly, as reviewed in the case study at the end of Chapter 4. Indeed, income growth rates have varied greatly in different developing regions and countries, with rapid growth in East Asia, slow or even no growth in sub-Saharan Africa, and intermediate levels of growth in other regions. Problems of igniting and then sustaining economic growth are examined in depth in Chapters 3 and 4.

One common misperception is that low incomes result from a country's being too small to be self-sufficient or too large to overcome economic inertia. However, there is no necessary correlation between country size in population or area and economic development (in part because each has different advantages and disadvantages that can offset each other).[15]

FIGURE 2.3   (a) Shares of Global Income, 2008. (b) Developing regions lag far behind the developed world in productivity measured as output per worker.

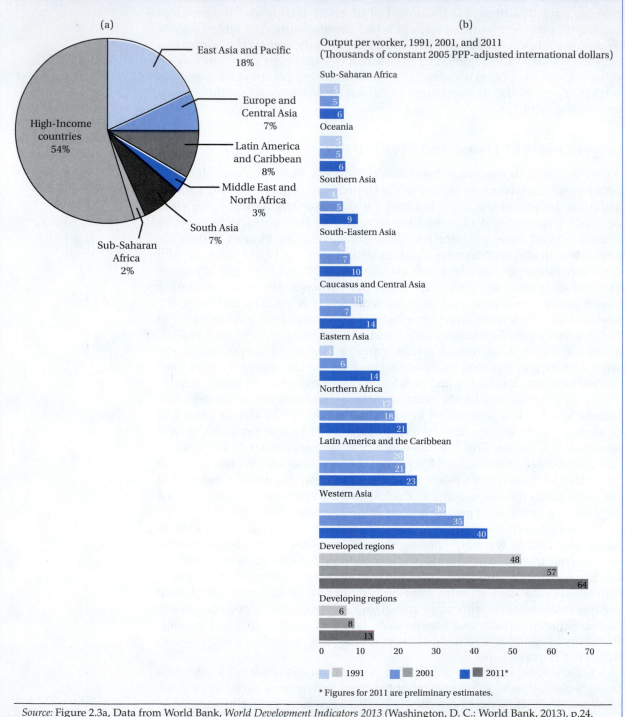

(a)

East Asia and Pacific
18%

Europe and
Central Asia
7%

Latin America
and Caribbean
8%

Middle East and
North Africa
3%

South Asia
7%

Sub-Saharan
Africa
2%

High-Income
countries
54%

(b)

Output per worker, 1991, 2001, and 2011
(Thousands of constant 2005 PPP-adjusted international dollars)

Sub-Saharan Africa
5
5
6

Oceania
5
5
6

Southern Asia
4
5
9

South-Eastern Asia
6
7
10

Caucasus and Central Asia
10
7
14

Eastern Asia
3
6
14

Northern Africa
17
18
21

Latin America and the Caribbean
20
21
23

Western Asia
30
35
40

Developed regions
48
57
64

Developing regions
6
8
13

0   10   20   30   40   50   60   70

■ 1991   ■ 2001   ■ 2011*

* Figures for 2011 are preliminary estimates.

Source: Figure 2.3a, Data from World Bank, *World Development Indicators 2013* (Washington, D. C.: World Bank, 2013), p.24. Figure 2.3b, United Nations, *Millenium Development Goals Report 2012*, p.9.

TABLE 2.5 The 12 Most and Least Populated Countries and Their Per Capita Income, 2008

Most Populous	Population (millions)	GNI Per Capita (U.S. $)	Least Populous[a]	Population (thousands)	GNI Per Capita (U.S. $)
1. China	1,325	2,940	1. Palau	20	8,630
2. India	1,140	1,040	2. St. Kitts and Nevis	49	10,870
3. United States	304	47,930	3. Marshall Islands	60	3,270
4. Indonesia	227	1,880	4. Dominica	73	4,750
5. Brazil	192	7,300	5. Antigua and Barbuda	87	13,200
6. Pakistan	166	950	6. Seychelles	87	10,220
7. Bangladesh	160	520	7. Kiribati	97	2,040
8. Nigeria	151	1,170	8. Tonga	104	2,690
9. Russian Federation	142	9,660	9. Grenada	104	5,880
10. Japan	128	38,130	10. St. Vincent and the Grenadines	109	5,050
11. Mexico	106	9,990	11. Micronesia	110	2,460
12. Philippines	90	1,890	12. São Tomé and Príncipe	160	1,030

[a]Criteria for inclusion in the least-populous rankings: United Nations member as of mid-2010, with 2008 comparable population and GNI per capita data in tab. 1.6 in the source.

Source: The World Bank, *World Development Indicators, 2010* (Washington, D.C.: World Bank, 2010), tabs 1.1 and 1.6.

The 12 most populous countries include representatives of all four categories: low-, lower-middle-, upper-middle-, and high-income countries (see Table 2.5). The 12 least populous on the list include primarily lower-middle- and upper-middle-income countries, although the 12th least populous country, São Tomé and Príncipe, has a per capita income of just $1,030. And four very small but high-income European countries that are UN members (Andorra, Monaco, Liechtenstein, and San Marino) would appear on the list if comparable World Bank income data were available.

Lower Levels of Human Capital

Human capital—health, education, and skills—is vital to economic growth and human development. We have already noted the great disparities in human capital around the world while discussing the Human Development Index. Compared with developed countries, much of the developing world has lagged in its average levels of nutrition, health (as measured, for example, by life expectancy or undernourishment), and education (measured by literacy), as seen in Table 2.3. The under-5 mortality is 17 times higher in low-income countries than in high-income countries, although great progress has been made since 1990, as shown graphically in Figure 2.4.

Table 2.6 shows primary school enrollment rates (percentage of students of primary age enrolled in school) and the primary school pupil-to-teacher ratio for the four country income groups and for six major developing regions. Enrollments have strongly improved in recent years, but student attendance and completion, along with attainment of basic skills such as functional literacy, remain problems. Indeed, *teacher* truancy remains a serious problem in South Asia and sub-Saharan Africa.[16]

Moreover, there are strong synergies (complementarities) between progress in health and education (examined in greater depth in Chapter 8). For

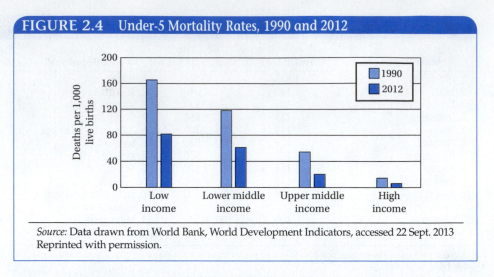

FIGURE 2.4   Under-5 Mortality Rates, 1990 and 2012

Source: Data drawn from World Bank, World Development Indicators, accessed 22 Sept. 2013
Reprinted with permission.

example, under-5 mortality rates improve as mothers' education levels rise, as seen in the country examples in Figure 2.5.

The well-performing developing countries are much closer to the developed world in health and education standards than they are to the lowest-income countries.[17] Although health conditions in East Asia are relatively good, sub-Saharan Africa continues to be plagued by problems of malnourishment, malaria, tuberculosis, AIDS, and parasitic infections. Despite progress, South Asia continues to have high levels of illiteracy, low schooling attainment, and undernourishment. Still, in fields such as primary school completion, low-income countries are also making great progress; for example, enrollments in India are up from 68% in the early 1990s to a reported 94% by 2008.

Higher Levels of Inequality and Absolute Poverty

Globally, the poorest 20% of people receive just 1.5% of world income. The lowest 20% now roughly corresponds to the approximately 1.2 billion people

TABLE 2.6   Primary School Enrollment and Pupil-Teacher Ratios, 2010

Region or Group	Net Primary School Enrollment (%)	Primary Pupil-Teacher Ratio
Income Group		
Low	80	45
Lower Middle	87	23[a]
Upper Middle	94	22
High	95	15
Region		
East Asia and Pacific	93[a]	19
Latin America and the Caribbean	94	25
Middle East and North Africa	91	24
South Asia	86	40[a]
Sub-Saharan Africa	73	49
Europe and Central Asia	92	16

[a]Data for 2009.
Source: Data from World Bank, *World Development Indicators, 2010* (Washington, D.C.: World Bank, 2010), tabs 2.11 and 2.12.

FIGURE 2.5 Correlation between Under-5 Mortality and Mother's Education

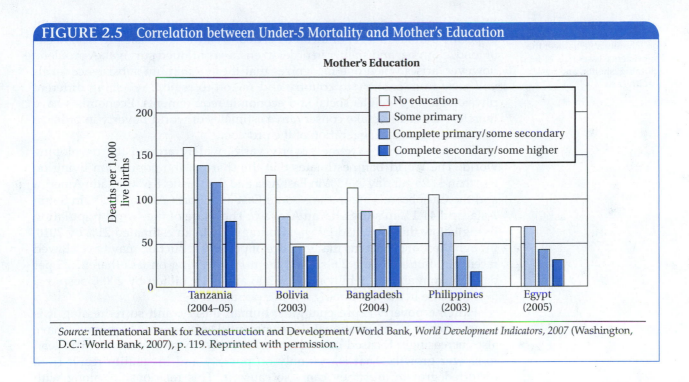

Mother's Education

Legend:
- ☐ No education
- Some primary
- Complete primary/some secondary
- Complete secondary/some higher

y-axis: Deaths per 1,000 live births

x-axis: Tanzania (2004–05), Bolivia (2003), Bangladesh (2004), Philippines (2003), Egypt (2005)

Source: International Bank for Reconstruction and Development/World Bank, *World Development Indicators, 2007* (Washington, D.C.: World Bank, 2007), p. 119. Reprinted with permission.

living in extreme poverty on less than $1.25 per day at purchasing power parity.[18] Bringing the incomes of those living on less than $1.25 per day up to this minimal poverty line would require less than 2% of the incomes of the world's wealthiest 10%.[19] Thus, the scale of global inequality is also immense.

But the enormous gap in per capita incomes between rich and poor nations is not the only manifestation of the huge global economic disparities. To appreciate the breadth and depth of deprivation in developing countries, it is also necessary to look at the gap between rich and poor *within* individual developing countries. Very high levels of inequality—extremes in the relative incomes of higher- and lower-income citizens—are found in many middle-income countries, partly because Latin American countries historically tend to be both middle-income and highly unequal. Several African countries, including Sierra Leone, Lesotho, and South Africa, also have among the highest levels of inequality in the world.[20] Inequality is particularly high in many resource-rich developing countries, notably in the Middle East and sub-Saharan Africa. Indeed, in many of these cases, inequality is substantially higher than in most developed countries (where inequality has in many cases been rising). But inequality varies greatly among developing countries, with generally much lower inequality in Asia. Consequently, we cannot confine our attention to averages; we must look within nations at how income is distributed to ask who benefits from economic development and why.

Corresponding to their low average income levels, a large majority of the extreme poor live in the low-income developing countries of sub-Saharan Africa and South Asia. Extreme poverty is due in part to low human capital but also to social and political exclusion and other deprivations. Great progress has already been made in reducing the fraction of the developing world's population living on less than $1.25 per day and raising the incomes of those still below that level, but much remains to be done, as we examine in detail in Chapter 5.

Absolute poverty The situation of being unable or only barely able to meet the subsistence essentials of food, clothing, shelter, and basic health care.

Development economists use the concept of **absolute poverty** to represent a specific minimum level of income needed to satisfy the basic physical needs of food, clothing, and shelter in order to ensure continued survival. A problem, however, arises when one recognizes that these minimum subsistence levels will vary from country to country and region to region, reflecting different physiological as well as social and economic requirements. Economists have therefore tended to make conservative estimates of world poverty in order to avoid unintended exaggeration of the problem.

The incidence of extreme poverty varies widely around the developing world. The World Bank estimates that the share of the population living on less than $1.25 per day is 9.1% in East Asia and the Pacific, 8.6% in Latin America and the Caribbean, 1.5% in the Middle East and North Africa, 31.7% in South Asia, and 41.1% in sub-Saharan Africa.[21] The share of the world population living below this level had fallen encouragingly to an estimated 21% by 2010, though there are concerns that the pace of poverty reduction may have slowed recently.[22] But as Figure 2.6 shows, the number living on less than $1.25 per day fell from about 1.9 billion in 1981 to about 1.2 billion by 2008, despite a 59% increase in the developing world's population.

Extreme poverty represents great human misery, and so redressing it is a top priority of international development. Development economists have also increasingly focused on ways in which poverty and inequality can lead to slower growth. That is, not only do poverty and inequality result from distorted growth, but they can also cause it. This relationship, along with

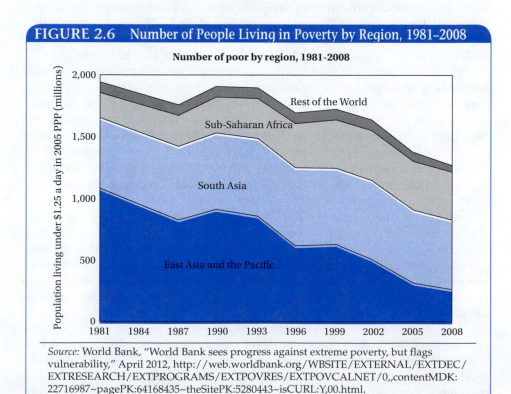

FIGURE 2.6   Number of People Living in Poverty by Region, 1981–2008

Number of poor by region, 1981-2008

Source: World Bank, "World Bank sees progress against extreme poverty, but flags vulnerability," April 2012, http://web.worldbank.org/WBSITE/EXTERNAL/EXTDEC/EXTRESEARCH/EXTPROGRAMS/EXTPOVRES/EXTPOVCALNET/0,,contentMDK:22716987~pagePK:64168435~theSitePK:5280443~isCURL:Y,00.html.

measurements of inequality and poverty and strategies to address these problems, is examined in depth in Chapter 5; because of their central importance in development, poverty reduction strategies are examined throughout the text.

Higher Population Growth Rates

Global population has skyrocketed since the beginning of the industrial era, from just under 1 billion in 1800 to 1.65 billion in 1900 and to over 6 billion by 2000. World population topped 7 billion by 2012. Rapid population growth began in Europe and other now developed countries. But in recent decades, most population growth has been centered in the developing world. Compared with the developed countries, which often have birth rates near or even below replacement (zero population growth) levels, the low-income developing countries have very high birth rates. More than five-sixths of all the people in the world now live in developing countries; and some 97% of net population growth (births minus deaths) in 2012 took place in developing regions.

But population dynamics varies widely among developing countries. Populations of some developing countries, particularly in Africa, continue to grow rapidly. From 1990 to 2008, population in the low-income countries grew at 2.2% per year, compared to 1.3% in the middle-income countries (the high-income countries grew at 0.7% per year, reflecting both births and immigration).[23]

Middle-income developing countries show greater variance, with some having achieved lower birth rates closer to those prevailing in rich countries. The birth rate is about three times as high in the low-income countries as in the high-income countries. In sub-Saharan Africa, the annual birth rate is 39 per 1,000—four times the rate in high-income countries. Intermediate but still relatively high birth rates are found in South Asia (24), the Middle East and North Africa (24), and Latin America and the Caribbean (19). East Asia and the Pacific have a moderate birth rate of 14 per 1,000, partly the result of birth control policies in China. The very wide range of **crude birth rates** around the world is illustrated in Table 2.7. As of 2010, the average rate of population growth was about 1.4% in the developing countries.

Crude birth rate The number of children born alive each year per 1,000 population.

A major implication of high birth rates is that the active labor force has to support proportionally almost twice as many children as it does in richer countries. By contrast, the proportion of people over the age of 65 is much

TABLE 2.7	Crude Birth Rates Around the World, 2012
45+	Chad, Dem. Rep. of Congo, Mali, Niger, Uganda, Zambia
40–44	Afghanistan, Angola, Benin, Burkina Faso, Liberia, Malawi, Mozambique, Nigeria, Somalia, South Sudan, Tanzania
35–39	Central African Republic, Côte d'Ivoire, Eritrea, Iraq, Jordan, Kenya, Madagascar, Senegal, Sierra Leone, Yemen
30–34	Ethiopia, Ghana, Papua New Guinea, Sudan, Timor-Leste, Vanatu, Zimbabwe
25–29	Algeria, Bolivia, Cambodia, Egypt, Guatemala, Haiti, Honduras, Kyrgyzstan, Pakistan, Philippines, Samoa, Tonga
20–24	Dominican Republic, El Salvador, India, Libya, Mexico, Peru, Saudi Arabia, South Africa, Venezuela
15–19	Argentina, Brazil, Colombia, Costa Rica, Indonesia, Jamaica, Sri Lanka, Turkey, Vietnam
10–14	Australia, Canada, China, France, Russia, United Kingdom, United States
<10	Austria, Croatia, Germany, Hungary, Italy, Japan, South Korea, Serbia, Portugal, Taiwan

Source: Population Reference Bureau, *Population Data Sheet*, 2012.

Dependency burden   The proportion of the total population aged 0 to 15 and 65+, which is considered economically unproductive and therefore not counted in the labor force.

greater in the developed nations. Both older people and children are often referred to as an economic **dependency burden** in the sense that they must be supported financially by the country's labor force (usually defined as citizens between the ages of 15 and 64). In low-income countries, there are 66 children under 15 for each 100 working-age (15–65) adults, while in middle-income countries, there are 41 and in high-income countries just 26. In contrast, low-income countries have just 6 people over 65 per 100 working-age adults, compared with 10 in middle-income countries and 23 in high-income countries. Thus, the total dependency ratio is 72 per 100 in low-income countries and 49 per 100 in high-income countries.[24] But in rich countries, older citizens are supported by their lifetime savings and by public and private pensions. In contrast, in developing countries, public support for children is very limited. So dependency has a further magnified impact in developing countries.

We may conclude, therefore, that not only are developing countries characterized by higher rates of population growth, but they must also contend with greater dependency burdens than rich nations, though with a wide gulf between low- and middle-income developing countries. The circumstances and conditions under which population growth becomes a deterrent to economic development is a critical issue and is examined in Chapter 6.

Greater Social Fractionalization

Fractionalization   Significant ethnic, linguistic, and other social divisions within a country.

Low-income countries often have ethnic, linguistic, and other forms of social divisions, sometimes known as **fractionalization**. This is sometimes associated with civil strife and even violent conflict, which can lead developing societies to divert considerable energies to working for political accommodations if not national consolidation. It is one of a variety of governance challenges many developing nations face. There is some evidence that many of the factors associated with poor economic growth performance in sub-Saharan Africa, such as low schooling, political instability, underdeveloped financial systems, and insufficient infrastructure, can be statistically explained by high ethnic fragmentation.[25]

The greater the ethnic, linguistic, and religious diversity of a country, the more likely it is that there will be internal strife and political instability. Some of the most successful development experiences—South Korea, Taiwan, Singapore, and Hong Kong—have occurred in culturally homogeneous societies.

But today, more than 40% of the world's nations have more than five significant ethnic populations. In most cases, one or more of these groups face serious problems of discrimination, social exclusion, or other systematic disadvantages. Over half of the world's developing countries have experienced some form of interethnic conflict. Ethnic and religious conflicts leading to widespread death and destruction have taken place in countries as diverse as Afghanistan, Rwanda, Mozambique, Guatemala, Mexico, Sri Lanka, Iraq, India, Kyrgyzstan, Azerbaijan, Somalia, Ethiopia, Liberia, Sierra Leone, Angola, Myanmar, Sudan, the former Yugoslavia, Indonesia, and the DRC.

Conflict can derail what had otherwise been relatively positive development progress, as in Côte d'Ivoire since 2002 (see Chapter 14 and the case study for Chapter 5). There is, however, a heartening trend since the late 1990s toward more successful resolution of conflicts and fewer new conflicts.

If development is about improving human lives and providing a widening range of choice to all peoples, racial, ethnic, caste, or religious discrimination is pernicious. For example, throughout Latin America, indigenous populations have significantly lagged behind other groups on almost every measure of economic and social progress. Whether in Bolivia, Brazil, Peru, Mexico, Guatemala, or Venezuela, indigenous groups have benefited little from overall economic growth. Being indigenous makes it much more likely that an individual will be less educated, in poorer health, and in a lower socioeconomic stratum than other citizens.[26] This is particularly true for indigenous women. Moreover, descendants of African slaves brought forcefully to the western hemisphere continue to suffer discrimination in countries such as Brazil.

Ethnic and religious diversity need not necessarily lead to inequality, turmoil, or instability, and unqualified statements about their impact cannot be made. There have been numerous instances of successful economic and social integration of minority or indigenous ethnic populations in countries as diverse as Malaysia and Mauritius. And in the United States, diversity is often cited as a source of creativity and innovation. The broader point is that the ethnic and religious composition of a developing nation and whether or not that diversity leads to conflict or cooperation can be important determinants of the success or failure of development efforts.[27]

Larger Rural Populations but Rapid Rural-to-Urban Migration

One of the hallmarks of economic development is a shift from agriculture to manufacturing and services. In developing countries, a much higher share of the population lives in rural areas, and correspondingly fewer in urban areas, as seen in Table 2.8. Although modernizing in many regions, rural areas are poorer and tend to suffer from missing markets, limited information, and social stratification. A massive population shift is also under way as hundreds of millions of people are moving from rural to urban areas, fueling rapid urbanization, with its own attendant problems. The world as a whole has just crossed the 50% threshold: For the first time in history, more people live in cities than

TABLE 2.8   The Urban Population in Developed Countries and Developing Regions

Region	Population (millions, 2009)	Urban Share (%)
World	6,810	50
More developed countries	1,232	75
Less developed countries	5,578	44
Sub-Saharan Africa	836	35
Northern Africa	205	50
Latin America and the Caribbean	580	77
Western Asia	231	64
South-central Asia	1,726	31
Southeast Asia	597	43
East Asia	1,564	51
Eastern Europe	295	69

Source: Population Reference Bureau, *2009 World Data Sheet.*

in rural areas. But sub-Saharan Africa and most of Asia remain predominantly rural. Migration and agriculture issues are examined in Chapters 7 and 9.

Lower Levels of Industrialization and Manufactured Exports

One of the most widely used terminologies for the original Group of Seven (G7) countries[28] and other advanced economies such as smaller European countries and Australia is the "industrial countries." Industrialization is associated with high productivity and incomes and has been a hallmark of modernization and national economic power. It is no accident that most developing-country governments have made industrialization a high national priority, with a number of prominent success stories in Asia.

Table 2.9 shows the relationship between employment and share of GDP in agriculture, industry, and services in selected developing and developed countries, in the 2004 to 2008 period. Generally, developing countries have a far higher share of employment in agriculture than developed countries. Moreover, in developed countries, agriculture represents a very small share of both employment and output—about 1% to 2% in Canada, the United States and United Kingdom—although productivity is not below the average for these economies as a whole. This is in sharp contrast to a majority of developing nations, which have relatively low productivity in agriculture in comparison

TABLE 2.9 Share of the Population Employed in the Agricultural, Industrial, and Service Sectors in Selected Countries, 2004–2008 (%)

	Agriculture			Industry			Services		
	Males	Females	Share of GDP (2008)	Males	Females	Share of GDP (2008)	Males	Females	Share of GDP (2008)
Africa									
Egypt	28	43	13	26	6	38	46	51	49
Ethiopia	12	6	44	27	17	13	61	77	42
Madagascar	82	83	25	5	2	17	13	16	57
Mauritius	10	8	4	36	26	29	54	66	67
South Africa	11	7	3	35	14	34	54	80	63
Asia									
Bangladesh	42	68	19	15	13	29	43	19	52
Indonesia	41	41	14	21	15	48	38	44	37
Malaysia	18	10	10	32	23	48	51	67	42
Pakistan	36	72	20	23	13	27	41	15	53
Philippines	44	24	15	18	11	32	39	65	53
South Korea	7	8	3	33	16	37	60	74	60
Thailand	43	40	12	22	19	44	35	41	44
Vietnam	56	60	22	21	14	40	23	26	38
Latin America									
Colombia	27	6	9	22	16	36	51	78	55
Costa Rica	18	5	7	28	13	29	54	82	64
Mexico	19	4	4	31	18	37	50	77	59
Nicaragua	42	8	19	20	18	30	38	73	51
Developed Countries									
United Kingdom	2	1	1	32	9	24	66	90	76
United States	2	1	1	30	9	22	68	90	77

Note: Ethiopia agricultural employment reflects limited coverage.

Source: World Bank, *World Development Indicators, 2010* (Washington, D.C.: World Bank, *2010*), tabs. 2.3 and 4.2.

to other sectors of their own economies—particularly industry. Madagascar is a dramatic example: while about 82% of both men and women worked in agriculture, it represented only a quarter of total output. In Indonesia, 41% of both men and women worked in agriculture, but it represented just 14% of output. The proportion of women who work in the agricultural sector varies greatly across the developing world. Generally, in Latin America a significantly higher proportion of men work in agriculture than women; but in numerous countries in Africa and Asia, a larger proportion of women work in agriculture.

Table 2.10 reveals the structural transformation of employment that has been occurring in developing countries. Where available, the table shows employment shares in both 1990–1992 and 2008–2011 periods. There have been substantial declines over this two-decade period in the share in employment in agriculture in most developing countries for which comparable data is available. For example, in Indonesia the proportion of men who work in agriculture fell from 54% to 37%; and the proportion of women who work in agriculture fell from 57% to 35%. Partial exceptions include Pakistan and Honduras, for which the share of women's agricultural employment rose by approximately as much as that of men fell.

At the same time, the share of employment in industry in many developed countries is smaller now than in some developing countries, particularly among women, as developed countries continue their secular trend to switch to from industry to service sector employment. However, many developed-country industrial jobs require high skills and pay high wages.

Relatively few countries managed a substantial gain of the fraction in manufacturing in this period; Indonesia, Turkey, and Mexico showed modest gains, particularly for men. (Other evidence indicates that a large fraction of global manufacturing jobs were gained in one country—China—during this period; but comparable data for China were unavailable for comparison.) The share of industrial employment in Africa remains low for both men and women in most countries.

Along with lower industrialization, developing nations tended to have a higher dependence on primary exports. Most developing countries have diversified away from agricultural and mineral exports to some degree. The middle-income countries are rapidly catching up with the developed world in the share of manufactured goods in their exports, even if these goods are typically less advanced in their skill and technology content. However, the low-income countries, particularly those in Africa, remain highly dependent on a relatively small number of agricultural and mineral exports. Africa will need to continue its efforts to diversify its exports. We examine this topic in Chapter 12.

Adverse Geography

Many analysts argue that geography must play some role in problems of agriculture, public health, and comparative development more generally. Landlocked economies, common in Africa, often have lower incomes than coastal economies.[29] As can be observed on the map on the inside cover, developing countries are primarily tropical or subtropical, and this has meant that they suffer more from tropical pests and parasites, endemic diseases such as malaria, water resource constraints, and extremes of heat. A great concern

TABLE 2.10 Share of the Population Employed in the Agricultural, Industrial, and Service Sectors in Selected Countries, 1990–92 and 2008–2011 (%)

	Agriculture				Industry				Services				
	Males % of Male Employment		Females % of Female Employment		Males % of Male Employment		Females % of Female Employment		Males % of Male Employment		Females % of Female Employment		Region
	1990–92	2008–11	1990–92	2008–11	1990–92	2008–11	1990–92	2008–11	1990–92	2008–11	1990–92	2008–11	
Cameroon	..	49	..	58	..	13	..	12	..	38	..	30	Africa
Egypt, Arab Rep.	35	28	52	46	25	27	10	6	41	44	37	49	Africa
Liberia	..	50	..	48	..	14	..	5	..	37	..	47	Africa
Mauritius	15	9	13	7	36	32	48	21	48	59	39	73	Africa
Namibia	45	23	52	8	21	24	8	9	34	53	40	83	Africa
Indonesia	54	37	57	35	15	24	13	15	31	40	31	50	Asia
Malaysia	23	16	20	9	31	31	32	21	46	53	48	71	Asia
Pakistan	45	37	69	75	20	22	15	12	35	41	16	13	Asia
Philippines	53	41	32	23	17	18	14	10	29	41	55	68	Asia
Thailand	60	41	62	37	18	23	13	18	22	37	25	45	Asia
Turkey	33	18	72	39	26	31	11	15	41	51	17	45	Asia
Chile	24	14	6	5	32	31	15	10	45	55	79	85	Latin America
Costa Rica	32	20	5	4	27	25	25	11	41	55	69	84	Latin America
Dominican Republic	26	19	3	2	23	21	21	7	52	47	76	60	Latin America
Honduras	53	50	6	12	18	19	25	21	29	31	69	67	Latin America
Mexico	34	19	11	4	25	30	19	18	41	51	70	78	Latin America
Canada	6	3	2	1	31	32	11	10	64	65	87	89	Developed
Japan	6	4	7	4	40	33	27	15	54	62	65	80	Developed
United Kingdom	3	2	1	1	41	29	16	8	55	69	82	91	Developed
United States	4	2	1	1	34	25	14	7	62	72	85	92	Developed

Note: Country selection reflects that only a limited number of countries are covered or have data over time. Data represent most recent in timeframe if average for the period is not available.

Source: World Bank, *World Development Indicators, 2013* (Washington, D.C.: World Bank, 2013), tab. 2.3.

going forward is that global warming is projected to have its greatest negative impact on Africa and South Asia (see Chapter 10).[30]

The extreme case of favorable physical **resource endowment** is the oil-rich Persian Gulf states. At the other extreme are countries like Chad, Yemen, Haiti, and Bangladesh, where endowments of raw materials and minerals and even fertile land are relatively minimal. However, as the case of the DRC shows vividly, high mineral wealth is no guarantee of development success. Conflict over the profits from these industries has often led to a focus on the distribution of wealth rather than its creation and to social strife, undemocratic governance, high inequality, and even armed conflict, in what is called the "curse of natural resources."

Clearly, geography is not destiny; high-income Singapore lies almost directly on the equator, and parts of southern India have exhibited enormous economic dynamism in recent years. Prior to colonization, some tropical and subtropical regions had higher incomes per capita than Europe. However, the presence of common and often adverse geographic features in comparison to temperate zone countries means it is beneficial to study tropical and subtropical developing countries together for some purposes. Redoubled efforts are now under way to extend the benefits of the green revolution and tropical disease control to sub-Saharan Africa. In section 2.7 of this chapter, we add further perspectives on the possible indirect roles of geography in comparative development.

Underdeveloped Markets

Imperfect markets and incomplete information are far more prevalent in developing countries, with the result that domestic markets, notably but not only financial markets, have worked less efficiently, as examined in Chapters 4, 11, and 15. In many developing countries, legal and institutional foundations for markets are extremely weak.

Some aspects of market underdevelopment are that they often lack (1) a legal system that enforces contracts and validates property rights; (2) a stable and trustworthy currency; (3) an **infrastructure** of roads and utilities that results in low transport and communication costs so as to facilitate interregional trade; (4) a well-developed and efficiently regulated system of banking and insurance, with broad access and with formal credit markets that select projects and allocate loanable funds on the basis of relative economic profitability and enforce rules of repayment; (5) substantial market information for consumers and producers about prices, quantities, and qualities of products and resources as well as the creditworthiness of potential borrowers; and (6) social norms that facilitate successful long-term business relationships. These six factors, along with the existence of economies of scale in major sectors of the economy, thin markets for many products due to limited demand and few sellers, widespread externalities (costs or benefits that accrue to companies or individuals not doing the producing or consuming) in production and consumption, and poorly regulated common property resources (e.g., fisheries, grazing lands, water holes) mean that markets are often highly imperfect. Moreover, information is limited and costly to obtain, thereby often causing goods, finances, and resources to be misallocated. And we have come to understand that small externalities can interact in ways that add up to very large distortions in an economy and present the real possibility of an

Resource endowment A nation's supply of usable factors of production, including mineral deposits, raw materials, and labor.

Infrastructure Facilities that enable economic activity and markets, such as transportation, communication and distribution networks, utilities, water, sewer, and energy supply systems.

Imperfect market   A market in which the theoretical assumptions of perfect competition are violated by the existence of, for example, a small number of buyers and sellers, barriers to entry, and incomplete information.

Incomplete information   The absence of information that producers and consumers need to make efficient decisions resulting in underperforming markets.

Property rights   The acknowledged right to use and benefit from a tangible (e.g., land) or intangible (e.g., intellectual) entity that may include owning, using, deriving income from, selling, and disposing.

underdevelopment trap (see Chapter 4). The extent to which these **imperfect markets** and **incomplete information** systems justify a more active role for government (which is also subject to similar problems of incomplete and imperfect information) is an issue that we will be dealing with in later chapters. But their existence remains a common characteristic of many developing nations and an important contributing factor to their state of underdevelopment.[31]

Lingering Colonial Impacts and Unequal International Relations

Colonial Legacy   Most developing countries were once colonies of Europe or otherwise dominated by European or other foreign powers, and institutions created during the colonial period often had pernicious effects on development that in many cases have persisted to the present day. Despite important variations that proved consequential, colonial era institutions often favored extractors of wealth rather than creators of wealth, harming development then and now. Both domestically and internationally, developing countries have more often lacked institutions and formal organizations of the type that have benefited the developed world: Domestically, on average, **property rights** have been less secure, constraints on elites have been weak, and a smaller segment of society has been able to gain access to and take advantage of economic opportunities.[32] Problems with governance and public administration (see Chapter 11), as well as poorly performing markets, often stem from poor institutions.

Decolonization was one of the most important historical and geopolitical events of the post–World War II era. More than 80 former European colonies have joined the United Nations. But several decades after independence, the effects of the colonial era linger for many developing nations, particularly the least developed ones.

Colonial history matters not only or even primarily because of stolen resources but also because the colonial powers determined whether the legal and other institutions in their colonies would encourage investments by (and in) the broad population or would instead facilitate exploitation of human and other resources for the benefit of the colonizing elite and create or reinforce extreme inequality. Development-facilitating or development-inhibiting institutions tend to have a very long life span. For example, when the conquered colonial lands were wealthier, there was more to steal. In these cases, colonial powers favored extractive (or "kleptocratic") institutions at the expense of ones that encouraged productive effort. When settlers came in large numbers to live permanently, incomes ultimately were relatively high, but the indigenous populations were largely annihilated by disease or conflict, and descendants of those who survived were exploited and blocked from advancement. A growing body of evidence demonstrates that practices such as forced labor had pernicious effects on human development even centuries after they were discontinued (see Box 2.3).

In a related point of great importance, European colonization often created or reinforced differing degrees of inequality, often correlated with ethnicity, which have also proved remarkably stable over the centuries. In some respects, postcolonial elites in many developing countries largely took over the exploitative role formerly played by the colonial powers. High inequality sometimes emerged as a result of slavery in regions where comparative advantage in crops

BOX 2.3 FINDINGS The Persistent Effects of Colonial Forced Labor on Poverty and Development

In a 2010 study, Melissa Dell used historical district-level data to examine the long-run impacts of the *mita* forced labor system in Peru and Bolivia, which "required over 200 indigenous communities to send one-seventh of their adult male population to work in the Potosi silver and Huancavelica mercury mines between 1573 and 1812." Forced labor can severely harm subjected communities. But Dell finds even today—two centuries later—districts covered by the *mita* system have lower household consumption and higher probability of stunting in children.

Can development economists conclude with confidence that a colonial system ending two centuries ago is the *cause* of worse performance in the districts it affected? In principle, such correlations could be due to observed or unobserved factors other than the *mita*. For example, households in *mita* districts may have been less well off to begin with. To address this question, Dell employed an important tool used by development economists to establish causal effects, known as regression discontinuity design (RDD).

RDD has many uses, including evaluation of development programs. In evaluating a program, if each individual is associated with an "assignment variable," z, and a "treatment" is assigned to individuals with a value of z less than or equal to a cutoff level z_0, then the impact of the treatment on an outcome variable, y, can be identified by comparing observations of those who started just below the threshold z_0 with those who started just above it. For this group, any difference in the outcome variable between people on each side of the discontinuity would be caused by the treatment. The assignment z can represent many types of threshold variables, including income, birth date, test scores, or a geographic boundary. And it turns out that a very wide range of impacts can be considered as a treatment—whatever impacts only people who are on one side of a threshold, provided that all relevant influences other than treatment vary smoothly across the threshold. Economists have learned that RDD estimates have statistically reliable properties that in

some circumstances can make these studies virtually as informative as a randomized trial.

One basic assumption of RDD is that individuals just below and just above the cutoff are otherwise similar and have the same potential outcomes in the absence of the treatment. This assumption means that individuals cannot "sort themselves" to be just under the cutoff (or over the cutoff, if that is the incentive). For example, people cannot pretend to be poorer in order to get into a poverty program. Otherwise, the estimated effect can be compounded with the characteristics of those people who respond by sorting themselves (e.g., people with higher cognitive skills).

Dell's RDD strategy was to use longitude-latitude, or simply distance to mines, as the assignment variable to predict the *mita* coverage. The effect of the *mita* system on social or economic outcomes can be estimated by comparing districts with and without the *mita* system among those close to the *mita* coverage boundary. These districts were considered likely to be similar in all respects except for the *mita*; and indeed, Dell found that prior to the *mita* system, factors such as tax rates, steepness of terrain, and ethnic distribution were similar across the boundaries that she studies. Using this strategy, Dell concluded that the "*mita* effect" lowers household consumption by approximately 25% and that it increases child stunting "by around 6 percentage points." These are really striking findings: Two centuries have passed since the *mita* boundary line carried any legal meaning whatsoever.

Dell then asked, "Why would the *mita* affect economic prosperity nearly 200 years after its abolition?" While "there exist many potential channels," Dell proposed, "the *mita*'s influence has persisted through its impacts on land tenure and public good provision." Outside the *mita* district boundaries, the Spanish *hacienda* system emerged—it was a feudal system, not a market in which labor was free. While the measured impact of the *mita* likely would have been even worse in comparison with "secure, enfranchised smallholders," Dell contrasted the two actual historical experiences in this region. Some exploitive conditions are worse than land inequality. Dell pointed out that the land tenure system in non-*mita* districts was more stable compared to *mita* districts, where there was no system of enforceable peasant titling even after the *mita* ended. For example, Dell cites a judicial procedure used in *mita* districts to seize land from peasants by falsely claiming their land was abandoned. Large landowners also had a profit incentive and the political influence to get more roads built in their districts. Dell argued that in this region of Peru, "large landowners—while they did not aim to promote economic prosperity for the masses—did shield individuals from exploitation by a highly extractive state and did ensure public goods."

Source: Melissa Dell. "The Persistent Effects of Peru's Mining Mita." *Econometrica* 78(2010): 1863–1903.

such as sugarcane could be profitably produced on slave plantations. It also emerged where a large, settled indigenous population could be coerced into labor. This history had long-term consequences, particularly in Latin America.[33] Where inequality was extreme, the result was less movement toward democratic institutions, less investment in public goods, and less widespread investment in human capital (education, skills, and health). These are among the ways in which extreme inequality is harmful to development and so is also an important long-term determinant of comparative development. We return to these themes later in this chapter.

The European colonial powers also had a dramatic and long-lasting impact on the economies and political and institutional structures of their African and Asian colonies by their introduction of three powerful and tradition-shattering ideas: private property, personal taxation, and the requirement that taxes be paid in money rather than in kind. These innovations were introduced in ways that facilitated elite rule rather than broad-based opportunity. The worst impact of colonization was probably felt in Africa, especially if one also considers the earlier slave trade. Whereas in former colonies such as India local people played a role in colonial governance, in Africa most governance was administered by expatriates. Other well-documented impacts included lasting damage to social trust.[34]

In Latin America, a longer history of political independence plus a more shared colonial heritage (Spanish and Portuguese) has meant that in spite of geographic and demographic diversity, the countries possess relatively similar economic, social, and cultural institutions and face similar problems, albeit with particular hardships for indigenous peoples and descendants of slaves. Latin American countries have long been middle-income but rarely have advanced to high-income status—reflecting a situation now known as the "middle-income trap." In Asia, different colonial heritages and the diverse cultural traditions of the people have combined to create different institutional and social patterns in countries such as India (British), the Philippines (Spanish and American), Vietnam (French), Indonesia (Dutch), Korea (Japanese), and China (not formally colonized but dominated by a variety of foreign powers).[35] To a widely varying degree, newly independent nations continued to experience foreign domination by former colonial powers and the United States, and in a number of countries by the Soviet Union, particularly during the Cold War period. The diversity of colonial experiences is one of the important factors that help explain the wide spectrum of development outcomes in today's world.

External Dependence Relatedly, developing countries have also been less well organized and influential in international relations, with sometimes adverse consequences for development. For example, agreements within the World Trade Organization (WTO) and its predecessors concerning matters such as agricultural subsidies in rich countries that harm developing-country farmers and one-sided regulation of intellectual property rights have often been relatively unfavorable to the developing world. The "Doha Development Round" of trade negotiations that began in 2001 was supposed to rectify some of these imbalances, but talks have been essentially stalled since 2008 (see Chapter 12). During debt crises in the 1980s and 1990s, the interests of international banks often prevailed over those of desperately indebted nations (discussed in Chapter 13). More generally, developing nations have weaker bargaining positions than developed nations in international economic relations. Developing nations often also voice great concern over various forms of cultural dependence, from news and entertainment to business practices, lifestyles, and social values. The potential importance of these concerns should not be underestimated, either in their direct effects on development in its broader meanings or indirect impacts on the speed or character of national development.

Developing nations are also dependent on the developed world for environmental preservation, on which hopes for sustainable development depend. Of greatest concern, global warming is projected to harm developing regions more than developed ones; yet both accumulated and current greenhouse gas emissions still largely originate in the high-income countries, despite the role of developing-country deforestation and growing emissions from lower-middle-income countries such as China and India. Thus the developing world endures what may be called *environmental dependence*, in which it must rely on the developed world to cease aggravating the problem and to develop solutions, including mitigation at home and assistance in developing countries. This topic is explored further in Chapter 10.

2.5 How Low-Income Countries Today Differ from Developed Countries in Their Earlier Stages

The position of developing countries today is in many important ways significantly different from that of the currently developed countries when they embarked on their era of modern economic growth. We can identify eight significant differences in initial conditions that require a special analysis of the growth prospects and requirements of modern economic development:

1. Physical and human resource endowments

2. Per capita incomes and levels of GDP in relation to the rest of the world

3. Climate

4. Population size, distribution, and growth

5. Historical role of international migration

6. International trade benefits

7. Basic scientific and technological research and development capabilities

8. Efficacy of domestic institutions

We will discuss each of these conditions with a view toward formulating requirements and priorities for generating and sustaining economic growth in developing countries.

Physical and Human Resource Endowments

Contemporary developing countries are often less well endowed with natural resources than the currently developed nations were at the time when the latter nations began their modern growth. Some developing nations are blessed with abundant supplies of petroleum, minerals, and raw materials for which world demand is growing; most less developed countries, however—especially in Asia, where more than half of the world's population resides—are poorly endowed with natural resources. Moreover, in parts of Africa, where natural resources are more plentiful, and geologists anticipate that there is far more yet to be discovered, heavy investments of capital are needed to exploit them, which until very recently has been strongly inhibited by domestic conflict and perhaps Western attitudes. A new wave of investments from China and other "nontraditional investors" has begun to change the picture, though critics are raising concerns about the process and foreign appropriation of gains.

The difference in skilled human resource endowments is even more pronounced. The ability of a country to exploit its natural resources and to initiate and sustain long-term economic growth is dependent on, among other things, the ingenuity and the managerial and technical skills of its people and its access to critical market and product information at minimal cost.[36] Paul Romer argues that today's developing nations "are poor because their citizens do not have access to the ideas that are used in industrial nations to generate economic value."[37] For Romer, the technology gap between rich and poor nations can be divided into two components, a physical object gap, involving factories, roads, and modern machinery, and an idea gap, including knowledge about marketing, distribution, inventory control, transactions processing, and worker motivation. This idea gap, and what Thomas Homer-Dixon calls the ingenuity gap (the ability to apply innovative ideas to solve practical social and technical problems), between rich and poor nations lies at the core of the development divide. There were no comparative human resource gaps for the now developed countries on the eve of their industrialization.

Relative Levels of Per Capita Income and GDP

The people living in low-income countries have, on average, a lower level of real per capita income than their developed-country counterparts had in the nineteenth century. First of all, nearly 40% of the population of developing countries is attempting to subsist at bare minimum levels. Obviously, the average standard of living in, say, early-nineteenth-century England was nothing to envy or boast about, but it was not as economically debilitating or precarious as it is today for a large fraction of people in the 40 or so least developed countries, the people now often referred to as the "bottom billion."

Second, at the beginning of their modern growth era, today's developed nations were economically in advance of the rest of the world. They could therefore take advantage of their relatively strong financial position to widen the income gaps between themselves and less fortunate countries in a long period of income divergence. By contrast, today's developing countries began their growth process at the low end of the international per capita income scale.

Climatic Differences

Almost all developing countries are situated in tropical or subtropical climatic zones. It has been observed that the economically most successful countries are located in the temperate zone. Although social inequality and institutional factors are widely believed to be of greater importance, the dichotomy is more than coincidence. Colonialists apparently created unhelpful "extractive" institutions where they found it uncomfortable to settle. But also, the extremes of heat and humidity in most poor countries contribute to deteriorating soil quality and the rapid depreciation of many natural goods. They also contribute to the low productivity of certain crops, the weakened regenerative growth of forests, and the poor health of animals. Extremes of heat and humidity not only cause discomfort to workers but can also weaken their health, reduce their desire to engage in strenuous physical work, and generally lower their levels of productivity and efficiency. As you will see in Chapter 8, malaria and other serious parasitic diseases are often concentrated in tropical areas. There is evidence that tropical geography does pose significant problems for economic development and that special attention in development assistance must be given to these problems, such as a concerted international effort to develop a malaria vaccine.[38]

Population Size, Distribution, and Growth

In Chapter 6, we will examine in detail some of the development problems and issues associated with rapid population growth. At this point, it is sufficient to note that population size, density, and growth constitute another important difference between less developed and developed countries. Before and during their early growth years, Western nations experienced a very slow rise in population growth. As industrialization proceeded, population growth rates increased primarily as a result of falling death rates but also because of slowly rising birth rates. However, at no time did European and North American countries have natural population growth rates in excess of 2% per annum, and they generally averaged much less.

By contrast, the populations of many developing countries have been increasing at annual rates in excess of 2.5% in recent decades, and some are still rising that fast today. Moreover, the concentration of these large and growing populations in a few areas means that many developing countries have considerably higher person-to-land ratios than the European countries did in their early growth years. Finally, in terms of comparative absolute size, no country that embarked on a long-term period of successful economic growth approached the present-day population size of India, Egypt, Pakistan, Indonesia, Nigeria, or Brazil. Nor were their rates of natural increase anything like that of present-day Kenya, the Philippines, Bangladesh, Malawi, or Guatemala. In fact, many observers doubt whether the Industrial Revolution and the high long-term growth rates of contemporary developed countries could have been achieved or proceeded so fast and with so few setbacks and disturbances, especially for the very poor, had their populations been expanding so rapidly.

The Historical Role of International Migration

In the nineteenth and early twentieth centuries, a major outlet for rural populations was international migration, which was both widespread and large-scale. More than 60 million people migrated to the Americas between 1850 and 1914, a time when world population averaged less than a quarter of its current levels. In countries such as Italy, Germany, and Ireland, periods of famine or pressure on the land often combined with limited economic opportunities in urban industry to push unskilled rural workers toward the labor-scarce nations of North America and Australia. In Brinley Thomas's famous description, the "three outstanding contributions of European labor to the American economy—1,187,000 Irish and 919,000 Germans between 1847 and 1855, 418,000 Scandinavians and 1,045,000 Germans between 1880 and 1885, and 1,754,000 Italians between 1898 and 1907—had the character of evacuations."[39]

Whereas the main thrust of international emigration up to World War I was both distant and permanent, the period since World War II witnessed a resurgence of international migration within Europe itself, which is essentially over short distances and to a large degree temporary. However, the economic forces giving rise to this migration are basically the same; that is, during the 1960s, surplus rural workers from southern Italy, Greece, and Turkey flocked into areas of labor shortages, most notably western Germany and Switzerland. Similar trends have been observed following the expansion of the European Union. The fact that this later migration from regions of surplus labor in southern and southeastern Europe was initially of both a permanent and a nonpermanent nature provided a valuable dual benefit to the relatively poor areas from which these unskilled workers migrated. The home governments were relieved of the costs of providing for people who in all probability would remain unemployed, and because a large percentage of the workers' earnings were sent home, these governments received a valuable and not insignificant source of foreign exchange.[40]

Historically, at least in the case of Africa, migrant labor both within and between countries was rather common and did provide some relief for locally depressed areas. Until recently, considerable benefits accrued and numerous potential problems were avoided by the fact that thousands of unskilled laborers in Burkina Faso were able to find temporary work in neighboring Côte d'Ivoire.

The same was true for Egyptians, Pakistanis, and Indians in Kuwait and Saudi Arabia; Tunisians, Moroccans, and Algerians in southern Europe; Colombians in Venezuela; and Haitians in the Dominican Republic. However, there is far less scope for reducing the pressures of growing populations in developing countries today through massive international emigration, largely due to the very restrictive nature of immigration laws in modern developed countries.

Despite these restrictions, well over 50 million people from the developing world have managed to migrate to the developed world since 1960. The pace of migration from developing to developed countries—particularly to the United States, Canada, and Australia—has picked up since the mid-1980s to between 2 and 3 million people per year. And the numbers of undocumented or illegal migrants have increased dramatically since 1980. Some people in recipient industrialized nations feel that these migrants are taking jobs away from poor, unskilled citizen workers. Moreover, illegal migrants and their families are often believed to be taking unfair advantage of free local health, educational, and social services, causing upward pressure on local taxes to support these services—despite emerging evidence that legalizing immigration actually provides a net positive effect on reducing deficits as well as to overall economic activity.[41] As a result, major debates are now under way in both the United States and Europe regarding the treatment of illegal migrants. Many citizens want severe restrictions on the number of immigrants that are permitted to enter or reside in developed countries.[42] The anti-immigration law passed in Arizona in 2010 reinforced the deterrent effect of the Mexico-U.S. border fence and also led many legal immigrants to feel vulnerable; a vociferous political debate surrounded proposed immigration reform legislation in the United States in 2013. In Europe, anti-immigrant parties have scored major gains, as in the Netherlands and Sweden in 2010.

The irony of international migration today, however, is not merely that this traditional outlet for surplus people has effectively been closed off but that many of the people who migrate from poor to richer lands are the very ones that developing countries can least afford to lose: the highly educated and skilled. Since the great majority of these migrants move on a permanent basis, this perverse **brain drain** not only represents a loss of valuable human resources but could also prove to be a serious constraint on the future economic progress of developing nations. For example, between 1960 and 1990, more than a million high-level professional and technical workers from the developing countries migrated to the United States, Canada, and the United Kingdom. By the late 1980s, Africa had lost nearly one-third of its skilled workers, with up to 60,000 middle- and high-level managers migrating to Europe and North America between 1985 and 1990. Sudan, for example, lost 17% of its doctors and dentists, 20% of its university teachers, 30% of its engineers, and 45% of its surveyors. The Philippines lost 12% of its professional workers to the United States, and 60% of Ghanaian doctors came to practice abroad.[43] India has been concerned that it may be unable to meet its burgeoning requirements for information technology workers in its growing high-tech enclaves if emigration to the United States, Canada, and the United Kingdom continues at its current pace.[44] Globally, remittances from illegal and legal migrants have been topping $100 million annually in this century and approached $200 billion in 2006.[45] Migration, when it is permitted, reduces poverty for migrants

Brain drain The emigration of highly educated and skilled professionals and technicians from the developing countries to the developed world.

and their families, and most of the poverty-reducing benefits of migration for those remaining in the origin countries come through remittances.[46] This is an extremely important resource (see Chapter 14).

Paradoxically, a *potential* benefit is that the mere possibility of skilled emigration may encourage many more workers to acquire information technology or other skills than are ultimately able to leave, leading to a net *increase* in labor force skills. At least in theory, the result could actually be a "brain gain."[47] The fundamental point remains, however, that the possibility of international migration of unskilled workers on a scale proportional to that of the nineteenth and early twentieth centuries no longer exists to provide an equivalent safety valve for the unskilled contemporary populations of Africa, Asia, and Latin America.

The Growth Stimulus of International Trade

Free trade Trade in which goods can be imported and exported without any barriers in the forms of tariffs, quotas, or other restrictions.

International **free trade** has been called the "engine of growth" that propelled the development of today's economically advanced nations during the nineteenth and early twentieth centuries. Rapidly expanding export markets provided an additional stimulus to growing local demands that led to the establishment of large-scale manufacturing industries. Together with a relatively stable political structure and flexible social institutions, these increased export earnings enabled the developing countries of the nineteenth century to borrow funds in the international capital market at very low interest rates. This capital accumulation in turn stimulated further production, made increased imports possible, and led to a more diversified industrial structure. In the nineteenth century, European and North American countries were able to participate in this dynamic growth of international exchange largely on the basis of relatively free trade, free capital movements, and the unfettered international migration of unskilled surplus labor.

In the twentieth century, the situation for many developing countries was very different. With the exception of a few very successful Asian countries, the non-oil-exporting (and even some oil-exporting) developing countries faced formidable difficulties in trying to generate rapid economic growth on the basis of world trade. For much of the past century, many developing countries experienced a deteriorating trade position. Their exports expanded, but usually not as fast as the exports of developed nations. Their **terms of trade** (the price they receive for their exports relative to the price they have to pay for imports) declined over several decades. Export volume therefore had to grow faster just to earn the same amount of foreign currency as in previous years. Moreover, it is unclear whether the commodity price boom of the early twenty-first century, which reversed only a portion of the long-term price declines, and fueled by the spectacular growth in China, can be maintained. Commodity prices are also subject to large, potentially destabilizing price fluctuations (see Chapter 13).

Terms of trade The ratio of a country's average export price to its average import price.

Where developing countries are successful at becoming lower-cost producers of competitive products with the developed countries (e.g., textiles, clothing, shoes, some light manufactures), the latter have often resorted to various forms of tariff and nontariff barriers to trade, including "voluntary" import quotas, excessive sanitary requirements, intellectual property claims, antidumping "investigations," and special licensing arrangements. But in recent years, an increasing number of developing countries, particularly China and others in East and Southeast Asia, have benefited from expanded manufactures exports to developed countries. We will discuss the economics of international trade and finance in the development context in detail in Part Three.

Basic Scientific and Technological Research and Development Capabilities

Basic scientific research and technological development have played a crucial role in the modern economic growth experience of contemporary developed countries. Their high rates of growth have been sustained by the interplay between mass applications of many new technological innovations based on a rapid advancement in the stock of scientific knowledge and further additions to that stock of knowledge made possible by growing surplus wealth. And even today, the process of scientific and technological advance in all its stages, from basic research to product development, is heavily concentrated in the rich nations, despite the emergence of China and India as destinations for **research and development (R&D)** activities of multinational corporations. Moreover, research funds are spent on solving the economic and technological problems of concern to rich countries in accordance with their own economic priorities and resource endowments.[48]

> **Research and development (R&D)** Scientific investigation with a view toward improving the existing quality of human life, products, profits, factors of production, or knowledge.

In the important area of scientific and technological research, low-income developing nations in particular are in an extremely disadvantageous position vis-à-vis the developed nations. In contrast, when the latter countries were embarking on their early growth process, they were scientifically and technologically greatly in advance of the rest of the world. They could consequently focus on staying ahead by designing and developing new technology at a pace dictated by their long-term economic growth requirements.

Efficacy of Domestic Institutions

Another difference between most developing countries and most developed countries at the time of their early stages of economic development lies in the efficacy of domestic economic, political, and social institutions. By the time of their early industrialization, many developed countries, notably the United Kingdom, the United States, and Canada, had economic rules in place that provided relatively broad access to opportunity for individuals with entrepreneurial drive. Earlier in the chapter, we noted that high inequality and poor institutions facilitating extraction rather than providing incentives for productivity were often established by colonial powers. Today such extraction may be carried out by powerful local interests as well as foreign ones. But it is very difficult to change institutions rapidly. As Douglass North stresses, even if the formal rules "may be changed overnight, the informal rules usually change only ever so gradually."[49] We will return to the question of economic institutions later in the chapter.

The developed countries also typically enjoyed relatively stronger political stability and more flexible social institutions with broader access to mobility. States typically emerged more organically over a longer period of time in the developed regions, and consolidation as nation-states generally occurred before the industrial era. In contrast, particularly in Africa, national boundaries were more arbitrarily dictated by colonial powers. The "failed state," and states in danger of becoming so, is a phenomenon of the postcolonial period, with roots in imperial and colonial practices. Although many developing nations have roots in ancient civilizations, a long hiatus often existed between autonomous regimes.

2.6 Are Living Standards of Developing and Developed Nations Converging?

At the dawn of the industrial era, average real living standards in the richest countries were no more than three times as great as those of the poorest. Today, the ratio approaches 100 to 1. So as noted by Lant Pritchett, there is no doubt that today's developed countries have enjoyed far higher rates of economic growth averaged over two centuries than today's developing countries, a process known as **divergence**. Theories of economic growth are discussed in Chapter 3. But in comparing development performance among developing nations and between developed and developing countries, it is appropriate to consider whether, with strenuous economic development efforts being made throughout the developing world, living standards of developing and developed nations are exhibiting **convergence**.

If the growth experience of developing and developed countries were similar, there are two important reasons to expect that developing countries would be "catching up" by growing faster on average than developed countries. The first reason is due to technology transfer. Today's developing countries do not have to "reinvent the wheel"; for example, they do not have to use vacuum tubes before they can use semiconductors. Even if royalties must be paid, it is cheaper to replicate technology than to undertake original R&D, partly because one does not have to pay for mistakes and dead ends along the way. This should enable developing countries to "leapfrog" over some of the earlier stages of technological development, moving immediately to high-productivity techniques of production. As a result, they should be able to grow much faster than today's developed countries are growing now or were able to grow in the past, when they had to invent the technology as they went along and proceed step by step through the historical stages of innovation. (This is known as an "advantage of backwardness," a term coined by economic historian Alexander Gerschenkron.) In fact, if we confine our attention to cases of successful development, the later a country begins its modern economic growth, the shorter the time needed to double output per worker. For example, Britain doubled its output per person in the first 60 years of its industrial development, and the United States did so in 45 years. South Korea once doubled per capita output in less than 12 years, and China has done so in less than 9 years.

The second reason to expect convergence if conditions are similar is based on factor accumulation. Today's developed countries have high levels of physical and human capital; in a production function analysis, this would explain their high levels of output per person. But in traditional neoclassical analysis,

Divergence   A tendency for per capita income (or output) to grow faster in higher-income countries than in lower-income countries so that the income gap widens across countries over time (as was seen in the two centuries after industrialization began).

Convergence   The tendency for per capita income (or output) to grow faster in lower-income countries than in higher-income countries so that lower-income countries are "catching up" over time. When countries are hypothesized to converge not in all cases but *other things being equal* (particularly savings rates, labor force growth, and production technologies), then the term *conditional convergence* is used.

the marginal product of capital and the profitability of investments would be lower in developed countries where capital intensity is higher, provided that the law of diminishing returns applied. That is, the impact of additional capital on output would be expected to be smaller in a developed country that already had a lot of capital in relation to the size of its workforce than in a developing country where capital was scarce. As a result, we would expect higher investment rates in developing countries, either through domestic sources or through attracting foreign investment (see Chapter 14). With higher investment rates, capital would grow more quickly in developing countries until approximately equal levels of capital and (other things being equal) output per worker were achieved.[50]

Given one or both of these conditions, technology transfer and more rapid capital accumulation, incomes would tend toward convergence in the long run as the faster-growing developing countries would be catching up with the slower-growing developed countries. Even if incomes did not eventually turn out to be identical, they would at least tend to converge *conditional on* (i.e., after also taking account of any systematic differences in) key variables such as population growth rates and savings rates (this argument is formalized in the neoclassical growth model examined in Chapter 3 and Appendix 3.2). Given the huge differences in capital and technology across countries, if growth conditions were similar, we should see tendencies for convergence in the data.

Whether there is now convergence in the world economy depends on two levels of how the question is framed: whether across average country incomes or across individuals (considering the world as if it were one country); and whether focusing on relative gaps or absolute gaps.

Relative Country Convergence   The most widely used approach is simply to examine whether poorer countries are growing faster than richer countries. As long as this is happening, poor countries would be on a path to eventually "catch up" to the income levels of rich countries. In the meantime, the *relative* gap in incomes would be shrinking, as the income of richer countries would become a smaller multiple of income of poorer countries (or looked at from the other perspective, incomes of poor countries would become an increasingly large fraction of income of rich countries). This can be seen on a country-by-country basis. Although China's average income was just 3% that of the United States in 1980, it was estimated to have reached 14% of U.S. income by 2007. But in the same period, the income of the DRC fell from about 5% of U.S. levels to just 1%. But globally, evidence for relative convergence is weak, even for the most recent decades.

Figure 2.7a illustrates the typical findings of this literature. On the *x*-axis, income data are plotted from the initial year, in this case 1980; while on the *y*-axis, the average growth rate of real per capita income is plotted, in this case, over the subsequent 27 years to 2007. If there were unconditional convergence, there would be a tendency for the points plotted to show a clear negative relationship, with the initially lower-income countries growing faster. But as seen in Figure 2.7a there is no apparent tendency toward convergence across countries. In fact, even in this recent period, about 60% of countries grew more slowly than the United States. Looking just at the developing countries, as in Figure 2.7b, it is clear that divergence is occurring: middle-income countries are

FIGURE 2.7   Relative Country Convergence: World, Developing Countries, and OECD

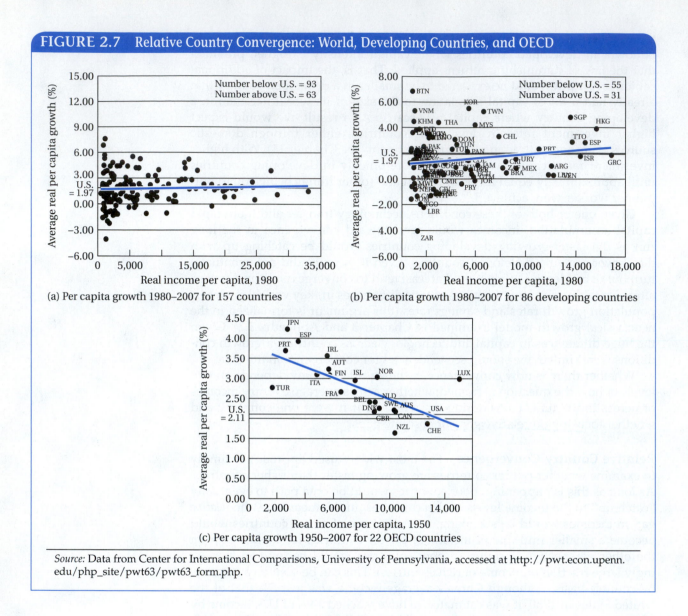

(a) Per capita growth 1980–2007 for 157 countries

(b) Per capita growth 1980–2007 for 86 developing countries

(c) Per capita growth 1950–2007 for 22 OECD countries

Source: Data from Center for International Comparisons, University of Pennsylvania, accessed at http://pwt.econ.upenn.edu/php_site/pwt63/pwt63_form.php.

growing faster than low-income countries, so there is a growing gap among developing countries. Many nations, especially among the 49 least developed countries, remain in relative stagnation. Poor developing countries have not been catching up as a group.[51]

In Figure 2.7c, growth of high-income OECD countries is examined separately for 1950–2007. The picture here is one of convergence, and we need to interpret it carefully. One explanation is that all of these countries have similar features, including a relatively early start at modern economic growth. This makes the countries more able to borrow technology from each other, as well as trade with and invest in each other's economies. We might conjecture that if developing countries closely followed the institutions and policies of these OECD economies, they might converge as well. However, as noted earlier, there are many institutional and other differences between low- and high-income economies today, some of which may be very difficult to change; we explore these further in the next section. Moreover, a poor country cannot force a rich country to lower its trade barriers. In any case, one must draw conclusions from the results with great caution because of *selection bias*. That is, among today's rich countries, some were relatively rich in the past and some relatively poor; in order for them all to be rich countries today, the poor countries *had* to have grown faster than the rich ones, simply as a matter of logic. Confining attention just to the rich countries thus commits the statistical error of selection bias.[52] Nevertheless, the strong evidence for convergence among the OECD countries, together with the failure at least until very recently to find compelling evidence for longer-term convergence for the world as a whole, particularly divergence for the least developed countries, is likely one reflection of the difference in growth conditions between now developed and developing countries.

Absolute Country Convergence   With the recent rapid growth in China, and the acceleration of growth in South Asia as well, these regions are currently on a path of relative country convergence. For example, in the 1990–2003 period, while income grew 24% in high-income OECD countries, it grew 56% in South Asia and 196% in China. But due to their relatively low starting income levels, despite higher growth, income gains were still smaller in absolute amount than in the OECD, as illustrated in Figure 2.8. That is, even when the average income of a developing country is becoming a larger fraction of developed

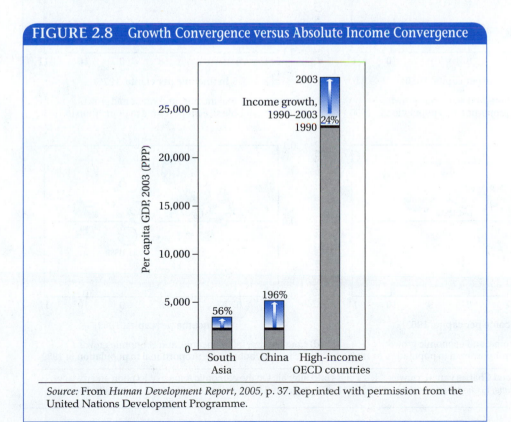

FIGURE 2.8   Growth Convergence versus Absolute Income Convergence

Source: From *Human Development Report, 2005*, p. 37. Reprinted with permission from the United Nations Development Programme.

country average incomes, the difference in incomes can still continue to widen for some time before they finally begin to shrink. A process of absolute country convergence is a stronger standard than (and appears only with a lag after) a process of relative country convergence.[53]

Population-Weighted Relative Country Convergence   The high growth rate in China and India is particularly important, because more than one-third of the world's people live in these two countries. This approach frames the question so as to weight the importance of a country's per capita income growth rate proportionately to the size of its population. A typical study of this type is depicted in Figure 2.9a–d. Instead of points representing the data for each country, bubble sizes are used to depict the relative size of countries'

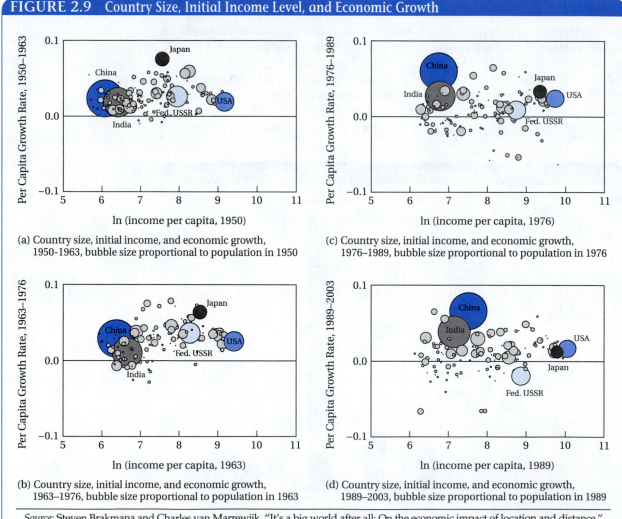

FIGURE 2.9   Country Size, Initial Income Level, and Economic Growth

(a) Country size, initial income, and economic growth, 1950-1963, bubble size proportional to population in 1950

(b) Country size, initial income, and economic growth, 1963–1976, bubble size proportional to population in 1963

(c) Country size, initial income, and economic growth, 1976–1989, bubble size proportional to population in 1976

(d) Country size, initial income, and economic growth, 1989–2003, bubble size proportional to population in 1989

Source: Steven Brakmana and Charles van Marrewijk, "It's a big world after all: On the economic impact of location and distance," *Cambridge Journal of Regions, Economy and Society* 1 (2008): 411–437. Reprinted by permission of Oxford University Press.

populations. To get a sense of how the acceleration of growth in China and India, along with a few other countries, have changed the picture, the data are broken up into four time periods. Figures 2.9a and 2.9b reflect that there was relative per capita *divergence* from 1950 through 1976, but Figure 2.9d reflects relative per capita convergence since 1989 (and less unambiguously but plausibly from 1977 to 1989 as well—see Figure 2.9c). If current trends continue (a "big if" given widespread predictions for a slowing of their growth rates), then China, India, and Brazil will account for nearly 40% of global output by 2050, compared with about 10% in 1950.[54] Although it is true that conditions have remained stagnant or even deteriorated in many of the least developed countries, because of their smaller population sizes with the population-weighted approach, this divergence effect is more than compensated for by growth in countries with large populations. Note that all such trends may be subject to change. For example, the population growth rates of the 49 least developed countries and other low-income countries are much higher than those of the middle- and upper-income countries; so their population-weights are increasing over time. African countries may see a furtherance of their recent trend to faster growth magnifying the new trend to global convergence; or they and other developing regions may see a growth slowdown, with commodity prices falling again and continuing governance problems; and the global economy could return to a period of divergence. These trends will be watched closely.

World-as-One-Country Convergence   An alternative approach to the study of convergence is to think of the world as if it were one country. In the first such study, Branko Milanovic stitched together household data sets from around the world and concluded that global inequality rose significantly in the period 1988 to 1993.[55] Studies of this kind are difficult to carry out. The most important difference from population-weighted country convergence is that a world-as-one-country convergence study can take into account changes in inequality *within* countries as well as between them. In particular, the widening gulf between incomes in rural and urban China had a major effect on the finding of global divergence using this method. But most researchers and policymakers frame development as a process that occurs on the national level, something rather different from global inequality; and country convergence studies remain the standard.

Sectoral Convergence   Despite evidence that economies are not converging unconditionally, there can be cross-national convergence of economic sectors, which in turn may signal the potential for future convergence. In particular, Dani Rodrik found evidence that there has been convergence in manufacturing, with implications that the failure to find overall convergence across countries is due to the small share and slow growth of manufacturing employment in low-income countries.[56]

2.7 Long-Run Causes of Comparative Development

What explains the extreme variations in development achievement to date among developing and developed countries? The next two chapters examine theories of economic growth and development processes and policy challenges;

here we present a schematic framework for appreciating the major long-run causes of comparative development[57] that have been argued in some of the most influential research literature of this century.[58] (Bear in mind that research on this important subject is still at a relatively early stage; scholars have legitimate disagreements about emphasis and substance, and new findings are being reported regularly.)

First, in the very long run, few economists doubt that physical geography, including climate, has had an important impact on economic history. *Geography* was once truly exogenous, even if human activity can now alter it, for better or worse. But the economic role played by geography, such as tropical climate, today is less clear. Some research suggests that when other factors, notably inequality and institutions, are taken into account, physical geography adds little to our understanding of current development levels. However, some evidence is mixed. For example, there is some evidence of an independent impact of malaria and indications that in some circumstances, landlocked status may be an impediment to economic growth; indeed, a direct link is argued by some economists,[59] so this possible effect is reflected in **Arrow 1** connecting geography to *income and human development* on the left side of Figure 2.10. Recently, the debate on comparative economic development has been widened further with some evidence that an intermediate degree of genetic diversity (heterozygosity) of human populations is most conducive to long-run economic development.[60]

Economic institutions, which play an important role in comparative development, are defined by Nobel laureate Douglass North as the "rules of the game" of economic life. As such, institutions provide the underpinning of a market economy by establishing the rules of property rights and contract enforcement; improving coordination;[61] restricting coercive, fraudulent, and anticompetitive behavior; providing access to opportunities for a broad population; constraining the power of elites; and managing conflict more generally. Moreover, institutions include social insurance (which also serves to legitimize market competition) and the provision of predictable macroeconomic stability.[62] Countries with higher incomes can afford better institutions, so it is challenging to identify the impact of institutions on income. But recently, development economists have made influential contributions toward achieving this research goal.

As noted earlier, most developing countries were once colonies. Geography affected the types of colonies established (**Arrow 2**), with one of the now best known geographic features being settler mortality rates, whose impact[63] was examined in work by Daron Acemoglu, Simon Johnson, and James Robinson. In this argument, when potential settlers faced higher mortality rates (or perhaps other high costs), they more often ruled at arm's length and avoided large, long-term settlement. Their interest could be summarized as "steal fast and get out" or "get locals to steal for you." Unfavorable institutions were therefore established, favoring extraction over production incentives. But where mortality was low, populations were not dense, and exploitation of resources required substantial efforts by colonists, institutions broadly encouraging investments, notably constraints on executives and protection from expropriation, were established (sometimes as a result of agitation from settlers who had the bargaining power to demand better treatment). These effects are reflected by **Arrow 3**. Acemoglu and colleagues present evidence that after

Economic Institutions
"Humanly devised" constraints that shape interactions (or "rules of the game") in an economy, including formal rules embodied in constitutions, laws, contracts, and market regulations, plus informal rules reflected in norms of behavior and conduct, values, customs, and generally accepted ways of doing things.

FIGURE 2.10   Schematic Representation of Leading Theories of Comparative Development

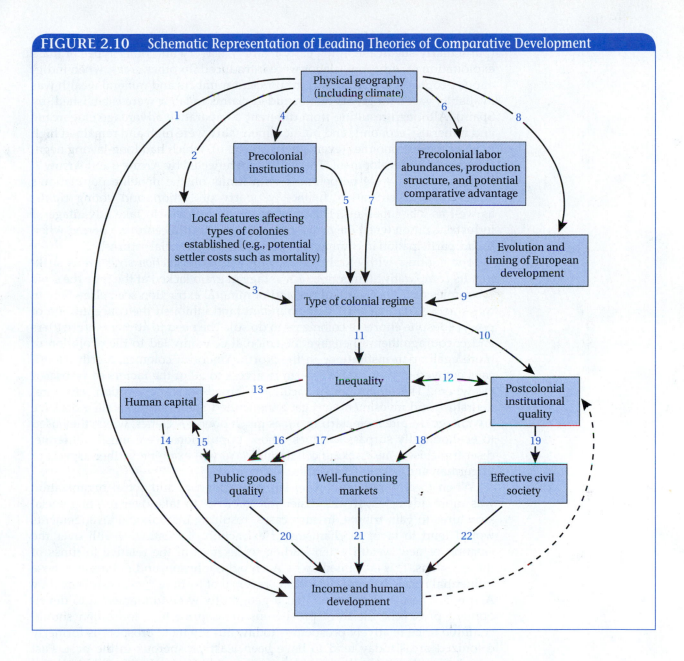

accounting for institutional differences, geographic variables (e.g., closeness to the equator) have little influence on incomes today.[64] Their statistical estimates imply large effects of institutions on per capita income.

The influence of geography on *precolonial institutions* is captured by **Arrow 4**. Precolonial institutions also mattered to the extent that they had influence on the *type of colonial regime* established. This possible effect is reflected by **Arrow 5**.

Precolonial comparative advantage and evolving *labor abundances* in the Americas and their relation to the institutions established have been examined in the pioneering work of Stanley Engerman and Kenneth Sokoloff.[65] When climate was suitable for a *production structure* featuring plantation agriculture (particularly sugarcane in the early history), slavery and other types of mass exploitation of indigenous labor were introduced. In other areas, when indigenous peoples survived contact in sufficient numbers and mineral wealth was available, vast land grants that included claims to labor were established (by Spain). Although resulting from different comparative advantage (sugarcane and minerals), economic and political inequality were high and remained high in all of these economies (even among freemen), which had long-lasting negative effects on development. These links are reflected by **Arrow 6** and **Arrow 7**. Early inequities were perpetuated with limits on the nonelite population's access to land, education, finance, property protection, and voting rights, as well as labor markets. This inhibited opportunities to take advantage of industrialization when they emerged in the nineteenth century, a period when broad participation in commercial activity had high social returns.

The contrast with North American potential *production structure* is striking. Its comparative (emerging) advantage in grain lacked at the time the scale economies of tropical agriculture and of mineral extraction seen elsewhere in the Americas. Scarce labor with abundant land inhibited the concentration of power (despite efforts of colonizers to do so). The need to attract more settlers and encourage them to engage the colonial economy led to the evolution of more egalitarian institutions in the North American colonies. North Americans enjoyed greater egalitarianism in access to all of the factors so restricted elsewhere. This environment facilitated broad-based innovation, entrepreneurship, and investment and gave the United States and Canada a decisive advantage despite their starting out as much poorer societies, which they used to economically surpass societies whose populations were mostly illiterate, disenfranchised, and lacking collateral.[66] (We will examine further aspects of Engerman and Sokoloff's analysis shortly.)

When local populations were larger and denser and social organization was more advanced, it was easier for colonists to take over existing social structures to gain tribute. In such cases, resulting institutional arrangements would tend to favor mechanisms of extraction of existing wealth over the creation of new wealth, often leading to declines in the relative fortunes of these regions. This is pointed up by Acemoglu, Johnson, and Robinson, whose influential research on this historical "reversal of fortune"[67] is also reflected by **Arrow 5**. These authors stress that if geography were fundamental to development prospects, the most prosperous areas prior to colonization should continue to be relatively prosperous today. But the most prosperous formerly colonized areas today tend to have been least prosperous in the past. Past population density and past urbanization, which are positively correlated with past income, are *negatively* correlated with current income, these authors show.[68] There is evidence that Europeans set up more *extractive institutions* (ones designed to extract more surplus from colonized populations) in prosperous areas and that these institutions have often persisted to the contemporary period.[69]

Geography undoubtedly influenced early economic history in Europe.[70] This is reflected by **Arrow 8**, leading to *evolution and timing of European development*. Early development in Europe gave it advantages over most other regions—advantages that were used to colonize much of the world. But the types of colonial regimes implemented varied considerably, depending on conditions prevailing at the time of colonization both in the different parts of the world colonized and within the colonizer's home country. The timing of European development influenced the *type of colonial regime* established, reflected by **Arrow 9**. For example, it has been argued that for various reasons, earlier colonization generally involved more plunder and less active production than later colonization, although both occurred at the expense of the indigenous populations.[71]

Precolonial comparative advantage may also have interacted with the timing of European development in influencing institutions in that settlers in later-colonized temperate zones arrived with more knowledge and more advanced technology. In particular, Europeans brought better agricultural techniques to the later-settled areas such as North America. As noted by David Fielding and Sebastian Torres, by the eighteenth century, population growth in Europe and technical change had produced a large supply of people with temperate-zone agricultural skills in products such as wheat and dairy. They were able to gain higher incomes using these skills in temperate colonies and former colonies (the so-called neo-Europes).[72] Thus, precolonial (potential) comparative advantage again mattered. This link is reflected in the flow through **Arrow 6** and **Arrow 7**. The possible role played by specific skills also points up the importance of human capital investments for development, reflected by **Arrow 14**.

Thus, the types of colonial regimes established, while always designed for the benefit of the colonizers, were influenced by local and European supply and demand factors. The type of regime had enormous influence on *postcolonial institutional quality*, reflected by **Arrow 10**. For example, the depraved rule of Belgium's King Leopold II over the Congo (today's Democratic Republic of Congo) was arguably an ultimate cause of the oppressive Mobutu reign after independence. Of course, not all influences of colonialism were necessarily bad. Along with enslavement, subjugation, exploitation, loss of cultural heritage, and repression, colonists also brought modern scientific methods in fields such as medicine and agriculture. Note that this can be no apologia for colonialism, because these advances could have been gained without the societies' becoming colonized, as in Japan. Still, there is some evidence that countries and territories that spent a longer time as colonies (at least in the case of islands) have higher incomes than those that experienced shorter colonial periods, with this effect greater for entities colonized later (perhaps because earlier colonial activity had more pernicious effects than later ones). Even so, there are strong caveats to this finding.[73]

Besides creating specific institutions, European colonization created or reinforced differing degrees of *inequality* (often correlated with ethnicity), ultimately leading to diminished prospects for growth and development, notably in Latin America and the Caribbean. This is reflected by **Arrow 11**. High inequality often emerged as a result of slavery in regions where crops could be "efficiently" produced on slave plantations. They also emerged where a large, settled indigenous population could be coerced into labor. Such histories had long-term consequences, particularly in Latin America. As Engerman and Sokoloff have argued, the degree of inequality itself can shape the evolution of institutions as well as specific policies. Where inequality was extreme, there was less investment in *human capital* (**Arrow 13**) and other public goods

(**Arrow 16**) and, as reflected by the bidirectional **Arrow 12**, a tendency of *less* movement toward democratic institutions (which could also have facilitated movement to other constructive institutions).[74]

Thus, extreme inequality is likely to be a long-term factor in explaining comparative development. This is raised in the striking historical contrast between the states of North America and the states of Central and South America. There was greater egalitarianism in North America, though the inhuman treatment of Native Americans and of slaves in the southern colonies (later the United States) reflects the fact that this is not because the English settlers were inherently "nicer masters" than the Spanish. Still, much of the North American experience contrasts strongly with the extreme inequality of Central and South America and the Caribbean.[75] Engerman and Sokoloff argued that high inequality in Latin America led to low *human capital* investments, again in contrast to North America;[76] this mechanism is again reflected by **Arrow 13**. Elites in Latin America then loosened their control only when their returns to increased immigration, and thus to creating more attractive conditions for immigrants, were high. Besides creating specific institutions, then, European colonization created or reinforced different degrees of inequality, often cor-related with ethnicity. This history had long-term consequences, particularly in Latin America. In the direction from inequality to *postcolonial institutional quality*, **Arrow 12** reflects what has been termed the social conflict theory of institutions. Box 2.4 presents findings that inequality does negatively affect per capita income much in the way predicted by Engerman and Sokoloff.

Cultural factors may also matter in influencing the degree of emphasis on education, postcolonial institutional quality, and the effectiveness of civil society, though the precise roles of culture are not clearly established in relation to the economic factors surveyed in this section and so are not included in the diagram. In addition, institutional quality affects the amount and quality of investments in education and health, via the mediating impact of inequality. In countries with higher levels of education, institutions tend to be more dem-ocratic, with more constraints on elites. The causality between education and institutions could run in either direction, or both could be caused jointly by still other factors. Some scholars argue that some countries with bad institu-tions run by dictators have implemented good policies, including educational investments, and subsequently, after reaping the benefits in terms of growth, those countries have changed their institutions.[77] They argue that human cap-ital is at least as fundamental a source of long-run development as institu-tions. In the diagram, this would suggest adding an arrow from human capital back to postcolonial institutional quality; this is intuitively plausible, although additional evidence for this link will be needed for it to become more fully established.[78] Clearly, however, in some cases extractive colonial institutions left a legacy that resulted in poor health and education decades after indepen-dence; an example from India is examined in Box 2.5.

For the relatively small number of developing countries never colonized, such as Thailand, *type of colonial regime* can be reinterpreted in the diagram as institutional quality at an early stage of development (or as cultural influ-ences not shown)—but note that the evidence for causality patterns is not as convincing in these cases. However, the diversity of development experiences of never-colonized countries caution us not to place complete emphasis on the choices of colonizers; preexisting social capital may matter at least as much.[79]

BOX 2.4 FINDINGS Instruments to Test Theories of Comparative Development: Inequality

In a 2007 study, William Easterly used cross-country data to examine the Engerman and Sokoloff hypothesis. His research confirmed that "agricultural endowments predict inequality and inequality predicts development." Specifically, Easterly finds that inequality negatively affects per capita income; it also negatively affects institutional quality and schooling, which are "mechanisms by which higher inequality lowers per capita income." That the negative relationship between income and inequality is present in the data is clear—but how do development economists take the step to prediction and assignment of causality when measurement error and many confounding factors are present, such as the possible link that underdevelopment itself is a cause of inequality?

Sometimes development economists run field experiments—but obviously, we cannot randomly assign countries various levels of inequality to see what happens! In the many cases when field experiments are impossible, development economists frequently try to understand causality by searching for an instrumental variable (or "instrument"); in fact, many researchers in development economics invest a lot of their time in this search. This is a topic covered in classes in econometrics. But the basic idea is that to identify the effect of a potential causal variable c (such as inequality) on a development outcome variable d (such as income or educational attainment), the hunt is on for an elusive instrumental variable e that affects d only through e's effect on c. So an instrument has no independent effect on the outcome variable of interest. You saw earlier that Acemoglu, Johnson, and Robinson used settler mortality as an instrument for early institutions. Easterly uses "the abundance of land suitable for growing wheat relative to that suitable for growing sugarcane" as an instrument for inequality. Using this strategy, Easterly concludes that high inequality of the Engerman and Sokoloff variety is independently "a large and statistically significant barrier to prosperity, good quality institutions, and high schooling." Schooling and institutional quality are precisely the mechanisms proposed by Engerman and Sokoloff by which higher inequality leads to lower incomes. Like a leprechaun, a good instrumental variable is hard to get hold of but when caught can give the researcher's equivalent of a pot of gold. Though active debate on inequality and development continues, the interplay between the careful institutional analysis and economic history scholarship of Engerman and Sokoloff and the study of causality with larger data sets as used by Easterly gives a window into how the field of development economics continues to make progress.

Sources: William Easterly, "Inequality does cause underdevelopment," *Journal of Development Economics* 84 (2007): 755–776; Joshua D. Angrist and Jorn-Steffen Pischke, *Mostly Harmless Econometrics: An Empiricist's Companion* (Princeton, N.J.: Princeton University Press, 2008). For an important critique of the use and interpretation of instrumental variables (and also of randomization) in development economics research see Angus Deaton, "Instruments, randomization, and learning about development," *Journal of Economic Literature,* 48, no. 2 (2010): 424–455.

Never-colonized countries also show a dramatic range in performance; Ethiopia and Afghanistan remain very poor, Thailand is in the lower-middle range, Turkey is in the upper-middle range, and Japan is among the very wealthiest countries; China, starting among the poorest countries 30 years ago, is now rapidly ascending the income tables. The quality of institutions (and inequality) undoubtedly mattered in noncolonized societies; it is just harder to conclude that institutions led to income rather than only vice versa.

Clearly, human capital has a direct impact on *income and on human development* more broadly, as reflected by **Arrow 14**. The depth and breadth of education in the population will help determine the effectiveness of government as a force for development, reflected by **Arrow 15**. This is due not only

BOX 2.5 FINDINGS   Legacy of Colonial Land Tenure and Governance Systems

Substantial evidence on the importance of institutions is provided in a study of the impact of land revenue institutions established by the British Raj in India conducted by Abhijit Banerjee and Lakshmi Iyer. Because areas where land revenue collection was taken over by the British between 1820 and 1856 (but not before or after) were much more likely to have a non-landlord system, the authors used being conquered in this period as an instrument for having a non-landlord system. They also used other statistical tests that showed the results were robust. They found that historical differences in property rights institutions led to sustained differences in economic outcomes, in that the regions in which property rights to land were given to landlords have had significantly lower agricultural investments and productivity in the postindependence period than regions in which property rights were given to cultivators. The authors concluded that the divergence occurred because historical differences in institutions led to different policy choices. Tellingly, the regions in which landlords received the proprietary rights also had significantly lower investments in health and education in the postcolonial period.

In subsequent research, Lakshmi Iyer compared economic outcomes across areas in India that experienced direct versus indirect British colonial rule, controlling for the apparent colonial preference to annex higher-quality lands using another instrumental variable strategy. She found evidence that colonial governance quality had persistent effects on postcolonial outcomes; areas under direct rule received significantly less access to schools, health centers, and roads in the postcolonial period, with higher levels of poverty and infant mortality.

Sources: Abhijit Banerjee and Lakshmi Iyer, "History, institutions, and economic performance: The legacy of colonial land tenure systems in India," *American Economic Review* 95 (2005): 1190–1213; and Lakshmi Iyer, "Direct versus indirect colonial rule in India: Long-term consequences," *Review of Economics and Statistics* 92 (2010): 693–713. Preparation of this box also benefited from a manuscript, Lakshmi Iyer, "The long-run consequences of colonial institutions," draft, Harvard Business School, 2013.

to a better-qualified civil service but also to the understanding of citizens of poor government performance and the knowledge of how to work for a better outcome and capacity to organize.[80] Of course, education could also independently affect the organization and functioning of markets per se (arrow omitted), but the literature to date has primarily viewed the productive impact of human capital on market outcomes as a direct one, reflected by **Arrow 14**. These impacts are explored further in Chapter 8.

The type and quality of global integration (particularly trade) have been stressed as a boon to long-run growth and development in many World Bank reports. Trade may be beneficial in that it provides various kinds of access to technology.[81] And some economists argue that greater openness to trade beneficially affects the subsequent evolution of institutions. On the other hand, critics argue that the wrong kind of integration or the failure to complement integration with appropriate policies could be harmful to development. In fact, evidence suggests that once institutions are accounted for, trade itself explains very little, so for simplicity, integration is left out of the diagram.[82]

Postcolonial institutional quality has a strong impact on the effectiveness of the private, public, and citizen (or civil society) sectors. Democratic governance, rule of law, and constraints on elites will encourage more and better quality public goods, reflected by **Arrow 17**. Better property rights protections and contract enforcement for ordinary citizens and broad access to economic opportunities will spur private investments, reflected by **Arrow 18**. And institutions will affect the ability of civil society to organize and act effectively as a force independent of state and market, reflected by **Arrow 19**. Clearly, the activities of the three sectors will each have an influence on productivity and incomes, and on human development more generally, as reflected by **Arrows 20**, **21**, and **22**, respectively.[83] These factors are explored further in Chapter 11.

It is not yet entirely clear which economic institutions are most important in facilitating development or the degree to which strength in one institution can compensate for weakness in another.[84] Clearly, there are multiple paths to economic development (see, e.g., the case study of China at the end of Chapter 4). But a key finding of recent research is that forces that protect narrow elites in ways that limit access of the broader population to opportunities for advancement are major obstacles to successful economic development. If institutions are highly resistant to attempts at reform, this helps clarify why development is so challenging.

Nevertheless, in most countries with poor institutions, there is still much that can be done to improve human welfare and to encourage the development of better institutions. Indeed, economic institutions do change over time, even though political institutions such as voting rules sometimes change without altering the real distribution of power or without leading to genuine reform of economic institutions. Although the evidence of the impact of democracy on growth in the short to medium term is not strong (see Chapter 11), in the long run democratic governance and genuine development do go hand in hand, and the steady spread of more genuinely democratic institutions in the developing world is a very encouraging sign.[85] As Dani Rodrik has noted, "Participatory and decentralized political systems are the most effective ones we have for processing and aggregating local knowledge. We can think of democracy as a meta-institution for building other good institutions."[86] In addition, development strategies that lead to greater human capital, improve access to new technologies, produce better-quality public goods, improve market functioning, address deep-rooted problems of poverty, improve access to finance, prevent environmental degradation, and foster a vibrant civil society all promote development.

2.8 Concluding Observations

History matters. We have learned that conditions prevailing in a developing nation when European colonialism began had a large impact on the subsequent history of inequality and institutional development in the nation in ways that either facilitated or thwarted participation in modern economic growth after the Industrial Revolution arrived in the late eighteenth century. And poor institutions have generally proved very resistant to efforts at reform. But the new perspectives do not imply that development is impossible! Instead, they serve to clarify the nature of the great challenges facing many developing nations. The phenomenon of underdevelopment is best viewed in both a national and an international context. Problems of poverty, inequality, low productivity, population growth, unemployment, primary-product export dependence, and international vulnerability have both domestic and global origins and potential solutions.

It should be remembered that most developing nations have succeeded in raising incomes significantly. And most developing countries have had notable successes in lowering infant mortality, improving educational access, and narrowing gender disparities.[87] By pursuing appropriate economic and social policies both at home and abroad and with effective assistance from developed nations, even the least developed countries do indeed have the means to realize their development aspirations. Parts Two and Three will discuss the ways in which these hopes and objectives can be attained.

But concomitant and complementary human capital, technological, social, and institutional changes must take place if long-term economic growth is to be realized. Such transformations must occur not only within individual developing countries but also in the international economy. In other words, unless there is some major structural, attitudinal, and institutional reform in the world economy, one that accommodates the rising aspirations and rewards the outstanding performances of individual developing nations, particularly the least developed countries, internal economic and social transformation within the developing world may be insufficient.[88]

There may be some "advantages of backwardness" in development, such as the ability to use existing, proven technologies rather than having to reinvent the wheel and even leapfrogging over older technology standards that developed countries have become locked into. One can also learn valuable lessons from economic policies that have been tried in various countries around the world. These advantages are especially helpful if an economy can successfully manage to get sustained modern economic growth under way, as, for example, in Taiwan, South Korea, China, and a few other cases. However, for most very poor countries, backwardness comes with severe disadvantages, many of which have been compounded by legacies of colonialism, slavery, and Cold War dictatorships. In either case, countries will generally have to do more than simply emulate policies followed by today's developed countries while they were in their early stages of development.

Despite the obvious diversity of these countries, and growing gaps between middle- and low-income countries, most developing nations share a set of common and well-defined goals. These include a reduction in poverty, inequality, and unemployment; the provision of basic education, health, housing, and food to every citizen; the broadening of economic and social opportunities; and the forging of a cohesive nation-state. Related to these economic, social, and political goals are the common problems shared in varying degrees by most developing countries: chronic absolute poverty, high levels of unemployment and underemployment, wide disparities in the distribution of income, low levels of agricultural productivity, sizable imbalances between urban and rural levels of living and economic opportunities, discontent on the part of the segments of the population not benefiting from economic growth, serious and worsening environmental decay, antiquated and inappropriate educational and health systems, and substantial dependence on foreign technologies, institutions, and value systems. It is therefore also possible and useful to talk about the similarities of critical development problems and to analyze these problems in a broad developing world perspective.

Economic and social development will often be impossible without corresponding changes in the social, political, legal, and economic institutions of a nation, such as land tenure systems, forms of governance, educational structures, labor market relationships, property rights, contract law, civic freedoms, the distribution and control of physical and financial assets, laws of taxation and inheritance, and provision of credit. But fundamentally, every developing country confronts its own constraints on feasible policy options and other special circumstances, and each will have to find its own path to effective economic and social institutions. Examples offered by developed countries' earlier experiences and current institutions, as well as those of other countries in the developing world, provide important insights for policy formulation. Economic institutions of Europe and North America are in most cases closer to efficient than those of many developing countries, although all countries have room for further institutional innovations. But developing countries cannot assume without additional investigation that patterning their policies and institutions on those of developed countries will always provide the fastest route to successful economic development; transitional institutions are likely to be the most effective route to rapid economic growth for at least some developing countries (see the case study of China at the end of Chapter 4).

In sum, this chapter has pointed up some important similarities across most developing countries, in contrast to contemporary and historical characteristics of developed countries. It has also shown that developing nations are very heterogeneous, differing in many critical respects. Looming large in explaining the root causes in the levels of incomes and human development are the higher inequality, weaker institutions, and lower levels of education and health. But even starting with these weaknesses, there is much that developing countries can undertake through appropriate policy strategies and at least incremental improvements in institutions to speed economic and social progress.

Indeed, the experience of the past 50 years shows that while development is not inevitable and poverty traps are quite real, it is possible to escape from poverty and initiate sustainable development. Before examining specific policies for doing so, in the next chapters we will set the context further by examining important theories and models of development and underdevelopment. In Chapter 3, we examine classic theories that remain influential and useful in many respects, and in Chapter 4, we consider models of coordination failures and other constraints and conceptual strategies for escaping from them.

Comparative Economic Development: Pakistan and Bangladesh

In 1971, Bangladesh declared independence from Pakistan. Previously, Bangladesh had been known as East Pakistan, and what is now Pakistan was called West Pakistan. Though more than 1,000 miles apart, both were part of a single country, with economic and political power concentrated in West Pakistan. Because they were once the same country, Pakistan and Bangladesh make for an interesting exercise in comparative development, in that the two shared a common national policy in the early years, even if they did not benefit from it equally. Pakistan and Bangladesh had a similar population in 2012: an estimated 180 million in Pakistan and 153 million in Bangladesh (Population Reference Bureau). They are located in the South Asian region, are both overwhelmingly Islamic, and were both once part of the colonial British Raj of India. Bangladesh was for a long time the global symbol of suffering, from the Bengal famine of 1943 to the 1971 Concert for Bangladesh featuring George Harrison, Eric Clapton, and Bob Dylan to the horrors of the 1974 postindependence famine.

But analysts such as William Easterly have declared Pakistan a leading example of "growth without development," with low social indicators for its income and growth. Meanwhile, Bangladesh, though still very poor and afflicted with many of the social problems found in Pakistan, has been transforming itself from a symbol of famine to a symbol of hope.

When Bangladesh gained its independence, it was viewed as lagging insurmountably behind Pakistan. Indeed, its poor social and economic development in comparison with West Pakistan was a major impetus behind the independence movement, which complained that Bangladesh was being drained of tax revenues to benefit West Pakistan. The war for independence itself and the economic destruction deliberately visited on Bangladesh's industry left an even wider gap, while abuses left serious psychological scars, and a terrible famine followed. One U.S. statesman undiplomatically dubbed Bangladesh the "international basket case." Others somewhat more tactfully called it the "test case for development"—meaning that if development could happen in Bangladesh, it could happen anywhere. Four decades later, Bangladesh is confounding the skeptics; it actually looks like it may pass this test. Although Pakistan still has 44% higher income than Bangladesh according to UNDP estimates, the two countries nonetheless received an identical New HDI ranking for 2013, with Bangladesh 9 places higher on NHDI than predicted for its income level, while Pakistan is 9 places below what would be predicted by income alone.

Not that Bangladesh has dramatically outperformed Pakistan. Bangladesh continues to have serious development problems. It is rather that Bangladesh has made *relatively* better progress than Pakistan, particularly on social development indicators, despite its handicaps at independence and expectations that it would continue to fare badly. Bangladesh started at a much lower level of social development and still has lower income. But in achieving more progress on social development, Bangladesh now also has the conditions for accelerating economic progress in the coming years, particularly if continuing problems of governance can be overcome.

Growth

PPP-adjusted income estimates vary, but all show average income remains higher in Pakistan than in

Bangladesh ($2,880 in Pakistan in 2011 and $1,910 in Bangladesh according to World Bank estimates). In Pakistan, per capita income grew at about 2.2% per year in the half-century from 1950 to 2000. As a result, per capita income tripled. But the growth rate declined decade by decade, even as it rose in other countries, including India. The decline in the growth rate may be a result of the poor performance on social indicators. From 2000 to 2011, GDP growth in Pakistan averaged 4.9% (World Bank); with population growth of 1.8%, per capita GDP growth was about 3.1%. It remains to be seen whether Pakistan's moderately increased growth rate will be sustainable. Indications are that Pakistan has experienced much less inclusive (pro-poor) growth in comparison with Bangladesh.

In Bangladesh, GDP growth averaged 6% from 2000 to 2011 (World Bank). With a 1.3% population growth in this period, per capita GDP growth was about 4.7%, substantially outpacing Pakistan in this period. Farm yields are up dramatically. When the international textiles quota system of the Multifiber Arrangement ended in 2005, Bangladesh garment factory jobs—a major source of job creation—were at ongoing risk. The speed and astuteness of the market response has been a major test of the resiliency of the Bangladeshi economy. So far, the outcome is better than many predicted; and the impact of the global crisis on employment in the sector is comparatively modest. But recent factory deaths resulting from disastrous negligence of owners put future growth of this sector in jeopardy—if only because of the resulting global public relations disaster.

Poverty

The World Bank 2013 WDI reports (albeit based on only 2005 data) that 23% of the population lives below the $1.25 per-day poverty line in Pakistan, compared with 51% in Bangladesh. But poverty progress has been impressive in the onetime "basket case" of Bangladesh, and incomes of the poorest people are rising. Many factors have contributed to the relatively rapid decrease in extreme poverty in the country, including the early and quickly disseminating green revolution, the impressive role of indigenous nongovernmental organizations (NGOs) fighting poverty in rural areas, opportunities for women's employment in export industries,

and remittances from relatives working abroad. Bangladesh remains a significantly poorer country, with 80% of Bangladeshis living on less than $2 per day, while the figure is a still very high 61% for Pakistan. But the two countries received much more similar scores on the UNDP's 2010 multidimensional poverty index (discussed in Chapter 5). Pakistan was only slightly less poor, ranking No. 70 with a score of 0.275, while Bangladesh ranked No. 73 with a score of 0.291, when aspects of poverty broader than income are considered.

Education and Literacy

According to UNESCO, in Pakistan in 2011, the female literacy rate was just 40% (the male rate was 69%) for those 15 and older. In some regions of the country, particularly Baluchistan and the Northwest Frontier, it is far lower. Although female literacy is not high in Bangladesh either, it is clearly better than Pakistan by both absolute and relative (gender parity) standards—the UNESCO estimate for Bangladesh in 2011 was 53% literacy for all women over age 15 (the male rate was 62%). Thirty times as many public education dollars are spent per pupil for university education as for primary school education. Primary school expenditures are extremely unequal, with the lion's share of funds going to schools that more often train the few students who will eventually go on to universities. Many teachers are hired for political reasons rather than professional competence, and "teacher truancy" is a serious problem. Easterly and other analysts such as Ishrat Husain believe that Pakistan's poor performance on education and literacy may result from the incentives of the elite to keep the poor from gaining too much education.

Looking to the future, Bangladesh has the clear edge in school enrollments; for example, in 2011 Bangladesh had a 52% enrollment in secondary school, compared with just 35% in Pakistan (2013 World Bank WDI, Table 2.11). Despite school quality problems in both countries, this differential will translate to higher literacy rates and general knowledge in Bangladesh in a few years. In Bangladesh just 30 years ago, attending school was an almost unimaginable luxury for most of the poor. Whereas only half of students completed primary school in 1990, more than two-thirds do today. And recent estimates showed that Bangladesh actually has a

female-to-male primary and secondary enrollment ratio of 1.07 to 1, while in Pakistan it is just 0.83. Thus, as we look ahead, then, we can also expect much greater parity in male and female literacy levels in Bangladesh. The nonformal education programs of NGOs such as BRAC provide a major contribution to this progress (see the case study in Chapter 11). But both countries are now making real progress.

Health

Life expectancy in Bangladesh is now 69 years, compared with only 65 in Pakistan (2012 Population Reference Bureau); but in 1970 life expectancy was 54 in Pakistan and only 44 in Bangladesh. Since 1990, the prevalence of child malnutrition in Bangladesh has fallen from two-thirds to less than half. Nutrition in Bangladesh has benefited from a successful green revolution. But child malnutrition remains lower in Pakistan, at about 38%.

Under-5 mortality in Bangladesh has fallen dramatically. On the eve of independence in 1970, the under-5 mortality rate in Bangladesh was 239 per 1,000 live births; the rate in Pakistan was 180 per 1,000. In 1990, the rate in Bangladesh had fallen to 139, and in Pakistan to 122. By 2011, both countries continued to make strong progress, but again their positions were reversed, with the Bangladesh under-5 mortality rate falling to 46 per 1,000, but that in Pakistan only to 72 per 1,000 (2013 WDI, Table 1.2). Thus, both countries have made progress on health, but the edge is strongly with Bangladesh.

Population

Bangladesh has made much greater progress than Pakistan in reducing fertility. Shortly after independence in 1971, both countries had an extremely high level of over 6 births per woman. In Bangladesh, fertility fell to 2.2 by 2011. But for Pakistan, fertility has fallen only to 3.3 (2013 WDI data), with much of Pakistan's decline very recent. These changes reflect both cause and effect. Fertility tends to fall as social and economic progress increases. Women perceive better economic opportunities and less need to rely on having several children for security. But with lower fertility, more can be invested in each child in health and education, by families, by governments, and by NGOs. Thus the productivity of the next generation is higher. A virtuous cycle can take

hold as the country passes through its demographic transition (see Chapter 6). Looked at differently, given the negative relationship between population growth and income per capita growth (see Chapter 6), continuing high fertility augurs relatively poorly for Pakistan as we look ahead (though fertility is falling in Pakistan as well). Rather than simply converging, Bangladesh is actually on a trend to pull ahead of Pakistan as they follow divergent paths, with greater human capital investment in Bangladesh. The early and strong emphasis on an effective family planning strategy was an important factor in the progress of Bangladesh.

Understanding the Divergence

What explains the unexpectedly poor performance of Pakistan in social development and recent growth even in relation to Bangladesh, and what might be done to improve it? The most commonly cited examples of countries exhibiting "growth without development" are the Middle Eastern oil-exporting economies of the Persian Gulf states. Elites contest control of natural resources, an enclave economy develops with relatively few strong links to other sectors of the economy, and social spending is crowded out by national defense expenditures—both to ward off external attack, as exemplified by Iraq's brief conquest of Kuwait in 1990, and at least implicitly also to control the domestic population. In contrast, Pakistan has minimal oil reserves, has to import about four-fifths of its crude oil requirements, and may have to begin importing natural gas.

It is important to note that it is *not* true that there has been no social progress at all in Pakistan. Rather, the concern is that less progress has been made than in many other countries, even in many that grew much more slowly or experienced negative growth. Why has there been such slow progress?

Geography

To the degree that geography constrains development success, Bangladesh would seem to be at a considerable disadvantage. Tropical countries such as Bangladesh have done more poorly around the world, other things being equal. Pakistan, though facing some geographic disadvantages, would seem to hold the edge here. Moreover, aside from a few city-states and islands, Bangladesh is the

most densely populated country in the world. For perspective, the Netherlands is famous for its crowding and has 495 people per square kilometer. But Bangladesh is more than double as densely populated, with 1,174 people per square kilometer (World Bank WDI). Bangladesh has more than half the population of the United States, squeezed into an area less than the size of Wisconsin. (A partial countervailing factor is the greater ease of connecting people and economic activity, facilitating the benefits of the division of labor, for example.)

William Easterly and Ross Levine propose that countries with a multitude of social divisions, ethnic groups, and languages tend to have lower social development and growth rates, although the result is largely muted if the regime is democratic. There is no iron rule here; Mauritius is very diverse but has experienced successful development; India is diverse but has done better than either Pakistan or Bangladesh. Bangladesh is quite homogeneous; as much as 98% of the population is considered ethnic Bangla (Bengali) and speaks the Bangla language. Pakistan has a very high level of ethnic and language diversity. Even its name derives from a compound of *Punjab*, *Afghanistan*, *Kashmir*, and *Baluchistan*. The official language is Urdu, but it is spoken as a first language by only 7% of the population (the largest language group is Punjabi, at 48%). The failure to provide a fair allocation of revenues and services and resolve other issues for one of the largest ethnic groups, the Bangla, led to the division of Bangladesh from Pakistan in the first place. Easterly concludes that part of the cause of Pakistan's "fractionalism lies in ethnolinguistic fractionalization" and argues that "Pakistan is the poster child for the hypothesis that a society polarized by class, gender, and ethnic group does poorly at providing public services."

Gender Equity

According to the *Social Watch Report, 2013*, Bangladesh received a gender equity index ranking of 0.55, much higher than the Pakistan score of just 0.29. In Pakistan, as of 2008, only 60% as many women as men were literate—a figure that is little higher in the 15–24 age group. This is a key age group to consider because it represents those old enough to have had a full chance to gain literacy in school yet not be weighted down by past practices, which tend to perpetuate illiteracy in older groups. In Bangladesh, a significantly higher ratio of female to male literacy of 83% was found in 2008. As already seen, today in Bangladesh, more girls than boys are enrolled in primary education, while in Pakistan, the enrollment level of girls is less than three-quarters that of boys. But both countries have a male-to-female ratio of 1.05, an indicator of gender inequality (higher mortality of girls).

The availability of opportunities for work outside the home, notably in garment factories, has probably increased the autonomy of women. Improved safety is the most urgent priority. Conditions are harsh in other ways by Western standards, and many workers are paid below the official minimum wage; unions are often suppressed. At the same time, incomes are still far higher than alternatives such as domestic work, and the factory jobs have offered a way out for hundreds of thousands of formerly impoverished Bangladeshi women. Ongoing risks facing women factory workers were brought into public view with a factory fire that killed 112 people in November 2012, and a building collapse in April 2013 that killed 1,127 people—the most deadly garment factory disaster in history. More than half of those killed were women; some of their children also died in the buildings. The factory owners may be punished for knowingly subjecting garment workers to risky factory conditions; sustained government, union, and civil society action will be needed to help ensure that safety can be instituted before others die needlessly. Fortunately, rather than simply treating this as a public relations disaster and shifting contracts to other countries, in 2013 a group of major European retailers set up an "Accord," and a grouping of North American retailers set up an "Initiative," to set standards and monitor workplaces producing their contract garment orders. Of the two programs, the European Accord was viewed by many civil society and union observers as being more legally binding than the North American Initiative—and hence more effective (U.S. retailers claim this is because they could face lawsuit risks). In any case, Bangladeshi workers would benefit from enhanced cooperation and coordination between these two alliances.

Meanwhile, conditions do not seem to be much if any better in Pakistan; for example, in less publicized incidents, more than 300 garment workers died in factory fires in Pakistan in September 2012.

Aid

Pakistan has received a great deal of aid. Since independence in 1947, it has been one of the top aid-earning countries. In the aftermath of the terrorist attacks on the United States of September 11, 2001, Pakistan assumed great importance as a strategic ally of the United States in the struggle against terrorism. Sanctions were lifted, and various forms of aid were greatly increased. Although this should be an opportunity for Pakistan to spur development, and growth has accelerated since 2003 apparently in part as a result, history suggests caution. The country was a major Cold War ally of the United States, but the poor seemed to derive little benefit from that association. Bangladesh has also benefited considerably from aid. Effectiveness in the use of aid may be important, particularly the active involvement of effective NGOs in Bangladesh. The major indigenous NGOs and similar groups in Bangladesh generally placed a central emphasis on empowerment of women, and the impacts are generally viewed as having been very strong.

Governance and the Role of the Military

The military has always played a prominent role in Pakistan, and from 1999 to 2008, the nation was governed by a military ruler, General Pervez Musharraf. Pakistan's long-standing rivalry with India and territorial dispute with it over Kashmir since 1947 have diverted resources as well as government attention from social priorities while reinforcing the influence of the military.

The conflicts in northwest Pakistan and neighboring Afghanistan also emphasize a military role. On the other hand, in a heartening sign that democracy is taking firmer root, the May 2013 elections were widely considered fair and represented the first time that Pakistan has seen a civilian transfer of power after successful completion of a full term in office of a democratically elected government.

Although the military was very active in Bangladeshi politics for nearly two decades after independence in 1971, the military's relative withdrawal from politics and government after 1990 probably has been a factor in the country's subsequent progress. Military involvement as the backer of a caretaker government in Bangladesh in 2007 and 2008 was widely viewed as relatively benign, and the country returned to elected civilian rule in 2009,

but political polarization and violence escalated dangerously in late 2013 and early 2014. Neither country has been particularly transparent or free from corruption. In fact, in its 2012 Corruption Perceptions Index, Transparency International gave an essentially equally poor score (out of a possible 100) to the two countries, with 27 for Pakistan and only 26 for Bangladesh.

Civil Society

Given the weak government and the private sector, one must look to the third sector, variously referred to as the "nongovernmental, nonprofit, or citizen sector." Here the difference is dramatic. Bangladesh has one of the most vibrant NGO sectors in the world, the most highly developed in Asia. This will be explored in more detail in the end-of-chapter case studies in Chapter 11, where different approaches of NGOs to poverty action in Bangladesh will be discussed in the cases of BRAC and of the Grameen Bank. If a larger NGO sector could be developed in Pakistan, perhaps led by the many educated Pakistanis living in the United Kingdom, the United States, and Canada, it might play a similar catalyzing role.

Ishrat Husain proposes that Pakistan has experienced an "elitist growth model," which he identifies as combining a powerful leader or succession of leaders operating without checks and balances, a bureaucratic class that unquestioningly implements the wishes of the leader, and a passive and subservient population. He argues that "failure of governance and the consistent domination of political power and state apparatus by a narrowly based elite seeking to advance private and family interests to the exclusion of the majority of the population lies at the root of the problem." Husain shows that Pakistan has exhibited these characteristics since independence and points out that "this combination of strong autocratic leaders, a pliant bureaucracy, and a subservient population made it possible for the benefits of growth to be unequally distributed and concentrated." He concludes that "the ruling elites found it convenient to perpetuate low literacy rates. The lower the proportion of literate people, the lower the probability that the ruling elite could be replaced." One reason is that while girls' education is a boon for development as a whole, it is not necessarily in the economic and political interests of some of the elites now in powerful positions, especially at

the local or regional level. The dominance of large landowners over tenants in the social, political, and economic spheres is all too apparent in rural Pakistan. With education, as some landlords and business operators well know, workers, especially women, may finally demand that laws that are in place to protect them be enforced. It is sometimes in the owners' interest to see that this does not happen.

Concluding Remarks

The differences in social development in Bangladesh and Pakistan are not as overwhelming as would be found in a comparison with Sri Lanka, which has had favorable human development statistics for its low-income level despite enduring civil conflict, or even as dramatic as found between low-income states in India, such as the relatively high human development state of Kerala and the low-development state of Bihar. But Pakistan's growth has been higher than many countries that have made much greater social improvements and has done much better with available aid. The alternative interpretation of Pakistan's experience is that economic growth is after all possible even without high investment in health and education. But the long-term trends are for slower growth in Pakistan and higher growth in Bangladesh, making this interpretation simply untenable. As Easterly conjectured:

> It may be that a certain degree of development and growth was attainable with a skilled managerial elite and unskilled workers, but over time this strategy ran into diminishing returns, as human capital did not grow at the same rate as the other factors. This is consistent with the slowdown in growth from the mid-1980s to the present…. Agricultural growth may have also been possible with the landlord elite taking advantage of the immense potential of the irrigation network and the green revolution, using only unskilled agricultural laborers. But agricultural growth may also have run into diminishing returns, as irrigated land and human capital did not grow at the same rate as other factors of production.

The current development levels of these two countries are not dramatically different. But this itself is the dramatic finding, given the wide disparity when the countries separated in 1971.

Sources

Alderman, Harold, and Marito Garcia. "Food security and health security: Explaining the levels of nutrition in Pakistan." World Bank Working Paper PRE 865. Washington, D.C.: World Bank, 1992.

Easterly, William. "The political economy of growth without development: A case study of Pakistan." In *In Search of Prosperity: Analytic Narratives on Economic Growth,* ed. Dani Rodrik. Princeton, N.J.: Princeton University Press, 2003.

Easterly, William, and Ross Levine. "Africa's growth tragedy: Policies and ethnic divisions." *Quarterly Journal of Economics* 112 (1997): 1203–1250.

Heston, Alan, Robert Summers, and Bettina Aten. *Penn World Table*, version 6.3, August 2009. http://pwt. econ.upenn.edu/php_site/pwt63/pwt63_form.php.

Husain, Ishrat. *Pakistan: The Economy of an Elitist State.* New York: Oxford University Press, 1999.

Hussain, Neelam. "Women and literacy development in Pakistan." Working paper.

Instituto del Tercer Mundo. *Social Watch Report, 2004.* Montevideo, Uruguay: Instituto del Tercer Mundo, 2004.

Population Reference Bureau, *World Population Datasheet, 2012,* and earlier years.

Razzaque, Muhammad Abdur. "Vision 2021: Bangladesh charts a path toward food security." *IFPRI 2012 Global Food Policy Report*, pp 80–82.

Sen, Amartya. *Development as Freedom.* New York: Knopf, 1999.

Smith, Stephen C. "The miracle of Bangladesh: From basket case to case in point." *World Ark*, May/June 2009, pp. 13–21.

Summers, Lawrence H. "Investing in all the people." World Bank Working Paper PRE 905. Washington D.C.: World Bank, 1992.

UNICEF. *State of the World's Children, 2010.* New York: UNICEF, 2010.

United Nations. *Human Development Report*, various years. New York: Oxford University Press.

World Bank. *World Development Indicators*, various years. Washington, D.C.: World Bank.

——— *World Development Report*, various years. New York: Oxford University Press. ∎

Concepts for Review

Absolute poverty	Free trade	Middle-income countries
Brain drain	Gross domestic product (GDP)	Newly industrializing countries
Capital stock	Gross national income (GNI)	(NICs)
Convergence	Human capital	Property rights
Crude birth rate	Human Development Index	Purchasing power parity (PPP)
Dependency burden	(HDI)	Research and development
Depreciation (of the capital stock)	Imperfect market	(R&D)
Diminishing marginal utility	Incomplete information	Resource endowment
Divergence	Infrastructure	Terms of trade
Economic institutions	Least developed countries	Value added
Fractionalization	Low-income countries (LICs)	World Bank

Questions for Discussion

1. For all of their diversity, many less developed countries are linked by a range of common problems. What are these problems? Which do you think are the most important? Why?

2. Explain the distinction between low levels of living and low per capita incomes. Can low levels of living exist simultaneously with high levels of per capita income? Explain and give some examples.

3. Can you think of other common (not necessarily universal but widespread) characteristics of less developed countries not mentioned in the text? See if you can list four or five and briefly justify them.

4. Do you think that there is a strong relationship among health, labor productivity, and income levels? Explain your answer.

5. What is meant by the statement that many developing nations are subject to "dominance, dependence, and vulnerability" in their relations with rich nations? Can you give some examples?

6. Explain the many ways in which developing countries may differ in their economic, social, and political structures.

7. What are some additional strengths and weaknesses of the Human Development Index as a comparative measure of human welfare? If you were designing the HDI, what might you do differently, and why?

8. "Social and institutional innovations are as important for economic growth as technological and scientific inventions and innovations." What is meant by this statement? Explain your answer.

9. Why do many economists expect income convergence between developed and developing countries, and what factors would you look to for an explanation of why this has occurred for only a limited number of countries and in such a limited degree so far?

10. What are good economic institutions, why do so many developing countries lack them, and what can developing countries do to get them? Justify your answer.

11. Which measure shows more equality among countries around the world—GNI calculated at exchange rates or GNI calculated at purchasing power parity? Explain.

12. "South Asia has a lower income per capita than sub-Saharan Africa." Comment on the validity of this statement.

13. What is the meaning of a "colonial legacy"? Discuss any disadvantages and possible advantages.

14. State five characteristics of the developing world. Discuss diversity *within* the developing world on these characteristics in relation to the developed world.

15. Discuss the differences between the traditional HDI (examined in Appendix 2.1) in comparison to the New NHDI formulation. In what ways do you think either one is a better measure of human development? In your answer, consider the significance of computing with a geometric mean, instead of an arithmetic mean.

16. What were the central findings of Melissa Dell's research on the *mita* system, and what is their significance for the study of economic development?

Notes

1. Alan Heston, Robert Summers, and Bettina Aten, *Penn World Table*, version 6.3, Center for International Comparisons of Production, Income and Prices, University of Pennsylvania, August 2009, http://pwt.econ.upenn.edu/php_site/pwt63/pwt63_form.php. Data for 2007.

2. World Bank, *World Development Indicators, 2013*. (Washington, D.C.: World Bank, 2010), tab. 1.1. Data for 2011. These real measures reflect purchasing power parity (explained later in the chapter).

3. United Nations Development Programme (UNDP), *Human Development Report*, 2005 (New York: Oxford University Press, 2005), p. 38. The global Gini coefficient is reported at 0.67 (for details on this measure of inequality, see Chapter 5).

4. World Bank, *World Development Indicators, 2010*, various tables. Some of these contrasts are summarized in Table 2.3 of this text.

5. For more information on country classification systems and other key comparative data, go to the World Bank Web site at http://www.worldbank.org/data, the OECD Web site at http://www.oecd.org/oecd, and the United Nations Development Programme Web site at http://www.undp.org. See http://www.unohrlls.org/en/home/ and http://www.unohrlls.org/en/ldc/related/59/. Some least developed countries such as Equatorial Guinea are on an "identified for graduation" list; but Equatorial Guinea does not meet "graduation criteria" on human assets or economic vulnerability.

6. Adjustments are made because otherwise the resulting PPP measure would essentially assume that the relative prices prevailing in the United States (i.e., the numeraire currency) also prevailed elsewhere (which would mean that the resulting total incomes would not be "base-country invariant"; that is, they would differ if, for example, the conversions were made to the UK pound sterling). Accounting for relative price differences recognizes the substitutions people make toward lower-priced goods in their market basket and thus gives a more accurate comparison of living standards. For details on calculations of PPP incomes, see the 2011 International Comparison Program site at http://siteresources.worldbank.org/ICPEXT/Resources/ICP_2011.html, the UN Statistics Division at http://unstats.un.org/unsd/methods/icp/ipc7_htm.htm, and the *Penn World Table* site at http://pwt.econ.upenn.edu/about-pwt2.html. These unadjusted figures do provide a useful indicator of the ability of a nation to buy goods and services in dollars abroad, but they are misleading regarding the ability to buy domestically.

   There are also other limitations of GNI (and PPP) calculations as measures of economic performance and welfare. For example, GNI does not take account of the depletion or degradation of natural resources; it assigns positive values to expenditures resulting from repair and cleanup costs following natural disasters (e.g., earthquakes, hurricanes, floods), to polluting activities, and to the costs of environmental cleanups (see Chapter 10). It frequently ignores nonmonetary transactions, household unpaid labor, and subsistence consumption (see Chapter 9). Products consumed by people living in poverty and prices they pay for them differ from the nonpoor. Finally, GNI figures take no account of income distribution (Chapter 5) or capabilities other than income.

7. This is accomplished in a special way. First, Equation 2.1 is applied to each of the two subcomponents, just as in Equations 2.3 and 2.4. Then, as explained by the UNDP, "a geometric mean of the resulting indexes is created and and, finally, Equation 2.1 is reapplied to the geometric mean of the indexes using 0 as the minimum and the highest geometric mean of the

resulting indexes for the time period under consideration as the maximum. This is equivalent to applying Equation 2.1 directly to the geometric mean of the two subcomponents." For further details, see http://hdr.undp.org/en/media/HDR%202013%20technical%20notes%20EN.pdf.

8. There is still substitutability across the three components in the NHDI, but not perfect substitutability as in the HDI. Regarding the calculation in the last equation of Box 2.1, recall that a geometric mean for the case of three variables is equivalent to the cube root of the product (by the properties of exponents). You can see how a geometric mean is used to build up the overall education index from its two components in the fourth equation in Box 2.1. For an interesting critique of the use of a geometric mean rather than a different functional form that also allows for imperfect substitutability, see Martin Ravallion, "Troubling tradeoffs in the Human Development Index," World Bank Policy Research Working Paper No. 5484, 2010.

9. The new UNDP measures can be found at http://hdr.undp.org.

10. It is possible that low income is supplemented by tapping into savings (broadly defined), which would reflect the unsustainable nature of such a low income.

11. See, for example, Jeffrey D. Sachs, *The End of Poverty: Economic Possibilities for Our Time* (New York: Penguin, 2005).

12. World Bank *World Development Indicators, 2013*.

13. Gunnar Myrdal, *Asian Drama* (New York: Pantheon, 1968), app. 2.

14. Recent debates on the incidence of national poverty traps and their causes is examined in Chapter 4. Economic growth is of course another area of wide variations in the developing world, with historically unprecedented growth in East Asia alongside chronic stagnation—at least until recently—in most of sub-Saharan Africa. Economic growth is a major subject of the next chapter.

15. For a discussion of the relative benefits and costs of country size, see Alberto Alesina and Enrico Spolaore, "On the number and size of nations," *Quarterly Journal of Economics* 112 (1997): 1027–1056.

16. For an interesting look at this problem in the context of India, see Kaushik Basu, "Teacher truancy

in India: The role of culture, norms and economic incentives," January 2006, http://ssrn.com/abstract=956057. We return to this topic in Chapters 8 and 11.

17. See Table 2.3, columns 3, 4, and 5. See also World Bank, *World Development Indicators, 2007*, tabs. 2.14 through 2.20, and World Health Organization, *World Health Report, 2006*, http://www.who.int/whr/2006/en/index.html.

18. This widely used benchmark is an updated value for the dollar-a-day level. The standard of $1.25 is increasingly used for reasons described in Chapter 5. The 1.2 billion figure, corresponding to 21% of global population, is based on the 2013 World Bank poverty numbers update of April 2013, downloaded July 10, 2013 from: http://www.worldbank.org/content/dam/Worldbank/document/State_of_the_poor_paper_April17.pdf.

19. UNDP, *Human Development Report, 2006*, p. 269.

20. World Bank, *World Development Indicators, 2007*, tab. 2.7.

21. World Bank, *Global Monitoring Report, 2007* (Washington, D.C.: World Bank, 2007), tab. A.1. For recent evidence, please see Shaohua Chen and Martin Ravallion, "The developing world is poorer than we thought, but no less successful against poverty." Policy Research Working Paper 4703, World Bank, August 2008.

22. Ibid. and pp. 40–41; World Bank, *World Development Report, 2000/2001* (New York: Oxford University Press, 2000); *World Development Indicators, 2007*, tab. 2.1; Population Reference Bureau, *2006 World Data Sheet*, http://www.prb.org/pdf06/06WorldDataSheet.pdf. Some economists argue that these figures understate poverty incidence, but the trend has been clearly favorable, at least until 2006. Since then, the World Bank reports, significantly higher food prices and other consequences of the global economic crisis have slowed the pace of poverty reduction substantially.

23. Population Reference Bureau, *World Population Trends 2012*; World Bank, *World Development Indicators, 2010*, tab. 2.1; Population Reference Bureau, *2009 World Data Sheet*, http://www.prb.org/pdf10/10WorldDataSheet.pdf. For the population projections, see United Nations, Population Division, "World Population Prospects: The 2008

Revision," June 2009, http://www.un.org/esa/population/publications/popnews/Newsltr_87.pdf.

24. Population Reference Bureau, *2010 World Data Sheet*.

25. See William Easterly and Ross Levine, "Africa's growth tragedy: Policies and ethnic divisions," *Quarterly Journal of Economics* 112 (1997): 1203–1250, and Alberto Alesina et al., "Fractionalization," *Journal of Economic Growth* 8 (2003): 155–194.

26. For a discussion of these issues and the most careful attempt at generating the needed data, see Gillette Hall and Harry Anthony Patrinos, eds., *Indigenous Peoples, Poverty and Human Development in Latin America: 1994–2004* (New York: Palgrave Macmillan, 2006); Haeduck Lee, *The Ethnic Dimension of Poverty and Income Distribution in Latin America* (Washington, D.C.: World Bank, 1993); and Paul Collier, "The political economy of ethnicity," *Annual World Bank Conference on Development Economics, 1998* (Washington, D.C.: World Bank, 1999).

27. For a review of the complex statistical issues in sorting out the possible impact of ethnic, religious, and linguistic fractionalization, see Alesina et al., "Fractionalization." An earlier paper drawing somewhat different conclusions using less comprehensive measures is Easterly and Levine, "Africa's growth tragedy."

28. The United States, United Kingdom, Japan, Germany, France, Italy, and Canada formed the original Group of Seven (G7) industrial countries, considered the world's leading economies, to meet annually to deliberate global economic policy; the group was later expanded to include Russia as the Group of Eight (G8).

29. See David Landes, *The Wealth and Poverty of Nations: Why Some Are So Rich and Some So Poor* (New York: Norton, 1998); Jared Diamond, *Guns, Germs, and Steel: The Fates of Human Societies* (New York: Norton, 1997); John Luke Gallup, Jeffrey D. Sachs, and Andrew D. Mellinger, "Geography and economic development," *Annual World Bank Conference on Development Economics, 1998* (Washington, D.C.: World Bank, 1999), pp. 127–178; and Paul Collier, *The Bottom Billion* (Oxford: Oxford University Press, 2007), who emphasizes the combination of being landlocked with "bad neighbors."

30. See, for example, Intergovernmental Panel on Climate Change, "Fourth assessment report: Climate change 2007," http://www.mnp.nl/ipcc/pages_edia/AR4-chapters.html. The IPCC was established by the World Meteorological Organization (WMO) and the United Nations Environment Program (UNEP) to "assess available scientific, technical, and socioeconomic information relevant for the understanding of climate change, its potential impacts, and options for adaptation and mitigation." The group won the Nobel Peace Prize in 2007. For more details, see Chapter 10.

31. For a detailed analysis of the importance of information acquisition, its absence in many developing countries, and the consequent role of governments in promoting knowledge and information in the context of limited markets, see World Bank, *World Development Report, 1998/99: Knowledge for Development* (New York: Oxford University Press, 1998), pp. 1–15.

32. These three factors are identified as critically important in the research by Daron Acemoglu and James A. Robinson; see their *Economic Origins of Dictatorship and Democracy* (New York: Cambridge University Press, 2005). See also note 58. As Dani Rodrik noted, a caveat is that the institutions generally viewed as favorable are correlated with each other; it is unclear which of these institutions matter most or how specific in form these institutions have to be to fulfill their main functions.

33. See Kenneth L. Sokoloff and Stanley L. Engerman, "Factor endowments, institutions, and differential paths of growth among New World economies: A view from economic historians of the United States," in *How Latin America Fell Behind: Essays on the Economic Histories of Brazil and Mexico* ed. Stephen Haber, (Stanford, Calif.: Stanford University Press, 1997); see also additional works by these authors cited in note 58.

34. See Nathan Nunn and Leonard Wantchekon, "The slave trade and the origins of mistrust in Africa," *American Economic Review* 101, No. 7 (December 2011): 3221–3252.

35. Having avoided formal colonization is no guarantee of development success; Afghanistan and Ethiopia are frequently cited examples. However, it should also be noted that although it was not successfully colonized, Afghanistan was subjected to extensive indirect control with British and Russian invasions from the early nineteenth to the early twentieth century (and later by Soviet

armies with ongoing consequences), and Ethiopia was subject to invasions and intrigue by Italy and Britain. (Liberia, the other frequently cited example, was also subject to major influence from the developed world.)

36. For an interesting and provocative analysis of the critical role of "ideas" and "ingenuity" in long-term economic growth, see Paul M. Romer, "Idea gaps and object gaps in economic development," *Journal of Monetary Economics* 32 (1993): 543–573, and Thomas Homer-Dixon, "The ingenuity gap: Can poor countries adapt to resource scarcity?" *Population and Development Review* 21 (1995): 587–612.

37. Romer, "Idea gaps," 543.

38. See, for example Gallup, Sachs, and Mellinger, "Geography and economic development," pp. 127–178; Desmond McCarthy, Holger Wolf, and Yi Wu, "The growth costs of malaria," NBER Working Paper No. W7541, February 2000; and John Luke Gallup and Jeffrey D. Sachs, "The economic burden of malaria," Harvard University CID Working Paper No. 52, July 2000. See also p. 85.

39. Brinley Thomas, *Migration and Economic Growth* (London: Cambridge University Press, 1954), p. viii.

40. For an interesting contemporaneous description of the process and implications of international migration from the Mediterranean area to western Europe, see W. R. Böhnung, "Some thoughts on emigration from the Mediterranean basin," *International Labour Review* 14 (1975): 251–277.

41. Congressional Budget Office study, June 18, 2013, http://www.cbo.gov/publication/44225.

42. For an analysis of this issue, see Douglas Massey, "The new immigration and ethnicity in the United States," *Population and Development Review* 21 (1995): 631–652.

43. UNDP, *Human Development Report, 1992* (New York: Oxford University Press, 1992), p. 57.

44. On the emigration of Indian information technology workers, see "India's plan to plug the brain drain," *Financial Times*, April 24, 2000, p.17.

45. World Bank, "Migration and development briefs," http://go.worldbank.org/R88ONI2MQ0.

46. For an excellent overview of these issues, see UNDP, *Human Development Report, 2009*, http://hdr.undp.org/en.

47. For a discussion, see Simon Commander, Mari Kangasniemi, and L. Alan Winters, "The brain drain: Curse or boon? A survey of the literature," in *Challenges to Globalization: Analyzing the Economics* (Chicago: University of Chicago Press, 2004), pp. 235–272. See also C. Simon Fan and Oded Stark, "International migration and 'educated unemployment,'" *Journal of Development Economics* 83 (2007): 76–87.

48. A theoretical contribution to the literature on historical growth and its relevance to contemporary developing countries can be found in Marvin Goodfriend and John McDermott, "Early development," *American Economic Review* 85 (1995): 116–133. Goodfriend and McDermott argue that long-term economic development involves four fundamental processes: the exploitation of increasing returns to specialization, the transition from household to market production, knowledge and human capital accumulation, and industrialization. With regard to developing countries, they argue that "the continuing widespread use of primitive production processes alongside relatively modern techniques is the most striking feature of less-developed countries" (p. 129).

49. Douglass C. North, "Economic performance through time," *American Economic Review* 84 (1994): 359–368, and Douglass C. North, *Institutions, Institutional Change and Economic Performance* (New York: Cambridge University Press, 1990). For a provocative analysis of the historical links between economic development and political development, including democratization and the extension of human and legal rights, drawing on economic theory and 500 years of the global historical record, see Acemoglu and Robinson, *Economic Origins of Dictatorship and Democracy*, and Acemoglu and Robinson, *Why Nations Fail*, 2012.

50. In Chapters 3 and 4, we examine economic growth more after including the contending views about whether such diminishing returns apply to aggregate growth experience. For an appealingly intuitive discussion of these two effects, see Eli Berman, "Does factor-biased technological change stifle international convergence? Evidence from manufacturing," NBER Working Paper, rev. September 2000. Note, however, that other factors such as institutional quality may be at least as important as capital per worker in explaining

income per capita, as you will see later in this chapter and in Chapters 3 and 4. On the long-term divergence between developed and developing nations, see Pritchett, "Divergence, big time."

51. Note that earlier and longer periods tend to show more divergence due to "divergence big time" effect of inequalities growing since the start of the industrial era. Note also that there is evidence of convergence taking place for the years 2001 to 2007 (a shorter period than entertained in this literature but an encouraging and intriguing short-term trend that will bear watching closely); data are awaited to determine if this continued or even amplified after the financial crisis. The sample criteria for the diagrams in Figure 2.8 were as follows. All data are constructed from the Penn World Table using PPP values (which extended through 2007 when the graphs were constructed in 2010). To be included, a country had to have data available in the PWT database for the sample period; by starting in 1980, a relatively small number of countries had to be omitted. For the world diagram, six countries were excluded as 1980 base-period outliers that had very high income in that year due to a temporary oil price increase (Brunei, Qatar, UAE, Libya, Saudi Arabia, and Kuwait). The criterion for inclusion as a developing country in the 1980 base year was classification as a low- or middle-income country in the 1980 World Bank's *World Development Report*; use of this early classification (in the base year of the study) avoided the bias of excluding countries that had grown fast enough to become high-income countries during this period. An implication of this criteria, however, is the exclusion of centrally planned and oil-exporting countries; these two groupings had separate classification categories in the 1980 WDR not based on income level, and for consistency, China is excluded from this group as a centrally planned economy. As it is only one data point, this exclusion does *not* affect the failure to find country convergence in this period. (But the finding of population-weighted convergence since 1989 is substantially driven by the rapid per capita income growth of China, where China is included; note that China is also included in the world sample in Figure 2.8a). For the purpose of the OECD convergence diagram,

the inclusion criteria was all original members plus Japan, Finland, Australia, and New Zealand, the four countries that joined after its founding but before 1973 (after which no new countries were admitted until Mexico in 1994), but with the exclusion of West Germany due to the statistical problem presented by its 1990 unification with East Germany.

52. For a detailed discussion, see J. Bradford De Long, "Productivity growth, convergence, and welfare: Comment," *American Economic Review* 78 (1988): 1138–1154.

53. Figure from *Human Development Report, 2005*, ch. 1. For graphs showing relative versus absolute income convergence for China in relation to the United States, see Stephen C. Smith, http://www.gwu.edu/~iiep/G2/. Note that in the 2008-2012 period, continued rapid growth in China, in combination with very slow growth in a majority of high-income OECD countries, led to estimates that China achieved higher per capita GDP absolute gains than OECD high-income countries. (Such absolute inequality measures can be used to address other kinds of questions about convergence or divergence, but this is rarely done. For example, it could be used in the size distribution of income at national or even international scale; but the usual preferred property for inequality measures is to make relative income comparisons. Details are discussed in Chapter 5.)

54. UNDP, *Human Development Report 2013*, p.13.

55. Branko Milanovic, "True world income distribution, 1988 and 1993: First calculation based on household surveys alone," *Economic Journal* 112, (2002) 51–92.

56. See Dani Rodrik, "Unconditional convergence in manufacturing," *Quarterly Journal of Economics* 128, No. 1 (2012): 165–204.

57. We thank Daron Acemoglu, Shahe Emran, Stanley Engerman, and Karla Hoff for their helpful comments on this section. Not all of the causal links described here are supported by the same type of evidence. Some are underpinned by widely (if not universally) accepted statistical (econometric) evidence. Other causal links emerge from historical studies. All links discussed are argued in the development economics literature to be

underlying factors leading to divergent development outcomes. The discussion follows the numbering of the arrows in Figure 2.11, which is arranged for concise display.

58. For very readable introductions to this research, see Daron Acemoglu, Simon Johnson, and James A. Robinson, "Understanding prosperity and poverty: Geography, institutions, and the reversal of fortune," in *Understanding Poverty*, eds. Abhijit Banerjee, Roland Benabou, and Dilip Mookherjee (New York: Oxford University Press, 2006), pp. 19–36, and Stanley L. Engerman and Kenneth L. Sokoloff, "Colonialism, inequality, and long-run paths of development," in *Understanding Poverty*, pp. 37–62. See also Daron Acemoglu, Simon Johnson, and James A. Robinson, "The colonial origins of comparative development: An empirical investigation," *American Economic Review* 91 (2001): 1369–1401, and Kenneth L. Sokoloff and Stanley L. Engerman, "History lessons: Institutions, factor endowments, and paths of development in the New World," *Journal of Economic Perspectives* 14 (2000): 217–232. For an excellent review of the work of these authors, see Karla Hoff, "Paths of institutional development: A view from economic history," *World Bank Research Observer* 18 (2003): 205–226. See also Dani Rodrik, Arvind Subramanian, and Francesco Trebbi, "Institutions rule: The primacy of institutions over geography and integration in economic development," *Journal of Economic Growth* 9 (2004): 135–165, and Dani Rodrik and Arvind Subramanian, "The primacy of institutions, and what this does and does not mean," *Finance and Development* (June 2003), http://www.imf.org/external/pubs/ft/fandd/2003/06/pdf/rodrik.pdf.

59. On the role of geography, see Diamond, *Guns, Germs, and Steel*; Gallup, Sachs, and Mellinger, "Geography and economic development"; Jeffrey D. Sachs, "Institutions don't rule: Direct effects of geography on per capita income," NBER Working Paper No. 9490, 2003; and Jeffrey D. Sachs, "Institutions matter, but not for everything," *Finance and Development* (June 2003), http://www.imf.org/external/pubs/ft/fandd/2003/06/pdf/sachs.pdf. See also Douglas A. Hibbs and Ola Olsson, "Geography, biogeography and why some countries are rich and others poor," *Proceedings of the National Academy of Sciences* (2004): 3715–3740; for a discussion on landlocked status as it affects poor African economies, see Paul Collier, *The Bottom Billion: Why the Poorest Countries Are Failing and What Can Be Done about It* (Oxford: Oxford University Press, 2007), pp. 53–63, 165–166, and 179–180.

60. See Quamrul Ashraf and Oded Galor, "The 'Out of Africa' hypothesis, human genetic diversity, and comparative economic development," *American Economic Review* 103 (2013): 1-46. It is doubtful whether there could be any meaningful policy implications.

61. See Chapter 4 for an analysis of problems of coordination failure and the importance of mechanisms to correct it.

62. For accessible discussions, see North, *Institutions, Institutional Change and Economic Performance*; Justin Lin and Jeffrey Nugent, "Institutions and economic development," *Handbook of Economic Development*, vol. 3A (Amsterdam: North Holland, 1995); Dani Rodrik, "Institutions for high-quality growth: What they are and how to acquire them," *Studies in Comparative International Development* 35, No. 3 (September 2000): 3–31; and Acemoglu, Johnson, and Robinson, "Understanding prosperity and poverty." Note that the quality of many of the institutions described in this paragraph of the text is correlated, and it is disputed which ones matter most and the degree to which they are substitutes for each other in spurring growth.

63. As an instrument for the types of institutions established (note that scholars have widely debated this instrument). For a discussion, with some important caveats, see Rodrik, Subramanian, and Trebbi, "Institutions rule."

64. This is after the problem of simultaneity between income and institutions is controlled for by taking advantage of the exogeneity of initial settler mortality risk (other approaches using different data still find some role for geography; see the papers by Sachs in note 59). See Acemoglu, Johnson, and Robinson, "Colonial origins of comparative development." The schema on page 1370 in their paper corresponds to links 3-10-18-21 or 3-10-19-22 in Figure 2.10 in this text. See also Daron Acemoglu, Simon Johnson, James A. Robinson, and Yunyong

Thaicharoen, "Institutional causes, macroeconomic symptoms: Volatility, crises and growth," *Journal of Monetary Economics* 50 (2003): 49–123. For a summary, see Daron Acemoglu, "Root causes: A historical approach to assessing the role of institutions in economic development," *Finance and Development* (June 2003), http://www.imf .org/external/pubs/ft/fandd/2003/06/pdf/Acemoglu.pdf. It is also worth noting, however, that in the early colonial period, potential settlers who did wish to emigrate to Latin America and the Caribbean (and perhaps to some other colonies in later times) were sometimes restricted by immigration rules. See Stanley L. Engerman and Kenneth L. Sokoloff, "Factor endowments, inequality, and paths of development among New World economies," *Journal of LACEA Economia* 3, No. 1 (Fall) (2002): 41–109. There is also some question about the use of largely eighteenth-century mortality data, which may possibly differ from earlier (but unavailable) mortality rates. These points may suggest some possible limitations to the mortality data-based research, although the results show considerable robustness. For a debate, see David Y. Albouy, "The colonial origins of comparative development: An empirical investigation: Comment." *American Economic Review*, 102, No. 6 (2012): 3059—3076, and Acemoglu, Johnson, and Robinson, "The colonial origins of comparative development: An empirical investigation: Reply." *American Economic Review*, 102, No. 6 (2012): 3077–3110. See also Rodrik et al., "Institutions rule," and Pranab Bardhan, "Institutions matter, but which ones?" *Economics of Transition* 13 (2005): 499–532.

65. Sokoloff and Engerman, "History lessons"; Engerman and Sokoloff, "Colonialism, inequality, and long-run paths of development."

66. Engerman and Sokoloff, "Colonialism, inequality, and long-run paths of development." On the role of labor scarcity in the development of institutions in North America, see David Galenson, "The settlement and growth of the colonies: Population, labor and economic development," in *The Cambridge Economic History of the United States*, vol. 1, eds. Stanley L. Engerman and Robert Gallman (New York: Cambridge University Press, 1996).

67. See Daron Acemoglu, Simon Johnson, and James A. Robinson, "Reversal of fortune: Geography and institutions in the making of the modern world income distribution," *Quarterly Journal of Economics* 118 (2002): 1231–1294. Although the reversal is now associated with this article, similar historical observations were a theme of the "dependency theory" literature, described in Chapter 3.

68. In fact, the Acemoglu-Johnson-Robinson theory could be said to turn dependency theory on its head. The neo-Marxist dependency theory (see Chapter 3) views development constraints as coming from foreign nationals, but in the Acemoglu et al. theory, the underlying development problem is the presence of extractive institutions, whether the extractors are nationals or foreigners, and the corrective is investment-encouraging institutions, whoever implements them. The preferred institutions include some that are clearly non-Marxist, such as broader respect for private property rights. The implication of their argument is that it is at best no more important to get today's rich countries to change their current behavior toward developing countries than it is to achieve reforms in local institutions, although former colonial powers might reasonably be asked to pay for costs of changing over to better domestic institutions, assuming that such change is possible. Inequality makes reform difficult to achieve.

69. This evidence is presented in Acemoglu, Johnson, and Robinson, "Reversal of fortune." The evidence has been criticized by some economists on the grounds that measures of modern institutions actually show great variability rather than persistence and may follow rather than lead growth; see, for example, Edward L. Glaeser, Rafael La Porta, Florencio Lopez de Silanes, and Andrei Shleifer, "Do institutions cause growth?" *Journal of Economic Growth* 91 (2004): 271–303, who argue that human capital is a more fundamental factor. But for a theoretical analysis of how change in specific political institutions is consistent with stability in economic institutions, see Daron Acemoglu and James A. Robinson, "De facto political power and institutional persistence, *American Economic Review* 96 (2006): 326–330. For an empirical analysis providing evidence that education does not, in fact, lead to democracy within countries over time, see Daron Acemoglu, Simon Johnson, James A. Robinson, and Pierre Yared, "From

education to democracy?" *American Economic Review* 95 (2005): 44–49. Other critical commentary is found in Pranab K. Bardhan, "Institutions matter, but which ones?" *Economics of Transition* 13 (2005): 499–532.

70. The primary evidence for this is historical. See Landes, *Wealth and Poverty of Nations.* For example, the fragmentation of a continent divided by mountains, sea lanes, and rivers facilitated political competition that fueled institutional development. See also Diamond, *Guns, Germs, and Steel.*

71. See David Fielding and Sebastian Torres, "Cows and conquistadors: A contribution on the colonial origins of comparative development," *Journal of Development Studies* 44 (2008): 1081–1099, and James Feyrer and Bruce Sacerdote, "Colonialism and modern income: Islands as natural experiments," *Review of Economics and Statistics* 91 (2009): 245–262. Both build on the pioneering research of Acemoglu, Johnson, and Robinson.

72. Fielding and Torres, "Cows and conquistadors." The neo-Europes are primarily the United States, Canada, Australia, and New Zealand.

73. See Feyrer and Sacerdote, "Colonialism and modern income." The authors use wind direction and wind speed as instruments for length and type of colonial experience of islands. They identify a positive relationship between colonization length and both income and child survival rates. They also use their evidence to argue that "time spent as a colony after 1700 is more beneficial to modern income than years before 1700, consistent with a change in the nature of colonial relationships over time." Note, however, that some islands included in this research are still colonies, such as overseas French departments with large European populations, and that in other independent former colonies with high incomes, the original inhabitants were largely wiped out—facts that weaken the case for benefits of longer colonization from the viewpoint of those who were colonized. But on a positive historical note, Stanley Engerman pointed out that in the later colonial period, Europeans were often responsible for ending slavery in Africa (personal communication with the authors).

74. Engerman and Sokoloff, "Colonialism, inequality, and long-run paths of development." For supporting econometric evidence on the negative effects of inequality using an identification strategy inspired by the Engerman and Sokoloff hypothesis, see Box 2.2. See also William Easterly and Ross Levine, "Tropics, germs, and crops: The role of endowments in economic development," *Journal of Monetary Economics* 50 (2003): 3–39. For a different argument, see Edward L. Glaeser, Giacomo Ponzetto, and Andrei Shleifer, "Why does democracy need education?" NBER Working Paper No. 12128, March 2006; however, see also Acemoglu et al., "From education to democracy?" For alternative perspectives, see Acemoglu and Robinson, *Economic Origins of Dictatorship and Democracy.* It remains unclear whether economic or political inequality is more fundamental, as politicians often amass wealth when their power is secure. For an interesting study suggesting that the latter is important, see Daron Acemoglu, Maria Angelica Bautista, Pablo Querubin, and James A. Robinson, "Economic and political inequality in development: The case of Cundinamarca, Colombia," June 2007, http://econ-www.mit.edu/faculty/download_pdf.php?id=1510.

75. Although in this century so far inequality has been rising in North America and falling somewhat in some Latin American countries, the contrast remains extreme. For a set of excellent analyses on recent trends, see Luis F. López-Calva and Nora Lustig, eds., *Declining Inequality in Latin America: A Decade of Progress?* (Washington, D.C.: Brookings Institution, 2010).

76. Engerman and Sokoloff, "Colonialism, inequality, and long-run paths of development." See also Edward L. Glaeser, "Inequality," in *The Oxford Handbook of Political Economy*, eds. Barry R. Weingast and Donald Wittman (New York: Oxford University Press, 2006), pp. 624–641.

77. See Glaeser et al., "Do institutions cause growth?"

78. Acemoglu et al., "From education to democracy?" esp. pp. 47–48. Evidence for the intuitive idea that migrants to the "neo-Europes" settled by Britain embodied not just better institutions but also higher human capital levels is not well established; see Acemoglu, Johnson, and Robinson, "Colonial

origins of comparative development." The effects of institutions held even when excluding these countries. Another possible channel, recently introduced by Gregory Clark, is that institutions affect preferences, which in turn directly or indirectly affect the quality of the workforce. For his provocative and controversial assessment, see *A Farewell to Alms: A Brief Economic History of the World* (Princeton, N.J.: Princeton University Press, 2007).

79. See, for example, Bardhan, "Institutions matter." This article also argues some limitations of the empirical methods of Acemoglu and colleagues.

80. Glaeser et al., "Do institutions cause growth?"

81. See Jeffrey Frankel and David Romer, "Does trade cause growth?" *American Economic Review* 89 (1999): 379–399.

82. Not surprisingly, trade effects are complex. Geography can influence the pattern and amount of trade. And as countries develop and incomes rise, countries trade in greater amounts and in a wider range of goods. See Rodrik, Subramanian, and Trebbi, "Institutions rule." They provide a diagram of the effects outlined in this paragraph in their Figure 1.

83. Of course, the effectiveness of each sector may also affect the effectiveness of the other sectors. This is not shown in the diagram.

84. Bardhan, "Institutions matter"; Rodrik, "Getting institutions right." For a provocative analysis of the historical links between economic development and political development, including democratization and the extension of human and legal rights, drawing on economic theory and 500 years of the global historical record, see Daron Acemoglu and James A. Robinson, *Economic Origins of Dictatorship and Democracy*. For an insightful analysis of diverging development paths, see Kenneth L. Sokoloff and Stanley L. Engerman, "History lessons: Institutions, factor endowments, and paths of development in the New World," *Journal of Economic Perspectives* 14 (2000): 217–232.

85. See, for example, UNDP, *Human Development Report, 2005.*

86. Dani Rodrik, "Institutions for high-quality growth: What they are and how to acquire them," *Studies in Comparative International Development* 35, No. 3 (2000), 3–31, DOI: 10.1007/BF02699764, p. 5

87. For an elaboration of this point, see Chapter 8 and also Lawrence H. Summers and Vinod Thomas, "Recent lessons of development," *World Bank Research Observer* 8 (1993): 241–254; Pam Woodall, "The global economy," *Economist*, October 1, 1994, pp. 3–38; World Bank, *World Development Indicators, 1998* (Washington, D.C.: World Bank, 1998), pp. 3–11; and UNDP, *Human Development Report, 2003.*

88. Similar conclusions can be found in Irma Adelman and Cynthia Taft Morris, "Development history and its implications for development theory," *World Development* 25 (1997): 831–840.

Appendix 2.1

The Traditional Human Development Index (HDI)

Like the New HDI, the Traditional HDI ranks all countries on a scale of 0 (lowest human development) to 1 (highest human development). The Traditional HDI, the UNDP centerpiece until 2010, is still widely referenced, and in this Appendix we present it in detail with calculations and comparative examples. The Traditional HDI is based on three goals or end products of development, corresponding to health, education, and income: *longevity* as measured by life expectancy at birth, *knowledge* as measured by a weighted average of adult literacy (two-thirds) and gross school enrollment ratio (one-third), and *standard of living* as measured by real per capita gross domestic product adjusted for the differing purchasing power parity of each country's currency to reflect cost of living and for the assumption of diminishing marginal utility of income. Using these three measures of development and applying a formula to data for 177 countries, the HDI ranks countries into four groups: low human development (0.0 to 0.499), medium human development (0.50 to 0.799), high human development (0.80 to 0.90), and very high human development (0.90 to 1.0).

Adjusted income is found by taking the log of current income. Then, to find the income index, one subtracts the log of 100 from the log of current income, on the assumption that real per capita income cannot possibly be less than $100 PPP.[1] The difference gives the amount by which the country has exceeded this "lower goalpost." To put this achievement in perspective, consider it in relation to the maximum that a developing country might reasonably aspire to over the coming generation. The UNDP sets this maximum at $40,000 PPP. So we then divide by the difference between the log of $40,000 and the log of $100 to find the country's relative income achievement. This gives each country an index number that ranges between 0 and 1. For example, for the case of Bangladesh, whose 2007 PPP GDP per capita was estimated by the UNDP to be $1,241, the income index for that year is calculated as follows:

$$\text{Income index} = \frac{[\log(1{,}241) - \log(100)]}{[\log(40{,}000) - \log(100)]} = 0.420 \qquad \text{(A2.1)}$$

The effect of diminishing marginal utility is clear. An income of $1,241, which is just 3% of the maximum goalpost of $40,000, is already enough to reach more than two-fifths of the maximum value that the index can take. Note that a few countries have already exceeded the $40,000 PPP income target; in such cases, the UNDP assigned the maximum value of $40,000 PPP income, and so the country gets the maximum income index of 1.

To find the life expectancy (health proxy) index, the UNDP starts with a country's current life expectancy at birth and subtracts 25 years. The latter is the lower goalpost, the lowest that life expectancy could have been in any country over the previous generation. Then the UNDP divides the result by 85 years minus 25 years, or 60 years, which represents the range of life expectancies expected over the previous and next generations. That is, it is anticipated that 85 years is a maximum reasonable life expectancy for a country to try to achieve over the coming generation. For example, for the case of Bangladesh, whose population life expectancy in 2007 was 65.7 years, the life expectancy index is calculated as follows:

$$\text{Life expectancy index} = \frac{65.7 - 25}{85 - 25} = 0.678 \qquad \text{(A2.2)}$$

Notice that no diminishing marginal utility of years of life are assumed; the same holds for the education index. The education index is made up of two parts, with two-thirds weight on literacy and one-third weight on school enrollment. Because gross school enrollments can exceed 100% (because of older students going back to school), this index is also capped at 100%. For the case of Bangladesh, adult literacy is estimated (rather uncertainly) at 53.5%, so

$$\text{Adult literacy index} = \frac{53.5 - 0}{100 - 0} = 0.535 \qquad \text{(A2.3)}$$

For the gross enrollment index, for Bangladesh it is estimated that 52.1% of its primary, secondary, and tertiary age population are enrolled in school, so the country receives the following value:

$$\text{Gross enrollment index} = \frac{52.1 - 0}{100 - 0} = 0.521 \qquad \text{(A2.4)}$$

Then, to get the overall education index, the adult literacy index is multiplied by two-thirds and the gross enrollment index is multiplied by one-third. This choice reflects the view that literacy is the fundamental characteristic of an educated person. In the case of Bangladesh, this gives us

$$\text{Education index} = \frac{2}{3}(\text{adult literacy index}) + \frac{1}{3}(\text{gross enrollment index})$$
$$= \frac{2}{3}(0.535) + \frac{1}{3}(0.521) = 0.530 \qquad \text{(A2.5)}$$

In the final index, each of the three components receives equal, or one-third, weight. Thus,

$$\text{HDI} = \frac{1}{3}(\text{income index}) + \frac{1}{3}(\text{life expectancy index}) + \frac{1}{3}(\text{education index}) \quad \text{(A2.6)}$$

For the case of Bangladesh,

$$\text{HDI} = \frac{1}{3}(0.420) + \frac{1}{3}(0.678) + \frac{1}{3}(0.530) = 0.543 \qquad \text{(A2.7)}$$

One major advantage of the HDI is that it does reveal that a country can do much better than might be expected at a low level of income and that substantial income gains can still accomplish relatively little in human development.

Moreover, the HDI reminds us that by *development*, we clearly mean broad human development, not just higher income. Many countries, such as some of the higher-income oil producers, have been said to have experienced "growth without development." Health and education are inputs into the national production function in their role as components of human capital, meaning productive investments embodied in persons. Improvements in health and education are also important development goals in their own right (see Chapter 8). We cannot easily argue that a nation of high-income individuals who are not well educated and suffer from significant health problems that lead to their living much shorter lives than others around the globe has achieved a higher level of development than a low-income country with high life expectancy and widespread literacy. A better indicator of development disparities and rankings might be found by including health and education variables in a weighted welfare measure rather than by simply looking at income levels, and the HDI offers one very useful way to do this.

There are other criticisms and possible drawbacks of the HDI. One is that gross enrollment in many cases overstates the amount of schooling, because in many countries, a student who begins primary school is counted as enrolled without considering whether the student drops out at some stage. Equal (one-third) weight is given to each of the three components, which clearly has some value judgment behind it, but it is difficult to determine what this is. Note that because the variables are measured in very different types of units, it is difficult even to say precisely what equal weights mean. Finally, there is no attention to the role of quality. For example, there is a big difference between an extra year of life as a healthy, well-functioning individual and an extra year with a sharply limited range of capabilities (such as being confined to bed). Moreover, the quality of schooling counts, not just the number of years of enrollment. Finally, it should be noted that while one could imagine better proxies for health and education, measures for these variables were chosen partly on the criterion that sufficient data must be available to include as many countries as possible.

Table A2.1.1 shows the 2009 Traditional Human Development Index (using 2007 data) for a sample of 24 developed and developing nations ranked from low to very high human development (column 3) along with their respective real GDP per capita (column 4) and a measure of the differential between the GDP per capita rank and the HDI rank (column 5). A positive number shows by how much a country's relative ranking rises when HDI is used instead of GDP per capita, and a negative number shows the opposite. We see from Table A2.1.1 that the country with the lowest HDI (0.340) in 2007 was Niger, and the one with the highest (0.971) was Norway.

The HDI has a strong tendency to rise with per capita income, as wealthier countries can invest more in health and education, and this added human capital raises productivity. But what is so striking is that despite this expected pattern, there is still such great variation between income and broader measures of well-being, as seen in Tables A2.1.1 and A2.1.2. For example, Senegal and Rwanda have essentially the same average HDI despite the fact that real income is 92% higher in Senegal. And Costa Rica has a higher HDI than Saudi Arabia, despite the fact that Saudi Arabia has more than double the real per capita income of Costa Rica. Many countries have an HDI significantly different from that predicted by their income. South Africa has an HDI of 0.683, but it ranks just 129th, 51 places lower than to be expected from its middle-income ranking. But similarly ranked São Tomé and Príncipe (number 131) ranks 17 places higher than expected from its income level.

For the countries listed in Table A2.1.2 with GDP per capita near $1,000, the HDI ranges dramatically from 0.371 to 0.543. Correspondingly, literacy rates

TABLE A2.1.1	2009 Traditional Human Development Index for 24 Selected Countries (2007 Data)			
Country	Relative Ranking	Human Development Index (HDI)	GDP Per Capita (PPP, U.S. $)	GDP Rank Minus HDI Rank
Low Human Development				
Niger	182	0.340	627	−6
Afghanistan	181	0.352	1,054	−17
Dem. Rep. Congo	176	0.389	298	5
Ethiopia	171	0.414	779	0
Rwanda	167	0.460	866	1
Côte d'Ivoire	163	0.484	1,690	−17
Malawi	160	0.493	761	12
Medium Human Development				
Bangladesh	146	0.543	1,241	9
Pakistan	141	0.572	2,496	−9
India	134	0.612	2,753	−6
South Africa	129	0.683	9,757	−51
Nicaragua	124	0.699	2,570	6
Gabon	103	0.755	15,167	−49
China	92	0.772	5,383	10
Iran	88	0.782	10,955	−17
Thailand	87	0.783	8,135	−5
High Human Development				
Saudi Arabia	59	0.843	22,935	−19
Costa Rica	54	0.854	10,842	19
Cuba	51	0.863	6,876	44
Chile	44	0.878	13,880	15
Very High Human Development				
United Kingdom	21	0.947	35,130	−1
United States	13	0.956	45,592	−4
Canada	4	0.966	35,812	14
Norway	1	0.971	53,433	4

Source: Data from United Nations Development Programme, *Human Development Report, 2009,* tab. 1.

range from just 26% to 71%. Life expectancy ranges from only 44 to 61. Among countries with GDP per capita near $1,500, literacy ranges from 32% to 74% and enrollment, from 37% to 60%, with corresponding variations in the HDI. For the countries in Table A2.1.1 with GDP per capita near $2,000, the HDI ranges, from 0.511 to 0.710. Life expectancy ranges from 48 to 68. The literacy rate ranges from 56% to 99%. For countries listed in Table A2.1.1 with GDP per capita near $4,000, the HDI index ranges from 0.654 to 0.768. Life expectancy ranges from 65 to 74, and literacy rates range strikingly from 56% in Morocco to essentially universal literacy in Tonga. These dramatic differences show that the Human Development Index project is worthwhile. Ranking countries only by income—or for that matter only by health or education—causes us to miss important differences in countries' development levels.

Average income is one thing, but sometimes even in a middle-income country, many people live in poverty. When the aggregate HDI for various countries was adjusted for income distribution, the relative rankings of many developing nations also changed significantly.[2] For example, Brazil had such a highly unequal distribution that its ranking slipped, while Sri Lanka saw its HDI ranking rise due to its more egalitarian distribution.

TABLE A2.1.2   2009 Human Development Index Variations for Similar Incomes (2007 Data)

Country	GDP Per Capita (U.S. $)	HDI	HDI Rank	Life Expectancy (years)	Adult Literacy (%)	Combined Gross Enrollment Ratio
GDP Per Capita near PPP $1,000						
Madagascar	932	0.543	145	59.9	70.7	61.3
Haiti	1,140	0.532	149	61.0	62.1	52.1
Rwanda	866	0.460	167	49.7	64.9	52.2
Mali	1,083	0.371	178	48.1	26.2	46.9
Afghanistan	1,054	0.352	181	43.6	28.0	50.1
GDP Per Capita near PPP $1,500						
Kenya	1,542	0.541	147	53.6	73.6	59.6
Ghana	1,334	0.526	152	56.5	65.0	56.5
Côte d'Ivoire	1,690	0.484	163	56.8	48.7	37.5
Senegal	1,666	0.464	166	55.4	41.9	41.2
Chad	1,477	0.392	175	48.6	31.8	36.5
GDP Per Capita near PPP $2,000						
Kyrgyzstan	2,006	0.710	120	67.6	99.3	77.3
Laos	2,165	0.619	133	64.6	72.7	59.6
Cambodia	1,802	0.593	137	60.6	76.3	58.5
Sudan	2,086	0.531	150	57.9	60.9	39.9
Cameroon	2,128	0.523	153	50.9	67.9	52.3
Mauritania	1,927	0.520	154	56.6	55.8	50.6
Nigeria	1,969	0.511	158	47.7	72.0	53.0
GDP Per Capita near PPP $4,000						
Tonga	3,748	0.768	99	71.7	99.2	78.0
Sri Lanka	4,243	0.759	102	74.0	90.8	68.7
Honduras	3,796	0.732	112	72.0	83.6	74.8
Bolivia	4,206	0.729	113	65.4	90.7	86.0
Guatemala	4,562	0.704	122	70.1	73.2	70.5
Morocco	4,108	0.654	130	71.0	55.6	61.0

Source: Data from United Nations Development Programme, *Human Development Report, 2009*, tab. 1.

The HDI also ranges greatly for groups within countries. The impact of social exclusion can be seen vividly in Guatemala, where the Q'eqchi ethnic group had an HDI rank similar to Cameroon, and the Poqomchi ranked below Zimbabwe, as seen in Figure A2.1.1a. Regional differences across districts can be seen in Kenya, where the HDI of the capital area of Nairobi ranks as high as Turkey, but Kenya's Turkana district's HDI is lower than that of any country average, as shown in Figure 2.3b. Rural-urban differences are illustrated in China, where as Figure A2.1.1c shows, urban Shanghai's HDI is nearly as high as that of Greece, while rural Gansu has an HDI on a par with India, and the HDI of rural Guizhou is below that of Cambodia. An earlier UN study found similarly that in South Africa, whites enjoy a high HDI level, while that for blacks was much lower.[3]

Among other things, the Traditional HDI had a large impact on encouraging conceptualization of development in a holistic way, elevating health and education to the same rank as income as development indicators; and broadening the types of measures, both individual and composite, that were calculated and reported on a regular basis.

FIGURE A2.1.1   Human Development Disparities within Selected Countries

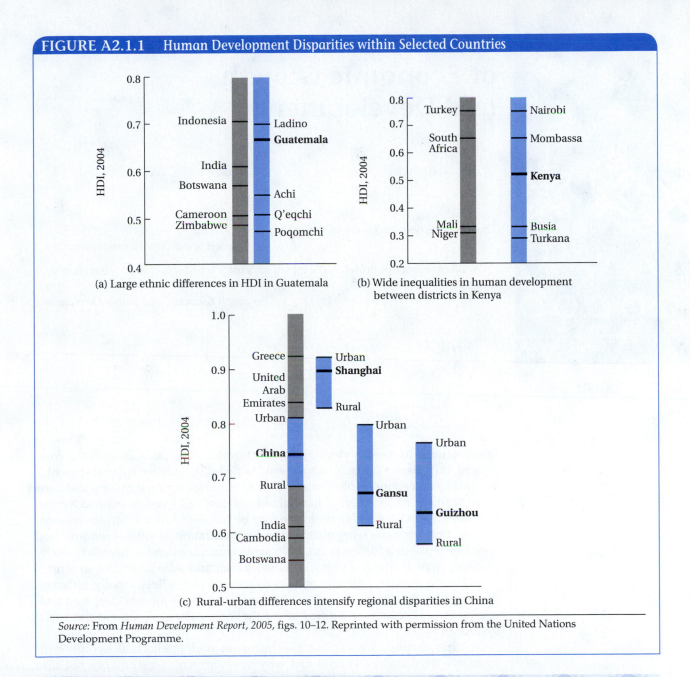

(a) Large ethnic differences in HDI in Guatemala

(b) Wide inequalities in human development between districts in Kenya

(c) Rural-urban differences intensify regional disparities in China

Source: From *Human Development Report, 2005,* figs. 10–12. Reprinted with permission from the United Nations Development Programme.

Notes

1. In fact, Lant Pritchett argues persuasively, considering available country data and the cost of minimum nutrients, that $250 is a more realistic lower bound for per capita income. See Lant Pritchett, "Divergence, big time," *Journal of Economic Perspectives* 11, No. 3 (1997): 3–17. The logarithms used in the Traditional HDI income index formula are common (base 10) logs rather than natural logs.

2. UNDP, *Human Development Report, 1994* (New York: Oxford University Press, 1994).

3. All but the South Africa example are drawn from *Human Development Report, 2006* (New York: Oxford University Press, 2006). An earlier *Human Development Report* gave South Africa an overall ranking of 0.666, with whites at 0.876 and blacks at 0.462.

3

Classic Theories of Economic Growth and Development

There is no Economic Theory of Everything,

—*Robert Solow, Nobel laureate in economics*

[In] modern economic growth...the rate of structural transformation of the economy is high.

—*Simon Kuznets, Nobel laureate in economics*

Every nation strives after development. Economic progress is an essential component, but it is not the only component. As noted in Chapter 1, development is not purely an economic phenomenon. In an ultimate sense, it must encompass more than the material and financial side of people's lives, to expand human freedoms. Development should therefore be perceived as a multidimensional process involving the reorganization and reorientation of entire economic and social systems. In addition to improvements in incomes and output, it typically involves radical changes in institutional, social, and administrative structures as well as in popular attitudes and even customs and beliefs. Finally, although development is usually defined in a national context, its more widespread realization may necessitate modification of the international economic and social system as well.

In this chapter, we explore the historical and intellectual evolution in scholarly thinking about how and why development does or does not take place. We do this by examining four major and often competing development theories. You will see that each offers valuable insights and a useful perspective on the nature of the development process. Some newer models of development and underdevelopment draw eclectically on the classic theories, and we consider them in Chapter 4.

Approaches to the analysis of economic growth are introduced throughout this review of alternative theories of development and are then amplified in three chapter appendixes.

3.1 Classic Theories of Economic Development: Four Approaches

The classic post–World War II literature on economic development has been dominated by four major and sometimes competing strands of thought: (1) the linear-stages-of-growth model, (2) theories and patterns of structural change, (3) the international-dependence revolution, and (4) the neoclassical, free-market counterrevolution. In recent years, an eclectic approach has emerged that draws on all of these classic theories.

Theorists of the 1950s and 1960s viewed the process of development as a series of successive stages of economic growth through which all countries must pass. It was primarily an economic theory of development in which the right quantity and mixture of saving, investment, and foreign aid were all that was necessary to enable developing nations to proceed along an economic growth path that had historically been followed by the more developed countries. Development thus became synonymous with rapid, aggregate economic growth.

This linear-stages approach was largely replaced in the 1970s by two competing schools of thought. The first, which focused on theories and patterns of structural change, used modern economic theory and statistical analysis in an attempt to portray the internal process of structural change that a "typical" developing country must undergo if it is to succeed in generating and sustaining rapid economic growth. The second, the international-dependence revolution, was more radical and more political. It viewed underdevelopment in terms of international and domestic power relationships, institutional and structural economic rigidities, and the resulting proliferation of dual economies and dual societies both within and among the nations of the world. Dependence theories tended to emphasize external and internal institutional and political constraints on economic development. Emphasis was placed on the need for major new policies to eradicate poverty, to provide more diversified employment opportunities, and to reduce income inequalities. These and other egalitarian objectives were to be achieved within the context of a growing economy, but economic growth per se was not given the exalted status accorded to it by the linear-stages and structural-change models.

Throughout much of the 1980s and 1990s, a fourth approach prevailed. This neoclassical (sometimes called *neoliberal*) counterrevolution in economic thought emphasized the beneficial role of free markets, open economies, and the privatization of inefficient public enterprises. Failure to develop, according to this theory, was not due to exploitive external and internal forces as expounded by dependence theorists. Rather, it was primarily the result of too much government intervention and regulation of the economy. Today's eclectic approach draws on all of these perspectives, and we will highlight the strengths and weaknesses of each.

3.2 Development as Growth and the Linear-Stages Theories

When interest in the poor nations of the world really began to materialize following World War II, economists in the industrialized nations were caught off guard. They had no readily available conceptual apparatus with which to analyze the process of economic growth in largely agrarian societies that lacked modern economic structures. But they did have the recent experience of the Marshall Plan, under which massive amounts of U.S. financial and technical assistance enabled the war-torn countries of Europe to rebuild and modernize their economies in a matter of years. Moreover, was it not true that all modern industrial nations were once undeveloped agrarian societies? Surely their historical experience in transforming their economies from poor agricultural subsistence societies to modern industrial giants had important lessons for the "backward" countries of Asia, Africa, and Latin America. The logic and simplicity of these two strands of thought—the utility of massive injections of capital and the historical experience of the now developed countries—was too irresistible to be refuted by scholars, politicians, and administrators in rich countries, to whom people and ways of life in the developing world were often no more real than UN statistics or scattered chapters in anthropology books. Because of its emphasis on the central role of accelerated capital accumulation, this approach is often dubbed "capital fundamentalism."

Rostow's Stages of Growth

Stages-of-growth model of development A theory of economic development, associated with the American economic historian Walt W. Rostow, according to which a country passes through sequential stages in achieving development.

The most influential and outspoken advocate of the **stages-of-growth model of development** was the American economic historian Walt W. Rostow. According to Rostow, the transition from underdevelopment to development can be described in terms of a series of steps or stages through which all countries must proceed. As Rostow wrote in the opening chapter of *The Stages of Economic Growth*:

> This book presents an economic historian's way of generalizing the sweep of modern history.…It is possible to identify all societies, in their economic dimensions, as lying within one of five categories: the traditional society, the preconditions for takeoff into self-sustaining growth, the take-off, the drive to maturity, and the age of high mass consumption.…These stages are not merely descriptive. They are not merely a way of generalizing certain factual observations about the sequence of development of modern societies. They have an inner logic and continuity.…They constitute, in the end, both a theory about economic growth and a more general, if still highly partial, theory about modern history as a whole.[1]

The advanced countries, it was argued, had all passed the stage of "takeoff into self-sustaining growth," and the underdeveloped countries that were still in either the traditional society or the "preconditions" stage had only to follow a certain set of rules of development to take off in their turn into self-sustaining economic growth.

Harrod-Domar growth model A functional economic relationship in which the growth rate of gross domestic product (g) depends directly on the national net savings rate (s) and inversely on the national capital-output ratio (c).

One of the principal strategies of development necessary for any takeoff was the mobilization of domestic and foreign saving in order to generate sufficient investment to accelerate economic growth. The economic mechanism by which more investment leads to more growth can be described in terms of the **Harrod-Domar growth model**,[2] today often referred to as the *AK* model because it is based on a linear production function with output given by the capital stock *K* times a constant, often labeled *A*. In one form or another, it has frequently been applied to policy issues facing developing countries, such as in the two-gap model examined in Chapter 14.

The Harrod-Domar Growth Model

Every economy must save a certain proportion of its national income, if only to replace worn-out or impaired capital goods (buildings, equipment, and materials). However, in order to grow, new investments representing net additions to the capital stock are necessary. If we assume that there is some direct economic relationship between the size of the total capital stock, K, and total GDP, Y—for example, if \$3 of capital is always necessary to produce an annual \$1 stream of GDP—it follows that any net additions to the capital stock in the form of new investment will bring about corresponding increases in the flow of national output, GDP.

Suppose that this relationship, known in economics as the **capital-output ratio**, is roughly 3 to 1. If we define the capital-output ratio as k and assume further that the national **net savings ratio**, s, is a fixed proportion of national output (e.g., 6%) and that total new investment is determined by the level of total savings, we can construct the following simple model of economic growth:

1. Net saving (S) is some proportion, s, of national income (Y) such that we have the simple equation

$$S = sY \tag{3.1}$$

2. Net investment (I) is defined as the change in the capital stock, K, and can be represented by ΔK such that

$$I = \Delta K \tag{3.2}$$

But because the total capital stock, K, bears a direct relationship to total national income or output, Y, as expressed by the capital-output ratio, c,[3] it follows that

$$\frac{K}{Y} = c$$

or

$$\frac{\Delta K}{\Delta Y} = c$$

or, finally,

$$\Delta K = c\Delta Y \tag{3.3}$$

1/c is a measure of the efficiency of capital utilization.

3. Finally, because net national savings, S, must equal net investment, I, we can write this equality as

$$S = I \tag{3.4}$$

But from Equation 3.1 we know that $S = sY$, and from Equations 3.2 and 3.3 we know that

$$I = \Delta K = c\Delta Y$$

It therefore follows that we can write the "identity" of saving equaling investment shown by Equation 3.4 as

$$S = sY = c\Delta Y = \Delta K = I \tag{3.5}$$

Capital-output ratio A ratio that shows the units of capital required to produce a unit of output over a given period of time.

Net savings ratio Savings expressed as a proportion of disposable income over some period of time.

or simply as

$$sY = c\Delta Y \qquad (3.6)$$

Dividing both sides of Equation 3.6 first by Y and then by c, we obtain the following expression:

$$\frac{\Delta Y}{Y} = \frac{s}{c} \qquad (3.7)$$

Note that the left-hand side of Equation 3.7, $\Delta Y/Y$, represents the rate of change or rate of growth of GDP.

Equation 3.7, which is a simplified version of the famous equation in the Harrod-Domar theory of economic growth, states simply that the rate of growth of GDP ($\Delta Y/Y$) is determined jointly by the net national savings ratio, s, and the national capital-output ratio, c. More specifically, it says that in the absence of government, the growth rate of national income will be directly or positively related to the savings ratio (i.e., the more an economy is able to save—and invest—out of a given GDP, the greater the growth of that GDP will be) and inversely or negatively related to the economy's capital-output ratio (i.e., the higher c is, the lower the rate of GDP growth will be). Equation 3.7 is also often expressed in terms of gross savings, s^G, in which case the growth rate is given by

$$\frac{\Delta Y}{Y} = \frac{s^G}{c} - \delta \qquad (3.7')$$

where δ is the rate of capital depreciation.[4]

The economic logic of Equations 3.7 and 3.7′ is very simple. To grow, economies must save and invest a certain proportion of their GDP. The more they can save and invest, the faster they can grow. But the actual rate at which they can grow for any level of saving and investment—how much additional output can be had from an additional unit of investment—can be measured by the inverse of the capital-output ratio, c, because this inverse, $1/c$, is simply the output-capital or output-investment ratio. It follows that multiplying the rate of new investment, $s = I/Y$, by its productivity, $1/c$, will give the rate by which national income or GDP will increase.

In addition to investment, two other components of economic growth are labor force growth and technological progress. The roles and functioning of these three components are examined in detail in Appendix 3.1. In the context of the Harrod-Domar growth model, labor force growth is not described explicitly. This is because labor is assumed to be abundant in a developing-country context and can be hired as needed in a given proportion to capital investments (this assumption is not always valid). In a general way, technological progress can be expressed in the Harrod-Domar context as a decrease in the required capital-output ratio, giving more growth for a given level of investment, as follows from Equation 3.7 or 3.7′. This is obvious when we realize that in the longer run, this ratio is not fixed but can change over time in response to the functioning of financial markets and the policy environment. But again, the focus was on the role of capital investment.

Obstacles and Constraints

Returning to the stages-of-growth theories and using Equation 3.7 of our simple Harrod-Domar growth model, we learn that one of the most fundamental strategies of economic growth is simply to increase the proportion of national income saved (i.e., not consumed). If we can raise s in Equation 3.7, we can increase $\Delta Y/Y$, the rate of GDP growth. For example, if we assume that the national capital-output ratio in some less developed country is, say, 3 and the aggregate net saving ratio is 6% of GDP, it follows from Equation 3.7 that this country can grow at a rate of 2% per year because

$$\frac{\Delta Y}{Y} = \frac{s}{c} = \frac{6\%}{3} = 2\% \tag{3.8}$$

Now if the national net savings rate can somehow be increased from 6% to, say, 15%—through some combination of increased taxes, foreign aid, and general consumption sacrifices—GDP growth can be increased from 2% to 5% because now

$$\frac{\Delta Y}{Y} = \frac{s}{c} = \frac{15\%}{3} = 5\% \tag{3.9}$$

In fact, Rostow and others defined the takeoff stage in precisely this way. Countries that were able to save 15 to 20% of GDP could grow ("develop") at a much faster rate than those that saved less. Moreover, this growth would then be self-sustaining. The mechanisms of economic growth and development, therefore, would be simply a matter of increasing national savings and investment.

The main obstacle to or constraint on development, according to this theory, is the relatively low level of new capital formation in most poor countries. But if a country wanted to grow at, say, a rate of 7% per year and if it could not generate savings and investment at a rate of 21% of national income (assuming that c, the final aggregate capital-output ratio, is 3) but could only manage to save 15%, it could seek to fill this "savings gap" of 6% through either foreign aid or private foreign investment.

Thus, the "capital constraint" stages approach to growth and development became a rationale and (in terms of Cold War politics) an opportunistic tool for justifying massive transfers of capital and technical assistance from the developed to the less developed nations. It was to be the Marshall Plan all over again, but this time for the nations of the developing world.

Necessary versus Sufficient Conditions: Some Criticisms of the Stages Model

Unfortunately, the mechanisms of development embodied in the theory of stages of growth did not always work. And the basic reason they didn't work was not because more saving and investment isn't a **necessary condition** for accelerated rates of economic growth but rather because it is not a **sufficient condition**. The Marshall Plan worked for Europe because the European countries receiving aid possessed the necessary structural, institutional, and

Necessary condition A condition that must be present, although it need not be in itself sufficient, for an event to occur. For example, capital formation may be a necessary condition for sustained economic growth (before growth in output can occur, there must be tools to produce it). But for this growth to continue, social, institutional, and attitudinal changes may have to occur.

Sufficient condition A condition that when present causes or guarantees that an event will or can occur; in economic models, a condition that logically requires that a statement must be true (or a result must hold) given other assumptions.

attitudinal conditions (e.g., well-integrated commodity and money markets, highly developed transport facilities, a well-trained and educated workforce, the motivation to succeed, an efficient government bureaucracy) to convert new capital effectively into higher levels of output. The Rostow and Harrod-Domar models implicitly assume the existence of these same attitudes and arrangements in underdeveloped nations. Yet, in many cases, they are lacking, as are complementary factors such as managerial competence, skilled labor, and the ability to plan and administer a wide assortment of development projects. There was also insufficient focus on another strategy for raising growth that is apparent from Equation 3.7: reducing the capital-output ratio, c, which entails increasing the efficiency with which investments generate extra output—a theme we take up later.

3.3 Structural-Change Models

Structural-change theory

The hypothesis that *underdevelopment* is due to underutilization of *resources* arising from structural or institutional factors that have their origins in both domestic and international *dualism. Development* therefore requires more than just accelerated *capital* formation.

Structural-change theory focuses on the mechanism by which underdeveloped economies transform their domestic economic structures from a heavy emphasis on traditional subsistence agriculture to a more modern, more urbanized, and more industrially diverse manufacturing and service economy. It employs the tools of neoclassical price and resource allocation theory and modern econometrics to describe how this transformation process takes place. Two well-known representative examples of the structural-change approach are the "two-sector surplus labor" theoretical model of W. Arthur Lewis and the "patterns of development" empirical analysis of Hollis B. Chenery and his coauthors.

Structural transformation

The process of transforming an economy in such a way that the contribution to national income by the manufacturing sector eventually surpasses the contribution by the agricultural sector. More generally, a major alteration in the industrial composition of any economy.

The Lewis Theory of Economic Development

Basic Model One of the best-known early theoretical models of development that focused on the **structural transformation** of a primarily subsistence economy was that formulated by Nobel laureate W. Arthur Lewis in the mid-1950s and later modified, formalized, and extended by John Fei and Gustav Ranis.[5] The **Lewis two-sector model** became the general theory of the development process in surplus-labor developing nations during most of the 1960s and early 1970s, and it is sometimes still applied, particularly to study the recent growth experience in China and labor markets in other developing countries.[6]

Lewis two-sector model A theory of development in which surplus labor from the traditional agricultural sector is transferred to the modern industrial sector, the growth of which absorbs the surplus labor, promotes industrialization, and stimulates sustained development.

In the Lewis model, the underdeveloped economy consists of two sectors: a traditional, overpopulated, rural subsistence sector characterized by zero marginal labor productivity—a situation that permits Lewis to classify this as **surplus labor** in the sense that it can be withdrawn from the traditional agricultural sector without any loss of output—and a high-productivity modern, urban industrial sector into which labor from the subsistence sector is gradually transferred. The primary focus of the model is on both the process of labor transfer and the growth of output and employment in the modern sector. (The modern sector could include modern agriculture, but we will call the sector "industrial" as a shorthand). Both labor transfer and modern-sector employment growth are brought about by output expansion in that sector. The speed with which this expansion occurs is determined by the rate

Surplus labor The excess supply of labor over and above the quantity demanded at the going free-market wage rate. In the Lewis two-sector model of economic development, *surplus labor* refers to the portion of the rural labor force whose marginal productivity is zero or negative.

of industrial investment and capital accumulation in the modern sector. Such investment is made possible by the excess of modern-sector profits over wages on the assumption that capitalists reinvest all their profits. Finally, Lewis assumed that the level of wages in the urban industrial sector was constant, determined as a given premium over a fixed average subsistence level of wages in the traditional agricultural sector. At the constant urban wage, the supply curve of rural labor to the modern sector is considered to be perfectly elastic.

We can illustrate the Lewis model of modern-sector growth in a two-sector economy by using Figure 3.1. Consider first the traditional agricultural sector portrayed in the two right-hand diagrams of Figure 3.1b. The upper diagram shows how subsistence food production varies with increases in labor inputs. It is a typical agricultural **production function** in which the total output or product (TP_A) of food is determined by changes in the amount of

Production function A technological or engineering relationship between the quantity of a good produced and the quantity of inputs required to produce it.

FIGURE 3.1 The Lewis Model of Modern-Sector Growth in a Two-Sector Surplus-Labor Economy

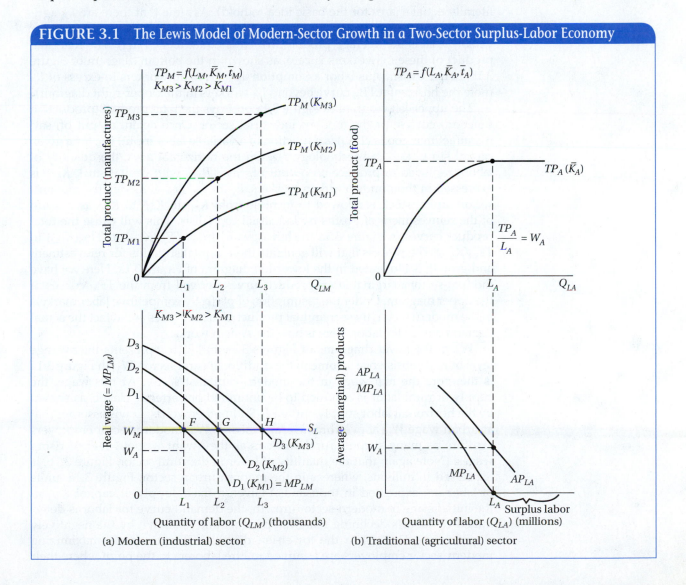

(a) Modern (industrial) sector

(b) Traditional (agricultural) sector

Average product Total output or product divided by total factor input (e.g., the average product of labor is equal to total output divided by the total amount of labor used to produce that output).

Marginal product The increase in total output resulting from the use of one additional unit of a variable factor of production (such as labor or capital). In the Lewis two-sector model, *surplus labor* is defined as workers whose marginal product is zero.

the only variable input, labor (L_A), given a fixed quantity of capital, $\overline{K}_A$, and unchanging traditional technology, $\bar{t}_A$. In the lower-right diagram, we have the **average** and **marginal product** of labor curves, AP_{LA} and MP_{LA}, which are derived from the total product curve shown immediately above. The quantity of agricultural labor (Q_{LA}) available is the same on both horizontal axes of the right-hand side of the figure and is expressed in millions of workers, as Lewis is describing an underdeveloped economy where much of the population lives and works in rural areas.

Lewis makes two assumptions about the traditional sector. First, there is surplus labor in the sense that MP_{LA} is zero, and second, all rural workers share *equally* in the output so that the rural real wage is determined by the average and not the marginal product of labor (as will be the case in the modern sector). Metaphorically, this may be thought of as passing around the family rice bowl at dinnertime, from which each person takes an equal share (this need not be literally equal shares for the basic idea to hold). Assume that there are L_A agricultural workers producing TP_A food, which is shared equally as W_A food per person (this is the average product, which is equal to TP_A/L_A). The marginal product of these L_A workers is zero, as shown in the bottom diagram of Figure 3.1b; hence the surplus-labor assumption applies to all workers in excess of L_A (note the horizontal TP_A curve beyond L_A workers in the upper-right diagram).

The upper-left diagram of Figure 3.1a portrays the total product (production function) curves for the modern industrial sector. Once again, output of, say, manufactured goods (TP_M) is a function of a variable labor input, L_M, for a given capital stock $\overline{K}_M$ and technology, $\bar{t}_M$. On the horizontal axes, the quantity of labor employed to produce an output of, say, TP_{M1}, with capital stock K_{M1}, is expressed in thousands of urban workers, L_1. In the Lewis model, the modern-sector capital stock is allowed to increase from K_{M1} to K_{M2} to K_{M3} as a result of the reinvestment of profits by industrial capitalists. This will cause the total product curves in Figure 3.1a to shift upward from $TP_M(K_{M1})$ to $TP_M(K_{M2})$ to $TP_M(K_{M3})$. The process that will generate these capitalist profits for reinvestment and growth is illustrated in the lower-left diagram of Figure 3.1a. Here we have modern-sector marginal labor product curves derived from the TP_M curves of the upper diagram. Under the assumption of perfectly competitive labor markets in the modern sector, these marginal product of labor curves are in fact the actual demand curves for labor. Here is how the system works.

W_A in the lower diagrams of Figures 3.1a and 3.1b represents the average level of real subsistence income in the traditional rural sector. W_M in Figure 3.1a is therefore the real wage in the modern capitalist sector. At this wage, the supply of rural labor is assumed to be unlimited or perfectly elastic, as shown by the horizontal labor supply curve $W_M S_L$. In other words, Lewis assumes that at urban wage W_M above rural average income W_A, modern-sector employers can hire as many surplus rural workers as they want without fear of rising wages. (Note again that the quantity of labor in the rural sector, Figure 3.1b, is expressed in millions, whereas in the modern urban sector, Figure 3.1a, units of labor are expressed in thousands.) Given a fixed supply of capital K_{M1} in the initial stage of modern-sector growth, the demand curve for labor is determined by labor's declining marginal product and is shown by the negatively sloped curve $D_1(K_{M1})$ in the lower-left diagram. Because profit-maximizing modern-sector employers are assumed to hire laborers to the point where their marginal physical product is equal to the real wage (i.e., the point F of intersection between the labor demand and supply curves), total modern-sector employment will be equal to L_1. Total modern-sector output, TP_{M1}, would be given by the area bounded by points $0D_1FL_1$. The share of this total output paid to workers in the form of wages would be equal, therefore, to the area of the rectangle $0W_MFL_1$. The balance of the output shown by the area W_MD_1F would be the total profits that accrue to the capitalists. Because Lewis assumes that all of these profits are reinvested, the total capital stock in the modern sector will rise from K_{M1} to K_{M2}. This larger capital stock causes the total product curve of the modern sector to shift to $TP_M(K_{M2})$, which in turn induces a rise in the marginal product demand curve for labor. This outward shift in the labor demand curve is shown by line $D_2(K_{M2})$ in the bottom half of Figure 3.1a. A new equilibrium modern-sector employment level will be established at point G with L_2 workers now employed. Total output rises to TP_{M2} or $0D_2GL_2$, while total wages and profits increase to $0W_MGL_2$ and W_MD_2G, respectively. Once again, these larger (W_MD_2G) profits are reinvested, increasing the total capital stock to K_{M3}, shifting the total product and labor demand curves to $TP_M(K_{M3})$ and to $D_3(K_{M3})$, respectively, and raising the level of modern-sector employment to L_3.

This process of modern-sector **self-sustaining growth** and employment expansion is assumed to continue until all surplus rural labor is absorbed in the new industrial sector. Thereafter, additional workers can be withdrawn from the agricultural sector only at a higher cost of lost food production because the declining labor-to-land ratio means that the marginal product of rural labor is no longer zero. This is known as the "Lewis turning point." Thus, the labor supply curve becomes positively sloped as modern-sector wages and employment continue to grow. The structural transformation of the economy will have taken place, with the balance of economic activity shifting from traditional rural agriculture to modern urban industry.

> **Self-sustaining growth** Economic growth that continues over the long run based on saving, investment, and complementary private and public activities.

Criticisms of the Lewis Model Although the Lewis two-sector development model is simple and roughly reflects the historical experience of economic growth in the West, four of its key assumptions do not fit the institutional and economic realities of most contemporary developing countries.

First, the model implicitly assumes that the rate of labor transfer and employment creation in the modern sector is proportional to the rate of modern-sector capital accumulation. The faster the rate of capital accumulation, the higher the growth rate of the modern sector and the faster the rate of new job creation. But what if capitalist profits are reinvested in more sophisticated laborsaving capital equipment rather than just duplicating the existing capital, as is implicitly assumed in the Lewis model? (We are, of course, here accepting the debatable assumption that capitalist profits are in fact reinvested in the local economy and not sent abroad as a form of "capital flight" to be added to the deposits of Western banks.) Figure 3.2 reproduces the lower, modern-sector diagram of Figure 3.1a, only this time the labor demand curves do not shift uniformly outward but in fact cross. Demand curve $D_2(K_{M2})$ has a greater negative slope than $D_2(K_{M1})$ to reflect the fact that additions to the capital stock embody laborsaving technical progress— that is, KM_2 technology requires much less labor per unit of output than KM_1 technology does.

**FIGURE 3.2   The Lewis Model Modified by Laborsaving Capital
Accumulation: Employment Implications**

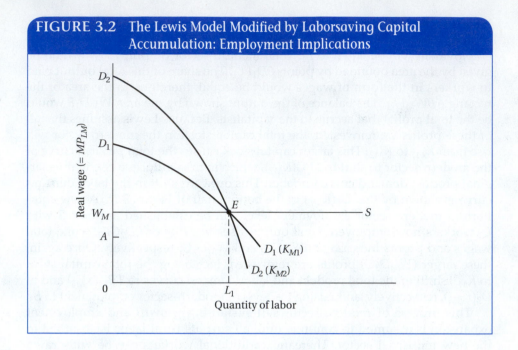

We see that even though total output has grown substantially (i.e., $0D_2EL_1$ is significantly greater than $0D_1EL_1$), total wages ($0W_MEL_1$) and employment (L_1) remain unchanged. All of the extra output accrues to capitalists in the form of profits. Figure 3.2 therefore provides an illustration of what some might call "antidevelopmental" economic growth—*all* the extra income and output growth are distributed to the few owners of capital, while income and employment levels for the masses of workers remain largely unchanged. Although total GDP would rise, there would be little or no improvement in aggregate social welfare measured, say, in terms of more widely distributed gains in income and employment.

The second questionable assumption of the Lewis model is the notion that surplus labor exists in rural areas while there is full employment in the urban areas. Most contemporary research indicates that there is little surplus labor in rural locations. True, there are both seasonal and geographic exceptions to this rule (e.g., at least until recently in parts of China and the Asian subcontinent, some Caribbean islands, and isolated regions of Latin America where land ownership is very unequal), but by and large, development economists today agree that Lewis's assumption of rural surplus labor is generally not valid.

The third dubious assumption is the notion of a competitive modern-sector labor market that guarantees the continued existence of constant real urban wages up to the point where the supply of rural surplus labor is exhausted. Prior to the 1980s, a striking feature of urban labor markets and wage determination in almost all developing countries was the tendency for these wages to rise substantially over time, both in absolute terms and relative to average rural incomes, even in the presence of rising levels of open modern-sector unemployment and low or zero marginal productivity in agriculture. Institutional factors such as union bargaining power, civil service wage scales, and multinational corporations' hiring practices tend to negate competitive forces in modern-sector labor markets in developing countries.

The fourth concern with the Lewis model is its assumption of diminishing returns in the modern industrial sector. Yet there is much evidence that increasing returns prevail in that sector, posing special problems for development policymaking that we will examine in Chapter 4.

We study the Lewis model because, as many development specialists still think about development in this way either explicitly or implicitly, it helps students participate in the debates. Moreover, the model is widely considered relevant to recent experiences in China, where labor has been steadily absorbed from farming into manufacturing, and to a few other countries with similar growth patterns. The Lewis turning point at which wages in manufacturing start to rise was widely identified with China's wage increases starting in 2010 (see the case study for Chapter 4).

However, when we take into account the laborsaving bias of most modern technological transfer, the existence of substantial capital flight, the widespread nonexistence of rural surplus labor, the growing prevalence of urban surplus labor, and the tendency for modern-sector wages to rise rapidly even where substantial open unemployment exists, we must acknowledge that the Lewis two-sector model—though valuable as an early conceptual portrayal of the development process of sectoral interaction and structural change and a description of some historical experiences, including some recent ones such as China—requires considerable modification in assumptions and analysis to fit the reality of most contemporary developing nations.

Structural Change and Patterns of Development

Like the earlier Lewis model, the **patterns-of-development analysis** of structural change focuses on the sequential process through which the economic, industrial, and institutional structure of an underdeveloped economy is transformed over time to permit new industries to replace traditional agriculture as the engine of economic growth. However, in contrast to the Lewis model and the original stages view of development, increased savings and investment are perceived by patterns-of-development analysts as necessary but not sufficient conditions for economic growth. In addition to the accumulation of capital, both physical and human, a set of interrelated changes in the economic structure of a country are required for the transition from a traditional economic system to a modern one. These structural changes involve virtually all economic functions, including the transformation of production and changes in the composition of consumer demand, international trade, and resource use as well as changes in socioeconomic factors such as urbanization and the growth and distribution of a country's population.

Empirical structural-change analysts emphasize both domestic and international constraints on development. The domestic ones include economic constraints such as a country's resource endowment and its physical and population size, as well as institutional constraints such as government policies and objectives. International constraints on development include access to external capital, technology, and international trade. Differences in development level among developing countries are largely ascribed to these domestic and

Patterns-of-development analysis An attempt to identify characteristic features of the internal process of structural transformation that a "typical" developing economy undergoes as it generates and sustains modern economic growth and development.

international constraints. However, it is the international constraints that make the transition of currently developing countries differ from that of now industrialized countries. To the extent that developing countries have access to the opportunities presented by the industrial countries as sources of capital, technology, and manufactured imports, as well as markets for exports, they can make the transition at an even faster rate than that achieved by the industrial countries during the early periods of their economic development. Thus, unlike the earlier stages model, the structural-change model recognizes the fact that developing countries are part of an integrated international system that can promote (as well as hinder) their development.

The best-known model of structural change is the one based largely on the empirical work of the late economist Hollis B. Chenery and his colleagues, who examined patterns of development for numerous developing countries during the postwar period. (This approach also built on research by Nobel laureate Simon Kuznets on modern economic growth of developed countries.)[7] Their empirical studies, both cross-sectional (among countries at a given point in time) and time-series (over long periods of time), of countries at different levels of per capita income led to the identification of several characteristic features of the development process. These included the shift from agricultural to industrial production, the steady accumulation of physical and human capital, the change in consumer demands from emphasis on food and basic necessities to desires for diverse manufactured goods and services, the growth of cities and urban industries as people migrate from farms and small towns, and the decline in family size and overall population growth as children lose their economic value and parents substitute what is traditionally labeled child quality (education) for quantity (see Chapter 6), with population growth first increasing and then decreasing in the process of development. Proponents of this school often call for development specialists to "let the facts speak for themselves" rather than get bogged down in the arcana of theories such as the stages of growth. This is a valuable counterbalance to empty theorizing, but it also has its own limits.

Conclusions and Implications

The structural changes that we have described are the "average" patterns of development that Chenery and his colleagues observed among countries in time-series and cross-sectional analyses. The major hypothesis of the structural-change model is that development is an identifiable process of growth and change, whose main features are similar in all countries. However, as mentioned earlier, the model does recognize that differences can arise among countries in the pace and pattern of development, depending on their particular set of circumstances. Factors influencing the development process include a country's resource endowment and size, its government's policies and objectives, the availability of external capital and technology, and the international trade environment.

One limitation to keep in mind is that by emphasizing patterns rather than theory, this approach runs the risk of leading practitioners to draw the wrong conclusions about causality—in effect, to "put the cart before the horse." Observing developed-country patterns such as the decline of the share of the labor force in agriculture over time, many developing-country policymakers have been inclined to neglect that vital sector. But as you will see in Chapter 9, that is precisely the opposite conclusion to the one that should be drawn. Observing the important role of higher education in developed countries, policymakers may be inclined to emphasize the development of an advanced university system even before a majority of the population has gained basic literacy, a policy that has led to gross inequities even in countries at least nominally committed to egalitarian outcomes, such as Tanzania.

Empirical studies on the process of structural change lead to the conclusion that the pace and pattern of development can vary according to both domestic and international factors, many of which lie beyond the control of an individual developing nation. Yet despite this variation, structural-change economists argue that one can identify certain patterns occurring in almost all countries during the development process. And these patterns, they argue, may be affected by the choice of development policies pursued by governments in developing countries as well as the international trade and foreign-assistance policies of developed nations. Hence, structural-change analysts are basically optimistic that the "correct" mix of economic policies will generate beneficial patterns of self-sustaining growth. The international-dependence school to which we now turn is, in contrast, much less sanguine and is in many cases downright pessimistic.

3.4 The International-Dependence Revolution

During the 1970s, international-dependence models gained increasing support, especially among developing-country intellectuals, as a result of growing disenchantment with both the stages and structural-change models. While this theory to a large degree went out of favor during the 1980s and 1990s, versions of it have enjoyed a resurgence in the twenty-first century as some of its views have been adopted, albeit in modified form, by theorists and leaders of the antiglobalization movement.[8] Essentially, international-dependence models view developing countries as beset by institutional, political, and economic rigidities, both domestic and international, and caught up in a **dependence** and **dominance** relationship with rich countries. Within this general approach are three major streams of thought: the neocolonial dependence model, the false-paradigm model, and the dualistic-development thesis.

The Neocolonial Dependence Model

The first major stream, which we call the **neocolonial dependence model**, is an indirect outgrowth of Marxist thinking. It attributes the existence and continuance of **underdevelopment** primarily to the historical evolution of a highly unequal international capitalist system of rich country–poor country relationships. Whether because rich nations are intentionally exploitative or unintentionally neglectful, the coexistence of rich and poor nations in an international system dominated by such unequal power relationships between the **center** (the developed countries) and the **periphery** (the developing countries) renders attempts by poor nations to be self-reliant and independent difficult and sometimes even impossible.[9] Certain groups in the developing countries (including landlords, entrepreneurs, military rulers, merchants, salaried public officials, and

Dependence   The reliance of developing countries on developed-country economic policies to stimulate their own economic growth. Dependence can also mean that the developing countries adopt developed-country education systems, technology, economic and political systems, attitudes, consumption patterns, dress, and so on.

Dominance   In international affairs, a situation in which the developed countries have much greater power than the less developed countries in decisions affecting important international economic issues, such as the prices of agricultural commodities and raw materials in world markets.

Neocolonial dependence model   A model whose main proposition is that underdevelopment exists in developing countries because of continuing exploitative economic, political, and cultural policies of former colonial rulers toward less developed countries.

Underdevelopment   An economic situation characterized by persistent low levels of living in conjunction with absolute poverty, low income per capita, low rates of economic growth, low consumption levels, poor health services, high death rates, high birth rates, dependence on foreign economies, and limited freedom to choose among activities that satisfy human wants.

Center   In dependence theory, the economically developed world.

Periphery   In dependence theory, the developing countries.

trade union leaders) that enjoy high incomes, social status, and political power constitute a small elite ruling class whose principal interest, knowingly or not, is in the perpetuation of the international capitalist system of inequality and conformity in which they are rewarded. Directly and indirectly, they serve (are dominated by) and are rewarded by (are dependent on) international special-interest power groups, including multinational corporations, national bilateral-aid agencies, and multilateral assistance organizations like the World Bank or the International Monetary Fund (IMF), which are tied by allegiance or funding to the wealthy capitalist countries. The elites' activities and viewpoints often serve to inhibit any genuine reform efforts that might benefit the wider population and in some cases actually lead to even lower levels of living and to the perpetuation of underdevelopment. In short, the neo-Marxist, neocolonial view of underdevelopment attributes a large part of the developing world's continuing poverty to the existence and policies of the industrial capitalist countries of the northern hemisphere and their extensions in the form of small but powerful elite or **comprador groups** in the less developed countries.[10] Underdevelopment is thus seen as an *externally* induced phenomenon, in contrast to the linear-stages and structural-change theories' stress on *internal* constraints, such as insufficient savings and investment or lack of education and skills. Revolutionary struggles or at least major restructuring of the world capitalist system is therefore required to free dependent developing nations from the direct and indirect economic control of their developed-world and domestic oppressors.

> **Comprador group** In dependence theory, local elites who act as fronts for foreign investors.

One of the most forceful statements of the international-dependence school of thought was made by Theotonio Dos Santos:

> Underdevelopment, far from constituting a state of backwardness prior to capitalism, is rather a consequence and a particular form of capitalist development known as dependent capitalism....Dependence is a conditioning situation in which the economies of one group of countries are conditioned by the development and expansion of others. A relationship of interdependence between two or more economies or between such economies and the world trading system becomes a dependent relationship when some countries can expand through self-impulsion while others, being in a dependent position, can only expand as a reflection of the expansion of the dominant countries, which may have positive or negative effects on their immediate development. In either case, the basic situation of dependence causes these countries to be both backward and exploited. Dominant countries are endowed with technological, commercial, capital and sociopolitical predominance over dependent countries—the form of this predominance varying according to the particular historical moment—and can therefore exploit them, and extract part of the locally produced surplus. Dependence, then, is based upon an international division of labor which allows industrial development to take place in some countries while restricting it in others, whose growth is conditioned by and subjected to the power centers of the world.[11]

A similar but obviously non-Marxist perspective was expounded by Pope John Paul II in his widely quoted 1988 encyclical letter (a formal, elaborate expression of papal teaching) *Sollicitudo rei socialis* (The Social Concerns of the Church), in which he declared:

> One must denounce the existence of economic, financial, and social mechanisms which, although they are manipulated by people, often function almost automatically, thus accentuating the situation of wealth for some and poverty for the rest. These mechanisms, which are maneuvered directly or indirectly by the more

developed countries, by their very functioning, favor the interests of the people manipulating them. But in the end they suffocate or condition the economies of the less developed countries.

The False-Paradigm Model

A second and less radical international-dependence approach to development, which we might call the **false-paradigm model**, attributes underdevelopment to faulty and inappropriate advice provided by well-meaning but often uninformed, biased, and ethnocentric international "expert" advisers from developed-country assistance agencies and multinational donor organizations. These experts are said to offer complex but ultimately misleading models of development that often lead to inappropriate or incorrect policies. Because of institutional factors such as the central and remarkably resilient role of traditional social structures (tribe, caste, class, etc.), the highly unequal ownership of land and other property rights, the disproportionate control by local elites over domestic and international financial assets, and the very unequal access to credit, these policies, based as they often are on mainstream, neoclassical (or perhaps Lewis-type surplus-labor or Chenery-type structural-change) models, in many cases merely serve the vested interests of existing power groups, both domestic and international.

In addition, according to this argument, leading university intellectuals, trade unionists, high-level government economists, and other civil servants all get their training in developed-country institutions where they are unwittingly served an unhealthy dose of alien concepts and elegant but inapplicable theoretical models. Having little or no really useful knowledge to enable them to come to grips in an effective way with real development problems, they often tend to become unknowing or reluctant apologists for the existing system of elitist policies and institutional structures. In university economics courses, for example, this typically entails the perpetuation of the teaching of many "irrelevant" Western concepts and models, while in government policy discussions, too much emphasis is placed on attempts to measure capital-output ratios, increase savings and investment ratios, privatize and deregulate the economy, or maximize GDP growth rates. As a result, proponents argue that desirable institutional and structural reforms, many of which we have discussed, are neglected or given only cursory attention.

The Dualistic-Development Thesis

Implicit in structural-change theories and explicit in international-dependence theories is the notion of a world of dual societies, of rich nations and poor nations and, in the developing countries, pockets of wealth within broad areas of poverty. **Dualism** is the existence and persistence of substantial and even increasing divergences between rich and poor nations and rich and poor peoples on various levels. Specifically, although research continues, the traditional concept of dualism embraces four key arguments:[12]

1. Different sets of conditions, of which some are "superior" and others "inferior," can coexist in a given space. Examples of this element of dualism

False-paradigm model The proposition that developing countries have failed to develop because their development strategies (usually given to them by Western economists) have been based on an incorrect model of development, one that, for example, overstresses capital accumulation or market liberalization without giving due consideration to needed social and institutional change.

Dualism The coexistence of two situations or phenomena (one desirable and the other not) that are mutually exclusive to different groups of society—for example, extreme poverty and affluence, modern and traditional economic sectors, growth and stagnation, and higher education among a few amid large-scale illiteracy.

include Lewis's notion of the coexistence of modern and traditional methods of production in urban and rural sectors; the coexistence of wealthy, highly educated elites with masses of illiterate poor people; and the dependence notion of the coexistence of powerful and wealthy industrialized nations with weak, impoverished peasant societies in the international economy.

2. This coexistence is chronic and not merely transitional. It is not due to a temporary phenomenon, in which case, time could eliminate the discrepancy between superior and inferior elements. In other words, the international coexistence of wealth and poverty is not simply a historical phenomenon that will be rectified in time. Although both the stages-of-growth theory and the structural-change models implicitly make such an assumption, to proponents of the dualistic development thesis, growing international inequalities seem to refute it.

3. Not only do the degrees of superiority or inferiority fail to show any signs of diminishing, but they even have an inherent tendency to increase. For example, the productivity gap between workers in developed countries and their counterparts in most developing countries seems to widen.

4. The interrelations between the superior and inferior elements are such that the existence of the superior elements does little or nothing to pull up the inferior element, let alone "trickle down" to it. In fact, it may actually serve to push it down—to "develop its underdevelopment."

Conclusions and Implications

Whatever their ideological differences, the advocates of the neocolonial-dependence, false-paradigm, and dualism models reject the exclusive emphasis on traditional neoclassical economic theories designed to accelerate the growth of GDP as the principal index of development. They question the validity of Lewis-type two-sector models of modernization and industrialization in light of their questionable assumptions and developing-world history. They further reject the claims made by Chenery and others that there are well-defined empirical patterns of development that should be pursued by most poor countries. Instead, dependence, false-paradigm, and dualism theorists place more emphasis on international power imbalances and on needed fundamental economic, political, and institutional reforms, both domestic and worldwide. In extreme cases, they call for the outright expropriation of privately owned assets in the expectation that public asset ownership and control will be a more effective means to help eradicate absolute poverty, provide expanded employment opportunities, lessen income inequalities, and raise the levels of living (including health, education, and cultural enrichment) of the masses. Although a few radical neo-Marxists would even go so far as to say that economic growth and structural change do not matter, the majority of thoughtful observers recognize that the most effective way to deal with these diverse social problems is to accelerate the pace of economic growth through domestic and international reforms, accompanied by a judicious mixture of both public and private economic activity.

Dependence theories have two major weaknesses. First, although they offer an appealing explanation of why many poor countries remain underdeveloped, they give no insight into how countries initiate and sustain development. Second and perhaps more important, the actual economic experience of developing countries that have pursued revolutionary campaigns of industrial nationalization and state-run production has been mostly negative.

If we are to take dependence theory at face value, we would conclude that the best course for developing countries is to become entangled as little as possible with the developed countries and instead pursue a policy of **autarky**, or inwardly directed development, or at most trade only with other developing countries. But large countries that embarked on autarkic policies, such as China and, to a significant extent, India, experienced stagnant growth and ultimately decided to open their economies, China beginning this process after 1978 and India, after 1990. At the opposite extreme, economies such as Taiwan and South Korea, and China more recently, which have most emphasized exports to developed countries, have grown strongly. Although in many cases close ties to metropolitan countries during the colonial period apparently produced damaging outcomes—as in Peru under Spain, the Congo under Belgium, India under Great Britain, and West Africa under France—in a majority of cases, this relationship appeared to have significantly altered during the postcolonial period. Clearly, however, conflicts of interest between the developed and developing worlds, such as took center stage at the Copenhagen climate summit in December 2009 and have played a role in recent WTO and G20 meetings, are genuine and cannot be ignored.

We next consider the view that the keys to development are found in free markets. For perspective, as will be noted in later chapters, governments can succeed or fail just as markets can; the key to successful development performance is achieving a careful balance among what government can successfully accomplish, what the private market system can do, and what both can best do working together.

While the international-dependence revolution in development theory was capturing the imagination of many Western and developing country scholars, a reaction was emerging in the late 1970s and early 1980s in the form of a neoclassical free-market counterrevolution. This very different approach would ultimately dominate Western (and to a lesser extent developing country) theories of economic development during the 1980s and early 1990s.

> **Autarky** A closed economy that attempts to be completely self-reliant.

3.5 The Neoclassical Counterrevolution: Market Fundamentalism

Challenging the Statist Model: Free Markets, Public Choice, and Market-Friendly Approaches

In the 1980s, the political ascendancy of conservative governments in the United States, Canada, Britain, and West Germany came with a **neoclassical counterrevolution** in economic theory and policy. In developed nations, this counterrevolution favored supply-side macroeconomic policies, rational expectations theories, and the privatization of public corporations. In developing

> **Neoclassical counterrevolution** The 1980s resurgence of neoclassical free-market orientation toward development problems and policies, counter to the interventionist dependence revolution of the 1970s.

countries, it called for freer markets and the dismantling of public ownership, statist planning, and government regulation of economic activities. Neoclassicists obtained controlling votes on the boards of the world's two most powerful international financial agencies—the World Bank and the International Monetary Fund. In conjunction and with the simultaneous erosion of influence of organizations such as the International Labor Organization (ILO), the United Nations Development Programme (UNDP), and the United Nations Conference on Trade and Development (UNCTAD), which more fully represent the views of delegates from developing countries, it was inevitable that the neoconservative, free-market challenge to the interventionist arguments of dependence theorists would gather momentum.

Free markets The system whereby prices of commodities or services freely rise or fall when the buyer's demand for them rises or falls or the seller's supply of them decreases or increases.

The central argument of the neoclassical counterrevolution is that underdevelopment results from poor resource allocation due to incorrect pricing policies and too much state intervention by overly active developing-nation governments. Rather, the leading writers of the counterrevolution school, including Lord Peter Bauer, Deepak Lal, Ian Little, Harry Johnson, Bela Balassa, Jagdish Bhagwati, and Anne Krueger, argued that it is this very state intervention in economic activity that slows the pace of economic growth. The neoliberals argue that by permitting competitive **free markets** to flourish, privatizing state-owned enterprises, promoting free trade and export expansion, welcoming investors from developed countries, and eliminating the plethora of government regulations and price distortions in factor, product, and financial markets, both economic efficiency and economic growth will be stimulated. Contrary to the claims of the dependence theorists, the neoclassical counterrevolutionaries argue that the developing world is underdeveloped, not because of the predatory activities of the developed world and the international agencies that it controls, but rather because of the heavy hand of the state and the corruption, inefficiency, and lack of economic incentives that permeate the economies of developing nations. What is needed, therefore, is not a reform of the international economic system, a restructuring of dualistic developing economies, an increase in foreign aid, attempts to control population growth, or a more effective development planning system. Rather, it is simply a matter of promoting free markets and laissez-faire economics within the context of permissive governments that allow the "magic of the marketplace" and the "invisible hand" of market prices to guide resource allocation and stimulate economic development. They point both to the success of economies like South Korea, Taiwan, and Singapore as "free-market" examples (although, as we shall see later, these Asian Tigers are far from the laissez-faire neoconservative prototype) and to the failures of the public-interventionist economies of Africa and Latin America.[13]

Free-market analysis Theoretical analysis of the properties of an economic system operating with free markets, often under the assumption that an unregulated market performs better than one with government regulation.

The neoclassical counterrevolution can be divided into three component approaches: the free-market approach, the public-choice (or "new political economy") approach, and the "market-friendly" approach. **Free-market analysis** argues that markets alone are efficient—product markets provide the best signals for investments in new activities; labor markets respond to these new industries in appropriate ways; producers know best what to produce and how to produce it efficiently; and product and factor prices reflect accurate scarcity values of goods and resources now and in the future. Competition is effective, if not perfect; technology is freely available and nearly costless to absorb; information is also perfect and nearly costless to obtain. Under these circumstances, any government intervention in the economy is by definition distortionary and counterproductive. Free-market development economists have tended to assume that developing-world markets are efficient and that whatever imperfections exist are of little consequence.

Public-choice theory, also known as the **new political economy approach**, goes even further to argue that governments can do (virtually) nothing right. This is because public-choice theory assumes that politicians, bureaucrats, citizens, and states act solely from a self-interested perspective, using their power and the authority of government for their own selfish ends. Citizens use political influence to obtain special benefits (called "rents") from government policies (e.g., import licenses or rationed foreign exchange) that restrict access to important resources. Politicians use government resources to consolidate and maintain positions of power and authority. Bureaucrats and public officials use their positions to extract bribes from rent-seeking citizens and to operate protected businesses on the side. Finally, states use their power to confiscate private property from individuals. The net result is not only a misallocation of resources but also a general reduction in individual freedoms. The conclusion, therefore, is that minimal government is the best government.[14]

The **market-friendly approach** is a variant on the neoclassical counterrevolution associated principally with the 1990s writings of the World Bank and its economists, many of whom were more in the free-market and public-choice camps during the 1980s.[15] This approach recognizes that there are many imperfections in developing-country product and factor markets and that governments do have a key role to play in facilitating the operation of markets through "nonselective" (market-friendly) interventions—for example, by investing in physical and social infrastructure, health care facilities, and educational institutions, and by providing a suitable climate for private enterprise. The market-friendly approach also differs from the free-market and public-choice schools of thought by accepting the notion that **market failures** (see Chapters 4 and 11) are more widespread in developing countries in areas such as investment coordination and environmental outcomes. Moreover, phenomena such as missing and incomplete information, externalities in skill creation and learning, and economies of scale in production are also endemic to markets in developing countries. In fact, the recognition of these last three phenomena gives rise to newer schools of development theory, the endogenous growth approach, to which we turn in Appendix 3.3 at the end of this chapter, and the coordination failure approach, discussed in Chapter 4.

Traditional Neoclassical Growth Theory

Another cornerstone of the neoclassical free-market argument is the assertion that liberalization (opening up) of national markets draws additional domestic and foreign investment and thus increases the rate of capital accumulation. In terms of GDP growth, this is equivalent to raising domestic savings rates, which enhances **capital-labor ratios** and per capita incomes in capital-poor developing countries.

Public-choice theory (new political economy approach) The theory that self-interest guides all individual behavior and that governments are inefficient and corrupt because people use government to pursue their own agendas.

Market-friendly approach The notion historically promulgated by the World Bank that successful development policy requires governments to create an environment in which markets can operate efficiently and to intervene only selectively in the economy in areas where the market is inefficient.

Market failure A market's inability to deliver its theoretical benefits due to the existence of market imperfections such as monopoly power, lack of factor mobility, significant externalities, or lack of knowledge. Market failure often provides the justification for government intervention to alter the working of the free market.

Capital-labor ratio The number of units of capital per unit of labor.

Solow neoclassical growth model   Growth model in which there are diminishing returns to each factor of production but constant returns to scale. Exogenous technological change generates long-term economic growth.

The **Solow neoclassical growth model** in particular represented the seminal contribution to the neoclassical theory of growth and later earned Robert Solow the Nobel Prize in economics.[16] It differed from the Harrod-Domar formulation by adding a second factor, labor, and introducing a third independent variable, technology, to the growth equation. Unlike the fixed-coefficient, constant-returns-to-scale assumption of the Harrod-Domar model, Solow's neoclassical growth model exhibited diminishing returns to labor and capital separately and constant returns to both factors jointly. Technological progress became the residual factor explaining long-term growth, and its level was assumed by Solow and other neoclassical growth theorists to be determined exogenously, that is, independently of all other factors in the model.

More formally, the standard exposition of the Solow neoclassical growth model uses an aggregate production function in which

$$Y = K^\alpha (AL)^{1-\alpha} \tag{3.10}$$

where Y is gross domestic product, K is the stock of capital (which may include human capital as well as physical capital), L is labor, and A represents the productivity of labor, which grows at an exogenous rate. For developed countries, this rate has been estimated at about 2% per year. It may be smaller or larger for developing countries, depending on whether they are stagnating or catching up with the developed countries. Because the rate of technological progress is given exogenously (at 2% per year, say), the Solow neoclassical model is sometimes called an "exogenous" growth model, to be contrasted with the endogenous growth approach (discussed in Appendix 3.3). In Equation 3.10, α represents the elasticity of output with respect to capital (the percentage increase in GDP resulting from a 1% increase in human and physical capital). Since α is assumed to be less than 1 and private capital is assumed to be paid its marginal product so that there are no external economies, this formulation of neoclassical growth theory yields diminishing returns both to capital and to labor.

The Solow neoclassical growth model implies that economies will converge to the same level of income per worker "conditionally"—that is, other things equal, particularly savings rates, depreciation, labor force growth, and productivity. The Solow neoclassical growth model is examined in detail in Appendix 3.2.

According to traditional neoclassical growth theory, output growth results from one or more of three factors: increases in labor quantity and quality (through population growth and education), increases in capital (through saving and investment), and improvements in technology (see Appendix 3.1). **Closed economies** (those with no external activities) with lower savings rates (other things being equal) grow more slowly in the short run than those with high savings rates and tend to converge to lower per capita income levels. **Open economies** (those with trade, foreign investment, etc.), however, experience income convergence at higher levels as capital flows from rich countries to poor countries where capital-labor ratios are lower and thus returns on investments are higher. Consequently, by impeding the inflow of foreign investment, the heavy-handedness of many developing countries' governments, according to neoclassical growth theory, will retard growth

Closed economy   An economy in which there are no foreign trade transactions or other economic contacts with the rest of the world.

Open economy   An economy that practices foreign trade and has extensive financial and nonfinancial contacts with the rest of the world.

in the economies of the developing world. In addition, openness is said to encourage greater access to foreign production ideas that can raise the rate of technological progress.

Conclusions and Implications

Whereas dependence theorists (many, but not all, of whom were economists from developing countries) saw underdevelopment as an externally induced phenomenon, neoclassical revisionists (most, but not all, of whom were Western economists) saw the problem as an internally induced phenomenon of developing countries, caused by too much government intervention and bad economic policies. Such finger-pointing on both sides is not uncommon in issues so contentious as those that divide rich and poor nations.

But what of the neoclassical counterrevolution's contention that free markets and less government provide the basic ingredients for development? On strictly efficiency (as opposed to equity) criteria, there can be little doubt that market price allocation usually does a better job than state intervention. The problem is that many developing economies are so different in structure and organization from their Western counterparts that the behavioral assumptions and policy precepts of traditional neoclassical theory are sometimes questionable and often incorrect. Competitive free markets generally do not exist, nor, given the institutional, cultural, and historical context of many developing countries, would they necessarily be desirable from a long-term economic and social perspective (see Chapter 11). Consumers as a whole are rarely sovereign about what goods and services are to be produced, in what quantities, and for whom. Information is limited, markets are fragmented, and much of the economy in low-income countries is still nonmonetized.[17] There are widespread externalities of both production and consumption as well as discontinuities in production and indivisibilities (i.e., economies of scale) in technology. Producers, private or public, have great power in determining market prices and quantities sold. The ideal of competition is typically just that—an ideal with little substance in reality. Although monopolies of resource purchase and product sale are pervasive in the developing world, the traditional neoclassical theory of monopoly also offers little insight into the day-to-day activities of public and private corporations. Decision rules can vary widely with the social setting so that profit maximization may be a low-priority objective, especially in state-owned enterprises, in comparison with, say, the creation of jobs or the replacement of foreign managers with local personnel. Finally, the invisible hand often acts not to promote the general welfare but rather to lift up those who are already well-off while failing to offer opportunities for upward mobility for the vast majority.

Much can be learned from neoclassical theory with regard to the importance of elementary supply-and-demand analysis in arriving at "correct" product, factor, and foreign-exchange prices for efficient production and resource allocation. However, enlightened governments can also make effective use of prices as signals and incentives for influencing socially optimal resource allocations. Indeed, we will often demonstrate the usefulness of various tools of neoclassical theory in our later analysis of problems such as population growth, agricultural stagnation, unemployment and underemployment, child labor, educational demands, the environment, export promotion versus import substitution, devaluation, project planning, monetary policy, microfinance, and economic privatization. Nevertheless, the reality of the institutional and political structure of many developing-world economies—not to mention their differing value systems and ideologies—often makes the attainment of appropriate economic policies based either on markets or on enlightened public intervention an exceedingly difficult endeavor. In an environment of widespread institutional rigidity and severe socioeconomic inequality, *both* markets and governments will typically fail. It is not simply an either-or question based on ideological leaning; rather, it is a matter of assessing each individual country's situation on a case-by-case basis. Developing nations need to adopt local solutions in response to local constraints.[18] Development economists must therefore be able to distinguish between textbook neoclassical theory and the institutional and political reality of contemporary developing countries.[19] They can then choose the traditional neoclassical concepts and models that can best illuminate issues and dilemmas of development and discard those that cannot. Approaches to making these distinctions and choices in key policy applications will feature centrally in Parts Two and Three.

3.6 Classic Theories of Development: Reconciling the Differences

In this chapter, we have reviewed a range of competing theories and approaches to the study of economic development. Each approach has its strengths and weaknesses. The fact that there exists such controversy—be it ideological, theoretical, or empirical—is what makes the study of economic development both challenging and exciting. Even more than other fields of economics, development economics has no universally accepted doctrine or paradigm. Instead, we have a continually evolving pattern of insights and understandings, reflecting in part improved data and emergence of new technologies and new institutions, that together provide the basis for examining the possibilities of contemporary development of the diverse nations of Africa, Asia, and Latin America.

You may wonder how consensus could emerge from so much disagreement. Although it is not implied here that such a consensus exists today or will ever emerge when such sharply conflicting values and ideologies prevail, we do suggest that something of significance can be gleaned from each of the four approaches that we have described. For example, the linear-stages model emphasizes the crucial role that saving and investment play in promoting sustainable long-run growth. The Lewis two-sector model of structural change underlines the importance of transfers of resources from low-productivity to high-productivity activities in the process of economic development, attempting to analyze the many linkages between traditional agriculture and modern industry, and clarifying recent growth experiences such as that of China. The empirical research of Chenery and his associates seeks to document precisely how economies undergo structural change while identifying the numerical values of key economic parameters involved in that process. The thoughts of international-dependence theorists alert us to the importance of the structure and workings of the world economy and the many ways in which decisions made in the developed world can affect the lives of millions of people in the developing world. Whether or not these activities are deliberately designed to maintain developing nations in a state of dependence is often beside the point. The very fact of their dependence and their vulnerability to key economic decisions made in the capitals of North America, western Europe, or Japan (not to mention those made by the IMF and the World Bank) forces us to recognize the importance of some of the insights of the international-dependence school. The same applies to arguments regarding the dualistic structures and the role of ruling elites in the domestic economies of the developing world.

Although a good deal of conventional neoclassical economic theory needs to be modified to fit the unique social, institutional, and structural circumstances of developing nations, there is no doubt that promoting efficient production and distribution through a proper, functioning price system is an integral part of any successful development process. Many of the arguments of the neoclassical counterrevolutionaries, especially those related to the inefficiency of state-owned enterprises and the failures of development planning (see Chapter 11), and the harmful effects of government-induced domestic and international price distortions (see Chapters 7, 12, and 15), are as well taken as those of the dependence and structuralist schools. By contrast, the unquestioning exaltation of free markets and open economies along with the universal disparagement of public-sector leadership in promoting growth with equity in the developing world is open to serious challenge. As the chapters in Parts Two and Three reveal, successful development requires a skillful and judicious balancing of market pricing and promotion where markets can exist and operate efficiently, along with intelligent and equity-oriented government intervention in areas where unfettered market forces would lead to undesirable economic and social outcomes. Great strides have been made in modern development economic analysis in clarifying the logic of how well-formulated government policy can facilitate the development of markets and shared growth, as will be explained in Chapter 4.

In summary, each of the approaches to understanding development has something to offer. Their respective contributions will become clear later in the book when we explore in detail both the origins of and possible solutions to a wide range of problems such as poverty, population growth, unemployment, rural development, international trade, and the environment. They also inform contemporary models of development and underdevelopment, to which we turn in the next chapter.

Schools of Thought in Context: South Korea and Argentina

A closer examination of two countries confirms the conclusion that each of the first four broad approaches to development—stages of growth, structural patterns of development, dependence, and neoclassical—provides important insights about development processes and policy. South Korea and Argentina are reasonably well matched for such a comparison; for example, both are midsize in population (41 million in Argentina and 50 million in South Korea in 2011), and both were long classified as middle-income countries. But South Korea, now designated by the World Bank as a high-income country with about $31,000 PPP in 2008, has nearly double the per capita income of Argentina, with about $17,000 PPP in 2011, whereas 30 years earlier the reverse was true. Can the four classic approaches to development explain this reversal?

South Korea

Stages of Growth South Korea confirms some linear-stages views, albeit in a limited way. Its share of investment in national income has been among the highest in the world, and this is a crucial part of the explanation of the nation's rapid ascent. To understand just how rapid this ascent has been, consider that the country did not even rate a mention in Rostow's *Stages of Economic Growth* in 1960, when the book was published, and few of the "preconditions for takeoff" were in place. Investment has been very high since then, but as a share of GNI, the investment ratio, at 15%, was still below takeoff levels in 1965. Yet it rose dramatically to 37% of GNI by 1990 and remained close to 40% in the 2000–2007 period (though the ratio has fallen in the last few years). Still, South Korea's ascent has seemed to epitomize Rostow's notion of an economy in the midst of a "drive to

maturity," well on its way toward mastering the range of currently available technologies; and appears to be entering an "age of high mass consumption."

Rostow claimed that maturity is attained some 60 years after takeoff begins, but he never denied unique experiences for each country, and it may well be that the gap between traditional and advanced technology can actually be crossed more quickly at later stages of development. The larger the productivity gap is between countries, the quicker income can grow once takeoff has been achieved. South Korea certainly meets the "maturity" criterion of becoming integrated with the world economy through new types of exports and imports. Although the fact that India, rather than South Korea, was picked by Rostow for takeoff shows the limits of the predictive powers of the stages theory, the case of South Korea nonetheless offers some confirmation of their value.

Structural Patterns South Korea also confirms some patterns-of-development structural-change models. In particular, South Korea's rise over the past generation has been characterized by rapidly increasing agricultural productivity, shifts of labor from agriculture to industry, the steady growth of the capital stock and of education and skills, and the demographic transition from high to low fertility. These changes have occurred while South Korea's per capita income has grown by more than 7% annually for the whole 1965–1990 period. Even in the 1990–2002 period, as a more mature economy and in the face of the Asian financial crisis of 1997–1998, the economy grew at a 5.8% rate. In 2002–2011, it grew at less than 4% on average, still substantially higher than most other high-income countries. In the late 1940s and 1950s, South Korea carried out a thoroughgoing land reform, so agriculture was not neglected;

but otherwise its growth through rapid expansion of the percentage of the labor force in industry has broadly conformed with the Lewis model of development. After about 1970, productivity growth in agriculture also increased rapidly, owing in part to a successful integrated rural development program.

Dependence Revolution But South Korea poses a serious challenge to the dependence revolution models. Here is a poor country that became tied in with the international economy: It was strongly dependent in international relations—it was a Japanese colony until 1945 and thereafter wholly dependent on maintaining the goodwill of the United States for defense against invasion by North Korea. It received a large part of its national budget in the form of U.S. aid in the 1950s and both exported and imported a great deal from developed countries, especially the United States and Japan. The shape of the nation's development was thus "conditioned" in large part by export opportunities to developed countries, and dependence theory would predict that retarded development opportunities should result. Yet South Korea today is an OECD member and is widely considered a "graduate" to developed-country status. Of course, dependence theorists could and do claim that South Korea is an exception because of the magnitude of aid it received and the self-interests of the advanced countries in seeing its full successful development because of its role as a bulwark against communism. And the Korean government pursued some particular policies that the dependence school would by and large applaud, including carrying out an extremely active industrial upgrading policy, sharply limiting the role of multinational corporations and deliberately establishing indigenous industries as an alternative, and using debt rather than direct foreign equity investment to finance extraordinary levels of investment. South Korea also implemented one of the most ambitious land reform programs in the developing world and placed strong emphasis on primary rather than university education, two policies of exceptional importance. But this does not explain how South Korea was able to adopt such policies to break out of dependence in the first place.

Neoclassical Counterrevolution South Korea likewise poses a strong challenge to the neoclassical counterrevolution models. The nation was highly interventionist at home and in international trade, with the government making extensive use of development planning, using a wide range of tax breaks and incentives to induce firms to follow government directives and interventions, setting individual company export targets, orchestrating efforts in various industries to upgrade the average technological level, coordinating foreign technology licensing agreements, using monopoly power to get the best deal from competing multinationals, and generally inducing firms to move rapidly up the ladder of (dynamic) comparative advantage (see Chapter 12). These policies addressed real technology and skill-raising market failure problems of development, and at least prior to the 1997 Asian currency crisis, from which Korea quickly recovered, very few cases of glaring government failure can be pointed to in this experience. Of course, it does confirm that firms respond to economic incentives. But it may also be claimed with at least equal force that South Korea provides a compelling example of government's role in overcoming coordination failures, as examined in Chapter 4 and applied to South Korea in the end-of-chapter case study for Chapter 12.

Argentina

In contrast, for Argentina, stages and patterns theories illuminate relatively little economic history, whereas the dependence revolution and neoclassical counterrevolution theories together offer important insights. It remains unclear whether Argentina has now relaunched onto a new growth episode following its 2002 default, as growth has been erratic, foreign exchange reserves falling, and political uncertainty returning.

Stages of Growth The history of Argentina poses a strong challenge to the linear-stages approach. Rostow defined *takeoff* as "the interval when the old blocks and resistances to steady growth are finally overcome....Growth becomes its normal condition." In 1870, Argentina ranked 11th in the world in per capita income (ahead of Germany); today, it is not even in the top 60. Although Rostow said that in determining a country's stage, technology absorption, not income per inhabitant, is what matters, he dated Argentina's preconditions for takeoff as an extended period before 1914 and concluded that takeoff "in some sense" began in World War I, but "in the mid 1930s...a sustained takeoff was inaugurated, which by and large can now [1960] be

judged to have been successful," concluding that "in Latin America the takeoff has been completed in two major cases (Mexico and Argentina)." Rostow attributes the fact that preconditions were there for some time before takeoff to excessive import of foreign capital over too long a period without increasing domestic savings. (But South Korea was also a heavy foreign borrower until recently.) Argentina certainly met Rostow's criterion of developing manufacturing sectors at a rapid rate.

But now let's look at what happened in Argentina since Rostow put the country forward as an example. According to World Bank data, Argentina had a *negative* growth rate throughout the 1965–1990 period, and in the 1980s, domestic investment shrank at a −8.3% rate, falling back well below Rostow's threshold takeoff investment levels. Although Argentina grew at 3.6% in 1990–2001, it defaulted on its debt in 2002, and the economy shrank 11%, followed by a recovery and resumed if erratic growth. Argentina's share of investment in GDP from 2000 to 2007 was 17%, well under half that of South Korea. Like many other Latin American and African countries in the 1970s, 1980s, and 1990s, Argentina demonstrated that development progress is not irreversible and that sustained growth can come to an end. It remains unclear whether Argentina has now relaunched onto a new growth episode following its 2002 default, as growth has been erratic, foreign exchange reserves falling, and political uncertainty returning.

Structural Patterns Argentina did exhibit many of the usual structural patterns of development as agricultural productivity rose, industrial employment grew (albeit slowly), urbanization took place, fertility fell, and so on. But the fact that many structural regularities of development were observed even as living standards in the country stagnated illustrates some of the shortcomings of relying too much on selected pieces of data without the assistance of guiding theory on how the parts fit together.

Dependence Revolution In contrast to South Korea, the case of Argentina offers some vindication for dependence theories in that the country relied to a large extent on exporting primary goods, and the real prices of these goods fell compared to imports. Multinational corporations played a large role, and Argentina was unable to create its own viable manufacturing *export* industries, ultimately having to submit to stringent structural-adjustment programs, sell state industries to foreign companies, and other constraints. Dependence theorists can claim with some justification that Argentina's conditioned development fell victim to developed-country economic interests, especially those of British and American corporations.

Neoclassical Counterrevolution But Argentina also offers some vindication for neoclassical counterrevolution theory in that faulty interventionist restrictions, inefficient state enterprise, bias against production for exports, and unnecessary red tape ended up hurting industry and entrepreneurship. Government policy consistently seemed to support privileged interests rather than broad goals of development, and government failure was usually worse than market failure in the country. In the mid-1990s, a large-scale liberalization and privatization program seemed to be beginning to reinvigorate growth in Argentina. Unfortunately, by 2002, four years of recession culminated in economic implosion as the economy collapsed under the weight of rising internal fiscal and external trade deficits, caused in part by the linking of the peso to a strong U.S. dollar. Dependence theorists claimed vindication. The recovery and comparatively rapid growth since 2004, despite Argentina's 2002 debt default, showed that single explanations for development success and failure are rarely adequate. Yet Argentina's economic recovery remains vulnerable—for example, growth dropped from about 9% in 2010 and 2011 to under 2% in 2012—and political institutions remain somewhat unsettled.

Summary

It is interesting that as South Korea provides a challenge to both dependence and neoclassical theory—the starkest opposites in many ways—Argentina can be viewed more as a vindication for these two theories. And whereas South Korea serves more to confirm linear stages of growth and conclusions about structural patterns of development, Argentina poses challenges to their universal importance. Yet each of these four approaches has added something vital to our understanding of development experiences and prospects in just these two countries. South Korea also illustrates the role of government in overcoming coordination failures, while Argentina illustrates how government can become part of a bad equilibrium, topics explored in depth in the next chapter. ∎

Sources

Fishlow, Albert, et al. *Miracle or Design? Lessons from the East Asian Experience*. Washington, D.C.: Overseas Development Council, 1994.

Heston, Alan, Robert Summers, and Bettina Aten. *Penn World Table*, version 6.3. Center for International Comparisons of Production, Income and Prices, University of Pennsylvania, August 2009, http://pwt.econ.upenn.edu/php_site/pwt63/pwt63_form.php.

Porter, Michael. *Competitive Advantage of Nations*. New York: Free Press, 1990.

Rodrik, Dani. "Coordination failures and government policy: A model with applications to East Asia and Eastern Europe." *Journal of International Economics* 40 (1996): 1–22.

Rostow, Walt W. *The Stages of Economic Growth: A Non-Communist Manifesto*. London: Cambridge University Press, 1960.

Smith, Stephen C. *Industrial Policy in Developing Countries: Reconsidering the Real Sources of Expert-Led Growth*. Washington, D.C.: Economic Policy Institute, 1991.

Thurow, Lester. *Head to Head*. New York: Morrow, 1992.

World Bank. *Korea: Managing the Industrial Transition*. Washington, D.C.: World Bank, 1987.

World Bank, *World Development Indicators*, various years.

World Bank, *World Development Reports*, various years.

Concepts for Review

Autarky	Harrod-Domar growth model	Production function
Average product	Lewis two-sector model	Public-choice theory
Capital-labor ratio	Marginal product	Self-sustaining growth
Capital-output ratio	Market failure	Solow neoclassical growth
Center	Market-friendly approach	model
Closed economy	Necessary condition	Stages-of-growth model
Comprador groups	Neoclassical counterrevolution	of development
Dependence	Neocolonial dependence model	Structural-change theory
Dominance	Net savings ratio	Structural transformation
Dualism	Open economy	Sufficient condition
False-paradigm model	Patterns-of-development	Surplus labor
Free market	analysis	Underdevelopment
Free-market analysis	Periphery	

Questions for Discussion

1. Explain the essential distinctions among the stages-of-growth theory of development, the structural-change models of Lewis and Chenery, and the theory of international dependence in both its neo-Marxist and false-paradigm conceptualizations. Which model do you think provides the best explanation of the situation in most developing nations? Explain your answer.

2. Explain the meaning of *dualism* and *dual societies*. Do you think that the concept of dualism adequately portrays the development picture in most developing countries? Explain your answer.

3. Some people claim that international dualism and domestic dualism are merely different manifestations of the same phenomenon. What do you think they mean by this, and is it a valid conceptualization? Explain your answer.

4. What is meant by the term *neoclassical counterrevolution*? What are its principal arguments, and how valid do you think they are? Explain your answer.

5. Given the diversity of developing countries, do you think that there could ever be a single, unified theory of development? Explain your answer.

6. Is the neoclassical, free-market theory necessarily incompatible with dependence theory? How might these two approaches work together?

7. In what ways do developing countries depend on rich countries? In what ways is the opposite true?

Notes

1. *The Stages of Economic Growth: A Non-Communist Manifesto*, 3rd Edition by W. W. Rostow. Copyright © 1960, 1971, 1990 Cambridge University Press. Reprinted with permission.

2. This model is named after two economists, Sir Roy Harrod of England and Professor Evesey Domar of the United States, who separately but concurrently developed a variant of it in the early 1950s.

3. In traditional presentations, including of this text, the symbol k has been used for this capital-*output* ratio, rather than the symbol c as used here. However, we use the symbol c to make sure it is not misidentified with the use (also traditional) of the symbol k in the Solow growth model (which stands there for the capital-*labor* ratio), discussed later in this chapter. Note also that in practice a developing economy may utilize capital inefficiently, that is, more than strictly required from an engineering standpoint.

4. To see this simply, note that $Y = K/c$, so $\Delta Y = (1/c) \Delta K$. But ΔK by definition is net investment, I^N, which is given by gross investment, I^G, less allowance for depreciation, which in turn is given by the rate of depreciation times the capital stock, δK. That is, $\Delta K = I^G - \delta K$. But gross investment is identically equal to gross savings, S^G. So $\Delta Y = (1/c)[S^G - \delta K]$. (Note that the gross savings rate, s^G, is given by S^G/Y.) Dividing both sides by Y and simplifying gives $\Delta Y / Y = s^G/c - \delta$, the result in the text.

5. W. Arthur Lewis, "Economic development with unlimited supplies of labour," *Manchester School* 22 (1954): 139–191; John C. H. Fei and Gustav Ranis, *Development of the Labor Surplus Economy: Theory and Policy* (Homewood, Ill.: Irwin, 1964). See also Ragnar Nurkse, *Problems of Capital Formation in Underdeveloped Countries* (New York: Oxford University Press, 1953).

6. For interesting applications to the recent growth experience of China, see Nazrul Islam and Kazuhiko Yokota, "Lewis growth model and China's industrialization," *Asian Economic Journal* 22 (2008): 359–396; Xiaobo Zhang, Jin Yang, and Shenglin Wang, "China has reached the Lewis turning point," IFPRI discussion paper No. 977 (Washington, D.C.: International Food Policy Research Institute, 2010). Cai

Fang, "A turning point for China and challenges for further development and reform," *Zhongguo shehui kexue (Social Sciences in China)*, 3 (2007) 4–12; and Huang Yiping and Jiang Tingsong, *What Does the Lewis Turning Point Mean for China? A Computable General Equilibrium Analysis,* China Center for Economic Research Working Paper 2010-03, March 2010. See also Gary Fields, "Dualism in the labor market: A perspective on the Lewis model after half a century," *Manchester School* 72 (2004): 724–735. Research on models of structural change continues; for an interesting contribution, see Douglas Gollin, Stephen L. Parente, and Richard Rogerson, "The food problem and the evolution of international income levels," *Journal of Monetary Economics* 54 (2007): 1230–1255.

7. See Hollis B. Chenery, *Structural Change and Development Policy* (Baltimore: Johns Hopkins University Press, 1979); Hollis B. Chenery and Moshe Syrquin, *Patterns of Development, 1950–70* (London: Oxford University Press, 1975); Moshe Syrquin, "Patterns of structural change," in *Handbook of Development Economics*, eds. Hollis B. Chenery and T. N. Srinivasan (Amsterdam: Elsevier, 1989), vol. 1, pp. 205–273; and Hollis B. Chenery, Sherman Robinson, and Moshe Syrquin, *Industrialization and Growth: A Comparative Study,* (New York: Oxford University Press, 1986). For a succinct summary of research by Simon Kuznets, see his "Modern economic growth, findings and reflections," *American Economic Review* 63 (1973): 247–258.

8. See, for example, Sarah Anderson, John Cavanagh, Thea Lee, and the Institute for Policy Studies, *Field Guide to the Global Economy* (New York: New Press, 2000); Robin Broad, ed., *Global Backlash: Citizen Initiatives for a Just World Economy* (Lanham, Md.: Rowman & Littlefield, 2002); and John Gray, *False Dawn: The Delusions of Global Capitalism* (New York: New Press, 2000).

9. See Paul Baran, *The Political Economy of Neo-Colonialism* (London: Heinemann, 1975). An outstanding literature review is contained in Keith Griffin and John Gurley, "Radical analysis of imperialism, the Third World, and the transition to socialism: A survey article," *Journal of Economic*

Literature 23 (1985): 1089–1143. See also Ted C. Lewellen, *Dependency and Development: An Introduction to the Third World* (Westport, Conn.: Bergin & Garvey, 1995).

10. A provocative and well-documented application of this argument to the case of Kenya can be found in Colin Leys, *Underdevelopment in Kenya: The Political Economy of Neo-Colonialism* (London: Heinemann, 1975).

11. Theotonio Dos Santos, "The crisis of development theory and the problem of dependence in Latin America," in *Underdevelopment and Development,* ed. Henry Bernstein (Harmondsworth, England: Penguin, 1973), pp. 57–80. See also Benjamin J. Cohen, *The Question of Imperialism: The Political Economy of Dominance and Dependence* (New York: Basic Books, 1973).

12. Hans W. Singer, "Dualism revisited: A new approach to the problems of dual societies in developing countries," *Journal of Development Studies* 7 (1970): 60–61. Domestic dualism models continue to be developed. For example, see Arup Banerji and Sanjay Jain, "Quality dualism," *Journal of Development Economics* 84 (2007): 234–250. For an interesting empirical study, see Niels-Hugo Blunch and Dorte Verner, "Shared sectoral growth versus the dual economy model: Evidence from Côte d'Ivoire, Ghana, and Zimbabwe," *African Development Review* 18, No. 3 (2006): 283–308; Jonathan Temple and Ludger Woessmann, "Dualism and cross-country growth regressions," *Journal of Economic Growth*, 11, No. 3 (2006): 187–228.

13. For examples of the literature of neoclassical counterrevolutionaries, see Peter T. Bauer, *Reality and Rhetoric: Studies in the Economics of Development* (London: Weidenfield & Nicolson, 1984); Deepak Lal, *The Poverty of Development Economics* (Cambridge, Mass.: Harvard University Press, 1985); Ian Little, *Economic Development: Theories, Policies, and International Relations* (New York: Basic Books 1982); and any mid-1980s issue of the World Bank's *World Development Report* and the International Monetary Fund's *Annual World Economic Outlook.* An outstanding critique of this literature can be found in John Toye, *Dilemmas of Development: Reflections on the Counter-Revolution in Development Theory and Policy* (Oxford: Blackwell, 1987). See also

Ziya Onis, "The limits of neoliberalism: Toward a reformulation of development theory," *Journal of Economic Issues* 29 (1995): 97–119; Lance Taylor, "The revival of the liberal creed: The IMF and the World Bank in a globalized economy," *World Development* 25 (1997): 145–152; and Alexandro Portes, "Neoliberalism and the sociology of development: Emerging trends and unanticipated facts," *Population and Development Review* 23 (1997): 229–259.

14. For a good explication of the tenets of the public-choice theory, see Merilee S. Grindle and John W. Thomas, *Public Choices and Public Policy Change: The Political Economy of Reform in Developing Countries* (Baltimore: Johns Hopkins University Press, 1991). The classic article in the field is by Nobel laureate James M. Buchanan, "Social choice, democracy and free markets," *Journal of Political Economy* 62 (1954): 114–123. For a critique, see Paul P. Streeten, "Markets and states: Against minimalism," *World Development* 21 (1993): 1281–1298, and Amartya Sen, "Rationality and social choice," *American Economic Review* 85 (1995): 1–24.

15. See any of the 1990s *World Development Reports*. For a critique of this approach, see Ajit Singh, "State intervention and 'market-friendly' approach to development: A critical analysis of the World Bank theses," in *The States, Markets and Development*, eds. Amitava K. Dutt, Kwan S. Kim, and Ajit Singh (London: Elgar, 1994). The World Bank has since added further nuance to its approach, for example, by encouraging use of the "growth diagnostics" approach described at the end of Chapter 4.

16. The Solow model is set forth in Robert Solow, "A contribution to the theory of economic growth," *Quarterly Journal of Economics* 70 (1956): 65–94.

17. For a discussion of these and related issues, see Heinz W. Arndt, "'Market failure' and underdevelopment," *World Development* 16 (1988): 210–229.

18. On identifying and addressing local constraints, see Ricardo Hausmann, Dani Rodrik, and Andrés Velasco, "Growth diagnostics," *One Economics, Many Recipes: Globalization, Institutions, and Economic Growth*, by Dani Rodrik (Princeton, N.J.: Princeton University Press, 2007). See Chapter 4 for more details.

19. An additional approach, reviewed in Chapter 2, is the new institutionalism. It has been alternatively

viewed as a component of the neoclassical counter-revolution or of the postneoclassical mainstream development economics. The institutions include property rights, prices and market structures, money and financial institutions, firms and industrial organization, and relationships between government and markets. The basic message of the new institutionalism is that even in a neoclassical world, the success or failure of development efforts will depend on the nature, existence, and proper functioning of a country's fundamental institutions. The origins of the new institutionalism can be found in the theory of institutions pioneered by the work of Nobel laureate Ronald Coase. See Ronald H.

Coase, "The institutional structure of production," *American Economic Review* 82 (1992): 713–719; Oliver E. Williamson, "The institutions and governance of economic development and reform," in *Proceedings of the World Bank Annual Conference on Development Economics, 1994* (Washington, D.C.: World Bank, 1995); and Jean-Jacques Laffont, "Competition, conformation and development," *Annual World Bank Conference on Development Economics, 1998* (Washington, D.C.: World Bank, 1999). Writings of Nobel laureate Douglass North have been particularly influential, notably *Institutions, Institutional Change, and Economic Performance* (New York: Cambridge University Press, 1990).

Appendix 3.1

Components of Economic Growth

Three components of economic growth are of prime importance:

1. Capital accumulation, including all new investments in land, physical equipment, and human resources through improvements in health, education, and job skills

2. Growth in population and hence eventual growth in the labor force

3. Technological progress—new ways of accomplishing tasks

In this appendix, we look briefly at each.

Capital Accumulation

Capital accumulation results when some proportion of present income is saved and invested in order to augment future output and income. New factories, machinery, equipment, and materials increase the physical **capital stock** of a nation (the total net real value of all physically productive capital goods) and make it possible for expanded output levels to be achieved. These directly productive investments are supplemented by investments in what is known as social and **economic infrastructure**—roads, electricity, water and sanitation, communications, and the like—which facilitates and integrates economic activities. For example, investment by a farmer in a new tractor may increase the total output of the crops he can produce, but without adequate transport facilities to get this extra product to local commercial markets, his investment may not add anything to national food production.

There are less direct ways to invest in a nation's resources. The installation of irrigation systems may improve the quality of a nation's agricultural land by raising productivity per hectare. If 100 hectares of irrigated land can produce the same output as 200 hectares of nonirrigated land using the same other inputs, the installation of such irrigation is the equivalent of doubling the quantity of nonirrigated land. Use of chemical fertilizers and the control of insects with pesticides may have equally beneficial effects in raising the productivity of existing farmland. All these forms of investment are ways of improving the quality of existing land resources. Their effect in raising the total stock of productive land is, for all practical purposes, indistinguishable from the simple clearing of hitherto unused arable land.

Similarly, investment in human resources can improve its quality and thereby have the same or even a more powerful effect on production as an increase in human numbers. Formal schooling, vocational and on-the-job training programs, and adult and other types of informal education may all be made more effective in augmenting human skills as a result of direct investments in buildings, equipment, and materials (e.g., books, film projectors, personal computers, science equipment, vocational tools, and machinery such as lathes and grinders). The advanced and relevant training of teachers, as

Capital accumulation Increasing a country's stock of real *capital* (net *investment* in fixed assets). To increase the production of capital *goods* necessitates a reduction in the production of consumer goods.

Capital stock   The total amount of physical goods existing at a particular time that have been produced for use in the production of other goods and services.

Economic infrastructure The amount of physical and financial capital embodied in roads, railways, waterways, airways, and other transportation and communications, plus other facilities such as water supplies, financial institutions, electricity, and public services such as health and education.

well as good textbooks in economics, may make an enormous difference in the quality, leadership, and productivity of a given labor force. Improved health can also significantly boost productivity. The concept of investment in human resources and the creation of **human capital** is therefore analogous to that of improving the quality and thus the productivity of existing land resources through strategic investments.

All of these phenomena and many others are forms of investment that lead to capital accumulation. Capital accumulation may add new resources (e.g., the clearing of unused land) or upgrade the quality of existing resources (e.g., irrigation), but its essential feature is that it involves a trade-off between present and future consumption—giving up a little now so that more can be had later, such as giving up current income to stay in school.

Population and Labor Force Growth

Population growth, and the associated eventual increase in the labor force, have traditionally been considered a positive factor in stimulating economic growth. A larger labor force means more productive workers, and a large overall population increases the potential size of domestic markets. However, it is questionable whether rapidly growing supplies of workers in developing countries with a surplus of labor exert a positive or a negative influence on economic progress (see Chapter 6 for an in-depth discussion of the pros and cons of population growth for economic development). Obviously, it will depend on the ability of the economic system to absorb and productively employ these added workers—an ability largely associated with the rate and kind of capital accumulation and the availability of related factors, such as managerial and administrative skills.

Given an initial understanding of these first two fundamental components of economic growth and disregarding for a moment the third (technology), let us see how they interact via the **production possibility curve** to expand society's potential total output of all goods. For a given technology and a given amount of physical and human resources, the production possibility curve portrays the *maximum* attainable output combinations of any two commodities—say, rice and radios—when all resources are fully and efficiently employed. Figure A3.1.1 shows two production possibility curves for rice and radios.

Initial possibilities for the production of rice and radios are shown by the curve *PP*. Now suppose that without any change in technology, the quantity of physical and human resources were to double as a result of either investments that improved the quality of the existing resources or investment in new resources—land, capital, and, in the case of larger families, labor. Figure A3.1.1 shows that this doubling of total resources will cause the entire production possibility curve to shift uniformly outward from *PP* to *P'P'*. More radios and more rice can now be produced.

Because these are assumed to be the only two goods produced by this economy, it follows that the gross domestic product (the total value of all goods and services produced) will be higher than before. In other words, the process of economic growth is under way.

Note that even if the country in question is operating with underutilized physical and human resources, as at point *X* in Figure A3.1.1, a growth

Production possibility curve A curve on a graph indicating alternative combinations of two commodities or categories of commodities (e.g., agricultural and manufactured goods) that can be produced when all the available factors of production are efficiently employed. Given available resources and technology, the curve sets the boundary between the attainable and the unobtainable.

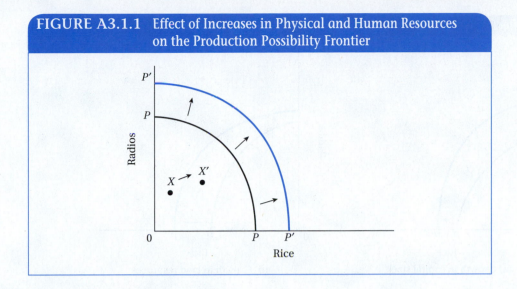

FIGURE A3.1.1   Effect of Increases in Physical and Human Resources on the Production Possibility Frontier

of productive resources can result in a higher total output combination, as at point X', even though there may still be widespread unemployment and underutilized or idle capital and land. But note also that there is nothing deterministic about resource growth leading to higher output growth. This is not an economic law, as attested by the poor growth record of many contemporary developing countries. Nor is resource growth even a necessary condition for *short-run* economic growth because the better utilization of idle existing resources can raise output levels substantially, as portrayed in the movement from X to X' in Figure A3.1.1. Nevertheless, in the *long run*, the improvement and upgrading of the quality of existing resources and new investments designed to expand the quantity of these resources are principal means of accelerating the growth of national output.

Now, instead of assuming the proportionate growth of *all* factors of production, let us assume that, say, only capital or only land is increased in quality and quantity. Figure A3.1.2 shows that if radio manufacturing is a relatively large user of capital equipment and rice production is a relatively land-intensive process, the shifts in society's production possibility curve will be more pronounced for radios when capital grows rapidly (Figure A3.1.2a) and for rice when the growth is in land quantity or quality (Figure A3.1.2b). However, because under normal conditions both products will require the use of both factors as productive inputs, albeit in different combinations, the production possibility curve still shifts slightly outward along the rice axis in Figure A3.1.2a when only capital is increased and along the radio axis in Figure A3.1.2b when only the quantity or quality of land resources is expanded.

Technological Progress

It is now time to consider the third, and to many economists the most important, source of economic growth, **technological progress**. In its simplest form, technological progress results from new and improved ways of accomplishing traditional tasks such as growing crops, making clothing, or building

Technological progress Increased application of new scientific knowledge in the form of inventions and innovations with regard to both physical and human capital.

FIGURE A3.1.2   Effect of Growth of Capital Stock and Land on the Production Possibility Frontier

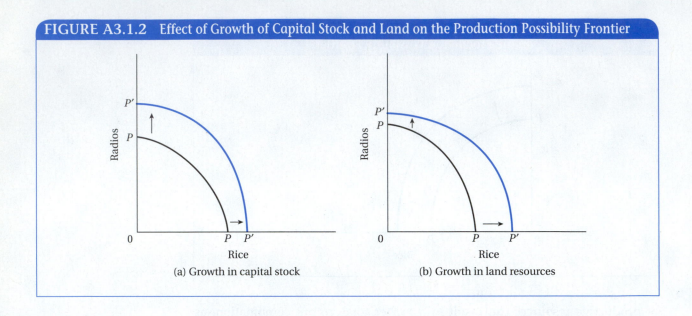

(a) Growth in capital stock

(b) Growth in land resources

a house. There are three basic classifications of technological progress: neutral, laborsaving, and capital-saving.

Neutral technological progress occurs when higher output levels are achieved with the same quantity and combinations of factor inputs. Simple innovations like those that arise from the division of labor can result in higher total output levels and greater consumption for all individuals. In terms of production possibility analysis, a neutral technological change that, say, doubles total output is conceptually equivalent to a doubling of all productive inputs. The outward-shifting production possibility curve of Figure A3.1.1 could therefore also be a diagrammatic representation of neutral technological progress.

By contrast, technological progress may result in savings of either labor or capital (i.e., higher levels of output can be achieved with the same quantity of labor or capital inputs). Computers, the Internet, automated looms, high-speed electric drills, tractors, mechanical ploughs—these and many other kinds of modern machinery and equipment can be classified as products of **laborsaving technological progress**. Technological progress since the late nineteenth century has consisted largely of rapid advances in laborsaving technologies for producing everything from beans to bicycles to bridges.

Capital-saving technological progress is a much rarer phenomenon. But this is primarily because most of the world's scientific and technological research is conducted in developed countries, where the mandate is to save labor, not capital. In the labor-abundant (capital-scarce) developing countries, however, capital-saving technological progress is what is needed most. Such progress results in more efficient (lower-cost) labor-intensive methods of production—for example, hand- or rotary-powered weeders and threshers, foot-operated bellows pumps, and back-mounted mechanical sprayers for small-scale agriculture. The indigenous development of low-cost, efficient, labor-intensive (capital-saving) techniques of production is one of the essential

Neutral technological progress Higher output levels achieved with the same quantity or combination of all factor inputs.

Laborsaving technological progress The achievement of higher output using an unchanged quantity of labor inputs as a result of some invention (e.g., the computer) or innovation (such as assembly-line production).

Capital-saving technological progress Technological progress that results from some invention or innovation that facilitates the achievement of higher output levels using the same quantity of inputs of capital.

ingredients in any long-run employment-oriented development strategy (see Appendix 5.1).

Technological progress may also be labor- or capital-augmenting. **Labor-augmenting technological progress** occurs when the quality or skills of the labor force are upgraded—for example, by the use of videotapes, televisions, and other electronic communications media for classroom instruction. Similarly, **capital-augmenting technological progress** results in the more productive use of existing capital goods—for example, the substitution of steel for wooden plows in agricultural production.

We can use our production possibility curve for rice and radios to examine two very specific examples of technological progress as it relates to output growth in developing countries. In the 1960s, agricultural scientists at the International Rice Research Institute in the Philippines developed a new and highly productive hybrid rice seed, known as IR-8, or "miracle rice." These new seeds, along with later further scientific improvements, enabled some rice farmers in parts of South and Southeast Asia to double or triple their yields in a matter of a few years. In effect, this technological progress was "embodied" in the new rice seeds (one could also say it was "land-augmenting"), which permitted higher output levels to be achieved with essentially the same complementary inputs (although more fertilizer and pesticides were recommended). In terms of our production possibility analysis, the higher-yielding varieties of hybrid rice could be depicted, as in Figure A3.1.3, by an outward shift of the curve along the rice axis with the intercept on the radio axis remaining essentially unchanged (i.e., the new rice seeds could not be directly used to increase radio production).

In terms of the technology of radio production, the invention of transistors has probably had as significant an impact on communications as the development of the steam engine had on transportation. Even in the remotest parts of Africa, Asia, and Latin America, the transistor radio has become a prized possession. The introduction of the transistor, by obviating the need

Labor-augmenting technological progress Technological progress that raises the productivity of an existing quantity of labor by general education, on-the-job training programs, and so on.

Capital-augmenting technological progress Technological progress that raises the productivity of capital by innovation and inventions.

FIGURE A3.1.3 Effect of Technological Change in the Agricultural Sector on the Production Possibility Frontier

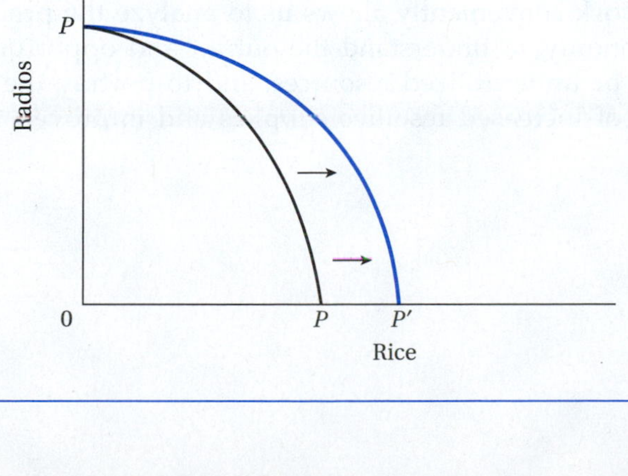

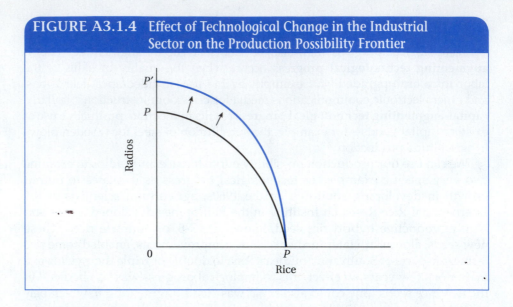

FIGURE A3.1.4   Effect of Technological Change in the Industrial
                Sector on the Production Possibility Frontier

for complicated, unwieldy, and fragile tubes, led to an enormous growth
of radio production. The production process became less complicated,
and workers were able to increase their total productivity significantly.
Figure A3.1.4 shows that as in the case of higher-yielding rice seeds, the technology of the transistor can be said to have caused the production possibility
curve to rotate outward along the vertical axis. For the most part, the rice
axis intercept remains unchanged (although perhaps the ability of rice paddy
workers to listen to music on their transistor radio while working may have
made them more productive!).

Conclusion

The sources of economic progress can be traced to a variety of factors, but
by and large, investments that improve the quality of existing physical and
human resources, increase the quantity of these same productive resources,
and raise the productivity of all or specific resources through invention, innovation, and technological progress have been and will continue to be primary
factors in stimulating economic growth in any society. The production possibility framework conveniently allows us to analyze the production choices
open to an economy, to understand the output and opportunity cost implications of idle or underutilized resources, and to portray the effects on economic growth of increased resource supplies and improved technologies of
production.

Appendix 3.2

The Solow Neoclassical Growth Model

The Solow neoclassical growth model, for which Robert Solow of the Massachusetts Institute of Technology received the Nobel Prize, is probably the best-known model of economic growth.[1] Although in some respects Solow's model describes a developed economy better than a developing one, it remains a basic reference point for the literature on growth and development. It implies that economies will conditionally converge to the same level of income if they have the same rates of savings, depreciation, labor force growth, and productivity growth. Thus, the Solow model is the basic framework for the study of convergence across countries (see Chapter 2). In this appendix, we consider this model in further detail.

The key modification from the Harrod-Domar (or AK) growth model, considered in this chapter, is that the Solow model allows for substitution between capital and labor. In the process, it assumes that there are diminishing returns to the use of these inputs.

The aggregate production function, $Y = F(K, L)$ is assumed characterized by constant returns to scale. For example, in the special case known as the Cobb-Douglas production function, at any time t we have

$$Y(t) = K(t)^\alpha (A(t)L(t))^{1-\alpha} \qquad \text{(A3.2.1)}$$

where Y is gross domestic product, K is the stock of capital (which may include human capital as well as physical capital), L is labor, and $A(t)$ represents the productivity of labor, which grows over time at an exogenous rate.

Because of constant returns to scale, if all inputs are increased by the same amount, say 10%, then output will increase by the same amount (10% in this case). More generally,

$$\gamma Y = F(\gamma K, \gamma L)$$

where γ is some positive amount (1.1 in the case of a 10% increase).

Because γ can be any positive real number, a mathematical trick useful in analyzing the implications of the model is to set $\gamma = 1/L$ so that

$$Y/L = f(K/L, 1) \; or \; y = f(k) \qquad \text{(A3.2.2)}$$

Lowercase variables are expressed in per-worker terms in these equations. The concave shape of $f(k)$—that is, increasing at a decreasing rate—reflects diminishing returns to capital per worker, as can be seen in Figure A3.2.1.[2] In the Harrod-Domar model, this would instead be a straight, upward-sloping line.

This simplification allows us to deal with just one argument in the production function. For example, in the Cobb-Douglas case introduced in Equation A3.2.1,

$$y = Ak^\alpha \qquad \text{(A3.2.3)}$$

This represents an alternative way to think about a production function, in which everything is measured in quantities per worker. Equation A3.2.3 states that output per worker is a function that depends on the amount of capital per worker. The more capital with which each worker has to work, the more output that worker can produce. The labor force grows at rate n per year, say,

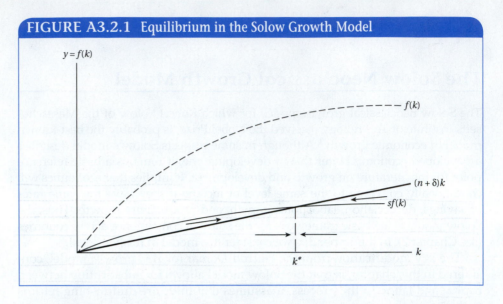

FIGURE A3.2.1 Equilibrium in the Solow Growth Model

and labor productivity growth, the rate at which the value of A in the production function increases, occurs at rate λ. The total capital stock grows when savings are greater than depreciation, but capital per worker grows when savings are also greater than what is needed to equip new workers with the same amount of capital as existing workers have.

The Solow equation (Equation A3.2.4) gives the growth of the capital-labor ratio, k (known as capital deepening), and shows that the growth of k depends on savings $sf(k)$, after allowing for the amount of capital required to service depreciation, δk, and after capital widening, that is, providing the existing amount of capital per worker to net new workers joining the labor force, nk. That is,

$$\Delta k = sf(k) - (\delta + n)k \qquad (A3.2.4)$$

Versions of the Solow equation are also valid for other growth models, such as the Harrod-Domar model.

For simplicity, we are assuming for now that A remains constant. In this case, there will be a state in which output and capital per worker are no longer changing, known as the *steady state*. (If A is increasing, the corresponding state will be one in which capital per effective worker is no longer changing. In that case, the number of effective workers rises as A rises; this is because when workers have higher productivity, it is as if there were extra workers on the job.) To find this steady state, set $\Delta k = 0$:

$$sf(k^*) = (\delta + n)k^* \qquad (A3.2.5)$$

The notation k^* means the level of capital per worker when the economy is in its steady state. That this equilibrium is stable can be seen from Figure A3.2.1.[3]

The capital per worker k^* represents the steady state. If k is higher or lower than k^*, the economy will return to it; thus k^* is a stable equilibrium. This stability is seen in the diagram by noting that to the left of k^*, $k < k^*$. Looking at the diagram, we see that in this case, $(n + \delta)k < sf(k)$. But now looking at the Solow equation (Equation A3.2.4), we see that when $(n + \delta)k < sf(k)$, $\Delta k > 0$. As a result, k in the economy is growing toward the equilibrium point k^*. By similar reasoning to the right of k^*, $(n + \delta)k > sf(k)$, and as a result, $\Delta k < 0$

(again refer to Equation A3.2.4), and capital per worker is actually shrinking toward the equilibrium k^*.[4] Note that in the Harrod-Domar model, $sf(k)$ would be a straight line, and provided that it was above the $(n + \delta)k$ line, growth in capital per worker—and output per worker—would continue indefinitely.

Equation (A3.2.5) has an interpretatation that the savings per worker, $sf(k^*)$, is just equal to δk^*, the amount of capital (per worker) needed to replace depreciating capital, plus nk^*, the amount of capital (per worker) that needs to be added due to population (labor force) growth.

The Solow model has a (single) equilibrium income per worker, again given by Equation (A3.2.5) above. In contrast, the Harrod Domar equilibrium is (constant, balanced) growth—there is no equilibrium income per worker. Essentially, this is because $f(k)$—and hence $sf(k)$—does not exhibit diminishing returns; rather, it is a straight line. That is, growth continues as long as the line $sf(k)$ stays above the line $(\delta + n)k$.

It is instructive to consider what happens in the Solow neoclassical growth model if we increase the rate of savings, s. A temporary increase in the rate of output growth is realized as we increase k by raising the rate of savings. We return to the original steady-state growth rate later, though at a higher level of output per worker in each later year. The key implication is that unlike in the Harrod-Domar (AK) analysis, in the Solow model an increase in s will not increase growth in the long run; it will only increase the equilibrium k^*. That is, after the economy has time to adjust, the capital-labor ratio increases, and so does the output-labor ratio, but not the rate of growth. The effect is shown in Figure A3.2.2, in which savings is raised to s'. In contrast, in the Harrod-Domar model, an increase in s raises the growth rate. (This is because in the Harrod-Domar model, $sf(k)$ becomes a straight line from the origin that does not cross $(n + \delta)k$; and so, as we assume that $sf(k)$ lies above $(n + \delta)k$, growth continues at the now higher Harrod-Domar rate—a result that was represented, for example, in the comparison of Equations 3.8 and 3.9.)

Note that the neoclassical growth model (Equation A3.2.5 and Figure A3.2.1) implies that while economies will (conditionally) converge to the same level of income per worker *other things equal*, it does not imply unconditional convergence. This can be seen clearly in Figure A3.2.2: We can interpret the alternative savings rates (s and s') in the figure as corresponding to those prevailing in two different countries; the country with the higher savings rate converges to a higher equilibrium income per worker.

Note carefully that in the Solow model, an increase in s does raise equilibrium output per person—which is certainly a valuable contribution to development—just not the equilibrium rate of growth. And the growth rate does increase temporarily as the economy kicks up toward the higher equilibrium capital per worker. Moreover, simulations based on cross-national data suggest that if s is increased, the economy may not return even halfway to its steady state for decades.[5] That is, for practical purposes of policymaking in developing countries, even if the Solow model is an accurate depiction of the economy, an increase in savings may substantially increase the growth rate for many decades to come. (Both theoretically and empirically, the link between the rate of savings and the rate of growth remains controversial.)

Finally, it is possible that the rate of savings (and hence investment) is positively related to the rate of technological progress itself so that the growth of A depends on s. This could be the case if investment uses newer-vintage

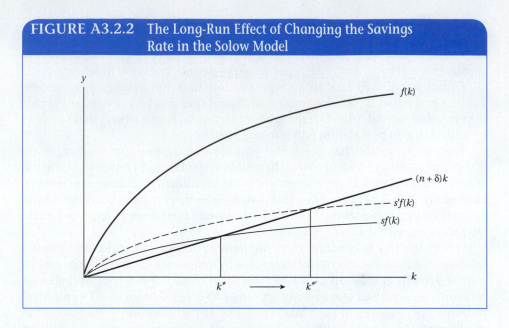

FIGURE A3.2.2   The Long-Run Effect of Changing the Savings Rate in the Solow Model

capital and hence is more productive, if investment represents innovation in that it solves problems faced by the firm, and if other firms see what the investing firm has done and imitate it ("learning by watching"), generating externalities. This leads to a model between the standard Solow model and the endogenous growth models such as the one examined in Appendix 3.3.

Notes

1. Robert M. Solow, "A contribution to the theory of economic growth," *Quarterly Journal of Economics* 70 (1956): 65–94.

2. Note that the symbol k is used for K/L and not for K/Y, as it is used in many expositions (including previous editions of this text) of the AK or Harrod-Domar model.

3. Readers with more advanced mathematical training may note that Figure A3.2.1 is a phase diagram, which applies given that the Inada conditions hold: that the marginal product of k goes to infinity as k goes to zero and goes to zero as k goes to infinity (this follows from Inada conditions assumed separately for capital and labor inputs). This diminishing-returns feature drives results of the Solow model.

4. Note that in the Solow model with technological progress, that is, growth of A, the capital-labor ratio grows to keep pace with the effective labor force, which is labor power that is augmented by its increasing productivity over time.

5. See N. Gregory Mankiw, David Romer, and David N. Weil, "A contribution to the empirics of economic growth," *Quarterly Journal of Economics* 107 (1992): 407–437. This article shows that when human capital is accounted for, as well as physical capital, the Solow model does a rather good job of explaining incomes and growth across countries. For a critical view, see William Easterly and Ross Levine, "It's not factor accumulation: Stylized facts and growth models," *World Bank Economic Review* 15 (2001): 177–219, with the reply by Robert M. Solow, "Applying growth theory across countries," *World Bank Economic Review* 15 (2001): 283–288. For time-series evidence that the Solow model does a good job of explaining even the case of South Korean growth, see Edward Feasel, Yongbeom Kim, and Stephen C. Smith, "Investment, exports, and output in South Korea: A VAR approach to growth empirics," *Review of Development Economics* 5 (2001): 421–432.

Appendix 3.3

Endogenous Growth Theory

Motivation for Endogenous Growth Theory

The mixed performance of neoclassical theories in illuminating the sources of long-term economic growth has led to dissatisfaction with traditional growth theory. In fact, according to traditional theory, there is no intrinsic characteristic of economies that causes them to grow over extended periods of time. The literature is instead concerned with the dynamic process through which capital-labor ratios approach long-run equilibrium levels. In the absence of external "shocks" or technological change, which is not explained in the neoclassical model, all economies will converge to zero growth. Hence, rising per capita GNI is considered a temporary phenomenon resulting from a change in technology or a short-term equilibrating process in which an economy approaches its long-run equilibrium.

Any increases in GNI that cannot be attributed to short-term adjustments in stocks of either labor or capital are ascribed to a third category, commonly referred to as the **Solow residual**. This residual is responsible for roughly 50% of historical growth in the industrialized nations.[1] In a rather ad hoc manner, neoclassical theory credits the bulk of economic growth to an exogenous or completely independent process of technological progress. Though intuitively plausible, this approach has at least two insurmountable drawbacks. First, using the neoclassical framework, it is impossible to analyze the determinants of technological advance because it is completely independent of the decisions of economic agents. And second, the theory fails to explain large differences in residuals across countries with similar technologies.

According to neoclassical theory, the low capital-labor ratios of developing countries promise exceptionally high rates of return on investment. The free-market reforms impressed on highly indebted countries by the World Bank and the International Monetary Fund should therefore have prompted higher investment, rising productivity, and improved standards of living. Yet even after the prescribed liberalization of trade and domestic markets, many developing countries experienced little or no growth and failed to attract new foreign investment or to halt the flight of domestic capital. The frequently anomalous behavior of developing-world capital flows (from poor to rich nations) helped provide the impetus for the development of the concept of **endogenous growth theory** or, more simply, the **new growth theory**.

The new growth theory provides a theoretical framework for analyzing endogenous growth, persistent GNI growth that is determined by the system governing the production process rather than by forces outside that system. In contrast to traditional neoclassical theory, these models hold GNI growth to be a natural consequence of long-run equilibrium. The principal motivations of the new growth theory are to explain both growth rate differentials across countries and a greater proportion of the growth observed. More succinctly, endogenous growth theorists seek to explain the factors that determine the size of λ, the rate of growth of GDP that is left unexplained and exogenously determined in the Solow neoclassical growth equation (i.e., the Solow residual).

Solow residual The proportion of long-term economic growth not explained by growth in labor or capital and therefore assigned primarily to exogenous technological change.

Endogenous growth theory (new growth theory) Economic growth generated by factors within the production process (e.g., increasing returns or induced technological change) that are studied as part of a growth model.

Models of endogenous growth bear some structural resemblance to their neo-classical counterparts, but they differ considerably in their underlying assumptions and the conclusions drawn. The most significant theoretical differences stem from discarding the neoclassical assumption of diminishing marginal returns to capital investments, permitting increasing returns to scale in aggregate production, and frequently focusing on the role of externalities in determining the rate of return on capital investments.[2] By assuming that public and private investments in human capital generate external economies and productivity improvements that offset the natural tendency for diminishing returns, endogenous growth theory seeks to explain the existence of increasing returns to scale and the divergent long-term growth patterns among countries. And whereas technology still plays an important role in these models, exogenous changes in technology are no longer necessary to explain long-run growth.

A useful way to contrast the new (endogenous) growth theory with traditional neoclassical theory is to recognize that many endogenous growth theories can be expressed by the simple equation $Y = AK$, as in the Harrod-Domar model. In this formulation, A is intended to represent any factor that affects technology, and K again includes both physical and human capital. But notice that there are no diminishing returns to capital in this formula, and the possibility exists that investments in physical and human capital can generate external economies and productivity improvements that exceed private gains by an amount sufficient to offset diminishing returns. The net result is sustained long-term growth—an outcome prohibited by traditional neoclassical growth theory. Thus, even though the new growth theory reemphasizes the importance of savings and human capital investments for achieving rapid growth, it also leads to several implications for growth that are in direct conflict with traditional theory. First, there is no force leading to the equilibration of growth rates across closed economies; national growth rates remain constant and differ across countries, depending on national savings rates and technology levels. Furthermore, there is no tendency for per capita income levels in capital-poor countries to catch up with those in rich countries with similar savings and population growth rates. A serious consequence of these facts is that a temporary or prolonged recession in one country can lead to a permanent increase in the income gap between itself and wealthier countries.

But perhaps the most interesting aspect of endogenous growth models is that they help explain anomalous international flows of capital that exacerbate wealth disparities between developed and developing countries. The potentially high rates of return on investment offered by developing economies with low capital-labor ratios are greatly eroded by lower levels of **complementary investments** in human capital (education), infrastructure, or research and development (R&D).[3] In turn, poor countries benefit less from the broader social gains associated with each of these alternative forms of capital expenditure.[4] Because individuals receive no personal gain from the positive externalities created by their own investments, the free market leads to the accumulation of less than the optimal level of complementary capital. (We examine these issues further in Chapter 4.)

Where complementary investments produce social as well as private benefits, governments may improve the efficiency of resource allocation. They can do this by providing public goods (infrastructure) or encouraging private

Complementary investments Investments that complement and facilitate other productive factors.

investment in knowledge-intensive industries, where human capital can be accumulated and subsequent increasing returns to scale generated. Unlike the Solow model, new growth theory models explain technological change as an endogenous outcome of public and private investments in human capital and knowledge-intensive industries. Thus, in contrast to the neoclassical counter-revolution theories examined in Appendix 3.2, models of endogenous growth suggest an active role for public policy in promoting economic development through direct and indirect investments in human capital formation and the encouragement of foreign private investment in knowledge-intensive industries such as computer software and telecommunications.

The Romer Model

To illustrate the endogenous growth approach, we examine the **Romer endogenous growth model** in detail because it addresses technological spillovers (in which one firm or industry's productivity gains lead to productivity gains in other firms or industries) that may be present in the process of industrialization. Thus, it is not only the seminal model of endogenous growth but also one of particular relevance for developing countries. We use a simplified version of Romer's model that keeps his main innovation—in modeling technology spillovers—without presenting unnecessary details of savings determination and other general equilibrium issues.

The model begins by assuming that growth processes derive from the firm or industry level. Each industry individually produces with constant returns to scale, so the model is consistent with perfect competition; and up to this point it matches assumptions of the Solow model. But Romer departs from Solow by assuming that the economy-wide capital stock, $\overline{K}$, positively affects output at the industry level so that there may be increasing returns to scale at the economy-wide level.

It is valuable to think of each firm's capital stock as including its knowledge. The knowledge part of the firm's capital stock is essentially a **public good**, like A in the Solow model, that is spilling over instantly to the other firms in the economy. As a result, this model treats learning by doing as "learning by investing." You can think of Romer's model as spelling out—endogenizing—the reason why growth might depend on the rate of investment (as in the Harrod-Domar model). In this simplification, we abstract from the household sector an important feature of the original model, in order to concentrate on issues concerning industrialization.[5] Formally,

$$Y_i = AK_i^{\alpha}L_i^{1-\alpha}\overline{K}^{\beta} \qquad (A3.3.1)$$

We assume symmetry across industries for simplicity, so each industry will use the same level of capital and labor. Then we have the aggregate production function:

$$Y = AK^{\alpha+\beta}L^{1-\alpha} \qquad (A3.3.2)$$

To make endogenous growth stand out clearly, we assume that A is constant rather than rising over time; that is, we assume for now that there is

Romer endogenous growth model An endogenous growth model in which technological spillovers are present; the economy-wide capital stock positively affects output at the industry level, so there may be increasing returns to scale at the economy-wide level.

Public good An entity that provides benefits to all individuals simultaneously and whose enjoyment by one person in no way diminishes that of anyone else.

no technological progress. With a little calculus,[6] it can be shown that the resulting growth rate for per capita income in the economy would be

$$g - n = \frac{\beta n}{1 - \alpha - \beta} \qquad \text{(A3.3.3)}$$

where g is the output growth rate and n is the population growth rate. Without spillovers, as in the Solow model with constant returns to scale, $\beta = 0$, and so per capita growth would be zero (without technological progress).[7]

However, with Romer's assumption of a positive capital externality, ($\beta > 0$), we have that $g - n > 0$ and Y/L is growing. Now we have endogenous growth, not driven exogenously by increases in productivity. If we also allowed for technological progress, so that λ in the Solow model is greater than zero, growth would be increased to that extent.[8]

Criticisms of Endogenous Growth Theory

An important shortcoming of the new growth theory is that it remains dependent on a number of traditional neoclassical assumptions that are often inappropriate for developing economies. For example, it assumes that there is but a single sector of production or that all sectors are symmetrical. This does not permit the crucial growth-generating reallocation of labor and capital among the sectors that are transformed during the process of structural change.[9] Moreover, economic growth in developing countries is frequently impeded by inefficiencies arising from poor infrastructure, inadequate institutional structures, and imperfect capital and goods markets. Because endogenous growth theory overlooks these very influential factors, its applicability for the study of economic development is limited, especially when country-to-country comparisons are involved. For example, existing theory fails to explain low rates of factory capacity utilization in low-income countries where capital is scarce. In fact, poor incentive structures may be as responsible for sluggish GNI growth as low rates of saving and human capital accumulation. Allocational inefficiencies are common in economies undergoing the transition from traditional to commercialized markets. However, their impact on short- and medium-term growth has been neglected due to the new theory's emphasis on the determinants of long-term growth rates. Finally, empirical studies of the predictive value of endogenous growth theories have to date offered only limited support.[10]

Notes

1. Oliver J. Blanchard and Stanley Fischer, *Lectures on Macroeconomics* (Cambridge, Mass.: MIT Press, 1989).

2. For a short history of the evolution of theoretical models of growth, see Nicholas Stern, "The determinants of growth," *Economic Journal* 101 (1991): 122–134. For a more detailed but technical discussion of endogenous growth models, see Robert

Barro and Xavier Sala-i-Martin, *Economic Growth*, 2nd ed. (Cambridge, Mass.: MIT Press, 2003), and Elhanan Helpman, "Endogenous macroeconomic growth theory," *European Economic Review* 36 (1992): 237–268.

3. See Paul M. Romer, "Increasing returns and long-run growth," *Journal of Political Economy* 94 (1986): 1002–1037; Robert E. Lucas, "On the mechanics of

economic development," *Journal of Monetary Economics* 22 (1988): 3–42; and Robert Barro, "Government spending in a simple model of endogenous growth," *Journal of Political Economy* 98 (1990): 5103–5125.

4. For a concise technical discussion of the importance of human capital as a complementary input, see Robert B. Lucas, "Why doesn't capital flow from rich to poor countries?" *AEA Papers and Proceedings* 80 (1990): 92–96.

5. The specific functional form in Equation A3.3.1, known as Cobb-Douglas production functions, will be assumed for simplicity.

6. By the chain rule,

$$\dot{Y} = \frac{dY}{dt} = \frac{\partial Y}{\partial K}\frac{\partial K}{\partial t} + \frac{\partial Y}{\partial L}\frac{\partial L}{\partial t}$$

By the exponent rule, we know that

$$\frac{\partial Y}{\partial K} = A(\alpha + \beta)K^{\alpha+\beta-1}L^{1-\alpha}$$

$$\frac{\partial Y}{\partial L} = AK^{\alpha+\beta}(1 - \alpha)L^{1-\alpha-1}$$

Combining these three equations, we have

$$\dot{Y} = dY/dt = \left[AK^{\alpha+\beta}L^{1-\alpha}\right]\left[(\alpha + \beta)\frac{\dot{K}}{K} + (1 - \alpha)\frac{\dot{L}}{L}\right]$$

The first term in brackets in the preceding expression is of course output, *Y*. For a steady state, $\dot{K}/K$, $\dot{L}/L$, and $\dot{Y}/Y$ are all constant. From earlier discussion of the Harrod-Domar and Solow models, we know that

$$\dot{K} = I - \delta K = sY - \delta K$$

where δ stands for the depreciation rate.

Dividing this expression through by *K*, we have

$$\frac{\dot{K}}{K} = \frac{sY}{K} - \delta$$

For $\dot{K}/K$ constant in the preceding expression, we must have *Y*/*K* constant. If this ratio is constant, we have

$$\frac{\dot{K}}{K} = \frac{\dot{Y}}{Y} = g, \text{ a constant growth rate}$$

So from the expression for *dY*/*dt* above, for the aggregate production function, with $\dot{L}/L = n$, which is also a constant, we have

$$\frac{\dot{Y}}{Y} = (\alpha + \beta)\frac{\dot{K}}{K} + (1 - \alpha)\frac{\dot{L}}{L} \to g$$
$$= (\alpha + \beta)g + (1 - \alpha)n \to g - n$$
$$= \left[\frac{(1 - \alpha) + (\alpha + \beta) - 1}{1 - (\alpha + \beta)}\right]n$$

which is Equation A3.3.3. This may also be expressed as

$$g = \frac{n(1 - \alpha)}{1 - \alpha - \beta}$$

7. Recall that there is no technological progress, so λ in the Solow model is zero.

8. In a more complex model, decisions about, and effects of, factors such as research and development investment can be modeled explicitly. Firms would decide on general investment and R&D investment. The effect of the latter on overall output would enter in a manner similar to $\overline{K}$ in Equation A3.3.1. For a discussion and references, see Gene M. Grossman and Elhanan Helpman, "Endogenous innovation in the theory of growth" in the symposium on new growth theory in the *Journal of Economic Perspectives* 8 (1994): 3–72.

9. Syed Nawab Haider Naqvi, "The significance of development economics," *World Development* 24 (1996): 977.

10. For an excellent review and empirical critique of the new growth theory, see Howard Pack, "Endogenous growth theory: Intellectual appeal and empirical shortcomings," *Journal of Economic Perspectives* 8 (1994): 55–72. See also articles by Paul M. Romer and Robert M. Solow in the same issue. For an argument that endogenous theory performs well in explaining differences in growth rates among countries, see Barro and Sala-i-Martin, *Economic Growth*. An excellent survey of quantitative growth research disputing this claim and indicating widening gaps between rich and poor countries can be found in Jonathan Temple, "The new growth evidence," *Journal of Economic Literature* 37 (1999): 112–156.

Contemporary Models of Development and Underdevelopment

Individuals need not make the right tradeoffs. And whereas in the past we thought the implication was that the economy would be slightly distorted, we now understand that the interaction of these slightly distorted behaviors may produce very large distortions. The consequence is that there may be multiple equilibria and that each may be inefficient.

—*Karla Hoff and Joseph E. Stiglitz,* Frontiers in Development Economics, *2002*

Governments can certainly deter entrepreneurship when they try to do too much; but they can also deter entrepreneurship when they do too little.

—*Dani Rodrik,* One Economics, Many Recipes, *2007*

After more than a half century of experience with attempting to encourage modern development, we have learned that development is both possible and extremely difficult to achieve. Thus, an improved understanding of impediments and catalysts of development is of the utmost importance. Since the late 1980s, significant strides have been made in the analysis of economic development and underdevelopment. In some cases, ideas of the classic theories reviewed in Chapter 3 have been formalized, and in the process, their logical structure and their significance for policy have been clarified and refined. At the same time, the analysis has also led to entirely new insights into what makes development so hard to achieve (as witnessed in sub-Saharan Africa) but also possible to achieve (as witnessed in East Asia). Indeed, this is what makes the study of economic development so very important: It does not happen automatically; it requires systematic effort. But development is far from a hopeless cause; we know it can be done. Theory helps us think systematically about how to organize our efforts to help achieve development—a goal second to none in its importance to humanity.

In this chapter, we review a sample of some of the most influential of the new models of economic development. In some ways, these models show that development is harder to achieve, in that it faces more barriers than had previously been recognized. But greater understanding itself facilitates improvements in development strategy, and the new models have already influenced development policy and modes of international assistance. The chapter concludes with a framework for appraising the locally **binding constraints** on the ability of a developing nation to further close the gap with the developed world.

The new research has broadened considerably the scope for modeling a market economy in a developing-country context. One of its major themes is incorporating problems of coordination among **economic agents**, such as among groups of firms, workers, or firms and workers together. Other key themes, often but not always in conjunction with the coordination problem, include the formal exploration of situations in which increasing returns to scale, a finer division of labor, the availability of new economic ideas or knowledge, learning by doing, information externalities, and monopolistic competition or other forms of industrial organization other than perfect competition predominate. The new perspective frequently incorporates work in the "new institutional economics," such as that of Nobel laureate Douglass C. North, and introduced in Chapter 2. All of these approaches depart to some degree from conventional neoclassical economics, at least in its assumptions of perfect information, the relative insignificance of externalities, and the uniqueness and optimality of equilibria.[1]

Binding constraint The one limiting factor that if relaxed would be the item that accelerates growth (or that allows a larger amount of some other targeted outcome).

Economic agent An economic actor—usually a firm, worker, consumer, or government official—that chooses actions so as to maximize an objective; often referred to as "agents."

4.1 Underdevelopment as a Coordination Failure

Many newer theories of economic development that became influential in the 1990s and the early years of the twenty-first century have emphasized **complementarities** between several conditions necessary for successful development. These theories often highlight the problem that several things must work well enough, at the same time, to get sustainable development under way. They also stress that in many important situations, investments must be undertaken by many agents in order for the results to be profitable for any individual agent. Generally, when complementarities are present, an action taken by one firm, worker, or organization increases the incentives for other agents to take similar actions.

Complementarity An action taken by one firm, worker, or organization that increases the incentives for other agents to take similar actions. Complementarities often involve investments whose return depends on other investments being made by other agents.

Models of development that stress complementarities are related to some of the models used in the endogenous growth approach (described in Appendix 3.3), in ways we will point out later in the chapter, but the **coordination failure** approach has evolved relatively independently and offers some significant and distinct insights.[2] Put simply, a coordination failure is a state of affairs in which agents' inability to coordinate their behavior (choices) leads to an outcome (equilibrium) that leaves all agents worse off than in an alternative situation that is also an equilibrium. This may occur even when all agents are fully informed about the preferred alternative equilibrium: They simply cannot get there because of difficulties of coordination, sometimes because people hold different expectations and sometimes because everyone is better off waiting for someone else to make the first move. This section spells out the meaning and implications of these perspectives in detail, through both simple models and examples.

Coordination failure A situation in which the inability of agents to coordinate their behavior (choices) leads to an outcome (equilibrium) that leaves all agents worse off than in an alternative situation that is also an equilibrium.

When complementarities are present, an action taken by one firm, worker, organization, or government increases the incentives for other agents to take

Big push   A concerted, economy-wide, and typically public policy–led effort to initiate or accelerate economic development across a broad spectrum of new industries and skills.

O-ring model   An economic model in which production functions exhibit strong complementarities among inputs and which has broader implications for impediments to achieving economic development.

Middle-income trap   A condition in which an economy begins development to reach middle-income status but is chronically unable to progress to high-income status. Often related to low capacity for original innovation or for absorption of advanced technology, and may be compounded by high inequality.

similar actions. In particular, these complementarities often involve investments whose return depends on other investments being made by other agents. In development economics, such network effects are common, and we consider some important examples later in this chapter, including the model of the **big push**, in which production decisions by modern-sector firms are mutually reinforcing, and the **O-ring model**, in which the value of upgrading skills or quality depends on similar upgrading by other agents. Curiously, such effects are also common in analyses of frontier technologies in developed countries, particularly information technologies, in which the value of using an operating system, word-processing program, spreadsheet program, instant messaging, and other software or product standard depends on how many other users also adopt it. In both cases, the circular causation of positive feedback is common.[3] This framework may also be used in analyses of the **middle-income trap**, in which countries develop to a degree but chronically fail to reach high-income status, often due to lack of innovation capacity.

An important example of a complementarity is the presence of firms using specialized skills and the availability of workers who have acquired those skills. Firms will not enter a market or locate in an area if workers do not possess the skills the firms need, but workers will not acquire the skills if there are no firms to employ them. This coordination problem can leave an economy stuck in a bad equilibrium—that is, at a low average income or growth rate or with a class of citizens trapped in extreme poverty. Even though all agents would be better off if workers acquired skills and firms invested, it might not be possible to get to this better equilibrium without the aid of government. As we will see, such coordination problems are also common in initial industrialization, as well as in upgrading skills and technologies, and may extend to issues as broad as changing behavior to modern "ways of doing things." Such problems are further compounded by other market failures, particularly those affecting capital markets.[4]

Another example typical of rural developing areas concerns the commercialization of agriculture. As Adam Smith already understood, specialization is one of the sources of high productivity. Indeed, specialization and a detailed division of labor are hallmarks of an advanced economy. But we can specialize only if we can trade for the other goods and services we need. Producers must somehow get their products to markets while convincing distant buyers of their quality. As Shahe Emran and Forhad Shilpi stress, in the development of agricultural markets, middlemen play a key role by effectively vouching for the quality of the products they sell; they can do this because they get to know the farmers from whom they buy as well as the products. It is difficult to be an expert in the quality of many products, so in order for a specialized agricultural market to emerge, there needs to be a sufficient number of concentrated producers with whom a middleman can work effectively. But without available middlemen to whom the farmers can sell, they will have little incentive to specialize in the first place and will prefer to continue producing their staple crop or a range of goods primarily for personal consumption or sale within the village. The result can be an **underdevelopment trap** in which a region remains stuck in subsistence agriculture.[5]

Underdevelopment trap   A poverty trap at the regional or national level in which underdevelopment tends to perpetuate itself over time.

In many cases, the presence of complementarities creates a classic "chicken and egg" problem: Which comes first, the skills or the demand for skills? Often the answer is that the complementary investments must come at the same time, through coordination. This is especially true when, as is generally the case, there is a lag between making an investment and realizing the return on that investment.[6] In this case, even if, for some reason, all parties expect a change to a better equilibrium, they will still be inclined to wait until other parties have made their investments. Thus, there can be an important role for government policy in coordinating joint investments, such as between the workers who want skills that employers can use and the employers who want equipment that workers can use. Neither may be in a position (or find it in their self-interest) to take the first step; each may be better off waiting for the other parties to invest first.

As another example, a new or modernizing firm using new technologies may provide benefits to other firms that the adopting firm cannot capture; so each firm has an incentive to underinvest in the new technology unless a sufficient number of others invest. Some of these benefits may include raising demand for key industrial products such as steel, helping pay for the fixed costs of an essential infrastructure such as railroads or container ports, or learning from others' experiences. We will take a closer look at this problem later in the chapter.

The new work expands the scope for potentially valuable government policy interventions, but it does not take their success for granted. Rather, government itself is increasingly analyzed in contemporary development models as one of the components of the development process that may contribute to the problem as well as to the solution; government policy is understood as partly determined by (endogenous to) the underdeveloped economy (see Chapter 11). For example, a dictator such as Mobutu Sese Seko, the former ruler of the Democratic Republic of Congo when it was known as Zaire, may prefer to keep his country in an underdevelopment trap, knowing full well that as the economy develops, he will lose power. But rather than concluding that government generally exacerbates underdevelopment rather than facilitates development (as in extreme versions of the neoclassical counterrevolution school), many development specialists look actively for cases in which government policy can still help, even when government is imperfect, by pushing the economy toward a self-sustaining, better equilibrium. Such **deep interventions** move an economy to a preferred equilibrium or even to a higher permanent rate of growth in which there is no incentive to go back to the behavior associated with the bad equilibrium. In these cases, government has no need to continue the interventions, because the better equilibrium will be maintained automatically. Government can then concentrate its efforts on other crucial problems in which it has an essential role (e.g., in addressing problems of public health). This onetime-fix character of some multiple-equilibrium problems makes them worthy of special focus because they can make government policy that much more powerful in addressing problems of economic development. But it also makes the policy choices more momentous, because a bad policy today could mire an economy in a bad equilibrium for years to come.

In much of economics, such complementarities are not present. For example, in competitive markets, when there is excess demand, there is counterpressure for prices to rise, restoring equilibrium. Whenever **congestion** may be present, these counterpressures are very strong: The more people there are fishing in one lake, the more fishers try to move to another lake that is less crowded; the more people there are using one road, the more commuters

Deep intervention A government policy that can move the economy to a preferred equilibrium or even to a higher permanent rate of growth, which can then be self-sustaining so that the policy need no longer be enforced because the better equilibrium will then prevail without further intervention.

Congestion The opposite of a complementarity; an action taken by one agent that decreases the incentives for other agents to take similar actions.

try to find an alternative route. But in the process of economic development, joint externalities are common: Underdevelopment begets underdevelopment, while processes of sustainable development, once under way, tend to stimulate further development.

Where-to-meet dilemma A situation in which all parties would be better off cooperating than competing but lack information about how to do so. If cooperation can be achieved, there is no subsequent incentive to defect or cheat.

Coordination problems are illustrated by the **where-to-meet dilemma**: Several friends know that they will all be in Buenos Aires on a certain day but have neglected to settle on a specific location within the city. Now they are out of communication and can arrive at a common meeting point only by chance or by very clever guessing. They want to meet and consider themselves better off if they can do so; there is no incentive to "cheat." Thus, the where-to-meet problem is quite different from that of **prisoners' dilemma**, another problem often encountered in theories of economic development.[7] But the fact that all gain from coordination does not make the where-to-meet dilemma easy to solve. There are many famous places in Buenos Aires: the Plaza de Mayo, the Cathedral, the colorful Caminito neighborhood, the Café Tortoni, the Cementerio de la Recoleta, even the casino. Only with luck would the friends end up making the same guesses and meeting in the same place. Arriving at, say, the center of Caminito and not finding the others there, one of our travelers might decide to try the Plaza de Mayo instead. But en route she might miss another of the other travelers, who at that moment might be on his way to check out the Cementerio. So the friends never meet. Something analogous happens when farmers in a region do not know what to specialize in. There may be several perfectly good products from which to choose, but the critical problem is for all the farmers to choose *one* so that middlemen may profitably bring the region's produce to market.

Prisoners' dilemma A situation in which all parties would be better off cooperating than competing, but once cooperation has been achieved, each party would gain the most by cheating, provided that others stick to cooperative agreements—thus causing any agreement to unravel.

The story may lose a bit of its power in the age of texting, cell phones, and e-mail. For example, as long as the friends have each other's contact information, they can come to an agreement about where to meet. Sometimes what seems at first a complex problem of coordination is really a simpler one of communication. But anyone who has tried to establish a meeting time by phone or e-mail with a large number of participants with no formal leader knows that this can be a slow and cumbersome process. Without a clear leader and with a large enough number of participants, no meeting place may be agreed to on short notice before it is too late. And in real economic problems, the people who need to "meet"—perhaps to coordinate investments—do not even know the identity of the other key agents.[8] However, our example does point up possibilities for improved prospects for development with the advent of modern computing and telecommunications technology. Of course, peasant farmers may not have access to cell phones or e-mail (but see the case study for Chapter 11 on the Grameen Bank).

4.2 Multiple Equilibria: A Diagrammatic Approach

Multiple equilibria A condition in which more than one equilibrium exists. These equilibria sometimes may be ranked, in the sense that one is preferred over another, but the unaided market will not move the economy to the preferred outcome.

The standard diagram to illustrate **multiple equilibria** with possible coordination failure is shown in Figure 4.1. This diagram, in one version or another, has become almost as ubiquitous in discussions of multiple equilibria as the famous supply-and-demand ("Marshallian scissors") diagram in discussions of single equilibrium analysis.[9]

FIGURE 4.1 Multiple Equilibria

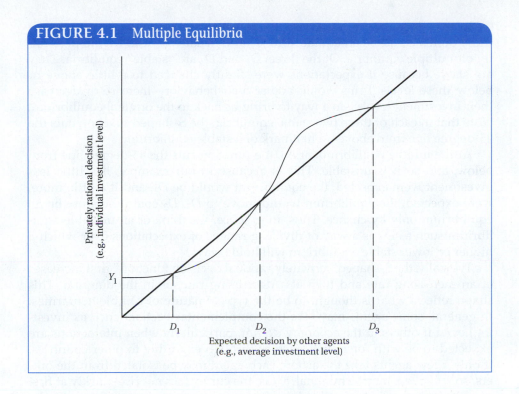

The basic idea reflected in the S-shaped function of Figure 4.1 is that the benefits an agent receives from taking an action depend positively on how many other agents are expected to take the action or on the extent of those actions. For example, the price a farmer can hope to receive for his produce depends on the number of middlemen who are active in the region, which in turn depends on the number of other farmers who specialize in the same product.

How do we find the equilibria in this type of problem? In the Marshallian supply-and-demand scissors diagram, equilibrium is found where the supply and demand curves cross. In the multiple-equilibria diagram, equilibrium is found where the "privately rational decision function" (the S-shaped curve in Figure 4.1) crosses the 45-degree line. This is because in these cases, agents observe what they expected to observe. Suppose that firms expected no other firms to make investments, but some firms did anyway (implying a positive vertical intercept in the diagram). But then, seeing that some firms did make investments, it would not be reasonable to continue to expect no investment! Firms would have to revise their expectations upward, matching their expectations to the level of investment they actually would see. But if firms now expected this higher level of investment, firms would want to invest even more. This process of adjustment of expectations would continue until the level of actual investment would just equal the level of expected investment: At that level, there would be no reason for firms to adjust their expectations any further. So the general idea of an equilibrium in such cases is one in which all participants are doing what is best for them, given what they expect others to do, which in turn matches what others are actually doing. This happens when the function crosses the 45-degree line. At these points, the values on the x-axis and y-axis are equal, implying in our example that the level of investment expected is equal to the level that all agents find best (e.g., the profit-maximizing level).

In the diagram, the function cuts the 45-degree line three times. Any of these points could be an equilibrium: That is what we mean by the possibility of multiple equilibria. Of the three, D_1 and D_3 are "stable" equilibria. They are stable because if expectations were slightly changed to a little above or below these levels, firms would adjust their behavior—increase or decrease their investment levels—in a way to bring us back to the original equilibrium. Note that in each of these two stable equilibria, the S-shaped function cuts the 45-degree line from above—a hallmark of a stable equilibrium.

At the middle equilibrium at D_2, the function cuts the 45-degree line from below, and so it is unstable. This is because in our example, if a little less investment were expected, the equilibrium would be D_1, and if a little more, were expected, the equilibrium would move to D_3. D_2 could therefore be an equilibrium only by chance. Thus, in practice, we think of an unstable equilibrium such as D_2 as a way of dividing ranges of expectations over which a higher or lower stable equilibrium will hold sway.

Typically, the S-shaped "privately rational decision function" first increases at an increasing rate and then at a decreasing rate, as in the diagram. This shape reflects what is thought to be the typical nature of complementarities. In general, some agents may take the complementary action (such as investing) even if others in the economy do not, particularly when interactions are expected to be with foreigners, such as through exporting to other countries. If only a few agents take the action, each agent may be isolated from the others, so spillovers may be minimal. Thus, the curve does not rise quickly at first as more agents take the action. But after enough agents invest, there may be a snowball effect, in which many agents begin to provide spillover benefits to neighboring agents, and the curve increases at a much faster rate. Finally, after most potential investors have been positively affected and the most important gains have been realized, the rate of increase starts to slow down.

In many cases, the shape of the function in Figure 4.1 could be different, however. For example, a very "wobbly" curve could cut the 45-degree line several times. In the case of telephone service, getting on e-mail or instant messaging, or buying a fax machine, where the value of taking the action steadily increases with the number of others in the network, the function may only increase at an increasing rate (like a quadratic or exponential function). Depending on the slope of the function and whether it cuts the 45-degree line, there can be a single equilibrium or multiple equilibria, including cases in which either no one ever adopts a new technology or virtually everyone does. In general, the value (utility) of the various equilibria (two in this case) is not the same. For example, it is very possible that everyone is better off in the equilibrium in which more people use the network. In this case, we say the equilibria are Pareto-ranked, with the higher rank to the equilibrium giving higher utility to everyone; in other words, moving to this equilibrium represents a **Pareto improvement** over the equilibrium with fewer users.

Pareto improvement A situation in which one or more persons may be made better off without making anyone worse off.

The classic example of this problem in economic development concerns coordinating investment decisions when the value (rate of return) of one investment depends on the presence or extent of other investments. All are better off with more investors or higher rates of investment, but the market may not get us there without the influence of certain types of government policy (but note that we may also not arrive at the preferred solutions if we have the wrong kinds of government policy). The difficulties of investment coordination give rise to various government-led strategies for industrialization that we consider both in this chapter and later in the text (see especially Chapter 12).

The investment coordination perspective helps clarify the nature and extent of problems posed when technology spillovers are present, such as seen in the Romer model described in Appendix 3.3.[10] Given what was learned in examining endogenous growth theory about the possible relation between investment and growth, you can see that an economy can get stuck in a low growth rate largely because the economy is expected to have a low investment rate. Strategies for coordinating a change from a less productive to a more productive set of mutually reinforcing expectations can vary widely, as the example in Box 4.1 and the findings in Box 4.2 illustrate. However, changing expectations may not be sufficient if it is more profitable for

BOX 4.1 Synchronizing Expectations: Resetting "Latin American Time"

Kaushik Basu and Jorgen Weibull argue that while the importance of culture is undeniable, the innateness of culture is not. They present a model that shows that punctuality may be "simply an equilibrium response of individuals to what they expect others to do" and that the same society can benefit from a "punctual equilibrium" or get caught in a lateness equilibrium.

Estimates suggested that Ecuador lost between 4% and 10% of its GDP due to chronic lateness. As one commentator put it, "Tardiness feeds on itself, creating a vicious cycle of *mañana, mañana.*" Lately, Ecuador has tried to make up for lost time. Inspired by some in the younger generation who are fed up with "Latin American time," government and business have joined in a private-sector-funded drive to get people to show up at their scheduled appointment times. The country has launched a national *campaña contra la impuntualidad* (campaign against lateness), coordinated by Participación Ciudadana (Citizen Participation). The result is a test of the idea that a society can consciously switch from a bad to a good equilibrium through a change in expectations.

The campaign is a timely one. A newspaper is publishing a list each day of officials who are late for public events. A popular poster for the campaign against lateness describes the disease and says, "Treatment: Inject yourself each morning with a dose of responsibility,

respect and discipline. Recommendation: Plan, organize activities and repair your watches." Hundreds of public and private institutions have signed up to a promise to be punctual. A popular notice for meeting rooms in the style of hotel "Do Not Disturb" signs has been making the rounds. On one side it says, "Come in: You're on time." When the meeting begins at its scheduled time, it is turned around to the other side, which reads, "Do not enter: The meeting began on time."

In Peru, a similar campaign is under way. If the campaign against lateness proves successful, it will be about more than time. If a social movement to change expectations about punctuality can be made to work, something similar might be tried around the world for fixing even more pernicious problems, such as public corruption.

Sources: Kaushik Basu and Jorgen Weibull, "Punctuality: A cultural trait as equilibrium," in *Economics for an Imperfect World: Essays in Honor of Joseph Stiglitz*, ed. Richard Arnott et al. (Cambridge, Mass.: MIT Press, 2003); Scott Wilson, "In Ecuador, a timeout for tardiness drive promotes punctuality," *Washington Post Foreign Service*, November 4, 2003, p. A22; "The price of lateness," *Economist*, November 22, 2003, p. 67; "Punctuality pays," *New Yorker*, April 5, 2004, p. 31. For an interesting critique, see Andrew M. Horowitz, "The punctuality prisoners' dilemma: Can current punctuality initiatives in low-income countries succeed?" Paper presented at the Northeast Universities Development Consortium Conference, Harvard University, October 2007.

BOX 4.2 FINDINGS   Village Coordination and Monitoring for Better Health Outcomes

Chapter 4 explains the important role of improved information, shared expectations, and coordination across agents in making development progress. Coordination across households potentially can improve outcomes, for example, by changing norms toward lower fertility and ending harmful practices, and enforcing noncorrupt and efficient public-service provisions. A recent study by Martina Björkman and Jakob Svensson shows how these mechanisms may work by drawing on evidence from a randomized control trial. The researchers found that initially, villagers had little information about the scope of health problems in their village compared with outside standards, nor about what to reasonably expect from government-funded health workers. The program provided villagers with the knowledge and resources to enable them to monitor health workers individually and through their community organization. This is important to do as a community because both information gathering and monitoring have features of public goods. The results suggest that such a program can improve the behavior of health workers and lead to measurably better health outcomes—all for apparently very modest cost outlays.

The study questions were whether the intervention *caused* an increased quantity and quality of health care provision; and whether this resulted in improved health outcomes. The researchers were checking for impacts along the hypothesized "accountability chain" that treatment communities became more involved in monitoring health workers and that the intervention changed the behavior of health workers. The initial intervention had three components: first, a meeting of villagers; second, a meeting with health care workers; and finally, a meeting including both groups. This was followed by a plan of action and monitoring organized by villagers.

Initially, a "report card" comparing performance of the local health facility with others was prepared. Then facilitators in conjunction with local community leaders and community-based organizations organized a village meeting to hear and discuss the results and develop an action plan. (This is similar to the process of many community-based development activities in Africa and elsewhere.) Participation in the two-afternoon event was carefully planned to include—and hear from—diverse representatives to avoid elite capture. The facilitators "encouraged community members to develop a shared view on how to improve service delivery and monitor the provider," which were "summarized in an action plan." In these meetings, researchers observed some common concerns that "included high rates of absenteeism, long waiting-time, weak attention of health staff, and differential treatment."

The health facility meeting was a one-afternoon, all-staff event where facilitators contrasted the facility's information on service provision with findings from a household survey. Finally, an "interface meeting" was held with community representatives chosen at the community meetings and health workers, where rights, responsibilities, and suggestions for improvements were discussed, resulting in a "shared action plan...on what needs to be done, how, when and by whom." Then, "after the initial meetings, the communities were themselves in charge of establishing ways of monitoring the provider."

The program was associated with (and apparently caused) positive health outcomes, including relatively higher weights of infants, fewer deaths of children less than five years old, and greater utilization of health facilities. Evidence showed that as a result of the program, treatment practices also improved the "quality and quantity of health care provision," suggesting that increases "are due to behavioral changes." In particular, equipment (such as a thermometer) was used more often; waiting time was reduced; clinic cleanliness improved; better information was provided to patients; appropriate supplements and vaccines for children were provided more often; and absenteeism by health workers declined. The program was estimated to improve health outcomes to a degree similar to findings from high-impact medical trials. However, such trials assume the health system is working fine and only benefits from improved procedures and medications; in contrast, this approach focused on getting health workers to do what they were supposed to do in the first place.

Some checks confirmed the program more likely had its impact through community participation rather than other mechanisms, but it is still possible that other mechanisms such as health workers responding to learning about patient rights rather than community pressure played some role; so we may not yet be certain how the program worked. This type of question is important to investigate because understanding mechanisms helps with designing other programs effectively.

Overall, the researchers surmised that "lack of relevant information and failure to agree on, or coordinate expectations of, what is reasonable to demand from the provider were holding back individual and group action to pressure and monitor the provider."

The authors caution that: "Before scaling up, it is also important to subject the project to a cost-benefit analysis....A back-of-the-envelope calculation suggests that....The estimated cost of averting the death of a child under five is around $300." If this estimate holds up to more systematic analysis, it would be an unusually cost-effective program. The authors concluded by noting that "future research should address long-term effects, identify which mechanisms or combination of mechanisms that are important, and study the extent to which the results generalize to other social sectors."

There remain some other questions. As hinted, it is uncertain whether these improvements can be sustained over time—at least without periodic outside facilitation—for example, if the initial interest for participants is in being part of a foreign-sponsored program and this motive fades over time, or if long-term threats to collective organization including free riding and capture rear their heads. So it would be valuable to return to these villages to look at conditions after a few years. It is not clear yet how well or how cost-effectively this approach would work elsewhere—the "external validity" question again. Even if the program does indeed work through the mechanism of empowerment, as seems quite likely, the real powers that be may not have allowed such outcomes if material interests of rulers were threatened by the program. Moreover, as the researchers note, an approach that combined more monitoring from the top of the health ministry in combination with the bottom-up monitoring of communities, as done in this program, could have even larger positive impacts. Finally, people and their communities have limited time; so inducing a shift of time to the health system monitoring activity in this program could cause a decrease in the amount of other valuable community activities.

But in sum, this is an exemplary design and evaluation of a community-based development program that provides substantive evidence of what can work to improve health (and empowerment) of villagers in a low-income rural area.

Sources: Martina Björkman and Jakob Svensson, "Power to the People: Evidence from a Randomized Field Experiment on Community-Based Monitoring in Uganda," *Quarterly Journal of Economics*, 124 (2), pp 735–769, May 2009; and supplementary appendix.

a firm to wait for others to invest rather than to be a "pioneer" investor. In that case, government policy is generally needed in addition to a change of expectations. This explains why attention to the potential presence of multiple equilibria is so important. Market forces can generally bring us to one of the equilibria, but they are not sufficient to ensure that the best equilibrium will be achieved, and they offer no mechanism to become unstuck from a bad equilibrium and move toward a better one.

A similar multiple-equilibria situation will be encountered in our analysis of the Malthus population trap in Chapter 6. In this population trap, fertility decisions need in effect to be coordinated across families—all are better off if the average fertility rate declines, but any one family may be worse off by being the only one to have fewer children. We also see coordination failures in processes of urbanization and other key elements of economic development.

In general, when jointly profitable investments may not be made without coordination, multiple equilibria may exist in which the same individuals with access to the same resources and technologies can find themselves in either a good or a bad situation. In the view of many development economists, it is very plausible that many of the least developed countries, including many in sub-Saharan Africa, are essentially caught in such circumstances. Of course, other problems are also present. For example, political pressures from potential losers in the modernization process can also prevent shifts to better equilibria. In addition, modern technology may not yet be available in the country. The technology transfer problem is another important concern in economic development. In fact, another problem illustrated by the graph in Figure 4.1 could be that the amount of effort each firm in a developing region expends to increase the rate of technology transfer depends on the effort undertaken by other firms; bringing in modern technology from abroad often has spillover effects for other firms. But the possibility of multiple equilibria shows that making better technology available is generally a necessary but not a sufficient condition for achieving development goals.

4.3 Starting Economic Development: The Big Push

Whether an economy has been growing sustainably for some time or has been stagnant seems to make a very big difference for subsequent development. If growth can be sustained for a substantial time, say, a generation or more, it is much more unusual for economic development to later get off track for long (though, of course, there will be setbacks over the business cycle as the economy is affected by temporary shocks). Certainly, we have had too many disappointing experiences to assume, with Rostow, that once economic development is under way, it can in effect never be stopped. As noted in the case study in Chapter 3, a century ago, Argentina was regarded as a future powerhouse of the world economy, yet it later experienced relative stagnation for more than half a century. A look at the record, however, allows us to agree with Rostow at least in that it is very difficult to get modern economic growth under way in the first place and much easier to maintain it once a track record has been established.

Why should it be so difficult to start modern growth? Many models of development that were influential in earlier years, such as the Lewis model examined in Chapter 3, assume perfectly competitive conditions in the industrial sector. Under perfect competition, it is not clear why starting development would be so difficult, provided at least that the needed human capital is developed, the technology transfer problem is adequately addressed, and government provides other essential services. But development seems hard to initiate even when better technologies are available—they often go unused. Apparently, people do not have the incentives to put the new technology to work. Beyond this, perfect competition does not hold under conditions of increasing returns to scale. And yet, looking at the Industrial Revolution, it is clear that taking advantage of returns to scale has been key. Many development economists have concluded that several market failures work to make economic development difficult to initiate, notably **pecuniary externalities**, which are spillover effects on costs or revenues.

Pecuniary externality   A positive or negative spillover effect on an agent's costs or revenues.

Perhaps the most famous coordination failures model in the development literature is that of the "big push," pioneered by Paul Rosenstein-Rodan, who first raised some of the basic coordination issues.[11] He pointed out several problems associated with initiating industrialization in a subsistence economy, of the type introduced in Chapter 1. The problem is easiest to perceive if we start with the simplifying assumption that the economy is not able to export. In this case, the question becomes one of who will buy the goods produced by the first firm to industrialize. Starting from a subsistence economy, no workers have the money to buy the new goods. The first factory can sell some of its goods to its own workers, but no one spends all of one's income on a single good. Each time an entrepreneur opens a factory, the workers spend some of their wages on other products. So the profitability of one factory depends on whether another one opens, which in turn depends on its own potential profitability, and that in turn depends on the profitability of still other factories. Such circular causation should now be a familiar pattern of a coordination failure problem. Moreover, the first factory has to train its workers, who are accustomed to a subsistence way of life. The cost of training puts a limit on how high a wage the factory can pay and still remain profitable. But once the first firm trains its workers, other entrepreneurs, not having to recoup training costs, can offer a slightly higher wage to attract the trained workers to their own new factories. However, the first entrepreneur, anticipating this likelihood, does not pay for training in the first place. No one is trained, and industrialization never gets under way.

The big push is a model of how the presence of market failures can lead to a need for a concerted economy-wide and probably public-policy-led effort to get the long process of economic development under way or to accelerate it. Put differently, coordination failure problems work against successful industrialization, a counterweight to the push for development. A big push may not always be needed, but it is helpful to find ways to characterize cases in which it will be.

Rosenstein-Rodan's arguments became a major part of the way development economists thought about development problems in the 1950s and 1960s, and they have continued to be taught in development courses. But while some of the basic intuition has thus been around for decades, the approach received a huge boost following the 1989 publication of a technical paper by Kevin Murphy, Andrei Shleifer, and Robert Vishny, which for the first time demonstrated the formal logic of this approach more clearly.[12] Its recent appeal is also due in part to its perceived value in explaining the success of the East Asian miracle economies, notably that of South Korea. One value of using a formal model is to get a clearer sense of when the need for coordination is more likely to present a serious problem. The approach of these authors was in turn simplified and popularized by Paul Krugman in his 1995 monograph, *Development, Geography, and Economic Theory*, and became the classic model of the new development theories of coordination failure of the 1990s.[13]

The Big Push: A Graphical Model

Assumptions   In any model (indeed, in any careful thinking), we need to make some assumptions, sometimes seemingly large assumptions, to make any progress in our understanding. The analysis of the big push is no exception to this rule. The assumptions we use for the big push analysis here can be relaxed somewhat, though at the expense of requiring more mathematical technique, but it should be noted that we cannot relax our assumptions as much as we are accustomed to doing in simpler microeconomic problems, such as those that assume perfect competition. Here we cannot meaningfully assume perfect competition in the modern sector, where increasing returns to scale and hence natural monopoly, or at least monopolistic competition, prevail. To paraphrase Paul Krugman, if we think development has something significant to do with increasing returns to scale, then we will have to sacrifice some generality to address it. We will make six types of assumptions.

1. *Factors.* We assume that there is only one factor of production—labor. It has a fixed total supply, L.

2. *Factor payments.* The labor market has two sectors. We assume that workers in the traditional sector receive a wage of 1 (or normalized to 1, treating the wage as the numeraire; that is, if the wage is 19 pesos per day, we simply call this amount of money "1" to facilitate analysis using the geometry in Figure 4.2). Workers in the modern sector receive a wage $W > 1$ (that is, some wage that is greater than 1).

   As a stylized fact, this wage differential is found in every developing country, even if it needs some explanation (see Chapter 7). The underlying reason for this differential *may be* a compensation for disutility of modern factory types of work. If so, in equilibrium, workers would receive no net utility benefits from switching sectors during industrialization; but if economic profits are generated, this will represent a Pareto improvement (in this case because investors are better off and no one is worse off), and average income would rise (there can also be income redistribution so that everyone may be made better off, not just no one worse off). Moreover, if there is surplus labor in the economy or if modern wages are higher than opportunity costs of labor for some other reason,[14] the social benefits of industrialization are all the greater.[15] Finally, note that we are examining one example of a model in which a driving force for an underdevelopment trap is the relatively high wages that have to be paid in the modern sector. We do this because it is an approach that is easy to characterize graphically and that has received a lot of attention. As will be described later, however, high modern wages is only one circumstance in which a coordination problem may exist. In fact, we will see that there may be coordination failure problems even if modern-sector wages are no higher than those in the traditional sector.

3. *Technology.* We assume that there are N types of products, where N is a large number.[16] For each product in the traditional sector, one worker produces one unit of output (this is a less stringent assumption than it

FIGURE 4.2 The Big Push

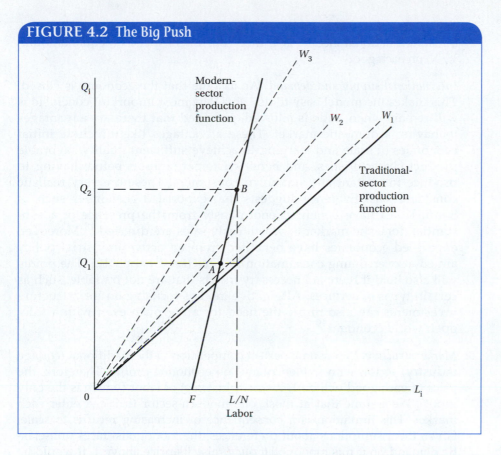

appears because again we have a certain freedom in choosing our unit of measurement; if a worker produces three pairs of shoes per day, we call this quantity one unit). This is a very simple example of constant-returns-to-scale production. In the modern sector, there are increasing returns to scale. We want to introduce increasing returns in a very simple way. Assume that no product can be produced unless a minimum of, say, F workers are employed. This is a fixed cost. Because we are keeping things simple to facilitate analysis of the core issues, we have not put capital explicitly in the model; thus the only way to introduce a fixed cost is to require a minimum number of workers. After that, there is a linear production function in which workers are more productive than those in the traditional sector. Thus labor requirements for producing any product in the modern sector take the form $L = F + cQ$, where $c < 1$ is the marginal labor required for an extra unit of output. The trade-off is that modern workers are more productive, but only if a significant cost is paid up front. As this fixed cost is amortized over more units of output, average cost declines, which is the effect of increasing returns to scale. We assume symmetry: The same production function holds for producing any product in the modern sector.

4. *Domestic demand.* We assume that each good receives a constant and equal share of consumption out of national income. The model has only one

period and no assets; thus there is no saving in the conventional sense. As a result, if national income is Y, then consumers spend an equal amount, Y/N, on each good.[17]

5. *International supply and demand.* We assume that the economy is closed. This makes the model easy to develop. The most important conclusions will remain when trade is allowed, provided that there are advantages to having a domestic market. These advantages likely include initial economies of scale and learning to achieve sufficient quality, favorable product characteristics, and better customer support before having to produce for distant and unknown consumers. These are very realistic considerations: Evidence suggests that export-led economies such as South Korea have benefited enormously from the presence of a substantial domestic market to which early sales are directed.[18] Moreover, export-led economies have benefited from an active industrial policy aimed at overcoming coordination failures (see Chapter 12). The points will also hold if there are necessary inputs that are not tradable, such as certain types of services. Alternative models focusing on infrastructure investments can also imply the need for a big push even with a fully open world economy.[19]

6. *Market structure.* We assume perfect competition in the traditional (cottage industry) sector, with free entry and no economic profits. Therefore, the price of each good will be 1, the marginal cost of labor (which is the only input). We assume that at most, one modern-sector firm can enter each market. This limitation is a consequence of increasing returns to scale. Given the assumptions about preferences, the monopolist faces unit-elastic demand, so if this monopolist *could* raise its price above 1, it would be profitable to do so.[20] However, if price is raised above 1, competition from the traditional-sector producers will cause the modern-sector firm to lose all of its business. Therefore, the monopolist will also charge a price of 1 if it decides to enter the market.[21] Because the monopolist charges the same price, it will monopolize this particular market if it enters but will also produce the same quantity that was produced by the traditional producers. Because this firm is the only one using modern techniques and, in producing all other products, workers receive a wage of 1, national income will be essentially the same, so more units of output cannot be sold.[22] We also assume that at the point the monopolist would choose to produce, it is able to produce at least as much output as the traditional producers for that same level of labor; otherwise, it would make no sense to switch out of the traditional techniques.

Conditions for Multiple Equilibria   With these six assumptions, we can characterize cases that will require a big push. To begin, suppose that we have a traditional economy with no modern production in any market. A potential producer with modern technology (i.e., a technology like the one described previously, with fixed costs and increasing returns) considers whether it is profitable to enter the market. Given the size of the fixed cost, the answer depends on two considerations: (1) how much more efficient the modern sector is than the traditional sector and (2) how much higher wages are in the modern sector than in the traditional sector.

In Figure 4.2, production functions are represented for the two types of firms for any industry.[23] The traditional producers use a linear technique with slope 1, with each worker producing one unit of output. The modern firm requires F workers before it can produce anything, but after that, it has a linear technique with slope $1/c > 1$. Price is 1, so revenues PQ can be read off the Q axis. For the traditional firm, the wage bill line lies coincident with the production line (both start at the origin and have a slope of 1). For the modern firm, the wage bill line has slope $W > 1$. At point A, we see the output that the modern firm will produce if it enters, provided there are traditional firms operating in the rest of the economy. Whether the modern firm enters depends, of course, on whether it is profitable to do so.

Using Figure 4.2, first consider a wage bill line like W_1 passing below point A. With this relatively low modern wage, revenues exceed costs, and the modern firm will pay the fixed cost F and enter the market. In general, this outcome is more likely if the firm has lower fixed costs or lower marginal labor requirements as well as if it pays a lower wage. By assumption, production functions are the same for each good, so if a modern firm finds it profitable to produce one good, the same incentives will be present for producing all goods, and the whole economy will industrialize through market forces alone; demand is now high enough that we end up at point B for each product. This shows that a coordination failure need not always happen: It depends on the technology and prices (including wages) prevailing in the economy.

If a wage bill line like W_2 holds, passing between points A and B, the firm would not enter if it were the only modern firm to do so in the economy because it would incur losses. But if modern firms enter in each of the markets, then wages are increased to the modern wage in all markets, and income expands. We may assume that price remains 1 after industrialization. Note that the traditional technique still exists and would be profitable with a price higher than 1. So to prevent traditional firms from entering, modern firms cannot raise prices above 1.[24] The modern firm can now sell all of its expanded output (at point B), produced by using all of its available labor allocation (L/N), because it has sufficient demand from workers and entrepreneurs in the other industrializing product sectors. As can be seen in Figure 4.2, with prevailing wage W_2, point B is profitable after industrialization because it lies above the W_2 line. Workers are also at least as well off as when they worked in the traditional sector because they can afford to purchase an additional quantity of goods in proportion to their increased wage,[25] and they have changed sectors (from traditional to modern) voluntarily. All of the output is purchased because all of national income is spent on output; national income is equal to wages plus profits, the value of which is output of each product times the number of products N.[26]

Thus, with a prevailing wage like W_2, there are two equilibria: one in which producers with modern techniques enter in all markets, and profits, wages, and output are higher than before; and one in which no modern producer enters, and wages and output remain lower. The equilibrium with higher output is unambiguously better, but in general, the market will not get there by itself.

A final possibility is found in a wage bill line like W_3, passing above point B. In this case, even if a modern producer entered in all product sectors, all of these firms would still lose money, so again the traditional technique would continue to be used. In general, whenever the wage bill line passes below point A, the market will lead the economy to modernize, and whenever it passes above A, it will not. The steeper (i.e., more efficient) the modern-sector production technique or the lower the fixed costs, the more likely it is that the wage bill will pass below the corresponding point A. If the line passes above B, it makes no sense to industrialize. But if the wage line passes between points A and B, it is efficient to industrialize, but the market will not achieve this on its own. Be sure to note that these are three different wages that might exist, depending on conditions in a particular economy at one point in time, not three wages that occur successively.

Again, the problematic cases occur when the wage bill line passes between A and B, thus creating two equilibria: one in which there is industrialization and the society is better off (point B) and one without industrialization (point A). However, the market will not get us from A to B because of a coordination failure.[27] In this case, there is a role for policy in starting economic development. There is no easy test to determine where a traditional economy, such as Mozambique, is located on this continuum. But at least we can begin to understand why development often has not gotten under way, even when technology is available.

Note that in general, it is not necessary for all product sectors to industrialize to get a sufficient push for some to do so. It is only necessary that a sufficient number industrialize in order to generate enough national income (through the higher industrial wage and positive profits from the industrialized product sectors) to make industrialization minimally profitable. Also note that each firm's failure to take into account the impact of its investments on demand for other firms' goods represents a very small distortion by itself. But when added up across all of the product sectors, the resulting distortion—namely, the failure to industrialize at all—is very large indeed.

We could also have cases of semi-industrialization, in which benefits or costs accrue in different amounts to different product sectors or in which there are different types of spillovers from firm to firm. For example, this is plausible when the level of required fixed costs declines the more product sectors industrialize, because there are more local examples from which to learn.[28] With this alternative type of externality, no wage premium is necessary for multiple equilibria to be present. In this case, if there are clusters of two or more firms that have large effects on each other's fixed costs, F, but not on firms outside of the cluster, the result can be an equilibrium in which only the industries in this cluster change to modern techniques. Thus, in this circumstance, we could have three or more equilibria; we could also have enclave economies, in which a modern sector exists side by side with traditional cottage industries in other product sectors.[29]

Notice that this model has not assumed the existence of any type of **technological externality**, in which the presence of one advanced firm can, through "learning by watching" other firms' production methods or some similar effect, generate spillovers to other firms that can raise their productivity as well as lower their costs. This is another type of market failure that can

Technological externality A positive or negative spillover effect on a firm's production function through some means other than market exchange.

also lead to inefficiently low investment; we considered one such possibility when we examined the Romer endogenous growth model in Appendix 3.3.

Other Cases in Which a Big Push May Be Necessary

The need for a big push can result from four conditions beyond those described previously.

1. *Intertemporal effects.* Even if the industrial wage rate is 1 (i.e., the same as the traditional-sector wage), multiple equilibria can occur if investment must be undertaken in the current period to get a more efficient production process in the next period.[30] Investment in the first period depresses aggregate demand in the first period but increases it in the second (or later) period. But investment will be undertaken only if it is profitable, that is, if demand is expected to be high enough in the second period, and this may require that many product sectors invest simultaneously. Once again, however, the market does not ensure that industrialization will occur, even when it is (Pareto-)preferred, because of pecuniary externalities. Again the source of the multiple equilibria is that one firm's profits do not capture its external contribution to overall demand for modern-sector products because it also raises wage income in the future periods when other entering modern firms will be seeking to sell their own products. When there is a case for a big push, industrialization makes the society better off (is Pareto-preferred) because first-period income is decreased only by the fixed cost, but second-period income is sufficiently increased by both the wage and profits in other product sectors to more than offset this.[31] Note once again that a part of the profits can, in principle, also be subject to income redistribution so that everyone may be made better off rather than just some people made better off and no one made worse off.

2. *Urbanization effects.* If some of the traditional cottage industry is rural and the increasing-returns-to-scale manufacturing is urban, urban dwellers' demand may be more concentrated in manufactured goods (e.g., foods must be processed to prevent spoilage due to the time needed for transportation and distribution). If this is the case, one needs a big push to urbanization to achieve industrialization.[32]

3. *Infrastructure effects.* By using infrastructure, such as a railroad or a port, an investing modern firm helps defray the large fixed costs of that infrastructure. The existence of the infrastructure helps investing firms lower their own costs. But investing firms thereby contribute indirectly to lowering the costs of other firms (by lowering the average cost of infrastructure use). Infrastructure, such as roads, railroads, and ports, is not tradable; by definition, it is located in a particular region. And openness to foreign investment cannot always solve the problem because investors do not know whether firms will develop to make use of the infrastructure.[33] The critical point is that when one product sector industrializes, it increases the size of the market for the use of infrastructure services that would be used by other product sectors and so makes the provision of these services more profitable. But it is also possible that efficient industrialization

may not take place, even if the infrastructure is built, if other coordination problems are present.

4. *Training effects.* There is underinvestment in training facilities because entrepreneurs know that the workers they train may be enticed away with higher wages offered by rival firms that do not have to pay these training costs. There is also too little demand by workers for training because they do not know what skills to acquire. (In addition to not knowing whether firms will make investments requiring these skills, people are not born with perfect information about their comparative advantage; basic education helps workers discover it.) This is part of the economic case for mandatory public education. Note that in this case, openness to trade cannot resolve the coordination failure unless there is free mobility of labor across borders, which has yet to develop perfectly even within the European Union, where there are few formal barriers to such mobility, and is far from emerging for any developing country. In any case, relying on expatriate skilled workers is hardly an adequate solution to a country's own underdevelopment. Actually, infrastructure and trained workers are subsets of a general case of jointly used intermediate goods. Another example is joint research facilities for small firms in an "industrial district" (see Chapter 7).

Why the Problem Cannot Be Solved by a Super-Entrepreneur

Some readers may wonder, why can't one agent solve the coordination failure problems by capturing all the rent? In other words, why not have a super-entrepreneur who enters into all of the markets that need to be coordinated and receives the profits from all of them? For some types of coordination failures, this solution is ruled out in advance. For example, regarding education and skill development, there is a legal constraint on bonded labor. But in terms of our industrialization problem, why can't one agent become a super-entrepreneur in each of the N markets simultaneously? There are at least four significant theoretical answers and one decisive empirical answer.

First, there may be capital market failures. How could one agent assemble all the capital needed to play the super-entrepreneur role? Even if this were logistically imaginable, how would lenders have confidence in their investments? In particular, how could a penalty for default be imposed?

Agency costs   Costs of monitoring managers and other employees and of designing and implementing schemes to ensure compliance or provide incentives to follow the wishes of the employer.

Second, there may be costs of monitoring managers and other agents and designing and implementing schemes to ensure compliance or provide incentives to follow the wishes of the employer; these are often referred to as **agency costs**. Monitoring is too expensive once the scale of a firm gets too large. Even if the plan is to sell off the industries, these industries must be developed simultaneously. The super-entrepreneur is likely to know more about the firms than the potential buyers do. In other words, if the firm is so profitable, why would its owners be selling? Thus, potential purchasers of the industries face a problem of **asymmetric information**, often known as the "lemons problem."[34]

Asymmetric information   A situation in which one party to a potential transaction (often a buyer, seller, lender, or borrower) has more information than another party.

Third, there may be communication failures. Suppose someone says to you, "I am coordinating investments, so work with me." Should you do so?

How do you know this person will eventually be the coordinator? There is a potentially huge profit to be made by assuming the super-entrepreneur role, so many agents might wish to play it. If many try to claim the role, with which one should you coordinate? Even if each agent personally encounters only one pretender to the super-entrepreneur role, that pretender may still not be the right one (i.e., the coordinator with whom you can make money).

Fourth, there are limits to knowledge. Even if we stipulate that the economy as a whole has access to modern technological ideas, this does not mean that one individual can gain sufficient knowledge to industrialize (or even gain enough knowledge about whom to hire to industrialize).

Finally, there is the empirical reason that no private agent has been observed playing the role of super-entrepreneur. Whether because of problems of monitoring, knowledge, capital markets, or other diseconomies of scope, "solving" problems with ever-larger firms clearly provides no answer. For example, it is rare enough to find a firm producing steel and even a significant fraction of the products using steel, let alone one firm owning all the industries backwardly linked from steel or forwardly linked from steel-using industries to industries further down the production chain. Nor can the problem be solved by direct government production (at least without unacceptable cost), as the extreme case of the former Soviet Union demonstrates. Rather, public coordination of actions of private investors is generally needed to solve the problem, a common interpretation of the role of industrial policy in East Asia.

In a Nutshell   Thus we have seen that under some conditions, pecuniary externalities associated with the development process can lead to multiple equilibria, which may create a case for a big push policy. Our main example (the moderate wage premium case) and each of the other examples have as a common feature a process by which an investing (industrializing) firm captures only part of the contribution of its investment to the profits of other investing firms. In these examples, firms adopting increasing-returns-to-scale technologies are having one or more of the following effects: raising total demand, shifting demand toward manufactured goods, redistributing demand toward the (later) periods in which other industrializing firms sell, reducing the fixed costs of later entrants, or helping defray the fixed costs of an essential infrastructure. Each of these has external beneficial effects on other industrializing firms.

4.4 Further Problems of Multiple Equilibria

Inefficient Advantages of Incumbency

The presence of increasing returns in modern industries can also create another kind of bad equilibrium. Once a modern firm has entered, it has an advantage over any rivals because its large output gives it low average costs. So if an even better modern technology becomes available to a potential rival, it may not be easy for the new technology to supplant the old. Even though the new technique has a lower per-unit cost for any given level of output, the firm with the old technique has an advantage because its large output lets it produce at a lower per-unit cost than that of the new technique, which starts out with a small customer base and a large fixed cost. As a result, firms may need access to significant amounts of capital to cover losses while they build their customer base. If capital markets do not work well, as they often do not in developing countries (see Chapter 15), the economy may be stuck with backward, less cost-effective industries.[35]

Behavior and Norms

Movement to a better equilibrium is especially difficult when it involves many individuals changing their behavior from one of rent seeking or corruption to honesty and the value of building a reputation to reap the gains from cooperation (e.g., with business partners). Your choice of partner may determine much. If you naively cooperate with an opportunistic, predator type, you may be worse off than by going it alone. Only by cooperating with other good-willed cooperators may you reach the best outcome. Moreover, past experience may lead people to expect opportunistic behavior at least among certain groups of potential business partners, which in turn raises the incentives for the potential partners to actually act that way. If there is nothing to be gained and something to be lost by being honest, the incentives lie in being dishonest. On the other hand, in some settings, individuals take it on themselves to enforce norms rather than leaving this task to government. If many people work to enforce a norm such as honesty, each individual's enforcement burden is relatively low. You can have equilibria where most people resist corruption, and so corruption is rare; and you can have equilibria where few resist corruption, and corruption is common.

We cannot rely on good organizations to prevail in competition if the rules of the game tend to reward the bad organizations. Rather, the critical importance of policies for developing or reforming institutions is highlighted, such as reform of the framework of property rights, antitrust, clean government rules, and other laws, regulations, and industry association norms that set the rules of the game for economic life. Once the new behavior assumes the status of a norm, it is much easier to maintain. Some neoclassical theorists have at times implied that good institutions would be developed through the market mechanism. Bad institutions would be outcompeted by good institutions. But reform of institutions aiding and abetting coordination failure—for example, by permitting or encouraging corruption—is itself subject to coordination failure.

Once cooperative relationships (e.g., in business) become a norm, more people may adopt cooperative behavior. But norms of all kinds are subject to inertia. Although norms may have been adaptive when they originated, they are hard to change, even when they become dysfunctional. An example is a value such as that to be a good citizen (or a good Hindu, Muslim, Christian, animist, etc.) one must have a large number of children. This value may have been adaptive at a premodern stage, but today it inhibits development. Another example may be to distrust anyone who is not a member of your family. This may be helpful in a tribal context, and caution is always advisable, but this extreme injunction hardly encourages the formation of successful business partnerships in a modern economy.

Linkages

There are several ways to undertake a big push, encouraging the simultaneous expansion of the modern sector in many industries. One strategy for solving coordination problems is to focus government policy on encouraging the development of industries with key backward or forward **linkages**. This could mean subsidies or quid pro quos for domestic industries to enter these key industries, as was done in South Korea; it could mean incentives for multinational firms to enter in key industries and provide advanced training, a policy followed in Singapore; or it could mean establishing a few key public enterprises to act as pioneers in an industry (that could later be sold), as was done in South Korea and Taiwan.[36] The theory of linkages stresses that when certain industries are developed first, their interconnections or linkages with other industries will induce or at least facilitate the development of new industries. Backward linkages raise demand for an activity, while forward linkages lower the costs of using an industry's output; both may involve interactions between the size of the market and increasing returns to scale and hence pecuniary externalities. In other words, linkages are especially significant for industrialization strategy when one or more of the industries involved have increasing returns to scale, of which a larger market may take advantage. For example, when the manufacture of power looms expands, enabling a reduction in the price of power looms, there are forward linkage effects due to increased output of woven cloth made by the power looms. When increased demand for chemicals used in textile manufacture causes expansion of the chemical industry that enables it to produce at a larger scale and hence lower cost, a backward linkage can occur. Both examples illustrate a pecuniary externality effect (a lowering of cost) when there are increasing returns in the linked industry.

The linkage approach targets investment in a key linkage as a start to overcoming a coordination failure and generating positive feedback. Such a policy would select industries with a larger number of links to other industries and greater strength of those links. In choosing among industries with several strong links (and passing a cost-benefit test), one policy would generally select industries that have a smaller likelihood of private investment, because that is where the most intransigent bottlenecks are most likely to be found. If an investment is profitable, it is more likely that an entrepreneur will come along to fill that niche.[37] This observation provides a reason to interpret with some caution studies that show state-owned enterprises to be less efficient than private ones. If government systematically enters vital but less profitable industries because of their beneficial effects on development, it is unreasonable to hold these enterprises to the same profit standards as those of the private firms. This is certainly not to say that state-owned enterprises are generally as efficient as privately owned ones; in fact, there is much evidence to the contrary.[38] We can say, however, that a blanket statement, such as has often been made in publications from agencies such as the World Bank, that government should never be in the business of production, even temporarily or in any industry, is sometimes unreasonable in the light of linkages and other strategic complementarities that a developing economy needs to address.

Linkages Connections between firms based on sales. A backward linkage is one in which a firm buys a good from another firm to use as an input; a forward linkage is one in which a firm sells to another firm. Such linkages are especially significant for industrialization strategy when one or more of the industries (product areas) involved have increasing returns to scale that a larger market takes advantage of.

Inequality, Multiple Equilibria, and Growth

Other important work being done on growth and multiple equilibria addresses the impact of inequality on growth. The traditional view has been that some inequality may enhance growth because the savings of the rich are higher than those of the poor. If at least some savings to be mobilized for investment purposes must come from within a country, then according to this view, too high a degree of equality could compromise growth. However, the poor save at much higher rates than previously believed, when savings are properly measured to include expenditures on health, children's education, and improvements on a home.

Moreover, where inequality is great, the poor may not be able to obtain loans because they lack collateral; indeed, one definition of what it means to be poor is to be entirely or mostly lacking in a source of collateral. Poor persons unable to get a loan to start a business due to such capital market imperfections may get stuck in subsistence or wage employment, although they (and perhaps potential employees) could do much better if they had access to financing or if there were a more even distribution of income. For example, Abhijit Banerjee and Andrew Newman show that multiple equilibria, including equilibria involving outcomes with virtually all citizens enjoying high incomes and outcomes with predominantly low-income people, can exist when imperfect credit markets provide too few people with the opportunity to become entrepreneurs.[39]

Similarly, if the poor lack access to credit, they may not be able to obtain loans to finance otherwise very productive schooling. If the poor are unable to bequeath much to their next generation, families can be trapped in poverty from generation to generation; however, if schooling could somehow be achieved, they could escape from this **poverty trap**. It is best to keep in mind a rather expansive definition of what is meant by a *transfer* from parents to be used for human capital accumulation by their children. It is more than tuition and more than forgone wages or work on the farm to help the family because it goes well beyond the cost of formal schooling and may be thought of as the building of a whole array of "capabilities" (see Chapter 1) that one acquires almost as a simple by-product of growing up in an affluent, educated family.

In a formal model of this problem, Oded Galor and Joseph Zeira examined the implications of missing credit markets for growth and the distribution of both income and human capital. They developed an endogenous growth model that points up the importance of both human capital and distribution, and of the interaction between the two, for economic growth and development as well as for more short-term macroeconomic adjustments. Their analysis contains two critical assumptions: (1) imperfect capital markets, which, as will be described in detail in Chapter 15, is a typical condition of these markets, and (2) indivisibilities in human capital investment, which means that markets treat investment in human capital as coming in discrete packages, such as a year of school, if not larger blocks, such as primary, secondary, and tertiary education. The second assumption does not seem unreasonable, both because of the nature of learning and because of the screening nature of markets for human capital. A threshold level of knowledge is necessary before an employer will be willing to pay for it. Further, because education acts as a screen for inherent ability, as will be discussed in Chapter 8, we have the well-known "sheepskin effect"; that is, there is a very large jump in the return

Poverty trap A bad equilibrium for a family, community, or nation, involving a vicious circle in which poverty and underdevelopment lead to more poverty and underdevelopment, often from one generation to the next.

to human capital when an individual passes primary school and again when the person obtains a secondary school diploma and so on. This is not because the last course taken conveys so much more knowledge than the ones preceding it but because the degree itself is what enables the individual to prove that an entire regimen of requirements has been met. Note that indivisibilities in amounts of investment imply a region of increasing returns to scale, as in the fixed costs of the big push model. Once again, increasing returns play a key role in generating multiple equilibria.[40] Empirically, many studies have found a negative impact of inequality on growth, especially for the period after 1980.[41]

4.5 Michael Kremer's O-Ring Theory of Economic Development

Another innovative and influential model that provides important insights into low-level equilibrium traps was provided by Michael Kremer.[42] The notion is that modern production (especially in contrast to traditional crafts production) requires that many activities be done well together in order for any of them to amount to a high value. This is a form of strong complementarity and is a natural way of thinking about specialization and the division of labor, which along with economies of scale is another hallmark of developed economies in general and industrial production in particular. The name for Kremer's model is taken from the 1986 *Challenger* disaster, in which the failure of one small, inexpensive part caused the space shuttle to explode. The O-ring theory is interesting in part because it explains not only the existence of poverty traps but also the reasons that countries caught in such traps may have such exceptionally low incomes compared with high-income countries.

The O-Ring Model

The key feature of the O-ring model is the way it models production with strong complementarities among inputs. We start by thinking of the model as describing what is going on inside a firm, but as we will see, this model also provides valuable insights into the impact of complementarities across firms or industrial (product) sectors of the economy.

Suppose that a production process is broken down into n tasks. There are many ways of carrying out these tasks, which for simplicity we order strictly by level of skill, q, required, where $0 \leq q \leq 1$. The higher the skill is, the higher the probability that the task will be "successfully completed" (which may mean, for example, that the part created in this task will not fail). Kremer's concept of q is quite flexible. Other interpretations may include a quality index for characteristics of the good: Consumers would be willing to pay more for higher-quality characteristics. For example, suppose that $q = 0.95$. Among other interpretations, this can mean (1) that there is a 95% chance that the task is completed perfectly, so the product keeps maximum value, and a 5% chance that it is completed so poorly that it has no value; (2) that the task is always completed well enough that it keeps 95% of its maximum value; or (3) that the product has a 50% chance of having full value and a 50% chance of an error reducing the value of the product to 90%. For simplicity, assume that the probability of mistakes by different workers is strictly independent. The production function assumed is a simple one: Output is given by multiplying the q values of each of the n tasks together, in turn multiplied by a term, say, B, that depends on the characteristics of the firm and is generally larger with a larger number of tasks. Suppose also that each firm hires only two workers. Then the **O-ring production function** looks like this:[43]

$$BF(q_i q_j) = q_i q_j \qquad (4.1)$$

That is, to make things simple, for this exposition we let the multiplier, B, equal 1. In addition to the form of the production function, we make three other significant types of simplifying assumptions: (1) Firms are risk-neutral, (2) labor markets are competitive, and (3) workers supply labor inelastically (i.e., they work regardless of the wage). If we consider capital markets, we assume that they are competitive as well. For now, we also assume that the economy is closed.

One of the most prominent features of this type of production function is what is termed *positive assortative matching*. This means that workers with high skills will work together and workers with low skills will work together. When we use the model to compare economies, this type of matching means that high-value products will be concentrated in countries with high-value skills. In this model, everyone will like to work with the more productive workers, because if your efforts are multiplied by those of someone else, as they are in Equation 4.1, you will be more productive when working with a more productive person. In competitive markets, your pay is based on how productive you are. A firm with a higher-productivity worker can more afford to pay a higher wage and has the incentive to bid higher to do so, because the value of output will be higher with two productive workers, say, than with one low- and one high-productivity worker. As a result, there will be a strong tendency for the most productive workers to work together.

This can be seen easily if we imagine a four-person economy. Suppose that this economy has two high-skill q_H workers and two low-skill q_L workers. The four workers can be arranged either as matched skill pairs or unmatched skill pairs. Total output will always be higher under a matching scheme because

$$q_H^2 + q_L^2 > 2 q_H q_L \qquad (4.2)$$

Recall that $(x - y)^2 > 0$ for any x that is not the same as y, so let x stand for q_H and y stand for q_L. Then $x^2 + y^2 > 2xy$, the same as in Equation 4.2. (Or try this by plugging in any values $q_H > q_L$.) This generalizes to larger numbers of workers in the firms and the economy; the result is that workers sort out by skill level.[44]

Because total value is higher when skill matching rather than skill mixing takes place, the firm that starts with high-productivity workers can afford to bid more to get additional high-productivity workers, and it is profitable to do so. Of course, every firm would like to hire the most productive worker, but it would be in that worker's interest to team up with other high-productivity workers. Think of firms being formed while workers try to determine for which firm they want to work. After the high-productivity workers pair off, they are out of the picture. The less productive workers are then stuck with each other. If there are many classes of skill or productivity, first the highest-skill workers

O-ring production function
A production function with strong complementarities among inputs, based on the products (i.e., multiplying) of the input qualities.

get together, then the next highest, and so on, such that skill matching results as a cascading process. For example, a symphony orchestra will be adversely affected as a whole by hiring one single poor performer. So an otherwise excellent orchestra has every incentive to bid the most for an outstanding performer to replace the poor performer. Similarly, the best jazz performers play and record together rather than each leading a group of poorer players. The restaurant with the very best chef also hires mature, highly trained, full-time waiters, while a fast-food restaurant does not hire a famous chef.

This sorting process is perhaps most vividly easy to remember by analogy to Nobel laureate Gary Becker's famous "marriage market" model, which is a somewhat different case[45] but offers some additional intuition. If prospective spouses care only about attractiveness, every man wants to marry the most attractive woman, and every woman wants to marry the most attractive man, so the most attractive man and woman will marry. They are now out of the picture, so next, the second most attractive man and woman marry. This process continues until the least attractive man and woman marry. Of course, beauty is in the eye of the beholder, and most people care about things besides attractiveness in a mate such as kindness, intelligence, wealth, beliefs, interests, commitment, and sense of humor; but the marriage model serves as a memorable analogy. The result in the business world is that some firms and workers, even an entire low-income economy, can fall into a trap of low skill and low productivity, while others escape into higher productivity.

Although this model may seem abstract, a numerical example can show how the firms with high-skill workers can and will pay more to get other high-skill workers or will have more incentive to upgrade skills among existing workers. Suppose that there are six workers; three have $q = 0.4$ and are grouped together in equilibrium, while the other three have $q = 0.8$. Now suppose that the q of one of the workers in the first firm rises from 0.4 to 0.5 (perhaps due to training). Similarly, suppose the q of one worker in the second firm rises from 0.8 to 1.0. In each case, we have a 25% increase in the quality of one worker. As you may expect, a 25% increase in the quality of one worker leads to a 25% increase in output quality. But starting from a higher level of quality, that 25% clearly translates into a much larger point increase: In the example, the first firm goes from $(0.4)(0.4)(0.4) = 0.064$ to $(0.4)(0.4)(0.5) = 0.080$; this is a difference of $0.080 - 0.064$, which is a point change of 0.016; and $0.016/0.064 = 0.25$, which is a 25% increase. For the second firm, we move from $(0.8)(0.8)(0.8) = 0.512$ to $(0.8)(0.8)(1.0) = 0.640$; the change in this case is 0.128, which is again 25%. However, the point value of the increase is much greater—eight times greater—for a doubled point-value investment (0.2 in the second firm versus 0.1 in the first firm). If a firm can increase quality in percentage terms at constant marginal cost or even a not too quickly rising cost, there is a virtuous circle in that the more the firm upgrades overall, the more value it obtains by doing so. Accordingly, *wages will increase at an increasing rate as skill is steadily raised*. As Kremer shows, the O-ring model is consistent with competitive equilibrium.

The O-ring result of positive assortative matching relies on some rather strong assumptions. How important are each of these, and how much can they be relaxed? Two points are crucial: (1) Workers must be sufficiently imperfect substitutes for each other, and (2) we must have sufficient complementarity of tasks. As long as these conditions hold, the basic results will follow.

To see why workers must be imperfect substitutes, suppose they were perfect substitutes. Specifically, suppose there are two skill levels, q_L and $q_H = 2q_L$, so every q_H worker can be replaced by two q_L workers with no other change. Thus q_H workers will be paid twice the amount that q_L workers are paid. We can draw no predictions about what combination of worker skill levels a firm—or an economy—will use, so we can learn nothing about low-skill-level equilibrium traps. In fact, there is empirical evidence for imperfect substitutability across worker types in firms.

To see why we must have complementarity of tasks, suppose that there were two tasks indexed by g and h but with no complementarity between them. To be specific, suppose that our q_H worker is hired for the g task, and a q_L worker is hired for the h task; then

$$F(q_H q_L) = g(q_H) + h(q_L)$$

Here skills are imperfect substitutes for each other, because only one type of worker can be hired for each task (i.e., no two-for-one type of substitution is possible here). However, because tasks are not complementary, the optimal choice of skill for the g task is independent of that of the h task, and again no strategic complementarities are present.[46]

Implications of the O-Ring Theory

The analysis has several important implications:

- Firms tend to employ workers with similar skills for their various tasks.

- Workers performing the same task earn higher wages in a high-skill firm than in a low-skill firm.

- Because wages increase in q at an increasing rate, wages will be more than proportionally higher in developed countries than would be predicted from standard measures of skill.

- If workers can improve their skill level and make such investments, and if it is in their interests to do so, they will consider the level of human capital investments made by other workers as a component of their own decision about how much skill to acquire. Put differently, when those around you have higher average skills, you have a greater *incentive* to acquire more skills. This type of complementarity should by now be a familiar condition in which multiple equilibria can emerge; it parallels issues raised in our analysis of the big push model. Kremer shows that a graph like Figure 4.1 can apply to choices about how much skill to acquire.

- One can get caught in economy-wide, low-production-quality traps. This will occur when there are (quite plausibly) O-ring effects across firms as well as within firms. Because there is an externality at work, there could thus be a case for an industrial policy to encourage quality upgrading, as some East Asian countries have undertaken in the past (see Chapter 12, section 12.6, and its end-of-chapter case study of South Korea). This could be relevant for a country trying to escape the middle-income trap.

- O-ring effects magnify the impact of local production bottlenecks because such bottlenecks have a multiplicative effect on other production.

- Bottlenecks also reduce the incentive for workers to invest in skills by lowering the expected return to these skills.

Following Kremer, consider a simple illustration of these bottleneck effects. Suppose that n tasks are required to produce a good. Let q be the standard skill level of these n tasks. But now let the actual skill level of two workers be cut in half in all firms. With an O-ring production function, output would fall by 75% (the result of cutting output in half once and then again). But then the marginal product of quality also falls by 75% for all the remaining $n - 2$ tasks, and thus so does the incentive to invest in increasing skill. The strong assumption of our simple O-ring production function may overstate the case, but the point that strategic complementarities can cause low-skill equilibria remains.

As workers reduce their planned skill investments, this further reduces the level of skill in the economy and thereby lowers further the incentive to invest in skill. To some extent, such bottlenecks could be ameliorated by international trade and investment, because foreign inputs and investors provide an alternative source of inputs from outside the bottlenecked economy. One explanation of why economies that have cut themselves off from the international economy, such as India or China before the 1980s, have not fared as well as those that are more integrated, such as South Korea, could well be their failure to take advantage of foreign inputs or investments; the O-ring analysis helps explain why the impact could be so great. Trade cannot solve all problems of industrialization, but the O-ring model helps explain why trade can play a key role as a part of an industrialization strategy.

The model also has implications for the choice of technology. When skill is scarce, a firm is less likely to choose a technique with higher value but complicated production technology with many tasks, because the costs of doing any one of those tasks poorly are magnified. In this way, the value of production is increasing in the complexity of the product, assuming that the product is completed successfully. Given positive assortative matching, firms producing products or using technologies that must be deployed at large scale or many steps will be induced to employ high-quality employees. Mistakes are costly to firms with large numbers of workers and production steps; therefore, such firms place exceptional value on high-quality, skilled workers who are unlikely to make mistakes.[47] This indicates one reason why rich countries with high-skill workers tend to have larger firms and specialize in more complex products; it also helps explain why firm size and wages are positively correlated within and across countries.

Finally, under some additional assumptions, the model can also help explain the international brain drain. It is often observed that when a worker of any given skill moves from a developing to a developed country, he or she immediately receives a higher wage for using those same skills. A version of the O-ring model is one way of explaining this.

Thus Kremer's O-ring model points out many of the implications of strong complementarities for economic development and the distribution of income across countries. As Kremer concludes, "If strategic complementarity is sufficiently strong, microeconomically identical nations or groups within nations could settle into equilibria with different levels of human capital."[48]

4.6 Economic Development as Self-Discovery

In simple models with perfect information, it is assumed that firms, and developing economies as a whole, already know their comparative advantage. But individuals must discover their own comparative advantage in labor markets; for example, no one is born knowing they are well suited to become an economist or international development specialist. Somewhat analogously, nations must learn what activities are most advantageous to specialize in. As Ricardo Hausmann and Dani Rodrik show, this is a complex task—and one prone to market failure.[49] It is not enough to tell a developing nation to specialize in "labor-intensive products," because even if this were always true, there are a vast number of such products in the world economy of today, and underlying costs of production of specific products can differ greatly from country to country. So it is socially valuable to discover that the true direct and indirect domestic costs of producing a particular product or service in a given country are low or can be brought down to a low level. It is valuable in part because once an activity is shown to be profitable, it can usually be imitated, at least after some lag, spawning a new domestic industry. An example is the ready-made garment industry in Bangladesh, which spread from the first pioneers as dozens of entrepreneurs entered the market. But as markets are eventually open to competing firms, they will take away potential profits from the original innovator. And since, due to this **information externality**, innovators do not reap the full returns generated by their search for profitable activities, there will be too little searching for the nation's comparative advantage—too much time carrying on with business as usual and too little time devoted to "self-discovery." The term *self-discovery* somewhat whimsically expresses the assumption that the products in question have already been discovered by someone else (either long ago, or recently in a developed economy); what remains to be discovered is which of these products a local economy is relatively good at making.

Hausmann and Rodrik also point out another market failure: There can be too much diversification after the point where the nation discovers its most advantageous products to specialize in. This is because there may be an extended period in which entry into the new activity is limited. Hausmann and Rodrik conclude that in the face of these market failures, government policy should counteract the distortions by encouraging broad investments in the modern sector in the discovery phase. In fact, they also argue that policy should in some cases work to rationalize production afterward, encouraging movement out of higher-cost activities and into the lower-cost activities, paring down industries to the ones with the most potential for the economy. The authors draw parallels with some of the successful export and industrial policy experiences of East Asia, a topic to which we will return in Chapter 12.

The authors note three "building blocks" of their theory: There is uncertainty about what products a country can produce efficiently; there is a need for local adaptation of imported technology so that it cannot be used productively "off the shelf"; and once these two obstacles have been overcome, imitation is often rapid (reducing the profitability of pioneers). They present a number of case examples that show the reasonableness of each of these assumptions

Information externality   The spillover of information—such as knowledge of a production process—from one agent to another, without intermediation of a market transaction; reflects the public good characteristic of information (and susceptibility to free riding)—it is neither fully excludable from other uses, nor nonrival (one agent's use of information does not prevent others from using it).

in practice, such as the unexpected emergence of the information technology industry in India and the surprising differences in the exports from various countries with similar apparent comparative advantages, such as Bangladesh (hats but not bedsheets) and Pakistan (bedsheets but not hats); the history of local adaptations of various types of Western technology in East Asia (such as shipbuilding in South Korea); and the rapid diffusion of new products and techniques in the local economy (often facilitated by the movement of personnel across firms), as seen in the growth of the cut-flower export industry in Colombia.

4.7 The Hausmann-Rodrik-Velasco Growth Diagnostics Framework

Encouraging efficient investment and widespread entrepreneurship plays a prominent role in accelerating growth and promoting development more broadly. But the once popular idea of finding a "one size fits all" policy for economic development is now generally recognized as a myth. Different countries face different binding constraints on achieving faster rates of growth and economic development. A key mission for economic development specialists is to help determine the nature of the constraints for each country. Ricardo Hausmann, Dani Rodrik, and Andrés Velasco (HRV) propose a **growth diagnostics** decision tree framework for zeroing in on a country's most binding constraints on economic growth. HRV explain that targeting the most binding constraint has important advantages over other approaches to policy selection.[50]

Growth diagnostics A decision tree framework for identifying a country's most binding constraints on economic growth.

If a developing nation experiences a relatively low level of private investment and entrepreneurship, what steps should it take? The basic decision tree for addressing this question is seen in Figure 4.3, with arrows leading to the ten bottom boxes (that is, the boxes from which no arrows extend further). At the first stage of the tree, the analyst seeks to divide countries between those for which the main problem is a low underlying rate of return and those for which the problem is an abnormally high cost of finance. Let us consider the former case first, following the left arrow pointing to *Low return to economic activity*.

Low returns to investors may be due to the fact that there are intrinsically low underlying **social returns** to economic activities. Alternatively, low returns may be caused by what is termed *low private appropriability*, meaning limited ability of investors to reap an adequate share of the rewards of their otherwise profitable investments. Considering these cases in turn, *low social returns* may be caused by one of three factors.

Social returns The profitability of an investment in which both costs and benefits are accounted for from the perspective of the society as a whole.

First, as noted in Chapter 2, *poor geography* such as tropical pests, mountains, and other physical barriers, distance to world markets, and landlocked status (which may render port access politically dubious or economically costly) may limit the ability of a low-income country to initiate and sustain economic development, especially when other compounding factors are present. When these constraints are most binding, development policy must initially focus on strategies for overcoming them. Second, *low human capital*—skills and education as well as health of workers—are complementary with other factors in production, affecting the returns to economic activity. For

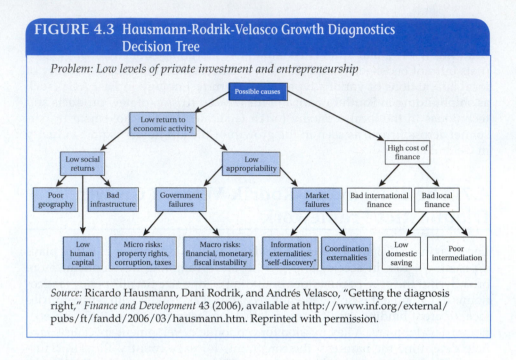

FIGURE 4.3 Hausmann-Rodrik-Velasco Growth Diagnostics Decision Tree

Problem: Low levels of private investment and entrepreneurship

Source: Ricardo Hausmann, Dani Rodrik, and Andrés Velasco, "Getting the diagnosis right," *Finance and Development* 43 (2006), available at http://www.inf.org/external/pubs/ft/fandd/2006/03/hausmann.htm. Reprinted with permission.

example, if economic returns are most affected by lack of literacy and numeracy, this becomes a development policy priority. (The importance of health and education was also stressed in Chapter 2, and this will be examined in depth in Chapter 8.) Third, every developing nation must provide the vital infrastructure needed to achieve and sustain a modern economy, beginning with basic physical structures such as roads, bridges, railroads, ports, telecommunications, and other utilities. With *bad infrastructure*, otherwise high-return economic activities may prove unprofitable. In some countries, inadequate and imbalanced infrastructure is the main factor preventing an acceleration of growth, and in such cases, policies focusing on providing it would boost investment and growth the most.

But the problem may lie not with the underlying social return to economic activities but with *low appropriability*, meaning that investors cannot reap an adequate share of returns to investment. We get to low appropriability from the right arrow emanating from Low return to economic activity. In turn, appropriability problems can be due to either *government failures* or *market failures*. In the HRV diagram, government failures are divided between *micro risks* and *macro risks*. Micro risks address fundamental institutional weaknesses such as inadequacy of property rights, government corruption, and excessively high effective taxation. That is, the return to economic activity may be high enough, but elites rather than investors may capture a large fraction of the returns and make investments unattractive. Despite the difficulty of effectively reforming institutions when reform threatens the interests of elites (see Chapter 2), such reform must become the development priority when micro risks are binding. As the case study of China at the end of this chapter demonstrates, reform can sometimes be accomplished in stages through transitional institutions. Appropriability may also be limited by macro risks—the failure of government to provide financial, monetary, and fiscal stability.

The fundamental problem may also be large-scale market failures of the type stressed in this chapter. These may include the *self-discovery* problems pointed up by Hausmann and Rodrik and reviewed in section 4.6. They may also take the form of *coordination externalities*, such as seen in the big push model of underdevelopment, examined in section 4.3. Other types of market failure and government failure are examined in Chapter 11.

In yet other cases, the main problem may not be underlying low rates of return but rather an abnormally *high cost of finance*. The possibilities are outlined following the right arrow from the top box in Figure 4.3 to *High cost of finance*. Here the problem may be *bad international finance*—inadequate access to foreign sources of capital or problems with debt, examined in Chapter 13; or the problem may reside in *bad local finance*, due either to low availability of loanable funds through domestic financial markets, traced to low *domestic saving*, or to *poor intermediation* owing to an inadequate or overregulated banking system that is unable or unwilling to channel funds to the economic activities with high returns. These also lead to other policy challenges, examined in Chapter 15.

In sum, one size does not fit all in development policy. Economic development strategies focusing on resource mobilization through foreign assistance and other capital flows, along with increased domestic national saving, can be most effective when domestic returns are both high *and* privately appropriable. In contrast, strategies focusing on market liberalization and opening up the economy can be most effective when social returns are high and the most serious obstacle to private appropriation are government-imposed excessive taxes and restrictions. Finally, strategies focusing on industrial policy (elaborated on in Chapter 12) can be most effective when private returns are low, not because of what a government does (errors of commission), but because of what a government does not do (errors of omission).

HRV illustrate their approach with case studies of El Salvador, Brazil, and the Dominican Republic. They argue that each case exhibits a different "diagnostic signal" of the most binding constraint, as seen in Box 4.3. HRV stress that an approach to development strategy that determines one or two policy priorities on this diagnostic basis will be more effective than pursuing a long laundry list of institutional and governance reforms that may not be targeted toward the most binding constraints.

It is often difficult to observe a binding constraint directly. In practice, growth diagnostics usually involves some economic detective work. To evaluate whether a proposed constraint is binding, a growth diagnostician looks for evidence on its implications. If the constraint is excessive taxation, we can expect to see high movement into the informal sector or underground economy. If the constraint is infrastructure, we can expect to see significant congestion. If the constraint is education, we can expect to see high rates of return to education. In general, the analyst looks for economic behavior consistent with agents trying to get around a constraint.

Growth diagnostics is also subject to some limitations and criticisms. One implicit assumption is that development can be equated with growth, which

BOX 4.3 FINDINGS   Three Country Case Study Applications of Growth Diagnostics

El Salvador

HRV argue that this economy is constrained by a lack of productive ideas. The binding constraint is a lack of innovation and demand for investment to replace the traditional cotton, coffee, and sugar sectors, or low "self-discovery." So the best strategy focus for El Salvador would be to encourage more entrepreneurship and development of new business opportunities.

Brazil

HRV identify the country's binding constraint as lack of sufficient funds to invest despite an abundance of productive ideas. They argued that private returns in Brazil are high, and therefore other flaws (inadequate business environment, a low supply of infrastructure, high taxes, high prices for public services, weak contract enforcement and property rights, and inadequate education) are not as binding in Brazil. So investment is instead constrained by Brazil's inability to mobilize sufficient domestic and foreign savings to finance needed investments at reasonable interest rates. Although Brazil could increase national savings to a degree by reducing government expenditure, this might not be politically feasible. If so, HRV suggest that higher taxes and user fees and lower infrastructure and human capital subsidies might work. "If the country can move to a faster growth path and if waste does not grow with GDP, it may outgrow its burdens and gradually improve its tax and spending system as fiscal resources become more abundant." In subse-

quent work, Hausmann has emphasized the importance of "creating a financially viable state that does not over-borrow, over-tax or under-invest" to successfully raise domestic savings.

Dominican Republic

HRV conclude that the Dominican Republic is constrained by core public goods in product sectors key for growth. The country began a new reform sequence during the 1980s, after it could no longer rely on sugar and gold exports. It followed a narrow strategy of investing in needed public goods for two emerging product (or service) sectors with high potential, tourism and *maquila* assembly manufacturing. The keys were security and infrastructure near the main tourist destinations and special trade policy benefits for the light manufacturing assembly (*maquila*) sector. As the economy grew from these sources, other constraints were hit, notably in the financial sector; getting past them (particularly a costly financial crisis) was bumpy, but the binding constraints stayed or became visible, so policymakers could focus on relaxing them to keep growth going.

Sources: Ricardo Hausmann, Dani Rodrik, and Andrés Velasco, "Growth diagnostics," in *One Economics, Many Recipes: Globalization, Institutions, and Economic Growth*, by Dani Rodrik (Princeton, N.J.: Princeton University Press, 2007), ch. 2; Ricardo Hausmann, "In search of the chains that hold Brazil back," October 31, 2008, http://papers.ssrn.com/sol3/papers.cfm?abstract_id=1338262. An excellent practicum is found in "Doing Growth Diagnostics in Practice: A 'Mindbook.'" See http://www.cid.harvard.edu/cidwp/177.html. The World Bank offers a set of growth diagnostics exercises at its Web site, http://web.worldbank.org/.

in turn is held back by investment. This is a useful analytical assumption for this and a range of other purposes, but it does not and cannot provide a complete understanding of development purposes, mechanisms, and constraints. And of course, it is often not a simple matter to find a single binding constraint. There can be uncertainty about the "position" of each constraint in the economy, so we can only make a probabilistic assessment of which one is binding. If there are important complementarities between two investments, combining them (in some sense) should be considered. Further, the fact that one constraint is not binding today does not mean that we can neglect it when there are long gestation periods before current investments become productive. For example, consider investments in education: Students require several years of schooling followed by experience before these investments become productive. So although education may not be binding for a particular country such as Bolivia at a particular point in time, this does not mean that it will not become binding at a later time; in response, we may need to make investments today. Clearly, identifying and addressing constraints that are likely to become binding in the future is even more challenging than targeting today's more visible bottlenecks.

Growth diagnostics has already had an effect on the work of development agencies. For example, the Inter-American Development Bank (IDB), the regional development bank for the western hemisphere, has been commissioning growth diagnostic studies of many member economies while training staff and nationals in the skills needed to conduct their own growth diagnostics. World Bank economists have applied the method in a dozen country pilot studies in Africa, Asia, and Latin America. And developing country scholars have applied the approach to their own countries. Although growth diagnostics might be criticized as "more art than science," at the very least this new approach forces the analyst to focus on country-specific circumstances and thus to get to know the individual country very well. This is one of the reasons that growth diagnostics offers a valuable complement to econometric studies.

4.8 Conclusions

The important point is not that people keep doing inefficient things. This is not in itself very surprising. The deeper point is that people keep doing inefficient things because it is rational to keep doing them, and it will remain rational as long as others keep doing inefficient things. This leads to a fundamental problem of coordination failure. Sometimes firms and other economic agents will be able to coordinate to achieve a better equilibrium on their own. But in many cases, government policy and aid will be necessary to overcome the resulting vicious circles of underdevelopment.

The purpose of economic development theory is not only to understand underdevelopment but also to devise effective policies to redress it. The analysis of coordination failure problems in this chapter affirmed that early development theorists such as Paul Rosenstein-Rodan identified important potential problems that are ignored in conventional competitive equilibrium models.[51] The new perspectives offer some important overall lessons for policy, but they are not simple lessons with easy applicability, and indeed they present something of a two-edged sword. On one side, the analysis shows that the potential for market failure, especially as it affects the prospects for economic development, is broader and deeper than had been fully appreciated in the past. Rather than the small "deadweight triangle losses" of conventional economic analysis of monopoly, pollution externalities, and other market failures, coordination failure problems can have more far-reaching effects and consequently much greater costs.[52] For example, the interactions of slightly distorted behaviors by potential investors failing to consider the income effects of the wages they pay may produce very large distortions, such as the outright failure to industrialize. This makes the potential benefit of an active role for government larger in the context of multiple equilibria.

The coordination failures that may arise in the presence of complementarities highlight potential policies for deep interventions that move the economy to a preferred equilibrium or even to a higher permanent rate of growth that can then be self-sustaining. For example, once a big push has been undertaken, government coordination may no longer be necessary. The unaided market can often maintain industrialization once it is achieved, even when it cannot initiate or complete the process of industrialization. For another example, we will see in Chapter 8 that in some cases, the presence of child labor represents a kind of bad equilibrium among the families with children who work, one that might be fixed with appropriate policy. After successfully abolishing child labor, it is possible that the regulations will not have to be actively enforced to keep child labor from making a resurgence (because most parents send their children to work only because they have to). If there is no incentive to go back to the behavior associated with the bad equilibrium, government has no need to continue the interventions. Instead, government can concentrate its efforts on other crucial problems in which it has an essential role (e.g., problems of public health). This onetime-fix character of some multiple-equilibria problems makes them worthy of special focus because they can make government policy much more powerful in addressing problems of economic development. Among other implications, the prospect of deep interventions can mean that the costs of implementing policy can be reduced and that carefully targeted development assistance could have more effective results.

The other edge of the sword, however, is that with deep interventions, the potential costs of a public role become much larger. Policy choices are more momentous because a bad policy today could push an economy into a bad equilibrium for years to come. This is because government can be a major part of the problem, playing a key role in perpetuating a bad equilibrium such as a high-corruption regime, in part because some government officials and politicians may benefit personally from it. Bad policy can even initiate a move to a worse equilibrium than a country began with. To expect government to be the source of reform that moves the economy to a better equilibrium in countries where government has been part of the complex nexus of a bad equilibrium can be naive. For example, as the 2001 Nobel laureate Joseph Stiglitz pointed out, development officials should have been more suspicious of corrupt government officials' embracing of the World Bank's doctrine of thoroughgoing privatization in the late 1980s and early 1990s. Why would corrupt officials have done so if they benefited from a stream of rents captured from public enterprises? The answer, Stiglitz suggests, is that these officials found that by corrupting the process of privatization, they could get not only a stream of corrupt rents from the annual operations of the enterprise but also a share of the present discounted value of the whole future operations of the enterprise.[53] The results of corrupt privatization in Russia in particular have been devastating for its economy, preventing it from enjoying the benefits of the market and potentially keeping it in a suboptimal equilibrium for many years to come. Even when a government is not corrupt, the potential impact of a well-intentioned but flawed government policy is much greater when it can push the economy to a fundamentally different equilibrium, which may be difficult to reverse. This is all the more problematic in the many cases in which "history matters" in a developing economy—that is, when past conditions determine what is possible today.

Both government failure and market failure (including coordination problems and information externalities) are real, but public- and private-sector contributions to development are also vital. Therefore, we need to work toward the development of institutions in which actors in the public and private sectors have incentives to work productively together (directly and indirectly) in such a way as to create the conditions necessary to break out of poverty traps. In achieving this goal, the international community also has a vital role to play, providing ideas and models and serving as a catalyst for change, as well as providing some of the necessary funding.

The growth diagnostics approach is a valuable tool for domestic and international analysts who start with a detailed understanding of a developing country; it can be helpful in identifying binding constraints on national growth and the policy priorities to address them.

In sum, the contributions of the new theories of development reviewed in this chapter include a better understanding of the causes and effects of poverty traps, achieved by more precisely pinning down roles of different types of strategic complementarities, explaining the role of expectations, clarifying the importance of externalities, illuminating the potential scope for deep interventions, and improving our understanding of both the potential role of government and the constraints on the effectiveness of that role—when government itself becomes a player in an underdevelopment trap. Finally, the new approaches point out more clearly the real potential contributions of outside development assistance that extend beyond provision of capital to modeling new ways of doing things.

As democratic government spreads in the developing world, the new understandings of underdevelopment traps can make for a more effective guide to policy design than was available even a few years ago. As Karla Hoff has aptly summarized, "Governments fail, even in democracies, just as markets do. But a positive development of recent years is to try more limited interventions to harness the spillovers among agents, and to try to sequence policy reforms in a way that makes it more likely for good equilibria to emerge."[54]

In Parts Two and Three, as we consider pressing issues affecting developing countries today, we will be using the insights provided by both the classic theories and the new models of development and underdevelopment to inform our understanding of both the nature of the problems faced and the potential benefits and pitfalls of policies designed to help overcome them.

Understanding a Development Miracle: China

An Extraordinary Performance

From 1978 to 2011, the economy of China grew at an average rate of close to 9% a year, an unprecedented achievement for any economy in history, let alone the world's most populous nation, with over 19% of global population. China's income per capita by 2012 was approaching *six times* what it was in 1978, when reforms began. Growth was three times the rate that would be considered respectable by the recent standards of most low-income countries.

China has also experienced the world's most dramatic reductions in poverty. The World Bank's most recent estimate is that just 12% of China's population lives on less than $1.25 per day (27% below $2 per day). This means that hundreds of millions fewer people were living in extreme poverty in a span of just three decades. Reductions in extreme poverty in China are far faster and greater than anywhere else in the world.

Debate on Sources of Success

For such a stunning record, the roots of China's success remain a source of disagreement. The Chinese experience seems to change everything—but does it? And if so, in what ways? Success has a thousand fathers, and all the major traditional and new schools of thought on development want to claim China as their most important case in point. China is hailed as an example of the benefits of markets, trade, and globalization. Yet by conventional measures, institutions in China remain quite weak. For example, the World Bank's 2013 "Ease of Doing Business" index ranks China poorly, at No. 96—worse than Russia, Mongolia, Zambia, or Serbia. Manufactured exports are a key to China's growth, and market incentives have played a primary motivational role in

business decisions. But China has also adopted activist industrial policies, pushing exports of increasingly higher skill and technology content, and it embarked on its period of rapid growth around 1980, more than a decade before significant trade liberalization. But often overlooked is that China's agricultural productivity growth was also very high. Moreover, much of China's growth in the 1980s and early 1990s was due to rural township and village enterprises, which had a quasi-cooperative and quasi-municipally owned character. There has been less privatization of state-owned enterprises than in most developing countries. In the meantime, countries in Africa, Latin America, and elsewhere that have most closely followed the free-market model have generally not done particularly well. While all schools may find something in China to let them claim it as vindication of their favored development policies, it is also clear that if China were performing dismally, each could (and likely would) find reasons why its own theories, including free-market theory, predicted such a failure.

There have been many special explanations for China's remarkable success. Many of them contain part of the truth, but such dramatic success is more than the sum of these parts. Let us review some of the explanations.

Regional "Demonstrations." The presence of regional "demonstration" models has been crucial. Japan was emulated by other countries in the East Asian region. Hong Kong provided an additional example for China, as did China's archrival Taiwan. Taiwan, Hong Kong, and South Korea focused on export-oriented industrialization strategy at a time when world trade was growing rapidly (see the end-of-chapter case studies for Chapters 12 and 13).

Leveraging the Lure of a Billion Consumers By the late 1980s, the locus of regional growth shifted to China as investors began to pour investments into China in large part because of the allure of its eventual market of more than 1.3 billion consumers. Government played off potential investors who wanted access to China's consumers, demanding and getting extensive technology transfer, public and private Chinese business partnerships, local content, and other concessions in exchange for the right to sell to Chinese citizens. Although the market was limited at first by both low incomes and government policies, early investors found high incentives to export from several special economic zones on the southeast coast. These investors discovered that China offered very cheap labor with unusually high skills and work habits for its income level.

Export-Led Investment and Growth Once early investments built up a sufficient critical mass, agglomeration benefits of concentrated economic activity kicked in (see Chapter 7). The more producers located in China, the greater the benefits for an increasing number of suppliers to operate there. At this point, investments started to feed on themselves in a cumulative causation. In the meantime, when wages began to rise, companies could set up production farther west, or migrants from the west could move to the new industrial centers. Given China's population of hundreds of millions of low-income farmers, expectations were formed that this process of wage restraint could continue for an extended time—although a string of wage increases beginning in 2010 began to challenge these expectations as financial analysts argued that the Lewis turning point had been reached (see Chapter 3).

Coordination After the bloody crackdown on Tiananmen Square protests in 1989, there was considerable doubt about whether the reforms would continue and therefore whether investment and growth would remain high (making other investments profitable). The Chinese leader Deng Xiaoping paid a 1991 visit to the southern China regions that had been leading in growth and reform and proclaimed, "You should be bolder and develop faster." A rapid burst of investment and growth, as well as policy reform, followed his speech and its subsequent publication. It has been suggested that in effect this served to coordinate expectations and led to the shift from a lower-growth to a higher-growth equilibrium. But much more generally, the government of China has used its centralized authority to coordinate investments across industries. Moreover, government negotiation of licenses and other business agreements helped ensure that China got more favorable deals than many other developing countries that relied on private company-level business transactions, although in this, the role model lessons from South Korea was also a benefit.

Health and Education Investments The central planning of China's first decades after its 1949 Communist revolution were by most measures a failure. Industry was highly inefficient. As many as 30 million people died in a late-1950s famine caused by poor central planning decisions and political pressures that led party and government officials to regularly overstate the harvest prospects. As Amartya Sen stresses, famines rarely occur in democratic countries with a free press. Such disasters were only partly offset by the early and ongoing emphasis on basic health and education in China and then on reductions of fertility through China's one-child policy (see the case study for Chapter 6). But these basic first steps on education, health, and eventually fertility helped set the stage for growth and poverty reduction when later combined with market incentives. One of the results is the apparently higher educational and skill level of factory workers for given wages in China in comparison to its competitor countries.

Productivity Growth There has been considerable debate about whether rapid growth in other East Asian countries is the result of capital accumulation or productivity gains. Alwyn Young, Paul Krugman, and others have concluded that South Korea and other Asian Tigers grew more from investing heavily in capital assets such as machinery and factories than by improved worker efficiency. Wing Thye Woo concluded that most of China's growth came from the reallocation of labor, particularly from agriculture to other activities, and that sustainable total factor productivity progress was much lower, on the order of 2% per year.

But for the case of China, Zuliu Hu and Mohsin Khan concluded that productivity gains explained more than 42% of China's growth in the formative

1979–1994 period and that productivity had over-taken investment by the early 1990s as the largest source of growth. This was considered surprising, in part because of the breathtaking pace of capital investments in China. But on the other hand, when China's rapid growth began in the late 1970s in the areas close to Hong Kong, while it was clear that a large volume of investment funds was flowing from capital-abundant Hong Kong (a British crown colony at the time) to capital-scarce China, the bigger story was the flow of productive ideas over the Hong Kong border, a barrier that had long prevented the transfer of both capital and know-how. Of these two factors, it often seemed that the ideas were more important than the finance.

There is widespread concern that by now, China has entered an investment bubble stage in which many investments are of dubious quality, particularly in real estate and some infrastructure and industrial sectors. Even so, the rapid pace of development in China has been unprecedented.

Recent research by Xiaodong Zhu, Loren Brandt, and their coauthors has provided new documentation that productivity growth, rather than mere factor accumulation, has been a very important source of China's rapid growth of output. In particular, Zhu has presented well-regarded evidence that productivity growth in the nonagricultural, non-state-owned sector is the most important source of growth in China. Noting that productivity is still well below that of the United States, he argues that there should still be significant opportunities for productivity to continue to grow rapidly in China by adopting foreign technology, learning best production practices, and improving institutions and policies, particularly to allocate capital more efficiently.

In another study, Ashoka Mody and Fang-Yi Wang of the World Bank examined the causes of industrial growth in China and concluded:

…much of the action came from region-specific influences and regional spillovers. Regional influences included the open-door policies and special economic zones that successfully attracted investments from overseas Chinese to particular locations. Existing regional strengths, especially high-quality human capital and infrastructure, also contributed to growth. Our results illuminate the interplay between conditions conducive for growth—for example, the contribution of foreign expertise is greatly enhanced by available human capital. China made judicious use of the advantages of backwardness by targeting areas that were less developed and less encumbered by the legacy of existing institutions, although it was fortunate in this regard that the backward regions were in close proximity to Hong Kong and Taiwan.

Thus, the China case also illuminates complementarities, a recurrent theme of this chapter.

Reform on the Margin

As examined in detail in Chapter 2, developing inclusive institutions that protect property rights and enforce contracts, and place checks on executive authority and the power of elites such as through the rule of law, have demonstrated importance in long-term economic development. China appears to be an outlier, in that such protections are demonstrably weak. Yet it is extremely difficult to navigate the course from bad to good institutions. It is rarely possible to follow a straight line on the map, as a vortex of obstacles are encountered, and the ship of state itself may be the cause of many of the problems. The process of getting the institutions right is one of starting with a clear understanding of both formal and informal local rules, and moving toward an eventual goal even when it cannot be seen clearly—in the presence of initial and then newly emerging constraints and opportunities, chartering what may seem to outsiders as large deviations off-course. A metaphor used by the post-Mao paramount leader Deng Xiaoping may also reflect in part this type of step-by-step, graduated process—"crossing the river by feeling the stones."

In China, the *way* that market incentives were introduced and used seems to have been almost as important as the fact that they were introduced at all. One of the most important features of the past quarter century of economic history in China has been the very gradual implementation of reforms. China's approach has been the opposite of that of many eastern European countries such as Russia and Poland, which opted for a "big bang," a sudden comprehensive changeover to a free-market economy. (Hungary and Slovenia are two countries in that region that pursued a more gradualist strategy.) China has introduced new and transitional institutions that exist side by side with previous institutions of central planning for extended

periods. In the former Soviet Union and eastern Europe, central planning was abolished almost immediately, and economic depression, with drops in output of up to 50%, ensued before gradual recovery. In contrast, China kept the central planning system partially intact for an extended period. Previous quotas for buyers and sellers at fixed planned prices were maintained. Reform was instead introduced on the margin. After filling their quotas, producers were free to buy and sell at market-determined prices; resales were generally not prohibited. This "dual-track" system simulated the allocational efficiency of a more competitive market economy and created strong incentives for firms to improve efficiency and increase output, in a manner less threatening to the status quo.

Moreover, while in other transition and developing countries state-owned enterprises (SOEs) were sold off to private investors fairly quickly, in China these remained in government hands for an extended period. The government tried to reform them internally, with limited success. But at the same time, China has allowed and encouraged a new, more efficient sector to grow up around them. In recent years, China has privatized or closed many of the smaller SOEs. Many larger SOEs continue to operate in a relatively inefficient manner, and some economists have suspected for years that their accumulating indebtedness will eventually pose significant financial risks to the economy. But the counterargument proposes that if the economy can continue to grow rapidly, it is also possible that China may stay ahead of this problem without experiencing a financial crash. Eventually, as employment opportunities continue to expand, more of the larger SOEs can be privatized or closed.

Further, for the first nearly two decades of reform, from the late 1970s to the mid-1990s, at the local level, township and village enterprises (TVEs) were encouraged. The TVEs were vaguely owned by local government, but their private entrepreneurs and employees held "vaguely defined" property rights, as Martin L. Weitzman and Chenggang Xu termed them. These TVEs accounted for a very large share of industrial output growth in China. Finally, after the Chinese economy had grown nearly fourfold, the majority of these TVEs were privatized in the late 1990s—by this point the private entrepreneurs had triumphed (or their underlying control became clarified). But the TVEs played a unique role in spurring growth and spreading the benefits of development to rural areas.

Reforms in the late 1970s and 1980s favored agriculture and entrepreneurship in the rural areas where most of the poor lived, and poverty fell as income rose. From at least the early to mid-1990s, the terms of trade shifted toward industry and urban areas. Yasheng Huang makes a strong case that this represented an important turning point, associated with growing inequality and other serious challenges.

Still, strong average growth continued through many changes. As outlined by Yingyi Qian, China's transitional institutions have served a dual purpose: to improve efficiency while compensating the losers (and thereby preserving legitimacy or at least reducing the chance of political backlash). Provided that the quotas were enforced—and for the most part they seem to have been in the transition in China—the dual-track allocation system protected the interests of those who had benefited from and planned on receiving inputs at fixed, low prices. As a result, these agents did not oppose or undermine reforms and indeed could benefit further to the degree they could learn to produce more efficiently and operate in markets effectively. The system was largely phased out many years later, after the economic landscape had changed dramatically.

The vague local-government ownership of the TVEs provided protection for investors who feared government hostility toward private property and worried about expropriation. The impression that these companies were owned by the township or village protected the de facto private owners. Once reform proceeded to a certain point, these de facto owners were able to "take off the red hat," as the saying went in China, and assume full ownership in exchange for considerations to local government, and taxes replaced direct revenue transfer out of the TVEs. Qian shows how similar arguments apply to fiscal and financial reforms. Under the reforms, local government continued to have a responsibility to provide revenue to the central government, but local government was allowed to keep a large share of collections on the margin before local and central revenue collection was fully separated. Government also allowed anonymous banking accounts for a long transition period, to credibly constrain

the ability of the government to arbitrarily impose high individual taxes on successful entrepreneurs; Qian judged the program a success despite the fact that this diverges from what is considered normal best practice in advanced Western countries.

Yingyi Qian's insightful explanation is:

> The difference between China and Russia is not at all that China has established best-practice institutions and Russia has not. The difference lies in the institutions in transition....The real challenge in reform facing transition and developing countries is not so much knowing where to end up, but searching for a feasible path toward the goal. Therefore, it focuses on transitional institutions, not best-practice institutions....The general principle of efficiency-improving and interest-compatible institutional change is simple, but the specific forms and mechanisms of transitional institutions often are not. Successful institutional forms usually are not a straightforward copy of best-practice institutions. They need not be and sometimes should not be. They need not be because room exists for efficiency improvement that does not require fine tuning at the beginning. They should not be because the initial conditions are country- and context-specific, requiring special arrangements....Understanding these mechanisms sometimes needs an appeal to the counterintuitive second best argument, which states that removing one distortion may be counterproductive in the presence of another distortion.

Finally, for peasants in parts of China where the rural sector has done well, earlier land reforms have been among the causes—with the revolution setting the stage and the late-1970s reforms giving greater incentives to individual farmers. Land reform has been notoriously difficult to implement in other parts of the world. Remittances from migrant workers have fueled a service-sector boom in some rural areas, and prices received by farmers have generally risen, particularly near urban areas.

China's Coming Challenges

China's successes do need to be kept in perspective. Since 1980, China has grown about 4½ times faster than the United States, as measured by per capita output. As a result, China has been closing the *relative* gap in living standards. In 1980, China's income per person was only 2% of that in the United States, but by 2012, it had grown to over 15%. But even if China's output per person continued to grow at its unprecedented recent rate of 8.4% and the United

States at its long-run rate of just 1.9%, China would still not catch up until close to 2040.

A high rate of domestic saving is associated with a trade surplus. Savings have been extremely high and rising in China. As of 2011, China was saving nearly half of its national income—an astounding and unprecedented rate compared to the country's own past rates (already a high 35% in 1990) and in relation to the high rates that have generally prevailed in East Asia. Such high rates are not consistent with the pivot toward increasing local consumption as an engine of growth.

It is now generally accepted in China and internationally that continuing to grow at such high rates is essentially impossible. Before China grew rapidly, South Korea did so, and before South Korea, Japan did. The later a country starts modern economic growth, the faster it can grow because the distance from traditional methods to the frontier technology of the day grows greater over time. But the pace of catch-up generally slows as an economy gets closer to the technology frontier and needs to innovate. Policymakers in China are actively preparing for this challenge. Despite its extraordinary record to date and considerable resources at its disposal, the substantial challenges that China faces in its attempt to reach developed country status should not be underestimated. There are some other limits and caveats to China's success and to the lessons that other countries can learn from it.

Poverty and Vulnerability Life can indeed be harder than ever for the millions remaining in extreme poverty, such as rural peasants in some parts of the country facing the loss of security; official corruption, including reports of official land grabs from peasants; rising local taxes; and minimal improvements in technology or skills. At the same time, despite the growth in average wages, inequality in China—once quite low—has been rising dramatically; inequality has now reached approximately the same level as in the United States, worst among the developed countries.

Environment and Pollution Moreover, the environmental crisis in China is reaching epic proportions. A majority of the most polluted cities in the world are located in China, and health problems are growing. Water resource problems, erosion, and loss of habitat undermine the prospects for sustainable development. The extreme air pollution is now

causing not just misery but deaths and other serious and growing health problems. This reached historic proportions in the so-called Beijing "airpocalypse" of January 2013, when pollution indicators exceeded 40 *times* World Health Organization standards; many other cities such as Tianjin and Harbin have been severely affected. There are very few historical precedents for prolonged pollution exposure of this magnitude. But a 2013 joint study by China, United States, and Israel university researchers estimated that air pollution in China has already decreased live expectancy north of the Huai River by an amazing 5.5 years, including increases in lung cancer, heart attack, and stroke.

Moreover, China's looming water shortages threaten to curtail industry, coal production, and agriculture. Some of China's environmental challenges result from global climate change; but many if not most result from poor national management of the environment. Although China produces about one-tenth of global output, it consumes nearly one-fifth of the world's energy production. Coal accounts for more than 70% of China's electricity production. Coal generates more greenhouse gases than any other significant energy source. Coal production also uses a lot of water. The rapid expansion of coal use is placing major demands on China's increasingly scarce water supply, adding to the growing demands stemming from irrigation and expanding cities. China is now the world's largest emitter of greenhouse gases such as CO_2, and emissions have been growing rapidly (see Chapter 10).

Product and worker safety Since 2007, highly publicized scandals concerning the safety of food, drugs, and other consumer products threatened the international public image of Chinese-made products. Indeed, product safety standards are low, and their regulation is lax. Foreign and local investors, and government, all share in the blame. China's regulatory institutions will need to catch up with the progress made in other aspects of national economic development.

Avoiding the Middle-Income Trap Chinese officials and researchers are also concerned about susceptibility to the "middle-income trap" and are engaging discussions with Latin American countries on this topic; Huang Yiping and Jiang Tingsong stressed that what "really trapped many Latin America and Middle East middle-income countries was lack of innovation capability. They failed to move up

the industrial ladder beyond resource-based activities. This will also be the real test for China." As the IMF concluded in its October 2013 *World Economic Outlook*, "There is strengthening conviction that China will grow more slowly over the medium term than in the recent past." The alternative is probably wasteful and unsustainable investment that would result in serious economic crises. The question for China will be how it can maintain somewhat more modest but historically still high growth, of perhaps 6.5%, sustainably over the next three decades. An economy growing at this rate must have a different structure of investment than an economy growing at 10% (as China did in 2010). Making these adjustments will not be easy. Developing innovative capacity will be an important part of the answer; first steps are being taken, but better institutions may be needed to sustain the momentum.

Addressing Structural Imbalances There are several other imbalances in China's economy that may lead to problems going forward. The World Bank pointed out in its 2013 *Global Economic Prospects* that "ongoing rebalancing efforts remain a priority, as does engineering a gradual decline in its unsustainably high investment rate." The report also stressed that "should investments prove unprofitable, the servicing of existing loans could become problematic—potentially sparking a sharp uptick in nonperforming loans that could require state intervention."

China's very large export surplus has come under great criticism, as this was widely argued to be one of the underlying causes of the global financial crisis. One cause of the surpluses is probably the undervaluation of China's exchange rate, estimated to be at least 20%. Undervaluation has been used by a number of East Asian economies as an industrial strategy for encouraging expansion of the manufacturing sector (notably in the 1960s and 1970s by South Korea and Taiwan; see Chapter 12), but those economies were much smaller than that of China. Note, however, that as recently as 2009 analysts estimated rates of overvaluation of up to 40%, approximately double the estimates of just four years later; and the external surplus as a share of GDP has decreased to a correspondingly degree since then (see Chapter 12 for details on measurement and analysis of international trade). Indeed, by 2013, some manufacturers found themselves struggling to adapt to a less overvalued currency.

Inevitably, more China-based firms will engage in direct foreign investment in their export destination countries such as the United States, just as Japan and South Korea did before them; but this will be a drawn-out process due to China's still relatively low (if strongly growing) average productivity level, and also probably national security worries arising in Europe and Japan as well as in the United States.

Another factor in the large trade surplus is China's high rate of savings, mentioned earlier, where the savings rate, long well above international averages, increased dramatically in the 1998–2010 period (when it peaked at approximately 49% of national income).

In parallel, investment as a share of GDP, long over 40%, reached an unprecedented 48% by 2010, before moderating slightly. Part of the uptick in recent years was due to an active response to the 2008 global economic crisis. The adjustment to sustainable investment and growth rates will be extremely difficult to accomplish without major and possibly prolonged disruptions. Yet in one sense the scope of the problem may also be somewhat exaggerated by the way national statistics are prepared, which as Jun Zhang and Tian Zhu argued in a 2013 study does not account for hidden consumption by the growing number of high-income citizens, the rent-equivalent consumption of owner-occupied housing, and reported corporate expenses that are actually more like private consumption. On the other hand, on the other side of the balance sheet, the extraordinarily high investment—with evidence showing that a significant amount of it is at very low productivity—has not been challenged, and these statistics (including international trade and finance data) must be considered and better understood as a whole.

The huge indebtedness of the state-owned enterprise (SOE) sector and other public debt (such as local government loans using land collateral) is thought by some financial commentators to be likely to eventually lead to a significant financial crisis—though other analysts argue that China can "grow its way out of" these problems.

For years, analysts have expressed concerns about the risk of "bubbles" (see Chapter 13) developing in financial and housing markets, due to very high rates of debt-financed investment. The potential problem has only worsened: just from 2008 to 2013, the over-all credit to GDP ratio increased from about 120% in 2008 to close to 200%. This again connects to China's unprecedentedly high investment rate and low consumption rate; adjustment is now essential, and indeed has begun, but the extent of the imbalances suggests that the transition from investment-led to consumption-led growth will be unusually long and difficult, and is very unlikely to be entirely smooth.

Political Weaknesses There are also political weaknesses. On the one hand, some analysts make a case for the strengths of more authoritarian regimes, at least in early stages of development and when leadership fosters a developmental state. But on the other hand, this may make for a less flexible response to changing circumstances and difficulties in escaping a possible middle-income trap. Some leaders in China have called for urgent political reforms. And the dramatically worsened inequality in China may undermine not just political stability but ultimately opportunities for future growth (for details on the challenges of rising inequality for growth and development, see Chapter 5).

Relatedly, China will need to find a way to continue its ongoing institutional reforms, whether through implementing new and productive transitional institutions or more fundamental change. In their 2012 book, *Why Nations Fail*, Daron Acemoglu and James Robinson make an extraordinary argument that institutional weaknesses will ultimately stall development in China. In their argument, institutions in China closely resemble the "extractive" political systems of other failed states where crony capitalism is the norm, vested interests are protected, and potentially disruptive entrepreneurs are blocked. They conclude that growth in China will ultimately be "unlikely to translate into sustained economic development." While relatively few analysts think the challenges are this steep, undoubtedly the needed reforms will be politically difficult to undertake.

The much-anticipated economic and social policy changes announced at the Third Plenum in November 2013 promised a further "unleashing" of market forces with their rhetoric promotion from a "basic" to "decisive" role—even if some details were left vague, and some predictions for reform were not realized (particularly in the field of finance). But left unambiguous was that the

Communist Party monopoly on political control remained unchallenged—and indeed seemed to have been reinforced.

Finally, despite the extraordinary economic growth in China, Richard Easterlin has found that improvements in happiness and satisfaction in the country simply have not kept pace, particularly among the bottom third.

Managing Urbanization The scope of urbanization in China has been called the largest migration in human history, and indeed it has been breathtaking. For the first time in its history, China has become a more urban than rural society, with the halfway mark believed to have been crossed sometime in 2011; as recently as 1980, more than 80% of Chinese citizens lived in rural areas. Before 2030, China may reach the "Urban Billion" mark. Chongqing featured in the vignette in Chapter 1, growing from 200,000 in the 1930s, to about 2 million during the Cultural Revolution of the 1970s, to now over 30 million people in the metropolitan area. In the south, Shenzhen was transformed from a fishing village near Hong Kong to another megacity in just a couple of decades. But conditions of ordinary people in many cities do not correspond to the media images of postmodern skyscrapers, as most are moving to large tracts of sometimes bleak, uniform apartment buildings, crawling in epic traffic jams through a vast urban sprawl—and indeed inhaling the "breathtaking" air pollution—in a picture simultaneously of public overinvestment in some areas and underinvestment in others.

Demographic Challenges

China also has a rapidly aging population. For the last decade of the twentieth century and first decade and a half of the twenty-first century, China has benefited from a *demographic dividend* (see Chapter 6), in which by global standards an unusually large fraction of its population has been of working age (neither too young nor too old to be active in the workforce). This "dividend" occurs in the process of economic development after the drop in births per woman but before the previous larger cohorts retire, allowing for rapid income growth. China is now entering a phase in which a large fraction of its working population will begin to retire. One challenge is the need to implement a modern pension system. Another is to respond to a shrinking workforce and the need to support a large retired population. It is a challenge common to many modern societies but may be particularly acute in China due to its one-child policy that has been in effect since about 1980, which has greatly accelerated the demographic transition. There was a slight relaxation of this policy at the Third Plenum in November 2013, to allow urban families for which either husband or wife is an only child to have a second child (previously this was allowed only if each was an only child). But this change may have very limited impact on fertility because of the high cost of raising children in China's cities. The very high ratio of males to females (see Chapter 8) remains another serious demographic challenge that may lead to continued distortions.

There are several explanations of China's historically unprecedented high savings rates (approaching 50% by some measures), but many of them relate to the unusual demographic challenges; they include "life-cycle" saving for retirement by an aging population that lacks social security, precautionary savings due to increased income uncertainty because of fears about catastrophic family events such as major illnesses or layoffs, poor financial intermediation, and—in an influential new theory of Shang-Jin Wei and Xiaobo Zhang—competitive saving by parents of sons who now greatly outnumber daughters due to China's growing sex-ratio imbalance and compete for prospective wives by offering larger houses and other wealth. High savings may be associated with the apparent property bubble that some economists in China believe has become dangerous—yet China has demonstrated a capacity for managing challenges, and considerable reserves for addressing crises.

Other Limits to Emulating China's Policies

There are other limits to the lessons of China's growth for other developing countries. China is quite homogeneous, overwhelmingly populated by members of the Han ethnic group. In Africa and other parts of the world, ethnic diversity is associated with slower growth, though only in countries that also have incomplete or nonexistent political freedoms. Clearly, China is lacking in many freedoms. There may be limits to the ability of other countries to carry out China's brand of centrally

designed and implemented policies for transition and directed growth when either broader democratic freedoms are in place or greater ethnic diversity is present. Finally, China, like much of the rest of East Asia, has a relatively poor endowment of natural resources. Many development specialists have concluded that this lack is actually more of a benefit than a drawback. Natural resource abundance encourages political infighting for control over the revenues, while manufacturing success is more important when a country does not have natural resources to fall back on. It requires more initiative and more efforts to upgrade technology and skill. In terms of geographic advantages, East Asia is also much less plagued than Africa and other developing regions by problems such as malaria and other tropical diseases for which medicines are not readily available, the difficulties and disadvantages of tropical agriculture, and the problems of landlocked countries.

The experience of China assures us that the East Asian miracle is not a fluke due to special local factors in economies such as South Korea and Taiwan. It gives us much greater confidence when we say that "real development is possible." On the other hand, there are clear limits to the ability of other developing regions to emulate the success of China. Not only do other developing countries differ in geography, demography, institutions, and allure to foreign investors, but also other regions may find themselves starved for investments that are redirected to China while remaining unable to compete with China's impressive combination of low wages, high skills and know-how, and agglomeration of economic activity. Some East Asian countries have greatly benefited from the surge in import demand from China. The commodity price boom of recent years, which has stimulated demand in several countries in Africa, is significantly attributable to growth in China. And China itself has a good chance of continued high, albeit moderated growth, provided it manages the next phase of its transition carefully. In the meantime, many developing countries that have hoped to rely more on manufactured exports view the success of China as much as a threat as an opportunity. Growth in China will continue to be a central theme in the global development drama—both in its huge economic impact and the policy debate spurred by its extraordinary achievements. ∎

Sources

Acemoglu, Daron, and James Robinson, *Why Nations Fail: The Origins of Power, Prosperity, and Poverty.* New York: Crown Business, 2012

Asian Development Bank. *The National Accounts of the People's Republic of China: Measurement Issues, Recent Developments, and the Way Forward.* Manila, Philippines: Asian Development Bank, 2007.

Brandt, Loren, and Xiaodong R. Zhu. "Distribution in a decentralized economy: Growth and inflation in China under reform." *Journal of Political Economy* 108 (2000): 422–439.

Byrd, William, and Lin Qingsong, eds. *China's Rural Industry: Structure, Development, and Reform.* New York: Oxford University Press, 1990.

Chen, B., and Y. Feng. "Determinants of economic growth in China: Private enterprise, education, and openness." *China Economic Review* 11 (2000): 1–15.

Chen, Shaohua, and Martin Ravallion. "China's (uneven) progress against poverty." *Journal of Development Economics* 82 (2007): 1–42.

———. "Learning from success: Understanding China's (uneven) progress against poverty." *Finance and Development* 41 (2004): 16–19.

Easterlin, Richard A. "When growth outpaces happiness." *New York Times*, September 27, 2012, http://www.nytimes.com/2012/09/28/opinion/in-china-growth-outpaces-happiness.html?_r=0.

Financial Times, numerous issues: the authors acknowledge the general contribution of the in-depth daily reporting on China by the *Financial Times* in informing the development of this case study over more than a decade.

George Washington University, Institute for International Economic Policy. "G2 at GW: Annual Conferences on China's Economic Development and U.S.-China Economic Relations", 2008–2013; "virtual conference volumes" at http://www.gwu.edu/~iiep/G2_at_GW/.

Hu, Zuliu, and Mohsin S. Khan. "Why is China growing so fast?" IMF Working Paper No. 96/75, 1996.

Huang, Yasheng, *Capitalism with Chinese Characteristics*. New York: Cambridge University Press, 2008.

Islam, Nazrul, and Kazuhiko Yokota. "Lewis growth model and China's industrialization." *Asian Economic Journal* 22 (2008): 359–396.

Krugman, Paul. "The myth of Asia's miracle." *Foreign Affairs* 73, No. 6 (1994): 62–78.

Lau, Lawrence J., Yingyi Qian, and Gérard Roland. "Pareto-improving economic reforms through dual-track liberalization." *Economics Letters* 55 (1997): 285–292.

———. "Reform without losers: An interpretation of China's dual-track approach to transition." *Journal of Political Economy* 108 (2000): 120–143.

Lu, D. "Industrial policy and resource allocation: Implications of China's participation in globalization." *China Economic Review* 11 (2000): 342–360.

Miller, Tom. *China's Urban Billion: The Story Behind the Biggest Migration in Human History*. London: Zed Books, 2012.

Mody, Ashoka, and Fang-Yi Wang. "Explaining industrial growth in coastal China: Economic reforms…and what else?" *World Bank Economic Review* 11 (1997): 293–325.

Qian, Yingyi. "How reform worked in China." In *In Search of Prosperity: Analytic Narratives on Economic Growth*, ed. Dani Rodrik. Princeton, N.J.: Princeton University Press, 2003.

Rawski, Thomas. "Measuring China's recent GDP growth: Where do we stand?" October 2002. http://www.pitt.edu/~tgrawski/papers2002/measuring.pdf.

Romer, Paul M. "Idea gaps and object gaps in economic development." *Journal of Monetary Economics* 32 (1993): 543–573.

———. "Two strategies for economic development: Using ideas versus producing ideas." *Proceedings of the Annual World Bank Conference on Development Economics, 1992*. Washington D.C. World Bank, 1993, pp. 63–91.

Sen, Amartya. *Development as Freedom*. New York: Knopf, 1999.

Smith, Stephen C. "Employee participation in China's township and village enterprises." *China Economic Review* 6 (1995): 157–167.

Smith, Stephen C. "Industrial policy and export success: Third World development strategies reconsidered." In *U.S. Trade Policy and Global Growth*, ed. Robert Blecker. New York: Sharpe, 1996.

Smith, Stephen C., and Yao Pan, "US-China Economic Relations," in *Oxford Companion to the Economics of China*, eds.: Shenggen Fan, Ravi Kanbur, Shang-Jin Wei, and Xiaobo Zhang. Oxford University Press.

United Nations Development Programme. *Human Poverty Report, 2000*. New York: United Nations, 2000.

Vogel, Ezra. *One Step Ahead in China*. Cambridge, Mass.: Harvard University Press, 1989.

Wei, Shang-Jin, and Xiaobo Zhang. "The competitive saving motive: Evidence from rising sex ratios and savings rates in China." NBER Working Paper No. 15093, 2009.

Weitzman, Martin L., and Chenggang Xu. "Chinese township and village enterprises as vaguely defined cooperatives." *Journal of Comparative Economics* 20 (1994): 121–145.

Woetzel, Jonathan, et al. *Preparing for China's Urban Billion*. McKinsey Global Institute, February 2009.

Woo, Wing Thye. "Chinese economic growth: Sources and prospects." In *The Chinese Economy*, ed. Michel Fouquin and Françoise Lemoine. London: Economica, 1998.

Yiping, Huang, and Jiang Tingsong. "What does the Lewis turning point mean for China? A computable general equilibrium analysis." China Center for Economic Research Working Paper No. E2010005, March 2010.

Young, Alwyn. "The tyranny of numbers: Confronting the statistical realities of the East Asian growth experience." *Quarterly Journal of Economics* 110 (1995): 641–680.

Zhang, Jun, and Tian Zhu. "Re-Estimating China's Underestimated Consumption." Working paper, China Europe International Business School, September 7, 2013.

Zhou, Ning, Yunshi Wang, and Lester Thurow. "The PRC's real economic growth rate." Unpublished report. Cambridge, Mass.: Massachusetts Institute of Technology, 2002.

Zhu, Xiaodong, "Understanding China's growth: Past, present and future. *Journal of Economic Perspectives* (Fall 2012).

Concepts for Review

Agency costs
Asymmetric information
Big push
Binding constraint
Complementarity
Congestion
Coordination failure
Deep intervention

Economic agent
Growth diagnostics
Information externality
Linkages
Middle-income trap
Multiple equilibria
O-ring model
O-ring production function

Pareto improvement
Pecuniary externality
Poverty trap
Prisoners' dilemma
Social returns
Technological externality
Underdevelopment trap
Where-to-meet dilemma

Questions for Discussion

1. Can you think of additional examples of complementarities from everyday life? Does the S-shaped curve of Figure 4.1 shed any light on them? Do you think your examples help as a metaphor for economic development problems?

2. What role do you think international trade and foreign investment can play in solving some of the problems identified in the big push model? In the O-ring model? What limitations to your arguments can you think of?

3. The word *trap* suggests that there may be a way to escape. Do you think developing countries can escape all of the traps described in this chapter? Which ones would be most difficult to escape? How could the developed world be of assistance in these cases? Could developed countries do more?

4. Why might high levels of inequality lead to lower rates of growth and development? Why might it be difficult to get out of this kind of trap?

5. Why is the government sometimes a part of the problem of coordination failure rather than the solution? Does this make the problem hopeless? What could be done in this case?

6. One of the characteristics of some developing economies is the relatively low level of trust of people outside one's extended family. How might the models explored in this chapter shed light on this problem?

7. Can you think of an example of O-ring production from everyday life? Do you think your example is a good metaphor for development problems?

8. Modern economic models sometimes require strong assumptions. What do you think are some of the trade-offs between a more rigorous, logically cohesive model with strong assumptions but clear inferences and a description of problems followed by a verbal discussion of possible implications? Do you think the two approaches can be used together to inform each other?

9. As you read later chapters, think about whether the models described in this chapter are useful in shedding additional light on the nature of the problems considered. Some of the later problems you might consider are child labor, poor health and nutrition among the poor, high fertility, environmental degradation, availability of credit for the poor, urbanization, protectionism in international trade by developed and developing countries, reform of government, and land reform.

10. Select a developing country that interests you and search for evidence suggesting which factors are the binding constraint on growth. (For inspiration, see the sources in Box 4.3.)

11. What kinds of market failures are present in the economic self-discovery framework, and how may they be overcome?

12. Consider the most recent economic performance in China. To what extent do you think it confirms, and to what extent calls for adjustments in, the analysis in the China case study?

Notes

1. See Karla Hoff and Joseph E. Stiglitz, "Modern economic theory and development," in *Frontiers in Development Economics*, eds. Gerald M. Meier and Joseph E. Stiglitz (New York: Oxford University Press, 2000). The Hoff and Stiglitz epigram (header quote) is drawn from this source, p. 390.

2. For example, the two approaches have converged when low-growth paths resulting from a coordination failure have been explicitly examined within an endogenous growth framework. See Oded Galor and Joseph Zeira, "Income distribution and macroeconomics," *Review of Economic Studies* 60 (1993): 35–52.

3. For an insightful discussion of how many of the perspectives of this approach are applied to "new economy" issues, see Carl Shapiro and Hal Varian, *Information Rules: A Strategic Guide to the Network Economy* (Boston: Harvard Business School Press, 1999).

4. The problems cannot be solved even by perfect labor contracting (which is generally impossible in any case) if there is a risk of involuntary separations between firms and their employees (e.g., firm bankruptcies or death or serious illness of an employee). For a particularly insightful formal model, see Daron Acemoglu, "Training and innovation in an imperfect labour market," *Review of Economic Studies* 64 (1997): 445–464.

5. For an interesting formal model of this problem with supporting empirical evidence from rural Bangladesh, see Shahe Emran and Forhad Shilpi, "Marketing externalities, multiple equilibria, and market development," a paper presented at the Northeast Universities Development Conference, Boston University, September 2001. See also Shahe Emran and Forhad Shilpi, "The extent of the market and stages of agricultural specialization," *Canadian Journal of Economics* 45, No. 3 (2012): 1125–1153.

6. Alicia Adsera and Debraj Ray, "History and coordination failure," *Journal of Economic Growth* 3 (1998): 267–276; Debraj Ray, *Development Economics* (Princeton, N.J.: Princeton University Press, 1998), ch. 5.

7. For an introductory overview of the prisoners' dilemma problem, see Robert Gibbons, *Game Theory for Applied Economists* (Princeton, N.J.: Princeton University Press, 1992), pp. 2–7.

8. Even under perfect information conditions, however, coordination can remain a problem.

9. Technically, Figure 4.1 assumes that agents are homogeneous and depicts a symmetrical Nash equilibrium, but this can be generalized to cases in which agents differ. An example of an upward-sloping supply curve intersecting a downward-sloping demand curve—to produce a single equilibrium—can be seen in Figure 5.5, for the case of a labor market.

10. Technically, what is depicted is a set of symmetrical Nash equilibria. The S-shaped curve is the reaction curve of a representative agent to the average behavior of the other agents.

11. Paul Rosenstein-Rodan, "Problems of industrialization of eastern and southeastern Europe," *Economic Journal* 53 (1943): 202–211.

12. Kevin M. Murphy, Andrei Shleifer, and Robert W. Vishny, "Industrialization and the big push," *Journal of Political Economy* 97 (1989): 1003–1026.

13. Paul Krugman, *Development, Geography, and Economic Theory* (Cambridge, Mass.: MIT Press, 1995), ch. 1. For an alternative exposition and an algebraic development of the model, see Kaushik Basu, *Analytical Development Economics* (Cambridge, Mass.: MIT Press, 1997), pp. 17–33.

14. One reason could be an efficiency wage effect, in which workers work harder to avoid being fired when paid a high wage, thereby raising productivity enough to pay for the higher wage.

15. We are assuming that modern-sector workers would be changing the sectors (from traditional to modern) in which they work voluntarily; that is, they are not slave labor.

16. In the formal model of Murphy, Shleifer, and Vishny, there is a continuum of products, but that need not concern us here.

17. This consumption pattern means that there is unit-elastic demand; this is the type of demand function

that follows from a Cobb-Douglas utility function with equal preference weights for all goods, such as a utility function given by the products of the amounts of each type of good consumed. Technically, Murphy, Schleifer, and Vishny assume that there is one representative consumer who supplies all labor and receives all profits and, with their other assumptions, set up the model so that Figure 4.2 and other parts of the analysis can be thought of either as the economy as a whole or as any particular market, but these considerations need not concern us here.

18. See, for example, Hollis B. Chenery, Sherman Robinson, and Moshe Syrquin, *Industrialization and Growth: A Comparative Study* (New York: Oxford University Press, 1986).

19. For work in this field, see, for example, Andrés Rodriguez-Clare, "The division of labor and economic development," *Journal of Development Economics* 49 (1996): 3–32. Rodriguez-Clare starts with three plausible conditions that have had wide theoretical and empirical support since Adam Smith in the first two cases and Alfred Marshall in the third: There are productivity gains from the division of labor, the division of labor is limited by the extent of the market, and, as explained in Chapter 7, efficiency gains are derived from the proximity of suppliers and users of certain inputs. Given these assumptions, Rodriguez-Clare then shows that a small, open economy may be caught in an underdevelopment trap in which a "shallow division of labor" (i.e., a low variety of specialized inputs) is self-reinforcing. This in turn leads to a low rate of return to capital, so foreign investment or domestic capital accumulation may not materialize to help solve the problem. For another illustration, see Dani Rodrik, "Coordination failures and government policy: A model with applications to East Asia and Eastern Europe," *Journal of International Economics* 40 (1996): 1–22. See also Murphy, Shleifer, and Vishny, "Industrialization," sec. 6.

20. Recall from microeconomics that we can write marginal revenue as $P(Q)[1 - 1/\eta]$, where P is price and η is the (absolute value of) price elasticity of demand. With unit elasticity, $\eta = 1$; then note that this producer has positive constant marginal costs. Therefore, profits may be indefinitely increased by decreasing output and raising price accordingly.

21. In other words, the producer acts as a limit-pricing monopolist.

22. Wages have risen to w, but this product sector is by definition a very small part of the economy, so we can ignore income effects, which are negligible.

23. The graph was suggested by Krugman. See *Development, Geography, and Economic Theory*.

24. Thus conditions for monopoly limit pricing are still present.

25. With a price of 1, the quantity of goods purchased by workers is equal to the wage bill.

26. To see this, note that after the big push, total wages in the economy are $w_2(L/N)N$, and total profits are $[1Q_2 - w_2(L/N)]N$. Summing these, we get $1Q_2N$, the value of total output.

27. Expressed differently, the problem is that market failure is present. In particular, as Krugman points out, the interaction between a firm's internal economies of scale and the existence of perfectly elastic labor supplies at low wages together generate pecuniary externalities that inhibit the entry of modern firms. In other words, by generating an increase in aggregate demand, each firm makes a contribution to a mutually profitable big push to industrialization, even though individually each firm would lose money by industrializing alone. Thus, although the economies of scale are internal to the firm, when combined with the presence of a traditional sector paying low wages, de facto external *pecuniary* positive externalities are generated. Again, this is because each firm's production has the effect of raising other firms' revenues, making them more profitable. A simple characterization of the conundrum is that if there is only one modern firm, profits are greater in the traditional sector, but if there is a modern firm in every activity, profits are greater in the modern sector.

28. Formally, $F = F(N)$, where F is falling as N rises.

29. For details of one insightful formal model that casts the big push model in relatively accessible algebraic terms, see Stefano Paternostro, "The poverty trap: The dual externality model and its policy implications," *World Development* 25 (1997): 2071–2081.

30. Note that formally, in this case, *efficient* means "laborsaving," but the point is more general.

31. As Murphy, Schleifer, and Vishny show, there is also a plausible equilibrium condition that an increased interest-rate effect is not too large.

32. Openness to trade will not resolve this problem because the development of cities in *other* countries does not generally assist with national development. Urbanization is discussed further in Chapter 7.

33. In principle, if it is known that a sufficient number of modern firms will enter, the infrastructure problem can be solved by using perfect price discrimination, but if firms have different fixed costs that are not observable by the infrastructure provider or if perfect price discrimination is not possible for some other reason, the infrastructure may not be built, even when it is efficient to do so. See Murphy, Shleifer, and Vishny, "Industrialization," sec. 6. For an accessible algebraic derivation using a diagram similar to Figure 4.2, see Pranab Bardhan and Chris Udry, *Development Microeconomics* (New York: Oxford University Press, 1999), pp. 208–211.

34. The term *lemons* derives from poor-quality used cars. As is well known, new cars lose a significant part of their value as soon as they leave the showroom. This is because the mere fact that a car is offered for sale is taken as valuable information about the car in itself. People wanting to buy a car are generally not expert mechanics, so they need to search for some shorthand information to help them decide what a car is worth; obviously, owners of a poor-quality car are more likely to offer it for sale. Analogies to this "lemons problem" have many other applications in economics, such as in financial markets (see Chapter 15). Also see George Akerlof, "The market for lemons," *Quarterly Journal of Economics* 84 (1970): 488–500.

35. For an excellent survey of some of the new developments covered in this section, see Hoff and Stiglitz, "Modern economic theory and development." Another good discussion of this and related topics is found in Ray, *Development Economics*, ch. 5.

36. See Alice Amsden, *Asia's Next Giant: South Korea and Late Industrialization* (Oxford: Oxford University Press, 1989) and *The Rise of the Rest* (New York: Oxford University Press, 2001); Carl J. Dahlman, Bruce Ross-Larson, and Larry E. Westphal, "Managing technical development: Lessons from the newly industrializing countries," *World Development* 15 (1987): 759–775; Richard Luedde-Neurath, *Import Controls and Export-Oriented Development: A Reassessment of the South Korean Case* (Boulder, Colo.: Westview Press, 1986); Howard Pack and Larry E. Westphal, "Industrial strategy and technological change: Theory versus reality," *Journal of Development Economics* 22 (1986): 87–128; Joseph Stern et al., *Industrialization and the State: The Korean Heavy and Chemical Industry Drive* (Cambridge, Mass.: Harvard University Press, 1995); Gordon White, ed., *Developmental States in East Asia* (New York: St. Martin's Press, 1988); and Stephen C. Smith, "Industrial policy and export success: Third World development strategies reconsidered," in *U.S. Trade Policy and Global Growth*, ed. Robert Blecker (New York: Sharpe, 1996), pp. 267–298. On linkages, see also Masahisa Fujita, Paul Krugman, and Anthony J. Venables, *The Spatial Economy: Cities, Regions, and International Trade* (Cambridge, Mass.: MIT Press 1999).

37. This perspective helps account for the popularity of input-output analysis in development planning and policy formulation, especially in earlier years, although it is an imperfect tool for this purpose (see Chapter 11).

38. For some evidence, see William L. Megginson and Jeffry M. Netter, "From state to market: A survey of empirical studies on privatization," *Journal of Economic Literature* 39 (2001): 321–390.

39. See Abhijit V. Banerjee and Andrew F. Newman, "Occupational choice and the process of development," *Journal of Political Economy* 101 (1993): 274–298.

40. Galor and Zeira's model rests on an alternative way to characterize imperfect capital markets—that the rate of interest for borrowers is greater than that for lenders. One can verify the reasonableness of this assumption with a brief visit to any bank. The model is a simple two-period, overlapping-generations model. See Galor and Zeira, "Income distribution and macroeconomics."

41. Torsten Persson and Guido Tabellini, "Is inequality harmful for growth?" *American Economic Review* 84 (1994): 600–621; see also Chapter 5 of this text.

42. Michael Kremer, "The O-ring theory of economic development," *Quarterly Journal of Economics* 108 (1993): 551–575. A good exposition of the model, which provides alternative proofs to the ones found in Kremer, is found in Basu, *Analytical Development Economics*.

43. More generally, there are *n* tasks; for simplicity, we continue to assume that one, and only one, worker must perform each of the *n* tasks,

but conceptually, n should be thought of as tasks rather than number of workers. If, and only if, all tasks are performed successfully, output per worker is given by B, which is given in value terms (or if thought of in quantity terms, price is normalized to 1). Conventional capital, k, may also be used (if not, simply set $k = 1$), which is introduced in the formula, with diminishing returns (of course, capital might also be of varying quality). Expected output y is given by

$$E(y) = K^\alpha \left(\prod_{i=1}^{n} q_i \right) nB$$

In general, we must multiply by n because otherwise the firm can only lose value by adding more differentiated tasks. In the O-ring theory, Kremer analyzes what happens when $B = B(n)$, where $B'(n) > 0$, as a way of endogenizing technology choice.

44. For a more formal and more general demonstration that firms would choose to employ workers of the same skill level (or as close to identical as possible), let us continue the example from note 43. A necessary condition for a maximum with respect to each of the labor qualities q is

$$\frac{dw(q_i)}{dq_i} \equiv \frac{dy}{dq_i} = \left(\prod_{j \neq i} q_j \right) nBK^\alpha$$

This equation tells us that in equilibrium, the value of the marginal product of skill is equal to the marginal cost of skill in wage payments. In other words, the firm finds that the added value of replacing one worker with another with higher skill while leaving the skill levels of all other workers constant is equal to the resulting increase in the wage bill. Next, note that the second derivative, or the derivative of the marginal product of skill for the ith worker with respect to the skill level of the other workers, is positive; that is,

$$\frac{d^2y}{dq_i d} = \left(\prod_{j \neq i} q_j \right) = nBK^\alpha > 0$$

This positive cross-derivative indicates that firms with high-skilled workers in all but one task receive the greatest benefits from having a high-skilled worker in the remaining task, and so they can and would bid the most for high-skilled workers.

45. Technically, this type of marriage market matching process does not depend on the presence of positive cross-derivatives, as in note 44, but results only from individual preferences, along with the assumption of nontransferable utility (meaning that there can be no side payments). Thus there are two types of situations in which positive assortative matching may occur.

46. See Michael Kremer and Eric Maskin, "Wage inequality and segregation by skill," NBER Working Paper No. 5718, 1996.

47. See Kremer, "O-ring theory," for a formal statement of this result and for extensions to cases of endogenous skill investments under imperfect information.

48. Ibid., p. 574. The multiple equilibrium analysis is found on pp. 564–571.

49. Ricardo Hausmann and Dani Rodrik, "Economic development as self-discovery," *Journal of Development Economics* 72 (2003): 603–633. A related and insightful earlier analysis was provided by Karla Hoff, "Bayesian learning in an infant industry model," *Journal of International Economics* 43 (1997): 409–436.

50. Ricardo Hausmann, Dani Rodrik, and Andrés Velasco, "Growth diagnostics," in *One Economics, Many Recipes: Globalization, Institutions, and Economic Growth,* by Dani Rodrik (Princeton, N.J.: Princeton University Press, 2007), ch. 2.

51. Paul Krugman, *Development, Geography, and Economic Theory,* (Cambridge: MIT Press, 1995.)

52. Hoff and Stiglitz, "Modern economic theory and development."

53. Seminar presentation by Joseph E. Stiglitz at the World Bank, May 27, 1999; and ibid., p. 421.

54. Karla Hoff, "Beyond Rosenstein-Rodan: The modern theory of coordination problems in development," in *Annual World Bank Conference on Development Economics, 1999* (Washington, D.C.: World Bank, 2000), p. 146.

PART TWO

Problems and Policies: Domestic

Poverty, Inequality, and Development

5

No society can surely be flourishing and happy, of which by far the greater part of the numbers are poor and miserable.

—*Adam Smith, 1776*

Viewed through the lens of human development, the global village appears deeply divided between the streets of the haves and those of the have-nots.
—*United Nations Development Programme*, Human Development Report, 2006

Social protection directly reduces poverty and helps make growth more pro-poor.
—*Organization for Economic Cooperation and Development, 2010*

The coincidence of severe and persistent poverty and hunger indicates the presence of poverty traps—conditions from which individuals or groups cannot emerge without the help of others.

—*International Food Policy Research Institute, 2007*

The World Bank Group has adopted two new goals: end extreme poverty by 2030 and boost shared prosperity by maximizing income growth for the poorest 40 percent in every country.

—*Jim Yong Kim, President, World Bank, 2013*

Chapters 1 and 2 introduced the problem that despite significant improvements over the past half century, extreme poverty remains widespread in the developing world. In 2010, more than 1.2 billion people lived on less than $1.25 per day at 2005 U.S. purchasing power parity (2013 World Bank estimate). Some 2.4 billion—more than one-third of the world's population—lived on less than $2 a day. As you will see in the next few chapters, often these impoverished people suffer from undernutrition and poor health, have little or no literacy, live in environmentally degraded areas, have little political voice, are socially excluded, and attempt to earn a meager living on small and marginal farms (or as day laborers) or in dilapidated urban slums. In this chapter, we set the stage with an in-depth examination of the problems of poverty and of highly unequal distributions of income.

That development requires a higher gross national income (GNI), and hence sustained growth, is clear. The basic issue, however, is not only how to make GNI grow but also who would make it grow: the few or the many. If it were the rich, it would most likely be appropriated by them, and progress against poverty would be slow, and inequality would worsen. But if it were generated by the many, they would be its principal beneficiaries, and the fruits of economic growth would be shared more evenly. Thus, many developing countries that had experienced relatively high rates of economic growth by historical standards discovered that such growth often brought little in the way of significant benefits to their poor.

216

Because the elimination of widespread poverty and high and even growing income inequality are at the core of all development problems and in fact define for many people the principal objective of development policy, we begin Part Two by focusing on the nature of the poverty and inequality problem in developing countries. Although our main focus is on economic poverty and inequalities in the distribution of incomes and assets, it is important to keep in mind that this is only part of the broader inequality problem in the developing world. Of equal or even greater importance are inequalities of power, prestige, status, gender, job satisfaction, conditions of work, degree of participation, freedom of choice, and many other dimensions of the problem that relate more to our second and third components of the meaning of development, self-esteem, and freedom to choose. As in most social relationships, we cannot really separate the economic from the noneconomic manifestations of inequality. Each reinforces the other in a complex and often interrelated process of cause and effect.

After introducing appropriate measures of inequality and poverty, we define the nature of the poverty and income distribution problem and consider its quantitative significance in various developing nations. We then examine in what ways economic analyses can shed light on the problem and explore possible alternative policy approaches directed at the elimination of poverty and the reduction of excessively wide disparities in the distributions of income in developing countries. A thorough understanding of these two fundamental economic manifestations of underdevelopment provides the basis for analysis in subsequent chapters of more specific development issues, including population growth, education, health, rural development, environmental degradation and climate change, and foreign assistance.

In this chapter, therefore, we will examine the following critical questions about the relationship among economic growth, income distribution, and poverty:

1. How can we best measure inequality and poverty?

2. What is the extent of relative inequality in developing countries, and how is this related to the extent of absolute poverty?

3. Who are the poor, and what are their economic characteristics?

4. What determines the nature of economic growth—that is, who benefits from economic growth, and why?

5. Are rapid economic growth and more equal distributions of income compatible or conflicting objectives for low-income countries? To put it another way, is rapid growth achievable only at the cost of greater inequalities in the distribution of income, or can a lessening of income disparities contribute to higher growth rates?

6. Do the poor benefit from growth, and does this depend on the type of growth a developing country experiences? What might be done to help the poor benefit more?

7. What is so bad about extreme inequality?

8. What kinds of policies are required to reduce the magnitude and extent of absolute poverty?

We begin the chapter by defining *inequality* and *poverty*, terms that are commonly used in informal conversation but need to be measured more precisely to provide a meaningful understanding of how much progress has already been made, how much remains to be achieved, and how to set incentives for government officials to focus on the most pressing needs. You will see that the most important measures of poverty and inequality used by development economists satisfy properties that most observers would agree are of fundamental importance. After a discussion of why attention to inequality as well as poverty is important, we then use the appropriate measures of poverty and inequality to evaluate the welfare significance of alternative patterns (or "typologies") of growth. After reviewing the evidence on the extent of poverty and inequality in the developing world, we conclude with an overview of the key issues in poverty policy. Some important principles of effective poverty policies are considered, together with some initial examples of programs that have worked well in practice. We conclude the chapter with a comparative case study of Ghana and Côte d'Ivoire, which illustrates, issues of the quality of growth and the difficulties of achieving it.

5.1 Measuring Inequality

In this section, we define the dimensions of the income distribution and poverty problems and identify some similar elements that characterize the problem in many developing nations. But first we should be clear about what we are measuring when we speak about the distribution of income and absolute poverty.

Economists usually distinguish between two principal measures of income distribution for both analytical and quantitative purposes: the personal or size distribution of income and the functional or distributive factor share distribution of income.

Size Distributions

Personal distribution of income (size distribution of income)   The distribution of income according to size class of persons—for example, the share of total income accruing to the poorest specific percentage or the richest specific percentage of a population—without regard to the sources of that income.

Quintile   A 20% proportion of any numerical quantity. A population divided into quintiles would be divided into five groups of equal size.

Decile   A 10% portion of any numerical quantity; a population divided into deciles would be divided into ten equal numerical groups.

The **personal** or **size distribution of income** is the measure most commonly used by economists. It simply deals with individual persons or households and the total incomes they receive. The way in which they received that income is not considered. What matters is how much each earns irrespective of whether the income is derived solely from employment or comes also from other sources such as interest, profits, rents, gifts, or inheritance. Moreover, the locational (urban or rural) and occupational sources of the income (e.g., agriculture, manufacturing, commerce, services) are ignored. If Ms. X and Mr. Y both receive the same personal income, they are classified together irrespective of the fact that Ms. X may work 15 hours a day as a doctor while Mr. Y doesn't work at all but simply collects interest on his inheritance.

Economists and statisticians therefore like to arrange all individuals by ascending personal incomes and then divide the total population into distinct groups, or sizes. A common method is to divide the population into successive **quintiles** (fifths) or **deciles** (tenths) according to ascending income levels and then determine what proportion of the total national income is received

		Share of Total Income (%)	
Individuals	**Personal Income (money units)**	**Quintiles**	**Deciles**
1	0.8		
2	1.0		1.8
3	1.4		
4	1.8	5	3.2
5	1.9		
6	2.0		3.9
7	2.4		
8	2.7	9	5.1
9	2.8		
10	3.0		5.8
11	3.4		
12	3.8	13	7.2
13	4.2		
14	4.8		9.0
15	5.9		
16	7.1	22	13.0
17	10.5		
18	12.0		22.5
19	13.5		
20	15.0	51	28.5
Total (national income)	100.0	100	100.0

TABLE 5.1 Typical Size Distribution of Personal Income in a Developing Country by Income Shares—Quintiles and Deciles

by each income group. For example, Table 5.1 shows a hypothetical but fairly typical distribution of income for a developing country. In this table, 20 individuals, representing the entire population of the country, are arranged in order of ascending annual personal income, ranging from the individual with the lowest income (0.8 units) to the one with the highest (15.0 units). The total or national income of all individuals amounts to 100 units and is the sum of all entries in column 2. In column 3, the population is grouped into quintiles of four individuals each. The first quintile represents the bottom 20% of the population on the income scale. This group receives only 5% (i.e., a total of 5 money units) of the total national income. The second quintile (individuals 5 through 8) receives 9% of the total income. Alternatively, the bottom 40% of the population (quintiles 1 plus 2) is receiving only 14% of the income, while the top 20% (the fifth quintile) of the population receives 51% of the total income.

A common measure of **income inequality** that can be derived from column 3 is the ratio of the incomes received by the top 20% and bottom 40% of the population. This ratio, sometimes called a *Kuznets ratio* after Nobel laureate Simon Kuznets, has often been used as a measure of the degree of inequality between high- and low-income groups in a country. In our example, this inequality ratio is equal to 51 divided by 14, or approximately 3.64.

To provide a more detailed breakdown of the size distribution of income, decile (10%) shares are listed in column 4. We see, for example, that the bottom 10% of the population (the two poorest individuals) receives only 1.8% of the total income, while the top 10% (the two richest individuals) receives 28.5%. Finally, if we wanted to know what the top 5% receives, we would divide

Income inequality The disproportionate distribution of total national income among households.

the total population into 20 equal groups of individuals (in our example, this would simply be each of the 20 individuals) and calculate the percentage of total income received by the top group. In Table 5.1, we see that the top 5% of the population (the twentieth individual) receives 15% of the income, a higher share than the combined shares of the lowest 40%.

Lorenz Curves

Lorenz curve   A graph depicting the variance of the size distribution of income from perfect equality.

Another common way to analyze personal income statistics is to construct what is known as a **Lorenz curve**.[1] Figure 5.1 shows how it is done. The numbers of income recipients are plotted on the horizontal axis, not in absolute terms but in *cumulative percentages*. For example, at point 20, we have the lowest (poorest) 20% of the population; at point 60, we have the bottom 60%; and at the end of the axis, all 100% of the population has been accounted for. The vertical axis shows the share of total income received by each percentage of population.

It is also cumulative up to 100%, meaning that both axes are the same length. The entire figure is enclosed in a square, and a diagonal line is drawn from the lower left corner (the origin) of the square to the upper right corner. At every point on that diagonal, the percentage of income received is *exactly equal* to the percentage of income recipients—for example, the point halfway along the length of the diagonal represents 50% of the income being distributed to exactly 50% of the population. At the three-quarters point on the diagonal, 75% of the income would be distributed to 75% of the population. In other words, the diagonal line in Figure 5.1 is representative of "perfect equality" in size distribution of income. Each percentage group of income recipients is receiving

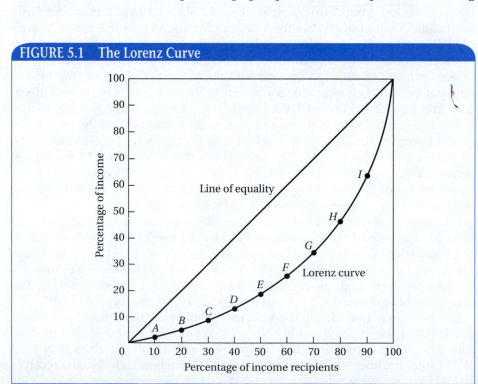

FIGURE 5.1   The Lorenz Curve

that same percentage of the total income; for example, the bottom 40% receives 40% of the income, while the top 5% receives only 5% of the total income.[2]

The Lorenz curve shows the *actual* quantitative relationship between the percentage of income recipients and the percentage of the total income they did in fact receive during, say, a given year. In Figure 5.1, we have plotted this Lorenz curve using the decile data contained in Table 5.1. In other words, we have divided both the horizontal and vertical axes into ten equal segments corresponding to each of the ten decile groups. Point *A* shows that the bottom 10% of the population receives only 1.8% of the total income, point *B* shows that the bottom 20% is receiving 5% of the total income, and so on for each of the other eight cumulative decile groups. Note that at the halfway point, 50% of the population is in fact receiving only 19.8% of the total income.

The more the Lorenz line curves away from the diagonal (line of perfect equality), the greater the degree of inequality represented. The extreme case of perfect inequality (i.e., a situation in which one person receives all of the national income while everybody else receives nothing) would be represented by the congruence of the Lorenz curve with the bottom horizontal and right-hand vertical axes. Because no country exhibits either perfect equality or perfect inequality in its distribution of income, the Lorenz curves for different countries will lie somewhere to the right of the diagonal in Figure 5.1. The greater the degree of inequality, the greater the bend and the closer to the bottom horizontal axis the Lorenz curve will be. Two representative distributions are shown in Figure 5.2, one for a relatively equal distribution (Figure 5.2a) and the other for a relatively unequal distribution (Figure 5.2b). (Can you explain why the Lorenz curve could not lie above or to the left of the diagonal at any point?)

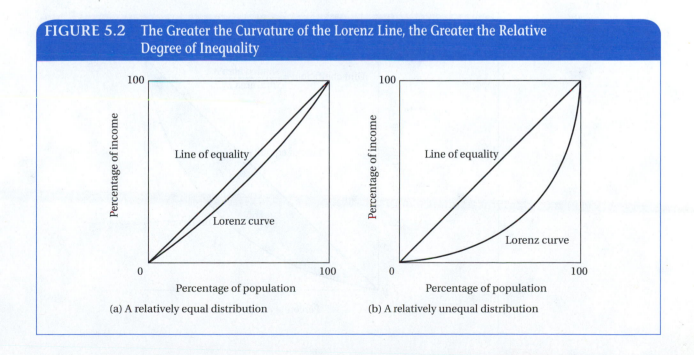

FIGURE 5.2 The Greater the Curvature of the Lorenz Line, the Greater the Relative Degree of Inequality

(a) A relatively equal distribution

(b) A relatively unequal distribution

Gini Coefficients and Aggregate Measures of Inequality

A final and very convenient shorthand summary measure of the relative degree of income inequality in a country can be obtained by calculating the ratio of the area between the diagonal and the Lorenz curve divided by the total area of the half-square in which the curve lies. In Figure 5.3, this is the ratio of the shaded area *A* to the total area of the triangle *BCD*. This ratio is known as the *Gini concentration ratio* or **Gini coefficient**, named after the Italian statistician who first formulated it in 1912.

Gini coefficients are aggregate inequality measures and can vary anywhere from 0 (perfect equality) to 1 (perfect inequality). In fact, as you will soon discover, the Gini coefficient for countries with highly unequal income distributions typically lies between 0.50 and 0.70, while for countries with relatively equal distributions, it is on the order of 0.20 to 0.35. The coefficient for our hypothetical distribution of Table 5.1 and Figure 5.1 is approximately 0.44—a relatively unequal distribution.

Four possible Lorenz curves such as might be found in international data are drawn in Figure 5.4. In the "Lorenz criterion" of income distribution, whenever one Lorenz curve lies above another Lorenz curve, the economy corresponding to the upper Lorenz curve is more equal than that of the lower curve. Thus, economy *A* may unambiguously be said to be more equal than economy *D*. Whenever two Lorenz curves cross, such as curves *B* and *C*, the Lorenz criterion states that we "need more information" or additional assumptions before we can determine which of the underlying economies is more equal. For example, we might argue on the grounds of the priority of addressing problems of poverty that curve *B* represents a more equal economy, since the poorest are richer, even though the richest are also richer (and hence the middle class is "squeezed"). But others might start with the assumption that

Gini coefficient An aggregate numerical measure of income inequality ranging from 0 (perfect equality) to 1 (perfect inequality). It is measured graphically by dividing the area between the perfect equality line and the Lorenz curve by the total area lying to the right of the equality line in a Lorenz diagram. The higher the value of the coefficient is, the higher the inequality of income distribution; the lower it is, the more equal the distribution of income.

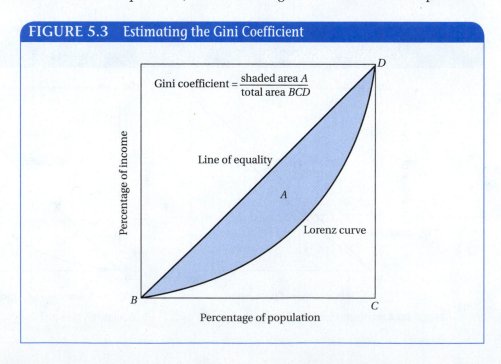

FIGURE 5.3   Estimating the Gini Coefficient

Gini coefficient = $\dfrac{\text{shaded area } A}{\text{total area } BCD}$

Line of equality

A

Lorenz curve

Percentage of income

Percentage of population

FIGURE 5.4   Four Possible Lorenz Curves

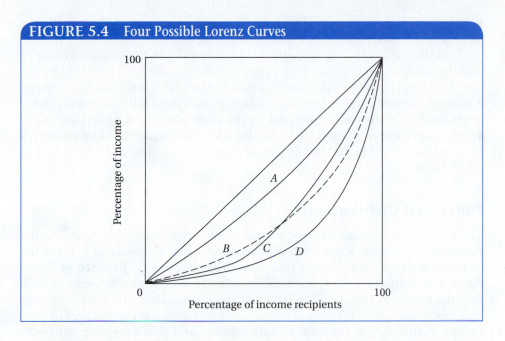

an economy with a stronger middle class is inherently more equal, and those observers might select economy C.

One could also use an aggregate measure such as the Gini coefficient to decide the matter. As it turns out, the Gini coefficient is among a class of measures that satisfy four highly desirable properties: the anonymity, scale independence, population independence, and transfer principles.[3] The *anonymity principle* simply means that our measure of inequality should not depend on who has the higher income; for example, it should not depend on whether we believe the rich or the poor to be good or bad people. The *scale independence principle* means that our measure of inequality should not depend on the size of the economy or the way we measure its income; for example, our inequality measure should not depend on whether we measure income in dollars or in cents or in rupees or rupiahs or for that matter on whether the economy is rich on average or poor on average—because if we are interested in inequality, we want a measure of the dispersion of income, not its magnitude (note that magnitudes are very important in poverty measures). The *population independence principle* is somewhat similar; it states that the measure of inequality should not be based on the number of income recipients. For example, the economy of China should be considered no more or less equal than the economy of Vietnam simply because China has a larger population than Vietnam. Finally, we have the *transfer principle* (sometimes called the *Pigou-Dalton principle* after its creators); it states that, holding all other incomes constant, if we transfer some income from a richer person to a poorer person (but not so much that the poorer person is now richer than the originally rich person), the resulting new income distribution is more equal. If we like these four criteria, we can measure the Gini coefficient in each case and rank the one with the larger Gini as more unequal. However, this is not always a perfect solution. For example, the Gini coefficient can, in theory, be identical for two Lorenz curves that cross; can you see why by looking at curves *B* and *C* in Figure 5.4? And sometimes different inequality measures that satisfy our four properties can give different answers as to which of two economies are more unequal.[4]

Note that a measure of dispersion common in statistics, the coefficient of variation (CV), which is simply the sample standard deviation divided by the sample mean, is another measure of inequality that also satisfies the four criteria. Although the CV is more commonly used in statistics, the Gini coefficient is often used in studies of income and wealth distribution due to its convenient Lorenz curve interpretation. Note, finally, that we can also use Lorenz curves to study inequality in the distribution of land, in education and health, and in other assets.

Functional Distributions

Functional distribution of income (factor share distribution of income) The distribution of income to factors of production without regard to the ownership of the factors.

Factors of production Resources or inputs required to produce a good or a service, such as land, labor, and capital.

The second common measure of income distribution used by economists, the **functional** or **factor share distribution of income**, attempts to explain the share of total national income that each of the **factors of production** (land, labor, and capital) receives. Instead of looking at individuals as separate entities, the theory of functional income distribution inquires into the percentage that labor receives as a whole and compares this with the percentages of total income distributed in the form of rent, interest, and profit (i.e., the returns to land and financial and physical capital). Although specific individuals may receive income from all these sources, that is not a matter of concern for the functional approach.

A sizable body of theoretical literature has been built up around the concept of functional income distribution. It attempts to explain the income of a factor of production by the contribution that this factor makes to production. Supply and demand curves are assumed to determine the unit prices of each productive factor. When these unit prices are multiplied by quantities employed on the assumption of efficient (minimum-cost) factor utilization, we get a measure of the total payment to each factor. For example, the supply of and demand for labor are assumed to determine its market wage. When this wage is then multiplied by the total level of employment, we get a measure of total wage payments, also sometimes called the *total wage bill*.

Figure 5.5 provides a simple diagrammatic illustration of the traditional theory of functional income distribution. We assume that there are only two factors of production: capital, which is a fixed (given) factor, and labor, which is the only variable factor. Under competitive market assumptions, the demand for labor will be determined by labor's marginal product (i.e., additional workers will be hired up to the point where the value of their marginal product equals their real wage). But in accordance with the principle of diminishing marginal products, this demand for labor will be a declining function of the numbers employed. Such a negatively sloped labor demand curve is shown by line D_L in Figure 5.5. With a traditional, neoclassical, upward-sloping labor supply curve S_L, the equilibrium wage will be equal to W_E and the equilibrium level of employment will be L_E. Total national output (which equals total national income) will be represented by the area $0REL_E$.[5] This national income will be distributed in two shares: $0W_EEL_E$ going to workers in the form of wages and W_ERE remaining as capitalist profits (the return to owners of capital). Hence, in a competitive market economy with constant-returns-to-scale

FIGURE 5.5   Functional Income Distribution in a Market Economy: An Illustration

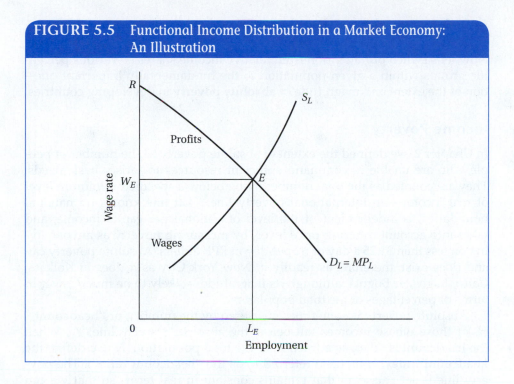

production functions (a doubling of all inputs doubles output), factor prices are determined by factor supply and demand curves, and factor shares always combine to exhaust the total national product. Income is distributed by function—laborers are paid wages, owners of land receive rents, and capitalists obtain profits. It is a neat and logical theory in that each and every factor gets paid only in accordance with what it contributes to national output, no more and no less. In fact, as you may recall from Chapter 3, this model of income distribution is at the core of the Lewis theory of modern-sector growth based on the reinvestment of rising capitalist profits.

Unfortunately, the relevance of the functional theory is greatly diminished by its failure to take into account the important role and influence of nonmarket forces such as power in determining these factor prices—for example, the role of collective bargaining between employers and trade unions in the setting of modern-sector wage rates, and the power of monopolists and wealthy landowners to manipulate prices on capital, land, and output to their own personal advantage. Appendix 5.1 examines the economic implications of factor price distortions, and we return to consider their implications for policy at the end of this chapter.

The Ahluwalia-Chenery Welfare Index (ACWI)

A final approach to accounting for the distribution of income in assessing the quality of growth is to value increases in income for all individuals but to assign a higher weight to income gains by lower-income individuals than to gains by higher-income individuals. Perhaps the best-known example is the Ahluwalia-Chenery Welfare Index (ACWI), which is explained in Appendix 5.2.

5.2 Measuring Absolute Poverty

Now let's switch our attention from relative income shares of various percentile groups within a given population to the fundamentally important question of the extent and magnitude of **absolute poverty** in developing countries.

Income Poverty

In Chapter 2, we defined the extent of absolute poverty as the number of people who are unable to command sufficient resources to satisfy basic needs. They are counted as the total number living below a specified minimum level of real income—an international poverty line. That line knows no national boundaries, is independent of the level of national per capita income, and takes into account differing price levels by measuring poverty as anyone living on less than $1.25 a day or $2 per day in PPP dollars. Absolute poverty can and does exist, therefore, as readily in New York City as it does in Kolkata, Cairo, Lagos, or Bogotá, although its magnitude is likely to be much lower in terms of percentages of the total population.

Absolute poverty is sometimes measured by the number, or "headcount," H, of those whose incomes fall below the absolute poverty line, Y_p. When the headcount is taken as a fraction of the total population, N, we define the **headcount index**, H/N (also referred to as the "headcount ratio"). The poverty line is set at a level that remains constant in real terms so that we can chart our progress on an absolute level over time. The idea is to set this level at a standard below which we would consider a person to live in "absolute human misery," such that the person's health is in jeopardy.

Of course, to define a minimum health standard that is invariant across historical epochs is an impossibility, in part because technology changes over time. For example, today we have 15-cent oral rehydration therapy packets that can save the life of a child in Malawi. Not long ago, the death of a child after a diarrheal disease would be taken as a sad but inevitable part of life, whereas today we regard such a death as a catastrophic moral failure of the international community. We simply come as close as we can to establishing a reasonable minimum standard that might hold over a few decades so that we can estimate more carefully how much progress we have made on a (more) absolute rather than a (highly) relative scale.

Certainly one would not accept the international poverty level of $1.25 a day in an unquestioning way when planning local poverty work. One practical strategy for determining a local absolute poverty line is to start by defining an adequate basket of food, based on nutritional requirements from medical studies of required calories, protein, and micronutrients. Then, using local household survey data, one can identify a typical basket of food purchased by households that just barely meet these nutritional requirements. One then adds other expenditures of this household, such as clothing, shelter, and medical care, to determine the local absolute poverty line. Depending on how these calculations are done, the resulting poverty line may come to more than $1.25 per day at PPP.

However, simply counting the number of people below an agreed-on poverty line has serious limitations. For example, if the poverty line is set at U.S. $450 per person, it makes a big difference whether most of the absolute

Absolute poverty The situation of being unable or only barely able to meet the subsistence essentials of food, clothing, and shelter.

Headcount index The proportion of a country's population living below the poverty line.

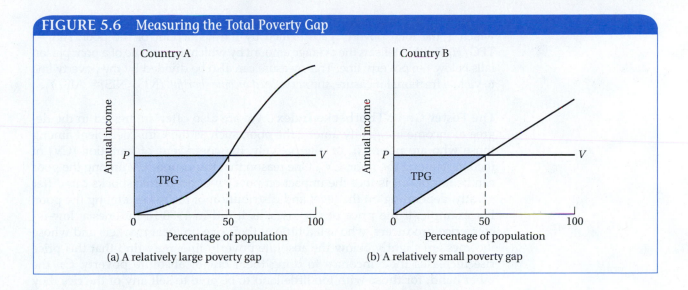

FIGURE 5.6 Measuring the Total Poverty Gap

(a) A relatively large poverty gap

(b) A relatively small poverty gap

poor earn $400 or $300 per year. Both are accorded the same weight when calculating the proportion of the population that lies below the poverty line; clearly, however, the poverty problem is much more serious in the latter instance. Economists therefore attempt to calculate a **total poverty gap (TPG)** that measures the total amount of income necessary to raise everyone who is below the poverty line up to that line. Figure 5.6 illustrates how we can measure the total poverty gap as the shaded area between poverty line, *PV*, and the annual income profile of the population.

> **Total poverty gap (TPG)**
> The sum of the difference between the poverty line and actual income levels of all people living below that line.

Even though in both country A and country B, 50% of the population falls below the same poverty line, the TPG in country A is greater than in country B. Therefore, it will take more of an effort to eliminate absolute poverty in country A.

The TPG—the extent to which the incomes of the poor lie below the poverty line—is found by adding up the amounts by which each poor person's income, Y_i, falls below the absolute poverty line, Y_p, as follows:

$$\text{TPG} = \sum_{i=1}^{H} (Y_p - Y_i) \qquad (5.1)$$

We can think of the TPG in a simplified way (i.e., no administrative costs or general equilibrium effects are accounted for) as the amount of money per day it would take to bring every poor person in an economy up to our defined minimum income standards. On a per capita basis, the *average poverty gap (APG)* is found by dividing the TPG by the total population:

$$\text{APG} = \frac{\text{TPG}}{N} \qquad (5.2)$$

Often we are interested in the size of the average poverty gap in relation to the poverty line, so we would use as our income shortfall measure the *normalized poverty gap (NPG)*: NPG = APG/Y_p; this measure lies between 0 and 1 and so can be useful when we want a unitless measure of the gap for easier comparisons.

Another important poverty gap measure is the *average income shortfall (AIS)*, which is the total poverty gap divided by the headcount of the poor: AIS = TPG/H. The AIS tells us the average amount by which the income of a poor person falls below the poverty line. This measure can also be divided by the poverty line to yield a fractional measure, the *normalized income shortfall (NIS)*: NIS = AIS/Y_p.

The Foster-Greer-Thorbecke Index   We are also often interested in the degree of income inequality among the poor, such as the Gini coefficient among those who are poor, G_p, or alternatively, the coefficient of variation (CV) of incomes among the poor, CV_p. One reason that the Gini or CV among the poor can be important is that the impact on poverty of economic shocks can differ greatly, depending on the level and distribution of resources among the poor. For example, if the price of rice rises, as it did in 1998 in Indonesia, low-income rice producers, who sell a little of their rice on local markets and whose incomes are slightly below the absolute poverty line, may find that this price rise increases their incomes to bring them out of absolute poverty. On the other hand, for those with too little land to be able to sell any of the rice they grow and who are net buyers of rice on markets, this price increase can greatly worsen their poverty. Thus, the most desirable measures of poverty would also be sensitive to the distribution of income among the poor.

As is the case with inequality measures, there are criteria for a desirable poverty measure that are widely accepted by development economists: the anonymity, population independence, monotonicity, and distributional sensitivity principles. The first two principles are very similar to the properties we examined for inequality indexes: Our measure of the extent of poverty should not depend on who is poor or on whether the country has a large or small population. The monotonicity principle means that if you add income to someone below the poverty line, all other incomes held constant, poverty can be *no greater* than it was.[6] The distributional sensitivity principle states that, other things being equal, if you transfer income from a poor person to a richer person, the resulting economy should be deemed strictly poorer. The headcount ratio measure satisfies anonymity, population independence, and monotonicity, but it fails on distributional sensitivity. The simple headcount fails even to satisfy the population independence principle.

A well-known poverty index that in certain forms satisfies all four criteria is the **Foster-Greer-Thorbecke (FGT) index**, often called the $P\alpha$ class of poverty measures.[7] The $P\alpha$ index is given by

Foster-Greer-Thorbecke (FGT) index   A class of measures of the level of absolute poverty.

$$P_\alpha = \frac{1}{N} \sum_{i=1}^{H} \left(\frac{Y_p - Y_i}{Y_p} \right)^\alpha \tag{5.3}$$

where Y_i is the income of the ith poor person, Y_p is the poverty line, and N is the population. Depending on the value of α, the $P\alpha$ index takes on different forms. If $\alpha = 0$, the numerator is equal to H, and we get the headcount ratio, H/N. Unfortunately, this measure is the same whether those in poverty earn 90 cents per day or 50 cents per day, so it cannot reveal the depth of poverty.

If $\alpha = 1$, we get the normalized (per capita) poverty gap. An alternative formula that can be derived for P_1 is given by $P_1 = (H/N)*(NIS)$, that is, the headcount ratio (H/N) times the normalized income shortfall (NIS). So, P_1 has the properties that poverty goes up whenever either the fraction of people in poverty goes up or the fractional income deficits (poverty depth) go up (or both)—in general, this makes it a better measure than P_0.

If $\alpha = 2$, we account for poverty severity, in that the impact on measured poverty of a gain in income by a poor person increases in relation to the square of the distance of the person from the poverty line. For example, raising the income of a person from a household living at half the per capita poverty line by, say, one penny per day would have five times the impact on poverty reduction as would raising by the same amount the income of a person living at 90% of the poverty line; this differing magnitude results from squaring the poverty gaps, so the P_2 measure captures the *severity* of poverty.

As a numerical example of the calculation of P_2, consider an 8-person economy with a poverty line of 1, and a hypothetical income distribution of: (0.6, 0.6, 0.8, 0.8, 2, 2, 6, 6). The headcount is 4, because two people have incomes of 0.6 and two people have incomes of 0.8; but the others have incomes above the poverty line. Using these numbers, we can find the P_2 level of poverty from equation 5.3:

$$P_2 = (1/8)[0.4^2 + 0.4^2 + 0.2^2 + 0.2^2] = (1/8)\,[0.16 + 0.16 + 0.04 + 0.04] = 0.4/8 = 0.05$$

Note that P_2 can be expressed in an alternative form to add further intuition. If $\alpha = 2$, the resulting measure, P_2, can be rewritten as[8]

$$P_2 = \left(\frac{H}{N}\right)[\,\mathrm{NIS}^2 + (1 - \mathrm{NIS})^2(\mathrm{CV}_P)^2\,] \tag{5.4}$$

As Equation 5.4 shows, P_2 contains the CV_p measure, and it satisfies all four of the poverty axioms.[9] Clearly, P_2 increases whenever H/N, NIS, or CV_p increases. Note from the formula that there is a greater emphasis on the distribution of income among the poor (CV_p) when the normalized income shortfall is small and a lesser emphasis when the NIS is large.

The **P_2 poverty measure**, also known as the *squared poverty gap index*, has become a standard of income poverty measure used by the World Bank and other agencies, and it is used in empirical work on income poverty because of its sensitivity to the depth and severity of poverty. Mexico uses the P_2 poverty measure to allocate funds for education, health, and welfare programs for the poor (in particular in the Progresa/Oportunidades Program, described at the end of Chapter 8), in accordance with the regional intensity of poverty.[10]

Another reason to prefer P_2 (or at least P_1) over P_0 is that standard headcount measures also have the perverse property of creating incentives for officials to focus efforts on the poor who are closest to the poverty line—because that is the easiest and cheapest way for them to demonstrate progress. We encountered a version of this problem in Chapter 1—a critique of the Millennium Development Goals focus on reducing the fraction of those living below the poverty line.

Values of P_0 and P_2 for selected developing countries are found in Table 5.6 later in this chapter.

Person-Equivalent Headcounts Although P_1 and P_2 are more informative measures, which provide better incentives to poverty programs than P_0, many agencies (including U.S. Agency for International Development—USAID) continue to report progress primarily if not exclusively in terms of P_0 head-count measures—apparently responding to public and legislative expectations to discuss poverty in terms of numbers of people. Given a political need to feature "headline" headcount measures, a partial improvement is to convert changes in the poverty gap into its headcount-equivalent (based on the initial average income shortfall). If aid agencies featured a supplementary headcount-equivalent, they could report in terms of numbers of people while accounting for changes in poverty depth. Estimates using this approach show progress against poverty in many countries is significantly greater than revealed using conventional headcount measures alone. [11]

Multidimensional Poverty Measurement Poverty cannot be adequately measured with income alone, as Amartya Sen's capability framework, examined in Chapter 1, makes apparent. To fill this gap, Sabina Alkire and James Foster have extended the FGT index to multiple dimensions.[12]

As always, the first step in measuring poverty is to know which people are poor. In the multidimensional poverty approach, a poor person is identified through what is called the "dual cutoff method": first, the cutoff levels within each of the dimensions (analogous to falling below a poverty line such as $1.25 per day if income poverty were being addressed) and second, the cutoff of the number of dimensions in which a person must be deprived (below the line) to be deemed multidimensionally poor. Using calculations analogous to the single-dimensional $P\alpha$ index, the multidimensional $M\alpha$ index is constructed. The most basic measure is the fraction of the population in multidimensional poverty—the multidimensional headcount ratio H_M.

The most common measure in practice is M_0, the *adjusted* headcount ratio, which uses ordinal data and is similar conceptually to the poverty gap P_1 (which again can be expressed as the headcount ratio times the normalized income shortfall). M_0 may be represented by the product of the multidimensional headcount ratio times the average fraction of dimensions in which the poor are deprived (or "average intensity of poverty" A, that is, $M_0 = H_M * A$. (In contrast to the simple multidimensional headcount ratio, the adjusted multidimensional headcount ratio satisfies the desirable property (called "dimensional monotonicity") that if the average fraction of deprivations increases, so does M_0).

In applied studies, proxy measures, called *indicators*, are used for each of the selected dimensions. Details of the way this measure has been constructed and applied in the UNDP Multidimensional Poverty Index and findings across countries are reported in Section 5.4, when we apply the poverty measures to examine the extent of poverty in different countries and regions. Another wisely used application is the Women's Empowerment in Agriculture Index, referred to in Chapter 9.

5.3 Poverty, Inequality, and Social Welfare

What's So Bad about Extreme Inequality?

Throughout this chapter, we are assuming that social welfare depends positively on the level of income per capita but negatively on poverty and negatively on the level of inequality, as these terms have just been defined. The problem of absolute poverty is obvious. No civilized people can feel satisfied with a state of affairs in which their fellow humans exist in conditions of such absolute human misery, which is probably why every major religion has emphasized the importance of working to alleviate poverty and is at least one of the reasons why international development assistance has the nearly universal support of every democratic nation. But it may reasonably be asked, if our top priority is the alleviation of absolute poverty, why should *relative inequality* be a concern? We have seen that inequality among the poor is a critical factor in understanding the severity of poverty and the impact of market and policy changes on the poor, but why should we be concerned with inequality among those *above* the poverty line?

There are three major answers to this question. First, extreme income inequality leads to economic inefficiency. This is partly because at any given average income, the higher the inequality is, the smaller the fraction of the population that qualifies for a loan or other credit. Indeed, one definition of *relative poverty* is the lack of collateral. When low-income individuals (whether they are absolutely poor or not) cannot borrow money, they generally cannot adequately educate their children or start and expand a business. Moreover, with high inequality, the overall rate of savings in the economy tends to be lower, because the highest rate of marginal savings is usually found among the middle classes. Although the rich may save a larger dollar amount, they typically save a smaller fraction of their incomes, and they almost always save a smaller fraction of their marginal incomes. Landlords, business leaders, politicians, and other rich elites are known to spend much of their incomes on imported luxury goods, gold, jewelry, expensive houses, and foreign travel or to seek safe havens abroad for their savings in what is known as *capital flight*. Such savings and investments do not add to the nation's productive resources; in fact, they represent substantial drains on these resources. In short, the rich do not generally save and invest significantly larger proportions of their incomes (in the real economic sense of productive domestic saving and investment) than the middle class or even the poor.[13] Furthermore, inequality may lead to an inefficient allocation of assets. As you will see in Chapter 8, high inequality leads to an overemphasis on higher education at the expense of quality universal primary education, which not only may be inefficient but is also likely to beget still more inequality in incomes. Moreover, as you will see in Chapter 9, high inequality of land ownership—characterized by the presence of huge *latifundios* (plantations) alongside tiny *minifundios* that are incapable of supporting even a single family—also leads to inefficiency because the most efficient scales for farming are family and medium-size farms. The result of these factors can be a lower average income and a lower rate of economic growth when inequality is high.[14]

The second reason to be concerned with inequality above the poverty line is that extreme income disparities undermine social stability and solidarity. Also, high inequality strengthens the political power of the rich and hence their economic bargaining power. Usually this power will be used to encourage outcomes favorable to themselves. High inequality facilitates *rent seeking*, including actions such as excessive lobbying, large political donations, bribery, and cronyism. When resources are allocated to such rent-seeking behaviors, they are diverted from productive purposes that could lead to faster growth. Even worse, high inequality makes poor institutions very difficult to improve, because the few with money and power are likely to view themselves as worse off from socially efficient reform, and so they have the motive and the means to resist it (see Chapter 2). Of course, high inequality may also lead the poor to support populist policies that can be self-defeating. Countries with extreme inequality, such as El Salvador and Iran, have undergone upheavals or extended civil strife that have cost countless lives and set back development progress by decades. High inequality is also associated with pathologies such as higher violent crime rates. In sum, with high inequality, the focus of politics often tends to be on supporting or resisting the redistribution of the existing economic pie rather than on policies to increase its size (Chapter 11 examines these concerns in more detail).[15]

Finally, extreme inequality is generally viewed as unfair. The philosopher John Rawls proposed a thought experiment to help clarify why this is so.[16] Suppose that before you were born into this world, you had a chance to select the overall level of inequality among the earth's people but not your own identity. That is, you might be born as Bill Gates, but you might be born as the most wretchedly poor person in rural Ethiopia with equal probability. Rawls calls this uncertainty the "veil of ignorance." The question is, facing this kind of risk, would you vote for an income distribution that was more equal or less equal than the one you see around you? If the degree of equality had no effect on the level of income or rate of growth, most people would vote for nearly perfect equality. Of course, if everyone had the same income no matter what, there would be little incentive to work hard, gain skills, or innovate. As a result, most people vote for *some* inequality of income outcomes, to the extent that these correspond to incentives for hard work or innovation. But even so, most vote for *less* inequality than is seen in the world (or in virtually any country) today. This is because much of the inequality we observe in the world is based on luck or extraneous factors, such as the inborn ability to kick a football or the identity of one's great-grandparents.

For all these reasons, for this part of the analysis we will write welfare, W, as

$$W = W(Y, I, P) \tag{5.5}$$

where Y is income per capita and enters our welfare function positively, I is inequality and enters negatively, and P is absolute poverty and also enters negatively. These three components have distinct significance, and we need to consider all three elements to achieve an overall assessment of welfare in developing countries. (A similar framework can be applied to health and education.)

Dualistic Development and Shifting Lorenz Curves: Some Stylized Typologies

As introduced by Gary Fields, Lorenz curves may be used to analyze three limiting cases of dualistic development:[17]

1. The *modern-sector enlargement* growth typology, in which the two-sector economy develops by enlarging the size of its modern sector while maintaining constant wages in both sectors. This is the case depicted by the

Lewis model in Chapter 3. It corresponds roughly to the historical growth pattern of Western developed nations and, to some extent, the pattern in East Asian economies such as China, South Korea, and Taiwan.

2. The *modern-sector enrichment* growth typology, in which the economy grows but such growth is limited to a fixed number of people in the modern sector, with both the numbers of workers and their wages held constant in the traditional sector. This roughly describes the experience of many Latin American and African economies.

3. The *traditional-sector enrichment* growth typology, in which all of the benefits of growth are divided among traditional-sector workers, with little or no growth occurring in the modern sector. This process roughly describes the experiences of countries whose policies focused on achieving substantial reductions in absolute poverty even at very low incomes and with relatively low growth rates, such as Sri Lanka, and the state of Kerala in southwestern India.

Using these three special cases and Lorenz curves, Fields demonstrated the validity of the following propositions (reversing the order just presented):

1. In the *traditional-sector enrichment* typology, growth results in higher income, a *more equal* relative distribution of income, and less poverty. Traditional-sector enrichment growth causes the Lorenz curve to shift uniformly upward and closer toward the line of equality, as depicted in Figure 5.7.

2. In the *modern-sector enrichment* growth typology, growth results in higher incomes, a *less equal* relative distribution of income, and no change in poverty.

FIGURE 5.7   Improved Income Distribution under the Traditional-Sector Enrichment Growth Typology

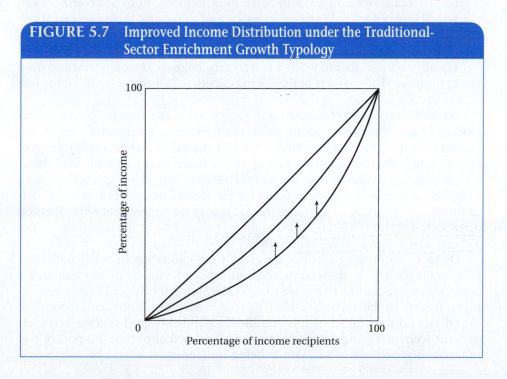

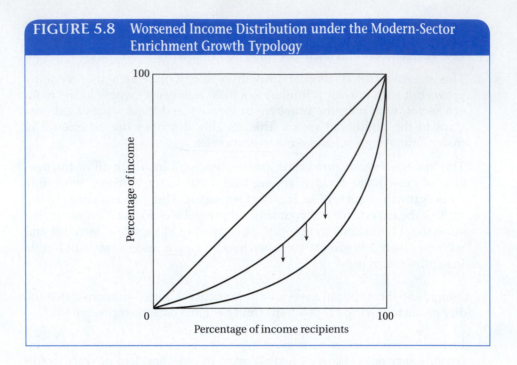

FIGURE 5.8   Worsened Income Distribution under the Modern-Sector Enrichment Growth Typology

Modern-sector enrichment growth causes the Lorenz curve to shift downward and farther from the line of equality, as shown in Figure 5.8.

3. Finally, in the case of Lewis-type, *modern-sector enlargement* growth, absolute incomes rise and absolute poverty is reduced, but the Lorenz curves will always cross, indicating that we cannot make any unambiguous statement about changes in relative inequality: It may improve or worsen. Fields shows that if, in fact, this style of growth experience is predominant, inequality is likely first to worsen in the early stages of development and then to improve. The crossing of the Lorenz curves is demonstrated in Figure 5.9.

The explanation for the crossing in Figure 5.9 is as follows: The poor who remain in the traditional sector have their incomes unchanged, but these incomes are now a smaller fraction of the larger total, so the new Lorenz curve, L_2, lies below the old Lorenz curve, L_1, at the lower end of the income distribution scale. Each modern-sector worker receives the same absolute income as before, but now the share received by the richest income group is smaller, so the new Lorenz curve lies *above* the old one at the higher end of the income distribution scale. Therefore, somewhere in the middle of the distribution, the old and new Lorenz curves must cross.[18]

These three typologies offer different predictions about what will happen to inequality in the course of economic growth. With modern-sector enrichment, inequality rises steadily, while under traditional-sector enrichment, inequality falls steadily. Under modern-sector enlargement, inequality first rises and then falls;[19] if this admittedly highly stylized process of development were occurring, we would not be concerned about the temporary rise in inequality, because in addition to being temporary, it would be reflecting a

FIGURE 5.9   Crossing Lorenz Curves in the Modern-Sector Enlargement Growth Typology

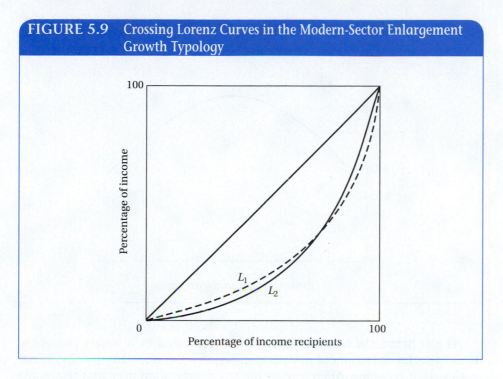

process in which citizens are, one by one, achieving incomes above the absolute poverty line.[20]

These observations tell us that we have to qualify our conclusion that a rise in inequality is inherently bad. In some cases, inequality may increase on a temporary basis due to causes that will eventually make everyone better off and ultimately lower inequality. However, with modern-sector enrichment growth, the increase in inequality is not later reversed, and the poor do not escape their poverty.[21] So we need to be careful about drawing conclusions from short-run changes in economic statistics before we know more about the underlying changes in the real economy that have given rise to these statistics. The process of modern-sector enlargement growth suggests a possible mechanism that can give rise to Kuznets's "inverted-U" hypothesis, so we turn to this question next.

Kuznets's Inverted-U Hypothesis

Simon Kuznets suggested that in the early stages of economic growth, the distribution of income will tend to worsen; only at later stages will it improve.[22] This observation came to be characterized by the "inverted-U" **Kuznets curve** because a longitudinal (time-series) plot of changes in the distribution of income—as measured, for example, by the Gini coefficient—seemed, when per capita GNI expanded, to trace out an inverted U-shaped curve in some of the cases Kuznets studied, as illustrated in Figure 5.10.

Explanations as to why inequality might worsen during the early stages of economic growth before eventually improving are numerous. They almost always relate to the nature of structural change. Early growth may, in accordance with the Lewis model, be concentrated in the modern industrial sector, where employment is limited but wages and productivity are high.

Kuznets curve   A graph reflecting the relationship between a country's income per capita and its inequality of income distribution.

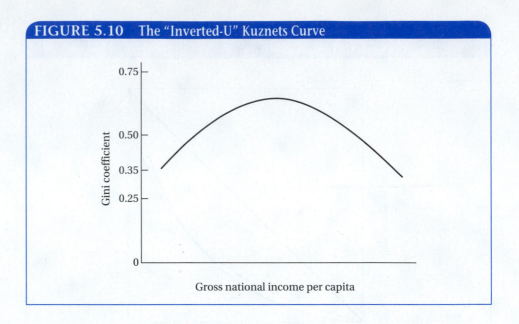

FIGURE 5.10 The "Inverted-U" Kuznets Curve

As just noted, the Kuznets curve can be generated by a steady process of modern-sector enlargement growth as a country develops from a traditional to a modern economy. Alternatively, returns to education may first rise as the emerging modern sector demands skills and then may fall as the supply of educated workers increases and the supply of unskilled workers falls. So while Kuznets did not specify the mechanism by which his inverted-U hypothesis was supposed to occur, it could in principle be consistent with a sequential process of economic development. But as shown earlier, traditional- and modern-sector enrichment would tend to pull inequality in opposing directions, so the net change in inequality is ambiguous, and the validity of the Kuznets curve is an empirical question.

Disregarding the merits of the methodological debate, few development economists would argue that the Kuznets sequence of increasing and then declining inequality is inevitable. There are now enough case studies and specific examples of countries such as Taiwan, South Korea, Costa Rica, and Sri Lanka to demonstrate that higher income levels can be accompanied by falling and not rising inequality. It all depends on the nature of the development process.

Evidence on the Inverted-U Hypothesis Let us look at data collected from 18 countries on the percentage shares in total national income going to different percentile groups (see Table 5.2). Though methods of collection, degree of coverage, and specific definitions of personal income may vary from country to country, the figures recorded in Table 5.2 give a first approximation of the magnitude of income inequality in developing countries. For example, we see that in Zambia, the poorest 20% (first quintile) of the population receives only 3.6% of the income, while the highest 10% and 20% (fifth quintile) receive 38.9% and 55.2%, respectively. By contrast, in a relatively equal developed country like Japan, the poorest 20% receives a much higher 10.6% of the income, while the richest 10% and 20% get only 21.7% and 35.7%, respectively.

gives a first approximation of the magnitude of income inequality in developing countries

TABLE 5.2	Selected Income Distribution Estimates							
		Quintile						
Country	Lowest 10%	1st	2nd	3rd	4th	5th	Highest 10%	Year
Bangladesh	4.3	9.4	12.6	16.1	21.1	40.8	26.6	2005
Brazil	1.1	3.0	6.9	11.8	19.6	58.7	43.0	2007
China	2.4	5.7	9.8	14.7	22.0	47.8	31.4	2005
Colombia	0.8	2.3	6.0	11.0	19.1	61.6	45.9	2006
Costa Rica	1.6	4.4	8.5	12.7	19.7	54.6	38.6	2007
Guatemala	1.3	3.4	7.2	12.0	19.5	57.8	42.4	2006
Honduras	0.7	2.5	6.7	12.1	20.4	58.4	42.2	2006
India	3.6	8.1	11.3	14.9	20.4	45.3	31.1	2005
Jamaica	2.1	5.2	9.0	13.8	20.9	51.2	35.6	2004
Namibia	0.6	1.5	2.8	5.5	12.0	78.3	65.0	1993
Pakistan	3.9	9.1	12.8	16.3	21.3	40.5	26.5	2005
Peru	1.3	3.6	7.8	13.0	20.8	54.8	38.4	2007
Philippines	2.4	5.6	9.1	13.7	21.2	50.4	33.9	2006
South Africa	1.3	3.1	5.6	9.9	18.8	62.7	44.9	2000
Tanzania	3.1	7.3	11.8	16.3	22.3	42.3	27.0	2001
Zambia	1.3	3.6	7.8	12.8	20.6	55.2	38.9	2005
Japan	4.8	10.6	14.2	17.6	22.0	35.7	21.7	1993
United States	1.9	5.4	10.7	15.7	22.4	45.8	29.9	2000

Source: based on World Bank, *World Development Indicators, 2010.* (Washington, D.C.: World Bank, 2010), tab. 2.9.

The income distribution of the United States, a relatively less equal developed country, is given for comparison in Table 5.2.

Consider now the relationship, if any, between levels of per capita income and degree of inequality. Are higher incomes associated with greater or lesser inequality, or can no definitive statement be made? Table 5.3 on page 240 provides data on income distribution in relation to per capita GNI for a sampling of countries, arranged from lowest to highest in terms of per capita income. What clearly emerges from Table 5.3 is that per capita incomes are not necessarily related to inequality. The very poorest countries, such as Ethiopia, may have low inequality simply because there is so little income. But even very poor countries such as Mozambique and Zambia have extremely high inequality by international standards. Although many high-inequality Latin American countries are found in the middle-income range, this range also includes countries such as Egypt and Indonesia, as well as eastern European countries, with low inequality. High-income countries do tend to be somewhat more equal than middle-income countries, but again, there is wide variation in inequality levels. In recent years, there has even been a tendency for inequality to rise in high-income countries and to fall at least somewhat in several Latin American countries.

In fact, the Kuznets curve that is seen in the data is now understood to be partially a statistical fluke resulting from the fact that for extraneous historical reasons, most Latin American countries just happen to have both a middle level of income and a high level of inequality (see Box 5.1).

Detailed longitudinal studies of developing countries show a very mixed pattern. Juan Luis Lonondro found an inverted U for Colombia, but Harry Oshima found no particular pattern among several Asian countries.[23] In fact, for many

BOX 5.1   The Latin America Effect

Gary Fields and George Jakubson used a combination of both cross-sectional and longitudinal (time-series) data to consider whether the inverted-U could result from the Latin American effect and how patterns might differ across countries. Figure 5.11 plots a combination of data from the 35 countries in Fields and Jakubson's data set, where reliable estimates of the Gini coefficient have been available for various developing countries at different points in time. The inverted-U relationship, tracing the triangles, is a computer-generated parabola that best fits the data under standard statistical criteria. Observations on Latin American countries are circled: All of the highest-inequality countries in their data come from that region. Statistically, when the Latin American identity of the country is controlled for, the inverted-U drawn in Figure 5.11 tends to disappear in this data set and others as well.[24]

So the question is, what happens over time? In Figure 5.12 on page 239, selected countries from the data in Figure 5.11 have been isolated. As can be seen, the data from Brazil, which have the label *1* in the diagram, do plainly show an inverted-U pattern. Data from Hong Kong and Singapore, in contrast, labeled *4* and *5* in the diagram, appear to reflect a U-shaped pattern. But when these separate experiences are merged into one picture, the eyes (and the computer) misleadingly trace an inverted U in the data taken as a whole. This reinforces the great importance of understanding what gives rise to the statistical patterns in the data rather than taking them at face value.

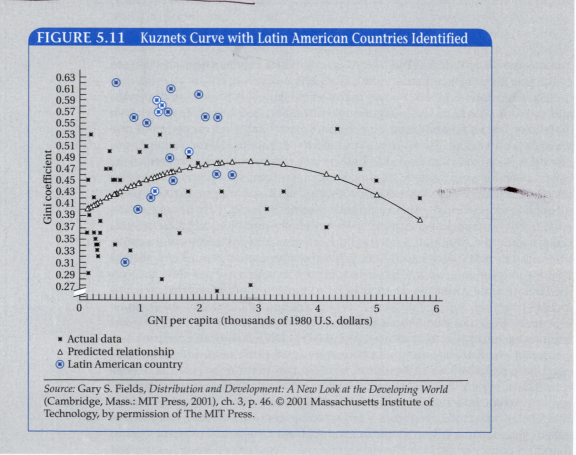

FIGURE 5.11   Kuznets Curve with Latin American Countries Identified

* Actual data
△ Predicted relationship
⊛ Latin American country

Source: Gary S. Fields, *Distribution and Development: A New Look at the Developing World* (Cambridge, Mass.: MIT Press, 2001), ch. 3, p. 46. © 2001 Massachusetts Institute of Technology, by permission of The MIT Press.

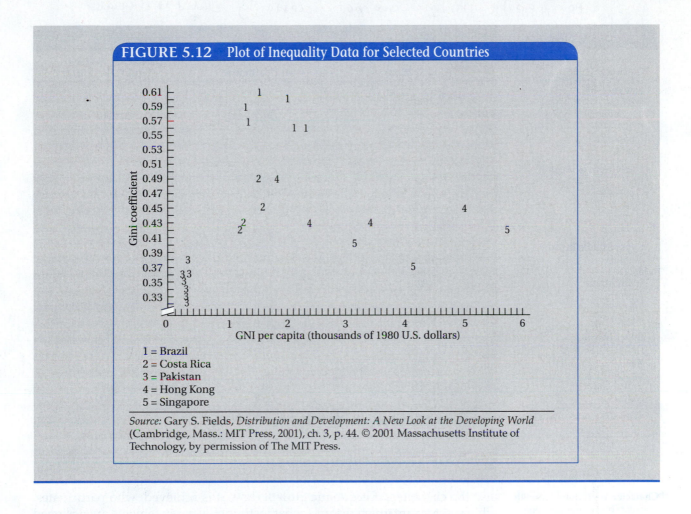

FIGURE 5.12   Plot of Inequality Data for Selected Countries

1 = Brazil
2 = Costa Rica
3 = Pakistan
4 = Hong Kong
5 = Singapore

Source: Gary S. Fields, *Distribution and Development: A New Look at the Developing World* (Cambridge, Mass.: MIT Press, 2001), ch. 3, p. 44. © 2001 Massachusetts Institute of Technology, by permission of The MIT Press.

countries, there is no particular tendency for inequality to change in the process of economic development. Inequality seems to be a rather stable part of a country's socioeconomic makeup, altered significantly only as a result of a substantial upheaval or systematic policies. East Asia achieved its relatively low inequality largely from exogenous forces: the U.S. occupation of Japan, the Nationalist takeover of Taiwan, and the expulsion of the Japanese from South Korea. In all three cases, land reform that had far-reaching effects on inequality was implemented (we examine land reform in Chapter 9). But inequality can be gradually reduced through well-implemented policies to promote pro-poor growth over time. With regressive policies, inequality may rise over time.

Growth and Inequality

Having examined the relationship between inequality and levels of per capita income, let us look now briefly at the relationship, if any, between economic growth and inequality. During the 1960s and 1990s, per capita growth in East Asia averaged 5.5% while that of Africa declined by 0.2%, yet both Gini coefficients remained essentially unchanged. Once again, it is not just the rate but

Per capita incomes are not necessarily related to inequality

TABLE 5.3 Income and Inequality in Selected Countries			
Country	Income Per Capita (U.S. $, 2008)	Gini Coefficient	Survey Year for Gini Calculation
Low Income			
Ethiopia	280	29.8	2005
Mozambique	380	47.1	2003
Nepal	400	47.3	2004
Cambodia	640	40.7	2007
Zambia	950	50.7	2005
Lower Middle Income			
India	1,040	36.8	2005
Cameroon	1,150	44.6	2001
Bolivia	1,460	57.2	2007
Egypt	1,800	32.1	2005
Indonesia	1,880	37.6	2007
Upper Middle Income			
Namibia	4,210	74.3	1993
Bulgaria	5,490	29.2	2003
South Africa	5,820	57.8	2000
Argentina	7,190	48.8	2006
Brazil	7,300	55.0	2007
Mexico	9,990	51.6	2008
Upper Income			
Hungary	12,810	30.0	2004
Spain	31,930	34.7	2000
Germany	42,710	28.3	2000
United States	47,930	40.8	2000
Norway	87,340	25.8	2000

Source: data from World Bank, *World Development Indicators, 2010* (Washington, D.C.: World Bank, 2010), tabs. 1.1 and 2.9.

Character of economic growth
The distributive implications of economic growth as reflected in such factors as participation in the growth process and asset ownership.

also the **character of economic growth** (how it is achieved, who participates, which sectors are given priority, what institutional arrangements are designed and emphasized, etc.) that determines the degree to which that growth is or is not reflected in improved living standards for the poor. Clearly, it is not necessary for inequality to increase for higher growth to be sustained.

5.4 Absolute Poverty: Extent and Magnitude

Like so much in economic development, the critical problem of eradicating absolute poverty is one of bad news and good news—of a glass that may be seen as either half empty or half full.

It is extremely difficult to arrive at a tight estimate of the extent of global poverty at any point in time. Major World Bank reports issued within a couple of years of each other have provided estimates of the dollar-a-day headcount that differ by tens of millions of people. This reflects the difficulty of the task. Another difficulty is determining the most appropriate cutoff income for extreme poverty. The $1-a-day line was first set in 1987 dollars, and for years the standard was $1.08 in 1993 U.S. purchasing power parity. In 2008, the equivalent line was reset at $1.25 at 2005 U.S. purchasing power. This (along with improved estimates of prices faced by the poor) resulted in an increase in the estimated number of the poor but did not change the conclusion that the number in poverty has been falling markedly since 1990, most conspicuously due to progress in China. Even as updated to today's dollars, the poverty line is to some degree arbitrary (although it has corresponded roughly to what many developing countries use and is at least related to expenditures of people who barely meet minimum nutrition).

The most recent systematic poverty estimates (available as of early 2014) show that in 2010 some 1.22 billion people lived below $1.25 per day, and some 2.36 billion below $2 per day (see Figure 5.13). The number of people living in $1.25 per day income poverty fell from about 1.94 billion in 1981 – a 37% reduction in the headcount. The drop in the number living on less than $2 per day was much smaller – under 8% - but this more modest decline was partly due to people whose incomes actually had crossed above the $1.25 per day, though still remained below $2 per day. These achievements in reducing the number of people living in poverty are all the more impressive when we note that world population rose by 2.39 billion people (53%) between 1981 and 2010 (UN estimates). Thus the headcount ratio (fraction) living on less than $1.25 per day fell to about 18% by 2010 – approaching half (55%) of its 1990 level of 33%. Thus, the MDG of halving $1.25 per day poverty was close to having been met by 2010; and preliminary estimates show that this goal had been met – and indeed exceeded – by the end of 2013. Global and regional poverty trends are summarized in Figure 5.13. Note that the numbers of the poor who live in sub-Saharan Africa rose steadily throughout this three-decade period; but the headcount of the poor declined in other regions.

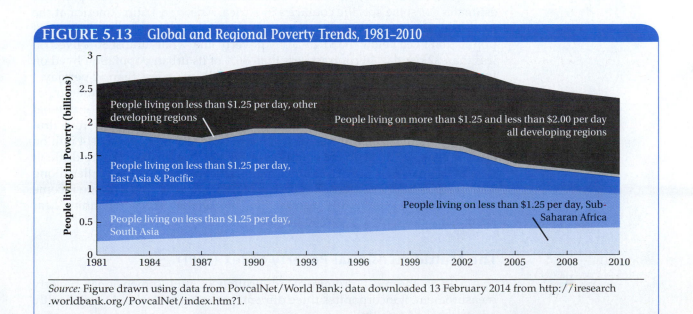

FIGURE 5.13 Global and Regional Poverty Trends, 1981–2010

Source: Figure drawn using data from PovcalNet/World Bank; data downloaded 13 February 2014 from http://iresearch.worldbank.org/PovcalNet/index.htm?1.

TABLE 5.4 Regional Poverty Incidence, 2010

Region	Headcount Ratio (P_0)	Poverty Gap (P_1)	Squared Poverty Gap (P_2)
Regional Aggregation at $1.25 per Day			
East Asia and the Pacific	12.48	2.82	0.93
Europe and Central Asia	0.66	0.21	0.13
Latin America and the Caribbean	5.53	2.89	2.12
Middle East and North Africa	2.41	0.55	0.23
South Asia	31.03	7.09	2.36
Sub-Saharan Africa	48.47	20.95	11.85
Total	20.63	6.3	2.92
Regional Aggregation at $2 per Day			
East Asia and the Pacific	29.14	9.42	4.05
Europe and Central Asia	2.27	0.64	0.3
Latin America and the Caribbean	10.18	4.67	3.13
Middle East and North Africa	11.55	2.66	0.99
South Asia	65.8	22.86	10.19
Sub-Saharan Africa	69.31	35.22	22.03
Total	40.08	15.32	7.79

Source: data from World Bank, "PovcalNet," http://iresearch.worldbank.org/PovcalNet, accessed 13 February 2014.

The incidence of extreme poverty is very uneven around the developing world. Household survey–based estimates are regarded as the most accurate ways to estimate poverty incidence. Table 5.4 provides some survey-based poverty estimates by region at the $1.25 and $2 poverty lines. As can be seen, poverty incidence is very high in both South Asia, with about 40% below $1.25 per day, and in sub-Saharan Africa, with 51% below. But poverty severity is far higher in sub-Saharan Africa, with a squared poverty gap index P_2 (in percentage terms) at 11.05, far above that of South Asia at 3.64. Table 5.5 provides estimates for some specific countries in Africa, Asia, and Latin America at the $1.25 and $2 poverty lines. It can be seen that about 44% of India's 2004 rural population lived below the $1.25-a-day poverty line, while almost 80% lived on less than $2 per day. In contrast, less than 36% of its urban population lived on less than $1.25 per day, although about 66% still lived on less than $2 per day.

Unfortunately, sub-Saharan Africa has shown far less progress than other developing regions. While the fraction living in poverty has fallen somewhat in the last decade, the headcount of individuals living in poverty rose dramatically in the 1981–2010 period, from about 205 million to about 414 million (World Bank, 2013). The concentration of poverty may make it more difficult to redress. In most countries in other regions, the poverty gap has fallen along with the poverty headcount. But between 1981 and 2010, the average income of the extremely poor hardly increased in sub-Saharan Africa, remaining near an appalling 70 cents per person per day.

The Multidimensional Poverty Index (MPI)

The MPI is the most prominent application of multidimensional poverty measurement; it incorporates three dimensions at the household level: health, education, and wealth.

TABLE 5.5   Income Poverty Incidence in Selected Countries

Country	Year	Per Capita Monthly Income (2005 PPP)	Headcount Ratio (%)	Poverty Gap (%)	Squared Poverty Gap (%)	Gini Index (%)
Incidence at $1.25 a Day; Poverty Line at 38 (monthly equivalent)						
Bangladesh	2005	48.27	50.47	14.17	5.20	33.22
Benin	2003	52.77	47.33	15.73	6.97	38.62
Brazil	2007	346.64	5.21	1.26	0.44	55.02
Burkina Faso	2003	46.85	56.54	20.27	9.38	39.6
China—Rural	2005	71.34	26.11	6.46	2.26	35.85
China—Urban	2005	161.83	1.71	0.45	0.24	34.8
Côte d'Ivoire	2002	101.11	23.34	6.82	2.87	48.39
Guatemala*	2006	191.7	12.65	3.83	1.63	53.69
Honduras*	2006	184.45	18.19	8.19	5.00	55.31
India—Rural	2004	49.93	43.83	10.66	3.65	30.46
India—Urban	2004	62.43	36.16	10.16	3.80	37.59
Indonesia—Rural	2005	62.79	24.01	5.03	1.61	29.52
Indonesia—Urban	2005	89.1	18.67	4.06	1.29	39.93
Madagascar	2005	44.82	67.83	26.52	13.23	47.24
Mexico	2006	330.37	0.65	0.13	0.05	48.11
Mozambique	2002	36.58	74.69	35.4	20.48	47.11
Nicaragua*	2005	151.18	15.81	5.23	2.54	52.33
Nigeria	2003	39.46	64.41	29.57	17.2	42.93
Pakistan	2004	65.76	22.59	4.35	1.28	31.18
Peru	2006	216.82	7.94	1.86	0.61	49.55
Philippines	2006	98.99	22.62	5.48	1.74	44.04
Rwanda	2000	33.76	76.56	38.21	22.94	46.68
Senegal	2005	66.86	33.5	10.8	4.67	39.19
Incidence at $2 a Day; Poverty Line at 60.84 (monthly equivalent)						
Bangladesh	2005	48.27	80.32	34.35	17.55	33.22
Benin	2003	52.77	75.33	33.51	18.25	38.62
Brazil	2007	346.64	12.70	4.15	1.85	55.02
Burkina Faso	2003	46.85	81.22	39.26	22.58	39.60
China—Rural	2005	71.34	55.63	19.47	8.94	35.85
China—Urban	2005	161.83	9.38	2.12	0.81	34.8
Côte d'Ivoire	2002	101.11	46.79	17.62	8.78	48.39
Guatemala*	2006	191.7	25.71	9.63	4.84	53.69
Honduras*	2006	184.45	29.73	14.15	8.91	55.31
India—Rural	2004	49.93	79.53	30.89	14.69	30.46
India—Urban	2004	62.43	65.85	25.99	12.92	37.59
Indonesia—Rural	2005	62.79	61.19	19.55	8.27	29.52
Indonesia—Urban	2005	89.1	45.85	14.85	6.39	39.93
Madagascar	2005	44.82	89.62	46.94	28.5	47.24
Mexico	2006	330.37	4.79	0.96	0.31	48.11
Mozambique	2002	36.58	90.03	53.56	36.00	48.07
Nicaragua*	2005	151.18	31.87	12.26	6.44	52.33
Nigeria	2003	39.46	83.92	46.89	30.8	42.93
Pakistan	2004	65.76	60.32	18.75	7.66	31.18
Peru	2006	216.82	18.51	5.95	2.54	49.55
Philippines	2006	98.99	45.05	16.36	7.58	44.04
Rwanda	2000	33.76	90.3	55.69	38.5	44.11
Senegal	2005	66.86	60.37	24.67	12.98	39.19

Source: data from World Bank, "PovcalNet," http://iresearch.worldbank.org/PovcalNet.

Income is imperfectly measured, but even more important, the advantages provided by a given amount of income greatly differ, depending on circumstances. To capture this idea, the United Nations Development Programme (UNDP) used its *Human Poverty Index*[26] from 1997 to 2009.

Multidimensional Poverty Index (MPI) A poverty measure that identifies the poor using dual cutoffs for levels and numbers of deprivations, and then multiplies the percentage of people living in poverty times the percent of weighted indicators for which poor households are deprived on average.

In 2010, the UNDP replaced the HPI with its **Multidimensional Poverty Index (MPI)**; by building up the index from the household level, the MPI takes into account that there are negative interaction effects when people have multiple deprivations—worse poverty than can be seen by simply adding up separate deprivations for the whole country, then taking averages, and only then combining them.

The index's creators report that they selected the three dimensions (health, education, and standard of living) and each of their corresponding indicators because they reflect problems often mentioned by the poor, they have been long considered important by the development community particularly as reflected in the Millennium Development Goals (see Chapter 1), and they are well established philosophically as human rights or basic needs; naturally, reliable data also had to be available for enough countries when selecting specific indicators for the index.

With respect to health, two indicators—whether any child has died in the family and whether any adult or child in the family is malnourished—are weighted equally (so each counts one-sixth toward the maximum possible deprivation in the MPI). Regarding education also, two indicators—whether not even one household member has completed five years of schooling and whether any school-age child is out of school for grades one through eight—are given equal weight (so again, each counts one-sixth toward the MPI). Finally, in terms of standard of living, equal weight is placed on six deprivations (each counting one-eighteenth toward the maximum possible): lack of electricity, insufficiently safe drinking water, inadequate sanitation, inadequate flooring, unimproved cooking fuel, and lack of more than one of five assets—telephone, radio, television, bicycle, and motorbike or similar vehicle.

Calculating deprivation in this way, individuals are then identified as "multidimensionally poor" when their family is deprived by a "weighted sum" of 0.3 or more (3 out of 10 points as calculated in practice). For concreteness, consider three examples of families whose members would be classified as multidimensionally poor. First, a person would get a value of 33% and thus be considered poor by having a child in the family who was malnourished, while at the same time the most educated person in the family received only three years of schooling. Second, a multidimensionally poor person might live in a household that had experienced a child's death and was also deprived in at least three of the six living standard indicators, which also would sum to $1/6 + 1/18 + 1/18 + 1/18 = 1/3$, or 33%. Third, they could live in a household that was deprived in the other three living standard indicators and in which there was a school-age child not attending school. But if there were no health or education deprivations, a person would have to live in a family which was deprived in all six standard-of-living indicators to be deemed poor. Thus, the MPI approach identifies the very poor by measuring a range of important household deprivations directly, rather than only indirectly through income, then building the index from household measures up to the aggregate measure. Rather than using already aggregated statistics in an index, the approach takes into account the *multiplied or interactive harm* done when multiple deprivations are experienced by *individuals in the same family*. In essence, the approach assumes that an individual's lack of capability in one area can to a degree be made up for by other capabilities—but only to a degree. (Put differently, capabilities are treated as substitutes up to a point but then as complements.) This greatly augments measures used previously.

Finally, the actual MPI for the country (or region or group) is computed with the adjusted headcount ratio; as noted previously, a convenient way to express the resulting value is the product of the headcount ratio, H_M (the percentage of people living in multidimensional poverty) and the average intensity of deprivation, A (the percentage of weighted indicators for which poor households are deprived on average). The adjusted headcount ratio, $H_M A$, is a special case of the broader class of multidimensional poverty measures developed by Sabira Alkire and James Foster introduced earlier; $H_M A$ is readily calculated, and it also satisfies some desirable properties, including *dimensional monotonicity,* meaning that when a person deemed poor becomes deprived in another indicator, he or she is deemed even poorer.[27]

In its 2013 *Human Development Report*, the UNDP presents the MPI for 104 developing countries, based on the currently available data; some examples are given in Table 5.6. Brazil and Mexico have very low MPI levels of just 0.011 and 0.015, respectively, while the world's most impoverished country for which data were available to compute the MPI, Niger, ranks 104th, with an MPI value of 0.642. The UNDP reports that there are nearly 1.6 billion people living in multidimensional poverty—several hundred million more than the estimated number living on an income of less than $1.25 per day. At the broadest level, the results are not out of line with what one might expect; sub-Saharan Africa has the highest *proportion* of people living in poverty, and South Asia has the largest *number* of people living in poverty.

The poorest country is Niger, the only country with an MPI higher than 0.6. Six other countries had an MPI higher than 0.5, all in sub-Saharan Africa: Ethiopia, Mali, Burkina Faso, Burundi, Mozambique, and Guinea (available earlier data also show Angola, the Central African Republic, and Somalia with an MPI greater than 0.5).

Countries outside Africa with high levels of multidimensional poverty for their regions include Bangladesh (with an MPI of 0.292), Cambodia (0.212), Haiti (0.299), Honduras (0.159), India (0.283), Lao PRD (0.267), Nepal (0.217) Pakistan (0.264), Timor-Leste (0.360), and Yemen (0.283).

The results show that knowing income poverty is not enough if our concern is with multidimensional poverty. For example, multidimensionally, Bangladesh is substantially less poor and Pakistan substantially poorer than would be predicted by these countries' income poverty (this finding may be related to some of the comparisons in the end-of-chapter case study in Chapter 2). In Africa, Ethiopia is far more multidimensionally poor and Tanzania much less so than predicted by income poverty. Most Latin American countries studied rank worse on multidimensional poverty than on income poverty, but Colombia's income and MPI poverty ranks are about the same.

The severity of poverty in Africa is also highlighted by some of the findings. In Guinea, Mali, and Niger, more than 50% are poor and live in a household in which at least one child has died. In Mozambique, Guinea, Burundi, Mali, Ethiopia, Burkina Faso, and Niger, more than 50% live in a poor household where no one has completed five years of education. Outside of Africa, 39% in India and 37% in Bangladesh live in a poor household where at least one child or woman is undernourished.[28]

Different regions in the same country can have very different MPIs. In Kenya, the MPI for Nairobi is close to that of Brazil. Central Kenya's MPI is similar to

TABLE 5.6   Multidimensional Poverty Index, Data for 2007–2011

Country and Survey Year	MPI	Percent Poor	Thousands Poor	Poverty Intensity (A)
Bangladesh 2007 (D)	0.292	57.8	83,207	50.4
Brazil 2006 (N)	0.011	2.7	5,075	39.3
Burundi 2005 (M)	0.530	84.5	6,128	62.7
Bolivia, PS 2008 (D)	0.089	20.5	1,972	43.7
Burkina Faso 2010 (D)	0.535	84.0	13,834	63.7
Cambodia 2010 (D)	0.212	45.9	6,415	46.1
Colombia 2010 (D)	0.022	5.4	2,500	40.9
Congo, DR 2010 (M)	0.392	74.0	48,815	53.0
Côte d'Ivoire 2005 (D)	0.353	61.5	11,083	57.4
Dominican Republic 2007 (D)	0.018	4.6	439	39.4
Egypt 2008 (D)	0.024	6.0	4,699	40.7
Ethiopia 2011 (D)	0.564	87.3	72,415	64.6
Ghana 2008 (D)	0.144	31.2	7,258	46.2
Guinea 2005 (D)	0.506	82.5	7,459	61.3
Haiti 2005/2006 (D)	0.299	56.4	5,346	53.0
Honduras 2005/2006 (D)	0.159	32.5	2,281	48.9
India 2005/2006 (D)	0.283	53.7	612,203	52.7
Indonesia 2007 (D)	0.095	20.8	48,352	45.9
Kenya 2008/2009 (D)	0.229	47.8	18,863	48.0
Lao PRD 2006 (M)	0.267	47.2	2,757	56.5
Liberia 2007 (D)	0.485	83.9	3,218	57.7
Mali 2006 (D)	0.558	86.6	11,771	64.4
Mexico 2006 (N)	0.015	4.0	4,313	38.9
Madagascar 2008/2009 (D)	0.357	66.9	13,463	53.3
Malawi 2010 (D)	0.334	66.7	9,633	50.1
Mozambique 2009 (D)	0.512	79.3	18,127	64.6
Nepal 2011 (D)	0.217	44.2	13,242	49.0
Niger 2006 (D)	0.642	92.4	12,437	69.4
Nigeria 2008 (D)	0.310	54.1	83,578	57.3
Pakistan 2006/2007 (D)	0.264 d	49.4 d	81,236 d	53.4 d
Peru 2008 (D)	0.066	15.7	4,422	42.2
Philippines 2008 (D)	0.064	13.4	12,083	47.4
Rwanda 2010 (D)	0.350	69.0	6,900	50.8
Senegal 2010/2011 (D)	0.439	74.4	7,642	58.9
Sierra Leone 2008 (D)	0.439	77.0	4,321	57.0
South Africa 2008 (N)	0.057	13.4	6,609	42.3
Tanzania, 2010 (D)	0.332	65.6	28,552	50.7
Timor-Leste 2009/2010 (D)	0.360	68.1	749	52.9
Uganda 2011 (D)	0.367	69.9	24,122	52.5
Vietnam 2010/2011 (M)	0.017	4.2	3,690	39.5
Yemen 2006 (M)	0.283	52.5	11,176	53.9

Key: D indicates data are from Demographic and Health Surveys, M indicates data are from Multiple Indicator Cluster Surveys, d indicates lower bound estimate, and N indicates data are from national surveys. Not all indicators were available for all countries; caution should thus be used in cross-country comparisons. Where data are missing, indicator weights are adjusted to total 100%.

Source: UNDP, *Human Development Report, 2013*, pp. 160–161.

that of Bolivia. And northeastern Kenya has a worse MPI even than Niger. There are also great inequalities across ethnic groups in Kenya, with 29% of the Embu considered multidimensionally poor, compared with a staggering 96% of the Turkana and Masai peoples. Great inequalities are also found in India, in which indigenous ("tribal") peoples and low-ranked ("scheduled") castes are far poorer than people from high-ranking castes. In the Delhi and Kerala regions, just 14 to 16% are MPI poor, but in Jharkhand and Bihar, 77 to 81% are MPI poor. Finally, changes in the MPI over time are examined for three countries: Ghana saw its MPI halved from 0.29 to 0.14; Bangladesh saw its MPI reduced by a more modest 22%; and in Ethiopia, the MPI fell by 16% in the periods studied.

As with all indexes, the MPI has some limitations. As mentioned, data are from the household rather than the individual level (such as whether *any* child of school age is out of school or whether *any* family member is undernourished). It does not fully distinguish between past and present conditions (because its measure is whether a child has *ever* died). It does not distinguish differences within households (such as who may use the bicycle or whether the undernourished individuals are females). Proxies are imperfect; for example, nourishment does not capture micronutrient deficiencies. Sometimes a person has to be labeled nondeprived if data are missing, so the numbers may understate poverty somewhat. Education considers only inputs such as enrolling or attending for five years, not outputs such as being able to read. And the choice of basic assets is questionable; for example, even where a radio and a simple bicycle are present, a woman may have just one dress and the children may sleep on a rough concrete floor.

The MPI provides a new and fundamentally important way to measure poverty, to help us understand how poverty levels differ across and within countries, and also how the dimensions (or composition) of poverty can differ greatly in different settings. Ultimately, this should assist with better design and targeting of programs and policies and help us evaluate their performance more quickly and effectively.

For now, because of the way living standards and human development surveys are conducted, most of the usable data is at the household level, making it difficult to "drill down" to the individual level. Household data are far better than what used to be available; in fact, the availability of household data has already had a substantial impact on improving the study of development economics. It is a great improvement to be able to focus on what is happening at the family rather than the national level. Well-designed income poverty measures such as P_2 will always be used for many purposes; but the MPI is likely to help usher in an era in which multidimensional poverty is examined in most assessments.

Chronic Poverty Research suggests that approximately one-third of all people who are income poor at any one time are chronically (always) poor. Andrew McKay and Bob Baulch provide a well-regarded "guesstimate" that about 300 to 420 million people were chronically poor at the $1-per-day level in the late 1990s. The other two-thirds are made up of families that are vulnerable to poverty and become extremely poor from time to time. These may be divided between families usually poor but occasionally receiving enough income to cross the poverty line and families usually nonpoor but occasionally experiencing a shock that knocks them temporarily below the poverty line. Chronic poverty is concentrated in India, where the largest numbers are found, and in Africa, where the severity of poverty among the chronically poor is greatest.[29]

Problems of the poorest of the poor pose particular challenges. *Ultrapoverty* differs from conventional poverty in terms of depth (degree of deprivation), length (duration of time), and breadth (the number of dimensions, such as illiteracy and malnutrition).[30] The mutual reinforcement among the different dimensions of poverty can potentially result in multiple mutually reinforcing poverty traps. This makes ultrapoverty a more difficult problem to address than conventional poverty, which can more often be redressed with simpler solutions such as microfinance (see Chapter 15) plus business training. The chronic nature and severity of ultrapoverty also make short-term policies more problematic. Poverty innovators such as Fazle Hasan Abed have concluded that conventional programs have often not reached the ultra-poor. An income-based definition of ultrapoverty is living on half the dollar-a-day poverty line, or 54 cents per day in 1993 dollars. According to International Food Policy Research Institute (IFPRI) estimates, 162 million people live below this stark income level, generally with malnutrition and other destitute conditions. The IFPRI study concluded:

> poverty just below $1 a day has fallen faster than poverty below 50 cents a day, suggesting that it has been easier to reach those living closer to the dollar-a-day line rather than those living well below it. . . .The slow progress of poverty reduction for the world's most deprived indicates the presence of poverty traps, or conditions from which the poorest individuals or groups cannot emerge without outside assistance.[31]

Some NGOs have responded to this problem, such as BRAC's Targeting the Ultra-Poor Program and Grameen's Beggars Program, both introduced in the case study for Chapter 11.

The prospect for ending poverty depends critically on two factors: first, the rate of economic growth—provided it is undertaken in a shared and sustainable way—and second, the level of resources devoted to poverty programs and the quality of those programs.

Growth and Poverty

Are the reduction of poverty and the acceleration of growth in conflict? Or are they complementary? Traditionally, a body of opinion held that rapid growth is bad for the poor because they would be bypassed and marginalized by the structural changes of modern growth. Beyond this, there had been considerable concern in policy circles that the public expenditures required for the reduction of poverty would entail a reduction in the rate of growth. The concerns that concentrated efforts to lower poverty would slow the rate of growth paralleled the arguments that countries with lower inequality would experience slower growth. In particular, if there were redistribution of income or assets from rich to poor, even through progressive taxation, the concern was expressed that savings would fall. However, while the middle class generally has the highest savings rates, the marginal savings rates of the poor, when viewed from a holistic perspective, are not small. In addition to financial savings, the poor tend to spend additional income on improved nutrition, education for their children, improvements in housing conditions, and other expenditures that, especially at poverty levels, represent investments rather than consumption. There are at least five reasons why policies focused toward reducing poverty levels need not lead to a slower rate of growth—and indeed could help to accelerate growth.

First, *widespread poverty creates conditions in which the poor have no access to credit*, are unable to finance their children's education, and, in the absence of physical or monetary investment opportunities, have many children as a source of old-age financial security. Moreover, lack of credit denies people living in poverty of opportunities for entrepreneurship that could otherwise help to spur growth. Together these factors cause per capita growth to be less than what it would be if there were less poverty.

Second, a wealth of empirical data bears witness to the fact that unlike the historical experience of the now developed countries, *the rich in many contemporary poor countries are generally not noted for their frugality or for their desire to save and invest* substantial proportions of their incomes in the local economy.

Third, the *low incomes and low levels of living for the poor, which are manifested in poor health, nutrition, and education, can lower their economic productivity and thereby lead directly and indirectly to a slower-growing economy.* Strategies to raise the incomes and levels of living of the poor will therefore contribute not only to their material well-being but also to the productivity and income of the economy as a whole.[32] (These issues are considered further in Chapter 8.)

Fourth, *raising the income levels of the poor will stimulate an overall increase in the demand for locally produced necessity products* like food and clothing, whereas the rich tend to spend more of their additional incomes on imported luxury goods. Rising demand for local goods provides a greater stimulus to local production, local employment, and local investment. Such demand thus creates the conditions for rapid economic growth and a broader popular participation in that growth.[33]

Fifth, *a reduction of mass poverty can stimulate healthy economic expansion by acting as a powerful material and psychological incentive to widespread public participation in the development process.* By contrast, wide income disparities and substantial absolute poverty can act as powerful material and psychological disincentives to economic progress. They may even create the conditions for an ultimate rejection of progress by the masses, impatient at the pace of progress or its failure to alter their material circumstances.[34] We can conclude, therefore, that promoting rapid economic growth and reducing poverty are not mutually conflicting objectives.[35]

That dramatic reductions in poverty need not be incompatible with high growth is seen both in case studies and in the cross-national comparisons of data. Countries where poverty has been reduced the most tend to have had sustained growth; at the same time, growth does not guarantee poverty reduction. Over the past 30 years, China has experienced the highest growth rate in the world and also the most dramatic reductions in poverty. The headcount of the poor in China fell from 634 million in 1981 to 128 million in 2004, with the corresponding headcount ratio falling from 64% to 10%. This did not occur merely as a result of high growth. Policies actively encouraged modern-sector enlargement. Moreover, China has worked with the World Bank and other development agencies to improve its poverty reduction programs and has built on its long-standing efforts to provide at least minimal education and health care for its people as a firm foundation for long-term progress. Although the plight of many peasants has worsened in recent years, especially in interior regions, and inequality has greatly increased, the positive overall results of China's efforts to fight extreme poverty are apparent. Recent dramatic reductions of poverty in Vietnam have followed a similar pattern.

Richer countries strongly tend to have low levels of absolute poverty. Through one means or another—the availability of employment and entrepreneurship opportunities and greater public and NGO assistance—people who live in rich countries tend to escape from poverty. Among developing countries, there is evidence that countries with faster overall rates of per capita income growth also tend on average to have faster rates of per capita income growth among those in the bottom quintile of the income distribution, though the proportions vary widely. While we cannot passively count on even sustainable growth by itself to end absolute poverty, ending poverty can be greatly facilitated through wise and shared stewardship of the various resources provided by growth.[36]

Certainly, the relationship between economic growth and progress among the poor does not by itself indicate causality. Some of the effect probably runs from improved incomes, education, and health among the poor to faster overall growth (as suggested by some of the arguments listed previously). Moreover, as we have noted, poverty reduction is possible without rapid growth. But whatever the causality, it is clear that growth and poverty reduction are entirely compatible objectives.

5.5 Economic Characteristics of High-Poverty Groups

So far we have painted a broad picture of the income distribution and poverty problem in developing countries. We have argued that the magnitude of absolute poverty results from a combination of low per capita incomes and highly unequal distributions of that income. Clearly, for any given distribution of income, the higher the level of per capita income is, the lower the numbers of the absolutely poor. But higher levels of per capita income are no guarantee of lower levels of poverty. An understanding of the nature of the size distribution of income is therefore central to any analysis of the poverty problem in low-income countries.

But painting a broad picture of absolute poverty is not enough. Before we can formulate effective policies and programs to attack poverty at its source, we need some specific knowledge of these high-poverty groups and their economic characteristics.[37]

Rural Poverty

Perhaps the most valid generalizations about the poor are that they are disproportionately located in rural areas, that they are primarily engaged in agricultural and associated activities, that they are more likely to be women and children than adult males, and that they are often concentrated among minority ethnic groups and indigenous peoples. Data from a broad cross section of developing nations support these generalizations. We find, for example, that about two-thirds of the very poor scratch out their livelihood from subsistence agriculture either as small farmers or as low-paid farmworkers. Some of the remaining one-third are also located in rural areas but engaged in petty services, and others are located on the fringes and in marginal areas of urban centers, where they engage in various forms of self-employment such as street hawking, trading, petty services, and small-scale commerce. On the average, we may conclude that in Africa and Asia, about 80% of all target poverty groups are located in the rural areas, as are about 50% in Latin America. Some data for specific countries are provided in Table 5.7.

TABLE 5.7 Poverty: Rural versus Urban

Region and Country	Survey Year	Percentage below National Poverty Line		
		Rural Population	Urban Population	National Population
Sub-Saharan Africa				
Benin	2003	46.0	29.0	39.0
Burkina Faso	2003	52.4	19.2	46.4
Cameroon	2007	55.0	12.2	29.9
Malawi	2005	55.9	25.4	52.4
Tanzania	2001	38.7	29.5	35.7
Uganda	2006	34.2	13.7	31.1
Zambia	2004	72.0	53.0	68.0
Asia				
Bangladesh	2005	43.8	28.4	40.0
India	2000	30.2	24.7	28.6
Indonesia	2004	20.1	12.1	16.7
Uzbekistan	2003	29.8	22.6	27.2
Vietnam	2002	35.6	6.6	28.9
Latin America				
Bolivia	2007	63.9	23.7	37.7
Brazil	2003	41.0	17.5	21.5
Dominican Republic	2007	54.1	45.4	48.5
Guatemala	2006	72.0	28.0	51.0
Honduras	2004	70.4	29.5	50.7
Mexico	2004	56.9	41.0	47.0
Peru	2004	72.5	40.3	51.6

Source: data from World Bank, *World Development Indicators, 2010* (Washington, D.C.: World Bank, 2010), tab. 2.7.

It is interesting to note, in light of the rural concentration of absolute poverty, that the majority of government expenditures in most developing countries over the past several decades has been directed toward the urban area and especially toward the relatively affluent modern manufacturing and commercial sectors. Whether in the realm of directly productive economic investments or in the fields of education, health, housing, and other social services, this urban modern-sector bias in government expenditures is at the core of many of the development problems that will be discussed in succeeding chapters. We need only point out here that in view of the disproportionate number of the very poor who reside in rural areas, any policy designed to alleviate poverty must necessarily be directed to a large extent toward rural development in general and the agricultural sector in particular (we will discuss this matter in detail in Chapter 9).

Women and Poverty

Women make up a substantial majority of the world's poor. If we compared the lives of the inhabitants of the poorest communities throughout the developing world, we would discover that virtually everywhere women and children experience the harshest deprivation. They are more likely to be poor and malnourished and less likely to receive medical services, clean water, sanitation, and other benefits.[38] The prevalence of female-headed households, the lower earning capacity of women, and their limited control over their spouses' income all contribute to this disturbing phenomenon. In addition, women have less access to education, formal-sector employment, social security, and government employment programs. These facts combine to ensure that poor women's financial resources are meager and unstable relative to men's.

A disproportionate number of the ultrapoor live in households headed by women, in which there are generally no male wage earners. Because the earning potential of women is considerably below that of their male counterparts, women are more likely to be among the very poor. In general, women in female-headed households have less education and lower incomes. Furthermore, the larger the household is, the greater the strain on the single parent and the lower the per capita food expenditure.

A portion of the income disparity between male- and female-headed households can be explained by the large earnings differentials between men and women. In addition to the fact that women are often paid less for performing similar tasks, in many cases they are essentially barred from higher-paying occupations. In urban areas, women are much less likely to obtain formal employment in private companies or public agencies and are frequently restricted to illegal, low-productivity jobs. The illegality of piecework, as in the garment industry, prevents it from being regulated and renders it exempt from minimum-wage laws or social security benefits. Even when women receive conventional wage payments in factory work, minimum wage and safety legislation may be flagrantly ignored. Similarly, rural women have less access to the resources necessary to generate stable incomes and are frequently subject to laws that further compromise earning potential. Legislation and social custom often prohibit women from owning property or signing financial contracts without a husband's signature. With a few notable exceptions, government employment or income-enhancing programs are accessible primarily if not exclusively by men, exacerbating existing income disparities between men and women.

But household income alone fails to describe the severity of women's relative deprivation. Because a higher proportion of female-headed households are situated in the poorest areas, which have little or no access to government-sponsored services such as piped water, sanitation, and health care, household members are more likely to fall ill and are less likely to receive medical attention. In addition, children in female-headed households are less likely to be enrolled in school and more likely to be working in order to provide additional income.

The degree of economic hardship may also vary widely within a household. We have already discussed the fact that GNI per capita is an inadequate measure of development because it fails to reflect the extent of absolute poverty. Likewise, household income is a poor measure of individual welfare because the distribution of income within the household may be quite unequal. In fact, among the poor, the economic status of women provides a better indication of their own welfare, as well as that of their children. Existing studies of intrahousehold resource allocation clearly indicate that in many regions of the world, there exists a strong bias against females in areas such as nutrition, medical care, education, and inheritance. Moreover, empirical research has shown that these gender biases in household resource allocation significantly reduce the rate of survival among female infants. This is one reason why recorded female-male sex ratios are so much below their expected values, primarily in Asian countries, that well over 100 million girls and women are said to be "missing."[39] The favor shown toward boys in part reflects the fact that men are perceived to have a greater potential for contributing financially to family survival. This is not only because well-paying employment for women is unavailable but also because daughters are often married to families outside the village, after which they become exclusively responsible to their in-laws and thus cease contributing to their family of origin.

The extent of these internal biases is strongly influenced by the economic status of women. Studies have found that where women's share of income within the home is relatively high, there is less discrimination against girls, and women are better able to meet their own needs as well as those of their children. When household income is marginal, most of women's income is contributed toward household nutritional intake. Since this fraction is considerably smaller for men, a rise in male earnings leads to a less than proportionate increase in the funds available for the provision of daily needs. It is thus unsurprising that programs designed to increase nutrition and family health are more effective when targeting women than when targeting men. In fact, significant increases in total household income do not necessarily translate into improved nutritional status (see Chapter 8). The persistence of low levels of living among women and children is common where the economic status of women remains low. Box 5.2 provides some views of the poor on gender relations.

Women's control over household income and resources is limited for a number of reasons. Of primary importance is the fact that a relatively large proportion of the work performed by women is unremunerated—for example, collecting firewood and cooking—and may even be intangible, as with parenting. Women's control over household resources may also be constrained by the fact that many women from poor households are not paid for the work they perform in family agriculture or business. It is common for the male head of household to control all funds from cash crops or the family business, even though a significant portion of the labor input is provided by his spouse. In addition, in many cultures, it is considered socially unacceptable for women to contribute significantly to household income, and hence women's work may remain concealed or unrecognized. These combined factors perpetuate the low economic status of women and can lead to strict limitations on their control over household resources.

Development policies that increase the productivity differentials between men and women are likely to worsen earnings disparities as well as further erode women's economic status within the household. Since government programs to alleviate poverty frequently work almost exclusively with men, they tend to exacerbate these inequalities. In urban areas, training programs to increase earning potential and formal-sector employment are generally geared to men, while agricultural extension programs promote male-dominated crops, frequently at the expense of women's vegetable plots (see Chapter 9). Studies have shown that development efforts can actually increase women's workload while at the same time reduce the share of household resources over which they exercise control. Consequently, women and their dependents remain the most economically vulnerable group in developing countries.

The fact that the welfare of women and children is strongly influenced by the design of development policy underscores the importance of integrating

BOX 5.2 Problems of Gender Relations in Developing Countries: Voices of the Poor

Sister, if you don't beat them, they'll stop being good. And if they're good and you beat them, they'll stay that way.

—A man in Bangladesh

When my husband died, my in-laws told me to get out. So I came to town and slept on the pavement.

—A middle-aged widow in Kenya

When I was working, I used to decide. When she is working, she owns her money and does anything she wishes.

—A man from Vila Junqueira, Brazil

Problems have affected our relationship. The day my husband brings in money, we are all right

together. The day he stays at home [out of work], we are fighting constantly.

—A woman from El Gawaber, Egypt

The unemployed men are frustrated because they can no longer play the part of family providers and protectors. They live on the money made by their wives and feel humiliated because of this.

—An elderly woman from Uchkun, Kyrgyzstan

When a woman gives her opinion, they [men] make fun of her and don't pay attention. If women go to a meeting, they don't give their opinion.

—A woman in Las Pascuas, Bolivia

women into development programs. To improve living conditions for the poorest individuals, women must be drawn into the economic mainstream. This would entail increasing female participation rates in educational and training programs, formal-sector employment, and agricultural extension programs. It is also of primary importance that precautions be taken to ensure that women have equal access to government resources provided through schooling, services, employment, and social security programs. Legalizing informal-sector employment where the majority of the female labor force is employed would also improve the economic status of women.

The consequences of declines in women's relative or absolute economic status have both ethical and long-term economic implications. Any process of growth that fails to improve the welfare of the people experiencing the greatest hardship, broadly recognized to be women and children, has failed to accomplish one of the principal goals of development. In the long run, the low status of women is likely to translate into slower rates of economic growth. This is true because the educational attainment and future financial status of children are much more likely to reflect those of the mother than those of the father. Thus, the benefits of current investments in human capital are more likely to be passed on to future generations if women are successfully integrated into the growth process. And considering that human capital is perhaps the most important prerequisite for growth, education and enhanced economic status for women are critical to meeting long-term development objectives. (We examine these issues in greater detail in Chapter 8.)

As feminist development economists have often expressed it, official poverty programs cannot simply "add women and stir." Women-centered poverty strategies often require us to challenge basic assumptions. The harsher conditions for women and women's crucial role in a community's escape from poverty mean that involvement of women cannot be left as an afterthought but will be most effective if it is the *first* thought—and the consistent basis for action—when addressing poverty.

Ethnic Minorities, Indigenous Populations, and Poverty

A final generalization about the incidence of poverty in the developing world is that it falls especially heavily on minority ethnic groups and indigenous populations. We pointed out in Chapter 2 that some 40% of the world's nation-states have more than five sizable ethnic populations, one or more of which faces serious economic, political, and social discrimination. In recent years, domestic conflicts and even civil wars have arisen out of ethnic groups' perceptions that they are losing out in the competition for limited resources and job opportunities. The poverty problem is even more serious for indigenous peoples, whose numbers exceed 300 million in over 5,000 different groups in more than 70 countries.[40]

Although detailed data on the relative poverty of minority ethnic and indigenous peoples are difficult to obtain (for political reasons, few countries wish to highlight these problems), researchers have compiled data on the poverty of indigenous people in Latin America.[41] The results clearly demonstrate that a majority of indigenous groups live in extreme poverty and that being indigenous greatly increases the chances that an individual will be malnourished, illiterate, in poor health, and unemployed. For example, the research has shown that in Mexico, over 80% of the indigenous population is poor, compared to 18% of the nonindigenous population. Table 5.8 shows that similar situations exist in countries such as Bolivia, Guatemala, and Peru (not to mention Native American populations in the United States and Canada). Moreover, a 2006 World Bank study confirmed that all too little progress had been made. Whether we speak of Tamils in Sri Lanka, Karens in Myanmar, Untouchables in India, or Tibetans in China, the poverty plight of minorities is as serious as that of indigenous peoples.

Poor Countries   Finally, it should be noted that the poor come from poor countries. Although this may seem like a trivial observation, it is actually a useful note of optimism. The negative relationship between poverty and per capita income suggests that if higher incomes can be achieved, poverty will be reduced, if only because of the greater resources that countries will have available to tackle poverty problems and the growth of civil society and the voluntary sector. Unfortunately,

TABLE 5.8   Indigenous Poverty in Latin America

	Population below the Poverty Line (%), Early 1990s		Change in Poverty (%), Various Periods		
Country	Indigenous	Nonindigenous	Period	Indigenous	Nonindigenous
Bolivia	64.3	48.1	1997–2002	0	−8
Guatemala	86.6	53.9	1989–2000	−15	−25
Mexico	80.6	17.9	1992–2002	0	−5
Peru	79.0	49.7	1994–2000	0	+3

Sources: Data for the left side of the table from George Psacharopoulos and Harry A. Patrinos, "Indigenous people and poverty in Latin America," *Finance and Development* 31 (1994): 41, used with permission; data for the right side of the table from Gillette Hall and Harry A. Patrinos, eds., *Indigenous Peoples, Poverty, and Human Development in Latin America, 1994–2004* (New York: Palgrave Macmillan, 2006).

as noted earlier, a high level of absolute poverty can also retard a country's growth prospects. Moreover, many of the poorest countries in sub-Saharan Africa experienced outright declines in per capita income throughout the 1980s and 1990s and in some cases during the first decade of this century. Among those that are growing, at current growth rates it would take decades to reach the levels of income at which poverty tends to be eradicated. After all, Brazil, which has been solidly middle-income for decades, still has 8% of its population living on less than $1.25 per day. Income poverty, malnutrition, low school attendance, and child labor in Brazil finally showed a substantial decline after the turn of this century, when antipoverty and social safety net programs were greatly expanded (see the case study at the end of Chapter 1). We can conclude that higher national incomes greatly facilitate poverty reduction, while at the same time, poverty still needs to be addressed directly.

5.6 Policy Options on Income Inequality and Poverty: Some Basic Considerations

Areas of Intervention

Developing countries that aim to reduce poverty and excessive inequalities in their distribution of income need to know how best to achieve their aim. What kinds of economic and other policies might governments in developing countries adopt to reduce poverty and inequality while maintaining or even accelerating economic growth rates? As we are concerned here with moderating the size distribution of incomes in general and raising the income levels of people living in poverty, it is important to understand the various determinants of the distribution of income in an economy and see in what ways government intervention can alter or modify their effect. The main focus of this section is on the relationship between income inequality and poverty. We examine the effects of policies and programs involving nonincome aspects of poverty in the subsequent chapters in Part Two—particularly with respect to health, nutrition, and education in Chapter 8.

We can identify four broad areas of possible government policy intervention, which correspond to the following four major elements in the determination of a developing economy's distribution of income.

1. *Altering the functional distribution*—the returns to labor, land, and capital as determined by factor prices, utilization levels, and the consequent shares of national income that accrue to the owners of each factor.

2. *Mitigating the size distribution*—the functional income distribution of an economy translated into a size distribution by knowledge of how ownership and control over productive assets and labor skills are concentrated and distributed throughout the population. The distribution of these asset holdings and skill endowments ultimately determines the distribution of personal income.

3. *Moderating (reducing) the size distribution at the upper levels* through progressive taxation of personal income and wealth. Such taxation increases government

revenues that decrease the share of disposable income of the very rich—revenues that can, with good policies, be invested in human capital and rural and other lagging infrastructure needs, thereby promoting inclusive growth. (An individual or family's **disposable income** is the actual amount available for expenditure on goods and services and for saving.)

4. *Moderating (increasing) the size distribution at the lower levels* through public expenditures of tax revenues to raise the incomes of the poor either directly (e.g., by conditional or unconditional cash transfers) or indirectly (e.g., through public employment creation such as local infrastructure projects or the provision of primary education and health care). Such public policies raise the real income levels of the poor above what their personal income levels would otherwise be, and, as will become clear in later chapters, can do so sustainably when they build the capabilities and assets of people living in poverty.

Disposable income The income that is available to households for spending and saving after personal income taxes have been deducted.

Altering the Functional Distribution of Income through Relative Factor Prices

Altering the functional distribution is a traditional economic approach. It is argued that as a result of institutional constraints and faulty government policies, the relative price of labor in the formal, modern, urban sector is higher than what would be determined by the free interplay of the forces of supply and demand. For example, the power of trade unions to raise minimum wages to artificially high levels (higher than those that would result from supply and demand) even in the face of widespread unemployment is often cited as an example of the "distorted" price of labor. From this it is argued that measures designed to reduce the price of labor relative to capital (e.g., through market-determined wages in the public sector or public wage subsidies to employers) will cause employers to substitute labor for capital in their production activities. Such factor substitution increases the overall level of employment and ultimately raises the incomes of the poor, who have been excluded from modern-sector employment and typically possess only their labor services. Put differently, artificially increased modern-sector wages reduce the rate of modern-sector enlargement growth, thus harming the poor. (For details of this analysis, see Appendix 5.1.)

However, in recent years, some scholars and practitioners, particularly from the developing world, argue that the impact of minimum wages on poverty is more nuanced in theory and practice, particularly when the possibility of income sharing among the poor is accounted for. In India, the Self-Employed Women's Association argues that minimum wages have beneficial effects even on informal-sector workers. And research by Darryl McLeod and Nora Lustig concludes that higher minimum wages are correlated with reductions in poverty.[42] Thus, actual impacts may vary, depending on local circumstances. These qualifications are particularly relevant for relatively low-skill and informal activities, such as garment stitching, beedi rolling, and incense rolling, in which workers have commonly held very low bargaining power, often due to monopsony, if not extramarket forces.

In addition, often the price of capital equipment is "institutionally" set at artificially low levels (below what supply and demand would dictate) through various public policies such as investment incentives, tax allowances, subsidized interest rates, overvalued exchange rates, and low tariffs on capital goods imports such as tractors and automated equipment relative to tariffs set on consumer goods. If these special privileges and capital subsidies were removed so that the price of capital would rise to its true "scarcity" level, producers would have a further incentive to increase their utilization of the abundant supply of labor and lower their uses of scarce capital. Moreover, owners of capital (both physical and financial) would not receive the artificially high economic returns they now enjoy.

Because factor prices are assumed to function as the ultimate signals and incentives in any economy, correcting these prices (i.e., lowering the relative price of labor and raising the relative price of capital) would, in general, not only increase productivity and efficiency but also reduce inequality by providing more wage-paying jobs for currently unemployed or underemployed unskilled and semiskilled workers. It would also lower the artificially high incomes of owners of capital. Removal of such *factor-price distortions* would therefore go a long way toward combining more growth, efficiently generated, with higher employment, less poverty, and greater equality (a more detailed analysis is presented in Appendix 5.1).

We may conclude that there is much merit to the traditional factor-price distortion argument and that correcting prices should contribute to a reduction in poverty and an improved distribution of income. How much it actually contributes will depend on the degree to which firms and farms switch to more labor-intensive production methods as the relative price of labor falls and the relative price of capital rises. These are important empirical questions, the answers to which will vary from country to country. Moreover, recent research would suggest that a close study of local conditions is needed before concluding that all minimum wages cause increases in poverty in all circumstances.

Modifying the Size Distribution through Increasing Assets of the Poor

Given correct resource prices and utilization levels for each type of productive factor (labor, land, and capital), we can arrive at estimates for the total earnings of each asset. But to translate this functional income into personal income, we need to know the distribution and ownership concentration of these assets among and within various segments of the population. Here we come to what is probably the most important fact about the determination of income distribution within an economy: The ultimate cause of the unequal distribution of personal incomes in most developing countries is the unequal and highly concentrated patterns of **asset ownership** (wealth) in these countries. The principal reason why 20% of their population often receives over 50% of the national income (see Table 5.2) is that this 20% probably owns and controls well over 90% of the productive and financial resources, especially physical capital and land but also financial capital (stocks and bonds) and human capital in the form of better education and health. Correcting factor prices is certainly not sufficient to reduce income inequalities substantially or to eliminate widespread poverty where physical and financial asset ownership—and education—are highly concentrated.

Asset ownership The ownership of land, physical capital (factories, buildings, machinery, etc.), human capital, and financial resources that generate income for owners.

It follows that the second and perhaps more important line of policy to reduce poverty and inequality is to focus directly on reducing the concentrated control of assets, the unequal distribution of power, and the unequal access to educational and income-earning opportunities that characterize many developing countries. A classic case of such **redistribution policies** as they relate to the rural poor, who comprise 70% to 80% of the target poverty group, is **land reform**. The basic purpose of land reform is to transform tenant cultivators into smallholders who will then have an incentive to raise production and improve their incomes. But as we explain in Chapter 9, land reform may be a weak instrument of income redistribution if other institutional and price distortions in the economic system prevent small farm holders from securing access to much needed critical inputs such as credit, fertilizers, seeds, marketing facilities, and agricultural education. Similar reforms in urban areas could include the provision of commercial credit at affordable rates (rather than through traditional, high-interest moneylenders) to small entrepreneurs (microcredit—for details, see Chapter 15 and the case study on the Grameen Bank at the end of that chapter) so that they can expand their business and provide more jobs to local workers.

In addition to the redistribution of existing productive assets, dynamic redistribution policies could be gradually pursued. For example, governments at least in developing countries that are growing could facilitate the transfer of a certain proportion of annual savings and investments to low-income groups so as to bring about a more gradual and perhaps politically more acceptable redistribution of additional assets as they accumulate over time. This is what is often meant by the expression "redistribution from growth." Whether such a gradual redistribution from growth is any more possible than a redistribution of existing assets is a moot point, especially in the context of very unequal power structures. But some form of asset redistribution, whether static or dynamic, seems to be a necessary condition for any significant reduction of poverty and inequality in most developing countries.

Human capital in the form of education and skills is another example of the unequal distribution of productive asset ownership. Public policy should therefore promote wider access to educational opportunities (for girls as well as boys) as a means of increasing income-earning potential for more people. But as in the case of land reform, the mere provision of greater access to additional education is no guarantee that the poor will be better off unless complementary policies—for example, the provision of more productive employment opportunities for the educated—are adopted to capitalize on this increased human capital. The relationship among education, employment, and development is discussed further in Chapter 8.

People living in poverty tend to have common problems, but the prevalent forms of deprivation and social exclusion can differ considerably even across regions within a country. Policymakers need to have a strong knowledge base. Essential to the process is a means to find out and utilize what the poor know about their own conditions of poverty. Practitioners stress that the more that people living in poverty are engaged in setting the agenda, the more effective programs to increase their assets and capabilities tend to be. But attention must be given to different segments of the local poor communities, as different priorities are often found between men and women, between ethnic groups, and between castes.

Redistribution policies Policies geared to reducing income inequality and expanding economic opportunities in order to promote development, including income tax policies, rural development policies, and publicly financed services.

Land reform A deliberate attempt to reorganize and transform existing agrarian systems with the intention of improving the distribution of agricultural incomes and thus fostering rural development.

Progressive Income and Wealth Taxes

Progressive income tax   A tax whose rate increases with increasing personal incomes.

Any national policy attempting to improve the living standards of the bottom 40% must secure sufficient financial resources to transform paper plans into program realities. The major source of such development finance is the direct and progressive taxation of both income and wealth. Direct **progressive income taxes** focus on personal and corporate incomes, with the rich required to pay a progressively larger percentage of their total income in taxes than the poor. Taxation on wealth (the stock of accumulated assets and income) typically involves personal and corporate property taxes but may also include progressive inheritance taxes. In either case, the burden of the tax is designed to fall most heavily on the upper-income groups.

Regressive tax   A tax structure in which the ratio of taxes to income tends to decrease as income increases.

Indirect taxes   Taxes levied on goods ultimately purchased by consumers, including customs duties (tariffs), excise duties, sales taxes, and export duties.

In reality, in many developing countries (and some developed countries), the gap between what is supposed to be a progressive tax structure and what different income groups actually pay can be substantial. Progressive tax structures on paper often turn out to be **regressive taxes** in practice, in that the lower- and middle-income groups often end up paying a proportionally larger share of their incomes in taxes than the upper-income groups. The reasons for this are simple. The poor are often taxed at the source of their incomes or expenditures (by withholding taxes from wages, general poll taxes, or **indirect taxes** levied on the retail purchase of goods such as cigarettes and beer). By contrast, the rich derive by far the largest part of their incomes from the return on physical and financial assets, which often go unreported. They often also have the power and ability to avoid paying taxes without fear of government reprisal. Policies to enforce progressive rates of direct taxation on income and wealth, especially at the highest levels, are what are most needed in this area of redistribution activity. (See Chapter 15 for a further discussion of taxation for development.)

Direct Transfer Payments and the Public Provision of Goods and Services

Public consumption   All current expenditures for purchases of goods and services by all levels of government, including capital expenditures on national defense and security.

The direct provision of tax-financed **public consumption** goods and services to the very poor is another potentially important instrument of a comprehensive policy designed to eradicate poverty. Examples include public health projects in rural villages and urban fringe areas, school lunches and preschool nutritional supplementation programs, and the provision of clean water and electrification to remote rural areas. Direct money transfers and subsidized food programs for the urban and rural poor, as well as direct government policies to keep the prices of essential foodstuffs low, represent additional forms of public consumption **subsidies**.

Subsidy   A payment by the government to producers or distributors in an industry to prevent the decline of that industry, to reduce the prices of its products, or to encourage hiring.

Direct transfers and subsidies can be highly effective, but they need to be designed carefully. Four significant problems require attention. First, when resources for attacking poverty are limited—as they always are—they need to be directed to people who are genuinely poor. Second, it is important that beneficiaries not become unduly dependent on the poverty program; in particular, we do not want to give the poor less incentive to build the assets, such as education, that can enable them to stay out of poverty. But a "safety net" can also be valuable to encourage the poor to accept a more entrepreneurial attitude toward their microenterprises. This is much more possible when the poor do not fear that their children will suffer terrible consequences if their small businesses fail. Third, we do not want to divert people who are productively engaged in alternative economic activities to participate in the poverty program instead. Finally, poverty policies are often limited by resentment from the nonpoor, including those who are working hard but are not very far above the poverty line themselves.

When a subsidy of goods consumed by the poor is planned, it should be targeted to the geographic areas where the poor are found and should emphasize goods that nonpoor people do not consume. This helps conserve resources for the program and minimizes efforts by nonpoor people to benefit from the program. For example, nutritional supplements can be provided for any woman who brings her baby to the neighborhood poverty program center located in villages and neighborhoods with a high incidence of absolute poverty. Although more affluent mothers could use the program, few would risk the stigma of venturing into the poorer villages and neighborhoods, let alone the center itself. The nutritional supplements help poor mothers and their small children stay healthy and thus help break the cycle of poverty.

In addition, it may be useful to impose a work requirement before food aid is provided. This is done in the well-known Bangladesh Food for Work Program and in the Maharashtra Employment Guarantee Scheme in India. More recently, the government of India has introduced a nationwide program to guarantee 100 days of employment to at least one family member each year; early reports suggest that the program has provided substantial benefits. In programs such as these, the poor are put to work building infrastructure, such as roads from outlying areas (where the poor live) to market towns, that will ultimately benefit the poor and others in the region. Although the administrative costs are generally higher and the skills of the workers significantly lower than would be the case with a commercially procured construction contract, in many cases these valuable infrastructure projects would never be tackled at all in the absence of the program. The high work requirement and very modest payment discourage the nonpoor from participating, thus conserving resources. This characteristic is known as the "screening" function of **workfare programs**. These requirements also help preserve the program's political sustainability: When people see that the poor are getting "a hand up rather than a handout," the programs tend to attract wider public support.

Workfare program A poverty alleviation program that requires program beneficiaries to work in exchange for benefits, as in a food-for-work program.

In sum, we can say that workfare, such as the Food for Work Program, represents a better policy than welfare or direct handouts when the following criteria are met:

- The program does not reduce or seriously undermine incentives for the poor to acquire human capital and other assets.

- There are greater *net* benefits of the work output of the program.

- It is harder to screen the poor without the workfare requirement.

- There is lower opportunity cost of time for poor workers (so the economy loses little output when they join the workfare program).

- There is higher opportunity cost of time for nonpoor workers (so they won't avail themselves of the benefits).

- The fraction of the population living in poverty is smaller (so the extra costs of a universal welfare program would be high).

- There is less social stigma attached to participating in a workfare program, so the poor do not suffer undue humiliation and are less deterred from seeking the help that their families need (otherwise, a discreet welfare transfer may be preferable to a highly visible workfare program).[43]

The poor often have low bargaining power in their communities, and while it is difficult politically to increase this power, well-designed programs can accomplish this indirectly by providing improved "outside options" such as guaranteed public employment programs when they are needed.

We will be continuing our examination of policies for poverty reduction throughout the remainder of this text. Appropriate agricultural development policies represent a crucial strategy for attacking poverty because such a high fraction of the poor are located in rural areas and engaged in agricultural pursuits. Strategies for agricultural development are examined in Chapter 9. In addition, the poor in urban as well as rural areas suffer from degraded environmental conditions, which lower opportunities for economic growth and also worsen the health of the poor; these problems are examined in Chapter 10.

Another set of viable policies involve targeted poverty programs to increase the capabilities and human and social capital of the poor. An important example centers on helping the poor develop their microenterprises, on which a large fraction of the nonagricultural poor depend for their survival. It has been found that credit is the binding constraint for many of these tiny firms. By building up the working capital and other assets of microenterprises, the poor can improve their productivity and incomes. The microfinance strategy for accomplishing this goal, as exemplified by the Grameen Bank of Bangladesh, is examined in Chapter 15. In addition, relatively new approaches to attacking poverty focus on an integrated approach to achieving higher incomes together with improved education, health, and nutrition among the poor, notably, conditional cash transfer (CCT) programs that transfer incomes to poor families conditional on behaviors such as keeping their children in school; these approaches are considered in Chapter 8 and its case study. Finally, strategies to assist the development of the urban informal sector are examined in Chapter 7.

5.7 Summary and Conclusions: The Need for a Package of Policies

To summarize our discussion of alternative policy approaches to the problems of poverty and inequality in development, the need is not for one or two isolated policies but for a "package" of complementary and supportive policies, including the following four basic elements.[44]

1. A policy or set of policies designed to correct factor price distortions (underpricing capital or overpricing modern-sector skilled wages) so as to ensure that market or institutionally established prices provide accurate signals and incentives to both producers and resource suppliers. Correcting distorted prices should contribute to greater productive efficiency, more employment,

and less poverty. The promotion of indigenous technological research and development of efficient, labor-intensive methods of production may also be valuable. (For a further analysis of factor price distortions, see Appendix 5.1.)

2. A policy or set of policies designed to bring about far-reaching structural changes in the distribution of assets, power, and access to education and associated income-earning (employment) opportunities. Such policies go beyond the realm of markets and touch on the whole social, institutional, cultural, and political fabric of the developing world. But such fundamental structural changes and substantive asset redistributions, whether immediately achieved (e.g., through public-sector interventions) or gradually introduced over time (through redistribution from growth), will increase the chances of improving significantly the living conditions of the masses of rural and urban poor.

3. A policy or set of policies designed to modify the size distribution of income at the upper levels through the enforcement of legislated progressive taxation on incomes and wealth; and at the same time, providing the poor with direct transfer payments and the expanded provision of publicly provided consumption goods and services, including workfare programs. The net effect is to create a social "safety net" for people who may be bypassed by the development process.

4. A set of targeted policies to directly improve the well-being of the poor and their communities, which goes beyond safety net schemes, to offer programs that build capabilities and human and social capital of the poor, such as microfinance, health, education, agricultural development, environmental sustainability, and community development and empowerment programs, as described throughout this text. These can be carried out either by government or by nongovernmental organizations through local and international support.

While providing a focus on ending extreme poverty and mitigating harmful inequality, such policies can be designed to encourage and accelerate inclusive economic growth targeted at the poor, while keeping in mind the inherently multidimensional nature of poverty. Key examples include growth-supporting investments in education, nutrition, health, and infrastructure that raise the incomes of those in the bottom deciles of the income distribution. Chapters 2 through 4 considered the sources of economic growth and basic policies to identify constraints and maintain growth that benefit people living in poverty. Additional supporting trade, macro, and financial policies are examined in more detail in Chapters 13 through 15. But when it is not inclusive, growth by itself is insufficient to eliminate extreme poverty, at least in any time frame that a nation—let alone people living in poverty—will find acceptable. So encouragement of inclusive growth goes hand in hand with active policies and programs to reduce poverty and to prevent nonpoor people from falling into poverty.

Though the task of ending extreme poverty will be difficult, it is possible, if we can only muster the will. As noted by James Speth, the executive director of the United Nations Development Programme, "Poverty is no longer inevitable. The world has the material and natural resources, the know-how and the people to make a poverty-free world a reality in less than a generation. This is not woolly idealism but a practical and achieveable goal."[45]

Institutions, Inequality, and Incomes: Ghana and Côte d'Ivoire

Ghana's development has exceeded expectations—at least after many disappointments. Côte d'Ivoire (CIV) started with many apparent advantages, but on many economic measures, Ghana has closed the development gap that existed between itself and CIV at independence.

It is recommended that you read Chapters 2 and 5 in conjunction with this case. These country illustrations provide further interpretation of the more general research discussed in those chapters.

A Natural Comparative Case Study

Ghana and Côte d'Ivoire border each other in West Africa. Their land area is similar in size at 92,456 square miles (239,450 km²) and 124,502 square miles (322,458 km²), respectively. Their populations are also similar, with 25.5 million people in Ghana and 20.6 million in Côte d'Ivoire in 2012. Becoming independent within three years of each other and also sharing similar geographies, these adjoining countries make for a natural comparison. One of the most striking differences is that Ghana was part of the British Empire from 1821 to 1957, and CIV was a French colony from 1842 until 1960. (Note, however, that full colonial rule took a long time to become established throughout the territories of these countries; the French were still fighting to extend their presence into the early years of the twentieth century.)

How did these colonial histories matter? Did their influences extend after independence, affecting later development policies for good or ill? Or have other, internal factors been more decisive? Can this help us to better understand why it is so challenging to sustain high growth, eliminate poverty and hunger, and to achieve other Millennium Development Goals?

The experiences of a half-century after independence illustrate some of the opportunities for and threats to development. This case study raises thought-provoking questions and presents the types of information one would weigh in addressing this and other comparative country studies. This case illustrates how the frameworks and many-country statistical studies of Chapters 2 and 5 can be applied to understanding development experiences in comparative perspective. The richness of culture and nuances of complex political histories are abstracted to feature some broad approaches and findings in development economics in a short space. Readers are encouraged to explore these leading African nations in detail.

Poverty and Human Development As reported in the UNDP's 2013 *Human Development Report*, Ghana is considered a medium human development country, with a New Human Development Index (NHDI) value of 0.558, while CIV is considered a low human development country, with an NHDI of just 0.432. Ghana's performance is 22 positions higher than predicted by income, while CIV's is 9 positions lower. In the 1990 *Human Development Report*, when the original HDI was introduced, the numbers were 0.393 for CIV and 0.360 for Ghana. Both made progress, but Ghana much more so. CIV's Multidimensional Poverty Index (MPI) as reported in the 2013 *Human Development Report* is very high at 0.353, while Ghana's MPI is substantially lower at 0.144. And the 2009 *Human Development Report* Human Poverty Index (see note 11) for CIV was 0.374, ranking 29 places lower in the country rankings based on human poverty than income poverty (the fraction under $1.25 per day). This suggested that what the UNDP termed *human poverty* is relatively worse in CIV than even

its income poverty would suggest. Ghana's HPI was significantly better, at 0.281 (with its ranking as predicted by its income poverty).

These outcomes would have surprised many who wrote at the time of independence. In 1960, Ghana had a real GDP per capita of just $594, far behind CIV's $1,675; but in 2007, according to the *Penn World Table*, Ghana had reached $1,653—a gain of 278% and nearly enough to close its original deficit—while CIV increased to $2,228, a modest gain of just 33% after 47 years. In 2011, Ghana's estimated income per capita PPP of $1,830 surpassed CIV's level of $1,780 (2013 World Development Indicators).

Ghana has a life expectancy of 64, while that of CIV is only 55 (2012 PRB estimates); in 1960, life expectancy in CIV was 51, to Ghana's 46, a dramatic reversal. In 2011, under-5 mortality was 115 in CIV and a still high but significantly lower 78 in Ghana.

Aysit Tansel showed that by 1987, Ghana was well ahead of CIV in mean years of schooling by each gender and across age groups. By 2008, the adult literacy rate reached 65.0% in Ghana versus 48.7% in CIV.

Highly credible information on the extent of extreme poverty in these countries is difficult to find, but it is not doubted that at the time of independence, poverty was far higher in Ghana. Using 1987 surveys, the World Bank put dollar-a-day poverty at just 3.28% in CIV that year but 46.51% in Ghana; a comparable figure for Ghana (from a 1998 study) was 36% and for CIV (2002) was 16%. The most recent available World Bank estimates are 28.6% below $1.25 per day in Ghana (2006 survey) and 23.8% (2008 survey) in CIV (2013 World Development Indicators). It appears that over time, poverty has fallen in Ghana and risen in CIV.

Progress in both countries is small in comparison to East Asia; but the differences between these countries are substantial. How can we begin to understand such differences? Sometimes even recent changes in the patterns of development can have long historical roots, and we consider this first.

Long-Run Factors in Comparative Development

The Colonial Impact and the Legacy of Institutions The Portuguese built a fortress on the coast of Ghana in 1482 and named it Elmina ("The Mine"). Later, the British named this area the Gold Coast, as it was known until independence in 1957.

Côte d'Ivoire (Ivory Coast) received its name from the French. These names apparently reflect how the colonial powers viewed the territories: as "coasts" rather than nations; as commodities for trade rather than people, or simply as a mine. The colonialists' priority of resources over people could not have been more obvious. Ghana suffered earlier and more from the impact of the slave trade. But CIV also suffered ill treatment, including a brutal campaign by the French to subdue the "interior" in the late nineteenth and early twentieth centuries and impose forced labor. How do we understand this terrible colonial experience and its possible aftermath? Settler mortality rates, which is correlated with the establishment of extractive institutions by the colonial power with long-term pernicious effects (see Chapter 2, section 2.7), was stunningly high in these two countries, each with an estimated 668 deaths per 1,000 per year, among the highest in the study by Acemoglu, Johnson, and Robinson (AJR); for comparison, the rate was just 15.5 in South Africa.*

Institutional Quality The expectation is that inherited institutions should be particularly bad in these two countries because colonialists would have had little incentive to protect property rights, encourage investment, or allow broad access to economic opportunities or political participation; instead, in stark terms, the incentive was to steal or have others steal for you. In their data for current institutional quality, the "average protection against expropriate risk" was 6.27 in Ghana and 7.00 in CIV, compared to a range from 3.50 in the Democratic Republic of Congo (known as Zaire at the time) to 10.00 in the United States—better, though not spectacularly better, investor protection. But a range of recent studies give higher marks to Ghana. Although all-country rankings of institutional quality should be used with caution, as they

---

*According to the AJR dataset, which is based on the work of the historian Philip Curtin, the other highest-mortality colonies were Togo, Gambia, Mali, and Nigeria. By contrast, the death rate was just 14.9 in Hong Kong, and 17.7 in Malaysia and Singapore. Settler mortality was used as an instrument for early institutions in the literature (see Chapter 2), and we examine two countries with identical settler mortalities giving attention to additional elements. (Conclusions of the research cited here are based on multicountry statistical analysis, not on case studies; we are taking such research as a starting point for issues to consider when conducting more in-depth comparative case studies.)

can contain subjective elements; when a group of independently produced indicators with different focuses all point in the same direction, they become suggestive (though still never substituting for careful country-specific appraisal). Regarding corruption perceptions, according to Transparency International, in 2012 Ghana ranked 64th and CIV 130th out of 176 countries ranked. Regarding "ease of doing business," the World Bank–International Finance Corporation 2010 rankings of 183 countries listed Ghana as 92nd (7th in sub-Saharan Africa) and CIV as 168th (32nd in the region). Regarding democracy, for 2012 the *Economist* listed Ghana (ranked 78th of 167) as a "flawed democracy" (two steps above authoritarian) and CIV (ranked 136th) as authoritarian. And on current property rights protections, a 2013 ranking sponsored by the *Wall Street Journal* and Heritage Foundation placed Ghana at 50 on a scale of 100 and CIV just 25. Critics point out limits and flaws of these various rankings, but they are consistent. So this, too, must be better understood. Is it because things had gotten so bad in Ghana that reform became the only option?

Ethnolinguistic Fractionalization Another feature associated in the economics literature with low incomes and growth is ethnolinguistic fractionalization, with some social scientists also pointing out the potential dangers of religious fractionalization. In fact, both countries are fairly highly fractionalized, but CIV more so. Both countries have an Akan majority (45% in Ghana and 42% in CIV) and many smaller groups. In Ghana, the population is 69% Christian and 16% Muslim, but in CIV, adherents are much more evenly divided, with 39% Muslim and 33% Christian. Although scholars debate the proper way to measure fractionalization, seven main measures are used, with CIV higher on six, in some cases substantially higher.[*] CIV was torn by civil war in 2002, which has split the country, and the opportunistic use of fractionalization by political figures is an important factor.

Population Patterns of population growth are often considered an important aspect of development, as discussed in Chapter 6. At independence in 1960,

*For example, according to the 1997 basic Easterly-Levine (ELF) measure, CIV was rated 0.86 and Ghana 0.71, with the range in Africa from 0.04 for Burundi to 0.9 for Congo and Uganda. On the widely cited 2003 Alesina et al. alternative measure, CIV is 0.82 and Ghana 0.67 in a range from 0 to 0.93. These are the usual baseline measures, but one measure of the seven points in the other direction: the 1999 measure of Fearon, on which CIV is 0.78 and Ghana 0.85.

the population of CIV was just 3.6 million, so it grew about 5½ times by 2007. In contrast, Ghana's population was already nearly 7 million in 1960, so it grew by less than 3⅓ times in the same period. Even now, the total fertility rate is a high 4.0 in Ghana but significantly higher at 4.9 in CIV, with one extra birth per woman. While just 8% of married women of childbearing age use modern contraceptives in CIV, 17% do in Ghana—still a small fraction but more than twice the incidence of CIV (the gap remains, at 24% to 13%, when considering both traditional and modern methods). High birth rates generally hinder economic development. Faster population growth is associated with slower per capita income growth and slower improvement in other development indicators; lower fertility increases family incentives and resources for education. But the geographic distribution of population does not seem to have particularly strong political implications. For example, Jeffrey Herbst classifies both Ghana and CIV as among just 7 of 40 sub-Saharan African countries with a "neutral political geography."

Extreme Inequality As explained in Chapter 5 (and introduced in Chapter 2), extreme inequality can retard the development process. The most recent World Bank Gini coefficient estimates for CIV and Ghana do not differ significantly (at 0.42 and 0.43). But Arnim Langer points out that the combination of relatively high and rising inequality in CIV, coupled with rising ethnic tensions that political actors had deliberately made worse, led to the conflict that broke out there in the early 2000s (ethnic inequalities as a factor in conflict is considered in Chapter 14, section 14.5).

Common Law versus Civil Law? As a former British colony, Ghana's legal system is based on common law, while the legal system in CIV is based on French civil law. Since the late 1990s, the view that common law legal systems provide a better foundation than civil law systems for the development of the financial system has been very influential. Authors in this literature such as Rafael La Porta and his colleagues argue either that common law better protects property rights, better enforces contracts, offers more predictability, or that it is better able to adapt to changes in economic conditions. Investment is generally necessary for economic growth (Chapters 3 and 4), and the development of an effective financial system encourages investment

(Chapter 15). Some evidence supports the prediction that civil law countries will experience less financial development and lower rates of investment. But differences between French and British institutions besides the legal system may be important.

French versus British Rule? The British Empire is commonly considered to have preferred indirect rule, relying on its ability to dominate local traditional political systems rather than to create new ones (possibly related to common law tradition). In contrast, the French are said to have tended to employ direct rule of their colonies, introducing their own centralized administrative structures, perhaps related to their own legal and historical traditions. Tactics might well have been similar regardless of the colonizer if conditions strongly favored central rule or indirect rule. But where starting conditions were similar in both colonies and when local advantages of either centralization or decentralization were not strong, a centralized French strategy and a decentralized British strategy might plausibly have been expected.

The evidence does reflect a more decentralized rule in British Ghana and more centralized rule in French Côte d'Ivoire. But if centralized rule is then transmitted to the postcolonial regime, the result can be a state with too few checks and balances. Decentralized rule, in contrast, provides better incentives and checks against large-scale government corruption (see Chapter 11). The postcolonial record is complex but shows continued strong tendencies toward centralization in CIV, although the aftermath of civil strife increases uncertainty about the future course (indeed there is some risk that CIV may face a prolonged period as a failed state). As Catherine Boone notes in her richly detailed study of both countries, the case of Ghana is subtle with initial but far from fully successful postcolonial government attempts at more centralization, probably in part to wrest a larger share of agricultural revenues, but in 1992 there was a reinstatement of at least a ceremonial role—and unofficially a much larger role—for chiefs and other traditional village governance. This built on long traditions that were not systematically undermined under the British the way they were under the French.

Finally, some observers view postindependence CIV as having a more dependent relationship with France. Besides colonial rule having negative effects in general, close CIV dependence on its former co-lonial ruler may have been a hindrance to its economic and political growth and development over the long run. In contrast, Ghana diversified more of its international relations, perhaps giving it somewhat higher bargaining power in pursuing its national development interests.

Education Some scholars consider education of central importance in explaining economic growth; Edward Glaeser and coauthors even argue that improved education can result in improved institutions. Educational attainment was abysmal in both nations at the time of independence. One of the most striking postcolonial differences between the countries is the higher level of educational attainment in Ghana, where there have been greater investments in education. In the early years after independence, there was strong policy attention to providing basic education in some of the poorer areas in Ghana. In 2010, according to the 2013 Human Development Report (HDR), the mean years of schooling was almost 3 years higher in Ghana (at 7.0) than in CIV (at 4.2). Moreover, expected schooling is now 11.4 years in Ghana, compared with only 6.5 years in CIV. Education is intrinsically valuable, as reflected in the HDI; it has apparently been a factor in faster growth and may even figure in later institutional improvements. Ghana has also had recent success scaling up basic health insurance.

Development Policies Development policies are often framed by a country's underlying economic institutions; this can place constraints on the types of beneficial reforms and policies that a country can successfully implement. The failure of a country to implement otherwise obvious policies (such as investing in quality primary education) may not reflect failures of understanding as much as the realities of political constraints. But when achieved, well-designed and implemented policies can have very positive effects on development outcomes; bad policies can have disastrous consequences.

Policies in Ghana Both nations started as (and still are) largely agrarian economies, with over half of the labor force working in rural areas. But the two countries have had somewhat different policy trajectories. The general scholarly view is that in the first quarter century after independence, Ghana chose many poorly conceived and often corrupt interventionist policies. Early policies have been described as oriented toward urban industry,

with inefficiently implemented import substitution to replace manufactured imports with locally produced ones (see Chapter 12). But one policy associated with the early rule of Kwame Nkrumah through 1966 was an emphasis on basic education, which may have left an enduring legacy through difficult subsequent swings. After disastrous policies and extreme instability, including coups in the mid-1960s to early 1980s, Ghana underwent a policy transformation to become a favorite country of liberalization promoters in the World Bank and elsewhere in the 1980s.

The development process is complex and rarely proceeds linearly. In Ghana, there was relative deterioration from independence until the early 1980s; much of its economic growth took place from the mid-1980s to the present. For example, cocoa had long been an important part of Ghana's economy, but it went into decline when state marketing boards (described in Chapter 9) limited the price farmers received for cocoa, so as to subsidize industrialization. After farmers were allowed to receive a much higher price and technical assistance was offered, output greatly increased, particularly in two spurts in the late 1980s and early 2000s. Fertilizer use and improved varieties have diffused among farmers (diffusion in Ghana for the case of pineapples is examined in Findings Box 9.1 in Chapter 9). Cocoa growing now provides a basic livelihood for over 700,000 farmers in Ghana.

By the early 1990s, World Bank analysts such as Ishrat Husain were pointing to Ghana as a country that had been doing a better job at following and implementing more of its recommended market-friendly policies than countries such as CIV.

A reason given for large-scale reform in Ghana (and in explaining other countries as well) is that things got so bad that there became no choice but to embrace reform. Naturally, when according to local conditions things become so bad that continued resistance to change is futile, *something* changes—perhaps not always for the better. Ghana became a classic example for proponents of the controversial view that duress "causes" reform. A criticism, to paraphrase Dani Rodrik, is that it is not clear how much duress is enough to "cause" reform; and as a result, it is not very convincing when analysts simply claim that a reform did not happen because the situation must not have been bad enough.

Policies in Côte d'Ivoire In contrast, CIV experienced relatively faster growth in the 1960s and 1970s and then decline from 1980 to the present (recently more pronounced due to civil conflict). Institutions that appear to perform serviceably for two decades can have underlying weaknesses that later emerge—for example, politicians treat weaknesses as a political opportunity or the system proves to have too little flexibility as new challenges emerge.

CIV is widely viewed as having started down a more market-based, export-oriented path in a way that should have helped the rural agricultural sector, where most of the population and most people living in poverty were located. But this did not prevent elites from extracting what they could from the rural areas. In fact, there were a number of policy lurches. An apparently favorable tactic might have been an early policy of effectively trying to keep all the ethnic groups engaged in and benefiting from growth in the national economy. There were large migrations into CIV, for example, including the forced labor brought into CIV from Burkina Faso (Upper Volta) by the French in the early 1940s. A more ethnically based politics in the late 1990s is viewed by specialists in the politics of CIV as helping to precipitate the disaster of regional and ethnic conflict in the 2000s.

Enduring Questions By 1990, Ghana was already being deemed a "success story" by the World Bank and others. Is it because the nation followed the right policies? And if so, what explains why Ghana chose good policies and CIV did not? How much benefit can be attributed to the volume of aid itself?

CIV fell into a period of severe conflict in 2002–2007; many lives were lost, and resources continue to be diverted into managing the problems, with perceptions of prospects still damaged. French military involvement reflected France's ongoing unique relationship with CIV. In contrast, Ghana has so far remained stable. Why? And can it continue to remain stable? It remains to be seen how well Ghana comes through its recent discovery and production of oil. In principle, new resources can help reduce poverty, directly and indirectly. But for many countries, a "resource curse" has resulted

from political conflict over resource revenues and an overspecialized or even "hollowed out" economy (see Chapter 14).

Have leadership differences mattered for development of these countries? Socialist Kwame Nkrumah constructively supported education but diverted resources from cocoa exports to local industry, leading to economic disaster; under duress, socialist Jerry Rawlings embraced market-oriented policy reforms that led to short-term pain but long-term gain. Subsequent leaders have been pragmatic and at least have done relatively little harm and perhaps some good. CIV's capitalist President Félix Houphouët-Boigny, backed by France ("Françafrique"), seemed early on to be leading his country to economic success but stole billions from the public purse and led the country to ruin while clinging to power for 33 years until his death in 1993. Subsequent leadership has impressed few observers. Of course, extraordinary leadership in government or civil society can play a decisive role in the course of development—think of Nelson Mandela in South Africa or Muhammad Yunus in Bangladesh. But in ordinary experience, is leadership the key, or is it underlying institutions? Or popular movements? Education? Imported ideas and technology? These remain enduring questions, and answers may depend on local circumstances.

As an examination of just two countries to illustrate more general evidence in the literature, it cannot be concluded beyond doubt that institutions set up by Great Britain in Ghana and France in Côte d'Ivoire had a dominant effect on the successes and failures of these nations in subsequent poverty reduction and economic growth. But there is support for factors identified in the large-sample statistical studies introduced in Chapter 2, notably institutions, inequality, and at least indirectly education. Colonial institutions apparently had negative effects, and within colonization, the degree of decentralization under colonial rule apparently also mattered. The reemergence of more decentralized governance in Ghana since 1992 may be related to less damaging British governance practices in this respect. At the same time, history is not destiny; Ghana has made progress that was not well predicted by instruments for colonial institutions. Nor are things necessarily bleak for CIV. Institutions and inequality are highly resistant to change. But the global trend is toward continued progress in human development, and other African nations such as Rwanda have made enormous economic strides that were very difficult to imagine just a few years earlier. But in CIV, the standoff following contaminated presidential elections in 2010 led to what has been called the Second Ivorian Civil War. Rather than simply blame CIV, it may be possible to trace the shape of policymaking to underlying institutions– doing so may be a way to help address deeper constraints. It is to be hoped that the international community can play a constructive role in facilitating improvements in CIV's underlying institutions, as well as to help secure the peace.

Sources

The authors would like to thank Gina Lambright, David Shinn, and Jennifer Spencer for their comments on the first draft of this case study, and Andrew Klein and Kevin Salador for their research assistance.

Acemoglu, Daron, Simon Johnson, and James A. Robinson. "The colonial origins of comparative development: An empirical investigation." *American Economics Review* 91 (2001): 1360–1401.

Adjibolosoo, Senyo. "Ghana at fifty years old: A critical review of the historical genesis of why Ghanaians are where they are today." *Review of Human Factor Studies.* 13 (2007): 6–40.

Alesina, Alberto, and Eliana La Ferrara. "Ethnic diversity and economic performance." *Journal of Economic Literature* 43 (2005): 762–800.

Alkire, Sabina, and Maria Emma Santos "Acute Multidimensional Poverty: A New Index for Developing Countries." OPHI Working Paper 38, 2010, at http://www.ophi.org.uk/acute-multidimensional-poverty-a-new-index-for-developing-countries/

Beck, Thorsten, Asli Demirguc-Kunt, and Ross Levine. "Law and finance: Why does legal origin matter?" *Journal of Comparative Economics* (2003): 663–675.

Blunch, Niels-Hugo, and Dorte Verner. "Shared sectoral growth versus the dual economy model: Evidence from Côte d'Ivoire, Ghana, and Zimbabwe." *Development Review* 18 (2006): 283–308.

Boone, Catherine. *Political Topographies of the African State. Territorial Authority and Institutional Choice*. Cambridge: Cambridge University Press, 2003.

Crook, Richard, Simplice Affou, Daniel Hammond, Adja F. Vanga, and Mark Owusu-Yeboah. "The law, legal institutions and the protection of land rights in Ghana and Côte d'Ivoire: Developing a more effective and equitable system." IDS Research Report 58. Brighton, U.K.: Institute of Development Studies at the University of Sussex, 2007.

Easterly, William. "Inequality does cause underdevelopment." *Journal of Development Economics* 84 (2007): 755–776.

Engelbert, Pierre. "Pre-colonial institutions, post-colonial states, and economic development in tropical Africa." *Political Research Quarterly* (2000): 7–36.

———. *State Legitimacy and Development in Africa*. Boulder, Colo.: Rienner, 2000.

Firmin-Sellers, Kathryn. "Institutions, context, and outcomes: Explaining French and British rule in West Africa." *Comparative Politics* 32 (2000): 253–272.

Glaeser, Edward L., Rafael La Porta, Florencio Lopez de Silanes, and Andrei Shleifer. "Do institutions cause growth?" *Journal of Economic Growth* 9 (2004): 271–303.

Herbst, Jeffrey. *States and Power in Africa. Comparative Lessons in Authority and Control*. Princeton, N.J.: Princeton University Press, 2000.

Heston, Alan, Robert Summers, and Bettina Aten. *Penn World Table*, vers. 6.3. Center for International Comparisons of Production, Income, and Prices at the University of Pennsylvania, August 2009.

Husain Ishrat. *"Why do some adjust more successfully than others? Lessons from seven African countries."* World Bank Africa Regional Office Policy Research Working Paper No. 1364, Office of the Chief Economist, 1994.

Husain, Ishrat, and Rashid Faruqee. *Adjustment in Africa: Lessons from Country Case Studies*. Washington, D.C.: World Bank, 1994.

La Porta, Rafael, Florencio Lopez-de-Silanes, Andrei Shleifer, and Robert W. Vishny. "Law and finance." *Journal of Political Economy* 106 (1998) 1113–1155.

Langer, Arnim, "Horizontal Inequalities and Violent Conflict" Côte d'Ivoire Country Paper, 2005. http://hdr.undp.org/en/reports.

MacLean, Lauren Morris. "Constructing a social safety net in Africa: An institutionalist analysis of colonial rule and state social policies in Ghana and Côte d'Ivoire." *Studies in Comparative International Development* 37 (2002): 64–90.

Office of the Chief Economist, Africa Region, World Bank. *Yes, Africa Can: Success Stories from a Dynamic Continent*. Washington, D.C.: World Bank, 2009.

Population Council. "Côte d'Ivoire, 1998–99 results from the Demographic and Health Survey source." *Studies in Family Planning* 34 (2003): 53–57.

Population Reference Bureau. *World Population Data Sheet, 2012.*

———. "Progress in Reducing Adolescent Childbearing: Ghana's Success Story," A PRB ENGAGE Snapshot, 2013 http://www.prb.org/Journalists/Webcasts/2013/ghana-adolescent-childbearing-engage-short.aspx.

Rodrik, Dani. "Understanding economic policy reform." *Journal of Economic Literature* 34 (1996): 9–41.

Stewart, Frances. "Horizontal inequalities: A neglected dimension of development." QEH Working Paper Series, No. 81. Oxford: University of Oxford, 2002.

Tansel, Aysit. "Schooling attainment, parental education, and gender in Côte d'Ivoire and Ghana." *Economic Development and Cultural Change* 45 (1997): 825–856.

Tsikata, Fui S. "National mineral policies in a changing world: The vicissitudes of mineral policy in Ghana." *Resources Policy* 23 (1997): 9–14.

United Nations Development Programme. *Human Development Report, 2009* and *2010*. New York: Oxford University Press, 2009 and 2010.

White, Howard. "Using household survey data to measure educational performance: The case of Ghana." *Social Indicators Research* 74 (2005): 395–422.

World Bank. "PovcalNet." http://iresearch.worldbank.org/PovcalNet.

———. *World Development Indicators, 2010, 2013*. Washington, D.C.: World Bank, 2010, 2013.

Yimam, Arega. *Social Development in Africa, 1950–1985: Methodological Perspectives and Future Prospects*. Brookfield, Vt.: Avebury, 1990.

Concepts for Review

Absolute poverty	Functional distribution of income	Personal distribution of income
Asset ownership	Gini coefficient	Progressive income tax
Character of economic growth	Headcount index	Public consumption
Decile	Income inequality	Quintile
Disposable income	Indirect taxes	Redistribution policies
Elasticity of factor substitution (Appendix 5.1)	Kuznets curve	Regressive tax
	Land reform	Subsidy
Factor price distortions (Appendix 5.1)	Lorenz curve	Total poverty gap (TPG)
	Multidimensional poverty index (MPI)	Workfare programs
Factors of production		
Foster-Greer-Thorbecke (FGT) index	Neoclassical price incentive model (Appendix 5.1)	

Questions for Discussion

1. Most development economists now seem to agree that the level and rate of growth of GNI and per capita income do not provide sufficient measures of a country's development. What is the essence of their argument? Give some examples.

2. Distinguish between size and functional distributions of income in a nation. Which do you conclude is the more appropriate concept? Explain your answer.

3. What is meant by absolute poverty? What measures of income poverty are favored by development economists? How do income poverty measures differ from the UNDP's Multidimensional Poverty Index? Why should we be concerned with the measurement of poverty in developing nations?

4. What are the principal economic characteristics of high-poverty groups? What do these characteristics tell us about the possible nature of a poverty-focused development strategy?

5. Describe Kuznets's inverted-U hypothesis. Discuss the conceptual merits and limitations of this hypothesis for contemporary developing countries.

6. In the text, when we examined statistics from a wide range of developing countries, we found that growth does not guarantee poverty reduction; while higher income is clearly associated with less poverty, economies can even reach upper-middle-income status but continue to struggle with a quite high incidence of extreme poverty. What does this tell us about the importance of the character of a nation's growth process and about its institutional structure?

7. What is the relationship between a Lorenz curve and a Gini coefficient? Give some examples of how Lorenz curves and Gini coefficients can be used as summary measures of equality and inequality in a nation's distribution of income.

8. "The major determinant of a country's income distribution is its distribution of productive and income-earning assets." Explain the meaning of this statement, giving examples of different kinds of productive and income-earning assets.

9. Are rapid economic growth (as measured by either GNI or per capita GNI) and a more equal distribution of personal income necessarily conflicting objectives? Summarize the arguments both for and against the presumed conflict of objectives, and state and explain your own view.

10. How might inequality lead to faster growth or development? How might it lead to slower growth or development?

11. Is progress being made in the fight against poverty? Why or why not?

12. What types of poverty policies have proved effective?

13. Economic growth is said to be a necessary but not sufficient condition to eradicate absolute poverty and reduce inequality. What is the reasoning behind this argument?

14. Outline the range of major policy options for a developing country to alter and modify its size distribution of national income. Which policies do you believe are absolutely essential? Explain your answer.

Appendix 5.1

Appropriate Technology and Employment Generation: The Price Incentive Model

Choice of Techniques: An Illustration

Neoclassical price incentive model A model whose main proposition is that if market prices are to influence economic activities in the right direction, they must be adjusted to remove factor price distortions by means of subsidies, taxes, or the like so that factor prices may reflect the true opportunity cost of the resources being used.

The basic proposition of the **neoclassical price incentive model** is quite simple and in the best tradition of the neoclassical theory of the firm. Following the principle of economy, producers (firms and farms) are assumed to face a given set of relative factor prices (e.g., of capital and labor) and to use the combination of capital and labor that minimizes the cost of producing a desired level of output. They are further assumed to be capable of producing that output with a variety of technological production processes, ranging from highly labor-intensive to highly capital-intensive methods. Thus, if the price of capital is very expensive relative to the price of labor, a relatively labor-intensive process will be chosen. Conversely, if labor is relatively expensive, our economizing firm or farm will use a more capital-intensive method of production—it will economize on the use of the expensive factor, which in this case is labor.

The conventional economics of technical choice is portrayed in Figure A5.1.1. Assume that the firm, farm, industry, or economy in question has only two techniques of production from which to choose: technique or process $0A$, which requires larger inputs of (homogeneous) capital relative to (homogeneous) labor, and technique or process $0B$, which is relatively labor-intensive. Points F and G

Figure A5.1.1   Choice of Techniques: The Price Incentive Model

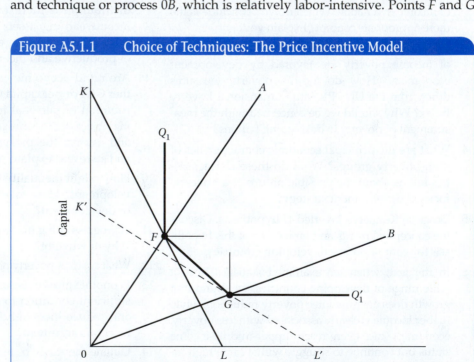

represent *unit* output levels for each process, and the line $Q_1 FGQ_1'$ connecting F and G is therefore a unit-output isoquant. (Note that in the traditional neoclassical model, an infinite number of such techniques or processes are assumed to exist so that the isoquant or equal-product line takes on its typical convex curvature.)

According to this theory, optimum (least-cost) capital-labor combinations (efficient or appropriate technologies) are determined by relative factor prices. Assume for the moment that market prices of capital and labor reflect their scarcity or shadow values and that the desired output level is Q_1 in Figure A5.1.1. If capital is cheap relative to labor (price line KL), production will occur at point F using capital-intensive process $0A$. Alternatively, if the market prices of labor and capital are such that labor is the relatively cheap (abundant) factor (line $K' L'$), optimal production will occur at point G, with the labor-intensive technique, $0B$, chosen. It follows that for any technique of production currently in use, a fall in the relative price of labor, all other things being equal, will lead to a substitution of labor for capital in an optimal production strategy. (Note that if capital-intensive process $0A$ "dominates" labor-intensive process $0B$—that is, if technology $0A$ requires less labor and less capital than $0B$ for all levels of output—then for any factor price ratio, the capital-intensive technique will be chosen.)

Factor Price Distortions and Appropriate Technology

Given that most developing countries are endowed with abundant supplies of labor but possess very little financial or physical capital, we would naturally expect production methods to be relatively labor-intensive. But in fact we often find production techniques in both agriculture and industry to be heavily mechanized and capital-intensive. Large tractors and combines dot the rural landscape of Asia, Africa, and Latin America, while people stand idly by. Gleaming new factories with the most modern and sophisticated automated machinery and equipment are a common feature of urban industries, while idle workers congregate outside the factory gates. Surely, this phenomenon could not be the result of a lesser degree of economic rationality on the part of farmers and manufacturers in developing countries.

The explanation, according to the price incentive school, is simple. Because of a variety of structural, institutional, and political factors, the actual market price of labor is higher and that of capital is lower than their respective true scarcity, or shadow, values dictate. In Figure A5.1.1, the shadow price ratio would be given by line $K' L'$, whereas the actual (distorted) market price ratio is shown by line KL. Market wage structures are relatively high because of trade union pressure, politically motivated minimum-wage laws, an increasing range of employee fringe benefits, and the high-wage policies of multinational corporations. In former colonial nations, high-wage structures are often relics of expatriate remuneration scales based on European levels of living and "hardship" premiums. By contrast, the price of (scarce) capital is kept artificially low by a combination of liberal capital depreciation allowances, low or even negative real interest rates, low or negative effective rates of protection on capital goods imports, tax rebates, and overvalued foreign-exchange rates (see Chapter 13).

The net result of these **factor price distortions** is the encouragement of inappropriate capital-intensive methods of production in both agriculture and

Factor price distortions
Situations in which factors of production are paid prices that do not reflect their true scarcity values (i.e., their competitive market prices) because of institutional arrangements that tamper with the free working of market forces of supply and demand.

manufacturing. Note that from the private-cost-minimizing viewpoint of individual firms and farms, the choice of a capital-intensive technique is correct. It is their rational response to the existing structure of price signals in the market for factors of production. However, from the viewpoint of society as a whole, the social cost of underutilized capital, and especially labor, can be very substantial. Government policies designed to "get the prices right"—that is, to remove factor price distortions—contribute not only to more employment but also to a better overall utilization of scarce capital resources through the adoption of more appropriate technologies of production.

The Possibilities of Labor-Capital Substitution

Elasticity of factor substitution A measure of the degree of substitutability between factors of production in any given production process when relative factor prices change.

The actual employment impact of removing factor price distortions will depend on the degree to which labor can be substituted for capital in the production processes of various developing-world industries. Economists refer to this as the **elasticity of factor substitution** and define it roughly as the ratio of the percentage change in the proportion of labor used relative to capital (labor-capital or L/K ratio) compared to a given percentage change in the price of capital relative to labor (P_K/P_L). Algebraically, the elasticity of substitution, η_{LK} can be defined as follows:

$$\eta_{LK} = \frac{d(L/K)(L/K)}{d(P_K/P_L)(P_K/P_L)} \qquad (A5.1.1)$$

For example, if the relative price of capital rises by 1% in the manufacturing sector and the labor-capital ratio rises as a result by, say, 1.5%, the elasticity of substitution in the manufacturing industry will be equal to 1.5. If P_K/P_L falls by, say, 10% while L/K falls by only 6%, the elasticity of substitution for that industry will be 0.6. Relatively high elasticities of substitution (ratios greater than about 0.7) are indicative that factor price adjustments can have a substantial impact on levels and combinations of factor utilization. In such cases, factor price modifications may be an important means of generating more employment opportunities.

In general, most empirical studies of the elasticity of substitution for manufacturing industries in less developed countries reveal coefficients in the range 0.5–1.0. These results indicate that a relative reduction in wages (either directly or by holding wages constant while letting the price of capital rise) of, say, 10% will lead to a 5% to 10% increase in employment.

Appendix 5.2

The Ahluwalia-Chenery Welfare Index

The necessity of reorienting development priorities away from an exclusive preoccupation with maximizing rates of GNI growth and toward broader social objectives such as the eradication of poverty and the reduction of excessive income disparities is now widely recognized throughout the developing world. Figures for GNI per capita give no indication of how national income is actually distributed and who is benefiting most from the growth of production. We have seen, for example, that a rising level of absolute and per capita GNI can camouflage the fact that the poor are no better off than before.

The calculation of the rate of GNI growth is largely a calculation of the rate of growth of the incomes of the upper 40% of the population, who receive a disproportionately large share of the national product. Therefore, the GNI growth rates can be a very misleading index of improved welfare. To give an extreme example, suppose that an economy consisted of only 10 people and that 9 of them had no income at all and the tenth received 100 units of income. The GNI for this economy would be 100 and per capita GNI would be 10. Now suppose that everyone's income increased by 20% so that GNI rose to 120 while per capita income grew to 12. For the 9 individuals with no income before and still no income now ($1.20 \times 0 = 0$), such a rise in per capita income would provide no cause for rejoicing. The one rich individual still would have all the income. And GNI, instead of being a welfare index of society as a whole, is merely measuring the welfare of a single individual!

The same line of reasoning applies to the more realistic situation where incomes are very unequally distributed, although not perfectly unequal as in our example. Taking the figures from Table 5.1, where we divided the population into quintiles that received 5%, 9%, 13%, 22%, and 51% income shares, respectively, we found that these income shares are a measure of the relative economic welfare of each income class and that the rate of income growth in each quintile is a measure of the economic welfare growth of that class. We can approximate the growth in the total welfare of society as the simple weighted sum of the growth of income in each class. This is in fact what the rate of GNI growth measures—the weights applied to each income class are their respective shares of national income. To be specific, in the case of a population divided into quintiles according to rising income levels, we have

$$G = w_1 g_1 + w_2 g_2 + w_3 g_3 + w_4 g_4 + w_5 g_5 \qquad (A5.2.1)$$

where G = a weighted index of growth of social welfare, g_i = the growth rate of income of the ith quintile (where the i quintiles are ordered 1, 2, 3, 4, and 5 in our example), and w_i = the "welfare weight" of the ith quintile (in our example, $w_1 = 0.05$, $w_2 = 0.09$, $w_3 = 0.13$, $w_4 = 0.22$, and $w_5 = 0.51$). As long as the weights add up to unity and are nonnegative, our overall measure of the growth of social welfare, G, must fall somewhere between the maximum and minimum income growth rates in the various quintiles. In the extreme case of all income accruing to one individual or one group of individuals in the highest quintile and where the welfare weights are the income shares (as they are with GNI growth calculations), Equation A5.2.1 would be written as

$$G = 0g_1 + 0g_2 + 0g_3 + 0g_4 + 1g_5 = 1g_5 \qquad \text{(A5.2.2)}$$

The growth of social welfare would therefore be associated exclusively with the growth of incomes of the top quintile of the population!

In the example derived from Table 5.1, the GNI-share-weighted index of social welfare would be written as

$$G = 0.05g_1 + 0.09g_2 + 0.13g_3 + 0.22g_4 + 0.51g_5 = 1g_5 \qquad \text{(A5.2.3)}$$

Now suppose that the income growth rate of the bottom 60% of the population was zero ($g_1 = g_2 = g_3 = 0$) while that of the top 40% was 10% ($g_4 = g_5 = 0.10$). Equation A5.2.3 could then be written as

$$G = 0.05(0) + 0.09(0) + 0.13(0.10) + 0.22(0.10) + 0.51(0.10) = 0.073 \qquad \text{(A5.2.4)}$$

and the social welfare index would rise by more than 7%, which is the rate of growth of GNI (i.e., GNI would rise from 100 in Table 5.1 to 107.3 if the incomes of the 4th and 5th quintiles grew by 10%). Thus, we have an illustration of a case where GNI rises by 7.3%, implying that social well-being has increased by this same proportionate amount even though 60% of the population is no better off than before. This bottom 60% still has only 5, 13, and 22 units of income, respectively. Clearly, the distribution of income would be worsened (the relative shares of the bottom 60% would fall) by such a respectable growth rate of GNI.

The numerical example given by Equation A5.2.4 illustrates our basic point. The use of the growth rate of GNI as an index of social welfare and as a method of comparing the development performance of different countries can be misleading, especially where countries have markedly different distributions of income. The welfare weights attached to the growth rates of different income groups are unequal, with a heavy social premium being placed on the income growth of the highest-quintile groups. In the example of Equation A5.2.3, a 1% growth in the income of the top quintile carries more than 10 times the weight of a 1% growth in the lowest quintile (0.51 compared with 0.05) because it implies an absolute increment that is 10 times larger. In other words, using the measure of GNI growth as an index of improvements in social welfare and development accords to each income group a welfare valuation that corresponds to its respective income share (i.e., a 1% increase in the income of the richest 20% of the population is implicitly assumed to be more than 10 times as important to society as a 1% increase in the income of the bottom 20%). It follows that the best way to maximize social welfare growth is to maximize the rate of growth of the incomes of the rich while neglecting the poor! If ever there was a case for *not* equating GNI growth with development, this example should provide a persuasive illustration.

Constructing a Poverty-Weighted Index of Social Welfare

An alternative to using a simple GNI growth rate or distributive share index of social welfare would be to construct an equal-weights or even a poverty-weighted index. Such indexes might be especially relevant for countries concerned with the elimination of poverty as a major development objective. As the name indicates, an equal-weights index weights the growth of income in each income class not by the proportion of total income in that class but rather by the proportion of the total population—that is, all people are treated (weighted) equally. In an economy divided into quintiles, such an index would give a weight of 0.2 to the growth of income in each quintile. So a 10% increase in the income of the lowest 20% of the population would have the same bearing on the overall measure of social welfare improvements as a 10% increase in the top 20% group or in any other quintile group, even though the absolute increase in income for the bottom group would be much smaller than for the upper groups.

Using an equal-weights index in our example of a 10% income growth of the top two quintiles with the bottom three remaining static, we would have

$$G = 0.20g_1 + 0.20g_2 + 0.20g_3 + 0.20g_4 + 0.20g_5 \qquad \text{(A5.2.5)}$$

or, inserting growth rates for g_1, through g_5,

$$G = 0.20(0) + 0.20(0) + 0.20(0) + 0.20(10) + 0.20(0.10) = 0.04 \quad \text{(A5.2.6)}$$

Social welfare would increase by only 4%, compared to the 7.3% increase recorded by using the distributive shares or GNI growth rate index. Even though recorded GNI still grew by 7.3%, this alternative welfare index of development would show only a 4% rise.

Finally, consider a developing country that is genuinely and solely concerned with improving the material well-being of, say, the poorest 40% of its population. Such a country might wish to construct a poverty-weighted index of development, which places "subjective" social values on the income growth rates of only the bottom 40%. In other words, it might arbitrarily place a welfare weight on w_1 of 0.60 and on w_2 of 0.40 while giving w_3, w_4, and w_5 zero weights. Using our same numerical example, the social welfare growth index for this country would be given by the expression

$$G = 0.60g_1 + 0.40g_2 + 0g_3 + 0g_4 + 0g_5 \qquad \text{(A5.2.7)}$$

which, when substituting $g_1 = g_2 = g_3 = 0$ and $g_4 = g_5 = 0.10$, becomes

$$G = 0.60(0) + 0.40(0) + 0(0) + 0(0.10) + 0(0.10) = 0 \qquad \text{(A5.2.8)}$$

The poverty-weighted index therefore records *no* improvement in social welfare (no development), even though recorded GNI has grown by 7.3%!

Although the choice of welfare weights in any index of development is purely arbitrary, it does represent and reflect important social value judgments about goals and objectives for a given society. It would certainly be interesting to know, if this were possible, the real implicit welfare weights of the various development strategies of different developing countries. Our main point, however, is that as long as the growth rate of GNI is explicitly or implicitly used to compare development performances, we know that a "wealthy weights" index is actually being employed.

To put some real-world flavor into the discussion of alternative indexes of improvements in economic welfare and to illustrate the usefulness of different weighted growth indexes in evaluating the economic performance of various countries, consider the data in Table A5.2.1 compiled by Montek Ahluwalia and Hollis Chenery. The table shows the growth of income in 12 countries as measured first by the rate of growth of GNI (GNI weights), second by an equal-weights index, and third by a poverty-weighted index where the actual weights assigned to income growth rates of the lowest 40%, the middle 40%, and the top 20% of the population are 0.6, 0.4, and 0.0, respectively. Some interesting conclusions emerge from a review of the last three columns of Table A5.2.1:

1. Economic performance as measured by equal-weights and poverty-weighted indexes was notably worse in some otherwise high-GNI-growth countries like Brazil, Mexico, and Panama. Because these countries all experienced a deterioration in income distribution and a growing concentration of income growth in the upper groups over this period, the equal-weights and poverty-weighted indexes naturally show a less impressive development performance than the simple GNI measure.

2. In five countries (Colombia, Costa Rica, El Salvador, Sri Lanka, and Taiwan), the weighted indexes show a better performance than GNI growth, because the relative income growth of lower-income groups proceeded more rapidly over the period in question in those five countries than that of the higher-income groups.

TABLE A5.2.1   Income Distribution and Growth in 12 Selected Countries

Country	Income Growth			Annual Increase in Welfare		
	Upper 20%	Middle 40%	Lowest 40%	GNI Weights	Equal Weights	Poverty Weights
Brazil	6.7	3.1	3.7	5.2	4.1	3.5
Colombia	5.2	7.9	7.8	6.2	7.3	7.8
Costa Rica	4.5	9.3	7.0	6.3	7.4	7.8
El Salvador	3.5	9.5	6.4	5.7	7.1	7.4
India	5.3	3.5	2.0	4.2	3.3	2.5
Mexico	8.8	5.8	6.0	7.8	6.5	5.9
Panama	8.8	9.2	3.2	8.2	6.7	5.2
Peru	3.9	6.7	2.4	4.6	4.4	3.8
Philippines	5.0	6.7	4.4	5.5	5.4	5.2
South Korea	12.4	9.5	11.0	11.0	10.7	10.5
Sri Lanka	3.1	6.3	8.3	5.0	6.5	7.6
Taiwan	4.5	9.1	12.1	6.8	9.4	11.1

3. In three countries (Peru, the Philippines, and South Korea), little change in income distribution during the period in question resulted in little variation between the GNI measure and the two alternative weighted indexes of social welfare.

We may conclude, therefore, that a useful summary measure of the degree to which economic growth is biased toward the relative improvement of high-income or low-income groups is the positive or negative divergence between a weighted social welfare index and the actual growth rate of GNI.

Notes

1. The Lorenz curve is named for Max Otto Lorenz, an American economist who in 1905 devised this convenient and widely used diagram to show the relationship between population groups and their respective income shares.

2. A more precise definition of perfect equality would take into account the age structure of a population and expected income variations over the life cycle of all households within that population. See Morton Paglin, "The measurement and trend of inequality: A basic revision," *American Economic Review* 65 (1975): 598–609.

3. For the details, see Gary S. Fields, *Distribution and Development: A New Look at the Developing World* (Cambridge, Mass.: MIT Press, 2001), ch. 2.

4. For more details on this and an alternative exposition of inequality properties, see Amartya Sen and James E. Foster, *On Economic Inequality,* expanded ed. (Oxford: Clarendon Press, 1997).

5. The sum of all workers' marginal product must equal total gross national income (GNI). Mathematically, GNI is simply the integral of the marginal product curve between 0 and L_E. This is because the marginal product function is the derivative of the GNI curve: $GNI = f(L, \overline{K}); MP_L = f'(L)$.

6. If measured poverty is always *strictly lower* after such transfers, this property is called *strong* monotonicity. The headcount ratio satisfies monotonicity but not strong monotonicity.

7. For technical details, see James Foster, Joel Greer, and Erik Thorbecke, "A class of decomposable poverty measures," *Econometrica* 52 (1984): 761–766.

8. For proof that Equation 5.4 follows from Equation 5.3, see Foster, Greer, and Thorbecke, "A class of decomposable poverty measures," Cornell University Discussion Paper No. 242, 1981.

9. It is similar in spirit to the Sen index, $S = (H/N)$ [NIS + (1 − NIS)G_p], where G_p stands for the Gini coefficient among the poor. For the technical details and derivations of the P_2 and S poverty measures, see Sen and Foster, *On Economic Inequality,* pp. 165–194, and ibid.

10. For the same reason, the P_2 measure has now become part of the Mexican constitution (chap. 5, art. 34). Interview with Erik Thorbecke, *Cornell Chronicle,* May 11, 2000.

11. For example, Uganda saw impressive reductions in poverty between 1999 and 2009, but the headcount decreased by only 1.9 million people. By the person-equivalent measure, poverty fell by 4.4 million poor person-equivalents. This measure adjusts for poverty depth, but still does not reflect poverty severity. For more details on the measure, along with applications to data from a number of developing countries, see Tony Castleman, James E. Foster, and Stephen C. Smith, "Person-Equivalent Poverty Measures," paper presented at the Brookings Institution, February 12, 2013.

12. The Alkire-Foster method, as it has become known, reduces to the FGT index when poverty is measured with just one dimension. See Sabina Alkire and James Foster, "Counting and multidimensional poverty measurement," *Journal of Public Economics* 95, No. 7 (2011): 476–487. For further intuition, see also Alkire and Foster "Understandings and misunderstanding of multidimensional poverty," *Journal of Economic Inequality* 9(2), pp. 289–314.

13. Various UN studies on sources of savings in developing nations show that small farmers and individuals seem to be among the highest savers. See Andrew Mason, "Savings, economic growth and demographic change," *Population and Development Review* 14 (1988): 113–144.

14. Two technical articles that address the mechanisms by which higher inequality may lead to lower growth or incomes are Abhijit V. Banerjee and Andrew F. Newman, "Occupational choice and the process of development," *Journal of Political Economy* 101 (1993): 274–298, and Oded Galor and Joseph Zeira, "Income distribution and macroeconomics," *Review of Economic Studies* 60 (1993): 35–52. See also Fields, *Distribution and Development*, ch. 10. The empirical literature remains mixed, however.

15. See, for example, Torsten Persson and Guido Tabellini, "Is inequality harmful for growth?" *American Economic Review* 84 (1994): 600–621, and Alberto Alesina and Dani Rodrik, "Distributive politics and economic growth," *Quarterly Journal of Economics* 109 (1994): 465–490. On the connection to violent crime, see Morgan Kelly, "Inequality and crime," *The Review of Economics and Statistics* 82, No. 4 (2000), pp. 530–539.

16. John Rawls, *A Theory of Justice* (Cambridge, Mass.: Belknap Press, 1971).

17. This approach was developed by Gary S. Fields, *Poverty, Inequality and Development* (Cambridge: Cambridge University Press, 1980), pp. 46–56.

18. Ibid., p. 52.

19. This can perhaps be visualized most easily by considering a traditional economy in which everyone is "equally poor," each claiming their share of, say, 50 cents per day. If the absolute poverty line is $1.25 per day, all are in absolute poverty. Then modernization begins, and the modern sector absorbs workers one by one, where the wage is, say, $2 per day. Starting from the line of perfect equality, the Lorenz curve bows out more and more until nearly half the people are in the modern sector. At that point, as more go to the modern sector, the Lorenz curve is less bowed in until finally everyone has been absorbed into the modern sector and all once again have equal incomes but now at a higher level of $2 per day. In the process, all of the people have been pulled out of poverty. (Try this as an exercise, plotting the Lorenz curves as this process takes place for an eight-person economy.) This exercise is adapted from Fields, ibid.

20. In fact, some would go further and say that an increase in relative inequality is not objectionable as long as everyone has a higher income, even though the rich get a larger share of the gains, even in proportion to their larger starting income. This situation is called "first-order stochastic dominance" in the literature. However, even in this case, incomes might be increased even more with less inequality.

21. Of course, in real economies, all three of these growth typologies may take place at the same time, and the net result may be little or no change in inequality. Or in more unfortunate cases, with economies with negative growth, like many of those in sub-Saharan Africa in the 1980s and 1990s, there may be modern- and traditional-sector impoverishment, accompanied by a shrinking modern sector.

22. Simon Kuznets, "Economic growth and income inequality," *American Economic Review* 45 (1955): 1–28, and "Quantitative aspects of the economic growth of nations," *Economic Development and Cultural Change* 11 (1963): 1–80. One of the cross-sectional studies supporting the Kuznets hypothesis is Montek S. Ahluwalia, Nicholas G. Carter, and Hollis B. Chenery, "Growth and poverty in developing countries," *Journal of Development Economics* 16 (1979): 298–323. Studies arguing against the hypothesis include Ashwani Saith, "Development and distribution: A critique of the cross-country U-hypothesis," *Journal of Development Economics* 13 (1983): 367–382, and Sudhir Anand and S. M. R. Kanbur, "The Kuznets process and the inequality-development relationship," *Journal of Development Economics* 40 (1993): 25–42.

23. The parabola plotted results from an ordinary least-squares regression. Fields reports results showing that in using a country fixed-effect specification, the estimated inverted U flips to an estimated U-pattern. For details, see Fields, *Distribution and Development*, ch. 3 (pp. 42–43).

24. Ibid., p. 35.

25. The 2008 and 2010 estimates are reported in the 2013 *World Development Indicators*. For an overview on the $1.25 a day estimation, see Martin

Ravallion, Shaohua Chen, and Prem Sangraula, *New Evidence on the Urbanization of Global Poverty* (Washington, D.C.: World Bank, 2007), and Martin Ravallion, Shaohua Chen, and Prem Sangraula, "Dollar a Day Revisited," World Bank, Policy Research Working Paper No. 4620, May 2008.

26. The HPI measured three deprivations—of life (as the percentage of people unlikely to live beyond 40 years of age), of basic education (as the percentage of adults who are illiterate), and of overall economic provisioning (as the percentage of people without access to safe water plus the percentage of children underweight for their age), giving them equal weight in a manner analogous to the original HDI. The 2009 HDR report ranked 135 countries from lowest to highest HPI and found this could differ substantially from income poverty rankings and the old HDI ranking. Since the HPI value indicates the proportion of the population adversely affected by the three deprivations, a higher HPI reflects greater deprivation. In the report, Côte d'Ivoire ranked 29 places higher (worse) in the country rankings based on income poverty than on human poverty; Morocco ranked 50 places higher; Iran, 44 higher; Algeria, 19 higher; Ethiopia, 30 higher. The implication is that human poverty is worse in these countries than headcount ratio income poverty measures indicate. In contrast, some of the countries that perform better on the human poverty ranking include Nigeria, 11 places lower; Ghana, 18 lower; Madagascar, 14 lower; Bolivia, 21 lower; and Tanzania, 37 lower. The MPI is strongly preferred because it aggregates up from the household level and allows for interactions of poverty dimensions; an index like the HPI may be used because it is familiar, can be applied to a larger number of countries, and can be extrapolated further back in time and at more frequent intervals.

27. The MPI was introduced in the 2010 *Human Development Report* (New York: United Nations Development Programme, 2010); for details, see Sabina Alkire and Maria Emma Santos, *Acute Multidimensional Poverty: A New Index for Developing Countries*, Human Development Research Paper No. 2010/11 (New York: United Nations Development Programme, 2010). The MPI is based on the increasingly used Alkire-Foster Method (AFM); for an introduction, see Sabina Alkire and

James Foster, "Counting and multidimensional poverty measurement," in *Oxford Poverty and Human Development Initiative*, Working Paper 07, 2008. Forthcoming *Journal of Public Economics*.

28. UNDP *Human Development Report, 2010*.

29. See Chronic Poverty Research Centre, *Chronic Poverty Report, 2004–05*, http://www.chronicpoverty.org/resources/cprc_report_2004-2005_contents.html, and Andrew McKay and Bob Baulch, "How many chronically poor people are there in the world? Some preliminary estimates," CPRC Working Paper No. 45, Chronic Poverty Research Centre, 2003.

30. We may also note that greater spatial concentration of poverty—a higher percentage of people in a given region who are poor—is an additional consideration for how ultrapoverty differs.

31. See International Food Policy Research Institute, *The World's Most Deprived* (Washington: D.C.: IFPRI, 2007).

32. Partha Dasgupta and Debraj Ray, "Inequality as a determinant of malnutrition and unemployment policy," *Economic Journal* 97 (1987): 177–188.

33. An empirical study of variables explaining growth in developing countries during the 1960–1973 period provide support for the argument that policies designed to promote better distribution and reduce poverty are, on balance, growth-stimulating rather than growth-retarding. See Norman L. Hicks, "Growth vs. basic needs: Is there a trade-off?" *World Development* 7 (1979): 985–994.

34. For empirical evidence on how improved distribution can increase domestic demand, promote political stability, and generate higher growth rates, see Alberto Alesina and Roberto Perotti, "The political economy of growth: A critical survey of the recent literature," *World Bank Economic Review* 8 (1994): 351–371, and Alberto Alesina and Dani Rodrik, "Distributive policies and economic growth," *Quarterly Journal of Economics* 109 (1994): 465–490.

35. See World Bank, *World Development Report, 2000/2001* (New York: Oxford University Press, 2000). See also World Bank, *World Development Report, 1990* (New York: Oxford University Press, 1990); Albert Fishlow, "Inequality, poverty, and growth: Where do we stand?" in *Proceedings of*

the World Bank Annual Conference on Development Economics, 1995, eds. Michael Bruno and Boris Pleskovic (Washington, D.C.: World Bank, 1996); Nancy Birdsall, David Ross, and Richard Sabot, "Inequality and growth reconsidered: Lessons from East Asia," *World Bank Economic Review* 9 (1995): 477–508; and George R. G. Clarke, "More evidence on income distribution and growth," *Journal of Development Economics* 47 (1995): 403–427.

36. A well-known study is David Dollar and Aart Kraay, "Growth is good for the poor," *Journal of Economic Growth* 7 (2002): 195–225. They find that on average, incomes of the bottom 20% grow about as fast as the overall average. However, critiques of the generality of this claim of rough proportionality have been summarized by the University of Manchester Chronic Poverty Research Center in its *Chronic Poverty Report 2004/05:* "It does not allow for variation around the average (which is known to be significant), it uses a relative concept of poverty, the data set used has been criticized, it does not consider poverty depth, and researchers using different econometric methods with the same data have produced contradictory findings." Clearly it is possible and sometimes does occur that inequality can increase with growth enough to offset any gains for the poor, including some cases in which rapid growth increases the incentive and opportunity of theft of natural resources from poor communities. The essential point is that growth is not guaranteed to automatically end absolute poverty or do so in an acceptable time frame, so targeted policies are generally also needed.

37. For a classic overview of the nature, magnitude, and incidence of poverty in the developing world, see World Bank, *World Development Report, 2000/2001.*

38. For a comprehensive analysis of how poverty directly affects women's lives in developing countries, see Irene Tinker, *Persistent Inequalities: Women and World Development* (New York: Oxford University Press, 1990); Judith Bruce and Daisy Dwyer, eds., *A Home Divided: Women and Income in the Third World* (Stanford, Calif.: Stanford University Press, 1988); Janet Momsen, *Women and*

Development in the Third World (New York: Routledge, 1991); and Diane Elson, "Gender-aware analysis and development economics," *Journal of International Development* 5 (1993): 237–247.

39. Amartya Sen, "Missing women," *British Medical Journal* 304 (1992): 587–588. A well-regarded 2003 analysis conclude that about 100 million or more women are "missing" in Asia alone. Stephan Klasen and Claudia Wink, "Missing Women: Revisiting the Debate," *Feminist Economics*, 9 (2–3), 2003, 263–299.

40. The International Fund for Agricultural Development provides basic statistics and links to key resources on indigenous peoples and development at http://www.iFad.org/pub/factsheet/ip/e.pdf.

41. See, for example, Haeduck Lee, *The Ethnic Dimension of Poverty and Income Distribution in Latin America* (Washington, D.C.: World Bank, 1993); George Psacharopoulos and Harry A. Patrinos, "Indigenous people and poverty in Latin America," *Finance and Development* 31 (1994): 41–43; and Gillette Hall and Harry Anthony Patrinos, eds., *Indigenous Peoples, Poverty and Human Development in Latin America; 1994–2004* (New York: Palgrave Macmillan, 2006).

42. Darryl McLeod and Nora Lustig, "Minimum wages and poverty in developing countries: Some empirical evidence," in *Labor Markets in Latin America: Combining Social Protection with Market Flexibility* (Washington, D.C.: Brookings Institution, 1997). An interesting theoretical contribution is found in Gary S. Fields and Ravi Kanbur, "Minimum wages and poverty with income-sharing," *Journal of Economic Inequality* 5 (2007): 135–147. Details of SEWA's in-house studies on minimum wages for poor informal workers are found at http://www.sewaresearch.org.

43. For the classic analytical treatment of the workfare-versus-welfare problem, see Timothy J. Besley and Stephen Coate, "Workfare versus welfare: Incentive arguments for work requirements in poverty alleviation programs," *American Economic Review* 82 (1992): 249–261.

44. For other discussions of poverty policies, see Arne Bigsten, "Poverty, inequality and development,"

in *Surveys in Development Economics,* ed. Norman Gemmell (Oxford: Blackwell, 1987), pp. 157–163; Jagdish N. Bhagwati, "Poverty and public policy," *World Development* 16 (1988): 539–555; World Bank, *World Development Report, 2000/2001*; Irma Adelman and Sherman Robinson, "Income distribution and development," in *Handbook of Development Economics,* vol. 2, eds. Hollis B. Chenery and

T. N. Srinivasan (Amsterdam: Elsevier, 1989), pp. 982–996; and Paul P. Streeten, *Strategies for Human Development: Global Poverty and Unemployment* (Copenhagen: Handelshojskølens Forlag, 1994).

45. James Speth, "Foreword," in United Nations Development Programme, *Human Development Report, 1997,* p. iii.

Population Growth and Economic Development: Causes, Consequences, and Controversies

6

Economic development may be far from "the best contraceptive" [that it is sometimes described as].... On the other hand, social development—especially women's education and employment—can be very effective indeed.

—*Amartya Sen, Nobel laureate in economics*

6.1 The Basic Issue: Population Growth and the Quality of Life

In 2013, the world's population reached about 7.2 billion people. In that year, the United Nations Population Division projected that population would rise to about 8.1 billion in 2025 and reach about 9.6 billion by the year 2050. The overwhelming majority of that population will inhabit the developing world. What will be the economic and social implications for development if such projections are realized? Is this scenario inevitable, or will it depend on the success or failure of development efforts? Finally, even more significant, is rapid population growth per se as serious a problem as many people believe, or is it a manifestation of more fundamental problems of underdevelopment and the unequal utilization of global resources between rich and poor nations, as others argue?

In this chapter, we examine many of the issues relating population growth to economic development. We begin, however, by looking at historical and recent population trends and the changing geographic distribution of the world's people. After explaining basic demographic concepts, we present some well-known economic models and hypotheses regarding the causes and consequences of rapid population growth in contemporary developing countries. Controversies surrounding the significance of the population factor in general and these models and hypotheses in particular are then explored.

Finally, we evaluate a range of alternative policy options that developing countries may wish to adopt to influence the size and growth of their populations, as well as ways in which industrialized countries can contribute to a more manageable global population and resource environment. Population policies in China and India, the nations with the largest populations in the world, are the focus of this chapter's case study.

Every year, more than 75 million people are being added to the world's population. Almost all of this net population increase—97%—is in developing countries. Increases of such magnitude are unprecedented. But the problem of population growth is not simply a problem of numbers. It is a problem of human welfare and of development, as defined in Chapter 1. Rapid population growth can have serious consequences for the well-being of all humanity. If development entails the improvement in people's levels of living—their incomes, health, education, and general well-being—and if it also encompasses their capabilities, self-esteem, respect, dignity, and freedom to choose, then the really important question about population growth is this: How does the contemporary population situation in many developing countries contribute to or detract from their chances of realizing the goals of development, not only for the current generation but also for future generations? In addressing this central issue, we examine the reasons and consequences for the positive relationship between poverty and family size. More broadly, we examine what drives high population growth in developing (particularly low-income) countries, why population growth in general subsequently falls as countries grow and develop, and the causes and implications of these patterns.

6.2 Population Growth: Past, Present, and Future

World Population Growth throughout History

For most of human existence on earth, humanity's numbers have been few. When people first started to cultivate food through agriculture some 12,000 years ago, the estimated world population was no more than 5 million (see Table 6.1). Two thousand years ago, world population had grown to nearly 250 million, less than a fifth of the population of China today. From year 1 on our calendar to the beginning of the Industrial Revolution around 1750, it tripled to 728 million people, less than three-quarters of the total number living in India today. During the next 200 years (1750–1950), an additional 1.7 billion people were added to the planet's numbers. But in just four decades thereafter (1950–1990), the earth's human population more than doubled again, bringing the total figure to around 5.3 billion. The world entered the twenty-first century with over 6 billion people.

As seen in Figure 6.1, in 1950 about 1.7 billion people lived in developing countries, representing about two-thirds of the world total; by 2050, the population of less developed countries will reach over 8 billion, nearly seven-eighths of the world's population. In the corresponding period,

	TABLE 6.1 Estimated World Population Growth		
Year	**Estimated Population (millions)**	**Estimated Annual Increase in the Intervening Period (%)**	**Doubling Time (years)**
10,000 B.C.E.	5		
1 C.E.	250	0.04	1,733
1650	545	0.04	1,733
1750	728	0.29	239
1800	906	0.45	154
1850	1,171	0.53	130
1900	1,608	0.65	106
1950	2,576	0.91	76
1970	3,698	2.09	33
1980	4,448	1.76	39
1990	5,292	1.73	40
2000	6,090	1.48	47
2010	6,892	1.22	57
2050 (projected)	9,600	0.98	71

Sources: Population Reference Bureau, *World Population Data Sheet* (Washington, D.C.: Population Reference Bureau, 2010 and previous annuals); Warren S. Thompson and David T. Lewis, *Population Problems*, 5th ed. (New York: McGraw-Hill, 1965), p. 384; United Nations, *Demographic Yearbook for 1971* (New York: United Nations, 1971); United Nations, *Report on the World Social Situation, 1997* (New York: United Nations, 1997), p. 14; and United Nations Population Division, *World Population Prospects: The 2012 Revision.* New York: United Nations (2013). An alternate system of broadly comparable and earlier estimates is found in Michael Kremer, "Population growth and technological change: One million B.C. to 1990," *Quarterly Journal of Economics* 108 (1993): 681–716.

the population of the least developed countries will increase by tenfold, from about 200 million to 2 billion people. In contrast, the population of the developed countries will grow very little between now and 2050, even accounting for immigration from developing countries.

Turning from absolute numbers to percentage growth rates, for almost the whole of human existence on earth until approximately 300 years ago, population grew at an annual rate not much greater than zero (0.002%, or 20 per million). Naturally, this overall rate was not steady; there were many ups and downs as a result of natural catastrophes and variations in growth rates among regions. By 1750, the population growth rate had accelerated to 0.3% per year. By the 1950s, the rate had again accelerated, tripling to about 1.0% per year. It continued to accelerate until around 1970, when it peaked at 2.35%.[1] Today the world's population growth rate remains at a historically high rate of nearly 1.2% per year, but the rate of increase is slowing. However, the population growth rate in Africa is still an extremely high 2.3% per year. (Note that estimates of population numbers and growth rates differ according to research methods, but the broad trends are similar across major studies.)

The relationship between annual percentage increases and the time it takes for a population to double in size, or **doubling time**,[2] is shown in the rightmost column of Table 6.1 (calculation of doubling time is explained in endnote 2). We see that before 1650, it took nearly 36,000 years, or about

Doubling time   Period that a given population or other quantity takes to increase by its present size.

FIGURE 6.1 World Population Growth, 1950–2050

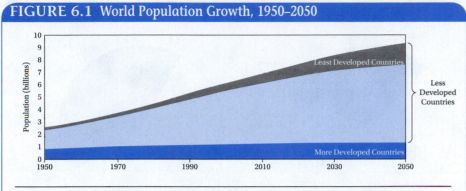

Source: Population Reference Bureau World Population Data Sheet 2012, page 4; data are drawn from United Nations Population Division, World Population Prospects: The 2010 Revision (2011), medium-variant estimates.

1,400 generations, for the world population to double. Today it would take about 58 years, or two generations, for world population to double at current growth rates. Moreover, whereas it took 1,750 years to add 480 million people to the world's population between year 1 and the onset of the Industrial Revolution, this same number of people is today being added in less than 7 years.

The reason for the sudden change in overall population trends is that for almost all of recorded history, the rate of population change, whether up or down, had been strongly influenced by the combined effects of famine, disease, malnutrition, plague, and war—conditions that resulted in high and fluctuating death rates. In the twentieth century, such conditions came increasingly under technological and economic control. As a result, human mortality (the death rate) is now lower than at any other point in human existence. It is this decline in mortality resulting from rapid technological advances in modern medicine, improved nutrition, and the spread of modern sanitation measures throughout the world, particularly within the past half-century, that has resulted in the unprecedented increases in world population growth, especially in developing countries. In short, population growth today is primarily the result of a rapid transition from a long historical era characterized by high birth and death rates to one in which death rates have fallen sharply but birth rates, especially in the least developed countries, have fallen more slowly from their historically high levels.

Structure of the World's Population

The world's population is very unevenly distributed by geographic region, by fertility and mortality levels, and by age structures.

Geographic Region   More than three-quarters of the world's people live in developing countries; fewer than one person in four lives in an economically developed nation. Figure 6.2 shows the regional distribution of the world's population as it existed in 2010 and as it is projected for 2050.

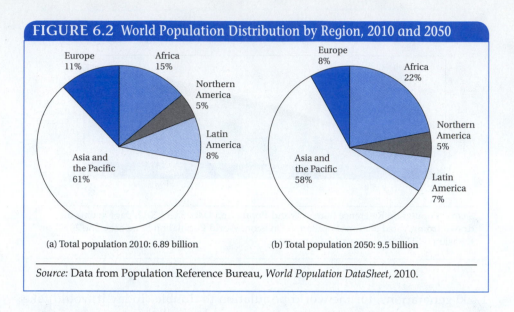

FIGURE 6.2 World Population Distribution by Region, 2010 and 2050

(a) Total population 2010: 6.89 billion

(b) Total population 2050: 9.5 billion

Source: Data from Population Reference Bureau, *World Population DataSheet*, 2010.

World population distribution is put into dramatic perspective by the map in Figure 6.3. Attention is drawn to the large size of India in comparison with Europe. China is bordered on the north and west by a thin strip of land that represents Russia. Mexico looms very large in comparison with Canada—a dramatic reversal of conventional maps; taken together, even the Caribbean islands are larger than Canada. Bangladesh, smaller in size than the state of Wisconsin, is larger than Germany and France combined. In Africa, the prominence of Nigeria stands out. Indonesia, which gets comparatively little

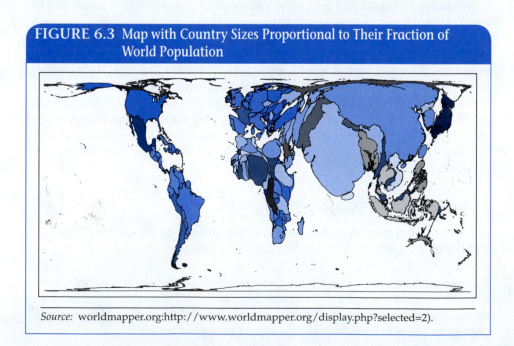

FIGURE 6.3 Map with Country Sizes Proportional to Their Fraction of World Population

Source: worldmapper.org:http://www.worldmapper.org/display.php?selected=2).

international attention, dwarfs its neighbor Australia while appearing nearly as large as the United States.

Fertility and Mortality Trends   The **rate of population increase** is quantitatively measured as the percentage yearly net relative increase (or decrease, in which case it is negative) in population size due to **natural increase** and **net international migration**. Natural increase simply measures the excess of births over deaths or, in more technical terms, the difference between fertility and mortality. Net international migration is of very limited, though growing, importance today (although in the nineteenth and early twentieth centuries it was an extremely important source of population increase in North America, Australia, and New Zealand and corresponding relative decrease in western Europe). Population increases in developing countries therefore depend almost entirely on the difference between their **crude birth rates** (or simply **birth rates**) and **death rates**.

Recall from Chapter 2 that most developing nations have birth rates ranging from 15 to 45 per 1,000. By contrast, in almost all developed countries, the rate is less than 15 per 1,000. Moreover, developing country birth rates today are still often higher than they were in preindustrial western Europe. But there has been a substantial decline in fertility over the past three decades, not only in countries like Taiwan, South Korea, and China, where rapid economic and social development have taken place, but also in nations where economic growth has been less rapid, including Mexico and Bangladesh, and in some where growth has stagnated, such as Zimbabwe. The **total fertility rate (TFR)**—the average number of children a woman would have, assuming that current age-specific birth rates remain constant throughout her childbearing years—has fallen dramatically in many countries since 1970, as the examples in Table 6.2 demonstrate, but remains high in sub-Saharan Africa (5.1 in 2012) and western Asia (2.9). Niger with 7.1 and Afghanistan with 6.2 were among the highest in the world.[3]

Modern vaccination campaigns against malaria, smallpox, yellow fever, and cholera as well as the proliferation of public health facilities, clean water supplies, improved nutrition, and public education have all worked together over the past three decades to lower death rates by as much as 50% in parts of Asia and Latin America and by over 30% in much of Africa and the Middle East. Death rates have fallen for all age groups. Nevertheless, the average life span remains about 12 years greater in the developed countries. This gap has been sharply reduced in recent decades. For example, in 1950, **life expectancy at birth** for people in developing countries averaged 35 to 40 years, compared with 62 to 65 years in the developed world. Considerable progress has been made on reducing the **under-5 mortality rate**. For example, according to UN compilations between 1990 and 2008, it fell from 121 per 1,000 to 74 per 1,000 in South Asia, from 73 to 38 per 1,000 in Southeast Asia and from 52 to 23 per 1,000 in Latin America and the Caribbean. Although the under-5 mortality rate declined from 184 to 144 per 1,000 in sub-Saharan Africa in this period, progress in the region continued to lag. In 2009, because of still relatively high under-5 mortality rates and the AIDS epidemic, sub-Saharan Africa had the lowest life expectancy, 51 years, while in the high-income countries, life expectancy at birth averaged nearly 78 years. In East Asia and Latin America, life

---

Rate of population increase   The growth rate of a population, calculated as the natural increase after adjusting for immigration and emigration.

Natural increase   The difference between the birth rate and the death rate of a given population.

Net international migration   The excess of persons migrating into a country over those who emigrate from that country.

Crude birth rate   The number of children born alive each year per 1,000 population (often shortened to *birth rate*).

Death rate   The number of deaths each year per 1,000 population.

Total fertility rate (TFR)   The number of children that would be born to a woman if she were to live to the end of her childbearing years and bear children in accordance with the prevailing age-specific fertility rates.

Life expectancy at birth   The number of years a newborn child would live if subjected to the mortality risks prevailing for the population at the time of the child's birth.

Under-5 mortality rate   Deaths among children between birth and 5 years of age per 1,000 live births.

TABLE 6.2   Fertility Rate for Selected Countries, 1970 and 2009

Country	Total Fertility Rate	
	1970	2012
Bangladesh	7.0	2.3
Colombia	5.3	2.1
Indonesia	5.5	2.3
Jamaica	5.3	2.1
Mexico	4.9	2.3
Thailand	5.5	1.6
Zimbabwe	7.7	4.1

Sources: World Bank, *World Development Report, 1994* (New York: Oxford University Press, 1994), tab. 26; Population Reference Bureau, *World Population Data Sheet* (Washington, D.C.: Population Reference Bureau, 2012).

expectancies have now reached an impressive 74 and 73 years, respectively. Finally, note that there remains a biological susceptibility for old people to die at higher rates than young people due to aging. Although death rates of children and younger people are higher on average in a developing country with rapid population growth, the fact that their populations are so youthful on average explains why they may have an overall population-average death rate that is lower than that of a developed country with a much older average population. You may notice this possibly unexpected relationship when you look at demographic statistics.

Some of the striking population projections issued by the United Nations in 2013 are reported in Box 6.1.

Age Structure and Dependency Burdens   Population is relatively youthful in the developing world. As of 2011, children under the age of 15 constitute more than 40% of the total population of the low-income countries, 32% of the lower-middle income countries, but just 17% of high-income countries.[4] In countries with such an age structure, the **youth dependency ratio**—the proportion of youths (under age 15) to economically active adults (ages 15 to 64)—is very high. Thus, the workforce in developing countries must support almost twice as many children as it does in the wealthier countries. In the United Sates, the workforce age group (15 to 64) amounts to about 67% of the total population, with 20% under age 15 and 13% over age 65 as of 2011; the corresponding ratios in the United Kingdom are similar: 66%, 18%, and 17% respectively. In the euro area, some 19% of the population is over age 65; and in Japan nearly one-quarter of the population already has reached age 65. The main problems in more developed countries relate more to their low population growth and old-age dependents (over age 65). By contrast, in sub-Saharan Africa, the economically active workforce makes up about 54% of the total population (just 3% of the population is over age 65) as of 2011. In general, the more rapid the population growth rate is, the greater the proportion of dependent children in the total population and the more difficult it is for people who

Youth dependency ratio The proportion of young people under age 15 to the working population aged 16 to 64 in a country.

BOX 6.1 FINDINGS   The 2012 Revised United Nations Population Projections

Here is a summary of some of the main findings found in the UN's *World Population Prospects 2012 Revision*, published in June 2013.

- World population is now projected at 8.1 billion by 2025; and 9.6 billion by 2050.
- Most population growth will continue to occur in developing regions where population will grow from 5.9 billion in 2013 to about 8.2 billion in 2050.
- "Give or take a billion": The projections depend on assumptions—the 2050 population could turn out to be as little as 8.3 billion or as many as 10.9 billion.
- Most population growth will occur in Africa.
- The 49 least developed countries are projected to double in size from 900 million in 2013 to 1.8 billion in 2050.
- Beyond Africa, projected population growth in the rest of world is just over 10% for 2013–2100.
- New projected total population is higher, particularly after 2075 because:
  - Current fertility level estimates are higher in some countries with better information (in particular, in 15 high-fertility sub-Saharan African countries, estimated births per woman were adjusted upwards more than 5%).
  - In some cases, the actual level of fertility appears to have risen in recent years.
  - In other cases, the previous estimate was too low.
- Other projections include:
  - Developed region population will be little changed at 1.3 billion–even with immigration.
  - India will become the world's most populous country, passing China around 2028, when each will have about 1.45 billion people.
  - The population of Nigeria could pass that of the United States by 2050; by 2100 it could rival China as the second most populous country.
  - By 2100, several other countries are projected to have populations over 200 million: Indonesia Tanzania, Pakistan, Congo, Ethiopia, Uganda, and Niger.

Source: United Nations Population Division, World Population Prospects: The 2012 Revision. New York: United Nations, Department of Economic and Social Affairs, 13 June 2013; downloaded from www.unpopulation.org. For a summary see http://www.un.org/apps/news/story. asp?NewsID=45165#.UlAkZmRVRz0.

are working to support those who are not. This phenomenon of youth dependency also leads to an important concept, the **hidden momentum of population growth**.

The Hidden Momentum of Population Growth

Perhaps the least understood aspect of population growth is its tendency to continue even after birth rates have declined substantially. Population growth has a built-in tendency to continue, a powerful momentum that, like a speeding automobile when the brakes are applied, tends to keep going for some time before coming to a stop. In the case of population growth, this momentum can persist for decades after birth rates drop.

Hidden momentum of population growth   The phenomenon whereby population continues to increase even after a fall in birth rates because the large existing youthful population expands the population's base of potential parents.

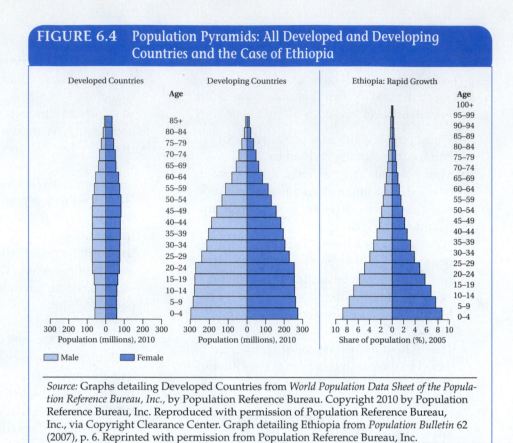

FIGURE 6.4   Population Pyramids: All Developed and Developing Countries and the Case of Ethiopia

Source: Graphs detailing Developed Countries from *World Population Data Sheet of the Population Reference Bureau, Inc.,* by Population Reference Bureau. Copyright 2010 by Population Reference Bureau, Inc. Reproduced with permission of Population Reference Bureau, Inc., via Copyright Clearance Center. Graph detailing Ethiopia from *Population Bulletin* 62 (2007), p. 6. Reprinted with permission from Population Reference Bureau, Inc.

There are two basic reasons for this. First, high birth rates cannot be altered substantially overnight. The social, economic, and institutional forces that have influenced fertility rates over the course of centuries do not simply evaporate at the urging of national leaders. We know from the experience of European nations that such reductions in birth rates can take many decades. Consequently, even if developing countries assign top priority to the limitation of population growth, it will still take many years to lower national fertility to desired levels.

The second and less obvious reason for the hidden momentum of population growth relates to the age structure of many developing countries' populations. Figure 6.4 illustrates the great difference between age structures in less developed and more developed countries by means of two **population pyramids** for 2010. Each pyramid rises by five-year age intervals for both males and females, with the total number in each age cohort measured on the horizontal axis. Panel A (the left and middle panels) show population pyramids for developed and developing countries, respectively (the age scale is that listed between these two figures). Expressed in millions of people, rather than percentages, the figure clearly reveals that most future population growth will take place in the developing world. The steeper bottom rungs for the developing world as a whole, in contrast to a very low-income country such as Ethiopia (right panel),

Population pyramid A graphic depiction of the age structure of the population, with age cohorts plotted on the vertical axis and either population shares or numbers of males and females in each cohort on the horizontal axis.

reflect the large declines in population growth in lower-middle income developing countries over the past quarter century, and particularly in China (see the case study at the end of this chapter). For developed countries, in the contemporary period the population in middle cohorts is typically greater than that of young cohorts; this is partly but certainly not exclusively viewed as a transitional feature of a period in which women have been delaying births until later in life.

From the Ethiopia pyramid (Panel B) expressed as share of population, young people greatly outnumber their parents (the age scale in this case is found to the right of the figure). When their generation reaches adulthood, the number of potential parents will inevitably be much larger than at present. It follows that even if these new parents have only enough children to replace themselves (two per couple, as compared with their parents, who may have had four or more children), the fact that the total number of couples having two children is much greater than the number of couples who previously had more children means that the total population will still increase substantially before leveling off.[5]

Panel A also focuses attention on the fact that some age brackets are increasing in size in some countries, while they are decreasing in others. This reflects that in the demographic transition, the fraction of the population of working age first rises and then falls. On the one hand, countries where the fraction of prime working-age citizens is rising face a potential crisis if many remain unemployed, as this is associated with inequality and (especially among males) social unrest, not to mention the potential output loss. On the other hand, this rise is also an important window of opportunity for strong income and productivity gains, referred to as the *demographic dividend*—a period in which there are fewer children to support, a larger fraction of women join or remain in the workforce for longer periods of time, and there are more available resources to invest in human capital (see Chapter 8).

In contrast, where the fraction of people of working age is falling as a result of population aging, the resources needed for old-age support are increasing. This is already a challenge for most high-income countries. Leading up to this period, a higher savings rate is required; but then allowing more immigration can also help. The transition is likely to pose an even greater challenge for some middle-income countries with big drops in fertility ahead of previous historical patterns, most notably China (see the case study at the end of the chapter), but also in several other Asian countries.[6]

6.3 The Demographic Transition

The process by which fertility rates eventually decline to low and stable levels has been portrayed by a famous concept in economic demography called the **demographic transition**.

The demographic transition attempts to explain why all contemporary developed nations have more or less passed through the same three stages of modern population history. Before their economic modernization, these countries for centuries had stable or very slow-growing populations as a result of a combination of high birth rates and almost equally high death rates. This was stage 1. Stage 2 began when modernization, associated with better

Demographic transition The phasing-out process of population growth rates from a virtually stagnant growth stage, characterized by high birth rates and death rates through a rapid-growth stage with high birth rates and low death rates to a stable, low-growth stage in which both birth and death rates are low.

public health methods, healthier diets, higher incomes, and other improvements led to a marked reduction in mortality that gradually raised life expectancy from under 40 years to over 60 years. However, the decline in death rates was not immediately accompanied by a decline in fertility. As a result, the growing divergence between high birth rates and falling death rates led to sharp increases in population growth compared to past centuries. Stage 2 thus marks the beginning of the demographic transition (the transition from stable or slow-growing populations first to rapidly increasing numbers and then to declining rates). Finally, stage 3 was entered when the forces and influences of modernization and development caused the beginning of a decline in fertility; eventually, falling birth rates converged with lower death rates, leaving little or no population growth.

Replacement fertility   The number of births per woman that would result in stable population levels.

This process implies movement from a relatively high number of births per woman to a population **replacement fertility** level that can be calculated to reach about 2.05 to 2.1 births per woman when nearly all women survive to the mean age of childbearing, as they do in developed countries. In developing countries with much lower survival rates, replacement fertility can be well over 3 births per woman.[7]

Figure 6.5 depicts the three historical stages of the demographic transition in western Europe. Before the early nineteenth century, birth rates hovered around 35 per 1,000, while death rates fluctuated around 30 per 1,000. This resulted in population growth rates of around 5 per 1,000, or less than 0.5% per year. Stage 2, the beginning of western Europe's demographic transition, was initiated around the first quarter of the nineteenth century by slowly falling death rates as a result of improving economic conditions and the gradual development of disease and death control through modern medical and public health technologies. The decline in birth rates (stage 3) did not really begin until late in the nineteenth century, with most of the reduction many decades occurring after modern economic growth had begun and long after death rates began their descent. But since the initial level of birth rates was generally low

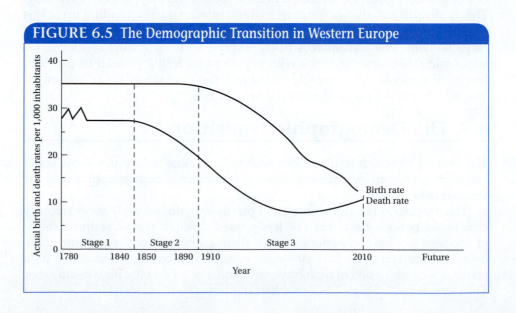

FIGURE 6.5 The Demographic Transition in Western Europe

in western Europe as a result of either late marriage or celibacy, overall rates of population growth seldom exceeded the 1% level, even at their peak. By the end of western Europe's demographic transition in the second half of the twentieth century, the relationship between birth and death rates that marked the early 1800s had reversed, with birth rates fluctuating and death rates remaining fairly stable or rising slightly. This latter phenomenon was simply due to the older age distributions of contemporary European populations. The patterns of the demographic transition in Europe are clear, though research continues to better identify the causal factors at work.[8]

Figure 6.6 shows the population histories of contemporary developing countries, which contrast with those of western Europe and fall into two patterns.

Birth rates in many developing countries today are considerably higher than they were in preindustrial western Europe. This is because women tend to marry at an earlier age. As a result, there are both more families for a given population size and more years in which to have children. In the 1950s and 1960s, stage 2 of the demographic transition occurred throughout most of the developing world. The application of highly effective imported modern medical and public health technologies caused death rates in developing countries to fall much more rapidly than in nineteenth-century Europe. Given their historically high birth rates (still over 35 per 1,000 in many countries), this has meant that stage 2 of the demographic transition has been characterized by peak population growth rates well in excess of 2.0% per annum in most developing countries.

With regard to stage 3, we can distinguish between two broad classes of developing countries. In case A in Figure 6.6, modern methods of death

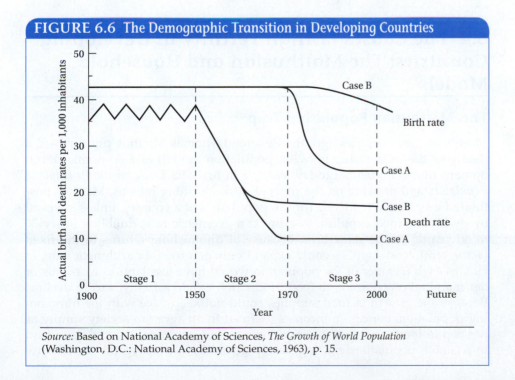

FIGURE 6.6 The Demographic Transition in Developing Countries

Source: Based on National Academy of Sciences, *The Growth of World Population* (Washington, D.C.: National Academy of Sciences, 1963), p. 15.

control, combined with rapid and widely distributed rises in levels of living, have resulted in death rates falling as low as 10 per 1,000 and birth rates also falling rapidly, to levels between 12 and 25 per 1,000. These countries, including Taiwan, South Korea, Costa Rica, China, Cuba, Chile, and Sri Lanka, have thus entered stage 3 of their demographic transition and have experienced rapidly falling rates of overall population growth.

But some developing countries fall into case B of Figure 6.6. After an initial period of rapid decline, death rates have failed to drop further, largely because of the persistence of widespread absolute poverty and low levels of living and more recently because of the AIDS epidemic. Moreover, the continuance of still quite high birth rates as a result of these low levels of living causes overall population growth rates to remain relatively high. These countries, including many of those in sub-Saharan Africa and the Middle East, are still in stage 2 of their demographic transition. Though fertility is declining, it remains very high in these parts of the world.

The important question, therefore, is this: When and under what conditions are developing nations likely to experience falling birth rates and a slower expansion of population? To answer this question, we need to ask a prior one. What are the principal determinants or causes of high fertility rates in developing countries, and can these determinants of the "demand" for children be influenced by government policy? To try to answer this critical question, we turn to a very old and famous classical macroeconomic and demographic model, the Malthusian "population trap," and a contemporary and highly influential neoclassical microeconomic model, the household theory of fertility.

6.4 The Causes of High Fertility in Developing Countries: The Malthusian and Household Models

The Malthusian Population Trap

More than two centuries ago, the Reverend Thomas Malthus put forward a theory of the relationship between population growth and economic development that is influential today. Writing in his 1798 *Essay on the Principle of Population* and drawing on the concept of diminishing returns, Malthus postulated a universal tendency for the population of a country, unless checked by dwindling food supplies, to grow at a geometric rate, doubling every 30 to 40 years.[9] At the same time, because of diminishing returns to the fixed factor, land, food supplies could expand only at a roughly arithmetic rate. In fact, as each member of the population would have less land to work, his or her marginal contribution to food production would actually start to decline. Because the growth in food supplies could not keep pace with the burgeoning population, per capita incomes (defined in an agrarian society simply as per capita food production) would have a tendency to fall so low as to lead to a stable population existing barely at or slightly above the subsistence level. Malthus therefore contended that the only way to avoid this condition of chronic low levels of living or absolute poverty was for people to engage in "moral restraint" and limit the number of their progeny. Hence, we might regard Malthus, indirectly and inadvertently, as the father of the modern birth control movement.

Modern economists have given a name to the Malthusian idea of a population inexorably forced to live at subsistence levels of income. They have called it the *low-level equilibrium population trap* or, more simply, the **Malthusian population trap**. Diagrammatically, the basic Malthusian model can be illustrated by comparing the shape and position of curves representing population growth rates and aggregate income growth rates when these two curves are each plotted against levels of per capita income. An example of this is presented in Figure 6.7.

On the vertical axis, we plot numerical percentage changes, both positive and negative, in the two principal variables under consideration (total population and aggregate income). On the horizontal axis are levels of per capita income. Figure 6.7 depicts the basic ideas. The *x*-axis shows the level of income per capita. The *y*-axis shows two rates—of population growth and of total income growth. Per capita income growth is, by definition, the difference between income growth and population growth—hence the vertical difference between these two curves. Thus, as we saw in Chapter 3 in our discussion of the Harrod-Domar (or AK) model, whenever the rate of total income growth is greater than the rate of population growth, income per capita is rising; this corresponds to moving to the right along the *x*-axis. Conversely, whenever the rate of total income growth is less than the rate of population growth, income per capita is falling, moving to the left along the *x*-axis. When these rates are equal, income per capita is unchanging. We can then explore the shapes of population growth and growth of income to understand potential implications of this relationship.

Malthusian population trap
The threshold population level anticipated by Thomas Malthus (1766–1834) at which population increase was bound to stop because life-sustaining resources, which increase at an arithmetic rate, would be insufficient to support human population, which would increase at a geometric rate.

FIGURE 6.7 The Malthusian Population Trap

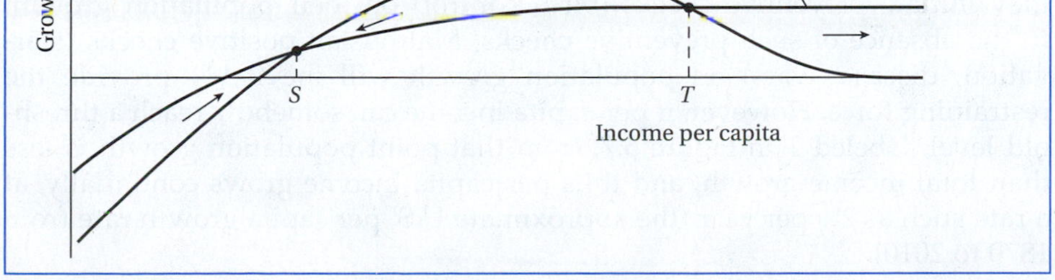

First consider population growth. When income is very low, say, below $250 per year at purchasing power parity, nutrition is so poor that people become susceptible to fatal infectious diseases; pregnancy and nursing become problematic; and, ultimately, outright starvation may occur. This is shown on the left in Figure 6.7. But after this minimum level of income per capita is reached, population begins to grow, eventually reaching a peak rate (perhaps at 3% to 4% per year); and then the population growth rate begins to fall until at last a fairly stable population is reached (a growth rate close to zero). Note that this pattern of population growth first increasing and then decreasing as per capita income rises corresponds to the pattern of the demographic transition, explained in section 6.3.

In Figure 6.7, total income growth becomes greater as the economy develops (and income per capita rises). An economic reason for this positive relationship is the assumption that savings vary positively with income per capita. Countries with higher per capita incomes are assumed to be capable of generating higher savings rates and thus more investment. Again, given a Harrod-Domar-type model of economic growth (see Chapter 3), higher savings rates mean higher rates of aggregate income growth. Eventually, however, growth levels off at a maximum. (Incomes of middle-income countries might grow fastest as they borrow technology to catch up—not shown in this diagram—but these higher rates cannot be continued once the technology frontier is reached.)

As drawn, the curves first cross at a low level of income, labeled S (for subsistence). This is a stable equilibrium: If per capita income levels become somewhat larger than (to the right of) S, it is assumed that population size will begin to increase in part because higher incomes improve nutrition and reduce death rates. But then, as shown in the figure, population is growing faster than income (the $\Delta P/P$ curve is vertically higher than the $\Delta Y/Y$ curve), so income per capita is falling, and we move to the left along the x-axis. The arrow pointing in the direction of S from the right therefore shows per capita income falling back to this very low level. On the other hand, if income per capita were a little less than S, the total income curve would be above the population growth curve and so income per capita would be rising. This corresponds to a move to the right along the x-axis. Thus, our conclusion is that point S represents a stable equilibrium (much as in our study of stable equilibria in Figure 4.1). This very low population growth rate along with a very low income per person is consistent with the experience of most of human history prior to the modern era.[10]

According to modern-day neo-Malthusians, poor nations will never be able to rise much above their subsistence levels of per capita income unless they initiate preventive checks (birth control) on their population growth. In the absence of such preventive checks, Malthusian positive checks (starvation, disease, wars) on population growth will inevitably provide the restraining force. However, if per capita income can somehow reach a threshold level, labeled T in Figure 6.7, from that point population growth is less than total income growth, and thus per capita income grows continually, at a rate such as 2% per year (the approximate U.S. per capita growth rate from 1870 to 2010).

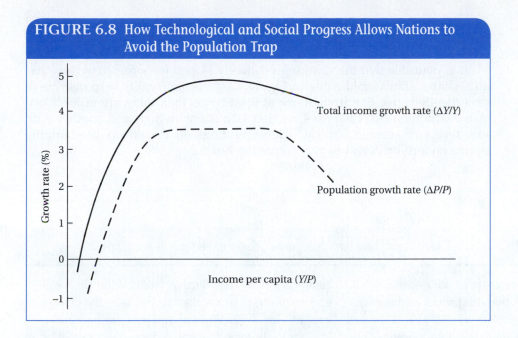

FIGURE 6.8 How Technological and Social Progress Allows Nations to Avoid the Population Trap

Countries or regions in such a population trap can also escape it by achieving technological progress that shifts the income growth rate curve up at any level of per capita income. And it may be able to achieve changes in economic institutions and culture ("social progress") that shifts the population growth curve down. In this way, the population trap equilibrium is eliminated altogether, and the economy is able to proceed with self-sustaining growth. An example of such a result is depicted in Figure 6.8. Total income growth is now greater than population growth at each level of per capita income. As a result, income per capita now grows steadily.

We have examined strategies for accelerating income growth in Chapters 3 (including its appendices) and 4, and we will examine specific growth policies further in Chapters 7, 9, 12, and 14. The main focus of the remainder of this chapter is on changes in economic institutions, economic power in households, and cultural norms, to reduce fertility to maintain population growth below income growth, and eventually to achieve population stability.

In addition to the classic Malthusian model, the multiple equilibrium analysis of Chapter 4, Figure 4.1, is also relevant to understanding high-fertility traps. In the diagram, we can take the x-axis to represent (expected) fertility and the y-axis, the family's own fertility decision. The upward-sloping response (along the S-shaped curve) of the individual family fertility decision to average fertility may be caused by at least two important complementarities—a basis for possible multiple equilibria. First, if others have high fertility, this may increase the number of formal-sector job seekers without (proportionally) increasing the number of (higher-paying) formal-sector jobs. Each family may feel it needs a larger number of children to raise the probability that at least one child will get a modern job. In addition, families often follow local social norms about fertility and tend to model their own behavior on the behavior of others in their community.

It is plausible that the resulting positively sloped response curve also has an S-shape, similar to the one in Figure 4.1[10a]. If the fertility response curve cuts the 45-degree line from above at least twice, then there are at least two stable equilibria (see Chapter 4, section 4.2): one with high and another with low levels of average fertility.[11] Some findings on the effects of changing norms on fertility decisions is presented in Box 6.2.

BOX 6.2 FINDINGS   Social Norms and the Changing Patterns of Fertility in Bangladesh

In this chapter, we describe an idea—presented in part by Partha Dasgupta—that social norms play a role in setting an equilibrium fertility rate: If families followed local customs about fertility—modeling their own behavior on that of their neighbors—the community might be trapped at a higher fertility rate than would prevail if they could manage a change in social expectations. The idea was also a starting point for empirical research by Kaivan Munshi and Jacques Myaux on the uneven transition to lower fertility in rural developing areas.

Munshi and Myaux applied their research to the experience of the Matlab area of Bangladesh. Fertility reduction varied greatly across apparently similar villages. In addition, response to the same family-planning program also varied greatly in the magnitude of their effects and time lags before these effects were realized. Data on fertility collected twice annually over an 11-year period offered a unique chance to learn about this process. (The data set included contraceptive use and demographic and socioeconomic characteristics for all women living in all 70 villages in the Matlab area who took part in the program and were followed throughout the 11-year period.)

Munshi and Myaux offered an explanation for widely varying local patterns: "Most societies have traditionally put norms into place to regulate fertility. When the economic environment changes, individuals gradually learn through their social interactions about the new reproductive equilibrium that will emerge in their community." In this case, the change was in the availability of modern contraception. There is likely some proportion of people who will be perpetually resistant to contraception; the remainder will be open-minded about it but may not want to behave too differently than local norms dictate. Until this process plays out, people will not know how many of their neighbors will be firmly resistant to change and thus whether contraceptive use will ultimately be socially acceptable overall. Munshi and Myaux propose that families' uncertainty about what potential new equilibrium (what level of contraceptive prevalence) in their villages will emerge leads to caution, giving rise to slow and different rates of fertility transition in otherwise apparently similar villages. They developed a model to demonstrate the underlying logic of this explanation and concluded that social norms do make a difference; the process of moving to a better equilibrium can be slow. In some cases, movement out of the high fertility equilibrium (too high for many who are stuck there) can be prevented indefinitely.

In rural Bangladesh, which has a large majority Muslim population but also a minority Hindu population, social norms correspond to religious groups. Women are secluded generally (through purdah) and almost never interact with anyone (including women) from another religious group.

In this context, the researchers studied an "exogenous economic intervention"—a thorough, long-term family-planning program introduced throughout the village areas, studied and promoted door to door to each religious group with equal intensity. This is the kind of quasi experiment needed to understand the effects of social interactions, a process of wide importance in development economics and one that presents great challenges for econometrics (statistical analysis). The authors examined the data and showed that a woman's contraception use "respond[s] strongly to contraceptive prevalence within their own religious group in the village, cross-religion effects are entirely absent in the data." This held despite the fact that "all individuals in the village have access to the same family-planning inputs" and even when the people are otherwise very similar. Thus, the findings are "consistent with the view that changing social norms are driving changes in reproductive behavior in these communities. "As in the model, uncertainty about the ultimate prevalence of contraception use "is slowly resolved over time as women in the village interact sequentially with each other from one period to the next, which explains the gradual change in contraceptive prevalence that we see in the data, as well as the convergence to different levels of contraceptive use across communities."

As societies gain the possibility of modern economic development, advantages of smaller family sizes grow both for families and for the societies of which they are a part. But multiple equilibria are possible. Many in communities with full knowledge of and access to contraception may still perpetuate high fertility rates when social norms and sanctions to contrary behavior prevail. Addressing situations like these requires attention to social aspects of the development process.

Source: Kaivan Munshi and Jacques Myaux, "Social norms and the fertility transition," *Journal of Development Economics* 80 (2006): 1–38. For further background on the issues involved, see also Partha Dasgupta, *An Inquiry into Well-Being and Destitution* (New York: Oxford University Press, 1993).

Criticisms of the Malthusian Model

The Malthusian population trap provides a theory of the relationship between population growth and economic development. Unfortunately, it is based on a number of simplistic assumptions and hypotheses that do not stand the test of empirical verification. We can criticize the population trap on two major grounds.

First, the model ignores the enormous impact of technological progress in offsetting the growth-inhibiting forces of rapid population increases. As we saw in Chapter 2, the history of modern economic growth has been closely associated with rapid technological progress in the form of a continuous series of scientific, technological, and social inventions and innovations. Increasing rather than decreasing returns to scale have been a distinguishing feature of the modern growth epoch. While Malthus was basically correct in assuming a limited supply of land, he did not—and in fairness could not at that time—anticipate the manner in which technological progress could augment the availability of land by raising its quality (its productivity) even though its quantity might remain roughly the same.

In terms of the population trap, rapid and continuing technological progress can be represented by an upward shift of the income growth (total product) curve so that at *all* levels of per capita income, it is vertically higher than the population growth curve. This is shown in Figure 6.8. As a result, per capita income will continue to grow over time. All countries therefore have the potential of escaping the Malthusian population trap.

The second basic criticism of the trap focuses on its assumption that national rates of population increase are directly (positively) related to the level of national per capita income. According to this assumption, at relatively low levels of per capita income, we should expect to find population growth rates increasing with increasing per capita income. But research indicates that there appears to be no clear correlation between population growth rates and levels of per capita income. As a result of modern medicine and public health programs, death rates have fallen rapidly and have become less dependent on the level of per capita income. Moreover, birth rates seem to show no rigid relationship with per capita income levels. Fertility rates vary widely for countries with the same per capita income, especially below $1,000. It is not so much the aggregate level of per capita income that matters for population growth but rather how that income is distributed. It is the level of household income, not the level of per capita income, that seems to matter most.

In sum, Malthusian and neo-Malthusian theories as applied to contemporary developing nations have severely limited relevance for the following reasons:

1. They do not take adequate account of the role and impact of technological progress.

2. They are based on a hypothesis about a macro relationship between population growth and levels of per capita income that does not stand up to empirical testing of the modern period.

3. They focus on the wrong variable, per capita income, as the principal determinant of population growth rates. A much better and more valid approach to the question of population and development centers on the microeconomics of family size decision making in which individual, and not aggregate, levels of living become the principal determinant of a family's decision to have more or fewer children.

We continue to study the Malthusian trap even though evidence shows that it is not currently relevant for three main reasons: First, because many people still believe it holds in poor countries today, despite the recent evidence; and people working in the development field should understand the model and the elements of it that do not currently apply so that they can engage the debate effectively. Second, because it seems clear that such traps have occurred in the historical past and may have been factors in population collapses, including in the pre-Columbian Americas. Third—as we will explore in the remainder of this chapter—the fact that this model no longer applies underlines the importance of factors that can prevent its emergence. These include efforts to continue steady and sustainable rises in agricultural productivity; moreover, they encompass increases in women's empowerment and freedom to choose—along with their incomes—which reduce the old-age security motive behind high fertility.

The Microeconomic Household Theory of Fertility

In recent years, economists have begun to look more closely at the microeconomic determinants of family fertility in an attempt to provide a better theoretical and empirical explanation for the observed falling birth rates associated with stage 3 of the demographic transition. In doing this, they have drawn on the traditional neoclassical theory of household and consumer behavior for their basic analytical model and have used the principles of economics and optimization to explain family size decisions.

The conventional theory of consumer behavior assumes that an individual with a given set of tastes or preferences for a range of goods (a "utility function") tries to maximize the satisfaction derived from consuming these goods subject to his or her own income constraint and the relative prices of all goods. In the application of this theory to fertility analysis, children are considered as a special kind of consumption (and in developing countries, particularly low-income countries, investment) good so that fertility becomes a rational economic response to the consumer's (family's) demand for children relative to other goods. The usual income and substitution effects are assumed to apply. That is, if other factors are held constant, the desired number of children can be expected to vary directly with household income (this direct relationship may not hold for poor societies; it depends on the strength of demand for children relative to other consumer goods and to the sources of increased income, such as female employment), inversely with the price (cost) of children, and inversely with the strength of tastes for other goods relative to children. Mathematically, these relationships can be expressed as follows:

$$C_d = f(Y, P_c, P_x, t_x), x = 1, \ldots, n \qquad (6.1)$$

where C_d, the demand for surviving children (an important consideration in low-income societies where infant mortality rates are high), is a function of the given level of household income (Y), the "net" price of children (the difference between anticipated costs, mostly the opportunity cost of a mother's time, and benefits, potential child income and old-age support, P_c), the prices of all other goods (P_x), and the tastes for goods relative to children (t_x). Under standard neoclassical conditions, we would expect the following (expressed both mathematically and in words):

$\partial C_d/\partial Y > 0$ The higher the household income, the greater the demand for children.

$\partial C_d/\partial P_c < 0$ The higher the net price of children, the lower the quantity demanded.

$\partial C_d/\partial P_x > 0$ The higher the prices of all other goods relative to children, the greater the quantity of children demanded.

$\partial C_d/\partial t_x < 0$ The greater the strength of tastes for goods relative to children, the fewer children demanded.

Figure 6.9 provides a simplified diagrammatic presentation of the **microeconomic theory of fertility**. The number of desired (surviving) children, C_d, is

Microeconomic theory of fertility The theory that family formation has costs and benefits that determine the size of families formed.

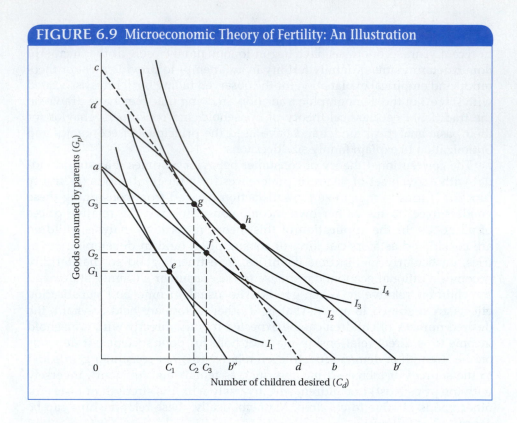

FIGURE 6.9 Microeconomic Theory of Fertility: An Illustration

measured along the horizontal axis, and the total quantity of goods consumed by the parents, G_p, is measured on the vertical axis.

Household desires for children are expressed in terms of an indifference map representing the subjective degree of satisfaction derived by the parents for all possible combinations of commodities and children. Each individual indifference curve portrays a locus of commodity-child combinations that yield the same amount of satisfaction. Any point (or combination of goods and children) on a "higher" indifference curve—that is, on a curve farther out from the origin—represents a higher level of satisfaction than any point on a lower indifference curve. But each indifference curve is a "constant satisfaction" locus.

In Figure 6.9, only four indifference curves, I_1 to I_4, are shown; in theory, there is an infinite set of such curves, filling the whole quadrant and covering all possible commodity-child combinations. The household's ability to "purchase" alternative combinations of goods and children is shown by the budget constraint line, ab. Thus, all combinations on or below line ab (within the triangular area $0ab$) are financially attainable by the household on the basis of its perceived income prospects and the relative prices of children and goods, as represented by the slope of the ab budget constraint. The steeper the slope of the budget line, the higher the price of children relative to goods.

According to the demand-based theory of fertility, the household chooses from among all attainable combinations the one combination of goods and children that maximizes family satisfaction on the basis of its subjectively determined preferences. Diagrammatically, this optimal combination is represented by point f, the tangency point between the budget constraint, ab, and indifference curve, I_2. Therefore, C_3 children and G_2 goods will be demanded.

A rise in family income, represented in Figure 6.9 by the parallel outward shift of the budget line from *ab* to *a'b'*, enables the household to attain a higher level of satisfaction (point *h* on curve I_4) by consuming more of *both* commodities and children—that is, if children, like most commodities, are assumed to be normal goods (demand for them rises with income), an important if in low-income countries where children are often in demand primarily as a source of future financial security. Note that as income rises, parents may spend more on each child, preferring a smaller number of children, each of higher "quality," for example, healthier and better educated.

Similarly, an increase in the price (opportunity cost) of children relative to other goods will cause households to substitute commodities for children. Other factors (namely, income and tastes) being constant, a rise in the relative price of children causes the household utility-maximizing consumption combination to occur on a lower indifference curve, as shown by the movement of the equilibrium point from *f* to *e* when the budget line rotates around point *a* to *ab"*.

Note, finally, that if there is a simultaneous increase in household income and net child price as a result of, say, expanding female employment opportunities and a rise in wages, coupled with a tax on children beyond a certain number per family, there will be *both* an outward shift and downward rotation of the budget constraint line of Figure 6.9 to, say, dashed line *cd*. The result is a new utility-maximizing combination that includes fewer children per family (point *g* compared with point *f*). In other words, higher levels of living for low-income families in combination with a relative increase in the price of children (whether brought about directly by fiscal measures or indirectly by expanded female employment opportunities) will motivate households to have fewer children while still improving their welfare. This is just one example of how the economic theory of fertility can shed light on the relationship between economic development and population growth as well as suggest possible lines of policy.

The Demand for Children in Developing Countries

The economic theory of fertility assumes that the household demand for children is determined by family preferences for a certain number of surviving (usually male) children (i.e., in regions of high mortality, parents may produce more children than they actually desire in the expectation that some will not survive), by the price or "opportunity cost" of rearing these children, and by levels of family income. Children in poor societies are seen partly as economic investment goods in that there is an expected return in the form of both child labor and the provision of financial support for parents in old age.[12] However, in many developing countries, there is a strong intrinsic psychological and cultural determinant of family size, so the first two or three children should be viewed as "consumer" goods for which demand may not be very responsive to relative price changes.

The choice mechanism in the economic theory of fertility as applied to developing countries is assumed, therefore, to exist primarily with regard to the additional ("marginal") children who are considered as investments. In deciding whether or not to have *additional* children, parents are assumed to weigh private economic benefits against private costs, where the principal benefits are the expected income from child labor, usually on the farm, and eventual financial support for elderly parents. Balanced against these benefits are the two principal elements of cost: the opportunity cost of the mother's time (the income she could earn if she were not at home caring for her children) and the cost of educating children—the financial trade-off between having fewer "high-quality," high-cost, educated children with high-income-earning potential versus more "low-quality," low-cost, uneducated children with much lower earning prospects.

Using the same thought processes as in the traditional theory of consumer behavior, the theory of family fertility concludes that when the price or cost of children rises as a result of, say, increased educational and employment opportunities for women or a rise in school fees or the establishment of minimum-age child labor laws or the provision of publicly financed old-age social security schemes, parents will demand fewer additional children, substituting, perhaps, quality for quantity or a mother's employment income for her child-rearing activities. It follows that one way to induce families to desire fewer children is to raise the price of child rearing by, say, providing greater educational opportunities and a wider range of higher-paying jobs for young women.

Recent research on household behavior has led to a major improvement of this theory. Households in developing countries generally do not act in a "unitary" manner, depicted with this traditional model. Instead, men and women have different objective functions; for example, husbands may prefer to have more children than wives. Household behavior is then explained as a result of *bargaining* between husbands and wives. Although the broad impacts we have just described continue to hold, the process includes increased bargaining power of women. Nonunitary, bargaining-based models of household behavior also improve our understanding of otherwise puzzlingly inefficient household behaviors, such as higher investment in husbands' farm plots than wives' farm plots even when a more even investment could lead to higher family incomes.[13]

Some Empirical Evidence   Statistical studies in a broad spectrum of developing countries have provided support for the economic theory of fertility.[14] For example, it has been found that high female employment opportunities outside the home and greater female school attendance, especially at the primary and secondary levels, are associated with significantly lower levels of fertility. As women become better educated, they tend to earn a larger share of household income and to produce fewer children. Moreover, these studies have confirmed the strong association between declines in child mortality and the subsequent decline in fertility. Assuming that households desire a target number of surviving children, increased female education and higher levels of income can decrease child mortality and therefore increase the chances that the firstborn will survive. As a result, fewer births may be necessary to attain the same number of surviving children. This fact alone underlines the importance of educating women and improving public health and child nutrition programs in reducing fertility levels.

Implications for Development and Fertility

All of the foregoing can be summarized by saying that the effect of social and economic progress in lowering fertility in developing countries will be the greatest when the majority of the population and especially the very poor share in its benefits. Specifically, birth rates among the very poor are likely to fall where the following socioeconomic changes come to pass:

1. An increase in the education of women and a consequent improvement in their role and status

2. An increase in female nonagricultural wage employment opportunities, which raises the price or cost of their traditional child-rearing activities

3. A rise in family income levels through the increased direct employment and earnings of a husband and wife or through the redistribution of income and assets from rich to poor

4. A reduction in infant mortality through expanded public health programs and better nutritional status for both mother and child, and better medical care

5. The development of old-age and other social security systems outside the extended family network to lessen the economic dependence of parents, especially women, on their offspring

6. Expanded schooling opportunities so that parents can better substitute child "quality" for large numbers of children

In short, expanded efforts to make jobs, education, and health more broadly available to poverty groups in general and women in particular will not only contribute to their economic and psychic well-being (i.e., to their development) but also contribute substantially to their motivation for smaller families (i.e., their freedom to choose), which is vital to reducing population growth rates. Where such motivation exists, well-executed **family-planning programs** can then be an effective tool.[15] But before discussing policy issues and what government might or might not do, we should point out that while there seems to be considerable agreement regarding the determinants or causes of population growth, substantial disagreement and controversy remain regarding its consequences.

Family-planning programs Public programs designed to help parents plan and regulate their family size.

6.5 The Consequences of High Fertility: Some Conflicting Perspectives

For many years, development economists and other social scientists have debated the seriousness of the consequences of rapid population growth.[16] On the one hand, we must recognize that population growth is not the only, or even the primary, source of low levels of living, eroding self-esteem, and limited freedom in developing nations. On the other hand, it would be equally naive to think that rapid population growth in many countries and regions is not a serious intensifier and multiplier of those integral components of underdevelopment, especially the first and third. The following discussion summarizes some of the main arguments for and against the idea that the consequences of rapid population growth lead to serious development problems. It then considers whether some consensus can be reached so that specific policy goals and objectives can be postulated.[17]

It's Not a Real Problem

We can identify three general lines of argument on the part of people who assert that population growth is not a cause for concern:

- The problem is not population growth but other issues.
- Population growth is a false issue deliberately created by dominant rich-country agencies and institutions to keep developing countries in their dependent condition.
- For many developing countries and regions, population growth is in fact desirable.

Other Issues   Many observers from both rich and poor nations argue that the real problem is not population growth per se but one or all of the following four issues.

1. *Underdevelopment.* If correct strategies are pursued and lead to higher levels of living, greater self-esteem, and expanded freedom, population will take care of itself. Eventually, it will disappear as a problem, as it has in all of the present economically advanced nations. According to this argument, underdevelopment is the real problem, and development should be the only goal. With it will come economic progress and social mechanisms that will more or less automatically regulate population growth and distribution. As long as people in developing countries remain impoverished, uneducated, and unhealthy and the social safety net remains weak, the large family will constitute the only real source of social security (i.e., parents will continue to be denied the freedom to choose a small family if they so desire). Some proponents of the underdevelopment argument then conclude that birth control programs will surely fail, as they have in the past, when there is no motivation on the part of poor families to limit their size.

2. *World Resource Depletion and Environmental Destruction.* Population can only be an economic problem in relation to the availability and utilization of scarce natural and material resources. The fact is that developed countries, with less than one-quarter of the world's population, consume almost 80% of the world's resources. In terms of the depletion of the world's limited resources, therefore, the addition of another child in the developed countries is as significant as the birth of many times as many additional children in the underdeveloped countries. According to this argument, developed nations should curtail their excessively high consumption standards instead of asking less developed nations to restrict their population growth. The latter's high fertility is really due to their low levels of living, which are in turn largely the result of the over-consumption of the world's scarce resources by rich nations. This combination of rising affluence and extravagant consumption habits in rich

countries and among rich people in poor countries, and not population growth, should be the major world concern. We will analyze issues of the environment and development in Chapter 10.

3. *Population Distribution.* According to this third argument, it is not the number of people per se that is causing population problems but their distribution in space. Many regions of the world (e.g., parts of sub-Saharan Africa) and many regions within countries (e.g., the northeastern and Amazon regions of Brazil) are viewed as underpopulated in terms of available or potential resources. Others simply have too many people concentrated in too small an area (e.g., central Java or most urban concentrations). Governments should therefore strive not to moderate the rate of population growth but rather to bring about a more natural spatial distribution of the population in terms of available land and other productive resources.

4. *Subordination of Women.* Perhaps most important, as noted previously, women often bear the disproportionate burdens of poverty, poor education, and limited social mobility. In many cases, their inferior roles, low status, and restricted access to birth control are manifested in their high fertility. According to this argument, population growth is a natural outcome of women's lack of economic opportunity. If women's health, education, and economic well-being are improved along with their role and status in both the family and the community, this empowerment of women will inevitably lead to smaller families and lower population growth.

It's a Deliberately Contrived False Issue

The second main line of argument denying the significance of population growth as a major development problem is closely allied to the neocolonial dependence theory of underdevelopment discussed in Chapter 3. Basically, it is argued that the overconcern in the rich nations with the population growth of poor nations is really an attempt by the former to hold down the development of the latter in order to maintain an international status quo that is favorable to the rich nations' self-interests. Rich nations are pressuring poor nations to adopt aggressive population control programs, even though they themselves went through a period of sizable population increase that accelerated their own development processes.

A radical neo-Marxist version of this argument views population control efforts by rich countries and their allied international agencies as racist or genocidal attempts to reduce the relative or absolute size of the poor, largely nonwhite populations of the world who may someday pose a serious threat to the welfare of the rich, predominantly white societies. Worldwide birth control campaigns are seen as manifestations of the fears of the developed world in the face of a possible radical challenge to the international order by the people who are its first victims.

It's a Desirable Phenomenon

A more conventional economic argument is that of population growth as an essential ingredient to stimulate economic development. Larger populations provide the needed consumer demand to generate favorable economies of scale in production, to lower production costs, and to provide a sufficient and low-cost labor supply to achieve higher output levels. Population "revisionist" economists of the neoclassical counterrevolution school argue, for example, that free markets will always adjust to any scarcities created by population pressures.[18] Such scarcities will drive up prices and signal the need for new cost-saving production technologies. In the end, free markets and human ingenuity (Julian Simon's "genius" as the "ultimate resource") will solve any and all problems arising from population growth. This revisionist viewpoint was clearly in contrast with the traditional "orthodox" argument that rapid population growth had serious economic consequences that, if left uncorrected, would slow economic development.

At the other end of the political spectrum, it has been argued by some developing-world neo-Marxist pronatalists that many rural regions in developing countries are in reality underpopulated in the sense that much unused but arable land could yield large increases in agricultural output if only more people were available to cultivate it. Many regions of tropical Africa and Latin America and even parts of Asia are said to be in this situation. With respect to Africa, for example, some observers have noted that many regions had larger populations in the remote past than after independence.[19] Their rural depopulation resulted not only from the slave trade but also from compulsory military service, confinement to reservations, and the forced-labor policies of former colonial governments. For example, the sixteenth-century Kongo kingdom is said to have had a population of approximately 2 million. But by the time of the colonial conquest, which followed 300 years of slave trade, the population of the region had fallen to less than one-third of that figure. After independence, parts of the Democratic Republic of Congo (formerly known as the Belgian Congo and later as Zaire) had barely caught up to the sixteenth-century numbers.[20] Other regions of western and eastern Africa provide similar examples—at least in the eyes of advocates of rapid population growth in Africa.

In terms of ratios of population to arable land (land under cultivation, fallow land, pastures, and forests), Africa south of the Sahara is said by these supporters of population expansion to have a total of 1.4 billion arable hectares. Land actually being cultivated amounts to only a fraction of this potential. Thus, only 12% of all potential arable land is under cultivation, and this low rural population density is viewed as a serious drawback to raising agricultural output.[21] Similar arguments have been expounded with regard to such Latin American countries as Brazil and Argentina.

Three other noneconomic arguments, each found to some degree in a wide range of developing countries, complete the "population growth is desirable" viewpoint. First, many countries claim a need for population growth to protect currently underpopulated border regions against the expansionist intentions of neighboring nations. Second, there are many ethnic, racial, and religious groups in less developed countries whose attitudes favoring large family size have to be protected for both moral and political reasons. Finally, military and political power are often seen as dependent on a large and youthful population.

Many of these arguments have a certain realism about them—if not in fact, then at least in the perceptions of vocal and influential individuals in both the developed and developing worlds. The important point is that they represent a considerable range of opinions and viewpoints and therefore need to be seriously weighed against the counterarguments of theorists who believe that rapid population growth is indeed a real and important problem for underdeveloped countries. Let us now look at some of these counterarguments.

It *Is* a Real Problem

Positions supporting the need to curtail population growth because of the negative economic, social, and environmental consequences are typically based on one of the following three arguments.

The Extremist Argument: Population and Global Crisis

The extreme version of the population-as-problem position attempts to attribute almost all of the world's economic and social evils to excessive population growth. Unrestrained population increase is seen as the major crisis facing humankind today. It is regarded as the principal cause of poverty, low levels of living, malnutrition, ill health, environmental degradation, and a wide array of other social problems. Value-laden and incendiary terms such as *population bomb* and *population explosion* are tossed around. Indeed, dire predictions of world food catastrophes and ecological disaster are often attributed almost entirely to the growth in population numbers.[22] Such an extreme position leads some of its advocates to assert that "world" (i.e., developing country) population stabilization or even decline is the most urgent contemporary task, even if it requires severe and coercive measures such as compulsory sterilization to control family size in some of the most densely populated developing countries, such as India and Bangladesh.

The Theoretical Argument: Population-Poverty Cycles and the Need for Family-Planning Programs

The **population-poverty cycle** theory is the main argument advanced by economists who hold that too rapid population growth yields negative economic consequences and thus should be a real concern for developing countries. Advocates start from the basic proposition that population growth intensifies and exacerbates the economic, social, and psychological problems associated with the condition of underdevelopment. Population growth is believed to retard the prospects for a better life for the already born by reducing savings rates at the household and national levels. It also severely draws down limited government revenues simply to provide the most rudimentary economic, health, and social services to the additional people. This, in turn, further reduces the prospects for any improvement in the levels of living of the existing generation and helps transmit poverty to future generations of low-income families.

Population-poverty cycle A theory to explain how poverty and high population growth become reinforcing.

Because widespread absolute poverty and low levels of living are thus seen as a major cause of large family size, and large families retard economic growth, it follows that economic and social development is a necessary condition for bringing about an eventual slowing or cessation of population growth at low levels of fertility and mortality. But according to this argument, it is not a sufficient condition—that is, development provides people with the incentives and motivations to limit their family size, but family-planning programs are needed to provide them with the technological means to avoid unwanted pregnancies. Even though countries such as France, Japan, the United States, Great Britain, and, more recently, Taiwan and South Korea were able to reduce their population growth rates without widespread family-planning clinics, it is argued that the provision of these services will enable other countries desiring to control excessive population growth to do so more rapidly than if these family-planning services were not available.

A Simple Model   A basic model that economists use to demonstrate these adverse consequences of rapid population growth is a simplification of the standard Solow-type neoclassical growth equation.[23] Using the standard production function, $Y = f(K,L,R,T)$—that is, output is a function of capital, labor, resources, and technology—and holding the resource base fixed, we can derive the result that

$$y - l = \alpha(k - l) + t \tag{6.2}$$

where y = rate of GNI growth $\Delta Y/Y$, l = rate of labor force (population) growth $\Delta L/L$, k = rate of growth of the capital stock $\Delta K/K$, α = capital elasticity of output (usually found to be constant), and t = the effect of technological change (the Solow residual in empirical studies of sources of economic growth).

Assuming constant returns to scale, Equation 6.2 simply states that the rate of per capita income growth $(y-l)$ is directly proportional to the rate of growth of the capital-labor ratio $(k-l)$ plus the residual effects of technological progress (including improved human and physical capital). Therefore, in the absence of technological change, the higher the rate of population growth (l), the more rapid the rate of capital stock growth (k) must be and thus the greater the concomitant savings and investment rate just to maintain constant levels of per capita income. Moreover, because k may not be independent of l, as is traditionally assumed in neoclassical growth models, but may in fact be inversely related due to the reduced savings impact implied by the higher dependency burden effects of rapid population growth, it follows that the negative economic impact of population growth may even be greater than these models imply. Finally, if low incomes induce poor families to have more children as a source of cheap labor and old-age security, then we have another vicious circle in progress—poor people have large families partly to compensate for their poverty, but large families mean greater population growth, higher dependency burdens, lower savings, less investment, slower economic growth, and ultimately greater poverty. In an extreme case, a neo-Malthusian population trap can emerge. Population growth is thus seen as both a cause and a consequence of underdevelopment!

However, keep in mind that, as you saw in Chapters 3 and 4, population growth can tell only part of the story of economic growth. In this regard, William Easterly argued that "even if population growth lowered per capita growth one for one (the general view of the population alarmists), this would explain only about one-third of the variation in per capita growth."[24] Growth in productivity, especially as spurred by structural transformation of the economy (Chapter 3), is usually more important in economic development outcomes.

Other Empirical Arguments: Seven Negative Consequences of Population Growth   According to the latest empirical research, the potential negative consequences of population growth for economic development can be divided into seven categories: its impact on economic growth, poverty and inequality, education, health, food, the environment, and international migration.[25]

1. *Economic Growth.* Evidence shows that although it is not the culprit behind economic stagnation, rapid population growth lowers per capita income growth in most developing countries, especially those that are already poor, dependent on agriculture, and experiencing pressures on land and natural resources.

2. *Poverty and Inequality.* Even though aggregate statistical correlations between measures of poverty and population growth at the national level are often inconclusive, at the household level the evidence is strong and compelling. The negative consequences of rapid population growth fall most heavily on the poor because they are the ones who are made landless, suffer first from cuts in government health and education programs, and bear the brunt of environmental damage. Poor women once again bear the greatest burden of government austerity programs, and another vicious circle ensues. To the extent that large families perpetuate poverty, they also exacerbate inequality.

3. *Education.* Although the data are sometimes ambiguous on this point, it is generally agreed that large family size and low incomes restrict the opportunities of parents to educate all their children. At the national level, rapid population growth causes educational expenditures to be spread more thinly, lowering quality for the sake of quantity. This in turn feeds back on economic growth because the stock of human capital is reduced by rapid population growth.

4. *Health.* High fertility harms the health of mothers and children. It increases the health risks of pregnancy, and closely spaced births have been shown to reduce birth weight and increase child mortality rates.

5. *Food.* Feeding the world's population is made more difficult by rapid population growth—a large fraction of developing country food requirements are the result of population increases. New technologies of production must be introduced more rapidly, as the best lands have already been cultivated. International food relief programs become more widespread.

6. *Environment.* Rapid population growth contributes to environmental degradation in the form of forest encroachment, deforestation, fuelwood depletion, soil erosion, declining fish and animal stocks, inadequate and unsafe water, air pollution, and urban congestion (see Chapter 10).

7. *International Migration.* Many observers consider the increase in international migration, both legal and illegal, to be one of the major consequences of developing countries' population growth. Though many factors spur migration (see Chapter 7), an excess of job seekers (caused by rapid

population growth) over job opportunities is surely one of them. However, unlike the first six consequences listed here, some of the economic and social costs of international migration fall on recipient countries, increasingly in the developed world. It is not surprising, therefore, that this issue has recently taken on political importance in North America and Europe (see Chapter 2).

Goals and Objectives: Toward a Consensus

In spite of what may appear to be seriously conflicting arguments about the positive and negative consequences of population growth, a common ground has emerged on which many people on both sides of the debate can agree. This position is characterized succinctly by Robert Cassen:

> After decades of controversy over the issue of population policy, there is a new international consensus among and between industrial and developing countries that individuals, countries, and the world at large would be better off if population were to grow more slowly. The consequences of rapid population growth should be neither exaggerated nor minimized. Some past expressions of alarm have been counterproductive, alienating the very audiences they were intended to persuade; at the same time, claims that population growth was not all that important have had the effect of diminishing a proper concern for the subject.[26]

The following three propositions constitute the essential components of this intermediate or consensus opinion.

1. Population growth is not the primary cause of low levels of living, extreme inequalities, or the limited freedom of choice that characterize much of the developing world. The fundamental causes of these problems must be sought, rather, in the plight of poor families, especially women, and the failure of other aspects of domestic and international development policy.

2. The problem of population is not simply one of numbers but involves the quality of life and material well-being. Thus, developing country population size must be viewed in conjunction with developed-country affluence in relation to the quantity, distribution, and utilization of world resources, not just in relation to developing countries' indigenous resources.

3. Rapid population growth does serve to intensify problems of underdevelopment and to make prospects for development that much more remote. As noted, the momentum of growth means that, barring catastrophe, the population of developing countries will increase dramatically over the coming decades, no matter what fertility control measures are adopted now. It follows that high population growth rates, though not the principal cause of underdevelopment, are nevertheless important contributing factors in specific countries and regions of the world.

In view of these three propositions, we may conclude that the following three policy goals and objectives might be included in any realistic approach to the issue of population growth in developing countries.

1. In countries or regions where population size, distribution, and growth are viewed as an existing or potential problem, the primary objective of any strategy to limit further growth must deal not only with the population variable per se but also with the underlying social and economic conditions of underdevelopment. Problems such as absolute poverty, gross inequality, widespread unemployment (especially among women), limited female access to education, malnutrition, and poor health facilities must be given high priority. Their amelioration is both a necessary concomitant of development and a fundamental motivational basis for the expanded freedom of the individual to choose an optimal—and in many cases, smaller—family size.

2. To bring about smaller families through development-induced motivations, family-planning programs providing both the education and the technological means to regulate fertility for people who wish to regulate it should be established.

3. Developed countries should help developing countries achieve their lowered fertility and mortality objectives, not only by providing contraceptives and funding family-planning clinics, but also, even more important, by curtailing their own excessive depletion of nonrenewable world resources through programs designed to cut back on the unnecessary consumption of products that intensively use such resources; by making genuine commitments to eradicating poverty, illiteracy, disease, and malnutrition in developing countries as well as their own; and by recognizing in both their rhetoric and their international economic and social dealings that development is the real issue, not simply population control.

6.6 Some Policy Approaches

In view of these broad goals and objectives, what kinds of economic and social policies might developing and developed-country governments and international assistance agencies consider to bring about long-term reductions in the overall rate of world population growth? Three areas of policy can have important direct and indirect influences on the well-being of present and future world populations:

1. General and specific policies that developing country governments can initiate to influence and perhaps even control their population growth and distribution

2. General and specific policies that developed-country governments can initiate in their own countries to lessen their disproportionate consumption of limited world resources and promote a more equitable distribution of the benefits of global economic progress

3. General and specific policies that developed-country governments and international assistance agencies can initiate to help developing countries achieve their population objectives

Let us deal with each of these areas in turn.

What Developing Countries Can Do

Earlier discussions have led to the conclusion that the principal variables influencing the demand for children at the family level are the ones most closely associated with the concept of development as we have defined it in Chapter 1. Thus, certain development policies are particularly crucial in the transition from a high-growth to a low-growth population. These policies aim at eliminating absolute poverty; lessening income inequalities; expanding educational opportunities, especially for women; providing increased job opportunities for both men and women; bringing the benefits of modern preventive medicine and public health programs, especially the provision of clean water and sanitation, to the rural and urban poor; improving maternal and child health through more food, better diets, and improved nutrition so as to lower infant mortality; and creating a more equitable provision of other social services to wide segments of the population. Again, it is not numbers per se or parental irrationality that is at the root of the "population problem." Rather, it is the pervasiveness of absolute poverty and low levels of living that provide the economic rationale for large families and burgeoning populations. And it is the spillover effects or negative social externalities of these private parental decisions (e.g., for education, health care, food supplies, environment and resource degradation, job creation, overall growth, and income distribution) that provide the strictly economic efficiency justification (in terms of "market failure" arguments) for government intervention in population matters. Clearly, there are noneconomic justifications as well.

Although long-run development policies of the kind just outlined are essential to ultimate population stabilization, there are five more specific policies that developing country governments might try to adopt to lower birth rates in the short run.[27]

First, they can try to *persuade people* to have smaller families through the media and the educational process, both formal (school system) and informal (adult education).

Second, they can *enhance family-planning programs* to provide health and contraceptive services to encourage the desired behavior. Such publicly sponsored or officially supported programs now exist in most developing countries. Today only a few countries do not have such publicly sponsored or officially endorsed family-planning programs. However, there remains substantial unmet demand for contraceptives, as seen in Box 6.3.

Third, they can deliberately *manipulate economic incentives and disincentives* for having children—for example, through the elimination or reduction of maternity leaves and benefits, the reduction or elimination of financial incentives, or the imposition of financial penalties for having children beyond a certain number; the establishment of old-age social security provisions and minimum-age child labor laws; the raising of fees and elimination of heavy public subsidies for higher education; and the subsidization of smaller families through direct money payments. Although some form of population-related *incentive or disincentive schemes* now exist in over 30 developing countries, Singapore, India, Bangladesh, South Korea, and China have been especially prominent in experimenting with policies to reduce family size. For example, Singapore allocated scarce public housing without giving consideration to

BOX 6.3 FINDINGS Contraceptives Need and Use in Developing Countries, 2003 to 2012

Jacqueline Darroch and Susheela Singh analyzed the use and need for contraceptives in developing countries, using data from comparable national surveys for married and unmarried women ages 15 to 49 in 2003, 2008, and 2012. Darroch and Singh estimated numbers and percentages of women wanting to avoid pregnancy, according to whether they were using modern contraceptives, or using either no method or only a traditional method. They found that "the number of women wanting to avoid pregnancy and therefore needing effective contraception increased substantially," from 716 million in 2003 to 867 million in 2012. Most of the increase corresponded to population growth. The percentage of women wishing to avoid pregnancy also rose, from 54% in 2003 to 57% in 2012. At the same time, the "use of modern contraceptive methods also increased, and the overall proportion" of all women ages 15-49 "with "unmet need for modern methods among those wanting to avoid pregnancy decreased," from 29% in 2003, to 26% in 2012 (although the number rose from 210 million to 222 million). The unmet need for modern contraceptives among those wanting to avoid pregnancy remained very high, "especially in sub-Saharan Africa (53 million [60%] of 89 million), south Asia (83 million [34%] of 246 million), and western Asia (14 million [50%] of 27 million)." The authors maintained that, "to meet the unmet need for modern contraception, countries need to increase resources, improve access to contraceptive services and supplies, and provide high-quality services and large-scale public education interventions to reduce social barriers."

Source: Jacqueline Darroch and Susheela Singh. "Trends in contraceptive need and use in developing countries in 2003, 2008, and 2012: An analysis of national surveys." *The Lancet* 381 (May 18, 2013): 1756–1762.

family size. It also limited paid maternity leave to a maximum of two children, scaling the delivery fee according to number of children and reducing income tax relief from five to three children. In 1984, it even went so far as to give special priority in school admission to all children born to women with university degrees while penalizing non-degree-holding women with more than two children. The presumed but dubious rationale was that educated women have brighter children whose births should be encouraged while discouraging the less educated (and presumably less intelligent) women from bearing more children. But fertility fell so dramatically that by 2004, the city-state had introduced incentives to *increase* fertility (as with Japan and Europe, relaxed controls on immigration would be more cost-effective). China has by far the most comprehensive set of state-enforced incentives and disincentives; they are described in the case study at the end of this chapter.

Fourth, governments can attempt to *coerce people* into having smaller families through the power of state legislation and penalties. For obvious reasons, few governments would attempt to engage in such coercion; not only is it often morally repugnant and politically unacceptable, but it is also almost always extremely difficult to administer. The defeat of Indian Prime Minister Indira Gandhi's government in 1977 was largely due to popular resentment of the government's forced-sterilization program.

Finally, no policy measures will be successful in controlling fertility unless efforts are made to *raise the social and economic status of women* and hence create conditions favorable to delayed marriage and lower marital fertility.[28] A crucial ingredient in any program designed to lower fertility rates is the increased education of women, followed by the creation of jobs for them outside the home. The availability of income-earning opportunities can lead young women to delay marriage by enabling them to become economically self-sufficient and therefore in a better position to exercise control over their choice of partner and the timing of marriage. It can also reduce family pressures for early marriage by allowing women to make a contribution to parental household income. An independent source of income also secures a stronger position for married women in the household, reducing their dependence on other family members, particularly male offspring, for economic security. Furthermore, it enables women to consider the opportunity costs of additional children when childbearing competes with income-generating activities. In general, the availability of outside sources of income offers women genuine alternatives to early marriage and frequent childbearing, which are often motivated by their lack of resources. An additional benefit of employment outside the home is that it reduces women's isolation, which is often an impediment to the provision of family-planning services, and can increase their household bargaining power.[29]

The importance of these policies to improve the role and status of women was underlined at the 1994 Cairo International Conference on Population and Development, where emphasis was placed on the general empowerment of women, especially in the area of **reproductive choice**. The Cairo Program of Action summarized this position in the following manner:

> The empowerment and autonomy of women and the improvement of their political, social, economic and health status . . . [are] essential for the achievement of sustainable development and . . . for the long-term success of population programs. Experience shows that population and development programs are most effective when steps have simultaneously been taken to improve the status of women.[30]

Reproductive choice   The concept that women should be able to determine on an equal status with their husbands and for themselves how many children they want and what methods to use to achieve their desired family size.

What the Developed Countries Can Do

When we view the problems of population from the perspective of global resources and the environment, as we should, the question of the relationship between population size and distribution and the depletion of many nonrenewable resources in developed and underdeveloped countries assumes major importance. In a world where 4.5% of the population, located in one country, the United States, accounts for nearly one-fifth of the annual world total energy use, we are clearly not dealing only or even primarily with a problem of population numbers when it comes to environment and resources. We must also be concerned with the impact of rising affluence and the very unequal worldwide distribution of incomes on the depletion of many nonrenewable resources such as petroleum, certain basic metals, and other raw materials essential for economic growth. The use of fossil fuel energy to power private automobiles, operate home and office air conditioners, and so on in the developed nations remains the major contributor of carbon dioxide (CO_2) gases into the atmosphere and to the phenomenon of greenhouse global warming (see Chapter 10).[31] It also means that there is potentially that much less to fertilize small family farms in the less developed nations. Alternatively, it means that poor families will have to pay more to obtain these valuable resource inputs.

Many similar examples could be given of the gross inequalities in global resource use. Perhaps more important, one could cite innumerable instances of the unnecessary and costly waste of many scarce and nonrenewable resources by the affluent developed nations. The point, therefore, is that any worldwide program designed to engender a better balance between resources and people by limiting developing-country population growth through social intervention and family planning must also include the responsibility of rich nations to simplify their own consumption demands and lifestyles. Such changes would free resources that could then be used by poor nations to generate the social and economic development essential to slowing population growth.

In addition to simplifying lifestyles and consumption habits, one other positive (if unlikely) internal policy that rich nations could adopt to mitigate current world population problems would be to liberalize the legal conditions for the international immigration of poor, unskilled workers and their families from Africa, Asia, and Latin America to North America, Europe, Japan, and Australia. The international migration of peasants from Europe to North America, Australia, and New Zealand in the nineteenth and early twentieth centuries was a major factor in moderating the problems of underdevelopment and population pressure in European countries. No such safety valve or outlet exists today for developing countries. In fact, what few outlets existed have over the past two decades been progressively closed. Yet clearly, many labor-scarce societies could benefit economically from international migration, and the benefits to developing countries would be enormous. For example, the United Nations has estimated that legal barriers to international migration from the developing to the developed world cost developing nations at least $250 billion a year.[32]

How Developed Countries Can Help Developing Countries with Their Population Programs

There are a number of ways in which the governments of rich countries and multilateral donor agencies can help the governments of developing countries achieve their population policy objectives sooner. The most important of these concerns the willingness of rich countries to be of genuine assistance to poor countries in their development efforts, particularly in sub-Saharan Africa. Such genuine support would consist not only of expanded public and private financial assistance but also of improved trade relations, such as tariff- and quota-free access to developed-country markets, more appropriate technology transfers, assistance in developing indigenous scientific research capacities, better international commodity-pricing policies, and a more equitable sharing of the world's scarce natural resources. (These and other areas of international economic relations between rich and poor countries will be examined in Part Three.)

There are two other activities more directly related to fertility moderation in which rich-country governments, international donor agencies, and private nongovernmental organizations (NGOs) can play an important assisting role. The first is the area of research into the technology of fertility control, the contraceptive pill, modern intrauterine devices (IUDs), voluntary sterilization procedures, and, particularly in the age of AIDS, effective barrier contraception. Research has been going on in this area for a number of years, almost all of it financed by international donor organizations, private foundations, and aid agencies of developed countries. Further efforts to improve the effectiveness of this low-cost contraceptive technology while minimizing the health risks should be encouraged.

The second area includes financial assistance from developed countries for family-planning programs, public education, and national population policy research activities in the developing countries. This has traditionally been the primary area of developed-country assistance in the field of population. Total resources devoted to these activities have risen dramatically. It remains an open question, however, whether such resources (especially those allocated to premature family-planning programs) might not have been more effectively used to achieve their fertility goals had they instead been devoted directly to helping low-income countries to raise the levels of living of their poorest people. As pointed out earlier, it is of little value to have sophisticated family-planning programs when people are not motivated to reduce family size.

We conclude with a note of optimism. Fertility rates in many of the poorest countries, such as Bangladesh and most of the countries in sub-Saharan Africa, have experienced an impressive decline. Population experts have lowered their estimates of world population growth for coming decades. In no small part, this decline is the result of more widespread availability of family planning. This change helps set the stage for an opportunity for successful development efforts in the coming years, but developed countries need to do their part in providing expanded development assistance, especially efforts focused on the need and opportunity to greatly reduce the incidence of poverty, which remains the biggest cause of high rates of fertility.

Population, Poverty, and Development: China and India

Two of the world's fastest growing economies, China and India, also happen to be the world's two most populous nations, with some 1.35 billion and 1.22 billion people, respectively. Both countries continue to grow, albeit at slower paces. According to the 2012 UN Population Division's medium-variant projections, by 2030 India will become the world's most populous nation, with 1.48 billion people. The United Nations projects a population of 1.45 billion in China by 2030, which is then projected to fall to about 1.28 billion by about 2065. In contrast, India's population is projected to continue growing until about 2065, reaching a peak of about 1.64 billion around 2065 before its population finally starts to decline.

India's 2013 population of more than 1.2 billion is well over triple the number at independence, despite introducing the world's first family-planning policy in 1950. At 1.35 billion, China's population remains larger, but its highly restrictive one-child policy, despite being fairly successful at slowing fertility, has apparently been less successful than approaches based on women's empowerment and education in some parts of India, such as the state of Kerala. What can we learn about population and development from the world's most populous countries?

In India, it is common to hear the view that "everything is growing faster in China than India, except for population." India, which had well under two-thirds of China's population half a century ago, is projected to surpass China's population by 200 million people by 2050. Like most developing countries, both countries' populations grew rapidly when their mortality rates fell and their birth rates fell much more slowly. Both countries have viewed population pressures as threatening prospects for future development.

It is well known that as incomes rise, fertility falls, due largely to the increased opportunity cost of women's time. The causality between fertility and growth runs in both directions. China's rapid economic growth since about 1980 has also been attributed in part to its lower fertility rate. India's increased growth rate since about 1990 may also be related to its more moderate decline in fertility. Both may reflect in part the "demographic dividend" examined earlier in the chapter. Thus, population policy can potentially play an important role in setting the stage for growth. Moreover, to the degree that we accept Nobel economics laureate Amartya Sen's view that development is freedom, the greater opportunities available to young women when fertility is reduced or delayed is itself a key indicator of development success, and population policy can help realize these goals.

Population Policy in China

China has been the world's most populous nation for centuries. After the Communist takeover in 1949, Chinese leaders led by Mao Zedong took a broadly pronatalist stance, believing that a communist society could solve any population problems and that a larger population would mean a more powerful country. Mao (whom China's leaders still call "60% right" about policy) went so far as to send advocates of population control to jail. However, in the face of famine in the late 1950s, these policies moderated.

In 1980, China initiated a tough new drive to deter births, with a goal of lowering the annual birth rate to 1% during the decade. Stringent and often

draconian measures to achieve that goal were introduced in 1982 and 1983 as the Chinese government adopted a policy of one child per family. Social and political pressures to limit family size to one child included requiring women to appeal to the neighborhood committee or council for formal permission to become pregnant. Although first births were routinely approved, second births were usually approved only if the first child had a serious birth defect or if the woman had remarried. Economic incentives included giving priority to one-child families in housing, medical care, and education. Mothers of two or more children were often denied promotions, and steep fines, sometimes in excess of 10 times China's per capita income, were levied for second and third children. Although a growing number of exceptions have been introduced in recent years, notably allowing a second child if the first child is a girl, and allowing a second child if *both* parents are themselves only children; at the Third Plenum in 2013, it was announced that the policy would be relaxed further, with a second child permitted if *either* parent is an only child (subject to verification by the government). Despite these adjustments, the policy remains probably the most restrictive in the world.

Given such rigid national policies and a strong cultural preference for boys, it is not surprising that there have been many reports of girls receiving less medical attention and also of selective abortion of female fetuses and even female infanticide ("gendercide").

Male-to-female ratios are higher than the normal level in many Asian countries, and gender bias is at least partly to blame. Amartya Sen's pioneering 1992 research estimated that 44 to 50 million women were already "missing" in China, depending on whether the comparison is to Western countries or to Africa. The most recent data confirm that these trends have continued, with Stephan Klasen and Claudia Wink calculating that well over 6% of women are "missing" in China. It is estimated that in 2010, there were 106 males for every 100 females in China overall; and in a trend pointing to a worsening of the problem, close to 118 boys were born for every 100 girls. Such balance is all but unprecedented in recorded world history. Of course, these current cultural preferences may change with further economic development. In fact, this ratio is now falling, albeit very, slightly, from a recent peak ratio of 120 boys to 100 girls, according to official government data.

The full impact of China's population control programs is uncertain. Only time will tell whether the benefits of reduced population growth achieved through severe social and economic pressures for one-child families will be worth the cost of a harsh break with traditional family norms and perceptions regarding the value of children. Resistance in rural areas, where well over 60% of the population still resides, was apparently so widespread that in August 1988, when the Chinese government discovered to its surprise that the population had already passed the 1 billion mark, it decided to increase its enforcement of the one-child norm in rural as well as urban areas. However, popular opposition again caused it to relax its stringent controls slightly and to focus more on elevating the status of women and providing greater old-age security.

By the mid-1990s, China's fertility rate reached 1.9 births per woman, and it fell further to below 1.6 by 2013. This rate is below replacement level and is consistent with a slow long-term decline in population growth. Because of population momentum, China's population has continued to grow as larger, younger cohorts replace smaller, older ones. However, the country's largest cohorts are now passing out of their childbearing years. The population growth rate has slowed dramatically, and the population is not expected to exceed 1.4 billion at its peak before starting to fall.

In practice, many families have two children rather than one, and others in rural areas, including ethnic minorities exempted from the one-child policy, have more than two children. But fertility rates are extremely low in the urban areas to which an increasing share of the rural population is moving. Typical estimates suggest that upward of 250 million fewer people were born in China than would have been born without the one-child policy—an enormous impact. There are now concerns that China will have to reevaluate the policy to prevent too high a dependency ratio of retired to working adults.

The apparent success of China's tough fertility policies has led some observers to see advantages of dictatorship rather than democracy in spurring development. But in fact there are several ways

in which the lack of a free press in particular and democracy more generally has held back China's development. In Mao's "Great Leap Forward," at least 30 million people died due to poor government decisions and incentives for bureaucrats to send overly optimistic reports from the field. Democratic India, by contrast, has not had a famine since independence in 1947. Amartya Sen attributes China's lead in economic growth to its massive investments in health and education, which India has lacked. Dictatorship can be good or bad for fertility programs or any other aspects of development. But the risks of a very bad outcome are probably much lower with democracy.

Successful population control in China comes with its own risks and unintended consequences as well as substantial rewards. By 2050, China will have almost twice as many people above age 50 as below age 20. In addition, while fertility has fallen, preference for boys over girls has actually intensified. Many Chinese families seem to feel that if they are to have only one child, it should be a boy, to carry on the family name and help support the parents in their old age. A 2007 report from China's State Population and Family Planning Commission concluded that the country may have about 30 million more men than women of marriageable age by 2020 and warned that the result could be social instability. A 2009 study by economists Shang-Jin Wei and Xiaobo Zhang provided robust evidence that China's recent new surge in savings is caused in large part by competitive investments in housing and other wealth accumulation by families seeking to attract brides for their sons. Such a savings surge even has potential implications for global imbalances (see Chapters 12 and 13).

The high fraction of the population now of working age has provided, in China's case at least, a "demographic dividend." But the next phase of the demographic transition is likely to pose major challenges for China, with its big drops in fertility ahead of historical patterns in other countries; hence the saying that "China must get rich before it gets old." But as far as is known, no society has ever faced such rapid population aging. By 2013, the labor force in China had already begun to slowly shrink.

In sum, although rapid economic growth and coercion and incentives in family planning account for part of China's drop in fertility, other factors include female literacy, improved child health, and greater economic opportunities for women. These have also been factors in the strong success in fertility reduction in the Indian state of Kerala.

Population Policy in India

In 1949, India became the first country to implement a national family-planning program. It has proved to be relatively ineffective and has proceeded in fits and starts. By the early 1970s, observers were becoming increasingly alarmed by the very high rate of population growth in India.

When Prime Minister Indira Gandhi tried to implement drastic population control in 1975–1977, a period during which she seized dictatorial powers, it was a failure. Reports of forced sterilizations, sometimes in mass "sterilization camps," and other coercive measures ended up giving family planning a bad reputation in many areas of the country. Indeed, public revulsion toward these coercive fertility policies helped bring the "emergency" period to an end more quickly, and when elections were held in 1977, Gandhi was voted out of office. Her return to power in the elections of 1980 was made possible in part by her commitment not to reintroduce coercive birth control policies. Years later, villagers in some parts of India avoided health workers out of fear of forced sterilization.

However, family planning did become more widely practiced. Some of the acceptance of limits on family size reflected rising income among the close to 250 million middle-class Indians and somewhat improved conditions among a significant fraction of the poor. Some of it reflected modest moves back to policy incentives to encourage smaller families. There have been variations from state to state. In Madhya Pradesh, individuals who had a third or subsequent child after January 2001 were banned from running for election to village council posts, spurring considerable controversy. In 2004, an uproar over reported higher fertility among Muslims than among Hindus—reports that turned out to be greatly exaggerated—revealed the continuing political sensitivity of the issue.

As fertility has fallen, a preference for boys over girls has developed, particularly in the "Hindi belt" in northern India. The result is a "missing women" problem parallel to China's. Stronger male bias is

actually found in the better-off states of India, and researchers Jean Drèze, Anne-Catherine Guio, and Mamta Murthi found that "female disadvantage in child survival is significantly lower in districts with higher poverty levels."

P. N. Mari Bhat and A. J. Francis Zavier analyzed data from the National Family Health Survey and estimated that "in northern India, girls currently constitute about 60% of the unwanted births and that the elimination of unwanted fertility has the potential to raise the sex ratio at birth to 130 boys per 100 girls." Such a dramatic imbalance seems likely to lead to future social stress. As of 2010, the ratio of males to females in India as a whole had reached 108 to 100, one of the highest in the world; the ratio at birth is now approximately 112 to 100. But this imbalance is not inevitable—social development can make all the difference.

Kerala, a state on India's southwest coast that has emphasized poverty reduction and human development, is an important case in point. By the mid-1990s, Kerala's fertility rate had fallen to just 1.7 births per woman and has remained low—still 1.7 in 2010 (Indian Planning Commission)—implying a slowly falling population over time (in the absence of in-migration). Thus, Kerala's fertility rate was until recently less than that of China, but unlike China, the dramatic reductions in fertility in Kerala were achieved without coercion, let alone China's huge direct economic incentives for lowered fertility. In India overall, the fertility rate is 2.5, and in Bihar, a socially backward state, the fertility rate in 2010 was 3.7, similar to that of Pakistan. Overall, there are actually slightly more females than males in Kerala.

Norms of behavior can be highly influential, and multiple equilibria resulting from different expected norms of behavior are possible, as explored in Chapter 4 and applied to population norms in this chapter in section 6.4. There has been a slow but steady movement in attitudes toward the notion that a happy family is a small family in the India of today. Amartya Sen has observed that sharp declines in the rate of fertility in India in literate states, particularly Kerala and Tamil Nadu, was greatly influenced by public discourse on the negative impacts of high fertility. Discussions have emphasized problems caused both for young women and for communities as a whole.

In addition, and especially more recently, greater awareness on the part of rural women of urban norms of women's empowerment, facilitated by village television and the Internet, may have made a big impact, proving that cultural awareness can be powerful. Robert Jensen and Emily Oster provide some evidence on the power of television in India.

While television, billboard, and other advertising in India has promoted family planning, and there is some evidence that these campaigns can have some positive impact on their own, such efforts have been far more successful when the social climate has changed enough to be receptive to the message. This helps explain why nongovernmental organizations working for comprehensive rural development have often apparently had more success than many government programs. In Kerala, if the official campaigns supporting small families have seemed more effective than elsewhere, it is largely because both social and economic conditions on the ground changed previously or simultaneously. More than 85% of women in Kerala are literate, which means they have more power in the household and opportunities in the workforce as well as the ability to read print materials about fertility and family planning. Some of Kerala's success is due to the traditionally higher status of women in the local culture. But there is no reason that Kerala's success cannot be duplicated elsewhere in India if there is the political and social will.

Sen concluded that Kerala's impressive results in fertility reduction were achieved through active public dialogue that resulted ultimately in the emergence of new social attitudes and values—and that such dialogues on this sensitive subject were possible only because of the very high level of female literacy in the state. Indeed, Sen pointed out that female literacy in Kerala was unmatched by any of China's provinces.

The success of Kerala suggests that fertility reduction may depend not on rapid economic growth or even, in its absence, on draconian governmental policies but rather on grassroots human development that emphasizes women's empowerment, in which civil society plays a leading role. ∎

Sources

Acharya, Keya. "Sterilisation in India." *Contemporary Review* 279 (2001): 26.

Amartya Sen, "What's the point of a development strategy," paper written for the United Nations Committee on Development Strategy and Management of the Market Economy, May 1996, page 20.

Barro, Robert J. *Determinants of Economic Growth: A Cross-Country Empirical Study.* Cambridge, Mass.: MIT Press, 1997.

"Can advertising create social change?" *Businessline*, January 20, 2000, p. 1.

Dasgupta, Partha. "The population problem: Theory and evidence." *Journal of Economic Literature* 33 (1995): 1879–1902.

Drèze, Jean, Anne-Catherine Guio, and Mamta Murthi. "Mortality, fertility, and gender bias in India: A district-level analysis." *Population and Development Review* 21 (1995): 745–782.

Drèze, Jean, and Mamta Murthi. "Fertility, education, and development: Evidence from India." *Population and Development Review* 27 (2001): 33–63.

Jensen, Robert, and Emily Oster. "The power of TV: Cable television and women's status in India." *Quarterly Journal of Economics* 124 (2009): 1057–1094.

Klasen, Stephan and Claudia Wink, "Missing women: Revisiting the debate." *Feminist Economics*, 9 (2–3), 2003, 263–299

Kremer, Michael. "Population growth and technological change: One million B.C. to 1990." *Quarterly Journal of Economics* 108 (1993): 681–716.

Mari Bhat, P. N., and Francis Zavier, A. J. "Fertility decline and gender bias in northern India." *Demography* 40 (2003): 637–657.

McElroy, Marjorie, and Dennis Tao Yang. "Carrots and sticks: Fertility effects of China's population policies." *American Economic Review* 90 (May 2000): 389–392.

Pritchett, Lant H. "Desired fertility and the impact of population policies." *Population and Development Review* 20 (1994): 1–55.

Sen, Amartya. *Development as Freedom.* New York: Knopf, 1999.

Sen, Amartya. "Missing women." *British Medical Journal* 304 (1992): 587–588.

Sunil, T. S., V. K. Pillai, and A. Pandey. "Do incentives matter? Evaluation of a family planning program in India." *Population Research and Policy Review* 18 (1999): 563–577.

Wei, Shang-Jin and Xiaobo Zhang. "The competitive saving motive: Evidence from rising sex ratios and savings rates in China.", *Journal of Political Economy* 119 (2011): 511–564.

Concepts for Review

Crude birth rate	Life expectancy at birth	Rate of population increase
Death rate	Malthusian population trap	Replacement fertility
Demographic transition	Microeconomic theory of fertility	Reproductive choice
Doubling time	Natural increase	Total fertility rate (TFR)
Family-planning programs	Net international migration	Under-5 mortality rate
Hidden momentum of population growth	Population-poverty cycle	Youth dependency ratio
	Population pyramid	

Questions for Discussion

1. Population growth in developing nations has proceeded at unprecedented rates over the past few decades. Compare and contrast the present rate of population growth in less developed countries with that of the modern developed nations during their early growth years. What has been the major factor contributing to rapid developing country population growth since the Second World War? Explain your answer.

2. What is the relationship between the age structure of a population and its dependency burden? Is the dependency burden higher or lower in developing countries? Why?

3. Explain the notion of the hidden momentum of population growth. Why is this an important concept for projecting future population trends in different developing nations?

4. Describe briefly the theory of the demographic transition. At what stage in this transition do most developing countries seem to be? Explain your answer.

5. How does the microeconomic theory of fertility relate to the theory of consumer choice? Do you think that economic incentives and disincentives influence family size decisions? Explain your answer, giving some specific examples of such incentives and disincentives.

6. "The world population problem is not just a matter of expanding numbers but also one of rising affluence and limited resources. It is as much a problem caused by developed nations as it is one deriving from developing countries." Comment on this statement.

7. List and briefly describe the principal causes of high population growth in developing countries and the major consequences.

8. Explain why fertility rates are falling much more rapidly in some developing countries than in others.

9. Outline and comment briefly on some of the arguments *against* the idea that population growth is a serious problem in developing nations.

10. Outline and comment briefly on some of the arguments *in support of* the idea that population growth is a serious problem in developing nations.

11. Outline and comment briefly on the various policy options available to developing countries' governments in their attempt to modify or limit the rate of population growth.

12. Suppose that a study finds that there is complementarity in fertility decisions. What would this mean? What are the possible implications?

13. What aspects of population policy alternatives—including their strengths and weaknesses—are illustrated by the cases of China and India?

Notes

1. The 1970s marked the apogee in the history of world population growth. By the end of the decade, rates had begun to decline in a large number of developing countries, and it became clear that the pace of world population growth had peaked. For some evidence of this turning point, see Bernard Berelson, W. Parker Mauldin, and Sheldon Segal, "Population: Current status and policy options," *Social Science and Medicine* 14c (1980): 71–97, and World Bank, *World Development Report, 1984* (New York: Oxford University Press, 1984), ch. 4.

2. A convenient shorthand method of calculating doubling time is simply to divide any growth rate into the number 70. For example, something (an asset, population, GNI, etc.) growing at 2% per year will double its value in approximately 35 years. You may recall from algebra that the doubling time of a value (such as the real GNI of an economy) growing at rate $p\%$ per year may be found with the formula $[1+p/100]^T = 2$. Taking natural logs of each side, T $ln[1+p/100]$ ln 2. The natural log of 2 is approximately 0.7. On the

left- hand side, for small p, $ln[1+p/100]$ is approximately equal to $p/100$. Substituting, $Tp/100 = 0.7$, or $T = 70/p$. For example, for reasonably small values of growth such as 4%, simply divide 70 by the percentage growth: After about $70/4 = 17.5$ years, national income would double. As an additional approximation, to find the growth of income per capita, simply subtract the rate of population growth. So if population is growing at 2% per year, in this example, income per capita would be growing at $4\% - 2\% = 2\%$ per year, and income per capita would double in approximately $70/2 = 35$ years.

3. Population Reference Bureau, *World Population Data Sheet, 2012* (Washington, D.C.: Population Reference Bureau, 2012).

4. The World Bank, *World Bank World Development Indicators 2013* (Washington, D.C.: The World Bank), tab. 2.1.

5. For more discussion, see John Bongaarts, "Population policy options in the developing world," *Science* 263 (1994): 771–776.

6. For an interesting reverse-population-alarmist perspective, see Philip Longman, "Think again: Global aging," *Foreign Policy* (2012).

7. Replacement fertility may be approximated by the value of TFRR $\approx$ (1+SRB)/p(A$_M$), where TFRR represents the replacement value for the total fertility rate, SRB represents the ratio of male to female births, and p(A$_M$) represents the probability of surviving to the mean age of the fertility schedule. See Samuel Preston, Patrick Heuveline, and Michel Guillo, *Demography: Measuring and Modeling Population Processes* (Oxford: Blackwell, 2001). Note that with gender balance and high female survival to mean fertility schedule (close to 30 years of age), the TFRR is close to 2.1. But when survival proportions are among the lowest in the world—close to 0.60 in the cases of Afghanistan, Burundi, and Sierra Leone; replacement total fertility rates above 3.3 are implied. Under these conditions, a fertility rate of 2.1 would actually result in population decline. See Thomas J. Espenshade, Juan Carlos Guzman, and Charles F. Westoff, "The surprising global variation in replacement fertility," *Population Research and Policy Review* 22, No. 5-6 (2003): 575–583, who calculate that the replacement rate across countries ranges from 2.05 to 3.43.

8. See Timothy W. Guinnane, "The historical fertility transition: A guide for economists," *Journal of Economic Literature* 49, No. 3 (2011): 589–614.

9. A geometric progression is simply a doubling (or some other multiple) of each previous number, as in 1, 2, 4, 8, 16, 32, 64, 128, 256, 512, 1,024, and so on. Like compound interest, geometric progressions have a way of reaching large numbers very rapidly.

10. Recent supporting evidence is found in Quamrul Ashraf and Oded Galor, "Dynamics and stagnation in the Malthusian epoch,"*American Economic Review* 101, No. 5 (2011): 2003–2041. The authors find that "technological superiority and higher land productivity had significant positive effects on population density but insignificant effects on the standard of living, during the time period 1–1500 CE."

10a. At lower levels of expected fertility, the slope of the S-shaped curve may increase at an *increasing* rate due to the presence of older children who can take care of younger siblings, together with a stronger family response to the negative impact of average fertility on wages and/or the decreased probability that any one child will gain formal-sector employment. But at higher levels of expected fertility, the slope of the S-shaped curve may increase at a *decreasing* rate due to worsening availability of education and health and increasing costs of raising additional children in relation to the benefits of doing so.

11. This interpretation is from Partha Dasgupta, *An Inquiry into Well-Being and Destitution* (New York: Oxford University Press, 1993), and is discussed in Pranab Bardhan and Chris Udry, *Development Microeconomics* (New York: Oxford University Press, 1999), p. 25.

12. The classic contribution is Simon Kuznets, *Fertility Differentials between Less Developed and Developed Regions: Components and Implications* (New Haven, Conn.: Economic Growth Center, Yale University, 1974).

13. See Chapter 9, and see Christopher Udry, "Gender, agricultural production, and the theory of the household," *Journal of Political Economy* 104 (1996): 1010–1046.

14. See, for example, Nancy Birdsall, "Economic approaches to population growth," in *Handbook of Development Economics*, vol. 1, eds. Hollis B. Chenery and T. N. Srinwasan (Amsterdam: Elsevier, 1988), pp. 478–542; Jean Drèze, Anne-Catherine Guio, and Mamta Murthi, "Mortality, fertility, and gender bias in India: A district-level analysis," *Population and Development Review* 21 (1995): 745–782; and Partha Dasgupta, "The population problem: Theory and evidence," *Journal of Economic Literature* 33 (1995): 1879–1902.

15. For empirical evidence that low fertility results mostly from economic, social, cultural, and educational improvements in a population and only slightly from the availability of family-planning programs, see Lant H. Pritchett, "Desired fertility and the impact of population policies," *Population and Development Review* 20 (1994): 1–55.

16. For an analysis of this conflict, see Jason L. Finkle and Barbara Crane, "The politics of Bucharest: Population, development, and the new international economic order," *Population and Development Review* 1 (1975): 87–114. Although this conflict was less visible in the Second World Population Conference held in Mexico City in August 1984 and was a minor issue beneath that of reproductive choice and the empowerment of women at the Third Conference held in Cairo in 1994, it remained prominent in the discussions of many developing-world delegates.

17. For a more detailed discussion of these divergent opinions, see Michael S. Teitelbaum, "Population and development: Is a consensus possible?" *Foreign Affairs* 52 (1974): 749–757. See also Timothy King and Allen Kelley, *The New Population Debate: Two Views on Population Growth and Economic Development* (Washington, D.C.: Population Reference Bureau, 1985), and Robert H. Cassen, *Population Policy: A New Consensus* (Washington, D.C.: Overseas Development Council, 1994).

18. See, for example, Colin Clark, "The 'population explosion' myth," *Bulletin of the Institute of Development Studies* 1 (1969); Julian Simon, *The Ultimate Resource* (Princeton, N.J.: Princeton University Press, 1981); Nick Eberstadt, "Population and economic growth," *Wilson Quarterly* (Winter 1986), pp. 95–129; and National Research Council, *Population Growth and Economic Development: Policy Questions* (Washington, D.C.: National Academy Press, 1986).

19. Samir Amin, "Underpopulated Africa," paper presented at the African Population Conference, Accra, Ghana, December 1971.

20. Ibid., fn. 2.

21. Ibid., p. 3. Of course, in the decades after these arguments were promulgated, population did dramatically increase in these regions. For another perspective on long-run benefits of greater population density via faster technological progress, see Michael Kremer, "Population growth and technological change: One million B.C. to 1990," *Quarterly Journal of Economics* 108 (1993): 681–716.

22. For example, see Paul R. Ehrlich and Anne H. Ehrlich, *Population, Resources, and Environment: Issues in Human Ecology*, 2nd ed. (New York: Freeman, 1972); Lester R. Brown, *In the Human Interest: A Strategy to Stabilize World Population* (New York: Norton, 1974); and Paul R. Ehrlich and Anne H. Ehrlich, *The Population Explosion* (New York: Simon & Schuster, 1990).

23. We are grateful to Professor Harold Votey for suggesting this illustration. Details on the Solow model are found in Chapter 3 and Appendix 3.2.

24. William Easterly made the very basic argument in 1999 that "population growth does not vary enough across countries to explain variations in per capita growth. GDP per capita growth varies between −2 and +7 percent for all countries between 1960 and 1992. Population growth varies only between 1 and 4 percent." Easterly, *The Elusive Quest for Growth* (Cambridge, Mass.: MIT Press, 1999), p. 92.

25. For a detailed review of this evidence, see Cassen, *Population Policy*, pp. 14–22; Dennis A. Ahlburg et al., *Population and Economic Development: A Report to the Government of the Commonwealth of Australia* (Canberra: Australian International Development Assistance Bureau, 1994); and Geoffrey McNicoll, "Effects of population growth: Visions and revisions," *Population and Development Review* 21 (1995): 307–340. As the Ahlburg report demonstrates, not all of these consequences are unambiguously negative. Much depends on the particular country and its demographic situation.

26. Robert Cassen, *Population Policy*, p. 12.

27. See Birdsall, "Economic approaches to population growth," pp. 523–529.

28. Sousan Abadian, "Women's autonomy and its impact on fertility," *World Development* 24 (1996): 1793–1809. See also Shireen J. Jeejeebhoy, *Women's Education, Autonomy, and Reproductive Behavior: Experiences from Developing Countries* (Oxford: Clarendon Press, 1995).

29. See Fenohasina Maret-Rakotondrazaka, "The effect of working outside the home on women's empowerment in Nigeria," Working Paper, George Washington University, 2014.

30. United Nations, *International Conference*, para. 4.1. See also Nancy Folbre, "Engendering economics: New perspectives on women, work, and demographic change," in *Proceedings of the World Bank Annual Conference on Development Economics, 1995,* eds. Michael Bruno and Boris Pleskovic (Washington, D.C.: World Bank, 1996).

31. The United Nations Population Fund's *State of the World's Population* 2009 edition (New York: United Nations, 2009) examines relationships between population and climate change. Cited energy data are from World Resources Institute, *World Resources, 2005* (New York: Oxford University Press, 2005), tab. 7.

32. More detail on the scale and benefits of remittances from international migration is provided in Chapter 14.

7

Urbanization and Rural-Urban Migration: Theory and Policy

Cities will increasingly become the main players in the global economy.
—*Kofi Annan, former secretary general of the United Nations and Nobel laureate for Peace*

The global economy is led by metropolitan economies.
—*Brookings Institution*, Global MetroMonitor, 2010

More than one billion persons are living in slums. With rapid urbanization it is expected that in the next two decades there will be nearly two billion new urban residents, 90% of them in developing countries.
—*World Bank,* Addressing the Urbanization Challenge, 2013

Any strategy for a less desperate and more deliberate urbanization must include efforts to improve public services in rural areas.
—*World Bank,* World Development Report, 2009

In this chapter, we focus on one of the most complex and nuanced dilemmas of the development process: the phenomenon of massive and historically unprecedented movements of people from the rural countryside to the burgeoning cities of Africa, Asia, and Latin America. In Chapter 6, we documented the extraordinary increase in world and especially developing-country populations over the past few decades. According to a 2013 UN estimate, by 2050 the world population is expected to reach 9.6 billion people, and nowhere will population growth be more dramatic than in the cities of the developing world. Indeed, according to estimates by the UN Population Division, for the first time in human history, in 2009 globally "the number of people living in urban areas (3.42 billion) had surpassed the number living in rural areas (3.41 billion)." The global urban majority is now widening with each passing year.[1]

After reviewing trends and prospects for overall urban population growth, we examine in this chapter the potential role of cities—both the modern sector and the urban informal sector—in fostering economic development. We then turn to a well-known theoretical model of rural-urban labor transfer in the context of rapid growth and high urban unemployment. In the final section, we evaluate various policy options that governments in developing countries may wish to pursue in their attempts to moderate the heavy flow of rural-to-urban migration and to ameliorate the serious unemployment problems that continue to plague their crowded cities. We also examine how the great potential dynamism and productivity of developing cities can be better harnessed for rapid and more inclusive economic development. This chapter's case study looks at patterns of migration in India and Botswana.

7.1 Urbanization: Trends and Living Conditions

While the world as a whole became majority urban in 2009, even the developing world is expected to become majority urban before 2020 (although the United Nations projects that the least developed countries will not reach this milestone until after 2050). Currently, most urban growth has occurred in cities in Asia and Africa. Indeed, in 2012 the United Nations projected that the urban population of Africa will grow from 414 million in 2012 to over 1.2 billion by 2050; and the urban population of Asia will grow from 1.9 billion to 3.3 billion. Thus taken together, the United Nations projects that Asia and Africa will account for some 86% of the global urban population increase in this period. In fact, there will be so much rural-to-urban migration in Asia that its rural population will actually decline in this period, as seen in Figure 7.1.[2]

Urbanization rates increase whenever urban population growth exceeds rural population growth. The positive association between urbanization and

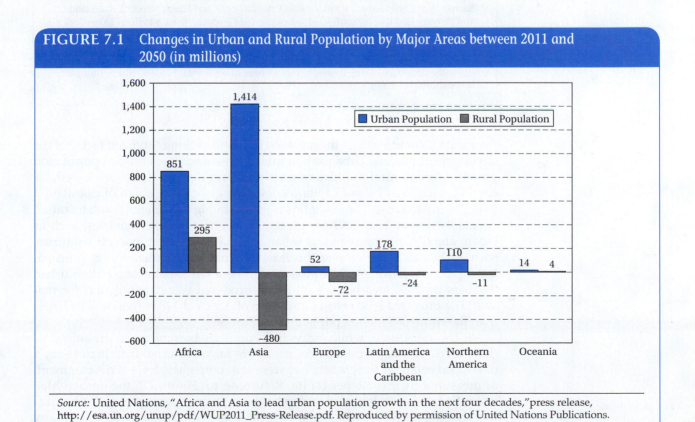

FIGURE 7.1 Changes in Urban and Rural Population by Major Areas between 2011 and 2050 (in millions)

Source: United Nations, "Africa and Asia to lead urban population growth in the next four decades,"press release, http://esa.un.org/unup/pdf/WUP2011_Press-Release.pdf. Reproduced by permission of United Nations Publications.

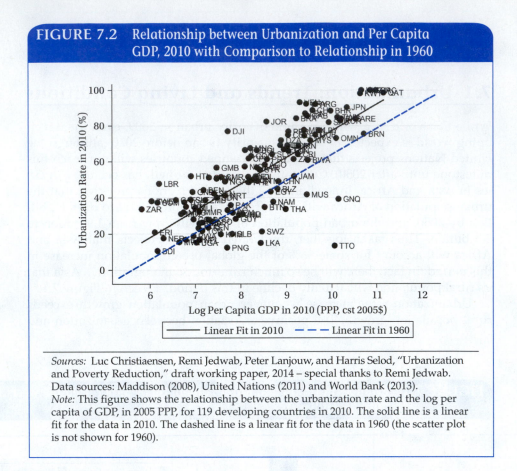

FIGURE 7.2   Relationship between Urbanization and Per Capita GDP, 2010 with Comparison to Relationship in 1960

Sources: Luc Christiaensen, Remi Jedwab, Peter Lanjouw, and Harris Selod, "Urbanization and Poverty Reduction," draft working paper, 2014 – special thanks to Remi Jedwab. Data sources: Maddison (2008), United Nations (2011) and World Bank (2013).
Note: This figure shows the relationship between the urbanization rate and the log per capita of GDP, in 2005 PPP, for 119 developing countries in 2010. The solid line is a linear fit for the data in 2010. The dashed line is a linear fit for the data in 1960 (the scatter plot is not shown for 1960).

per capita income is one of the most obvious and striking "stylized facts" of the development process. Urbanization rates increase whenever urban population growth exceeds rural population growth. Generally, the more developed the country, measured by per capita income, the greater the share of population living in urban areas. The black linear fit line in Figure 7.2 shows urbanization versus the log of 2010 GNI per capita; the highest-income countries, such as Japan, are also among the most urbanized, while the very poorest countries, such as Burundi, are among the least urbanized. Urbanization is proceeding rapidly. According to UN projections, there will be almost 5 billion urban dwellers by 2030, nearly five-eighths of projected world population for that year. The projected 2030 urban population of Africa of 748 million will be larger than the entire 685 million population of Europe.

At the same time, while individual countries become more urbanized as they develop, today's poorest countries are far more urbanized than today's developed countries were when they were at a comparable level of development, as measured by income per capita. Returning to Figure 7.2, the dashed blue linear fit line shows the relationship between income per capita and urbanization that prevailed in 1960. A comparison of the two lines reveals that for any given income in 2010, a country that had the identical income in 1960 was significantly less urbanized.

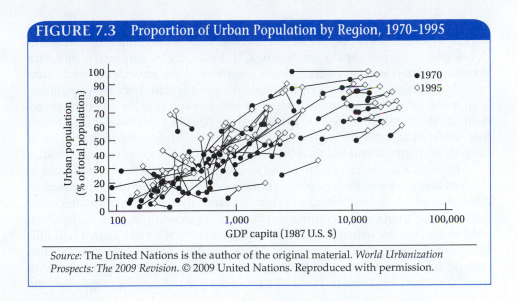

FIGURE 7.3   Proportion of Urban Population by Region, 1970–1995

Source: The United Nations is the author of the original material. *World Urbanization Prospects: The 2009 Revision.* © 2009 United Nations. Reproduced with permission.

In recent decades urbanization has continued in nearly all developing countries, even those that have experienced only minimal industrialization. Figure 7.3 shows urbanization over time and across income levels over the quarter century from 1970 to 1995. Each line segment represents the trajectory of one country, starting from the solid dots, which represent the 1970 income and urbanization level for a given country and ending at the end of the line segments (marked by a diamond), which represent the corresponding 1995 income and urbanization level for the same country. Although the World Bank caption to the figure stated that "urbanization is closely associated with economic growth," the figure may also be interpreted as showing that urbanization is occurring everywhere, at high and low levels of income and whether growth is positive or negative. Even when the lines point to the left, indicating shrinking incomes per capita over the period, they still generally point upward, indicating that urbanization continued. In short, urbanization is happening everywhere in the world, although at differing rates.

Thus, it becomes clear that urbanization is not driven solely by income. In addition, some countries with approximately the same income level are significantly more or less urbanized, partly due to differing domestic policies. So we need to consider urbanization carefully—is it only correlated with economic development, or is causation also at work?

Indeed, one of the most significant of all modern demographic phenomena is the rapid growth of cities in developing countries. In 1950, some 275 million people were living in cities in the developing world, 38% of the 724 million total urban population; by 2010, the world's urban population had surpassed 3.4 billion, with over three-quarters of all urban dwellers living in metropolitan areas of low- and middle-income countries.

While in a significant number of cases the speed at which the share of urban population has increased in developing countries in the late twentieth and early twenty-first century is not much faster than in many of the developed countries when they were urbanizing in the late nineteenth century, nonetheless shares of urban population are being reached, particularly in Africa, at lower levels of per capita income than at a comparable stage in developed countries (again see Figure 7.2). Relatedly, urbanization in Africa is not associated with industrialization, as it was in the now-developed countries. Moreover, in most regions of the developing world, because population is so much larger, the sheer numbers of people coming into the city is unprecedented. Also unprecedented are the very large sizes of individual cities at such low levels of income per capita. The largest cities in developed countries in the past were much smaller than the large cities of developing countries today.

Although a majority of developing-country urban growth will be found in cities of less than 5 million people, it is also the case that population growth in cities of over 5 million in population is more rapid than growth of smaller cities (under 500,000) in the developing world. In fact, according to the UN, by 2025, only about half the urban population will be in cities with less than a half million people, the lowest fraction ever. Moreover, the developing world is also coming to dominate the world's largest cities, including the megacities with over 10 million inhabitants. Figure 7.4 provides a map locating megacities, the

FIGURE 7.4   Megacities: Cities with 10 Million or More Inhabitants

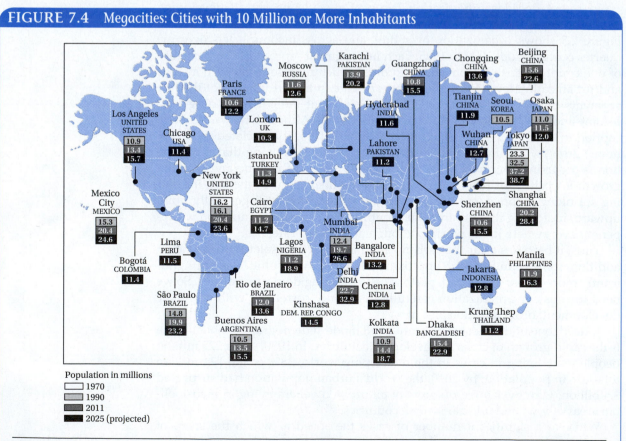

Source: Data drawn from United Nations Population Division, World Urbanization Prospects: The 2011 Revision (New York: United Nations, 2011), at http://esa.un.org/unup/pdf/WUP2011_Highlights.pdf

largest urban agglomerations in the world containing a population of at least 10 million people. As the figure shows, in 1970, there were only 2 megacities, but by 1990, there were 10, and by 2011, there were 23 such metropolises. Of these, 18 (over three-quarters) were located in the developing world. By 2025, 30 of the 37 megacities (more than 80%) will be in developing countries.

Based on numbers of people, the small and medium cities in developing countries have added more residents than the megacities. But while the number living in cities of fewer than 500,000 will more than double (grow by 2.4 times) from 1970 to 2025, the number in megacities will increase by *16 times*, from 39 million to 630 million. Figure 7.5 presents total urban populations in millions by different city sizes for 1970, 1990, and 2011, with projections to 2025. In 2011, more people lived in megacities of over 10 million than in cities from 5 to 10 million people in size. In principle, a megacity could offer large agglomeration economies, although congestion costs may rise rapidly. Another potential downside is that megacities tend to be more capital intensive, which does not match with the comparative advantage of most developing countries. Megacities, particularly in low-income countries, may also have outsized social and health problems. The relative balance of these factors is likely to differ across countries depending on the forces that led these cities to reach their megascales.

Moreover, as Figure 7.6 shows, going forward almost all of the increments to the world's population will be accounted for by the growth of urban areas as migrants continue to stream into the cities from rural areas and as

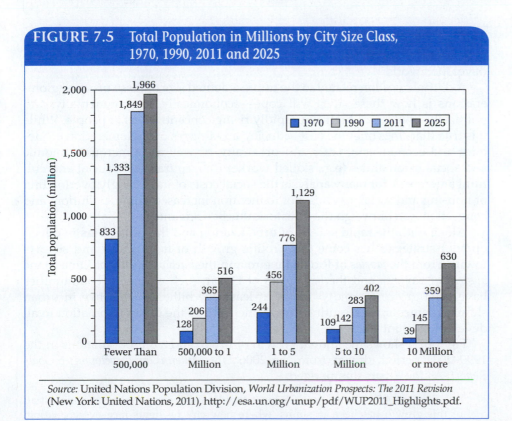

FIGURE 7.5 Total Population in Millions by City Size Class, 1970, 1990, 2011 and 2025

Source: United Nations Population Division, *World Urbanization Prospects: The 2011 Revision* (New York: United Nations, 2011), http://esa.un.org/unup/pdf/WUP2011_Highlights.pdf.

FIGURE 7.6   Estimated and Projected Urban and Rural Population of the More and Less Developed Regions, 1950–2050

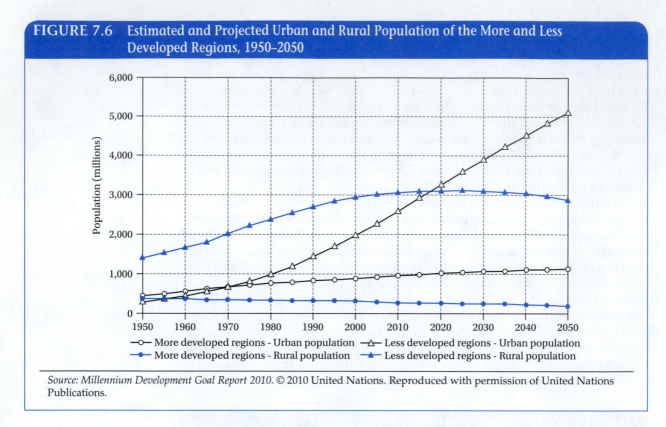

urbanization rates in the developing world continue to approach those of the developed world.

A central question related to the unprecedented size of these urban agglomerations is how these cities will cope—economically, environmentally, and politically—with such high and rapidly rising concentrations of people. While it is true that cities offer the cost-reducing advantages of agglomeration economies and economies of scale and proximity, as well as numerous economic and social externalities (e.g., skilled workers, cheap transport, social and cultural amenities), for many analysts the social costs of increasingly overloading of housing and social services, not to mention increased crime, pollution, and congestion, can outweigh these historical urban advantages.[3]

Urban bias   The notion that most governments in developing countries favor the urban sector in their development policies, thereby creating a widening gap between the urban and rural economies.

Along with the rapid spread of urbanization and the **urban bias** in development strategies has come this prolific growth of huge slums and shantytowns. From the *favelas* of Rio de Janeiro and the *pueblos jovenes* of Lima to the *bustees* of Kolkata and the *bidonvilles* of Dakar, such makeshift communities have been growing rapidly. Today, at least one billion people live in urban slum settlements, representing nearly one-third of the urban population in all developing countries.

Figure 7.7 shows the annual growth of urban and slum populations in the 1990–2001 period, drawn from the 2006 UN *Millennium Development Goals Report*. As the *Report* summarized:

Sub-Saharan Africa is the world's most rapidly urbanizing region, and almost all of this growth has been in slums, where new city residents face overcrowding,

FIGURE 7.7   Annual Growth of Urban and Slum Populations, 1990–2001

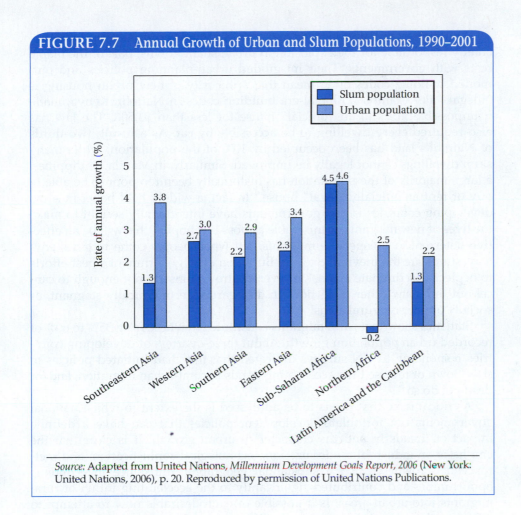

Source: Adapted from United Nations, *Millennium Development Goals Report, 2006* (New York: United Nations, 2006), p. 20. Reproduced by permission of United Nations Publications.

inadequate housing, and a lack of water and sanitation. In Western Asia, as well, most of the urban growth is occurring in slums. The rapid expansion of urban areas in Southern and Eastern Asia is creating cities of unprecedented size and complexity and new challenges for providing a decent environment for the poor. Northern Africa is the only developing region where the quality of urban life is improving."

The importance of addressing this problem has been enshrined in the Millennium Development Goals (MDGs —see Chapter 1), in which Target 11 of Goal 7 commits "to improve the lives of at least 100 million slum dwellers by the year 2020." Yet even though this number seems likely to be met, it represents only about one-tenth of all urban slum dwellers as of 2013! It is extremely difficult to provide reliable projections of slum populations further into the future because much depends on uncertain future policies and economic growth rates, as well as the extent of migration that occurs in response to growth and policy change. Allowing that simple extrapolation of trends would tend to significantly overstate the problem, UN-Habitat has noted that such trends would point to a slum population of as large as 3 billion people in 2050.

Rural-urban migration   The movement of people from rural villages, towns, and farms to urban centers (cities) in search of jobs.

Although population growth and accelerated **rural-urban migration** are chiefly responsible for the explosion in urban shantytowns, part of the blame rests with governments. Their misguided urban-planning policies and outmoded building codes often mean that a majority of new urban housing is "illegal." For example, colonial-era building codes in Nairobi, Kenya, made it impossible to build an "official" house for less than $3,500. The law has also required every dwelling to be accessible by car. As a result, two-thirds of Nairobi's land has been occupied by 10% of the population, while many slum dwellings cannot legally be improved. Similarly, in Manila, Philippines, a large majority of the population has historically been too poor to be able to buy or rent an officially "legal" house.[4] In fact, a widely held belief in some developing countries is that governments have intentionally sought to make the lives of new migrants as miserable as possible, hoping this will be an effective deterrent to prospective migrants; but when people come to cities anyway, slums are the inevitable result. But often even government's best efforts to neglect, discriminate against, or even destroy slums are not enough to cancel out the many other distortions in disregarded, economically stagnant, or socially oppressive rural areas.

Statistics show that rural migrants constitute anywhere from 35% to 60% of recorded urban population growth. About three-quarters of developing countries responding to UN surveys indicated that they had initiated policies to slow down or reverse their accelerating trends in rural-urban migration, and/or desire to do so.[5]

A critical issue that needs to be addressed is the extent to which national governments can formulate development policies that can have a definite impact on trends in and the character of urban growth. It is clear that the emphasis on industrial modernization, technological sophistication, and metropolitan growth created a substantial geographic imbalance in economic opportunities and contributed significantly to the accelerating influx of rural migrants into urban areas. Is it possible or even desirable now to attempt to influence these trends by pursuing a different set of population and development policies? With birth rates declining in many developing countries, rapid urban growth and accelerated rural-urban migration will undoubtedly be one of the most important development and demographic issues of the coming decades. And in urban areas, the growth and development of the informal sector, as well as its role and limitations for labor absorption and economic progress, will assume increasing importance.

Before examining other problems and policy approaches in developing-country cities more closely, let us first consider the potential advantages offered by cities. Urban areas have played a highly constructive role in the economies of today's developed countries, and they offer huge and still largely untapped potential to do the same for developing countries. A detailed look at the informal sector in developing cities will give an idea of its potential as an engine of growth. We also consider in more detail what has been different—and what has gone wrong—with urban development and the excessively rapid pace of rural-urban migration in many developing countries. We conclude with a look at constructive policies to help cities foster successful urban development while at the same time giving more balanced treatment to development in rural areas.

7.2 The Role of Cities

What explains the strong association between urbanization and development? To a large degree, cities are formed because they provide cost advantages to producers and consumers through what are called **agglomeration economies**. As noted by Walter Isard, these agglomeration economies come in two forms. **Urbanization economies** are effects associated with the general growth of a concentrated geographic region. **Localization economies** are effects captured by particular sectors of the economy, such as finance or automobiles, as they grow within an area. Localization economies often take the form of backward and forward linkages of the type introduced in Chapter 4. When transportation costs are significant, users of the outputs of an industry may benefit from a nearby location to save on these costs. This benefit is a type of forward linkage. In addition, firms of the same or related industries may benefit from being located in the same city, so they can all draw on a large pool of workers with the specific skills used in that sector or from specialized infrastructure. This is a type of backward linkage. Workers with specialized skills appropriate to the industry prefer to be located there as well so that they can easily find a new job or be in a position to take advantage of better opportunities.

Agglomeration economies Cost advantages to producers and consumers from location in cities and towns, which take the forms of urbanization economies and localization economies.

Urbanization economies Agglomeration effects associated with the general growth of a concentrated geographic region.

Localization economies Agglomeration effects captured by particular sectors of the economy, such as finance or autos, as they grow within an area.

Industrial Districts

An economic definition of a city is "an area with relatively high population density that contains a set of closely related activities." Firms often also prefer to be located where they can learn from other firms doing similar work. Learning takes place in both formal relationships, such as joint ventures, and informal ones, such as from tips learned in evening social clubs or over lunch. These spillovers are also agglomeration economies, part of the benefits of what Alfred Marshall called "industrial districts," and they play a big role in Michael Porter's "clusters" theory of competitive advantage.[6] Firms located in such industrial districts also benefit from the opportunity to contract out work easily when an unusually large order materializes. Thus, a firm of modest size does not have to turn down a big job due to lack of capacity, an arrangement that provides "flexible specialization."[7] Further, firms may wish to operate in well-known districts for the marketing advantages of locating where company procurers and household consumers of their goods know to shop to get the best selection.

It may not matter as much where such industrial districts are located as that they somehow got an early start there, perhaps because of a historical accident. For example, in the United States, many innovative computer firms located in Silicon Valley, California, simply because other such firms were already located there. Analogously, suppliers to shoe firms located in the Sinos Valley in southern Brazil and in Guadalajara in Mexico because so many shoe firms located in those regions. Some of the benefits are gained simply by the fact of location—Khalid Nadvi has termed this "passive collective efficiency"—but other benefits must be achieved through collective action, such as developing training facilities or lobbying government for needed infrastructure as an industry rather than as individual firms ("active collective efficiency").[8]

A growing body of evidence shows that industrial clusters are increasingly common in developing countries, at stages of industrial development ranging from cottage industry to advanced manufacturing techniques, and appear to be significant factors in emerging industrial competitiveness. Nevertheless, the dynamism of these clusters has varied widely. Some of the identified districts are traditional clusters of artisans that have shown little ability to innovate, export, or expand. But such groupings often remain one-family microenterprises with little division of labor or use of modern techniques. Producers in a village are better off sharing a common specialization than producing a random assortment of goods, in part because intermediaries work with villages with a high concentration of producers in their sector. But such traditional producers sometimes benefit little from "internal" divisions of labor within the firm, producing a largely complete product within the household and remaining at very low productivity and incomes. For example, a small town in Kenya may have a dozen or more families fabricating wheelbarrows, each family starting with timber and a few simple purchased metal inputs and producing a final product for sale. Nevertheless, clustering can generate more specialized employment in the rural nonfarm sector, as in the rural hand-loom weaver clusters of Ethiopia, in which microentrepreneurs share a work space, take part in a finer division of labor, and benefit from trade credits for working capital. Researchers also found that better electricity reliability and other infrastructure that are available to a cluster lead to better firm performance; in particular, "producers in electrified towns work longer hours than those in towns without electricity."[9]

In some cases, traditional township specializations have evolved into more developed clusters, with still modest-size but somewhat larger firms using a more detailed division of labor, such as a group of wheelbarrow producers with some specialization, each employing a few workers. Eventually, the cluster might expand in scope and become a low-tech metal products industrial district selling products throughout the country as the town grows into a small city. These clusters are reminiscent of the industrial districts of developed countries but require that sufficient financing be gathered to invest in core firms using somewhat larger-scale capital goods. But note that clusters of some sophistication can emerge in an otherwise fairly rural but densely populated area. As manufacturing has progressed in China, there has been a dramatic emergence of specialized clusters, to the point where they have now become pervasive, as detailed in Box 7.1.

As Hermine Weijland found in her study of Java, Indonesia, "It needs only a few fortunate years of market expansion to create gains from externalities and joint action."[10] She cites as examples local clusters that have upgraded and now competitively produce such goods as roof tiles, rattan furniture, cast metal, and textiles. Similarly, Dorothy McCormick concluded from a study of six representative clusters in Africa that "groundwork clusters prepare the way; industrializing clusters begin the process of specialization, differentiation, and technological development; and complex industrial clusters produce competitively for wider markets."[11] In some cases, the evidence suggests that coordination failures are not overcome, and so there may be a role for government policy in encouraging the upgrading of clusters. In other cases, it is the government itself that shares blame for cluster stagnation when it enforces irrational and stifling regulations, which are far more damaging than the usual policy of benign neglect toward nascent clusters in the informal sector. Examples of clusters in developing countries that are widely considered successful include surgical instruments in Sialkot, Pakistan, and software in the Bengaluru (Bangalore) area in India. Clusters of all kinds, however, and particularly those producing for the local market, face substantial challenges from globalization and trade liberalization.

BOX 7.1 FINDINGS   The Emergence of Industrial Districts or Clusters in China

Prior to the 1980s, industry in China was stateowned, and factories were dispersed geographically for military defense. Beginning in 1980, Special Economic Zones such as Shenzhen were created to attract foreign firms in many industries; domestic firms sold inputs to them, but not as clusters. Township and village enterprises (TVEs) then emerged, initiated outside of local governments but "vaguely owned" by them. TVE managers usually tried a variety of activities, and early 1990s field research found little evidence that firms in the same or related industries were locating in close proximity to each other. But starting in the mid-1990s, TVEs rapidly privatized, and a combination of competition, responses to credit constraints, an abundance of entrepreneurial talent, and supportive local policies led to the emergence of localized industrial clusters. But like other Chinese institutions (see the case study in Chapter 4), some may ultimately prove "transitional."

The Zhili Township children's garment cluster studied by Fleisher and colleagues saw "a significant rise in specialization and outsourcing among firms." Median investment to start a business more than doubled, but bank loans remained unnecessary as many entrepreneurs generated sufficient savings. Accordingly, many firms entered, and after 2000, wages rose and profitability fell. In response, firms selling directly to markets sought to "signal their commitment to product quality"—nearly half by establishing trademarks and nearly a fifth achieving International Organization for Standardization (ISO) certification. Meanwhile, quality of subcontractors was "monitored by their outsourcing

partners." Social capital is critical, Fleisher and colleagues concluded: "Clustering within established communities where long-time relationships among family and neighbors prevail offers an institutional substitute for court enforcement of contractual relationships among borrowers and lenders and between outsourcing firms and their subcontractors." They also reported that "township government has imposed safety regulations in response to major industrial accidents" and helped "prevent a destructive 'race to the bottom' in terms of product quality and employee safety" where markets failed to do so.

From firm surveys in the Puyuan cashmere sweater district, Ruan and Zhang found that state-owned banks rarely gave loans to small and medium-size enterprises. But small firms borrowed from relatives and friends and gave and received credit from buyers and sellers, so clusters lowered "capital barriers to entry through the division of labor, enabling individuals to choose the appropriate type of specialization according to their capital portfolio," while a deeper division of labor allowed "people with different talents and endowments to find their own positions." Similar conclusions followed from a study of the world's largest footwear cluster in Wenzhou.

With a detailed analysis of 1995 and 2004 firm census data, Long and Zhang confirmed that "China's rapid industrialization is marked by increased clustering." Their research supported the conclusion that clustering of firms relaxed credit constraints through "two mechanisms: (1) within a cluster, finer division of labor lowers the capital barriers to entry, and (2) closer proximity makes the provision of trade credit among firms easier." They found that clusters use more "entrepreneurs and labor, and less . . . capital, compared to nonclustered large factories" and thus followed comparative advantage. They noted that clusters could be useful in countries facing a "scarcity of capital and an inefficient financial system." However, they cautioned, "clustering may be a second-best solution to the financing problem when the local conditions do not permit easy access to regular financing." Thus clustering, like TVEs, might be a transitional form until financial markets deepened, formal contract enforcement could be provided, and larger investments would be needed.

Sources: Fleisher, Belton, Dinghuan Hu, William McGuire, and Xiaobo Zhang. "The evolution of an industrial cluster in China." *China Economic Review* 21, No. 3 (September 2010): 456–469; Huang, Zuhui, Xiaobo Zhang, and Yunwei Zhu. "The role of clustering in rural industrialization: A case study of Wenzhou's footwear industry." *China Economic Review* 19 (2008): 409–420; Long, Cheryl, and Xiaobo Zhang. "Cluster-based industrialization in China: Financing and performance." IFPRI Discussion Paper No. 937. Washington, D.C.: International Food Policy Research Institute, 2009; Ruan, Jianqing, and Xiaobo Zhang. "Credit constraints, organizational choice, and returns to capital: Evidence from a rural industrial cluster in China." IFPRI Discussion Paper No. 830. Washington, D.C.: International Food Policy Research Institute, 2008; Ruan, Jianqing, and Xiaobo Zhang. "Finance and cluster-based industrial development in China." *Economic Development and Cultural Change* 58 (2009): 143–164.

Social capital   The productive value of a set of social institutions and norms, including group trust, expected cooperative behaviors with predictable punishments for deviations, and a shared history of successful collective action, that raises expectations for participation in future cooperative behavior.

Again, not all of the collective efficiency advantages of an industrial district are realized through passive location. Others are actively created by joint investments and promotional activities of the firms in the district. One factor determining the dynamism of a district is the ability of its firms to find a mechanism for such collective action. While the government can provide financial and other important services to facilitate cluster development, **social capital** is also critical, especially group trust and a shared history of successful collective action, which requires time to develop. Government can help by bringing parties together and helping them gain experience in cooperating on more modest goals before tackling larger ones, but social capital normally grows organically in an economic community and cannot be created by fiat. Even with collective action to supplement passive benefits of agglomeration, traditional clusters may not survive in their current form into more advanced stages of industrialization. Nonetheless, as Hubert Schmitz and Khalid Nadvi note, even if transitional, districts in the informal sector may still play a crucial role in mobilizing underused human and financial resources. They argue that clustering enables entrepreneurs to focus on selected stages of the production process, while other producers focus on their own specialized stages. Thus, even though the overall capital needs of a cluster may be too large for individual investors, each small producer individually needs only raise rather modest quantities of investment and working capital.[12]

Statistical estimates show that benefits of agglomeration can be quite substantial in practice. For example, studies have demonstrated that "if a plant moves from a location shared by 1,000 workers employed by firms in the same industry to one with 10,000 such workers, output will increase an average of 15%, largely because the pool of specialized workers and inputs deepens." Moreover, "productivity rises with city size, so much so that a typical firm will see its productivity climb 5% to 10% if city size and the scale of local industry double."[13]

Efficient Urban Scale

Localization economies do not imply that it would be efficient for all of a country's industries to be located together in a single city. These economies extend across closely related industries, such as those with strong backward and forward linkages, but there are fewer productivity benefits for unrelated industries to locate together. One notable exception is the potential spillover from technological progress in one industry to its adaptation for different uses in another industry. But there are also some important **congestion** costs. The higher the urban density, the higher the costs of real estate. It is much more expensive to build vertically than horizontally, increasingly so as skyscraper scale is reached, so that when market forces work properly, tall buildings are built primarily when urban land costs become high. (Note that skyscrapers and other buildings of monumental scale are sometimes built for political show rather than for economic efficiency, such as the world's tallest buildings in Dubai, United Arab Emirates; Shanghai, China; Mecca, Saudi Arabia; Taipei, Taiwan; and Kuala Lumpur, Malaysia.) In large urban areas, workers may find themselves with longer and longer commutes and greater transportation costs and may demand higher wages to cover these costs. In addition, the costs of infrastructure such as water and sewer systems are higher in concentrated urban areas. In theory, if costs of transportation of finished goods are high and consumers wish to be located in the largest city to avoid paying those transportation costs as much as possible, economic activity could become indefinitely concentrated within a city (called the "black hole" effect), but it is generally much less costly to improve the transportation system of a country than to pay the costs of maintaining a gargantuan urban complex. Under competitive forces, and other things being equal, if workers are mobile, a worker in a large city with higher wages but higher costs of living (such as higher housing prices) is no better off in real material terms than a worker with comparable education, experience, ability, and health in a small city who has lower wages and lower costs of living.[14]

Thus, the concentrating, or "centripetal," forces of urban agglomeration economies are opposed by the dispersing, or "centrifugal," forces of diseconomies featuring increasing costs with greater concentration, because some of the factors of production, most obviously land, are not mobile. We can "create" more central city land by building skyscrapers, but only to a certain scale and only at substantial cost. Thus, it is normal for an economy to have a range of cities, with sizes dependent on the scale of the industries it sponsors and the extent of agglomeration economies found for that industry or cluster of industries.

Two well-known theories of city size are the urban hierarchy model (central place theory) and the differentiated plane model.[15] In the urban hierarchy model, originated by August Losch and Walter Christaller, plants in various industries have a characteristic market radius that results from the interplay of three factors: economies of scale in production, transportation costs, and the way the demand for land is spread over space. The larger the economies of scale in production and the lower the transportation costs, the larger the radius of territory that will be served by that industry to minimize costs. In contrast, if the price of real estate is bid up to high levels in the resulting cities, this will tend to create smaller radii. As a result, small cities contain activities

Congestion An action taken by one agent that decreases the incentives for other agents to take similar actions. Compare to the opposite effect of a complementarity.

with short market radii, while large cities emerge to contain activities of both small and large radii. Generally speaking, activities of a national scope, such as government and finance, will be located in a single city (though not necessarily the same large city because of the effect of congestion costs). Clearly, the urban hierarchy approach applies better to nonexport industries than to export industries. When countries have different specializations in the international market or are at different stages of economic development, the size distribution of cities may potentially differ. For example, a developing country that still overwhelmingly specializes in agriculture might reasonably have one or two large cities serving national industries such as finance and government and many smaller towns serving local agricultural areas. A country with a highly differentiated manufacturing and service base might have a large number of medium-size cities.

In the differentiated plane model, originated by Alfred Weber, Walter Isard, and Leon Moses, the limited number of transportation routes linking the industries within an economy plays a key role. The model predicts urban concentrations at the points where the scarce transportation routes cross, called "internal nodes." The hierarchy of urban sizes depends on the pattern of nodes and the industrial mix. Primary processing industries have few inputs and are usually located near the source of the primary resource. However, there will also be incentives for industries with strong backward or forward linkages to locate in the same city.

Of course, there is nothing inherently wrong with very large cities per se—even megacities have some special productive advantages in a global economy.[15a] But the *distortions* that have led to the outsize cities prevalent in developing countries have been costly and problematic.

7.3 The Urban Giantism Problem

In the case of developing countries, the main transportation routes are often a legacy of colonialism. Theorists of the dependence school (see Chapter 3) have compared colonial transportation networks to drainage systems, emphasizing ease of extraction of the country's natural resources. In many cases, the capital city will be located near the outlet of this system on the seacoast. This type of transportation system is also called a "hub-and-spoke system," which is especially visible when the capital city is located in the interior of the country. Many nations inherited a hub-and-spoke system from colonial times, including many in Africa and Latin America, which also facilitated movement of troops from the capital to the outlying towns to suppress revolts.

The differentiated plane approach emphasizes the lasting impact of historical accidents. In this case, it helps explain where the most oversized cities are found in the developing world and suggests where policies of urban decentralization may be most helpful. Note that not all countries inherited such a hub-and-spoke system; Germany did not; the United States did not, in part because it is the result of the merger of 13 separate British colonies, which retained some measure of local autonomy, as do the federal states of Germany. The recent development of the United States makes the emergence of cities such as Atlanta from the crossing of transportation routes especially clear, but the same principle has applied elsewhere over longer historical periods. Of course, as nations become wealthy, they generally build better transportation systems.

Sometimes one urban core becomes too large to keep the costs of the industries located there to a minimum. In developed countries, other cores are often developed within the broad metropolitan region, enabling the region as a whole to continue to receive benefits of agglomeration while lowering some of the costs; or new cities may develop in entirely different parts of the country. But this creation of new urban cores does not happen automatically if there are advantages to locating where other firms and residents are already present. This is another chicken-and-egg coordination problem of the type described in Chapter 4. Who will be the pioneer if it is less costly to stay where you are and wait for other pioneers to settle in the new city first? In economic terms, the agglomeration economies of cities are externalities, which must somehow be internalized or the market will fail. How can this be done?

In the United States, developers frequently internalize the externality by creating a new "edge city" within a metropolitan area, financing and building a new center where land is still relatively inexpensive, perhaps 10 to 50 kilometers from the original urban core. This takes place within a context of public oversight in the form of zoning regulations and inducements such as tax breaks. In developing countries, however, capital markets generally do not work well enough for this process of development to take place. In Europe, the public sector plays a much larger role in coordinating new towns and large developments.

In developing countries, however, governments are less involved in the dispersal of economic activity to more manageable sizes or, if they are involved, are often less effective. For example, government may seek to disperse industry without regard to the nature of agglomeration economies, giving incentives for dispersal but no attention to clustering relevant industries together, a problem seen in industrial parks in Pakistan. And all too often, the incentives are for firms to concentrate in the capital city or other "urban giants." A key problem of countries such as Peru and Argentina is that their giant capitals suffer from enormous levels of congestion, but adequate midsize cities that might provide alternative locations for growth are lacking. A well-designed infrastructure development program, including more efficient links between medium-size cities and better roads, utilities, and telecommunications within these cities, can help alleviate this problem.

A more detailed comparison of North and South America is instructive. The largest urban area in the United States, the New York metropolitan area, has about 6% of the national population. Toronto, the largest metropolitan area in Canada, has about 5 million residents, some 15% of the Canadian population. But Mexico City holds nearly one-fifth of the population of Mexico, Montevideo nearly half of the population of Uruguay, Lima over one-quarter of the population of Peru, and Buenos Aires and Santiago close to a third of the populations of Argentina and Chile, respectively.[16]

First-City Bias

A form of urban bias that has often caused considerable distortions might be termed *first-city bias*. The country's largest or first ("first-place") city receives a disproportionately large share of public investment and incentives for private investment in relation to the country's second-largest city and other smaller cities. As a result, the first city receives a disproportionately—and inefficiently—large share of population and economic activity.

Table 7.1 shows the largest and second-largest cities in the United States, Canada, and major Latin American countries. Notice that in all of the outsized capital cities—Buenos Aires, Santiago, Mexico City, and Lima—the first city also serves as the capital. Some other developing countries have remarkably outsized first cities, notably Thailand, where Bangkok has a population about 20 times the size of the second city. Further examples can be found in the Philippines (where Manila has over 7 times the population of the second city) and Congo (where Kinshasa has more than 5 times the second city's population). There are at least 10 other examples of relatively large first (primate) cities in developing nations with sizable populations.[17]

Causes of Urban Giantism

Why have first cities often swelled to such a large multiple of second cities in developing countries? Overall, urban giantism probably results from a combination of a hub-and-spoke transportation system and the location of the political capital in the largest city. This is further reinforced by a political culture of rent seeking and the capital market failures that make the creation of new urban centers a task that markets cannot complete. Other more detailed explanations also generally involve unfortunate consequences of political economy (see Chapter 11). One argument, featured in the work of Paul Krugman, stresses that under import substitution industrialization (see Chapter 12), with a high level of protection, there is much less international trade, and population and economic activity have an incentive to concentrate in a single city, largely to avoid transportation costs. Thus, firms wish to set up operations in the city where the most consumers already live, which attracts more people to the region in search of jobs and perhaps lower prices (made possible because there are fewer transport costs to be passed on to consumers and perhaps by economies of larger store size and specialized sales districts);

TABLE 7.1	Population of the Largest and Second-Largest Cities in Selected Countries (Millions)		
Country	**Largest-City Population**	**Second-Largest-City Population**	**Ratio**
Canada	Toronto, 5.035	Montreal, 3.603	1.40
United States	New York, 18.727	Los Angeles, 12.303	1.52
Argentina	Buenos Aires, 12.551	Cordoba, 1.423	8.82
Brazil	São Paulo, 18.647	Rio de Janeiro, 11.368	1.64
Chile	Santiago, 5.605	Valparaiso, 0.837	6.70
Mexico	Mexico City, 18.735	Guadalajara, 4.057	4.62
Peru	Lima, 8.081	Arequipa, 0.732	11.04

Note: Definitions of city size differ across studies.
Source: From *UN World Urbanization Prospects 2009 Revision.*

this concentration in turn attracts still more firms and consumers in a circle of causation. However, when trade barriers are reduced, the incentive to focus production on the home market is also reduced, and exporters and their suppliers have much less incentive to be located in the country's biggest population center. This moves production toward ports and borders, or elsewhere in the country, to escape the excessive congestion costs of the largest city.[18]

Another explanation for urban giants focuses on the consequences of dictators' efforts to remain in power. As Figure 7.8 shows, on average, a much larger share of a country's urbanized population (37%) lives in the first city in unstable dictatorships than in stable democracies (23%). In interpreting this finding, Alberto Ades and Edward Glaeser argue that unstable dictatorships (fearing overthrow) must provide "bread and circuses" for the first city (usually the capital) to prevent unrest; this extreme urban bias in turn attracts more migrants to the favored city and a still larger need for bread and circuses. It should be noted that although the authors attempt to control for reverse causality, it may still be the case that unstable dictatorships also tend to emerge in countries with high first-city concentrations.[19]

In the developing world, until recently, relatively few countries were effective democracies. Until the democratization waves beginning in the 1980s, most developing countries had authoritarian governments of one form or another. To remain in power and prevent popular uprisings and coups, which were generally thought to be most threatening when launched from the capital city, governments had an incentive to "buy off" the population of the largest city. This focus of national government spending on the capital city is the bread-and-circuses effect, recalling the phrasing of "rent-sharing" policies in ancient Rome in its period of expansion. The availability of better opportunities, whether the equivalent of the grain handouts in ancient Rome or jobs, wages, infrastructure,

---

FIGURE 7.8   Politics and Urban Concentration

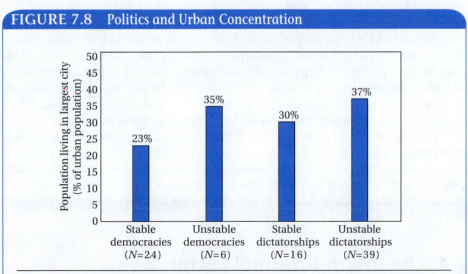

Source: Data from Alberto F. Ades and Edward L. Glaeser, "Trade and circuses: Explaining urban giants," *Quarterly Journal of Economics* 110 (1995): 196. Copyright © 1995 by the President and Fellows of Harvard College and the Massachusetts Institute of Technology. *Note:* N = number of countries in group.

and other government services concentrated in the capital city of many of today's developing countries, attracts an ever-growing migrant population, in turn leading to larger precautionary government spending as the fear of political instability grows.

Another political economy factor contributes to capital city giantism: It becomes advantageous for firms to be located where they have easy access to government officials, to curry political favor from a regime that can be induced to give companies special favors for a price or that simply demands bribes to function at all. The resulting first-city giantism may be viewed as a form of underdevelopment trap, which may be escaped fully only with a return to democratic rule together with a better balance of incentives to compete for exports as well as home consumption. Democracy does not eliminate political benefits of location in the national capital, but while lobbyists still congregate in the political capital, there may be less incentive for production to become overconcentrated there. Moreover, a free press tends to expose corruption and generate public pressure to root it out, as recent experience in many democratizing countries in Latin America and East Asia makes clear.

The explanations for urban giantism—production for the home market in the face of high protection and transport costs, few adequate smaller cities as alternative locations for firms reflecting infrastructure patterns, location of the capital in the largest city, and the political logic of unstable dictatorships—are complementary and help explain some of the advantages of democracies with more balanced economic policies, including well-planned investments in infrastructure. Such countries are able to avoid some of the costs of urban giantism.

Finally, special factors may lead to high costs of doing business elsewhere in the country. There is an incentive to locate in the capital where personal security is highest in countries in or emerging from conflict such as the Democratic Republic of Congo. And firms may be responding primarily to costs and risks resulting from extortion, greater corruption, or civil unrest in rural areas and small cities, as well as bad infrastructure. The swelling of the urban giant can therefore also be a symptom of binding constraints on development elsewhere in the country that growth diagnosticians can learn from (see Chapter 4). This may suggest priority policies to help overcome a nation's particular problems of high costs of operating outside the primate city. In recent years Mexico City has been growing more slowly than the Mexican population as a whole, so that its share of the national population is also slowly becoming reduced.

With our better understanding of the causes of outsized primate cities, it becomes clear that this feature is not inevitable. Indeed, if trends toward greater democracy, reduced incidence of coups, increased outward-looking policies, and improved prospects of solving and preventing civil conflicts are maintained, the ratios of largest to second-largest cities where urban giantism has prevailed are likely to continue to decrease.

7.4 The Urban Informal Sector

As noted in Chapter 3, a focus of development theory has been on the dualistic nature of developing countries' national economies—the existence of a modern urban capitalist sector geared toward capital-intensive, large-scale production and a traditional rural subsistence sector geared toward labor-intensive, small-scale production. This dualistic analysis has also been applied specifically to the urban economy, which has been decomposed into a formal and an informal sector.

The existence of an unorganized, unregulated, and mostly legal but unregistered **informal sector** was recognized in the 1970s, following observations in several developing countries that massive additions to the urban labor force failed to show up in formal modern-sector unemployment statistics. The bulk of new entrants to the urban labor force seemed to create their own employment or to work for small-scale family-owned enterprises. The self-employed were engaged in a remarkable array of activities, ranging from hawking, street vending, letter writing, knife sharpening, and junk collecting to selling fireworks, prostitution, drug peddling, and snake charming. Others found jobs as mechanics, carpenters, small artisans, barbers, and personal servants. Still others were highly successful small-scale entrepreneurs with several employees (mostly relatives) and higher incomes. Some could even eventually graduate to the formal sector, where they became legally registered, licensed, and subject to government labor regulations. With the unprecedented rate of growth of the urban population in developing countries expected to continue and with the increasing failure of the rural and urban formal sectors to absorb additions to the labor force, more attention is being devoted to the role of the informal sector in serving as a panacea for the growing unemployment problem.

The informal sector continues to play an important role in developing countries, despite decades of benign neglect and even outright hostility. In many developing countries, about half of the employed urban population works in the informal sector. Figure 7.9 shows the relative importance of informal unemployment in selected cities. Most of these cities reflect the typical range of informal-sector employment share, from about 30% to 70%. (The only exception is Ljubljana, a virtually developed city near Austria and Italy.) We find a similar pattern of high informal-sector employment in cities throughout the developing world. For example, in India, the urban informal sector comprises 28.5% of employment in Kolkata, 46.5% in Ahmedabad, 49.5% in Mumbai, 53.8% in Chennai, 61.4% in Delhi, and 65.5% in Bangaluru.

The informal sector is characterized by a large number of small-scale production and service activities that are individually or family-owned and use simple, labor-intensive technology. They tend to operate like monopolistically competitive firms with ease of entry, excess capacity, and competition driving profits (incomes) down to the average supply price of labor of potential new entrants. The usually self-employed workers in this sector have less formal education, are generally unskilled, and lack access to financial capital. As a result, worker productivity and income tend to be lower in the informal sector than in the formal sector. Moreover, workers in the informal sector do not enjoy the measure of protection afforded by the formal modern sector in terms of job security, decent working conditions, and old-age pensions. Many workers entering this sector are recent migrants from rural areas unable to find employment in the formal sector. Their motivation is often to obtain sufficient income for survival, relying on their own indigenous resources to create work. As many members of the household as possible are involved in income-generating activities, including women and children, and they often work very long

Informal sector The part of the urban economy of developing countries characterized by small competitive individual or family firms, petty retail trade and services, labor-intensive methods, free entry, and market-determined factor and product prices.

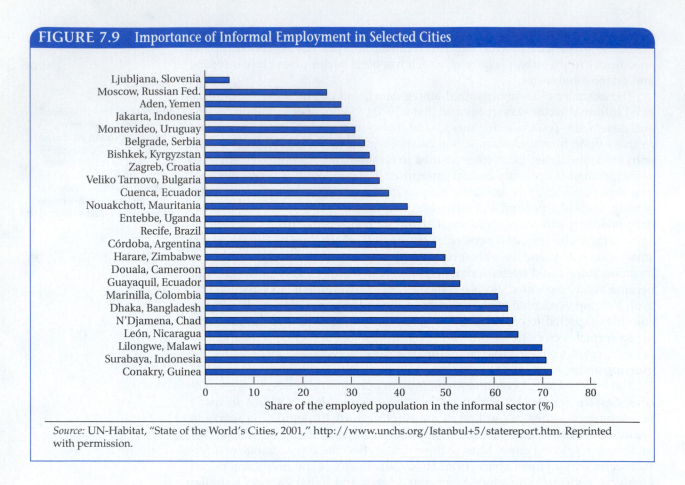

FIGURE 7.9   Importance of Informal Employment in Selected Cities

Share of the employed population in the informal sector (%)

Source: UN-Habitat, "State of the World's Cities, 2001," http://www.unchs.org/Istanbul+5/statereport.htm. Reprinted with permission.

hours. A large fraction inhabit shacks and small cinder-block houses that they themselves have built in slums and squatter settlements, which generally lack minimal public services such as electricity, water, drainage, transportation, and educational and health services. Many are vulnerable to cyclones (hurricanes), storm surges, mudslides, and other disasters caused by extreme weather—of the type predicted to substantially worsen with climate change (see Chapter 10). Others are even less fortunate, homeless, and living on the pavements. They find sporadic temporary employment in the informal sector as day laborers and hawkers, but their incomes are insufficient to provide even the most rudimentary shelter.

Policies for the Urban Informal Sector

In terms of its relationship with other sectors, the informal sector is linked with the rural sector in that it allows excess labor to escape from extreme rural poverty and underemployment, although under living and working conditions and for incomes that are often not much better. It is closely connected with the formal urban sector: The formal sector depends on the informal sector for cheap inputs and wage goods for its workers, and the informal sector in turn depends on the growth of the formal sector for a good portion of its income and clientele.

Informal-sector incomes have remained persistently higher than those in the poorest rural regions, despite the continued flow of rural-urban migration. The Nobel laureate Sir Arthur Lewis in the 1950s viewed traditional-sector workers, petty traders such as newspaper hawkers, as unproductive and essentially engaged in distractions from the main urban work of industrialization. But if wages are persistently higher in very competitive activities such as urban informal work than in rural work, this likely reflects higher productivities as well. Consequently, a revisionist view espousing the constructive role of cities (that includes their informal sectors) in economic development has taken hold. This approach has been championed by the Dar es Salaam–based UN-Habitat, in its "State of the World's Cities" reports.[20] The 2001 report systematically criticized what it termed the "anti-urban bias of the development agencies." Acting on the strong development tradition beginning with the Lewis skepticism of the urban informal sector, developed with the Todaro migration model (examined later in this chapter) emphasizing the negative consequences of urban bias for both efficiency and equity, continuing with the influential work of the integrated rural development school of the 1970s and recast and reemphasized under the Wolfensohn and subsequent presidencies at the World Bank, development agencies have indeed stressed rural development rhetorically. Many scholars have concluded, however, that this rhetoric often goes untranslated into real resources for the rural areas so that any pro-rural bias of development agencies is typically little more than a partial correction to the overriding forces for urban bias. However, the renewed focus on the development role of cities is an important trend. Besides UN-Habitat, the World Bank and other agencies have placed increasing emphasis on improved urban development.[21] The new focus is on how to make cities in developing countries more dynamic engines of growth and more livable environments, and it promises to be one of the more important streams of emerging research and policy analysis in economic development in coming years. In any case, while medium-size cities undoubtedly deserve greater attention for the constructive role they play in the development process, this does not obviate the problem of overconcentration of activities in first-city urban giantism.

The important role that the informal sector plays in providing income opportunities for the poor is clear. There is some question, however, as to whether the informal sector is merely a holding ground for people awaiting entry into the formal sector and as such is a transitional phase that must be made as comfortable as possible without perpetuating its existence until it is itself absorbed by the formal sector or whether it is here to stay and should in fact be promoted as a major source of employment and income for the urban labor force, or some combination. The answer is likely to differ by country. A 2012 study by Isabel Günther and Andrey Launov found that for the case of Cote d'Ivoire, about half of those working in the informal sector fell into each category of "opportunity" or "last resort."[22]

In support of the latter view, the formal sector in developing countries often has a small base in terms of output and employment. To absorb future additions to the urban labor force, the formal sector must be able to generate employment at a very high rate. This means that output must grow at an even faster rate, since employment in this sector increases less than proportionately in relation to output. This sort of growth seems highly unlikely in view of current trends. Thus, the burden on the informal sector to absorb more labor will continue to grow unless other solutions to the urban unemployment problem are provided. But young people face increasingly difficult job prospects, as can be seen in Figure 7.10.

The informal sector has demonstrated its ability to generate employment and income for the urban labor force. As pointed out earlier, it is already absorbing an average of 50% of the urban labor force. Some studies have shown the informal sector generating almost one-third of urban income.

Several other arguments can be made in favor of promoting the informal sector. First, scattered evidence indicates that the informal sector generates surpluses even in a hostile policy environment that denies it access to the advantages offered to the formal sector, such as credit, foreign exchange, and tax concessions. Thus, the informal sector's surplus could provide an impetus to growth in the urban economy. Second, as a result of its low capital intensity, only a fraction of the capital needed in the formal sector is required to employ a worker in the informal sector, offering considerable savings to developing countries so often plagued with capital shortages. Third, by providing access to training and apprenticeships at substantially lower costs than provided by formal institutions and the formal sector, the informal sector can play an important role in the formation of human capital. Fourth, the informal sector generates demand for semiskilled and unskilled labor, whose supply is increasing in both

FIGURE 7.10   Youth Unemployment Rates, 1995 and 2005

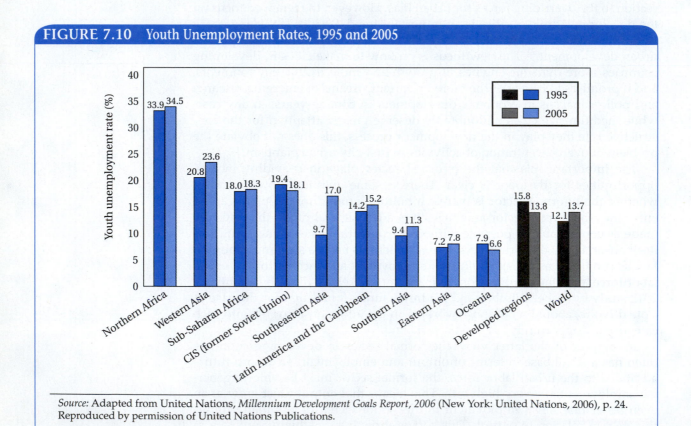

Source: Adapted from United Nations, *Millennium Development Goals Report, 2006* (New York: United Nations, 2006), p. 24. Reproduced by permission of United Nations Publications.

relative and absolute terms and is unlikely to be absorbed by the formal sector with its increasing demands for a skilled labor force. Fifth, the informal sector is more likely to adopt appropriate technologies and make use of local resources, allowing for a more efficient allocation of resources. Sixth, the informal sector plays an important role in recycling waste materials, engaging in the collection of goods ranging from scrap metals to cigarette butts, many of which find their way to the industrial sector or provide basic commodities for the poor. Finally, promotion of the informal sector would ensure an increased distribution of the benefits of development to the poor, many of whom are concentrated in the informal sector.

Promotion of the informal sector is not, however, without its disadvantages. One of the major disadvantages in promoting the informal sector lies in the strong relationship between rural-urban migration and labor absorption in the informal sector. Migrants from the rural sector have both a lower unemployment rate and a shorter waiting period before obtaining a job in the informal sector. Promoting income and employment opportunities in the informal sector could therefore aggravate the urban unemployment problem by attracting more labor than either the desirable parts of the informal or the formal sector could absorb. Furthermore, there is concern over the environmental consequences of a highly concentrated informal sector in the urban areas. Many informal-sector activities cause pollution and congestion (e.g., pedicabs) or inconvenience to pedestrians (e.g., hawkers and vendors). Moreover, increased densities in slums and low-income neighborhoods, coupled with poor urban services, could cause enormous problems for urban areas. Any policy measures designed to promote the informal sector must be able to cope with these various problems. Finally, it is an almost universal observation that when regular formal-sector employment becomes available, many informal-sector microentrepreneurs switch sectors to take these jobs—clear evidence of "revealed preference."

The International Labor Organization has made some general suggestions as to what sorts of measures might be adopted to promote the informal sector. To begin with, governments will have to abandon their hostility toward the informal sector and adopt a more positive and sympathetic posture. For example, in Latin America, although improving in many cases, bureaucratic red tape and an inordinate number of administrative procedures needed to register a new business result in delays of up to 240 days in Ecuador, 310 days in Venezuela, and 525 days in Guatemala. Until recently, Brazil, Mexico, and Chile all required more than 20 applications before a company could be approved to do business. Such procedures not only cause excessive delays but can also inflate the costs of doing business by up to 70% annually. So informal-sector businesses simply skirt the law. Fortunately, there has been progress in improving these policies; the 2013 *Doing Business* annual report explains that, "in the past 8 years the start-up process received more attention from policy makers than any other area of business regulation tracked by *Doing Business*— through 368 reforms in 149 economies. These worldwide efforts reduced the average time to start a business from 50 days to 30 and the average cost from 89% of income per capita to 31%. But other metrics indicate less progress."[23]

Because access to skills plays an important role in determining the structure of the informal sector, governments should facilitate training in the areas that are most beneficial to the urban economy. In this way, the government can play a role in shaping the informal sector so that it contains production and service activities that provide the most value to society. Specifically, such measures might promote legal activities and discourage illegal ones by providing proper skills and other incentives. They could also generate taxes that now go unpaid.

The lack of capital is a major constraint on activities in the informal sector. The provision of credit would therefore permit these enterprises to expand, produce more profit, and hence generate more income and employment. Microfinance institutions have been leading the way in providing enhanced credit access (see Chapter 15). Access to improved technology would have similar effects. Providing infrastructure and suitable locations for work (e.g., designating specific areas for stalls) could help alleviate some of the environmental and congestion consequences of an expanded informal sector. Finally, better living conditions must be provided, if not directly, then by promoting growth of the sector on the fringes of urban areas or in smaller towns where the population will settle close to its new area of work, away from the urban density. Promotion of the informal sector outside the urban areas may also help redirect the flow of rural-urban migration, especially if carried out in conjunction with the policies discussed later in this chapter.

Women in the Informal Sector

In some regions of the world, women predominate among rural-urban migrants and may even comprise the majority of the urban population. Though historically many of these women are simply accompanying their spouses, a growing number of women in Latin America, Asia, and Africa migrate to seek economic opportunity. With the exception of the export enclaves of East Asia and a few other cities, where everything from computers to clothing and running shoes are manufactured, only a small minority of these migrants is able to find employment in the formal sector, which is generally dominated by men. As a consequence, women often represent the bulk of the informal-sector labor supply, working for low wages at unstable jobs with no employee or social security benefits. The increase in the number of single female migrants has also contributed to the rising proportion of urban households headed by women, which tend to be poorer, experience tighter resource constraints, and retain relatively high fertility rates. The changing composition of migration flows has important economic and demographic implications for many urban areas of the developing world.

As UN-Habitat noted for its *State of Women in Cities 2012/2013*:

> Urban women supposedly enjoy greater social, economic, political opportunities and freedoms than their rural counterparts. However, the notable gender gaps in labor and employment, decent work, pay, tenure rights, access to and accumulation of assets, personal security and safety and representation in formal structures of urban governance, show that women are often the last to benefit from the prosperity of cities.[24]

Because members of female-headed households are generally restricted to low-productivity, informal-sector employment and experience higher dependency burdens, they are more likely to be poor and malnourished and less likely to obtain formal education, health care, or clean water and sanitation, often remaining effectively excluded from government services. Dropout rates among children from households headed by women are much higher because the children are more likely to be working to contribute to household income.

Many women run small business ventures or microenterprises that require little or no start-up capital and often involve the marketing of homemade foodstuffs and handicrafts. Though women's restricted access to capital leads to high rates of return on their tiny investments, the extremely low capital-labor ratios confine women to low-productivity undertakings. Studies in Latin America and Asia have found that where credit is available to women with informal-sector microenterprises, repayment rates have equaled or exceeded those for men (see Chapter 15) . And because women are able to make more productive use of capital and start from a much lower investment base, their rates of return on investments often surpass those for men.

Despite the impressive record of these credit programs, they remain limited. The majority of institutional credit is still channeled through formal-sector agencies, and as a result, women generally find themselves ineligible for even small loans. Government programs to enhance income in poor households will inevitably neglect the neediest households so long as governments continue to focus on formal-sector employment of men and allocation of resources through formal-sector institutions. To solve the plight of poor urban women and their children, it is imperative that efforts be made to integrate women into the economic mainstream. Ensuring that women benefit from development programs will require that women's special circumstances be considered in policy design.

The legalization and economic promotion of informal-sector activities, where the majority of the urban female labor force is employed, could greatly improve women's financial flexibility and the productivity of their ventures. However, to enable women to reap these benefits, governments must repeal laws that restrict women's rights to own property and conduct financial transactions. Likewise, barriers to women's direct involvement in technical training programs and extension services must be eradicated. Finally, the provision of affordable child care and family-planning services would lighten the burden of women's reproductive roles and permit them a greater degree of economic participation.

7.5 Migration and Development

As noted earlier in the chapter, rural-urban migration has been dramatic, and urban development plays an important role in economic development. Rates of rural-urban migration in developing countries have exceeded rates of urban job creation and thus have surpassed greatly the absorption capacity of both industry and urban social services.

Migration worsens rural-urban structural imbalances in two direct ways. First, on the supply side, internal migration disproportionately increases the growth rate of urban job seekers relative to urban population growth, which itself is at historically unprecedented levels because of the high proportion of well-educated young people in the migrant system. Their presence tends to swell the urban labor supply while depleting the rural countryside of valuable human capital. Second, on the demand side, urban job creation is generally more difficult and costly to accomplish than rural job creation because of the need for substantial complementary resource inputs for most jobs in the industrial sector. Moreover, the pressures of rising urban wages and compulsory employee fringe benefits in combination with the unavailability of appropriate, more labor-intensive production technologies means that a rising share of modern-sector output growth is accounted for by increases in labor productivity. Together this rapid supply increase and lagging demand growth tend to convert a short-run problem of resource imbalances into a long-run situation of chronic urban surplus labor.

But the impact of migration on the development process is much more pervasive than its exacerbation of urban unemployment and underemployment. In fact, the significance of the migration phenomenon in most developing countries is not necessarily in the process itself or even in its impact on the sectoral allocation of human resources. Rather, its significance lies in its implications for economic growth in general and for the character of that growth, particularly its distributional manifestations.

We must therefore recognize that migration in excess of job opportunities is both a symptom of and a contributor to underdevelopment. Understanding the causes, determinants, and consequences of internal rural-urban labor migration is thus central to understanding the nature and character of the development process and to formulating policies to influence this process in socially desirable ways. A simple yet crucial step in underlining the centrality of the migration phenomenon is to recognize that any economic and social policy that affects rural and urban real incomes will directly or indirectly influence the migration process. This process will in turn tend to alter the pattern of sectoral and geographic economic activity, income distribution, and even population growth. Because all economic policies have direct and indirect effects on the level and growth of urban or rural incomes, or both, they all will have a tendency to influence the nature and magnitude of the migration stream. Some policies may have a more direct and immediate impact, such as wages and income policies and employment promotion programs. There are other policies that, though less obvious, may in the long run be no less important. Included among these policies, for example, would be land tenure arrangements; commodity pricing policies; credit allocation; taxation; export promotion; import substitution; commercial policies; the geographic distribution of social services; the nature of public investment programs; attitudes toward private foreign investors; the organization of population and family-planning programs; the structure, content, and orientation of the educational system; the functioning of labor markets; and the nature of public policies toward international technology transfer and the location of new industries. There is thus a clear need to recognize the central importance of internal and, for many countries, even international migration and to integrate the two-way relationship between migration and population distribution on the one hand and economic variables on the other into a more comprehensive framework designed to improve development policy formulation.

In addition, we need to understand better not only why people move and what factors are most important in their decision-making process but also what the consequences of migration are for rural and urban economic and social development. If all development policies affect migration and are affected by it, which are the most significant, and why? What are the policy options and trade-offs among different and sometimes competing objectives (e.g., curtailing internal migration and expanding educational opportunities in rural areas)? Part of our task in the following sections will be to seek answers to these and other questions relating to migration, unemployment, and development.

Migration patterns are complex. The most important type of migration from the standpoint of long-run development is rural-urban migration, but a great deal of rural-rural, urban-urban, and even urban-rural migration also takes place. Rural-urban migration is most important because the population share of cities is growing, despite the fact that fertility is much lower in urban areas, and the difference is accounted for by rural-urban migration. It is also important because of the potential development benefits of economic activity of cities, due to agglomeration economies and other factors. However, urban-rural migration is important to understand because it usually occurs when hard times in cities coincide with increases in output prices from the country's cash crops, as occurred in Ghana not long ago. Thus, the overall picture is one of a remarkable amount of "churning," or continuous movements of people within developing countries, especially over short distances. These movements contradict the popular image of stasis in traditional societies. The composition of internal migration for several countries is shown in Figure 7.11.

In addition to wage differentials, age, and education, migration is also explained partly by relocation upon remarrying; prior emigration of family members; distance and costs of relocation; occurrence of famine, disease, violence, and other disasters; and relative standing in the origin community, with those lower on the social order more likely to migrate. Migration can also be a form of portfolio diversification for families who seek to settle some members in areas where they may not be affected by economic shocks in the same way as if they had stayed at home.[25]

7.6 Toward an Economic Theory of Rural-Urban Migration

The economic development of western Europe and the United States was closely associated with the movement of labor from rural to urban areas. For the most part, with a rural sector dominated by agricultural activities and an urban sector focusing on industrialization, overall economic development in these countries was characterized by the gradual reallocation of labor out of agriculture and into industry through rural-urban migration, both internal and international. Urbanization and industrialization were in essence synonymous. This historical model served as a blueprint for structural change in developing countries, as evidenced, for example, by the original Lewis theory of labor transfer (see Chapter 3).

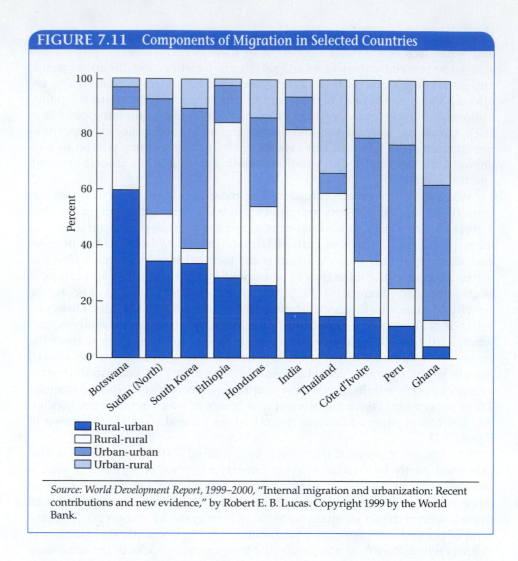

FIGURE 7.11   Components of Migration in Selected Countries

Legend:
- Rural-urban
- Rural-rural
- Urban-urban
- Urban-rural

Source: World Development Report, 1999–2000, "Internal migration and urbanization: Recent contributions and new evidence," by Robert E. B. Lucas. Copyright 1999 by the World Bank.

Todaro migration model
A theory that explains rural-urban migration as an economically rational process despite high urban unemployment. Migrants calculate (present value of) urban expected income (or its equivalent) and move if this exceeds average rural income.

Harris-Todaro model
An equilibrium version of the Todaro migration model that predicts that expected incomes will be equated across rural and urban sectors when taking into account informal-sector activities and outright unemployment.

But the overwhelming evidence of the past several decades, when developing nations witnessed a massive migration of their rural populations into urban areas despite rising levels of urban unemployment and underemployment, lessens the validity of the Lewis two-sector model of development.[26] An explanation of the phenomenon, as well as policies to address the resulting problems, must be sought elsewhere. One theory to explain the apparently paradoxical relationship of accelerated rural-urban migration in the context of rising urban unemployment has come to be known as the **Todaro migration model** and in its equilibrium form as the **Harris-Todaro model**.[27]

A Verbal Description of the Todaro Model

Starting from the assumption that migration is primarily an economic phenomenon, which for the individual migrant can be a quite rational decision despite the existence of urban unemployment, the Todaro model postulates that migration proceeds in response to urban-rural differences in expected income rather than actual earnings. The fundamental premise is that migrants consider the various labor market opportunities available to them in the rural and urban sectors and choose the one that maximizes their expected gains from migration.

In essence, the theory assumes that members of the labor force, both actual and potential, compare their expected incomes for a given time horizon in the urban sector (the difference between returns and costs of migration) with prevailing average rural incomes and migrate if the former exceeds the latter. (See Appendix 7.1 for a mathematical formulation.)

Consider the following illustration. Suppose that the average unskilled or semiskilled rural worker has a choice between being a farm laborer (or working his own land) for an annual average real income of, say, 50 units or migrating to the city, where a worker with his skill or educational background can obtain wage employment yielding an annual real income of 100 units. The more commonly used economic models of migration, which place exclusive emphasis on the income differential factor as the determinant of the decision to migrate, would indicate a clear choice in this situation. The worker should seek the higher-paying urban job. It is important to recognize, however, that these migration models were developed largely in the context of advanced industrial economies and hence implicitly assume the existence of full or near-full employment. In a full-employment environment, the decision to migrate can be based solely on the desire to secure the highest-paid job wherever it becomes available. Simple economic theory would then indicate that such migration should lead to a reduction in wage differentials through the interaction of the forces of supply and demand, in areas of both emigration and immigration.

Unfortunately, such an analysis is not realistic in the context of the institutional and economic framework of most developing nations. First, these countries are beset by a chronic unemployment problem, which means that a typical migrant cannot expect to secure a high-paying urban job immediately. In fact, it is much more likely that on entering the urban labor market, many uneducated, unskilled migrants will either become totally unemployed or will seek casual and part-time employment as vendors, hawkers, repairmen, and itinerant day laborers in the urban traditional or informal sector, where ease of entry, small scale of operation, and relatively competitive price and wage determination prevail. In the case of migrants with considerable human capital in the form of a secondary or university certificate, opportunities are much better, and many will find formal-sector jobs relatively quickly. But they constitute only a small proportion of the total migration stream. Consequently, in deciding to migrate, the individual must balance the probabilities and risks of being unemployed or underemployed for a considerable period of time against the positive urban-rural real income differential. The fact that a typical migrant who gains a modern-sector job can expect to earn twice the annual real income in an urban area than in a rural environment may be of little consequence if the actual probability of his securing the higher-paying job within, say, a one-year period is one chance in five. Thus, the actual probability of his being successful in securing the higher-paying urban job is 20%, and therefore his expected urban income for the one-year period is in fact 20 units and not the 100 units that an urban worker in a full-employment environment would expect to receive. So with a one-period time horizon and a probability of success of 20%, it would be irrational for this migrant to seek an urban job, even though the differential between urban and rural earnings capacity is 100%. However, if the probability of success were 60% and the expected urban income therefore 60 units, it would be entirely rational for our migrant with his one-period time horizon to try his luck in the urban area, even though urban unemployment may be extremely high.

If we now approach the situation by assuming a considerably longer time horizon—a more realistic assumption, especially in view of the fact that the vast majority of migrants are between the ages of 15 and 24—the decision to migrate should be represented on the basis of a longer-term, more permanent income calculation. If the migrant anticipates a relatively low probability of finding regular wage employment in the initial period but expects this probability to increase over time as he is able to broaden his urban contacts, it would still be rational for him to migrate, even though expected urban income during the initial period or periods might be lower than expected rural income. As long as the **present value** of the net stream of expected urban income over the migrant's planning horizon exceeds that of the expected rural income, the decision to migrate is justifiable.

Rather than equalizing urban and rural wage rates, as would be the case in a competitive model, we see that rural-urban migration in our model equates rural and urban expected incomes. For example, if average rural income were 60 and urban income were 120, a 50% urban unemployment rate would be necessary before further migration would no longer be profitable. Because expected incomes are defined in terms of both wages and employment probabilities, it is possible to have continued migration despite the existence of sizable rates of urban unemployment. In our example, migration would continue even if the urban unemployment rate were 30% to 40%.

A Diagrammatic Presentation

This process of achieving an unemployment equilibrium between urban expected wages and average rural income rather than an equalized rural-urban wage, as in the traditional neoclassical free-market model, can also be explained by a diagrammatic portrayal of the basic Harris-Todaro model. This is done in Figure 7.12.[28] Assume only two sectors, rural agriculture and urban manufacturing. The demand for labor (the marginal product of labor curve) in agriculture is given by the negatively sloped line AA. Labor demand in manufacturing is given by MM' (reading from right to left). The total labor force is given by line $O_A O_M$. In a neoclassical, flexible-wage, full-employment market economy, the equilibrium wage would be established at $W_A^* W_M^*$, with $O_A L_A^*$ workers in agriculture and $O_M L_M^*$ workers employed in urban manufacturing. All available workers are therefore employed.

But what if urban wages are institutionally determined (inflexible downward) as assumed by Todaro at a level $\overline{W}_M$, which is at a considerable distance above W_A^*? If for the moment we continue to assume that there is no unemployment, $O_M L_M$ workers would get urban jobs, and the rest, $O_A L_M$, would have to settle for rural employment at $O_A W_A^{**}$ wages (below the free-market level of $O_A W_A^*$). So now we have an urban-rural real wage gap of $\overline{W}_M - W_A^{**}$, with $\overline{W}_M$ institutionally fixed. If rural workers were free to migrate (as they

Present value   The discounted value at the present time of a sum of money to be received in the future.

FIGURE 7.12   The Harris-Todaro Migration Model

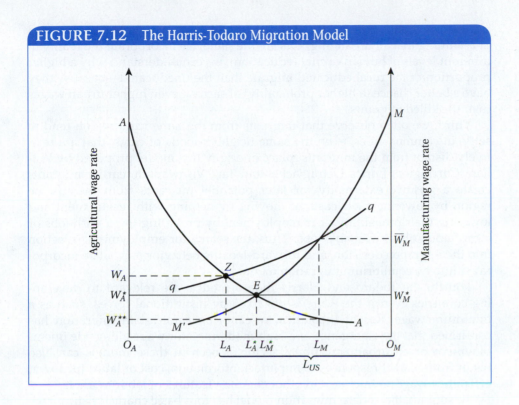

are almost everywhere except China), then despite the availability of only $O_M L_M$ jobs, they are willing to take their chances in the urban job lottery. If their chance (probability) of securing one of these favored jobs is expressed by the ratio of employment in manufacturing, L_M, to the total urban labor pool, L_{US}, then the expression

$$W_A = \frac{L_M}{L_{US}}(\overline{W}_M) \qquad (7.1)$$

shows the probability of urban job success necessary to equate agricultural income W_A with urban expected income $(L_M/L_{US})\ (\overline{W}_M)$, thus causing a potential migrant to be indifferent between job locations. The locus of such points of indifference is given by the qq' curve in Figure 7.12.[29] The new unemployment equilibrium now occurs at point Z, where the urban-rural actual wage gap is $\overline{W}_M - W_A$, $O_A L_A$ workers are still in the agricultural sector, and $O_M L_M$ of these workers have modern (formal)-sector jobs paying $\overline{W}_M$ wages. The rest, $O_M L_A - O_M L_M$, are either unemployed or engaged in low-income informal-sector activities. This explains the existence of urban unemployment and the private economic rationality of continued rural-to-urban migration, despite this high unemployment. However, although it may be privately rational from a cost-benefit perspective for an individual to migrate to the city despite high unemployment, it can, as will soon become clear, be socially very costly.

There are many ways to extend the model; here we mention four. First, Equation 7.1 simplifies by assuming that those who migrate and do not get a modern job receive no income; but if they instead receive urban informal-sector income, we modify expected income accordingly.[30] Second, note that if instead of assuming that all urban migrants are the same, we incorporate the reality of different levels of human capital (education), we can understand why a higher proportion of the rural educated migrate than the uneducated—because they have a better chance (a higher probability) of earning even higher urban wages than unskilled migrants.

Third, we often observe that migrants from the same rural region tend to settle in common cities, even the same neighborhoods of cities, that are relatively distant from the migrants' place of origin. In a model proposed by William Carrington, Enrica Detragiache, and Tara Vishwanath, earlier migrants create a positive externality for later potential migrants from their home region by lowering their costs of moving by helping with resettlement and lowering their probability of unemployment by providing them with jobs or information about available jobs. Thus, the search for employment, selection into the migration decision, and forward-looking behavior may all be incorporated into an equilibrium migration model.[31]

Fourth, the Todaro and Harris-Todaro models are relevant to developing countries even if the wage is not fixed by institutional forces, such as a minimum wage. Recent theoretical research on rural-urban migration has confirmed that the emergence of a high modern-sector wage alongside unemployment or an urban traditional sector as seen in these models can also result from market responses to imperfect information, cost of **labor turnover**, **efficiency wage** payments, and other common features of labor markets.[32]

To sum up, the Todaro migration model has four basic characteristics:

Labor turnover Worker separations from employers, a concept used in theory that the urban-rural wage gap is partly explained by the fact that urban modern-sector employers pay higher wages to reduce labor turnover rates and retain trained and skilled workers.

Efficiency wage The notion that modern-sector urban employers pay a higher wage than the equilibrium wage rate in order to attract and retain a higher-quality workforce or to obtain higher productivity on the job.

1. Migration is stimulated primarily by rational economic considerations of relative benefits and costs—mostly financial but also psychological.

2. The decision to migrate depends on expected rather than actual urban-rural real-wage differentials, where the expected differential is determined by the interaction of two variables, the actual urban-rural wage differential and the probability of successfully obtaining employment in the urban sector.

3. The probability of obtaining an urban job is directly related to the urban employment rate and thus inversely related to the urban unemployment rate.

4. Migration rates in excess of urban job opportunity growth rates are not only possible but also rational and even likely in the face of wide urban-rural expected income differentials. High rates of urban unemployment are therefore inevitable outcomes of the serious imbalance of economic opportunities between urban and rural areas in most underdeveloped countries.

Five Policy Implications

Although the Todaro theory might at first seem to devalue the critical importance of rural-urban migration by portraying it as an adjustment mechanism by which workers allocate themselves between rural and urban labor markets, it does have important policy implications for development strategy with regard to wages and incomes, rural development, and industrialization.

First, imbalances in urban-rural employment opportunities caused by the urban bias, particularly first-city bias, of development strategies must be reduced. Because migrants are assumed to respond to differentials in expected incomes, it is vitally important that imbalances between economic opportunities in rural and urban sectors be minimized. When urban wage rates rise faster than average rural incomes, they stimulate further rural-urban migration in spite of rising levels of urban unemployment. This heavy influx of people into urban areas not only gives rise to socioeconomic problems in the cities but may also eventually create problems of labor shortages and lack of entrepreneurship in rural areas. Thus, policy distortions that induce more rapid rural-to-urban migration than would otherwise occur generally reduce overall social welfare.

Second, urban job creation is an insufficient solution for the urban unemployment problem. The traditional (Keynesian) economic solution to urban unemployment (the creation of more urban modern-sector jobs without simultaneous attempts to improve rural incomes and employment opportunities) can result in the paradoxical situation in which more urban employment leads to higher levels of urban unemployment! Once again, the imbalance in expected income-earning opportunities is the crucial concept. Because migration rates are assumed to respond positively to *both* higher urban wages *and* higher urban employment opportunities (or probabilities), it follows that for any given positive urban-rural wage differential (in most developing countries, urban wages are typically three to four times as large as rural wages), higher urban employment rates will widen the expected differential and induce even higher rates of rural-urban migration. For every new job created, two or three migrants who were productively occupied in rural areas may come to the city. Thus, if 100 new jobs are created, there may be as many as 300 new migrants and therefore 200 more urban unemployed. Hence, a policy designed to reduce urban unemployment may lead not only to higher levels of urban unemployment but also to lower levels of agricultural output due to **induced migration**.

> **Induced migration** Process in which the creation of urban jobs raises expected incomes and induces more people to migrate from rural areas.

Third, indiscriminate educational expansion will lead to further migration and unemployment. The Todaro model also has important policy implications for curtailing public investment in higher education. The heavy influx of rural migrants into urban areas at rates much in excess of new employment opportunities necessitates rationing in the selection of new employees. Although within each educational group such selection may be largely random, many observers have noted that employers tend to use educational attainment or number of years of completed schooling as the typical rationing device. For the same wage, they will hire people with more education in preference to those with less, even though extra education may not contribute to better job performance. Jobs that could formerly be filled by those with a primary education (sweepers, messengers, filing clerks, etc.) now require secondary training; those formerly requiring a secondary certificate (clerks, typists, bookkeepers, etc.) must now have a university degree. It follows that for any given urban wage, if the probability of success in securing a modern-sector job is higher for people with more education, their expected income differential will also be higher, and they will be more likely to migrate to the cities. The basic Todaro model therefore provides an economic explanation for the observed fact in most developing countries that rural inhabitants with more education are more likely to migrate than those with less.

Wage subsidy   A government financial incentive to private employers to hire more workers, as through tax deductions for new job creation.

Fourth, wage subsidies and traditional scarcity factor pricing can be counterproductive. As noted in Chapter 5 and Appendix 5.1, a standard economic policy prescription for generating urban employment opportunities is to eliminate factor price distortions by using "correct" prices, perhaps implemented by wage subsidies (fixed government subsidies to employers for each worker employed) or direct government hiring. Because actual urban wages generally exceed the market or "correct" wage as a result of a variety of institutional factors, it is often argued that the elimination of wage distortions through price adjustments or a subsidy system will encourage more labor-intensive modes of production. Although such policies can generate more labor-intensive modes of production, they can also lead to higher levels of unemployment in accordance with our argument about induced migration. The overall welfare impact of a **wage subsidy** policy when both the rural and urban sectors are taken into account is not immediately clear. Much will depend on the level of urban unemployment, the size of the urban-rural expected-income differential, and the magnitude of induced migration as more urban jobs are created.

Finally, programs of integrated rural development should be encouraged. Policies that operate only on the demand side of the urban employment picture, such as wage subsidies, direct government hiring, elimination of factor price distortions, and employer tax incentives, are probably far less effective in the long run in alleviating the unemployment problem than policies designed directly to regulate the supply of labor to urban areas. Clearly, however, some combination of both kinds of policies is most desirable.

Conceptually, it may be useful to think of cities and their surrounding rural areas as integrated systems. There are significant complementarities between town and country (see Chapter 9). Agricultural and raw materials grown and extracted in rural areas are inputs for urban industry. Although there is some urban agriculture, most food consumed in urban areas is grown in agricultural regions. Towns are needed to allow sufficient agglomeration economies, as well as economies of scale, to produce and exchange many goods and services that are needed in rural areas. In turn, when rural incomes grow, markets for urban manufacturers expand. People come from their rural residences to work in the city by the day or the week. City residents temporarily migrate to nearby agricultural regions during peak planting and harvesting seasons. Thus, rural-urban linkages are extensive. And while investment in urban areas can accelerate migration to cities, investment in agriculture can raise productivity and incomes, making labor redundant, and also accelerate migration. As a result, for policy purposes, it may make a great deal of sense to take account of rural impacts when devising urban policies and vice versa.

At the same time, as globalization proceeds (see Chapter 12), cities tend to trade more with other cities, often in distant parts of the world, and less with nearby rural areas. Moreover, cities generally get the upper hand when urban and rural areas are treated as a bloc, reinforcing urban bias. And rural hinterlands, far from significant cities and from the attention of distant governments, whether national or regional, often suffer from benign neglect at best and systematic exploitation at worst, such as forced sale of food at low prices. Thus, rural areas need to retain their own autonomy, and poverty programs need to be tailored to the needs of rural citizens.

Every effort must be made to broaden the economic base of the rural economy. The present unnecessary economic incentives for rural-urban migration can be minimized through creative and well-designed programs of integrated rural development. These should focus on both farm and nonfarm income generation, employment growth, health care delivery, educational improvement, infrastructure development (electricity, water, roads, etc.), and the provision of other rural amenities. Successful rural development programs adapted to the socioeconomic and environmental needs of particular countries and regions seem to offer the only viable long-run solution to the problem of excessive rural-urban migration.

To assert, however, that there is an urgent need for policies designed to curb the excessive influx of rural migrants is not to imply an attempt to reverse what some observers have called inevitable historical trends. Rather, the implication of the Todaro migration model is that there is a growing need for a policy package that does not exacerbate these historical trends toward urbanization by artificially creating serious imbalances in economic opportunities between urban and rural areas.

7.7 Conclusion: A Comprehensive Urbanization, Migration, and Employment Strategy

Developing-country cities are projected to grow by more than 2 billion people over the next three decades. This presents enormous challenges for the developing world, but at the same time important economic development opportunities. The pattern of urban settlements tends to be very persistent, so the quality of planning now for this enormous transformation will have ramifications for decades to come.

Based on long-term trends, comparisons with developed countries, and still-strong individual incentives, continued urbanization and rural-urban migration are probably inevitable. Urban bias spurs migration, but focused investment in agriculture raises rural productivity sufficiently to require less labor; a majority of alternative types of employment expansion tend to be concentrated in urban areas because of agglomeration effects. Moreover, as education increases in rural areas, workers gain the skills they need, and perhaps the rising aspirations, to seek employment in the city. But the pace of rural-urban migration is still often excessive from the social viewpoint. At various points throughout this chapter, we have looked at possible policy approaches designed to improve the very serious migration and employment situation in developing countries. We conclude with a summary of what appears to be the growing consensus of most economists on the shape of a comprehensive migration and employment strategy.[33] These elements reflect the complex and nuanced nature of the topic, with potentially excessive migration relative to urban opportunities partly due to low productivity, poor rural institutions, and harsh social conditions; and the great and still not fully tapped opportunities for urban dynamism as an engine of economic development. We consider 10 key elements:

1. *Creating an appropriate rural-urban economic balance.* A more appropriate balance between rural and urban economic opportunities appears to be

indispensable to ameliorating both urban and rural unemployment problems and to slowing the pace of excessive rural-urban migration. The main thrust of this activity should be in the integrated development of the rural sector, the spread of rural nonfarm employment opportunities, improved credit access, better agricultural training, the reorientation of social investments toward rural areas, improving rural infrastructure, and addressing shortcomings of rural institutions (including corruption, discrimination, and stratification), the presence of which has the effect of raising the cost of delaying out-migration.

2. *Expansion of small-scale, labor-intensive industries.* The composition or "product mix" of output has obvious effects on the magnitude (and in many cases the location) of employment opportunities, because some products (often basic consumer goods) require more labor per unit of output and per unit of capital than others. Expansion of these mostly small-scale and labor-intensive industries in both urban and rural areas can be accomplished in two ways: directly, through government investment and incentives and improved access to credit, particularly for activities in the urban informal sector, and indirectly, through income redistribution (either directly or from future growth) to the rural poor, whose structure of consumer demand is both less import-intensive and more labor-intensive than that of the rich. Under the right conditions, such enterprises can agglomerate as industrial districts in ways that can generate exports, as pointed to by the findings on China in Box 7.1. Policies that effectively discourage clustering of specialized activities are likely to be harmful.

3. *Eliminating factor price distortions.* There is ample evidence to demonstrate that correcting factor price distortions—primarily by eliminating various capital subsidies and curtailing the growth of urban wages through market-based pricing—would increase employment opportunities and make better use of scarce capital resources. But by how much or how quickly these policies would work is not clear. Moreover, their migration implications would have to be ascertained. Correct pricing policies by themselves are insufficient to fundamentally alter the present employment situation.[34]

4. *Choosing appropriate labor-intensive technologies of production.* One of the principal factors inhibiting the success of any long-run program of employment creation in both urban industry and rural agriculture is the almost complete technological dependence on (typically laborsaving) machinery and equipment from the developed countries. Domestic and international efforts can help reduce this dependence by developing technological research and adaptation capacities in developing countries. Such efforts might first be linked to the development of small-scale, labor-intensive rural and urban enterprises. They could focus on developing low-cost, labor-intensive methods of meeting rural infrastructure needs, including roads, irrigation and drainage systems, and essential health and educational services. This is an area where scientific and technological assistance from the developed countries could prove extremely helpful.

5. *Modifying the linkage between education and employment.* The emergence of the phenomenon of the educated unemployed is calling into question the

appropriateness of the massive quantitative expansion of educational systems, especially at the higher levels. Formal education has become the rationing tunnel through which all prospective jobholders must pass. Although a full discussion of educational problems and policies must await the next chapter, one way to moderate the excessive demand for additional years of schooling (which in reality is a demand for modern-sector jobs) would be for governments, often the largest employers, to base their hiring practices and their wage structures on other criteria. Moreover, the creation of attractive economic opportunities in rural areas would make it easier to redirect educational systems toward the needs of rural development. At present, many of the skills needed for development remain largely neglected.

6. *Reducing population growth.* This is most efficiently accomplished through reductions in absolute poverty and inequality, particularly for women, along with the expanded provision of family-planning and rural health services. The labor force size for the next two decades is already determined by today's birth rates, and hidden momentum of population growth applies as well to labor force growth. Together with the demand policies identified in points 1 through 5, the population and labor supply reduction policies described in this chapter provide an essential ingredient in any strategy to combat the severe employment problems that developing countries face now and in future years.

7. *Decentralizing authority to cities and neighborhoods.* Experience shows that decentralization of authority to municipalities is an essential step in the improvement of urban policies and the quality of public services. Local conditions vary greatly among small and large cities, as well as across different national regions, and policies need to be designed to reflect these differences. Local officials have greater information about evolving local conditions; and when officials are held accountable for local fiscal performance and know they must answer to recipients of the services they provide, they also have greater incentives to carry out their responsibilities effectively. Decentralization, with increased authority of cities and regions, has been a major international trend in the organization of government (see Chapter 11) .

8. *Leveraging untapped opportunities for urban dynamism.* With strong, pro-poor rural development policies in place, many developing countries in Africa, Asia, and Latin America can still make gains in harnessing the growth potential of developing-country cities, with ongoing attention to preparing for its possible migration implications.

9. *Addressing the desperate poverty needs of the poor now living in urban slum conditions.* As poor rural residents continue to migrate to urban areas, there is a growing phenomenon of the "urbanization of global poverty," even if more than half of the poor will be found in rural areas for the next decades. As Martin Ravallion, Shaohua Chen, and Prem Sangraula concluded, "By fostering economic growth, urbanization helped reduce absolute poverty in the aggregate but did little for urban poverty."[35] For poor residents in slum communities, basic protection is needed. These residents face disease and death from unsanitary conditions and increasing vulnerability to severe weather events and other disasters. These citizens urgently need a

basic safety net, let alone an improvement in the actively hostile policies that have prevailed in many developing nations and regions by denying property rights (which has allowed the seizing of land and the demolishing of housing) and other forms of discrimination. A change in basic policies can lead to large improvements in living conditions in slums.

10. *Anticipating and assisting the new "climate migrants."* In a related point, one major response to climate change is rural-to-urban migration (see Chapter 10), section 10.3). This needs to be anticipated and planned for. A critical part of the solution is more effective rural development, from better access to sustainable irrigation to improved rural institutions. But "climate migrants" are already arriving in developing-country cities, and many of them end up on land that is highly vulnerable to disasters brought about by extreme weather, such as mudslides following heavy rains. As the World Bank has proposed:

> In facilitating migration as a response to climate impacts, it is better to formulate integrated migration and development policies that address the needs of voluntary migrants and support their entrepreneurial abilities and technical skills. To the extent possible, policies should discourage settlement of migrants in areas with high exposure to persistent climate hazards . . . forward-looking plans should identify alternative sites, apply compensation formulas that allow migrants to relocate and develop new sources of livelihoods, and build public and social infrastructure for community life.[36]

We return to the topic of rural development in Chapter 9 and environment and development in Chapter 10.

We conclude by noting that while a much higher urban share of population is inevitable, the tempo and pattern of urbanization will be key determinants of whether the deeper objectives of economic development are achieved. China and India, which together account for over one-third of the world's population, are in the midst of their most rapid migration and urbanization period. Several African and other Asian countries are entering this stage. Because of fixed costs, including infrastructure and land use patterns, the quality of policies toward urbanization and migration that are implemented now are thus of momentous importance for the character of economic development for many decades to come.

Rural-Urban Migration and Urbanization in Developing Countries: India and Botswana

About half of the world's population lives in cities; by 2025, nearly two-thirds will live in urban areas. Most of the urban growth is taking place in the developing world. The patterns of this growth and its implications are complex. Urban population growth in the developing world is far more rapid than population growth generally; about half the urban growth is accounted for by migrants from rural areas. Unchecked urbanization of the developing world is placing a strain on infrastructure and public health and threatens social stability. Shantytowns and similar makeshift settlements represent over one-third of developing-country urban residences. About half of the urban labor force works in the informal sector of low-skilled, low-productivity, often self-employed jobs in petty sales and services. Still, this sector may generate up to a third of urban income and features a low capital intensity, low-cost training, waste recycling, and employment creation. What drives migration? The cases of India and Botswana are instructive in showing the value of the probabilistic theory of migration and suggesting ways of extending it.

The scale of urbanization in these countries is dramatic. The UN Population Division projected in 2013 that India will surpass China as the world's largest nation in 2028, when India reaches a population of 1.45 billion; due largely to migration, the growth of the urban population will be much faster than that of the rural population. Botswana is a small country but represents one of Africa's relatively few long-term success stories (see the case study for Chapter 14); and as of 2012, its urbanization rate had already reached well over 60%, compared with an average of under one-third in sub-Saharan Africa as a whole.

Any economic or social policy that affects rural and urban incomes will influence migration; this, in turn, will affect sectoral and geographic economic activity, income distribution, and even population growth. Before the Todaro and Harris-Todaro migration models were introduced, migration was widely viewed as irrational or driven by noneconomic motivations, sometimes attributed to the lure of the "bright city lights." Noneconomic factors do influence migration decisions, but economic factors are now understood to be primary. In the economic version of the bright-city-lights theory, people rationally migrated on the basis of costs and benefits. In this approach, it was assumed that if migrants appeared to be worse off, this was because other benefits were being overlooked, with the effect of making the migrants feel better off (or raising their overall utility).

The Todaro migration models postulate that observed migration is individually rational but that migrants respond to urban-rural differences in expected rather than actual earnings. Urban modern-sector earnings are much higher than rural earnings, which may in turn be even higher than urban traditional-sector earnings. Migration occurs until average or expected rather than actual incomes are equal across regions, generating equilibrium unemployment or underemployment in the urban traditional sector. The extension of the model to consider equilibrium and effects of actions such as increases in wages and probability of employment in the urban areas, undertaken by Harris and Todaro, shows that under some conditions, notably elastic supply of labor, creation of employment opportunities in cities can actually lead to an *increase* in unemployment by attracting more migrants than there are new jobs. Despite being individually rational, extensive rural-urban migration generates social costs for crowded cities, while excessive migration also

imposes external costs on the rural areas emptied of better-educated, more venturesome young people, as well as external costs on urban infrastructure and lost output.

One set of relevant migration and employment policies emphasizes rural development, rural basic-needs strategies, elimination of factor price distortions, appropriate technology choice, and appropriate education. Each is intended to increase the incentives for rural residents to remain in rural areas rather than migrate to cities. But even if rural development is successful, fewer rural laborers will ultimately be needed, and demand for products of the cities will grow, which will fuel migration anyway. So other policies seek to influence the pace and pattern of urban development to gain the most benefits for the fewest costs from migration that is probably inevitable.

India provides an interesting setting for a case study because future urban migration is potentially so vast and because a number of interesting studies have been undertaken there. Botswana offers a good counterpoint because it has been the subject of some of the most interesting empirical research and represents one of the most rapidly urbanizing African countries as well as one of its most important success stories.

India

The growth of Delhi has been extraordinary: In 1950, Delhi was not even among the world's 30 largest cities, but by 2013 its population had soared to become second in size only to Tokyo.

One of the most detailed studies of rural-urban migration, providing some tests of the Todaro migration models and depicting the characteristics of migrants and the migration process, is Biswajit Banerjee's *Rural to Urban Migration and the Urban Labor Market: A Case Study of Delhi*.

Everyone who has been to a major city in a developing country has noticed the sharp inequality between residents with modern-sector jobs and those working in the informal sector. But can the informal sector be seen as a temporary way station on the road to the formal sector, or can the barriers between these sectors be explained by education and skill requirements that informal-sector workers cannot hope to meet? Banerjee found that the idea of segmented formal-informal rural labor markets could be substantiated statistically. After carefully controlling for

human capital variables, Banerjee was still left with earnings in the formal sector 9% higher than in the informal sector that were not explained by any standard economic factor. Even so, the earnings differences found in India were not nearly so dramatic as implied in some of the migration literature.

In much of the literature on urbanization, the typical laborer is characterized as self-employed or working on some type of piecework basis. But Banerjee found that only 14% of his informal-sector sample worked in nonwage employment. Interestingly, average monthly incomes of nonwage workers were 47% higher than those of formal-sector workers.

Banerjee argued that entry into nonwage employment was not easy in Delhi. Some activities required significant skills or capital. Those that did not were often controlled by cohesive "networks" of operators that controlled activities in various enterprises. Entry barriers to self-employment in petty services were probably lower in other developing-country cities.

Consistent with these findings, Banerjee found that mobility from the informal to the formal sector was low: There was little evidence that more than a very small minority of informal-sector workers were actively seeking jobs in the formal sectors, and only 5% to 15% of rural migrants in the informal sector had moved over to the formal sector in a year's time.

Moreover, the rate of entrance into the formal sector from the informal sector was just one-sixth to one-third that of the rate of direct entry into the urban formal sector from outside the area.

Informal-sector workers tended to work in the same job almost as long as those in the formal sector; the average informal-sector worker had worked 1.67 jobs over a period of 61 months in the city, while formal-sector workers averaged 1.24 jobs over an urban career of 67 months.

Banerjee's survey data suggested that a large number of informal-sector workers who had migrated to the city were attracted to the informal rather than the formal sector, coming to work as domestic servants, informal construction laborers, and salespeople. Of those who began nonwage employment upon their arrival, 71% had expected to do so. The fact that only a minority of informal-sector workers continued to search for formal-sector work was taken as further evidence that migrants had come to Delhi expressly to take up informal-sector work.

Workers who appear underemployed may not consider themselves as such, may perceive no possibility of moving into the modern sector, may be unable to effectively search for modern-sector work while employed in the informal sector, and hence do not create as much downward pressure on modern-sector wages as it may at first appear. This may be one factor keeping modern-sector wages well above informal-sector wages for indefinite periods of time despite high measured urban underemployment.

One reason for this focus on the informal sector was concluded to be the lack of contacts of informal-sector workers with the formal sector. About two-thirds of direct entrants into the formal sector and nearly as many of those switching from the informal to the formal sector found their jobs through personal contacts. This overwhelming importance of contacts explained why some 43% of Banerjee's sample migrated after receiving a suggestion from a contact, which suggests that job market information can become available to potential migrants without their being physically present in the city. An additional 10% of the sample had a prearranged job in the city prior to migration.

Finally, the duration of unemployment following migration is usually very short. Within one week, 64% of new arrivals had found employment, and although a few were unemployed for a long period, the average waiting time to obtain a first job was just 17 days.

Banerjee also found that migrants kept close ties to their rural roots. Some three-quarters of the migrants visited their villages of origin and about two-thirds were remitting part of their urban incomes, a substantial 23% of income on average. This indicates that concern for the whole family appeared to be a guiding force in migration. It also suggests a source of the rapid flow of job market information from urban to rural areas.

In a separate study, A. S. Oberai, Pradhan Prasad, and M. G. Sardana examined the determinants of migration in three states in India—Bihar, Kerala, and Uttar Pradesh. Their findings were consistent with the ideas that migrants often have a history of chronic underemployment before they migrate, migrate only as a measure of desperation, and have the expectation of participating in the informal urban sector even in the long run. Remittances were found to be substantial, and considerable levels of return migration were also documented, among other evidence of continued close ties of migrants to their home villages.

But Banerjee's fascinating findings do not necessarily represent a challenge to the applicability of Harris-Todaro or other "probabilistic migration models." Instead, they suggest that they need to be extended to accommodate the apparently common pattern of migrating with the ultimate aim of urban informal-sector employment. As Ira Gang and Shubhashis Gangopadhyay have noted, one can modify the model to include in the urban area not only a formal sector but also a highly paid informal sector, as well as a low-paid (or unemployed) sector. In this case, people will migrate looking for either a formal-sector job or a high-paying informal-sector job. This seems to be consistent with Banerjee's evidence. The assumption that keeps the essence of the probabilistic models intact is that the wage of the formal urban sector exceeds the high-paying informal wage, which in turn exceeds the agricultural wage, which in turn exceeds the low-paying informal (or unemployed) wage. In fact, if rural wages remain below all urban opportunities, this suggests that we are well out of equilibrium, and much additional migration must occur before expected incomes can be equalized across sectors. The particular formulations of the Todaro models are really no more than examples of a general principle: that migrants go where they expect in advance to do better, not where they do better after the fact. The basic ideas of the Todaro models do not depend on a particular notion of an informal or a formal sector.

Oded Stark's ideas on a family's use of migration can be a useful supplement to the Todaro models and may apply to some of Banerjee's findings. In his view, a family will send members to different areas as a "portfolio diversification" strategy, to reduce the risk that the family will have no income. This approach is useful to explain any observed migration from higher- to lower-wage areas and into higher-wage areas but not necessarily the area with the highest expected wage. The basic idea of the Todaro models still applies, but this approach looks at families rather than individuals and stresses risk aversion.

Other studies have shown that the Todaro migration models have held up well without modification in other parts of the world. A survey by Deepak Mazumdar confirmed that the evidence is overwhelming that migration decisions are made according to rational economic motivations.

Botswana

A study of migration behavior conducted by Robert E. B. Lucas in Botswana addressed such problems in one of the most careful empirical studies of migration in a developing country. His econometric model consisted of four groups of equations—for employment, earnings, internal migration, and migration to South Africa. Each group was estimated from microeconomic data on individual migrants and nonmigrants. Very detailed demographic information was used in the survey.

Rural migrants in Botswana moved to five urban centers (they would be called towns rather than cities in many parts of the world) as well as to neighboring South Africa. Lucas found that unadjusted urban earnings were much higher than rural earnings—68% higher for males—but these differences became much smaller when schooling and experience were controlled for.

Lucas's results confirm that the higher a person's expected earnings and the higher the estimated probability of employment after a move to an urban center, the greater the chances that the person will migrate. And the higher the estimated wage and probability of employment for a person in his or her home village, the lower the chances that the person will migrate. This result was very "robust"—not sensitive to which subgroups were examined or the way various factors were controlled for—and statistically significant. It represents clear evidence in support of Todaro's original hypothesis.

Moreover, Lucas estimated that at current pay differentials, the creation of one job in an urban center would draw more than one new migrant from the rural areas, thus confirming the Harris-Todaro effect. Earnings were also found to rise significantly the longer a migrant had been in an urban center, holding education and age constant. But the reason was because of increases in the rate of pay rather than in the probability of modern-sector employment.

Taken together, the best-conducted studies of urbanization confirm the value of probabilistic migration models as the appropriate place to start seeking explanations of rural-to-urban migration in developing countries. But these studies underscore the need to expand these explanations of migration, considering that many people today migrate to participate in the informal rather than the formal urban sector and that workers may face a variety of risks in different settings. ■

Sources

Banerjee, Biswajit. "The role of the informal sector in the migration process: A test of probabilistic migration models and labour market segmentation for India." *Oxford Economic Papers* 35 (1983): 399–422.

Banerjee, Biswajit. *Rural to Urban Migration and the Urban Labor Market: A Case Study of Delhi.* Mumbai: Himalaya Publishing House, 1986.

Cole, William E., and Richard D. Sanders. "Internal migration and urban employment in the Third World." *American Economic Review* 75 (1985): 481–494.

Corden, W. Max, and Ronald Findlay. "Urban unemployment, intersectoral capital mobility, and development policy." *Economica* 42 (1975): 37–78.

Gang, Ira N., and Shubhashis Gangopadhyay. "A model of the informal sector in development." *Journal of Economic Studies* 17 (1990): 19–31.

———. "Optimal policies in a dual economy with open unemployment and surplus labour." *Oxford Economic Papers* 39 (1987): 378–387.

Harris, John, and Michael P. Todaro. "Migration, unemployment, and development: A two-sector analysis." *American Economic Review* 60 (1970): 126–142.

Lucas, Robert E. B. "Emigration to South Africa's mines." *American Economic Review* 77 (1987): 313–330.

———. "Migration amongst the Batswana." *Economic Journal* 95 (1985): 358–382.

Mazumdar, Deepak. "Rural-urban migration in developing countries." In *Handbook of Regional and Urban Economics*, vol. 2. New York: Elsevier, 1987.

Oberai, A. S., Pradhan Prasad, and M. G. Sardana. *Determinants and Consequences of Internal Migration in India: Studies in Bihar, Kerala and Uttar Pradesh.* Delhi: Oxford University Press, 1989.

Stark, Oded. *The Migration of Labor.* Cambridge, Mass.: Blackwell, 1991.

Stark, Oded, and David Levhari. "On migration and risk in LDCs." *Economic Development and Cultural Change* 31, (1982): 191–196.

Todaro, Michael P. "A model of labor migration and urban unemployment in LDCs." *American Economic Review* 59 (1969): 138–148.

UN-Habitat, "State of the World's Cities, 2001," http://www.unchs.org/Istanbul+5/86.pdf.

United Nations. *An Urbanizing World: Global Report on Human Settlements*. Report presented to the Habitat II conference, Istanbul, 1996.

United Nations Population Division. *World Urbanization Prospects: The 1999 Revision*. New York: United Nations, 2000.

Concepts for Review

Agglomeration economies	Informal sector	Social capital
Congestion	Labor turnover	Todaro migration model
Efficiency wage	Localization economies	Urban bias
Harris-Todaro model	Present value	Urbanization economies
Induced migration	Rural-urban migration	Wage subsidy

Questions for Discussion

1. Why might the problem of rapid urbanization be a more significant population policy issue than curtailing population growth rates over the next two decades for most developing countries? Explain your answer.

2. Describe briefly the essential assumptions and major features of the Todaro model of rural-urban migration. One of the most significant implications of this model is the paradoxical conclusion that government policies designed to create more urban employment may in fact lead to more urban unemployment. Explain the reasons for such a paradoxical result.

3. "The key to solving the serious problem of excessive rural-urban migration and rising urban unemployment and underemployment in developing countries is to restore a proper balance between urban and rural economic and social opportunities." Discuss the reasoning behind this statement, and give a few specific examples of government policies that would promote a better balance between urban and rural economic and social opportunities.

4. For many years, the conventional wisdom of development economics assumed an inherent conflict between the objectives of maximizing output growth and promoting rapid industrial employment growth. Might these two objectives be mutually supportive rather than conflicting? Explain your answer.

5. What is meant by the expression "getting prices right"? Under what conditions will eliminating factor price distortions generate substantial new employment opportunities? (Be sure to define *factor price distortions*.)

6. The informal sector has become a very large part of the urban economy. Distinguish between the urban formal and informal sectors, and discuss both the positive and the negative aspects of the informal urban labor market.

7. Why are primary cities—generally the capital—often disproportionately large in many developing countries? Which factors can be addressed with better policies?

8. What is an industrial district? How might governments of developing countries help them succeed?

9. Suppose that potential migrants make decisions only based on comparisons of their expected incomes. Now suppose the rural wage is $1 per day. Urban modern sector employment can be obtained with 0.25 probability and pays $3 per day. The urban traditional sector pays $0.40 per day. Using this information, and making assumptions as needed, can you make a prediction about whether there will be any rural-to-urban or urban-to-rural migration? Explain your reasoning, stating explicitly any simplifying assumptions, and show all work. Consider an approach that calculates an expected income in the urban sector of 0.25(3) + (0.75)(0.40) = 1.05; and note that this

exceeds the rural wage of 1—would you predict that there will be rural-to-urban migration? What simplifying assumptions are needed to make this a valid conclusion? Now, what would the urban traditional sector daily income have to be to induce no net rural-urban migration? If wages in all sectors are inflexible, what else adjusts in this model to lead to equilibrium (how much does it adjust and what is the intuition)?

10. Explain the concept of urban bias. What policies are associated with it, and what are their likely effects on urban and rural areas?

11. Now explain the economic benefits of concentration of economic activity in cities. How are various costs of doing business likely to be affected? Why are some of the potential benefits of urbanization lost when congestion becomes substantial? What policies are likely to strengthen or weaken the opportunities to take advantage of the economic benefits of cities?

Appendix 7.1

A Mathematical Formulation of the Todaro Migration Model

Consider the following mathematical formulation of the basic Todaro model discussed in this chapter. Individuals are assumed to base their decision to migrate on considerations of income maximization and what they perceive to be their expected income streams in urban and rural areas. It is further assumed that the individual who chooses to migrate is attempting to achieve the prevailing average income for his or her level of education or skill attainment in the urban center of his or her choice. Nevertheless, the migrant is assumed to be aware of the limited chances of immediately securing wage employment and the likelihood that he or she will be unemployed or underemployed for a certain period of time. It follows that the migrant's expected income stream is determined by both the prevailing income in the modern sector and the probability of being employed there, rather than being underemployed in the urban informal sector or totally unemployed.

If we let $V(0)$ be the discounted present value of the expected "net" urban-rural income stream over the migrant's time horizon; $Y_u(t)$ and $Y_r(t)$ the average real incomes of individuals employed in the urban and the rural economy, respectively; n the number of time periods in the migrant's planning horizon; and r the discount rate reflecting the migrant's degree of time preference, then the decision to migrate or not will depend on whether

$$V(0) = \int_{t=0}^{n} [p(t)Y_u(t) - Y_r(t)]e^{-rt}dt - C(0) \qquad \text{(A7.1.1)}$$

is positive or negative, where $C(0)$ represents the cost of migration and $p(t)$ is the probability that a migrant will have secured an urban job at the average income level in period t.

In any one time period, the probability of being employed in the modern sector, $p(t)$, will be directly related to the probability π of having been selected in that or any previous period from a given stock of unemployed or underemployed job seekers. If we assume that for most migrants the selection procedure is random, then the probability of having a job in the modern sector within x periods after migration, $p(x)$, is $p(1) = \pi(1)$ and $p(2) = \pi(1) + [1 - \pi(1)]\pi(2)$ so that

$$p(x) = p(x - 1) + [1 - p(x - 1)]\pi(x) \qquad \text{(A7.1.2)}$$

or

$$p(x) = \pi(1) + \sum_{t=2}^{x} \pi(t) \prod_{s=1}^{t-1} [1 - \pi(s)] \qquad \text{(A7.1.3)}$$

where $\pi(t)$ equals the ratio of new job openings relative to the number of accumulated job aspirants in period t.

It follows from this probability formulation that for any given level of $Y_u(t)$ and $Y_i(t)$, the longer the migrant has been in the city, the higher his or her probability p of having a job and the higher, therefore, his or her expected income in that period.

Formulating the probability variable in this way has two advantages:

1. It avoids the "all or nothing" problem of having to assume that the migrant either earns the average income or earns nothing in the periods immediately following migration. Consequently, it reflects the fact that many underemployed migrants will be able to generate some income in the urban informal or traditional sector while searching for a regular job.

2. It modifies somewhat the assumption of random selection, since the probability of a migrant's having been selected varies directly with the time the migrant has been in the city. This permits adjustments for the fact that longer-term migrants usually have more contacts and better information systems so that their expected incomes should be higher than those of newly arrived migrants with similar skills.

Suppose that we now incorporate this behavioristic theory of migration into a simple aggregate dynamic equilibrium model of urban labor demand and supply in the following manner. We once again define the probability π of obtaining a job in the urban sector in any one time period as being directly related to the rate of new employment creation and inversely related to the ratio of unemployed job seekers to the number of existing job opportunities, that is:

$$\pi = \frac{\lambda N}{S - N} \qquad (A7.1.4)$$

where λ is the net rate of urban new job creation, N is the level of urban employment, and S is the total urban labor force. If w is the urban real wage rate and r represents average rural real income, then the expected urban-rural real-income differential d is

$$d = w\pi - r \qquad (A7.1.5)$$

or, substituting Equation A7.1.4 into Equation A7.1.5,

$$d = w\frac{\lambda N}{S - N} - r \qquad (A7.1.6)$$

The basic assumption of our model once again is that the supply of labor to the urban sector is a function of the urban-rural *expected* real-income differential, that is,

$$S = f_s(d) \qquad (A7.1.7)$$

If the rate of urban job creation is a function of the urban wage w and a policy parameter a, such as a concentrated governmental effort to increase employment through a program of import substitution, both of which operate on labor demand, we have

$$\lambda = f_d(w; a) \qquad (A7.1.8)$$

where it is assumed that $\partial\lambda/\partial a > 0$. If the growth in the urban labor demand is increased as a result of the governmental policy shift, the increase in the urban labor supply is

$$\frac{\partial S}{\partial a} = \frac{\partial S}{\partial d}\frac{\partial d}{\partial \lambda}\frac{\partial \lambda}{\partial a} \qquad (A7.1.9)$$

Differentiating Equation A7.1.6 and substituting into Equation A7.1.9, we obtain

$$\frac{\partial S}{\partial a} = \frac{\partial S}{\partial d}w\frac{N}{S-N}\cdot\frac{\partial \lambda}{\partial a} \qquad (A7.1.10)$$

The absolute number of urban employed will increase if the increase in labor supply exceeds the increase in the number of new jobs created, that is, if

$$\frac{\partial S}{\partial a} > \frac{\partial(\lambda N)}{\partial a} = \frac{N\partial \lambda}{\partial a} \qquad (A7.1.11)$$

Combining Equations A7.1.10 and A7.1.11, we get

$$\frac{\partial S}{\partial d}w\frac{N}{S-N}\cdot\frac{\partial \lambda}{\partial a} > \frac{N\partial \lambda}{\partial a} \qquad (A7.1.12)$$

or

$$\frac{\partial S/S}{\partial d/d} > \frac{d}{w}\cdot\frac{S-N}{S} \qquad (A7.1.13)$$

or, finally, substituting for d:

$$\frac{\partial S/S}{\partial d/d} > \frac{w\pi - r}{w}\cdot\frac{S-N}{S} \qquad (A7.1.14)$$

Equation A7.1.14 reveals that the absolute level of unemployment will rise if the elasticity of urban labor supply with respect to the expected urban-rural income differential $(\partial S/S)/(\partial d/d)$—what has been called elsewhere the "migration response function"—exceeds the urban-rural differential as a proportion of the urban wage times the unemployment rate, $(S-N)/S$. Alternatively, Equation A7.1.14 shows that the higher the unemployment rate, the higher must be the elasticity to increase the level of unemployment for any expected real-income differential. But note that in most developing nations, the inequality in Equation A7.1.14 will be satisfied by a very low elasticity of supply when realistic figures are used. For example, if the urban real wage is 60, average rural real income is 20, the probability of getting a job is 0.50, and the unemployment rate is 20%, then the level of unemployment will increase if the elasticity of urban labor supply is greater than 0.033; that is, substituting into Equation A7.1.14, we get

$$\frac{\partial S/S}{\partial d/d} = \frac{(0.5 \times 60) - 20}{60}(0.20) = \frac{2}{60} = 0.033 \qquad (A7.1.15)$$

Note that before one can realistically predict what the impact of a policy to generate more urban *employment* will be on the overall level of urban *unemployment*, one needs solid estimates of the empirical value of this elasticity coefficient prevailing in particular developing nations.

Notes

1. The estimate of 9.6 billion people was announced in June 2013; see *United Nations World Population Prospects: The 2012 Revision* (New York: United Nations, Department of Economic and Social Affairs, June 13, 2013). The mid-2009 estimate for the point when the urban population became the majority globally is found in *United Nations World Urbanization Prospects: The 2011 Revision*, 2012; the quote is from the UN Population Division 2009 chart at: http://www.un.org/en/development/desa/population/publications/urbanization/urban-rural.shtml.

2. See *United Nations World Urbanization Prospects: The 2011 Revision*, released April 5, 2012.

3. A well-known comment along these lines was made in 1984 by former World Bank president Robert McNamara, who expressed his skepticism that huge urban agglomerations could be made to work at all: "These sizes are such that any economies of location are dwarfed by costs of congestion. The rapid population growth that has produced them will have far outpaced the growth of human and physical infrastructure needed for even moderately efficient economic life and orderly political and social relationships, let alone amenity for their residents." See Robert S. McNamara, "The population problem: Time bomb or myth?" *Foreign Affairs* 62 (1984): 1107–1131. For additional arguments on problems caused by rapid urban population growth, see Bertrand Renaud, *National Urbanization Policy in Developing Countries* (New York: Oxford University Press, 1981). A less concerned viewpoint is expressed in Jeffrey G. Williamson, "Migration and urbanization," in *Handbook of Development Economics,* vol. 1, eds. Hollis B. Chenery and T. N. Srinivasan (Amsterdam: Elsevier, 1988), pp. 426–465.

4. United Nations Population Fund, *Population, Resources, and the Environment* (New York: United Nations, 1991), p. 61.

5. United Nations Population Division, *World Population Monitoring, 1987* (New York: United Nations, 1988). Those results were reiterated in the Program of Action of the 1994 International Conference on Population and Development, para. 9.1. More recently, the United Nations reported in 2006 that nearly three-quarters of developing-country officials indicated a strong desire to implement policies that would reduce rural-to-urban migration or to take actions to reverse rural-urban migration trends. See United Nations Population Division, *World Urbanization Prospects: The 2005 Revision.*

6. See Michael Porter, *The Competitive Advantage of Nations* (New York: Free Press, 1990); his theory is reviewed further in Chapter 12. Marshall introduced the industrial districts concept in his 1890 *Principles of Economics.*

7. See Michael Piore and Charles Sabel, *The Second Industrial Divide* (New York: Basic Books, 1984).

8. See Khalid Nadvi, "Collective efficiency and collective failure: The response of the Sialkot Surgical Instrument Cluster to global quality pressures," *World Development* 27 (1999): 1605–1626.

9. Gezahegn Ayele, Lisa Moorman, Kassu Wamisho, and Xiaobo Zhang, "Infrastructure and cluster development," International Food Policy Research Institute Discussion Paper No. 980, 2009.

10. The significance of industrial districts in developing countries is difficult to pin down, in part because such clusters overlap traditional political jurisdictions for which data are collected. An excellent source on this topic is Hubert Schmitz and Khalid Nadvi, eds., "Introduction: Clustering and industrialization," *World Development* 27 (1999): 1503–1514. See also Khalid Nadvi, "Collective efficiency and collective failure: The response of the Sialkot Surgical Instrument Cluster to global quality pressures," *World Development* 27 (1999): 1605–1626. Hermine Weijland, "Microenterprise clusters in rural Indonesia: Industrial seedbed and policy target," in ibid., p. 1519.

11. Dorothy McCormick, "African enterprise and industrialization: Theory and reality," in ibid., pp. 1531–1551.

12. Schmitz and Nadvi, "Introduction" ibid., pp. 1505–1506,

13. World Bank, *World Development Report, 1999–2000* (New York: Oxford University Press, 2000), ch. 6.

14. Ibid.

15. For an introductory overview of urban economics, see, for example, Arthur M. O'Sullivan, *Urban Economics*, 5th ed. (New York: McGraw-Hill/Irwin, 2002). Formal models of some of these ideas can be found in Masahisa Fujita, Paul Krugman, and Anthony J. Venables, *The Spatial Economy: Cities, Regions, and International Trade* (Cambridge, Mass.: MIT Press, 1999). We would like to thank Anthony Yezer for his very helpful suggestions on these sections.

15a. For a discussion, see World Bank, *World Development Report 2009: Reshaping Economic Geography*.

16. In this comparison, it is no accident that a relatively modest scale of the largest city tends to be found in countries in which the political capital is not found in the largest city, as will be explained shortly. This has been true in Canada and the United States nearly since their founding; it is more recently true in Brazil, where urban growth has been diverted to the new capital, Brasília, which was inaugurated in 1960 and has reached a population approaching 4 million. Comparative advantage and geography are other important factors; continent-sized countries are more plausible settings for multiple major hubs, as are also found in China and India. The picture also changes somewhat if one considers what the United Nations termed *megaregions* in a 2010 report, which include Hong Kong–Shenzhen–Guangzhou in China and Rio de Janeiro–São Paulo in Brazil.

17. With the exception of France and Britain, most ratios in Europe are small. Examples—Italy: Rome, 3.4 million; Milan, 2.9 million. Germany: Berlin, 3.4 million; Hamburg, 1.7 million. Netherlands: Rotterdam and Amsterdam, 1.0 million each. Portugal: Lisbon, 2.7 million; Porto, 1.3 million. Spain: Madrid, 5.4 million; Barcelona, 4.8 million. Other sizable developing countries where ratios of largest to second-largest city are relatively higher include Indonesia (about 4), Ethiopia (over 8), Afghanistan (over 6), and Côte d'Ivoire (over 6). Egypt, Iran, Iraq, Kenya, Nigeria, and Bangladesh all have ratios of about 3. Some ratios are higher with alternative metropolitan area estimates.

18. For example, while Mexico City continues to expand, it has a smaller share of industry than in decades past. A major reason is the growing concentration of export industries in northern Mexico along the U.S. border, especially following implementation of NAFTA and, even more recently, the move of some low-skill industries to southern Mexico.

19. Alberto F. Ades and Edward L. Glaeser, "Trade and circuses: Explaining urban giants," *Quarterly Journal of Economics* 110 (1995): 195–227. Urban concentration is defined as the average share of urbanized population living in the main city from 1970 to 1985. Stable countries are defined as those whose average number of revolutions and coups is below the worldwide median. Dictatorships are countries whose average Gastil democracy and freedoms index for the period is higher than 3. See also Rasha Gustavsson, "Explaining the phenomenon of Third World urban giants: The effects of trade costs," *Journal of Economic Integration* 14 (1999): 625–650.

20. UN-Habitat's annual "State of the World's Cities" reports are available at http://www.unhabitat.org.

21. See World Bank, *World Development Report, 2008–2009* (New York: Oxford University Press, 2008), on the often unrealized role of agriculture in development (discussed in Chapter 9); UN-Habitat on new developing-country perspectives on urbanization at http://www.unhabitat.org; and the World Bank on realizing more of the potential benefits of cities at http://www.worldbank.org/urban. See also World Bank, *World Development Report 2009: Reshaping Economic Geography* (New York: Oxford University Press, 2009).

22. For the 2012 CIV study, see Isabel Günther and Andrey Launov, "Informal employment in developing countries: Opportunity or last resort?" *Journal of Development Economics* 97, No. 1 (2012): 88–98; the authors use a parametric identification strategy. For a concise review of the overall debate, see Cathy A. Rakowski, "Convergence and divergence in the informal sector debate: A focus on Latin America, 1984–92," *World Development* 22 (1994): 501–516. See also Donald C. Mead and Christian Morrisson, "The informal sector elephant," *World Development* 24 (1996): 1611–1619, and Edward Funkhauser, "The urban informal sector in Central America: Household survey evidence," *World Development* 24 (1996): 1737–1751.

23. For updates on these and related indices, see International Finance Corporation, *Doing Business 2013, Smarter Regulations for Small and Medium-Size Enterprises*, http://www.doingbusiness.org/~/media/GIAWB/Doing%20Business/Documents/Annual-Reports/English/DB13-full-report.pdf.

24. UN-Habitat noted this for its *State of Women in Cities 2012/2013*, http://www.unhabitat.org/pmss/listItemDetails.aspx?publicationID=3457.

25. See Robert E. B. Lucas, "Internal migration and urbanization: Recent contributions and new evidence," background paper for World Bank, *World Development Report, 1999–2000*.

26. Although the *rate* of rural-urban migration slowed during the 1980s, especially in Latin America and sub-Saharan Africa, as a result of declining urban real wages and fewer formal-sector employment opportunities, the actual number of migrants continued to increase.

27. See Appendix 7.1 and Michael P. Todaro, "A model of labor migration and urban unemployment in less developed countries," *American Economic Review* 59 (1969): 138–148, and John R. Harris and Michael P. Todaro, "Migration, unemployment, and development: A two-sector analysis," *American Economic Review* 60 (1970): 126–142.

28. This graph was first introduced in W. Max Corden and Ronald Findlay, "Urban unemployment, intersectoral capital mobility, and development policy," *Economica* 42 (1975): 59–78. It reflects Harris and Todaro," Migration, unemployment, and development."

29. Note that qq' is a rectangular hyperbola, a unitary-elasticity curve showing a constant urban wage bill; that is, $L_M \yen W_M$ is fixed.

30. That is, if informal-sector income is greater than zero, we add to expected urban income (on the right side of Equation 7.1) the informal-sector wage W_{UI} times the probability of receiving it: $W_{UI}(1 - L_M/L_{US})$, where $(1 - L_M/L_{US})$ is the probability of not receiving the preferred urban formal wage. We can further distinguish wages and probabilities of receiving them in this period, or in a more general model in future periods; for a fully developed model, see Appendix 7.1.

31. William J. Carrington, Enrica Detragiache, and Tara Vishwanath, "Migration with endogenous moving costs," *American Economic Review* 86 (1996): 909–930.

32. Whereas the Todaro model focuses on the institutional determinants of urban wage rates above the equilibrium wage, several later analysts have sought to explain this phenomenon by focusing on the high costs of labor turnover (the so-called labor turnover model) in urban areas and the notion of an efficiency wage; an above-equilibrium urban wage enables employers to secure a higher-quality workforce and greater productivity on the job. For a review of these various models, see Joseph E. Stiglitz, "Alternative theories of wage determination and unemployment in LDCs: The labor turnover model," *Quarterly Journal of Economics* 88 (1974): 194–227, and Janet L. Yellen, "Efficiency wage models of unemployment," *American Economic Review* 74 (1984): 200–205. For evidence of the existence and importance of an institutionally determined urban-rural wage gap, see Francis Teal, "The size and sources of economic rents in a developing country manufacturing labour market," *Economic Journal* 106 (1996): 963–976. In an influential study, Valerie Bencivenga and Bruce Smith make the alternative assumption that urban modern firms do not know the productivity of migrants but that some potential migrants from rural areas are highly productive and others are unproductive within formal-sector (say, industrial) firms. In this scenario, firms will be motivated through competitive forces to (in effect) offer migrants a package of a wage and a probability of employment. Modern-sector firms hire labor until their marginal products are equal to the resulting high wage rate, and unemployment ensues. Moreover, if modern-sector labor demand increases, both modern- and traditional-sector workforces expand proportionately, inducing additional migration. See Valerie R. Bencivenga and Bruce D. Smith, "Unemployment, migration, and growth," *Journal of Political Economy* 105 (1997): 582–608. An alternative perspective in the economics-of-information framework, based on moral hazard problems, is offered by Hadi S. Esfahani and Djavad Salehi-Ifsahani, "Effort observability and worker productivity: Toward an explanation of economic dualism," *Economic Journal* 99 (1989): 818–836.

33. On problems of job creation, see World Bank, *World Development Report 2012*. For other perspectives on migration and urbanization policy, see, for example, Gary S. Fields, "Public policy and the labor market in less developed countries," in *The Theory of Taxation for Developing Countries*, eds. David P. Newbery and Nicholas Stern (New York: Oxford University Press, 1987); Charles M. Becker, Andrew M. Hammer, and Andrew R. Morrison, *Beyond Urban Bias in Africa: Urbanization in an Era of Structural Adjustment* (Portsmouth, N.H.: Heinemann, 1994), chs. 4–7; David Turnham, *Employment and Development: A New Review of Evidence* (Paris: Organization for Economic Coordination and Development, 1993), pp. 245–253; Paul P. Streeten, *Strategies for Human Development: Global Poverty and Unemployment* (Copenhagen: Handelshøjskolens Forlag, 1994), pp. 50–64; and Cedric Pugh, "Poverty and progress: Reflections on housing and urban policies in developing countries, 1976–96," *Urban Studies* 34 (1997): 1547–1595.

34. The literature has also examined strategies to eliminate excessive migration through wage subsidies; these would prove expensive and difficult to administer, but their analysis has yielded interesting insights into the nature of the Harris-Todaro migration model. See, for example, Ira Gang and Shubhashis Gangopadhyay, "Optimal policies in a dual economy with open unemployment and surplus labour," *Oxford Economic Papers* 39 (1987): 378–387, which also contains references to important earlier work.

35. Martin Ravallion, Shaohua Chen, and Prem Sangraula, "New evidence on the urbanization of global poverty," World Bank Research Working Paper 4199, 2008.

36. *World Bank World Development Report*, 2010, p. 110.

Human Capital: Education and Health in Economic Development

To end poverty and boost shared prosperity, countries need robust, inclusive economic growth. And to drive growth, they need to build human capital through investments in health, education and social protection for all their citizens.

—*Jim Yong Kim, World Bank President, 2013*

My work on human capital began with an effort to calculate both private and social rates of return to men, women, blacks, and other groups from investments in different levels of education.

—*Gary Becker, Nobel laureate in economics*

The slow improvement in the health status of our people has been a matter of great concern. There is no denying the fact that we have not paid adequate attention to this dimension of development thus far.

—*Manmohan Singh, prime minister of India, 2005*

8.1 The Central Roles of Education and Health

Education and health are basic *objectives of development*; they are important ends in themselves. Health is central to well-being, and education is essential for a satisfying and rewarding life; both are fundamental to the broader notion of expanded human capabilities that lie at the heart of the meaning of development (see Chapter 1). At the same time, education plays a key role in the ability of a developing country to absorb modern technology and to develop the capacity for self-sustaining growth and development. Moreover, health is a prerequisite for increases in productivity, and successful education relies on adequate health as well. Thus, both health and education can also be seen as vital *components of growth and development*—as inputs to the aggregate production function. Their dual role as both inputs and outputs gives health and education their central importance in economic development.

It is hard to overstate how truly dramatic the improvements in world health and education have been. In 1950, some 280 of every 1,000 children in the developing world as a whole died before their fifth birthday. By 2011, that number had fallen to 95 per 1,000 in low-income countries and 46 per 1,000 in middle-income countries (though now compared with 6 per 1,000 in high-income countries and just 4 in many European countries).[1] Some important killers have been completely or nearly eradicated. Smallpox used to kill more than 5 million people every year; the virus no longer exists outside a few laboratory samples. Major childhood illnesses such as rubella and polio have been largely controlled through the use of vaccines. In addition, recent decades have witnessed a historically unprecedented extension of **literacy** and other basic education to a majority of people in the developing world. The United Nations reports that although there were still a staggering 775 million illiterate people aged 15 or older in the world in 2010, the good news is that 82% of all people are literate today, compared to just 63% as recently as 1970.[2] But almost two-thirds of the world's illiterate people are women.

Literacy   The ability to read and write.

Despite such outstanding achievements, developing countries continue to face great challenges as they seek to continue to improve the health and education of their people. The distribution of health and education within countries is as important as income distribution; life expectancy may be quite high for better-off people in developing countries but far lower for the poor. Child mortality rates in developing countries remain more than 10 times higher than those found in the rich countries. These deaths generally result from conditions that are easily treatable, including millions who continue to die needlessly each year from dehydration caused by diarrhea. If child death rates in developing countries fell to those prevailing in the developed countries, the lives of nearly 7 million children would be saved each year. Many children who survive nonetheless suffer chronic problems of malnutrition, debilitating parasitic infections, and other recurrent illnesses. Problems caused by lack of key micronutrients such as iodine, as well as protein, affect up to 2 billion people, but children are particularly vulnerable. Whereas citizens in Europe, North America, or Japan have more than 12 years of schooling on average, the average citizen in sub-Saharan Africa and South Asia spends less than five years in school—before taking account of teacher absenteeism and making no adjustment for the lack of schoolbooks and other resources even when a teacher is present. The "voices of the poor" in Box 8.1 convey some of the impact of deprivation in health and education on people's lives.

In this chapter, we examine the roles of education and health in economic development. These two **human capital** issues are treated together because of their close relationship. There are dual impacts of the effects of health spending on the effectiveness of the educational system and vice versa; and when we speak of investing in a person's health and investing in a person's education, we are after all talking about the same person. We then consider the relationships between income on the one hand and health and education on the other. Despite their close relationship, you will see that higher household income is no guarantee of improved health and education: Human capital must be given direct attention in its own right, even in economies that are growing rapidly. Health and education may be distributed very unequally, just as income and wealth are. But improved health and education help families escape some of the vicious circles of poverty in which they are trapped. Finally, we take a close look at educational and health systems in developing countries, to identify the sources of the severe inequalities and inefficiencies that continue to plague them. The evidence reveals that investments in human capital have to be undertaken with both equity and efficiency for them to have their potential positive effects on incomes.

Human capital   Productive investments embodied in human persons, including skills, abilities, ideals, health, and locations, often resulting from expenditures on education, on-the-job training programs, and medical care.

BOX 8.1 Health and Education: Voices of the Poor

If you don't have money today, your disease will take you to your grave.

—An old woman from Ghana

The children keep playing in the sewage.

—Sacadura Cabral, Brazil

In the hospitals, they don't provide good care to the indigenous people like they ought to; because of their illiteracy they treat them badly. . . . They give us other medicines that are not for the health problem you have.

—A young man from La Calera, Ecuador

The school was OK, but now it is in shambles; there are no teachers for weeks. . . . There is no safety and no hygiene.

—Vila Junqueira, Brazil

If parents do not meet these payments, which are as high as 40 to 50 rupees per month, the teachers were reported to beat the student or submit a failing grade for her/him.

—Pakistan ("Voice of the Poor")

Teachers do not go to school except when it is time to receive salaries.

—Nigeria ("Voice of the Poor")

Before everyone could get health care, but now everyone just prays to God that they don't get sick because everywhere they just ask for money.

—Vares, Bosnia and Herzegovina

Education and Health as Joint Investments for Development

Health and education are closely related in economic development.[3] On one hand, greater health capital may improve the return to investments in education, in part because health is an important factor in school attendance and in the formal learning process of a child. A longer life raises the return to investments in education; better health at any point during working life may in effect lower the rate of depreciation of education capital. On the other hand, greater education capital may improve the return to investments in health, because many health programs rely on basic skills often learned at school, including personal hygiene and sanitation, not to mention basic literacy and numeracy; education is also needed for the formation and training of health personnel. Finally, an improvement in productive efficiency from investments in education raises the return on a lifesaving investment in health. Box 8.2 summarizes the linkages between investments in health and education.

The past half-century or so has witnessed unprecedented advances in human capital. Health and education levels improved in both developed and developing countries, but by most measures, they have improved more rapidly in developing countries. As a result, there has been some international convergence in these measures. Only in sub-Saharan Africa, where life expectancies fell due to the AIDS crisis, has some doubt been cast on the trend toward catching up in health. As primary enrollments rise in developing countries, education is catching up, though some observers believe that the quality gap may be larger than ever. Even though the health and education gap between developed and developing countries remains large and further improvements may prove difficult, the progress to date has been unmistakable.[4]

BOX 8.2 Linkages between Investments in Health and Education

- Health and education are investments made in the same individual.
- Greater health capital may raise the return on investment in education for several reasons:

  Health is an important factor in school attendance.

  Healthier children are more successful in school and learn more efficiently.

  Deaths of school-age children also increase the cost of education per worker.

  Longer life spans raise the return to investments in education.

  Healthier individuals are more able to productively use education at any point in life.

- Greater education capital may raise the return to investment in health in the following ways:

  Many health programs rely on skills learned in school (including literacy and numeracy).

  Schools teach basic personal hygiene and sanitation.

  Education is needed for the formation and training of health personnel.

  Education leads to delayed childbearing, which improves health.

- Improvements in productive efficiency from investment in education raise the return on a lifesaving investment in health.

Improving Health and Education: Why Increasing Income Is Not Sufficient

Health and education levels are much higher in high-income countries. There are good reasons to believe that the causality runs in both directions: With higher income, people and governments can afford to spend more on education and health, and with greater health and education, higher productivity and incomes are possible. Because of these relationships, development policy needs to focus on income, health, and education simultaneously. This conclusion is parallel to our conclusion in Chapter 5 that we need a multipronged strategy to address the stubborn problems of absolute poverty.

People will spend more on human capital when income is higher. But the evidence shows clearly that even if we were able to raise incomes without a large improvement in health and education, we could not count on that income increase being used to adequately invest in children's education and health. The market will not solve this problem automatically, and in many cases, household consumption choices themselves may lead to a surprisingly small link between income and nutrition, especially for children.[5] The income elasticity of the demand for calories (that is, the percentage change in calories consumed for a percentage change in family incomes) among low-income people range from near zero to about 0.5, depending on the region and the statistical strategy used by the researchers.[6] This less than proportional response is due to two factors: Income is spent on other goods besides food, and part of the increased food expenditures is used to increase food variety without necessarily increasing the consumption of calories. If the relationship between income and nutrition is indeed quite low, as some studies suggest, then development policies that emphasize increasing incomes of the poor without attention to the way these additional resources are expended within the family may not lead to improved health, and successful development more generally, at least not very quickly.[7] As discussed further in Chapter 15 and its case study, credit for microenterprises has been one of the most popular poverty alleviation strategies in recent years. In this case, credit may help the poor improve their nutrition, for example, because seasonal price fluctuations are also shown to be an important determinant of calorie consumption along with average income among the very poor, but credit will not be sufficient if nutrition remains inadequate and does not improve automatically with higher income.

Moreover, calories are not the same as nutrition, and the nutrition of earners is not the same as the nutrition of their children. The income elasticity of "convenience" foods is greater than unity.[8] An increase in income frequently allows families in developing countries to switch consumption from nutritious foods such as beans and rice to nonnutritious "empty calories" such as candy and soda, which may be perceived as modern and symbolic of economic success.[9] A major problem is that poor health (e.g., diarrheal diseases) can negate the health advantages of better nutrition.[10]

There is considerable evidence that the better the education of the mother, the better the health of her children (see Figure 2.5 on page 61 and Box 8.3).[11] There are still opportunities for improving health through simple activities in school that have not been utilized.

Health status, once attained, also affects school performance, as has been shown in studies of many developing countries. Better health and nutrition lead to earlier and longer school enrollment, better school attendance, and more effective learning.[12] Thus, to improve enrollments and the effectiveness of schooling, we must improve the health of children in developing countries.

BOX 8.3 FINDINGS   Mothers' Health Knowledge Is Crucial for Raising Child Health

Usually, formal education is needed in complementary relationship with ongoing access to current information. Paul Glewwe found in an analysis of data from Morocco that a mother's basic health knowledge had a positive effect on her children's health. Several mechanisms were possible, such as that "formal education directly teaches health knowledge to future mothers; literacy and numeracy skills acquired in school assist future mothers in diagnosing and treating child health problems; and exposure to modern society from formal schooling makes women more receptive to modern medical treatments." But,

Glewwe concludes, "Mother's health knowledge alone appears to be the crucial skill for raising child health. In Morocco, such knowledge is primarily obtained outside the classroom, although it is obtained using literacy and numeracy skills learned in school.... Teaching of health knowledge skills in Moroccan schools could substantially raise child health and nutrition in Morocco."

Source: Based on Paul Glewwe, "Why does mother's schooling raise child health in developing countries? Evidence from Morocco," *Journal of Human Resources* 34 (1999): 124–159.

Indeed, advances in statistical methods are showing that the links from health to educational attainment in developing countries are stronger than had been believed (see Box 8.4). These effects are large for both boys and often especially for girls.[13]

Finally, there are other important spillover benefits to investment in one's health or education. An educated person provides benefits to people around him or her, such as reading for them or coming up with innovations that benefit the community.[14] As a result, there are significant market failures in education. Moreover, a healthy person is not only less contagious but also can

BOX 8.4 FINDINGS   School Impact of a Low-Cost Health Intervention

A study in the Busia district in Kenya conducted by Edward Miguel of the University of California at Berkeley and Michael Kremer of Harvard University showed that inexpensive "deworming" drugs to eliminate parasitic infections in children are also very cost-effective in increasing school attendance. The order in which schools received the treatments was randomized, enabling identification of the causal effect of treatments by comparing outcomes with the not-yet-treated schools.

Their baseline survey showed 92% of schoolchildren were infected with at least one parasite, and 28% had at least three infections. A moderate to heavy infection was present in 31%. In fact, the prevalence was probably worse because "heavily infected children were more likely to be absent from school on the day of the survey."

As a result of the deworming, absenteeism decreased by about one-quarter (7 percentage points). Younger children typically had suffered more infection, and they now attended 15 more school days per year on average; older children attended about 10 more days. The program cost per additional year of schooling was about $3.50, much less than the alternative methods used to increase school participation. Treated children also had lower anemia, somewhat reduced reported illness, and better height-for-age scores.

Children can spread parasitic infections across school districts, notably when they swim in the same lake. This explains the study's finding that curing worm infections also led to substantial benefits for neighboring school districts that had not yet been dewormed—a classic externality. Reduced infection can also benefit adults, who can work more days.

Although academic test scores did not increase significantly, this may have been due to the larger school class size that resulted from greater participation rates, thereby increasing the student-to-teacher ratio. Evaluated over the course of the student's lifetime, the deworming drugs are not only inexpensive but also yield a very high rate of return, with the implied present discounted value of wage gains of more than $30 per treated child. The net benefit of the program is greater than the cost of hiring additional teachers to keep this ratio from rising—though this does depend on the political will to do so.

Despite its large benefits, families in impoverished Busia are very sensitive to the price of deworming treatments, suggesting that subsidies will be needed for some time. As one might hope from such clear findings, this study has had a substantial impact on health priorities of developing-country governments and international agencies, and deworming programs are expanding in many countries. This study's clear findings from carefully designed methods provide one of the important impetuses to the recent emphasis on and progress in deworming in schools.

Source: Edward Miguel and Michael Kremer, "Worms: Identifying impact on education and health in the presence of treatment externalities," *Econometrica* 72 (2004): 159–217. On deworming activities, see the links at http://www.dewormtheworld.org.

benefit the community in many ways that a sick person cannot. Because of such spillover effects, the market cannot be counted on to deliver the socially efficient levels of health and education. Thus, as the World Health Organization (WHO) concluded, "Ultimate responsibility for the performance of a country's health system lies with government."[15] Developing-country officials are drawing lessons from the many studies showing the interrelationships among health, education, and incomes and are devising integrated strategies. The case study of Mexico at the end of this chapter provides an important example.

8.2 Investing in Education and Health: The Human Capital Approach

The analysis of investments in health and education is unified in the human capital approach. *Human capital* is the term economists often use for education, health, and other human capacities that can raise productivity when increased. An analogy is made to conventional investments in physical capital: After an initial investment is made, a stream of higher future income can be generated from both expansion of education and improvements in health. As a result, a rate of return can be deduced and compared with returns to other investments. This is done by estimating the present discounted value of the increased income stream made possible by these investments and then comparing it with their direct and indirect costs. Of course, health and education also contribute directly to well-being. For example, education increases empowerment and autonomy in major matters in life, such as capacity for civic engagement, making decisions concerning one's own health care, and freedom to choose one's own spouse over an arranged marriage.[16] But the basic human capital approach focuses on the indirect ability to increase well-being by increasing incomes. In this section, we will generally illustrate points with educational investments, but the same principles apply to health investments.

The impact of human capital investments in developing countries can be quite substantial. Figure 8.1 shows the age-earnings profiles by levels of education in Venezuela.[17] The chart shows how incomes vary over the life cycle for people with various levels of education. Note that those with higher levels of education start full-time work at a later age, but as is shown, their incomes quickly outpace those who started working earlier. But such future income gains from education must be compared with the total costs incurred to understand the value of human capital as an investment. Education costs include any direct tuition or other expenditures specifically related to education, such as books and required school uniforms, and indirect costs, primarily income forgone because the student could not work while in school.

Formally, the income gains can be written as follows, where E is income with extra education, N is income without extra education, t is year, i is the **discount rate**, and the summation is over expected years of working life:

Discount rate In present-value calculations, the annual rate at which future values are decreased to make them comparable to values in the present.

$$\sum \frac{E_t - N_t}{(1 + i)^t} \qquad (8.1)$$

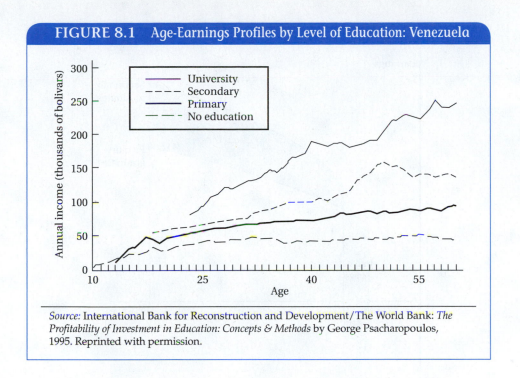

FIGURE 8.1   Age-Earnings Profiles by Level of Education: Venezuela

Source: International Bank for Reconstruction and Development/The World Bank: *The Profitability of Investment in Education: Concepts & Methods* by George Psacharopoulos, 1995. Reprinted with permission.

An analogous formula applies to health (such as improved nutritional status), with the direct and indirect cost of resources devoted to health compared with the extra income gained in the future as a result of higher health status.

Figure 8.2 provides a typical schematic representation of the trade-offs involved in the decision to continue in school.[18] It is assumed that the individual works from the time he or she finishes school until he or she is unable to work, retires, or dies. This is taken to be 66 years. Two earnings profiles are presented—for workers with primary school but no secondary education and for those with a full secondary (but no higher) education. Primary graduates are assumed to begin work at age 13, and secondary graduates, at age 17. For an individual in a developing country deciding whether to go on from primary to secondary education, four years of income are forgone. This is the indirect cost, as labeled in the diagram. The child may work part time, a possibility ignored here for simplicity, but if so, only part of the indirect-cost area applies. There is also a direct cost, such as fees, school uniforms, books, and other expenditures that would not have been made if the individual had left school at the end of the primary grades. Over the rest of the person's life, he or she makes more money each year than would have been earned with only a primary education. This differential is labeled "Benefits" in the diagram. Before comparing costs with benefits, note that a dollar today is worth more to an individual than a dollar in the future, so those future income gains must be discounted accordingly, as is done in Equation 8.1. The rate of return will be higher whenever the discount rate is lower, the direct or indirect costs are lower, or the benefits are higher.

This analysis was performed from the individual's point of view in the three right-hand columns of Table 8.1. Notice that in sub-Saharan Africa, the

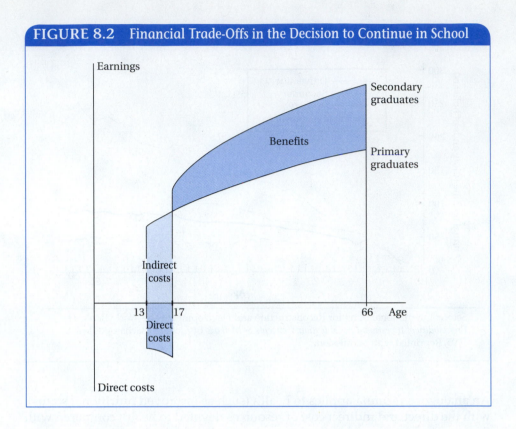

FIGURE 8.2   Financial Trade-Offs in the Decision to Continue in School

private rate of return to primary education is over 37%! Despite this extraordinary return, many families do not make this investment because they have no ability to borrow even the meager amount of money that a working child can bring into the family—the topic of the next section. Note that the higher rates of return for developing countries reflect that the income differential between those with more and less schooling is greater on average than for the developed countries.

The first three columns of Table 8.1 indicate the social rate of return. This is found by including the amount of public subsidy for the individual's education as part of the direct costs, because this is part of the investment from the social point of view (and also by considering pretax rather than after-tax incomes). Details of the calculations are presented in note 19.[19] It should be noted that these social returns are probably understated because they do not take into account the externality that educated people confer on others (e.g., being able to read for other family members and coworkers), not to mention other individual and social benefits such as increased autonomy and civic participation, being able to communicate more effectively, making more informed choices, and even being taken more seriously in public discussions, as stressed by Amartya Sen. Figure 8.2 can also be used to illustrate the benefit-cost trade-off from the public policy point of view by including fiscal costs and social welfare benefits; that is, adding the social costs of education such as subsidies to the direct costs part of the costs area below the x-axis and

TABLE 8.1   Returns to Investment in Education by Level, Regional Averages (%)

Region	Social			Private		
	Primary	Secondary	Higher	Primary	Secondary	Higher
Asia[a]	16.2	11.1	11.0	20.0	15.8	18.2
MENA[b]	15.6	9.7	9.9	13.8	13.6	18.8
Latin America/Caribbean	17.4	12.9	12.3	26.6	17.0	19.5
OECD	8.5	9.4	8.5	13.4	11.3	11.6
Sub-Saharan Africa	25.4	18.4	11.3	37.6	24.6	27.8
World	18.9	13.1	10.8	26.6	17.0	19.0

[a] Non-OECD.
[b] Europe/Middle East/North Africa, Non-OECD
Source: George G. Psacharopoulos and Harry A. Patrinos, "Returns to investment in education: A further update," *Education Economics* 12, No. 2 (August 2004), tab. 1.
Note: How these rates of return were calculated is explained in detail in note 19 at the end of this chapter.

adding in any net spillover benefits to the benefits area (not shown are such benefits as occur before graduation or after retirement).[19a]

8.3 Child Labor

Child labor is a widespread problem in developing countries. When children under age 15 work, their labor time disrupts their schooling and, in a majority of cases, prevents them from attending school altogether. Compounding this, the health of child workers is significantly worse, even accounting for their poverty status, than that of children who do not work; physical stunting among child laborers is very common. In addition, many laboring children are subject to especially cruel and exploitative working conditions.

The International Labor Organization (ILO), a UN body that has played a leading role on the child labor issue,[20] reported in its 2010 quadrennial report on child labor that as of 2008, there was a total of 306 million children between ages 5 and 17 doing some kind of work, but about one-third of this is considered permissible work based on national laws and existing ILO conventions. But 215 million are classified as "child laborers" because they "are either under the minimum age for work or above that age [through age 17] and engaged in work that poses a threat to their health, safety, or morals, or are subject to conditions of forced labor." This number is down about 3% from the 222 million estimated for 2004. There are over 9 million child laborers between the ages of 5 and 11, nearly a third of them doing *hazardous work*. More than half of child laborers, some 115 million children, are still exposed to hazardous work. More than half of all child laborers live in Asia and the Pacific, but sub-Saharan Africa has the highest rate of child labor. Among children doing hazardous work, over 48 million live in Asia and the Pacific, nearly 39 million live in sub-Saharan Africa, and over 9 million live in Latin America. Child labor remains a problem in the Arab states, where the issue has been largely ignored until very recently. And major progress has been made in some countries such as Brazil and some regions such as Kerala in India.

Working conditions are often horrendous; the ILO reports that some of its surveys show that more than half of child laborers toil for nine or more hours per day. The worst forms of child labor endanger health or well-being, involving hazards, sexual exploitation, trafficking, and debt bondage. In a 2011 publication, the ILO reported that every year, about 22,000 children die as a result of work-related accidents. Clearly, child labor is not an isolated problem but a widespread one, especially in Africa and South Asia.

Nevertheless, it is not obvious that an immediate ban on all forms of child labor is always in the best interests of the child. Without work, a child may become severely malnourished; with work, school fees as well as basic nutrition and health care may be available. But there is one set of circumstances under which both the child laborer and the family as a whole may be unambiguously better off with a ban on child labor: multiple equilibria. Kaushik Basu has provided such an analysis, and we shall first consider his simple model, which shows how this problem may arise.[21]

To model child labor, we make two important assumptions: First, a household with a sufficiently high income would not send its children to work. As one might hope, there is strong evidence that this is true, at least most of the time. Second, child and adult labor are substitutes. In fact, children are not as productive as adults, and adults can do any work that children can do. This assertion is not an assumption; it is a finding of many studies of the productivity of child laborers in many countries. It is important to emphasize this, because one rationalization for child labor often heard is that children have special productive abilities, such as small fingers, that make them important for the production of rugs and other products. However, there is no support for this view. In essentially every task that has been studied, including carpet weaving, adult laborers are significantly more productive. As a result, we can consider the supply of adult and child labor together in an economic analysis of the problem.

The child labor model is graphed in Figure 8.3. On the x-axis, we have the supply of labor in adult equivalents. Because we are interested in understanding the impact of the demand for labor, in a graph it is best to consider homogeneous units of labor. So if a child laborer is γ times as productive as an adult worker, we consider one child the productive equivalent of γ adult workers. According to our assumptions, $\gamma < 1$. For example, if a child laborer is half as productive as an adult worker, $\gamma = 0.5$.

We start with the assumption that in the region in question, all (unskilled) adults work, regardless of the wage. This gives us a perfectly inelastic, vertical adult labor supply curve, called AA' in the diagram. Highly inelastic supply is a very reasonable assumption among families so poor that their children must work. While the parents may not have modern-sector jobs, every adult is involved in some type of activity to help the family survive. This adult supply AA' is simply the number of unskilled adults. To understand the total labor supply curve, consider what happens if the wage falls. If the wage falls below w_H, then some families find they are poor enough that they have to send their children to work. At first wages are still high enough so that this affects only a few families and children, reflected in the fact that the S-shaped curve just below w_H is still quite steep. As the wage continued to fall, more families would do the same, and labor supply expands along the S-shaped curve, which becomes flatter as smaller drops in the wage lead many more families to send their children to work. If a wage of w_L were reached, all of the children

FIGURE 8.3 Child Labor as a Bad Equilibrium

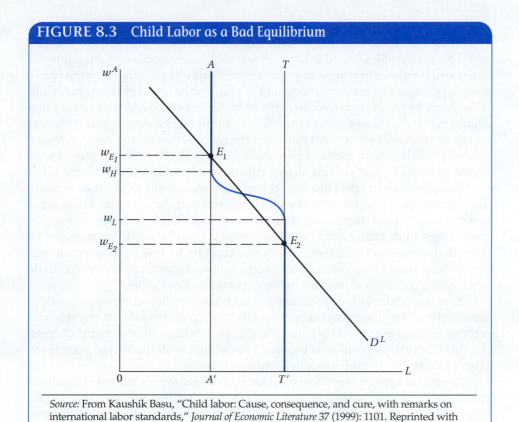

Source: From Kaushik Basu, "Child labor: Cause, consequence, and cure, with remarks on international labor standards," *Journal of Economic Literature* 37 (1999): 1101. Reprinted with the permission of the author and the American Economic Association.

would work. At this point, we are on the vertical line labeled TT', which is the aggregate labor supply of all the adults and all the children together. This sum is the number of adults plus the number of children, multiplied by their lower productivity, $\gamma < 1$. (An S shape in the middle portion is likely, but the analysis holds even if this is a straight line.) The resulting supply curve for children and adults together is very different from the standard ones that we usually consider in basic microeconomics, such as the upward-sloping supply curve seen in Figure 5.5 (in Chapter 5), but it is highly relevant for the developing-country child labor context. To summarize, as long as the wage is above w_H, the supply curve is along AA'; if the wage is below w_L, the supply curve is along TT', and in between, it follows the S-shaped curve between the two vertical lines.

Now consider the labor demand curve, D^L; if demand is inelastic enough to cut the AA' line above w_H and also cut the TT' line below w_L, there will be two stable equilibria, labeled E_1 and E_2, in the diagram.[22] When there are two equilibria, if we start out at the bad equilibrium E_2, an effective ban on child labor will move the region to the good equilibrium E_1. Moreover, once the economy has moved to the new equilibrium, the child labor ban will be self-enforcing, because by assumption, the new wage is high enough for no family to have to send its children to work. If poor families coordinate with each other and refuse to send their children to work, each will be better off; but in general, with a large number of families, they will be unable to achieve this.[23]

Banning child labor when there is an alternative equilibrium in which all children go to school might seem like an irresistible policy, but note that while all the families of child laborers are better off, employers may now be worse off, because they have to pay a higher wage. Thus, employers may use political pressure to prevent enactment of child labor laws. In this sense, child labor, even its worst forms, could actually be Pareto-optimal—a discovery that should remind us that Pareto optimality is sometimes a very weak condition on which to base development policy! In the same sense, many other problems of underdevelopment, including extreme poverty itself, may at times also be Pareto-optimal, in that solving these problems may make the rich worse off.

While these child labor models are probably reasonable depictions of many developing areas, we do not know enough about conditions in unskilled labor markets to say how significant these types of multiple equilibria and severe credit constraints really are as explanations for child labor. Thus, it would be potentially counterproductive, if even enforceable, to seek an immediate ban on all child labor in all parts of the world today. As a result, an intermediate approach is currently dominant in international policy circles.[24]

There are four main approaches to child labor policy current in development policy. The first recognizes child labor as an expression of poverty and recommends an emphasis on eliminating poverty rather than directly addressing child labor; this position is generally associated with the World Bank (poverty policy is discussed further in Chapters 5, 9, and 15).

Conditional cash transfer (CCT) programs Welfare benefits provided conditionally based on family behavior such as children's regular school attendance and health clinic visitations.

The second approach emphasizes strategies to get more children into school, including expanded school places, such as new village schools, and **conditional cash transfer** (CCT) incentives to induce parents to send their children to school, such as the Progresa/Oportunidades Program in Mexico, discussed in this chapter's case study, or the experimental Malawi program discussed in Box 8.5. This strategy has widespread support from many international agencies and development bodies. It is probably a more effective approach than making basic education compulsory, because without complementary policies, the incentives to send children to work would still remain strong and enforcement is likely to be weak, for the same reasons that regulation of the informal sector has proved almost impossible in many other cases. Compulsory schooling is a good idea, but it is not by itself a sufficient solution to the problem of child labor. Improving the quality of basic schooling and increasing accessibility are also very important; the fraction of national income spent on basic education in a majority of low-income countries remains problematic. As the ILO points out,

> In sub-Saharan Africa, about half of all low-income countries spend less than 4 per-cent of their national income on education. In South Asia, Bangladesh devotes only 2.6 per-cent of its national income to education and Pakistan, 2.7 per-cent. India invests a smaller proportion of GNP (around 3.3 per-cent) than the median for sub-Saharan Africa, even though average incomes are around one third higher. Even more worrying is that the share of national income devoted to education is stagnating or decreasing in key countries, including Bangladesh, India and Pakistan, which account for over 15 million out-of-school children.[25]

The third approach considers child labor inevitable, at least in the short run, and stresses palliative measures such as regulating it to prevent abuse and to provide support services for working children. This approach is most commonly associated with UNICEF, which has prepared a checklist of regulatory and

BOX 8.5 FINDINGS   Cash or Condition? Evidence from Malawi

What programs are effective at addressing the nexus of poverty and unmet health and education needs, especially for girls growing up in extreme poverty? As Sarah Baird, Craig McIntosh, and Berk Ozler note, school enrollment and effective learning, and marriage and fertility outcomes are of "central importance to the long-term prospects of school-age girls" living in poverty. What programs would be most cost-effective?

Findings from a randomized control trial study of a cash transfer program targeted to adolescent girls in Malawi offer important insights. Baird, McIntosh, and Ozler compared families who were randomly assigned to one of three groups: no cash transfer, unconditional cash transfers (UCTs), and cash transfers that were made conditional on the girls' continued school attendance (CCTs). Given this structure, the researchers examined education achievements and marriage and childbearing outcomes. They found both transfer programs led to higher rates of continued enrollment (avoiding dropouts); but CCTs had well over double (about 2.3 times) the impact as UCTs. On the other hand, some earlier studies (primarily in Latin America) had implied little or no effect of UCTs; perhaps the difference reflects conditions prevailing in low-income Africa. The research found that girls in the CCT program outperformed those in the UCT program on English reading comprehension (a "modest but significant" difference).

At the same time, the authors found that the CCTs were far more *cost-effective* in raising enrollment and attendance than the UCTs, even taking into account the extra expenses of running the more administratively complex CCT program. The authors examined different transfers and found that even the smallest amount studied—$4 per month to the parents and $1 per month to the school-age girl—"were sufficient to attain the average schooling impacts observed under the CCT arm."

On the other hand, the UCT program was found to have a strong impact on "delaying marriage and childbearing—by 44% and 27%, respectively, after 2 years." And while the CCTs worked better at keeping girls in school and learning effectively, they still "had no effect on reducing the likelihood of teenage pregnancies or marriages." The authors found this was "entirely due to the impact of UCTs on these outcomes among girls who dropped out of school" but whose families continued to receive the transfer benefits (because, after all, the transfer is unconditional). The authors concluded that the "offer of a CCT appears to have been ineffective in dissuading those with a high propensity to drop out of school from getting married and starting childbearing, especially among girls sixteen or older." Meanwhile, families living in poverty whose daughters did drop out of school ended up receiving nothing, precluding other poverty-reduction benefits.

These findings reflect the difficulties in identifying a single program design to effectively achieve poverty reduction, health, education, and social progress goals. As the authors conclude, "This study makes clear that while CCT programs may be more effective than UCTs in obtaining the desired behavior change, they can also undermine the social protection dimension of cash transfer programs."

Source: Based on Sarah Baird, Craig McIntosh, and Berk Ozler, "Cash or condition? Evidence from a cash transfer experiment," *Quarterly Journal of Economics* 126, No. 4 (2011): 1709–1753.

social approaches that could meet the "best interest of the child." The regulations included on UNICEF's checklist include expanding educational opportunities through "time off" for standard or workplace schooling, encouraging stricter law enforcement against illegal child labor trafficking, providing

Educational gender gap
Male-female differences in
school access and completion.

support services for parents and for children working on the streets, and working to develop social norms against the economic exploitation of children.

The fourth approach, most often associated with the ILO, favors banning child labor. If this is not possible, however, and recognizing that child labor may not always result from multiple equilibria problems, this approach favors banning child labor *in its most abusive forms.* The latter approach has received much attention in recent years; the ILO's "Worst Forms of Child Labor Convention" was adopted in 1999. The worst forms covered under the convention include "all forms of slavery or practices similar to slavery, such as the sale and trafficking of children, debt bondage and serfdom and forced or compulsory labor"; child prostitution and pornography; other illicit activities, such as drug trafficking; and work that "by its nature or the circumstances...is likely to harm the health, safety or morals of children." The ILO set a working target to completely eliminate the worst forms of child labor by 2016; significant progress has been made, but as of 2011, the ILO reported that progress was not fast enough to meet this goal.

A 2003 study by the ILO estimated that eliminating child labor and extending quality schooling for all children up to age 14 over a 20-year period would result in the baseline case of $5 trillion of economic gains (in present discounted value), after accounting for opportunity costs. Even when changing the assumptions of the study to be very conservative about the likely income gains, the result is an enormously productive economic investment with a 44% internal rate of return in the baseline case and 23% in a conservative case.[26]

Finally, many activists in developed countries have proposed the imposition of trade sanctions against countries that permit child labor or at least banning the goods on which children work. This approach is well intentioned, but if the objective is the welfare of children, it needs to be considered carefully, because if children cannot work in the export sector, they will almost certainly be forced to work in the informal sector, where wages and other working conditions are generally worse. Export restrictions may also make it more difficult for poor countries to grow their way out of poverty. Of course, the worst forms of child labor can never be tolerated. It seems clear that if efforts at banning imports from developing countries were channeled instead into working to secure more public and private development assistance for nongovernmental organizations that work with child laborers, much more would be accomplished to help these children.

8.4 The Gender Gap: Discrimination in Education and Health

Education and Gender

Young females receive less education than young males in most low-income developing countries. While youth literacy is now much higher than it was as recently as 1990, Figure 8.4 shows that in most regions, girls still lag behind boys. Large majorities of illiterate people and those who have been unable to attend school around the developing world are female. The **educational gender gap** is especially great in the least developed countries in Africa, where female literacy rates can be less than half that of men in countries such as Niger, Mali,

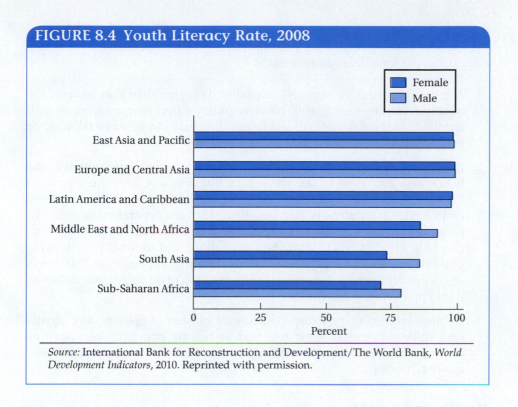

FIGURE 8.4 Youth Literacy Rate, 2008

Source: International Bank for Reconstruction and Development/The World Bank, *World Development Indicators*, 2010. Reprinted with permission.

Guinea, and Benin. The gap is also relatively large in South Asia; in India, the adult female literacy rate is just 47.8%, which is just 65% of the male rate (the female youth literacy rate is 67.7%, 80% of the male youth literacy rate). In Pakistan, the adult female literacy rate is just 36%, only 57% of the male rate (in this case, the female youth literacy rate is 54.7%, some 72% of the male rate). While globally, 123 million youth (aged 15 to 24) lack basic reading and writing skills; 61 per cent of them are young women.[27] Recall that the target for Millennium Development Goal 3 ("promote gender equality and empower women") is to "eliminate gender disparity in primary and secondary education preferably by 2005, and at all levels by 2015." Although the 2005 date was missed in many countries, progress has been dramatic in many others. In most low-income countries and many middle-income countries, women make up a minority—sometimes a small minority—of college students. But the long-term trend in higher-income countries for a significantly higher and growing share of female than male enrollment in tertiary (university) education has been extending recently to many upper-middle-income countries in the Middle East, Latin America, and elsewhere.

School completion is also subject to gender inequalities, and the gap is often particularly large in rural areas. For example, in rural Pakistan, 42% of males complete their primary education, while only 17% of females do. In the cities, the gender gap is smaller though still substantial, as 64% of males complete primary education versus 50% of females in urban areas.[28]

Empirical evidence shows that educational discrimination against women hinders economic development in addition to reinforcing social inequality.

Closing the educational gender gap by expanding educational opportunities for women, a key plank of the Millennium Development Goals, is economically desirable for at least three reasons:[29]

1. The rate of return on women's education is higher than that on men's in most developing countries. [This may partly reflect that, with fewer girls enrolled, the next (marginal) girl to enroll is likely to be more talented on average than the marginal boy.]

2. Increasing women's education not only increases their productivity (and hence also earnings) in the workplace but also results in greater labor force participation, later marriage, lower fertility, and greatly improved child health and nutrition, thus benefiting the next generation as well. The latter is because a mother's education directly increases knowledge that can help child survival, nutrition, education, and indirectly by making possible higher earnings for the family—noting in particular that mothers generally spend a somewhat larger fraction of an additional dollar on their children than do fathers.

3. Because women carry a disproportionate burden of poverty, any significant improvements in their role and status via education can have an important impact on breaking the vicious circles of poverty and inadequate schooling.

Health and Gender

Girls also face discrimination in health care in many developing countries, as discussed in Chapter 6. In South Asia, for example, studies show that families are far more likely to take an ill boy than an ill girl to a health center. Women are often denied reproductive rights, whether legally or illegally. Broadly, health spending on men is often substantially higher than that on women. And in many countries such as Nigeria, health care decisions affecting wives are often made by their husbands.

Female genital mutilation/cutting (FGM/C) is a health and gender tragedy, explained in an influential 2005 UNICEF report, *Changing a Harmful Social Convention: Female Genital Mutilation/Cutting*. FGM/C is most widely practiced in sub-Saharan Africa and the Middle East and is believed to have affected about 130 million women. This practice, which is dangerous and a violation of the most basic rights, does not only result from decisions made by men; many mothers who have undergone FGM/C also require their daughters to do so. If most other families practice FGM/C, it becomes difficult for any one family to refuse to take part, to avoid the perceived resulting "dishonor" to the daughter and her family and lost "marriageability." The general problem fits the model of multiple equilibria associated with social norms or conventions, such as foot binding, an interpretation suggested by Gerry Mackie drawing on work of Nobel laureate Thomas Schelling. This general framework was also applied earlier in the text in the analysis of whether women have high or low fertility (using Figure 4.1 on page 169, applied in a way similar to the discussion in Chapter 6 on pages 299–300). In an encouraging sign of progress, there are a growing number of experiences of "mass abandonment" of the practice of

FGM/C, sometimes started with an organized pledge of families in an intermarrying group that they will no longer follow the practice with their daughters. Thus, such coordination failures can be overcome, often with facilitation of locally based NGOs and similar organizations.[30]

Consequences of Gender Bias in Health and Education

Studies from around the developing world consistently show that expansion of basic education of girls earns among the very highest rates of return of any investment—much higher, for example, than most public infrastructure projects. One estimate is that the global cost of *failing* to educate girls is about $92 billion a year.[31] This is one reason why discrimination against girls in education is not just inequitable but also very costly from the standpoint of achieving development goals.

Education of girls has also been shown to be one of the most cost-effective means of improving local health standards. Studies by the United Nations, the World Bank, and other agencies have concluded that the social benefits alone of increased education of girls is more than sufficient to cover its costs—even before considering the added earning power this education would bring. However, evidence from Pakistan, Bangladesh, and other countries shows that we cannot assume that education of girls will increase automatically with increases in family income.

Inferior education and health care access for girls shows the interlinked nature of economic incentives and the cultural setting. In many parts of Asia, a boy provides future economic benefits, such as support of parents in their old age and possible receipt of a dowry upon marriage, and often continues to work on the farm into adulthood. A girl, in contrast, may require a dowry upon marriage, often at a young age, and will then move to the village of her husband's family, becoming responsible for the welfare of her husband's parents rather than her own. A girl from a poor rural family in South Asia will in many cases perceive no suitable alternatives in life than serving a husband and his family; indeed, a more educated girl may be considered "less marriageable." For the parents, treatment of disease may be expensive and may require several days lost from work to go into town for medical attention. Empirical studies demonstrate what we might guess from these perverse incentives: Often more strenuous efforts are made to save the life of a son than a daughter, and girls generally receive less schooling than boys.

The bias toward boys helps explain the "missing women" mystery. In Asia, the United Nations has found that there are far fewer females as a share of the population than would be predicted by demographic norms (see Chapter 6). Estimating from developed-country gender ratios, Nobel laureate Amartya Sen concludes that worldwide "many more than" 100 million women are "missing."[32] Evidence shows that these conditions are continuing to worsen in China and India, implying that tens of millions of young males will be unable to marry, increasing the chances of future social instability. As Sen notes, that dearth of women is not just a matter of poverty per se because in Africa, where poverty is most severe, there are actually about 2% more women than men. Although this number is not as high as in western Europe and North America, it is still much higher than in Asia, which has higher income on average. A large part of the explanation is poorer treatment of girls. As of 2010, the estimated ratio of males to females in China and India was 1.06 and 1.08, respectively, compared with 0.98 in the United States, United Kingdom, and Canada. The problem may be worsening in several countries, including China, where the Chinese Academy of Sciences estimated in a 2010 report that 119.5 boys were born for every 100 girls in 2009; sex-selective abortion is an important cause.[33] In India, this ratio is also a very high 112. These averages obscure much higher ratios in some regions. The evidence on gender bias in Africa is mixed, with some studies finding a small pro-female bias and others a small and possibly rising pro-male bias.[34]

Figure 8.5 shows the estimated percent of females missing in the populations of five Asian countries, along with the overall average for sub-Saharan Africa, drawing from the highly regarded research of Stephan Klasen and Claudia Wink.

Greater mothers' education, however, generally improves prospects for both their sons' and daughters' health and education, but apparently even more so for girls.[35]

Taken together, the evidence shows that increases in family income do not automatically result in improved health status or educational attainment. If higher income cannot be expected to necessarily lead to higher health and education, as we will show in subsequent sections, there are no guarantees that higher health or education will lead to higher productivities and incomes. Much depends on the context, on whether gains from income growth and also the benefits of public investments in health and education and other infrastructure are shared equitably.

In the remainder of this chapter, we will examine issues of education and health systems in turn. Even though the two topics will be examined separately, it is important to keep their mutually reinforcing roles in mind.

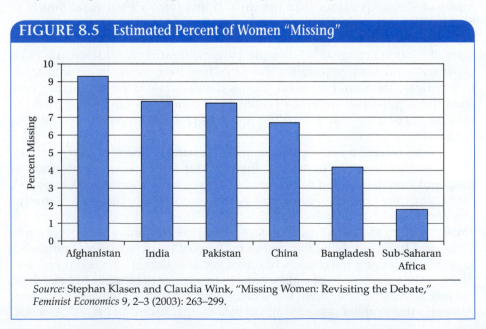

FIGURE 8.5   Estimated Percent of Women "Missing"

Source: Stephan Klasen and Claudia Wink, "Missing Women: Revisiting the Debate," *Feminist Economics* 9, 2–3 (2003): 263–299.

8.5 Educational Systems and Development

Much of the literature and public discussion about education and economic development, in general, and education and employment, in particular, revolves around two fundamental economic processes: (1) the interaction between economically motivated demands and politically responsive supplies in determining how many quality school places are provided, who gets access to these places, and what kind of instruction they receive, and (2) the important distinction between social and private benefits and costs of different levels of education, and the implications of these differentials for educational investment strategy.

The Political Economy of Educational Supply and Demand: The Relationship between Employment Opportunities and Educational Demands

The amount of schooling received by an individual, although affected by many nonmarket factors, can be regarded as largely determined by demand and supply, like any other commodity or service.[36] On the demand side, the two principal influences on the amount of schooling desired are (1) a more educated student's prospects of earning considerably more income through future modern-sector employment (the family's **private benefits** of education) and (2) the educational costs, both direct and indirect, that a student or family must bear. The amount of education demanded is thus in reality a **derived demand** for high-wage employment opportunities in the modern sector. This is because access to such jobs is largely determined by an individual's education.

On the supply side, the quantity of school places at the primary, secondary, and university levels is determined largely by political processes, often unrelated to economic criteria. Given mounting political pressure throughout the developing world for greater numbers of school places at higher levels, we can for convenience assume that the public supply of these places is fixed by the level of government educational expenditures. These are in turn influenced by the level of aggregate private demand for education.

Because the amount of education demanded largely determines the supply (within the limits of government financial feasibility), let us look more closely at the economic (employment-oriented) determinants of this derived demand.

The amount of schooling demanded that is sufficient to qualify an individual for modern-sector jobs appears to be related to or determined by the combined influence of four variables: the wage or income differential, the probability of success in finding modern-sector employment, the direct private costs of education, and the indirect or opportunity costs of education.

For example, suppose that we have a situation in a developing country where the following conditions prevail:

1. The modern-traditional or urban-rural wage gap is of the magnitude of, say, 100% for secondary versus primary school graduates.

Private benefits The benefits that accrue directly to an individual economic unit. For example, private benefits of education are those that directly accrue to a student and his or her family.

Derived demand Demand for a good that emerges indirectly from demand for another good.

2. The rate of increase in modern-sector employment opportunities for primary school dropouts is slower than the rate at which such individuals enter the labor force. The same may be true at the secondary level and even the university level in countries such as India, Mexico, Egypt, Pakistan, Ghana, Nigeria, and Kenya.

3. Employers, facing an excess of applicants, tend to select by level of education. They will choose candidates with secondary rather than primary education even though satisfactory job performance may require no more than a primary education.

4. Governments, supported by the political pressure of the educated, tend to bind the going wage to the level of educational attainment of jobholders rather than to the minimum educational qualification required for the job.

5. School fees decline at the university level, as the state bears a larger proportion of the college student's costs.

Under these conditions, which conform closely to the realities of the employment and education situation in many developing nations, we would expect the quantity of higher education demanded for the formal sector to be substantial. This is because the anticipated private benefits of more schooling would be high compared to the alternative of little schooling, while the direct and indirect private educational costs are relatively low. And the demand spirals upward over time. As job opportunities for the uneducated are limited, individuals must safeguard their position by acquiring increasingly more education.

The upshot is the chronic tendency for some developing nations to expand their higher-level educational facilities at a rate that is extremely difficult to justify either socially or financially in terms of optimal resource allocations. Supply and amount demanded are equated not by a price-adjusting market mechanism but rather institutionally, largely by the state. The **social benefits of education** (the payoff to society as a whole) for all levels of schooling fall short of the private benefits (see Table 8.1).

Governments and formal-sector private employers in many developing countries tend to reinforce this trend by **educational certification**—continuously upgraded formal educational entry requirements for jobs previously filled by less educated workers. Excess educational qualification becomes formalized and may resist downward adjustment. Moreover, to the extent that trade unions succeed in binding going wages to the educational attainments of jobholders, the going wage for each job will tend to rise (even though worker productivity in that job does not significantly increase). Existing distortions in wage differentials will be magnified, thus stimulating the amount of education demanded even further. Egypt presents a classic case of this phenomenon with its government-guaranteed and budget-busting employment in the public sector and its massive civil service overstaffing of overcredentialized school graduates.[37]

Note that this political economy process pulls scarce public resources away from the limited and often low-quality **basic education** available for the many and toward more advanced education for the few. This is both inequitable and economically inefficient.

Social benefits of education Benefits of the schooling of individuals, including those that accrue to others or even to the entire society, such as the benefits of a more literate workforce and citizenry.

Educational certification The phenomenon by which particular jobs require specified levels of education.

Basic education The attainment of literacy, arithmetic competence, and elementary vocational skills.

Social versus Private Benefits and Costs

Typically in developing countries, the **social costs of education** (the opportunity cost to society as a whole resulting from the need to finance costly educational expansion at higher levels when these limited funds might be more productively used in other sectors of the economy) increase rapidly as students climb the educational ladder. The **private costs** of education (those borne by students themselves) increase more slowly or may even decline.

This widening gap between social and private costs provides an even greater stimulus to the demand for higher education than it does for education at lower levels. But educational opportunities can be accommodated to these distorted demands only at full social cost.

Figure 8.6 provides an illustration of this divergence between private and social benefits and costs. It also demonstrates how this divergence can lead

Social costs of education
Costs borne by both the individual and society from private education decisions, including government education subsidies.

Private costs The costs that accrue to an individual economic unit.

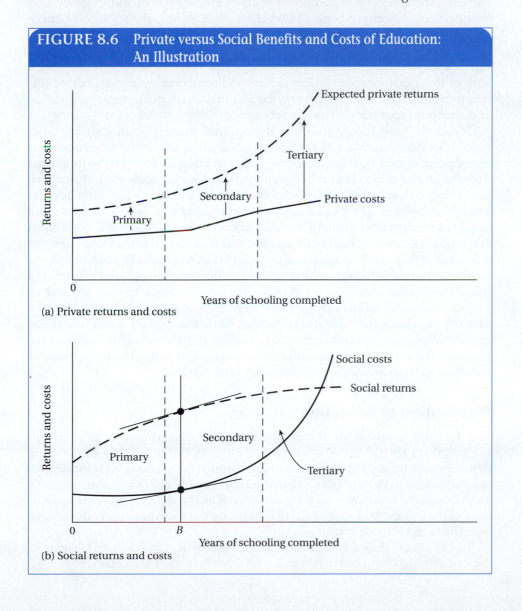

FIGURE 8.6 Private versus Social Benefits and Costs of Education: An Illustration

(a) Private returns and costs

(b) Social returns and costs

to a misallocation of resources when private interests supersede social invest-ment criteria. In Figure 8.6a, expected private returns and actual private costs are plotted against years of completed schooling. As a student completes more and more years of schooling, expected private returns grow at a much faster rate than private costs, for reasons explained earlier. To maximize the dif-ference between expected benefits and costs (and thereby the private rate of return to investment in education), the optimal strategy for a student would be to secure as much schooling as possible.

Now consider Figure 8.6b, where social returns and social costs are plot-ted against years of schooling. The social benefits curve rises sharply at first, reflecting the improved levels of productivity of, say, small farmers and the self-employed that result from receipt of a basic education and the attainment of literacy, arithmetic skills, and elementary vocational skills. Thereafter, the marginal social benefit of additional years of schooling rises more slowly, and the social returns curve begins to level off. By contrast, the social cost curve shows a slow rate of growth for early years of schooling (basic education) and then a much more rapid growth for higher levels of education. This rapid increase in the marginal social costs of postprimary education is the result both of the much more expensive capital and recurrent costs of higher educa-tion (buildings and equipment) and the fact that much postprimary education in developing countries is heavily subsidized.[38]

It follows from Figure 8.6b that the optimal strategy from a social view-point, the one that maximizes the net social rate of return to educational investment, would be one that focuses on providing all students with at least *B* years of schooling. Beyond *B* years, *marginal* social costs exceed *marginal* social benefits, so additional public educational investment in new, higher-level school places will yield a *negative* net social rate of return. The value of *B*, such as nine years of school, would vary according to economic conditions and would be controversial both because of difficulties in calculating earnings gains and debate over which types of social benefits should be considered.

Figure 8.6 also illustrates the inherent conflict between optimal private and social investment strategies—a conflict that will continue to exist as long as private and social valuations of investment in education continue to diverge as students climb the educational ladder, with the highest subsidies at the highest levels of education, commonly availed of by elites. This is one of the reasons why we must also consider the structure and pattern of that economic growth and its distribution implications—who benefits.

Distribution of Education

The forgoing analysis of forces operating for overeducation in develop-ing countries should not lead us to despair over the possibility of fostering development through greater education. Countries that have developed suc-cessfully have generally ensured that educational benefits are more broadly available in the economy—to the poor as well as the rich, in the rural areas as well as the urban. And so we turn to examining the distribution of educational benefits in developing countries.

Just as we can derive Lorenz curves for distribution of income (see Chapter 5), we can also develop Lorenz curves for the distribution of education. Figure 8.7

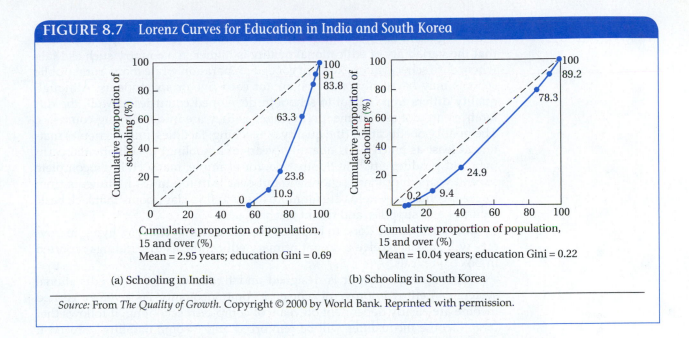

FIGURE 8.7   Lorenz Curves for Education in India and South Korea

(a) Schooling in India

Cumulative proportion of population, 15 and over (%)
Mean = 2.95 years; education Gini = 0.69

(b) Schooling in South Korea

Cumulative proportion of population, 15 and over (%)
Mean = 10.04 years; education Gini = 0.22

Source: From *The Quality of Growth.* Copyright © 2000 by World Bank. Reprinted with permission.

shows Lorenz curves for education in India and South Korea, using comparable data from 1990. By analogy with income Lorenz curves, we write the cumulative proportion of the population on the x-axis and the cumulative proportion of years of schooling on the y-axis. Along the 45-degree line of perfect equality, everyone in the economy would have the same number of years of schooling; for example, everyone would have finished a basic eight years of school, but no one would have started secondary education. In a highly unequal economy, many people might have no years of schooling at all, while a few might have received a Ph.D. from foreign universities. The closer the Lorenz curve is to the 45-degree line, the more equal the distribution of education.

As can be seen from Figure 8.7, South Korea had a much more equal distribution of education than India. For example, in the sample year 1990, well over half of the population of India had received no schooling at all. In South Korea, less than 10% had received no schooling. Yet both countries were producing significant numbers of Ph.D. diplomates. One may also derive an education Gini coefficient, again by analogy with the derivation of the Gini coefficient for income inequality examined in Chapter 5; it is given by the area A above the education Lorenz curve, divided by the whole area A + B below the 45-degree line of perfect equality. As you might guess from looking at the graph, India had a much higher educational inequality as measured by the education Gini (in fact, the Gini was 0.69) than South Korea did (0.22). Educational inequality (in relation to number of years of schooling) tends to fall as average years of education in the population rises. Nonetheless, for a given average years of schooling, some countries such as Sri Lanka have managed relatively equal access to education, and others such as India have managed relatively unequal access.[39]

There is also great inequality in school quality. Some secondary school systems, for example, do a much more effective job of teaching than others.

Certainly, educational quality is higher in high- than in low-income countries—higher in Europe than in Africa, for example. However, it is also likely that the variability of educational quality is higher in a country such as Mali, where elite schools offer excellent college preparation while many rural public schools may have only one textbook for each five or six students. Although quality differs from school to school in developed countries as well, the differences are not as extreme, on average, as they are in developing countries. The quality of education (the quality of teaching, facilities, and curricula) matters at least as much as its quantity (years of schooling) for differential earnings and productivity.[40] In South Asia, for example, many children complete several years in primary school without ever learning to read. Students from lower-income households are far more likely to find classrooms that lack basic facilities and supplies, and truant teachers.

But much can be done to improve the chances that children living in poverty will at least receive a decent primary education, as the findings reported in Box 8.6 reveals.

Depending on how it is designed and financed, a nation's educational system can either improve or worsen income inequality. As levels of earned income are clearly dependent on years of completed schooling, it follows that large income inequalities will be reinforced and income mobility reduced if students from the middle- and upper-income brackets are represented disproportionately in secondary and university enrollments. Despite the recent rapid proliferation of private schools for nonelites in South Asia and other developing regions, their quality is generally not high, and their teacher qualifications are often lower than those in the public schools. In many cases, parents do not appear to be getting what they think they are paying for. The cost of quality education therefore becomes prohibitive to lower-income families, who are often unable to borrow funds to finance their children's middle and secondary school education. Child labor can be understood as a substitute for a loan as a way to bring money to the family now at later cost—a very high cost in the case of child labor. This, in effect, amounts to a system of educational advancement and selection based not on merit but on family wealth. It thus perpetuates concentration of income within certain population groups.[41]

The inegalitarian nature of many developing-country educational systems is compounded even further at the university level, where the government may pay the full cost of tuition and fees and even provide university students with income grants in the form of stipends. Because most university students already come from the upper-income brackets (and were so selected at the secondary level), highly subsidized university education using public funds often amounts to a transfer payment from the poor to the wealthy in the name of "free" higher education![42]

8.6 Health Measurement and Disease Burden

World Health Organization (WHO) The key UN agency concerned with global health matters.

The **World Health Organization (WHO)**, the key UN agency concerned with global health matters, defines health as "a state of complete physical, mental, and social well-being and not merely the absence of disease and infirmity."[43] This approach may put us on a better conceptual foundation but does not in

BOX 8.6 FINDINGS   Impacts of Tutor and Computer-Assisted Learning Programs

Pratham is a large India-based nongovernmental organization (NGO); its name means "primary" or "beginning." Its motto is "To ensure that every child is in school...and learning well." This is of critical importance because "a large fraction of Indian children cannot read when they leave school." Randomized evaluations in urban schools found two of Pratham's programs to be highly cost-effective: tutoring poor children from slums and providing computer learning programs for children to set their own pace to catch up in math. Like many areas in India, in Vadodara, where the program was studied, children are usually on the school's books but often attend sporadically.

Targeted Tutoring

Enrolled children in grades (standards) three and four identified as at risk—lagging behind in first-grade literacy and numeracy—are tutored about two hours a day by young women. These *balsakhis,* meaning "children's friends," have managed to finish secondary school but typically live in the same slums as the children they tutor. *Balsakhis* provide patient attention to children who may find the school environment threatening. The presence of the program increased average test scores of all children in treatment schools by a substantial amount, normalized to 0.28 standard deviations (SDs) after two years. Children with low starting test grades—usually the ones taking part in the program—accounted for most of these gains. The cost is only about $5 per child per year. Results suggest that the program is 12 to 16 times more cost-effective than hiring new teachers. There could be spillover benefits from tutored to untutored children or from the program's presence, but evidence indicates that most gains were from children who worked with a *balsakhi.* Their

scores gained an average of 0.6 SDs in their second year in the program—more than half the gain from a year of school for a comparison child. *Balsakhi* salaries are the program's main cost, about 500 to 750 rupees per month, around $14 based on 2010 exchange rates—a good income for them, though far less than regular teachers make. Thus, the program costs about 107 rupees (about $2.25) per student per year.

Computer-Assisted Learning (CAL)

Pratham set up computers for fourth-grade (standard) children to review math skills—similar to learning programs seen in the United States, Canada, and Britain—for randomly selected participants. Math scores increased by 0.36 SDs the first year and by 0.54 SDs the second year. But some of the gains faded over time. The CAL program costs approximately 722 rupees (about $16) per student per year, including costs for computers.

Thus, both programs are relatively inexpensive and work well. But the *balsakhi* program is five to seven times more cost-effective than the CAL program (evaluated as costs incurred for a given gain in test scores). In fact, total benefits may be greater; for example, greater student learning may lead to higher earnings later in life. The *balsakhi* program has already included tens of thousands of children in India, and the CAL program should not be hard to replicate. Clearly, such programs can be expanded to a large scale. But more research is needed on conditions for helping students better retain what they learn.

Source: Based on Abhijit V. Banerjee, Shawn Cole, Esther Duflo, and Leigh Linden, "Remedying education: Evidence from two randomized experiments in India," *Quarterly Journal of Economics* 122 (2007): 1235–1264.

itself provide a better measure. An alternative measure of health promoted by the WHO is the *disability-adjusted life year* (DALY). There are doubts about the quality of data used in these measures, especially for some of the poorest countries, and the use of DALYs to compare health across countries is controversial. Premature deaths represented about two-thirds of lost DALYs, and disabilities accounted for the remaining third. Using a DALY measure, a World Bank study calculated that about one-quarter of the global burden of disease was represented by diarrhea, childhood diseases including measles, respiratory infections, parasitic worm infections, and malaria—all major health problems in developing countries.[44] Progress has continued to be made in most but not all of these disease categories.

However, average health levels can mask great inequality. For example, in some countries, minorities and indigenous populations can have life expectancies that are a decade or more shorter than the dominant groups, and their infant mortality rates can be more than triple the national average.[45] Thus, as is the case with income and education, the distribution of health among the population, not just averages, is what matters. As one might expect, the poor are significantly less healthy than the more affluent. Figure 8.8 shows that the children of the poor are much more likely to die than those of the rich. Figure 8.9 points to an important culprit. The proportion of children under age 5 who are underweight is far higher for poorer quintiles than for richer quintiles, particularly in South Asia and sub-Saharan Africa. Health inequality is a consistent pattern, whatever the measure of health outcomes used.

Health inputs are also very unequal, even when they are provided by public authorities rather than procured privately. Higher-quality medical facilities are concentrated in urban and richer areas, where the more affluent have the political clout to secure them. Even when public clinics are available in poor rural areas, they are typically underequipped and understaffed. Just as teacher truancy is a problem in schools, absenteeism of medical personnel can be pervasive. A World Bank study found that absentee rates among health care workers in primary health facilities on which the poorer population depends was 43% in India in 14 states studied, 42% in Indonesia, 35% in Bangladesh, 35% in Uganda, 26% in Peru, and 19% in Papua New Guinea.[46]

Developing countries face a much more crippling disease burden than developed countries, especially regarding infectious diseases. AIDS, malaria,

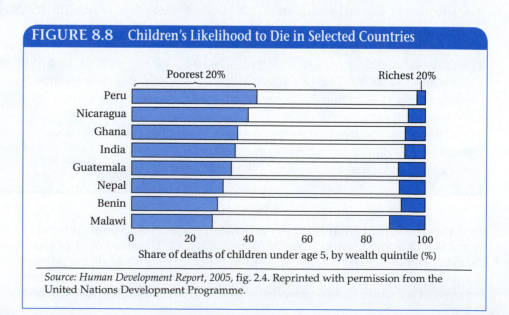

FIGURE 8.8   Children's Likelihood to Die in Selected Countries

Share of deaths of children under age 5, by wealth quintile (%)

Source: Human Development Report, 2005, fig. 2.4. Reprinted with permission from the United Nations Development Programme.

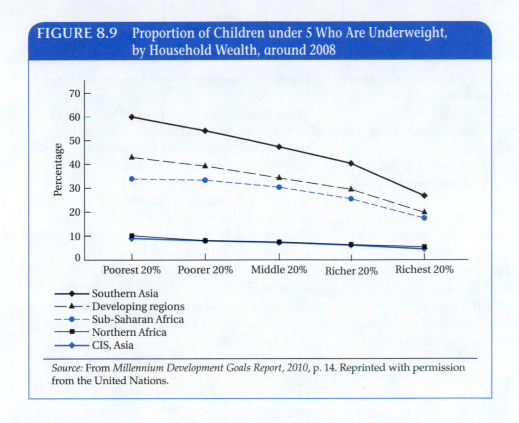

FIGURE 8.9 Proportion of Children under 5 Who Are Underweight, by Household Wealth, around 2008

Southern Asia
Developing regions
Sub-Saharan Africa
Northern Africa
CIS, Asia

Source: From *Millennium Development Goals Report, 2010*, p. 14. Reprinted with permission from the United Nations.

and parasites are three major problems that we consider in this section. These and other health challenges faced by developing countries are surveyed in Box 8.7.

In 2012, nearly 7 million children under the age of 5 died in developing countries. This means that under-5 child deaths accounted for about 12% of all deaths worldwide. Because most of these children died of causes that could be prevented at very low cost per child, it has been rightly claimed that their real underlying disease is poverty.

Health problems are particularly severe in sub-Saharan Africa. Water is often contaminated and scarce,[47] and under-5 mortality in 2011 was 109 deaths per 1,000 live births in these countries, though this represented a dramatic improvement from 1990, when the comparable number was 178 per 1,000. In at least a dozen sub-Saharan African countries, a child is more likely to die before the age of 5 than to attend secondary school. Life expectancy at birth in the region is only 55 years, kept down in part because of the impact of the AIDS epidemic, though this represents an increase from 50 years in 1990. Over 21% of children under 5 in sub-Saharan Africa are undernourished. In this case, the problem is actually less severe than that in South Asia, where child hunger among children under 5 has remained at extremely elevated levels— over 33%—despite better economic growth performance.

Some diseases are especially deadly when combined with other diseases. Malnutrition is a form of disease, and its presence is a major factor among children in both contracting disease and dying of it. While the death certificate may cite dehydration from diarrhea or a specific infectious disease, in many cases death would not have occurred without the contributing factor of malnutrition.

BOX 8.7   Health Challenges Faced by Developing Countries

- *Absolute poverty.* Poverty plays such a central role in most health problems faced by developing countries that it has its own designation in the International Classification of Diseases: code Z59.5—extreme poverty.

- *Malnutrition.* Many deaths attributed to a proximate cause of disease—particularly among children—have as their root cause malnutrition, which can weaken the immune system. About 800 million people suffer undernourishment, and up to 2 billion suffer one or more micronutrient deficiencies.

- *AIDS.* Now the leading cause of death of working-age adults in the developing world, if unchecked it may condemn many countries in sub-Saharan Africa, the hardest-hit region, to continued grinding poverty.

- *Malaria.* Once in retreat, its most deadly strain is now making a big comeback, particularly in Africa; it still kills well over 1 million people each year, 70% of them children under age 5.

- *Tuberculosis.* TB currently claims about 2 million lives each year. One-third of the world's population is infected with the TB bacillus, and each year, about 8 million new cases result from this "reservoir of infection." New multi-drug-resistant strains of TB, difficult and expensive to treat, are spreading in "TB hot zones" in the developing world.

- *Acute lower respiratory infections.* Lung infections, primarily pneumonia—generally preventable and curable—cause about 20% of all deaths in children under age 5.

- *Hepatitis B.* Hepatitis B may now kill as many as 1 million people each year.

- *Ascariasis. Ascaris* roundworm parasites affect some 10% of the population of the developing world, possibly as many as 1.2 billion people. The parasites most commonly infect children ages 3 to 8 years when they put their hands to their mouths after playing in contaminated soil or eat uncooked food grown in contaminated soil or irrigated with unsanitary water. The worst infections cause about 60,000 deaths per year, the overwhelming majority of whom are children.

- *Cholera.* Once largely in retreat, cholera has been on the upsurge in recent years in many countries in Africa, Asia, and Latin America. Untreated, dehydration from severe diarrhea causes death.

- *Dengue.* Dengue and dengue hemorrhagic fever are spreading rapidly, with millions of cases reported each year and thousands of deaths; about a half million cases require hospital treatment.

- *Leprosy (Hansen disease).* There are still about 400,000 new cases of leprosy each year. About 2 million people are disabled by leprosy, including those who have been cured but crippled prior to treatment, in India and many other developing countries.

- *Dracunculiasis (guinea worm disease).* This debilitating nematode infestation afflicts the poorest of the poor, who lack access to even minimally safe water.

- *Chagas disease.* This parasitic infection attacks an estimated 17 million people in Latin America, causing about 45,000 deaths annually.

- *Leishmaniasis.* This group of parasitic diseases infect about 12 million people. Visceral leishmaniasis, also known as *kala-azar*, is the most severe form. Fatal in 90% of untreated cases, it causes tens of thousands of deaths each year.

- *Lymphatic filariasis (elephantiasis).* This disfiguring parasitic disease still affects around 100 million people in the developing world, leaving 40 million of them seriously incapacitated and disfigured.

- *Other parasites.*Many other parasites are active, including *Trichuris* and hookworm, each of which affects about 600 million people.
- *Other diarrheal diseases.*Whether caused by infectious agents listed in this box or other bacterial, viral, or parasitic organisms, diarrhea

is often spread by contaminated water; untreated, it can lead to extreme dehydration, the proximate cause of death of close to 2 million people each year.

Source: World Health Organization.

Malnutrition among children is particularly consequential. Although child hunger has been declining in all developing regions, the rate of improvement is too slow to achieve even the fundamental Millennium Development Goal target of halving hunger between 1990 and 2015 (see Figure 8.10). And an increase in hunger caused by the global food price spike in 2007–2008 and the global crisis that followed highlighted continued vulnerability, as seen also in the upward push of food prices in 2010. The International Food Policy Research Institute has introduced an annual global hunger index to track progress and setbacks; the 2013 report found that 870 million people are still suffering from hunger.[48]

FIGURE 8.10   Proportion of Children under 5 Who Are Underweight, 1990 and 2005

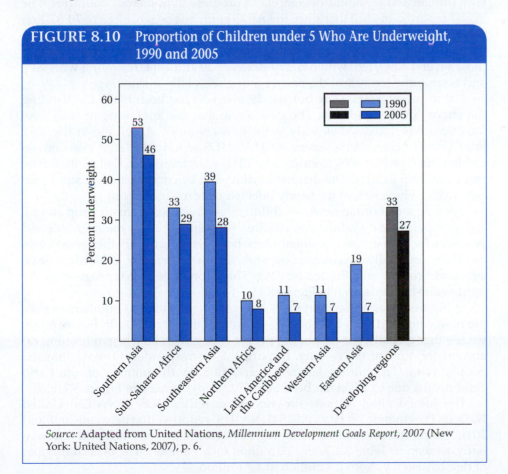

Source: Adapted from United Nations, *Millennium Development Goals Report, 2007* (New York: United Nations, 2007), p. 6.

The interaction between malaria and acute respiratory infections or anemia is also deadly. Another important lethal interaction is between AIDS and tuberculosis. Failure to control either of the diseases makes each more likely to be fatal. Moreover, the spread of HIV has been demonstrated to be significantly promoted by the presence of other sexually transmitted diseases, whose sores facilitate viral invasion.

To address problems of acute respiratory infections, diarrhea, measles, malaria, and malnutrition, the WHO, in cooperation with other major international agencies and national health authorities, has been implementing its Integrated Management of Childhood Illness (IMCI) program, aimed at improving the training and performance of national health organizations and personnel in disease prevention and the treatment of sick children. The program emphasizes education on practices such as breast-feeding and use of oral rehydration therapy.

We turn now to consider three major scourges of the developing world—AIDS, malaria, and parasitic worms.

HIV/AIDS

The AIDS epidemic has been threatening to halt or even reverse years of hard-won human and economic development progress in numerous countries. The WHO reported in 2013 that since the AIDS epidemic began, close to 70 million people have been infected with the HIV virus; and about half of them—about 35 million people—have already died of AIDS. Sub-Saharan Africa remains most severely affected, with nearly 1 in every 20 adults (4.9%) living with HIV and accounting for 69% of the people living with HIV worldwide.

But in recent years, slow but steady progress has been made in "bending the curve" of the epidemic. The data show that the annual number of new infections has decreased steadily in the new century.[49] According to the 2012 Joint United Nations Programme on HIV/AIDS report, new HIV infections in children dropped by 43% from 2003 to 2011, with more than half of that drop just from 2009 to 2011. The disease continues to be concentrated in sub-Saharan Africa, where 90% of the newly infected children live.

But new infections in newborn children had the most dramatic drop among any group, including adults and children—a result of better medical care and practices for HIV-positive women. There has been a flurry of other good news on AIDS, especially by comparison with the worst fears of a decade or two ago, and progress may be accelerating. The impressive global progress in the fight against AIDS is seen in Figure 8.11.

In Figure 8.11a, we see that there has been a global fall in numbers of people newly infected with HIV, beginning around the late 1990s. In Figure 8.11b, we see that globally, the number of people living with HIV began leveling off around the turn of the century. In part, this corresponded to some infected people dying. Now in the last few years, globally the number of adult and child deaths due to AIDS has been actually falling, as seen in Figure 8.11c.

The Joint United Nations Programme on HIV/AIDS (UNAIDS) United Nations Programme on HIV/AIDS (UNAIDS) reported that between 2001 and 2011, the number of people becoming newly infected with HIV fell substantially, as seen in Table 8.2, from 3.2 million to 2.5 million. The overall number of deaths also fell, from 2.3 million to 1.7 million.

FIGURE 8.11   Global HIV Trends, 1990–2011

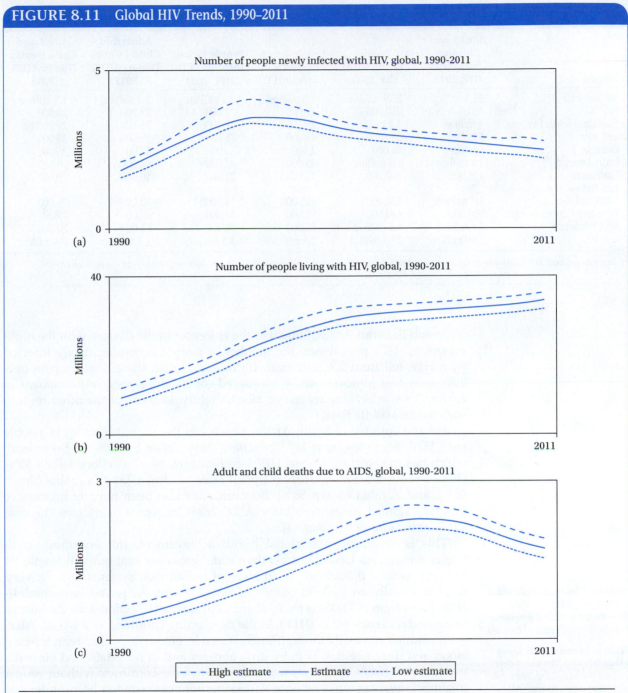

Number of people newly infected with HIV, global, 1990-2011

Number of people living with HIV, global, 1990-2011

Adult and child deaths due to AIDS, global, 1990-2011

– – – High estimate   ——— Estimate   ········· Low estimate

Source: 2012 UNAIDS Report on the Global AIDS Epidemic, Page 14; downloaded from http://www.unaids.org/en/resources/publications/2012/name,76121,en.asp.

TABLE 8.2   Regional HIV and AIDS Statistics, a Decade of Bending the Curve, 2011 versus 2001

Region	Adults and Children Living with HIV, 2011	People Living with HIV, 2001	People Newly Infected with HIV, 2011	People Newly Infected with HIV, 2001	Adult and Child Deaths Due to AIDS, 2011	Adult and Child Deaths Due to AIDS, 2005
Sub-Saharan Africa	23.5 million	20.9 million	1.8 million	2.4 million	1.2 million	1.8 million
MENA	300,000	210,000	37,000	27,000	23,000	20,000
South and South East Asia	4 million	3.7 million	280,000	370,000	250,000	290,000
East Asia	830,000	390,000	89,000	75,000	59,000	39,000
Oceania	59,000	38,000	2,900	3,700	1,300	2,300
Latin America	1.4 million	1.2 million	83,000	93,000	54,000	60,000
Caribbean	230,000	240,000	13,000	22,000	10,000	20,000
East Europe and Central Asia	1.4 million	970,000	140,000	130,000	92,000	76,000
West and Central Europe	900,000	640,000	30,000	29,000	7,000	7,800
North America	1.4 million	1.1 million	51,000	50,000	21,000	20,000
TOTAL	34.0 million	29.4 million	2.5 million	3.2 million	1.7 million	2.3 million

Source: Adapted from 2009 AIDS Epidemic Update, p. 11. © 2009 Joint United Nations Programme on HIV/AIDS (UNAIDS) and World Health Organization (WHO).

In sub-Saharan Africa, known as the epicenter of the disease with the highest overall HIV prevalence, the number of people becoming newly infected with HIV fell from 2.4 million to 1.8 million. Thus, the global drop in new infections was almost entirely accounted for by the strong improvement in Africa. New infections are rising, albeit slightly, in some of the other regions such as the Middle East.

For the country of South Africa, which has the largest number of people with HIV infections, new HIV infections have fallen by 41%. In Swaziland, which has the world's highest HIV infection rate, new infections fell by 37%. Other countries with big drops included Malawi (down 73%), Namibia (down 68%), and Zambia (down 58%). Botswana has also been making impressive progress against its extraordinary AIDS crisis in recent years (see the case study at the end of Chapter 14).

This is an impressive global health achievement, but enormous challenges remain. As UNAIDS recently put it, "gains are real but still fragile."[50] Though usually thought of as an issue of health care systems and delivery, AIDS is equally an issue of economic development. **Acquired immunodeficiency syndrome (AIDS)** is the final and fatal stage of infection with the **human immunodeficiency virus (HIV)**. In the developing countries as a whole, AIDS is transmitted primarily through heterosexual intercourse; contact with infected blood and drug needles, both by drug abusers and in hospitals; and perinatal transmission (from mother to fetus). In low-income countries, without proper treatment, average survival once AIDS symptoms appear has been under one year. There has been progress in making expensive antiretroviral medication available to low- and lower-middle-income countries at much reduced prices (or even free of charge); at the end of 2011, for the first time, a majority of HIV-positive people eligible for antiretroviral therapy treatment in low- and middle-income countries actually were receiving it—8 million people in all, up dramatically in recent years. Unfortunately, these lifesaving drugs are still

Acquired immunodeficiency syndrome (AIDS) Viral disease transmitted predominantly through sexual contact.

Human immunodeficiency virus (HIV) The virus that causes the acquired immunodeficiency syndrome (AIDS).

not available to millions infected in Africa and South Asia. Treatments have often otherwise been limited to aspirin, antibiotics for infections, and cortisone for skin rashes.

Initially, AIDS was widely perceived as a disease of developed countries, primarily affecting men who have sex with men. But in fact, more than 95% of all HIV cases and AIDS deaths occur in the developing world. Throughout the region of sub-Saharan Africa, AIDS is now the leading cause of death of adults in the economically active years. Although infectious childhood diseases still kill far more people in developing countries, AIDS strikes those who have successfully run this gauntlet of child killers. Their societies depend on the energies and skills of precisely the part of the population most afflicted.

Emily Oster presents evidence that the high incidence of HIV in Africa may result from higher rates of HIV viral transmission, which is facilitated by higher rates of other untreated sexually transmitted diseases. This provides another example of potential synergies among health problems to be taken into account in the design of successful programs.

According to the *UNAIDS Report on the Global AIDS Epidemic, 2010*, there were about 15 million AIDS orphans in sub-Saharan Africa as of 2009 (who had lost at least one parent to AIDS). Providing basic needs for these orphans, ensuring that they are not discriminated against because of irrational fears, and seeing that they are able to obtain the few years of schooling that will help rescue them from absolute poverty will be a major development challenge. It is not a challenge that Africa, with all its problems, is accustomed to. Extended family networks have provided privately for children who have lost their parents. In some parts of East Africa, this traditional family adaptation to death appears threatened due to the scope of the AIDS crisis. Political analysts claim that conditions are ripe not only for child abuse and exploitation but also for recruiting of children for guerrilla armies led by unscrupulous aspiring dictators or mercenary groups. The resulting destabilization and diversion of resources can have a devastating impact on social and economic development. An excellent strategy developed by church groups in Zimbabwe is to have volunteers visit and provide basic care for these orphans in the homes where they live, which can be homes of child-headed households, foster parents, grandparents, or other relatives. These visits provide a much needed combination of emotional and material support for these orphans.

The case of the AIDS crisis in Uganda and the response of government and civil society is presented in Box 8.8.

Malaria

Malaria directly causes over 1 million deaths each year, most of them among impoverished African children. Pregnant women are also at high risk. Severe cases of malaria leave about 15% of the children who survive the disease with substantial neurological problems and learning disabilities. A child dies from malaria every 30 seconds. Over 500 million people become severely ill with malaria each year. There is evidence that Malaria can lower productivity and possibly even reduce growth rates.[51]

The WHO's Roll Back Malaria Partnership seeks to eradicate this disease at its source. Eradication has been most successful where campaigns have combined

BOX 8.8 AIDS: Crisis and Response in Uganda

The AIDS pandemic in Uganda was the first to reach a large scale and then the first to register a significant decline in prevalence; as a result, the Ugandan experience has been widely studied. Although the picture is not completely clear, some important lessons have emerged. HIV was probably spreading in the late 1970s, and the first AIDS cases were diagnosed in the early 1980s. It was several years before a national response emerged, criticized as slow at the time but rapid in comparison with many other countries. A 1988 national survey of the epidemic found an HIV prevalence of 9%, unprecedented at that time. UNAIDS estimated that national prevalence peaked at 15% in 1991. But the national and international response also accelerated.

The Ugandan government introduced one of the most active and comprehensive AIDS prevention programs in Africa. Programs were coordinated by the Ugandan AIDS Commission Secretariat. Funding was provided by UNICEF, the WHO, USAID, the World Bank, and the UNDP. Donor countries, including the United States, were probably more active on AIDS in Uganda than other countries as a result of the extensive attention to the early epidemic there. The AIDS Support Organization (TASO), a Ugandan NGO, has played a crucial role in innovation and scaled-up service delivery in treatment, family assistance, and counseling, as well as education and awareness, since its founding in 1987. Civil society, including churches, played a major role in mobilizing a community response.

Mass media were employed in Uganda's HIV awareness efforts. The main slogan, "Zero Grazing," was a locally sophisticated way of saying "stay with one partner." At first, many people did not understand it, but once they did, its simple message—at a time when many knew infected Ugandans—was thought to have had some impact. The AIDS film, *It's Not Easy*, was viewed by some 90% of Uganda's formal-sector workforce. T-shirts with mottos like "Love Carefully" became popular. Abstinence was promoted but is estimated to have had a more limited effect. After

overcoming religious opposition, condom use was heavily promoted, a major factor in reduced transmission of HIV in Uganda. The spread of HIV has also been demonstrated to be significantly promoted by the presence of other sexually transmitted diseases which could also be reduced by condom use. In Uganda, the commercial sex industry in towns known to be highly infected dropped dramatically. Several studies showed that the rate of AIDS infection among teenagers in Uganda dropped steeply from 1990 to 1995, most likely due in part to the adoption of at least comparatively safer sex practices. However, some of this decrease might have been due to a decline in trade in this period. And the rate fell further when many of those previously infected began to die in larger numbers.

During the early spread of HIV, commercial controls were a factor leading to an active smuggling industry. Some highly paid truck smugglers, often stranded for days in towns along smuggling routes, made frequent visits to sex workers, encouraging the rapid spread of the disease. The decrease in economic activity in the 1990s may be a complementary explanation for the reduced HIV infection rates, along with behavior change.

The HIV prevalence rate appears to have risen somewhat since 2000. UNAIDS has estimated that 6.9% to 7.7% of Ugandan adults were infected in 2011. About 1.4 million people are HIV-positive in the country, with 62,000 deaths in 2011 alone. There are over 1 million AIDS orphans in the country. This has generated great concern. The apparent uptick may be partly due to complacency in sexual behavior after rates fell and antiretrovirals became more available. It may also not be a coincidence that economic activity has also picked up in Uganda in recent years. There is concern that previous estimates may have been somewhat low. Many Ugandans and aid officials are worried about the trend and are working to reverse it with renewed emphasis on the media and community mobilization strategies that are widely understood to have helped in the past.

Sources: Martha Ainsworth and Mead Over, "AIDS and African development," *World Bank Research Observer* 9 (1994): 203–240; Jill Armstrong, "Socioeconomic implications of AIDS in developing countries," *Finance and Development,* 28, No. 4 (1991): 14–17; Tony Barnett and Piers Blaikie, *AIDS in Africa: Its Present and Future Impact.* New York: Guilford Press, 1992; Gerard Kambou, Shanta Devarajan, and Mead Over, "The economic impact of AIDS in an African country: Simulations with a CGE model of Cameroon," *Journal of African Economies* 1 (1993): 109–130; Jean-Louis Lamboray and A. Edward Elmendorf, "Combating AIDS and other sexually transmitted diseases in Africa." World Bank Africa Technical Division Paper No. 181. Washington, D.C.: World Bank, 1994; Maureen A. Lewis et al., *AIDS in Developing Countries: Cost Issues and Policy Tradeoffs.* Washington, D.C.: Urban Institute, 1989; Mead Over, *The Macroeconomic Impact of AIDS in Sub-Saharan Africa.* Washington, D.C.: World Bank Africa Technical Division, 1993; *Population and Development,* special issue, "A Cultural Perspective on HIV Transmission," January 1993; Uganda AIDS Commission, http://www.aidsuganda.org; UNAIDS; http://www.unaids.org/en/HIV_data/epi2006/default.asp; United Nations Development Programme, *Human Development Report, 2001.* New York: Oxford University Press, 2001; World Bank, *Report on a Workshop on the Economic Impact of Fatal Adult Illness in Sub-Saharan Africa.* Washington, D.C.: World Bank, July 1993; Emily Oster, "Routes of infection: Exports and HIV incidence in sub-Saharan Africa." NBER Working Paper No. 13610, January 16, 2009, forthcoming in the *Journal of the European Economic Association*; Emily Oster, "Sexually transmitted infections, sexual behavior, and the HIV/AIDS epidemic," *Quarterly Journal of Economics* 120 (2005): 467–515; Note that an AIDS orphan is defined by UNAIDS as a child who has lost at least one parent to AIDS.

better targeted DDT spraying and draining swamps where malarial mosquitoes are breeding with using mosquito bed nets, improving nutrition to build resistance, and sealing houses against mosquito entry.[52]

In addition, major efforts are under way to increase international funding for a war on malaria, emphasizing the development of a malaria vaccine. With proper funding, specialists believe that an effective vaccine might be just a few years away, but because victims of malaria tend to come from low-income countries and cannot afford expensive drugs, there has been little incentive for pharmaceutical companies to emphasize research in this field. However, citizen and government pressure in developed countries and a desire to score public relations points, among other factors, have increasingly led drug companies to begin to offer drugs at lower costs in low-income countries, and this may expand to a more balanced portfolio of research.

Vaccines for other diseases have saved many children's lives in developing countries. For example, the WHO and UNICEF, in their 2005 report, *Global Immunization Vision and Strategy,* estimated that immunization of children carried out in 2003 alone saved 2 million lives (plus hundreds of thousands of additional lives saved in adulthood from complications of hepatitis B). Most vaccines (against diphtheria, tetanus, pertussis/whooping cough, polio, hepatitis B, and measles, for example) were first developed for use in high-income countries. There are other diseases—concentrated in the developing world rather than in both developing and developed countries—that could be controlled with vaccines that pose technical problems no more difficult than vaccines for other diseases previously developed. So why aren't there more vaccines for diseases of the developing world?

If the science is not necessarily the constraint, one reason is that the people who would most benefit are poor and therefore less able to pay. Governments and international assistance could help with subsidies. But as pointed out by Michael Kremer, two market failures are also at work. First, there is an incentive for governments to wait for other countries to spend the resources on vaccine R&D, after which the benefits will largely spill over as an externality to citizens in one's own country. Even if cooperation could be agreed to, there still would be an incentive for participating governments to "defect" and not pay their share. And second, whatever is claimed by aid agencies and governments in advance, companies developing vaccines fear that once they have succeeded, they will be pushed to lower their prices close to production costs, thereby making recouping their original R&D costs unlikely. This is a "time inconsistency problem."[53]

If such problems could be overcome, a potential vaccine would be one of the best solutions for malaria and many other tropical diseases. An idea that has received much attention to address market failure problems are guaranteed vaccine purchases, studied by the Advance Market Commitment Working Group led by Ruth Levine, Michael Kremer, and Alice Albright. In their report, *Making Markets for Vaccines: Ideas to Action,* the group proposed that international sponsors make a legally binding commitment to pay for 200 million malaria vaccine treatments at a guaranteed real price of $15 each, of which $14 would be paid by the sponsors and $1 by the recipient countries. The agreement would set up an independent adjudication committee (IAC) to determine that the required technical specifications for the vaccine had been met. If the IAC found that a later-developed product was superior, it too would be eligible for the price guarantee within the 200 million doses, according to the underlying demand. Firms would have to agree to offer further treatments after the 200 million had been subsidized at a price reflecting production costs, estimated at about $1 per treatment. The group estimated the market under these parameters at about $3 billion, which it found were approximately average revenues for new drugs developed for rich countries. This project has since been introduced. Funding for malaria vaccines is now substantially improving. A similar structure should work for vaccines for other diseases.[54]

Parasitic Worms and Other "Neglected Tropical Diseases"

Many health challenges of developing countries have received high-profile attention in recent years, epitomized by the relatively well-funded and central role of the Global Fund to Fight AIDS, Tuberculosis, and Malaria.[55] Recall from Chapter 1 that the sixth Millennium Development Goal is to combat "HIV-AIDS, malaria, and other diseases." Indeed, these "other" developing-country health problems, including several types of parasitic worms, have also had devastating impacts on the developing world but have long been comparatively neglected.

The incidence of debilitating parasitic worms has been vast with some 2 billion people affected—300 million severely. Among the many parasitic diseases plaguing people in the developing world, schistosomiasis (also called *bilharziasis,* or *snail fever*) is one of the worst in terms of its human and development impact (following malaria, which is also classified as a parasitic disease). Schistosomiasis in humans is caused by waterborne flatworms (also known as blood flukes) called *schistosomes.* According to WHO estimates, the disease infects about 200 million people in 74 developing countries, of whom about 120 million are symptomatic and some 20 million suffer severe consequences, including about 200,000 deaths each year. Half of those severely affected are school-age children. The disease retards their growth and harms their school performance if they are in school. The WHO reports that the stunting effects of schistosomiasis are 90% reversible with effective treatment, which is still all too often entirely lacking. Effects on adults can also be serious. According to the WHO, the work capacity of rural laborers in Egypt, Sudan, and northeastern Brazil, for example, is severely reduced due to weakness and lethargy caused by the disease. Liver and kidney damage can result. If this were not enough, the WHO's International Agency for Research on Cancer has determined that urinary schistosomiasis causes bladder cancer: In some areas of sub-Saharan Africa, the incidence of schistosomiasis-linked bladder cancer is about 32 times higher than the incidence of bladder cancer in the United States.

Another long-standing scourge, African trypanosomiasis, or sleeping sickness, still affects several hundred thousand people in sub-Saharan Africa, mostly in remote areas. Tragically, because the disease is endemic where health systems are weakest, most people who contract sleeping sickness die before they are even diagnosed. The WHO estimated that sleeping sickness kills some 55,000 people a year. The impact of trypanosomiasis on economic development can be severe; in addition to the loss of human life and vitality, the disease kills cattle and leads to the abandonment of fertile but infected land. In this case, the parasites (*Trypanosoma*) are protozoa transmitted to humans by tsetse flies. The disease is being attacked with drugs donated to international organizations from a pharmaceutical company. In recent years, public pressure and attention have played an important role in getting drug companies to be more active and constructive in developing countries and in making donations to key agencies such as the WHO. The sleeping sickness initiative is a good example, with Aventis Pharma providing three key drugs—pentamidine, melarsoprol, and eflornithine—that are each essential for treating sleeping sickness.

Table 8.3 shows the 13 major **neglected tropical diseases**, ranked by their global prevalence (number infected). Taken together, these diseases cause an estimated 534,000 deaths each year. But most of these diseases are curable, can be prevented with environmental improvements at their source, and can ultimately be inoculated against with vaccines. The cost of combating these diseases is relatively low in most cases, and the tragedy is that despite this, they have received relatively little attention. Yet research demonstrates that deworming of children can improve both their health and their school attendance—at very low cost (again, see the findings in Box 8.4 on page 387).

But these "neglected" tropical diseases are finally starting to get the focus they deserve. The Global Network for Neglected Tropical Diseases is coordinating a campaign to fight these scourges.

The net benefits of expanded support for other health programs in addition to HIV/AIDS, including child nutrition and the neglected tropical diseases, are very high and often show strong synergies. The moral and economic case for a much enhanced international response is clear.

Neglected tropical diseases Thirteen treatable diseases, most of them parasitic, that are prevalent in developing countries but receive much less attention than tuberculosis, malaria, and AIDS.

TABLE 8.3   Some Major Neglected Tropical Diseases

Neglected Disease	Symptoms and Effects	Global prevalance (millions)*	Regions with highest Prevalence/Risk
Roundworm (Ascariasis)	Malnutrition and intestinal obstruction in young children; Child stunting; Impaired cognition	820	East Asia and Pacific Islands, sub-Saharan Africa; India, South Asia, China, Latin America and Caribbean
Whipworm (Trichuriasis)	Colitis and inflammatory bowel disease; Child stunting and impaired cognition	465	Sub-Saharan Africa, East Asia and Pacific Islands, Latin America and Caribbean, India, South Asia
Hookworm infection	Severe iron deficiency anemia and protein malnutrition; anemia; Child stunting and impaired intellectual and cognitive development; Maternal morbidity and mortality in pregnancy	439	Sub-Saharan Africa, East Asia and Pacific Islands, India, South Asia, Latin America and Caribbean
Schistosomiasis	Bladder damage, intestine or liver inflammation; Chronic pain, anemia, malnutrition and stunting; Liver and intestinal fibrosis, kidney disease, female genital schistosomiasis	200+	Sub-Saharan Africa, Latin America and Caribbean
Lymphatic filariasis (elephantiasis)	Leg swelling, disfigurement, extreme pain	120	India, South Asia, East Asia and Pacific Islands, sub-Saharan Africa
Trachoma	Blindness	60 - 80	Sub-Saharan Africa, Middle East and North Africa
Onchocerciasis	Larvae in skin and eyes; Onchocerca skin disease; Blindness	30–40	Sub-Saharan Africa, Latin America and Caribbean
Leishmaniasis	Fever, weight loss, enlargement of the spleen and liver, and anaemia	12	India, South Asia, sub-Saharan Africa, Latin America and Caribbean
Chagas' disease	Heart and digestive problems	8+	Latin America and Caribbean
Trypanosomiasis (Human African)	Sleepiness, wwollen lymph nodes, weakness, psychiatric disorders, seizures	0.3	Sub-Saharan Africa

*Note: Population considered at risk generally much higher than current prevalence; Estimated DALYs are far higher than death rates

Sources: World Health Organization Website, Neglected Tropical Diseases website accessed Feb. 15, 2014: http://www.who.int/neglected_diseases/en/; infections in 2010 Rachel L Pullan, Jennifer L Smith, Rashmi Jasrasaria, and Simon J Brooke, "Global numbers of infection and disease burden of soil transmitted helminth infections in 2010", Parasites and Vectors, 2014; Peter Hotez, "A Plan to Defeat Neglected Tropical Diseases," Scientific American, Jan. 10, 2010, p90-96; Peter J Hotez, Alan Fenwick, Lorenzo Savioli, and David H Molyneux, "Rescuing the bottom billion through control of neglected tropical diseases, May 2, 2009 Lancet #379, p1570-75 ; Peter Hotez, "NTDs V.2.0: "Blue Marble Health"—Neglected Tropical Disease Control and Elimination in a Shifting Health Policy Landscape Blue Marble Health 2013 PLOS Neglected Tropical Diseases, www.plosntds.org, 1 November 2013, Vol. 7, No. 11 ,e2570; Peter Hotez et al., "Control of neglected tropical diseases," New England Journal of Medicine, 357: 1018–1027 (2007)

8.7 Health, Productivity, and Policy

Productivity

The devastating effects of poor health on child mortality are clear enough. But do poor health conditions in developing countries also harm the productivity of adults? The answer appears to be yes. Studies show that healthier people earn higher wages. For example, daily wage rates in Côte d'Ivoire have been estimated to be about 19% lower among men whose health status makes them likely to lose a day of work per month because of illness than daily wage rates of healthier men. Careful statistical methods have shown that a large part of the effect of health on raising earnings is due to productivity differences: It is not just the reverse causality that higher wages are used in part to purchase better health. A study in Bangladesh found that the higher productivity of healthier workers allows them to get better-paying jobs. In another study, the elimination of deformity from leprosy was estimated to more than triple earnings of workers in India.[56]

The Nobel laureate Robert Fogel has found that citizens of developed countries are substantially taller today than they were two centuries ago and has argued that stature is a useful index of the health and general well-being of a population. Increases in height have also been found in developing countries in recent decades as health conditions have improved. In most cases, rapid increases in average height earlier in the twentieth century gave way to smaller increases by midcentury.

If height is an indicator of general health status, to the extent that increases in health lead to higher productivity, taller people should earn more (unless height also proxies other productivity characteristics). John Strauss and Duncan Thomas found that taller men earn more money in Brazil, even after controlling for other important determinants of income such as education and experience (Figure 8.12, panels A1 and A2). A 1% increase in height is associated with a 7% increase in wages in that middle-income country. In the United States, there is also an association, but a much smaller one, with a 1% increase in height associated with a 1% increase in wages. Moreover, shorter individuals are more likely to be unemployed altogether. Height reflects various

FIGURE 8.12   Wages, Education, and Height of Males in Brazil and the United States

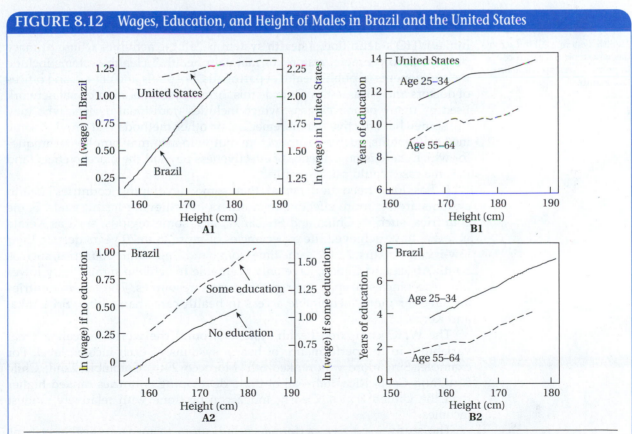

Source: "Health, nutrition, and economic development," by John Strauss and Duncan Thomas, *Journal of Economic Literature* 36 (1998): 766–817. Reprinted with permission.

Note: ln (wage) stands for natural log of wage.

benefits achieved early in life; thus one is not seeing just the impact of current income on current height. In particular, taller people receive significantly more education than shorter people (see Figure 8.12, panels B1 and B2). Note also that these relationships carry over to alternative health measures such as the body mass index, which reflects short-term as well as long-term health and nutrition. Strauss and Thomas draw on these results and a survey of the literature to conclude that health and nutrition do increase productivity, with the greatest improvements occurring for those who are initially least educated and poorest.[57]

Thus, the preponderance of the evidence is that health and nutrition do affect employment, productivity, and wages, and very substantially so among the poorest of the poor. This finding magnifies the policy priority of health in development; not only is health a major goal in itself, but also it has a significant impact on income levels. After their exhaustive review of the literature and its complex statistical and data problems, Strauss and Thomas conclude that "the balance of evidence points to a positive effect of elevated nutrient intakes on wages, at least among those who are malnourished."[58]

A healthy population is a prerequisite for successful development.

Health Systems Policy

Health system All the activities whose primary purpose is to promote, restore, or maintain health.

In the WHO's definition, a **health system** is "all the activities whose primary purpose is to promote, restore, or maintain health." Health systems include the components of public health departments, hospitals and clinics, and offices of doctors and paramedics. Outside this formal system is an informal network used by many poorer citizens, which includes traditional healers, who may use somewhat effective herbal remedies, or other methods that provide some medical benefits, such as acupuncture, but who also may employ techniques for which there is no evidence of effectiveness beyond the placebo effect (and in some cases could cause harm).

It has long been understood that some developing countries' health systems are far more effective than others in achieving health goals. Some countries, such as China and Sri Lanka, and some regions, such as Kerala in India, have achieved life expectancies of more than 70 years despite their low-income status. At the same time, some middle-income countries, such as South Africa and Gabon, have only been able to achieve significantly lower life expectancies despite their much greater resources. The latter countries all have far more inequitable access to health care than China, Sri Lanka, and Kerala.

The WHO compared health systems around the world, revealing great variability in the performance of health systems at each income level. For example, Singapore was ranked 6th, Morocco 29th, Colombia 22nd, Chile 33rd, and Costa Rica 36th—all of these developing countries ranked higher than the United States. Clearly, much can be done with relatively modest incomes.[59]

The study used five performance indicators to measure health systems in the 191 WHO member states: (1) the overall level of health of the population, (2) health inequalities within the population, (3) health system responsiveness (a combination of patient satisfaction and system performance), (4) the distribution of responsiveness within the population (how well people of varying economic status find that they are served by the health system), and (5) the distribution, or fairness, of the health system's financial burden within the population.

The WHO concluded that "dollar for dollar spent on health, many countries are falling short of their performance potential. The result is a large number of preventable deaths and lives stunted by disability. The impact of this failure is born disproportionately by the poor." At any given income level, there was wide variation in country performance, showing that a low-income country can achieve fairness in allocating the resources that it has. In fact, in equity of financial contribution, Colombia was the top-rated country overall. But several developing countries were judged to have the least fair financing of health systems, including Sierra Leone, Myanmar, Brazil, China, Vietnam, Nepal, the Russian Federation, Peru, and Cambodia. In Brazil and Peru, people make high out-of-pocket payments for health care, so poor households spend a large fraction of their income on health.

Formal public health measures have played a very important role in developing countries. Ministries of health, sometimes complemented by the services of nongovernmental organizations, have played vital roles in extending vaccines to remote rural areas, greatly reducing once-lethal diseases such as smallpox. But like educational systems, public health operations have often favored the wealthy and well connected. Partly as a result, health systems often use public funds inefficiently. In effect, subsidies turn out to be focused on expensive curative measures for older (and generally richer) patients, such as those with heart disease or cancer, who are influential enough to get into the right hospitals. Too often ignored or at best underfunded are cost-effective preventive health campaigns and basic medical care for those not currently attended to by any health professionals. Doctors trained with public subsidies often choose to practice a specialty in affluent areas of the cities or emigrate to developed countries. And as the World Bank concluded, "In some countries a single teaching hospital can absorb 20% or more of the budget of the ministry of health, even though almost all cost-effective interventions are best delivered at lower-level facilities."[60]

In addition to its direct positive effect on national health standards, basic health is also an effective means to achieve goals of poverty reduction. Although both parents may be employed or self-employed long hours, if parents are too weak, unhealthy, and unskilled to be productive enough to support their family, the children have to work. But if the children work, they cannot get the education they need, so when they grow up, they will have to send their own children to work. Thus, the bad equilibrium of child labor examined earlier in the chapter may extend across generations, as a family is effectively locked into a vicious circle of poverty. Calculations of benefits of health investments need to keep these long-term spillovers in mind.

An effective government role in health systems is crucial for at least four important reasons. First, health is central to poverty alleviation, because people are often uninformed about health, a situation compounded by poverty. Second, households spend too little on health because they may neglect externalities (such as, literally, contagion problems). Third, the market would invest too little in health infrastructure and research and development and technology transfer to developing countries due to market failures. Fourth, public health programs in developing countries have many proven successes. Government has different roles in different countries, but as the WHO concluded, "The careful and responsible management of the well-being of the population—stewardship—is the very essence of good government…. The health of people is always a national priority: Government responsibility for it is continuous and permanent."[61]

Broad Findings   We conclude that health and education play pivotal roles in economic development, as both inputs into production enabling higher incomes and outputs directly affecting human well-being. Many health and education problems plague developing countries, ranging from child labor to heavy disease burdens. Education and health will not always automatically improve with higher incomes. And market failures mean that too few investments in education and health will be made from the social point of view. Moreover, the wrong kinds of government policies have sometimes led to distortions in the educational system that have reinforced inequality; and inequities in health systems are common. Thus, government plays an essential role in health and education, and in most developing countries, considerable improvements in policy are needed.

Pathways Out of Poverty: Progresa/Oportunidades in Mexico

The Mexican Program on Education, Health, and Nutrition is widely known by its Spanish acronym, Progresa, though officially renamed the Oportunidades Human Development Program (http://www.oportunidades.gob.mx). Progresa/Oportunidades combats child labor, poor education, and health by ensuring that parents can feed their children, take them to health clinics, and keep them in school while providing financial incentives to do so.

Progresa/Oportunidades builds on the growing understanding that health, nutrition, and education are complements in the struggle to end poverty. The program features the promotion of an integrated package to promote the education, health, and nutritional status of poor families. It provides cash transfers to poor families, family clinic visits, in-kind nutritional supplements, and other health benefits for pregnant and lactating women and their children under the age of 5. Some of these benefits are provided conditionally on children's regular school and health clinic attendance, and so programs of this kind are commonly called conditional cash transfer (CCT) programs.

In effect, low-income parents are paid to send their children to school and clinics, and this is one of the recent tactics most widely believed by the donor and development community to be effective in sustainably reducing poverty. The benefits compensate parents for lost income or the lost value of work at home or in workplaces in the form of child labor. Such payments work to increase school enrollments, attendance, progress through grades, other schooling outcomes, and nutrition and health.

Before the program, Mexico operated a maze of inefficiently run food subsidy programs managed by as many as 10 different ministries. These programs were very blunt instruments against poverty and often failed to reach the very poor. For example, the better-off urban poor benefited far more than the hard-to-reach but worse-off rural poor. There was no mechanism to ensure that food subsidies benefited vulnerable children in poor households. Nor was there any clear exit strategy for sustainably helping poor families stay out of poverty. Malnutrition remained common in poor rural (especially indigenous) families, and educational achievements and health gains failed to reach the poor in the way they had benefited the better off in Mexico. For economic reasons, many poor children had to work rather than go to school. But poor health and education as a child are major determinants of lifelong poverty.

One solution has turned out to be Progresa/Oportunidades, an innovative developing-country-designed integrated poverty program. Its major architect was Santiago Levy, a development economist who led the design and implementation of the program in the 1990s while serving as deputy minister of finance. Levy describes the program and its development, implementation, and evaluation in his excellent 2006 book, *Progress against Poverty*.

From its inception in rural areas in August 1997, the Progresa program had grown to benefit some 5.8 million rural and urban households by 2012 (Government of Mexico website data).

It has been estimated that more than 21 million people benefit—approximately one-fifth of the Mexican population—in over 75,000 localities. In 2002, the program distributed 857 million doses of nutritional supplements and covered 2.4 million medical checkups. Over 4.5 million "scholarships" were provided to schoolchildren. By the end of

425

2005, the program had covered 5 million families, which contained almost one-quarter of the country's population and most people living in extreme poverty.

Progresa/Oportunidades affects child nutrition through four program components, called *pathways:* cash transfers, which may be used in part for improved nutrition; nutritional supplements given to all participating children under the age of 2, pregnant and breastfeeding mothers, and children between the ages of 2 and 5 who show signs of malnutrition; growth monitoring, which provides feedback to parents; and other preventive measures, including required participation in regular meetings where vital information about hygiene and nutrition is taught.

Participating families receive school program payments every other month. In addition, families receive grants for school supplies and food subsidies, on the proviso that they get regular public health care for the children, including medical checkups and immunizations. Payments are generally provided through the mother, because evidence shows that mothers use more of their available funds in support of their children's well-being than fathers do. The payments are supplied via a bank card, directly from the federal government and not through intermediaries, reducing chances of corruption, and mothers are taught how and where to cash in their payments.

Program payments are conditional on children in grades three through nine attending school regularly. In developing countries such as Mexico, children are often enrolled in school but do not attend for long. The payments increase as the child increases in grade level. This gives an incentive to keep children in school longer and helps the children continue into higher grades. Initially, parents of a third grader received a little over $10 per month; parents of girls in ninth grade got over $35 per month. This was close to two-thirds of the income the children would have received as laborers. The overall result was to break the trade-off that parents faced between higher consumption for the family today and the higher future consumption possible when the child completed school. Families of girls also receive slightly higher payments than boys, partly because girls are more likely to drop out, while the social benefits of keeping girls

in school are well known from development economics research to be very high. Provided that the school and health checkup conditions are met, the families, not the government, decide how to best spend these extra resources. Levy estimates that the average family participating in the program receives about $35 per month in combined cash and in-kind transfers, which is about 25% of average poor rural family income without the program.

The program is also more effective than standard alternatives. For example, evidence shows that Progresa/Oportunidades has a larger impact on enrollment and performance per dollar spent than building new schools.

The budget for even the much-expanded Progresa/Oportunidades Program in 2005 was still some $2.8 billion—fairly modest, even in Mexico's economy. This represented less than 0.4% of gross national income. Only Mexico's pension (social security) system is a larger social program. Progresa/Oportunidades is also organizationally efficient, with operating expenses of only about 6% of total outlays. This it owes in part to the direct provision of cash grants via bank cards to the beneficiaries, bypassing the sometimes ineffective and potentially corrupt administrative bureaucracy. Fully 82% goes to the direct cash transfers, and the remaining 12% goes to nutritional supplements and other in-kind transfers. Some additional costs for provision of health care and schooling are borne by the Mexican health and education ministries.

However, Progresa/Oportunidades is lauded not so much for its modest cost as for the fact that it works. It has been subject to one of the most rigorous randomized trials of any public poverty program in the world. The Washington-based International Food Policy Research Institute (IFPRI), with many affiliated researchers, has intensively studied the program, using a variety of methods. The most convincing evidence comes from the way the program was initially rolled out. Only some communities were to take part in the program at first, before it reached full scale, and the order in which initially targeted communities were included was randomized. Data were collected from both initially included and excluded families so that the impact of the program could be studied independently of the many possible confounding factors

that could otherwise distort the results of an evaluation. Participants in these rigorous studies have included some of the world's leading development microeconomists.

Evaluations of Progresa/Oportunidades indicate that its integrated approach has been highly successful, with large improvements in the well-being of participants. Malnutrition has measurably declined; family use of health care, including prenatal care, has increased, and child health indicators have improved; school attendance is up significantly, and the dropout rate has declined substantially, especially in the so-called transition grades six through nine, when children either get launched toward high school or drop out. In general terms, the research showed that Progresa/Oportunidades increased by some 20% the number of children who stay in school rather than drop out just before high school. Child labor decreased by about 15%. At first, there were some concerns that adults might work less when receiving the transfers, but the evidence is that no work reduction has occurred. Several of the most statistically reliable studies and their research methods and findings are reviewed in Emmanuel Skoufias's 2005 IFPRI report, *PROGRESA and Its Impacts on the Welfare of Rural Households in Mexico.* Other key research reports are listed among the sources at the end of this case study.

The lessons of Progresa/Oportunidades are spreading throughout Latin America, and some of its features are also found in the Bolsa Familia program in Brazil, Familias por la Inclusión Social in Argentina, Chile Solidario, Familias en Acción in Colombia, Superemonos in Costa Rica, Bono de Desarrollo Humano in Ecuador, Programa de Asignación Familiar in Honduras, Programa de Avance Mediante la Salud y la Educación in Nicaragua, Red de Oportunidades in Panama, and Proyecto 300 in Uruguay. By 2010, Progresa had been replicated in whole or in part in 29 countries.

Although the cost of a CCT program like Progresa/Oportunidades may be manageable in middle- to upper-middle-income countries, in low-income countries, outside financial assistance is needed, both for the payments themselves and to increase the number (and quality) of clinics and schools to be availed of in the program. Poverty reduction still requires complementary improvements, such as better roads to poor areas, public health investments, and local empowerment. The will to replace poorly performing but politically expedient programs with more effective ones is necessary. Administrative infrastructure may be a major challenge, and disbursing funds to beneficiaries electronically can prove problematic. But CCT pilot or larger-scale programs have been launched in recent years in several African countries, including Nigeria, Malawi, and Mali.

In conclusion, CCT programs focusing on improving health, nutrition, and education are a key component of a successful policy to end poverty—although in most cases, they will need to be part of a broader strategy to be fully effective. In Mexico, as in other countries, the broader package includes development of infrastructure so the poor can get their products to market and get access to safe water and electricity. It also includes integrated rural development programs of the type outlined in Chapter 9, along with provision of credit and some temporary employment programs. But by building the human capital of the poor, the program provides the essential foundation for the poor to increase their capabilities and take advantage of opportunities as the economy grows. It thereby also enhances the prospects for Mexico's own growth and development.

In sum, the Progresa/Oportunidades Program is a model of success in many ways. The rigorous program evaluations show that it has a substantial effect on human welfare. It was designed and implemented in the developing world with close attention given to local circumstances while making constructive use of what has been learned in development economics. It placed the crucial complementarities between education, health, and nutrition at the center of the program's design while paying close attention to the need for appropriate incentives for beneficiaries. Finally, its method of cash transfer and the move away from cumbersome and nontransparent in-kind transfer programs placed constraints on possible bureaucratic inefficiency as well as official corruption. Progresa/Oportunidades thus offers a model for providing health and educational progress for poor families and opportunities for their permanent escape from poverty. ∎

Sources

Baird Sarah, Craig McIntosh, and Berk Ozler. "Cash or condition? Evidence from a randomized cash transfer program." Policy Research Working Paper Series 5259. Washington, D.C.: World Bank, 2010.

Bando, Rosangela, Luis F. Lopez-Calva, and Harry Anthony Patrinos. "Child labor, school attendance, and indigenous households: Evidence from Mexico." World Bank Policy Research Working Paper No. 3487. Washington, D.C.: 2005.

Behrman, Jere R., and John Hoddinott. "Programme evaluation with unobserved heterogeneity and selective implementation: The Mexican PROGRESA impact on child nutrition." *Oxford Bulletin of Economics and Statistics* 67 (2005): 547–569.

Behrman, Jere R., Piyali Sengupta, and Petra Todd. "Progressing through PROGRESA: An impact assessment of a school subsidy experiment in rural Mexico." *Economic Development and Cultural Change* 54 (2005): 237–275.

Buddelmeyer, Hielke, and Emmanuel Skoufias. "An evaluation of the performance of regression discontinuity design on PROGRESA." World Bank Policy Research Working Paper No. 3386. Washington, D.C.: , 2004.

Cardenas-Rodriguez, Oscar J. "Do indigenous peoples benefit from poverty programs? Evidence from Mexico's 2000 census." *Estudios Economicos* 19 (2004): 125–135.

Coady, David P., and Susan W. Parker. "Cost-effectiveness analysis of demand- and supply-side education interventions: The case of PROGRESA in Mexico." *Review of Development Economics* 8 (2004): 440–451.

Davis, Benjamin, Sudhanshu Handa, and Humberto Soto. "Households, poverty and policy in times of crisis: Mexico, 1992–1996." *CEPAL Review* 82 (2004): 191–212.

Government of Mexico, Oportunidades website: http://www.oportunidades.gob.mx/Portal/wb/Web/introduction.

Hoddinott, John, and Emmanuel Skoufias. "The impact of PROGRESA on food consumption." *Economic Development and Cultural Change* 53 (2004): 37–61.

Levy, Santiago. *Progress against Poverty: Sustaining Mexico's Progresa-Oportunidades Program.* Washington, D.C.: Brookings Institution Press, 2006, available at: http://www.brookings.edu/global/progress/pap_total.pdf.

Parker, Susan W., and Graciela M. Teruel. "Randomization and social program evaluation: The case of Progresa." *Annals of the American Academy of Political and Social Science* 599 (2005): 199–219.

Schultz, T. Paul. "School subsidies for the poor: Evaluating the Mexican Progresa poverty program." *Journal of Development Economics* 74 (2004): 199–250.

Secretaría de Desarrollo Social (SEDESOL). "Programa de Educación, Salud y Alimentación (PROGRESA)," 2001, http://www.progresa.gob.mx.

Skoufias, Emmanuel. *PROGRESA and Its Impacts on the Welfare of Rural Households in Mexico.* Research Report No. 139. Washington, D.C.: International Food Policy Research Institute, 2005, http://www.ifpri.org/pubs/abstract/abstr139.htm.

Skoufias, Emmanuel, Benjamin Davis, and Sergio de la Vega. "Targeting the poor in Mexico: An evaluation of the selection of households into PROGRESA." *World Development* 29 (2001): 1769–1784.

Skoufias, Emmanuel, and Bonnie McClafferty. "Is PROGRESA working? Summary of the results of an evaluation by IFPRI," 2000, http://www.ifpri.org/themes/progresa/synthesis.htm.

Skoufias, Emmanuel, and Susan W. Parker, with comments by Jere R. Behrman and Carola Pessino. "Conditional cash transfers and their impact on child work and schooling: Evidence from the PROGRESA program in Mexico." *Economia* 2 (2001): 45–96.

Smith, Stephen C. *Ending Global Poverty: A Guide to What Works.* New York: Palgrave Macmillan, 2005.

Stecklov, Guy, Paul Winters, Marco Stampini, and Benjamin Davis. "Do conditional cash transfers influence migration? A study using experimental data from the Mexican PROGRESA program." *Demography* 42 (2005): 769–790.

Todd, Petra, and Kenneth Wolpin. "Using a social experiment to validate a dynamic behavioral model of child schooling and fertility: Assessing the impact of a school subsidy program in Mexico." Penn Institute for Economic Research Working Paper, Department of Economics, University of Pennsylvania, 2002.

Concepts for Review

Acquired immunodeficiency
  syndrome (AIDS)
Basic education
Conditional cash transfer (CCT)
  programs
Derived demand
Discount rate

Educational certification
Educational gender gap
Health system
Human capital
Human immunodeficiency virus
  (HIV)
Literacy

Neglected tropical diseases
Private benefits
Private costs
Social benefits of education
Social costs of education
World Health Organization
  (WHO)

Questions for Discussion

1. What reasons would you give for the rather sizable school dropout rates in developing countries? What might be done to lower these rates?

2. What are the differences between formal and non-formal education? Give some examples of each.

3. It is often asserted that educational systems in developing countries, especially in rural areas, are unsuited to the real social and economic needs of development. Do you agree or disagree with this statement? Explain your reasoning.

4. How would you explain the fact that relative costs of and returns to higher education are so much higher in developing than in developed countries?

5. What is the supposed rationale for subsidizing higher education in many developing countries? Do you think that it is a legitimate rationale from an economic viewpoint? Explain your answer.

6. Early-childhood environmental factors are said to be important determinants of school performance. What are some of these factors, how important do you think they are, and what might be done to ensure that these factors are not negative?

7. What do we mean by the *economics of education?* To what extent do you think educational planning and policy decisions ought to be guided by economic considerations? Explain, giving hypothetical or actual examples.

8. What is meant by the statement, "The demand for education is a 'derived demand' for high-paying modern-sector job opportunities"?

9. What are the links among educational systems, labor markets, and employment determination in many developing countries? Describe the process of educational job displacement.

10. Distinguish carefully between private and social benefits and costs of education. What economic factors give rise to the wide divergence between private and social benefit-to-cost valuations in most developing countries? Should governments attempt through their educational and economic policies to narrow the gap between private and social valuations? Explain.

11. Describe and comment on each of the following education development relationships:

    a. Education and economic growth: Does education promote growth? How?

    b. Education, inequality, and poverty: Do educational systems typical of most developing countries tend to reduce, exacerbate, or have no effect on inequality and poverty? Explain with specific reference to a country with which you are familiar or investigate.

    c. Education and migration: Does education stimulate rural-urban migration? Why?

    d. Education and fertility: Does the education of women tend to reduce their fertility? Why?

    e. Education and rural development: Do most formal educational systems in developing countries contribute substantially to the promotion of rural development? Explain.

12. Governments can influence the character, quality, and content of their educational systems by manipulating important economic and noneconomic factors or variables both outside of and

within educational systems. What are some of these external and internal factors, and how can government policies make education more relevant to the real meaning of development?

13. What explains the large gains in health and education in recent decades?

14. Why are health and education so closely linked in the development challenge?

15. What are the most pressing health and education challenges today? What makes them so difficult to solve?

16. What makes for (a) a good and fair health system and (b) a good and fair education system?

17. What are the consequences of gender bias in health and education? Can a large gap between male and female literacy affect development? Why?

18. What is the human capital approach to health and education? What do you think are its most important strengths and weaknesses?

19. What are the strategies being discussed to address the problem of child labor? What are the strengths and weaknesses of these approaches?

20. What are the relationships between health and education, on the one hand, and productivity and incomes, on the other?

21. What can government do to make health systems more equitable?

22. Here are some questions to review for the Progresa/Oportunidades Program examined in the end-of-chapter case study:

   a. What is the Progresa/Oportunidades Program, and what does it try to accomplish?

   b. How does it try to do so—what are the key program features and innovations?

   c. Why make transfers conditional? What are the possible benefits as well as drawbacks?

   d. Specifically, how does Progresa work to improve nutrition (with its "four pathways")?

   e. Specifically, how does Progresa work to improve education?

   f. What were the features of the original evaluation?

Notes

1. United Nations Development Programme, *Human Development Report, 2004* (New York: Oxford University Press, 2004), p. 171; World Bank, *World Development Indicators, 2013* (Washington, D.C.: World Bank, 2013). Note that the developing-country child mortality statistics in some cases actually *understate* progress, because some formerly middle-income countries have become high-income countries in recent years.

2. UNESCO, Institute for Statistics (UIS), *UIS Fact Sheet No. 20*, September 2012; UNESCO, *EFA Global Monitoring Report, 2007*, Statistical Annex, tab. 2, http://unesdoc.unesco.org/images/0014/001477/147794E.pdf.

3. See Selma Mushkin, "Health as an investment," *Journal of Political Economy* 70 (1962): 129–157.

4. See Randa Sab and Stephen C. Smith, "Human capital convergence: International evidence,"

http://www.imf.org/external/pubs/ft/wp/2001/wp0132.pdf. The paper presents evidence that the relative improvement in health and education in the developing world is pronounced enough to conclude that slow but steady convergence is taking place across countries. See also Randa Sab and Stephen C. Smith, "Human capital convergence: A joint estimation approach," *IMF Staff Papers* 49 (2002): 200–211, https://www.imf.org/external/pubs/ft/staffp/2002/02/pdf/sab.pdf, and Robert J. Barro and Jong-Wha Lee, "International comparisons of educational attainment," *Journal of Monetary Economics* 32 (1993): 363–394.

5. This discussion draws on Stephen C. Smith, "Microcredit and health programs: To integrate or not to integrate?" in *Microenterprise Development for Better Health Outcomes*, eds. Rosalia Rodriguez-Garcia, James A. Macinko, and William F. Waters (Westport, Conn.: Greenwood Press, 2001), pp. 41–50.

6. See Howarth E. Bouis and Lawrence J. Haddad, "Are estimates of calorie-income elasticities too high? A recalibration of the plausible range," *Journal of Development Economics* 39 (1992): 333–364; Jere Behrman and Anil Deolalikar, "Will developing country nutrition improve with income? A case study for rural South India," *Journal of Political Economy* 95 (1987): 108–138; and Shankar Subramanian and Angus Deaton, "The demand for food and calories," *Journal of Political Economy* 104 (1996): 133–162.

7. For a review of some of this literature, see Tonia Marek, *Ending Malnutrition: Why Increasing Income Is Not Enough* (Washington, D.C.: World Bank, 1992).

8. See Maurice Schiff and Alberto Valdes, "Nutrition: Alternative definitions and policy implications," *Economic Development and Cultural Change* 38 (1990): 281–292; and Marek, *Ending Malnutrition*.

9. Howarth Bouis found that intake of vitamins A and C was not positively associated with income in the Philippines and argued that consumer education was important. Moreover, morbidity (incidence of sickness) did not necessarily decrease significantly with income in that country. See Howarth E. Bouis, *The Determinants of Household-Level Demand for Micronutrients: An Analysis for Philippine Farm Households* (Washington, D.C.: International Food Policy Research Institute, 1991).

10. A study of the Gambia found that diarrhea is associated with reduced nutritional status even after calorie intake is controlled for; see Joachim von Braum, Detlev Peutz, and Patrick Webb, *Irrigation Technology and Commercialization of Rice in the Gambia: Effects on Income and Nutrition* (Washington, D.C.: International Food Policy Research Institute, 1989).

11. See Paul Glewwe, "Why does mother's schooling raise child health in developing countries? Evidence from Morocco," *Journal of Human Resources* 34 (1999): 124–159; and Ravi Kanbur and Lyn Squire, "The evolution of thinking about poverty," in *Frontiers of Development Economics: The Future in Perspective*, eds. Gerald M. Meier and Joseph E. Stiglitz (New York: Oxford University Press, 2001).

12. For example, it was found that the probability of attending school among nutritionally stunted children in Nepal was far lower than for nonstunted students; children with low height for their age, an indicator of undernutrition, were found to lag in school grade attainment in many parts of the world, including rural China and Thailand; and undernourished children were found to lag 20% in test score gains in northeast Brazil. See World Bank, *World Development Report, 1993* (New York: Oxford University Press, 1993), p. 18–19.

13. In addition to Box 8.4, see Ernesto Pollitt, *Malnutrition and Infection in the Classroom* (Paris: UNESCO, 1990); Harold Alderman, Jere Behrman, Victor Lavy, and Rekha Menon, "Child health and school enrollment: A longitudinal analysis," *Journal of Human Resources* 36 (2001): 185–201; Jere Behrman, "The impact of health and nutrition on education," *World Bank Researcher* 11 (1996): 23–37; and Paul Glewwe and Hanan G. Jacoby, "An economic analysis of delayed primary school enrollment in a low-income country: The role of early childhood nutrition," *Review of Economics and Statistics* 77 (1995): 156–169.

14. See Kaushik Basu and James Foster, "On measuring literacy," *Economic Journal* 108 (1998): 1733–1749.

15. World Health Organization, *World Health Report, 2000* (Geneva: World Health Organization, 2000), p. 4.

16. Amartya Sen, *Development as Freedom* (New York: Knopf, 1999), p. 294; M. Shahe Emran, Fenohasina Maret, and Stephen C. Smith, "Education and freedom of choice: Evidence from arranged marriages in Vietnam," forthcoming 2014 in the *Journal of Development Studies* [online version at: http://www.tandfonline.com/doi/abs/10.1080/00220388.2013.841884#.UrN2m2RDtWJ].

17. For an example, see Harry A. Patrinos and S. Metzger, "Returns to education in Mexico: An update," World Bank, World Bank/Universidad de las Americas, Mexico, 2004; and Dominic J. Brewer and Patrick J. McEwan, eds., *Economics of Education* (San Diego, Calif.: Elsevier, 2010).

18. The human capital analysis was introduced by Jacob Mincer, "Investment in human capital and personal income distribution," *Journal of Political Economy* 66 (1958): 281–302. Graphs similar to Figure 8.2 are also widely used in the labor economics literature. See, for example, Ronald Ehrenberg and Robert Smith, *Modern Labor Economics*, 2nd ed. (Glenview, Ill: Scott Foresman, 1985), fig. 9.1, p. 256; or Daniel Hamermesh and Albert Rees, *The Economics of*

432 PART TWO Problems and Policies: Domestic

Work and Play, 4th ed. (New York: HarperCollins, 1988), fig. 3.3, p. 70.

19. See George Psacharopoulos, "Returns to education: An updated international comparison," *Comparative Education* 17 (1981): 321–341, and "Returns to investment in education: A global update," *World Development* 22 (1994): 1325–1343; Christopher Colclough, "The impact of primary schooling on economic development: A review of the evidence," *World Development* 10 (1982): 167–185; and Rati Ram, "Level of development and rates of return to schooling: Some estimates from multicountry data," *Economic Development and Cultural Change* 44 (1996): 839–857. As Psacharopoulos explains in "Education as investment," *Finance and Development* (1982): 40 (Reprinted with permission from International Monetary Fund.): Estimates of the private rate of return to a given level of education are calculated by comparing the discounted benefits over the lifetime of an educational investment "project" to the costs of such a project. Thus, for a calculation of the private rate of return to four years of university education, benefits are estimated by taking the difference between existing statistics on the mean post-tax earnings of university graduates by age and those of a sample group of secondary school graduates. The earnings of the latter also represent the opportunity costs of staying in school. Direct costs are obtained from statistics on a student's out-of-pocket expenditures that are strictly due to the costs of college attendance. Given these data, the rate of return to investment in a college degree compared with a secondary school qualification is the rate of interest that reduces to zero the net present value of the discounted difference between the costs and benefits. A simple equation for the private rate of return is

A social rate of return to college education could be calculated in the same way, although earnings should be pretax (as taxes are a transfer from the point of view of society at large), and the direct cost should include the full amount of resources committed per student for higher education, rather than the usually smaller part of expenditures borne by the student.

19a. See Amartya Sen, op. cit. (note 16), Basu and Foster, op. cit. (note 14), and Ehrenberg and Smith, op. cit. (note 18).]

20. Child labor statistics are from the International Labor Organization; child labor Web site, http://www.ilo.org/ipec/index.htm. The latest updates may be found there. Specific statistics on child labor hazards are also drawn from ILO, *Employers and Workers Handbook on Hazardous Child Labour*. (Geneva: ILO, 2011). The 2010 report was accessed on August 1, 2010, at http://www.ilo.org/global/What_we_do/Officialmeetings/ilc/ILCSessions/99thSession/reports/lang–en/docName–WCMS_126752/index.htm.

21. For further details on the model and an excellent survey, see Kaushik Basu, "Child labor: Cause, consequence, and cure, with remarks on international labor standards," *Journal of Economic Literature* 37 (1999): 1083–1120.

22. Notice that the demand curve also cuts the labor supply curve a third time, through the S-shaped part of the supply curve, but this is an unstable equilibrium; see Chapter 4 for a discussion of unstable equilibria. Note also that it is not necessary for this part of the curve to be S-shaped for the result to occur. To see this, consider that, instead, the supply curve from the point at which AA' and W_H intersect to the point at which TT' and W_L intersect is just a straight line: There are still two stable equilibria and one unstable equilibrium. Either

$$\text{Private rate of return} = \frac{\begin{pmatrix}\text{Mean annual post-tax}\\\text{earnings of university}\\\text{graduates}\end{pmatrix} - \begin{pmatrix}\text{Mean annual post-tax}\\\text{earnings of secondary}\\\text{school graduates}\end{pmatrix}}{\begin{pmatrix}\text{Four}\\\text{years}\\\text{of study}\end{pmatrix} \times \begin{pmatrix}\text{Mean annual post-tax}\\\text{earnings of secondary}\\\text{school graduates}\end{pmatrix} + \begin{pmatrix}\text{Mean annual}\\\text{private direct}\\\text{cost of study}\end{pmatrix}}$$

way, this middle part of the curve slopes downward, characteristic of a "backward-bending supply curve" in labor economics, in which families use some of their extra earnings potential when wages are higher to "consume" more leisure, which in this case represents nonwork by the children. Note that the completely vertical adult labor supply curve is only a convenience to make the graph easier to read; results can hold even if the curve is less than perfectly inelastic. On the other hand, note that if the demand curve is sufficiently elastic, there will only be a single equilibrium; with high and elastic demand, the single equilibrium will be at a high wage with no child labor, while with low and elastic demand, there will be a low wage with child labor.

23. Another influential theoretical model was provided by Jean-Marie Baland and James Robinson, who point out that with highly imperfect capital markets such as those faced by many impoverished rural families, child labor is one of the few ways families have to borrow from the future. The result is that child labor, which reduces future earning opportunities because the working child receives less schooling, may exist only because of market failures. The authors formally derive conditions under which a ban on child labor may be Pareto-improving in general equilibrium. See Jean-Marie Baland and James A. Robinson, "Is child labor inefficient?" *Journal of Political Economy* 108 (2000): 663–679.

24. The following discussion draws on information obtained from the ILO, UNICEF, and the World Bank.

25. ILO, 2010 report, p. 50; data from UNICEF, *The State of the World's Children, 2008: Child Survival* (New York, United Nations, 2007), p. 140.

26. International Program on the Elimination of Child Labor, *Investing in Every Child. An Economic Study of the Costs and Benefits of Eliminating Child Labor* (Geneva: International Labor Organization, 2003).

27. On youth data, see United Nations 2013 MDG fact sheet accessed at http://www.un.org/millenniumgoals/education.shtml. Other data are drawn from United Nations Development Programme, *Human Development Report, 2004* (New York: Oxford University Press, 2004), tab. 26. For more on

the international response to educational gender disparity, go to the UN Millennium Campaign Web site, http://www.millenniumcampaign.org.

28. United Nations Development Programme, *Human Development Report, 2005* (New York: Oxford University Press, 2005), p. 60.

29. Wadi D. Haddad et al., *Education and Development: Evidence for New Priorities* (Washington, D.C.: World Bank, 1990), pp. 12–15. The Millennium Development Goals are described in Chapter 1.

30. See UNICEF Innocenti Centre, *Changing a Harmful Social Convention: Female Genital Mutilation/Cutting*, (New York: United Nations, 2005) and subsequent working papers; Gerry Mackie, "Female genital cutting: The beginning of the end," in *Female Circumcision: Multidisciplinary Perspectives*, eds. Bettina Shell-Duncan and Ylva Hernlund (Boulder, Colo.: Reinner, 2000), pp. 245–282; and Gerry Mackie, "Ending footbinding and infibulation: A convention account," *American Sociological Review* 61, no. 6(1996): 999–1017.

31. Plan International, *Paying the Price: The Economic Cost of Failing to Educate Girls* (Woking, England: Plan International, 2008). Although human capital investment rate of return estimates are often fraught with errors and problems of interpretation, results such as those on the benefits of educating girls, when consistent across time and space and methods of evaluation, offer useful guidance for policy. See, for example, George Psacharopoulos, "Education and development: A review," *World Bank Research Observer* 3 (January 1988): 99–116. As Psacharopoulos notes, potential benefits of education for development are broad ranging. Basic education, which has been steadily approaching the target of universal primary school enrollment, has made great contributions to development, broadly conceived. Moreover, despite the substantial distortions just reviewed, it seems clear that the expansion of educational opportunities has contributed to aggregate economic growth by (1) creating a more productive labor force and endowing it with increased knowledge and skills; (2) providing widespread employment and income-earning opportunities for teachers, school and construction workers, textbook and paper printers, school uniform manufacturers, and related workers; (3) creating a class of educated leaders to fill vacancies

left by departing expatriates or otherwise vacant or prospective positions in governmental services, public corporations, private domestic and foreign businesses, and professions; and (4) providing the kind of training and education that would promote literacy and basic skills while encouraging "modern" attitudes on the part of diverse segments of the population. Even if alternative investments in the economy could have generated greater growth, this would not detract from the important contributions, noneconomic as well as economic, that education can make and has made to promoting aggregate economic growth.

32. Amartya Sen, "Missing women," *British Medical Journal* 304 (1992): 587–588. See also Sen's *Development as Freedom*, p. 104.

33. Yuyu Chen, Hongbin Li, and Lingsheng Meng, "Prenatal sex selection and missing girls in China: Evidence from the diffusion of diagnostic ultrasound," Working Paper, Tsinghua University, May 2010. See also the Chinese Academy of Science book on gender imbalance reported in BBC News, "China faces growing gender imbalance," January 11, 2010, http://news.bbc.co.uk/2/hi/asia-pacific/8451289.stm. On the social instability and security implications of the 12% to 15% of the adult male population in China and India projected by 2020 to find itself unable to marry, see Valerie M. Hudson and Andrea M. den Boer, *Bare Branches: The Security Implications of Asia's Surplus Male Population* (Cambridge, Mass.: MIT Press, 2004.) Alternate estimates for most countries are available in the *CIA World Factbook* at https://www.cia.gov/library/publications/the-world-factbook/fields/2018.html.

34. For more on the Africa debate, see Stephan Klasen, "Nutrition, health, and mortality in sub-Saharan Africa: Is there a gender bias?" and "Rejoinder," *Journal of Development Studies* 32 (1996): 913–933, 944–948; and Peter Svedberg, "Gender biases in sub-Saharan Africa: Reply and further evidence," *Journal of Development Studies* 32 (1996): 934–943.

35. Studies show that mothers' education plays a decisive role in raising nutritional levels in rural areas. The level of child stunting, a valid indicator of child undernutrition, is much lower with higher education attainment of the mother at every income level. Harold Alderman and Marito Garcia report that the incidence of child stunting would be reduced by a quarter of current levels (from 63.6% to 47.1% in their sample in Pakistan) if women were to obtain a primary-level education. They note that this is almost 10 times the projected impact of a 10% increase in per capita income. Coupled with the result that in many countries, mothers' education tends to make a disproportionately larger health difference for daughters than for sons, as Duncan Thomas has reported, we can expect major benefits for girls. See Harold Alderman and Marito Garcia, *Food Security and Health Security: Explaining the Levels of Nutrition in Pakistan* (Washington, D.C.: World Bank, 1992); Duncan Thomas, *Gender Differences in Household Resource Allocations* (Washington, D.C.: World Bank, 1991).

36. Much of the material in this section is drawn from Michael P. Todaro and Edgar O. Edwards, "Educational demand and supply in the context of growing unemployment in less developed countries," *World Development* 1 (1973): 107–117.

37. See, for example, Ragui Assaad, "The effects of public sector hiring and compensation policies on the Egyptian labor market," *World Bank Economic Review* 11 (1997): 85–118.

38. For evidence of this, see Emmanuel Jimenez, "The public subsidization of education and health in developing countries: A review of equity and efficiency," *World Bank Research Observer* 1 (1986): 123.

39. See World Bank, *The Quality of Growth* (New York: Oxford University Press, 2000), pp. 56–66, and Vinod Thomas, Yan Wang, and Xibo Fan, *Measuring Education Inequality: Gini Coefficients of Education* (Washington, D.C.: World Bank Institute, 2000).

40. Jere Behrman and Nancy Birdsall, "The quality of schooling: Quantity alone is misleading," *American Economic Review* 73 (1983): 928–946. See also Eric A. Hanushek, "Interpreting recent research on schooling in developing countries," *World Bank Research Observer* 10 (1995): 227–246, and Paul Glewwe, "The relevance of standard estimates of rates of return to schooling for educational policy," *Journal of Development Economics* 51 (1996): 267–290.

41. Another explanation is that where perfect capital markets exist, all individuals can borrow for

their education in anticipation of high future earnings. But in developing countries with imperfect capital markets, limited information about individual abilities, and poor loan enforcement, it is extremely difficult for the poor to borrow to finance their education. This is not, however, a problem for the rich, who can rely on their own resources to invest in education. So the system of inequality has a built-in tendency to reproduce itself with each generation.

42. For some evidence of the regressive nature of educational subsidies in Latin America, see Jean-Pierre Jallade, *Public Expenditures on Education and Income Distribution in Colombia* (Baltimore: Johns Hopkins University Press, 1974), and *Basic Education and Income Inequality in Brazil: The Long-Term View* (Washington, D.C.: World Bank, 1977).

43. World Health Organization, "Frequently asked questions," http://www.who.int/suggestions/faq/en.

44. World Bank, *World Development Report, 1993* (New York: Oxford University Press, 1993).

45. The same types of measures used for studying the distribution of income (reviewed in Chapter 5) could also be used to examine the distribution of health; see, for example, R. Andrew Allison and James Foster, *Measuring Health Inequality Using Qualitative Data* (Cambridge, Mass.: Harvard Center for Population and Development Studies, 1999).

46. World Bank, *World Development Indicators, 2007* (Washington, D.C.: World Bank, 2007), fig. 2n.

47. See United Nations Development Programme, *Human Development Report, 2006* (New York: Oxford University Press, 2006), chs. 1–4.

48. Data from *World Development Indicators, 2010* (Washington, D.C.: World Bank, 2010), and http://stats.uis.unesco.org/unesco. See International Food Policy Research Institute, "2013 Global Hunger Index," http://www.ifpri.org/ghi/2013, accessed 15 Feb. 2014.

49. For this and updated reports, see the WHO AIDS page, http://www.who.int/gho/hiv/en/index.html (accessed July 20, 2013).

50. In 1996, the AIDS programs of several international agencies were merged into the Joint United Nations Programme on HIV/AIDS, commonly

referred to as UNAIDS, which is a kind of joint venture among the WHO, the UNDP, UNICEF, UNESCO, UNFPA, UNDCP, and the World Bank.

51. See, for example, Jeffrey D. Sachs, "Institutions don't rule: Direct effects of geography on per capita income," NBER Working Paper No. 9490, 2003; and John L. Gallup and Jeffrey D. Sachs, "The economic burden of malaria: Cause, consequence and correlation: Assessing the relationship between malaria and poverty," Commission on Macroeconomics and Health, World Health Organization, 2001; Gallup and Sachs, "The economic burden of malaria," *American Journal of Tropical Medicine and Hygiene* 64(2001): 85–96; and, Matthew A. Cole and Eric Neumayer, "The impact of poor health on total factor productivity," *Journal of Development Studies* 42 (2006): 918–938, and references therein.

52. For informative field reports, see the *Financial Times*, 2012.

53. Michael Kremer, "Creating markets for new vaccines: Part I: Rationale," in *Innovation Policy and the Economy*, vol. 1, eds. Adam B. Jaffe, Josh Lerner, and Scott Stern (Cambridge, Mass: MIT Press, 2001).

54. Note that even the $1 share could be supported internationally. A treatment might be administered in three doses (at $5 each, say) for a malaria vaccine. See Center for Global Development, Advance Market Commitment Working Group (Ruth Levine, Michael Kremer, and Alice Albright, co-chairs), *Making Markets for Vaccines: Ideas to Action* (Washington, D.C.: Center for Global Development, 2005). The underlying concepts are examined in Rachel Glennerster and Michael Kremer, "A World Bank vaccine commitment," Brookings Policy Brief No. 57, May 2000, and in Kremer, "Creating markets for new vaccines." A short overview is found in Rachel Glennerster, Michael Kremer, and Heidi Williams, "Creating markets for vaccines," *Innovations* (Winter 2006): 67–79.

55. The fund's Web site is http://www.theglobalfund.org.

56. World Bank, *World Development Report, 1993*; T. Paul Schultz and Aysit Tansel, "Wage and labor supply effects of illness in Côte d'Ivoire and

Ghana: Instrumental variable estimates for days disabled," *Journal of Development Economics* 53 (1997): 251–286; Emmanuel Max and Donald S. Shepard, "Productivity loss to deformity from leprosy in India," *International Journal of Leprosy* 57 (1989): 476–482.

57. John Strauss and Duncan Thomas, "Health, nutrition, and economic development," *Journal of Economic Literature* 36 (1998): 766–817; see also Strauss and Thomas, "Health wages: Evidence on men and women in urban Brazil," *Journal of Econometrics* 77 (1997): 159–185. Note, however, that height could be independently associated with physical strength (e.g., through muscle length), which would tend to overstate the effect of health per se.

58. Strauss and Thomas, "Health, nutrition, and economic development," p. 806. Note that some statements to the contrary were found in earlier literature reviews, but those reports fail to take into account more recent rigorous studies that do a better job of accounting for the joint determination of health and income.

59. World Health Organization, *World Health Report, 2000* (Geneva: World Health Organization, 2000), http://www.who.int/whr/2000/en/index.htm. The study ranked France in first place and found that the "U.S. health system spends a higher portion of its gross domestic product than any other country but ranks 37 out of 191 countries according to its performance."

60. World Bank, *World Development Report, 1993,* p. viii.

61. World Health Organization, *World Health Report, 2000.* For a review of public health successes in developing countries, see Ruth Levine and Molly Kinder, *Millions Saved: Proven Successes in Public Health* (Washington, D.C.: Center for Global Development, 2004).

Agricultural Transformation and Rural Development

9

It is in the agricultural sector that the battle for long-term economic development will be won or lost.

—*Gunnar Myrdal, Nobel laureate in economics*

Recent developments in the land, water, and energy sectors have been wake-up calls for global food security.

—*International Food Policy Research Institute, 2012*

Many development policies continue to wrongly assume that farmers are men.

—*World Bank, World Development Report, 2008*

Africa is the only region where overall food security and livelihoods are deteriorating. We will reverse this trend by working to create an environmentally sustainable, uniquely African Green Revolution. When our poorest farmers finally prosper, all of Africa will benefit.

—*Kofi Annan, former secretary general of the United Nations, Nobel laureate for peace, and first chairman of the Alliance for a Green Revolution in Africa*

9.1 The Imperative of Agricultural Progress and Rural Development

If the migration of people with and without school certificates to the cities of Africa, Asia, and Latin America is proceeding at historically unprecedented rates, a large part of the explanation can be found in the economic stagnation of outlying rural areas. Despite real progress, nearly 2 billion people in the developing world grind out a meager and often inadequate existence in agricultural pursuits. Over 3.1 billion people lived in rural areas in developing countries in 2013, about a quarter of them in extreme poverty. And despite the extraordinary urbanization taking place throughout the world (examined in Chapter 7), people living in the countryside make up more than 60% of the population in both low- and lower middle–income countries on average. Latin America is highly urbanized, having reached the same level of urbanization as the high-income Organization for Economic Cooperation and Development (OECD) countries by 2011. But in sub-Saharan Africa, rural dwellers constitute 64% of the total population; in South Asia, some 69% of the population live in rural areas as of 2011, with the result that more than half the workforce is concentrated in agriculture. Countries whose population is more than 80% rural include Ethiopia, Nepal, Niger, Papua New Guinea, Rwanda, South Sudan, Sri Lanka, and Uganda. India remains more than two-thirds rural.[1]

Of greater importance than sheer numbers is the fact that well over two-thirds of the world's poorest people are also located in rural areas and engaged primarily in subsistence agriculture. Their basic concern is survival. Many hundreds of millions of people have been bypassed by whatever economic progress their nations have attained. The United Nations Food and Agriculture Organization estimated that in 2012, about 870 million people did not have enough food to meet their basic nutritional needs.[2] In the daily struggle to subsist, behavior of poor farmers in developing countries often seemed irrational to many observers who until recently had little comprehension of the precarious nature of subsistence living and the importance of avoiding risks. If development is to take place and become self-sustaining, it will have to include the rural areas, in general, and the agricultural sector, in particular. The core problems of widespread poverty, growing inequality, and rapid population growth all originate in the stagnation and often retrogression of economic life in rural areas, particularly in Africa.

Traditionally in economic development, agriculture has been assumed to play a passive and supportive role. Its primary purpose is to provide sufficient low-priced food and manpower to the expanding industrial economy, which is thought to be the dynamic "leading sector" in any overall strategy of economic development. Lewis's famous two-sector model, discussed in Chapter 3, is an example of a theory of development that places heavy emphasis on rapid industrial growth, with an agricultural sector fueling this industrial expansion by means of its cheap food and surplus labor. Nobel laureate Simon Kuznets introduced an early schema, noting that agriculture made four "contributions to economic development": the product contribution of inputs for industry such as textiles and food processing, the foreign-exchange contribution of using agricultural export revenues to import capital equipment, the market contribution of rising rural incomes that create more demand for consumer products, and the factor market contribution, divided between the labor contribution (Lewis's manpower)—workers not needed on farms after agricultural productivity was raised could then work in industry—and the capital contribution (some farm profits could be reinvested in industry as agriculture became a steadily smaller fraction of national income). The capital contribution was misapplied as a "squeezing of the peasantry," but it meant investing first in agriculture and later reaping profits that would be partially reinvested in industry. As can be seen from this description, however, the framework implicitly—and ironically—still treats industrialization rather than rural modernization as the core development goal.[3]

Today, most development economists share the consensus that far from playing a passive, supporting role in the process of economic development, the agricultural sector, in particular, and the rural economy, in general, must play an indispensable part in any overall strategy of economic progress, especially for the low-income developing countries.

An agriculture- and employment-based strategy of economic development requires three basic complementary elements: (1) accelerated output growth through technological, institutional, and price incentive changes designed to raise the productivity of small farmers; (2) rising domestic demand for agricultural output derived from an employment-oriented, urban development strategy; and (3) diversified, nonagricultural, labor-intensive rural development activities that directly and indirectly support and are supported by the farming community.[4] To a large extent, therefore, agricultural and rural development has come to be regarded by many economists as the sine qua non of national development. Without such **integrated rural development**, in most cases, industrial growth either would be stultified or, if it succeeded, would create severe internal imbalances in the economy.

Seven main questions, therefore, need to be asked about agricultural and rural development as it relates to overall national development:

1. How can total agricultural output and productivity per capita be substantially increased in a manner that will directly benefit the average small farmer and the landless rural dweller while providing a sufficient food surplus to promote food security and support a growing urban, industrial sector?

2. What is the process by which traditional low-productivity (peasant) farms are transformed into high-productivity commercial enterprises?

3. When traditional family farmers and traditional (peasant) cultivators resist change, is their behavior stubborn and irrational, or are they acting rationally within the context of their particular economic environment?

4. What are the effects of the high risks faced by farmers in low-income countries, how do farm families cope with these risks, and what policies are appropriate to lessen risk?

5. Are economic and price incentives sufficient to elicit output increases among traditional (peasant) agriculturalists, or are institutional and structural changes in rural farming systems also required?

6. Is raising agricultural productivity sufficient to improve rural life, or must there be concomitant off-farm employment creation along with improvements in educational, medical, and other social services? In other words, what do we mean by *rural development*, and how can it be achieved?

7. How can countries most effectively address problems of national food security?

In this chapter, after a look at broad trends, we will examine the basic characteristics of agrarian systems in Latin America, Asia, and Africa. Although there is considerable diversity among developing nations, as well as within developing countries, each region tends to have a number of characteristics in common. First, these regions typically reflect the agricultural patterns of agriculture-based economies (in Africa), agriculturally transforming economies (in Asia), and urbanized economies (in Latin America). Relatedly, agriculture in these regions often typifies the stages of subsistence, mixed, and commercial farming, with important regional exceptions and varying success at inclusion of the poor. With successful development, countries tend to move toward commercialized agriculture, though with different trajectories and differing economic, social, and technical problems to solve along the way. Regions that have high concentrations of poverty also often reflect patterns of traditional agriculture (in Africa), high population density and subdivided smallholdings (in Asia), and the sharp inequalities of very large and very small farms (in Latin America). We will identify the various challenges facing

Integrated rural development The broad spectrum of rural development activities, including small-farmer agricultural progress, the provision of physical and social infrastructure, the development of rural nonfarm industries, and the capacity of the rural sector to sustain and accelerate the pace of these improvements over time.

each group of countries and look at countries that are typical of their region and some countries and districts that deviate from the pattern.

Over two-thirds of the world's extreme poor are involved in agricultural activities. We will therefore examine the economics of traditional (or peasant) subsistence agriculture and discuss the stages of transition from subsistence to commercial farming in developing nations. Our focus is not only the economic factors but also on the social, institutional, and structural requirements of small-farm modernization. We will then explore the meaning of *integrated rural development* and review alternative policies designed to raise levels of living in rural areas. The chapter concludes with a case study of problems of agricultural extension for women farmers in Africa.

9.2 Agricultural Growth: Past Progress and Current Challenges

Trends in Agricultural Productivity

The ability of agricultural production to keep pace with world population growth has been impressive, defying some neo-Malthusian predictions that global food shortages would have emerged by now. And it has actually been output gains in the developing world that have led the way. According to World Bank estimates, the developing world experienced faster growth in the value of agricultural output (2.6% per year) than the developed world (0.9% per year) during the period 1980–2004. Correspondingly, developing countries' share of global agricultural GDP rose from 56% to 65% in this period, far higher than their 21% share of world nonagricultural GDP. Since 2005, the growth gap has widened further. And research by the International Food Policy Research Institute points up that a wide range of successful programs have reduced hunger while raising agricultural productivity over the last several decades, including **Green Revolution** successes in Asia; containment of wheat rusts; improved maize and pest-resistant cassavas in sub-Saharan Africa; shallow tubewells for rice and homestead food production in Bangladesh; hybrid rice and mung bean improvement in East Asia; pearl millet and sorghum and smallholder dairy marketing in India; improved tilapia in the Philippines; successful land tenure reform in China and Vietnam; cotton reforms in Burkina Faso; and improvements of markets in Kenya.[5]

The degree to which general agricultural output grew significantly faster in developing countries in the 40-year period from 1970 to 2010 is reflected in Table 9.1. Output also grew in OECD regions; the sole exception was the poor performance in the transition countries. But growth in the value of output has not kept pace with population growth in Africa.

As Figure 9.1 shows, low-income countries tend to have the highest share of the labor force in agriculture, sometimes as much as 80 to 90%. The share of agriculture in GDP is lower but can represent as much as half of the value of output. These shares both tend to fall as GDP per capita rises: This is one of the broad patterns of economic development (see Chapter 3). But attention to the time paths of the share of agriculture in specific countries reveals a great deal of variation, which is also informative. In particular, sometimes the share of labor in agriculture declines greatly even when GDP per capita does not

Green Revolution The boost in grain production associated with the scientific discovery of new hybrid seed varieties of wheat, rice, and corn that have resulted in high farm yields in many developing countries.

TABLE 9.1 Average Annual Growth Rates of Agriculture, by Region (%)					
	1971–1980	**1981–1990**	**1991–2000**	**2001–2010**	**1971–2010**
High-income countries	1.83	0.97	1.25	0.47	1.14
Developing countries					
Latin America and Caribbean	2.93	2.35	3.09	3.21	2.89
Northeast Asia	3.23	5.04	5.04	3.39	4.19
South Asia	2.19	3.70	2.76	2.80	2.86
Southeast Asia	3.66	3.32	3.41	4.23	3.64
Sub-Saharan Africa	1.05	2.68	3.11	2.97	2.44
West Asia and North Africa	3.31	3.84	2.61	2.75	3.13
Transition countries	0.81	1.42	–4.03	2.28	0.04
World	2.08	2.42	2.09	2.42	2.25

Source: IFPRI (International Food Policy Research Institute). 2013. Global Food Policy Report, Table 1. Washington, DC.

increase much, if at all; examples are seen in the time paths of Nigeria and Brazil, as traced out in Figure 9.1. This finding parallels the observation in the Chapter 7, that urbanization is proceeding in many countries even when per capita income is falling or not rising much. Problems in the agricultural sector can suppress incomes, encouraging more migration to the urban informal sector. We will review the most important problems of developing-country agriculture in this chapter. Figure 9.1 also illustrates the time path of China, in which growth has been extremely rapid but the fall of the share of labor in agriculture has been unusually slow due in significant part to restrictions on rural-urban migration (though migration out of agriculture has greatly accelerated in the ensuing decade through 2013).

In marked contrast to the historical experience of advanced countries' agricultural output in their early stages of growth, which always contributed at least as much to total output as the share of the labor force engaged in these activities, the fact that contemporary agricultural employment in developing countries is much higher than agricultural output reflects the relatively low levels of labor productivity compared with those in manufacturing and commerce.

Agricultural production continues to rise around the world, broadly keeping pace with the rising population. But progress has been very uneven, as seen in Figure 9.2. In Asian developing countries, cereal yields per hectare in 2005 were nearly triple their 1960 levels. Production in Latin America also posted strong gains. Hunger in China fell. Agriculture in South Asia performed well, although hunger is thought to have increased in India in recent years. And in sub-Saharan Africa, yields increased by only about one-third. One of the causes is that in many areas of Africa, the population has reached a size where traditional slash-and-burn agricultural practices are no longer feasible without reusing land after too little rest, resulting in significant deterioration of soil nutrients. But subsistence farmers cannot purchase improved seeds, fertilizers, and other essentials of modern agriculture; the result can be a poverty trap in which farmers must work harder and harder just to stay in place.

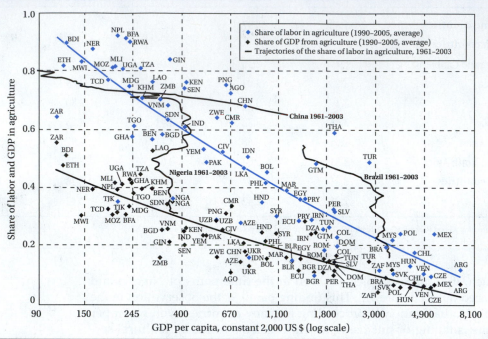

FIGURE 9.1   As Countries Develop, the Shares of GDP and Labor in Agriculture Tend to Decline, but with Many Idiosyncrasies

Source: International Bank for Reconstruction and Development/World Bank, *World Development Report, 2008.* Reprinted with permission.

Note: The list of 3-letter codes and the countries they represent can be found in Table 2.1 on pp. 43–44 of this text.

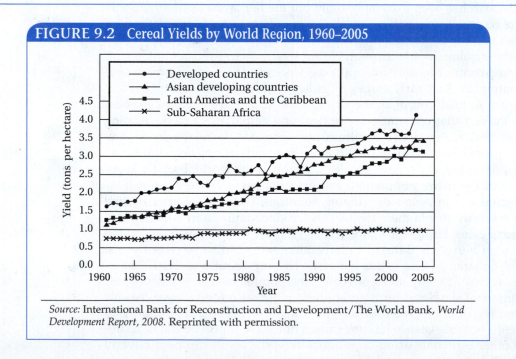

FIGURE 9.2   Cereal Yields by World Region, 1960–2005

Source: International Bank for Reconstruction and Development/The World Bank, *World Development Report, 2008.* Reprinted with permission.

Recurrent famine, regional famine, and catastrophic food shortages have repeatedly plagued many of the least developed countries, particularly in Africa. The 2011 drought and famine in the Horn of Africa, which affected over 13 million people, brought renewed attention to the problem (see Box 9.1). Of Africa's 750 million people, more than 270 million suffer from some form of malnutrition associated with inadequate food supplies. The severe famine of 1973–1974 took the lives of hundreds of thousands and left many more with permanent damage from malnutrition across the continent in the Sahelian belt that stretches below the Sahara from Cape Verde, off the coast of Senegal in the west, all the way to Ethiopia in the east. Four times in the 1980s and 1990s, at least 22 African nations faced severe famine. In the 2000s, famine again seriously affected African countries as widely separated as Mauritania in the northwest, Ethiopia and Eritrea in the east, and Angola, Zambia, Zimbabwe, Malawi, and Mozambique across the south.[6] The recent famine in the Horn of Africa is examined in Box 9.1.

Calls to mount a new Green Revolution in Africa like the successful one in Asia are now starting to get the hearing they deserve, with public, private, and nonprofit sector actors getting involved—including major support from the Alliance for a Green Revolution in Africa (AGRA), chaired by former UN secretary general Kofi Annan. Technical advances are clearly needed, and institutional and social transformation on the ground will also be needed to achieve the goals of rural development. The African Union's peer-review NEPAD initiative developed the Comprehensive Africa Agricultural Development Program to emphasize investments and regional cooperation in agriculture-led growth as a main strategy to achieve the first Millennium Development Goal of halving hunger and poverty. It targets the allocation of 10% of national budgets to agriculture and a 6% rate of growth in the agriculture sector at the national level.[7]

One early success is in work at the Africa Rice Center in Benin to develop varieties of New Rice for Africa (NERICA). These have so far proven beneficial in Benin, Uganda, and the Gambia, with apparently greater impact on women farmers than men farmers. It is not easy to replicate successes across Africa, however; for example, NERICA varieties have not helped in Guinea and Côte d'Ivoire. And food production will not automatically solve the problems of hunger among people living in poverty.

The food price spike of 2007–2008 and an additional spike in 2011 highlighted the continuing vulnerabilities. During the food price crisis, progress in reducing hunger ground to a halt and showed little improvement in the ensuing years. Some of the causes were temporary factors. But expert predictions are for high food prices in the longer term. Throughout the twentieth century, food prices fell at an average rate of 1% per year; but so far in the twenty-first century, food prices have risen on average. Figure 9.3 shows price trends for several key agricultural commodities; prices have generally returned to levels not seen since the late 1970s.[8]

As Nora Lustig has summarized, some of the causes of the 2007–2008 food price spike also reflect longer-term forces that will lead to high future food prices, including diversion of food to biofuels production, increase in the demand for food (particularly meat, which uses much more land than grain

BOX 9.1 Development Policy Issues: Famine in the Horn of Africa

On July 20, 2011, the United Nations declared formally that a famine was under way in two regions of Somalia, after horrific images of suffering were publicized.

Facts about the Famine

Somalia and neighboring countries faced a terrible drought, probably the worst in a half-century. More importantly, it took place in one of world's worst governance situations, which created a catastrophe for many women, children, and other noncombatants caught in the crossfire—metaphorically and sometimes literally. The situation was further compounded by rapidly increasing food prices. Tens of thousands of people died as a result of this famine according to UN estimates. The appalling images of the famine compare with similar catastrophes, and already 100,000 residents reportedly fled to refugee camps to seek shelter and food. Health and nutrition conditions in the camps were reportedly very dangerous. Malnutrition rates in southern Somalia are among the highest in the world, over 50% in some regions, with 6 deaths per 10,000 people per day. After famine was declared, some commentators said starvation in Somalia seemed like a never-ending story, but this was the first time in close to 20 years that conditions reached the point of a declared famine.

Drought afflicts not just Somalia but also parts of Ethiopia, Kenya, and South Sudan, and agencies report that about 11.5 million people are severely affected. A key to the drought seems to be an unusually strong Pacific La Niña, which has interrupted seasonal rains for the last two seasons. About half of all livestock has died in some areas. Staple food prices are soaring in affected areas, making the situation dire for the poor. Globally, food prices have risen greatly over the past few years with a new spike in 2011, which saw average global prices nearly double. Some causes are temporary including bad weather, but longer-term forces at work include diversion of food to biofuels production, increase in demand, including grain, for meat production for China, general population growth, higher energy prices

affecting agricultural costs, lack of new farmland, and impacts of climate change. Food prices have shot up more than the global average in this region, most dramatically in Somalia, where prices reportedly have tripled—just when the earnings capacity of most households has been falling. There are severe hardships in the other drought-stricken areas, such as northern Kenya, and people living there are at serious risk and need help. At the same time, more aid is getting to those who need it, and the suffering is not on the same scale, reflecting Somalia's "man-made" famine conditions.

Perspective on the Region

The East African "Horn" region is sometimes given a broad definition to include large parts of Ethiopia, Eritrea, Kenya, Djibouti, southern Sudan, and Uganda as well as Somalia. Taken as a region, the Horn is the poorest area in sub-Saharan Africa, though at least nine individual countries elsewhere in Africa are even poorer. Conditions in the region have historically been difficult; the record shows drought has intermittently afflicted the area. No doubt the region was seriously harmed by colonialism, with regions agglomerated arbitrarily, notably Eritrea to Ethiopia, and South Sudan to northern Sudan. This is a major reason the region has been plagued by conflict in the postcolonial era. The assumption in much of the press is that there must be something fundamentally different and special about the geography and climate of this region and the culture of its peoples to explain its recurrent plight. But, in fact, similar root problems are found in this area as in other regions that have failed to develop: poor institutions, ethnolinguistic fractionalization, and "fault lines" of regional inequality corresponding with ethnic or religious areas. Undoubtedly the area has some quite unfavorable geography; but other regions with unfavorable endowments have substantially overcome their disadvantages over time. However, adapting to future impacts of climate change projected for this region will be a challenge the international community will have to respond to.

Other conditions have compounded the problems; for example, Somalia's population was well under 3 million in 1960 but is well over 9 million today, and this is a factor putting strain on the food supply. However, as explained in Chapter 6, the poor have children as a survival necessity; rapid population is far more a symptom of poverty than its cause.

International Response

This famine has already reached a huge scale, and it would be difficult to reach all the affected people without a large, consolidated effort even under low-conflict conditions. But as with the last famine in Somalia in 1992, it will be one thing to rush food into the country and another to see that it reaches many of the people most in need. Al-Shabaab, a militant Islamist group linked to Al-Qaeda controls large parts of the declared famine areas. Some relief groups are getting through, but the militants have thwarted efforts by the UN'S World Food Program (WFP)—one of the most efficient food deliverers—from coming into these regions, claiming the WFP is biased and has a hidden agenda. The militants claim drought conditions have been exaggerated into famine proportions for political purposes, but the facts on the ground are too obvious to ignore; and there are indications they are reconsidering: There is little political gain in claiming dominance of an area depopulated by the escape of refugees and famine deaths. But governments, international organizations, and NGOs are now gearing up for a full-scale response to worsening famine. The problem is complex, because low incomes resulting from drought mean people cannot afford food, but dumping food on markets may keep prices so low that local growers find it unfavorable to produce for the market. In response, an important strategy is to purchase food for those suffering from local producers whenever possible.

The Entitlement Problem

Historically, a large majority of famines have been "man-made." Amartya Sen frames "the acquirement problem" as one of establishing "command over commodities." *Famine* is defined for international humanitarian and UN purposes as a combination of child malnutrition, deaths from hunger, and low food access, specifically: (1) more than 30% of children suffering from acute malnutrition; (2) more than two adults or four children dying of hunger each day per 10,000 people; and (3) the population overall having access to less than 2,100 kilocalories of food and 4 liters of water per day on average. This definition is not quite the same as Webster's "extreme scarcity of food; a great shortage." For example, in the Bangladesh famine in 1974, food output was actually there; it just wasn't getting to hungry people. According to Amartya Sen's research, also in Bengal in 1943, incomes were actually up as an average, which increased those more fortunate peoples' purchasing power, thus pushing food prices up, and then others such as laborers could not afford it in sufficient amounts.

In Somalia, and elsewhere in the region, output is drastically lower due to the severe drought. Commonly in famines, when many people are unable to buy as much locally grown food as they usually do, it becomes more attractive for sellers to export food out of the area. But if people had earning power, they could afford to buy food and traders would bring it to villages where they lived. The problem is that markets may not provide command over commodities, or entitlements, which people living in poverty need to survive in such conditions. While specific evidence of food exporting is not yet readily verifiable in Somalia, this problem is one of the reasons why public action is generally needed in a famine when entitlement is not established. There may be droughts and drastic declines in food output, but there never needs to be a famine.

Sources: Dreze, Jean, and Amartya Sen. *Hunger and Public Action.* New York: Oxford University Press, 1989; Amartya Sen. *Poverty and Famines: An Essay on Entitlement and Deprivation.* New York: Oxford University Press, 1981. For more details on the economics of conflict and development, see section 14.6, pages 708–717. For analysis of the importance of institutions and the historical legacy, see section 2.7, pages 83–91. On impact of and adaptation to climate change in developing countries, see section 10.3, pages 476–480

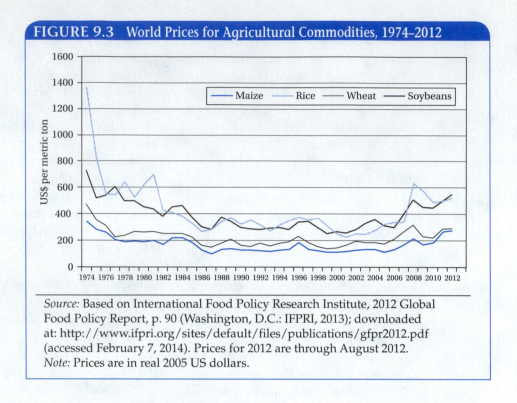

FIGURE 9.3   World Prices for Agricultural Commodities, 1974–2012

Source: Based on International Food Policy Research Institute, 2012 Global Food Policy Report, p. 90 (Washington, D.C.: IFPRI, 2013); downloaded at: http://www.ifpri.org/sites/default/files/publications/gfpr2012.pdf (accessed February 7, 2014). Prices for 2012 are through August 2012. *Note:* Prices are in real 2005 US dollars.

production) due to higher incomes in China and elsewhere, the slowdown in productivity growth of agricultural commodities, higher energy prices affecting agricultural input costs, running out of new land to be brought into farming, and the negative impact of climate change on developing-country food production. These are exacerbated by a number of unfavorable policies, including various forms of interference with food prices.[9]

Furthermore, there is not a large global market for food in relation to total demand. Most countries strive for food self-sufficiency, largely for national security reasons. Embargoes of food exports by such countries as Egypt, Vietnam, and Russia reflect this reluctance. In the late 2040s, the world will find itself having to manage to feed over 9 billion people. While highlighting impressive successes, we must also keep in mind looming challenges.

Market Failures and the Need for Government Policy

A major reason for the relatively poor performance of agriculture in low-income regions has been the neglect of this sector in the development priorities of their governments, which the initiatives just described are intended to overcome. This neglect of agriculture and the accompanying bias toward investment in the urban industrial economy can in turn be traced historically to the misplaced emphasis on rapid industrialization via import substitution and exchange rate overvaluation (see Chapter 12) that permeated development thinking and strategy during the postwar decades.[10]

If agricultural development is to receive a renewed emphasis, what is the proper role for government? In fact, one of the most important challenges for agriculture in development is to get the role of government right. A major theme of development agencies in the 1980s was to reduce government intervention in agriculture. Indeed, many of the early interventions did more harm than good; an extreme example is government requirements for farmers to sell at a low price to state marketing boards, an attempt to keep urban food prices low. Production subsidies, now spreading like a contagion from high-income to middle-income countries, are costly and inefficient.

Agriculture is generally thought of as a perfectly competitive activity, but this does not mean that there are no market failures and no role for government. In fact, market failures in the sector are quite common and include environmental externalities, the public good character of agricultural research and development and extension services, economies of scale in marketing, information asymmetries in product quality, missing markets, and monopoly power in input supply, in addition to the more general government roles of providing institutions and infrastructure. Despite many failures, sometimes government has been relatively effective in these roles, as in Asia during its Green Revolution.[11]

But government also has a role in agriculture simply because of its necessary role in poverty alleviation—and a large majority of the world's poor are still farmers. Poverty itself prevents farmers from taking advantage of opportunities that could help pull them out of poverty. Lacking collateral, they cannot get credit. Lacking credit, they may have to take their children out of school to work, transmitting poverty across generations. Lacking health and nutrition, they may be unable to work well enough to afford better health and nutrition. With a lack of information and missing markets, they cannot get insurance. Lacking insurance, they cannot take what might seem favorable risks for fear of falling below subsistence. Without middlemen, they cannot specialize (and without specialization, middlemen lack incentives to enter). Being socially excluded because of ethnicity, caste, language, or gender, they are denied opportunities, which keep them excluded. These poverty traps are often all but impossible to escape without assistance. In all of these areas, NGOs can and do step in to help (Chapter 11), but government is needed to at least play a facilitating role and to create the needed supporting environment.[12]

Policies to improve efficiency and alleviate poverty are closely related. Many market failures, such as missing markets and capital market failures, sharply limit the ability of poor farmers to take advantage of opportunities of globalization when governments liberalize trade, for example. If these problems are not addressed prior to deregulation or making other structural changes, the poor can remain excluded and even end up worse off. A key role for government, then, is to ensure that growth in agriculture is shared by the poor. In some countries, impressive agricultural growth has occurred without the poor receiving proportional benefits. Examples include Brazil, with its extremely unequal land distribution, and Pakistan, with its social injustices and inequality of access to key resources such as irrigation. But by including the poor, the human and natural resources of a developing nation are more fully employed, and that can result in an increased rate of growth as well as poverty reduction.[13]

9.3 The Structure of Agrarian Systems in the Developing World

Three Systems of Agriculture

A first step toward understanding what is needed for further agricultural and rural development progress is a clear perspective of the nature of agricultural systems in diverse developing regions and, in particular, of the economic aspects of the transition from subsistence to commercial agriculture.

One helpful way to categorize world agriculture, proposed by the agricultural development economist Alain de Janvry and his colleagues in the World Bank's 2008 *World Development Report,* is to see that alongside advanced agricultural systems in developed countries, three quite different situations are found among developing countries.

First, in what the report terms *agriculture-based countries*, agriculture is still a major source of economic growth—although mainly because agriculture makes up such a large share of GDP. The World Bank estimates that agriculture accounts for some 32% of GDP growth on average in these countries, in which 417 million people live. More than two-thirds of the poor of these countries live in rural areas. Some 82% of the rural population of sub-Saharan Africa lives in these countries. It also includes a few countries outside the region, such as Laos. And a few African countries, such as Senegal, are undergoing transformation.

Second, most of the world's rural people—some 2.2 billion—live in what the report categorizes as transforming countries, in which the share of the poor who are rural is very high (almost 80% on average) but agriculture now contributes only a small share to GDP growth (7% on average). Most of the population of South and East Asia, North Africa, and the Middle East lives in these countries, along with some outliers such as Guatemala.

Third, in what the report calls *urbanized countries*, rural-urban migration has reached the point at which nearly half, or more, of the poor are found in the cities, and agriculture tends to contribute even less to output growth. The urbanized countries are largely found in Latin America and the Caribbean, along with developing eastern Europe and Central Asia, and contain about 255 million rural dwellers.

In many cases, the position of countries within these groups is not stagnant. Many countries that were in the agriculture-based category moved to the transforming category in recent decades, most prominently India and China.

Figure 9.4 shows some of the country positions in each group, along with the movement over time for four major countries over an approximately three-decade period: China, India, Indonesia, and Brazil. For example, Brazil has moved from being a borderline transforming country to a solidly urbanized one according to the World Bank classification.

Agricultural productivity varies dramatically across countries. Table 9.2 shows variations in land productivity (measured as kilograms of grain harvested per hectare of agricultural land) between 3 developed countries (Canada, Japan, and the United States) and 12 developing countries, along with the averages for low-, middle-, and high-income countries. Despite the far smaller number of farmworkers per hectare in the United States, its grain yield per hectare was about 2.4 times that of India and almost 9 times that of the DRC

FIGURE 9.4 Agriculture's Contribution to Growth and the Rural Share in Poverty in Three Types of Countries

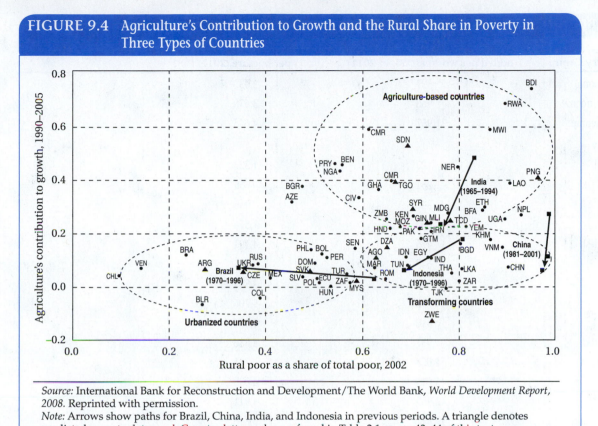

Source: International Bank for Reconstruction and Development/The World Bank, *World Development Report, 2008*. Reprinted with permission.

Note: Arrows show paths for Brazil, China, India, and Indonesia in previous periods. A triangle denotes predicted poverty data used. Country letter codes are found in Table 2.1 on pp. 43–44 of this text.

(Congo). The value added per worker in U.S. agriculture was over 75 times that of India and over 177 times that of Congo.

It is also important to note that regional disparities can be quite large *within* countries. India has regions that fall within each of the three classifications, from modernized Punjab to semifeudal Bihar. Even upper-middle-income, urbanized Mexico has regions in the south with substantial poverty and high dependence on agriculture. Moreover, within regions, large and small, rich and poor often exist side by side—though large does not necessarily mean efficient. Let us look at agricultural issues facing countries in Latin America, Asia, and sub-Saharan Africa in more detail.

Traditional and Peasant Agriculture in Latin America, Asia, and Africa

In many developing countries, various historical circumstances have led to a concentration of large areas of land in the hands of a small class of powerful landowners. This is especially true in Latin America and parts of the Asian subcontinent. In Africa, both historical circumstances and the availability of relatively more unused land have resulted in a different pattern and structure of agricultural activity.

Although the day-to-day struggle for survival permeates the lives and attitudes of impoverished peasants in both Latin America and Asia (and also

TABLE 9.2	Labor and Land Productivity in Developed and Developing Countries	
Country Group	**Agricultural Productivity (value added per worker, US$, in 2011)**	**Average Grain Yield (kilograms per hectare, 2011)**
Low-income	337	2,035
Middle-income	953	3,678
High-income	21,957	4,645
Country		
Burundi	123	1,326
Congo, DR	281	766
Senegal	346	966
Kenya	363	1,514
Bangladesh	475	4,191
Bolivia	629	2,365
India	657	2,883
China	713	5,706
Ghana	810	1,594
Indonesia	937	4,886
Mexico	4,028	3,241
Brazil	5,019	4,038
Japan	42,953	4,911
United States	49,817	6,818
Canada	59,818	3,527

Source: Based on data from World Bank, *World Development Indicators, 2013* (Washington, D.C.: World Bank, 2013), tab. 3.3.

Agrarian system   The pattern of land distribution, ownership, and management, and also the social and institutional structure of the agrarian economy.

Africa, although the rural structure and institutions are considerably different), the nature of their **agrarian systems** differs markedly. In Latin America, in a number of poorer and more backward areas, the peasants' plight is rooted in the *latifundio–minifundio* system (to be explained shortly). In Asia, it lies primarily in fragmented and heavily congested dwarf parcels of land. The average farm size in Latin America is far larger than in Asia; the countries included in Table 9.3 are typical. The average farm size for Latin American countries such as Ecuador, Chile, Panama, and Brazil are several *times* larger than farm size in Asian countries such as Bangladesh, Pakistan, Thailand, and India. But the variance of farm size is much higher in Latin America, with huge farmlands controlled by the largest farms in Latin America. As the table reveals, patterns are anything but uniform, with farms in some countries splitting into smaller sizes and in other countries consolidating to larger sizes, and some experiencing increasing and others showing decreasing inequality over time.

Just as we can draw income Lorenz curves from data on the distribution of income (see Figure 5.1), we can draw land Lorenz curves from data on the distribution of farmholds among farmers. In this case, the *x*-axis reports the proportion of total holdings, and the *y*-axis reports the proportion of total

TABLE 9.3 Changes in Farm Size and Land Distribution								
		Land Distribution Gini (percent)		Average Farm Size (hectares)		Change (%)		
Country	Period	Start	End	Start	End	Total Number of Farms	Total Area	Farm Size Definition Used
Smaller Farm Size, More Inequality								
Bangladesh	1977–1996	43.1	48.3	1.4	0.6	103	–13	Total land area
Pakistan	1990–2000	53.5	54.0	3.8	3.1	31	6	Total land area
Thailand	1978–1993	43.5	46.7	3.8	3.4	42	27	Total land area
Ecuador	1974–2000	69.3	71.2	15.4	14.7	63	56	Total land area
Smaller Farm Size, Less Inequality								
India	1990–1995	46.6	44.8	1.6	1.4	8	–5	Total land area
Egypt	1990–2000	46.5	37.8	1.0	0.8	31	5	Total land area
Malawi	1981–1993	34.4	33.2[a]	1.2	0.8	37	–8	Cultivated crop area
Tanzania	1971–1996	40.5	37.6	1.3	1.0	64	26	Cultivated crop area
Chile	1975–1997	60.7	58.2	10.7	7.0	6	–31	Arable land area
Panama	1990–2001	77.1	74.5	13.8	11.7	11	–6	Total land area
Larger Farm Size, More Inequality								
Botswana	1982–1993	39.3	40.5	3.3	4.8	–1	43	Cultivated crop area
Brazil	1985–1996	76.5	76.6	64.6	72.8	–16	–6	Total land area
Larger Farm Size, Less Inequality								
Togo	1983–1996	47.8	42.1	1.6	2.0	64	105	Cultivated crop area
Algeria	1973–2001	64.9	60.2	5.8	8.3	14	63	Arable land area

[a] Figure for 2004–2005

Source: World Development Report, 2008: Agriculture and Development by World Bank. Copyright © 2008 by World Bank. Reproduced with permission.

area. A land Gini may be calculated in a manner analogous to that of the income Gini: It is the ratio of the area between the land Lorenz curve and the 45-degree line, and the whole triangle. Table 9.3 presents land Gini coefficients and their change over time for representative developing countries.

One of the broadest trends is for farm sizes to become smaller over time in Asia as land is subdivided, and this trend is seen increasingly also in Africa.

Agrarian Patterns in Latin America: Progress and Remaining Poverty Challenges

In Latin America, as in Asia and Africa, agrarian structures are not only part of the production system but also a basic feature of the entire economic, social, and political organization of rural life. The agrarian structure that has existed in Latin America since colonial times and is still widespread in a substantial

Latifundio   A very large landholding found particularly in the Latin American agrarian system, capable of providing employment for more than 12 people, owned by a small number of landlords, and comprising a disproportionate share of total agricultural land.

Minifundio   A landholding found particularly in the Latin American agrarian system considered too small to provide adequate employment for a single family.

Family farm   A farm plot owned and operated by a single household.

Medium-size farm   A farm employing up to 12 workers.

Transaction costs   Costs of doing business related to gathering information, monitoring, establishing reliable suppliers, formulating contracts, obtaining credit, and so on.

part of the region is a pattern of agricultural dualism known as *latifundio-minifundio*.[14] Basically, **latifundios** are very large landholdings. They are usually defined as farms large enough to provide employment for more than 12 people, though some employ thousands. In contrast, **minifundios** are the smallest farms. They are defined as farms too small to provide employment for a single family (two workers) with the typical incomes, markets, and levels of technology and capital prevailing in each country or region.

Using Gini coefficients to measure the degree of land concentration, as seen in Table 9.3, researchers report that the coefficient for Brazil is 0.77, for Panama is 0.75, and for Ecuador is 0.71. Although estimates vary, changes in land inequality are limited in the case of Latin America (for example, see the data for Brazil and Ecuador in Table 9.3). Other countries are even more unequal; the Gini for Paraguay has been estimated to be an astoundingly unequal 0.94, and very high inequality has been estimated for Colombia and Uruguay, among others.[15] These are the highest regional Gini coefficients in the world, and they dramatically reflect the degree of land ownership inequality (and thus, in part, income inequality) throughout Latin America.

But *latifundios* and *minifundios* do not constitute the entirety of Latin American agricultural holdings. A considerable amount of production occurs on **family farms** and **medium-size farms**. The former provide work for two to four people (recall that the *minifundio* can provide work for fewer than two people), and the latter employ 4 to 12 workers (just below the *latifundio*). In Venezuela, Brazil, and Uruguay, these intermediate farm organizations account for almost 50% of total agricultural output and employ similar proportions of agricultural labor. These farms use a more efficient balance between labor and land, and studies show that they have a much higher total factor productivity than either *latifundios* or *minifundios,* as the law of diminishing returns would suggest. Indeed, evidence from a wide range of developing countries demonstrates that smaller farms are more efficient (lower-cost) producers of most agricultural commodities.[16]

A major explanation for the relative economic inefficiency of farming the fertile land on the *latifundios* is simply that the wealthy landowners often value these holdings not for their potential contributions to national agricultural output but rather for the considerable power and prestige that they bring. Much of the land is left idle or farmed less intensively than on smaller farms. Also, *latifundio* **transaction costs**, especially the cost of supervising hired labor, are much higher than the low effective cost of using family labor on family farms or *minifundios*. It follows that raising agricultural production and improving the efficiency of Latin American agrarian systems in traditional areas will require much more than direct economic policies that lead to the provision of better seeds, more fertilizer, less distorted factor prices, higher output prices, and improved marketing facilities.[17] It will also require a reorganization of rural social and institutional structures to provide Latin American peasants, particularly indigenous people who find it more challenging to migrate, a real opportunity to lift themselves out of their present state of economic subsistence and social subservience.[18]

Despite the fact that many *minifundio* owners remain in poverty, especially among indigenous and mixed-race populations, and many *latifundios* continue to operate well below their productivity potential, a more dynamic sector, including some larger farms, has emerged. Efficient family and medium-size farms are found throughout the region.

At an aggregate level, the agricultural sector in Latin America appears to be doing fairly well. Chile has led the way in "nontraditional exports," notably fresh fruits for the northern hemisphere winter markets and also aquaculture, vegetables, and wines; performance in Chile has benefited from an active and relatively efficient agricultural extension system that has included efforts to promote new exports. Diversification has reduced variance in export earnings. Productivity growth in cereals has been quite solid. Sugarcane-based biofuels and soybeans have played important roles in agricultural growth in Brazil. And in traditional exports, particularly coffee, Latin America has led the way in taking advantage of niche opportunities for higher-value-added activities such as organic and Fair Trade markets.[19]

Some Latin American countries, such as Guatemala and Honduras, are still in the mixed transition phase, and in such countries, the *latifundio-minifundio* pattern tends to remain particularly dominant. But much of this pattern still prevails in many other areas. As noted in Chapter 2, the extreme rural inequalities in Latin America typically stem from the Spanish and Portuguese colonial period, in which indigenous peoples were exploited in what often amounted to slavery (see Box 2.3 on continuing effects of the *mita* system in Peru) and African slaves were forcibly brought to the region. Overcoming this legacy has been a long and painful process, with much remaining to be achieved. Social discrimination continues, and improved access for the poor to agricultural land in countries such as Colombia is still in all too many cases suppressed.[20]

Areas with less favorable agricultural conditions, often with a concentration of minority populations, such as northeast Brazil, the Andean region, and parts of Mexico and Central America, tend to have persistently high poverty levels. Extreme rural inequality inhibits progress in these areas, both because of reduced access by the poor to credit and other inputs and because elites effectively continue to block political participation by the poor, who often receive low levels of government services. Moreover, rural-to-urban migration has been disproportionately among more educated people, and the result is that rural populations are becoming older, more female, and more indigenous. These are factors in poverty rates that remain high for middle-income countries and will require sustained action by government and civil society.[21]

Transforming Economies: Problems of Fragmentation and Subdivision of Peasant Land in Asia

If the major agrarian problem of Latin America, at least in traditional areas, can be identified as too much land under the control of too few people, the basic problem in Asia is one of too many people crowded onto too little land. For example, the average farm size is just 3.4 hectares in Thailand, 3.1 hectares in Pakistan, 1.4 hectares in India, and 0.6 hectares in Bangladesh; in each of these cases, farm sizes have been getting even smaller over time (see Table 9.3). The land is distributed more equally in Asia than in Latin America but still with substantial levels of inequality. As seen in Table 9.3, the estimated Gini coefficients for land distribution in Asia range from 0.448 in India, to 0.483 in Bangladesh and 0.467 in Thailand, to 0.540 in Pakistan.

Throughout much of the twentieth century, rural conditions in Asia typically deteriorated. Nobel laureate Gunnar Myrdal identified three major interrelated forces that molded the traditional pattern of land ownership into its present fragmented condition: (1) the intervention of European rule, (2) the progressive introduction of monetized transactions and the rise in power of the moneylender, and (3) the rapid growth of Asian populations.[22]

The traditional Asian agrarian structure before European colonization was organized around the village. Local chiefs and peasant families each provided goods and services—produce and labor from the peasants to the chief in return for protection, rights to use community land, and the provision of public services. Decisions on the allocation, disposition, and use of the village's most valuable resource, land, belonged to the tribe or community, either as a body or through its chief. Land could be redistributed among village members as a result of either population increase or natural calamities such as drought, flood, famine, war, or disease. Within the community, families had a basic right to cultivate land for their own use, and they could be evicted from their land only after a decision was made by the whole village.

The arrival of the Europeans (mainly the British, French, and Dutch) led to major changes in the traditional agrarian structure, some of which had already begun. As Myrdal points out, "Colonial rule acted as an important catalyst to change, both directly through its effects on property rights and indirectly through its effects on the pace of monetization of the indigenous economy and on the growth of population."[23] In the area of property rights, European land tenure systems of private property ownership were both encouraged and reinforced by law. One of the major social consequences of the imposition of these systems was, as Myrdal explains, the

> breakdown of much of the earlier cohesion of village life with its often elaborate, though informal, structure of rights and obligations. The landlord was given unrestricted rights to dispose of the land and to raise the tribute from its customary level to whatever amount he was able to extract. He was usually relieved of the obligation to supply security and public amenities because these functions were taken over by the government. Thus his status was transformed from that of a tribute receiver with responsibilities to the community to that of an absolute owner unencumbered by obligations toward the peasants and the public, other than the payment of land taxes.[24]

Landlord   The proprietor of a freehold interest in land with rights to lease out to tenants in return for some form of compensation for the use of the land.

Sharecropper   A tenant farmer whose crop has to be shared with the landlord, as the basis for the rental contract.

Tenant farmer   One who farms on land held by a landlord and therefore lacks ownership rights and has to pay for the use of that land, for example, by giving a share of output to the owner.

Contemporary **landlords** in India and Pakistan are able to avoid much of the taxation on income derived from their ownership of land. There are variations, but landlords in South Asia are often absentee owners who live in the town and turn over the working of the land to **sharecroppers** and other **tenant farmers**. Sharecropping is widespread in both Asia and Latin America but more pervasive in Asia. It has been estimated that of all tenanted land, some 84.5% is sharecropped in Asia but only 16.1% in Latin America. The institution is almost unknown in Africa, where the typical arrangement continues to be farms operated under tribal or communal tenures. For example, it has been estimated that about 48% of all tenanted land is sharecropped in India, 60% in Indonesia, and 79% in the Philippines. Though common in Colombia, sharecropping is unusual elsewhere in Latin America; for example, it has all but disappeared in Peru.[25]

2

The creation of individual titles to land made possible the rise to power of another dubious agent of change in Asian rural socioeconomic structures, the **moneylender**. Once private property came into effect, land became a negotiable asset that could be offered by peasants as security for loans and, in the case of default, could be forfeited and transferred to the often unscrupulous moneylender. At the same time, Asian agriculture was being transformed from a subsistence to a commercial orientation, both as a result of rising local demand in new towns and, more important, in response to external food demands of colonial European powers. With this transition from subsistence to commercial production, the role of the moneylender changed drastically. In the subsistence economy, his activities had been restricted to supplying the peasant with money to tide him over a crop failure or to cover extraordinary ceremonial expenditures such as family weddings or funerals. Most of these loans were paid in kind (in the form of food) at very high rates of interest. With the development of commercial farming, however, the peasant's cash needs grew significantly. Money was needed for seeds, fertilizer, and other inputs. It was also needed to cover his food requirements if he shifted to the production of cash crops such as tea, rubber, or jute. Often moneylenders were more interested in acquiring peasant lands as a result of loan defaults than they were in extracting high rates of interest. By charging exorbitant interest rates or inducing peasants to secure larger credits than they could manage, moneylenders were often able to drive the peasants off their land. They could then reap the profits of land speculation by selling this farmland to rich and acquisitive landlords. Largely as a consequence of the moneylenders' influence, Asian traditional peasant cultivators saw their economic status deteriorate.[26] And rapid population growth often led to fragmentation and impoverishment.[27]

To understand the deterioration of rural conditions in some Asian countries during the twentieth century, consider the cases of India, Indonesia, and the Philippines. In 1901, there were 286 million Indians; by 2013, there were more than quadruple that number. The Indonesian population grew from 28.4 million in 1900 to 210 million in 2000. The population of central Luzon in the Philippines increased more than tenfold from its level of 1 million from 1903 to 2003. In each case, severe fragmentation of landholdings inevitably followed so that today average peasant holdings in many areas of these countries are less than 1 hectare. As seen in Table 9.3, average farm size has fallen throughout South Asia and in Thailand.

For many impoverished families, as these holdings shrink even further, production falls below the subsistence level, and chronic poverty becomes a way of life for many. Peasants are forced to borrow even more from the moneylender at interest rates ranging from 50 to 200%. Most cannot repay these loans. They are then compelled to sell their land and become tenants with large debts. Because land is scarce, they are forced to pay high rents or sharecrop on unfavorable terms. And because labor is abundant, wages are extremely low. Peasants can thus get trapped in a vise of chronic poverty from which, in the absence of major rural reconstruction and reform, there is no escape. Thus, many rural Asians are gradually being transformed from small proprietors to tenant farmers and sharecroppers, then landless rural laborers, then jobless vagrants, and finally migrant slum dwellers on the fringes of modern urban areas.[28] At the same time, many other farmers have benefited from the

Moneylender A person who lends money at high rates of interest, for example to peasant farmers to meet their needs for seeds, fertilizers, and other inputs.

enormous productivity gains resulting from the Green Revolution; yet for an increasing number of them, environmental problems such as rapidly falling water tables represent new and looming challenges.

Again, as noted in Chapter 2, colonial practices often had long-lasting influences. In the case of India, regions in which property rights to land were given to landlords had significantly lower productivity and agricultural investments—and significantly lower investments in health and education—in the postindependence period than regions in which property rights were given to cultivators.[29]

Subsistence Agriculture and Extensive Cultivation in Africa

Subsistence farming on small plots of land is the way of life for the majority of African people living in agriculture-based economies. The great majority of farm families in tropical Africa still plan their output primarily for their own subsistence. There are important exceptions, including the sugar, cocoa, coffee, tea, and other plantations in East and West Africa; and farms devoted to such export crops as green beans in Niger, cut flowers in Kenya and Ethiopia, legumes in Tanzania, and other contract farming arrangements.

Since the basic variable input in traditional African agriculture is farm family and village labor, African agriculture systems are dominated by three major characteristics: (1) the importance of subsistence farming in the village community; (2) the existence of some (though rapidly diminishing) land in excess of immediate requirements, which permits a general practice of shifting cultivation and reduces the value of land ownership as an instrument of economic and political power; and (3) the rights of each family (both nuclear and extended) in a village to have access to land and water in the immediate territorial vicinity, excluding from such access use by families that do not belong to the community even though they may be of the same tribe. Where traditional systems are breaking down, inequality is often increasing.

The low-productivity subsistence farming characteristic of most traditional African agriculture results from a combination of three historical forces restricting the growth of output:

1. In spite of the existence of some unused and potentially cultivable land, only small areas can be planted and weeded by the farm family when it uses only traditional tools such as the short-handled hoe, the ax, and the long-handled knife, or *panga*. In some countries, use of animals is impossible because of the tsetse fly or a lack of fodder in the long, dry seasons, and traditional farming practices must rely primarily on the application of human labor to small parcels of land.

2. Given the limited amount of land that a farm family can cultivate in the context of a traditional technology, these small areas tend to be intensively cultivated. As a result, they are subject to rapidly diminishing returns to increased labor inputs. In such conditions, **shifting cultivation** is the most economic method of using limited supplies of labor on extensive tracts of land. Under shifting cultivation, once the minerals are drawn out of the soil as a result of numerous croppings, new land is cleared, and the process of planting and weeding is repeated. In the meantime, formerly

Subsistence farming Farming in which crop production, stock rearing, and other activities are conducted mainly for personal consumption.

Shifting cultivation Tilling land until it has been exhausted of fertility and then moving to a new parcel of land, leaving the former one to regain fertility until it can be cultivated again.

cropped land is allowed to recover fertility until it can be used again. Under such a process, manure and chemical fertilizers have been unnecessary, although in most African villages, some form of manure (mostly animal waste) is applied to nearby plots that are intensively cultivated in order to extend their period of fertility.

3. Labor is scarce during the busiest part of the growing season, planting and weeding times. At other times, much of the labor is underemployed. Because the time of planting is determined by the onset of the rains and because much of Africa experiences only one extended rainy season, the demand for workers during the early weeks of this rainy season usually exceeds all available rural labor supplies.

The net result of these three forces had been slow growth in agricultural labor productivity throughout much of Africa. As long as population size remained relatively stable, this historical pattern of low productivity and shifting cultivation enabled most African tribes to meet their subsistence food requirements. But the feasibility of shifting cultivation has now broken down as population densities increase. It has largely been replaced by sedentary cultivation on small owner-occupied plots. As a result, the need for other nonhuman productive inputs and new technologies grows, especially in the more densely populated agricultural regions of Kenya, Nigeria, Ghana, and Uganda. Farm size has also fallen in countries such as Malawi and Tanzania, as seen in Table 9.3. Moreover, with the growth of towns, the penetration of the monetary economy, soil erosion and deforestation of marginal lands, and the introduction of land taxes, pure subsistence-agricultural practices are no longer viable. And as land becomes increasingly scarce, land degradation is increasing in scope. The 2008 *World Development Report* concluded:

> Higher productivity is not possible without urgent attention to better soil and water management. Sub-Saharan Africa must replace the soil nutrients it has mined for decades. African farmers apply less than 10 kilograms of fertilizer per hectare, compared with more than 100 kilograms in South Asia. Programs to develop efficient fertilizer markets, and agroforestry systems to replenish soil fertility through legumes, need to be scaled up.[30]

Moreover, by 2007, only 4% of the cropland in sub-Saharan Africa was irrigated, in sharp contrast to 39% in South Asia and 29% in the East Asia and Pacific region. Despite some recent progress, just 22% of the cereal-growing farmland in sub-Saharan Africa is sown with improved varieties, which are used on a large majority of the land in all other developing regions. Dependence on unimproved seeds sown on unfertilized, rain-fed fields is a worsening problem for the region, given both the depletion of soils and the unreliability of rainfall (see Figure 9.5).

Of all the major regions of the world, Africa has suffered the most from its inability to expand food production at a sufficient pace to keep up with its rapid population growth.[31] As a result of declining production, African per capita food consumption fell dramatically during the 1980s and 1990s, while dependence on imports—particularly wheat and rice—increased.[32]

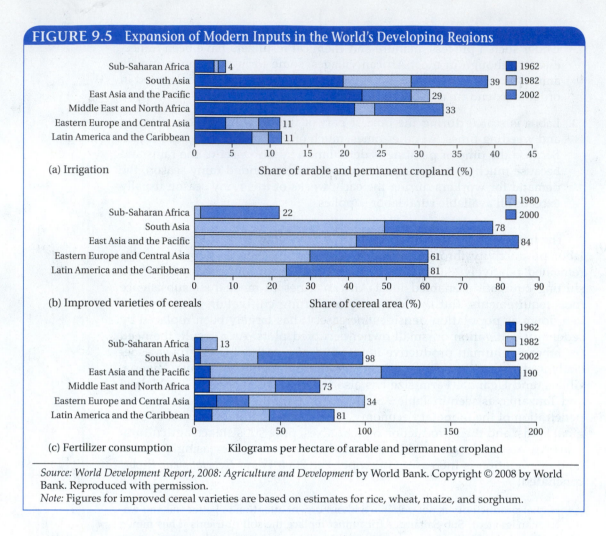

FIGURE 9.5 Expansion of Modern Inputs in the World's Developing Regions

(a) Irrigation   Share of arable and permanent cropland (%)

(b) Improved varieties of cereals   Share of cereal area (%)

(c) Fertilizer consumption   Kilograms per hectare of arable and permanent cropland

Source: World Development Report, 2008: Agriculture and Development by World Bank. Copyright © 2008 by World Bank. Reproduced with permission.
Note: Figures for improved cereal varieties are based on estimates for rice, wheat, maize, and sorghum.

9.4 The Important Role of Women

A major and until recently often overlooked feature of agrarian systems in the developing world, particularly in Africa and Asia, is the crucial role played by women in agricultural production.[33] In Africa, where subsistence farming is predominant and shifting cultivation remains important, nearly all tasks associated with subsistence food production are performed by women. Although men who remain home generally perform the initial task of cutting trees and bushes on a potentially cultivable plot of land, women are typically responsible for all subsequent operations, including removing and burning felled trees, sowing or planting the plot, weeding, harvesting, and preparing the crop for storage or immediate consumption. In her pioneering work on women and development, Ester Boserup examined many studies on African women's participation in agriculture and found that in nearly all cases recorded, women did most of the agricultural work. In some cases, they were found to do around 70% and in one case, nearly 80% of the total. Typically, these tasks are performed only with primitive tools and require many days of long, hard labor simply to produce enough output to meet the family's subsistence requirements, while the men often attempt to generate cash income through work on nearby plantations or in the cities.[34] Recent research confirms women's "time poverty" predicament.

Women do much of the labor for cash crop production, cultivate food for household consumption, raise and market livestock, generate additional income through cottage industries, collect firewood and water, and perform household chores, including the processing and cooking of food. Due to the time-consuming nature of their diverse responsibilities—and no doubt to their limited household bargaining power—women tend to work longer hours than their male counterparts. Studies concerning the allocation of women's time among different activities have greatly increased recognition of the importance of rural women's economic contribution. It has become clear that since women produce a large share of agricultural output and supply a large share of the labor—a share that has actually been increasing over time—successful agricultural reform will require raising women's productivity and ensuring that gender-specific policies are at the core of rural development strategy. The necessity of starting with women's activity when agricultural policy is designed is captured by the maxim of feminist economists that "you cannot just add women and stir."

The diversity of women's duties makes it difficult to determine their share of agricultural production, much less place an economic value on their work. However, current estimates underscore the importance of women's agricultural labor. It is estimated that in addition to work in the household, women provide 60 to 80% of agricultural labor in Africa and Asia and about 40% in Latin America. Much of this work, however, is statistically "invisible" in that women often receive no payment for the work they perform.

Women make an important contribution to the agricultural economy through the labor they supply in the cultivation of **cash crops**. Though the production and profits from commercial crops are generally controlled by men, women are usually responsible for the strenuous jobs of weeding and transplanting. As population density increases and land becomes more fragmented, the length of time that women must spend walking to and from the fields increases, often in very hot climates that make strenuous work exceedingly difficult. In addition to commercial crops, women frequently cultivate small vegetable gardens that provide food for family consumption. Though the cash value of produce from these gardens may be small, it often represents an important component of the total resources available to women.

Cash crops Crops produced entirely for the market.

Women's work in the low-income household involves a range of demanding tasks, including processing and pounding raw grains, tending livestock, cooking, and caring for children. Collecting increasingly scarce firewood and water from distant sources may add several hours to the workday. To raise additional income, it is common for women to engage in household production of goods for sale in village markets. These items are specific to each region, but a few examples are homemade beer, processed foods, handicrafts, and textiles.

Perhaps the most important role of women is providing food security for the household. This is accomplished through the supplementation of household earnings, diversification of household income sources, and raising of livestock to augment household assets. The production of vegetables for household consumption helps insulate households from swings in food prices and reduces cash outlays for the purchase of household necessities. Women's investments in revenue-generating projects and livestock are crucial to stabilizing household income, especially but not only in female-headed households, where resource constraints are the most severe.

However, financial investments are inherently risky, and the poorer the household, the more averse its members are to taking any kind of risk. When credit and resources are unavailable, reducing the variability of household earnings generally entails choosing less efficient methods of production and thus, lower average income. This trade-off occurs most frequently in female-headed households, where resource constraints are greatest. Thus, as a consequence of their restricted range of choices, women tend to retain traditional modes of economic activity. The upshot is that their productivity has stagnated while that of men has continued to improve.

Where the structure of agriculture is becoming more commercialized, women's roles and hence their economic status are changing. In many developing regions, women are still unremunerated for the long hours they contribute to the tending of commercial crops. As revenue-generating cash cropping rises in importance, the proportion of resources controlled by women tends to diminish. This is largely due to the fact that household resources, such as land and inputs, are transferred away from women's crops in order to promote the production of cash crops. Nonfarm activities are growing in importance and represent an important path for rural women's economic and social advancement.

Government extension programs that provide resources exclusively to men tend to exacerbate existing disparities between men's and women's access to resources (see the case study at the end of this chapter). If credit is provided solely or preferentially to men for the purpose of cash cropping, commercial production will increase at the expense of women's vegetable gardens. Since homegrown vegetables must be replaced by purchased substitutes, significant increases in a male spouse's cash contribution are necessary to offset a woman's losses. If the market price of vegetables increases markedly (there are now fewer producers) and the increase in the husband's contribution is not sufficient to compensate for the increased need for cash, the welfare of the woman and her children will decline.

This drop in the well-being of family members is due to the fact that a considerably higher proportion of women's income than men's is used for nutrition and basic necessities. Thus, if men's incomes rise at the expense of women's resources, as many studies have indicated, an increase in household income will not necessarily lead to improvements in health and nutrition. Changes in land use that increase household income but reduce women's economic status can be detrimental to the welfare of both women and children. Consequently, it is important that the design of government extension programs reflect the interests of all household members.

Recent economic studies have improved our understanding of these problems. A traditional economics assumption following Nobel laureate Gary Becker has been that households cooperate to maximize effectively shared objectives: the "unitary household" model. But development economics research has found that households engage in extensive bargaining, sometimes to the point where higher incomes would be possible if husbands and wives could cooperate more extensively. First, households spend differently, depending on whether the wealth or income is contributed to the family or otherwise controlled by the wife or the husband. Apparently, providing resources to the household increases bargaining power over how they will be used, contrary to what would be expected in a unitary household. When men control income from cash crops after development leads to new marketing opportunities, the perverse result can be to increase men's already high bargaining power.

The differing use of funds affects not only adults but also the children. Again, the evidence is clear that in most contexts, a larger fraction of income provided and controlled by the wife tends to be used for children's health and education than that by husbands. Moreover, evidence is growing that agricultural households could earn more by reallocating inputs such as manure from husbands' to wives' plots, for example. Thus, gender inequality also leads to significant losses in efficiency. Further gains could be had by shifting from subsistence crops to cash crops on wives' plots, though given different preferences for how cash income would be used, this could turn out to be at the expense of food for the wife and children. For example, in a detailed study of Burkina Faso, Christopher Udry found that "plots controlled by women have significantly lower yields than similar plots within the household planted with the same crop in the same year, but controlled by men." His detailed data enabled him to clearly identify the difference as due to "significantly higher labor and fertilizer inputs per acre on plots controlled by men." Udry's estimates showed that "about six percent of output is lost due to the misallocation of variable factors across plots within the household." In addition to the obvious social justice concerns, this efficiency argument forms part of the economic case for supporting programs that empower rural women.[35]

Yet many government-sponsored programs effectively continue to exclude women, often because women lack collateral for loans or are barred from owning property or conducting financial transactions without their husbands' permission. Agricultural inputs and training are rarely provided to female applicants. Even efforts to reduce poverty through land reforms have been found to reduce female income and economic status because they distribute land titles only to male heads of household. Cultural and social barriers to women's integration into agricultural programs remain strong because, in many countries, women's income is perceived as a threat to men's authority. While men are taught new agricultural techniques to increase their productivity, women, if involved at all, are trained to perform low-productivity tasks that are considered compatible with their traditional roles, such as sewing, cooking, and basic hygiene. Women's components of development projects are frequently little more than welfare programs that fail to improve economic well-being. Furthermore, these projects tend to depend on the unpaid work of women, while men are remunerated for their efforts.

Although efforts to increase the income of women by providing direct access to credit and inputs have experienced considerable success, programs that work indirectly with women have frequently fallen short of their stated goals. Studies have found that projects are most likely to elicit the engagement of women when resources are placed directly under their control. Clearly, projects that depend on the unremunerated labor of women are likely to obtain only minimal support. Adoption of new crops and technologies will be more effective where patterns of production are consistent with the interests of female household members. Because the active participation of women is critical to agricultural prosperity, policy design should ensure that women benefit equally from development efforts (this is examined further in the case study at the end of this chapter).

9.5 The Microeconomics of Farmer Behavior and Agricultural Development

The Transition from Traditional Subsistence to Specialized Commercial Farming

For expository convenience, we can identify three broad stages in the evolution of agricultural production.[36] The first stage is the pure, low-productivity, mostly subsistence-level traditional (peasant) farm, still prevalent in Africa. The second stage is what might be called *diversified* or *mixed family agriculture*, where a small part, of the produce is grown for consumption and a significant part for sale to the commercial sector, as in much of Asia. The third stage represents the modern farm, exclusively engaged in high-productivity, specialized agriculture geared to the commercial market, as in developed countries, and often found in the highly urbanized developing countries.

Agricultural modernization in mixed-market developing economies may be described in terms of the gradual but sustained transition from subsistence to diversified and specialized production. But such a transition involves much more than reorganizing the structure of the farm economy or applying new agricultural technologies. Transforming traditional agriculture often requires, in addition to adapting the farm structure to meet the demand for increased production, profound changes affecting the entire social, political, and institutional structure of rural societies. Without such changes, agricultural development will either continue to lag greatly behind or, more likely, simply widen the already sizable gap between the few wealthy large landholders and the masses of impoverished tenant farmers, smallholders, and landless laborers.

We first consider the evolution of the agricultural system of a developing nation over time from a predominantly traditional, subsistence-level and small-scale peasant orientation to more diversified operations and eventually to the rise of fully commercial enterprises, though still often family based.

Subsistence Farming: Risk Aversion, Uncertainty, and Survival

On the classic traditional (peasant) subsistence farm, most output is produced for family consumption (although some may be sold or traded in local markets), and a few **staple foods** (usually including cassava, wheat, barley, sorghum, rice, potatoes, or corn) are the chief sources of nutrition. Output and productivity are low, and only the simplest traditional methods and tools are used. Capital investment is minimal; land and labor are the principal factors of production. The law of diminishing returns is in operation as more labor is applied to shrinking (or shifting) parcels of land. The failure of the rains, the appropriation of the land, and the appearance of the moneylender to collect

Staple food A main food consumed by a large portion of a country's population.

outstanding debts are the banes of the peasant's existence. Labor is under-employed for most of the year, although workers may be fully occupied at seasonal peak periods such as planting and harvest. The traditional farmer (peasant) usually cultivates only as much land as his family can manage without the need for hired labor, although many traditional farmers intermittently employ one or two landless laborers. Much of the cash income that is generated comes from nonfarm wage labor.[37]

In much of sub-Saharan Africa, agriculture is still largely in this subsistence stage, as it is in pockets in Asia and even Latin America. The Green Revolution has bypassed much of Africa. But in spite of the relative backwardness of production technologies and the misguided convictions of some foreigners who attribute the peasants' resistance to change as a sign of incompetence or irrationality, the fact remains that given the nature of the peasants' environment, the uncertainties that surround them, the need to meet minimum survival levels of output, and the rigid social institutions into which many peasants, but particularly women, are locked, most farmers do behave in an economically rational manner when confronted with alternative opportunities.

Some insight into the economics of subsistence agriculture is provided by the traditional two-factor neoclassical theory of production in which land (and perhaps capital) is fixed, labor is the only variable input, and profit is maximized. Specifically, the theory provides an economic rationale for the observed low productivity of traditional agriculture in the form of the law of diminishing marginal productivity.

Unfortunately, this theory does not satisfactorily explain why small-scale farmers are often resistant to technological innovation in farming techniques or to the introduction of new seeds or different cash crops. According to the standard theory, a rational income or profit-maximizing farm or firm will always choose a method of production that will increase output for a given cost (in this case, the available labor time) or lower costs for a given output level. But the theory is based on the crucial assumption that farmers possess "perfect knowledge" of all technological input-output relationships as well as current information about prevailing factor and product prices. This is the point at which the simple theory loses a good deal of its validity when applied to the environment of subsistence agriculture. Furthermore, when access to information is highly imperfect, the transaction costs of obtaining this information are usually very high. Given price uncertainty, traditional (peasant) farmers often face a wide range of possible prices rather than a single input price. Along with limited access to credit and insurance, such an environment is not conducive to the type of behavior posited by neoclassical theory and goes a long way toward explaining the actual risk-averse behavior of peasant farmers, including their caution in the use of purchased inputs such as fertilizer.[38]

Subsistence agriculture is thus a highly risky and uncertain venture. It is made even more so by the fact that human lives are at stake. In regions where farms are extremely small and cultivation is dependent on the uncertainties of variable rainfall, average output will be low, and in poor years, the peasant family will be exposed to the very real danger of starvation. In such circumstances, the main motivating force in the peasant's life may be the maximization, not of income, but of the family's chances of survival. Accordingly, when risk and uncertainty are high, small farmers may be very reluctant to shift from a traditional technology and crop pattern that over the years they have come to

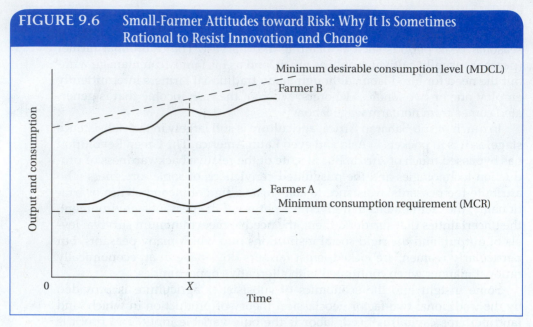

FIGURE 9.6   Small-Farmer Attitudes toward Risk: Why It Is Sometimes Rational to Resist Innovation and Change

know and understand to a new one that promises higher yields but may entail greater risks of crop failure. When sheer survival is at stake, it is more important to avoid a bad year (total crop failure) than to maximize the output in better years. Risk-avoiding traditional farmers are likely to prefer a technology of food production that combines a low *mean* per-hectare yield with low *variance* (fluctuations around the average) to alternative technologies and crops that may promise a higher mean yield but also present the risk of a greater variance.

Figure 9.6 provides a simple illustration of how attitudes toward risk among small farmers may militate against apparently economically justified innovations.[39] In the figure, levels of output and consumption are measured on the vertical axis and different points in time, on the horizontal axis, and two straight lines are drawn. The lower horizontal line measures the minimum consumption requirements (MCR) necessary for the farm family's physical survival. This may be taken as the starvation minimum fixed by nature. Any output below this level would be catastrophic for the peasant or subsistence farming family. The upper, positively sloped straight line represents the minimum level of food consumption that would be desirable, given the prevailing cultural or potential productivity factors affecting village consumption standards. It is assumed that this line rises over time.

Looking at Figure 9.6, we see that at time X, farmer A's output levels have been very close to the MCR. She is barely getting by and cannot take a chance of any crop failure. She will have a greater incentive to minimize risk than farmer B, whose output performance has been well above the minimum subsistence level and is close to the minimum desired consumption level (MDCL). Farmer B will therefore be more likely than farmer A to innovate and change. The result may be that farmer A remains in a self-perpetuating poverty trap.[40] Moreover, inequality is growing.

There is an alternative way to look at risk-aversion decisions of peasant farmers. In Figure 9.7, two curves portray hypothetical probabilities for crop yields. The higher curves (technique A) shows a production technology with a

FIGURE 9.7   Crop Yield Probability Densities of Two Different Farming Techniques

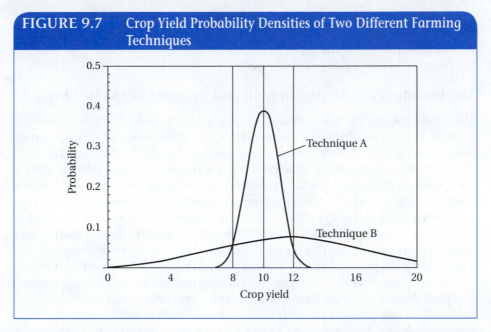

lower mean crop yield (10) than that of technique B (12), shown by the lower curve. But it also has a lower variance around that mean yield than technique B. Clearly, the chances of starving are much greater with technique B, so risk-averse peasant farmers would naturally choose technique A, the one with the lower mean yield.[41] Evidence is clear that farmers pay for "self-insurance" of this type with much lower average returns.[42]

Many programs to raise agricultural productivity among small farmers in Africa and elsewhere have suffered because of failure to provide adequate insurance (both financial credit and physical "buffer" stocks) against the risks of crop shortfalls, whether these risks are real or imagined. An understanding of the major role that risk and uncertainty play in the economics of subsistence agriculture would have prevented early and unfortunate characterizations of subsistence or traditional farmers as technologically backward, irrational producers with limited aspirations or just plain "lazy natives," as in the colonial stereotype. Moreover, in parts of Asia and Latin America where agriculture has performed poorly, a closer examination of why traditional (peasant) farmers have apparently not responded to an "obvious" economic opportunity will often reveal that (1) the landlord secured much if not all of the gain, (2) the moneylender captured the profits, (3) the government's "guaranteed" price was never paid, or (4) complementary inputs (fertilizers, pesticides, assured supplies of water, adequate nonusurious credit, etc.) were never made available or their use was otherwise more problematic than outsiders understood. In particular, when peasants have reason to be concerned about the risk of eviction or expropriation—whether by landlords or by the state—incentives for those who work the land to invest in it will be proportionately reduced.

Farmers will consider the expected value of the marginal product of any inputs they apply, such as fertilizer, which will be lowered in relation to the probability they place on expropriation. For example, if fertilizer lasts for two growing seasons but the peasant is sure her land will be expropriated as soon as someone with the power to do so sees that the land has already been fertilized, then too little fertilizer will be used from the social point of view, because the peasant will consider the benefits of the fertilizer as if it disappeared after just one season (while its price is not lowered). This type of effect has been confirmed by careful econometric evidence from China.[43]

The Economics of Sharecropping and Interlocking Factor Markets

The phenomenon of risk aversion among peasant farmers in the presence of high land inequality also helps explain the prevalence of sharecropping throughout much of Asia and parts of Latin America.[44] Although different types of relationships may arise between the owners of land and the people who work on them (e.g., the farmers could rent or act as wage laborers), sharecropping is widespread. Sharecropping occurs when a peasant farmer uses the landowner's farmland in exchange for a share of food output, such as half of the rice or wheat grown. The landlord's share may vary from less than a third to more than two-thirds of output, depending on local labor availability and the other inputs (such as credit, seeds, and tools) that the landlord provides.

The poor incentive structure of sharecropping lends itself to inefficiency. Alfred Marshall observed that the farmer was, in effect, paid only part, rather than all, of his marginal product and would rationally reduce work effort accordingly.[45] This effect can be seen graphically in Figure 9.8. Labor input is found along the x-axis, which may be interpreted as number of hours of work or of total effort; value of output per unit of labor is found along the y-axis. A farmer who owned his own farm would work until his value marginal product of labor (VMP$_L$) was equal to his alternative wage, or opportunity cost of labor, w^A, and so would put in an

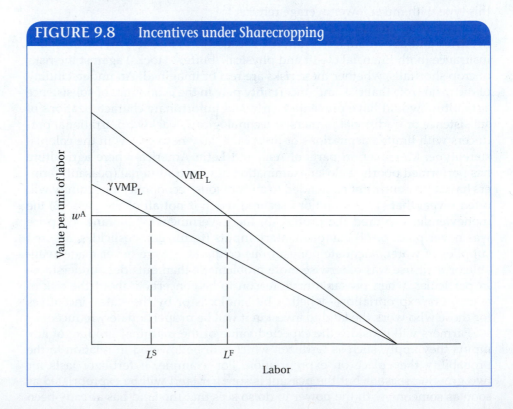

FIGURE 9.8   Incentives under Sharecropping

efficient amount of labor effort, L^F. However, a sharecropper receives only a fraction, γ, of his effort; for example, under 50–50 sharecropping, the sharecropper's share would be $\gamma = 0.5$. Thus, the sharecropper would receive only γ of his value marginal product, or γVMP_L. As a result, the sharecropper would have an incentive to put in an inefficiently low level of effort, L^S, as seen in Figure 9.8.

This view was challenged in the 1960s by Steven Cheung, who argued that profit-maximizing landlords would establish contracts requiring adequate work effort from the tenant as well as stipulating each party's share of the output. If, as Cheung argued, effort was not too difficult to monitor, then if one tenant failed to live up to his part of the bargain, he would be replaced by another tenant who was willing to work harder; as a result, sharecropping would be as efficient as any other contractual form. Cheung's theory is known as the *monitoring approach*, in contrast to the *Marshallian approach* to the analysis of sharecropping illustrated in Figure 9.8; Cheung argued that labor effort, L^F, would also obtain under sharecropping.[46]

The monitoring approach was popular for two decades, and it was difficult to test because of endogeneity. For example, only low-productivity people may choose to enter into sharecropping contracts. In fact, some scholars believe that landlords may offer tenants an option of either sharecropping or pure rental contracts precisely because higher-ability people more often choose pure rental arrangements: High-ability farmers are able to get the full value of their high marginal product, while this is not as attractive to lower-ability farmers. If landlords are not sure which farmers have high ability, they may find out by observing which ones choose the pure rental contract. The motivation may be to enable landlords to squeeze more profits out of the renters, charging higher effective rents for pure rental contracts than for sharecropping contracts—but not *too* high or even high-ability farmers would choose sharecropping. This approach is known as the *screening hypothesis* of sharecropping.[47]

However, Radwan Ali Shaban identified farmers who farmed plots that they owned and who also leased out additional farmland under a sharecropping contract. By comparing the *same* farmers' behavior under different contractual arrangements, Ali Shaban controlled for factors specific to individual farmers that cannot be easily observed. He found that farmers used fewer inputs and produced less output on the sharecropped land than on their own land, all else being equal. These results provide evidence that sharecropping is less efficient than farming one's own land, just as Marshall predicted.[48]

A final approach suggests that sharecropping is relatively efficient after all, in that it makes the best out of an inherently uncertain and risky situation for both parties.[49] If the landlord paid the tenant a straight wage, which would be efficient if the tenant always gave his full effort and it didn't cost the landlord anything to make sure of this, the tenant would have every incentive to accept the money and not work hard. If the tenant paid a straight rent for the land, he would face the appalling risk that there would be a particularly lean year, such as a drought, and there would not be enough food left after the rent was paid to prevent starvation. Thus, sharecropping represents a compromise between the risk to the landlord that the tenant will not do much work and the risk to the tenant that a fixed rent will in some years leave him no income. So even though sharecropping, with its poor work incentives, would be inefficient in a world of perfect certainty, in the real world, with inequality in land ownership as well as uncertainty, it is "as efficient as we can get." However, this arrangement is necessary only because of extreme inequality of land ownership. Farmers who own their own farms do not generally choose sharecropping contracts for themselves. As a result, the enormous efficiency loss, as seen in Figure 9.8, is not negated by this important explanation of why sharecropping arises.[50]

Where tenancy reform is well designed and enforced, giving sharecroppers a larger share of the produce and security of tenure on the land, the result can be not only higher income for the tenants but also greater overall efficiency. A clear example is the tenancy reform policy implemented in the Indian state of West Bengal in the late 1970s.[51] The explanation is clear from what we have just established: that a higher product share gives greater work effort incentives, and greater security of tenure gives greater investment incentives. Land reform that distributes ownership of "land to the tiller" can provide similar and superior improvements in incentives, if needed complementary inputs are provided.

More broadly, the economic and social framework in which sharecropping takes place is one of extraordinary social inequality and far-reaching market failure. When the peasant faces his landlord, he often faces not only the individual whom he must persuade to rent him productive land but at the same time his prospective employer, his loan officer, and even his ultimate customer for any crops he wishes to sell. Such conditions, an example of **interlocking factor markets**, provide the rural landlord with abundant sources of monopoly and monopsony power. Under some conditions—in particular, the availability of a perfectly elastic supply of tenants and the ability of the landlord to subdivide his land into as many plots as he chooses—the peasant is forced to his *reservation utility level*, or next-best income opportunity. (In practice, on one hand, peasants are sometimes prevented from learning about some of the alternatives available to them; on the other hand, subdivision may be restricted.) Interlocked-factor-market sharecropping does have the resource allocation advantage that it is in the landlord's interest to see to it that his sharecropper receives credit from the lowest-cost source. At the same time, the personal nature of interlinkage gives the dominant party far-ranging leverage and acts as a barrier to entry that restricts competition that might ultimately benefit the peasant. In this regard, as an observation applying to interlinkage and to other rural institutions, Pranab Bardhan and Christopher Udry make the important point that "the thin line between *understanding* an institution and *justifying* it is often blurred, particularly by careless interpreters of the theory."[52]

For many analysts, a study of interlinkage involving a dominant landlord often concludes that nothing short of land reform will reliably affect the tenant's welfare. We discuss land reform more fully later in the chapter.[53]

Interlocking factor markets
Factor markets whose supply functions are interdependent, frequently because different inputs are provided by the same suppliers who exercise monopolistic or oligopolistic control over resources.

The Transition to Mixed or Diversified Farming

It is neither realistic nor necessarily desirable to think of instantly transforming a traditional agrarian system that has prevailed for many generations into a highly specialized commercial farming system. Attempts to introduce cash crops indiscriminately in subsistence farms have often resulted in the peasants' loss of land to moneylenders or landlords. Subsistence living is merely substituted for subsistence production. For small farmers, exclusive reliance on cash crops can be even more precarious than pure subsistence agriculture because the risks of price fluctuations are added to the uncertainty of nature.

Diversified or **mixed farming** therefore represents a logical intermediate step in the transition from subsistence to specialized production. In this stage, the staple crop no longer dominates farm output, and new cash crops such as fruits, vegetables, coffee, tea, and pyrethrum are established, together with simple animal husbandry. These new activities can take up slack in farm workloads during times of the year when disguised unemployment is prevalent.

For example, if the staple crop occupies the land only during parts of the year, new crops can be introduced in the slack season to take advantage of both idle land and family labor. And where labor is in short supply during peak planting seasons, simple laborsaving devices (such as small tractors, mechanical seeders, or animal-operated steel plows) can be introduced to free labor for other farm activities. Finally, the use of better seeds, fertilizers, and simple irrigation to increase yields of staple crops such as wheat, maize, and rice can free part of the land for cash crop cultivation while ensuring an adequate supply of the staple food. The farm operator can thus have a marketable surplus, which she can sell to raise her family's consumption standards or invest in farm improvements. Diversified farming can also minimize the impact of staple crop failure and provide a security of income previously unavailable.

The success or failure of such efforts to transform traditional agriculture will depend not only on the farmer's ability and skill in raising his productivity but also, even more important, on the social, commercial, and institutional conditions under which he must function. Specifically, if he can have reasonable and reliable access to credit, fertilizer, water, crop information, and marketing facilities; if he receives a fair market price for his output; and if he can feel secure that he and his family will be the primary beneficiaries of any improvements, there is no reason to assume that the traditional farmer will not respond to economic incentives and new opportunities to improve his standard of living. Evidence from such diverse countries as Colombia, Mexico, Nigeria, Ghana, Kenya, India, Pakistan, Thailand, and the Philippines shows that under the proper conditions, small farmers are responsive to price incentives and economic opportunities and will make radical changes in what they produce and how they produce it.[54] Lack of innovation in agriculture, as noted earlier, is usually due not to poor motivation or fear of change but to inadequate or unprofitable opportunities. In Africa, lack of information is often a constraint, but farmers learn from each other when valuable new crops and techniques are introduced locally. This facilitates dissemination of new technologies, as a study in Ghana revealed (see Box 9.2).

> **Diversified (mixed) farming** The production of both staple crops and cash crops and simple animal husbandry typical of the first stage in the transition from subsistence to specialized farming.

From Divergence to Specialization: Modern Commercial Farming

The specialized farm represents the final and most advanced stage of individual holding in a mixed market economy. It is the most prevalent type of farming in advanced industrial nations. It has evolved in response to and parallel with development in other areas of the national economy. General rises in living standards, biological and technical progress, and the expansion of national and international markets have provided the main impetus for its emergence and growth.

BOX 9.2 FINDINGS   Learning about Farming: The Diffusion of Pineapple Growing in Ghana

Agricultural experts cannot train millions of farmers—who sometimes also know constraints and opportunities that trainers do not. So farmers must partly learn new products and techniques from each other, and social learning is very difficult to identify. But Timothy Conley and Christopher Udry collected detailed information from farmers in the Akwapim South district of Ghana, asking them whom they know and talk to about farming, to better understand and test for "social learning in the diffusion of a new agricultural technology."

In Akwapim South, farmers traditionally grew maize and cassava, which they sold to urban consumers. But a transformation was under way toward farmers cultivating pineapples for export to Europe. Doing so required intensive fertilizer use—adoption of a new technology. Pineapple technologies were spreading geographically through the region. But a farmer might adopt a new technology soon after his neighbor, not from learning, but just because neighbors tend to be similar in other ways. Conley and Udry collected information on geography, soil and agronomics, credit, and family relationships to control for similarities that previous studies had been unable to observe. Then the researchers tested "whether farmers adjust their inputs to align with those of their information neighbors who were surprisingly successful in previous periods," and they found robust evidence to support this idea: "We find strong effects of news about input productivity in the information neighborhood of a farmer on his innovations in input use."

Data on inputs used and output harvested by each farmer let Conley and Udry infer the information conveyed by each "experiment" with pineapples and fertilizer by any of their respondents. They utilize data on "information flow between farmers to trace the impact of the information revealed by each experiment on the future input decisions of other farmers who are in the information neighborhood of the cultivator who conducted the experiment."

Important findings include the following:

- A farmer is "more likely to change his fertilizer use after his information neighbors who use similar amounts of fertilizer achieve lower than expected profits."

- A farmer "increases (decreases) his use of fertilizer after his information neighbors achieve unexpectedly high profits when using more (less) fertilizer than he did."

- A farmer's "responsiveness to news about the productivity of fertilizer in his information neighborhood is much greater if he has only recently begun cultivating pineapple."

- A farmer "responds more to news about the productivity of fertilizer on plots cultivated by veteran farmers and farmers with wealth similar to his."

Since novice farmers "are most responsive to news in their information neighborhoods," the results probably reflect learning. This conclusion is reinforced because there is no evidence of learning when the authors' research methods are "applied to a known maize-cassava technology." Sometimes a neighbor's surprising lower profit leads a farmer to make the wrong decision by lowering his own fertilizer use. But this is also part of the ongoing learning process.

The evidence implies that information "has value in these villages, as do the network connections through which that information flows." But forming and maintaining a connection has real costs; and such costs—as well as benefits—generally depend on factors such as religion, gender, wealth, or family ties. This implies that "measurement of the extent of social learning is not sufficient for adequate evaluation of policy regarding the diffusion of technology." Moreover, the paper highlights that network connections are endogenous; this is a very important consideration for policy analysis.

Source: Based on Timothy G. Conley and Christopher R. Udry, "Learning about a new technology: Pineapple in Ghana," *American Economic Review* 100 (2010): 35–69. Copyright © 2010 by the American Economic Association. Used with permission.

In **specialized farming**, the provision of food for the family with some marketable surplus is no longer the basic goal. Instead, pure commercial profit becomes the criterion of success, and maximum per-hectare yields derived from synthetic (irrigation, fertilizer, pesticides, hybrid seeds, etc.) and natural resources become the object of farm activity. Production, in short, is entirely for the market. Economic concepts such as fixed and variable costs, saving, investment and rates of return, optimal factor combinations, maximum production possibilities, market prices, and price supports take on quantitative and qualitative significance. The emphasis in resource utilization is on capital formation, technological progress, and scientific research and development in stimulating higher levels of output and productivity.

Specialized farms vary in both size and function. They range from intensively cultivated fruit and vegetable farms to the vast wheat and corn fields of North America. In most cases, sophisticated laborsaving mechanical equipment, ranging from huge tractors and combine harvesters to airborne spraying techniques, permits a single family to cultivate many thousands of hectares of land.

The common features of all specialized farms, therefore, are their emphasis on the cultivation of one particular crop, their use of capital-intensive and in many cases laborsaving techniques of production, and their reliance on economies of scale to reduce unit costs and maximize profits. In some ways, specialized farming is no different in concept or operation from large industrial enterprises. In fact, some of the largest specialized farming operations in both the developed and the less developed nations are owned and managed by large, multinational, corporate agribusiness enterprises. Large, modern farms are now found in many middle-income countries such as Brazil. But for smallholder farmers where subsistence farming predominates, strategies for dealing with risk, and in some cases overcoming coordination failures in specialization as described in Chapter 4, remain prerequisites for successful specialization.

Although we can find all three types of farms—subsistence, mixed, and specialized commercial—coexisting in almost all developing countries at any given time, for the majority of low-income countries, particularly in Africa, contemporary agricultural systems are still dominated by small-scale mixed and even subsistence-based family farms. The further transition to a preponderance of commercial enterprises may be difficult to achieve, depending as it does on the solution to many other short- and intermediate-term problems. But there is wide agreement that the improvement of small- and medium-scale mixed farming practices that will not only raise farm incomes and average yields but, if labor-intensive, also effectively absorb underutilized rural labor offers the major immediate avenue toward the achievement of real people-oriented rural development.

Specialized farming The final and most advanced stage of the evolution of agricultural production in which farm output is produced wholly for the market.

9.6 Core Requirements of a Strategy of Agricultural and Rural Development

If the major objective of agricultural and rural development in developing nations is the progressive improvement in rural levels of living achieved primarily through increases in small-farm incomes, output, and productivity, along with genuine food security, it is important to identify the principal sources of agricultural progress and the basic conditions essential to its achievement.

Improving Small-Scale Agriculture

Technology and Innovation   In most developing countries, new agricultural technologies and innovations in farm practices are preconditions for sustained improvements in levels of output and productivity. In many parts of Africa, however, increased output in earlier years was achieved without the need for new technology simply by extending cultivation into unused but potentially productive lands. Almost all of these opportunities have by now been exploited, and there is little scope for further significant or sustainable expansion.

Two major sources of technological innovation can increase farm yields. Unfortunately, both have somewhat problematic implications for agricultural development. The first is the introduction of mechanized agriculture to replace human labor. The introduction of laborsaving machinery can have a dramatic effect on the volume of output per worker, especially where land is extensively cultivated and labor is scarce. For example, one man operating a huge combine harvester can accomplish in a single hour what would require hundreds of workers using traditional methods.

But in the rural areas of many developing nations, where land parcels are small, capital is scarce, and labor is abundant, the introduction of heavily mechanized techniques is often ill suited to the physical environment and has the effect of creating more rural unemployment without necessarily lowering per-unit costs of food production.[55] Importation of such machinery can require large tracts of land (and thus the consolidation of small holdings) and tends to exacerbate the already serious problems of rural poverty and underemployment. And if mechanized techniques exclude women, the male-female productivity gap could widen further, with serious repercussions.[56]

Biological (hybrid seeds and biotechnology), water control (irrigation), and chemical (fertilizer, pesticides, insecticides, etc.) innovations—the second major source—are not without their own problems. They are land-augmenting; that is, they improve the quality of existing land by raising yields per hectare. Only indirectly do they increase output per worker. Improved seeds; advanced techniques of irrigation and crop rotation; the increasing use of fertilizers, pesticides, and herbicides; and new developments in veterinary medicine and animal nutrition represent major scientific advances in modern agriculture. These measures are often technologically **scale-neutral**; theoretically, they can be applied equally effectively on large and small farms. They do not necessarily require large capital inputs or mechanized equipment. They are therefore particularly well suited for tropical and subtropical regions, and offer enormous potential for raising agricultural output in developing nations and have been highly effective in doing so, particularly in Asia. Again, the major challenge is to extend this success to sub-Saharan Africa, which will in some cases need new innovations. There are also important environmental challenges in many parts of the developing world, including risks posed by a falling water table, salination, and other resource degradation for which well-designed government policy and in some cases restored collective action mechanisms are usually necessary.

Scale-neutral Unaffected by size; applied to technological progress that can lead to the achievement of higher output levels irrespective of the size (scale) of a firm or farm.

Institutional and Pricing Policies: Providing the Necessary Economic Incentives

Unfortunately, although the green revolution varieties of wheat, corn, and rice, together with needed irrigation and chemicals, are scale-neutral and thus offer the potential for continued small-farm progress, the social institutions and government economic policies that accompany their introduction into the rural economy are often *not* scale-neutral.[57] On the contrary, they often merely serve the needs and vested interests of the wealthy landowners. Because the new hybrid seeds require access to complementary inputs such as irrigation, fertilizer, insecticides, credit, and agricultural extension services, if these are provided only to a small minority of large landowners, one impact of the green revolution can be (as in parts of South Asia and Mexico) the further impoverishment of many peasants. Large landowners, with their disproportionate access to these complementary inputs and support services, are able to gain a competitive advantage over smallholders and eventually drive them out of the market. Large-scale farmers obtain access to low-interest government credit, while smallholders are forced to turn to moneylenders. The result has all too often been the further widening of the gap between rich and poor and the increased consolidation of agricultural land in the hands of a very few so-called progressive farmers. A developmental innovation with great potential for alleviating rural poverty and raising agricultural output can thus turn out to be antidevelopmental if public policies and social institutions militate against the active participation of the small farmer in the evolving agrarian structure.[58]

Another critical area of many past and some continued failures in government policies relates to the pricing of agricultural commodities, especially food grains and other staples produced for local markets. Many governments in developing nations, in their headlong pursuit of rapid industrial and urban development, maintained low agricultural prices in an attempt to provide cheap food for the urban modern sector. Farmers were paid prices below either world competitive or free-market internal prices. The relative internal price ratio between food and manufactured goods (the domestic terms of trade) thus turned against farmers and in favor of urban manufacturers. With farm prices so low—in some cases below the costs of production—there was no incentive for farmers to expand output or invest in new productivity-raising technology. As a result, local food supplies continually fell short of demand, and many developing nations, especially in sub-Saharan Africa, that were once self-sufficient in food production had to import food.

Many development economists therefore argue that if governments are to promote further increases in agricultural production that make a larger impact on poverty reduction through Green Revolution technologies, they must make not only the appropriate institutional and credit market adjustments but also continued progress to provide incentives for small and medium-size farmers by implementing pricing policies that truly reflect internal market conditions.[59]

Adapting to New Opportunities and New Constraints

As a route out of poverty and toward genuine rural development, enhanced cereal productivity (the classic Green Revolution characteristic) represents only a small part of the agricultural opportunities. The best opportunities for sales to growing urban areas are generally found in higher value-added activities, particularly horticulture (fruits, vegetables, and cut flowers) and aquaculture. These products, along with organic and perhaps Fair Trade versions of some otherwise traditional developing country exports such as coffee and spices, also provide good opportunities for higher-value exports. But small farmers will need special organization and assistance to take advantage of new opportunities. As the 2008 *World Development Report* concludes, "Smallholders can bargain better as a group than as individuals. So a high priority is to facilitate collective action through producer organizations to reach scale in marketing and bargain for better prices."[60] Otherwise, the risk is large that these developments will benefit mainly the larger farmers.

An opportunity—which also poses a potential threat—is the growing activity of foreign investment in developing country farmland, also known as *land grabbing*. An IFPRI report estimated that from 2006 to 2009, 15 to 20 million hectares of developing country farmland had been transferred. An example is the 2008 deal of South Korea to acquire 690,000 hectares in Sudan. Foreign ownership and long-term leasing of farmland can lead to some better-paying job creation, training, access to better techniques, and new export markets. But there is a real threat that many farmers will lose access to their traditional rights to use land, that there may be net job losses, and that water shortages and environmental degradation of adjacent lands may accelerate, at least without adequate oversight. These and other potential risks are greater when there are governance shortcomings, including corruption, and when women and other poor and vulnerable claimants are not empowered. This is a topic that will be followed closely.[61]

One of the biggest constraints looking ahead is the looming environmental problems driven by global warming and climate change, which are expected to most negatively affect sub-Saharan Africa and South Asia. Smaller and poorer farmers are likely to be affected severely, because of their lower access to irrigation and other inputs and generally lesser capacity to adapt—although, ironically, with their smaller use of irrigation and different crop mix, their absolute income declines may be less than those of richer farmers. Although the majority of global warming problems are caused by developed countries, to the extent that cultivated areas in developing countries continue to increase by means of eliminating remaining forested areas, climate change problems will only worsen. This "agricultural extensification," not only in forests but also in drier and other sensitive lands, further brings the risk of local soil degradation and lost environmental services such as maintaining water and air quality. The losses of wetlands and of biodiversity also lead to substantial national (as well as international) costs. Moreover, intensification of agriculture has often brought with it the misuse of agrochemicals, which can entail large human and ecosystem costs.[62] We return to these problems of environmental sustainability in the next chapter.

Conditions for Rural Development

We can draw three conclusions regarding the necessary conditions for the realization of a people-oriented agricultural and rural development strategy.[63]

Land Reform

> *Conclusion 1: Farm structures and land tenure patterns must be adapted to the dual objectives of increasing food production and promoting a wider distribution of the benefits of agrarian progress, allowing further progress against poverty.*

Agricultural and rural development that benefits the poor can succeed only through a joint effort by the government and *all* farmers, not just the large farmers. A first step in any such effort, especially in Latin America and Asia, is the provision of secured tenure rights to the individual farmer. The small farm family's attachment to their land is profound. It is closely bound up with their innermost sense of self-esteem and freedom from coercion. When they are driven off their land or they are gradually impoverished through accumulated debts, not only is their material well-being damaged, but so is their sense of self-worth.

It is for these humane reasons as well as for reasons of higher agricultural output and the simultaneous achievement of both greater efficiency and more equity that **land reform** is often proposed as a necessary first condition for agricultural development in many developing countries. In most countries, the highly unequal structure of land ownership is a key determinant of the existing highly inequitable distribution of rural income and wealth. It is also the basis for the character of agricultural development. When land is very unevenly distributed, in quality as well as in quantity, rural peasants can have little hope for economic advancement through agriculture.

Land reform usually entails a redistribution of the rights of ownership or use of land away from large landowners in favor of cultivators with very limited or no landholdings. It can take many forms: the transfer of ownership to tenants who already work the land to create family farms (Japan, South Korea, Taiwan); transfer of land from large estates to small farms or rural cooperatives (Mexico); or the appropriation of large estates for new settlement (Kenya). All go under the heading of "land reform" and are designed to fulfill one central function: the transfer of land ownership or control directly or indirectly to the people who actually work the land. Tenancy reform as in West Bengal can also yield favorable efficiency and distributional benefits.

There is widespread agreement among economists and other development specialists on the need for land reform. Inequality is increasing in Africa. The Economic Commission for Latin America (ECLA) has repeatedly identified land reform as a necessary precondition for poverty-reducing agricultural and rural progress. A Food and Agriculture Organization (FAO) report concluded that in many developing regions, land reform remains a prerequisite for development. The report argued that such reform was more urgent today than ever before, primarily because (1) income inequalities and unemployment in rural areas have worsened, (2) rapid population growth threatens to exacerbate existing inequalities, and (3) recent and potential technological breakthroughs in agriculture (the Green Revolution) can be exploited primarily by large and powerful rural landholders and hence can result in an increase in their power, wealth, and capacity to resist future reform.[64] Finally, as noted earlier, from a strict view of economic efficiency and growth, there is ample empirical evidence that land redistribution not only increases rural employment and raises rural incomes but also leads to greater agricultural production and more efficient resource utilization. Significant though often limited land reforms have already been implemented in many countries, but some countries have still seen little reform.

Unfortunately, very small or landless farmers cannot directly purchase land from the big landowners because of market failures. Credit markets do not function well enough to provide a potentially efficient family farmer with

Land reform A deliberate attempt to reorganize and transform agrarian systems with the intention of fostering a more equal distribution of agricultural incomes and facilitating rural development.

a loan; even if they did, the price of *latifundio* and other estate and plantation land is too high because land ownership confers many benefits beyond the income from farming activities, such as disproportionate political influence.

If programs of land reform can be legislated and effectively implemented by the government, the basis for improved output levels and higher standards of living for rural peasants will be established. Unfortunately, many land reform efforts have failed because governments (especially those in Latin America) bowed to political pressures from powerful landowning groups and failed to implement the intended reforms.[65] But even an egalitarian land reform program alone is no guarantee of successful agricultural and rural development.[66] This leads to our second conclusion.

Supportive Policies

Conclusion 2: The full benefits of small-scale agricultural development cannot be realized unless government support systems are created that provide the necessary incentives, economic opportunities, and access to needed credit and inputs to enable small cultivators to expand their output and raise their productivity.

Though land reform is essential in many parts of Asia and Latin America, it is likely to be ineffective and perhaps even counterproductive unless there are corresponding changes in rural institutions that control production (e.g., banks, moneylenders, seed and fertilizer distributors), in supporting government aid services (e.g., technical and educational extension services, public credit agencies, storage and marketing facilities, rural transport and feeder roads), and in government pricing policies with regard to both inputs (e.g., removing factor price distortions) and outputs (ensuring market-value prices for farmers). Even where land reform is less necessary but where productivity and incomes are low (as in parts of Africa and Southeast Asia), this broad network of external support services, along with appropriate governmental pricing policies related to both farm inputs and outputs, is an essential condition for sustained agricultural progress.[67]

Integrated Development Objectives

Conclusion 3: Rural development, though dependent primarily on small-farmer agricultural progress, implies much more. It encompasses (a) efforts to raise both farm and nonfarm rural real incomes through job creation, rural industrialization, and other nonfarm opportunities and the increased provision of education, health and nutrition, housing, and a variety of related social and welfare services; (b) a decreasing inequality in the distribution of rural incomes and a lessening of urban-rural imbalances in incomes and economic opportunities; (c) successful attention to the need for environmental sustainability—limiting the extension of farmland into remaining forests and other fragile areas, promoting conservation, and preventing the harmful misuse of agrochemicals and other inputs; and (d) the capacity of the rural sector to sustain and accelerate the pace of these improvements over time.

The achievement of these four objectives is vital to national development. More than half of the population of the developing world is still located in rural areas. By restoring a proper balance between urban and rural economic opportunities and by creating the conditions for broad popular participation in national development efforts and rewards, developing nations will have taken a giant step toward the realization of the true meaning of development.

The Need to Improve Agricultural Extension for Women Farmers: Kenya

As noted in Chapter 5, absolute poverty is disproportionately concentrated among women, in rural areas, and in the agricultural sector. Improvements in the productivity and incomes of women farmers are therefore key to a strategy for poverty reduction. The role of women in agriculture is particularly important in sub-Saharan Africa. But this is also the region that has benefited least from the Green Revolution of high-yielding crop varieties and other modern farming practices that have had such a large productivity impact in many parts of Asia over the past half-century.

The crucial importance of a solid agricultural extension program for successful rural development and increased yields has been appreciated by development specialists for decades. Support for agricultural extension has played a central role in the activities of most multilateral and bilateral development agencies. Historically, agricultural extension programs have played a vital development role in the United States, one of the world's great agricultural productivity success stories.

Traditionally, agricultural extension programs in developing countries were aimed almost exclusively at training men, even though women do most of the agricultural work. In sub-Saharan Africa, women are responsible for well over two-thirds of staple food production. They are also active in growing and marketing cash crops, in food processing, and in animal husbandry. But women's roles have expanded in recent years as men have increasingly migrated to urban areas and taken nonagricultural jobs. Where men and women both do agricultural work, there still tends to be a gender-based division of labor. As a result, techniques relevant to the work of men are often not relevant to the work of women. Where they are relevant, men in the region have, for various reasons, tended to pass on to their wives ("trickle across") surprisingly little of what they have learned.

The focus on training men has generally been more by default than by design. For example, training has been copied from developed countries like the United States, where men do the majority of agricultural work. There may be religious or cultural constraints on men training women, and male extension agents may simply be more comfortable talking to men. A World Bank study showed that most male African extension agents have perceived women as "wives of farmers" rather than as farmers in their own right. And almost all extension agents have been male. Female agents must be trained. A major problem is the segregation and exclusion of women in large parts of Africa and Asia.

The success of women in agriculture in sub-Saharan Africa is at the very core of prospects for genuine development and poverty reduction. But the agricultural extension program response to the problem has been slow. And in some countries, program design is said to reflect a bias against providing women with too much independence.

One important strategy of the past 30 years has been to make use of radio, audiotapes, television, videotapes, DVDs, and more recently SMS (texting). Women may listen to or watch the materials in groups in homes or village centers. Katrin Saito and her colleagues reported that female farmers question extension agents in Ghana about subjects they have heard discussed on the radio.

Agricultural extension programs for women are interconnected with a number of other important rural development and women in development issues. Five key issues are the following:

1. *Human capital.* Women have less education than men on average in most rural developing areas. The bias in agricultural extension programs may in some part be a bias to train the more educated spouse, but the practice has also exacerbated this relative deficiency.

2. *Appropriate technology.* Because women tend to be involved in different farm activities than men, they will often have different technology requirements. Most technology development has been focused on activities of men.

3. *Land reform and agrarian design.* On average, women farm on much smaller, more fragmented plots than men; are less likely to have secure ownership; and often cultivate less fertile soil. This distribution is likely to be inefficient as well as distributionally inequitable.

4. *Credit.* Women have little access, if any, to financial credit, a key input in efficient agriculture.

5. *Work requirements.* Many women who work as many or more hours per day as men in agricultural pursuits also have to perform several hours of domestic work that men do not do. The workday of a poor woman farmer in Africa has been estimated at 16 to 19 hours. The attention mothers can give to their children is limited by long agricultural working hours. The implication may be that women should receive an even higher priority for technical education and technology development and access.

As Rekha Mehra has noted, one intent of structural adjustment programs in many African countries has been to encourage the shift to exportable cash crops. But these are the crops over which men tend to exercise control. A woman's profit share after working with these crops may be as little as 5%. But she is still responsible for growing consumption crops and feeding her children. Mehra concludes that structural adjustment programs tend to place even more time requirements on women already burdened with 16-hour workdays. The irony is that as the husband controls the cash, his "say" in the family may actually *increase* as a result.

Removal of agricultural price controls in Africa, allowing the prices that farmers receive for their crops to move toward world market levels, has provided more accurate price signals to farmers and encouraged a switch to more economically productive crops. But an IFPRI study showed that after diversification to commercial crops, Kenyan women still try to grow the same amount of consumption crops. Thus, more is needed than price adjustments featured under structural adjustment programs; reform must address structural problems faced by women that will prevent them from responding to price signals efficiently. A good example is the larger profit share taken by the husband and often not shared with his wife or wives.

None of these problems is limited to Africa. For example, Carmen Diana Deere, in a review of 13 Latin American agrarian reform experiences, found that most have benefited only men. This was mostly because farmers were thought of as men and the reforms were designed to target only men as beneficiaries. Her review found that women benefit only in the rare instances when their well-being is a specific objective of the reform and rural women are made an explicit part of the design of programs from the outset.

Taken as a whole, these points show why women farmers need the help of extension programs. It is also efficient to do this because of an application of the law of diminishing returns to training for men. The evidence suggests that the trickle-across theory—that trained husbands will in turn train their wives—all too rarely occurs in practice, at least in sub-Saharan Africa.

In Kenya, the ministry of agriculture operates a national extension system (NES) in concert with its agricultural research efforts. Before 1983, the NES worked almost exclusively with male farmers, while a separate "home economics branch" advised women on household and cottage industry management and domestic hygiene, but only peripherally on farming matters. Research by the Institute of Development Studies in Nairobi and other agencies confirmed that extension programs were much more likely to have reached men than women farmers. In 1983, Kenya's training and visit (T&V) system was established with the express purpose of training women as well as men in efficient agricultural practices. The case provides an example of the necessary ingredients of progress and also of how very much remains to be accomplished.

The design of the T&V system is based on providing "technical messages" to selected "contact farmers," who are regularly visited on their farms.

Unfortunately, resources are insufficient to reach all farmers, and even if the T&V system did try to reach all farmers, the quality of training would be poor. As a result, only 10% of all farmers are chosen to adopt advice brought to them in these messages and then to help spread this new technical knowledge by persuading other farmers in the villages to adopt them as well. A number of "follower farmers" are expected to attend meetings with T&V officials on the contact farmer's land. In this way, it is hoped that technical "diffusion" is maximized in a cost-effective manner. The selection process is vital. Farmers must be selected who are capable, likely to diligently follow through on new information, and locally respected so as to encourage emulation. In choosing contact farmers, T&V officials meet with farmers and consult with local communities and their leaders. In recent years, T&V outreach has focused more on working with traditional community farmer self-help groups, which can provide greater flexibility, better diffusion, and group reinforcement.

At first, messages focused on procedures offering the prospect of significant productivity gains but not requiring cash expenditure, such as ground preparation, spacing, seed varieties, and pruning. The messages being diffused in any one month are linked to farm activities under way in the annual crop cycle, such as planting or harvesting the crops being cultivated at any given point in the course of the year. The training process builds step by step: Simpler messages are imparted in early stages, and more complex messages, later in the program. Moreover, only after farmers see results from this initial advice and so come to trust the T&V messages, are measures requiring modest cash outlays introduced, such as fertilizer use and crop spraying. In a later stage, measures requiring purchase of capital goods may be introduced. Increasing numbers of women function officially as contact farmers. Even more serve unofficially in this role, as their husbands farm only part time or not at all.

The messages of the T&V program, ideally, are supposed to be transmitted in both directions. T&V agents are supposed to gather information about how well previous advice has worked in practice and about continued problems in order to guide research efforts. This is in the spirit of the often touted but seldom fulfilled development participation ideal.

T&V-type programs received substantial encouragement and financial support from the World Bank from the mid-1970s through the 1990s. But in most countries, performance was disappointing.

In 1997, Vishva Bindlish and Robert Evenson reported that T&V-type extension programs operated in more than 30 countries in sub-Saharan Africa. They concluded from their statistical evidence that the experience of "Kenya and Burkina Faso shows that T&V management enhances the effectiveness of extension and that such programs support agricultural growth and produce high returns on investments." They found that "areas served by extension have higher yields and that within these areas the highest yields are achieved by farmers who participate directly in extension activities. As a result, extension helps to close the gap between the yields attainable with existing technologies and those actually realized by farmers." But they found that while this makes improvements in the short run, there are limits to what the program can achieve without "the development of improved technologies that are relevant to local conditions."

A study by Robert Evenson and Germano Mwabu found that the impact of T&V in Kenya on productivity was positive but, interestingly, strongest among farmers of highest and lowest ability (measured by the portion of productivity unexplained by the use of farm inputs). They hypothesized that high ability overcame diminishing returns to inputs. Perhaps extension is complementary with high (unobserved) management ability. But the relatively high impact on the lower-ability farmers is noteworthy, even if data drawing conclusions about possible impacts such as on poverty are not available.

Economic advancement of women farmers is also important for promoting environmentally sustainable development. In addition to their responsibility for agriculture, especially on more marginal and often ecologically fragile lands, women have a customary role in traditional societies as the guardians of natural resources such as the water supply. This is also an important domain for agricultural extension work with women. In Kenya, the T&V system is not yet strongly involved in environmental problems.

Christina Gladwin and Della McMillan argue that much more must be done; for example, women should be consulted at the design stage of technology development, extension specialists should receive training on how to approach a male farmer about training his wife or wives, and governments should target funds to women's organizations and clubs.

Another shortcoming of the T&V system is that it has made too little progress in the field of women's credit. A study by Kathleen Staudt found that of 84 female farm managers interviewed in the Kakamega District in Kenya's Western Province, only one knew about the credit program, and no female manager had received any credit. Informal indications are that this is the area that has improved least over the subsequent years. But rural credit, often run by local NGOs, has recently been expanding in Kenya at a rapid rate that has surprised many long-term observers.

The strategy of involving women in public agriculture initiatives has shown some results in environment and credit as well as agricultural productivity. For example, the United Nations Population Fund reports that "women are now the principal participants in Kenya's National Soil Conservation Program. Since the mid-1980s, women have terraced more than 360,000 small farms, or 40 per cent of the country's total. Rural collectives, run by women, are now getting bank loans and agricultural extension services tailored to their specific needs and interests."

The Women in Development Service of the FAO reports that "in Kenya, following a national information campaign targeted at women under a National Extension Project, yields of corn increased by 28 percent, beans by 80 percent and potatoes by 84 percent." The way forward also includes a greater emphasis on more general knowledge. The FAO also reports on a study in Kenya that showed that farm "yields among rural women could be increased by 24 percent if all women farmers completed primary school."

Nevertheless, the agricultural extension program in Kenya has remained weak by international standards. The World Bank audited its programs in this field in 1999 and found it severely wanting in many respects, including low cost-effectiveness. The audit called for more efficient targeting of extension services where the impact is likely to be greatest, using improved information systems, and empowering farmer clients by giving them a greater voice in the design of the services. The World Bank also called for more cost recovery, but this is likely to prove controversial. Kenya eliminated user fees on primary education in 2002, making it at least nominally free for all, despite 1980s-era encouragement by the World Bank and other agencies to seek "cost recovery" from impoverished parents of primary pupils. As a vital part of poverty alleviation, cost recovery from impoverished women farmers is a dubious strategy. It may also be noted that structural adjustment in Kenya is cited by other critics as a cause of declining T&V budgets in the late 1980s and 1990s, severely crippling the capacities of this program.

In Kenya and elsewhere in sub-Saharan Africa, public extension programs have also been supplemented in recent years by a growing presence of nongovernmental organizations (see Chapter 11). For example, in western Kenya, the NGO Africa Now is actively recruiting and training farmers to participate in beekeeping as an alternative means of income generation. Broad participation of many civil society actors with diverse knowledge bases and connections with various ethnic and other social groupings is essential to success in an ecologically and socially diverse region such as sub-Saharan Africa.

Regarding government extension, a World Bank evaluation concluded that "progress on gender issues has been mixed. The earlier bias against women farmers has been rectified, but some bias persists in the selection of contact farmers. The proportion of female field-extension agents has remained largely unchanged since 1982." Though a better performance than many African and Asian countries and than Kenya exhibited in the past, it leaves much to be desired. Real progress has been made, but there is a pressing need for systematic follow-up and expansion.

A hopeful sign is that in decentralizing extension to more local levels, opportunities for active participation are increasing. Kenya's National Agricultural and Livestock Program has established stakeholder forums to decide on extension service priorities at the district and subdistrict levels, in which farmers are to be given a substantial say. But it is too early

to determine how much more responsive the new system will be to the needs of women farmers or whether the long-run impact will be greater than past efforts.

In another development, Esther Duflo, Michael Kremer, and Jonathan Robinson presented intriguing evidence, from the Busia district in Kenya, that farmers also have a "commitment problem" in using returns from produce sales to purchase fertilizer for next season. Although still at an early stage, this pioneering research may open up new avenues for more effective agricultural program design.

But the role of women is strengthening throughout Kenya. Thousands of women are taking part in the Green Belt Movement (GBM), established in 1977 by the National Council of Women in Kenya at the behest of the visionary leader Wangari Maathai. Its simple objective, in Maathai's words, is to "halt desertification by encouraging tree planting and soil and water conservation in rural communities." The GBM also works to promote sustainable development and poverty alleviation in parallel projects. Although the program is run through the NGO or citizen sector, seedlings are provided by the government at low prices, and GBM volunteers receive advice and support from government forestry officials. For her work in supporting sustainable agriculture and forestry that benefits women and children, Maathai was awarded the 2004 Nobel Prize for Peace.

The GBM emphasizes grassroots participation and self-help and strives to educate people on the link between deforestation, erosion, poor soil quality, and subsequent low crop yields. With the help of outside funding, women are paid to work at about 1,000 nurseries. Seedlings grown at these nurseries are given to small farmers, schools, and churches, which have planted tens of millions of trees. The estimated survival rate is 70 to 80%. The GBM has had striking success in scalability, that is, bringing the model throughout Kenya and then disseminating it widely in Africa. This success was noted by the Nobel committee when awarding the prize to Maathai. ■

Sources

Anderson, Jock R. "Agricultural Advisory Services, Background paper for 2008 World Development Report." Washington, D.C.: World Bank, 2007.

Bindlish, Vishva, and Robert E. Evenson. *Evaluation of the Performance of T&V Extension in Kenya.* Washington, D.C.: World Bank, 1994.

———. "The impact of T&V extension in Africa: The experience of Kenya and Burkina Faso." *World Bank Research Observer* 12 (1997): 183–201.

Davison, Jean, ed. *Agriculture, Women, and Land: The African Experience.* Boulder, Colo.: Westview Press, 1989.

Deere, Carmen Diana. "The division of labor by sex in agriculture: A Peruvian case study." *Economic Development and Cultural Change* 30 (1982): 795–781.

———. "Rural women and state policy: The Latin American agrarian reform experience." *World Development* 13 (1985): 1037–1053.

Due, Jean M., and Christina H. Gladwin. "Impacts of structural adjustment programs on African women farmers and female-headed households." *American Journal of Agricultural Economics* 73 (1991): 1431–1439.

Duflo, Esther, Michael Kremer, and Jonathan Robinson. "How high are rates of return to fertilizer? Evidence from field experiments in Kenya." *American Economic Review* 98 (May 2008): 482–488.

———. "Nudging farmers to use fertilizer: Theory and experimental evidence from Kenya." *American Economic Review* 101, No. 6 (October 2011): 2350–2390.

Evenson, Robert E., and Germano Mwabu. "The effect of agricultural extension on farm yields in Kenya." *African Development Review* 13 (2001): 1–23.

Gautam, Madhur. *Agricultural Extension: The Kenya Experience: An Impact Evaluation.* Washington, D.C.: World Bank, 2000.

Gladwin, Christina H., and Della McMillan. "Is a turnaround in Africa possible without helping African women to farm?" *Economic Development and Cultural Change* 37 (1989): 345–369.

Kennedy, Eileen T., and Bruce Cogill. *Income and Nutritional Effects of the Commercialization of Agriculture in Southwestern Kenya.* Research Report No. 63. Washington, D.C.: International Food Policy Research Institute, 1987.

Maathai, Wangari. "Kenya's Green Belt Movement, ecological movement headed by women." *UNESCO Courier*, March 1992.

Mehra, Rekha. "Can structural adjustment work for women farmers?" *American Journal of Agricultural Economics* 73 (1991): 1440–1447.

Sahn, David E., and Lawrence Haddad. "The gendered impacts of structural adjustment programs in Africa: Discussion." *American Journal of Agricultural Economics* 73 (1991): 1448–1451.

Saito, Katrin, Hailu Mekonnen, and Daphne Spurling. "Raising the productivity of women farmers in Sub-Saharan Africa." World Bank Discussion Paper No. 230. Washington, D.C.: World Bank, 1994.

Saito, Katrin, and C. Jean Weidemann. *Agricultural Extension for Women Farmers in Sub-Saharan Africa.* Washington, D.C.: World Bank, 1990.

Staudt, Kathleen K. *The Effects of Government Agricultural Policy on Women Farmers: Preliminary Findings from Idakho Location in Kakamega District*. Nairobi, Kenya: Institute of Development Studies, 1975.

———. "Women farmers and inequities in agricultural services." In *Women and Work in Africa*, ed. Edna Bay. Boulder, Colo.: Westview Press, 1982.

United Nations Food and Agriculture Organization. *Improving Extension Work with Rural Women.* Rome: United Nations Food and Agricultural Organization, 1996.

United Nations Population Fund. *Women as Land Stewards.* New York: United Nations, n.d.

von Braun, Joachim. *Commercialization of Smallholder Agriculture: Policy Requirements for Capturing Gains for the Malnourished Poor.* Washington, D.C.: International Food Policy Research Institute, 1989.

World Bank. "Agricultural extension: The Kenya experience." *Précis*, Winter 1999.

———. *World Bank Agricultural Extension Projects in Kenya.* Washington, D.C.: World Bank, 1999.

Concepts for Review

Agrarian system	Landlord	Shifting cultivation
Cash crops	Land reform	Specialized farming
Diversified farming	*Latifundio*	Staple food
Diversified (mixed) farming	Medium-size farm	Subsistence farming
Family farm	*Minifundio*	Tenant farmer
Green revolution	Moneylender	Transaction costs
Integrated rural development	Scale-neutral	
Interlocking factor markets	Sharecropper	

Questions for Discussion

1. Why should any analysis of development problems place heavy emphasis on the study of agricultural systems, especially peasant agriculture, and the rural sector?

2. What are the principal reasons for the relative stagnation of developing-country agriculture in Africa? How can this disappointing performance be improved on in the future? Explain your answer.

3. Discuss three main systems of agriculture found in the developing world. To what extent are these systems concentrated in three major developing regions?

4. Compare and contrast the nature of peasant or small-scale traditional agriculture in Asia, Africa, and Latin America. How do overall agricultural systems differ among these regions? What are the common characteristics?

5. Explain the meaning of Gunnar Myrdal's quote at the beginning of this chapter: "It is in the agricultural sector that the battle for long-term economic development will be won or lost."

6. It is sometimes asserted that small, traditional (peasant) farmers are backward and ignorant because they seem to resist agricultural innovations that could raise farm yields substantially. Does this resistance stem from an inherent irrationality on their part, or might it be attributable to some other factors often overlooked by traditional economic analysis? Explain your answer.

7. We described three stages in the transition from subsistence to specialized agriculture. What are the principal characteristics of each of these stages?

8. There appears to be widespread agreement that in regions where the distribution of land ownership is highly unequal (mainly Latin America but also parts of Asia), land reform is a necessary but not sufficient condition for promoting and improving small-scale agriculture. What is meant by this statement and by the concept of land reform?

Give some examples of supportive policy measures that might accompany land reform.

9. What is meant by comprehensive or integrated rural development? What criteria would you use to decide whether or not such integrated rural development was or was not taking place?

10. What explains sharecropping? To what extent do you think your explanation justifies the practice?

11. If land reform is efficient, why do you think it is not more commonly implemented?

12. Why is a proper understanding of risks faced by smallholder farmers of such fundamental importance to agricultural development policy?

13. Explain the argument that effective agricultural policies center around the role of women.

14. The poorest farmers tend to work on farms with the poorest soil and water conditions. Do you think this is the cause, the effect, or both?

15. What basic problems does the case study evoke on agricultural extension for women in Kenya? What special strategies may be used to address them?

Notes

1. Regional and national figures are drawn from World Bank, *World Development Indicators 2013*.

2. See United Nations Food and Agriculture Organization, "Economic growth is necessary but not sufficient to accelerate reduction of hunger and malnutrition," 2012, http://www.fao.org/docrep/016/i2845e/i2845e00.pdf. In 2009, the UN FAO estimated that for the first time, over 1 billion people did not have enough food to meet their basic nutritional needs as a result of a world food price spike, showing the high vulnerability many people face. See United Nations Food and Agriculture Organization, "The state of food insecurity in the world, 2012, and 2009," http://www.fao.org/docrep/012/i0876e/i0876e00.htm. See also, http://www.fao.org/publications/sofi/en; and International Food Policy Research Institute, "2012 Global Hunger Index: The challenge of hunger: Ensuring sustainable food security under land, water, and energy stresses," and "2009 Global Hunger Index," http://www.ifpri.org/publication/2009-global-hunger-index.

3. Simon Kuznets, "Economic growth and the contribution of agriculture," in *Agriculture in Economic Development*, eds. C. K. Eicher and L. W. Witt (New York: McGraw-Hill, 1964).

4. Ibid. See also John W. Mellor, "Agriculture on the road to industrialization," in *Development Strategies Reconsidered*, eds. John P. Lewis and Valeriana Kallab (Washington, D.C.: Overseas Development Council, 1986), pp. 67–89; Subrata Ghatak, "Agriculture and economic development," in *Surveys in Economic Development*, ed. Norman Gemmell (Oxford: Blackwell, 1987), ch. 10; Charles P. Timmer, "The agricultural transformation," in *Handbook of Development Economics*, vol. 1, eds. Hollis B. Chenery and T. N. Srinivasan (Amsterdam: Elsevier, 1988), pp. 276–331.

5. For data see World Development Indicators, Table 4.1, columns 3 and 4, which show growth in low- and middle-income areas accelerating in the 2001–2011 period over the 1990–2000 period, but slightly decelerating in high-income countries. On successful agricultural development and hunger programs and projects, see International Food Policy Research Institute, "Millions fed," 2009, http://www.ifpri.org/publication/millions-fed. Regarding high developing country productivity gains, see World Bank, *World Development Report, 2008* (New York: Oxford University Press, 2007), p. 69, and Mette Wik, Prabhu Pingali, and Sumiter Broca, "Global agricultural performance: Past trends and future prospects," WDR background paper, 2007.

6. See the United Nations Food and Agriculture Organization (FAO), *State of Food Insecurity*, 2012, http://www.fao.org/publications/sofi/2012/en; the *OECD-FAO Agricultural Outlook 2013–2022*, June 2013, http://www.oecd.org/site/oecd-faoagriculturaloutlook; and previous issues of these annual series.

7. Rockefeller Foundation Web page, http://www.rockfound.org/initiatives/agra/agra.shtml. The AGRA home page is http://www.agra-alliance.org. For information on the NEPAD initiative, gotohttp://www.nepad.org/2005/files/documents/172.pdf.

8. On NERICA, see Office of the Chief Economist, Africa Region, World Bank, *Yes, Africa Can: Success Stories from a Dynamic Continent* (Washington D.C.: World Bank, 2009), p. 9. On the 2008 food price spike and an explanation of short- and long-term forces for price increases, see the OECD-FAO reports, op. cit. (endnote 5). For more analysis on progress and challenges in reducing global hunger, see International Food Policy Research Institute, *2012 Global Food Policy Report* (Washington, D.C.: IFPRI, 2013); and K. O. Fuglie and S. L. Wang, "New evidence points to robust but uneven productivity growth in global agriculture," *Amber Waves* 10 (September 2012). Note that 30 countries imposed food export restrictions by the peak of the food price spike, at the same time as many food-importing developing nations were making efforts to rebuild stocks. This kind of panic can be expectations driven and raise prices above what is consistent with long-run equilibrium.

9. See Nora Lustig, "Thought for food: The challenges of coping with rising food prices," CGD Working Paper at http://www.cgdev.org/content/publications/detail/967250. Later in the chapter we consider further the impact of food prices on poverty; poor smallholders and agricultural workers may receive benefits from rising demand as well as face higher food costs.

10. E. F. Sczepanik, *Agricultural Capital Formation in Selected Developing Countries* (Rome: FAO, 1970).

11. See World Bank, *World Development Report, 2008*, ch. 11.

12. Stephen C. Smith, *Ending Global Poverty: A Guide to What Works* (New York: Palgrave Macmillan, 2005); Sungil Kwak and Stephen C. Smith, "Regional agricultural endowments and shifts of poverty trap equilibria: Evidence from Ethiopian panel data," *Journal of Development Studies* 47, No. 7 (July 2013): 955–975.

13. For an excellent survey of recent developments in agricultural development economics, see Alain de Janvry and Elisabeth Sadoulet, "Progress in the modeling of rural households' behavior under market failures," in de Janvry and Kanbur, eds., *Poverty, Inequality, and Development: Essays in Honor of Erik Thorbecke* (New York: Kluwer, 2006). See also World Bank, "Pakistan: Promoting rural growth and poverty reduction," 2007, http://siteresources.worldbank.org/PAKISTANEXTN/Resources/293051-1177200597243/ruralgrowthandpovertyreduction.pdf.

14. Beginning in the early 1960s, many countries in Latin America initiated land reform programs that did not alter the highly unequal distribution of land ownership but did do away with some of the more feudal patron-client social relationships associated with *latifundios* and *minifundios*. For pedagogical purposes, we will continue to use these terms more as a designation of the dualistic agrarian structure that still permeates Latin America than as a description of contemporary rural social relationships. For an early analysis, see also Celso Furtado, *Economic Development in Latin America* (New York: Cambridge University Press, 1970). The Latin America data in Table 9.3 also reflect the extreme inequality of the region.

15. United Nations Development Programme, *Human Development Report, 1996* (New York: Oxford University Press, 1996), p. 98. For other country estimates, see Keijiro Otsuka, Hiroyuki Chuma, and Yujiro Hayami, "Land and labor contracts in agrarian economies: Theories and facts," *Journal of Economic Literature* 30 (1992): 1965–2018.

16. For a summary of the empirical evidence on this point, see the *World Development Report, 2008*; and R. Albert Berry and William Cline, *Agrarian Structure and Productivity in Developing Countries* (Baltimore: Johns Hopkins University Press, 1979), ch. 3 and app. B; G. A. Cornia, "Farm size, land yields and the agricultural production function: An analysis of fifteen developing countries," *World Development* 13 (1985): 513–534; Nancy L. Johnson and Vernon Ruttan, "Why are farms so small?" *World Development* 22 (1994): 691–705; and United Nations Development Programme, *Human Development Report, 1996*, p. 95.

17. For evidence that land redistribution is likely to lead to greater output and higher productivity levels, see Cornia, "Farm size, land yields and the agricultural production function."

18. Francis M. Foland, "Agrarian unrest in Asia and Latin America," *World Development* 2 (1974): 57.

19. See *World Development Report, 2008*, ch. 10, and Cathy Farnworth and Michael Goodman, "Growing ethical networks: The Fair Trade market for raw and processed agricultural products (in five parts) with associated case studies on Africa and Latin America," November 2006, http://www.rimisp.org/getdoc.php?docid=6442.

20. Kenneth L. Sokoloff and Stanley L. Engerman, "History lessons: Institutions, factor endowments, and paths of development in the New World," *Journal of Economic Perspectives* 14 (2000): 217–232, and Stanley L. Engerman and Kenneth L. Sokoloff, "Colonialism, inequality, and long-run paths of development," in *Understanding Poverty*, eds. Abhijit V. Banerjee, Roland Benabou, and Dilip Mookherjee (New York: Oxford University Press, 2006), pp. 37–62. On Colombia, see *World Development Report, 2008*, box 11.1, and Klaus Deininger, Ana Maria Ibañez, and Pablo Querubin, "Determinants of internal displacement and desire to return: Micro-level evidence from Colombia," working paper, World Bank, 2007.

21. See World Bank, *World Development Report, 2003*, ch. 10.

22. Gunnar Myrdal, *Asian Drama* (New York: Pantheon, 1968), pp. 1033–1052.

23. Ibid., p. 1035.

24. Ibid.

25. Otsuka, Chuma, and Hayami, "Land and labor contracts," tab. 1.

26. A somewhat more positive view of the efficiency of land leases and access to credit through moneylenders and other informal sources of credit in Asia (and Latin America) was the focus of the "new agrarian economics" of the late 1970s and 1980s. In general, the position of this school of thought was that land contracting and usurious moneylending are efficient given the existence of other market failures, imperfect information, high transaction costs, moral hazards, and the like. Whether or not they were as efficient as these theorists claimed was far from clear, but their ultimate exploitive nature is difficult to deny. For examples of this literature, see Pranab K. Bardhan, *Land, Labor, and Rural Poverty: Essays in Development Economics* (New York: Columbia University Press, 1984); Keijiro Otsuka and Yujiro Hayami, "Theories of shared tenancy: A critical survey," *Economic Development and Cultural Change* 37 (1988): 31–68; Karla Hoff and Joseph E. Stiglitz, "Imperfect information and rural credit markets: Puzzles and policy perspectives," *World Bank Economic Review* 4 (1990): 235–250; and Timothy Besley, "How do market failures justify interventions in rural credit markets?" *World Bank Research Observer* 9 (1994): 27–47.

27. Myrdal, *Asian Drama*, p. 1048.

28. For a discussion of the phenomenon of landlessness in developing countries with a particular emphasis on Asia, see Mahmood H. Khan, "Landlessness and rural poverty in underdeveloped countries," *Pakistan Development Review* 25 (1986): 371–394.

29. Abhijit V. Banerjee and Lakshmi Iyer, "History, institutions, and economic performance: The legacy of colonial land tenure systems in India," *American Economic Review* 95 (2005): 1190–1213.

30. World Bank, *World Development Report, 2008*, p. 233 and fig. 2.2.

31. See World Bank, *World Development Indicators, 2003*, p. 131, and *2004*, tabs. 2.1, 3.3, and 4.1 (Washington, D.C.: World Bank, 2003, 2004) and Figure 9.2 in this chapter.

32. World Resources Institute, *World Resources, 1996–97*, tab. 10.1, and *World Resources, 1987* (New York: Basic Books, 1987).

33. See Carolyn Sachs, *The Invisible Farmers: Women in Agriculture* (Totowa, N.J.: Rowman & Littlefield, 1983). The classic and still influential treatment of the subject can be found in Ester Boserup, *Women's Role in Economic Development* (New York: St. Martin's Press, 1970).

34. Boserup, *Women's Role*. For a valuable collection of reviews and studies, see C. Mark Blackden and Quentin Wodon, eds., *Gender, Time Use, and Poverty in Sub-Saharan Africa* (Washington, D.C.: World Bank, 2006).

35. See Christopher Udry, "Gender, agricultural production, and the theory of the household," *Journal of Political Economy* 104 (1996): 1010–1046; Udry examines detailed data from Burkina Faso and finds that "plots controlled by women have significantly lower yields than similar plots within the household planted with the same crop in the same year, but controlled by men. The yield differential is attributable to significantly higher labor and fertilizer inputs per acre on plots controlled by men. These results contradict the Pareto efficiency of resource allocation within the household. Production function estimates imply that about six percent of output is lost due to the misallocation of variable factors across plots within the household." See also Christopher Udry, John Hoddinott, Harold Alderman, and Lawrence Haddad, "Gender differentials in farm productivity: Implications for household efficiency and agricultural policy," *Food Policy* 20 (1995): 407–423; Michael Carter and Elizabeth Katz, "Separate spheres and the conjugal contract: Understanding gender-biased development," in *Intrahousehold Resource Allocation in Developing Countries: Methods, Models, and Policy*, eds. Lawrence Haddad, John Hoddinott, and Harold Alderman (Baltimore: Johns Hopkins University Press, 1997); Pierre Chiappori, Lawrence Haddad, John Hoddinott, and Ravi Kanbur, "Unitary versus collective models of the household: Time to shift the burden of proof?" World Bank Policy Research Working Paper No. 1217; James Warner and D. A. Campbell, "Supply response in an agrarian economy with non-symmetric gender relations," *World Development* 28 (2000): 1327–1340; and Kaushik Basu, "Gender and say: A model of household behavior with endogenous balance of power," *Economic Journal* 116 (2006): 558–580.

36. For the classic treatment, see Raanan Weitz, *From Peasant to Farmer: A Revolutionary Strategy for Development* (New York: Columbia University Press, 1971), pp. 15–28, from which much of the following material is drawn. The three stages of farm evolution outlined in this section should not be interpreted as inevitable periods or sequences implying that all farms are in one of these stages before moving on to the next. In reality, of course, all three types of farms exist in every developing country at all points in time.

37. See Carmen Diana Deere and Alain de Janvry, "A conceptual framework for the empirical analysis of peasants," *American Journal of Agricultural Economics* 61 (1979): 602–612. See also Alain de Janvry, Elisabeth Sadoulet, and Linda Wilcox Young, *Rural Labor in Latin America* (Geneva: International Labor Organization, 1986), tab. 24.

38. See World Bank, *World Development Report 2014, Risk and Opportunity: Managing Risk for Development*, Washington DC: World Bank, 2013; and Marcel Fafchamps, *Rural Poverty, Risk, and Development* (Northampton, Mass.: Elgar, 2004). Important earlier contributions include Alain de Janvry, Marcel Fafchamps, and Elisabeth Sadoulet, "Peasant household behavior with missing markets: Some paradoxes explained," *Economic Journal* 101 (1991): 1400–1417, and Alain de Janvry and Elisabeth Sadoulet, "Structural adjustment under transaction costs," in *Food and Agricultural Policies under Structural Adjustment*, eds. F. Heidhues and B. Knerr (Frankfurt, Germany: Lang, 1995).

39. See Marvin P. Miracle, "Subsistence agriculture: Analytical problems and alternative concepts," *American Journal of Agricultural Economics* 50 (1968): 292–310.

40. For a rigorous analysis of how related farmer productivity traps operate, see Frederick J. Zimmerman

and Michael R. Carter, "Asset smoothing, consumption smoothing, and the reproduction of inequality under risk and subsistence constraints," *Journal of Development Economics* 71 (2003): 233–260. See also the two special issues on poverty traps in *Journal of Development Studies* in 2006 (Volume 42, No. 2) and 2013 (Volume 47, No. 7).

41. We are grateful to Professor Frank Thompson for this suggestion.

42. See Marcel Fafchamps and John Pender, "Precautionary saving, credit constraints, and irreversible investment: Theory and evidence from semiarid India," *Journal of Business and Economic Statistics* (1997): 180–194; Hans P. Binswanger and Mark Rosenzweig, "Wealth, weather risk, and the composition and profitability of agricultural investments, *Economic Journal* 103 (1993): 56–78; and Harold Alderman and Christina Paxson, "Do the poor insure? A synthesis of the literature on risk and consumption in developing countries," World Bank Policy Research Paper No. 1008, 1994.

43. Hanan G. Jacoby, Guo Li, and Scott Rozelle, "Hazards of expropriation: Tenure insecurity and investment in rural China," *American Economic Review* 92 (2002): 1420–1447. For broader background, see also Keith Griffin, "Agrarian policy. The political and economic context," *World Development* 1 (1973): 6.

44. Joseph E. Stiglitz first formulated the argument that sharecropping represents a compromise between landlord and tenant in which the landlord assumes some of the production risk but the tenant accepts some degree of work incentive given that monitoring is costly; see Stiglitz, "Incentives and risk sharing in sharecropping," *Review of Economic Studies* 41 (1974): 219–255.

45. Alfred Marshall, *Principles of Economics*, 8th ed. (London: Macmillan, 1920).

46. Steven N. S. Cheung, "Private property rights and sharecropping," *Journal of Political Economy* 76 (1968): 1107–1122. Of course, the contract would somehow have to provide an effective total compensation to the employee that matched the opportunity cost of providing the efficient level of effort, or the potential sharecropper would choose an alternative activity instead.

47. The classic article in this literature is William S. Hallagan, "Self-selection by contractual choice and the theory of sharecropping," *Bell Journal of Economics* 9 (1978): 344–354.

48. Radwan Ali Shaban, "Testing between competing models of sharecropping," *Journal of Political Economy* 95 (1987): 893–920. Some of the input results may not be fully free of confounding of expropriation risk.

49. See, for example, Nirviker Singh, "Theories of sharecropping," in *The Economic Theory of Agrarian Institutions*, ed. Pranab K. Bardhan (Oxford: Clarendon Press, 1989), pp. 33–72; David M. Newberry, "Risk-sharing, sharecropping, and uncertain labor markets," *Review of Economic Studies* (1977): 585–594; and Joseph E. Stiglitz, "Sharecropping," in *Economic Development*, eds. John Eatwell, Murray Milgate, and Peter Newman (London: Macmillan, 1989), pp. 308–315.

50. A succinct but rather technical overview of the competing theories is found in Singh, "Theories of sharecropping." The point that sharecropping results from inequality and that it remains inefficient in the Marshallian sense despite the potentially reduced inefficiency relative to straight wage or rental contracts was made by Joseph Stiglitz at a World Bank lecture in Washington, D.C., September 1997.

51. See Abhijit V. Banerjee, Paul Gertler, and Maitresh Ghatak, "Empowerment and efficiency: Tenancy reform in West Bengal," *Journal of Political Economy* 110 (2002): 239–280. Of course, in general, enforcement of tenancy and land reform is problematic in settings in which large landowners wield substantial power. For a simple and intuitive model of investment incentives (including fertilizer that is effective for more than one growing season) in the face of eviction risk, see Jacoby, Li, and Rozelle, "Hazards of expropriation."

52. Pranab K. Bardhan and Christopher Udry, *Development Microeconomics* (New York: Oxford University Press, 1999), p. 111.

53. See Pranab K. Bardhan, "Interlocking factor markets and agrarian development: A review of issues," *Oxford Economic Papers* 32 (1980): 82–98. See also Bardhan and Udry, *Development Microeconomics*. They note that while interlinkage can have

some positive efficiency implications in informal rural markets, "personalized interlinking may at the same time act as a formidable barrier to entry for other parties and may give the dominant partner in a transaction some additional leverage" (p. 111). Note that other forms of interlinkage exist in which the peasant retains ownership of his land. An example is contract farming in parts of Africa, in which a contractor who has "cultivated" export marketing channels provides seeds, fertilizer, and other inputs to a farmer to produce an output such as legumes that the contractor buys at an agreed price at harvest time.

54. For an interesting analysis of the process of agricultural specialization, see M. Shahe Emran and Forhad Shilpi, "The extent of the market and stages of agricultural specialization," *Canadian Journal of Economics* 45, No. 3 (2012): 1125–1153. An analysis of the impact of market access is presented in M. Shahe Emran and Zhaoyang Hou, "Access to markets and rural poverty: Evidence from household consumption in China," *Review of Economics and Statistics* 95, No. 2 (2013): 682–697. For a detailed analysis of the responsiveness of farmers in developing countries to price incentives, see World Bank, *World Development Report, 1986* (New York: Oxford University Press, 1986), chs. 4 and 5. A more cautious assessment is found in the 2008 *World Development Report,* however. For an analysis of the role of risk, see also Fafchamps, *Rural Poverty, Risk, and Development,* p. 28.

55. For an analysis of the adverse effects of premature mechanization, see Yujiro Hayami and Vernon Ruttan, *Agricultural Development: An International Perspective* (Baltimore: Johns Hopkins University Press, 1985).

56. Two informative articles on appropriate mechanization for development are Hans P. Binswanger, "Agricultural mechanization: A comparative historical perspective," *World Bank Research Observer* 1 (1986): 81–98, and Hans P. Binswanger and Prabhu Pingali, "Technological priorities for farming in sub-Saharan Africa," *World Bank Research Observer* 3 (1988): 81–92.

57. See World Bank, *World Development Report, 2008,* esp. chs. 6 and 11. An excellent analysis of the role of institutions in rural development can be found in Brian van Arkadie, "The role of institutions in development," *Proceedings of the World Bank Annual Conference on Development Economics, 1989* (Washington, D.C.: World Bank, 1989), pp. 153–192.

58. For an early analysis of the impact of the green revolution in the developing world, see Keith Griffin, *The Political Economy of Agrarian Change* (London: Macmillan, 1974); Chris Manning, "Rural employment creation in Java: Lessons from the green revolution and oil boom," *Population and Development Review* 14 (1988): 17–18; and Donald K. Freebairn, "Did the green revolution concentrate incomes? A quantitative study of research reports," *World Development* 23 (1995): 265–279.

59. World Bank, *World Development Report, 2008,* ch. 11. An informative discussion of the important role of appropriate pricing policies in stimulating agricultural production can be found in A. Drazen and Z. Eckstein, "On the organization of rural markets and the process of economic development," *American Economic Review* 78 (1988): 431–443. A massive five-volume research report, *The Political Economy of Agrarian Pricing Policy,* published by the World Bank in 1991, found similar results in the 18 developing countries investigated. For an extensive critique of inappropriate government policies hindering agricultural development in sub-Saharan Africa as well as elsewhere in the developing world, see Hans P. Binswanger and Klaus Deininger, "Explaining agricultural and agrarian policies in developing countries," *Journal of Economic Literature* 35 (1997): 1958–2005.

60. World Bank, *World Development Report, 2008,* p. 338.

61. See Oxfam UK, "Our land, our lives: Time out on the global land rush," Oxfam Briefing Note, October 2012, http://www.oxfam.org/sites/www.oxfam.org/files/bn-land-lives-freeze-041012-en_1.pdf; and Joachim von Braun, and Ruth Suseela Meinzen-Dick, "'Land grabbing' by foreign investors in developing countries: Risks and opportunities," *IFPRI Policy Briefing No. 12,* 2009.

62. For a survey of the connections between agriculture and environmental sustainability issues, see World Bank, *World Development Report, 2008,* ch. 8 and the references cited therein.

63. For a more comprehensive review of integrated programs for rural development, see World Bank, *World Development Report, 2008*, ch. 6, and Alain de Janvry, *The Economics of Investment in Rural Development: Private and Social Accounting Experiences from Latin America* (Berkeley: Department of Agricultural and Resource Economics, University of California, 1988).

64. United Nations Food and Agriculture Organization, "Land reform: Land settlement and cooperatives," 2007, http://www.fao.org/sd/Ltdirect/landrF. htm. For the seminal analysis see Myrdal, Gunnar, "The equality issue in world development," in *Nobel Lectures, Economics, 1969–1980*, ed. Assar Lindbeck (Singapore: World Scientific Publishing, 1992).

65. See Alain de Janvry, *The Agrarian Question and Reformism in Latin America* (Baltimore: Johns Hopkins University Press, 1981).

66. For an analysis of the successes and failures of various reform efforts, see World Bank, *World Development Report, 2008;* World Bank, *World Development Report, 1990* (New York: Oxford University Press, 1990), pp. 64–73; and Peter Dorner, *Latin American Land Reforms in Theory and Practice: A Retrospective Analysis* (Madison: University of Wisconsin Press, 1992).

67. See, for example, World Bank, *World Development Report, 2008*, and Jock R. Anderson, "Agricultural advisory services," Background paper for 2008 World Development Report. World Bank, 2007.

10

The Environment and Development

The poorest developing countries will be hit earliest and hardest by climate change, even though they have contributed little to causing the problem.
—*Nicholas Stern*, The Stern Review on the Economics of Climate Change, *2006*

Inequality in capacity to adapt to climate change is emerging as a potential driver of wider disparities in wealth, security and opportunities for human development.
—*United Nations Development Programme*, Human Development Report, *2007/2008*

Development co-operation should promote "pro-poor green growth," i.e., environmentally sustainable growth in which poor women and men can participate, contribute and benefit.
—*Organization for Economic Cooperation and Development,*
Development Assistance Committee, 2010

Each generation shall reap what the former generation has sown.

—*Ancient Proverb of China*

The road ahead is long and hard.

—*UN Secretary General Ban Ki-Moon, at Rio+20 Earth Summit, 2012*

The livelihood of more than half of the economically active population in the developing world directly depends in whole or part on the environment through agriculture, as well as animal husbandry, hunting, fishing, forestry, and foraging. This alone underscores the importance of the seventh Millennium Development Goal MDG: to "ensure environmental sustainability," and the central place of environment in the emerging post-2015 Sustainable Development Goals. Environmental quality strongly affects, and is affected by, economic development.

10.1 Environment and Development: the Basic Issues

Economics and the Environment

In recent years, economists have increasingly focused on the important implications of environmental issues for the success of development efforts. It is clear that classic market failures lead to too much environmental degradation. We now also understand that the interaction between poverty and environmental degradation can lead to a self-perpetuating process in which, as a result of ignorance or economic necessity, communities may inadvertently destroy or exhaust the resources on which they depend for survival. Rising pressures on environmental resources in developing countries can have severe consequences for self-sufficiency, income distribution, future growth potential, and the fundamental quality of life.

Environmental degradation can also detract from the pace of economic development by imposing high costs on developing countries through health-related expenses and the reduced productivity of resources. The poorest 20% of the poor in both rural and urban areas will experience the consequences of environmental ills most acutely. Severe environmental degradation, due to population pressures on marginal land, has led to falling farm productivity and per capita food production. Since the cultivation of marginal land is largely the domain of lower-income groups, the losses are suffered by those who can least afford them. Similarly, the inaccessibility of sanitation and clean water mainly affects the poor and is believed to be responsible for a preponderance of infectious disease worldwide. Because the solutions to these and many other environmental problems involve enhancing the productivity of resources and improving living conditions among the poor, achieving environmentally sustainable growth is synonymous with our definition of economic development.

Although the environmental costs associated with various economic activities are disputed, development economists agree that environmental considerations should form an integral part of policy initiatives.[1] Damage to soil, water supplies, and forests resulting from unsustainable methods of production can greatly reduce long-term national productivity but paradoxically can show up as having a positive impact on current GNI figures. It is thus very important that the long-term implications of environmental quality be considered in economic analysis. Rapid population growth and expanding economic activity in the developing world are likely to do extensive environmental damage unless steps are taken to mitigate their negative consequences.

The growing consumption needs of people in developing countries may have global implications as well. There is increasing concern that the destruction of the world's remaining forests, which are concentrated in a number of highly indebted developing countries in Africa as well as such countries as Indonesia, Brazil, Peru, and the Philippines, will greatly contribute to climate change caused by **global warming** through the greenhouse effect. At the same time, developing countries, particularly those in sub-Saharan Africa and South Asia, are predicted by climate models to suffer most from future global warming and **climate change**. Yet to date, most of the greenhouse gases causing the problem have been emitted in developed countries, creating what may be termed *environmental dependence:* Developing nations will be reliant on the developed world to take immediate steps to reduce emissions, as well as to develop new technologies that will enable further reductions and successful adaptation to the already inevitable warming and resulting climate change. However, developing countries, most prominently China at this stage, will also have to reduce emissions well below current forecasts, or any reductions in the developed world will only delay the possibly catastrophic consequences.

In this chapter, we examine the economic causes and consequences of environmental crises and explore potential solutions to the cycle of poverty

Global warming Increasing average air and ocean temperatures. Used in reference to the trend that began in the mid-twentieth century and attributed largely to human industrial, forestry, and agricultural activities emitting greenhouse gases.

Climate change Nontransient altering of underlying climate, such as increased average temperature, decreased annual precipitation, or greater average intensity of droughts or storms. Used in reference to the impact of the global warming phenomenon. Note the distinction between changes in weather (which varies within a climate) and changes in climate that alter underlying probabilities of weather outcomes.

and resource degradation. We begin with a survey of basic issues, including discussions of sustainable development and the linkages among population, poverty, economic growth, rural development, urbanization, and the environment in developing countries. We next look at the applicability of traditional economic models of the environment, depict some typical environmental situations, and provide some relevant data. We then broaden our scope to examine the global environment and explore policies for seeking worldwide sustainable development. The end-of-chapter comparative case study of Haiti and the Dominican Republic—two nations sharing one island—examines the role of environment as one of the dimensions of their very different development outcomes.

Eight basic issues define the environment of development. Many grow out of the discussions in the preceding chapters. The first is the concept of sustainable development; the others involve linkages between the environment and population and resources, poverty, economic growth, rural development, urbanization, the global economy, and the nature and pace of greenhouse gas–induced climate change. We briefly discuss each in turn.

Sustainable Development and Environmental Accounting

The term *sustainability* reflects the need for careful balance between economic growth and environmental preservation. Although many definitions exist,[2] *sustainability* generally refers to "meeting the needs of the present generation without compromising the needs of future generations."[3]

Sustainable development can be studied using long-standing concepts of economic analysis. These include three tools: using an appropriate valuation of future social benefits (generally placing more weight on the future than does the market); paying proper attention to market failures (focusing on externalities and public goods); and explicitly valuing natural resources as a form of capital stock rather than just a stream of consumption. We turn first to the problem of properly valuating the environment in national income accounting.

In a classic definition, a development path is sustainable "if and only if the stock of overall capital assets remains constant or rises over time."[4] But in this regard, natural resources and other forms of capital are substitutes only at a limited scale and to a limited degree. Rather, after the environment has been degraded to some extent, *natural resources and other forms of capital likely act as complements*. Manufactured capital is generally unproductive without a minimum of available environmental services. While future technological fixes may be imagined, there is certainly no guarantee that they will emerge.[5]

Implicit in these statements is the fact that future growth and overall quality of life are critically dependent on the quality of the environment. The natural resource base of a country and the quality of its air, water, and land represent a common heritage for all generations. To destroy that endowment indiscriminately in the pursuit of short-term economic goals penalizes both present and, especially, future generations. It is therefore important that development policymakers incorporate some form of **environmental accounting** into their decisions. For example, the preservation or loss of valuable environmental resources should be factored into estimates of economic growth and human well-being. Alternatively, policymakers may set a goal of no net loss

Environmental accounting The incorporation of environmental benefits and costs into the quantitative analysis of economic activities.

of environmental assets. In other words, if an environmental resource is damaged or depleted in one area, a resource of equal or greater value should be regenerated elsewhere.

Overall capital assets are meant to include not only manufactured capital (machines, factories, roads) but also human capital (knowledge, experience, skills) and **environmental capital** (forests, soil quality, rangeland). By this definition, **sustainable development** requires that these overall capital assets not be decreasing and that the correct measure of **sustainable net national income (NNI*)** is the amount that can be consumed without diminishing the capital stock. Symbolically,

$$NNI^* = GNI - D_m - D_n \qquad (10.1)$$

where NNI* is sustainable national income, D_m is depreciation of manufactured capital assets, and D_n is depreciation of environmental capital—the monetary value of environmental decay over the course of a year. NNI* includes costs of activities to reverse or avert environmental decay.

An even better measure, though more difficult to calculate with present data collection methods, would be

$$NNI^{**} = GNI - D_m - D_n - R - A \qquad (10.2)$$

where D_m and D_n are as before, R is expenditure required to restore environmental capital (forests, fisheries, etc.), and A is expenditure required to avert destruction of environmental capital (air pollution, water and soil quality, etc.). (Note that NNI includes R and A as economic activities, but these are then subtracted as forms of "allowance for depreciation" in arriving at NNI**.)[6]

In light of rising consumption levels worldwide, combined with high rates of population growth, the realization of sustainable development will be a major challenge. We must ask ourselves, "What are realistic expectations about sustainable standards of living"? From present information concerning rapid destruction of many of the world's resources, it is clear that meeting the needs of a world population that is projected to grow by about 2 billion in the next 35 years will require radical and early changes in consumption and production patterns. We discuss these needed changes later in the chapter.

Environment Relationships to Population, Poverty, and Economic Growth

Population, Resources, and the Environment   Much of the concern over environmental issues stems from the perception that we may reach a limit to the number of people whose needs can be met by the earth's finite resources. We may or may not reach this point, given the potential for new technological discoveries, but it is clear that continuing on our present path of accelerating environmental degradation would severely compromise the ability of present and future generations to meet their needs. A slowing of population growth rates would help ease the intensification of many environmental problems. However, the rate and timing of fertility declines, and thus the eventual size of world population, will largely depend on the commitment of governments to creating economic and institutional conditions that are conducive to limiting fertility (see Chapter 6).

Environmental capital   The portion of a country's overall capital assets that directly relate to the environment—for example, forests, soil quality, and ground water.

Sustainable development   A pattern of development that permits future generations to live at least as well as the current generation, generally requiring at least a minimum environmental protection

Sustainable net national income (NNI*)   An environmental accounting measure of the total annual income that can be consumed without diminishing the overall capital assets of a nation (including environmental capital).

Rapidly growing populations have led to land, water, and fuelwood shortages in rural areas and to urban health crises stemming from lack of sanitation and clean water.[7] In many of the poorest regions of the globe, it is clear that increasing population density has contributed to severe and accelerating degradation of the very resources that these growing populations depend on for survival. To meet expanding needs in developing countries, environmental devastation must be halted and the productivity of existing resources stretched further so as to benefit more people. If increases in GNI and food production are slower than population growth, per capita levels of production and food self-sufficiency will fall. Ironically, the resulting persistence of poverty would be likely to perpetuate high fertility rates, given, as noted in Chapter 6, that the poor are often dependent on large families for survival.

Poverty and the Environment   The poor are usually the main victims of environmental degradation. The poor suffer more from environmental decay because they must often live on degraded lands that are less expensive because the rich avoid them. Moreover, people living in poverty have less political clout to reduce pollution where they live. And living in less productive polluted lands gives the poor less opportunity to work their way out of poverty. But in some cases they are also its agents, typically as a result of the constraints of their poverty. Too often, again, high fertility is blamed for problems that are attributable to poverty itself. For example, China's population density per acre of arable land is twice that of India, yet yields are also twice as high. Though it is clear that environmental destruction and high fertility go hand in hand, they are both direct outgrowths of a third factor, absolute poverty. For environmental policies to succeed in developing countries, they must first address the issues of landlessness, poverty, and lack of access to institutional resources. Insecure land tenure rights, lack of credit and inputs, and absence of information often prevent the poor from making resource-augmenting investments that would help preserve the environmental assets from which they derive their livelihood. Hence, preventing environmental degradation includes as a key component the provision of institutional support to the poor, rather than fighting an inevitable process of decay.[8] For this reason, many goals on the international environmental agenda are very much in harmony with the three objectives of development articulated in Chapter 1.

Growth versus the Environment?   If, in fact, it is possible to reduce environmental destruction by increasing the incomes of the poor, is it then possible to achieve growth without further damage to the environment? Evidence indicates that the very poor cause considerable environmental destruction as a direct result of their poverty. It follows that increasing the economic status of the poorest group would provide an environmental windfall. However, as the income and consumption levels of everyone else in the economy also rise, there is likely to be a net increase in environmental destruction. Meeting increasing consumption demand while keeping environmental degradation at a minimum will be no small task.

At one point, it was widely believed that as per capita incomes rose, pollution and other forms of environmental degradation would first rise and then fall in an inverted-U pattern. (This idea is referred to as the **environmental Kuznets curve** because Kuznets's hypothesis that inequality would first rise and then fall as incomes increased, as detailed in Chapter 5, also traces such an inverted-U pattern.) According to the theory, as incomes rise, societies will have both the means and the willingness to pay for environmental protection. Indeed, there is evidence that this inverted-U relationship holds for at least some local pollutants, such as particulate matter in the air, sulfur dioxide, and nitrogen oxides. Other environmental problems, such as unsafe water and poor sanitation, begin to improve as income rises even from very low levels.

These are average patterns that vary across countries. And to the extent an income-pollution relationship holds, the patterns by themselves are not informative about causality. Environmental pollution itself may cause slow economic growth; or third factors, such as bad institutions, can lead to both high pollution and low income per capita. Moreover, better environmental regulation does not spring into existence automatically with higher income; this largely depends on the political process. Nevertheless, whatever the shape—inverted-U, or falling, or even rising—more effective environmental policies can shift the pollution curve downward (illustrated for the case of the inverted-U pattern in Figure 10.1).[9]

Moreover, we note that there is no convincing evidence that other environmental damage decreases with higher incomes. As we will see, this is a particular problem when it comes to global public goods, such as greenhouse gases. Finally, even if the inverted-U environmental Kuznets curve relationship does hold for such global public goods in the very long term, some damage, such as loss of biodiversity, may well prove to be irreversible. Active international policy will be needed.

Environmental Kuznets curve   A graph reflecting the concept that pollution and other environmental degradation first rises and then falls with increases in income per capita. There is evidence that this holds for some pollutants, such as sulfur dioxide and particulate matter in the air, but not for others, such as emissions of greenhouse gases.

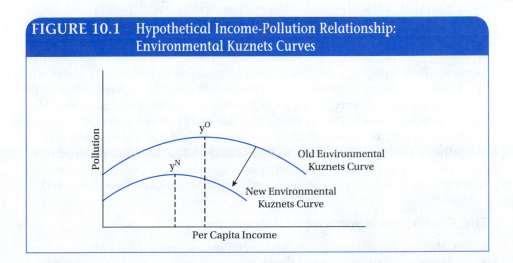

FIGURE 10.1   Hypothetical Income-Pollution Relationship: Environmental Kuznets Curves

Environment and Rural and Urban Development

Rural Development and the Environment   To meet the expanded food needs of rapidly growing populations, it is estimated that food production in developing countries will have to increase by at least 50% in the next three decades. Because land in many areas of the developing world is being unsustainably overexploited by existing populations, meeting this output target will require radical changes in the distribution, use, and quantity of resources available to the agricultural sector. And because women are frequently the caretakers of rural resources such as forests and water supplies and provide much of the agricultural supply of labor, it is of primary importance that environmental programs be designed around their role—not considered as an afterthought. In addition, poverty alleviation efforts must target women's economic status, in particular, to reduce their dependence on unsustainable methods of production.

The increased accessibility of agricultural inputs to small farmers and the introduction (or reintroduction) of sustainable methods of farming will help create attractive alternatives to current environmentally destructive patterns of resource use. Land-augmenting investments can greatly increase the yields from cultivated land and help ensure future food self-sufficiency.

Urban Development and the Environment   Chapter 7 demonstrated that rapid population increases, accompanied by heavy rural-urban migration, are leading to unprecedented rates of urban population growth, sometimes at twice the rate of national growth. Consequently, few governments are prepared to cope with the vastly increased strain on existing urban water supplies and sanitation facilities. The resulting environmental ills pose extreme health hazards for the growing numbers of people exposed to them. Such conditions threaten to precipitate the collapse of the existing urban infrastructure and create circumstances ripe for epidemics and national health crises. These conditions are exacerbated by the fact that under existing legislation, much urban housing is illegal. This makes private household investments risky and renders large portions of urban populations ineligible for government services.

Congestion, vehicular and industrial emissions, and poorly ventilated household stoves also inflate the tremendously high environmental costs of urban crowding. Lost productivity of ill or diseased workers, contamination of existing water sources, and destruction of infrastructure, in addition to increased fuel expenses incurred by people's having to boil unsafe water, are just a few of the costs associated with poor urban conditions. Research reveals that the urban environment appears to worsen at a faster rate than urban population size increases, with the result that the marginal environmental cost of additional residents rises over time. However, for a given income, the carbon footprint of a city resident tends to be lower than that of a suburban or rural resident.[10] The importance of urban as well as rural environmental protection is recognized in the seventh Millennium Development Goal (see Chapter 1).

The Global Environment and Economy

As total world population grows and incomes rise, net global environmental degradation is likely to worsen. Some trade-offs will be necessary to achieve sustainable world development. By using resources more efficiently, a number of environmental changes will actually provide economic savings, and others will be achieved at relatively minor expense. However, because many essential changes will require substantial investments in pollution abatement technology and resource management, significant trade-offs between output and environmental improvements will occasionally become necessary. The poorer the country, the more difficult it will be to absorb these costs. Yet a number of issues, including biodiversity, rain forest destruction, and population growth, will focus international attention on some of the most economically strapped countries in the world. In the absence of substantial assistance to low-income countries, environmental efforts will necessarily have to be funded at the expense of other social programs, such as education, health services, and employment programs, which themselves have important implications for the preservation of the global environment.

Most cumulative environmental destruction to date has been caused by the developed world. However, with high fertility rates, rising average incomes, and increasing greenhouse gas emissions in the developing world, this pattern is likely to reverse in the coming years. China is now the world's largest greenhouse gas emitter, albeit still lower on a per capita basis than most rich countries.[11] It is a matter of ongoing debate how the costs of global reform should be divided.

The divisions were very clear at Earth Summit 2012, also known as Rio+20, as it occurred 20 years after the original 1992 Earth Summit, which also took place in Rio de Janeiro, Brazil. The summit was intended to be a milestone meeting with most UN member states participating, but although some 57 heads of state and 31 heads of government attended, along with many private-sector and nongovernmental organization (NGO) observers, many key leaders including U.S. President Barack Obama and U.K. Prime Minister David Cameron did not. Despite some optimistic rhetoric, many analysts concluded the summit was a disappointment if not a major failure. The final statement, "The Future We Want," covered important areas such as increased protection of oceans and food security but was nonbinding and added little to previous declarations that had led to few results. And although hundreds of voluntary commitments for sustainable development were made by various UN member states, many were essentially restatements of existing policies. There was confirmation of plans to follow up on the MDGs, expiring in 2015, with new Sustainable Development Goals (see Chapter 1). Ban Ki-moon, the UN secretary general, summarized the mood when he said, "The road ahead is long and hard."

The Nature and Pace of Greenhouse Gas–Induced Climate Change Environmental scientists and economists are increasingly appreciating that the impacts of global warming are likely to be felt earlier than expected—indeed, are already beginning to be felt in parts of Africa—and that the window within which very large future costs can be averted is starting to close. The developed countries will have to take the lead and bear most of the costs in funding both remediation and adaptation in low-income countries, but developing countries will also need to play a significant role in limiting global warming to safeguard their own futures. We examine this issue in greater depth later in the chapter.

Natural Resource–Based Livelihoods as a Pathway Out of Poverty: Promise and Limitations

As noted at the start of this chapter, more than half of the economically active people in the developing world depend on agriculture, hunting, fishing, or forestry.[12] This environmental income, along with foraging and other activities, is vitally important to a majority of the poor and under the right policy conditions can offer a pathway out of poverty. But access to the benefits of environmental resources is often highly inequitable and in some cases increasingly so. In many countries, the poor have been losing control of some of their traditional natural resource commons, including forests, fields, and fishing areas, to new private property rights arrangements or to corrupt public land management. This trend is being widely resisted by communities and their supporters in NGOs, agencies, and local governments. Many of the rural poor lacking access to adequate farmland or to resources for earning adequate livelihoods from nature, such as access to forests, cattle to graze, or boats and equipment for fishing, have seen few gains or have suffered setbacks.[13]

In developing countries, much natural resource exploitation has been locally unsustainable and has occurred in a manner and on a scale that often bypasses the poor. In Africa and Asia, what had been common village lands may be "spontaneously" privatized. Governments may grant or allow (or overlook) foreign or national companies' logging, fishing, and mining without regard to the people who depend on these lands and resources for their livelihoods and way of life. Or they may designate common lands used by the poor to be "protected" areas—although corruption and poaching may negate any ecological gains—thereby banning the livelihood and way of life of the poor, giving them no incentive to take part in protection. Part of the solution is "pro-poor governance," with the genuine empowerment of poor people and their communities to assert their rights. This magnifies the impact of training that helps fuse scientific management with traditional community practices.[14] The empowerment of women in their communities is often a key aspect of program success. Many outstanding examples, such as the Suledo Forest Community and the HASHI project in Tanzania, are found among winners and runners-up of the United Nations Equator Prize, which recognizes "local efforts to reduce poverty through the conservation and sustainable use of biodiversity."[15]

The Centrality of Water　In policy circles, it has become common to hear the view that "water is the new oil." Clearly, water has become increasingly scarce and valuable.

The poor often talk about problems of water availability and quality in ways that make it clear that they think of water problems at the center of their experience of poverty. They speak of the lack of clean water, of what happens when people in their family and village drink contaminated water, of the large fraction of their time spent collecting water, of the high cost per liter of water when they have to buy it.

Conflict over water has also become a source of friction between developing countries, which otherwise have so much to gain through cooperation. One of the most serious and disconcerting examples is the growing tension between China and India. Other potential flashpoints include Ethiopia and Egypt.[16]

The Scope of Domestic-Origin Environmental Degradation

Environmental challenges in developing countries caused by poverty include health hazards created by lack of access to clean water and sanitation, indoor air pollution from biomass stoves, and deforestation and severe soil degradation—all most common where households lack economic alternatives to unsustainable patterns of living. The principal health and productivity consequences of environmental damage include water pollution and scarcity, air pollution, solid and hazardous wastes, soil degradation, deforestation, loss of biodiversity, and global warming–caused climate change.

It is estimated that over 60% of the poorest people residing in developing countries struggle for survival on agriculturally marginal soils. This trend is greatly worsened in some areas of the developing world by strong inequalities in the distribution of land, which force landless workers onto increasingly taxed, ecologically sensitive soils. The growing intensification of cultivation on fragile lands leads to rapid soil degradation and loss of productivity. It has been estimated that roughly 270,000 square kilometers of soil lose virtually all of their productivity each year. An area greater than the size of India and China combined has been significantly degraded. The resulting annual loss in agricultural productivity is estimated to be between 0.5% and 1.5% of annual worldwide GNI. As a result of rapid population increases and the failure of agricultural production to keep pace, per capita food production declined in sub-Saharan Africa during the 1980s and 1990s (see Chapter 9).[17]

The higher commodity prices of this century have apparently encouraged poaching and illegal logging in countries such as Indonesia. High fish prices have been associated with overfishing in restricted areas and environmentally destructive fishing practices. Runoffs and collateral damage have resulted from expansion of mining activities into sensitive areas. In many of these cases, indigenous and poor people dependent on natural resources for their survival have suffered.

An environmental problem shared by both the urban and the rural poor is the prevalence of unhealthy conditions created by the lack of clean water and sanitation. This in turn contributes greatly to the spread of infectious diseases. It has been estimated that waterborne pathogens that cause typhoid, cholera, amoebic infections, bacillary dysentery, and diarrhea account for 80% of all disease in developing countries and at least in part for up to 90% of the approximately 7 million child deaths each year. Deteriorating environmental conditions were cited as a contributing factor to the spread of cholera epidemics and other health problems in a number of countries in Latin America and Africa in the 1990s (see Chapter 8). And as noted in Chapter 7, rapid population growth and heavy rural-urban migration make it difficult to extend urban services to many people who need them.

Airborne pollutants also take a high toll on the health of citizens in developing countries. Dependence on **biomass fuels** such as wood, straw, and manure is closely related to poverty. The burning of biomass fuels for cooking and the boiling of water create dangerously high levels of indoor pollution to which 400 million to 700 million people, mostly women and children, are exposed each year. Smoke and fumes from indoor stoves are

Biomass fuels Any combustible organic matter that may be used as fuel, such as firewood, dung, or agricultural residues.

believed to contribute significantly to some 4 million childhood deaths each year from respiratory diseases and to an ever-larger number of chronic respiratory illnesses.[18]

In urban areas, other sources of pollution pose serious threats to physical well-being. According to the World Health Organization, 1.3 billion people live in urban areas with unsafe levels of airborne pollutants. Yet it has been projected that by 2030, manufacturing in developing countries will expand to 600% of 2000 levels, vastly increasing potential concentrations of pollutants. Just to maintain current urban air standards until 2030 (which means conceding to conditions much worse than those existing in the urban centers of developed countries), average emissions from industries and electric generators in developing countries would have to be reduced by 90 to 95% per unit of output.

Rural Development and the Environment: A Tale of Two Villages

To clarify how rural poverty and environmental degradation interact, let us take a brief look at two hypothetical developing-world villages, one in Africa and the other in South America.

A Village in Sub-Saharan Africa   The residents of the African village, located in a semiarid landscape, have been warned by international experts that cutting the remaining trees and cultivating marginal land will only worsen the hardships that they already endure. The advice runs counter to each family's first priority, which remains obtaining the basic necessities for survival. Here trees serve many functions, the most important of which is to provide firewood for cooking. Without wood, it would be impossible to prepare many foods, make cornmeal, or boil water. As a result of the intensification of land use by a rapidly growing population, the cutting of trees for firewood, and the clearing of marginal land for cultivation, the soil is increasingly exposed to destructive environmental forces. The loss of vegetation, which helps mitigate the destructive impact of heavy winds, rain, and desiccation by the sun, leads to more rapid erosion of precious topsoil needed for cultivation. Good yields are more difficult to obtain, and the consequences of drought years are more intense. **Desertification**—encroachment of the desert into areas where erosion has been most severe—threatens to consume even the more productive land.

As a result of the loss of precious topsoil and declining output, there are fewer crops to bring to market to barter for necessities. In many households, there is less food for the children. Yet the family must spend longer hours trying to obtain enough income to survive. Paid work is scarce, although some households earn a small amount of additional income by sending family members to work on larger, more prosperous farms.

It is generally the job of women to collect enough firewood for the day's cooking. It may take hours to walk to and from an area where it is available, adding considerably to the day's work. But no alternative forms of fuel are available in the local market, and even if they were, household funds would be insufficient to purchase them. In fact, many women spend additional time collecting precious firewood to make charcoal, which can then be sold in the

Desertification The transformation of a region into dry, barren land with little or no capacity to sustain life without an artificial source of water.

cities for the equivalent of a few pennies, which helps buy household necessities. The low opportunity cost of a woman's time perpetuates the wasteful use of forests and worsens local environmental conditions.[19]

A Settlement Near the Amazon   Consider now the other hypothetical village, on the edge of a vast rain forest in South America. The great majority of farmers here are newcomers, drawn by government promises of land and prosperity. The public resettlement program, which distributes property titles to settlers willing to clear the land, is designed to reduce the overcrowding of cities and stem the flow of rural-to-urban migrants. In contrast to the African village, this settlement has no shortage of rainfall, wildlife, or trees. In fact, the forest is an obstacle for migrant farmers and is regularly burned to make room for cultivation.

Though burning the forest may temporarily provide the landless with a modest source of income, the land, like 90% of rain forest soil worldwide, is not very fertile and can sustain intensive cultivation for only a few years. Complementary inputs and farming know-how that might help improve levels of output are in short supply, and yields begin to drop rapidly after the first few years. Settlers are then forced to burn their way deeper into the forest. Because the settlers are located on marginal soils and must constantly seek new arable ground, with little prospect of rising above a subsistence existence, the government program may be antidevelopmental in the long run. Household incomes remain low and unstable, there is little gain in average productivity, and the migrating population leaves environmental devastation in its wake, further reducing the productivity of all.

Environmental Deterioration in Villages

Although heavy urbanization is leading to rapid demographic changes, the majority of the very poor live in rural areas similar to the two villages just described. Economic necessity often forces small farmers to use resources in ways that guarantee short-term survival but reduce the future productivity of environmental assets. Unsustainable patterns of living may be imposed by economic necessity. In periods of prolonged and severe food shortages, desperately hungry farmers have been known to eat the seeds with which they would have planted the next year's crop, knowingly paving the way for future disaster. Because it happens more slowly, the tendency of impoverished people to degrade agricultural resources on which they depend for survival is less dramatic, but it is motivated by similar circumstances.

The causes and consequences of rural environmental destruction vary greatly by region. However, persistent poverty is frequently the root of much locally caused damage. The majority of the poor in developing countries survive on the meager yield obtained from cultivation of small plots of land whose soil may be too shallow, too dry, or too sandy to sustain permanent agriculture. If the land is not in some way replenished through either shifting cultivation or the use of manufactured fertilizers, it becomes exhausted, and yields decrease with successive harvests. But the poor generally do not have the wherewithal to increase the productivity of the land by allowing it to lay fallow or by making investments in irrigation and fertilizer. In addition, where fertility rates are high and children provide a vital economic contribution through wages or on-farm labor, population and the intensity of cultivation are likely to increase over time, speeding the rate at which the soil becomes exhausted.

Soil erosion Loss of valuable topsoils resulting from overuse of farmland, and deforestation and consequent flooding of farmland.

One immediate result of this type of environmental pressure is **soil erosion**. With little plant cover to protect it from wind and water, precious topsoil may be blown or washed away, further reducing the productivity of the land. This process of environmental degradation leads to persistent declines in local per capita food production and may eventually lead to desertification. This phenomenon is likely to spur increases in rural-to-urban migration or may force the remaining local population onto even less fertile land, where the process is repeated.

Deforestation The clearing of forested land either for agricultural purposes or for logging and for use as firewood.

Another factor in the cycle of rural poverty and environmental destruction is **deforestation**. The vast majority of wood cut in the developing world is used as fuel for cooking. Loss of tree cover has two potentially devastating environmental implications for predominantly poor rural populations. Deforestation can lead to a number of environmental maladies that over time can greatly lower agricultural yields and increase rural hardships. On a day-to-day basis, however, the increasing scarcity of firewood means that women must spend large portions of the day in search of fuel, diverting time from other important activities such as income generation and child care. In the worst cases, fuel shortages are sufficient to require the burning of biomass or natural fertilizers, such as manure, which are important farm inputs for maintaining crop yields. In extreme cases, deforestation can facilitate the spread of disease, such as malaria in Borneo.

Environmental degradation that begins on a local scale can quickly escalate into a regional problem. For example, clearing of vegetation at high elevations may increase the exposure of cultivated lands at lower altitudes. Soil that has been carried away by heavy rains may silt rivers and pollute drinking water. Plants help retain rainfall, which percolates down through the soil into underground reserves of groundwater. The water is, in turn, tapped by a variety of plants during dry seasons in arid regions. The loss of vegetation and forest leads to a decrease in the rate at which groundwater is replenished and can even cause a decrease in local rainfall. The subsequent drop in the water level leads to the death of plants with shallow root systems, including young trees. This self-perpetuating process can spread the malady to previously unaffected regions. Not surprisingly, the increase in natural disasters associated with local environmental degradation, including floods, droughts, and mudslides, can have a devastating impact on both the local and the regional agricultural economy. These problems are expected to be severely exacerbated by climate change associated with global warming in coming decades.

10.2 Global Warming and Climate Change: Scope, Mitigation, and Adaptation

Scope of the Problem

The Intergovernmental Panel on Climate Change (IPCC)[20] is the United Nations–sponsored international scientific body analyzing climate change and its impacts. In late 2013 the IPCC released *Climate Change 2013: The*

Physical Science Basis, which reinforced its earlier conclusions; and new reports on *Impacts, Adaptation and Vulnerability*, and *Mitigation of Climate Change*, are coming out in 2014.

In 2007, the IPCC released its fourth assessment report. It concluded that the developing world, particularly the poorest countries, can expect major consequences from global warming, involving larger and more severe heat waves and higher average temperatures, hurricanes, floods from heavy rains, prolonged droughts, losses of valuable species, and crop and fishing losses. These conclusions have been strongly reinforced by subsequent research. The IPCC identified four zones highly vulnerable to greenhouse gas–induced climate change: sub-Saharan Africa because of drying, Asian megadeltas because of flooding, small islands due to multiple sensitivities, and the Arctic.

Sub-Saharan Africa will be hit particularly hard. The IPCC report concluded that by 2020, although adaptations would help, and certain regions such as Ethiopian highlands would gain from lengthened growing seasons, conditions will already worsen:

> agricultural production, including access to food, in many countries and regions in Africa is projected to be severely compromised by climate variability and change. The area suitable for agriculture, the length of growing seasons and yield potential, particularly along the margins of semi-arid and arid areas, are expected to decrease. This would further adversely affect food security and exacerbate malnutrition in the continent. In some countries, yields from rain-fed agriculture could be reduced by up to 50% by 2020.

The study projected that 75 to 250 million people in Africa will be exposed to increased "water stress due to climate change" by 2020.[21] Coastal fisheries, mangroves, and coral reefs will be further degraded and threatened by projected rises in sea level and storms. Freshwater lakes will also be negatively affected.

In Asia, millions of people live in low-lying areas in the path of typhoons of expected increasing frequency and intensity or otherwise at greater risk of ocean or river flooding.[22] Glacier melting is projected to increase flooding, but after a few decades, once the glaciers have receded, there will be decreased flow, especially in the summer, when seasonal melt had been normal and beneficial. Decreased freshwater availability could affect a billion people in Asia by the 2050s. With moderate warming, crop yields are projected to rise in some northern areas in Asia but fall in many tropical and subtropical areas. Increased flooding also threatens both rural and urban infrastructure. Later in the century, South Asia faces further droughts, water shortages, and declines in agricultural productivity.[23]

In Latin America, warming was projected to cause further losses of Amazon forest and biodiversity by midcentury, while agriculture will be harmed in drier areas. Finally, many small islands are at risk because of sensitivity and vulnerability to ocean flooding, erosion, and loss of freshwater, fishing, and tourism.

In sum, prolonged droughts; expanded desertification; increased severity of storms with heavy precipitation and flooding and consequent erosion; longer and more severe heat waves; reduced summer river flow and water shortages; decreased grain yields; climate-induced spreading ranges of pests and disease; lost and contaminated groundwater; deteriorated freshwater lakes, coastal fisheries, mangroves, and coral reefs; and coastal flooding—one or more of these impacts are expected to affect most of the world's poorest countries during this century, and sooner than once believed. Other likely ecological damage includes loss of essential species such as pollinators and soil organisms, forest and crop fires, and rising surface ozone levels.[24] These problems mean that productivity gains can be lost just trying to keep pace with the deterioration.

That greenhouse gas–induced climate change has arrived and that much more is coming are beyond any reasonable doubt. While weather and average annual temperatures fluctuate, as an average, there is confirmation that some of these changes have already arrived. In 2010, the U.S. National Oceanic and Atmospheric Administration (NOAA) released a study drawing on 11 indicators of climate and found that each one showed evidence of global warming due to the influence of greenhouse gases. The study was able to draw on data not yet available when the IPCC released its report. A 2013 study in the journal *Science* concluded that climate change can now be expected to unfold at a rate "orders of magnitude more rapid" than at any other time over the past 65 million years.[25]

And as the World Bank concluded in its 2009 *World Development Report*:

> The effects of climate change are already visible in higher average air and ocean temperatures, widespread melting of snow and ice, and rising sea levels. Cold days, cold nights, and frosts have become less frequent while heat waves are more common. Globally, precipitation has increased even as Australia, Central Asia, the Mediterranean basin, the Sahel, the western United States, and many other regions have seen more frequent and more intense droughts. Heavy rainfall and floods have become more common, and the damage from—and probably the intensity of—storms and tropical cyclones have increased.[26]

Global warming is likely to present an unprecedented environmental challenge for the developing world. The 2006 *Stern Review on the Economics of Climate Change* concluded that "the poorest developing countries will be hit earliest and hardest by climate change, even though they have contributed little to causing the problem. Their low incomes make it difficult to finance adaptation. The international community has an obligation to support them in adapting to climate change. Without such support there is a serious risk that development progress will be undermined."[27] The *Review* also concluded, consistent with other studies, that food production in the tropics would be harmed: "In tropical regions, even small amounts of warming will lead to declines in yield." The greater the degree of warming, the larger the predicted global agricultural and water impact will be. But generally, the *Review* found that effective remediation is surprisingly affordable—if decisive action is taken soon.

The World Bank published a sobering 2012 study, *Turn Down the Heat*, which presented a case that the world will face a 4-degree increase in average global temperatures this century, which will result in dire consequences. Its 2013 follow-up study, *Turn Down the Heat II: Climate Extremes, Regional Impacts, and the Case for Resilience*, focused on impacts already felt after just a 0.8 degree (Celsius) temperature rise to date, such as extreme weather events and sea level rise. The report also highlighted that the expected 2 degree rise in 20 to 30 years will create food shortages in Africa and water crises in South Asia. As the temperature rises above 2 degrees, approaching 4 degrees, there will be extreme heat waves, rising sea levels, storms, droughts, floods, and losses of grasslands, farmlands, and marine ecosystem.[28]

The worst impact will likely be felt by the very poor, who depend most on natural resources, including rain-fed agriculture. Moreover, the housing of the poor in urban as well as rural areas is often poorly constructed and located in the most environmentally stressed and risky areas—largely because the rich do not want to live there. Houses of the poor constructed of mud, bamboo, straw, and other inexpensive or gatherable materials are the most vulnerable to extreme weather events. They are vulnerable to heat waves, flooding, mudslides, and diseases. Floods on the scale of the 2010 humanitarian disaster in Pakistan could become common. The poor cannot get insurance against the risks to which they are most exposed. The World Health Organization estimated that by 2004, over 140,000 excess deaths per year had been caused by the global warming that had taken place since the 1970s, largely due to diarrhea, malaria, and malnutrition. Mosquito-carried malaria is expected to migrate further to higher altitudes, newly threatening Nairobi, Harare, and other cities. Already, heat waves have claimed more lives in many developing nations such as India. [29]

Some analysts predict that in addition to the direct environmental impacts, social strains caused by increased resource scarcity may lead to greater conflict, with the poor again being the most likely victims. The crisis in the Darfur region of Sudan is believed by some analysts to have been triggered by environmental stress.[30]

Thus, environmental catastrophe would have sweeping consequences for the poor and their human development. The *2013 Human Development Report* compares the UNDP's baseline forecasts with those living under environmental disaster. They projected that "some 2.7 billion more people would live in extreme income poverty under the environmental disaster scenario than under the base case scenario," reflecting about 1.9 billion people entering poverty and 800 million failing to escape poverty who otherwise would likely have done so.

Mitigation

Many strategies have been proposed for mitigation of emissions, including development of "carbon markets," taxes on carbon, and subsidies to encourage faster technological progress. For regulation, given uncertainties in both benefits and costs of emissions reductions, there are difficult economic questions in devising the most efficient permit or emissions tax regimes. As a policy strategy, the *Stern Review* suggests establishing a long-term quantity cap on greenhouse gases in the atmosphere to guard against environmental catastrophe. This would involve long-term limits on the amount of greenhouse emissions equal to a quantity that the earth could absorb. In the short term, policies could be designed to limit the economic burden if abatement costs turned out initially to be unexpectedly high.[31]

Global warming is primarily but not exclusively a developed-country-caused problem. Although much of the accumulated greenhouse gases to date has been emitted by the high-income countries, even if the developed world were to drastically reduce greenhouse gas pollution now, we would still have to act to contain greenhouse gas emissions of the developing world, which are projected to grow at alarming rates. This has many causes, but the rapid industrial growth in Asia is already a major contributor, and this is expected to worsen substantially with the planned expansion of coal-fired electrical generation in China, India, and elsewhere. Policies and mechanisms have been introduced essentially to pay for costs of avoiding emissions in developing countries. Deforestation in developing countries contributes over 20% of harmful greenhouse gases, in addition to the losses it causes of valuable biodiversity and the environmental services of cleaning air and water. Helping developing countries reduce greenhouse gas emissions has emerged as an important dimension for foreign aid. Indeed, the need to develop and implement a mechanism for paying developing countries for forest preservation has long been an active topic of international negotiations on climate change. The Reducing Emissions from Deforestation and Forest Degradation (REDD) mechanism, along with enhanced incentives for reestablishing and maintaining forests with engagement of indigenous communities that depend on them (known as REDD-plus), has slowly made some progress.[32]

Adaptation

While immediate action on mitigation is necessary, a significant amount of climate change is now essentially inevitable. Even if drastic mitigation begins immediately, lags in the climate system mean change will unfold for many years. Thus, adaptation to climate change in developing countries is critical for protecting livelihoods and continuing to make development gains.

The UNDP has defined climate change adaptation as "a process by which strategies to moderate, cope with and take advantage of the consequences of climatic events are enhanced, developed and implemented."

Adaptation takes place in two forms: "planned" (or policy) adaptation undertaken by governments and "autonomous" (or private) adaptation undertaken directly by households, farms, and firms in response to climate change they experience or anticipate. The distinction between autonomous or private and planned or policy adaptation is not a sharp one—governments respond to citizens, and government incentives affect what individuals choose to do—but the categories are useful for analysis of adaptation. These responses are in some ways complements and in other ways substitutes. If autonomous adaptation increases the marginal benefit of planned adaptation and vice versa, they are considered complements—for example, when farmers respond to increasing temperature by planting new varieties and government research institutes develop new heat-resistant seeds. But if autonomous adaptation reduces the need for planned adaptation and vice versa, then they are substitutes—for example, if government builds reservoirs and irrigation systems, farmers have less incentive to change crops or conserve water.[33]

As suggested by Arun Agrawal and Nicolas Perrin, depending on how risks are reduced or avoided, four classes of adaptation strategies can be identified. Mobility avoids risks across space. Storage reduces risks experienced over time. Diversification reduces risks across assets owned by households or collectives. Communal pooling involves joint ownership of assets and resources; sharing of wealth, labor, or incomes from particular activities across households or mobilization and use of resources held collectively during time of scarcity. Exchange can substitute for any of these four classes of adaptation strategies.[34]

National and local public health agencies can respond with citizen awareness campaigns to build public knowledge of how to adapt as well as emergency health infrastructure. For example, in Odisha state in India, ongoing emergency preparedness efforts implemented with UN assistance are credited for reducing loss of life from heat waves and from the massive Cyclone Phailin that hit the region in October 2013.[35]

Policy adaptations can help make the "livelihood assets" of the poor more resilient to environmental stresses while providing other development benefits; examples include [36]

- Inventorying and tracking ecological resources of the poor; addressing environmental deprivations including susceptibility to ecological stresses in poverty assessments and programs

- Implementing early warning systems to anticipate environmental emergencies and to prevent disasters (preserving funds for development efforts)

- Restoring and expanding natural ecosystem barriers (such as reforestation and mangrove expansion) to extreme events such as flooding and water shortages

- Constructing infrastructure to serve the poor while accounting for likely climate change (including storm shelters and flood barriers as well as protected roads and bridges, with a margin for safety); and establishing microinsurance systems for farmers

- Ensuring better voice and empowerment of the poor and their organizations—in part, to get information about the environmental stresses they face to government, media, and the public and to make it more likely that the poor will get a fair share of government services; sharing economic growth more equitably

- And supporting all this, demanding more government transparency and accountability

In addition to the long-term trends caused by global warming, climate also fluctuates and changes for other reasons, and rural people in developing countries naturally take steps to adapt. Many adaptations to the different types of climate change have already been observed; some of these are described in Box 10.1.

Governmental and international efforts to adapt to climate change will remain indispensable; Box 10.2 reviews the efforts of Niger to adapt to climate change and the modest but growing assistance role being played by development agencies.

BOX 10.1 Autonomous Adaptation to Climate Change by Farmers in Africa

Siri Eriksen, Karen O'Brien, and Lynn Rosentrater observed a number of "indigenous" adaptation strategies to climate change impacts in eastern and southern Africa. First is livelihood diversification; for example, fishers in Uganda also cultivate crops, raise livestock, collect firewood, engage in trade, and practice temporary migration. Second, livestock herding is an adaptation to frequent droughts in Namibia and Botswana. Third is ecological diversification—for example, farmers in Mozambique use plots on high ground when there is a lot of rain and on low ground when there is little rain.

David Thomas and his colleagues found several adaptation strategies by farmers in South Africa. Many change farming practices by planting drought-resistant varieties, switching to more livestock and less crops, and building cattle shelters. Others diversify livelihood sources by getting off-farm work and starting small businesses or using networks, including cooperatives and community horticultural projects.

Ariel Dinar and his colleagues examined adaptation activities in 11 African countries and found that changing planting dates, adopting shorter growing seasons, increasing the use of irrigation, and actively practicing water conservation and soil conservation techniques were found in several countries. In addition, farmers in Egypt reported increased use of weather insurance, in addition to moving to nonfarming activities. The researchers found that more experienced and better-educated farmers were more likely to take adaptive measures. Farmers working on rented land were less likely to adapt, at least partly because of tenure insecurity (see Chapter 9). Heads of household were also more likely to practice adaptation, possibly because they controlled household resources. David Maddison noted that using different varieties of the same crop was considered one of the most important adaptation activities in 9 of the 11 countries.

Sources: Siri Eriksen, Karen O'Brien, and Lynn Rosentrater, *Climate Change in Eastern and Southern Africa: Impacts, Vulnerability and Adaptation*, Global Environmental Change and Human Security Report No. 2008:2 (Oslo, Norway: University of Oslo, 2008), http://www.gechs.org/downloads/reports/2008-2.pdf; David S. G. Thomas et al., "Adaptation to climate change and variability: Farmer responses to intra-seasonal precipitation trends in South Africa," *Climatic Change* 83 (2007): 301–322; David Maddison, *The Perception of and Adaptation to Climate Change in Africa*, CEEPA Discussion Paper No. 10 (Pretoria, South Africa: Centre for Environmental Economics and Policy in Africa, 2006), http://www.ceepa.co.za/docs/CDPNo10.pdf; Ariel Dinar et al., *Climate Change and Agriculture in Africa: Impact Assessment and Adaptation Strategies* (London: Earthscan, 2008).

10.3 Economic Models of Environmental Issues

Privately Owned Resources

We will review some common economic models of the environment. In each model, the market's failure to account for environmental externalities is the exception rather than the rule, and neoclassical theory is then applied in order to cure or circumvent an inefficiency.[37] Neoclassical theory has been applied to environmental issues to determine what conditions are necessary for the efficient allocation of resources and how market failures lead to inefficiencies, and to suggest ways in which these distortions can be corrected.

BOX 10.2 One of the World's Poorest Countries Tries to Prepare for Climate Change: Niger

Niger is one of the world's poorest nations, as measured by almost any indicator of well-being and as seen at a glance in the following table.

Niger also has a very challenging natural environment. Almost twice the size of France, Niger is subtropical, hot, and dry. A majority of its land is in

Niger Indicators

Indicator	Value
Income per capita	$330 (WDI, 2011)
PPP income per capita	$600 (WDI, 2011)
Percent below $1.25 per day	43.6% (WDI, 2008)
Mean years of schooling (Adults)	1.4 (WDI, 2010)
Literacy, male	42.9% (CIA, 2005)
Literacy, female	15.1% (CIA, 2005)
Primary completion rate (2011)	46% (WDI, 2011)
Life expectancy at birth	58 (PRB, 2012)
Malnutrition (under-5 underweight)	39.9 (WDI, 2005–2011)
Under-5 mortality rate (per 1,000 live births)	125 per thousand (WDI, 2011)
Total fertility rate (births per woman)	7.2 (world's highest, PRB, 2012)
Crude birth rate	46 (among 3 highest) (PRB, 2012)
New Human Development Index (New HDI)	0.304 (lowest in world, HDR, 2013)
Multidimensional Poverty Index (MPI)	0.642 (world's poorest, HDR, 2013)
Population	16.3 million (2012, PRB)
Projected population, 2050	54.2 million (3.3x increase, PRB)
Percent rural	82% (PRB)

Note: Data from 2013 World Development Indicators, except where otherwise noted.

Niger faces many other conditions that make development challenging. It is landlocked and borders seven countries, most of them also having stability, development, and environmental challenges: Nigeria, Benin, Burkina Faso, Mali, Algeria, Libya, and Chad. Niger struggles with needed improvements in governance, the private sector, and civil society. The colonial period left Niger with a difficult institutional legacy. French colonizing efforts began before 1900 with "pacification campaigns," and the nation became an official colony of France from 1922 until its formal independence in 1960. Despite some periods of democratic openings, the country has been under military or single-party rule, or unstable, including a series of coups and regional rebellions at least until the 2011 elections. But risks continue, including from ethnic strife, spillovers from conflicts in Mali and potentially Libya, and unresolved border issues.

the Sahara desert, and the remaining area has been plagued by recurring droughts. Yet it has a predominantly rural and agricultural economy. Now, its already precarious natural environment is deteriorating. As in most countries, some impacts are due to poor domestic practices, while some of Niger's problems reflect secular desertification along the Sahel. But an increasingly prominent factor is the worsening impact of climate change brought about by global warming. Temperatures have already increased in Niger by over 0.7 degrees Celsius (1.25 degrees Fahrenheit). Climate change is worsening water scarcity and food insecurity. Most farmers in Niger understand something about climate change and say they are experiencing it in decreasing rainfall. Yet at the same time, research suggests that Niger has considerable potential for improved agricultural and livestock practices and increased productivity.

Niger has been actively trying to respond to threats of climate change. By 1997, Niger first set up its National Technical Committee on Climate Changes and Variability (CNCVC). From there, Niger worked with support from the Global Environment Fund and other agencies to complete in 2006 its National Adaptation Program of Action (NAPAs), an official United Nations Framework Convention on Climate Change (UNFCCC) process for least developed countries like Niger to "identify priority activities that respond to their urgent and immediate needs to adapt to climate change" for which delay would increase vulnerability and costs. NAPAs then provide a basis for special assistance. Niger's NAPA priorities include introducing fodder crops in pastoral areas, creating livestock food banks, improving crop irrigation, promoting peri-urban market gardening, promoting income-generating activities and mutual benefit societies, water control, and producing and disseminating meteorological data.

Niger applied and became one of the 20 developing countries in the Pilot Program for Climate Resilience (PPCR). Building on its NAPA, in 2010 Niger developed a Strategic Program for Climate Resilience (SPCR) with PPCR funding and assistance, to identify and justify the uses to be made of PPCR grants and loans. Niger's SPCR has three parts: a climate resilience Community Action Project (CAPCR); sustainable management and control of water resources; and climate forecasting and early warning systems. CAPCR has two major focuses; first, to make climate change and variability resilience a "mainstream" part of development strategies at national and local levels; second, to integrate resilience practices into local populations' combined forestry, grazing, and agriculture activities, with a goal of improved productivity and sustainability, while creating needed social protection measures for people working in these activities.

PPCR does not administer funds directly; to save money and speed implementation, it works through existing multilateral development agencies. For example, for Niger the World Bank is channeling $35 million in PPCR grants and $28 million in PPCR loans for the CAPCR program. Each use is matched with a funding source and financing "modality."

The CAPCR project targets areas that face severe climate risks, promotes use of climate-sensitive technologies, combines sustainable land and water management with social protection measures, and emphasizes local government planning leadership. Investment activities include soil/moisture conservation methods, water harvesting, reduced tillage, agro-forestry, nutrient-enhancing rotation systems, and animal health and nutrition. Nigerien women traditionally play an important role in natural resource management, and part of the program is to be specially focused on improvements for women working in these activities. Planned assistance for people living in poverty as part of the overall program includes matching grants for targeted communes, a cash transfer system for vulnerable households, workfare, and food stamp distribution.

Most farming in Niger is rain-fed, despite the great variability of rainfall; improved irrigation will be an essential part of climate adaptation. PPCR is also planning to fund water resource activities, including large- and small-scale irrigation development, and related expansion of agricultural extension and funding sources for farmers.

Meanwhile, the International Finance Corporation (IFC) is working with Niger to fund its climate information platform through PPCR loans; the program is predicted to more than pay for itself with subscriptions and indirect benefits, and the results will be watched closely. The IFC found that most farmers and pastoralists in Niger already seek and use forecasts, particularly of rain, but also of temperature, wind, and pests; an IFC survey found a majority of farmers would benefit from more weather information and might be willing to pay for it. The IFC is also planning for a weather index insurance program.

Niger is eligible to accept PPCR loans as well as grants because it is not deemed to be in debt distress. The loans are highly "concessionary," typically at one-tenth of 1% interest over 40 years, with a 10-year grace period—yet they must eventually be repaid. Thus, it makes sense for loan uses to be matched with activities that have a revenue stream and where there are clear assurances that benefits will not go to the rich while the burden of repayment falls upon the poor. Thus far at least, there do not seem to be any reasons for concern.

The experience in Niger raises many questions about environment and development—the problems, their impact on the poor, and potential solutions; and who will benefit from the responses, and who will pay. Niger's initiative offers a model for other countries in the region.

Sources: African Development Bank Group, *Water Resources Mobilization and Development Project, Republic of Niger, Project Appraisal Report*, March 2012; Climate Investment Funds, PPCR page, https://www.climateinvestmentfunds .org/cif/node/4; International Finance Corporation, *Niger Climate Information Platform Final Report*, 2011; United Nations Framework Convention on Climate Change, National Adaptation Programmes of Action (NAPAs) page, https://unfccc.int/national_reports/napa/items/2719.php; World Bank Group, *Project Appraisal Document, Republic of Niger Community Action Project for Climate Resilience (CAPCR)*, December 19, 2011.

Figure 10.2 demonstrates how the market determines the optimal consumption of a natural resource. Finding the optimal market outcome involves maximizing the total net benefits to society from a resource, which is the difference between the total benefits derived from a resource and the total costs to producers of providing it. This is equal to the shaded area in Figure 10.2. **Total net benefit** is maximized when the **marginal cost** of producing or extracting one more unit of the resource is equal to its marginal benefit to the consumer. This occurs at Q^*, where the demand and supply curves intersect. In a perfectly competitive market, the "invisible hand" will ensure that Q^* is the quantity produced. The marginal cost curve in Figure 10.2 is upward-sloping because extraction costs increase as a resource becomes more scarce. The resulting **producer surplus** is area aPb, and the **consumer surplus** is area DPb. Together they yield a maximum net benefit equal to Dab.

If resources are scarce and are rationed over time, **scarcity rents** may arise; these may obtain even when the marginal cost of production is constant, as

Total net benefit   The sum of net benefits to all consumers.

Marginal cost   The addition to total cost incurred by the producer as a result of increasing output by one more unit.

Producer surplus   Excess of what a producer of a good receives and the minimum amount the producer would be willing to accept because of a positive-sloping marginal cost curve.

Consumer surplus   Excess utility over price derived by consumers because of a negative-sloping demand curve.

Scarcity rent   The premium or additional rent charged for the use of a resource or good that is in fixed or limited supply.

FIGURE 10.2 Static Efficiency in Resource Allocation

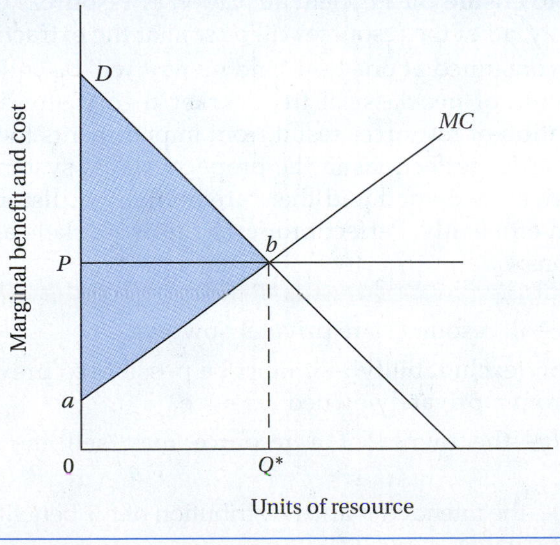

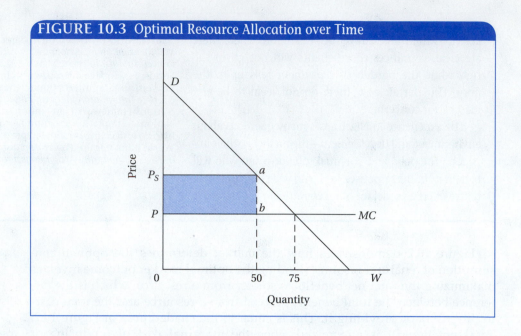

FIGURE 10.3 Optimal Resource Allocation over Time

Present value The discounted value at the present time of a sum of money to be received in the future.

Marginal net benefit The benefit derived from the last unit of a good minus its cost.

Property rights The acknowledged right to use and benefit from a tangible (e.g., land) or intangible (e.g., intellectual) entity that may include owning, using, deriving income from, selling, and disposing.

in Figure 10.3. The owner of a scarce resource has a finite volume of a resource X to sell (75 units) and knows that by saving a portion of it for future sales, he or she can charge a higher price today. The price of a good that is being rationed intertemporally (over time) must equate the **present value** of the **marginal net benefit** of the last unit consumed in each period. That is, the consumer must be indifferent between obtaining the next unit today and obtaining it tomorrow. In Figure 10.3, assume that a resource owner has 75 units available. If he or she is willing to offer only 50 units for sale today, the market price for the scarce resource is P_s. The scarcity rent collected by the owner of the resource is equal to P_sabP, the shaded region in the diagram between price and marginal cost. It is the owner's ability to collect this rent that creates the rationing effect to ensure the efficient allocation of resources over time. In the absence of scarcity, all of the resource will be sold at the extraction cost $P = MC$, 75 units will be consumed at one time, and no rent will be collected.

The proponents of neoclassical free-market theory stress that inefficiencies in the allocation of resources result from impediments to the operation of the free market or imperfections in the property rights system. So long as all resources are privately owned and there are no market distortions, resources will be allocated efficiently. Perfect **property rights** markets are characterized by four conditions:

1. *Universality*—all resources are privately owned.
2. *Exclusivity* or "excludability"—it must be possible to prevent others from benefiting from a privately owned resource.
3. *Transferability*—the owner of a resource may sell the resource when desired.
4. *Enforceability*—the intended market distribution of the benefits from resources must be enforceable.

   Under these conditions, the owner of a scarce resource has an economic incentive to maximize the net benefit from its sale or use. For example, a farmer who owns his land will choose the levels of investment, technology, and output that maximize the net yield from the land. Because the value of the land may be used as collateral, any viable farm investment can be financed by obtaining a loan at the prevailing market rate of interest.

   If the forgoing conditions are not met simultaneously, inefficiencies are likely to arise. Thus, the way to correct the misallocation of resources is generally to remove any market distortions. A number of models have been designed to explain apparent inefficiencies in resource allocation and to evaluate alternative remedies. We next look at two simple models of inefficiency arising from imperfections in property markets.

Common Property Resources

If a scarce resource (such as arable land) is publicly owned and is freely available to all (for, say, farming or grazing animals), as is the case with a **common property resource**, any potential profits or scarcity rents will be competed away (unless efficient social conventions are binding, as will be discussed shortly). As we have noted, neoclassical theory suggests that in the absence of scarcity rents, inefficiencies will arise. Using a somewhat different framework, we will investigate the misallocation of resources under a common property system. Figure 10.4 describes the relationship between the value per unit of labor on a given piece of land and the number of laborers cultivating it.

   Suppose for the moment that this piece of land is privately held. Conventional wisdom tells us that the landowner will hire additional labor to work the land until the marginal product of the last worker is equal to the market or alternative wage, W^A, at point L^*. The workload is shared equally among the

Common property resource   A resource that is collectively or publicly owned and allocated under a system of unrestricted access, or as self-regulated by users.

FIGURE 10.4 Common Property Resources and Misallocation

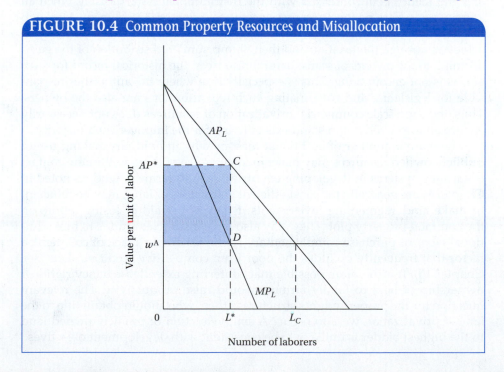

employees, each of whom produces the *average* product. However, assuming decreasing returns to labor, each new worker hired reduces the average product of all workers. The *marginal* product of each additional worker is thus equal to his average product minus the decrease in the average product across all other workers. If an additional employee is hired beyond L^*, his cost to the producer, W^A, will be greater than his marginal product, and the difference will represent a net loss to the landowner. A profit maximizer will thus hire L^* workers, with a total output equal to average product, AP^*, multiplied by the number of workers, L^*. Scarcity rents collected by the landowner will equal AP^*CDW_A.

Society's total net benefit from land will be lower under a system of common property unless workers can coordinate their resource use decisions in a cooperative manner. Generally, if land is commonly owned, each worker is able to appropriate the entire product of his work, which is equal to the average product of all workers. Worker income will continue to exceed the wage until enough workers are attracted so that the average product falls to the level of the wage, at which point the labor force equals L_C. Though total output may either rise or fall (depending on whether MP_L is positive or negative—it is negative as drawn in Figure 10.4), the marginal product of the additional workers is below the wage. Because we are assuming that all workers can be employed elsewhere with productivity equal to or greater than W_A, it follows that social welfare must fall when marginal product falls below W^A. This situation is sometimes referred to as the "tragedy of the commons." No scarcity rent is collected at L_C. The implication of the common property resource model is that where possible, privatization of resources will lead to an increase in aggregate welfare and an efficient allocation of resources.

Note that these neoclassical models are strictly concerned with efficiency and do not address issues related to equity. Income distribution is not considered, and the theory is unconcerned with the distributional issues arising when all scarcity rents from national resources accrue to a few private owners. Although neoclassical theorists have sometimes suggested that an optimal outcome may be achieved through the taxation and then "lump sum" redistribution of the gains accruing to the owners of scarce natural resources, the historical record for such efforts is not encouraging. This is especially true where the authorities responsible for legislating and coordinating such redistributions are also the owners. Thus, the large-scale commercial privatization of resources does not necessarily ensure an improvement in standards of living for the impoverished majority.

There are a number of additional reasons why individuals making use of publicly owned resources may make inefficient use of them within the context of farming systems in developing countries. Family farmers, who, as noted in Chapter 9, are generally the most efficient cultivators of land, may be reluctant to make land-augmenting investments if they are afraid of losing tenure on the common property plot. They may also have insufficient funds to hire additional labor or purchase complementary resources due to a lack of collateral, a factor that frequently excludes the poor from competitive credit markets (see Chapter 15). It is therefore possible that conferring extended tenancy rights or ownership of land to family farmers would raise productivity. The relevant question for the property rights structure is then, who should obtain title to the land if privatization were to occur? A simple auction of publicly owned land to the highest bidder is unlikely to be consistent with development objectives.

Elinor Ostrom, the 2009 Nobel laureate in economics, discovered that under some conditions, a fair and efficient management of common property can be achieved by the people who depend on it. She and other researchers have also found thousands of historical and contemporary examples where this is achieved in practice. Out of this experience she drew out the "design principles" found in Box 10.3. Traditional societies have often been successful at devising and enforcing stable social norms and formal rules for cooperative natural resource management and even restoring cooperation after it has broken down. However, vigilance is needed because the underlying incentives for defection remain. In fact, as development proceeds, there are generally greater opportunities and incentives for individuals to appropriate common property for their own use, so in some cases, increased vigilance and external support could play a vital role; a subset of common property systems will be unlikely to endure.[38]

Public Goods and Bads: Regional Environmental Degradation and the Free-Rider Problem

In the preceding discussion, the core economic problem was that each additional worker who joined those cultivating commonly held land created a negative **externality** by lowering the returns to all other workers without providing any compensation. An externality occurs when one person's consumption or production behavior affects that of another without any compensation. The benefits and costs of one's actions are said to be internalized when one is made to bear them in full. In the previous common property problem, the externalities associated with decreasing average product were easily internalized by reestablishing perfect property markets through the privatization of public property. In many cases, the **internalization** of externalities is not so easily accomplished. This is especially the case where the consequences of an individual's actions constitute a public good or a public bad. A **public good** is anything that provides a benefit to everyone and the availability of which is in no way diminished by its simultaneous enjoyment by others. Common examples include clean air, economic institutions, and national defense. A **public bad** is any product or condition that decreases the well-being of others in a nonexhaustive manner. Air pollution and water pollution are examples. Intuitively, it is clear that given the fact that individuals do not pay the full costs associated with their actions, too much of a public bad will be produced. The result is a socially nonoptimal outcome. We will demonstrate this shortly using a diagrammatic representation. Public goods can be local, national, or, as with greenhouse gases, even global in scope.[39]

Let us consider the case of a particular public bad, regional environmental degradation caused by deforestation. Increased exposure to the forces of erosion, excessive drying of the soil, regional loss of groundwater, silting or pollution of public water supplies, and potential climatic changes are all public bads associated with the clear-cutting or burning of trees. Whether these trees are on private or commonly held property, the clearing of protective ground cover, either for cultivation or for the extraction of timber, may lead to more widespread regional environmental degradation. To simplify our analysis, we will translate this public-bad problem into a public-good framework. Environmental conservation through the protection of trees provides a benefit to all and is thus a public good.

Externality   Any benefit or cost borne by an individual economic unit that is a direct consequence of another's behavior.

Internalization   The process whereby external environmental or other costs are borne by the producers or consumers who generate them, usually through the imposition of pollution or consumption taxes.

Public good   An entity that provides benefits to all individuals simultaneously and whose enjoyment by one person in no way diminishes that of another.

Public bad   An entity that imposes costs on groups of individuals simultaneously. Compare with public good.

BOX 10.3 FINDINGS   Elinor Ostrom's Design Principles Derived from Studies of
Long-Enduring Institutions for Governing Sustainable Resources

Elinor Ostrom, 2009 Nobel laureate in economics, has summarized findings from research on common property resource management, in the form of eight conditions facilitating fair and efficient management of common property by those who depend upon it. These are:

1. *Clearly defined boundaries.* The boundaries of the resource system (e.g., irrigation system or fishery) and the individuals or households with rights to harvest resource units are clearly defined.

2. *Proportional equivalence between benefits and costs.* Rules specifying the amount of resource products that a user is allocated are related to local conditions and to rules requiring labor, materials, and money inputs.

3. *Collective-choice arrangements.* Many of the individuals affected by the harvesting and protection rules are included in the group who can modify these rules.

4. *Monitoring.* Monitors, who actively audit biophysical conditions and user behavior, are at least partially accountable to the users or are the users themselves.

5. *Graduated sanctions.* Users who violate rules are likely to receive graduated sanctions (depending on the seriousness and context of the offense) from other users, from officials accountable to these users, or from both.

6. *Conflict resolution mechanisms.* Users and their officials have rapid access to low-cost, local arenas to resolve conflicts among users or between users and officials.

7. *At least minimal recognition of rights to organize.* The rights of users to devise their own institutions are not challenged by external governmental authorities, and users have long-term tenure rights to the resource.

8. *For resources that are parts of larger systems: nested enterprises.* Appropriation, provision, monitoring, enforcement, conflict resolution, and governance activities are organized in multiple layers of nested enterprises.

Ostrom notes, "The design principles are not blueprints....They describe the broad structural similarities among those self-organized systems that have been able to adapt and learn so as to be robust to the many social, economic and ecological disturbances that occur over time."

Source: Ostrom, Elinor. *Understanding Institutional Diversity.* Princeton, N.J.: Princeton University Press, 2005. © 2005 by Princeton University Press. Reprinted by permission of Princeton University Press.

The most obvious difference between a public good and a purely private good is that aggregate demand for the public resource is determined by summing individual demand curves vertically, as in Figure 10.5a, rather than horizontally, as is the case for private goods as illustrated in Figure 10.5b. The difference results from the fact that many individuals may enjoy the same unit of a public good but only one may benefit from a unit of a normal, private-consumption good. Through vertical summation, we are sure to capture all benefits accruing to all individuals from each unit of a public good. The marginal cost associated with the preservation of an additional tree is equal to the forestry maintenance cost plus the opportunity cost of the tree, that is, the most valuable alternative use of the tree, such as for firewood, charcoal, animal fodder, or lumber. Figure 10.5 illustrates the problem of pricing public goods.

FIGURE 10.5 Public Goods, Private Goods, and the Free-Rider Problem

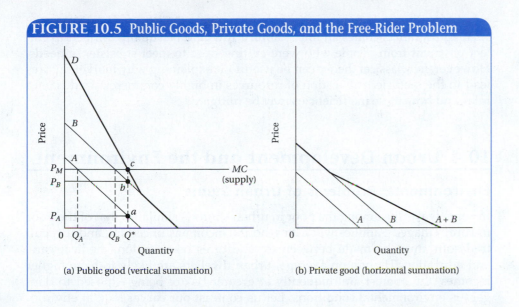

(a) Public good (vertical summation)   (b) Private good (horizontal summation)

In Figure 10.5a, the socially optimal number of trees is Q^*. It is determined by the intersection of the (vertically summed) aggregate demand curve with the supply (MC) curve. At Q^*, total net benefits to society from the public good are maximized. However, due to what we call the **free-rider problem**, the free market will not lead to this optimal quantity. Because individuals are able to enjoy the benefits of trees provided by others, each will contribute less than what he or she would if acting independently. At a price of P_M, the free market will satisfy person B's demand, Q_B, while not denying person A's requirements of Q_A; that is, A can free ride on B's contribution. The market will therefore provide a suboptimal level of forest preservation, Q_B. To restore optimality (Q^* of the public good), some form of government intervention is required. The most effective solution is to charge each consumer just enough per unit, P_A and P_B for individuals A and B, respectively, to entice each of them to demand the preservation of the optimal quantity of trees, Q^*. Their joint payments, $P_A \times Q^*$ for A plus $P_B \times Q^*$ for B, represent a total contribution equal to $P_M \times Q^*$, exactly the sum required to purchase the socially optimal level of preservation.

Free-rider problem The situation in which people can secure benefits that someone else pays for.

Limitations of the Public-Good Framework

The problem with the public-good pricing mechanism is, of course, how to know which prices to charge. People have no incentive to divulge how much they really benefit from a public good because by shirking they may free ride on the contributions of others and avoid paying their full share. A government may be capable of reducing market inefficiencies, but it is unlikely to be able to produce a perfect allocation of resources due to deficiencies in the information available to it. Hypothetically, collected fees can be used to provide a public good by preserving existing forests or managing a sustainable timber production program that will supply the community's needed timber. Although charging fees to the people benefiting from the preservation of a resource may sound practical, it is exceedingly difficult. In a development context, the problems become even more complicated. When the collection of fees entails taxing deeply impoverished populations with little or no cash income, such a program becomes an impossibility. It would be equally difficult to collect payment from people who were cutting trees to meet subsistence needs. However, neoclassical theory can be useful for explaining why market failures lead to the inefficient allocation of resources in highly commercialized economies and how these inefficiencies may be mitigated.

10.4 Urban Development and the Environment

Environmental Problems of Urban Slums

In some ways, life among the poor in urban slums is similar to that of the poor in rural villages: Families work long hours, income is uncertain, and difficult trade-offs must be made between expenditures on nutrition, medical care, and education. Though on average, urban dwellers are likely to have higher incomes, the poorest are frequently at greater risk of being exposed to dangerous environmental conditions. Let us contrast our earlier look at environmental conditions in an African and a South American rural community with those of an Asian urban shanty.

In a typical urban slum in an Asian metropolis, health-threatening pollutants are commonplace both inside and outside the home. Many women are unaware that the smoke from the fuels they burn in the home to cook and boil water may have severe long-term consequences for the health of their children (though public health programs and NGOs have recently been encouraging cooking with better alternatives, with some success). Conditions resulting from poor ventilation in the home can be equivalent to smoking several packs of cigarettes per day, and women and their children are exposed to these fumes for long portions of each day. Though some children actually avoid much of this exposure by attending school, many are kept out of school to assist their mothers in market work or the production of goods at home. Thus, from an early age, chronic and acute bronchitis is a cruel fact of life. Debilitating and ultimately fatal respiratory infections among the poor are commonplace.

But it is not only in the home that individuals are exposed to harmful pollutants. Street vendors and market workers are constantly exposed to high levels of other pollutants. Untreated sewage runs in open drains along the roads, providing a conduit for infectious diseases. Because food and drinking water are frequently contaminated, diarrhea is common, especially in young children. Frequent spells of the illness cause malnourishment, even when food is more plentiful, making the young more susceptible to other diseases. Many of the weakest children die from severe dehydration. Because the fuels used to cook foods and boil water must be purchased in the market and consume a large portion of the daily earnings, there is sometimes insufficient fuel to boil the household's drinking water, increasing the chance of infection. The costs associated with obtaining medical treatment for sick children may be very high, involving the opportunity cost of time spent traveling to and from clinics and long hours in crowded waiting rooms, in addition to medical fees. For many households, the forgone earnings can be ill afforded. In many of the poorest households, only boys receive medical attention because they are expected to contribute more to household income. It is thus not surprising that they are more likely than their sisters to survive to adulthood.

Children playing in the streets and others working outdoors are also exposed to the combined emissions from automobiles and factories. Dangerously high levels of atmospheric lead are common because few cars are equipped with the expensive catalytic converters now mandated in the West. Due both to physical and mental impairments suffered as a result of exposure to environmental factors and to repeated absence from school, children in the poorest neighborhoods may find it difficult to meet basic academic standards. It is no wonder that improvement in the lives of slum dwellers is a key part of the Millennium Development Goals.

Because the urban poor are much less able than the wealthy to insulate themselves from the negative effects of a tainted environment, they are more likely to suffer serious consequences resulting from environmental degradation. In addition, malnutrition and poor health among a large proportion of urban dwellers in shantytowns tend to reduce individual resistance to environmental hazards.[40]

To explore viable solutions, it is necessary to have a clear understanding of the sources of problems and the ways in which they interact. The causes of severe urban environmental problems are numerous, but for simplicity of analysis, we will divide these factors into two categories: those associated with urbanization and industrial growth, and those that must be dealt with in any community but tend to be exacerbated by the congestion of urban settings.

Industrialization and Urban Air Pollution

The early stages of urbanization and industrialization in developing countries are generally accompanied by rising incomes and worsening environmental conditions. Cross-sectional analysis of numerous countries at different levels of income suggests that some types of urban pollution tend first to rise with national income levels and then to fall.[41] As noted earlier, this effect has been dubbed the *environmental Kuznets curve*. According to the World Bank, pollution levels for even the worst quartile of high-income cities are better than for the best quartile of low-income cities.[42] Indeed, at higher incomes, it is easier to afford expensive **clean technologies**. However, there is nothing inevitable about the trend. Air (and water) quality is closely related to the extent of government regulation, in both high- and low-income countries. Moreover, some environmental resources may be irretrievably lost unless action is taken immediately.

Clean technologies Technologies that by design produce less pollution and waste and use resources more efficiently.

The principal sources of air pollution, which pose the greatest health threat associated with modernization, are energy use, vehicular emissions, and industrial production. Industrialization can lead to increases in waste either directly through emissions or indirectly by altering patterns of consumption and boosting demand for manufactured goods. The production of manufactured goods generally entails the creation of by-products that may be detrimental to the environment. The extent to which they degrade the environment will depend on a number of factors, including the type of by-products produced, their quantities, and their means of disposal. Unfortunately, in the absence of regulation, the cheapest way to dispose of unwanted by-products is usually to release them untreated into the air and waterways or to dump them on the ground where runoff is free to sink into groundwater or wash into rivers. Due to the broader transmission of ideas, greater availability of goods, and increased incomes, changes in patterns of consumption and their environmental consequences are likely to appear first in cities. Until technologies and infrastructures capable of coping with environmental consequences are introduced, modernization is likely to lead to high urban environmental costs.

We have already looked briefly at the issue of externalities and the fact that many of the costs of pollutants are borne by someone other than the polluter. This suggests that the price paid for the consumption of a good is below the social cost associated with the good. Figure 10.6 depicts the typical supply and demand curves. In this case, however, we have labeled the supply curve $S = MC_P$ because it represents the marginal **private costs** associated with producing good X. The free-market equilibrium output and price are Q_M and P_M, respectively. If there are externalities associated with the consumption or production of each unit of good X, the MC_P curve does not represent the true costs of the good to society. If each unit of good X imposes a cost of $2 on a third party, we can obtain the true marginal social cost curve, MC_S, by legislating a $2-per-unit sales tax on the output. This **pollution tax** shifts the private cost curve upward by $2 at every point to MC_S in Figure 10.6. At the new intersection between the demand curve and the marginal **social cost** curve, Q^* is the efficient outcome and P^* is the price. Therefore, by incorporating the social costs of pollution into the analysis, the actual output of the polluting product is reduced to the socially optimal level, while the price charged to the consumer rises from P_M to P^* and the price received by the producer falls from P_M to P_C. Depending on the relative elasticities of the demand and supply curves, the burden of the pollution tax is shared by both consumers and producers. In Figure 10.6, the consumer pays ab and the producer pays bc of the ac tax.

Private costs   The direct monetary outlays or costs of an individual economic unit.

Pollution tax   A tax levied on the quantity of pollutants released into the physical environment.

Social cost   The full cost of an economic decision, whether private or public, to society as a whole.

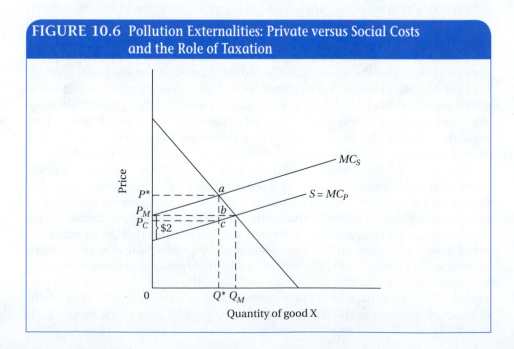

FIGURE 10.6 Pollution Externalities: Private versus Social Costs and the Role of Taxation

FIGURE 10.7 Increasing Pollution Externalities with Economic Growth

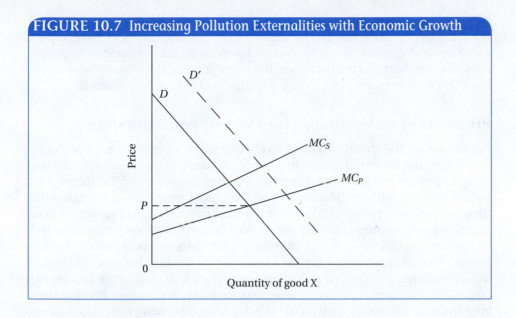

At sufficiently high levels, most emissions will be toxic to humans or otherwise damaging to the environment, whereas at low levels, per-unit costs may be insignificant. This is due to the fact that humans have some tolerance for most toxins, although the ability to tolerate exposure may rapidly decline as concentrations in drinking water and air increase. The environment also has an **absorptive capacity** that enables it to assimilate a quantity of most pollutants. Once this critical quantity has been exceeded, however, concentrations and hence toxicity are likely to rise rapidly. A more realistic marginal social cost curve is drawn in Figure 10.7. As concentrations of pollutants increase (as total output increases), the gap between the social and private cost curves increases. While aggregate demand remains low, this differential will be small. However, as the demand curve shifts outward from D to D' with rapid urbanization and rising incomes, the importance of externalities rises at an increasing rate. This suggests that the costs associated with curing urban ills caused by congestion will increase faster than the rate of increase of the population.

Health hazards are created by toxic air emissions as well as increasing volumes of waste that contaminate water supplies and land. The World Health Organization (WHO) has estimated that 1.5 billion people live in cities with unsafe levels of airborne particulate matter and 1 billion have been exposed to unacceptably high levels of sulfur dioxide.[43] Other compounds, such as nitrous oxides and organic compounds, rise in importance as industrialization proceeds. By contaminating water supplies, contributing to dangerous levels of air pollution, and damaging public and private property, industrial pollution can exact a high toll in terms of human health and economic prosperity.

A number of case studies indicate the potential severity of industrial pollution. In Bangkok, high levels of airborne lead caused such severe consequences for the development of small children that the average child's IQ was lowered by four or more points by the age of 7. Seventy percent of children

Absorptive capacity The capacity of an ecosystem to assimilate potential pollutants.

in Mexico City had abnormally high blood levels of lead. Health complications caused by smog tend to be worse in developing countries, where poor nutrition and general ill health greatly lower individual tolerance to pollutants. The implications for health are the worst for young children, who inhale roughly twice as many pollutants per unit of body weight as adults do.

Problems of Congestion, Clean Water, and Sanitation

As serious as the threat of rising levels of industrial emissions of pollution may be to the health of urban inhabitants in developing countries, the two most important environmental factors affecting the health of the urban poor are the inaccessibility of clean water and the lack of sanitation. Although much progress has been made, in 2009, over a billion people still had no access to an improved water source, and 1.5 billion had no improved sanitation. The lack of sanitary conditions in urban slums often presents severe threats to human health. The urban statistics can be somewhat misleading because millions of urban residents are counted as having access if they share a single faucet with over 1,000 residents at a considerable distance from their homes. Because there are no alternative sources, many of the poor collect drinking water from rivers, streams, and canals that are polluted with human excreta and chemicals.

Although the poorest urban dwellers experience many of the same adverse environmental conditions as the rural poor, including heavy indoor pollution and unsanitary conditions, crowding can intensify exposure. Raw sewage runs in many streets, mixing with garbage and contributing to the spread of disease. This is reflected in the fact that death rates in urban shanties are occasionally higher than in rural areas, even though the latter generally have fewer services.

The health and economic costs associated with these conditions are enormous (see Chapter 8) and represent formidable obstacles to the improvement of living standards. But children in households with adequate facilities are 60% less likely to die from diarrhea than those in households without such facilities.

The enormous economic costs resulting from lost productivity and expensive medical care represent a drag on economic development. Chronic ill health is both a consequence and a cause of poverty. It can contribute to poor nutrition, poor school performance, reduced productivity, and permanent disability, and thus give little hope for economic advancement (see Chapter 8). In addition to averting fatalities, improvements in the supply of water and sanitation reduce the incidence and severity of illnesses, thereby reducing other costs associated with waterborne disease.

Although higher-income households generally have access to either publicly or privately provided services, the poorest are generally without services. This is frequently due to the illegal status of much low-income housing, which renders it ineligible for government services and makes it risky for private individuals to invest in upgrading equipment. As a result, the majority of the poor must purchase water, often contaminated, from vendors at an average of 10 times the cost of piped water.

Postponement of investments in the infrastructure required for provision of urban water and sanitation can lead to much greater costs in the future. Poor access to water has led to widespread systems of private wells, which can overtax existing groundwater supplies. In a number of large cities, including Bangkok,

Mexico City, and Jakarta, this phenomenon has led to the collapse of existing infrastructure and the destruction of property through subsidence of the land and flooding. In coastal areas, overuse can draw salt water into supplies, leading to their permanent salinization. Where raw sewage is untreated and is improperly disposed of, underground and surface water is frequently contaminated, creating long-term shortages of clean water and threatening public health.

Foreign-exchange earnings may also be severely threatened by contaminated water supplies. Health standards in developed countries may prohibit the importation of agricultural goods produced with potentially contaminated water.

In light of these problems, it is not surprising that the costs of preventive measures are typically lower than those associated with lost revenues, resources, and infrastructure.

10.5 The Local and Global Costs of Rain Forest Destruction

Changes in patterns of land use in the developing countries currently make their largest contribution to global concentrations of **greenhouse gases**. It is estimated that deforestation alone accounts for roughly 20% of carbon dioxide (CO_2) emissions worldwide.[44] Because trees consume carbon dioxide and release oxygen during the process of photosynthesis, the tropical rain forests represent an important mechanism through which the ecosystem regenerates itself. Clearing rain forests reduces the environment's absorptive capacity for CO_2. In addition, accelerating extinctions pose a dangerous threat to **biodiversity**, with an estimated 12% of the world's bird species, 24% of mammal species, and 30% of fish species vulnerable or in immediate danger of extinction, largely in rain forest areas.[45]

Deforestation continues at a massive scale. Globally, the loss of forests can stem from several causes, including severe droughts with fires, and invasive pest species. However, most deforestation is caused by the clearing of tropical rain forests for agricultural purposes.

The UN Food and Agriculture Organization estimates that about 13 million hectares of forest were lost each year on average for the decade 2000–2010, which represents some improvement when compared to the annual loss of 16 million hectares in the historical peak decade of deforestation in the 1990s. Forest expansion, including large-scale tree planting and natural expansion in other areas of the world, partially compensates (these are usually not rain forests), but the net annual global loss remains a very high 5.2 million hectares.[46]

The majority of tropical rain forest destroyed, about 60%, is cleared for cultivation by small farmers. Much of it, like 90% of rain forest land worldwide, is so infertile that it will be cultivable for no more than a few years. The land is then frequently sold to large farmers who use it for grazing cattle, often under heavy government subsidy, leading to further desertification. The previous tenants are then forced to clear additional forest areas in a desperate attempt to derive a livelihood for the next few years. In the past, rain forest settlement programs have regularly been encouraged and financed by governments in several developing nations, often with the assistance of international development banks. A review by the World Bank of its own support for settlement

Greenhouse gases Gases that trap heat within the earth's atmosphere and can thus contribute to global warming.

Biodiversity The variety of life forms within an ecosystem.

programs found that they were exceptionally expensive—on average, $10,000 per household—and could be environmentally destructive. Policymakers in countries with large rain forests, including Brazil, Bolivia, the Philippines, and Ecuador, are therefore experiencing increasing pressure from foreign public and private agencies to implement policies that will reduce the rate of tropical forest destruction. It is argued that the resulting decrease in the growth of concentration of greenhouse gases and protection of biodiversity will be in everyone's interests. Thus, rain forest preservation provides a public good.

Because the political and economic costs of preserving the rain forests are often masked or ambiguous, maintaining a rain forest may appear to be an almost costless venture. In fact, because of the important roles that rain forests play in the domestic economies of many developing nations, the true costs of preserving all remaining rain forest may be extraordinarily high. The opportunity costs arising from the preservation of rain forests will involve the loss of an important source of domestic fuel, forgone foreign-exchange earnings from timber and beef, and the loss of a temporary solution to the problem of land shortages and population pressures. It is therefore unreasonable to assume that the few developing countries that contain the majority of remaining rain forests should be responsible for single-handedly providing this **global public good**. Indeed, when foreign countries are allowed a free ride—that is, if they are allowed to benefit from rain forest preservation without contributing to it—deforestation will continue at an undesirable pace. To reduce the resulting inefficiencies, the public-goods model would suggest lowering the relative price per unit of protected forest for the developing country and increasing it for the outside beneficiaries. For the latter, this would entail the contribution of fees earmarked for the preservation of rain forests.

Global public good A public good, whose benefits reach across national borders and population groups.

Several steps must be taken to preserve the rain forests. Long-term solutions include increasing the accessibility of alternative fuels, managing sustainable timber programs, and providing economic opportunities for impoverished peoples now resorting to clearing tracts of fragile rain forest land. Developing countries could vastly increase the efficiency of their economic use of rain forests by managing them (less than 1% of rain forests have been replanted or cut in a sustainable manner) and by developing alternative markets for other rain forest products, such as nuts, fruits, oils, sweeteners, resins, tannin, fibers, construction materials, and natural medicinal compounds. Much of the timber burned to open land for cultivation could be harvested for financial gain. For example, it was estimated that in the 1990s, Brazil lost some $2.5 billion annually in the burning of rain forest timber. Sustainable timber production for fuel or export can be achieved through the restriction of cutting cycles to 30-year intervals and the careful maintenance of new growth. It is extremely costly, if not impossible, to regenerate a rain forest that has been clear-cut, so proper maintenance and supervision of logging are necessary. More careful oversight of timber concessions by developing country governments can prevent clear-cutting, reduce careless destruction of uncut trees, and increase the efficiency of revenue collection from concessions. There are also undervalued services from forests, including climate regulation, rain (and water cycling), flood control, and soil conservation.

The international community should also assist in the preservation effort. By reducing trade barriers to the alternative goods just mentioned, developed countries reduce the dependence of many developing countries on unsustainable modes of production. Debt-for-nature swaps (to be explained shortly) also reduce the need for the rapid exploitation of forests to raise foreign exchange. Finally, funds for the preservation and maintenance of tropical rain forests are necessary to guarantee the success of conservation programs that provide global public goods. It is important that such funds not be viewed as aid, because the ultimate benefits are to be shared by all in natural heritage, biodiversity, and containment of global warming. The Global Environmental Facility has played a significant role in rain forest protection. The global REDD-plus program to help developing countries preserve forests was discussed earlier in the chapter. The continued indebtedness of a number of developing nations with substantial forests, particularly in Africa, may make it exceptionally difficult for governments with large debt burdens to finance the expenses of environmental programs designed to protect natural resources.

In recent years, a number of international assistance agencies have established environmental divisions to promote more environmentally conscientious patterns of lending. They have also initiated programs to address environmental issues directly. Their success in the future may largely depend on the compatibility of such efforts with the economic realities confronting governments in the developing world.[47]

People from countries with significant rain forests sometimes object to the strong pressure they feel to protect rain forests by asking, "Didn't developed countries grow by cutting down forests? So why should you pressure us in the developing world not to do so now? Do you want us not to develop?" To the first question, development probably did not arise from cutting forests; productivity gains were primarily responsible, not unsustainable timbering and extended use of more land. But even so, there are many technology alternatives not available in past decades. Of course, it would indeed be better to emphasize local benefits and pay for global costs, rather than to pressure or bully developing countries, which have a long history of unequal relations with the developed world. But there are indeed at least four other significant differences:

- First, tropical and deciduous forests differ in nutrients and restorability—in the former, nutrients are more in the biomass, less in the soil; rain forests do not regenerate the way deciduous forests do.

- Second, tropical rain forest destruction generates much larger externalities—local and especially global.

- Third, forests have more value now due to opportunities for payments for carbon protection and genetic diversity funds.

- Fourth, there is also more value now in fields, such as sources of new antibiotics and other drugs. In addition, expanded forest use and elimination is a strange target for industrial policy because productivity gains are focused in the manufacturing sector; from a fiscal standpoint, it makes basic economic sense to eliminate subsidies and tax breaks for doing so. And carving bean farms out of rain forests is an unfortunate substitute for land reform (for example, indigenous people already live and depend on these forests).

10.6 Policy Options in Developing and Developed Countries

What Developing Countries Can Do

A range of policy options is available for governments in developing countries. Seven stand out: (1) proper resource pricing, (2) community involvement, (3) clearer property rights and resource ownership, (4) improving economic alternatives for the poor, (5) raising the economic status of women, (6) policies to abate industrial emissions, and (7) taking a proactive stance toward adapting to climate change. Let's briefly examine each in turn.[48]

Proper Resource Pricing   The most obvious area for reform is probably government pricing policy, including subsidies, which can exacerbate resource shortages or encourage unsustainable methods of production. Often programs that were ostensibly designed to reduce hardships for the very poor have had little impact on poverty and have worsened existing inequalities. High-income households have frequently been the predominant beneficiaries of environmentally damaging energy, water, and agricultural subsidies. For example, on average in developing countries, the price paid for piped water is less than the total cost of supplying it. Due to rationing, such subsidies frequently benefit only people with higher incomes. Much public water is simply stolen—often by wealthy individuals. The result has often been a wasteful and unsustainable use of resources. Even though elimination of misdirected subsidies is a relatively costless (or profitable) way of protecting the environment, the political stakes are high where powerful elites stand to lose lucrative government transfers.

Community Involvement   Programs to improve environmental conditions are likely to be most effective when they work in tandem with community networks, ensuring that program design is consistent with both local and national objectives. The experience of development agencies has demonstrated that grassroots efforts can be more cost-effective because they generally involve the use of low-cost alternatives and provide jobs to local populations. When poor communities truly benefit from public-works programs, residents are often willing and able to contribute much of the program costs. Institutions facilitating cooperative management of common property resources can also be encouraged.

Clearer Property Rights and Resource Ownership   Investments in household sanitation and water and on-farm improvements often represent a large portion of lifetime savings for the poor, the loss of which can impose harsh economic consequences on households. Hence, the lack of secure tenure on rural or urban property can greatly hinder investment in environmental upgrading. Legalization of tenure can lead to improved living conditions for the poor and increases in agricultural investments.

In many cases, however, land reform may be necessary (see Chapter 9). It is not uncommon for renters or sharecroppers to lose the economic gains from their farm investments because it is relatively easy for landlords to extract higher rents once the productivity of the land has been improved. Transferring title to tenants may be the only means of ensuring that financial rewards from land-augmenting investments accrue to the investor. Land reform may also be required where unequal distribution of land has led to large tracts of uncultivated high-quality land in close proximity to overexploited marginal lands cultivated by large numbers of landless workers. If equitable and efficient common property resource use is to continue, well-designed facilitating policies will be needed, taking into account what has been learned about the conditions in which they are most effective (see Box 10.3).

Programs to Improve the Economic Alternatives of the Poor   Further environmental devastation in rural areas may be avoidable in many cases through on-farm investments in irrigation and sustainable farming techniques, the use of alternative fuels, and the creation of barriers to erosion. However, the economic costs of each of these alternatives are prohibitive for the vast majority of impoverished family producers. Ironically, the greater the environmental devastation, the less likely that a rural population will be able to afford alternative methods of production. It is therefore important that government programs make credit and land-augmenting inputs accessible to small farmers. By providing rural economic opportunities outside the home, governments can also create alternative employment opportunities so that the very poor are not forced to cultivate marginal lands; for example, programs to build rural infrastructure (roads, storage facilities, etc.) create local jobs, alleviate population pressures on ecologically sensitive land, stimulate rural development, and reduce the flow of rural-to-urban migration.

Raising the Economic Status of Women   Improving the educational attainment of women and increasing their range of economic alternatives raise the opportunity cost of their time and may lead to decreases in desired family size (see Chapter 6). Education also tends to increase women's access to information concerning child nutrition and hygiene, a factor that has been linked to rapid declines in child mortality. It is important that community-based environmental programs work closely with women because their own day-to-day activities may largely determine patterns of resource use and their ability to meet the needs of their families is dependent on the sustainable management of water and fuel supplies.

Industrial Emissions Abatement Policies   A range of policy options is available to developing-country governments for the purpose of limiting industrial pollution, including the taxation of emissions, tradable emissions permits, quotas, and standards. There is some evidence to suggest that the first two policies, which are market-based, are more effective because they tend to reward the more efficient producers, allow greater flexibility for firms, and are generally easier to enforce. Regulations should be as simple as possible and must be enforceable. Additional incentives to adopt clean technologies may be provided through tax credits and subsidies specifically tied to the purchase or development of pollution abatement technologies. Ironically, the hardest industries to regulate are those run by governments themselves because the profit motive is often not a consideration and, as a general rule, it is difficult for any group to regulate itself.[49]

Proactive Stance toward Climate Change and Environmental Degradation   Proactive policies can help make the developing economy, in general, and the poor, in particular, more resilient and able to adapt to climate change, much of which is already inevitable. Developing nations can implement and continuously improve early warning systems to anticipate environmental emergencies; promote reforestation; restore natural ecosystem barriers such as mangroves; improve microinsurance programs; and construct storm shelters, flood barriers, and protected roads and bridges. To protect forest cover, it may be effective to employ the poor as guardians of these resources. Living on site, they are more likely than absentee owners to pay attention to poaching and illegal logging. In many countries, more government transparency and accountability are also needed. The empowerment of the poor and their organizations can play an important role in protecting the natural resources on which many of the poor depend for their livelihoods and in seeing that government helps meet their generally greater needs for assistance with adaptation.

How Developed Countries Can Help Developing Countries

Industrial countries can help developing nations in their efforts to improve the environment of development in three areas: (1) trade liberalization, (2) debt relief, and (3) financial and technological assistance.

Trade Policies   The focus of much current discussion concerning the environment is the desperate need to break the cycle of poverty and environmental destruction in developing countries. However, protectionism in agricultural and other goods has caused international markets and thus earning capacity for these developing-country products to shrink dramatically (see Chapter 12).[50] Eliminating trade barriers against developing-country exports by stimulating economic growth in the developing world, creating new jobs, and encouraging rural development could significantly reduce the level of absolute poverty.

In addition to trade barriers, the industrialized countries penalize developing-country exports by heavily subsidizing their own agricultural sectors. The resulting large surpluses are often dumped on international markets, unfairly undercutting the agricultural exports of developing countries in markets for which they are presumed to have a comparative advantage. Reducing the estimated $500 billion in annual agricultural subsidies in developed countries could help guarantee the success of rural development efforts in developing nations by reducing poverty and the environmental decay that it causes. Developing countries would thereby reduce their dependence on the unsustainable exploitation of rain forests and other resources to raise foreign exchange.

Debt Relief   Wider access to international markets not only raises incomes but also improves the ability of heavily indebted countries to service their debt. Heavy debt servicing drastically reduces funds available to developing-country governments for domestic social programs, including those designed to alleviate poverty and reduce environmental degradation (see Chapter 13). Debt forgiveness may be required if governments particularly in heavily indebted poor countries are to be given the flexibility to make the sweeping changes necessary to achieve sustainable development.

Debt-for-nature swaps offer an attractive and mutually beneficial way for the developing world to retire its foreign-denominated debt while guaranteeing the protection of tropical rain forests.[51] In a debt-for-nature swap, a foreign, private environmental organization such as the U.S.-based Rainforest Alliance or the Nature Conservancy, working in conjunction with a local environmental organization, purchases developing-country debt on financial markets at a fraction, say, 30%, of the face value. The debt is then exchanged for government bonds denominated in the debtor-country currency but worth the full value of the original foreign debt. The environmental organization purchasing the debt is thus able to leverage its funds by 230%. Income from the securities is used to maintain rain forest or wildlife reserves. In this way, the developing country no longer owes debt in scarce hard currencies and is able to set up endowments for the preservation of national resources. The foreign donor is able to make an effective contribution several times larger than the actual outlay of cash and obtains a verbal guarantee that the endowment will be used to protect natural resources. Although debt-for-nature swaps provided an exciting, albeit partial, solution to tropical deforestation, a number of persistent economic and political obstacles has limited the potential scope of such programs, not the least of which is fear of foreign control over domestic resource decisions.[52]

Debt-for-nature swap The exchange of foreign debt held by an organization for a larger quantity of domestic debt that is used to finance the preservation of a natural resource or environment in the debtor country.

Development Assistance   Substantial new development assistance is necessary in developing countries to achieve sustainable development. These investments would be used for a variety of programs to alleviate poverty, provide services, and promote sustainable patterns of production. Additional aid from developing countries earmarked for these purposes could have a positive impact on developing-country environments (see Chapter 14). Even greater sums would be necessary to maintain tropical rain forests, which provide benefits to the entire international community through reduced CO_2 emissions. There are many tactics that can be evaluated on a case-by-case basis for cost-effectiveness. The most general approach is to support programs to alleviate landlessness and poverty, to help eliminate the socioeconomic causes of some of the tropical deforestation. Specific tactics include purchase of timber rights by national and international agencies, together with paying indigenous communities to monitor forest preservation (as originally proposed by Conservation International, an NGO). Preservation efforts could be paid for by the international community as a global public good.

Assistance with adaptation to climate change is a critical element where assistance is needed. Provision of greener technology to developing countries can help reduce greenhouse gases generally but will not in themselves help developing countries adapt to climate change. Programs such as the GEF (Global Environment Facility) and REDD-plus, discussed earlier, are important steps.

What Developed Countries Can Do for the Global Environment

Perhaps most important, developed countries, which currently consume over 70% of the earth's resources, can directly contribute to global environmental improvement through their own efforts to (1) reduce harmful emissions,

FIGURE 10.8 The Earth at Night, Reflecting Inequality of Energy Use across High-, Middle-, and Low-Income Countries; and Concentration of Economic Activity along Seacoasts

Craig Mayhew and Robert Simmon, NASA GSFC

including greenhouse gases, (2) undertake R&D to develop green technologies and pollution control for themselves and for developing countries, and (3) alter their own environmentally harmful patterns of demand.

The composite photo in Figure 10.8 dramatically illustrates the unequal global pattern of resource use. This image is a composite of hundreds of photos of the earth at night taken by satellite. Human-made lights draw attention to high-income (as well as densely populated) regions, particularly Europe, the United States, and Japan. Highly populated and now upper-middle-income coastal China also stands out. India is clearly seen, if less brightly; India is a lower-middle-income country, but with high population density. The lack of electric lighting in sub-Saharan Africa, the poorest region, compares dramatically with other population centers. Middle-income areas of very low population density, such as the central parts of South America and Asia, are also dark. As the map suggests, much economic activity is located near seacoasts largely for the simple economic reason that people can exchange goods utilizing low-cost shipping; for example the big cities of Brazil stand out. Differences in economies with good and poor institutions also show up—most vividly across the border between North and South Korea. Note that the per capita use of lighting parallels the overall use of electric power and other resources. Thus, the image also provides a vivid picture of the extraordinary unequal distribution of resource use that still prevails across high-, upper-middle-, lower-middle-, and low-income countries.

The United States and other developed countries produce a majority of the greenhouse gas emissions and consume a disproportionate share of environmentally sensitive products such as ocean fish; their consumption of energy, wood products, and raw materials is even more strikingly disproportionate.[53] A substantial part of developed-country consumption is wasteful. It seems clear that the world as a whole cannot consume at current U.S. or other developed-country levels; responsible consumption on the part of the developed countries is not just setting a good example but an ecological necessity. This does not mean that economies cannot continue to grow indefinitely—clearly they can, as more consumption becomes knowledge-based and more modest in its use of raw materials. It is rather that the patterns of consumption must change. As we have seen, price signals alone will not guide resource use when substantial externalities and public goods are involved.

Emission Controls Beyond responsible consumption, perhaps the greatest contribution that the developed world can make to the global environment will be through a clear demonstration of their own commitment to a cleaner environment. Because they remain the main polluters of air and sea, developed countries must lead the way to global changes in current and future patterns of production. If wealthy nations do not achieve significant and sustained reductions in the production of greenhouse gases, it will be difficult to convince the developing world to do so, considering that per capita emissions levels are far below those in the industrialized countries.

Research and Development The high-income countries must also take a leadership role in research and development efforts. Growing public support for stricter environmental regulation in the industrialized world is likely to lead to the development of both cheaper emissions abatement technologies and cleaner (or "greener") production processes. Innovations resulting from research and development will enhance efforts to reduce emissions if they are adopted in developing countries. Currently, many clean technologies are prohibitively expensive for the developing world's industries. It is thus unrealistic to expect low-income countries to attain standards set in high-income countries. However, it is not necessary for developing countries to reproduce environmental debacles endured during the onset of industrialization in the developed world. Making cheaper, cleaner abatement technologies accessible to developing countries can help limit a principal source of global emissions—the rapid industrialization of the developing world. Availability of low-carbon technologies will be crucial in the fight to limit climate change.

Import Restrictions Through its importation of products that are associated with environmentally unsustainable production, the developed world has an indirect but important impact on the global environment. International treaties to limit the destruction of endangered resources will have little effect if wealthy nations continue to provide lucrative markets for the sale of such goods. Import restrictions are an effective way of reducing undesired international trade. Consumer sovereignty expressed through boycotts and other forms of pressure on corporations can be effective. However, they require strong leadership and tend to focus on large firms, which represent only a relatively small portion of the overall problem.

Of course, it is important to make certain that such environmental restrictions applied by government or civil society are not merely disguised protectionism against developing countries and to ensure that the poor are provided opportunities to preserve their livelihoods through their environmental wealth in a sustainable and equitable manner.

A World of Contrasts on One Island: Haiti and the Dominican Republic

The terrible earthquake that struck Haiti in January 2010 brought to public awareness an immediate crisis of horrific proportions—and also an ongoing slow-motion disaster of poverty and suffering in a nation of 10 million people, including an environmental crisis. News reports showed its neighbor, the Dominican Republic (DR), also with a population of just over 10 million in 2012, with higher incomes, less poverty, and much better environmental conditions.

Haiti's environmental disaster could have been substantially averted with better domestic policies. And so it is not the root cause of Haiti's problems. But why were better environmental (and other supporting) policies not in place? That is, what were the limits of Haiti's institutions in this respect? And are Haiti's environmental problems caused by the country's great poverty? Has environmental degradation itself now also become one of the causes of continued economic and human development stagnation? What could have been done with well-targeted aid, and what role can aid play now?

Travelers to Haiti who flew across the border from the DR saw an astonishing contrast: Haiti to the west is barren, while the DR to the east is lush forest—except where Haitians desperate for fuelwood for income from charcoal production have made forays across the border. In 2004, the United Nations Development Programme (UNDP) commented on this scene, noting "a cycle of poverty and environmental destruction has denuded hillsides." In 2005, Jared Diamond wrote eloquently that "the border looks like a sharp line with bends, cut arbitrarily across the island by a knife, and abruptly dividing a darker and greener landscape east of the line (the Dominican side) from a paler and browner landscape west of the line (the Haitian

side)." He added, "On the ground, one can stand on the border at many places, face east, and look into pine forest, then turn around, face west, and see nothing except fields almost devoid of trees." Years after this helpful publicity, little to address the problems was being accomplished.

On the eastern (nearly) two-thirds of the island of Hispaniola that the two nations share, the DR finds itself with a medium human development ranking, at number 96 on the 2012 New HDI. On the western third of Hispaniola, Haiti has a low human development ranking, at number 161—using data that do not yet reflect the full impact of the earthquake.

The contrasts between the two nations sharing the island of Hispaniola were not always as stark as today. In 1960, real incomes in these two countries were not very far apart, about \$2,345 for the DR and \$1,877 for Haiti in the Penn World Table estimates—that is, approximately 25% higher in the DR. Haiti had about 12% of average U.S. income levels at the time, while the DR had 16% of average U.S. income. But by 2007, real GDP in the DR had risen to \$9,664; but it actually fell in Haiti to \$1,581. That is, income in the DR is now over *six times* that of Haiti. U.S. incomes grew in this period such that Haiti's average income by 2007 was less than 4% of U.S. levels. But the DR, which had grown somewhat faster than the United States, now reached an average income that was more than 22% of that in the United States. (While estimates differ across methods, the qualitative comparisons are similar; Angus Maddison's research indicates almost identical incomes for the two countries in 1950, but by 2008, the DR incomes were over *seven* times that of Haiti.) This fact suggests that important clues are to be found in events and policies since 1960. On the other hand, to understand opportunities and

constraints so that it becomes clearer why policies diverged, it is often helpful to start with the beginnings of colonial times.

Hispaniola was "discovered" in 1492 by Christopher Columbus, but a large majority of its hundreds of thousands of Arawak and Taino people soon died—of diseases brought by the Spaniards, overwork in enslavement, and genocide. Slaves were then forcibly brought in from Africa. Since that hideous period, the economic histories of Haiti and the DR have been a tale of contrasts.

Haiti soon became one of the highest-income countries in the world, albeit with one of the highest extremes of inequality in history, with a large, impoverished, and brutalized slave population supporting a small, wealthy elite. In contrast, the DR, with fewer slave plantations, was more the tortoise to Haiti's hare. The better performance of the DR seems to offer further confirmation of the analysis of Chapter 2 (and of the case study for Chapter 5) of how differences in earlier institutions can have a big effect on economic development outcomes. This experience also reveals how influences of deep, structural inequality and education (or its lack) can shape the evolution of institutions over time, as was also first introduced in Chapter 2 and explored in Chapters 5 and 8. And it is also suggestive as to how each of these three factors can, through the quality of policies, affect the extent of environmental decay and how that can, in turn, worsen human capabilities and development prospects. What can we learn from the long-term record?

Geography and Original Environments

Hispaniola is a subtropical island of about 76,482 square kilometers—smaller than Cuba but larger than Jamaica or Puerto Rico. Sharing the same island, both Haiti and the DR seem to have started with similar geographies and environments, with some modest differences. The DR occupies about 64% of the land area; with the remaining 36%, Haiti is about the size of the Hawaiian Islands. Rainfall is slightly higher in the DR because the rain typically comes from the east; Haiti is more mountainous, and its mountains block the rain. The rivers flow mostly eastward from these mountains, providing water for the DR. These modest initial environmental differences may have put Haiti at some disadvantage, but Haiti has done

well economically in comparison to the DR in some periods. Both countries were once largely covered with forests. But environmental damage was already under way under colonial rule, with deforestation due to extensive logging and overuse of the soil. Adverse human influence has had a bigger impact in Haiti.

Institutions: Historical Legacy

Clearly, neither country started with favorable institutions. The abundance of resources and the island's suitability for sugar production led the Spanish to create institutions designed for extraction. The Spanish New World *repartimiento* system, in which Spanish-born *peninsulares* received land tracts and the right to use native labor, was first implemented in Hispaniola. When importing slaves became too expensive for the Spanish, the French gained control of Haiti in 1697. The colony became a major slaveholding plantation economy and the wealthiest European colony in the New World. But a large majority of the population were slaves. A slave revolt led Haiti to independence in 1804. Both Haiti and the DR suffered subsequent attempts to reinstate slavery and fought wars against each other, including an 1821–1843 attempt at reunification (known as the Haitian occupation in the DR, whose Independence Day celebrates freedom from Haiti).

The period of revolt in Haiti led to much death and to the destruction of wealth as sugar plantations burned. And while the brutality of slavery ended, extreme inequality persisted in Haiti under a new mulatto and black privileged class for whom the French elite were the cultural reference point. But the French invaded and received a huge ransom, allegedly for lost wealth from expropriation. Fear of invasion and alienation from white slaveholding countries and colonies kept the country inward looking; this was reinforced by a policy of isolation imposed by slaveholding countries, including the United States. The mutual distrust between Haiti and its potential trading partners is one cause of the resulting autarkic development, including reluctance to allow foreign ownership. The people of Haiti also spoke Creole, an obstacle for potential trading partners; Spanish was spoken in the DR. Europeans tended to view the DR as Spanish but Haiti as African and hence "inferior."

Haiti then evolved into a subsistence farming economy but continued to have a larger population than the DR on far less land. The DR had more extensive cattle-based activities.

The DR became fully independent only after 1843. It was undermined by war and intrigue, such as restoration of Spanish authority briefly in the 1860s and occupation by the United States from 1916 to 1924. During the occupation, significant infrastructure was built, including schools, roads, and ports—projects continued and extended to hydropower under the subsequent brutal Trujillo dictatorship; this helped facilitate a relatively higher growth rate, though inequality was reinforced while freedoms were repressed.

The United States occupied Haiti from 1915 to 1934. Basic security and order were restored, and road construction, expanded public health, education services, and other infrastructure improved. However, after U.S. occupation, the dictator François "Papa Doc" Duvalier—a brutal ruler like Trujillo in the DR—did not focus on modernizing Haiti, in some contrast to Trujillo. As Laura Jaramillo and Cemile Sancak concluded, Duvalier was only interested in short-term rent-seeking opportunities instead of maintaining the country's infrastructure. The DR has emerged as a much more democratic nation since the 1978 elections, while at least until very recently Haiti has made far less progress.

Human Capital

Haiti has the highest illiteracy rate in the western hemisphere, estimated at more than half the population. The school system is badly underfunded and disorganized. Health conditions are equally bad and include high under-5 mortality, hunger, and a large HIV/AIDS problem. The 2010 cholera outbreak was a symptom of a broken health system. The DR, although not without serious education problems, has done a far better job than Haiti at providing its people with the human capital they need to compete in a globalizing economy.

Policy Effects

In the 1990s, growth rates accelerated in the DR due to improvements in education, trade policies, and infrastructure. Remittances and tourism grew to become nearly a quarter of the country's GDP, and net manufacturing exports per capita doubled. Haiti, however, suffered from political instability during the same period. The army overthrew President Aristide in 1991 and began a violent regime that damaged the economy directly and also indirectly through subsequent UN and U.S. trade embargoes. Haiti also failed to diversify its economy; its continued focus on sugar has left Haiti not only contending with volatile sugar prices but also competing against sugar-subsidizing rich countries (most prominently the United States). The DR's diversification into tourism depended on a clean environment—both on its beaches and in its forests—for ecotourism. Policy in the DR actively sought out foreign investment for manufacturing that provided higher-wage employment. The DR has long had far more nature reserves and national parks; Trujillo's insistence on forest preservation had long-run positive effects on the environment and development. The DR has clearly had better policies, and apparently, a long legacy of institutions mattered for the policy differences between the DR and its neighbor.

Poverty can cause environmental damage, and the poor can, in turn, become its victims. Haiti's agricultural expansion has been poorly managed. Deforestation has, in turn, led to the massive loss of fertile soil, lowering productivity of farms. Currently, more than a quarter of the DR is forested, compared to only 1% forest cover in Haiti. A similar cover existed in Haiti as in the DR just a few decades ago. Other low-income countries have introduced and enforced helpful environmental regulations; had Haiti done the same, despite deep historical roots, the environmental disaster might at some level have been averted. The case of Haiti adds to the growing evidence that environmental destruction can retard the development process more generally and needs to be a bigger priority.

Both countries have faced serious environmental challenges, including hurricanes and earthquakes. It is critical to manage the risk of extreme events before they become full-blown humanitarian disasters; this is something the DR has done much more effectively than Haiti. The UNDP explained it this way in its 2007–2008 *Human Development Report*:

> In 2004, the Dominican Republic and Haiti were simultaneously struck by Hurricane Jeanne. In the Dominican Republic, some 2 million people were affected and a

major town was almost destroyed, but there were just 23 deaths and recovery was relatively swift. In Haiti, over 2,000 people were killed in the town of Gonaives alone. And tens of thousands were left trapped in a downward spiral of poverty. The contrasting impacts were not the product of meteorology. In Haiti, a cycle of poverty and environmental destruction has denuded hillsides of trees and left millions of people in vulnerable slums. Governance problems, low levels of finance and a limited disaster response capacity left public agencies unable to initiate rescue and recovery operations on the scale required. In the Dominican Republic, national laws have limited deforestation and the civil defence force has a staff 10 times larger than its counterpart in Haiti to cater for a population of similar size.

Poverty cannot always be contained by national boundaries. There is a large-scale emigration of Haitians over the border to the DR, despite the harsh welcome they often receive there. Dominicans, in turn, are emigrating to the United States in significant numbers. The reported illegal logging by Haitians across the border in the DR, believed to be largely for charcoal production, is a challenge for the DR's emphasis on environmental preservation as a development strategy. Currently, the DR is investing in replanting trees along its border with Haiti.

It is clear that environmental deterioration results from bad economic and regulatory policies. Poverty, too, remains severe in significant measure due to poor policies. Severe poverty, in turn, leads to environmental deterioration, which perpetuates poverty directly and through reduced overall growth.

Most of the causality has run from poverty to environment (as well as from rapacious, unsustainable economic policies dating from the French colonial period). But today, addressing environment is a vital step in Haiti's start toward development. Improved environmental policies have greatly aided countries such as Costa Rica—and increasingly the DR—that have invested in the land. Unfortunately, as noted in this chapter, global warming will bring much more substantial climate change. The future is expected to see more and deadlier hurricanes and other challenges that will require adaptation and resilience. To the extent that adaptation capacity and resilience are synonymous with human development, this gives the edge for the DR to build on its already large lead going forward. There is a strong case for the international community to respond to Haiti's plight with well-implemented aid, with attention that does not dissipate as the earthquake disaster recedes in the world's memory. ■

Sources

Diamond, Jared. *Collapse: How Societies Choose to Fail or Succeed*. New York: Penguin Books, 2005.

Dupuy, Alex. *Haiti in the World Economy: Class, Race, and Underdevelopment since 1700*. Boulder, Colo.: Westview Press, 1989.

Fielding, David, and Sebastian Torres. "Cows and conquistadores: A contribution to the colonial origins of comparative development." *Journal of Development Studies* 44 (2008): 1081–1099.

Gronewold, Nathanial. "Haiti: Environmental destruction, chaos bleeding across border." *Greenwire*, December 14, 2009. http://www.eenews.net/public/Greenwire/2009/12/14/5.

Hartlyn, Jonathan. *The Struggle for Democratic Politics in the Dominican Republic*. Chapel Hill: University of North Carolina Press, 1998.

Hausmann, Ricardo, Dani Rodrik, and Andrés Velasco. "Growth diagnostics," 2005. http://ksghome.harvard.edu/~drodrik/barcelonafinalmarch2005.pdf.

Howard, Philip. "Environmental scarcities and conflict in Haiti: Ecology and grievances in Haiti's troubled past and uncertain future." Paper prepared for the Canadian International Development Agency, June 1998.

Jaramillo, Laura, and Cemile Sancak. "Why has the grass been greener on one side of Hispaniola? A comparative growth analysis of the Dominican Republic and Haiti." *IMF Staff Papers* 56 (2009): 323–349.

Logan, Rayford W. *Haiti and the Dominican Republic*. New York: Oxford University Press, 1968.

Lundahl, Mats. "Poorest in the Caribbean: Haiti in the twentieth century." *Integration and Trade* 5 (2001): 177–200.

Maddison Project, http://www.ggdc.net/maddison/maddison-project/home.htm, accessed 16 February 2014.

Martinez, Samuel. "From hidden hand to heavy hand: Sugar, the state, and migrant labor in Haiti and the Dominican Republic." *Latin American Research Review* 34 (1999): 57–84.

Matibag, Euginio. *Haitian-Dominican Counterpoint: Nation, State, Race on Hispaniola*. New York: Palgrave Macmillan, 2003.

Penn World Table, http://pwt.econ.upenn.edu.

Roc, Nancy. "Haiti-environment: From the 'Pearl of the Antilles' to desolation." *FRIDE*, September 19, 2008.

United Nations Development Programme. *Human Development Report, 2007–2008*. New York: Oxford University Press, 2007.

Walter, Ingo, and Judith L. Ugelow. "Environmental policies in developing countries." *Ambio* 8 (1979): 102–109.

World Resources Institute. *World Resources 2005: The Wealth of the Poor—Managing Ecosystems to Fight Poverty*. Washington, D.C.: World Resources Institute, 2005. ∎

Concepts for Review

Absorptive capacity
Biodiversity
Biomass fuels
Clean technologies
Climate change
Common property resource
Consumer surplus
Debt-for-nature swap
Deforestation
Desertification
Environmental accounting
Environmental capital

Environmental Kuznets curve
Externality
Free-rider problem
Global public good
Global warming
Greenhouse gases
Internalization
Marginal cost
Marginal net benefit
Pollution tax
Present value
Private costs

Producer surplus
Property rights
Public bad
Public good
Scarcity rent
Social cost
Soil erosion
Sustainable development
Sustainable net national income (NNI*)
Total net benefit

Questions for Discussion

1. Is sustainable development a practical and feasible goal for nations? What might be some of the difficulties and possible trade-offs? Explain your answer.

2. In what ways does poverty lead to environmental degradation? In what way are the poor victims? Specifically, provide two examples of how the poor sometimes degrade the natural resources on which they depend. Why does this happen, and what might be done to escape this trap?

3. What types of environmental problems do the rural and urban poor share? What are some differences in the conditions they face?

4. How are population growth, poverty, and land pressures interrelated? Explain how these problems can create a vicious circle of events.

5. What steps might governments in less developed countries take to reduce overexploitation of natural resources? What impact do pricing policies have?

6. Why are national environmental concerns in developing countries likely to focus increasingly on urban problems in the future? How are urban conditions related to rural-to-urban migration?

7. Why are the objectives of economic development and sustainable growth mutually reinforcing?

8. In what ways does neoclassical theory provide a useful framework for analyzing environmental issues? What are some of its limitations?

9. What are some of the costs associated with environmental degradation? How might they detract from economic growth? What are the developmental implications?

10. Why are children more susceptible than adults to health risks posed by their environment?

11. In what ways can developed nations best contribute to the alleviation of global and domestic environmental problems? Be specific.

12. Explain the difference between purely private and public goods and how it applies to environmental problems faced by developing countries. What are the implications of the free-rider problem for allocation of a public good?

13. What is the environmental Kuznets curve? What factors may make it plausible? In what cases does it seem implausible?

14. How is climate change expected to impact countries in Latin America, Asia, and Africa? What policies in developed and developing countries may help address these problems?

15. How do farmers in developing countries adapt to climate change that they experience?

16. What are the main ideas of environmental accounting? If practiced, what effects would you expect to see?

17. What are natural resources–based livelihoods, and how are they threatened?

18. What are common property resources; what economic incentive problems do they face; and how have some communities successfully overcome these problems?

19. What is the international community doing to assist the least developed countries (such as Niger) with resilience to climate change? Can you identify any limitations to this assistance?

20. What insights can be found from a comparison of Haiti and the DR for the potential role of environment in economic development?

Notes

1. For a comprehensive view of the range of issues linking the environment to economic development, see World Bank, *World Development Report, 1992* and *2003* (New York: Oxford University Press, 1992, 2003); John M. Antle and Gregg Heidebrink, "Environment and development: Theory and international evidence," *Economic Development and Cultural Change* 43 (1995): 603–625; and Herman E. Daly, *Beyond Doubt: The Economics of Sustainable Development* (Boston: Beacon Press, 1996).

2. For a comparative analysis of various definitions of sustainable development, see Sharachchandra A. Lele, "Sustainable development: A critical review," *World Development* 19 (1991): 607–621, and Lance Taylor, "Sustainable development: An introduction," *World Development* 24 (1996): 215–225.

3. World Commission on Environment and Development, *Our Common Future* (New York: Oxford University Press, 1987), p. 4.

4. David W. Pearce and Jeremy J. Warford, *World without End: Economics, Environment, and Sustainable Development—A Summary* (Washington, D.C.: World Bank, 1993), p. 2. As we will see, policies for achieving sustainable development also involve utilizing an appropriate social discount rate and creating incentives internalization of negative environmental and health externalities.

5. See World Bank, *World Development Report, 2003* (New York: Oxford University Press, 2003), pp. 18 ff. for a brief introduction to the complementarity of environmental assets with other assets.

6. David Pearce and Jeremy Warford provide a good example of environmental accounting, on which this presentation is largely based, in *World without End*, pp. 2–3. See also World Bank, *ibid.*, ch. 2. Regarding the reformulation of NNI**, note that R and A are also part of basic net national income (NNI) because they represent economic activity (for which labor and other factors are paid). Thus, while R and A were also included as part of NNI*, they are being subtracted to arrive at NNI**, because R and A are now treated as part of the broader allowance for depreciation. Their deployment may be highly cost-effective, however.

7. See United Nations Population Fund, *Population, Resources, and the Environment: The Critical*

Challenge (New York: United Nations, 1991), for a review and an analysis of these critical population-environment linkages. See also Maureen L. Cropper and Charles Griffiths, "The interaction of population growth and environmental quality," *American Economic Review* 84 (1994): 250–254, and World Bank, *World Development Report, 2003*.

8. For analysis of these issues, see Karl-Göran Mäler, "Environment, poverty and growth," in World Bank, *Annual World Bank Conference on Development Economics, 1997* (Washington, D.C.: World Bank, 1998), pp. 251–284, and, in the same volume, Ramon E. Lopez, "Where development can or cannot go: The role of poverty-environment linkages," pp. 285–306.

9. Cynthia C. Y. Lin, "Endogeneity in the environmental Kuznets curve: An instrumental variables approach," *American Journal of Agricultural Economics* 95, No. 2(2013): 268–274; and Susmita Dasgupta, Benoit Laplante, Hua Wang and David Wheeler, "Confronting the Environmental Kuznets Curve," *Journal of Economic Perspectives*, 16, 1, Winter 2002, Pages 147–168.

10. See World Resources Institute, *World Resources, 1996–97: The Urban Environment* (New York: Oxford University Press, 1996).

11. A description of the factors leading to the production of greenhouse gases in developing countries is offered in World Bank, *World Development Report, 2009* (New York: Oxford University Press, 2009), and John Bongaarts, "Population growth and global warming," *Population and Development Review* 18 (1992): 299–319.

12. See United Nations Food and Agriculture Organization, *The State of Food and Agriculture, 2006* (Rome: United Nations Food and Agricultural Organization, 2006), tab. A-4, p. 127.

13. For an excellent overview, see United Nations Development Programme, United Nations Environment Program, World Bank, and World Resources Institute, *World Resources, 2005: The Wealth of the Poor: Managing Ecosystems to Fight Poverty* (Washington, D.C.: World Resources Institute, 2005).

14. Ibid.

15. For reports on these and other projects, go to the Equator Initiative Web site, http://www.equatorinitiative.org. A fine review of the HASHI project can be found in United Nations Development Programme et al., *World Resources, 2005*, pp. 131–138; other informative case studies are also presented there in ch. 5.

16. See e.g. http://www.circleofblue.org/waternews/2012/world/choke-point-china-ii-introduction/Poor.

17. United Nations Development Programme et al., *World Resources, 2005*. See also World Resources Institute, *World Resources, 1994–95* and *1998–99* (New York: Oxford University Press, 1994, 1998); World Bank, *World Development Report, 1992, 2003*, and *2009*; United Nations, *Population, Resources, and the Environment*; and World Resources Institute, *World Resources, 2000–2001* (New York: Oxford University Press, 2000). For likely impacts due to global warming, see the references in notes 18, 22, and 28.

18. An interesting analysis of the market for biomass fuels is Elizabeth M. Remedio and Terrence G. Bensel, "The woodfuel supply system for Cebu City, Philippines: A preliminary analysis," *Philippine Quarterly of Culture and Society* 20 (1992): 157–169. See also World Bank, *World Development Report, 1992*, tab. 1.

19. For a provocative look at the issue of gender and the environment, see Cecile Jackson, "Doing what comes naturally: Women and environment in development," *World Development* 21 (1993): 1947–1963.

20. The World Meteorological Organization (WMO) and the United Nations Environment Program (UNEP) established the Intergovernmental Panel on Climate Change (IPCC) in 1988 to address the problem of potential global climate change. It is open to all members of the United Nations and WMO. The IPCC won the Nobel Peace Prize in 2007. The impact study referred to in the text is *Fourth Assessment Report: Climate Change, 2007*, available at http://www.ipcc-wg2.org. This site also provides links to other IPCC reports on climate change.

21. Ibid., pp. 13, 435. This assessment has been subject to some debate. Timing and details of rainfall changes remain subject to uncertainty.

22. The IPCC identifies as at risk the megadeltas of the Huanghe/Yellow (China), Changjiang/Yangtze (China), Pearl (China), Red (Vietnam), Mekong

(Indochina), Chao Phraya (Thailand), Irrawaddy (Burma), Ganges-Brahmaputra (India and Bangladesh), and Indus (Pakistan) river systems.

23. IPCC, *Fourth Assessment Report*, pp. 479–482. Some crops may show some temporarily increased productivity, but these gains are not expected to last.

24. See ibid. and also Nicholas Stern, *The Stern Review on the Economics of Climate Change*, http://www .hm-treasury.gov.uk/independent_reviews/stern_ review_economics_climate_change/sternreview_ index.cfm.

25. Although climate has changed as drastically in the distant past as that now predicted for the coming century, those past changes unfolded over many thousands or millions of years; see Noah S. Diffenbaugh and Christopher B. Field, "Changes in ecologically critical terrestrial climate conditions," *Science* 341, No. 6145 (August 2, 2013): 486–492. For details of the NOAA study and recent results of ongoing monitoring see http://www.noaa.gov.

26. World Bank, *World Development Report, 2009*, p. 4.

27. Stern, *Stern Review*.

28. See World Bank, *Turn Down the Heat, Why a 4°C Warmer World Must Be Avoided*, 2012, http://documents .worldbank.org/curated/en/2012/11/17097815 /turn-down-heat-4%C2%B0c-warmer-world-must -avoided; and *Turn Down the Heat II: Climate Extremes, Regional Impacts, and the Case for Resilience*, 2013, http://documents.worldbank.org/curated /en/2013/06/17862361/turn-down-heat-climate -extremes-regional-impacts-case-resilience-full -report.

29. For details, see World Bank, *Turn Down the Heat* reports; World Health Organization, *Climate Change and Human Health*, http://www.who .int/globalchange/en/index.html, accessed August 13, 2013; Juliet Eilperin, "Climate shift tied to 150,000 fatalities; most victims are poor, study says," *Washington Post*, November 17, 2005, p. A20; IPCC, *Fourth Assessment Report*, pp. 446–447; and United Nations Economic and Social Council, Economic Commission for Africa, "State of the environment in Africa," November 2001, http:// www.uneca.org/panafcon/State_Environ_Afri.pdf.

30. See United Nations Environment Programme, "Sudan: Post-conflict environmental assessment,

2007,"http://sudanreport.unep.ch/UNEP_Sudan .pdf.

31. Stern, *Stern Review*, pp. 312–322.

32. See the official REDD Web site at http://www.un- redd.org.

33. See "Adaptation policy frameworks for climate change: Developing strategies, policies and measures: Annexes," 2010, http://www.undp.org /gef/documents/publications/apf-annexes-a-b.pdf. See also World Bank and others, *Economics of Adaptation to Climate Change Social Synthesis Report*, Final Consultation Draft, August 2010, available at http://siteresources.worldbank.org. In addition, see Arun Malik and Stephen C. Smith, "Adaptation to climate change in low-income countries: Lessons from current research and needs from future research," *Climate Change Economics* 3, No. 2 (May 2012). See also Arun Malik, Jonathan Rothbaum, and Stephen C. Smith, "Climate change, uncertainty, and decision-making," IIEP Working Paper 2010-4, at http://www.gwu.edu/~iiep/adaptation.

34. Arun Agrawal and Nicolas Perrin, "Climate adaptation, local institutions and rural livelihoods," in *Adapting to Climate Change: Thresholds, Values, Governance*, eds. W. Neil Adger, Irene Lorenzoni, and Karen L. O'Brien (New York: Cambridge University Press, 2009), pp. 350–367.

35. IPCC, *Fourth Assessment Report*, pp. 446–447. See also United Nations Economic and Social Council, Economic Commission for Africa, "State of the environment in Africa," November 2001, http:// www.uneca.org/panafcon/State_Environ_Afri.pdf. For an example of a heat wave program, see Saudamini Das and Stephen C. Smith, "Awareness as an adaptation strategy for reducing mortality from heat waves: Evidence from a disaster risk management program in India," *Climate Change Economics* 3, No. 2 (May 2012).

36. For more detail, see African Development Bank et al., *Poverty and Climate Change: Reducing the Vulnerability of the Poor through Adaptation*, 2003, http://siteresources.worldbank.org/INTCC /8173721115381292846/20480623/PovertyAnd ClimateChangeReportPart12003.pdf.

37. For a presentation of models of environmental economics, see Tom Tietenberg, *Environmental and*

Natural Resources Economics (Glenview, Ill.: Scott, Foresman, 1990); John M. Hartwick and N. Olewiler, *The Economics of Natural Resource Use* (New York: Harper & Row, 1986); G. Tyler Miller, *Living in the Environment* (Belmont, Calif.: Wadsworth, 1990); and Maureen L. Cropper and Wallace E. Oates, "Environmental economics: A survey," *Journal of Economic Literature* 30 (1992): 675–740.

38. See Elinor Ostrom, "Beyond markets and states: Polycentric governance of complex economic systems," *American Economic Review* 100 (2010): 641–672, *Understanding Institutional Diversity* (Princeton, N.J.: Princeton University Press, 2005), and *Governing the Commons: Evolution of Institutions for Collective Action* (New York: Cambridge University Press, 1990). See also Jean-Marie Baland and Jean Philippe Plateau, *Halting Degradation of Natural Resources: Is There a Role for Rural Communities?* (Rome: United Nations Food and Agricultural Organization, 1996). For a case example of restored cooperative resource management in Tanzania, see Stephen C. Smith, *Ending Global Poverty,* pp. 117–120.

39. For an excellent overview of global public goods, see Inge Kaul, Isabelle Grunberg, and Marc A. Stern, eds., *Global Public Goods: International Cooperation in the 21st Century* (New York: Oxford University Press, 1999).

40. See UN-Habitat, *The Challenge of Slums: Global Report on Human Settlements, 2003* (New York: United Nations, 2003).

41. World Bank, *World Development Report, 1992,* fig. 4. Note that for the most part, the Coase theorem does not apply to these discussions due to the high transaction costs involved.

42. Ibid.

43. Ibid., fig. 2.4.

44. World Bank, *World Development Indicators, 2010* (New York: Oxford University Press, 2010), tab. 1.3 and pp. 20–21. See also United Nations, *Millennium Development Goals Report, 2005* (New York: United Nations, 2005).

45. Excellent sources of information concerning tropical deforestation drawn on in this section are World Resources Institute, *World Resources, 1994–95,* ch. 7;

2005 *Millennium Ecosystem Assessment,* http://www.millenniumassessment.org/en/Synthesis.aspx; Lester Brown, *Eco-Economy: Building an Economy for the Earth* (New York: Norton, 2001); and World Bank, *World Development Report, 1992* and *2003.*

46. See the FAO's excellent *Global Forest Resources Assessment 2010,* accessed August 12, 2013, at http://www.fao.org/forestry/fra/fra2010/en.

47. United Nations Development Programme et al., *World Resources, 2005.* For an analysis of the effects of changes in economic policies and parameters on deforestation, see Joachim von Amsberg, "Economic parameters of deforestation," *World Bank Economic Review* 12 (1998): 133–153. For more on the Global Environmental Facility, go to http://www.thegef.org/gef.

48. For extensive discussions of public environment policies that in developing countries governments might pursue, see World Bank, *World Development Report, 1992,* chs. 3 and 7; World Resources Institute, *World Resources, 1992–93,* chs. 3 and 14; World Bank, *World Development Report, 2003;* and Stern, *Stern Review.*

49. An interesting discussion of government policy options in this area can be found in Stephen W. Salant, "The economics of natural resource extraction: A primer for development economists," *World Bank Research Observer* 10 (1995): 93–111.

50. According to a 2001 UN estimate, annual losses in the developing world due to the lack of access to the goods markets of the developed world were more than double the total amount of aid received in 2000 from all sources. If lack of access to capital and labor markets is also included, losses totaled about $500 billion.

51. For more information concerning debt-for-nature swaps, see World Resources Institute, *World Resources, 1992–93,* pp. 122–123 and tab. 20.6. See also Chapter 14.

52. See World Bank, *Global Development Finance, 1998* (Washington, D.C.: World Bank, 1998).

53. The reports of the World Resources Institute and its Web site (http://earthtrends.wri.org) are excellent sources of data and information on global environmental and resource trends.

Development Policymaking and the Roles of Market, State, and Civil Society

11

My research showed that one needed to find a balance between markets, government, and other institutions, including not-for-profits and cooperatives, and that the successful countries were those that had found that balance.

—*Joseph Stiglitz, Nobel laureate in economics, 2009*

A core goal of public policy should be to facilitate the development of institutions that bring out the best in humans.

—*Elinor Ostrom, Nobel laureate in economics, "Beyond Markets and States," 2010*

11.1 A Question of Balance

National governments have played an important role in the successful development experiences of the countries in East Asia. In other parts of the world, including some countries in Africa, Latin America, the Caribbean, and the transition countries, government often appears to have been more of a hindrance than a help, stifling the market rather than facilitating its role in growth and development. This chapter examines the balance of and relationships between states and markets in the process of economic development.

Achieving the proper balance between private markets and public policy is a challenge. In early years of development following World War II and decolonization, a perception of the state as a benevolent supporter of development held sway, at least implicitly, but the record of corruption, poor governance, and state capture by vested interests in so many developing countries has made this view untenable. More recently, a negative view of government has predominated, but it too has been based more on theory than fact and has failed to explain the important and constructive role that the state has played in many successful development experiences, particularly in East Asia. Now a middle ground has emerged, recognizing both the strengths and the weaknesses of the public and private roles, providing a more empirically grounded analysis of what goes wrong with governance in development and the conditions under which these flaws can be rectified, and incorporating an appreciation of the role of civil society. More subtle shadings between the sectors are also becoming more appreciated. Not only do the private and public sectors work together constructively surprisingly often, but also the lines between the sectors are not always sharp. Indeed, as pointed out by the late Elinor Ostrom, 2009 Nobel laureate in economics, we must appreciate that some phenomena "do not fit in a dichotomous world of 'the market' and 'the state.'"[1]

In this chapter, we examine the roles and limitations of planning and development policymaking as practiced in developing nations, consider the problems of economic transition to more competitive market economies, and ask fundamental questions as to the proper role of the state and how public and private economic activity can best be made mutually supporting. We start with a brief review of the nature of development planning and a summary of general planning issues. After examining the main arguments for and against the role of planning in developing societies and briefly reviewing different models of planning and project appraisal, we examine the requirements for getting the most social benefits from market economies and evaluate the arguments for and against a relatively broader or narrower role of the state in contemporary developing nations.

In particular, we examine the once dominant "Washington consensus" on development policy and its limitations and discuss ongoing progress toward an emerging new consensus. Then we examine some recent theories of development policy formulation, including studies of the impact of political processes on the quality of policy decisions. We next examine three important trends in governance and reform: tackling the problem of corruption, implementing decentralization, and encouraging broad-based development participation. Finally, we examine the nature of the third sector—the civil society or citizen sector, encompassing NGOs—and its growing role in economic development. The chapter concludes with a comparative case study of two of the largest and most innovative developing country–based development NGOs, both based in Bangladesh but with global reach: BRAC and the Grameen Bank.

11.2 Development Planning: Concepts and Rationale

The Planning Mystique

In the initial decades after World War II and decolonization, the pursuit of economic development was reflected in the almost universal acceptance of development planning as the surest and most direct route to economic progress. Until the 1980s, few people in the developing world would have questioned the advisability or desirability of formulating and implementing a national development plan. Planning had become a way of life in government ministries, and every five years or so, the latest development plan was paraded out with great fanfare.

National planning was widely believed to offer the essential and perhaps the only institutional and organizational mechanism for overcoming the major obstacles to development and for ensuring a sustained high rate of economic growth. To catch up with their former rulers, poor nations were persuaded that they required a comprehensive national plan. The planning record, unfortunately, did not live up to its advance billing. But a comprehensive development policy framework can play an important role in accelerating growth, reducing poverty, and reaching human development goals.

The Nature of Development Planning

Economic planning may be described as a deliberate governmental attempt to coordinate economic decision making over the long run and to influence, direct, and in some cases even control the level and growth of a nation's principal economic variables (income, consumption, employment, investment, saving, exports, imports, etc.) to achieve a predetermined set of development objectives.[2] An **economic plan** is simply a specific set of quantitative economic targets to be reached in a given period of time, with a stated strategy for achieving those targets. Economic plans may be comprehensive or partial. A **comprehensive plan** sets its targets to cover all major aspects of the national economy. A **partial plan** covers only a part of the national economy—industry, agriculture, the public sector, the foreign sector, and so forth. Finally, the **planning process** itself can be described as an exercise in which a government first chooses social objectives, then sets various targets, and finally organizes a framework for implementing, coordinating, and monitoring a development plan.[3]

Proponents of economic planning for developing countries argue that the uncontrolled market economy can, and often does, subject these nations to economic dualism, unstable markets, low investment in key sectors, and low levels of employment. In particular, they claim that the market economy is not geared to the principal operational task of poor countries: mobilizing limited resources in a way that will bring about the structural change necessary to stimulate a sustained and balanced growth of the entire economy. Planning has come to be accepted, therefore, as an essential and pivotal means of guiding and accelerating economic growth in almost all developing countries.

Planning in Mixed Developing Economies

Most development plans have been formulated and carried out within the framework of the mixed economies of the developing world. These economies are characterized by the existence of an institutional setting in which some of the productive resources are privately owned and operated and some are controlled by the public sector. The actual proportionate division of public and private ownership and control varies from country to country, and neither the private nor the public sector can really be considered in isolation from the other. However, mixed economies are often distinguished by a substantial amount of government ownership and control. The private sector in developing countries typically comprises four traditional forms of private ownership and a more recent emerging one:

1. The subsistence sector, consisting of small-scale private farms and handicraft shops selling a part of their production to local markets

2. Small-scale individual or family-owned commercial business and service activities in the formal and informal urban sectors

Economic planning   A deliberate and conscious attempt by the state to formulate decisions on how the factors of production will be allocated among different uses or industries, thereby determining how much of total goods and services will be produced in one or more ensuing periods.

Economic plan   A written document containing government policy decisions on how resources will be allocated among various uses so as to attain a targeted rate of economic growth or other goals over a certain period of time.

Comprehensive plan   An economic plan that sets targets to cover all the major sectors of the national economy.

Partial plan   A plan that covers only a part of the national economy (e.g., agriculture, industry, tourism).

Planning process   The procedure for drawing up and carrying out a formal economic plan.

3. Medium-size commercial enterprises in agriculture, industry, trade, and transport owned and operated by local entrepreneurs

4. Large jointly owned or completely foreign-owned manufacturing enterprises, mining companies, and plantations, catering primarily to foreign markets but sometimes with substantial local sales (the capital for such enterprises usually comes from abroad, and a good proportion of the profits tends to be transferred overseas)

5. A growing number of relatively large, domestic-based firms, primarily locally managed and largely locally owned, often listed on national stock markets in countries such as Brazil, Russia, India, and China but much more common in middle-income than low-income countries and rare in the least developed countries

In the context of such an institutional setting, we can identify two principal components of development planning in mixed economies:

Economic infrastructure
The capital embodied in roads, railways, waterways, airways, and other forms of transportation and communication plus water supplies, electricity, and public services such as health and education.

1. The government's deliberate use of domestic saving and foreign finance to carry out public investment projects and to mobilize and channel scarce resources into areas that can be expected to make the greatest contribution toward the realization of long-term economic objectives (e.g., the construction of railways, schools, hydroelectric projects, and other components of **economic infrastructure**, as well as the creation of import-substituting industries or projected future export sectors)

2. Governmental economic policy (e.g., taxation, industrial licensing, the setting of tariffs, and the manipulation of quotas, wages, interest rates, and prices) to stimulate, direct, and in some cases even control private economic activity so as to ensure a harmonious relationship between the desires of private business operators and the social objectives of the central government

Thus, even when development planning is quite active, there is almost always a balance between the extremes of market inducement and central control, as is readily evident from our simplified characterization of planning in mixed market economies.

The Rationale for Development Planning

The early widespread acceptance of planning as a development tool rested on a number of fundamental economic and institutional arguments. Of these we can single out four as the most prominent.

Market Failure   Markets in developing economies are permeated by imperfections of structure and operation. Commodity and factor markets are often badly organized, and the existence of distorted prices often means that producers and consumers are responding to economic signals and incentives that are a poor reflection of the real cost to society of these goods, services, and resources. It is therefore argued that governments have an important role to play in integrating markets and modifying prices. Moreover, the failure of the market to price factors of production correctly is further assumed to lead to gross disparities between social and private valuations of alternative investment projects. In the absence of governmental interference, therefore, the market is said to lead to a misallocation of present and future resources or, at least, to an allocation that may not be in the best long-run social interests. This **market failure** argument is perhaps the most often quoted reason for the expanded role of government in less developed countries.[4]

Various kinds of market and government failures are examined in several of the earlier chapters, but a brief review is in order here. There are three general forms in which market failure can be observed: The market cannot function properly or no market exists; the market exists but implies an inefficient allocation of resources; the market produces undesirable results as measured by social objectives other than the allocation of resources. Market failures can occur in situations in which social costs or benefits differ from the private costs or benefits of firms or consumers; public goods, externalities, and market power are the best-known examples. With public goods, "free riders" who do not pay for the goods cannot be excluded except at high cost; it is economically inefficient to exclude nonpaying individuals from consuming these goods. With externalities, consumers or firms do not have to pay all the costs of their activities or are unable to receive all the benefits. Coordination failures occur when several agents would be better off if they could cooperate on actions if all or most agents participated but worse off taking the action if too few participated. Moreover, economic development is a process of structural change. The market may be efficient in allocating resources at the margin, allowing certain industries to emerge and others to fail, but may be ineffective in producing large discontinuous changes in the economic structure that may be crucial to the country's long-term development (see Chapter 4).[5] Market power occurs when firms can influence price by restricting quantity, a power most common under increasing returns to scale. Capital markets are particularly prone to failure due to their intrinsic connection to information generation and transmittal; information has public-good properties (see Chapter 15). A more equal distribution of income itself can be considered a public good when it is an agreed social objective. There may be concern for the well-being of future generations, who cannot participate in today's economic or political markets. Merit goods, such as health, education, and basic welfare, can also be considered public goods or social entitlements guaranteed by government. But concerns about distribution and merit goods are often treated as separate rationales for policy because their levels are generally viewed as outside the realm of economic efficiency.

Unfortunately, we cannot jump to the conclusion that if economic theory says policy can fix market failures, it will do so in practice. Government failure may also occur in the many cases in which politicians, bureaucrats, and the individuals or groups who influence them give priority to their own private interests rather than to the public interest. Analysis of incentives for government failure helps guide reforms such as constitution design and civil service rules. Developing countries tend to have both high market failure and government failure.[6] (As noted later in the chapter, the NGO sector can also be subject to what is termed *voluntary failure*.").

Market failure A phenomenon that results from the existence of market imperfections (e.g., monopoly power, lack of factor mobility, significant externalities, lack of knowledge) that weaken the functioning of a market economy.

Resource Mobilization and Allocation   This argument stresses that developing economies cannot afford to waste their very limited financial and skilled human resources on unproductive ventures. Investment projects must be chosen not solely on the basis of partial productivity analysis dictated by individual industrial capital-output ratios but also in the context of an overall development program that takes account of external economies, indirect repercussions, and long-term objectives. Skilled workers must be employed where their contribution will be most widely felt. Economic planning is assumed to help by recognizing the existence of particular constraints and by choosing and coordinating investment projects so as to channel these scarce factors into their most productive outlets. In contrast, it is argued, competitive markets will tend to generate less investment and to direct that investment into areas of low social priority (e.g., consumption goods for the rich).

Attitudinal or Psychological Impact   It is often assumed that a detailed statement of national economic and social objectives in the form of a specific development plan can have an important attitudinal or psychological impact on a diverse and often fragmented population. It may succeed in rallying the people behind the government in a national campaign to eliminate poverty, ignorance, and disease or to boost national prowess. By mobilizing popular support and cutting across class, caste, racial, religious, or tribal factions with the plea to all citizens to work together toward building the nation, it is argued that an enlightened central government, through its economic plan, can best provide the needed incentives to overcome the inhibiting and often divisive forces of sectionalism and traditionalism in a common quest for widespread material and social progress.

Foreign Aid   The formulation of detailed development plans has often been a necessary condition for the receipt of bilateral and multilateral foreign aid. With a shopping list of projects, governments are better equipped to solicit foreign assistance and persuade donors that their money will be used as an essential ingredient in a well-conceived and internally consistent plan of action. The requirement that developing countries must put an approved plan in place to receive various forms of assistance remains at least as true in this century as it was in the last.[7]

11.3 The Development Planning Process: Some Basic Models

Three Stages of Planning

Most development plans have traditionally been based initially on some more or less formalized macroeconomic model. Such economy-wide planning models can be divided into two basic categories: (1) aggregate growth models, involving macroeconomic estimates of planned or required changes in principal economic variables, and (2) multisector input-output, social accounting, and computable general equilibrium (CGE) models, which ascertain (among other

things) the production, resource, employment, and foreign-exchange implications of a given set of final demand targets within an internally consistent
framework of interindustry product flows. Finally, probably the most important component of plan formulation is the detailed selection of specific investment projects within each sector through the technique of project appraisal
and social cost-benefit analysis. These three "stages" of planning—aggregate,
sectoral, and project—provide the main intellectual tools of the planning
authority. All of these tools have been, and still are, extensively used by the
World Bank and other development agencies, as well as developing country
governments. We now turn to examine each of these stages and their associated models.

Aggregate Growth Models: Projecting Macro Variables

The first and most elementary planning model used in almost every developing country is the **aggregate growth model**. It deals with the entire economy in
terms of a limited set of macroeconomic variables deemed most critical to the
determination of levels and growth rates of national output: savings, investment, capital stocks, exports, imports, foreign assistance, and so on. Aggregate
growth models provide a convenient method for forecasting output (and perhaps also employment) growth over a three- to five-year period. Almost all
such models represent some variant of the basic Harrod-Domar (or AK) model
described in Chapter 3.

> **Aggregate growth model**   A formal economic model describing growth of an economy in one or a few sectors using a limited number of variables.

Given targeted GDP growth rates and a national capital-output ratio, the
Harrod-Domar model is used to specify the amount of domestic saving necessary to generate such growth. Typically, this necessary amount of domestic
saving is not likely to be realized on the basis of existing savings functions,
and so the basic policy problem of how to generate additional domestic savings
or foreign assistance comes into play. For planning purposes, the Harrod-
Domar model has been typically formulated along the following lines.[8]

We start with the assumption that the ratio of total output to reproducible
capital is constant so that

$$K(t) = cY(t) \tag{11.1}$$

where $K(t)$ is capital stock at time t, $Y(t)$ is total output (GDP) at time t, and c is
the average (equal to the marginal) capital-output ratio. We assume next that a
constant share (s) of output (Y) is always saved (S) so that

$$I(t) = K(t + 1) - K(t) + \delta K(t) = sY = S(t) \tag{11.2}$$

where $I(t)$ is gross investment at the time t and δ is the fraction of the capital
stock depreciated in each period. Now if g is the targeted rate of growth of
output such that

$$g = \frac{Y(t + 1) - Y(t)}{Y(t)} = \frac{\Delta Y(t)}{Y(t)} \tag{11.3}$$

then capital must be growing at the same rate, because from Equation 11.1 we know that

$$\frac{\Delta K}{K} = \frac{c\Delta Y}{K} = \frac{(K/Y)\Delta Y}{K} = \frac{\Delta Y}{Y} \qquad (11.4)$$

Using Equation 11.2, we therefore arrive once again at the basic Harrod-Domar growth formula (with the capital depreciation parameter):

$$g = \frac{sY - \delta K}{K} = \frac{s}{c} - \delta \qquad (11.5)$$

Finally, because output growth can also be expressed as the sum of labor force growth (n) and the rate of growth of labor productivity (p), Equation 11.5 can be rewritten for planning purposes as

$$n + p = \frac{s}{c} - \delta \qquad (11.6)$$

Of course, much development policymaking does not take productivity as exogenous but is actively focused on raising it. But given an expected rate of labor force and productivity growth (labor force growth can be calculated from readily available demographic information, and productivity growth estimates are usually based either on extrapolations of past trends or on an assumed constant rate of increase), Equation 11.6 can then be used to estimate whether domestic savings will be sufficient to provide an adequate number of new employment opportunities to a growing labor force. One way of doing this is to disaggregate the overall savings function ($S = sY$) into at least two component sources of saving, normally, the propensity to save out of wage income, W, and profit income, π. Thus, we define

$$W + \pi = Y \qquad (11.7)$$

and

$$s_\pi \pi + s_W W = I \qquad (11.8)$$

where s_π and s_W are the savings propensities from π and W, respectively. By manipulating Equation 11.5 and substituting Equations 11.7 and 11.8 into it, we arrive at a modified Harrod-Domar growth equation:

$$c(g + \delta) = (s_\pi - s_W)\left(\frac{\pi}{Y}\right) + s_W \qquad (11.9)$$

which can then serve as a formula for ascertaining the adequacy of current saving out of profit and wage income. For example, if a 4% growth rate is desired and if $\delta = 0.03, c = 3.0$, and $\pi/Y = 0.5$, Equation 11.9 reduces to $0.42 = s_\pi + s_W$.[9] If savings out of capital income amount to 25%, wage earners must save at a 17% rate to achieve the targeted rate of growth. In the absence of such a savings rate out of labor income, the government could pursue a variety of policies to raise domestic saving or seek foreign assistance.

In countries where inadequate foreign-exchange reserves are believed to be the principal constraint on economic growth, the aggregate growth model typically employed is some variant of the two-gap model, which will be described, along with their limits, in Chapter 14. (Two-gap models are simply Harrod-Domar models generalized to take foreign-trade problems into account.) In either case, aggregate growth models can provide only a rough first approximation of the general directions an economy might take. Thus, they rarely constitute the operational development plan. Perhaps more important, the simplicity and relatively low data collection cost of using aggregate growth models can often blind us to their very real limitations, especially when carried out in too mechanical a fashion. Average capital-output ratios are notoriously difficult to estimate and may bear little relation to marginal capital-output ratios, which are the relevant ratios for forecasting purposes, and savings rates can be highly unstable. The operational plan requires a more disaggregated multisector model of economic activity like the well-known input-output approach.

Multisector Models and Sectoral Projections

A much more sophisticated approach to development planning is to use some variant of the **interindustry** or **input-output model**, in which the activities of the major industrial sectors of the economy are interrelated by means of a set of simultaneous algebraic equations expressing the specific production processes or technologies of each industry. All industries are viewed both as producers of outputs and users of inputs from other industries. For example, the agricultural sector is both a producer of output (e.g., wheat) and a user of inputs from, say, the manufacturing sector (e.g., machinery, fertilizer). Thus, direct and indirect repercussions of planned changes in the demand for the products of any one industry on output, employment, and imports of all other industries can be traced throughout the entire economy in an intricate web of economic interdependence. Given the planned output targets for each sector of the economy, the interindustry model can be used to determine intermediate material, import, labor, and capital requirements with the result that a comprehensive economic plan with mutually consistent production levels and resource requirements can, in theory, be constructed.

Input-output model (interindustry model) A formal model dividing the economy into sectors and tracing the flow of interindustry purchases (inputs) and sales (outputs).

Interindustry models range from simple input-output models, usually consisting of 10 to 30 sectors in the developing economies and 30 to 400 sectors in advanced economies, to more complicated linear programming or activity analysis models where checks of feasibility (what is possible given certain resource constraints) and optimality (what is best among different alternatives) are also built into the model. But the distinguishing characteristic of the interindustry or input-output approach is the attempt to formulate an internally consistent, comprehensive development plan for the entire economy.[10]

Input-output analysis is often extended in two ways. First, by including data on factor payments, sources of household income, and the pattern of household goods consumption across various social groups (such as urban and rural households), a social accounting matrix (SAM) is created. This is accomplished by adding data from the system of national accounts, balance of payments, and flow-of-funds databases, often supplemented with household survey data, to the basic input-output table. A SAM therefore provides a comprehensive and detailed quantitative description of the interrelationships in an economy as they exist at a point in time, making it well suited as a tool for evaluating the impact of alternative development policies. SAMs for many countries can be found online. SAMs are often further elaborated with CGE models, which assume that households maximize utility and firms maximize profits. Utility (or demand) and production functions are assumed or estimated from national data. The resulting impact of the policy is then simulated using standard computer programs. The CGE approach is more complicated than a SAM, but its value lies in enabling policymakers to take into account the possible reactions of consumers and firms to the alternative policies being considered rather than assume that they will behave the way they did before the new policies were implemented.[11]

Project Appraisal and Social Cost-Benefit Analysis

The vast majority of day-to-day operational decisions with regard to the allocation of limited public investment funds are based on a microeconomic technique of analysis known as **project appraisal**. The intellectual as well as the operational linkage among the three major planning techniques, however, should not be overlooked. Macro growth models set the broad strategy, input-output analysis ensures an internally consistent set of sectoral targets, and project appraisal is designed to ensure the efficient planning of individual projects within each sector.

Project appraisal The quantitative analysis of the relative desirability (profitability) of investing a given sum of public or private funds in alternative projects.

Basic Concepts and Methodology   The methodology of project appraisal rests on the theory and practice of social **cost-benefit analysis**,[12] which is also used in the United States and other developed countries. The basic idea of cost-benefit analysis is simple: To decide on the worth of projects involving public expenditure (or, indeed, in which public policy can play a crucial role), it is necessary to weigh the advantages (benefits) and the disadvantages (costs) to society as a whole. The need for social cost-benefit analysis arises because the normal yardstick of commercial profitability that guides the investment decisions of private investors may not be an appropriate guide for public-investment decisions. Private investors are interested in maximizing private profits and therefore normally take into account only the variables that affect net profit: receipts and expenditures. Both receipts and expenditures are valued at prevailing market prices for inputs and outputs.

Cost-benefit analysis A tool of economic analysis in which the actual and potential private and social costs of various economic decisions are weighed against actual and potential private and social benefits.

The point of departure for social cost-benefit analysis is that it does not accept that actual receipts are a true measure of social benefits or that actual expenditures are a true measure of social costs. Not only will actual market prices often diverge from their true value, but also private investors do not take into account the external effects of their decisions. These externalities can be sizable and pervasive.[13] In other words, where social costs and benefits diverge from private costs and benefits, investment decisions based entirely on the criterion of commercial profitability may lead to wrong decisions from the point of view of social welfare, which should be the government's primary concern. Although social valuations may differ significantly from private valuations, the practice of cost-benefit analysis is based on the assumption that these divergences can be adjusted for by public policy so that the difference between social benefit and cost will properly reflect social profitability, just as the difference between actual receipts and expenditures measures the private profitability of an investment.

Thus, we can define **social profit** in any period as the difference between social benefits and social costs where these are measured both directly (the real costs of inputs and the real value of outputs) and indirectly (e.g., employment effects, distributional effects). The calculation of the social profitability of an investment is then a three-step process.[14]

Social profit The difference between social benefits and social costs, both direct and indirect.

1. We must first specify the objective function to be maximized—ordinarily, net social benefit—with some measure of how different benefits (e.g., per capita consumption, income distribution) are to be calculated and what the trade-off between them might be.

2. To arrive at calculations of net social benefit, we need social measures of the unit values of all project inputs and outputs. Such social measures are often called **accounting prices** or **shadow prices** of inputs and outputs to distinguish them from actual **market prices**.[15] In general, the greater the divergence is between shadow and market prices, the greater the need for social cost-benefit analysis in arriving at public investment decision rules.

Shadow prices (or accounting prices) Prices that reflect the true opportunity costs of resources.

Market prices Prices established by demand and supply in markets.

3. Finally, we need some decision criterion to reduce the stream of projected social benefit and cost flows to an index, the value of which can then be used to select or reject a project or to rank it relative to alternative projects.

Let us briefly examine each of these steps of project appraisal.

Setting Objectives Given the difficulty of attaching numerical values to such objectives as national cohesion, self-reliance, political stability, modernization, and quality of life, economic planners typically measure the social worth of a project in terms of the degree to which it contributes to the net flow of future goods and services in the economy—that is, by its impact on future levels of consumption.

Recently, a second major criterion, the project's impact on income distribution, has received increased attention. If preference is to be given to raising the consumption standards of low-income groups, the social worth of a project must be calculated as a weighted sum of the distribution of its benefits, where additional consumption by low-income groups may receive a disproportionately high weight in the social welfare objective function. (This procedure is analogous to that of constructing a poverty-weighted index of economic growth, discussed in Appendix 5.2.) Beginning in 1991, project analysis at the World Bank also included an environmental impact evaluation as a third criterion, along with future consumption and income distribution.

Computing Shadow Prices and Social Discount Rates The core of social cost-benefit analysis is the calculation or estimation of the prices to be used in determining the true value of benefits and the real magnitude of costs. There are many reasons for believing that in developing countries, market prices of outputs and inputs do not give a true reflection of social benefits and costs. Five such reasons, in particular, are often cited.

1. *Inflation and currency overvaluation.* Many developing countries are still beset by inflation and varying degrees of price controls. Controlled prices do not typically reflect the real opportunity cost to society of producing these goods and services. Moreover, in many countries, the government manages the price of foreign exchange. With inflation and unaltered foreign **exchange rates**, the domestic currency becomes overvalued (see Chapters 12 and 13), with the result that import prices underestimate the real cost to the country of purchasing foreign products and export prices (in local currency) understate the real benefit accruing to the country from a given volume of exports. Bubbles and crises can also lead to larger distortions. Public investment decisions based on this price will therefore tend to be biased against export industries and to favor import substitutions. The reverse holds with systematically undervalued exchange rates.

2. *Wage rates, capital costs, and unemployment.* Almost all developing countries exhibit factor price distortions resulting in modern-sector wage rates exceeding the social opportunity cost (or shadow price) of labor and interest rates understating the social opportunity cost of capital. This leads to widespread unemployment and underemployment and the excessive capital intensity of industrial production technologies. If governments were to use unadjusted market prices for labor and capital in calculating the costs of alternative public investment projects, they would underestimate the real costs of capital-intensive projects and tend to promote these at the expense of the socially less costly labor-intensive projects that would be more favorable to the poor.

3. *Tariffs, quotas, subsidies, and import substitution.* The existence of high tariffs, in combination with import quotas and overvalued exchange rates, discriminates against the agricultural export sector and favors the import-substituting manufacturing sector (see Chapter 12). It also encourages socially wasteful **rent seeking** on the part of competing exporters and importers. They vie with each other (often through bribes and threats as well as direct lobbying efforts) to capture the extra profits that can accrue to traders with import licenses, export subsidies, tariff protection, and industrial preferences.

4. *Savings deficiency.* Given the substantial pressures for providing higher immediate consumption levels to the masses of poor people, the level and rate of domestic savings in most developing countries is often thought to be suboptimal. According to this argument, governments should use a discount rate that is lower than the market rate of interest in order to promote projects that have a longer payoff period and generate a higher stream of investible surpluses in the future.[16]

5. *The social rate of discount.* In our discussion of the shadow price of savings, we mentioned the need for governments to choose appropriate discount rates in calculating the worth of project benefits and costs that occur over time.

Exchange rate   Rate at which the domestic currency may be converted into (sold for) a foreign currency such as the U.S. dollar.

Rent seeking   Efforts by individuals and businesses to capture the economic rent arising from price distortions and physical controls caused by excessive government intervention, such as licenses, quotas, interest rate ceilings, and exchange control.

The **social rate of discount** (also sometimes referred to as *social time preference*) is essentially a price of time—the rate used to calculate the **net present value** of a time stream of project benefits and costs, where the net present value (NPV) is calculated as

$$\text{NPV} = \sum_t \frac{B_t - C_t}{(1 + r)^t} \qquad (11.10)$$

where B_t is the expected benefit of the project at time t, C_t is the expected cost (both evaluated using shadow prices), and r is the government's social rate of discount. Social discount rates may differ from market rates of interest (normally used by private investors to calculate the profitability of investments), depending on the subjective evaluation placed on future net benefits: The higher the future benefits and costs are valued in the government's planning program—for example, if government also represents future, unborn citizens—the lower the social rate of discount will be.

In view of these five forces leading to considerable product, factor, and money price distortions, as well as considerations of external economies and diseconomies of production and consumption (by definition, factors not taken into account in private-investment decisions), it has been widely argued and generally agreed that a strong case can be made for concluding that a project's actual anticipated receipts and expenditures often do *not* provide an accurate measure of its social worth. It is primarily for this reason that the tools of social cost-benefit analysis for project appraisal are essential to an efficient process of project selection in developing countries.

Choosing Projects: Some Decision Criteria Having computed relevant shadow prices, projected a time stream of expected benefits and costs (including indirect or external effects), and selected an appropriate social discount rate, planners are in a position to choose from a set of alternative investment projects those thought to be most desirable. They therefore need to adopt a decision criterion to be followed. Normally, economists advocate using the NPV rule in choosing investment projects; that is, projects should be accepted or rejected according to whether their NPV is positive or negative. As noted, however, NPV calculations are very sensitive to the choice of a social discount rate. An alternative approach is to calculate the discount rate that gives the project an NPV of zero; compare this **internal rate of return** with either a predetermined social discount rate or, with less justification, an estimate of either the marginal product of capital in the economy or the market rate of interest; and choose projects whose internal rates exceed the predetermined or market rate. This approach is widely used in evaluating educational investments.

Because most developing countries face substantial capital constraints, the choice of investment projects will normally also involve a ranking of all projects that meet the NPV rule. Projects are ranked by descending net present value (more precisely, by their benefit-cost ratios, which are arrived at by dividing NPV by the constraint on total capital cost, K—that is, an NPV/K ratio is calculated for each project). The project or set of projects (some investments should be considered as a package of projects) with the highest NPV/K ratio is chosen first, then the next highest, and so on down the line until all available capital investment funds have been exhausted.[17]

Social rate of discount The rate at which a society discounts potential future social benefits to find out whether such benefits are worth their present social cost.

Net present value The value of a future stream of net benefits discounted to the present by means of an appropriate discount (interest) rate.

Internal rate of return The discount rate that causes a project to have a net present value of zero, used to rank projects in comparison with market rates of interest.

Conclusions: Planning Models and Plan Consistency   The process of formulating a comprehensive, detailed development plan is obviously a more complicated process than that described by our three-stage approach. It involves a constant dialogue and feedback mechanism between national leaders who set priorities and planners, statisticians, research workers, and departmental or ministry officials. Internal rivalries and conflicting objectives (not to mention political pressure from powerful vested-interest groups) are always to be reckoned with. Nevertheless, our presentation should at least serve to provide a feel for the mechanics of planning and to demonstrate the ways in which aggregate, input-output, and project planning models have been used to attempt to formulate an internally consistent and comprehensive development plan.

11.4 Government Failure and Preferences for Markets Over Planning

Problems of Plan Implementation and Plan Failure

The results of development planning have been generally disappointing.[18] The widespread rejection of comprehensive development planning based on poor performance has had a number of practical outcomes, the most important of which is the adoption in a majority of developing countries of a more market-oriented economic system.

What went wrong? Why has the early euphoria about planning gradually been transformed into disillusionment and dejection? We can identify two interrelated sets of answers—one dealing with the gap between the theoretical economic benefits and the practical results of development planning, and the other associated with more fundamental defects in the planning process, especially as they relate to administrative capacities, political will, and plan implementation.

Theory versus Practice   The principal economic arguments for planning briefly outlined earlier in this chapter—market failure, divergences between private and social valuations, resource mobilization, investment coordination, and the like—have often turned out to be weakly supported by the actual planning experience. Commenting on this planning failure, Tony Killick has noted that

> it is doubtful whether plans have generated more useful signals for the future than would otherwise have been forthcoming; governments have rarely, in practice, reconciled private and social valuations except in a piecemeal manner; because they have seldom become operational documents, plans have probably had only limited impact in mobilizing resources and in coordinating economic policies.[19]

To take the specific case of the market failure argument and the presumed role of governments in reconciling the divergence between private and social valuations of benefits and costs, the experience of government policy in many developing countries has been one of often *exacerbating* rather than reconciling these divergences—**government failure** rather than market failure. Government policy often tends to increase rather than reduce the divergences

Government failure   A situation in which government intervention in an economy worsens outcomes.

between private and social valuations. For example, public policies have raised the level of wages above labor's shadow price or scarcity value by various devices such as minimum-wage legislation, tying wages to educational attainment, and structuring rates of remuneration at higher levels on the basis of international salary scales. Similarly, investment depreciation and tax allowances, overvalued exchange rates, low effective rates of protection, quotas, and credit rationing at low interest rates all serve to drop the private cost of capital far below its scarcity or social cost. The net effect of these factor price distortions has been to encourage private and public enterprises to adopt more capital-intensive production methods than would exist if public policy attempted to correct the prices.

As another example, we noted in Chapter 8 that economic signals and incentives in many developing countries have served to exaggerate the private valuations of the returns to education at the secondary and tertiary levels to a point where the private demand for ever more years of schooling greatly exceeds the social payoff. The tendency to ration scarce high-paying employment opportunities by level of completed education and the policy of most governments in the developing world to subsidize the private costs of education at the higher levels together have led to a situation in which the social returns to investment in further quantitative educational expansion seem hardly justified in comparison with alternative investment opportunities.

In view of the forgoing examples, we may conclude that the gap between the theoretical economic benefits of planning and its practical results in most developing countries has been quite large. The gap between public rhetoric and economic reality has been even greater. While supposedly concerned with eliminating poverty, reducing inequality, and lowering unemployment, many planning policies in developing countries have in fact unwittingly contributed to their perpetuation. Some of the major explanations for this have to do with failures of the planning process itself; these failures in turn arise out of certain specific problems.[20]

Deficiencies in Plans and Their Implementation   Plans are often overambitious. They try to accomplish too many objectives at once without consideration that some of the objectives are competing or even conflicting. They are often grandiose in design but vague on specific policies for achieving stated objectives. In this they have much in common with the excessive lists of 60 to 100 or more issue areas in conditionality agreements set out by the World Bank and the International Monetary Fund (IMF). Finally, the gap between plan formulation and implementation is often enormous (many plans, for reasons to be discussed, are never implemented).

Insufficient and Unreliable Data   The economic value of a development plan depends to a great extent on the quality and reliability of the statistical data on which it is based. When these data are weak, unreliable, or nonexistent, as in many poor countries, the accuracy and internal consistency of economy-wide quantitative plans are greatly diminished. And when unreliable data are compounded by an inadequate supply of qualified economists, statisticians, and other planning personnel (as is also the situation in most poor nations), the attempt to formulate and carry out a comprehensive and detailed development plan is likely to be frustrated at all levels.

Unanticipated Economic Disturbances, External and Internal   Because most developing countries have open economies that are dependent on the vicissitudes of international trade, aid, "hot" speculative capital inflows, and private foreign investment, it becomes exceedingly difficult for them to engage in even short-term forecasting, let alone long-range planning. The oil price increases of the 1970s caused havoc in most development plans. But the energy crisis was only an extreme case of a general tendency for economic factors over which most governments in the developing world had little control to determine the success or failure of their development policies.

Institutional Weaknesses   The institutional weaknesses of the planning processes of most developing countries include the separation of the planning agency from the day-to-day decision-making machinery of government; the failure of planners, administrators, and political leaders to engage in continuous dialogue and internal communication about goals and strategies; and the international transfer of institutional planning practices and organizational arrangements that may be inappropriate to local conditions. In addition, there has been much concern about incompetent and unqualified civil servants; cumbersome bureaucratic procedures; excessive caution and resistance to innovation and change; interministerial personal and departmental rivalries (e.g., finance ministries and planning agencies are often conflicting rather than cooperative forces in governments); lack of commitment to national goals as opposed to regional, departmental, or simply private objectives on the part of political leaders and government bureaucrats; and in accordance with this lack of national as opposed to personal interest, the political and bureaucratic corruption that is pervasive in many governments.[21]

Political will   A determined effort by persons in political authority to achieve certain economic objectives through various reforms.

Lack of Political Will   Poor plan performance and the wide gap between plan formulation and plan implementation are also attributable to a lack of commitment and **political will** on the part of many developing-country leaders and high-level decision makers.[22] Political will entails much more than high-minded purposes and noble rhetoric. It requires an unusual ability and a great deal of political courage to challenge powerful elites and vested-interest groups and to persuade them that development is in the long-run interests of *all* citizens even though some of them may suffer short-term losses. In the absence of their support, be it freely offered or coerced, a will to develop on the part of politicians is likely to meet with staunch resistance, frustration, and internal conflict.

Conflict, Postconflict, and Fragile States   In extreme cases, violent conflict or the large-scale failure of a state to otherwise function meaningfully has resulted in catastrophic failure of even the most basic development objectives. In these cases, development assistance is usually essential. This topic will be examined in Chapter 14, section 14.6.

The 1980s Policy Shift toward Free Markets

As a result of the disenchantment with planning and the perceived failure of government intervention, many economists, some finance ministers in developing countries, and the heads of the major international development organizations advocated increased use of the market mechanism as a key instrument for promoting greater efficiency and more rapid economic growth. U.S. President Ronald Reagan made a famous reference to the "magic of the marketplace" in a 1981 speech at Cancun, Mexico. If the decade of the 1970s could be described as a period of increased public-sector activity in the pursuit of more equitable development, the 1980s and 1990s witnessed the reemergence of free-market economics.

As part of their domestic-market liberalization programs, a majority of developing countries, with differing degrees of seriousness of purpose, generally sought to reduce the role of the public sector, encourage greater private-sector activity, and eliminate distortions in interest rates, wages, and the prices of consumer goods. The intent of such changes was to lubricate the wheels of the market mechanism, thereby achieving a more productive allocation of investments. In addition, these "liberalizing" developing countries sought to improve their comparative advantage in the international economy by lowering exchange rates, promoting exports, and eliminating trade barriers.

Among the international organizations preaching the virtues of the free market were the IMF and the World Bank, in addition to several bilateral donors such as U.S. Agency for International Development (USAID). The IMF required substantial market liberalization programs and policies to improve comparative advantage and promote macroeconomic stabilization as conditions for access to its higher credit windows. The World Bank carefully scrutinized its project lending to ensure that the projects proposed could not otherwise be undertaken by the private sector.

Government Failure

Just as markets are permeated by imperfections, so too is government subject to a variety of failures.[23] Thus, while in theory government can correct a market failure, sometimes in practice it fails to do so despite costly expenditure—and in some cases might only make matters worse. Thus, government regulations may improve industry efficiency, such as by breaking monopoly power; and it may otherwise improve social welfare, such as by limiting pollution (as we saw in Chapter 10). But poorly designed regulations could stifle emerging industries or even facilitate corruption. And once established, special interest groups may spring up, which find ways to benefit from regulations through rent seeking. Such groups may resist modifications in regulations even long after conditions that led to them have changed; this problem is examined in more detail below in Section 11.7.

There is a general presumption that when markets are functioning well, government should not intervene—on efficiency grounds there is generally no case for doing so. Instead, often there are great benefits to allowing decisions to be made on a decentralized basis. In general, individuals and families know more about their preferences and conditions than government can know.

As government failures are sometimes serious even regarding rather specific interventions, with overall development planning the scope for failure is larger. As we saw in Chapter 4, government can help by pushing an economy toward a better equilibrium, which the unaided market cannot attain; but government could potentially make things that much worse by pushing the economy into a bad equilibrium. Similarly, government programs can reduce social risks; but it has been observed that development planning could increase risks because of problems of correcting mistakes: Markets may make serious mistakes; but through its decentralized decision making mechanisms, often markets can more easily self-correct. And while markets generally cannot overcome coordination failures (see Chapter 4), coordination across government departments—or national and regional levels of government—cannot always be readily achieved.

More generally, development planning, which sometimes relies on seeking broad consensus, may be more rigid than markets, which can have a more agile response to unexpected shocks such as changes in global markets. In other cases, rather than resulting from consensus, development planning may be heavily influenced by powerful interest groups. The result may be the augmentation of the power of elites, rather than achievement of more egalitarian development goals. Development planning also faces the broad problem of *incentive compatibility*, meaning that the goals and mechanisms of the plan may be inconsistent with the self-interest of many of the key actors in the economy. Even when workers are employed directly for government, their incentives for hard or creative work may be less than for private sector workers.

But just as market failure does not always justify public intervention (because governments, as noted, can often make things worse), so too government failure is not necessarily an argument for private markets. For example, in South Korea, the Pohang Steel Company was publicly operated and highly efficient until its privatization in 2000, whereas the Steel Authority in India, also publicly owned and operated, has been a model of inefficiency. Subsidized interest rates exist in both East Asia, where growth accelerated, and in Latin America, where it stagnated. Unproductive rent-seeking activities can just as easily be found in poorly functioning private markets as in inefficient state operations. Simple judgments about the relative merits of public versus private economic activities cannot therefore be made outside the context of specific countries and concrete situations. But for developing countries intent on extending market reforms, either because of their dissatisfaction with the performance of their public sectors or because of IMF or World Bank pressure, a number of sociocultural preconditions and economic practices must be met.

11.5 The Market Economy

Sociocultural Preconditions and Economic Requirements

Markets accomplish many positive things, not least of which is delivering goods that consumers want, where and when they want them, and providing incentives for innovation. Amartya Sen has pointed out that to be generically against markets is almost as strange as to be generically against conversations.[24] As he says, some conversations do harm, even to those doing the conversing, but this is not a reason to be against conversations in general. To underpin a well-functioning market system requires special social, institutional, legal, and cultural conditions that are often very limited, if not absent, in developing nations. Fraud, corruption, monopoly, and other market failures do not disappear with the wave of a magic neoclassical wand.

A well-functioning market system depends on at least the following 12 market-facilitating legal and economic practices:[25]

1. Property rights clearly established and demarcated; procedures for establishing property rights and transferring them

2. Commercial laws and an independent judiciary to enforce them, especially contract and bankruptcy laws

3. Freedom to establish businesses in all sectors except those with significant externalities, without excessive licensing requirements; analogous freedom to enter trades and professions and to attain government offices (equal economic opportunity)

4. A stable currency and banking system, including a reliable and efficient system for making transfers

5. Public supervision or operation of natural monopolies (industries with increasing returns to scale) as occurs in industries where technological efficiency requires that a firm be large enough to supply a substantial fraction of the national market

6. Provision of adequate information in every market about the characteristics of the products offered and the state of supply and demand, to both buyers and sellers

7. Autonomous tastes—protection of consumers' preferences from influence by producers and purveyors

8. Public management of externalities (both harmful and beneficial) and provision of public goods

9. Instruments for executing stabilizing monetary and fiscal policies (see Chapter 15)

10. Safety nets—provisions for maintaining adequate consumption for individuals affected by certain economic misfortunes, especially involuntary unemployment, industrial injuries, and work disabilities

11. Encouragement of innovation, in particular, issuance and enforcement of patents and copyrights

12. Security from violence, the most basic of all social foundations

It is clear that market reforms involve much more than merely eliminating price distortions, privatizing public enterprises, and declaring markets free. The setbacks to market reforms in many transition economies is in no small measure attributable to the absence of some (or many) of the institutional preconditions and market practices. Thus, governments have important limits, and so do markets, as the earlier review of market failures makes clear.[26] Again, the question is one of balance. This is reflected in the move away from the once dominant "Washington Consensus."

11.6 The Washington Consensus on the Role of the State in Development and Its Subsequent Evolution

For much of the 1980s and into the 1990s, the so-called Washington Consensus on development policy held sway. This consensus, encapsulated by John Williamson, reflected the free-market approach to development followed in those years by the IMF, World Bank, and key U.S. government agencies, along with some other developed countries at the time. It contained 10 points, summarized in column 1 of Box 11.1.

The 10 points of the Washington Consensus are striking at least as much for what they do not contain as for what they do. There is no mention of shared growth, of the central need to focus on eliminating absolute poverty to achieve development in any meaningful sense, or of reducing inequality, as central ends in themselves as well as instruments of economic growth.[27] Driving the several components of the consensus was the conviction that government was more likely to make things worse than better. Prevalent also was the view that poverty would be taken care of by growth and was not a major obstacle in itself to growth and development; but this view, as noted in Chapter 5, is no longer considered adequate by most development specialists.

The Washington Consensus list is also striking in its free-market approach, even in fields in which market failure is prevalent, such as the financial sector

BOX 11.1 The Washington Consensus and East Asia

Elements of the Washington Consensus	South Korea	Taiwan
1. Fiscal discipline	Yes, generally	Yes
2. Redirection of public expenditure priorities toward health, education, and infrastructure	Yes	Yes
3. Tax reform, including the broadening of the tax base and cutting marginal tax rates	Yes, generally	Yes
4. Unified and competitive exchange rates	Yes (except for limited time periods)	Yes
5. Secure property rights	President Park starts his rule in 1961 by imprisoning leading businessmen and threatening confiscation of their assets	Yes
6. Deregulation	Limited	Limited
7. Trade liberalization	Limited until the 1980s	Limited until the 1980s
8. Privatization	No. Government established many public enterprises during 1950s and 1960s.	No. Government established many public enterprises during 1950s and 1960s.
9. Elimination of barriers to direct foreign investment (DFI)	DFI heavily restricted	DFI subject to government control
10. Financial liberalization	Limited until the 1980s	Limited until the 1980s

Source: From "Understanding economic policy reform," by Dani Rodrik. *Journal of Economic Literature* 34 (1996): 17. Reprinted with permission from the American Economic Association and courtesy of Dani Rodrik.

(examined in Chapter 15). Moreover, the list is striking in its limited applicability to two of the most successful cases in the history of economic development, South Korea and Taiwan. These cases not only represent among the highest rates of economic growth over the past half-century but also have often been cited as examples of shared growth, in which absolute poverty was eliminated early on, and the lower-income groups have continued to benefit from the development process, despite an upturn in inequality since the late 1990s. The historical record of high growth in China reflects the combination of various incentives for entrepreneurship and an extremely active industrial policy and other government activity. Indeed, as Dani Rodrik summarizes in Box 11.1, for about half of its elements, the Washington Consensus is at best of limited applicability to South Korea and Taiwan. It can be concluded that the state has had a broader role in the most successful development experiences than encapsulated by the Washington Consensus.

Toward a New Consensus

In recent years, major changes in the Washington Consensus worldview have occurred in Washington D.C and elsewhere. In the Americas, the new views were sometimes referred to as the *New Consensus*, which began to take shape at the April 1998 Summit of the Americas in Santiago, Chile. Other important contributions to attempts to describe an expanded and more balanced consensus—albeit with a focus solely on growth rather than broader human development—include the Commission on Growth and Development's 2008 *Growth Report: Strategies for Sustained Growth and Inclusive Development* (commonly referred to as the *Spence Report*) and the broader scope suggested by Dani Rodrik. A final example including infrastructure and industrialization was articulated in the 2010 Seoul G20 communique.[28] Note that the scholarly tradition in Europe and Japan, as well as in many parts of the developing world, such as India, has remained more positive toward the role of the state throughout the period but has to a large degree also converged toward the New Consensus. The broad elements of the New Consensus are summarized in Box 11.2.

Given that developing-country governments are highly constrained in their available resources, some of these New Consensus objectives will have to receive less emphasis than others. An important dimension of the New Consensus is the emphasis on government's responsibility to focus on poverty alleviation. This is in part a return to the focus of the 1970s; one reason for this renewed focus is that free-market policies of the 1980s and early 1990s were viewed as inadequately helping the poor. The New Consensus also appears to reflect a growing sentiment that the goal of poverty eradication is finally achievable, especially given recent progress in health, education, and other areas. But the New Consensus on the role of government in development borrows some important lessons from the Washington Consensus period. In particular, the stress on market-based development and limiting government's role in direct production continues to be the consensus view. And the new elements are not based on an assumption that government is a benevolent provider of social welfare. A sober view continues but emphasizes the importance of building state capacity and responsiveness by reacting to government failure with judiciously designed reforms, seeking feasible improvements in economic institutions, and encouraging a deepened civil society role.

BOX 11.2   The New Consensus

1. Development must be market-based, but there are large market failures that cannot be ignored.
2. Government should not be in the business of direct production, as a general rule.
3. Nevertheless, there is a broad, eclectic role for government in the following areas:

   - Providing a stable macro environment
   - Infrastructure, though in fewer sectors than thought necessary in the past
   - Public health
   - Education and training
   - Technology transfer (and for advanced developing economies, the beginnings of original R&D)

- Ensuring environmentally sustainable development and ecological protection
- Providing export incentives
- Helping the private sector overcome coordination failures
- Ensuring "shared growth" by acting to reduce poverty and inequality and to ensure that as the economy grows, the poor share substantially in the benefits
- Prudential supervision and regulation of the financial sector
- Provision of fundamental public goods, including institutions such as protection of property rights and broad access to opportunity

The New Consensus also does not include some features that many commentators have considered significant to East Asian success, such as an active or at least a highly targeted industrial policy—picking winners—to overcome coordination failures, because these remain controversial. There are doubts about the replicability of industrial policy experiences—specifically in encouraging particular industrial activities—of these countries, and the most widely held perspective is that industrial policy is generally ineffective when government is less capable or more constrained (though some specialists conclude from this problem that it should be a priority to raise government capabilities in these fields in other countries).

The New Consensus view represents in part a renewed recognition that markets do fail; that at times these failures cannot be addressed without a significant and ongoing role for government—that market failure can be significantly worse than government failure after all; and that when governance is poor, it can often be improved. Indeed, a key part of government's role is to help secure the foundations for economic development by ensuring that the requirements for an effective market-based economy are met.

11.7 Development Political Economy: Theories of Policy Formulation and Reform

Until recently, two extreme views seem often to have dominated the discussions of the role of government in economic development. The first view has been that effective government was not only necessary due to market failure but possibly even sufficient to achieve economic development. At least implicit in this view is the argument that if a particular regime could not be counted on to perform competently and honestly in this process, either the regime would eventually be forced to do so as a result of building political pressures or else it would lose power, through elections if available or through other means if not.

The second view, associated with the neoclassical counterrevolution or new orthodoxy school, which has its roots in Nobel laureate Friedrich von Hayek, was developed in the ideas of Nobel laureate James Buchanan and was applied to development policy by Anne Krueger, Deepak Lal, and others. In this view, participants in government, such as politicians and bureaucrats, were as selfish and self-interested as owners of companies but lacked the market to restrain them. Even when the economy was locked in a poverty trap, government itself played a key role in that bad equilibrium. While these points might enjoy broad agreement under some circumstances, this approach drew the strong conclusion that as a rule, at least beyond a minimum role, governments could only make things worse.[29]

It is easy to see how such extreme views became popular: At least they offered a guiding framework. Development specialists with a more nuanced view of government's role seemed to lack a clear theory. At the same time, most countries seemed to follow a particular "model" of development year after year, decade after decade, many reacting to colonial experiences: Governments in newly independent countries often either continued colonial policies or seemed to choose policies in angry reaction to those of the colonial period by emulating either Soviet policies or more moderate versions of them, as in India. In short, there was all too little on which to base a meaningful theory of development policy formulation.

The questions are insistent ones. Why did some developing countries reform quickly and effectively and others remain stuck year after year in an obviously counterproductive set of policies? Why did some adopt a course of aggrandizement for the rulers and others focus successfully on shared growth? Why did some reform programs become bogged down in squabbling among interest groups and others reach compromises that allowed for relatively efficient and equitable outcomes? Why were apparently good policy reforms abandoned in some countries after their adoption and stuck to diligently and unswervingly in others? Moreover, why did some governments that seemed to be following good advice on reform end up with an unequal and slow-growth outcome when they led to better outcomes elsewhere? Why were some countries such as Chile able to make a transition to a centrist, shared-growth regime after being stuck first in a stagnant import substitution mode and then in a dictatorship for which reducing poverty and inequality was not a priority? What makes for the dynamism of a Mauritius rather than the stagnation of a Guinea-Bissau, the recent progress of a Mozambique rather than the impasse of an Angola, a South Korea rather than a Philippines, a Thailand rather than a Myanmar? There are better questions than answers, but a start has been made.

A foundation is to focus on the quality of incentives provided by the underlying economic institutions as examined in detail in Chapter 2. Beyond this, the general framework of political economy analysis is that people may be assumed to oppose policy changes if they think they are likely to personally lose by them. Obviously, people do at times support policies that they believe are morally right, even if they will prove materially costly to them. As a rule of thumb, however, most work in this field begins with the assumption of material self-interest, the so-called *self-interest standard of rationality*. For example, an economic reform that benefits most people may not be adopted if the losers are relatively few in number but have a lot to lose and so have a great incentive to take actions—ranging from lobbying to bribery—to block the reform, while the many gainers each stand individually to benefit relatively little, so they do not have much of an incentive to take comparable political action in support of the reform.

As a simple numerical example, suppose that nine people each gain $100 from a reform, and one person loses rents worth $300, for a net gain of $600. It sounds like a winner—but in some contexts, political participation can require time, effort, and money. Suppose that the opportunity cost of political engagement to influence the decision is $200, so the nine gainers do not politically engage. But the last person retains a net gain (or put differently, avoids a loss) of $300 − $200 = $100, and so determines the decision—not to reform. This pattern of diffuse gainers and concentrated losers has been identified repeatedly in postmortems of reform failure.[30]

Understanding Voting Patterns on Policy Reform

Sometimes reform is designed to maximize the benefits of the few. It is natural that the majority would oppose this, if they have the power to do so. Or they may think it likely that they will lose in the process of reform and, perhaps reflecting their previous experience, not believe that they will be adequately compensated through redistribution. But sometimes a majority of the public opposes policies that the majority would likely gain from. This may in part be due to lack of understanding of the nature of economic policy choices among the general public. It may be due to uncertainty over who will likely gain or lose from the policy. It is easy to understand that if voters are risk-averse, they may oppose a policy if they see a risk that they may turn out to be among those who will lose from it.

Raquel Fernandez and Dani Rodrik, however, demonstrated why even risk-neutral voters may rationally vote against a policy from which a majority will benefit. The basic idea is that if a significant number, but still a minority, of voters know with certainty that they will gain from a policy, they will vote for the policy. But what of the majority who do not know? For example, most may be unsure what skills they will need in order to be successful in the still obscure postreform environment and therefore how competitive they can be. Suppose that these remaining voters can only estimate their chances of gaining. Even if the percentage of gainers is fully known—say, 55% will gain—in many cases, if the uncertain voters estimate their chances of gaining as equal to that of the other uncertain voters, it will be rational to vote no.[31] A simple numerical example of this "status quo bias" will illustrate.

Suppose that 60% of the people will gain $100 each from the proposed reform, while 40% will lose $80 each. The expected gain for this population is given by $0.6(100) − 0.4(80) = 28$. If no one knows who any of the gainers are, this reform passes (because people are not averse to risk). But if a fraction *x* are known beforehand with certainty to be among the gainers, a majority of risk-neutral voters (who still do not know if they are one of the remaining winners) may have an incentive to vote no. In this case, if 40% of the people know that they will be winners, this leaves 60% who do not know; when they recalculate with this greater chance of being one of the losers, they find it in their interests to vote no.[32]

Although this is a specific case, the result is quite general. Students can verify that in many cases, a large majority of 60% or more can gain from a policy, but when a sufficient number are already known with certainty to gain, this leaves a majority of voters with an expected loss, and they then block the policy.

In contrast to our relatively clearer understanding of the obstacles to constructive reform, we still understand too little about why constructive change takes place at all. If progress were rare, this would not be much of an empirical problem, because there would be little to explain. It would, of course, remain an important development problem because it would leave an important sphere of policy unaddressed. Fortunately, progress appears to be much more common than political economy theory would suggest. Democratization has been sweeping the developing world, as reflected in governance indices such as those in Figure 11.1. In more countries, attention to shared growth and development participation has been strengthening. Reforms that benefit the majority are sometimes implemented even over the strenuous resistance of powerful social and economic forces that stand to lose. This is what we need to understand better if successful development policy reform is to spread further in the developing world.[33]

FIGURE 11.1 Global Trends in Governance, 1946–2008

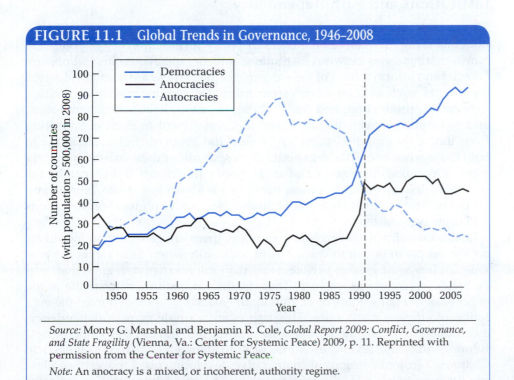

Source: Monty G. Marshall and Benjamin R. Cole, *Global Report 2009: Conflict, Governance, and State Fragility* (Vienna, Va.: Center for Systemic Peace) 2009, p. 11. Reprinted with permission from the Center for Systemic Peace.

Note: An anocracy is a mixed, or incoherent, authority regime.

A widely favored approach to understanding policy formation has been to examine the trade-off between short-term costs of reform and its long-term benefits, to both politicians and the economy. Politicians in particular are viewed as having a very short time horizon because of their limited time in office. Only when crises become sufficiently serious do discounted net benefits of reform become sufficiently large to induce change. The limitation of this literature is that the short-term costs of reform are rarely quantified, and the precise causes of increased growth remain difficult to identify.

It has been noted that reforms are often instituted after a crisis, and so the literature has considered whether "crisis can cause reform." Only when conditions are very serious, one view has it, will risk-averse politicians and voters be willing to try a different strategy. The debt crisis in Latin America is viewed as the catalyst to the adoption of more market-friendly policies, moving away from what had been, in most Latin American countries, failed experiments in import substitution. However, left unexplained is why even more severe debt crises in Africa did not promote analogous reforms. One part of the answer may be that greater outside pressure and resources were brought to bear on Latin America because of the greater threat its insolvency represented to major banks. But as Rodrik notes, "What we surely need to understand is why South Korea's politicians are ready to change course at the slightest hint of a crisis, while Brazil's will bring their economy to the brink of hyperinflation several times before they tackle the problem."[34] The political-economy literature recognizes this issue but is largely silent on it.

Institutions and Path Dependency

The framework suggested by Nobel laureate Douglass North is useful for understanding qualitative differences in policy formulation across countries. North distinguishes between institutions and organizations. Institutions are "formal and informal rules of the economic game." These are humanly devised constraints, such as contract enforcement, that define incentives for savings, investment, production, and trade. These, in turn, affect benefits and costs, and economic behavior that may lead to development or decline. Following from this, organizations spring up around the property rights, designed to help those who control the organization prosper under these existing property rights. Organizations emerge that are in large part defined and shaped by the incentives that emerge from these rules. In a widely cited quote, North says, "If the institutional matrix rewards piracy, then [only] piratical organizations will come into existence."[35]

Once these inefficient rights are in place, there are generally no incentives for the people in power to change them, especially when these rights can provide leaders with greater private gains than an alternative regime that may be better for society as a whole. Thus, inefficient institutions continue at the expense of overall welfare or of growth; the market cannot guarantee the evolution of efficient institutions. This trap is an example of **path dependency**, a condition in which the past condition of an individual or economy affects future conditions. Several examples of path dependency were examined in Chapters 2 (colonial origins of comparative development), 4 (poverty and low productivity traps), 6 (Malthusian traps), and 8 (child labor traps). Specifically,

Path dependency A condition in which the past condition of an individual or economy, measured by the level of one or more variables, affects future conditions.

North argues that the "inability of societies to develop effective low-cost enforcement of contracts is the most important source of both historical stagnation and contemporary underdevelopment."[36]

The individuals who control the state have the incentive to use it for private gain rather than for the public interest. But North argues that historically, on occasion, the interests of those with high bargaining power have coincided with the public interest; when this occurs, effective institutions emerge, which prove very difficult to roll back once established.

In addition, although there is no way to ensure that this will happen, it appears that the more examples of successful institutions in neighboring countries, the greater the pressure on governments to adopt similar institutions. Clearly, the adoption of certain institutions, including human rights, property rights protection, and democracy, has spread over the objections of dictators because of their popular appeal. An example of the outward spread of democracy to neighbors can be seen in Europe from core advanced countries toward less developed areas—first to Spain, Portugal, and Greece and then to eastern Europe from the fall of the Berlin Wall to some of the "color revolutions" and recent "Arab Spring" revolts. Other examples are the spread of democracy across Latin America from the 1980s, from Japan outward to other East Asian countries after their middle classes reached a certain size, and in a cascade of freer elections in Africa. A final approach argues that democratization can emerge as a commitment device, that is, a reform accepted by elites who need to prevent revolution but can do so only by guaranteeing in this way that they will not renege on their concessions. Of course, democracies make serious policy errors too, but the chance that very bad policies will be implemented and go unchecked are much reduced. Unfortunately, even after democracy emerges, societies sometimes revert to autocracy, as long-standing political forces reassert themselves—the process can be more like the proverbial "two steps forward, one step backward."

An improved understanding of the political economy of successful policy reform and implementation will probably require continued and extensive interactions between political scientists, sociologists, and economists, each of whom have valuable insights to contribute from their research. In the process, more will have to be done to base theory on the experiences of the governments of developing countries, which in many cases will be struggling with the early stages of democratization and expanding avenues for development participation, with higher levels of conflict and in some cases an ongoing threat of return to military government or other autocratic rule. As Merilee Grindle has noted, further progress in this field will require moving beyond political-economy models that were developed primarily to study political processes in advanced economies with stable democratic traditions.[37]

Democracy versus Autocracy: Which Facilitates Faster Growth?

The comparative merits of democratic or autocratic regimes for development performance (especially economic growth) have been much debated. These debates have presented some of the trade-offs starkly. Under democracy, politicians seeking reelection have an incentive to reflect the will and interests of a majority of the people. On the other hand, a looming election gives an incentive to pursue short-term accomplishments that can be pointed to during a campaign, rather than what is necessarily good for long-term development. Worse, the corrupt politician who knows he or she will soon be voted out of office has an interest to steal as much as possible in the meantime. Under autocracy, there are fewer constraints on what can be stolen and for how long. But the politician who is reasonably confident of remaining in power for a long time can pursue long-term development strategies (at the very least, to have more to steal from).

Some high-growth but autocratic countries such as Singapore, along with South Korea and Taiwan prior to their transitions to democracy, appear to have enjoyed some of the potential benefits of autocracy for development. In these cases, corruption was present but to no greater extent than in most other developing countries and probably somewhat less than average. The positive effect of autocracy on growth-enhancing policies seems to have worked best when a regime sees that its greatest chance of remaining in power lies in achieving a maximum rate of growth; this is the case with South Korea, which has historically viewed economic development as a bulwark against the aggressive designs of North Korea, or of Taiwan, with its concern over possible invasion from the People's Republic of China. For that matter, China's current rulers have staked their political legitimacy and dreams of political recognition as a world power on a drive to modernization, so far with success. But autocrats also have the power to use the state for strictly private gains, as Mobutu did in the Democratic Republic of Congo (which he had named Zaire), following the example of the ruthless Belgian colonial rule of that unfortunate country. And those who fear overthrow will have an incentive both to "steal fast" and to focus resources on fortifying their own power and crushing opponents rather than using state resources to develop institutions and make investments that foster development.

Some dictatorships have been explained as "necessary" phases in the economic development of countries, as in the "Lee thesis," named after longtime Singapore prime minister Lee Kuan Yew. Amartya Sen would disagree, arguing that market freedoms and political freedoms are both valuable development outcomes in their own right and also are complements in encouraging economic development. For every example of a development star under dictatorship, other examples of development disasters under dictatorship can be provided. And many democracies have prospered; Botswana is a democracy, and over the long run has been the fastest-growing country in Africa. Sen also argues for a *constructive* role of political and other human rights in achieving pro-poor development: that people only become aware of important information (such as the plight of poverty of an ethnic minority) or understand the importance of some fundamental values (such as the right to a basic education) in the *process* of free public debate. Moreover, people only frame their own preferences in the context of *dialogue*. Although decision making may be slower, the best choices—including in the evolution of institutions—are likely to be made under conditions of freedom, Sen argues. For example, famines are unlikely when there is a free press to report on them. The greater capacity for the poor to organize their communities under democracy may give rise to many benefits in addressing local problems of poverty. Corruption is more likely to be rooted out more quickly. And fertility declined more in Kerala, with its emphasis on political dialogue, than in China, with its administrative mandates.[38]

In the face of such nuanced problems, it is no wonder that the empirical results are closely divided. It seems that about a third of studies find a positive effect for democracy, a third a neutral effect, and the remaining third a negative effect. Ahmed Mobarak has proposed that democratic regimes will be less volatile than autocratic ones. As a result, because more volatile economies are known to grow more slowly than more stable economies, the positive effect of democracy on growth may operate through this channel. But these benefits may be canceled by negative direct effects of democracy on growth.[39]

Jakob de Haan and Clemens Siermann point out that despite the arguments and also some evidence in the literature of a negative relationship between growth and democracy, such studies report that a *lack* of civil and political liberties is also negatively correlated with growth. They propose using better measures of democracy, including how deeply rooted it has become in the society, suggesting a measure based on the number of years that a country can be regarded as a democracy. They then offer various statistical tests of direct and indirect effects of "democratic liberties." Their main conclusion may speak for the literature in general: "The relationship between democracy and economic growth is not robust."[40] However, a widespread view is that democracy is good for broader development objectives, such as equity, education, health, and famine prevention.

11.8 Development Roles of NGOs and the Broader Citizen Sector

It is increasingly recognized that development success depends not only on a vibrant private sector and an efficient public sector but on a vigorous citizen sector as well. Relying on the former sectors alone has been compared to trying to sit on a two-legged stool. Organizations of the citizen sector are usually termed **nongovernmental organizations (NGOs)** in the development context but are also referred to as *nonprofit, voluntary, independent, civil society*, or *citizen organizations*.

A wide range of organizations fall under the NGO banner. The United Nations Development Programme defines an NGO as

> any non-profit, voluntary citizens' group which is organized on a local, national or international level. Task-oriented and driven by people with a common interest, NGOs perform a variety of services and humanitarian functions, bring citizens' concerns to governments, monitor policies and encourage political participation at the community level. They provide analysis and expertise, serve as early warning mechanisms and help monitor and implement international agreements. Some are organized around specific issues, such as human rights, the environment or health.[41]

Whereas governments rely on authority to achieve outcomes, and private-sector firms rely on market mechanisms to provide incentives for mutually beneficial exchange, civil society actors, working through NGOs, rely on independent

Nongovernmental organizations (NGOs) Nonprofit organizations often involved in providing financial and technical assistance in developing countries.

voluntary efforts and influence to promote their values and to further social and economic development.

Cooperatives also play significant and important roles in economic development in many developing countries; but the experience has been mixed. In some countries and regions co-ops have assisted farmers with getting more reliable and lower-cost inputs, better access to credit, and higher prices and better marketing channels for their output. In other regions, co-ops have been subject to manipulation by the state, paving the way for corruption as well as inefficiency. Richard Simmons and Johnston Birchall concluded that in many cases, cooperatives in developing countries historically "failed to live up to expectations; having been created by governments they remained controlled by the interests of government, party and civil service"; however, "some new, more genuine co-operative sectors are now emerging."[42]

The emergence of civil-society actors such as NGOs as key players in global affairs is recognized by Nobel Peace Prizes given to the Campaign to Ban Landmines in 1997, Doctors Without Borders in 1999, and the Grameen Bank in 2006 (see the case study at the end of this chapter), as well as individual Nobel laureates who have played key roles in establishing NGOs and other citizen organizations.[43] A good example is the late 2004 Nobel laureate, Wangari Maathai, who launched the Kenyan and now Africa-wide Green Belt Movement.

Some 3,051 NGOs had consultative status with the United Nations as of 2010; the number of international NGOs grew by 20% in the 1990s and grew 20-fold from 1964 to 1998.[44] The potential impact of NGOs is also seen in their wide scope in activities and issues and their size as measured by number of employees as well as their large and growing budgets.

In contrast to private goods, public goods are nonexcludable (it is impossible to prevent individuals from consuming them except at excessive cost) and nonrival (consumption by individuals does not reduce the amount of the good available for consumption by others). Activities in which NGOs have comparative advantage typically lie between conventional private and public goods in these dimensions. In particular, they tend to be partially rival, partially excludable, rival but not excludable, or excludable but not rival. Figure 11.2 reflects this range of activities in these two dimensions. The result is a typology that includes "private goods" (high excludability, high rivalry) in the upper right-hand corner, referred to here as Type I goods, and "public goods" (low excludability, low rivalry) in the lower left-hand corner, referred to here as Type III goods. The production and distribution of these Type I and Type III goods are generally assigned to the market and the public sector, respectively. The other two corners represent goods that are hybrids of the other two.[45]

In the lower right-hand corner are found common-pool (or common-property) resources, characterized by low excludability but high rivalry. Examples of such Type II goods are natural resources such as fisheries, pastures, and forests, with open access. As explained in Chapter 10, unless well-managed (see Box 10.3, page 516), these resources often tend to be overused (and underinvested).[46] Common-property resources can be allocated through institutions in both public and private sectors, but NGOs play an important and growing role. Historically, common-property resources were allocated by traditional (e.g., tribal) mechanisms, but these often broke down under colonialism and postcolonial government control in many developing countries.[47] Increasingly,

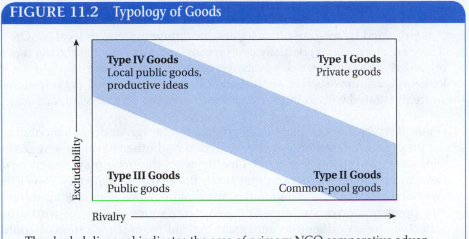

FIGURE 11.2   Typology of Goods

Type IV Goods
Local public goods,
productive ideas

Type I Goods
Private goods

Type III Goods
Public goods

Type II Goods
Common-pool goods

Excludability

Rivalry

The shaded diagonal indicates the area of primary NGO comparative advantage in dimensions of rivalry and excludability. When, based on local conditions (such as government failure), NGOs are in a position to supply public or private goods at a lower price or higher quality, they may be found expanding into these nonshaded areas as well (Type I and Type III goods).

NGOs are helping community-based organizations (CBOs) reclaim this role in common-property resource allocation. Because they are organizations based on trust rather than coercion (government) or individual self-interest (market), NGOs may be able to arrive at efficient and socially acceptable allocations of common-property resources at relatively low transaction costs.

Finally, in the upper left-hand corner are found another hybrid, Type IV goods. For example, productive ideas can be used by all without their becoming used up or degraded and so are nonrival, but they can often be effectively kept secret, so they are excludable.[48] A related example is technology transfer to developing countries. Technical knowledge is not a rival good once it is transferred and absorbed into the local economy, as ideas may often spread rather freely across firms within a locality, but it is excludable in that without active intervention, productive ideas often do not cross national boundaries (especially between developed and developing countries). One reason is the free-rider problem: One firm might pay to learn a new technology, but its local rivals could likely find a way to absorb their knowledge (such as hiring away employees) without sharing the cost. Type IV goods exhibit high excludability but low rivalry and are typically assigned to government-regulated private-sector or civil-society actors.[49] For example, productive but basic and general ideas are often developed by nonprofit universities and other research centers, and technology transfer in areas such as public health is often undertaken by specialized NGOs or nonprofit industry associations or consortia.

A special form of public good that operates at the local level or in a specialized subgroup of a wider society is known as a *local public good*. Under some conditions, a decentralized solution to allocation problems for such goods may be found.[50] Local public goods are excludable from those outside the area but generally not for those in the local area. One can find all three sectors active in producing and allocating local public goods. For example, local amenities may be provided by for-profit developers, local government, or local NGOs.

There are at least seven partially overlapping and mutually reinforcing types of organizational comparative advantage for international or national NGOs or local organizations such as federations of community-based organizations; these are illustrated with examples from the field of poverty alleviation.

1. *Innovation.* NGOs can play a key role in the design and implementation of programs focused on poverty reduction and other development goals. For example, NGOs that work directly with the poor may design new and more effective programs that reach the poor, facilitated by this close working relationship. Individual profit-making firms may lack incentives for poverty innovation, especially when the innovations that would be effective are so difficult to anticipate that no request for proposal could be written to draw them out. In many cases, government has an advantage in scaling up established programs. But government has been relatively less successful at significant program innovation, compared to (or at least without a prod from) the NGO sector. Often government programs have not reached the poorest families. More broadly, government tends to offer uniform services, whereas the poor may have special needs that are different from mainstream populations. Some of the most important innovations in poverty programs (such as microfinance) have been conceptualized and initially developed by domestic and international NGOs. In the sphere of education, for example, NGOs have played the pioneering role in such areas as nonformal education, community literacy campaigns, educational village theater, use of computer technology in urban slums, and subtitling of community center music videos for educational purposes.[51] A key question is whether the government or private sector is then capable of scaling up NGO innovations, once they have become established as working models, as effectively as or better than the innovating NGO. In any case, if governments or private-sector firms are unable or unwilling, the experience of BRAC (see the case study at the end of this chapter) shows that NGOs may do this scaling up to a substantial degree, at least until the government is finally ready to step in. Such innovations are nonrival but are potentially excludable, particularly if detailed information is not transmitted easily.

2. *Program flexibility.* An NGO can address development issues that are viewed as important for the communities in which it works. In principle, an NGO is not constrained by the limits of public policy or other agendas such as those of donor-country, foreign-assistance priorities or by domestic national or local governmental programs. Indeed, national NGOs (such as BRAC, in this chapter's case study) are in principle also unconstrained by the preferences of the international NGOs (and vice versa). Moreover, once a potential solution to a development problem has been identified, NGOs may have greater flexibility in altering their program structure accordingly than would be the case for a government program. Flexibility can be interpreted as localized innovations or minor adaptations of program

innovations to suit particular needs. NGOs may be better able to make use of participation mechanisms, unconstrained by limits placed on individual rights or prerogatives for elites that prevail in the public sphere. However, there are limits to this flexibility, as NGOs may have a tendency to tailor their programs to fit the available funding, a phenomenon known as *donor capture*.

3. *Specialized technical knowledge.* National and international NGOs may be greater repositories of technical expertise and specialized knowledge than local governments (or businesses). In particular, international NGOs can draw on the experiences of many countries that may offer possible models for problems of poverty faced by any one country, as well as possible solutions. Of course, this forms part of the basis for credibility. These technical skills may be used for developing effective responses to locally binding poverty traps and coordination problems. Specialized knowledge is acquired in the process of doing specialized work with local citizen groups, including those of the poor. Consider the Grameen phone lady model, in which microcredit and training are provided to village women to purchase and operate a cell phone available to community members on a fee basis (see the case study on the Grameen Bank). This program reflects innovations coupled with local NGO advantages in technical knowledge. Knowledge, understood as an economic good, is also excludable but nonrival.

4. *Targeted local public goods.* Goods and services that are rival but excludable, including those targeted to socially excluded populations, may be best designed and provided by NGOs that know and work with these groups. Possible examples include local public health facilities, nonformal education, provision of specialized village telecommunications and computing facilities, codification and integration of traditional legal and governance practices, creating local markets, community mapping and property registration, and community negotiations with governments. Some examples of these goods may lie along the shaded diagonal of Figure 11.2, but local public goods are generally locally nonrival but excludable from those outside the local area.

5. *Common-property resource management design and implementation.* NGOs, including federations of local CBOs, can play an important role in common-property management and targeted local public-good provision. Throughout the developing world, both governments and the private sector have a poor track record in ensuring sustainability of forests, lakes, coastal fishing areas, pasturelands, and other common-property resources, also known as "commons." But a large fraction of the world's people still rely on local natural resources for most of their income and consumption. Targeted NGO and CBO programs, including training, assistance with organizational development, efforts to change noncooperative cultural characteristics, and initiating measures such as community and common-property policing, can help address common-property mismanagement and related problems. Common-property resources are rival but nonexcludable.

6. *Trust and credibility.* In practice, NGOs may have other advantages over government in gaining the trust of, and providing effective services to,

groups with special needs, notably those in extreme poverty. NGOs' local presence and relationships, frequent interaction and communication, and greater avenues for participation may generate greater trust among the poor and other citizens. Although in a decentralized and socially inclusive democratic setting, an elected government might be at least as trusted as "unelected" NGOs, government in many developing countries may be democratic in name only. But even majority rule can be of little benefit to the socially excluded, particularly when the majority population or its representatives actively marginalize the poor. When government resources are limited, trade-offs between benefits for established or excluded groups can take on added significance. Democracy may also provide little benefit to the socially excluded when they experience benign neglect and a lack of established communication channels with the government. Once such a history is established, it may be difficult for even a new and well-meaning government to overcome this legacy. NGOs, in contrast, may enjoy greater trust in assumed competence, benevolence, reliability, responsiveness, established personal contacts, and perception of consistent behavior in various settings that may not be possible to monitor. To the degree that NGOs follow explicit bylaws requiring democratic practice, accountability, and responsiveness, credibility is enhanced over time. Partly as a result, NGOs may also be more trusted by local government than less responsive or less accessible official donors. At the same time, if governments are perceived as corrupt or incompetent, foundations and certain other donors may trust only NGOs to address poverty, environment, local health and education delivery, and other services. Thus, NGOs help mobilize resources that would otherwise not be available for local residents, including those in structural poverty. Finally, the private sector may prefer to partner with NGOs than with governments or other official actors to gain credibility in socially responsible investment activities.[52] In sum, NGOs may enjoy higher trust than other organizations among all the major parties concerned, including the poor, developing-country local and national governments, and donors. Trust is related to the capability for effective advocacy.

7. *Representation and advocacy.* NGOs may hold advantages in understanding the needs of the poor, who otherwise are often excluded from political processes and even local community deliberations. NGOs may play a role in the aggregation of preferences and hence of representation of community needs. To the degree that NGOs have a better understanding of locally binding poverty traps, they should be in a position to represent the needs of the poor more effectively. This responsibility reflects the advocacy role of NGOs, including federations of CBOs, in advocating for the needs of poor and socially excluded peoples. Minorities may need special protections in majority-rule representative democracies, and existing constitutional protections are not always sufficient. It is not a comparative advantage of either the private or the public sector to advocate for the poor or the excluded. The private sector is less likely to hold the trust of those whose interests are to be advocated. Individual donors, foundations, agencies, or other funders of advocacy will want to ensure that the

advocates they sponsor are working with a broad understanding of the mission. Finally, if it is government that needs to be lobbied or influenced, it is unlikely to be in the comparative advantage of government to fulfill this function—particularly to the degree that trust is at issue—although an ombudsman or citizen protection office can play a valuable role. Advocacy for a given group is partly nonrival and nonexcludable.

Sometimes exceptional failures of either government or the private sector create situations under which NGOs can, and perhaps should, temporarily step in to fill the void through "sector extension." For example, BRAC is involved with producing private goods such as chalk, shoes, and seeds, under conditions of a dysfunctional private sector, at least in rural areas (see the case study at the end of this chapter). In Africa, in the face of government neglect, the international NGO Africare is involved in what are normally government responsibilities such as road building. But in such cases, NGOs may eventually turn these functions over to local CBOs, to the private sector, or to government (through a transfer agreement) when conditions warrant. For example, Africare helps government and CBOs take over responsibility for road maintenance after construction of a road has been completed.

As noted, in the developing countries, both government and markets can be weak, and strengthening their capacity is essential. But unfortunately, the citizen sector is often even weaker in these countries, in part because people have less money and time to donate, because skills are lacking, and because sometimes the citizen sector is actively undermined by the government and business sectors. Short of embezzlement or other outright lawbreaking, NGOs are also vulnerable to weaknesses, termed **voluntary failure**. Instead of realizing their potential, NGOs may be insignificant (owing to limited resources or small scale and reach), selective and exclusionary, elitist, and or ineffective.[53] One potential pitfall is the lack of adequate incentives to ensure effectiveness, which requires careful organizational design. Another is the ever-present danger of capture by the goals of funders rather than intended beneficiaries. This can reach the point where NGOs change their priorities from one year to the next.[54] NGOs can fail to live up to their organizational potential when means—such as fund-raising—become ends in themselves or when means are given too little attention, as when poor fund-raising keeps NGOs from realizing the scale they need to have a real impact. There are sometimes inadequate checks and balances to prevent these flaws. NGOs may not receive the immediate feedback from the market that private firms receive or that elected governments receive at the polls. This lack of rapid feedback can encourage these weaknesses or at least let them go on for some time before being corrected. Such problems must be addressed if NGOs are to achieve their potential for facilitating development and poverty alleviation. Research findings on tactics to improve NGO performance are found in Box 11.3. In this case, the program focused on an NGO-run school system whose leaders were motivated to improve performance, but this could become an example of innovations in the NGO sector that can spill over to the public sector.

In addition to the rapid rise to prominence of NGOs as key players in the development drama, three other major trends in governance have emerged: tackling corruption, fostering decentralization, and facilitating development participation in both the government and NGO sectors.

Voluntary failure The inability of nongovernmental organizations and the citizen sector more broadly to efficiently achieve social objectives in their areas of supposed comparative advantage.

BOX 11.3 FINDINGS   Reducing Teacher Absenteeism in an NGO School

Teacher "truancy" (absenteeism) helps explain why effective literacy skills have remained so poor in South Asia despite increases in enrollments. Esther Duflo, Rema Hanna, and Stephen Ryan studied one-teacher nonformal primary schools run by the NGO Seva Mandir in rural Udaipur, in the Indian state of Rajasthan. In half the schools, which were randomly selected, teachers were told to have a student photograph them with the rest of the class at the beginning and end of each school day. A tamperproof time stamp showed which days the school was open and at what times the classes began and ended. The teachers' salaries directly depended on their attendance for at least a five-hour day. Thus, the study examined the combined effect of direct monitoring with financial incentives. The impact was strong, with teacher absenteeism rates dropping by half, from 42% to 21%. The teachers' measured effort while at the school did not decline, so students benefited from about 30% more instruction time. These students had somewhat higher exam scores (by 0.17 standard deviations after one year) and were more able to gain admittance to formal government schools. This simple technological monitoring proved cost-effective for monitoring teacher attendance, because staff visits could be reduced from daily to periodically. Duflo, Hanna, and Ryan used economic analysis to conclude that the financial incentives alone could explain the difference of monitored teachers, and they argued that the incentives, rather than being monitored per se, caused the improvements. The researchers used the information to estimate cost-effective compensation policies. NGO schools might be different, for example, by providing better training, but the study team argued that such a program should also be workable in government schools; in any event, the team noted, the results supported hiring more "parateachers" such as those studied.

Source: Based on Esther Duflo, Rema Hanna, and Stephen P. Ryan, "Incentives work: Getting teachers to come to school," *American Economic Review*, 102(4): 1241–78, June 2012.

11.9 Trends In Governance and Reform

Tackling the Problem of Corruption

Corruption The appropriation of public resources for private profit and other private purposes through the use and abuse of official power or influence.

Corruption is the abuse of public trust for private gain; it is a form of stealing. Indexes of corruption regularly rate the incidence of corruption far higher in developing countries than in developed countries. This is understood to reflect both cause and effect. An absence of corruption encourages investment and efforts to expand the pie rather than merely fight over its distribution, and thus encourages growth; to this extent, improvements in governance, in general, and reduction of corruption, in particular, could be means to accelerate the process of development. In addition, as societies grow wealthier, good governance becomes more widely demanded by the population. This latter effect makes simple correlations between income and good governance difficult to interpret: Which causes which? Poor governance practices, such as bribery, controls over the press, and limits on civil liberties, are often found together and are clearly mutually reinforcing. As pointed out in Chapter 2, there is clear evidence that good institutions such as rule of law and constraints on elites lead to higher growth and incomes. But reform can also beget reform. For example, when Taiwan's press obtained substantial freedoms, many public scandals became publicized, which in turn helped generate public pressures for reform; the introduction of elections provided a mechanism to enforce this popular will.

The elimination of corruption is important for development for several reasons. First of all, as just noted, honest government may promote growth and sustainably high incomes. In addition, the association of eliminating corruption with public empowerment suggests that it is a direct objective of development (see Chapter 1). Finally, the effects of corruption fall disproportionately on the poor and are a major restraint on their ability to escape from poverty.[55]

The elimination of corruption and improvement of governance, in general, can thus also be viewed as part of an antipoverty strategy. While the rich may pay large bribes under corrupt regimes, the poor generally pay much larger fractions of their incomes in bribes and other forms of extortion. In other words, corruption may be viewed as a regressive tax on the absolutely poor. In addition, government for sale means government for the highest bidder. The poor find fewer services in their communities, including poor education and health facilities, when corruption is rife. This makes it more difficult to accumulate the means to escape from poverty traps. In addition, microenterprises of the poor pay a much higher fraction of their sales in bribes than larger firms do, and low-income households pay a much larger percentage of their incomes in bribes than higher-income households, as Figure 11.3 illustrates for the case of Ecuador.

Countries that have avoided or successfully tackled corruption have tended, on average, to promote competition and entry in the economy, avoiding too much power in the hands of large monopolies such as those in the energy sector in many countries, and have ensured that privatized firms faced competition; promoted civil service professionalism, with improved pay and incentives for public servants; made public expenditures more transparent, with clearer rules of procurement and budgeting; reduced immunity from prosecution of executive, legislative, and judicial figures; provided judicial independence; established and enforced meritocratic, transparent promotion policies; and eliminated inefficient regulations and made needed ones more transparent.[56]

With many forms of corruption and differences across nations and localities, there is no single best way to fight it. Basic public monitoring even by itself may matter, in procurement, or in local government public funds receipts and disbursements.[57]

Recent experience also suggests that even in broadly corrupt environments, real progress in overcoming government shortcomings is achievable, at least in some contexts, through focused reform efforts at the local level. This may threaten some local interests but need not threaten (or may even benefit) more national-level interests. For example, on net urban elites probably do not benefit from village power abuses, or from rural teacher and health worker truancy, and may back reforms that address such problems. A potential example of locally based popular reforms is the community monitoring of local health facilities in Uganda as examined in Box 4.2. Such examples also raise the broader tantalizing prospect that higher-level institutions eventually can be reformed from the bottom up.

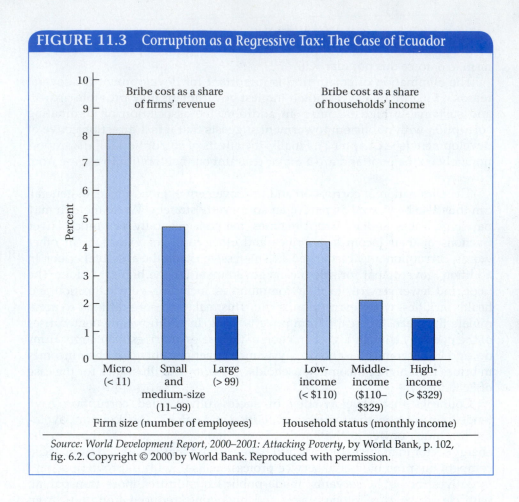

FIGURE 11.3   Corruption as a Regressive Tax: The Case of Ecuador

Source: World Development Report, 2000–2001: Attacking Poverty, by World Bank, p. 102, fig. 6.2. Copyright © 2000 by World Bank. Reproduced with permission.

The relationship between the rule of law and per capita GDP is shown in Figure 11.4.

Decentralization

Decentralization has been a long-term trend in developed countries. The United States, Canada, and Germany have had significant powers at the state and local level enshrined in their constitutions. The European Union has been proceeding—officially, at least—on the principle of "subsidiarity," meaning that feasible decisions are made at the most local level. The United Kingdom has decentralized authority to Scotland and Wales and also to local authorities in England. In Italy, power has been transferred to the 20 regions and their provinces. Local governments are closer to the urban and rural problems they must address.

Recently, trends toward decentralization and greater urban self-government have been growing in the developing world as democracy has spread in Latin America and elsewhere, and the political process has allowed for providing greater autonomy, notably more fiscal autonomy, for regional and local levels of

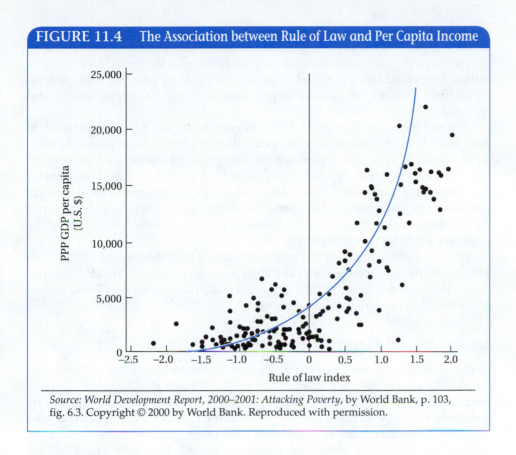

FIGURE 11.4   The Association between Rule of Law and Per Capita Income

government. The constitutional reform that has frequently accompanied democratization has in many cases provided an opportunity to codify greater local autonomy. A major motivation of the central government has often been to share fiscal burdens with regions and cities, but decentralization has sometimes taken on a life of its own that has been difficult to contain.

Decentralization in Brazil to its 26 states and some 5,000 municipalities dates at least to the 1891 constitution, but the recent period of devolution of authority started with the constitutional reform of 1989, which gave new authority and responsibilities to the states and developed fiscal federalism, increasing the local share of government resources. The fiscal decentralization occurred in the wake of the debt crisis of the 1980s and the perceived need to carry out structural adjustment by lowering the federal budget deficit and spread some of the adjustment burden to the regions. However, many observers consider the resources available to states and cities too small in relation to responsibilities, with still more burden than opportunity.

A wave of decentralization in Mexico also began in the late 1980s in the wake of the debt crisis, alongside programs of privatization, liberalization, and deregulation. Constitutional reforms transferred additional power—and responsibilities—to the states and municipalities. But as in Brazil, local governments complain that they have insufficient resources to carry out their added mandates. (The debt crisis is examined in Chapter 13.)

A third Latin American example is the Bolivia decentralization of 1994, which recognized local forms of organization and citizen participation; indigenous and peasant organizations have sought an active role under the new system, although conflict has continued. The decentralization resulted from a combination of pressures from local government and popular organizations and from international agencies.

The experience of Senegal is a well-known example of decentralization in Africa. In 1996, presidents of rural councils were made more accountable to their constituencies, and regional governments were established to develop and carry out regional development policy. However, the fiscal limitations of local government in Latin America are small compared to those faced in Senegal, and thoroughgoing fiscal reform remains a top priority. There were high hopes for the democratically elected government that came to power in 2013, and the experience will be watched closely.

In Asia, decentralization has proceeded apace with democratization, while long-standing democracies such as India have also provided greater local control, notably under India's 74th Constitutional Amendment. In China, decentralization has occurred to some extent.

Development Participation

If the goal of economic growth is human development, then without participation, we could have economic growth without development. Indeed, participation—a say in development policies by the people most affected by them—is arguably in itself a chief end of development. Participation is also a means to further human capabilities and other goals of development, as defined in Chapter 1. Moreover, economic growth is greatly facilitated by human development and impossible to sustain without it. Development participation has been shown to make projects work better. With genuine and full participation by beneficiaries on what projects are chosen and in the way that development assistance gets used more generally, we should expect less corruption and greater development results per dollar of aid spent.

Development participation has been discussed for decades. The United Nations has been promoting it since the 1970s; it was an academic fad in the early 1980s; and in the late 1990s, the World Bank came out vocally for development participation. Critics have complained that when the World Bank uses the term *participation*, it often seems meant as a strategy to reduce project costs or to deflect criticism. But the World Bank has clearly discovered the merits of getting governments and civil society to take ownership of development projects and reforms. Only then are reforms undertaken in a serious and sustainable way.

What are the potential objections to the principle of genuine participation? First, the poorest countries need to make some policy decisions and get some relief operations up and running immediately. The highly indebted poor countries that need immediate debt relief feel pressure to prepare plans quickly and provide little more than nominal time for civil-society participation. Even if the mechanisms of participation are already in place, it takes time to operate them, to make sure there is sufficient voice, to aggregate the preferences voiced, and to work out a means of implementation. But in most cases, mechanisms of genuine participation are not in place; doing so may take years, even with the full cooperation of national government and local power brokers.

Second, unhealthy and unskilled people are probably not able to participate effectively in development projects, let alone have a full voice in the decisions that affect them. A third objection is the costs of time: The poor are busy trying to survive. They may receive a low market wage, but that does not mean they have time available for volunteer work. This is especially true of women. They work long hours in both economic activity and at home because they cannot afford alternatives to household production. They may reasonably view expectations that they participate as unremunerated labor. Donors and developing-country governments need to develop ways to reward participation, but a big part of the problem is the superficiality of what passes for participation in the field. These three objections suggest that participation may have limits.

Distinctions between different types of participation are a valuable starting point and have been suggested by a number of authors. For example, John Cohen and Norman Uphoff examine degrees of participation along three dimensions: kinds of participation (in decision making, implementation, benefits, and evaluation), identity of participants (including residents, leaders, government personnel, and foreign personnel), and how participation occurs (the basis, form, extent, and effect of participation).[58] David Deshler and Donald Sock distinguish "genuine participation," which can include either citizen control or cooperation, with delegated power or partnership agreements between citizens and agencies, from "pseudo-participation," which can include placation, consultation, or information without power sharing, as well as "therapy" and manipulation.[59] The deeper problem is that genuine participation is often not in the interests of national or local government officials and other elites.

Many NGOs are committed, at least on paper, to the more complete forms of participation, and aid is often channeled through these organizations. But NGO staff often perceive, rightly or wrongly, that beneficiaries do not have the skills and experience needed to make fundamental decisions or administer projects efficiently. Administrative competence of beneficiaries is a less tangible outcome than, for example, the percentage of farmers who get linked up to irrigation canals; so staff, even with the best of motives, may not view genuine participation as a priority but more as a distraction. It is also obvious that staff owe their livelihoods to development work and do not have a material interest in working themselves out of a job. Thus, voluntary failure may again be present, and staff are motivated to encourage participation as long as it increases the efficiency of the project, but not necessarily beyond that point. Such a level of participation may bring benefits, but not normally the socially transformative benefits of genuine participation.

Sarah White reports on an NGO in the Philippines that was committed to genuine participation in theory and enabled local people to develop and control their own organization. But when this organization wanted to bypass the NGO and interact directly with donors, the NGO would not allow it to do so.[60] Victoria Michener reports on a nonformal education project run by an NGO (Save the Children/FDC in Burkina Faso). Participation itself is one of the six objectives of the project, to "increase community participation in educational decision making, and in the management of educational activities." Participants are expected to play an active role in recruiting teachers and students, determining curriculum, building and maintaining the schoolhouse, and paying costs such as teacher salaries. Overall, the projects would rank very high in participation typologies such as that of Cohen and Uphoff, providing for substantial participation in decision making, implementation, benefits, and evaluation. But at the same time, Michener notes an undertone of "planner-centered participation," especially in the emphasis on the responsibilities of beneficiaries. To fieldworkers, participation comes with an obligation that recipients give something in return—payment, in a sense—for the benefits of a project: financial, in-kind, or at least the donation of time. But participants naturally resent this requirement, at least in a context of paternalism. Typically, villagers cannot afford to repudiate the NGO; they do benefit from the assistance but lack the resources to continue the project on their own.[61]

Genuine public participation at all levels provides a foundation for democratic and responsive government. Participation will not cure all of the ills of government, including the limits of democracy itself, but it will go some distance to alleviating the ills of the politics of development policy reform. Unfortunately, the rhetoric is still well ahead of the reality on the ground.

A Three-legged Stool   We may conclude, then, that successful economic development requires improved functioning of the public, private, and citizen sectors. Each has serious weaknesses that must be addressed. Each leg of this "three-legged stool" needs strengthening. At the same time, each plays an essential and complementary role in attaining balanced, shared, and sustainable development.

The Role of Development NGOs: BRAC and the Grameen Bank

In this case study, we examine two of the largest, most innovative, and most acclaimed developing-country-based development NGOs in the world, both based in Bangladesh but with global reach: BRAC, a quintessential multidimensional development organization, and Grameen Bank, like BRAC a microfinance pioneer that has engaged in other innovative initiatives.

The BRAC Model

BRAC, previously known as the Bangladesh Rural Advancement Committee, is an extraordinary NGO whose mission is poverty reduction. The BRAC model illuminates how comparative advantages of NGOs can function to support poverty reduction and illustrates conditions under which NGOs extend their activities in the face of deficiencies of government and private-sector actors. BRAC is consistently ranked as among the top-rated NGOs in the world, number one in a 2012 *Global Journal* survey.

BRAC was founded in the early 1970s to aid displaced persons in the aftermath of civil war and famine. The organization's leaders soon understood that the problems of the rural poor were chronic and structural, and they turned their attention to long-term development and poverty alleviation efforts. BRAC originally operated in the rural areas of Bangladesh, where government is characterized by low capacity and high corruption. In contrast, BRAC has grown steadily, attracting funds because of its reputation for competence, dedication, innovativeness, accountability, and effectiveness.

With tens of millions of people and some regions of Bangladesh caught in complex poverty traps, BRAC has had to innovate continuously to bring needed services to the poor. Through helping the poor identify their own needs and priorities, BRAC has developed high-impact and widely emulated program innovations in education, nutrition, health, credit, legal rights, advocacy, and other fields.

By some measures, BRAC is now the largest NGO in the world. BRAC's activities contribute more than half of 1% of Bangladesh's GDP. As of 2013, BRAC had over 120,000 employees, making it the country's second-largest employer. Just over half of BRAC employees are primary teachers in its widely emulated nonformal BRAC Education Program. While BRAC programs such as "microcredit-plus" have been widely replicated in other countries, none operate on BRAC's scale. BRAC is a complex organization, with over 8 million grassroots members (usually one woman per household) and over 6 million microfinance borrowers. These members participate in BRAC's basic units, the Village Organization (VO). There are nearly 300,000 VOs, each consisting of 35 to 50 women from a village or neighborhood. BRAC currently works in most of the country's 80,000 villages through a system of 14 training centers and over 2,800 branch offices, with a budget of approximately half a billion U.S. dollars.

Once highly dependent on donors, BRAC has responded to donor demands for greater self-reliance. BRAC is now more than 70% self-supporting. The major source of its internal revenue is a growing network of productive enterprises that it has established, with the twin aims of poverty reduction and net income generation for its poverty programs. BRAC owns or co-owns and operates several small and medium-size enterprises with the explicit aim of direct or indirect poverty reduction as well as its

income-generating mission. BRAC rural enterprises produce goods such as chalk, seeds, shoes, and sanitary napkins. Although these are all classic private goods, an extended role for NGOs has emerged due to Bangladesh's often dysfunctional private sector. BRAC's activities supply needed inputs for nonformal schools and farms and more affordable basic consumer goods for local people while providing employment for poor women.

Fazle Hasan Abed originally founded BRAC to provide assistance to victims of famine and displacement. Soon, however, Abed and his organization concluded that poverty was a chronic and entrenched problem, and they turned their attention to development and poverty alleviation. Abed has won international recognition for his work, including the Ramon Magsaysay Award, the Noma Prize for Literacy, the Feinstein World Hunger Award, UNICEF's Maurice Pate Award, and the 2004 Gates Prize. Aware of the need for sustained leadership, BRAC is developing a new generation of professionals who continue to innovate in poverty alleviation programs while increasing the efficiency and effectiveness of existing programs.

BRAC has helped fill the vacuum sometimes left by government, taking on many of the functions of good governance—targeting public goods, providing common-pool (or common-property) goods, and advocating for the poor. The influence of BRAC has been so great that a popular saying in Bangladesh is that "we have two governments," the formal government and BRAC. Despite its size, BRAC remains very flexible. When catastrophic flooding hit the country in August 2004, BRAC temporarily reassigned virtually its entire organization relief activities.

The linchpin program, microfinance for the poor, started two years before the Grameen Bank. The program is targeted to individuals owning very little land and typically involved in rural nonfarm activities such as door-to-door sales and small-scale vending from their homes or markets. These women borrowers often had very little inventory because they could afford to hold little; thus their sales would be so low that they could afford no more inventory the next day.

But people stuck in working-capital poverty traps may face several other types of poverty traps at the same time. Thus, BRAC has designed a strategy that it calls *microcredit-plus-plus* to convey the scope of its

interrelated village programs seeking to meet a variety of poverty reduction goals. As Ian Smillie shows, although some of the programs in credit, health, and education evolved somewhat separately, they have been packaged together effectively.

In Bangladesh 30 years ago, attending school was an unimaginable luxury for most of the poor. Even in 1990, fewer than half of all children in the country completed primary school. By 2003, about two-thirds were completing school. BRAC has been one of the major driving forces in this transformation through its education program. BRAC began establishing highly innovative village nonformal primary schools in 1984, in response to the needs and requests of the village women with whom it works. A major reason that parents do not send their children to school is that their work is needed at home and on the small family farm plot to help the family survive. A second reason is the intimidation and alienation that uneducated parents and their children feel in traditional school settings. A third is harassment of girls.

The program structure was developed to respond to schooling problems identified by mothers taking part in other BRAC programs. BRAC schools teach the children of poor, often landless families. Well over two-thirds of the students are girls. In the earlier years of the program, the schools typically operated for only a few hours a day so that the children can help at home and in farm or nonfarm activities. Parents decide whether classes will be held in the morning or the evening, depending on the nature of the village's needs. Little homework assigned, as homework requirements were identified as a major stumbling block to keeping children in school. BRAC hoped to make up for shorter school hours with a higher-quality education featuring a significantly smaller class size of about 30 to 35, engaging teaching styles, and the care shown for the pupils.

The school program has grown steadily, and today there are over 1 million pupils enrolled in some 8,000 schools, with over 65,000 teachers. There are now also about 700,000 students in BRAC's preprimary school program.

Many BRAC schools have bamboo walls and a thatched roof; others are bamboo-framed, with tin sheets for walls and roof. Inside, decorations are hung from the roof. Lessons and papers are posted on the walls. The children typically sit around the

periphery of the room. In addition to lessons, all are expected to participate in recitations, traditional dances, and other engaging activities.

Nearly all the teachers (about 97%) are village women who are trained and supervised by professional staff. They are required to have had nine years of education, less than required by public schools but sufficient for the materials being taught. Outside evaluators of the program have concluded that the quality of teacher supervision is one of the keys to the program's consistent success. This paraprofessionals-based program design keeps costs low and quality high while providing useful employment for village women who have obtained somewhat more education.

The education program has evolved over the years to reflect the changing needs of the rural poor. At first, the program lasted three years, usually between the ages of 8 and 10. This was a year or two later than students start public school; the reason for this, BRAC officials explain, is to identify students who would for some reason likely never start public school or would drop out almost immediately. The greatest emphasis is on literacy and numeracy, health and hygiene, basic science, and social studies. The program was designed in part to establish a foundation from which students could enter the fourth grade of the public school system. There is also a system of basic education for somewhat older children, aged 11 to 14.

In 1998, the schools expanded to a four-year program, covering the five-year primary curriculum in less time. This redesign was in response to the large number of BRAC graduates interested in continuing their education at the secondary level. BRAC says that today more than 90% of its graduates continue in the formal system.

BRAC is also well known for its health care innovations and programs. Here, too, BRAC used paraprofessionals from the villages in which it works—for example, in large-scale activities such as the directly observed treatment short course (DOTS) for TB and training for oral rehydration therapy (ORT). The DOTS program exemplifies the roles in BRAC of monitoring and evaluation, waiting until a program is working smoothly and shows clear evidence of positive impact before replicating it so as to reach a very wide population. BRAC then proceeds to relentlessly work to reach a very wide population, a process known as "bringing to scale."

To bring needed services to the poor, BRAC has had to innovate. Many of BRAC's programs, including its "microcredit-plus," nonformal primary education, health, and legal education programs, have been emulated in other countries, though not yet on the same scale. BRAC continues to innovate with new ventures such as the Targeting the Ultrapoor program.

Ian Smillie depicts BRAC as a "learning organization." He quotes David Korten as saying that BRAC "comes as near to a pure example of a learning organization as one is likely to find." Smillie describes remarkable cases of BRAC's honesty to funders and others about the organization's failures rather than the usual defensiveness and exaggerations. Of course, being able to explain the causes of failure convincingly, made possible by careful investigation, and offering credible next steps that put into practice the lessons learned from failure were necessary conditions for getting further funding under such circumstances. Success stories can be helpful, but so can failure stories. Smillie describes several, such as the purchase of poorly designed motorcycles from China and ventures such as production of silk, tubewells, and pumps. This honesty and behavior as a learning organization were both effective and of great appeal to donors, who provided critical resources to implement what had been learned. Smillie reports that some foundations, including smaller ones, provided funds for experiments, and larger funders helped bring successes to scale.

Though one can question how it is possible for BRAC to do so many things without losing its management discipline and poverty focus, BRAC can hardly be blamed for taking so seriously the insistence of donors that it become more self-sufficient. And rather than charge the poor for "full cost recovery" of basic medical and other services for the poor, as the development agencies advised in earlier years, BRAC views it as a better option to subsidize services for the desperately poor with profits from productive enterprises that themselves provide employment and guarantee inputs that poor farmers need and help find markets for the products of the poor. There are very strong penalties for unethical behavior, and BRAC is considered to hold to an unusually high standard of probity. However, it is difficult for an outsider to be sure where all the

cross-subsidies are going under the current system of accounts.

One of the most important factors in BRAC's success has been the high quality of BRAC management. Abed is one of the most impressive management talents in the country, and BRAC has been able to recruit many other highly competent managers from all sectors of Bangladesh. It seems that BRAC is so much better than management in the private sector that it has repeatedly been able to find untapped opportunities and to profit from them. (This is true not just of BRAC but of other leading NGOs such as the Grameen Bank.) The most effective scope for a company depends not just on the type of activities it specializes in but on the management skills available in the rest of the country. If one organization's talent is high while that of its competitors is low, one company or NGO can participate in many activities that in another country would constitute an inefficient distraction away from its "core competencies." But one can find no hint of a negative attitude toward the private sector at BRAC; instead, BRAC is actively working to foster its growth.

BRAC is working to improve the efficacy of government as well. For example, although the public schools are in some sense competitors of its education program, BRAC is working actively with interested government officials to infuse the public schools with some of the ingredients of its own success.

Among its ventures, BRAC has established a university, a bank, and a program for assisting private small and medium-size enterprises. Finally, it has established international affiliates in Afghanistan, Sri Lanka, Uganda, southern Sudan, Tanzania, Pakistan, Siera Leone, and Liberia. Launched in June 2006, BRAC Uganda is already one of the largest NGOs in that country, working in microfinance, primary education, health, and agriculture. Most staff are Ugandan nationals.

The low cost of BRAC's activities in Africa is remarkable; for the case of Tanzania, Smillie describes how the organization saves money while maintaining quality. He notes that staff all are "experienced, top-notch professionals in their fields." He stresses that "BRAC's overheads are minuscule in comparison to other international NGOs because all of their staff lives together in shared accommodation, and they do not bring their families with them. [Staff] get sizable premiums for working abroad

and home leave every six months," but "they are still paid on the basis of their Bangladeshi salaries, so BRAC's staff costs are tiny in comparison with other agencies." BRAC has demonstrated that it can thrive inside and outside Bangladesh; it remains to be seen how many other developing-country-based NGOs can go national in scale, widen in scope, and even eventually go global.

BRAC faces several challenges. As BRAC's first generation of founders retires, replacements must be found who have the same special combination of talents and commitment. As BRAC continues to grow and diversify, it will confront management problems that would prove challenging in any environment, but particularly for a poverty-focused organization operating in rural areas of low-income nations. But BRAC has consistently served as a pioneer, both in innovation of specific programs and in widening the vision of development practitioners around the world about the possible range and scope for the work of NGOs in developing countries.

Making Microfinance Work for the Poor: The Grameen Bank of Bangladesh

One of the major obstacles facing the poor and those not far above the poverty line is access to credit (see Chapter 15). The Grameen Bank of Bangladesh is an excellent illustration of how credit can be provided to the poor while minimizing the risk that resources will be wasted. Microfinance institutions (MFIs) targeting the poor such as the Grameen Bank have expanded rapidly throughout the developing world since the 1980s. But nowhere has this expansion been more striking than in Bangladesh, which has been transforming itself from a symbol of famine to a symbol of hope, due in part to the success of its MFIs.

Muhammad Yunus conceived of the Grameen Bank in the mid-1970s when he was a Chittagong University economics professor. Yunus had become convinced from his research that the lack of access to credit on the part of the poor was one of the key constraints on their economic progress, a conclusion that has been supported by later studies from around the developing world. Yunus wanted to demonstrate that it was possible to lend to the poor without collateral. To determine the best system for doing so, he created the Grameen Bank as an "action and research project." Today the Grameen Bank is a

chartered financial institution with over 8.25 million borrowers among the poor and formerly poor.

Yunus said in an interview that "all human beings are born entrepreneurs. Some get the opportunity to find this out, but some never get this opportunity. A small loan can be a ticket to exploration of personal ability. All human beings have a skill—the survival skill. The fact that they are alive proves this. Just support this skill and see how they will choose to use it."

Yunus began the operation in 1976 after convincing the Bangladeshi agricultural development bank to provide initial loan money, the first loans guaranteed personally by Yunus. A series of expansions convinced the government of the Grameen Bank's value, and the Grameen Bank was formally chartered as a financial institution in 1983.

Today, a public-cooperative bank 94% owned by its borrowers, the Grameen Bank continues to grow rapidly and now has over 2,400 branch offices throughout the country. It works in about 78,000 villages. Today, the Grameen Bank finances all its outstanding loans from borrowers' deposits. The branch office, covering 15 to 20 villages, is the basic organizational unit and is responsible for its profits and losses. Each branch has a number of village or neighborhood centers, comprised of about 8 solidarity groups. Each solidarity group has 5 members, so there are about 40 borrowers in each center. The 5-person group size was not decided arbitrarily but on the basis of experimentation. Initially, loans were awarded directly to individuals, but this required too much staff time to control the use and repayment of the loan. After the idea of mutual responsibility was developed, groups of 10 or more were tried at first, but this proved too large for intimate and informal peer-to-peer monitoring to be effective. Groups of 5 proved in practice to work best. Since 1998, the Grameen Bank has been placing greater emphasis on individual liability.

Since its founding, the Grameen Bank has enabled several million poor Bangladeshis to start or upgrade their own small businesses. Ninety-seven percent of the borrowers are women. Borrowers are generally limited to those who own less than half an acre, and this seems to hold for 96% of borrowers. Representatives of the Grameen Bank's branches often go door to door in the villages they cover to inform people, who are often illiterate and very reticent about dealing with banks, about the Grameen Bank's services.

Before opening a branch, the new branch manager is assigned to prepare a socioeconomic report covering the economy, geography, demographics, transportation and communications infrastructure, and politics of the area. Among other things, this ensures that the branch manager becomes familiar with the region and its potential borrowers before the branch begins operations.

The Grameen Bank (*grameen* means "rural" in Bengali) is incorporated as a publicly supported credit union, with borrowers owning 94% of the bank's stock and the government owning the remainder. Once borrowers reach a certain borrowing level, they are entitled to purchase one share of Grameen Bank stock. The bank sets its own policy with strong borrower input, independent of government control. The Grameen Bank's total annualized interest rate on its basic working-capital loans has been kept at 20% (on a declining basis). The current interest rate is 8% on home loans and 5% on student loans. A special recent program provides zero-interest loans for beggars.

To qualify for uncollateralized loans, potential borrowers form five-member groups. Each member must undergo a two-week training session before any member can secure a loan, and the training sessions are followed up with weekly group meetings with a bank officer. Many microfinance providers rely on what could be called the "collateral of peer pressure." However, under Grameen Bank II, the redesigned and more flexible payment system introduced in 1998, borrowers in the solidarity groups do *not* have to cosign or jointly guarantee each other's loans. Observers have nevertheless reported that strong social pressure is placed on members to repay. Members know the character of other group members and generally join groups with members who they believe are likely to repay their loans.

In its early period, peer oversight contributed to the Grameen Bank's high repayment rate, reported to be 98%. Although the exact repayment rate has been a matter of some controversy in the literature, there is no doubt that repayment has been far higher than the national average for bank loans to much wealthier borrowers.

There are also additional financial incentives to repay loans in a timely manner. Each individual

borrower can increase by 10% the amount she can borrow each year if she has repaid loans in a timely manner. For the group, if there is 100% attendance at meetings and all loans are repaid, each borrower can increase her borrowing by an additional 5%, thus raising her borrowing ceiling at a rate of 15% per year. An additional increment is provided when there is a perfect record from each of the eight or so borrowing groups in a center. The desire of many borrowers to take advantage of these higher borrowing ceilings presumably does lead to some peer pressure for all to repay in a timely manner.

A member who is unable to repay is allowed to restructure her loan, repaying at a slower rate, with some limited refinancing as needed. This has reduced defaults to essentially zero, according to the Grameen Bank. In addition to peer pressure, most borrowers wish to reestablish their credit and resume their rights to borrow increasing sums, so they work hard to get and keep their loans up to date.

The group structure facilitates the formation of cooperative ventures among the participants, permitting the undertaking of ventures too large or too risky for poor individuals to shoulder alone. Grameen also works to facilitate the accumulation of savings among its members through savings requirements or incentives for its borrowers to save.

Group members are trained in such practical matters as bank procedures, the group savings program, the role of the center chief and the chairperson of the five-member group, and even how to write their signatures. In addition, training has a moral component, stressing the bank's 16 principles, known as "decisions," to be adhered to by each member. These decisions were formulated in a national conference of 100 female center chiefs in 1984. They emphasize mutual assistance and other modern values, including self-discipline and hard work, hygiene, and refusal to participate in backward practices such as demanding dowries. Adherence to these principles and attendance at rallies featuring the chanting of the decisions were not formal requirements for receiving loans but in the late 1980s and 1990s were said to have become effective, implicit requirements.

The 16 decisions cover a wide range of activities. Here are a few:

3. We shall not live in dilapidated houses. We shall repair our houses and work toward constructing new houses as soon as possible.

4. We shall grow vegetables all the year round. We shall eat plenty of them and sell the surplus.

6. We shall plan to keep our families small.

8. We shall always keep our children and the environment clean.

11. We shall not take any dowry in our sons' weddings, neither shall we give any dowry in our daughters' weddings. We shall not practice child marriage.

13. For higher income, we shall collectively undertake higher investments.*

A major debate in the microfinance community concerns whether microcredit institutions should limit themselves to making loans or also engage in other social development activities. The Grameen Bank, which is technically a type of bank rather than an NGO, is usually grouped among the minimalist institutions, but the 16 decisions show that there is a much broader social component at the Grameen Bank as well. Other institutions have sought to actively combine very different activities; BRAC, examined earlier in this case study, is one of the world's most comprehensive NGOs.

As of 2010, the average loan size was $384. Mahmoub Hossain found that 46% of loans went for livestock and poultry raising, 25% for processing and light manufacturing, and 23% for trading and shopkeeping; thus, almost no loans went to finance farm crop activities. Grameen Bank borrowers have had notable success in capital accumulation. Cattle raising is a major activity of borrowers. Hossain found that the number of cattle owned increased by 26% per year. Though the numbers involved are small—going from 61 per 100 borrowers before becoming a Grameen Bank member to 102 per 100 borrowers at the time of the survey—these are impressive improvements for Bangladesh's poor. The working capital of borrowers tripled on average within 27 months.

But completely landless agricultural laborers appear to remain significantly underrepresented in the pool of borrowers: Hossain found that they represent 60% of the Grameen Bank's target group but only 20% of its actual borrowers—and this includes those who reported hired agricultural

*The full list, with their pictorial presentation for villagers, can be found on the Grameen Bank Web site at http://www.grameen-info.org.

labor as a secondary economic activity as well as those who reported it as a primary economic activity. Note that in Bangladesh, most laborers own a small plot of land for their house but too little to form the basis for a viable farm. Some 60% of Bangladeshis are "functionally landless" in this sense. Landless farm laborers are extremely hard to reach for any development program in any country. They also tend to be the least educated and are probably the least well prepared to move into viable entrepreneurial activities.

The Grameen Bank's emphasis on serving poor women is especially impressive. According to Hossain's survey, half the women borrowers said they were unemployed at the time they became Grameen Bank members (compared with less than 7% of the men). An impact evaluation carried out by Mark Pitt and Shahidur Khandker concluded that microcredit for women from the Grameen Bank and two other lenders had a larger effect on the behavior of poor households in Bangladesh than for men. In a representative finding, they concluded that annual household consumption expenditure increases 18 taka for every additional 100 taka borrowed by women from credit programs, compared with just 11 taka for men. In addition, availability of microcredit also helps households smooth consumption over time so that family members can reduce suffering during lean periods. In other research, Pitt and his collaborators found that credit for women had a positive effect on children's health in Bangladesh, but credit for men had no comparable effect. (Related issues were examined in Chapter 8.)

Mir Salim presents econometric evidence that both the Grameen Bank and BRAC act in ways not predicted by purely profit-maximizing behavior, but instead tilt in favor of poverty alleviation.

Is Grameen subsidized, and how much subsidy makes sense? Some analysts argue that microfinance institutions should not provide loans at subsidized rates so that as many total loans can be made as possible, plowing back all the profits into new loans. Others argue that the poorest of the poor cannot afford to borrow at unsubsidized rates because they do not yet have access to sufficiently profitable activities. Although the Grameen Bank seems uneasy with the idea that they provide, or pass through, any subsidies, Jonathan Morduch has examined the evidence and has concluded that

there have indeed been subsidies. For example, he calculated that total subsidies in 1996, evaluated at the economic opportunity cost of capital, amounted to between $26 million and $30 million. The Grameen Bank insists that no subsidies remain at this time. Over half of the Grameen Bank's loans are made possible by members' savings accounts.

Costs at the Grameen Bank are quite high by commercial bank standards. They have been estimated at 26.5% of the value of loans and advances. This is some 10% higher than the nominal interest rate charged, meaning that 39% of the costs of lending are subsidized from all sources. Adding in estimated opportunity costs, Hossain has calculated an effective subsidy of 51%. About half of the excess of costs over interest receipts is attributable to the expense of opening new branches, which should be treated as a capital cost. Whether a significant fraction of poor borrowers could pay higher interest rates and remain profitable remains uncertain.

Since funds for subsidies are limited, the more the subsidy per loan, the fewer subsidized loans can be made. There may be some combination of reduced operating costs, modest increases in interest rates, and continued subsidy that is optimal for creating the most welfare gains with the available resources. However, a public subsidy of Grameen Bank loans may be justified on the basis of the loans' effect on absolute poverty alleviation and positive externalities.

The Grameen Bank does face some challenges. Bangladesh remains subject to environmental shocks such as severe flooding that will continue to test the resiliency of the Grameen Bank's borrowers and the Grameen Bank itself. As MFIs expand and new private and quasiprivate credit providers enter the market, competition among microcredit providers is growing. Adapting to this new environment will be challenging. In Bolivia, another country where microfinance is highly developed, increases in competition, especially from private consumer credit companies eager to piggyback on MFI membership lists, were widely viewed as at least partly responsible for a financial crisis there.

Cultural challenges are also important. Rising women's incomes, self-esteem, and business clout have caused some backlash in the conservative Islamic culture of rural Bangladesh, in which women are expected to be secluded from social activities.

The Grameen Bank and other programs, such as the nontraditional schools run by BRAC, are seen as a challenge to this traditional status quo over which men have traditionally presided. Schools have been burned, and women have been driven out of their villages or even harmed for challenging traditional cultural norms, including participating in market activities. Yunus has stated that some husbands have viewed the Grameen Bank as a threat to their authority. In some cases, "the husband thought we had insulted him and were destroying his family. We had cases of divorce just because the woman took loans." A fundamentalist cleric in Dhaka claimed that "we have no objection to improving the lot of women, but the motives of the Grameen Bank and other organizations are completely different. They want to eradicate Islam, and they want to do this through women and children." The future of the Grameen Bank will depend on a creative response to this difficult environment of economic and cultural change in which many development problems remain.

The Grameen Bank has been highly innovative—for example, by bringing cell phones to rural Bangladesh via its phone ladies loan and service program. This program played the key facilitating role in the now remarkably high penetration of cell phones throughout rural Bangladesh, even among quite poor people.

The Grameen Bank has also proved flexible and responsive to the borrowing needs of its members. For example, the Grameen Bank has established a life insurance program, as well as a loan insurance program. The Grameen Bank housing program finances houses being built or rebuilt—adding iron roofs, cement pillars, and sanitary latrines. The houses generally have mud walls, but these are thick and, properly maintained, can last many years. The houses are substantial in size, with an electric fan overhead and usually other basic appliances in electrified villages. Grameen has also started offering higher education loans for its members. An increasing number of parents are witnessing the first members of their families to ever go to college and graduate in fields such as computer science and accounting. It is a remarkable transformation.

In 2006, the Grameen Bank and its founder, Muhammad Yunus, were jointly awarded the Nobel Peace Prize, a well-deserved honor. ■

Sources

BRAC. http://www.brac.net.

Banerjee, Abhijit V., Timothy Besley, and Timothy W. Guinnane. "Thy neighbor's keeper: The design of a credit cooperative with theory and a test." *Quarterly Journal of Economics* 109 (1994): 491–515.

Emran, M. Shahe, Virginia Robano, and Stephen C. Smith, "Assessing the frontiers of ultra-poverty reduction: Evidence from CFPR/TUP, an Innovative program in Bangladesh," *Economic Development and Cultural Change*, 62 (2), 339–380, February 2014.

Ghatak, Maitreesh, and Timothy W. Guinnane. "The economics of lending with joint liability: A review of theory and practice." *Journal of Development Economics* 60 (1999): 195–228.

Grameen Bank Web page, http://www.grameen-info.org.

Hossain, Mahmoub. *Credit for Alleviation of Rural Poverty: The Grameen Bank in Bangladesh.* Washington, D.C.: International Food Policy Research Institute, 1988.

Khandker, Shahidur R. *Fighting Poverty with Microcredit: Experience in Bangladesh.* New York: Oxford University Press, 1998.

Khandker, Shahidur R., Hussain A. Samad, and Zahed H. Khan. "Income and employment effects of microcredit programs: Village-level evidence from Bangladesh." *Journal of Development Studies* 35 (1998): 96–124.

Khandker, Shahidur R., and Baqui Khalily. *The Bangladesh Rural Advancement Committee's Credit Programs: Performance and Sustainability.* Washington, D.C.: World Bank, 1996.

Lovell, Catherine H., and Kaniz Fatema. *BRAC: Non-Formal Primary Education in Bangladesh.* New York: United Nations Children's Fund, 1989.

Matin, Imran. *Stories of Targeting: The BRAC Targeting the Ultrapoor Program.* Dhaka, Bangladesh: BRAC Research and Evaluation Division, 2003.

Matin, Imran, and David Hulme. "Programs for the poorest: Learning from the IGVGD program in Bangladesh." *World Development* 31 (2003): 647–665.

Morduch, Jonathan. "The microfinance promise." *Journal of Economic Literature* 37 (1999): 1569–1614.

———. "The microfinance schism." *World Development* 28 (2000): 617–629.

———. "The role of subsidies in microfinance: Evidence from the Grameen Bank." *Journal of Development Economics* 60 (1999): 229–248.

Osmani, S. R. "Limits to the alleviation of poverty through non-farm credit." *Bangladesh Development Studies* 17 (1989): 1–17.

Pitt, Mark M., and Shahidur R. Khandker. "Credit programs for the poor and seasonality in rural Bangladesh." *Journal of Development Studies* 39, No. 2 (2002): 1–24.

———. "The impact of group-based credit programs on poor households in Bangladesh: Does the gender of participants matter?" *Journal of Political Economy* 106 (1998): 958–996.

Pitt, Mark M., Shahidur R. Khandker, Omar Haider Choudhury, and Daniel Millimet. "Credit programs for the poor and the health status of children in rural Bangladesh." *International Economic Review* 44 (2003): 87–118.

Quelch, John, and Nathalie Laidler. *The BRAC and Aarong Commercial Brands.* Cambridge, Mass.: Harvard Business School, 2003.

Salim, Mir M., "Revealed objective functions of microfinance institutions: Evidence from Bangladesh,"

Journal of Development Economics 104 (September 2013): 34–55.

Singh, Inderjit. *The Great Ascent: The Rural Poor in South Asia.* Baltimore: Johns Hopkins University Press, 1990.

Smillie, Ian. *Freedom from Want: The Remarkable Success Story of BRAC, the Global Grassroots Organization That's Winning the Fight against Poverty.* Bloomfield, Conn.: Kumarian Press, 2009.

Smith, Stephen C. "Review of Smillie, *Freedom from Want.*" *Economic Development and Cultural Change* 58 (2010): 808–814.

———. *Ending Global Poverty: A Guide to What Works.* New York: Palgrave Macmillan, 2005.

Wahid, Abu N. M. "The Grameen Bank and poverty alleviation in Bangladesh: Theory, evidence, and limitations." *American Journal of Economics and Sociology* 53 (1994): 1–15.

———. *The Grameen Bank: Poverty Alleviation in Bangladesh.* Boulder, Colo.: Westview, 1993.

Yunus, Muhammad. *Grameen II.* Dhaka, Bangladesh: Grameen Bank, 2001.

———. Speech and interview at the World Bank, October 4, 1995.

Yunus, Muhammad, and Alan Jolis. *Banker to the Poor: Micro-Lending and the Battle against World Poverty.* New York: Public Affairs, 1999.

Concepts for Review

Aggregate growth model
Comprehensive plan
Corruption
Cost-benefit analysis
Economic infrastructure
Economic plan
Economic planning
Exchange rate
Government failure

Input-output model (interindustry model)
Internal rate of return
Market failure
Market prices
Net present value
Nongovernmental organizations (NGOs)
Partial plan

Path dependency
Planning process
Political will
Project appraisal
Rent seeking
Shadow prices (or accounting prices)
Social profit
Social rate of discount
Voluntary failure

Questions for Discussion

1. Why do you think so many developing countries were convinced of the necessity of development planning? Were the reasons strictly economic? Comment.

2. Explain and comment on some of the major arguments or rationales, both economic and noneconomic, for planning in developing economies.

3. Planning is said to be more than just the formulation of quantitative economic targets. It is often described as a process. What is meant by the planning process, and what are some of its basic characteristics?

4. Compare and contrast the three basic types of planning models: aggregate growth models, input-output analysis, and project appraisal. What do you think are some of the strengths and weaknesses of these models from the standpoint of planning in developing nations?

5. There is much talk today about the demise of development planning. Many observers assert that development planning has been a failure. List and explain some of the major reasons for plan failures. Which reasons do you think are the most important? Explain your thinking.

6. Distinguish between market failure and government failure. Does rent-seeking behavior occur only as a result of government failure? Explain your answer.

7. What are some of the difficulties associated with the establishment of market economies in developing countries? In what type of country is the market more likely to succeed? Why?

8. What do you think should be the role of the state in contemporary developing countries? Is the choice between markets and government an either-or choice? Explain your answer.

9. What features of the political process make effective development policymaking so difficult?

10. Why is development participation not used more often, despite its potentially decisive role in ensuring the success of development policies?

11. Do you think that setting goals for development could in itself help a developing nation to achieve those goals? Why or why not?

12. Discuss the potential role of NGOs in relation to the government and private sectors. What are the most important potential areas of comparative advantage of NGOs? What are the most important "voluntary failures" that can inhibit NGOs from realizing their comparative advantages in development activities?

13. Discuss the components of the original Washington Consensus. What do you think was most lacking from this framework? What important factors have achieved widespread acceptance in the evolution toward a new consensus?

14. If a reform improves everyone's income on average, why might people vote against it? You may wish to provide one or more numerical examples to illustrate your answer.

15. Explain the differences between characteristics of public goods and private goods and services. How can goods and services provided by nongovernmental organizations be considered in this framework?

Notes

1. Elinor Ostrom, "Beyond markets and states: Polycentric governance and complex economic systems," *American Economic Review* 100, (2010): 641. See also Joseph Stiglitz, "Moving beyond market fundamentalism to a more balanced economy," *Annals of Public and Cooperative Economics* 80, No. 3 (2009): 345–360.

2. For a more detailed discussion of planning and planning models, see Michael P. Todaro, *Development Planning: Models and Methods* (Nairobi, Kenya: Oxford University Press, 1971), and J. Price Gittinger, *Economic Analysis of Agricultural Projects,* 2nd ed. (Baltimore: Johns Hopkins University Press, 1984).

3. United Nations Department of Economic Affairs, *Measures for the Economic Development of Underdeveloped Countries* (New York: United Nations Department of Economic Affairs, 1951), p. 63.

4. United Nations, *Planning the External Sector: Techniques, Problems, and Policies* (New York: United Nations, 1965), p. 12; R. Helfgoth and S. Schiavo-Campo, "An introduction to development planning," *UNIDO Industrialization and Productivity Bulletin* 16 (1970): 11. A more sophisticated version of the market failure argument can be found in Heinz W. Arndt, "Market failure and underdevelopment," *World Development* 16 (1988): 219–229. For a concise explication of the economic rationale for state intervention, stressing not only market failure and externalities but also public goods, natural monopolies, incomplete markets, and imperfect information, see World Bank, *World Development Report, 1997* (New York: Oxford University Press, 1997), box 1.4.

5. These failures differ from the familiar prisoner's dilemma model, in which there is an incentive to defect after coordination is achieved.

6. See Anthony Atkinson and Joseph E. Stiglitz, *Lectures on Public Economics* (New York: McGraw-Hill, 1980); Karla Hoff and Joseph E. Stiglitz, "Modern economic theory and development," in *Frontiers in Development Economics*, eds. Gerald M. Meier and Joseph E. Stiglitz (New York: Oxford University Press, 2001); Oliver Williamson, *The Economic Institutions of Capitalism* (New York: Free Press, 1985); Stephen C. Smith, *The Firm, Human Development, and Market Failure* (Geneva, Switzerland: International Labor Office, 1995); and Carl Shapiro and Hal Varian, *Information Rules: A Strategic Guide to the Network Economy* (Boston: Harvard Business School Press, 1999).

7. Recent examples include climate change adaptation assistance, notably the Strategic Programs for Climate Resilience (see Box 10.2), the IMF/World Bank Poverty Reduction Strategy Paper (PSPR) process, and the U.S. Millennium Challenge Corporation (MCC) Compacts. (The role of foreign aid in theory and practice is examined in Chapter 14, section 14.4).

8. Lance Taylor, "Theoretical foundations and technical implications," in *Economy-Wide Models and Development Planning*, eds. Charles R. Blitzer, Paul B. Clark, and Lance Taylor (Oxford: Oxford University Press, 1975), pp. 37–42.

9. Ibid., p. 39.

10. For an introductory discussion of the nature and use of input-output models, see Todaro, *Development Planning*, ch. 5.

11. For good surveys, see F. Graham Pyatt and Erik Thorbecke, *Planning Techniques for a Better Future* (Geneva, Switzerland: International Labor Office, 1976), and Shantayanan Devarajan, Jeffrey D. Lewis, and Sherman Robinson, *Getting the Model Right: The General Equilibrium Approach to Adjustment Policy* (Washington, D.C.: World Bank, 1994). The International Food Policy Research Institute is a major contributor to recent work in this field; go to http://www.ifpri.cgiar.org/divs/tmd/method/sam.htm.

12. For a good introduction to cost-benefit analysis stressing links with economic theory, see Ajit K. Dasgupta and David W. Pearce, *Cost-Benefit Analysis: Theory and Practice* (London: Macmillan, 1972).

13. For an excellent assessment of the magnitude and policy significance of externalities in developing countries, see Frances Stewart and Ejaz Ghani, "How significant are externalities for development?" *World Development* 19 (1991): 569–591. Large-scale externalities were discussed in Chapter 4.

14. The classic analysis of project appraisal issues is Partha Dasgupta, Stephen Marglin, and Amartya Sen, *UNIDO Guidelines for Project Evaluation* (New York: United Nations Industrial Development Organization, 1972). Excellent survey of various techniques of project appraisal can be found in Ivy Papps, "Techniques of project appraisal," in *Surveys in Development Economics*, ed. Norman Gemmell (Oxford: Blackwell, 1987), pp. 307–338, and Ian Little and James Mirrlees, "Project appraisal and planning twenty years on," *Proceedings of the World Bank Annual Conference on Development Economics, 1990* (Washington, D.C.: World Bank, 1991), pp. 351–382.

15. If you are familiar with the techniques of linear programming, you will recognize that shadow prices are merely the solution values of the dual to a linear-programming output or profit maximization problem; see Todaro, *Development Planning*, ch. 5.

16. This approach is advocated by Ian Little and James Mirrlees in *Project Appraisal and Planning in Developing Countries* (New York: Basic Books, 1974).

17. For a complete discussion, see Gittinger, *Economic Analysis of Agricultural Projects*. On social discount rates, see Dasgupta, Marglin, and Sen, *UNIDO Guidelines*.

18. Derek T. Healey, "Development policy: New thinking about an interpretation," *Journal of Economic Literature* 10 (1973): 761; Ian Little, *Economic Development* (New York: Basic Books, 1982).

19. Tony Killick, "Possibilities of development planning," *Oxford Economic Papers* 41 (1976): 163–164.

20. Ibid., 164.

21. For an overview, see World Bank, *World Development Report, 2002* (New York: Oxford University Press, 2002). For an analysis of the effects of corruption, see M. Shahid Alam, "Some economic costs of corruption in LDCs," *Journal of Development Studies* 27 (1990): 89–97; Susan Rose-Ackerman, "Corruption and development," *Annual World Bank Conference on Development Economics, 1997* (Washington, D.C.: World Bank, 1998), pp. 35–68; and Pranab K. Bardhan, "Corruption and development: A review of issues," *Journal of Economic Literature* 35 (1997): 1320–1346.

22. Albert Waterston, *Development Planning: Lessons of Experience* (Baltimore: Johns Hopkins University Press, 1965), p. 367.

23. For perspectives of problems of government failure, see Anne Krueger, "Government failures in development," *Journal of Economic Perspectives* 4 (1990): 9–24; Nicholas Stern, "The economics of development: A survey," *Economic Journal* 99 (1989): 597–685; Roger E. Backhouse and Steven G. Medema, "Laissez-faire economists and," *New Palgrave Dictionary of Economics*, Second Edition, 2008, Steven N. Durlauf and Lawrence E. Blume, eds.

24. Amartya Sen, *Development as Freedom* (New York: Knopf, 1999), p. 6.

25. This framework draws from Nathan Keyfitz and Robert A. Dorfman, *The Market Economy Is the Best but Not the Easiest* (mimeograph, 1991), pp. 7–13. See also Robert Klitgaard, *Adjusting to Reality: Beyond "State versus Market" in Economic Development* (San Francisco: ICS Press, 1991), pp. 5–6.

26. For further analysis on this subject, see Arndt, "Market failure and underdevelopment," and Bruce C. Greenwald and Joseph E. Stiglitz, "Externalities in economies with imperfect information and incomplete markets," *Quarterly Journal of Economics* 101 (1986): 229–264. For an in-depth analysis of the role of infrastructure in development, see World Bank, *World Development Report, 1994* (New York: Oxford University Press, 1994). An interesting commentary was provided by Alice Amsden, who noted that when the operations evaluation division of the World Bank reported that South Korea and Taiwan used extensive government intervention to industrialize, the bank refused to publish this analysis. See Alice H. Amsden, "From P.C. to E.C.," *New York Times*, January 12, 1993, p. A15, as well as Richard Grabowski, "The successful development state: Where does it come from?" *World Development* 22 (1994): 413–422; Ajit Singh, "Openness and market-friendly approach to development: Learning the right lessons from development experience," *World Development* 22 (1994): 1811–1823; and Jene Kwon, "The East Asia challenge to neoclassical orthodoxy," *World Development* 22 (1994): 635–644. See also Alejandro Foxley, "Latin American development after the debt crisis," *Journal of Development Economics* 27 (1987): 211–212.

27. John Williamson, the original compiler of the list, has indicated that he would have wanted to add distributional considerations as a component of development policy but did not observe it as part of the consensus he sought to summarize.

28. See http://www.growthcommission.org/index and Dani Rodrik, *One Economics, Many Recipes: Globalization, Institutions, and Economic Growth* (Princeton, N.J.: Princeton University Press, 2007). These contributions focus on growth rather than capabilities and human development, so they do not fully reflect the broader consensus. Lord Nicholas Stern, chief economist of the World Bank from 2000 to 2002, was an early proponent of parts of what later became the New Consensus; see his "Public policy and the economics of development," *European Economic Review* 35 (1991): 250–257. For the Seoul "consensus" declaration, see http://media.seoulsummit.kr.

29. Anne Krueger, "Government failures in development," *Journal of Economic Perspectives* 4 (1990):

9–24; Deepak Lal, *The Poverty of Development Economics* (Cambridge, Mass.: Harvard University Press, 1995); Friedrich A. Hayek, *The Road to Serfdom* (Chicago: University of Chicago Press, 1994).

30. Note that, in principle at least, the majority might win their reform if they could coordinate with each other at low cost or somehow provide a "side payment" to the person who lost the rents, but this is often problematic. For a broader discussion, see Dani Rodrik, "Understanding economic policy reform," *Journal of Economic Literature* 34 (1996): 9–41, and Merilee S. Grindle, "In quest of the political: The political economy of development policymaking," in *Frontiers in Development Economics*, eds. Gerald M. Meier and Joseph E. Stiglitz (New York: Oxford University Press, 2001). See also the classic work by Mancur Olsen, *The Logic of Collective Action* (Cambridge, Mass.: Harvard University Press, 1965).

31. See Raquel Fernandez and Dani Rodrik, "Resistance to reform: Status quo bias in the presence of individual specific uncertainty," *American Economic Review* 81 (1991): 1146–1155.

32. In our particular example, if $x = 0.4$, $EV(0.4) = [(0.6 - 0.4)100]/0.6 - 0.4(80)/0.6 = -20$, so the remaining 60% would vote no. You can find the cutoff fraction for this example by setting this expression to zero: For $0.28 < x < 0.5$, the "rational" vote for someone who does not know whether he or she will gain is no. For another numerical example, see Dani Rodrik, "Understanding economic policy reform," *Journal of Economic Literature* 34 (1996): 9–41.

33. The development political-economy literature has often examined the process by which Washington Consensus policies become adopted. Again, see the surveys of Rodrik and Grindle cited in note 30. This has posed some difficulties for formulating a general theory of the establishment of good governance, because not all development specialists have agreed that all of these policies are best for development broadly construed. However, future studies might focus on a few variables that virtually all specialists agree to be good policies for development. One example, an element of the Washington Consensus, is the "redirection of public expenditure priorities toward health, education,

and infrastructure."

34. Rodrik, "Understanding economic policy reform," p. 26.

35. Douglass C. North, "Economic performance through time," *American Economic Review* 84 (1994): 361.

36. Douglass C. North, *Institutions, Institutional Change, and Economic Performance* (New York: Cambridge University Press, 1990), p. 54.

37. Grindle, "In quest of the political." On democratization as a commitment device, see Daron Acemoglu and James Robinson, *Economic Origins of Dictatorship and Democracy* (New York: Cambridge University Press, 2006).

38. On the "Lee thesis," see Amartya Sen, *Development as Freedom* (New York, Knopf 1999), pp. 148–149. Sen's analysis of this topic is developed in much further detail in *The Idea of Justice,* Part IV (Cambridge: Harvard, 2009).

39. Ahmed Mobarak, "Democracy, volatility, and economic development," *Review of Economics and Statistics* 87 (2005): 348–361.

40. Jakob de Haan and Clemens L. J. Siermann, "New evidence on the relationship between democracy and economic growth," *Public Choice* 86 (1996): 175. See also Sen, *Development as Freedom* (New York: Knopf, 1999).

41. United Nations Development Programme, *Human Development Report, 2003* (New York: Oxford University Press, 2003). The difficulty in sharply defining NGOs is reflected in the broad and diverse sector these actors have come to constitute. With a plethora of terms and acronyms to describe them—from *people's organizations* to *briefcase* or *nongovernmental individuals*—NGOs run the gamut from profit-seeking entrepreneurs to well-intentioned catalyst organizations to professional, streamlined, efficient service deliverers. Overall, while many NGOs retain their philanthropic origin and orientation, they have evolved into strategically managed development specialists, treading the fine line between the technical language and processes of the development industry, on the one hand, and responsiveness to developing-country clientele and individual contributors, on the other. See Jennifer Brinkerhoff,

Partnership for Development: Rhetoric or Results? (Boulder, Colo.: Rienner, 2002). Parts of this discussion draw on Jennifer Brinkerhoff, Stephen C. Smith, and Hildy Teegen, "Beyond the 'non': The strategic space for NGOs in development," and Stephen C. Smith, "Organizational comparative advantages of NGOs in eradicating extreme poverty and hunger: Strategy for escape from poverty traps," chs. 4 and 8, respectively, in *NGOs and the Millennium Development Goals: Citizen Action to Reduce Poverty,* eds. Jennifer Brinkerhoff, Stephen C. Smith, and Hildy Teegen (New York: Palgrave Macmillan, 2007), and the 2003 Brinkerhoff, Smith, and Teegen framing paper on which this book was based. An interesting paper that develops related themes is Inge Kaul's, "Achieving the Millennium Development Goals: A global public goods perspective—reflections on the debate," GpgNet Discussion Forum Paper No. 5, United Nations Development Programme, December 2003. See also Stephen C. Smith, "The scope of nongovernmental organizations and development program design: Application to problems of multidimensional poverty," *Public Administration and Development* 32, Nos. 4–5 (2012): 357–370 for an examination of the market and other forces that affect the likelihood of wider or narrower organizational scope, or breadth of concerns within a single program or initiative, and of when the degree of observed diversification may be inefficient (either too much or too little specialization).

42. See, for example, Johnston Birchall, *Co-operatives and the Millennium Development Goals* (Geneva: ILO, 2004); Johnston Birchall and Richard Simmons, "The role of co-operatives in poverty reduction: Network perspectives, *Journal of Socio-Economics* 37, No. 6 (2008): 2131–2140; and Stephen C. Smith and Jonathan Rothbaum, "Cooperatives in a global economy: Key economic issues, recent trends, and potential for development," IZA Policy Paper No. 68, 2013: http://www.iza.org /en/webcontent/publications/policypapers/view Abstract?policypaper_id=68.

43. These include the 2003 Nobel laureate, Shirin Ebadi, who founded and served as first director of the Association for Protection of Children Rights in Iran, and 2002 Nobel laureate Jimmy Carter, the former U.S. president who has been active in Habitat for Humanity as well as in resolving developing-country conflicts through the Carter Center.

44. See http://www.un.org/esa/coordination/ngo/faq .htm. See also United Nations Development Programme, *Human Development Report, 2001* and *2003* (New York: Oxford University Press, 2001, 2003), and Susan Raymond, "The nonprofit piece of the global puzzle," *On Philanthropy,* October 15, 2001.

45. See Jennifer Brinkerhoff, Stephen C. Smith, and Hildy Teegen, "Beyond the 'non': The strategic space for NGOs in development," in Brinkerhoff, Smith, and Teegen, eds. *NGOs and the Millennium Development Goals: Citizen Action to Reduce Poverty* (New York: Palgrave Macmillan, 2007),

46. Other examples include modern-sector jobs in the Harris-Todaro migration model and effort expended in other types of winner-take-all markets.

47. Elinor Ostrom, *Governing the Commons: The Evolution of Institutions for Collective Action* (New York: Cambridge University Press, 1990).

48. See Paul Romer, "Idea gaps and object gaps in economic development," *Journal of Monetary Economics* 32 (1993): 543–573, and Paul Romer, "Two strategies for economic development: Using ideas vs. producing ideas," *World Bank Economic Review Annual Supplement,* 1992.

49. Vincent Ostrom and Elinor Ostrom, "Public goods and public choice," in *Alternatives for Delivering Public Services,* ed. E. S. Savas (Boulder, Colo.: Westview Press, 1977), pp. 7–49; David L. Weimar and Aidan R. Vining, Policy *Analysis: Concepts and Practice,* 2nd ed. (Englewood Cliffs, N.J.: Prentice Hall, 1992).

50. Charles M. Tiebout, "A pure theory of local expenditures," *Journal of Political Economy* 64 (1956): 416–424; James M. Buchanan, "An economic theory of clubs," *Economica* 32 (1965): 1–14. Club goods may be thought of as a form of hybrid of private goods and local public goods that exhibit some degree of rivalry in the form of congestion as well as excludability.

51. In addition to the Grameen Bank and BRAC in Bangladesh, international NGOs such as ACCION and FINCA pioneered village banking in Latin America. See Stephen C. Smith, *Ending Global Poverty* (New York: Palgrave Macmillan, 2005), where

examples of NGO educational innovations are also detailed.

52. For a broad analysis, see Jonathan P. Doh and Hildy Teegen, *Globalization and NGOs: Transforming Business, Government, and Society* (Westport, Conn.: Praeger, 2003).

53. The citizen sector (including NGOs) relies on voluntary action, hence the term *voluntary failure*—though despite its logic, the term is unfortunate to the extent that it seems to suggest intentional failure. Ralph Kramer identifies four characteristic vulnerabilities: (1) institutionalization, or "a process of creeping formalization"; (2) goal deflection, or the displacement of ends by means, such as fund-raising; (3) minority rule, in which NGOs reflect their philanthropic origins (i.e., funders) rather than their clientele; and (4) ineffectuality. Lester Salamon outlines four similar voluntary failures: (1) philanthropic insufficiency, rooted in NGOs' limited scale and resources; (2) philanthropic particularism, reflecting NGOs' choice of clientele and projects; (3) philanthropic paternalism, where those who control the most resources are able to control community priorities; and (4) philanthropic amateurism. See Ralph M. Kramer, *Voluntary Agencies in the Welfare State* (Berkeley: University of California Press, 1981), and Lester M. Salamon, "Of market failure, voluntary failure, and third-party government: Toward a theory of government-nonprofit relations in the modern welfare state," *Journal of Voluntary Action Research* 16 (1987): 29–49.

54. Ian Smillie and Henny Helmich call this phenomenon the "alms bazaar" (i.e., the development industry). See Smillie and Helmich, eds., *Non-Governmental Organisations and Governments: Stakeholders for Development* (Paris: Development Center of the Organization for Economic Cooperation and Development, 1993).

55. The literature has been mixed on this question and has been plagued with statistical identification difficulties. However, recent evidence suggests that when endogeneity is accounted for, the extent of regressivity can be very strong: see M. Shahe Emran, Asadul Islam, and Forhad Shilpi, "Admission is free only if your dad is rich! Distributional effects of corruption in schools in developing countries," http://

dx.doi.org/10.2139/ssrn.2214550. This paper also provides a good literature review of this topic.

56. World Bank, *The Quality of Growth* (New York: Oxford University Press, 2000), ch. 6. The actual extent to which bribery is regressive remains somewhat controversial. In addition to Emran, Islam, and Shilpi, "Admission is free only if your dad is rich!," op. cit., other useful surveys and findings include Abhijit V. Banerjee, Rema Hanna, and Sundhil Mullainathan, "Corruption," in *The Handbook of Organizational Economics*, edited by Robert Gibbons, John Roberts (Princeton 2013). Jakob Svensson, "Eight questions about corruption," *Journal of Economic Perspectives* 19, No. 5 (2005): 19–42; J. Hunt and S. Laszlo "Is bribery really regressive? Bribery's costs, benefits and mechanisms," *World Development* 40, No. 2 (2012): 223–436; J. Hunt, "How corruption hits people when they are down," *Journal of Development Economics* 84, No. 2 (2007): 574–589; and Jakob Svensson, " Who must pay bribes and how much? Evidence from a cross section of firms," *Quarterly Journal of Economics* 118, No. 1 (2003): 207–230.

57. See, for example, Benjamin A. Olken, "Monitoring corruption: Evidence from a field experiment in Indonesia," *Journal of Political Economy* 115, No. 2 (2007): 200–249; and Ritva Reinikka and Jakob Svensson, "Fighting Corruption to Improve Schooling: Evidence from a Newspaper Campaign in Uganda," *Journal of the European Economic Association* 3, Nos. 2-3 (April-May 2005): 259–267.

58. John M. Cohen and Norman T. Uphoff, "Participation's place in rural development: Seeking clarity through specificity," *World Development* 8 (1980): 213–235.

59. David Deshler and Donald Sock, "Community development participation: A concept review of the international literature," paper presented at the conference of the International League for Social Commitment in Adult Education, Ljungskile, Sweden, July 22–26, 1985.

60. Sarah C. White, "Depoliticising development: The uses and abuses of participation," *Development in Practice* 6 (1996): 6–15.

61. Victoria J. Michener, "The participatory approach: Contradiction and cooption in Burkina Faso," *World Development* 26 (1998): 2105–2118.

PART THREE

Problems and Policies: International and Macro

12 International Trade Theory and Development Strategy

The South needs the North, and increasingly the North needs the South.
—*United Nations Development Programme,* Human Development Report, 2013

Diversification and industrialization remain the best means in the long run for countries to reduce their vulnerability to the adverse growth effects of commodity price volatility.
—*UNCTAD, 2012*

You become what you export.

—*Ricardo Hausmann and Dani Rodrik, 2006*

However misguided the old model of blanket protection intended to nurture import substitute industries, it would be a mistake to go to the other extreme and deny developing countries the opportunity of actively nurturing the development of an industrial sector.
—*Report of the High-Level Panel on Financing for Development (Zedillo Commission), 2001*

The upshot is an agricultural trading system in which success depends less on comparative advantage than on comparative access to subsidies.
—*Kevin Watkins and Joachim von Braun, 2002–2003 IFPRI Annual Report Essay*

12.1 Economic Globalization: An Introduction

Over the past several decades, the economies of the world have become increasingly linked, through expanded international trade in services as well as primary and manufactured goods, through portfolio investments such as international loans and purchases of stock, and through direct foreign investment, especially on the part of large multinational corporations. At the same time, foreign aid has increased much less in real terms and globally has become dwarfed by the now much larger flows of both private capital and remittances. These linkages have had a marked effect on the developing world. But developing countries are importing and exporting more from each other, as well as from the developed countries, and in some parts of the developing world, most prominently East Asia but also Latin America and in this century, investments have poured in from developed countries such as the United States, the United Kingdom, and Japan. We shall review how developing countries have been affected by these trends and examine theories of the effects of expanded international linkages for the prospects of development.

Globalization is one of the most frequently used words in discussions of development, trade, and international political economy.[1] As the form of the word implies, globalization is a *process* by which the economies of the world become more integrated, leading to a global economy and, increasingly, global economic policymaking, for example, through international agencies such as the **World Trade Organization (WTO)**. *Globalization* also refers to an emerging "global culture," in which people consume similar goods and services across countries and use a common language of business, English; these changes facilitate economic integration and are, in turn, further promoted by it. But in its core economic meaning, *globalization* refers to the increased openness of economies to international trade, financial flows, and direct foreign investment, which are topics of this and the following two chapters. The growing interconnection of all kinds across national governments and firms and directly between peoples is a process that affects everyone in the world, even if so far it still seems more visible in the developed countries. But globalization can in many ways have a greater impact in developing countries.

For some people, the term *globalization* suggests exciting business opportunities, efficiency gains from trade, more rapid growth of knowledge and innovation, and the transfer of such knowledge to developing countries, facilitating faster growth, or the prospect of a world too interdependent to engage in war. In part, globalization may well turn out to be all of these things.

For other people, however, globalization raises troubling concerns: that inequalities may be accentuated both across and within countries, that environmental degradation may be accelerated, that the international dominance of the richest countries may be expanded and locked in, and that some peoples and regions may be left further behind. Nobel laureate Muhammad Yunus captured some of these sentiments when he wrote in 2008, "Global trade is like a hundred-lane highway criss-crossing the world. If it is a free-for-all highway, with no stop lights, speed limits, size restrictions, or even lane markers, its surface will be taken over by the giant trucks from the world's most powerful economies."[2] Appropriate policies and agreements are needed to forestall such potential problems.

Thus, globalization carries benefits and opportunities as well as costs and risks. This is true for all peoples in all countries but especially for poor families in low-income countries, for whom the stakes are much higher. The potential upside is perhaps also greatest for developing countries; globalization does present new possibilities for broad-based economic development. By providing many types of interactions with people in other countries, globalization can potentially benefit developing countries directly and indirectly through cultural, social, scientific, and technological exchanges, as well as through conventional trade and finance. A faster diffusion of productive ideas, such as a shorter time between innovation and adoption of new technologies around the world, might help developing countries catch up more quickly. In short, globalization makes it possible, at least in principle, for the less developed countries to more effectively absorb the knowledge that is one of the foundations of the wealth of developed countries. In addition, as Adam Smith wrote in 1776, "the division of labor is limited by the extent of the market." The larger the market that can be sold to, the greater the gains from trade and the division of labor. Moreover, the greater is the incentive for innovation, because the potential return is much larger.

Globalization The increasing integration of national economies into expanding international markets.

World Trade Organization (WTO) Geneva-based watchdog and enforcer of international trade agreements since 1995; replaced the General Agreement on Tariffs and Trade (GATT).

The potential downside of globalization is also greater for poorer countries if they become locked into a pattern of dependence, if dualism within developing countries sharpens, or if some of the poor are entirely bypassed by globalization. Critics have raised the legitimate worry that many people living in poverty could find it all the harder to break out of poverty traps without concerted public action—for example, if human capital fell below the minimum needed to engage the global economy. The share of international investment received by the poorest countries has been on a long-term trend of falling rather than rising. All countries may be affected by increased vulnerability to capital flows, as the 2008 financial crisis has seemed to confirm, but developing countries more so. All countries may experience certain threats to their cultural identities, but developing countries the most.

Certainly, some very important developing countries, accounting for a large fraction of the world's population, notably China and India, have recently been using globalization as an opportunity to accelerate their rate of catch-up by growing faster than the developed world, thereby reducing some international inequalities. But by other measures, inequality may be accentuated both across and within countries. The two-decade decline in Africa from the early 1980s to the beginning of this century and the extreme disparities that opened up between coastal and inland China are important cases in point.

Widespread and understandable concerns about globalization are based on the fact that previous great waves of globalization, associated with the colonial period, were extraordinarily uneven in their impact. The worst affected areas, such as Africa, are still reeling. The argument that there will be widespread general benefits from at least some form of globalization today must rest on what is different about this current wave. It is not enough simply to say that previous waves were associated with conquest and subordination by colonialism. Critics can and do contend that today's globalization is only superficially different. A claim that "things are different this time" must stand or fall on evidence that there are now effective rules of the game for international trade, investment, finance, and assistance to the poor—or if not, that these rules are steadily, convincingly, and irreversibly being put into place.

Formal processes of trade liberalization have been key to the encouragement of globalization thus far. A significant series of rounds of trade negotiations were held under the **General Agreement on Tariffs and Trade (GATT)**, initiated in 1947, which led eventually to the creation of the WTO in 1995. The trade rules negotiated under the auspices of the WTO are key examples of how rules of the game are being created. So far, however, the rules have not been balanced. They have greatly benefited some countries but have benefited less the poor countries still trying to gain a foothold in growth and development through agriculture and facing barriers put up by the very countries that are most promoting the benefits of trade openness: Trade protectionism as practiced by developed countries tends to fall most heavily on the poorest developing countries because developed-country protection focuses on agriculture. Tariffs placed by developed countries on imports from developing countries—though currently not very high by historical standards—were by 2010 still about double those placed on imports coming from other developed countries. The Organization for Economic Cooperation and Development (OECD) estimates that in 2010, its members' agricultural producer support was $227 billion; although this was about 10% less than the

General Agreement on Tariffs and Trade (GATT) An international body set up in 1947 to explore ways and means of reducing tariffs on internationally traded goods and services; replaced in 1995 by the World Trade Organization.

previous three years, it far exceeded the level of aid from these countries, which was about $130 billion in 2010. And nontariff barriers are also much higher.[3] The damage this tactic does to developing countries is immense.

To create genuinely fair as well as efficient rules of the game, much more needs to be done. International agreements are needed to level the globalization playing field for the poor. Some of this leveling process involves international change, and some involves national changes that can be facilitated by the international community—for example, to prevent propping up corrupt governments that violate human rights, and violent and exploitative rebels that stay in power through international trade in legal goods such as diamonds (which may be mined under conditions that violate the most basic of rights) as well as in illegal goods such as narcotics. Codes of conduct for multinational corporations, regarding political and other behavior, can be developed further. And reasonable limits on the applicability of international property rights must be agreed to, such as those concerning provision of life-threatening medicines in poor countries that cannot afford to pay monopoly **rent**, prices that far exceed production costs. In Chapter 14, you will see that direct foreign investment by multinational corporations (MNCs) may contribute to development, but a country also eventually needs its own modern-sector firms or at least a way of inducing international firms to treat the country as a home base.

It has also been asked whether more cannot be done for the poorest countries than merely leveling the playing field. Many development advocates are calling for more genuine and fuller opening of developed-country markets to exports from the poorest countries. It may also be said that among the worst possible outcomes for a poor country is for the current round of globalization to bypass the country entirely. This is largely the situation in much of sub-Saharan Africa—although a number of countries have benefited substantially from the commodity boom of recent years. Nevertheless, adversely affected by previous waves of globalization, most countries in this region have been much less affected by the present wave.

> **Rent** In macroeconomics, the share of national income going to the owners of the productive resource, land (i.e., landlords). In everyday usage, the price paid for the use of property (e.g., buildings, housing). In microeconomics, economic rent is the payment to a factor of production over and above its highest opportunity cost. In public choice theory, rent refers to those excess payments that are gained as a result of government laws, policies, or regulations.

12.2 International Trade: Some Key Issues

International trade has often played a central role in the historical experience of the developing world. As with many other topics in development, there is a great deal of diversity in developing countries' experiences with trade. In recent years, much of the attention to trade and development issues has been focused on understanding the spectacular export success of East Asia. Taiwan, South Korea, and other East Asian economies pioneered this strategy, which has been successfully followed by their much larger neighbor, China. The experiences of these economies are an important plotline in the unfolding trade and development drama and will be examined later in the chapter.

At the same time, throughout Africa, the Middle East, and Latin America, primary product exports have traditionally accounted for a sizable proportion of individual gross domestic products. In some of the smaller countries, a substantial percentage of the economy's income is derived from the overseas sale of agricultural and other **primary products** or commodities such as coffee, cotton, cacao, sugar, palm oil, bauxite, and copper. In the special circumstances of the

> **Primary products** Products derived from all extractive occupations—farming, lumbering, fishing, mining, and quarrying, foodstuffs, and raw materials.

oil-producing nations in the Persian Gulf and elsewhere, the sale of unrefined and refined petroleum products to countries throughout the world accounts for over 70% of their national incomes—despite obvious benefits, specialization in oil production frequently has brought with it substantial, if sometimes hidden, economic costs, including both economic and political distortions. Many other developing countries must still depend on nonmineral primary-product exports for a relatively large fraction of their foreign-exchange earnings. This is a particularly serious problem in sub-Saharan Africa. Because the markets and prices for these exports are often unstable, primary-product **export dependence** carries with it a degree of risk and uncertainty that few nations desire. This is an important issue, because despite strength since 2002 and some rebounding after the 2008 crisis, the long-term trend for prices of primary goods is downward, as well as very volatile (as we examine later in this section).

Export dependence   A country's reliance on exports as the major source of financing for development activities.

Some African countries, including Burkina Faso, Burundi, Central African Republic, Gambia, Niger, and São Tomé and Príncipe, received 8% or less of their merchandise export earnings from manufactures in 2011 (WDI); none of these countries received more than 2% of their export earnings from fossil fuels in 2011. Some other countries such as Nicaragua have similarly low manufacturing export shares.

Indeed, some developing countries have been receiving at least two-fifths of their export earnings from one or two agricultural or nonfuel mineral products. And as noted by David Harvey and his coauthors, "For 40 countries, the production of three or fewer commodities explains all export earnings."[4] And the United Nations Conference on Trade and Development (UNCTAD) reported in 2006 that "out of 141 developing countries, 95 are more than 50% dependent on commodity exports.... In most sub-Saharan African countries, the figure is 80%."[5]

Some developing countries are overwhelmingly dependent on fuel exports. For example, in 2011, Venezuela, Yemen, and Algeria each received 97% of their export earnings from fossil fuels; Nigeria and Iran each received 89% of their export earnings from fossil fuels. Despite the apparent bonanza, high reliance on oil and other fuel exports has also brought with it substantial, if often hidden, economic costs and political distortions. An outsize oil sector often acts as an enclave in the economy, benefiting relatively few citizens, yet resulting in reduced exports from other sectors of the economy that might do more to benefit development in the long term.

Export dependence also extends to services, notably tourism, which is "exported" when foreign visitors purchase domestically produced services, including hotel stays, restaurant meals, local transportation, theme park admissions, tour packages, and value added in retail (such as wages of workers in stores when tourists purchase goods). These expenditures are paid for by money from other countries, such as the dollars that Americans spend in destinations like beaches in Grenada and wildlife parks in Tanzania. This dependence is clearest in Small Island Developing States (SIDS), a special UN category. But a sudden loss of income from service exports can be as devastating as the loss of other export revenues. This happened in 2011 in the Middle East and North Africa (MENA) region during and after the conflicts associated with the "Arab Spring," which heavily affected tourism. In Egypt, which is highly dependent on earnings from tourism, "tourist arrivals" fell by 32% in 2011, and tourist expenditures correspondingly fell from about $51 billion to about

$43 billion, and remained at depressed levels. In 2011, tourism revenues in Tunisia fell by nearly 30%.[6] In addition to demonstrating the economic advantages of democratic political institutions that do not rely upon repression and violence, such experiences also illustrate the benefits of diversification.

In addition to their export dependence, many developing countries rely, generally to an even greater extent, on the importation of raw materials, machinery, capital goods, intermediate producer goods, and consumer products to fuel their industrial expansion and satisfy the rising consumption aspirations of their people. For a majority of developing nations, import demands exceeded their capacity to generate sufficient revenues from the sale of exports for much of the post–World War II period. This led to chronic deficits on their balance of payments position vis-à-vis the rest of the world. Whereas such deficits on the **current account** (an excess of import *payments* over export *receipts* for goods and services) were compensated for on their balance of payments table by a surplus on the **capital account** (a receipt of foreign private and public lending and investment in excess of repayment of principal and interest on former loans and investments), the debt burden of repaying earlier international loans and investments often becomes acute. In a number of developing countries, severe deficits on current and capital accounts have led to a depletion of international monetary reserves, currency instability, and a slowdown in economic growth.

In the 1980s and 1990s, this combination of rising trade deficits, growing foreign debts, accelerated capital flight, and diminished international reserves led to the widespread adoption of fiscal and monetary austerity measures, especially in Africa and Latin America (often with the involvement of the International Monetary Fund, or IMF), which may have further exacerbated the slowdown in economic growth and the worsening of poverty and unemployment in much of the developing world. These various concepts of international economics will be explained in more detail later in this chapter and in the next. Here the point is merely that a chronic excess of foreign expenditures over receipts (which may have nothing to do with a developing country's inability to handle its financial affairs but rather may be related to its vulnerability to global economic disturbances) can significantly retard development efforts. It can also greatly limit a low-income nation's ability to determine and pursue its most desirable economic strategies.

Many indebted countries went into surplus as they paid down some of their debt. In the new century, a pattern of trade surpluses has strengthened for many, though by no means all, developing countries. Developing countries have sought to avoid repeats of the crisis conditions of Latin America in the 1980s, sub-Saharan Africa in the 1980s and 1990s, and East Asia in 1997–1998. The sudden collapse of export earnings during the 2008 financial crisis provided a glimpse of the dangers. This pattern carries its own risks; for example, it means that developing countries are effectively exporting capital, and it leaves economies vulnerable to a sharp correction when the large and chronic U.S. balance of payments deficits are reversed.[7]

But international trade and finance must be understood in a much broader perspective than simply the intercountry flow of commodities and financial resources. By opening their economies and societies to global trade and commerce and by looking outward to the rest of the world, developing countries

Current account   The portion of a country's balance of payments that reflects the market value of the country's "visible" (e.g., commodity trade) and "invisible" (e.g., shipping services) exports and imports.

Capital account   The portion of a country's balance of payments that shows the volume of private foreign investment and public grants and loans that flow into and out of the country.

invite not only the international transfer of goods, services, and financial resources but also the developmental or antidevelopmental influences of the transfer of production technologies; consumption patterns; institutional and organizational arrangements; educational, health, and social systems; and the more general values, ideals, and lifestyles of the developed nations of the world. The impact of such technological, economic, social, and cultural transfers on the character of the development process can be either consistent or inconsistent with broader development objectives. Much will depend on the nature of the political, social, and institutional structure of the recipient country and its development priorities. Whether it is best for developing countries to look primarily outward (as single economies or as blocs) and promote more exports, either passively or actively; to emphasize looking inward and substitute domestic production for imports, as the protectionists and cultural nationalists propose; or to be simultaneously and strategically outward- and inward-looking in their international economic policies cannot be stated a priori. Individual nations must appraise their present and prospective situations in the world community realistically in the light of their specific development objectives. Only thus can they determine how to design the most beneficial trade strategy. Although participation in the world economy is all but inevitable, there is ample room for policy choice about what *kind* of participation to promote and what policy strategies to pursue. As you will see, WTO membership comes with prohibitions or restrictions on some policies, but there remains a great deal of scope for policy choice for developing countries.

Five Basic Questions about Trade and Development

Our objective in the next few sections is to focus on traditional and more contemporary theories of international trade in the context of five basic themes or questions of particular importance to developing nations.

1. How does international trade affect the rate, structure, and character of economic *growth*? This is the traditional "trade as an engine of growth" controversy, set in terms of contemporary development aspirations.

2. How does trade alter the *distribution* of income and wealth within a country and among different countries? Is trade a force for international and domestic equality or inequality? In other words, how are the gains and losses distributed, and who benefits?

3. Under what conditions can trade help a nation to achieve its *development* objectives?

4. Can a developing country by its own actions determine how much it trades or which products and services it sells?

5. In the light of past experience and prospective judgment, should a developing country adopt an outward-looking policy (freer trade, expanded flows of capital and human resources, etc.) or an inward-looking one (protectionism in the interest of self-reliance), or some combination of both, for example, in the form of regional economic cooperation and strategic export policies? What are the arguments for and against these alternative trade strategies for development?

Clearly, the answers or suggested answers to these five questions will not be uniform throughout the diverse economies of the developing world. The whole economic basis for international trade rests on the fact that countries do differ in their resource endowments, their preferences and technologies, their scale economies, their economic and social institutions, and their capacities for growth and development. Developing countries are no exception to this rule. Some are rapidly ascending through the income rankings as they expand their industrial capacities. Some are very populous yet deficient in both natural resources and human skills, at least in large regions of the country. Others are sparsely populated yet endowed with abundant mineral and raw material resources. Yet others are small and economically weak, still having at present neither adequate human capital nor the material resources on which to base a sustained and largely self-sufficient strategy of economic and social development.

We begin with a statistical summary of recent trade performance of developing countries and patterns. There follows a simplified presentation of the basic neoclassical theory of international trade and its effect on efficiency, equity, stability, and growth (four basic economic concepts related to the central questions outlined here). We then provide a critique of the relevance of pure free-trade theories for developing countries in the light of both historical experience and the contemporary realities of the world economy. Like free markets, **free trade** has many desirable theoretical features, not the least of which is the promotion of static economic efficiency and optimal resource allocation. But also like free markets and perfect competition, free trade exists more in theory than in practice—and today's developing nations have to function in the imperfect and often highly unequal real world of international commerce. Consequently, we will briefly discuss alternative trade models that focus on imperfect competition, unequal trade, and the dynamic effects of differential human resource and technological growth. Later in the chapter and in the next chapter, we examine the balance of payments, review some issues in international finance, engage in an in-depth analysis of debt crises, and explore the range of commercial policies (tariffs, subsidies, quotas, exchange-rate adjustments, etc.) that a developing country might wish to adopt within the broader context of the ongoing debate about the relative merits of export promotion versus import substitution. We then examine a wide range of commercial policies used in developing countries, including import tariffs, physical quotas, export promotion versus import substitution, policies to directly or indirectly influence exchange rates, bargaining over technology licensing and market access, strategy for export upgrading, international commodity agreements, and economic integration. Our objective is to ascertain the conditions under which these policies might help or harm developing countries in their dealings with the developed world and with one another. We then summarize the various positions in the ongoing debate between the "trade optimists" and "trade pessimists," and between outward- and inward-looking strategies of development. Finally, we look at the trade policies of developed countries to see in what ways they directly and indirectly affect the economies of the developing world. An outstanding example of the benefits of world trade is illustrated at the conclusion of this chapter, where the sources of the pioneering success of now high-income Taiwan are examined.

Free trade The importation and exportation of goods without any barriers in the form of tariffs, quotas, or other restrictions.

Importance of Exports to Different Developing Nations

Although the overall figures for export volumes and values of developing countries are important indicators of patterns of trade for the group as a whole, we will see throughout this chapter that *what* a country exports can matter as much as the *dollar value* of its exports. Table 12.1 has been compiled to provide a capsule picture of the relative importance of merchandise export earnings to various developing nations of different sizes and in different regions. For purposes of comparison, some developed countries are included.

As with most development topics, there is high diversity among developing countries. Traditionally, however, developing countries are typically are more dependent on trade than developed countries. As Table 12.1 indicates, while large countries are understandably less dependent on trade than small countries, at any given size, many developing countries tend to devote a large share of their output as merchandise exports. We see that some large countries, most importantly Brazil, which have had unusually closed economies, tend to be less dependent on foreign trade in terms of national income than most relatively small countries.

And some very low income countries, such as Burundi and Ethiopia, remain markedly divorced from the global economy. As a group, however, less developed nations are typically more dependent on foreign trade in terms of its share in national income than the very highly developed countries are. This is reflected in the case of traditionally export-oriented Japan, whose merchandise exports amounted to roughly 13% of GDP in 2012. In contrast, many developing countries with similar sized populations export a much higher share of output, including Nigeria, Bangladesh, Russia, Mexico, Philippines, and Vietnam, and have a merchandise export share that is substantially higher than that of Japan.

The greater recorded share of developing-country exports in GDP is probably due in part to the much higher relative prices of nontraded services in developed than in developing countries. Nevertheless, the point remains that developing countries are generally more dependent on trade in international economic relations because most trade is in merchandise, for which price disparities are smaller across countries. Moreover, in general, the exports of developing countries are much less diversified than those of the developed countries (though some upper-middle-income countries are very highly diversified). While total exports and the share of manufactures in merchandise exports have been rising for many developing countries, it is important to keep this rise in perspective. A few newly industrializing countries (NICs) still command a dominant position in developing-country exports. For example, in 2011, South Korea alone exported far more merchandise than either all of South Asia (including India) or all of sub-Saharan Africa; and, in fact, South Korea exported more manufactured goods than South Asia and sub-Saharan Africa *combined*.[8] At the same time, the emergence of China as "workshop of the world" highlights the connection between manufactured export share and high growth in developing countries, as examined further in section 12.6 and explored in the China, Taiwan, and Southe Korea case studies in Chapters 4, 12, and 13, respectively.

The composition of exports differs markedly across countries. For developed countries such as Japan, the United Kingdom, and the United States, manufactures comprise 90%, 66%, and 63% of merchandise exports, respectively—higher than the developing country average. But developing countries are also diverse in their exports. For example, among the five so-called BRICS countries,

TABLE 12.1 Structure of merchandise exports: Selected Countries, 2012

Country	GDP, $ billions, 2012	Merchandise exports, $ billions, 2012	Merchan-dise Exports, % of GDP, 2012	Food, % of Total, 2012	Agricul-tural raw materials, % of total, 2012	Fuels, % of to-tal, 2012	Ores and Metals, % of total, 2012	Manufac-tures, % of totals, 2012
Algeria	205.8	74.0	36	0	0	97	0	2
Benin	7.6	1.4	18	61	24	0	1	15
Bolivia	27.0	10.9	40	14	1	55	25	5
Brazil	2252.7	242.6	11	32	4	11	16	35
Burkina Faso	10.4	2.4	23	38	52	0	1	8
Burundi	2.5	0.1	5	74	5	0	8	13
Central African Republic	2.2	0.2	10	1	31	1	62	4
China	8227.1	2048.8	25	3	0	2	1	94
Cote d'Ivoire	24.7	12.4	50	51	13	26	0	10
Ecuador	84.0	23.9	28	30	4	58	1	8
Egypt, Arab Rep.	262.8	29.4	11	14	2	32	6	45
Ethiopia	41.6	3.0	7	78	9	0	1	10
Gambia, The	0.9	0.1	11	82	2	0	9	7
Ghana	40.7	12.0	29	48	2	39	2	9
India	1841.7	293.2	16	11	2	19	3	65
Indonesia	878.0	188.1	21	18	6	34	6	36
Iran, Islamic Rep.	514.1	95.5	19	4	0	70	2	12
Japan	5959.7	798.6	13	1	1	2	3	90
Malawi	4.3	1.3	30	76	5	0	9	9
Malaysia	305.0	227.4	75	13	2	20	2	62
Mexico	1178.1	370.9	31	6	0	14	4	74
Mozambique	14.2	4.1	29	20	5	16	51	7
Nicaragua	10.5	2.7	25	90	2	1	2	6
Niger	6.8	1.5	22	14	3	1	76	6
Nigeria	262.6	114.0	43	2	6	89	0	3
Peru	203.8	45.6	22	21	1	14	50	14
Philippines	250.2	52.0	21	9	1	2	5	83
Russian Federation	2014.8	529.3	26	3	2	70	4	14
Rwanda	7.1	0.5	7	51	5	0	34	10
South Africa	384.3	87.3	23	8	2	12	32	45
United Kingdom	2471.8	468.4	19	6	1	14	4	66
United States	16244.6	1547.3	10	10	2	10	4	63
Vietnam	155.8	114.6	74	19	4	11	1	65
Yemen, Rep.	35.6	8.5	24	7	0	89	0	3

Source: World Bank, World Development Indicators, 2013, Table 4.4, at: http://wdi.worldbank.org/table/4.4, accessed 18 February 2014.

for India and especially China, manufactures make up a substantial majority of exports; but Brazil, South Africa, and especially Russia are much more specialized (and dependent) in commodity exports. Manufactured exports themselves are highly diverse in the extent of their skill and technology content.

As introduced earlier in the chapter, many developing countries are also dependent on one or a few commodity exports. In addition to losing the bene-fits of maintaining a competitive manufacturing sector, this carries substantial risks of facing falling relative prices in the long run and highly unstable prices in the short run.

Demand Elasticities and Export Earnings Instability

Most statistical studies of world demand patterns for different commodity groups reveal that in the case of primary products, the **income elasticity of demand** is relatively low: The percentage increase in quantity of primary agricultural products and most raw materials demanded by importers (mostly rich nations) will rise by less than the percentage increase in their gross national incomes (GNIs). By contrast, for fuels, certain raw materials, and manufactured goods, income elasticity is relatively high.[9] For example, it has been estimated that a 1% increase in developed-country incomes will normally raise their imports of foodstuffs by a mere 0.6% and of agricultural raw materials such as rubber and vegetable oils by 0.5% but will raise imports of manufactures by about 1.9%. Consequently, when incomes rise in rich countries, their demand for food, food products, and raw materials from the developing nations goes up relatively slowly, whereas demand for manufactures goes up relatively rapidly. The net result of these low income elasticities of demand is the tendency for the relative price of primary products to decline over time.

Moreover, since the **price elasticity of demand** for (and supply of) primary commodities also tends to be quite low (i.e., inelastic), any shifts in demand or supply curves can cause large and volatile price fluctuations. Together these two elasticity phenomena contribute to what has come to be known as **export earnings instability**. A 2012 UNCTAD study found that commodity price volatility faced by developing countries clearly increased over the past half century—and in the post 2003 period, in particular—potentially increasing vulnerability for exporters dependent on commodity exports. And instability (or volatility) in export earnings and the terms of trade can lead to lower and less predictable rates of economic growth.[10]

While almost all attention goes to merchandise exports, there has been a slow rise in the share of commercial services in the exports of both developed and developing countries. For the former, these are more likely to represent highly skilled activities such as investment banking and management consulting, while for the latter, construction and other less skill-intensive activities are more common.

The Terms of Trade and the Prebisch-Singer Hypothesis

The question of changing relative price levels for different commodities brings us to another important quantitative dimension of the trade problems historically faced by developing nations. The total value of export earnings depends not only on the volume of these exports sold abroad but also on the price paid for them. If export prices decline, a greater volume of exports will have to be sold merely to keep total earnings constant. Similarly, on the import side, the total foreign exchange expended depends on both the quantity and the price of imports.

Clearly, if the price of a country's exports is falling relative to the prices of the products it imports, it will have to sell that much more of its exports and enlist more of its scarce productive resources merely to secure the same level of imported goods that it purchased in previous years. In other words, the real or social opportunity costs of a unit of imports will rise for a country when its export prices decline relative to its import prices.

Economists have a special name for the relationship or ratio between the price of a typical unit of exports and the price of a typical unit of imports. This relationship is called the **commodity terms of trade**, and it is expressed as P_x/P_m, where P_x and P_m represent the export and import price indexes, respectively, calculated on the same base period (e.g., 2012 = 100). The commodity terms of trade are said to deteriorate for a country if P_x/P_m falls, that is, if export prices decline *relative to* import prices, even though both may rise. Most scholarship has broadly confirmed that historically, the prices of primary commodities have declined relative to manufactured goods.[11] As a result, the terms of trade have on the average tended to worsen over time for the non-oil-exporting developing countries while showing a relative improvement for the developed countries. Moreover, recent empirical studies suggest that real primary-product prices declined at an average annual rate of 0.6% in the twentieth century, although the commodity price boom prior to the financial crisis was the largest boom since 1900. But the strong increases since 2002 have not nearly negated the long-term trends; and this period of price rises already may have peaked.[12]

The main theory for the declining commodity terms of trade is known as the **Prebisch-Singer hypothesis**, after two famous development economists who first explored its implications in the 1950s.[13] They argued that there was and would continue to be a secular (long-term) decline in the terms of trade of primary-commodity exporters due to a combination of low income and price elasticities of demand. This decline would result in an ongoing transfer of income from poor to rich countries that could be combated only by efforts to protect domestic manufacturing industries through a process that came to be known as *import substitution*, considered later in this chapter. As noted in Box 12.1, recent research has added new evidence in support of the hypothesis.

Both because of this theory and because of the unfavorable terms-of-trade trends, developing countries have been doing their utmost over the past several decades to diversify into manufactures exports. After a slow and costly start, these efforts have resulted in a dramatic shift in the composition of developing-country exports, especially among middle-income countries. Led at first by the East Asian Tiger economies of South Korea, Taiwan, Hong Kong, and Singapore and now followed by many other countries, including China, the share of merchandise exports accounted for by manufactured goods has risen strongly in many developing countries.

Unfortunately, this structural change has not brought as many benefits to most developing countries as they had hoped, because relative prices within manufactures have also diverged: Over the past few decades, the prices of the basic manufactured goods exported by developing countries fell relative to the advanced products exported by rich countries. The price of textiles fell especially precipitously, and low-skilled electronic goods were not far behind.

Using alternative methods, the United Nations found that the real decline in developing-country export prices of manufactures in the 1980s was about 3.5% per year, or about 30% for the decade. In a detailed study, Alf Maizels discovered that the terms of trade in manufacturing goods for developing countries vis-à-vis the United States deteriorated over the 1981–1997 period.[14] The declines in textile prices accelerated dramatically starting in the late 1990s.

Commodity terms of trade The ratio of a country's average export price to its average import price.

Prebisch-Singer hypothesis The argument that the commodity terms of trade for primary-product exports of developing countries tends to decline over time.

BOX 12.1 FINDINGS   Four Centuries of Evidence on the Prebisch-Singer Hypothesis

There is a broad consensus among development economists that if a long-term negative trend in prices of a developing country's main commodity exports *relative* to its imports can be confirmed, diversification of the nation's mix of exports should be encouraged. Traditionally, developing economies, and particularly the least developed countries, have exported commodities and imported manufactures. Commodity prices are so volatile—and some hypothesized commodity price cycles potentially so long—that it is difficult to prove a long-term trend, but studies have generally tended to confirm the broad outlines of the Prebisch-Singer hypothesis (including a well-known 1994 International Monetary Fund study). But even though the unanticipated boom in commodity prices in the first years of this century has a long way to go before it will reverse the twentieth-century trend, some have questioned whether the decline in the relative price of commodities to manufactures can be reversed.

To obtain a reliable answer, it is best to have longer periods of data than have previously been available. To make matters even more difficult, empirical work has also been challenging because most tests depend on assumptions about the statistical properties of the data over time.[a] In a 2010 article in the *Review of Economics and Statistics*, David Harvey and his colleagues applied new techniques that require fewer statistical assumptions and also collected data going

remarkably farther back in time—in some cases, back to 1650. This makes it much easier to disentangle long-term trends from cycles.

In a striking example of their findings, the authors concluded that "the relative price of an important commodity like coffee has been declining at an annual rate of 0.77% for approximately 300 years!" More generally, they found that "overall, eleven major commodities show new and robust evidence of a long-run decline in their relative price." These commodities are aluminum, coffee, hides, jute, silver, sugar, tea, tobacco, wheat, wool, and zinc.

As the authors summarize:

In our opinion, this provides much more robust support that the Prebisch-Singer hypothesis is relevant for commodity prices. For the remaining fourteen commodities, no positive and significant trends could be detected over all or some fraction of the sample period. These zero-trending commodities suggest that the Lewis hypothesis may also play a part in explaining the behavior of certain commodity prices;…conversely, however, in the very long run, there is simply no statistical evidence that relative commodity prices have ever trended upward.

[a]Testing issues include whether the time series contains a unit root and whether there have been structural breaks.

Source: Based on David I. Harvey, Neil M. Kellard, Jakob B. Madsen, and Mark E. Wohar, "The Prebisch-Singer hypothesis: Four centuries of evidence," *Review of Economics and Statistics* 92 (2010): 367–377.

Having reviewed some of the international trade issues that developing countries face, we turn next to consider alternative theories of the role that trade plays in economic development.

12.3 The Traditional Theory of International Trade

The phenomenon of transactions and exchange is a basic component of human activity throughout the world. Even in the most remote villages of Africa, people regularly meet in the marketplace to exchange goods, either for money or for other goods through simple **barter transactions**. A transaction is an exchange of two things—something is given up in return for something else. In an African village, women may barter food such as cassava for cloth or simple jewelry for clay pots. Implicit in all transactions is a price. For example, if 20 kilos of cassava are traded for 1 meter of bark cloth, the implicit price (or terms of trade) of the bark cloth is 20 kilos of cassava. If 20 kilos of cassava can also be exchanged for one small clay pot, it follows that clay pots and 1-meter pieces of bark cloth can be exchanged on a one-to-one basis. A price system is already in the making.

> **Barter transactions** The trading of goods directly for other goods in economies not fully monetized.

Comparative Advantage

Why do people trade? Basically, because it is profitable to do so. Different people possess different abilities and resources and may want to consume goods in different proportions. Diverse preferences as well as varied physical and financial endowments open up the possibility of profitable trade. People usually find it profitable to trade the things they possess in large quantities relative to their tastes or needs in return for things they want more urgently. Because it is virtually impossible for individuals or families to provide themselves with all the consumption requirements of even the simplest life, they usually find it profitable to engage in the activities for which they are best suited or have a **comparative advantage** in terms of their natural abilities or resource endowments. They can then exchange any surplus of these home-produced commodities for products that others may be relatively more suited to produce. The phenomenon of **specialization** based on comparative advantage arises, therefore, to some extent in even the most subsistence economies.

> **Comparative advantage** Production of a commodity at a lower opportunity cost than any of the alternative commodities that could be produced.
>
> **Specialization** Concentration of resources in the production of relatively few commodities.

These same principles of specialization and comparative advantage have long been applied by economists to the exchange of goods between individual nations. In answer to the questions of what determines which goods are traded and why some countries produce some things while others produce different things, economists since the time of Adam Smith have sought the answers in terms of international differences in costs of production and prices of different products. Countries, like people, specialize in a limited range of production activities because it is to their advantage to do so. They specialize in activities where the gains from specialization are likely to be the largest.

But why, in the case of international trade, should costs differ from country to country? For example, how can Germany produce cameras, electrical appliances, and automobiles cheaper than Kenya and exchange these manufactured goods for Kenya's relatively cheaper agricultural produce (fruits, vegetables, cut flowers, coffee, and tea)? Again, the answer is to be found in international differences in the structure of costs and prices. Some things (manufactured goods) are relatively cheaper to produce in Germany and can profitably be exported to other countries like Kenya; other things (agricultural goods) can be produced in Kenya at a lower relative cost and are therefore imported into Germany in exchange for its manufactures.

The concept of *relative* cost and price differences is basic to the theory of international trade. The *principle of comparative advantage*, as it is called, asserts that a country should, and under competitive conditions will, specialize in the export of the products that it can produce at the lowest *relative cost*. Germany may be able to produce cameras and cars as well as fruits and vegetables at lower *absolute* unit costs than Kenya, but because the commodity cost differences between countries are greater for the manufactured goods than for agricultural products, it will be to Germany's advantage to specialize in the production of manufactured goods and exchange them for Kenya's agricultural produce. So even though Germany may have an **absolute advantage** in the cost of both commodities, its comparative cost advantage lies in manufactured goods. Conversely, Kenya may be at an absolute disadvantage vis-à-vis Germany in both manufacturing and agriculture in that its absolute unit costs of production are higher for both types of products. It can nevertheless still engage in profitable trade because it has a comparative advantage in agricultural specialization (or alternatively, because its absolute disadvantage is less in agriculture). It is this phenomenon of differences in comparative advantage that gives rise to beneficial trade even among the most unequal trading partners.

Absolute advantage Production of a commodity with the same amount of real resources as another producer but at a lower absolute unit cost.

Relative Factor Endowments and International Specialization: The Neoclassical Model

The classical comparative advantage theory of free trade is a static model based strictly on a one-variable-factor (labor cost), complete-specialization approach to demonstrating the gains from trade. This nineteenth-century free-trade model, primarily associated with David Ricardo and John Stuart Mill, was modified and refined in the twentieth century by two Swedish economists, Eli Hecksher and Bertil Ohlin, to take into account differences in factor supplies (mainly land, labor, and capital) on international specialization. The Hecksher-Ohlin neoclassical (or variable-proportions) **factor endowment trade theory** also enables us to describe analytically the impact of economic growth on trade patterns and the impact of trade on the structure of national economies and on the differential returns or payments to various factors of production.

Factor endowment trade theory The neoclassical model of free trade, which postulates that countries will tend to specialize in the production of the commodities that make use of their abundant factors of production (land, labor, capital, etc.).

Unlike the classical labor cost model, however, where trade arises because of fixed but differing labor productivities for different commodities in different countries, the neoclassical factor endowment model assumes away inherent differences in relative labor productivity by postulating that all countries have access to the same technological possibilities for all commodities. If domestic factor prices were the same, all countries would use identical methods of production and would therefore have the same relative domestic product price ratios and factor productivities. The basis for trade arises not because of inherent technological differences in labor productivity for different commodities between different countries but because countries are endowed with different factor supplies. Given relative factor endowments, relative factor prices will differ (e.g., labor will be relatively cheap in labor-abundant countries), and so will domestic commodity price ratios and factor combinations. Countries with cheap labor will have a relative cost and price advantage over countries with relatively expensive labor in commodities that make intensive use of labor (e.g., primary products). They should therefore focus on the production of these labor-intensive products and export the surplus in return for imports of capital-intensive goods.

Conversely, countries well endowed with capital will have a relative cost and price advantage in the production of manufactured goods, which tend to require relatively large inputs of capital compared with labor. They can thus benefit from specialization in, and export of, capital-intensive manufactures in return for imports of labor-intensive products from labor-abundant countries. Trade therefore serves as a vehicle for a nation to capitalize on its abundant resources through more intensive production and export of commodities that require large inputs of those resources while relieving its factor shortage through the importation of commodities that use large amounts of its relatively scarce resources.

To summarize, the factor endowment theory is based on two crucial propositions:

1. *Different products require productive factors in different relative proportions.* For example, agricultural products generally require relatively greater proportions of labor per unit of capital than manufactured goods, which require more machine time (capital) per worker than most primary products. The proportions in which factors are actually used to produce different goods will depend on their relative prices. But no matter what factor prices may be, the factor endowment model assumes that certain products will always be relatively more capital-intensive while others will be relatively more labor-intensive. These relative factor intensities will be no different in India than in the United States; primary products will be the relatively labor-intensive commodities compared with secondary manufactured goods in both India and the United States.

2. *Countries have different endowments of factors of production.* Some countries, like the United States, have large amounts of capital per worker and are therefore designated capital-abundant countries. Others, like India, Egypt, or Colombia, have little capital and much labor and are designated labor-abundant countries. In general, developed countries are relatively capital-abundant (one could also add that they are well endowed with skilled labor), while most developing countries are labor-abundant.

The factor endowment theory goes on to argue that capital-abundant countries will tend to specialize in such products as automobiles, aircraft, sophisticated electronics, communication goods, and computers, which use capital intensively in their technology of production. They will export some of these capital-intensive products in exchange for the labor- or land-intensive products like food, raw materials, and minerals that can best be produced by countries that are relatively well endowed with labor or land.

This theory, which played a predominant role in the early literature and policy advice on trade and development, encouraged developing countries to focus on their labor- and land-intensive primary-product exports. It was argued that by trading these primary commodities for the manufactured goods that developed countries were theoretically best suited to produce, developing nations could realize the enormous potential benefits to be had from free trade with the richer nations of the world. Little attention was given in this literature to diversification as an objective or the productivity benefits of expanding manufactures' share.

The mechanism whereby the benefits of trade are transmitted across national boundaries under the factor endowment approach is analogous to that of the classical labor cost approach. However, in the factor endowment case, with the possibility of differing factor combinations for producing different commodities, nations are assumed to be operating initially at some point on their concave (or increasing opportunity cost) production possibility frontier, determined by domestic demand conditions. For example, consider the standard two-country, two-commodity model. Let the two countries be "Less Developed World" and "Rest of World" and the two commodities be agricultural goods and manufactured goods. Figure 12.1 portrays the theoretical benefits of free trade with Less Developed World's domestic (no-trade) production possibility frontier shown in Figure 12.1a and Rest of World's frontier in Figure 12.1b. Point A on the Less Developed World production possibility frontier PP in Figure 12.1a provides the illustration. With full employment of all resources and under perfectly competitive assumptions, Less Developed World will be producing and consuming at point A, where the relative price ratio, P_a/P_m, will be given by the slope of the dotted line, $(P_a/P_m)_L$, at point A.[15]

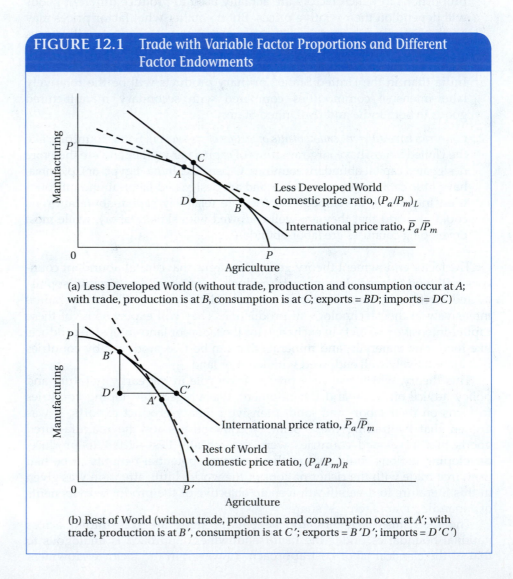

FIGURE 12.1   Trade with Variable Factor Proportions and Different Factor Endowments

(a) Less Developed World (without trade, production and consumption occur at A; with trade, production is at B, consumption is at C; exports = BD; imports = DC)

(b) Rest of World (without trade, production and consumption occur at A'; with trade, production is at B', consumption is at C'; exports = $B'D'$; imports = $D'C'$)

Similarly, Rest of World may be producing and consuming at point A' in Figure 12.1b, with a domestic price ratio, $(P_a/P_m)_R$, that differs (agricultural goods are relatively more costly, or conversely, manufactured goods are relatively cheaper) from that of Less Developed World. Note that with a closed economy, both countries will be producing both commodities. However, Less Developed World, being poorer, will produce a greater proportion of food products in its (smaller) total output.

The relative difference in costs of production and prices at points A and A' (i.e., their different slopes) gives rise once again to the possibilities of profitable trade. As in the classical labor cost model, the international free-trade price ratio, $\overline{P}_a/\overline{P}_m$, will settle somewhere between $(P_a/P_m)_L$ and $(P_a/P_m)_R$, the domestic price ratios of Less Developed World and Rest of World, respectively. The lines $\overline{P}_a/\overline{P}_m$ in both graphs in Figure 12.1 denote the common world price ratio. For Less Developed World, this steeper slope of $\overline{P}_a/\overline{P}_m$ means that it can get more manufactured goods for a unit of agriculture than in the absence of trade; that is, the world price of agricultural goods in terms of manufactures is higher than Less Developed World's domestic price ratio. It will therefore reallocate resources away from its costly capital-intensive manufacturing sector and specialize more in labor-intensive agricultural production. Under perfectly competitive assumptions, it will produce at point B on its production frontier, where its relative production (opportunity) costs are just equal to relative world prices. It can then trade along $\overline{P}_a/\overline{P}_m$, the prevailing international price line, exporting BD agricultural products in return for DC manufactured imports and arrive at a final consumption point C with more of *both* goods than before trade. To give a numerical example, suppose that the free-trade international price ratio, $\overline{P}_a/\overline{P}_m$, were 2 to 1. In other words, a unit of agricultural goods sells at a price twice that of a unit of manufactured goods. This means that for every unit of agriculture that Less Developed World exports to Rest of World, it can import 2 units of manufactured goods. The slope of the international price line graphically portrays this trading ratio, these terms of trade. If Less Developed World exports BD agriculture (say, 30 units), it will receive DC manufactures (60 units) in return.

Similarly, for Rest of World, the new international price ratio means more agricultural products in exchange for manufactured goods than at domestic prices. Graphically, the international price ratio has a lesser slope than Rest of World's domestic price ratio (see Figure 12.1b). Rest of World will therefore reallocate its abundant capital resources so as to produce more manufactured goods and less agriculture, as at point B', where its relative domestic production costs are just equal to relative world prices. It can then trade $B'D'(=DC)$ of these manufactures for $D'C'(=BD)$ of Less Developed World's agricultural products. Rest of World can therefore also move outside the confines of its production frontier and end up consuming at a point like C' in Figure 12.1b. Trade is balanced—the value of exports equals the value of imports for both regions. Moreover, it has resulted in increased consumption of both goods for both regions, as shown by a comparison between free-trade points C and C' and no-trade points A and A' in Figure 12.1.

The main conclusions of the neoclassical model of free trade are that all countries gain from trade and world output is increased. However, there are several others in addition to these two basic conclusions. First, due to increasing opportunity costs associated with resource shifting among commodities with different factor intensities of production, complete specialization will not occur as in the classical comparative-advantage model. Countries will tend to specialize in products that use their abundant resources intensively. They will compensate for their scarce resources by importing products that use these scarce resources most intensively. But rising domestic costs and therefore prices in excess of world prices will prevent complete specialization from occurring.

Second, given identical technologies of production throughout the world, the equalization of domestic product price ratios with the international free-trade price ratio will tend to **factor price equalization** across trading countries. Wage rates, for example, will rise in labor-abundant Less Developed World as a result of the more intensive use of human resources in the production of additional agricultural output. But the price of scarce capital will decline due to the diminished production of manufactured goods, which are heavy users of capital. In Rest of World, the price of its abundant capital will rise relative to its scarce labor as more emphasis is placed on the production of capital-intensive manufactured goods and less on labor-intensive agriculture.

> **Factor price equalization** In factor endowment trade theory, the proposition that because countries trade at a common international price ratio, factor prices among trading partners will tend to equalize.

The neoclassical factor endowment theory therefore makes the important prediction that international real wage rates and capital costs will gradually tend toward equalization. Much of the direct competition is in the low-skilled labor that developing countries have in relative abundance; many low-skilled manufacturing jobs have indeed been lost outright in developed countries, and wage growth has at best been slow, if not declining, in real terms. In recent years, many highly paid manufacturing workers in the more developed countries have been concerned that freer trade and greater international competition would drive their wages down to developing-country levels. However, on average, with the exception of a few Asian economies, the wage gap between developed and less developed country manufacturing workers has remained persistently wide. This is due in part to higher skills and in part to complementary factors such as the higher general knowledge base embedded within corporations, so wages can remain higher commensurate with the resulting higher productivity.[16] But some part is likely due to protectionism.

Third, within countries, the factor endowment theory predicts that the economic return to owners of the abundant resources will rise in relation to owners of scarce resources as the abundant factor is more intensively used; in developing countries, this would generally mean a rise in the share of national income going to labor. In the absence of trade, labor's share might be smaller. Thus, trade tends to promote more equality in domestic income distributions.

Finally, by enabling countries to move outside their production possibility frontiers and secure capital as well as consumption goods from other parts of the world, trade is assumed to stimulate economic growth. If developed countries have the comparative advantage in producing higher-skill capital goods, trade would lower the price of equipment and machinery and stimulate investment and growth for developing countries. Developing-country exporters learn from their customers in developed countries, who may also alert them to other products they might produce given their mix of skills, as the experience of Taiwan shows. Trade also enables a nation to obtain the domestically expensive raw materials and other products (as well as knowledge, ideas, new technologies, etc.) with which it is relatively less well endowed at lower world market prices. It can thus create the conditions for a more broadly based and self-sustaining growth of its industrial output.

Trade Theory and Development: The Traditional Arguments

We are now in a position to summarize the theoretical answers to our five basic questions about trade and development, derived from the neoclassical free-trade model.

1. Trade is an important stimulator of economic growth. It enlarges a country's consumption capacities, increases world output, and provides access to scarce resources and worldwide markets for products without which developing countries would be unable to grow.

2. Trade tends to promote greater international and domestic equality by equalizing factor prices, raising real incomes of trading countries, and making efficient use of each nation's and the world's resource endowments (e.g., raising relative wages in labor-abundant countries and lowering them in labor-scarce countries).

3. Trade helps countries achieve development by promoting and rewarding the sectors of the economy where individual countries possess a comparative advantage, whether in terms of labor efficiency or factor endowments. It also lets them take advantage of economies of scale.

4. In a world of free trade, international prices and costs of production determine how much a country should trade in order to maximize its national welfare. Countries should follow the principle of comparative advantage and not try to interfere with the free workings of the market through government policies that either promote exports or restrict imports.

5. Finally, to promote growth and development, an outward-looking international policy is required. In all cases, self-reliance based on partial or complete isolation is asserted to be economically inferior to participation in a world of unlimited free trade.

12.4 The Critique of Traditional Free-Trade Theory in the Context of Developing-Country Experience

The conclusions of traditional international trade theory are derived from a number of explicit and implicit assumptions that in many ways are often contrary to the reality of contemporary international economic relations. This is not to deny the potential benefits of a world of free trade but rather to recognize that the real world is beset by national protectionism, international noncompetitive pricing policies, and other market failures.

What are the major and crucial assumptions of the traditional factor endowment theory of trade, and how are these assumptions violated in the real world? What are the implications for the trade and financial prospects of developing nations when a more realistic assessment of the actual mechanism of international economic and political relations is made?

Six basic assumptions of the traditional neoclassical trade model must be scrutinized:

1. All productive resources are fixed in quantity and constant in quality across nations, and are fully employed.

2. The technology of production is fixed (classical model) or similar and freely available to all nations (factor endowment model). Moreover, the spread of such technology works to the benefit of all. Consumer tastes are also fixed and independent of the influence of producers (international consumer sovereignty prevails).

3. Within nations, factors of production are perfectly mobile between different production activities, and the economy as a whole is characterized by the existence of perfect competition. There are no risks or uncertainties.

4. The national government plays no role in international economic relations; trade is carried out among many atomistic and anonymous producers seeking to minimize costs and maximize profits. International prices are therefore set by the forces of supply and demand.

5. Trade is balanced for each country at any point in time, and all economies are readily able to adjust to changes in the international prices with a minimum of dislocation.

6. The gains from trade that accrue to any country benefit the nationals of that country.

We can now take a critical look at each of these assumptions in the context of the contemporary position of developing countries in the international economic system. Some of these criticisms form the rationale for other, non-neoclassical theories of trade and development, including vent-for-surplus, structuralist, and North-South models.

Fixed Resources, Full Employment, and the International Immobility of Capital and Skilled Labor

Trade and Resource Growth: North-South Models of Unequal Trade   This initial assumption about the static nature of international exchange—that resources are fixed, fully utilized, and internationally immobile with product production functions everywhere identical—is central to the traditional theory of trade and finance. In reality, the world economy is characterized by rapid change, and factors of production are fixed neither in quantity nor in quality. Critics point out that this is especially true with respect to resources that are most crucial to growth and development, such as physical capital, entrepreneurial abilities, scientific capacities, the ability to carry out technological research and development, and the upgrading of technical skills in the labor force.

It follows, therefore, that relative factor endowments and comparative costs are not given but are in a state of constant change. Moreover, they are often determined by, rather than themselves determine, the nature and character of international specialization. Any initial state of unequal resource endowments may be reinforced and exacerbated by the very trade that these differing resource endowments were supposed to justify. Specifically, if rich nations (the *North*) as a result of historical forces, are relatively well-endowed with the vital resources of capital, entrepreneurial ability, and skilled labor, their continued specialization in products and processes that use these resources intensively can create the necessary conditions and economic incentives for their further growth. By contrast, developing-world countries (the *South*), endowed with abundant supplies of unskilled labor, by specializing in products that intensively use unskilled labor and for which world demand prospects and terms of trade may be very unfavorable, often find themselves locked into a stagnant situation that perpetuates their comparative advantage in unskilled, unproductive activities. This, in turn, inhibits the domestic growth of needed capital, entrepreneurship, and technical skills. As some developing-country scholars have effectively argued, static efficiency can become dynamic inefficiency, and a cumulative process is set in motion in which trade exacerbates already unequal trading relationships, distributes the benefits largely to the people who are already relatively well off, and perpetuates the physical and human resource underdevelopment that characterizes most low-income nations. As one well-known developing-country scholar put it, "With few exceptions, the technological distance between the developing and the developed countries is widening. Neoclassical international trade theory, by postulating identical production functions for different products in various countries, assumes this problem away."[17]

In recent years, some economists have therefore challenged the static neoclassical model with alternative dynamic models of trade and growth that emphasize the process of factor accumulation and uneven development along the lines suggested in the preceding paragraphs. These so-called **North-South trade models** focus specifically on trade relations between rich and poor countries, whereas the traditional model was assumed to apply to all nations. The typical North-South model argues, for example, that initial higher endowments of capital in the industrialized North generate external economies in manufacturing output and higher profit rates. This, in combination with the rise in monopoly power, stimulates higher Northern growth rates (in accordance with Harrod-Domar and factor share growth models discussed earlier) through further capital accumulation. As a result, the rapidly growing North develops a cumulative competitive advantage over the slower-growing South. If we then add differential income elasticities of demand (higher for Northern "capital goods" than for Southern "consumption goods") and capital mobility to the model (in the form of South-to-North capital flight, as occurred in the 1980s), the basis for the developing-world trade pessimism would be further enhanced. Nobel laureate Paul Krugman and other modern trade theorists have also introduced models incorporating imperfect competition and other more realistic features.[18]

Some economies, like the Four Asian Tigers (Taiwan, South Korea, Singapore, and Hong Kong), have succeeded in transforming their economies through

North-South trade models Trade and development theories that focus on the unequal exchange between the North developed countries and the South developing countries in an attempt to explain why the South gains less from trade than the North.

purposeful effort from unskilled-labor to skilled-labor to capital-intensive production. Other Asian countries, notably China, are following in their footsteps. However, for the vast majority of low-income nations, the possibility of trade itself stimulating similar structural economic changes is more remote without the application of judicious development policies.

Another interesting example of the new, postneoclassical genre of international trade models is contained in Michael Porter's *Competitive Advantage of Nations*.[19] Porter's fundamental departure from the standard, neoclassical factor endowment theory is to posit a *qualitative* difference between basic factors and advanced factors of production. He argues that standard trade theory applies only to basic factors like undeveloped physical resources and unskilled labor. For the advanced factors, which are more specialized and include highly trained workers with specific skills, and knowledge resources such as government and private research institutes, major universities, and leading industry associations, standard theory does not apply. Porter argues that "the central task facing developing countries is to escape from the straitjacket of factor-driven national advantage…where natural resources, cheap labor, locational factors and other basic factor advantages provide a fragile and often fleeting ability to export." He concludes that "creation of advanced factors is perhaps the first priority."[20]

Unemployment, Resource Underutilization, and the Vent-for-Surplus Theory of International Trade

The assumption of full employment in traditional trade models, like that of the standard perfectly competitive equilibrium model of microeconomic theory, violates the reality of unemployment and underemployment in developing nations. Two conclusions could be drawn from the recognition of widespread unemployment in the developing world. The first is that underutilized human resources create the opportunity to expand productive capacity and GNI at little or no real cost by producing for export markets products that are not demanded locally. This is known as the **vent-for-surplus theory of international trade**. First formulated by Adam Smith, it was expounded in the context of developing nations by the Burmese economist Hla Myint.

According to this theory, the opening of world markets to remote agrarian societies creates opportunities not to reallocate fully employed resources as in the traditional models but rather to make use of formerly *underemployed* land and labor resources to produce greater output for export to foreign markets. The colonial system of plantation agriculture, as well as the commercialization of small-scale subsistence agriculture, were made possible, according to this view, by the availability of unemployed and underemployed human resources. In terms of our production possibility analyses, the vent-for-surplus argument can be represented by a shift in production from point *V* to point *B* in Figure 12.2, with trade enlarging final domestic consumption from *V* to *C*.

We see that before trade, the resources of this closed developing-world economy were underutilized. Production was occurring at point *V*, well within the confines of the production possibility frontier, and 0*X* primary products and 0*Y* manufactures were being produced and consumed. The opening up of the nation to foreign markets (probably as a result of colonization) provides the economic impetus to utilize these idle resources (mostly excess land and

Vent-for-surplus theory of international trade The contention that opening world markets to developing countries through international trade allows those countries to make better use of formerly underutilized land and labor resources so as to produce larger primary-product outputs, the surpluses of which can be exported.

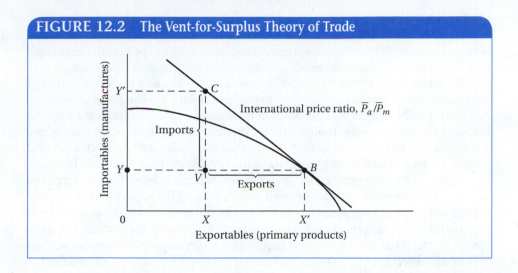

FIGURE 12.2 The Vent-for-Surplus Theory of Trade

labor) and expand primary-product exportable production from $0X$ to $0X'$ at point B on the production frontier. Given the international price ratio, $\overline{P}_a/\overline{P}_m$, $X' - X$ (equal to VB) primary products can now be exported in exchange for $Y' - Y$ (equal to VC) manufactures, with the result that the final consumption point, C, is attained with the same primary products (X) being consumed as before but with $Y' - Y$ more imported manufactures now available.

Unfortunately, in the short run, the beneficiaries of this process were often colonial and expatriate entrepreneurs rather than developing-country nationals. And, in the long run, the structural orientation of the developing-country economy toward primary-product exports in many cases created an export "enclave" and inhibited needed structural transformation in the direction of a more diversified economy.

Fixed, Freely Available Technology and Consumer Sovereignty

Just as capital resources are rapidly growing and being dispersed to maximize the returns of their owners throughout the world, rapid technological change is profoundly affecting world trading relationships. One of the most obvious examples of the impact of developed-country technological change on developing-country export earnings is the development of synthetic substitutes for many traditional primary products. Since World War II, **synthetic substitutes** for such diverse commodities as rubber, wool, cotton, sisal, jute, hides, and skins have been manufactured in increasing quantities. The developing world's market shares of these sectors have fallen steadily.

On the other side of the ledger, however, is the argument that the worldwide availability of new technologies developed in the West has given many newly industrializing countries the opportunity to capitalize on Western research and development expenditures. By first imitating products developed abroad but not on the frontiers of technological research, certain middle-income countries with sufficient human capital (e.g., the Asian NICs) can follow the **product cycle** of international trade. Using their relatively lower

Synthetic substitutes Commodities that are artificially produced but can be substituted for the natural commodities (e.g., manufactured rubber, cotton, wool, camphor, and pyrethrum).

Product cycle In international trade, the progressive replacement of more developed countries by less developed countries in the production of manufactures of increasing complexity.

wages, they move from low-tech to high-tech production, filling manufacturing gaps left vacant by the more industrialized nations. Eventually, the hope is to catch up with the developed countries, as in the case of Japan, Singapore, and South Korea. China has made striking progress through this strategy.

The assumption of fixed worldwide consumer tastes and preferences dictating production patterns to market-responsive atomistic producers is unrealistic. Not only are the capital and production technologies disseminated throughout the world by means of the multinational corporations often aided by their home governments, but also consumer preferences and tastes are often created and reinforced by the advertising campaigns that dominate local markets. By creating demands for imported goods, market-dominating international enterprises can create the conditions for increased profitability. This is particularly significant in developing countries, where limited and imperfect information in both production and consumption creates a situation of highly incomplete markets. For example, it has been estimated that in many developing nations, more than 90% of all advertising is financed by foreign firms selling in the local market.

Internal Factor Mobility, Perfect Competition, and Uncertainty: Increasing Returns, Imperfect Competition and Issues in Specialization

The traditional theory of trade assumes that nations are readily able to adjust their economic structures to the changing dictates of world prices and markets. Movements along production possibility frontiers involving the reallocation of resources from one industry to another may be easy to make on paper, but according to structuralist arguments, such reallocations are extremely difficult to achieve in practice. This is especially true in developing nations, where production structures are often rigid and factor movements are largely restricted. The most obvious example of this is plantation and small-farm commercial agriculture. In economies that have gradually become heavily dependent on a few primary-product exports, the whole economic and social infrastructure (roads, railways, communications, power locations, credit and marketing arrangements, etc.) may be geared to facilitate the movement of goods from production locations to shipping and storage depots for transfer to foreign markets. Over time, cumulative investments of capital may have been sunk into these economic and infrastructure facilities, and they cannot easily be transferred to manufacturing activities located elsewhere. Thus, the more dependent nations become on a few primary-product exports, the more inflexible their economic structures become, and the more vulnerable they are to the unpredictabilities of international markets. It may take many years to transform an underdeveloped economy from an almost exclusively primary-product, export-oriented reliance to a more diversified, multisector structure. More generally, structuralist critics argue that all kinds of politically and institutionally generated structural rigidities, including product supply inelasticities, lack of intermediate products, fragmented money markets, limited foreign exchange, government licensing, import controls, poor transport and distribution facilities, and scarcities of managerial and skilled labor, often inhibit a developing country's ability to respond to changing international price signals in the smooth and frictionless way of the neoclassical trade model.[21]

Thus, the internal processes of adjustment and resource reallocation that are necessary to capitalize on changing world economic conditions are much more difficult for the less diversified developing economies to realize than for their rich counterparts in the North. And yet, curiously enough, developing countries that begin to expand their capacities to produce low-cost, labor-intensive manufactured goods for export in industries such as textiles, shoes, sporting goods, handbags, processed foodstuffs, wigs, and rugs have often found these exports blocked by tariff and nontariff barriers erected by developed countries to restrict the entry of such low-cost goods into their home markets.[22] The reasons usually given by the North are that this low-cost foreign competition will create unemployment among the higher-cost domestic industries of the developed country and that the problems of internal economic adjustment are too serious to permit such unfettered foreign competition! And while notable improvements have been made through the WTO and bilateral offers (discussed later in the chapter), protectionism in various forms remains a serious impediment to growth in the developing world, especially for the least developed countries.

Moreover, by assuming either fixed or diminishing **returns to scale** (fixed or increasing production costs as output is expanded), the labor cost and factor endowment theories of trade neglect one of the most important phenomena in international economic relations. This is the pervasive and income-widening effect of increasing returns to scale and hence decreasing costs of production. Decreasing production costs mean simply that large existing firms are able to underprice smaller or new firms and thus exert monopolistic control over world markets. Far from being a rare exception, economies of scale are a common factor in determining trade patterns. Economies of large-scale production lead to monopolistic and oligopolistic control of world supply conditions (just as they do in domestic markets) for a wide range of products.

In addition, **monopolistic** and **oligopolistic market control** of internationally traded commodities, along with widespread product differentiation, intraindustry trade, and external economies of production, means that large individual corporations are able to manipulate world prices and supplies (and often demands as well) in their own private interest. Instead of competition, we find joint producer activities and oligopolistic bargaining among giant buyers and sellers as the most pervasive price- and quantity-determining force in the international economy.[23] But from the perspective of developing nations trying to diversify their economies and promote industrial exports in particular, the phenomenon of **increasing returns** and **product differentiation** (monopolistic competition), combined with the noneconomic power of large multinational corporations (their political influence with many governments—see Chapter 14), means that the first nations to industrialize (the rich nations) are often able to take advantage of these economies of scale and differentiated products to perpetuate their dominant position in world markets.[24]

The second major limitation of the perfectly competitive assumption of trade models is its exclusion of **risk** and **uncertainty** in international trading arrangements. It may not be in a low-income country's long-run interest to invest heavily in primary-product export promotion, given the historical instability of world markets for primary commodities in comparison with those for manufactured goods. As was already pointed out, concentration on one

Returns to scale How much output expands when all inputs are proportionately increased.

Monopolistic market control A situation in which the output of an industry is controlled by a single producer (or seller) or by a group of producers who make joint decisions.

Oligopolistic market control A situation in which a small number of rival but not necessarily competing firms dominate an industry.

Increasing returns A disproportionate increase in output that results from a change in the scale of production.

Product differentiation Attempts by producers to distinguish their product from similar ones through advertising or minor design changes.

Risk A situation in which the probabilities of the various possible outcomes are known, but the actual outcome is not known.

Uncertainty A situation in which neither the actual outcome nor even the precise probabilities of the various possible outcomes are known.

or two vital primary exports can play havoc with development plans when foreign-exchange earnings are largely unpredictable from one year to the next.

Patterns of specialization in the process of economic development are still not fully understood, and theory gives ambiguous answers. On the one hand, traditional theory suggests that developing nations can reach higher levels of income by specializing in the world economy according to comparative advantage and that as globalization proceeds, the opportunity and benefits of doing so increase. On the other hand, as countries develop, they gain a wider range of skills and technologies and can move beyond producing a few primary goods to become competitive in a range of relatively advanced goods. In fact, a careful empirical study by Jean Imbs and Romain Wacziarg found that sectoral concentration generally follows a U-shaped pattern in relation to the level of per capita income: "Countries first diversify, in the sense that economic activity is spread more equally across sectors, but there exists, relatively late in the development process, a point at which they start specializing again."[25] And this pattern goes well beyond the tendency to move from dependence on primary goods alone to manufacturing and services. The policy implications also remain ambiguous. But their results are consistent with the view that development is not driven by a simple process of gains from specialization.

The Absence of National Governments in Trading Relations

In domestic economies, the coexistence of rich and poor regions, of rapidly growing and stagnating industries, and of the persistent disproportionate regional distribution of the benefits of economic growth can all, at least in theory, be counteracted and ameliorated by the intervention of the state. Cumulative processes for inequality within nation-states by which **growth poles** may expand rapidly while other regions stagnate can be modified by government through legislation, taxes, transfer payments, subsidies, social services, regional development programs, and so forth. But since there is no effective international government to play a comparable role across countries, the highly uneven gains from trade can easily become self-sustaining. This result is then reinforced by the uneven power of national governments to promote and protect their own interests. Despite the advice to developing countries, the developed countries protect their own favored industries when they find it advantageous or politically expedient, as in the U.S. bailout of the auto industry in 2009, to name just one high-profile case. The protection of the financial industry in the United States and the United Kingdom protect not just the domestic financial system but an industry that generates high-paying jobs.

Government has also played a strong role in cases of successful rapid developments. Spectacular export successes such as South Korea were in no small way aided and abetted by government promotion of export industries. (See the case studies in Chapters 4, 12, and 13, respectively.) Governments are often partisan players whose activist interventions in this area of **industrial policy** (guiding the market through strategic coordination of business investments to increase export market shares) are specifically designed to create a comparative advantage where none existed before but where world demand is likely to rise in the future. The history of industrial growth in Japan in the 1950s and 1960s with its famous Ministry of International Trade and Industry (MITI) is a

Growth poles Regions that are more economically and socially advanced than others around them, such as urban centers versus rural areas or highway corridors in developing countries.

Industrial policy Deliberate effort by governments to guide the market by coordinating and supporting specific industrial activities.

widely cited example of industrial policy.[26] Yet, for various reasons, a majority of developing countries outside of East Asia have either not attempted, or have tried but failed to achieve, the potential advantages of applying this approach systematically. This approach to industrialization strategy as widely practiced in East Asia is examined later in this chapter.

Governments may also employ various instruments of commercial policy, such as **tariffs**, import **quotas**, and export **subsidies**, and can manipulate commodity prices and thus their trade position vis-à-vis the rest of the world. Moreover, when developed-nation governments pursue restrictive economic policies that are designed to deal with purely domestic issues like inflation or unemployment, these policies can have profound negative effects on the economies of developing nations. The reverse, however, is not true. Developing nations' domestic economic policies generally have little impact on the economies of rich nations.

Governments often serve to reinforce the unequal distribution of resources and **gains from trade** resulting from differences in size and economic power. Rich-country governments can influence world economic affairs by their domestic and international policies, shaped by their often common interests. Despite the growing role of the World Trade Organization, there is no superagency or world government to protect and promote the interests of the weaker parties—especially the least developed countries—in such international affairs. A trade and industrialization strategy must therefore take into account the powerful governmental forces of the developed world.

Balanced Trade and International Price Adjustments

The theory of international trade, like other perfectly competitive general-equilibrium models in economics, is not only a full-employment model but also one in which flexible domestic and international product and resource prices always adjust instantaneously to conditions of supply and demand. In particular, the terms of trade (international commodity price ratios) adjust to equate supply and demand for a country's exportable and importable products so that trade is always balanced; that is, the value of exports (quantity times price) is always equal to the value of imports. With **balanced trade** and no international capital movements, balance of payments problems never arise in the pure theory of trade. But in some periods, as seen following the rapid increase in international oil prices in the 1970s, balance of payments deficits and the consequent depletion of foreign reserves (or the need to borrow foreign funds to cover commodity deficits) become a major cause of concern for all nations, rich and poor.

Trade Gains Accruing to Nationals

The sixth and final major assumption of traditional trade theory, that trade gains accrue to nationals in the trading countries, is more implicit than the other five. It is rarely spelled out, nor need it be if we accept the assumption that factors are internationally immobile. But we need to examine the implicit notion that if developing countries benefit from trade, it is the people of these countries who reap the benefits. The issue thus revolves around the question of who owns the land, capital, and skills that are rewarded as a result of trade. Are they nationals or foreigners? If both, in what proportions are the gains distributed?

Tariff A fixed-percentage tax on the value of an imported commodity levied at the point of entry into the importing country.

Quota In international trade, a physical limitation on the quantity of any item that can be imported into a country.

Subsidy A payment by the government to producers or distributors in an industry for such purposes as preventing the decline of that industry, expanding employment, increasing exports, or reducing selected prices paid by consumers.

Gains from trade The increase in output and consumption resulting from specialization in production and free trade with other economic units, including persons, regions, or countries.

Balanced trade A situation in which the value of a country's exports and the value of its imports are equal.

Enclave economies Small, economically developed regions in developing countries in which the remaining areas have experienced much less progress.

In some **enclave economies** in developing countries, such as those with substantial foreign-owned mining and plantation operations, foreigners often pay very low rents for the rights to use land, bring in their own foreign capital and skilled labor, hire local unskilled workers at subsistence wages, and have a minimal effect on the rest of the economy, even though they may generate significant export revenues. Much depends on the bargaining power of multinational corporations and developing-country governments. There are still some foreign-owned mining and plantation enclaves and many "manufacturing export enclaves" (personal computer assembly, shoe and toy manufacture, etc.) with few linkages to the wider economy, run by or for multinational corporations. The distinction, therefore, between gross domestic product (GDP), which is a measure of the value of output generated within defined geographic boundaries, and gross national income (GNI), which measures the income actually earned by nationals of that country, becomes extremely important. As the 2009 Stiglitz-Sen-Fitoussi ("Sarkozy") Commission on the Measurement of Economic Performance and Social Progress put it, "GDP is the most widely used measure of economic activity....However, it has often been treated as if it were a measure of economic well-being....production can expand while income decreases or vice versa when account is taken of...income flows into and out of a country."[27] To the extent that the export sector, or, for that matter, any sector of the economy, is foreign owned and operated, GDP will be that much higher than GNI, and fewer of the benefits of trade will actually accrue to nationals of developing countries.

With the proliferation of multinational corporations and increasing foreign ownership of companies in a wide range of countries, aggregate statistics for developing-country export earnings (and, indeed, GDP) may mask the fact that a country's own citizens, especially those in lower income brackets, may not benefit from these exports. The major gains from trade may instead accrue to nonnationals, who often repatriate large proportions of these earnings. The inter- and intraindustry trade that is being carried out may look like trade between rich and poor nations. But, in reality, such trade may be conducted between rich nations and *other nationals of rich nations* operating in developing countries! Manufactures exports are generally more effective at generating modern-sector enlargement, but some export enclave manufacturing activities in developing countries may merely be masking the fact that a large proportion of the benefits are still being reaped by foreign enterprises. In short, a developing country's export performance can be deceptive unless we analyze the character and structure of export earnings by ascertaining who owns or controls the factors of production that are rewarded as a result of export expansion.

Some Conclusions on Trade Theory and Economic Development Strategy

We can now attempt to provide some preliminary general answers to the five questions posed early in the chapter. We must stress that our conclusions are general and set in the context of the diversity of developing countries.

First, with regard to the rate, structure, and character of economic growth, our conclusion is that trade can be an important stimulus to rapid economic growth. This has been amply demonstrated by the successful experiences over the past half century of countries like China, Malaysia, Thailand, Brazil,

Chile, Taiwan, Singapore, and South Korea. Access to the markets of developed nations (an important factor for developing nations bent on export promotion) can provide an important stimulus for the greater utilization of idle human and capital resources. Expanded **foreign-exchange earnings** through improved export performance also provide the wherewithal by which a developing country can augment its scarce physical and financial resources. In short, where opportunities for profitable exchange arise, foreign trade can provide an important stimulus to aggregate economic growth.[28]

Foreign-exchange earnings The sum total of all foreign currency receipts less expenditures during a given fiscal year.

But, as noted in earlier chapters, growth of national output may have little impact on development. An export-oriented strategy of growth, particularly in commodities with few linkages and when a large proportion of export earnings accrue to foreigners, may not only bias the structure of the economy in the wrong directions (by not catering to the real needs of local people) but also reinforce the internal and external dualistic and inegalitarian character of that growth. It all depends on the nature of the export sector, the distribution of its benefits, and its linkages with the rest of the economy and how these evolve over time.

Factors such as the widespread existence of increasing returns, the highly unequal international distribution of economic assets and power, the influence of large multinational corporations, and the combined ability of both governments and businesses to manipulate international prices, levels of production, and patterns of demand are crucial. Together, they lead us to the general conclusion that many developing countries have in the past benefited disproportionately less from their economic dealings with developed nations.

It should be apparent by now that the answer to the third question—the conditions under which trade can help a developing country achieve development aspirations—is to be found largely in the ability of developing nations— for example, as a caucus within WTO negotiations or G20 forums to extract and maintain favorable trade concessions from the developed nations. As we will address shortly, progress through the World Trade Organization and its predecessor, along with bilateral programs, such as the U.S. Africa Growth and Opportunity Act (AGOA) and the European Everything but Arms (EBA) initiative, provided a helpful but still very incomplete start. Also, the extent to which exports can efficiently utilize scarce capital resources while making maximum use of abundant but presently underutilized labor supplies will determine the degree to which export earnings benefit the ordinary citizen in developing countries. Again, links between export earnings and other sectors of the economy are crucial. Finally, much will depend on how well a developing nation can influence and control the activities of private foreign enterprises. The ability to deal effectively with multinational corporations in guaranteeing a fair share of the benefits to local citizens is extremely important. These issues are further examined later in this chapter and in Chapter 14.

The answer to the fourth question—whether developing countries can determine how much they trade—can only be speculative. For small and poor countries, the option of not trading at all, by closing their borders to the rest of the world, is obviously not realistic. Not only do they lack the resources and market size to be self-sufficient, but also their very survival, especially in the area of food production, often depends on their ability to secure foreign goods and resources. Some 32 of the least developed countries face annual threats of severe famine for which international assistance is not a choice but a necessity.

Whether to trade or to remain in isolation is not the issue; the real issue turns out to be the balance between selling for the domestic market and exporting and, if the latter is chosen, whether to encourage exporting across the board or to promote targeted sectors.[29]

Moreover, for most developing nations, the international economic system still offers the only real source of scarce capital and needed technological knowledge. The conditions under which such resources are obtained will greatly influence the character of the development process. Finally, for countries rich in mineral resources and raw materials, especially those that have been able to establish an effective international bargaining stance against the large corporations that purchase their exports (e.g., the members of OPEC), trade has been and continues to be a vital source of development finance.

The fifth question—whether on balance it is better for developing countries to look outward toward the rest of the world or more inward toward their own capacities for development—turns out not to be an either-or question at all.[30] While exploring profitable opportunities for trade with the rest of the world, developing countries can effectively seek ways to expand their share of world trade *and* extend their economic ties with one another. For example, by pooling their resources, small countries can overcome the limits of their small individual markets and their serious resource constraints while retaining an important degree of autonomy in pursuing their individual development aspirations. In this way, groups of small countries may have a better chance of achieving what China has been able to do in recent years: leveraging the bargaining power of its large market to insist on the best deal from potential foreign exporters and investors. Indeed, this strategy has likely been one of the factors helping China realize very high growth rates in recent decades. Benefits are still to be had from further expansion of trade among developing countries themselves.

Although the preceding argument is often overstated, it seems clear that if interregional political rivalries can be transcended, increased regional cooperation among developing nations offers an important component of a trade and industrialization strategy. Explicit developing-country policies, including free-trade areas such as the Association of Southeast Asian Nations (ASEAN) in Southeast Asia and Mercosur in South America, are at least partly responsible for this trend. Of course, the trend also reflects the development successes in Asia, many of whose economies have been growing faster than those in North America and Europe in recent years. Renewed efforts are being made in Africa, through the African Union and the New Partnership for Africa's Development (NEPAD) peer review program, but there is a long way to go.

We turn now to consider the advantages and disadvantages of alternative trade policies for developing countries in more detail.

12.5 Traditional Trade Strategies and Policy Mechanisms for Development: Export Promotion versus Import Substitution

A traditional way to approach the complex issues of appropriate trade policies for development is to set these specific policies in the context of a broader strategy of looking outward or looking inward.[31] In the words of Paul Streeten, **outward-looking development policies** "encourage not only free trade but also the free movement of capital, workers, enterprises and students..., the multinational enterprise, and an open system of communications." By contrast, **inward-looking development policies** stress the need for nations to evolve their own styles of development and to control their own destiny. This means setting policies to encourage indigenous "learning by doing" in manufacturing and developing technologies appropriate to a country's resource endowments. According to proponents of inward-looking trade policies, greater self-reliance can be accomplished, in Streeten's words, only if "you restrict trade, the movement of people, and communications and if you keep out the multinational enterprise, with its wrong products and wrong want-stimulation and hence its wrong technology."[32]

A lively debate regarding these two philosophical approaches has been carried on in the development literature since the 1950s. The debate pits the free traders, who advocate outward-looking export promotion strategies of industrialization, against the protectionists, who are proponents of inward-looking import substitution strategies. The latter predominated into the 1970s; the former gained the upper hand, especially among Western and World Bank economists, in the 1980s and early 1990s.

Basically, the distinction between these two traditional, trade-related development strategies is that advocates of **import substitution** (IS) believe that a developing economy should initially substitute domestic production of previously imported simple consumer goods (first-stage IS) and then substitute through domestic production for a wider range of more sophisticated manufactured items (second-stage IS)—all behind the protection of high tariffs and quotas on these imports. In the long run, IS advocates cite the benefits of greater domestic industrial diversification ("balanced growth") and the ultimate ability to export some previously protected manufactured goods as economies of scale, low labor costs, and the positive externalities of learning by doing cause domestic prices to become more competitive with world prices.

By contrast, advocates of **export promotion** (EP) of both primary and manufactured goods cite the efficiency and growth benefits of free trade and competition, the importance of substituting large world markets for narrow domestic markets, the distorting price and cost effects of protection, and the tremendous successes of such export-oriented economies as South Korea, Taiwan, Singapore, Hong Kong, China, and others in Asia. They stress that firms in these economies have learned a great deal from the firms in the United States, Japan, and other developed-country economies that have been their long-term customers. Sometimes a distinction is made between "strong export promotion," in which policies are explicitly geared to expansion of exports (in general, such as through a weak currency), rather than production for the domestic market, and "weak export promotion," which emphasizes free trade and a level playing field and is viewed by advocates as likely to promote exports by comparison with previous import substitution policies (which tend to discourage exports in relative terms). Beyond this, many Asian countries also have adopted a more nuanced approach that draws on some elements of both to develop targeted sectors, which will be examined later in the chapter.

Outward-looking development policies Policies that encourage exports, often through the free movement of capital, workers, enterprises, and students; a welcome to multinational corporations; and open communications.

Inward-looking development policies Policies that stress economic self-reliance on the part of developing countries, including domestic development of technology, the imposition of barriers to imports, and the discouragement of private foreign investment.

Import substitution A deliberate effort to replace consumer imports by promoting the emergence and expansion of domestic industries.

Export promotion Governmental efforts to expand the volume of a country's exports through increasing export incentives, decreasing disincentives, and other means in order to generate more foreign exchange and improve the current account of its balance of payments or achieve other objectives.

In practice, the distinction between IS and EP strategies is much less pronounced than many advocates would imply. Most developing economies have employed both strategies with different degrees of emphasis at one time or another. For example, in the 1950s and 1960s, the inward-looking industrialization strategies of the larger Latin American and Asian countries such as Chile, Peru, Argentina, India, Pakistan, and the Philippines were heavily IS-oriented. By the end of the 1960s, some of the key sub-Saharan African countries like Nigeria, Ethiopia, Ghana, and Zambia had begun to pursue IS strategies, and some smaller Latin American and Asian countries also joined in.[33] However, since the mid-1970s, the EP strategy has been increasingly adopted by a growing number of countries. The early EP adherents—South Korea, Taiwan, Singapore, and Hong Kong—were thus joined by the likes of Brazil, Chile, Thailand, and Turkey, which switched from an earlier IS strategy. It must be stressed, however, that most successful East Asian export promoters have pursued protectionist IS strategies sequentially and simultaneously in certain industries, so it is inaccurate to call them free traders, even though they are outward-oriented.[34]

Against this background, we can now examine the issue of outward-looking export promotion versus inward-looking import substitution in more detail by applying the following fourfold categorization:

1. Primary outward-looking policies (encouragement of agricultural and raw-materials exports)

2. Secondary outward-looking policies (promotion of manufactured exports)

3. Primary inward-looking policies (mainly agricultural self-sufficiency)

4. Secondary inward-looking policies (manufactured commodity self-sufficiency through import substitution)

Then we turn our attention to eclectic strategies, particularly export-oriented strategic industrialization, and South-South economic integration.

Export Promotion: Looking Outward and Seeing Trade Barriers

The promotion of primary or secondary exports has long been considered a major ingredient in any viable long-run development strategy. The colonial territories of Africa and Asia, with their foreign-owned mines and plantations, were classic examples of primary outward-looking regions. It was partly in reaction to this enclave economic structure and partly as a consequence of the industrialization bias of the 1950s and 1960s that most developing countries put great emphasis on the production of manufactured goods initially for the home market (secondary inward) and then for export (secondary outward).

Primary-Commodity Export Expansion: Limited Demand   As noted earlier in this chapter, many low-income countries still rely on primary products for a majority of their export earnings. With the notable exception of petroleum exports and a few needed minerals, primary-product exports have grown more slowly than total world trade.

On the demand side, there appear to be at least five factors working against the rapid expansion of primary-product and especially agricultural exports. First, the income elasticities of demand for agricultural foodstuffs and raw materials are relatively low compared with those for fuels, certain minerals, and manufactures. For example, the income elasticities of demand for sugar, cacao, tea, coffee, and bananas have all been estimated at less than 1, with most in the range of 0.3–0.6. Inelastic demand means that only a sustained high rate of per capita income growth in the developed countries can lead to even modest export expansion of these particular commodities from the developing countries. (Many primary exporters have benefited from the boom in China since about 2002—excepting the 2008–2009 debacle—and this will be followed carefully.)

Second, developed-country population growth rates are now at or near the replacement level, so little expansion can be expected from this source. Third, the price elasticity of demand for most primary commodities is relatively low. When relative agricultural prices are falling, as they have been during most of the past five decades, such low elasticities mean less total revenue for exporting nations.

With the exception of oil and a few minor commodities, **international commodity agreements** have not fared well. Such agreements are intended to set overall output levels, stabilize world prices, and assign quota shares to various producing nations for such items as coffee, tea, copper, lead, and sugar. To work effectively, they require cooperation and compromise among participants. Commodity agreements can also provide greater protection to individual exporting nations against excessive competition and the overexpansion of world production. Such overexpansion of supply tends to drive down prices and curtail the growth of earnings for all countries. In short, commodity agreements attempt to guarantee participating nations a relatively fixed share of world export earnings and a more stable world price for their commodity. But proposals by the United Nations Conference on Trade and Development (UNCTAD) for the establishment of a common fund to finance "buffer stocks" to support the prices of some 19 primary commodities (including sugar, coffee, tea, bauxite, jute, cotton, tin, and vegetable oil) produced by various developing nations have made little progress. Most existing non-oil commodity agreements have either failed (tin) or been largely ignored by producers (coffee, sugar). Even in the best scenarios, such agreements cannot be effective for perishable commodities. Imagine trying to operate a buffer stock of bananas!

The fourth and fifth factors working against the long-run expansion of primary-product export earnings—the development of synthetic substitutes and the growth of agricultural protection in the developed countries—are perhaps the most important. Synthetic substitutes for commodities like cotton, rubber, sisal, jute, hide, skins, and copper (replaced by glass fiber optics for communication networks) act both as a brake against higher commodity prices and as a direct source of competition in world export markets. The synthetic share of world market export earnings has generally risen over time, while the share of natural products has fallen. In the case of agricultural protection, which usually takes the form of tariffs, quotas, and, increasingly, nontariff barriers such as sometimes arbitrary sanitary laws regulating food and fiber imports, or

International commodity agreement   A formal agreement by sellers of a common internationally traded commodity (e.g., coffee, sugar) to coordinate supply to maintain price stability.

cryptic rules of origin, the effects can be devastating to developing countries' export earnings. Such nontariff barriers can all but negate the otherwise promising moves by rich countries to nearly abolish conventional exports for most developing-country exports. The common agricultural policy of the European Union (EU), for example, has resulted in greater subsidies that have harmed the competitiveness of developing countries.

On the supply side, a number of factors also work against the rapid expansion of primary-product export earnings. The most important is the structural rigidity of many rural production systems in developing countries. We discussed rigidities—such as limited resources; poor climate; bad soils; antiquated rural institutional, social, and economic structures; and nonproductive patterns of land tenure—in Chapter 9. Whatever the international demand situation for particular commodities (which will differ from commodity to commodity), little export expansion can be expected when rural economic and social structures militate against positive supply responses from peasant farmers who are averse to risk. Furthermore, in developing nations with markedly dualistic farming structures (i.e., large, corporate capital-intensive farms existing side by side with thousands of fragmented, low-productivity peasant holdings), any growth in export earnings is likely to be distributed very unevenly among the rural population. Small farmers have been further disadvantaged in countries (mostly in Africa) in which agricultural marketing boards act as middlemen between the farmers and export markets. These boards—or at least their practices of significantly suppressing prices that farmers can receive—have been largely dismantled in recent years.

Primary export growth has remained modest, partly due to the pernicious effects of developed-country trade policies (such as the United States' sugar and cotton subsidies) and foreign-aid policies that depress agricultural prices in the least developed countries and discourage production. For example, the EU's policy of selling subsidized beef to the nations of West Africa in the guise of foreign assistance has devastated cattle prices in those countries. As summarized by Kevin Watkins and Joachim von Braun of the International Food Policy Research Institute:

> Small farmers in developing countries suffer on several counts from rich-country farm policies. Northern production subsidies lower prices for farm produce. Unable to compete against subsidized competition, the world's poorest farmers are often pushed out of international and even domestic markets. The upshot is an agricultural trading system in which success depends less on comparative advantage than on comparative access to subsidies. Small farmers are efficient, innovative, and potentially competitive, and creatively combine farming with off-farm work. But the world's poorest farmers cannot compete against the world's richest treasuries, nor should they have to.[35]

We may conclude, therefore, that the successful promotion of primary-product exports in low-income countries and for the benefit of the poor cannot occur unless there is a reorganization of rural social and economic structures along the lines suggested in Chapter 9 to raise total agricultural productivity and distribute the benefits more widely. The primary objective of any rural development strategy is widely accepted to be *first* to provide sufficient food to feed local people and only then to be concerned about export expansion. Given the structure of world demands for primary products, the threat of local food shortages and thus the desire of potential importers to focus on agricultural self-sufficiency, the inevitability of the development of further synthetic substitutes, and the (tragic) unlikelihood of significantly lower levels of agricultural protection among developed nations in light of the stalled trade talks, the real scope for primary-product export expansion in individual developing nations seems limited.[36]

Expanding Exports of Manufactured Goods

The expansion of manufactured exports has been encouraged by the spectacular export performances of countries like South Korea, Singapore, Hong Kong, Taiwan, and China. For example, for decades, Taiwan's total exports grew at an annual rate of over 20%, and exports from South Korea grew even faster. In both cases, this export growth was led by manufactured goods, which contributed over 80% of both nations' foreign-exchange earnings. For the developing world as a whole, manufactured exports grew from 6% of their total merchandise exports in 1950 to almost 64% by 2000. Taken together, by 2011, the low- and middle-income countries accounted for about 29% of the world's manufactured exports; China commanded a fast-growing share. However, the low-income countries accounted for just under 1% of the world total.[37]

The export successes of recent decades, especially among the Asian Tigers, have provided impetus for arguments by market fundamentalists (see Chapter 3) that economic growth is best served by allowing market forces, free enterprise, and open economies to prevail while minimizing government intervention. However, evidence from East Asia does not support this view of how export success was achieved. In South Korea, Taiwan, and Singapore (as in Japan earlier and to a large degree China more recently), the production and composition of exports was not left to the market but resulted from planned intervention by the government while making ample use of the profit incentive.[38] We return to this consideration later in the chapter.

The demand problems for export expansion of many manufactured goods, though different in basic economic content from those for primary products, can still pose similar problems for developing countries. For many years, there was widespread protection in developed nations against the manufactured exports of developing countries, which was in part the direct result of the successful penetration of low-cost, labor-intensive manufactures from countries like Taiwan, Hong Kong, and South Korea during the 1960s and 1970s. And as noted earlier, relative prices of the most basic manufactured goods have also fallen.

Industrial-nation trade barriers have been extensive. During the 1980s, for example, 20 of the 24 industrialized countries *increased* their protection against developing countries' manufactured or processed products. Moreover, their rates of protection were considerably higher against developing-country exports than against those of high-income countries. Then there are the nontariff barriers, which came to form the main protection against manufactured exports from developing countries, affecting at least one-third of them. A major example was the **Multifiber Arrangement (MFA)**, in effect until 2005, a complex system of mostly bilateral quotas against exports of cotton, wool, and synthetic fiber products. The United Nations Development Programme

Multifiber Arrangement (MFA) A set of nontariff quotas established by developed countries on imports of cotton, wool, synthetic textiles, and clothing from individual developing countries.

estimated that the MFA cost the developing world $24 billion a year in lost textile and clothing export earnings. The end of the MFA has benefited China most, though some other developing countries, notably Bangladesh, have been able to hold their market share. Much-publicized initiatives for opening markets to the least developed countries, most prominently through the African Growth and Opportunities Act in the United States and Everything but Arms in the European Union, noted earlier, are bilateral offers that can later be withdrawn. These programs also have impediments such as a time horizon that is too short to be effective at encouraging investment or requiring costly and cumbersome documentation, which creates a high hurdle for low-income countries.[39]

Whether displaced high-wage workers in developed-country manufacturing (and now services) will continue to permit the unimpeded entry of low-wage products remains to be seen. WTO rules have eliminated many formal barriers, but many implicit barriers remain. The encouraging pace of tariff reductions at the time of the Uruguay Round and the early years of the WTO has in recent years slowed almost to a halt. Antidumping "investigations" increased significantly, reaching a peak in 1999, with the United States the largest user of these protectionist measures. Although the number of new investigations subsequently declined in the early years of the new century, they remain an important weapon in the protectionist arsenal. For example, as the global recession got underway in 2007, antidumping investigations surged until the end of 2009. Countervailing duty investigations are also on the rise: "Buy American" and analogous legislation that garnered much publicity in stimulus packages following the 2008 crisis are of dubious legality but can have major impacts on developing-country investments, at least for as long as they remain in place, and can also function in the protectionist arsenal as a deterrent. Regional trading agreements, including the North American Free Trade Agreement (NAFTA) and the EU, may also have the effect of discriminating against exports from nonmember developing countries.[40] Analysts also questioned how long the United States could continue to act as the "consumer of last resort" in the wake of its large and chronic **trade deficits** and how developing countries would respond to the apparently inevitable decline in the value of the U.S. dollar; the rebounding U.S. trade deficit after the financial crisis surprised many analysts, but at some point, this export opportunity for developing nations might well be reduced. It was also widely doubted how many other developed-country markets would open to the extent seen in the United States during this period (this topic is discussed further in Chapter 13).

Trade deficit   An excess of import expenditures over export receipts measured on the current account.

As in the case of agricultural and other primary production, the uncertain export outlook should be no cause for curtailing the needed expansion of manufacturing production to serve local markets. There is also great scope for mutually beneficial trade in manufactures among developing countries themselves within the context of the gradual economic integration of their national economies. South-South trade in minerals and agriculture has been rising much more quickly than South-South manufactures trade. China's primary-goods investments in, and exports from, Africa are the most visible, but the emergence of manufacturing zones in Africa working under contract with Chinese firms is also significant. On the other hand, antidumping and other trade complaints against China by other developing nations are rising rapidly.

Import Substitution: Looking Inward but Still Paying Outward

Observing weak world markets for their primary products and subscribing to the widespread belief in the magic of industrialization and the Prebisch-Singer hypothesis, developing nations turned to an import substitution strategy of urban industrial development in the post–World War II decades. Some countries still follow this strategy for both economic and political reasons, although pressure from the WTO, IMF, and World Bank imposes high opportunity costs on such endeavors. As noted earlier, import substitution entails an attempt to replace commodities that are being imported, usually manufactured consumer goods, with domestic sources of production and supply. The typical strategy is first to erect tariff barriers or quotas on certain imported commodities and then to try to set up a local industry to produce these goods—items such as radios, bicycles, or household appliances. Typically, this involves joint ventures with foreign companies, which are encouraged to set up their plants behind the wall of tariff protection and given all kinds of tax and investment incentives. Although initial costs of production may be higher than former import prices, the economic rationale put forward for the establishment of import-substituting manufacturing operations is either that the industry will eventually be able to reap the benefits of large-scale production and lower costs (the so-called **infant industry** argument for tariff protection) or that the balance of payments will be improved as fewer consumer goods are imported. Often a combination of both arguments is advanced. Eventually, it is hoped, the infant industry will grow up and be able to compete in world markets. It will then be able to generate net foreign-exchange earnings once it has lowered its average costs of production. Let us see how the theory of protection can be used to demonstrate this process.

Infant industry   A newly established industry, usually protected by a tariff barrier as part of a policy of import substitution.

Tariffs, Infant Industries, and the Theory of Protection

A principal mechanism of the import substitution strategy is the erection of protective tariffs (taxes on imports) or quotas (limits on the quantity of imports) behind which IS industries are permitted to operate. The basic economic rationale for such protection is the infant-industry argument. Tariff protection against the imported commodity is needed, so the argument goes, in order to allow the now higher-priced domestic producers enough time to learn the business and to achieve the economies of scale in production and the external economies of learning by doing that are necessary to lower unit costs and prices. With enough time and sufficient protection, the infant will eventually grow up, be directly competitive with developed-country producers, and no longer need this protection. Ultimately, as actually seen in the case of many formerly protected IS industries in South Korea and Taiwan, domestic producers hope to be able not only to produce for the domestic market without a tariff wall or government subsidies but also to export their now lower-cost manufactured goods to the rest of the world. Thus, for many developing-country industries, in theory, an IS strategy becomes the prerequisite for an EP strategy. It is for this reason, among others (including the desire to reduce dependence and attain greater self-reliance, the need to build a domestic industrial base, and the ease of raising substantial tax revenue from tariff collections),[41] that import substitution has been appealing to so many governments.

The basic theory of protection is an old and controversial issue in the field of international trade. It is relatively simple to demonstrate. Consider Figure 12.3. The top portion of the figure shows standard domestic supply and demand curves for the industry in question (say, shoes) if there were no international trade—that is, in a closed economy. The equilibrium home price and quantity would be P_1 and Q_1. If this country were then to open its economy to world trade, its small size in relation to the world market would mean that it would face a horizontal, perfectly elastic demand curve. In other words, it could sell (or buy) all it wanted at a lower world price, P_2. Domestic consumers would benefit from the lower price of imports and the resultant greater quantity purchased, while domestic producers and their employees would clearly suffer as they lost business to lower-cost foreign suppliers. Thus, at the lower world price, P_2, the quantity demanded would rise from Q_1 to Q_3, whereas the

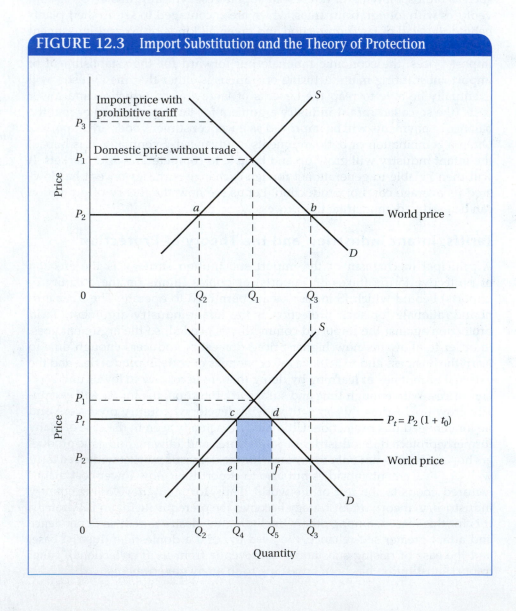

FIGURE 12.3   Import Substitution and the Theory of Protection

quantity supplied by domestic producers would fall from Q_1 to Q_2. The difference between what domestic producers would be willing to supply at the lower P_2 world price (Q_2) and what consumers would want to buy (Q_3) would be the amount that would be imported—shown as line ab in Figure 12.3.

Facing the potential loss of domestic production and jobs as a result of free trade and desiring to obtain infant-industry protection, local producers will seek tariff relief from the government. The effects of a tariff (equal to t_0) are shown in the lower half of Figure 12.3. The tariff causes the domestic price of shoes to rise from P_2 to P_t—that is, $P_t = P_2 (1 + t_0)$. Local consumers now have to pay the higher price and will reduce their quantity demanded from Q_3 to Q_5. Domestic producers can now expand production (and employment) up to quantity Q_4 from Q_2. The rectangular area $cdfe$ measures the amount of the tariff revenue collected by the government on imported shoes.

Clearly, the higher the tariff, the closer to the domestic price the sum of the world price plus the import tax will be. In the classic infant-industry IS scenario, the tariff may be so high that it raises the price of the imported product above P_1 to, say, P_3 in the upper diagram of Figure 12.3 so that imports are effectively prohibited and the local industry is allowed to operate behind a fully protective tariff wall, once again selling Q_1 output at P_1 price. In the short run, it is clear that the impact of such a prohibitive tariff is to penalize consumers, who are in effect subsidizing domestic producers and their employees through higher prices and lower consumption. Alternatively, we can say that a tariff redistributes income from consumers to producers. However, in the longer run, advocates of IS protection for infant industries argue that everyone will benefit as domestic and other shoe manufacturers reap the benefits of economies of scale and learning by doing so that ultimately the domestic price falls below P_2 (the world price). Production will then occur for *both* the domestic and world markets, domestic consumers as well as domestic producers and their employees will benefit, protective tariffs can be removed, and the government will be able to replace any lost tariff revenue with taxes on the now very much higher incomes of domestic manufactures. It all sounds logical and persuasive in theory. But how has it performed in practice?

The IS Industrialization Strategy and Results

Most observers agree that the import-substituting strategy of industrialization has been largely unsuccessful.[42] Specifically, there have been five undesirable outcomes. First, secure behind protective tariff walls and immune from competitive pressures, many IS industries (both publicly and privately owned) remain inefficient and costly to operate. Second, the main beneficiaries of the import substitution process have been the foreign firms that were able to locate behind tariff walls and take advantage of liberal tax and investment incentives. After deducting interest, profits, and royalty and management fees, much of which are remitted abroad, the little that may be left over usually accrues to the wealthy local industrialists with whom foreign manufacturers cooperate and who provide their political and economic cover.

Third, most import substitution has been made possible by the heavy and often government-subsidized importation of capital goods and intermediate products by foreign and domestic companies. In the case of foreign companies, much of this is purchased from parent and sister companies abroad. There are two immediate results. On the one hand, capital-intensive industries are set up, usually catering to the consumption habits of the rich while having a minimal employment effect. On the other hand, far from improving the developing nation's balance of payments situation and alleviating the debt problem, indiscriminate import substitution often worsens the situation by increasing a need for imported capital-good inputs and intermediate products while, as just noted, a good part of the profits is remitted abroad in the form of private transfer payments.

A fourth detrimental effect of many import substitution strategies has been their impact on traditional primary-product exports. To encourage local manufacturing through the importation of cheap capital and intermediate goods, **official exchange rates** (the rates at which the central bank of a nation is prepared to purchase specific foreign currencies) have often been artificially overvalued. This has had the effect of raising the price of exports and lowering the price of imports in terms of the local currency. For example, if the free-market exchange rate between Pakistani rupees and U.S. dollars was 20 to 1 but the official exchange rate was 10 to 1, an item that cost $10 in the United States could be imported into Pakistan for 100 rupees (excluding transport costs and other service charges). If the **free-market exchange rate** (the exchange rate determined by the supply and demand for Pakistani rupees in terms of dollars) prevailed, that item would cost 200 rupees. Thus, by means of an **overvalued exchange rate**, developing-country governments have effectively lowered the domestic currency price of their imports. At the same time, their export prices have increased—for example, at an exchange rate of 10 to 1, U.S. importers would have to pay 10 cents for every 1-rupee item rather than the 5 cents they would pay if the hypothetical free-market ratio of 20 to 1 were in effect.

The net effect of overvaluing exchange rates in the context of import substitution policies is to encourage capital-intensive production methods still further (because the price of imported capital goods is artificially lowered) and to penalize the traditional primary-product export sector by artificially raising the price of exports in terms of foreign currencies. This overvaluation, then, causes local farmers to be less competitive in world markets. In terms of its income distribution effects, the outcome of such government policies may be to penalize the small farmer and the self-employed while improving the profits of the owners of capital, both foreign and domestic. Industrial protection thus has the effect of taxing agricultural goods in the home market as well as discouraging agricultural exports. Import substitution policies have in practice often worsened the local distribution of income by favoring the urban sector and higher-income groups while discriminating against the rural sector and lower-income groups.

Fifth and finally, import substitution, which may have been conceived with the idea of stimulating infant-industry growth and self-sustained industrialization by creating "forward" and "backward" linkages with the rest of the economy, has often inhibited that industrialization. Many infant industries never grow up, content to hide behind protective tariffs and governments loath to force them to be more competitive by lowering tariffs. In fact, governments themselves often operate protected industries as state-owned enterprises.

Official exchange rate Rate at which the central bank will buy and sell the domestic currency in terms of a foreign currency such as the U.S. dollar.

Free-market exchange rate Rate determined solely by international supply and demand for domestic currency expressed in terms of, say, U.S. dollars.

Overvalued exchange rate An official exchange rate set at a level higher than its real or shadow value.

Moreover, by increasing the costs of inputs to potentially forward-linked industries (those that purchase the output of the protected firm as inputs or intermediate products in their own productive process, such as a printer's purchase of paper from a locally protected paper mill) and by purchasing their own inputs from overseas sources of supply rather than through backward linkages to domestic suppliers, inefficient import-substituting firms may in fact block the hoped-for process of self-reliant integrated industrialization.[43]

Tariff Structures and Effective Protection   Because import substitution programs are based on the protection of local industries against competing imports primarily through the use of tariffs and physical quotas, we need to analyze the role and limitations of these commercial policy instruments in developing nations. As we have already discussed, governments impose tariffs and physical quotas on imports for a variety of reasons. For example, tariff barriers may be erected to raise public revenue. In fact, given the administrative and political difficulties of collecting local income taxes, fixed-percentage taxes on imports collected at a relatively few ports or border posts often constitute one of the cheapest and most efficient ways to raise government revenue. In many developing countries, these foreign-trade taxes are thus a central feature of the overall fiscal system. **Nontariff trade barriers**, such as physical quotas on imports like automobiles and other luxury consumer goods, though more difficult to administer and more subject to delay, inefficiency, and rent-seeking corruption (e.g., with regard to the granting of import licenses), provide an effective means of restricting the entry of particularly troublesome commodities. Tariffs, too, may serve to restrict the importation of non-necessity products (usually expensive consumer goods). By restricting imports, both quotas and tariffs can improve the balance of payments. And like overvaluing the official rate of foreign exchange, tariffs may be used to improve a nation's terms of trade. However, in a small developing country that is unable to influence world prices of its exports or imports, this argument for tariffs (or devaluation) has little validity. Finally, as noted, tariffs may form an integral component of an import substitution policy of industrialization.

> **Nontariff trade barrier**   A barrier to free trade that takes a form other than a tariff, such as quotas or (possibly arbitrary) sanitary requirements.

Whatever the means used to restrict imports, such restriction always protects domestic firms from competition with producers from other countries. To measure the degree of protection, we need to ask by how much these restrictions cause the domestic prices of imports to exceed what their prices would be if there were no protection. There are two basic measures of protection: the nominal rate and the effective rate.

The **nominal rate of protection** shows the extent, in percentages, to which the domestic price of imported goods exceeds what their price would be in the absence of protection. Thus, the nominal (ad valorem) tariff rate, t, refers to the final prices of commodities and can be defined simply as

> **Nominal rate of protection** An ad valorem percentage tariff levied on imports.

$$t = \frac{p' - p}{p} \tag{12.1}$$

where p' and p are the unit prices of industry's output with and without tariffs, respectively.

For example, if the domestic price, p', of an imported automobile is \$5,000 whereas the CIF (cost plus insurance and freight) price, p, when the automobile arrives at the port of entry is \$4,000, the nominal rate of tariff protection, t, would be 25%. This is the kind of tariff depicted as t_0 in Figure 12.3.

By contrast, the **effective rate of protection** shows the percentage by which the **value added** at a particular stage of processing in a domestic industry can exceed what it would be without protection. In other words, it shows by what percentage the sum of wages, interest, profits, and depreciation allowances payable by local firms could, as a result of protection, exceed what this sum would be if these same firms had to face unrestricted competition (no tariff protection) from foreign producers.[44] The effective rate, ρ, can therefore be defined as the difference between value added (percent of output) in domestic prices and value added in world prices, expressed as a percentage of the latter, so that

$$\rho = \frac{v'-v}{v} \tag{12.2}$$

where v' and v are the value added per unit of output with and without protection, respectively. The result can be either positive or negative, depending on whether v' is greater or less than v. For most developing economies, it is highly positive.

The important difference between nominal and effective rates of protection can be illustrated by means of an example.[45] Consider a nation without tariffs in which automobiles are produced and sold at the international or world price of \$10,000. The value added by labor in the final assembly process is assumed to be \$2,000, and the total value of the remaining inputs is \$8,000. Assume for simplicity that the prices of these nonlabor inputs are equal to their world prices. Suppose that a nominal tariff of 10% is now imposed on imported automobiles, which raises the domestic price of cars to \$11,000 but leaves the prices of all the other importable intermediate units unchanged. The domestic process of automobile production can now spend \$3,000 per unit of output on labor inputs, as contrasted with \$2,000 per unit before the tariff. The theory of effective protection therefore implies that under these conditions, the nominal tariff of 10% on the final product (automobiles) has resulted in an effective rate of protection of 50% for the local assembly process in terms of its value added per unit of output. It follows that for any given nominal tariff rate, the effective rate is greater the smaller the value added of the process; that is, $\rho = t/(1-a)$, where t is the nominal rate on final product and a is the proportionate value of the importable inputs in a free market where these inputs are assumed to enter the country duty-free.

Most economists argue that the effective rate of protection is the more useful concept (even though the nominal or ad valorem rate is simpler to measure) for ascertaining the degree of protection and encouragement afforded to local manufacturers by a given country's tariff structure. This is because effective rates of protection show the net effect on a firm or industry of restrictions on the imports of both its outputs and its inputs. For most countries, developing and developed, the effective rate of protection normally exceeds the nominal rate of protection, sometimes by as much as 200%. For example, average levels of effective protection have exceeded 300% for Pakistan and Uruguay, 100% for Argentina and Brazil, 50% for the Philippines, and 25%

Effective rate of protection The degree of protection on value added as opposed to the final price of an imported product—usually higher than the nominal rate of protection.

Value added Amount of a product's final value that is added at each stage of production.

for Mexico.[46] However, effective rates of protection have fallen substantially since the mid-1980s.

Among the many implications of analyzing effective versus nominal tariff structures with regard to developing countries, two stand out as particularly noteworthy. First, it is clear that most developing countries have pursued import-substituting programs of industrialization with emphasis on the local production of final consumer goods for which a ready market was presumed to exist. Moreover, final goods production is generally less technically sophisticated than intermediate capital-goods production. The expectation was that in time, rising demand and economies of scale in finished-goods production would create strong backward linkages leading to the creation of domestic intermediate-goods industries. It is also clear that for most developing countries, the record of performance has been disappointing. Part of the reason for this lack of success has been that developing-country tariff structures have afforded exceedingly high rates of effective protection to final-goods industries while granting considerably less effective protection to intermediate and capital goods. The net result is an attraction of scarce resources away from intermediate-goods production and toward the often inefficient production of highly protected final consumer goods. Backward linkages do not develop, intermediate-good import costs rise, and the development of an indigenous capital-goods industry focusing on efficient, low-cost, labor-intensive techniques is severely impeded.

Second, even though nominal rates of protection in developed countries on imports from the developing countries may seem relatively low, effective protection rates can be quite substantial. As noted earlier in the cases of cacao and sugar, raw materials are usually imported duty-free, whereas processed products such as roasted and powdered coffee, coconut oil, and cocoa butter appear to have low nominal tariffs. The theory of effective protection suggests that in combination with zero tariffs on imported raw materials, low nominal tariffs on processed products can represent substantially higher effective rates of protection. For example, if a tariff of 10% is levied on processed coconut oil whereas copra (dried coconut) can be imported duty-free, and if the value added in making oil from copra is 5% of the total value of coconut oil, the *process* is actually being protected at 200%! This greatly inhibits the development of food and other raw-materials-processing industries in developing nations and ultimately cuts back on their potential earnings of foreign exchange.

Effective rates of protection are also considerably higher than of nominal rates protection in the developed countries, especially in goods where low-income countries can be most competitive. For example, until recently, the effective rate of protection on thread and yarn, textile fabrics, clothing, wood products, leather, and rubber goods has averaged more than twice the nominal rate of protection on these same items in the United States and the European Union. In the EU, effective rates of protection on coconut oil have been 10 times the nominal rate of protection (150% compared with 15%), and those on processed soybeans have been 16 times the nominal rate of protection (160% as opposed to 10%).

To sum up, the standard argument for tariff protection in developing countries has four major components:

1. Duties on trade are a major source of government revenue in a majority of developing countries because they are a relatively easy form of taxation to impose and even easier to collect.

2. Import restrictions represent an obvious response to chronic balance of payments and debt problems.

3. Protection against imports is said to be an appropriate means for fostering economies of scale, positive externalities, and industrial self-reliance as well as overcoming the pervasive state of economic dependence in which many or most developing countries understandably perceive themselves.

4. By pursuing policies of import restriction, developing countries can gain greater control over their economic destinies while encouraging foreign business interests to invest in local import-substituting industries, generating high profits and thus the potential for greater saving and future growth. They can also obtain imported equipment at relatively favorable prices and reserve an already established domestic market for local or locally controlled producers. Eventually, they may even become competitive enough to export to the world market.

Although these arguments can sound convincing and some protective policies have proved highly beneficial to the developing world, many have failed to bring about their desired results. Protection is a tool of economic policy that must be employed selectively and wisely, not as a panacea to be applied indiscriminately and without consideration of both short- and long-term ramifications.

Foreign-Exchange Rates, Exchange Controls, and the Devaluation Decision

We have already briefly discussed the question of foreign-exchange rates. Remember that a country's official exchange rate is the rate at which its central bank is prepared to transact exchanges of its local currency for other currencies in approved foreign-exchange markets. Official exchange rates are usually quoted in terms of U.S. dollars—so many pesos, reals, pounds, euros, rupees, bhat, or yen per dollar. For example, the official exchange rate of the South African rand for U.S. dollars in 1998 was approximately 5 rand per dollar, and the Indian rupee was officially valued at approximately 40 rupees per dollar. If a South African manufacturer wished to import fabrics from an Indian textile exporter at a cost of 40,000 rupees, he would need 5,000 rand to make the purchase. However, since most foreign-exchange transactions are conducted in U.S. dollars, the South African importer would need to purchase $1,000 worth of foreign exchange from the central bank of South Africa for his 5,000 rand and then transmit these dollars through official channels to the Indian exporter. Currently, few major economies operate traditional fixed exchange rates except those pegged to the Euro; China moved from a fixed exchange rate to a managed float (giving more flexibility) in 2005. Note that many developing countries with managed floats still use intervention to maintain significant control over their exchange rates.

Official foreign-exchange rates are not necessarily set at or near the economic equilibrium price for foreign exchange—that is, the rate at which the domestic demand for a foreign currency such as dollars would just equal its supply in the absence of governmental regulation or intervention. In fact, as noted earlier, historically the currencies of most developing countries have been overvalued by the exchange rate. Whenever the official price of foreign exchange is established at a level that in the absence of any governmental restrictions or controls would result in an excess of local demand over the available supply of foreign exchange, the domestic currency in question is said to be overvalued.

In situations of excess demand, developing-country central banks have three basic policy options to maintain the official rate of exchange. First, they can attempt to accommodate the excess demand by running down their reserves of foreign exchange (as Mexico did from 1991 to 1994 and Thailand, Malaysia, Indonesia, and the Philippines did from 1995 to 1997) or by borrowing additional foreign exchange abroad and thereby incurring further debts (as many African countries did in the 1980s and Indonesia and South Korea did in the 1990s). Second, they can attempt to curtail the excess demand for foreign exchange by pursuing commercial policies and tax measures that are designed to lessen the demand for imports (e.g., tariffs, physical quotas, licensing). Third, they can regulate and intervene in the foreign-exchange market by rationing the limited supply of available foreign exchange to "preferred" customers.[47] Such rationing is more commonly known as **exchange control**. The policy has been widely used throughout the developing world, although it is much less common than it once was.

Exchange control A governmental policy designed to restrict the outflow of domestic currency and prevent a worsened balance of payments position by controlling the amount of foreign exchange that can be obtained or held by domestic citizens.

The mechanism and operation of exchange control can be illustrated diagrammatically with the aid of Figure 12.4. Under free-market conditions, the equilibrium price of foreign exchange would be P_e, with a total of M units of foreign exchange demanded and supplied. If, however, the government maintains an artificially low price of foreign exchange (i.e., an overvaluation of its domestic currency) at P_a, the supply of foreign exchange will amount to only M' units because exports are overpriced. But at price P_a, the demand

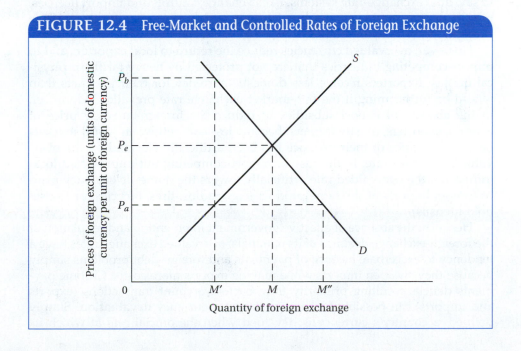

FIGURE 12.4   Free-Market and Controlled Rates of Foreign Exchange

for foreign exchange will be M'' units, with the result that there is an "excess demand" equal to $M'' - M'$ units. Unless foreigners are willing to lend to or invest in the country to make up the difference, some mechanism will have to be devised to ration the available supply of M'. If the government were to auction this supply, importers would be willing to pay a price of P_b for the foreign exchange. In such a case, the government would make a profit of $P_b - P_a$ per unit. However, such open auctions are rarely carried out, and limited supplies of foreign exchange are allocated through some administrative quota or licensing device. Opportunities for corruption, evasion, and the emergence of black markets are thus made possible because importers are willing to pay as much as P_b per unit of foreign exchange.

Why have a majority of developing-country governments at one time or another opted for an overvalued official exchange rate? Many have done so as part of widespread programs of rapid industrialization and import substitution. As mentioned earlier, overvalued exchange rates reduce the domestic currency price of imports below the level that would exist in a free market for foreign exchange (i.e., by the forces of supply and demand). Cheaper imports, especially capital and intermediate producer goods, are needed to fuel the industrialization process. But overvalued exchange rates also lower the domestic currency price of imported consumer goods, especially expensive luxury products. Developing countries wishing to limit such unnecessary and costly imports often need to establish import controls (mostly physical quotas) or to set up a system of **dual** or **parallel exchange rates**, with one rate, usually highly overvalued and legally fixed, applied to capital and intermediate-good imports and the other, much lower and illegal (or freely floating), for luxury consumption good imports. Such dual exchange-rate systems make the domestic price of imported luxury goods very high while maintaining the artificially low and thus subsidized price of producer good imports. Needless to say, dual exchange-rate systems, like exchange controls and import licenses, present serious problems of administration and can promote black markets, corruption, evasion, and rent seeking (see Chapter 11).[48]

However, overvalued currencies reduce the return to local exporters and to import-competing industries that are not protected by heavy tariffs or physical quotas. Exporters receive less domestic currency for their products than would be forthcoming if the free-market exchange rate prevailed. Moreover, in the absence of export subsidies to reduce the foreign-currency price of exports, exporters, mostly farmers, become less competitive in world markets because the price of their produce has been artificially elevated by the overvalued exchange rate. In the case of import-competing but unprotected local industries, the overvalued rate artificially lowers the domestic currency price of foreign imports of the same product (e.g., radios, tires, bicycles, or household utensils).

Hence, in the absence of effective government intervention and regulation of the foreign-exchange dealings of its nationals, overvalued exchange rates have a tendency to exacerbate balance of payments and foreign-debt problems simply because they cheapen imports while making exports more costly. Chronic payments deficits resulting primarily from current account transactions (exports and imports) can possibly be ameliorated by a currency **devaluation**. Simply defined, a country's currency is devalued when the official rate at which its

Dual exchange rate (parallel exchange rate) Foreign-exchange-rate system with a highly overvalued and legally fixed rate applied to capital- and intermediate-goods imports and a second, illegal (or freely floating) rate for imported consumption goods.

Devaluation A lowering of the official exchange rate between one country's currency and all other currencies.

central bank is prepared to exchange the local currency for dollars is abruptly increased. A currency **depreciation**, by contrast, refers to a gradual decrease in the purchasing power of a domestic currency in foreign markets relative to domestic markets; *appreciation* refers to a gradual increase.[49] For example, when these currencies were pegged, a devaluation of the South African rand and the Indian rupee would occur if their official exchange rates of approximately 5 rand and 40 rupees to the dollar were changed to, say, 8 rand and 50 rupees per dollar. Following these devaluations, U.S. importers of South African and Indian goods would pay fewer dollars to obtain the same products. But U.S. exports to South Africa and India would become more expensive, requiring more rand or rupees to purchase than before. In short, by lowering the *foreign*-currency price of its exports (and thereby generating more foreign demand) while raising the *domestic*-currency price of its imports (and thereby lowering domestic demand), developing countries that devalue their currency hope to improve their trade balance vis-à-vis the rest of the world. This is a principal reason why devaluation is always a key component of IMF stabilization policies when currencies are "pegged."

An alternative to a currency devaluation is to allow foreign-exchange rates to fluctuate freely in accordance with changing conditions of international demand and supply. Freely fluctuating or **flexible exchange rates** in the past were not thought to be desirable, especially in developing nations heavily dependent on exports and imports, because they are extremely unpredictable, subject to wide and uncontrollable fluctuations, and susceptible to foreign and domestic currency speculation. Such unpredictable fluctuations can wreak havoc with both short- and long-range development plans. Nevertheless, during the global balance of payments and debt crises of the 1980s, many developing countries, including Mexico, Argentina, Chile, and the Philippines, were heavily influenced by the IMF to let their exchange rates float freely in order to correct sizable payments imbalances and to prevent continued capital flight. The same phenomenon occurred again for Mexico in 1994 and for Thailand, the Philippines, South Korea, Malaysia, and Indonesia in 1997 and 1998 during the Asian currency crisis. In a matter of several months during 1997, the Thai baht lost one-third of its value against the dollar, and the Philippine peso, South Korean won, Malaysian ringgit, and Indonesian rupiah fell by almost 30%. In a recent if less consequential example, the Indian rupee suddenly fell beginning in May 2013, losing as much as 20% of its value against the U.S. dollar (9% in August 2013 alone); the central bank responded by raising interest rates, which temporarily reversed about half of the 2013 decline but at an apparent cost of economic growth, which was already slowing. Some analysts viewed this as a potential harbinger of a new set of crises involving more countries such as Brazil, as the "ultra-loose" U.S. monetary policy tightens; we return to related topics in Chapters 13 and 15.

The present international system of floating exchange rates, formally legalized at an IMF meeting in 1976, represents a compromise between a fixed (artificially pegged) and a fully flexible exchange-rate system. Under this "managed" floating system, major international currencies are permitted to fluctuate freely, but erratic swings are limited through central bank intervention. The trend for most developing countries is toward a **managed float** of their currencies.

One final point that should be made about currency devaluations concerns their probable effect on domestic prices. Devaluation has the immediate effect

Depreciation (of currency) The decline over time in the value or price of one currency in terms of another as a result of market forces of supply and demand.

Flexible exchange rate The exchange value of a national currency that is free to move up and down in response to shifts in demand and supply arising from international trade and finance.

Managed float A fluctuating exchange rate that allows central bank intervention to reduce erratic currency fluctuations.

Wage-price spiral A vicious cycle in which higher consumer prices (e.g., as a result of devaluation) cause workers to demand higher wages, which in turn cause producers to raise prices and worsen inflationary forces.

of raising prices of imported goods in terms of the local currency. Imported shirts, shoes, radios, records, foodstuffs, and bicycles that formerly cost x rupees now cost $(1 + d)x$ rupees, depending on the percentage magnitude of the devaluation, d. If, as a result of these higher prices, domestic workers seek to preserve the real value of their purchasing power, they are likely to initiate increased wage and salary demands. Such increases, if granted, will raise production costs and tend to push local prices up even higher. A **wage-price spiral** of domestic inflation can be thereby set in motion. For example, following the widespread IMF-induced currency devaluations during the 1997 Asian crisis, rates of inflation shot up in 1998 from 11% to 35% in Indonesia, from 6% to 12% in Thailand, and from 5% to 10% in the Philippines. Unemployment rates doubled, and workers took to the streets, demanding an end to the layoffs and a rise in wages to offset their lost purchasing power.

As for the distributional effects of a devaluation, it is clear that by altering the domestic price and returns of "tradable" goods (exports and imports) and creating incentives for the production of exports as opposed to domestic goods, devaluation will benefit certain groups at the expense of others. In general, urban wage earners, people with fixed incomes, the unemployed, and the small farmers and rural and urban small-scale producers and suppliers of services who do not participate in the export sector stand to be financially hurt by the domestic inflation that typically follows a devaluation. Conversely, large exporters (often large landowners and foreign-owned corporations) and medium- to large-size local businesses engaged in foreign trade stand to benefit the most.[50] For this reason and others, international commercial and financial problems (e.g., chronic balance of payments deficits) cannot be divorced from developing countries' domestic problems (e.g., poverty and inequality). Policy responses to alleviate one problem can either improve or worsen others.

Undervalued exchange rate An official exchange rate set at a level lower than its real or shadow value.

Finally, note that while a neutral exchange rate favors producing for neither the export market nor the domestic market, and free-market economists tend to favor it because of its "level playing field" in that respect, in contrast, an **undervalued exchange rate** is strongly export promoting. This is because it raises the local prices that firms receive for goods that can be exported *relative to* prices of nontradable goods that are sold only to domestic buyers, thus motivating a reorientation of firms toward the export market. If exports stimulate growth and if that growth is widely shared, many development economists expect that in the longer term, devaluation—and perhaps even undervaluation of exchange rates—can provide important development advantages. Proponents of industrial policy (and critics who consider it unfair currency manipulation) point to the long-term undervaluation of the Chinese renminbi and the earlier undervaluation of other East Asian currencies, particularly those of South Korea and Taiwan during their rapid catch-up phase; we return to this topic in the end-of-chapter case studies on Taiwan and South Korea in Chapters 12 and 13, respectively.

Trade Optimists and Trade Pessimists: Summarizing the Traditional Debate

We are now in a position to summarize the major issues and arguments in the great debate between advocates of free-trade, outward-looking development and export promotion policies—the **trade optimists**—and advocates of greater protection, more inward-looking strategies, and greater import substitution—the **trade pessimists**.[51] Let us begin with the latter school of thought.

Trade Pessimist Arguments   Trade pessimists tend to focus on four basic themes: (1) the limited growth of world demand for primary exports, (2) the secular deterioration in the terms of trade for primary producing nations, (3) the rise of "new protectionism" against manufactured and processed agricultural goods from developing countries, and (4) the presence of market failures that reduce the ability of developing countries to move up to export higher-value products.

The value of traditional developing-country exports to developed countries grow slowly because of (1) a shift in developed countries from low-technology, material-intensive goods to high-technology, skill-intensive products, which decreases the demand for raw materials; (2) increased efficiency in industrial uses of raw materials; (3) the substitution of synthetics for natural raw materials like rubber, copper, and cotton; (4) the low income elasticity of demand for primary products and light manufactured goods; (5) the rising productivity of agriculture in developed countries; and (6) relatively higher levels of protectionism for both agriculture and labor-intensive developed-country industries.

The terms of trade remain unfavorable or continue to deteriorate because of (1) oligopolistic control of factor and commodity markets in developed countries, combined with increasing competitive sources of supply of a developing country's exportables, and (2) a generally lower level of the income elasticity of demand for its exports.

The rise of **new protectionism** in the developed world results from the success of a growing number of developing countries in producing a wide range of both primary and secondary products at competitive world market prices, combined with the quite natural fears of workers in higher-cost developed-country industries that their jobs will be lost. They pressure their governments in North America, Europe, and Japan to curtail or prohibit competitive imports from the developing world. The form this takes changes over time; the 2010 proposals by the leaders of France and Italy for "carbon tariffs" to be levied on exports of developing countries that do not restrict greenhouse gases are a recent example: Surely, protectionism against developing countries is not the only way to help them to decrease greenhouse gas emissions.

Trade pessimists therefore conclude that trade opportunities are limited and even hurt developing countries for four reasons:

1. The slow growth in demand for their traditional exports means that export expansion results in lower export prices and a transfer of income from poor to rich nations.

2. Without import restrictions, the high elasticity of developing countries' demand for imports, combined with the low elasticity for their exports, means that developing countries must grow slowly to avoid chronic balance of payments and foreign-exchange crises.

Trade optimists   Theorists who believe in the benefits of free trade, open economies, and outward-looking development policies.

Trade pessimists   Theorists who argue that without tariff protection or quantitative restrictions on trade, developing countries gain little or nothing from an export-oriented, open-economy posture.

New protectionism   The erection of various nontariff trade barriers by developed countries against the manufactured exports of developing nations.

3. Developing nations have their "static" comparative advantage in primary products, which means that export-promoting free-trade policies tend to inhibit industrialization, which is in turn the major vehicle for the accumulation of technical skills and entrepreneurial talents.

4. Trade pessimists view trade liberalization under the WTO as limited in practice, with developing economies—particularly the least developed countries—lacking the high-powered lawyers and other resources needed to pry developed markets open.

Trade Optimist Arguments   Trade optimists tend to underplay the role of international demand in determining the gains from trade. Instead, they focus on the relationship between trade policy, export performance, and economic growth.[52] They argue that **trade liberalization** (including export promotion, currency devaluation, removal of trade restrictions, and generally "getting prices right") generates rapid export and economic growth because free trade provides a number of benefits:

Trade liberalization
Removal of obstacles to free trade, such as quotas, nominal and effective rates of protection, and exchange controls.

1. It promotes competition, improved resource allocation, and economies of scale in areas where developing countries have a comparative advantage. Costs of production are consequently lowered.

2. It generates pressures for increased efficiencies, product improvement, and technical change, thus raising factor productivity and further lowering costs of production.

3. It accelerates overall economic growth, which raises profits and promotes greater saving and investment and thus furthers growth.

4. It attracts foreign capital and expertise, which are in scarce supply in most developing countries.

5. It generates needed foreign exchange that can be used to import food if the agricultural sector lags behind or suffers droughts or other natural catastrophes.

6. It eliminates costly economic distortions caused by government interventions in both the export and foreign-exchange markets, and substitutes market allocation for the corruption and rent-seeking activities that typically result from an overactive government sector.

7. It promotes more equal access to scarce resources, which improves overall resource allocation.

8. It enables developing countries to take full advantage of reforms under the WTO.

Trade optimists argue, finally, that even though export promotion may at first be difficult with limited gains—especially in comparison with the easy gains of first-stage import substitution—over the longer run, the economic benefits tend to gain momentum, whereas import substitution faces rapidly diminishing returns.

12.6 The Industrialization Strategy Approach to Export Policy

Export-Oriented Industrialization Strategy

Since the mid-1980s, another important strand of thought has emerged concerning the relationship between trade and development. The **industrialization strategy approach** is outward-oriented and optimistic about export-led development but still envisions an active role for government in influencing the type and sequencing of exports as a country strives to produce more advanced products, adding higher value.

The industrialization strategy approach began primarily as an empirical literature but has developed a theory to help explain why an interventionist strategy toward exports can accelerate growth and improve development outcomes more than a strict free-trade approach. The theories developed in this approach are focused on identifying and redressing market failures encountered in the process of industrialization.

This strain of research has revealed that rather than operating on a free-market basis, leading export-oriented East Asian economies that are now high-income, in fact, had very active government interventions to encourage industrial exports and to attempt to move up the ladder of comparative advantage toward more advanced products, generating higher value added by employing higher skills and higher technology. Such programs are termed *industrialization strategies* or, more narrowly, *industrial policies*.[53]

Why might an economy be better off using such policies, and why might these policies be better than available alternatives for achieving development goals? It has long been recognized that there are market failures in original research and development; some of the benefits of these expenditures are captured by other firms. This is the rationale for government research programs in the developed countries (such as the National Institutes of Health in the United States). But analogous market failures apply to the transfer of technology from developed to developing countries. In particular, if one firm absorbs technology from outside the region but then other firms benefit from learning by watching and similar spillover effects, then without outside support, we can expect too little technology transfer and other firm upgrading from the social viewpoint. This market failure forms part of the explanation for why a government industrialization strategy centered on absorbing technology from abroad may improve efficiency. In part, government can help solve a coordination problem. More broadly, it has been argued that policy can improve on markets when they are incomplete; that is, market prices of local costs, as well as sales opportunity, provide signals to entrepreneurs only on existing products, not new ones. Unlike conventional regulation, industrial policies can be designed to attempt to complement market forces, providing incentives to sustainably undertake activities on a for-profit basis that are socially efficient but need some complementary inputs and initial conditions to get under way.

The question, then, is why an *export-oriented* industrialization strategy might be important. Of course, for small countries, one reason is to ensure a market of adequate size. But proponents argue that the full explanation goes

Industrialization strategy approach   A school of thought in trade and development that emphasizes the importance of overcoming market failures through government policy to encourage technology transfer and exports of progressively more advanced products.

well beyond this. The use of manufacturing exports of growing technological content as a yardstick of performance automatically emphasizes targets with very strong development benefits. In addition, the world export market is an arena in which performance is clearly, quickly, and rigorously tested while keeping government, whose resources and information capacities are inherently limited, tightly focused on relevant and manageable problems.

In this regard, export targets as a development policy mechanism hold the advantage of being easily observable. This fact has long been understood by developing-country fiscal authorities, who have taxed exports precisely because they are observable and therefore not subject to the tax evasion that is so rampant in the developing world. This distortion has a well-publicized (if not self-evident) antiexport bias effect. But proponents point out that East Asian countries put this "fiscal observability" to use as the centerpiece of their industrial policy system in a way that reversed the negative incentive effects of export taxes.

However, the literature has also stressed the continued importance of infant-industry support. Why might this sometimes be effective? First, empirically, import substitution often precedes export promotion. One influential study concluded that "periods of significant export expansion are almost always preceded by periods of strong import substitution."[54] This does not mean that across-the-board protection is viable today, even for large countries, but countries known primarily for their export prowess, such as South Korea, have often protected—for a limited time—the very industries in which they later became successful exporters.

In 2007 research, Ricardo Hausmann, Jason Hwang, and Dani Rodrik found that exporting a mix of goods that are more typical for a country with higher per capita income predicts higher subsequent growth. As they concluded, "Not all goods are alike in terms of their consequences for economic performance. Specializing in some products will bring higher growth than specializing in others." Or, as Hausmann and Rodrik put it, "You become what you export."[55]

Note that without proper attention to incentives (for both market and rent-seeking activities), these same industrial policies can prove counterproductive. Countries that cannot find the political will to use protection as a highly selective and strictly temporary instrument of industrial policy may be better off abandoning this instrument altogether.

Evidence shows that Singapore, Taiwan, and South Korea have had especially active government industrialization strategies and specific industrial policies over a period of several decades. The experience in South Korea is examined in the case study at the end of the next chapter. The specific policies differ across countries but have common features in encouraging indigenous skills, technologies, and firms and not just promoting labor-intensive manufactures but actively and systematically seeking to upgrade over time. Another feature is collaboration between the public and private sectors, with government playing a coordinating role but with ongoing effective communication and an attempt to understand the constraints faced by the private sector and how to relax them, and not trying to manage industry.

The East Asian success stories are interestingly characterized by Colin Bradford:

> What seems to distinguish the East Asian development experiences is not the dominance of market forces, free enterprise, and internal liberalization, but effective,

highly interactive relationships between the public and private sectors character-ized by shared goals and commitments embodied in the development strategy and economic policy of the government. The dichotomy between market forces and government intervention is not only overdrawn: it misconceives the fundamental dynamic at work. It is the *degree of consistency* between the two sectors—rather than the extent of implicit or explicit conflict—that has been important in the successful development cases. A coherent development strategy was not only formulated but followed by both the government and the private sector in providing an unusual degree of common direction to national energies in these cases.[56]

In a globalizing economy, opportunities to grow through exporting by rely-ing on free-market incentives are in some ways greater but in other ways less strong than before. For example, the end of the Multifiber Arrangement made it more likely that low-income countries will find it difficult to launch a man-ufactured-exports program via the traditional means of starting with textile exports. The growth of China as the "workshop of the world" suggests that it may become more difficult to break into exporting in other sectors as well. On the other hand, with wages beginning to increase in China, new opportunities may emerge for other regions.

Conditions for industrialization strategy also differ today from those that prevailed decades ago in that foreign investors are far more mobile and can quickly go wherever wages or other production costs are lowest. But as the late Sanjaya Lall argued, "Increasing mobility does not mean factors spread themselves evenly over poor countries. Efficient production requires local capabilities to complement the mobile factors. Thus globali-zation needs efficient 'localization': Countries must provide the technical, skill, quality, and reliability needs of competitive production." Lall further argued that:

> technologies cannot be effectively used by developing economies just by opening up to global trade, technology, or capital flows. Technology cannot be fully em-bodied in machines, licences, or people: It has strong tacit elements. These tacit elements need time, investment and effort: to understand, adapt, use and improve technologies—to build new capabilities. Such effort generally faces pervasive market and institutional failures: within the firm, between firms, and between enterprises and factor markets and institutions. Proactive strategies, often selective in nature, are essential for industrial success.[57]

As evidence has accumulated, the debate has shifted. Instead of opposing all government industrialization strategy, it has become a mainstream view to acknowledge the value of policies that effectively improve the position of all industrial exporters but to avoid what is termed "picking winners." In prac-tice, Lall argued, this distinction is difficult to make because often the needed new organizations, skills, and infrastructure are specific to a given sector. But as a general starting point, reasonably nonpreferential but active government support for manufactures exporting as a development policy has gained wide acceptance.

Another issue is whether and to what degree WTO rules permit such gov-ernment actions. Although general support for all industries that does not discriminate is permitted, and such support continues to be practiced by econ-omies sufficiently advanced and governments sufficiently skilled to do so, such as Taiwan and South Korea, some developing countries that might benefit from exporting strategically are not permitted to do so. There are, however, some important exceptions to these rules, notably for the least developed countries. There are also some gray areas. Governments may build infrastructure, and to a degree, this can be industry-specific. Governments can assist an emerging industry as long as it does not give domestic firms a significant advantage over foreign firms. Government can also promote some categories of foreign investment in selected sectors, specialized human capital formation, innovation priorities, and joint-venture agreements.

A third issue is whether other governments have the competence and political authority that South Korea did during its period of active industrial policy management. Where competence is lacking, advocates have argued that the World Bank and other agencies should help governments build this competence. But some observers argue that if governments lack the needed skills (and are unable to get international assistance to develop the needed capabilities), they may ultimately be better off using less interventionist strategies.

Moreover, as Dani Rodrik and others have pointed out, a government does not have to pick all industries correctly, only a sufficient number for the benefits of those successes to outweigh the costs of failure. As Rodrik puts it, "conducting policy in a manner that would ensure zero failure would make as much sense as a pharmaceutical company investing only in drugs that are guaranteed to be profitable from the outset."[58] Rodrik reviews examples cited in the literature of major industrial policy successes, for example, in Chile and Uruguay. He proposes that incentives for government agencies can be established, involving benchmarking and transparency, to help ensure that support for industrial sectors is limited and temporary. Rodrik suggests that the problems of carrying out industrial policy—such as imperfect government knowledge, avoiding rent seeking, and ceasing support of failed initiatives—are not fundamentally different from those faced by government activity in other sectors such as education, health, social insurance, and macroeconomic stabilization. Market failures in these sectors are hard to observe and prone to rent seeking, yet government's role is understood to be vital.

From Rodrik's research, other general principles are to target new activities, not existing ones; to use clear benchmarking to determine eligibility for continued support; to build in sunset clauses (or time limits for support); to give industrial policy authority to agencies with previously demonstrated competence that are, in turn, to be overseen by top political figures—essentially making their careers dependent on industrial policy success; and to employ active and transparent channels of communication with broad representatives of the private sector. In a challenge to some proponents of this school, Rodrik proposes to target broader activities and not narrow sectors (for example, English language training, not call centers or tourism as such).

It is also important to stress that these approaches are more likely to be effective if the public and private sectors are able work together cooperatively in ways consistent both with broad development objectives and with profitability for investors. Although the context of this debate has changed, with the far more competitive world environment and changes in trade rules, industrial policy considerations will continue to be important in the design of developing countries' export strategies.

The New Firm-level International Trade Research and the Developing Countries

In recent years, a new strand of literature in international trade theory has emerged that emphasizes the importance of differences (heterogeneity) among firms in understanding international trade patterns. An important topic is the impact of international trade on individual firms and the extent and nature of competition within domestic industries. The new research examines ways that firms respond to more open economies and the globalization process, and the implications of these responses for patterns of investment—and potentially for structural transformation. Relevant research topics have included "the higher productivity of exporters relative to nonexporters, within-industry realloca- tions of resources following trade liberalization, and patterns of trade partici- pation across firms and destination markets."[59]

To the extent that the new analysis is based on the behavior of firms, the results of further research with these models may ultimately offer a more real- istic framework for evaluating trade policies for developing countries. It is too early to judge the extent of the flexibility of these models to represent special developing-country circumstances, but the new approach holds the potential of important improvements over more aggregated models, reviewed earlier in the chapter. But a systematic empirical as well as theoretical application to special problems of economic development and particular developing coun- tries is needed.

One useful starting point may be another recent strand of development lit- erature focusing on analysis of the firm- and plant-level data from developing countries and regions. The new availability of firm- and plant-level data has provided a spur to new research. A good example is the Enterprise Surveys, including several on the African manufacturing sector carried out under the Regional Program on Enterprise Development (RPED).[60]

An important strand of this empirical research has focused on using firm- level data to identify what factors cause firms in developing countries to export—or at least to find the factors associated with export activity by par- ticular companies. Another related empirical research strand seeks to better understand what problems firms face at the microeconomic level in developing countries, including the degree of corruption, badly designed regulations, lack of key infrastructure, poor access to technical knowledge, or skill shortages, all of which may affect capacity to export. These emerging areas of research will be watched closely in the coming years for its lessons for development policy.[61]

12.7 South-South Trade and Economic Integration

Economic Integration: Theory and Practice

The United Nations Development Programme (UNDP) reported in its *2013 Human Development Report* that from 1981 to 2011, South-South trade increased from less than 8% to more than 26% of world merchandise trade.

South-South trade represents over one-third of all developing-world exports.[62] Exports to China have provided an important opportunity in recent years for some developing countries. Many pioneering development economists, such as Nobel laureate Sir Arthur Lewis, have argued that developing countries should orient more of their trade toward one another.[63] Variants of this theme have been taken up by many contemporary development economists. One argument, advanced in 2006 by Abhijit Banerjee, is that it is difficult for exporters from most low-income countries to break into developed markets because of the effects on their reputation. It is very costly to create and maintain a reputation as a country that exports high-quality products. Thus, it may be better to trade with other developing economies because reputation effects are not as important for exporting to these markets. They can also work together to establish quality standards and certify their achievement, as Pranab Bardhan has proposed.[64]

One strong variant of the South-South trade hypothesis is that developing countries should go beyond greater trade with one another and move in the direction of **economic integration**. Economic integration occurs whenever a group of nations in the same region join together to form an **economic union** or **regional trading bloc** by raising a common tariff wall against the products of nonmember countries while freeing internal trade among members. In the terminology of integration literature, nations that levy common external tariffs while freeing internal trade are said to have formed a **customs union**. If external tariffs against outside countries differ among member nations while internal trade is free, the nations are said to have formed a **free-trade area**. Finally, a **common market** possesses all the attributes of a customs union (common external tariffs and free internal trade) plus the free movement of labor and capital among the partner states.

The traditional theory of customs unions and economic integration focuses on the static resource and production reallocation effects. But the deeper economic rationale for the gradual integration of less developed economies is a long-term dynamic one: Integration provides the opportunity for industries that have not yet been established as well as for those that have to take advantage of economies of large-scale production made possible by expanded markets. In some cases, this is perceived as a defensive response to decreased access to export to other markets due to protectionism or the formation of other trading blocs, such as the European Union, that divert trade to their own group. Integration can be viewed as a mechanism to encourage a rational division of labor among a group of countries, each of which is too small to benefit from such a division by itself. In the absence of integration, each separate country may not provide a sufficiently large domestic market to enable local industries to lower their production costs through economies of scale. In such cases, import-substituting industrialization will typically result, as noted earlier, in the establishment of high-cost, inefficient local industries. Moreover, in the absence of integration, the same industry (e.g., textiles or shoes) may be set up in two or more adjoining small nations. Each will be operating at less than optimal capacity but will be protected against the imports of the other by high tariff or quota barriers. Not only does such duplication result in wasted scarce resources, but it also means that consumers are forced to pay a higher price for the product than if the market were large enough for high-volume, low-cost production to take place at a single location.

This leads to a second dynamic rationale for economic integration. By removing barriers to trade among member states, the possibility of coordinated industrial strategy is created, especially in industries where economies of scale

Economic integration   The merging to various degrees of the economies and economic policies of two or more countries in a region.

Economic union   The full integration of two or more economies into a single economic entity.

Regional trading bloc   An economic coalition among countries within a geographic region, usually characterized by liberalized internal trade and uniform restrictions on external trade, designed to promote regional economic integration and growth.

Customs union   A form of economic integration in which two or more nations agree to free all internal trade while levying a common external tariff on all nonmember countries.

Free-trade area   A form of economic integration in which free trade exists among member countries, but members are free to levy tariffs on nonmember countries.

Common market   A form of economic integration in which there is free internal trade, a common tariff, and the free movement of labor and capital among partner states.

are likely to exist. Examples include fertilizer and petrochemical plants, heavy industry like iron and steel, capital goods and machine tool industries, and small-farm mechanical equipment. But the coordination of industrial expansion that enables all member states to accelerate their rates of industrial growth by assigning given industries to different members takes the partners that much closer to full economic and eventual political union. Problems of sovereignty and national self-interest impinge at this stage. To date, they have overwhelmed the economic logic of a close and coordinated union. However, as developing countries, especially small ones, continue to experience the limitations of either development in isolation (**autarky**) or full participation in the highly unequal world economy, it is likely that interest will increase in the coming decades in the long-run benefits of some form of economic (and perhaps political) cooperation. The recent expansion and deepening of cooperation in the Association of Southeast Asian Nations (ASEAN) is a case in point.

Autarky A closed economy that attempts to be completely self-reliant.

In addition to these two long-term dynamic arguments for integration, there are also the standard static evaluative criteria known as **trade creation** and **trade diversion**. Trade creation is said to occur when common external barriers and internal free trade lead to a shift in production from high- to low-cost member states. For example, before integration, both country A and country B may produce textiles for their respective local markets. Country A may be a lower-cost producer, but its exports to country B are blocked by the latter's high tariffs. If A and B form a customs union by eliminating all barriers to internal trade, country A's more efficient low-cost textile industry will service both markets. Trade will have been created in the sense that the removal of barriers has led to a shift in country B's consumption from its own relatively high-cost textiles to the lower-cost textiles of country A.

Trade creation Shift, upon formation of a customs union, in the location of production from higher-cost to lower-cost member states.

In contrast, trade diversion is said to occur when the erection of external tariff barriers causes production and consumption of one or more member states to shift from lower-cost nonmember sources of supply (e.g., a developed country) to higher-cost member producers. Trade diversion is normally considered undesirable because both the world and member states are perceived to be worse off as a result of diversion of production from more efficient foreign suppliers to the less efficient domestic industries of member states. However, some advocates anticipate dynamic benefits analogous to some of the industrialization strategy arguments just discussed.

Trade diversion Shift, upon formation of a customs union, of the location of production of formerly imported goods from a lower-cost nonmember state to a higher-cost member nation.

Some other special advantages depend on local conditions. Landlocked developing countries may be viewed as safer locations for investment (in infrastructure as well as export industries) when they join a trading agreement with a group in which at least one country has access to the sea. For small-island developing countries, such groupings can offer a lifeline to greater capabilities. Some observers believe that regional economic integration reduces the chances of war or other strife (this belief was part of the original rationale for the creation of the European Union and, to some extent, its later expansion to the east).

Regional Trading Blocs, the Globalization of Trade, and Prospects for South-South Cooperation

Many European Union members use a single currency, the euro, requiring close monetary coordination and in effect creating the largest economic entity in the world. The North American Free Trade Agreement (NAFTA) represents a unique arrangement in that a large developing country, Mexico, has joined a developed-country trading bloc, Canada and the United States. (Chile, an NIC, is also seeking membership.)

A number of trading blocs have emerged in Latin America. Argentina, Brazil, Paraguay, Uruguay, and, following its accession in 2012, Venezuela, have formed a common market–style agreement called the Common Market of the South, also known as Mercosur. Having a "political" purpose as well as an economic purpose, Mercosur is frequently described as a divided or "fractious" bloc; Mercosur suspended Paraguay in 2012, and the addition of Venezuela was controversial. The other South American bloc, the Andean Group (consisting of Bolivia, Colombia, Ecuador, Peru, and Venezuela), established a full-fledged common market in 1995. The 2008 launch of a regional customs union, known as the Union of South American Nations (UNASUR), signaled a new impetus for this trend; UNASUR has an aspirational objective of integration on the scale of the European Union. The Caribbean and Central American states also have an agreement in place.

In Africa, moves are under way to promote regional economic integration, including the South African Development Community (SADC). Thanks to well-developed railroad and air links, the 10 members of SADC—Angola, Botswana, Lesotho, Malawi, Mozambique, Namibia, South Africa, Swaziland, Zambia, and Zimbabwe—anticipate new and much greater trading opportunities. East African countries are revitalizing the East African Community (EAC), originally established in the late 1960s but which fell victim to differing national policies and broke down just a decade after its founding. But it was revived in 2000 with a new trade agreement—now common market—among Burundi, Kenya, Rwanda, Tanzania, and Uganda. The EAC has aspirations of full political as well as economic union, but its 2012 target of a common currency was not achieved. More broadly, a Common Market for Eastern and Southern Africa (COMESA) provides an evolving umbrella for the process; by 2013, it was a free-trade area with 19 member nations. There is also a 15-member Economic Community of West African States (also known as CEDEAO, its French acronym); its focus is primarily on monetary union.

One unresolved question about these regional trading blocs, aspirational full-fledged common markets, and political unions is whether they will fragment the world economy and run counter to the globalization of trade. Another consideration concerns integration behind tariff barriers among developing countries at different stages of development. Anthony Venables argues through extensions of traditional trade theory that within customs unions, "countries with a comparative advantage between that of their partners and the rest of the world do better than countries with an 'extreme' comparative advantage. Consequently, integration between low income countries tends to lead to divergence of member country incomes, while agreements between high income countries cause convergence."[65] Thus, a customs union among developing countries could provide its biggest benefits to the highest-income nations within the group as they attract the manufacturing sector. Venables argues that developing countries are likely better off by entering into North-South than South-South agreements. The availability of North-South agreements is at best unclear for many low-income countries. More generally, the relevance of this theory depends on local conditions, such as opportunities for dynamic gains and the specifics of South-South agreements, which at their best are about more than merely setting common tariffs. Paul Collier offers a balanced starting point when he argues that "regional integration is a good idea, but not behind high external barriers."[66]

International trade patterns are evolving, if unevenly. The World Development Indicators show that from 2000 to 2010, developing-country merchandise exports to high-income countries approximately tripled, but at the same time, merchandise exports between developing countries expanded by more than six times. As a result, as noted at the outset, about one-third of the value of developing-country exports now goes to other developing countries. This trend is less pronounced among the low-income countries but is prevalent among upper-middle-income countries such as Brazil, which has greatly expanded its agricultural and resource exports to China, as well as expanded trade with its partners in the Common Market of the South. The special role of China as a resource importer and manufactures exporter stands out in South-South trade patterns. And as noted by UNIDO, "East Asia and the Pacific accounted for almost 70 percent of manufactured exports between developing countries over 2000-2009."[67]

Beyond this, although opportunities to benefit from solidarity across developing countries have improved in some ways, prospects remain uncertain. On one hand, leading developing countries have never had so much power in the councils of global economic policymaking, including the increasingly important G20, a willingness to exercise veto power in the WTO, beginnings of a power shift in the World Bank and IMF, and perhaps, most importantly, having more to offer one another—from better technology to transfer, to means to pay higher prices for primary products. The once-sharp ideological differences among many of them have narrowed—though these seem to have been replaced in some cases with religious differences. On the other hand, over the past two decades there has been steadily increasing inequalities *among* developing countries in rates of growth and of incomes per capita; this also tends to widen disparities in their priorities and interests.

12.8 Trade Policies of Developed Countries: The Need for Reform and Resistance to New Protectionist Pressures

It is clear that a major obstacle to export expansion, whether in primary products or manufactures, has been the various trade barriers erected by developed nations against the principal commodity exports of developing countries. In the absence of economic integration or even in support of that effort, the prospects for future trade and foreign-exchange expansion depend largely on the domestic and international economic policies of developed nations. Unfortunately, the integration among NAFTA and EU members may itself pose one of the biggest impediments to developing-world exports to North America and Europe. Although internal structural and economic reform may be essential to economic and social progress, an improvement in the competitive position of industries in which developing economies do have a dynamic comparative advantage will be of little benefit to them or the world as a whole so long as their access to major world markets is restricted by rich-country commercial policies.

Developed countries' economic and commercial policies are most important from the perspective of future developing-country foreign-exchange earnings in three major areas: tariff and nontariff barriers to their exports; adjustment assistance for displaced workers in developed-country industries hurt by freer access of labor-intensive, low-cost developing-country exports; and the general impact of rich-country domestic economic policies on developing economies.

The new protectionist tariff and nontariff trade barriers (e.g., excise taxes, quotas, "voluntary" export restraints, disingenuous sanitary regulations) imposed by rich nations on the commodity exports of poor ones have been major obstacles to the expansion of the latter's export-earning capacities, and the advent of the WTO has only partially eliminated these problems. As we have noted, many tariffs for both agricultural and nonagricultural goods increase with the degree of product processing; that is, they are higher for processed foodstuffs than for basic foodstuffs (e.g., peanut oil compared with peanuts)—higher for, say, shirts than for raw cotton. These high effective tariffs have inhibited many low-income nations from developing and diversifying their own secondary-export industries and thus have acted to restrain their industrial expansion. The overall effect of developed-country tariffs, quotas, and nontariff barriers has been to lower the effective price received by developing countries for their exports, reduce the quantity exported, and diminish foreign-exchange earnings.[68]

Uruguay Round   A round of the General Agreement on Tariffs and Trade negotiations, started in Uruguay in 1986 and signed in 1994, designed to promote international free trade.

The **Uruguay Round** agreement of 1995 substantially reduced tariff and nontariff trade barriers in many sectors. It also established the Geneva-based World Trade Organization to replace the 47-year-old General Agreement on Tariffs and Trade. The three major provisions from the perspective of developing nations are the following:[69]

1. Developed countries cut tariffs on manufactures by an average of 40% in five equal annual reductions. Developing countries in turn agreed to not raise tariffs by "binding" in recent trade reforms. Despite these reductions, developing countries still face tariffs that are 10% higher than the global average, while the least developed countries face tariffs that are 30% higher.[70]

2. Trade in agricultural products came under the authority of the WTO and were to be progressively liberalized. Although progress was made at first, agricultural subsidies subsequently returned to record highs.

3. For textiles and apparel, the Multifiber Arrangement quotas, which long penalized exports of developing countries, were phased out in 2005, with most of the progressive reductions taking effect toward the end of the period. But tariffs on textile imports were reduced only to an average of 12%—three times the average level of tariffs on other imports.

The reforms had other important limitations. Although average tariffs are generally quite low by historical standards, tariffs that "escalate" (increase the more processed the product becomes before it is exported) remain in place in many cases; low-income countries still face peak tariffs in some key products in agriculture, textiles, and clothing; and enormously distorting agricultural subsidies still cause great harm to many developing countries. As the United Nations Development Programme concluded:

> Developing countries, with three-quarters of the world's people, will get only a quarter to a third of the income gains generated—and most of that will go to a few powerful exporters in Asia and Latin America.[71]

Indeed, at the household level, the World Bank reported that the effective, trade-weighted tariffs faced by the poor are much higher than those faced by the nonpoor. Both those living on less than $1 a day and those living on between $1 and $2 a day faced effective tariffs of well over 14%, while those with higher incomes of over $2 a day faced trade-weighted tariffs of only just over 6% on average, as shown in Figure 12.5.

Partly as a result, many governments of developing countries, as well as companies and citizens, believe that they got a bad deal in the Uruguay Round negotiations that culminated in the establishment of the WTO. There is the widespread conviction in the developing world that the rich countries did not live up to their part of the bargain, failing to open their markets fairly. Developing nations complain that governments and corporations of the developed world have the most effective (and expensive) lawyers and other leverage to force developing countries to follow WTO requirements, while developing nations lack the resources to force the rich nations to do the same.

However, developing countries now represent about three-quarters of the 159-member WTO (as of 2013). And whereas India and Brazil played high-profile, vocal roles in trade negotiations under the GATT, with perhaps three dozen other developing countries taking active, if relatively quiet, roles in the new century, the situation has changed palpably. The WTO director's own

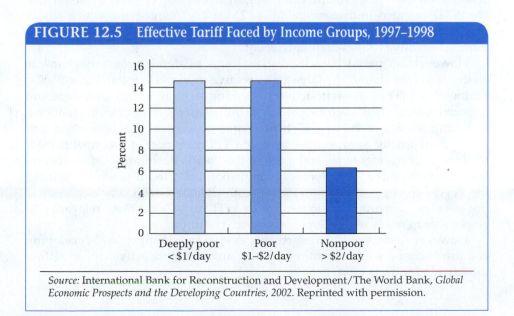

FIGURE 12.5   Effective Tariff Faced by Income Groups, 1997–1998

Source: International Bank for Reconstruction and Development/The World Bank, *Global Economic Prospects and the Developing Countries*, 2002. Reprinted with permission.

2001 report noted that after eight trade liberalization rounds over the past half century, trade barriers remain in place in textiles and agriculture, the goods most affecting the developing world. As the world's trading nations began consideration of a new round of negotiations on reducing trade barriers, the developing world was insisting on a larger say. Unlike the IMF and World Bank, the WTO operates on consensus, in effect giving even small, low-income nations an equal vote—and an effective veto. Developing-country governments say they are reluctant to extend negotiations to what they term the "nontrade" issues of investment, competition, environment, and labor standards. Thus, the developing countries do not appear to be without bargaining power if they can learn to use it effectively.

The most recent round of negotiations were dubbed the "Doha Development Round": *Doha* for the city in Qatar in which agreement on the agenda was reached in November 2001 and *Development* for the commitment to focus much more on the needs and aspirations of the developing world in this round of trade agreements. Whether this goal ultimately will be achieved remains to be seen. But these talks have been at a protracted impasse. For example, the 2006 talks ended in discord about reducing developed-country farm subsidies, and the 2008 talks collapsed over this and other issues of market access, and acrimony over the extent of permissible use of developing-countries' "special safeguard mechanisms" to protect poor farmers in countries such as India in the event of import surges. The outlook was cloudy after failure to conclude the round on the agreed timetable. Since the 2008 economic crisis, politicians in many countries have considered it inexpedient to be viewed as extending "concessions" on trade.

In what was widely viewed as new evidence of the increasing role and power of developing countries in international economic affairs, in May 2013, Brazilian diplomat Roberto Azevêdo was elected as the new WTO director-general—despite the fact that he was not the preferred candidate of the United States or the EU—after an unusually lengthy leadership contest. Subsequently, the WTO engaged in discussions for a "Doha lite" agreement, which would give a sense of progress on trade talks while avoiding more sensitive—albeit more substantive—areas of disagreement.[72]

However, on parallel tracks, regional and bilateral trade arrangements continue to take shape. The largest prospective example is for a "Trans-Pacific Partnership" (TPP), now in active discussion, which would include about a dozen mostly high-income countries but also some developing nations, including Mexico, Peru, and Vietnam. Some observers have concluded that rather than strictly a trade agreement, the TPP gets part of its impetus from the fear of China's growing influence in the Pacific Basin area. Other observers have viewed the TPP process as emblematic of a trend toward sidelining the WTO—the opposite of what many countries had originally envisaged.[73] But debates over proposals to reform the WTO to make it more relevant and responsive to needs of developing countries continue.[74]

However institutional arrangements evolve in coming years, developing countries seem certain to continue to play an ever more active role in setting the agenda for trade talks.

A Pioneer in Development Success through Trade: Taiwan

Taiwan is one of the original four "East Asian Tiger" economies whose dramatic economic successes of recent decades influenced the way economists think about development. The experience of Taiwan was a major impetus behind the changes in economic policy instituted in the People's Republic of China (PRC) beginning in 1978. With a population of about 23 million, Taiwan, which calls itself the Republic of China (ROC), is a mountainous, 36,000-square-kilometer (14,000-square-mile) island off the coast of the Chinese mainland, about the combined size of Maryland and Delaware, or a little less than that of the Netherlands.

Taiwan's claim to its status as a "development miracle" is strong. The island racked up a measured annual economic growth rate averaging about 7% over the four decades from 1960 to 2000. Taiwan's economy grew nearly 10% annually in the 1965–1980 period, faster than any other nation's. Despite its now high-income status, with a per capita income of $13,925 in 2000 at market exchange rates ($22,646 in 2000 at PPP), Taiwan continued to grow, at a rapid rate of 5.7% on average over the 1996–2000 period. Sustaining such high rates over such a long stretch of time was unprecedented until the subsequent growth of China itself (see the case study in Chapter 4). At least as important, Taiwan has achieved universal elementary and middle school education (nine years are mandatory), a healthy population with a life expectancy of 75 years, and an infant mortality rate of only 5 per 1,000 live births. Absolute poverty has essentially been eliminated, unemployment is extremely low, and relative inequality is modest even by developed-country standards.

Taiwan has had to adjust to some of the changes that economies that reach the threshold of high-income status must confront. The GDP growth rate fell to just 2% in the 2000–2010 decade. Like Japan, Taiwan has a below-replacement fertility rate, and its population growth rate has now dropped to less than a quarter of a percent per year. There has been a "hollowing out" of basic manufacturing as plants have moved to (mainland) China in search of lower-wage labor. Production that has remained has been forced to shift rapidly to high-tech products and processes in the face of rising competition in basic industries from other developing countries. Continued uncertainty clouds the island's political future, given the forceful response from China in response to any hint of Taiwan independence, as China regards Taiwan as a renegade province. The resulting business uncertainty has had at least some dampening effect on investment. But Taiwan has also transformed itself into a credibly and competitively democratic polity with a vigorously free press and far less corruption and greater government transparency than its neighbors.

Taiwan's achievement stands in contrast to many other economies that started in similar—or even better—circumstances in the postwar world.

Competing Explanations for Success

Taiwan's success has been ascribed to many factors, including an emphasis on education, extensive infrastructure development, early and thorough land reform, very high rates of saving and investment, a mixture of constructive foreign influences and diffusion of commercial ideas from Japan and the United States, an effective government industrialization strategy, the free market's release of

human energies and creativity, a 1960s boom resulting from the Vietnam War, the initiation of an export-led growth strategy in the midst of the rapidly expanding world economy of the early 1960s, direct American aid—and Taiwan's use of that aid for investment rather than consumption, the work ethic and productive attitudes of the Taiwanese labor force, a long history as an entrepreneurial culture, the movement into entrepreneurship of capable local islanders who sought opportunities for advancement but were blocked from the political arena, and the survival instinct—the necessity of economic development as a defense against attack from the PRC.

Instead of having to choose from just one or two of these factors, an alternative interpretation is that development success requires many things to work well together, and hence there may not be so many explanations after all. Many of the cited factors may reflect necessary but not sufficient conditions. In this view, the key is to understand the magnified impact of having many development factors operating successfully at the same time (see Chapter 4).

Let's examine the factors cited more closely.

Emphasis on Education

Consistent with the historical Chinese cultural veneration for education, six years of education became compulsory in Taiwan in 1950. Especially impressive were enrollment rates for girls, which surpassed 90% for those aged 6 to 11 by 1956. (The comparable figure for boys in that year was over 96%.) Emphasis on girls' education is widely viewed as one of the most important factors in successful development.

When compulsory education was expanded to nine years in 1968, there were doubts that the economy could afford it. Today, while 9 years remains a remarkable minimum educational standard for any developing economy, plans are being considered to expand compulsory schooling to 12 years.

Other features have also been in play. Students go to school seven hours a day, five and one-half days a week. In 2002, the overall student-teacher ratio was less than 20. Teacher salaries are relatively high, comparable to lower-middle management in Taiwan. Taiwan's models were the United States for general education and Japan for vocational education.

Greater emphasis is placed on general than on job-specific skills. But incentives for close relationships between education and business are also stressed. Tax breaks are given for company donations of personnel and equipment to schools.

Assuming that the world development community is serious in its Millennium Development Goal of enrolling all children in six years of elementary school by 2015, the early experience of Taiwan is instructive. Enrollment was real and not just on paper, students generally remained in school after they enrolled, teachers taught seriously, and corruption was kept to a minimum. The contrast in most of these respects to today's low-income countries is striking.

Extensive Infrastructure Development

Development of infrastructure has been widely cited as a crucial factor in successful development. A major highway, for example, is argued to represent a "growth pole" around which industrial and commercial development can consolidate and grow. From the period of Japanese colonial rule (1905–1945), Taiwan inherited an infrastructure system that was far superior to that of most poor countries. The Japanese built roads, ports, and railroads to facilitate their own acquisition of rice and other farm products from the island. But this same infrastructure became a vehicle for national industrial growth from the 1950s. This endowment was supplemented by the government's own extensive program in the 1950s and 1960s. Taiwan's army was too large for the island, a legacy of the pre-1949 control of the mainland by the governing Kuomintang, or Chinese Nationalists. Thousands of soldiers participated in a voluntary program to retire from active military service to build infrastructure, including the technically challenging east-west highway projects, a program reckoned in Taiwan to be a major factor in its subsequent success. In more recent years, the emphasis has moved to telecoms and other high-tech infrastructure.

There was some waste, fraud, and abuse in infrastructure spending, though apparently less than average. When the press was freed, a number of infrastructure scandals were uncovered, many affecting Taiwan's capital, Taipei. The political openings

have played a role in keeping infrastructure development and other development necessities on track, another reflection of the interactive roles played by several contributory factors in economic growth.

Early and Thorough Land Reform Not burdened by close political ties to landlords, the Taiwanese government implemented a thoroughgoing land-to-the-tiller reform program in the 1950s. Landowners received stock in state-owned enterprises in return for transferring land to peasants. This was a major factor in the extremely rapid growth of agricultural productivity in this period—a crucial foundation for later industrialization. Other countries with similar land reform efforts, such as South Korea and Japan, have seen impressive results. The United States had similarly benefited from nineteenth-century programs such as the Homestead Act. In contrast, development in Latin America, as well as in some Asian countries such as the Philippines, has been severely hampered by the lack of land reform.

Very High Rates of Saving and Investment Most analysts agree that capital formation is crucial to successful development. Developed countries have much higher levels of capital per head than less developed countries, one of the factors enabling developed countries to enjoy higher productivity and incomes. Taiwan's saving rates were among the highest ever recorded, reaching 30 to 40% in the 1950s and 1960s.

The saving ethic is deeply rooted in Taiwanese culture. Parents teach children the overriding need to save for a rainy day. Public policies keep real interest rates for savers relatively high and tax-free. Interestingly, like fellow Tiger South Korea, Taiwan has a relatively low foreign-capital share in total investment, about 10%. High rates of saving and investment are important factors in development but not sufficient ones. India has substantially increased its rate of investment since independence in 1947 but not until recently its growth rate, partly because capital equipment has been expensive there and partly because investments have not been made in the most productive sectors at any point in time.

Diffusion of Commercial Ideas High saving alone will not create a development miracle without productive ideas among entrepreneurs about what use to make of it. Taiwan has had considerable success in absorbing commercial ideas from Japan and the United States, largely due to the diligence of thousands of individual small companies. But government has also played a role, through agencies like the China External Trade Development Council (CETDC) that combed the world, especially the United States, for ideas on how Taiwanese firms could upgrade their technology and adapt to enter industrial markets. The World Bank's Donald Keesing has offered some fascinating insights into the CETDC's operation:

> Market research in CETDC's New York office as of 1980 was based on an active search for items that could be sold in the United States. The search began with an analysis of the size and origin of U.S. imports, followed by a preliminary study of the price and quality of the more competitive imported and U.S. products. From this the officers in New York reached an estimate of the likelihood of Taiwan, China, firms competing successfully against offerings already on the market. (They claimed to understand the manufacturing capabilities of Taiwan, China, firms well enough to do this.) Once a likely product was identified, the office asked firms in Taiwan, China, to send it samples of the product and price lists. Representatives of the office would then visit importers, wholesalers, and other traders with samples and price lists, prospecting for sales. They would try to get reactions to the product. If the buyers were interested, they would telex the manufacturers. If not, they would find out why and then suggest appropriate steps to the manufacturer.

These observations lead us to perhaps the most complex set of development issues, the roles of state and market in successful development.

Effective Government Industrial Policies A traditional explanation for Taiwan's success is the operation of the free market. In contrast, Robert Wade and others have shown that Taiwan employed extensive government industrial policies and have presented somewhat controversial evidence that Taiwan's success is due in large measure to the effectiveness of its industrial policy.

Taiwan has had active industrial policy systems in place to license exports, control direct foreign investment both in and from Taiwan, establish

export cartels, and provide fiscal incentives for investment in priority sectors and concessional credit for favored industries. The government plays a much less active role today, now that developed-country status has been nearly attained, but it is interesting to view the roles played in Taiwan's more formative development stages.

Taiwan's economic history began with a very highly dirigiste, or state-directed, import substitution–oriented industrialization in the 1949–1958 period. Reforms in 1958 switched intervention to export promotion and introduced market forces. But what emerged was not a free market but merely a less thoroughly planned economy. Into the 1980s, all imports and exports in Taiwan had to be covered by a license. Imports were categorized as "prohibited," "controlled," and "permissible." Controlled goods included luxuries and some goods produced locally with reasonable quality, in sufficient quantities, and whose prices were not more than a narrow margin (about 5%) above comparable import prices. Because the controlled list was larger than the published one, not all "permissibles" were automatically approved. As Wade shows, a potential importer of an item on the hidden list had to provide evidence that domestic suppliers could not meet foreign price, quality, and timing-of-delivery terms. Wade presents evidence that their function was to jump-start growth industries by providing domestic demand for products targeted by the government. Then aggressive incentives were provided to induce companies to begin to export these products.

Wade's interpretation of the relative success of this import substitution program is consistent with an emphasis on market incentives. He argues that because it controls quantities of foreign goods entering the local economy, the government can use international prices to discipline the price-setting behavior of protected domestic producers. The government demanded to know good reasons why domestic prices of protected items were significantly higher than international prices, especially in the case of inputs to be used for export production. In this way, domestic prices for controlled goods could be kept near world price levels through the threat of permitting imports, even without free trade of goods across national borders. Wade concluded that an effective government threat of allowing more goods in can itself be sufficient to hold prices down, despite trade protection. Thus, the argument is that government is able to play an active role in industrial policy without compromising the vitality of market incentives.

Clearly, Taiwan's economy has been far from a free market, but explanations for Taiwan's success other than its actively interventionist policies can be given. In particular, general policies such as support of basic education and encouragement of high rates of saving cannot be ruled out as more important factors in Taiwan's success. Many entrepreneurs of small businesses in Taiwan seemed to feel that government has done more to harass them than to help them. And the stable, consistent macroeconomic policies in Taiwan and elsewhere in East Asia also stand in dramatic contrast to much of the rest of the developing world, especially the poorest-performing regions.

Market Incentives Even if entrepreneurial dynamism is hard to measure precisely, it is in evidence throughout the island. Incentives to produce wealth rather than merely to seek a share of existing wealth (rent-seeking behavior) are established with solid property rights and not significantly undermined by other policies.

Taiwan's government has not always been a highly efficient engine of progress. The mere fact that the ROC administers both a central and a provincial government covering exactly the same territory presented many opportunities for inefficiency. This is a legacy of the Chinese civil war, which the ROC lost. Moreover, until 1991, the government ruled Taiwan under martial law, creating opportunities for corruption. Indeed, in the 1990s, new corruption scandals were reported almost daily in Taiwan's many independent newspapers. The free election of Lee Teng-hui as president in 1996 was the culmination of a smooth five-year transition to democratic governance. Elections have been highly competitive since then and are generally viewed as free and fair; power has changed hands peacefully.

Other Factors The other explanations listed earlier were also somewhat important but unlikely to have been critical, given the decisive role of the seven factors just discussed. They are also special features that other economies cannot easily encourage through policy measures. The 1960s Vietnam War boom affected countries such as the Philippines as much as, if not more than, Taiwan, without lasting

effect. American aid to Egypt has been far larger and substantially used for investment purposes but with less impressive results. Undoubtedly, the work ethic and attitudes of the labor force were important. At the same time, they could not be called into play without the right incentives in place and without the availability of economically productive ideas. And a work ethic can be stimulated by the right incentives. A long history as an entrepreneurial culture may also be important, but in the long run, these will similarly be influenced by incentives for entrepreneurship.

The fact that Taiwan benefited from beginning export-led growth in the early 1960s, a time of unequaled world growth and a wide-open American market, was an undoubted advantage. On the other hand, other countries such as Thailand successfully grew through manufactures exports in the 1980s, despite far slower U.S. and world income and trade growth rates. The PRC has grown faster over the past quarter century than Taiwan ever did, despite sometimes sluggish world trade growth. Many of the PRC's reform policies since 1978 have been copied from the experience of Taiwan.

The idea that local islanders had few opportunities outside of entrepreneurship has not been proved; in any case, Taiwan seems hardly to differ in this regard from the situation under many other authoritarian regimes around the developing world that have suffered negative per capita income growth.

As to the necessity of economic development as a defense strategy, one cannot single out Taiwan. The United States guaranteed Taiwan's defense after President Truman sealed off the island in 1950 in response to the Korean crisis. Other developing countries lacking the natural defenses of an island and as gravely threatened by hostile neighbors have made little development progress in the same period. Military necessity more often represents a diversion of resources needed for development than a productive stimulus.

Conclusion

A combination of factors underlies Taiwan's success. Among them are an emphasis on education, absorption of productive ideas from abroad, extensive infrastructure development, thoroughgoing land reform, very high rates of saving and investment, an effective industrial policy, and ensuring that marketplace incentives to produce wealth rather than to seek a share of existing wealth are established with solid property rights and not undermined by other policies.

Recently, the government of Taiwan has focused on collaborating with the private sector on more advanced research and development as Taiwan moves into high-technology fields. Taiwan's dynamic firms have invested vast sums in the PRC. Taiwan has been striving to adapt to a future in which relatively unskilled industrial jobs will no longer be available. The focus has been on education; high-technology production in several sectors, including computers, software, and biotechnology; and financial development. The focus continues to be on development through increasingly sophisticated exports. As Erik Thorbecke and Henry Wan point out, Taiwan launched its competitive semiconductor industry by using government laboratories to develop basic know-how and then formed private spin-off companies from these laboratories. And as noted by Thorbecke, Tung, and Wan, the government has also provided indirect but effective incentives to local firms that are providing key inputs to high-tech exporters and achieved success notably in the synthetic fiber and semiconductor industries. Thus, continued development of government competence and effectiveness in industrialization strategy may be critical as a developing economy approaches developed-country status. The economy may still face multiple equilibria (see Chapter 4) regarding its possible location on or below the world technology frontier. Haider Ali Khan provides an interesting analysis of Taiwan's efforts to transform its economy into a center of original research and development via a "positive feedback loop innovation system."

The fact that Taiwan weathered the enormous storms of the East Asian financial crisis in 1997–1998 strongly signaled the economy's development and resilience. The biggest problems looming for Taiwan are the resolution of the conflict with the PRC and the wholesale moves of Taiwan's industrial base to that country. The two issues are interrelated, most notably because greater interdependence between these economies is likely to raise the costs of war and lead to a peaceful resolution of the island's status. The resumption in 2008 of direct

mail and flights between Taiwan and mainland China, after 59 years, was a hopeful sign that violence can be avoided.

Are there any drawbacks to Taiwan's growth? Certainly environmental considerations have taken a backseat to economic growth until very recently. Taipei suffers from exceedingly noxious air pollution, for example. Despite a nominal beginning at land use planning, a drive down the island's west coast reveals a dizzying jumble of agricultural, industrial, commercial, and residential uses, defying any economic rationale, let alone aesthetics. Industrial sites sit perched on landfill over rice paddies and prawn pools, into which some waste products inevitably seep. Only after much Western pressure was attention given to endangered species. Even with increased government attention, as one Taiwanese official frankly put it, "the private sector is flexible and vibrant in Taiwan—where there is profit, there is activity."

For the most part, housing remains relatively small and basic in Taiwan. Again, with the opening of the PRC, many Taiwanese companies are moving lock, stock, and barrel to the mainland; some hollowing out of the economy, as has been seen in the United States and the United Kingdom, has occurred, but investment in the PRC by Taiwanese firms has arguably brought at least as much opportunity as problems. Taiwan was hit significantly by the global recession in 2008 and 2009, before rebounding. Although the caveats qualify Taiwan's success and point to some necessary future directions, they do not negate its impressive accomplishments.

In sum, Taiwan illustrates well the complex mix of factors behind the kind of rapid economic and social progress often termed *a development miracle*. The factors that stood out were education, infrastructure, land reform, high rates of saving and investment, absorption of commercial ideas, effective industrial policy in formative stages, market incentives, and policies and incentives for continued improvement and upgrading in skills, specialization in design skills, flexible production operations, productive knowledge, and efficiency. Thus, the transformation in Taiwan is not really a "mysterious" miracle; it can be understood as the result of policies consistent with the broader research on economic development. ■

Sources

Amsden, Alice H. "Taiwan's economic history: A case of *étatisme* and a challenge to dependency theory." *Modern China* 5 (1979): 341–380.

———. "Taiwan." *World Development* 12 (1984): 627–633.

Balassa, Bela. "The lessons of East Asian development: An overview." *Economic Development and Cultural Change* 36 (1988): S273–S290.

Bradford, Colin I. "Trade and structural change: NICs and next-tier NICs as transitional economies." *World Development* 15 (1987): 299–316.

Chenery, Hollis, Sherman Robinson, and Moses Syrquin. *Industrialization and Growth: A Comparative Study*. New York: Oxford University Press, 1986.

Chu, Wan-wen. "Export-led growth and import dependence: The case of Taiwan, 1969–1981." *Journal of Development Economics* 28 (1988): 265–276.

Dahlman, Carl J., and Ousa Sananikone. "Taiwan, China: Policies and institutions for rapid growth," in *Lessons from East Asia*, ed. Danny M. Leipziger. Ann Arbor: University of Michigan Press, 1997.

Dahlman, Carl J., Bruce Ross-Larson, and Larry E. Westphal. "Managing technical development: Lessons from the newly industrializing countries." *World Development* 15 (1987): 759–775.

Jacobsson, Steffan. "Technical change and industrial policy: The case of computer numerically controlled lathes in Argentina, Korea and Taiwan." *World Development* 10 (1982): 991–1014.

Keesing, Donald B. "The four successful exceptions: Official export promotion and support for export marketing in Korea, Hong Kong, Singapore and Taiwan, China." United Nations Development Programme–World Bank Trade Expansion Program Occasional Paper No. 2, 1988.

Khan, Haider Ali. "Innovation and growth: A Schumpeterian model of innovation applied to Taiwan." *Oxford Development Studies* 30 (2002): 289–306.

Mathews, John A. "The origins and dynamics of Taiwan's R&D consortia." *Research Policy* 31 (2002): 633–651.

Pack, Howard, and Larry E. Westphal. "Industrial strategy and technological change: Theory versus reality." *Journal of Development Economics* 22 (1986): 87–128.

Smith, Stephen C. *Industrial Policy in Developing Countries: Reconsidering the Real Sources of Export-Led Growth.* Washington, D.C.: Economic Policy Institute, 1991.

Taiwan Yearbook, 1993 and 2004. Taipei Government Information Office.

Thorbecke, Erik, and Henry Wan. "Revisiting East (and Southeast) Asia's development model." Paper presented at the Cornell University Conference on Seventy-Five Years of Development, Ithaca, N.Y., May 7–9, 2004.

Thorbecke, Erik, An-chi Tung, and Henry Wan. "Industrial targeting: Lessons from past errors and successes of Hong Kong and Taiwan." *World Economy* 25 (2002): 1047–1061.

Wade, Robert. *Governing the Market.* Princeton, N.J.: Princeton University Press, 1991.

———. "The role of government in overcoming market failure: Taiwan, Republic of Korea and Japan," in *Achieving Industrialization in East Asia,* ed. Helen Hughes. New York: Cambridge University Press, 1988.

———. "State intervention in outward-looking development: Neoclassical theory and Taiwanese practice," in *Developmental States in East Asia,* ed. Gordon White. New York: St. Martin's Press, 1988.

Concepts for Review

Absolute advantage
Autarky
Balanced trade
Barter transactions
Capital account
Commodity terms of trade
Common market
Comparative advantage
Current account
Customs union
Depreciation (of currency)
Devaluation
Dual exchange rate (parallel exchange rate)
Economic integration
Economic union
Effective rate of protection
Enclave economies
Exchange control
Export dependence
Export earnings instability
Export promotion
Factor endowment trade theory
Factor price equalization
Flexible exchange rate
Foreign-exchange earnings
Free-market exchange rate
Free trade

Free-trade area
Gains from trade
General Agreement on Tariffs and Trade (GATT)
Globalization
Growth poles
Import substitution
Income elasticity of demand
Increasing returns
Industrialization strategy approach
Industrial policy
Infant industry
International commodity agreement
Inward-looking development policies
Managed float
Monopolistic market control
Multifiber Arrangement (MFA)
New protectionism
Nominal rate of protection
Nontariff trade barrier
North-South trade models
Official exchange rate
Oligopolistic market control
Outward-looking development policies
Overvalued exchange rate

Prebisch-Singer hypothesis
Price elasticity of demand
Primary products
Product cycle
Product differentiation
Quota
Regional trading bloc
Rent
Returns to scale
Risk
Specialization
Subsidy
Synthetic substitutes
Tariff
Trade creation
Trade deficit
Trade diversion
Trade liberalization
Trade optimists
Trade pessimists
Uncertainty
Undervalued exchange rate
Uruguay Round
Value added
Vent-for-surplus theory of international trade
Wage-price spiral
World Trade Organization (WTO)

Questions for Discussion

1. The effects of international trade on a country's development are often related to four basic economic concepts: efficiency, growth, equity, and stability. Briefly explain what is meant by each of these concepts as it relates to the theory of international trade.

2. Compare and contrast the classical labor cost theory of comparative advantage with the neoclassical factor endowment theory of international trade. Be sure to include an analysis of both assumptions and conclusions.

3. Briefly summarize the major conclusions of the traditional theory of free trade with regard to its theoretical effects on world and domestic efficiency, world and domestic economic growth, world and domestic income distribution, and the pattern of world production and consumption.

4. Proponents of free trade, primarily developed-country economists, argue that the liberalization of trading relationships between rich and poor countries (the removal of tariff and nontariff barriers) would work toward the long-run benefit of *all* countries. Under what conditions might the removal of all tariffs and other impediments to trade work to the best advantage of developing countries? Explain.

5. Traditional free-trade theories are based on six crucial assumptions, which may or may not be valid for developing nations (or for developed nations for that matter). What are these crucial assumptions, and how might they be violated in the real world of international trade?

6. Traditional free-trade theory is basically a *static* theory of international exchange leading to certain conclusions about the benefits likely to accrue to all participants. Explain the dynamic elements that are also important.

7. Critics of international trade from developing countries sometimes claim that present trading relationships between developed and underdeveloped countries can be a source of "antidevelopment" for the latter and merely serve to perpetuate their weak and dependent status. Explain their argument. Do you tend to agree or disagree? Explain why.

8. Manufactures now account for a majority of exports from the developing world. What factors have limited the benefits that developing countries receive from this progress?

9. In what ways is the emergence of China as the "workshop of the world" an opportunity for other developing countries, and in what ways is it a threat?

10. Explain the distinction between primary and secondary inward- and outward-looking development policies.

11. Briefly summarize the range of commercial policies available to developing countries, and explain why some of these policies might be adopted.

12. What are the possibilities, advantages, and disadvantages of export promotion in developing nations with reference to specific types of commodities (e.g., primary food products, raw materials, fuels, minerals, manufactured goods)?

13. Most less developed countries in Latin America, Africa, and Asia pursued policies of import substitution as a major component of their development strategies. Explain the theoretical and practical arguments in support of import substitution policies. What have been some of the weaknesses of these policies in practice, and why have the results often not lived up to expectations?

14. Explain some of the arguments in support of the use of tariffs, quotas, and other trade barriers in developing countries.

15. What issues form the basis of the debate between trade optimists and trade pessimists? Explain your answer.

16. What are the basic static and dynamic arguments for economic integration in less developed countries? Briefly describe the various forms that economic integration can take (e.g., customs union, free-trade areas). What are the major obstacles to effective economic integration in developing regions?

17. How do the trade policies of developed countries affect the ability of less developed countries to benefit from greater participation in the world economy? How do nontrade domestic economic policies of rich nations affect the export earnings of developing countries?

18. What factors do you think are most important in implementing a successful, outward-looking industrialization strategy?

Notes

1. This discussion draws on World Bank, *Poverty in an Age of Globalization* (Washington, D.C.: World Bank, 2000); Sarah Anderson and John Cavanaugh, with Thea Lee, *Field Guide to the Global Economy* (New York: New Press, 2000); Jeffrey Sachs, *Making Globalization Work* (Washington, D.C.: George Washington University Press, 2000); the articles in *Symposium on Globalization in Perspective*, esp. Dani Rodrik, "An Introduction," *Journal of Economic Perspectives* 12 (1998): 3–8; and Dani Rodrik, "Globalisation, social conflict and economic growth," *World Economy* 21 (1998): 143–158.; Joseph Stiglitz, *Globalization and Its Discontents* (New York: W. W. Norton, 2007); and Jagdish Bhagwati, *In Defense of Globalization* (New York: Oxford University Press, 2007).

2. Muhammad Yunus, *Creating a World without Poverty: Social Business and the Future of Capitalism* (New York: Public Affairs, 2008), p. 5.

3. World Bank, *World Development Indicators, 2010* (New York: Oxford University Press, 2010), p. 381. The comparison of agricultural subsidies and aid is based on OECD data as reported in *World Development Indicators, 2012*, p. 16.

4. David I. Harvey, Neil M. Kellard, Jakob B. Madsen, and Mark E. Wohar, "The Prebisch-Singer hypothesis: Four centuries of evidence," *Review of Economics and Statistics* 92 (2010): 367.

5. United Nations Conference on Trade and Development (UNCTAD), "Commodity information," 2002, http://www.unctad.org/Templates/Page.asp?intltemelD=3599&lang=1. See also World Bank, *Can Africa Claim the 21st Century?* (Washington, D.C.: World Bank, 2000), ch. 7; Sarah Anderson, John Cavanagh, Thea Lee, and Barbara Ehrenreich, *Field Guide to the Global Economy* (New York: New Press, 2000), pp. 10–11; and *World Development Indicators 2010*, Figure 6h, p. 349.

6. Statistics on tourism services are available from the *Yearbook of Tourism Statistics and World Tourism* (2012 edition) from the World Tourism Organization.

7. See UNCTAD, *Trade and Development Report, 2006* (New York: United Nations, 2006), ch. 1.

8. Derived from World Bank, *World Development Indicators, 2013*, tab. 4.4 2012 data). On diversification patterns, see Jean Imbs and Romain Wacziarg, "Stages of diversification," *American Economic Review* 93 (2003): 63–86.

9. For data on relative income elasticities of demand for selected commodities in relation to manufactures, see World Bank, *1994 Global Economic Prospects and the Developing Countries* (Washington, D.C.: World Bank, 1994), tab. 2.5. A good discussion of primary-product export earnings instability can be found in ch. 2.

10. United Nations Conference on Trade and Development, "Excessive commodity price volatility: Macroeconomic effects on growth and policy options," Contribution from the UNCTAD secretariat to the G20 Commodity Markets Working Group," April 2012, at http://unctad.org/meetings/en/Miscellaneous%20Documents/gds_mdpb_G20_001_en.pdf.

The study found volatility increasing for all groups of developing countries and found that the effect is not only due to concentrating on only a couple of commodities—it is the type of commodity that mattered, not the variety of those commodities per se. On impacts, see, for example, Matthias Lutz, "The effect of volatility in the terms of trade on output growth: New evidence," *World Development* 22 (1994): 1959–1975. Related studies address terms of trade instability. See, for example, Teame Ghirmaya, Subhash C. Sharmaa, and Richard Grabowskia, "Export instability, income terms of trade instability and growth: causal analyses," *Journal of International Trade and Economic Development* 8, No. 2 (1999): 209–229; the authors' co-integration results indicate, "For most countries, instability in the income terms of trade is negatively related to output while the results for export instability are mixed." They inferred that "export instability and income terms of trade instability play a causal role in the development process via a variety of avenues." Other authors have concluded that there may be indirect effects through instability in investments and imports, for example. More research is needed to pin down circumstances under which different forms of instability impact different outcomes.

11. See Carmen M. Reinhart and Peter Wickham, "Commodity prices: Cyclical weakness or secular

decline?" *International Monetary Fund Staff Papers* 41 (1994): 175–213, and Rati Ram, "Trends in developing countries' commodity terms-of-trade since 1970," *Review of Radical Political Economics* 36 (2004): 241–253.

12. Somewhat reduced but relatively high prices despite recessions suggested supply constraints; as higher prices spur investments in extraction, relative commodity prices may drop again. See World Bank, *Global Economic Prospects 2009: Commodities at the Crossroads* (Washington, D.C.: World Bank, 2009), p. 55. And by 2013, even nominal commodity prices remained about 12% below their 2008 peak, with at best an uncertain trajectory. See UNCTAD, op. cit. An alternative measure of the terms of trade is the income terms of trade, which measures the relative purchasing power of a country's exports. Some economists argue that this gives a better picture of the relationship between exports (and export earnings instability) and growth because it abstracts from relative price movements. For example, Matthias Lutz found a strong negative relationship between income terms of trade volatility (see note 10) and economic growth rates, confirming some earlier studies that found a negative relationship between volatility in commodity terms of trade and economic growth.

13. See Raul Prebisch, *The Economic Development of Latin America and Its Principal Problems* (New York: United Nations, 1950), and Hans W. Singer, "The distribution of gains between borrowing and investing countries," *American Economic Review* 40 (1950): 473–485.

14. See Alf Maizels, *The Manufactures Terms of Trade of Developing Countries with the United States, 1981–97* (Oxford: Oxford University Press, 2000), and Sarkar Prabirjit and Hans W. Singer, "Manufactured exports of developing countries and their terms of trade since 1965," *World Development* 19 (1991): 333–340.

15. Recall that the slope of a line tangent to any point on the concave production possibility frontier will show the opportunity or real costs of reducing the output of one commodity in order to produce more of the other. In a world of perfect competition, these relative costs would also equal relative market prices. Therefore, the slope of the dotted line

tangent to point *A* also shows relative commodity prices. The steeper the slope, the higher would be the price of *a* relative to *m*. As we move from left to right (e.g., from point *A* to point *B* in Figure 12.1a), the slope of the tangent line becomes progressively steeper, indicating increasing opportunity costs of producing more food. Similarly, a right-to-left movement along the production frontier (from *B* to *A*) would represent increasing opportunity costs of producing more manufactured goods in terms of forgone food output.

16. The classic article on the theory of factor price equalization is Paul A. Samuelson, "International trade and equalization of factor prices," *Economic Journal* 48 (1948): 163–184. It should be noted that manufacturing workers who have permanently lost their jobs in this sector have on average experienced a net decline in incomes, according to research by the Economic Policy Institute.

17. Manmohan Singh, "Development policy research: The task ahead," *Proceedings of the World Bank Annual Conference on Development Economics, 1989* (Washington, D.C.: World Bank, 1990), p. 12. Singh was secretary general of the South Commission, Geneva, at the time of this address. In 2004, he became prime minister of India and still remained in power in late 2013.

18. For some representative literature on North-South trade models, as well as other nontraditional theories, see Paul Krugman, "Trade, accumulation and uneven development," *Journal of Development Economics* 8 (1981): 149–161; Graciella Chichilnisky, "A general equilibrium theory of North-South trade," in *Essays in Honor of Kenneth J. Arrow,* eds. Walter Heller et al. (New York: Cambridge University Press, 1986); Jose Antonio Ocampo, "New developments in trade theory and LDCs," *Journal of Development Economics* 22 (1986): 129–170; and Amitava K. Dutt, "Monopoly power and uneven development: Baran revisited," *Journal of Development Studies* 24 (1988): 161–176.

19. Michael E. Porter, *The Competitive Advantage of Nations* (New York: Free Press, 1990). The new trade theory that allows for increasing returns to scale and imperfect competition, pioneered by Paul Krugman, offers an analysis that is parallel in some ways and leads to some similar conclusions. For an overview, see Paul Krugman, "Increasing

returns, imperfect competition and the positive theory of international trade, in *Handbook of International Economics, Handbooks in Economics,* vol. 3 (New York: Elsevier, 1995), pp. 1243–1277.

20. Porter also notes that developing countries are also "vulnerable to exchange rate and factor cost swings. Many of these industries are also not growing, as the resource intensity of advanced economies falls and demand becomes more sophisticated." See Porter, *Competitive Advantage of Nations,* pp. 675–676.

21. See Heinz W. Arndt, "The origins of structuralism," *World Development* 13 (1985): 151–159.

22. The United Nations estimated in 2001 that such trade restrictions cost developing countries at least $100 billion annually—2% of their GDP.

23. For a review of how imperfect competition pervades international trading relations, see Elhanan Helpman, "The noncompetitive theory of international trade and trade policy," *Proceedings of the World Bank Annual Conference on Development Economics, 1989,* pp. 193–216, and David Greenaway, "New trade theories and developing countries," in *Current Issues in Development Economics,* eds. V. N. Balasubramanyam and Sanjaya Lall (New York: St. Martin's Press, 1991), pp. 159–169. On the costs of protection, see Intergovernmental Group of 24, "Communiqué on international monetary affairs and development," April 28, 2001, http://www.un.org/esa.

24. Helpman, "Noncompetitive theory," p. 196.

25. Jean Imbs and Romain Wacziarg, "Stages of diversification," *American Economic Review* 93 (2003): 63–86.

26. See Ajit Singh, "Openness and the market-friendly approach to development: Learning the right lessons from the development experience," *World Development* 22 (1994): 1814. See also the references in notes 35, 39, and 53.

27. Stiglitz-Sen-Fitoussi Commission on the Measurement of Economic Performance and Social Progress, 2009, http://www.stiglitz-sen-fitoussi.fr/en/index.htm.

28. For evidence that trade-oriented developing countries seem to have higher rates of aggregate economic growth (although, in many cases, it is difficult to isolate the true sources of that growth, and growth may lead to more trade), see World Bank,

World Development Report, 1992 (New York: Oxford University Press, 1992), and Jagdish N. Bhagwati, "Export-promoting trade strategy: Issues and evidence," *World Bank Research Observer* 3 (1988): 27–57.

29. Graciella Chichilnisky and Geoffrey Heal, *The Evolving International Economy* (New York: Cambridge University Press, 1986).

30. See, for example, the Santiago Declaration of Third World Economists, April 1973, and the Communiqué of the Third World Forum, Karachi, 1975. A later presentation of a similar, though less radical, view can be found in United Nations, *Development and International Economic Cooperation: An Agenda for Development* (New York: United Nations, 1994).

31. For an excellent discussion of inward versus outward development policies, see Paul P. Streeten, "Trade strategies for development: Some themes for the seventies," *World Development* 1 (1973): 1–10, and Donald B. Keesing, *Trade Policy for Developing Countries* (Washington, D.C.: World Bank, 1979). Among many informative reviews, two alternative perspectives are particularly noteworthy: Rudiger Dornbusch, "The case for trade liberalization in developing countries," *Journal of Economic Perspectives* 6 (1992): 69–85, and Dani Rodrik, "The limits of trade policy reform in developing countries," *Journal of Economic Perspectives* 6 (1992): 87–105.

32. Streeten, "Trade strategies," pp. 1, 2.

33. See Colin Kirkpatrick, "Trade policy and industrialization in LDCs," in *Surveys in Development Economics,* ed. Norman Gemmell (Oxford: Blackwell, 1987), pp. 71–72.

34. See, for example, Colin I. Bradford Jr., "East Asian 'models': Myths and lessons," in *Development Strategies Reconsidered,* eds. John P. Lewis and Valeriana Kallab (Washington, D.C.: Overseas Development Council, 1986), ch. 5; Stephen C. Smith, *Industrial Policy in Developing Countries: Reconsidering the Real Sources of Export-Led Growth* (Washington, D.C.: Economic Policy Institute, 1991); and Robert Wade, *Governing the Market: Economic Theory and the Role of Government in East Asian Industrialization* (Princeton, N.J.: Princeton University Press, 1990).

35. Kevin Watkins and Joachim von Braun, "Essay: Time to Stop Dumping on the World's Poor,"

in *International Food Policy Research Institute, 2002–2003 Annual Report* Washington, D.C., IFPRI, 2003, pp. 6–20; quote is from p. 9. This report contains an excellent review of problems of agricultural protectionism; unfortunately, in the years since it was written, no progress on trade talks has been made. Other indications of the serious problems caused by U.S. cotton, sugar, and other agricultural policies are found in Nicholas Minot and Lisa Daniels, "Impact of global cotton markets on rural poverty in Benin," IFPRI Discussion Paper No. 48, November 2002, http://www.ifpri .org/divs/mtid/dp/mssdp48.htm; Oxfam International, "Rigged rules and double standards," http://www.maketradefair.com/en/index.php? file=26032002105549.htm; Oxfam International, "Cultivating poverty," http://www.oxfam.org /eng/pdfs/pp020925_cotton.pdf; and the *New York Times'* "Harvesting Poverty" series, http:// nytimes.com/harvestingpoverty. See also Warren Vieth, "U.S. exports misery to Africa with farm bill," *Los Angeles Times*, May 27, 2002, p. Al, and "Sweet deals: 'Big sugar' fights threats from free trade and a global drive to limit consumption," *Financial Times*, February 27, 2004, p. 17. We thank Professor Andreas Savvides for his helpful suggestions regarding this topic.

36. For a review and summary of issues and evidence, see Watkins and von Braun, "2002–2003 IFPRI annual report essay." For classic earlier examinations of the difficulties that developing countries have had with primary-product exports, see United Nations Development Programme, *Human Development Report, 1992* (New York: Oxford University Press, 1992), pp. 59–62; World Bank, *World Development Report, 1991* (Washington, D.C.: World Bank, 1991), pp. 105–110; and World Bank, *Global Economic Prospects and the Developing Countries* (Washington, D.C.: World Bank, 1994), ch. 2.

37. World Bank, *World Development Indicators, 2013,* tab. 4.4 (Washington, D.C.: World Bank, 2013), and earlier WDI issues.

38. Bradford, "East Asian 'models'"; Stephen C. Smith, "Industrial policy and export success: Third World development strategies reconsidered," in *U.S. Trade Policy and Global Growth*, ed. Robert Blecker (New York: Sharpe, 1996), pp. 267–298; Jene Kwon, "The East Asian challenge

to neoclassical orthodoxy," *World Development* 22 (1994): 635–644; Paul Krugman, "The myth of Asia's miracle," *Foreign Affairs* 73 (1994): 62–78; Dani Rodrik, "Getting interventions right: How South Korea and Taiwan grew rich," *Economic Policy* 20 (1995): 53–97; Henry J. Bruton, "A reconsideration of import substitution," *Journal of Economic Literature* 36 (1998): 903–936; Sebastian Edwards, "Openness, trade liberalization, and growth in developing countries," *Journal of Economic Literature* 31 (1993): 1358–1393; Behzad Yaghmaian, "An empirical investigation of exports, development, and growth in developing countries: Challenging the neoclassical theory of export-led growth," *World Development* 22 (1994): 1977–1995; and Syed Nawab Haider Naqvi, "The significance of development economics," *World Development* 24 (1996): 978–980.

39. This problem is stressed by Africa expert Paul Collier. On limitations of AGOA and EBA, see Paul Collier, *The Bottom Billion: Why the Poorest Countries Are Falling Behind and What Can Be Done about It* (New York: Oxford University Press, 2007), pp. 168–170.

40. World Trade Organization, *Annual Report, 2001* (Geneva: World Trade Organization, 2001). See subsequent editions for annual trends. For a comprehensive exposition, see Judith Czako, Johann Human, and Jorge Miranda, *A Handbook of Anti-Dumping Investigations* (Cambridge: Cambridge University Press, 2003). On the antidumping surge, see World Trade Organization, "WTO Secretariat reports surge in new anti-dumping investigations" World Trade Organization Press/542, 20 October 2008; and Chad P. Bown, (2009) "Monitoring Update to the Global Antidumping Database," Brandeis working paper, http://www .brandeis.edu/~cbown/global_ad.

41. For many developing nations, trade taxes represent a major source of government revenue. For details, see Chapter 15.

42. For a classic critique of import substitution policies in developing countries, see Ian Little, Tibor Scitovsky, and Maurice Scott, *Industry and Trade in Some Developing Countries* (Oxford: Oxford University Press, 1970). See also Kirkpatrick, "Trade policy and industrialization," pp. 71–75; Hubert Schmitz, "Industrialization strategies in less developed countries: Some lessons of historical experience,"

Journal of Development Studies 21 (1984): 1–21; and Dornbusch, "Case for trade liberalization."

43. It should be mentioned, however, that in light of some of the new trade theories, with their emphasis on economies of scale, externalities, and human capital investments, the arguments for selective tariff protection came back into vogue. See Bruton, "Reconsideration of import substitution," for a summary of these issues.

44. Little et al., *Industry and Trade,* p. 39.

45. Herbert G. Grubel, "Effective tariff protection: A non-specialist introduction to the theory, policy implications and controversies," in *Effective Tariff Protection,* eds. Herbert G. Grubel and Harry Johnson (Geneva: GATT, 1971), p. 2.

46. Little et al., *Industry and Trade,* p. 4. See also David Greenaway and Chris Milner, "Trade theory and the less developed countries," in *Surveys in Development Economics,* ed. Norman Gemmel (Oxford: Blackwell, 1987), tab. 1.5.

47. Such preferred customers are often identified in the literature as "rent seekers" because they spend a great amount of time and effort engaged in activities, such as bribery, designed to capture the economic rent generated by government-induced price distortions like overvalued exchange rates. See Anne O. Krueger, "The political economy of the rent-seeking society," *American Economic Review* 64 (1974): 291–303.

48. For an analysis of multiple exchange rates and their effects on the economy, see Miguel Kiguel and Stephen A. O'Connell, "Parallel exchange rates in developing countries," *World Bank Research Observer* 10 (1995): 21–52. Black market premiums in the 1980s ranged from 66% in Mexico and 173% in Brazil to 4,264% in Ghana.

49. For example, in December 1994, the Mexican government *devalued* its currency, the peso, by 35% against the dollar. By February 1995, the peso had *depreciated* by another 15% before recovering some of its losses in the foreign-exchange market.

50. For a concise discussion of some issues related to devaluation, see Karim Nashashibi, "Devaluation in developing countries: The difficult choices," *Finance and Development* 20 (1983): 14–17.

51. For an excellent review and analysis of these issues, from which much of the following discussion is drawn, see Rostam M. Kavoussi, "International trade and economic development: The recent experience of developing countries," *Journal of Developing Areas* 19 (1985): 379–392. See also Dornbusch, "Case for trade liberalization," and Rodrik, "Limits of trade policy reform."

52. A statement of these views can be found in Deepak Lal and Sarath Rajapatirana, "Foreign trade regimes and economic growth in developing countries," *World Bank Research Observer* 2 (1987): 189–217, and Bhagwati, "Export-promoting trade strategy."

53. For a good recent review of economic issues and some evidence, see Mario Cimoli, Giovanni Dosi, and Joseph E. Stiglitz, *Industrial Policy and Development: The Political Economy of Capabilities Accumulation* (New York: Oxford University Press, 2009). Other key sources are Alice H. Amsden, *The Rise of "the Rest": Challenges to the West from Late-Industrializing Economies* (New York: Oxford University Press, 2001); Howard Pack and Larry Westphal, "Industrial strategy and technological change: Theory versus reality," *Journal of Development Economics* 22 (1986): 87–128; Robert Wade, *Governing the Market* (Princeton, N.J.: Princeton University Press, 1991); Dani Rodrik, "Getting interventions right: How South Korea and Taiwan grew rich," *Economic Policy* 20 (1995): 53–101; Sanjaya Lall, *Learning from the Asian Tigers* (London: Macmillan, 1996) and *The Role of Government Policy in Building Industrial Competitiveness in a Globalizing World* (Oxford: International Development Centre, Oxford University, 2003); Dani Rodrik, "Normalizing industrial policy," August 2007, http://ksghome.harvard.edu/~drodrik /Industrial%20Policy%20_Growth%20Commission_ .pdf; and Ricardo Hausmann and Dani Rodrik, "Doomed to choose: Industrial policy as predicament," September 2006, http://ksghome.harvard .edu/~drodrik/doomed.pdf. Parts of Rodrik's research on these topics have been published in his book *One Economics, Many Recipes* (Princeton, N.J.: Princeton University Press, 2007).

54. Hollis Chenery, Sherwin Robinson, and Moshe Syrquin, eds., *Industrialization and Growth: A Comparative Study* (New York: Oxford University Press, 1986), p. 178.

55. Ricardo Hausmann, Jason Hwang, and Dani Rodrik, "What you export matters," *Journal of Economic Growth* 12 (2007): 1, and Hausmann

and Rodrik, "Doomed to Choose: Industrial Policy as Predicament," Harvard University, 2006, downloaded at http://www.hks.harvard.edu/fs/drodrik/Research%20papers/doomed.pdf.

56. Excerpted from "East Asian 'models': Myths and lessons" by Colin I. Bradford, Jr. in *Development Strategies Reconsidered,* edited by John Lewis and Valeriana Kallab. Reprinted with permission from Transaction Publishers, Inc. On certification action, see Pranab Bardhan, "The Global Economy and the Poor," in *Understanding Poverty, Understanding Poverty,* eds. Abhijit Banerjee, Roland Benabou, and Dilip Mookherjee (New York: Oxford University Press, 2006) pp. 99–110.

57. Sanjaya Lall, "Globalization and industrial performance," presentation at the Globelics Academy, Lisbon, May 2004.

58. Rodrik, "Normalizing industrial policy"; See also Hausmann and Rodrik, "Doomed to choose."

59. The authors would like to thank Maggie Chen and Marc Melitz for helpful discussions. For an overview of this research area, see Marc J. Melitz and Stephen J. Redding, "Heterogeneous firms and trade," forthcoming in *Handbook of International Economics,* 4th ed. (available as a preliminary draft). A seminal article is Marc Melitz, "The impact of trade on intra-industry reallocations and aggregate industry productivity," *Econometrica* 71 (2003): 1695–1725. An interesting approach is provided in Alla Lileeva and Daniel Trefler, "Improved access to foreign markets raises plant-level productivity…for some plants," *Quarterly Journal of Economics* 125, No. 3 (2010): 1051–1099.

60. RPED is organized by the World Bank; some of these data are available at these sites: http://www.enterprisesurveys.org and http://microdata.worldbank.org/index.php/catalog/enterprise_surveys. Some developing-country, firm-level datasets such as the Enterprise Surveys are analogous to the household surveys that have had such a big impact on microeconomic research on poverty, health, education, and other development topics.

61. A paper in this emerging strand of literature is R. E. Baldwin and R. Forslid, "Trade liberalization with heterogeneous firms," *Review of Development Economics* 14 (2010): 161–176. Papers based on developing-country, firm- and plant-level survey data that could be connected to the new heterogeneous firm trade literature include Arne Bigsten and Mans Söderbom, "What have we learned from a decade of manufacturing enterprise surveys in Africa?" *World Bank Research Observer* 21, No. 2 (2006): 241–265; Arne Bigsten et al., "Do African manufacturing firms learn from exporting?" *Journal of Development Studies* 40, No. 3 (2004): 115–141; Neil Rankin et al., "Exporting from manufacturing firms in sub-Saharan Africa," *Journal of African Economies* 15, No. 4 (2006): 671–687; Mans Soderbom et al., "The determinants of survival among African manufacturing firms," *Economic Development and Cultural Change* 54, No. 3 (2006): 533–555; and Mans Soderbom et al., "Unobserved heterogeneity and the relation between earnings and firm size: Evidence from two developing countries," *Economics Letters* 87, No. 2 (2005): 153–159.

62. Different ways of treating unrecorded exports, such as those between sub-Saharan African countries, and varying definitions of which countries currently should be considered as part of the South (notably whether to include South Korea or a few other countries now classified by the World Bank as high-income) give very different estimates, ranging from just over one-fifth to just under two-fifths. A conservative estimate of 23.5% in 2002 may be derived from the presentation of data in World Bank, *World Development Indicators, 2004,* tab. 6.2. Detailed data for 1998 and 2008 by country and region can be found in the World Bank, *World Development Indicators, 2010,* tab. 6.5. These data reveal a substantial drop in the share of exports going to high-income economies (and hence a rise to middle- and low-income countries) for most developing countries in the 1998–2008 period. In fact, in recent years, developing economies have been increasingly trading with other developing economies in their same region: see World Bank, *2010 World Development Indicators* (Washington, D. C.: World Bank, 2010), fig. 6.5a, p. 370.

63. For the classic arguments for the benefits of encouraging trade among developing countries, see W. Arthur Lewis, "The slowing down of the engine of growth," *American Economic Review* 70 (1980): 555–564, and Frances Stewart, "The direction of international trade: Gains and losses for the Third World," in *A World Divided,* ed. Gerald K.

Helleiner (Cambridge: Cambridge University Press, 1976).

64. Abhijit V. Banerjee, "Globalization and all that," *Understanding Poverty*, eds. Abhijit V. Banerjee, Roland Bénabou, and Dilip Mookherjee (New York: Oxford University Press, 2006), pp. 85–98, and Pranab Bardhan "The global economy and the poor," in the same volume, pp. 99–110.

65. Anthony Venables, "Winners and losers from regional integration agreements," *Economic Journal* 113 (2003): 747.

66. Paul Collier, *The Bottom Billion*, p. 166. For a critique of these agreements in Africa, see pp. 164–166 of Collier's book.

67. United Nations Industrial Development Organization, *UNIDO Industrial Development Report 2011*, p. 160.

68. Although the burdens that developed-country tariffs imposed on primary- and secondary-product exports varied from commodity to commodity, it has been estimated that the net impact of trade barriers on all products reduced developing-world foreign-exchange earnings by more than $100 billion per year by 2000.

69. International Monetary Fund, *World Economic Outlook, May 1994* (Washington, D.C.: International Monetary Fund, 1994), annex 1.

70. For an analysis of the many ways that poor countries lose under the Uruguay Round, because the rules of the game are biased against them, see United Nations Development Programme, *Human Development Report, 1997* (New York: Oxford University Press, 1997), ch. 4.

71. United Nations Development Programme, *Human Development Report, 1997*, p. 85. A similar conclusion was reached by the IMF in its 1997 *World Economic Outlook* (Washington, D.C.: International Monetary Fund, 1997), p. 13. This discussion also draws on the 2010 Millennium Development Goals report.

72. See, for example, "India and US retreat from battle over food security," *Financial Times*, September 15, 2013.

73. For an overview of the process and some key issues, see "Ocean's 12," *Financial Times*, September 23, 2013, p. 9.

74. For example, see Bernard Hoekman, "WTO reform: A synthesis and assessment of recent proposals," in *The Oxford Handbook on the World Trade Organization*, eds. Amrita Narlikar, Martin Daunton and Robert Stern (Oxford: Oxford University Press, 2012), and Bernard Hoekman, "Proposals for WTO reform: A synthesis and assessment," World Bank Policy Research Working Paper No. 5525, 2011. The WTO Web site is updated regularly at http://www.wto.org.

13

Balance of Payments, Debt, Financial Crises, and Stabilization Policies

By the end of the 1970s African economies were plunged into what was to be known as the two "'lost decades."

— Encyclopedia of Twentieth-Century African History,
Dickson Eyoh and Paul Tiyambe Zeleza, editors

As the sovereign debt workout processes are political at their core, they tend to benefit the powerful at the expense of the powerless.
—*Barry Herman, José Antonio Ocampo, and Shari Spiegel, 2010*

Global growth is in low gear, the drivers of activity are changing, and downside risks persist.
—*International Monetary Fund*, World Economic Outlook
October 2013—Transitions and Tensions

13.1 International Finance and Investment: Key Issues for Developing Countries

In this chapter, after looking at a country's balance of payments accounts and recent trends in developing-country trade balances, we will examine the dimensions and effects of debt crises in developing countries. We will examine in depth how major debt crises emerged during the 1980s and into the 1990s, and why debt remained a serious impediment to growth in Africa for two decades or more after the crisis hit. These crises are of exceptional importance because of their scope and impact on slowing the development progress of dozens of developing nations over protracted periods; and much has been learned from years of careful study of the lessons from this experience. We appraise how the crisis was addressed first in Latin America (including a case study of Mexico in Box 13.3); how it was finally addressed much later in Africa; and in the process, who bore the burden of stabilization and structural adjustment programs induced by the International Monetary Fund (IMF) and supported by the World Bank. We next examine some of the smaller but significant international crises that emerged in developing countries over the subsequent decades, particularly the East Asian crisis of the late 1990s, and consider how adverse impacts of international debt crises on developing-country citizens might be minimized or prevented. We examine the international legal concept of odious debt and strategies to prevent it (Box 13.4). We conclude with an in-depth review of the 2008 global financial crisis that began in the United States but had major direct and indirect impacts on all developing regions. We see how ongoing conditions have potential to lead to future financial crises. Boxes 13.1 and 13.2 provide brief histories of the IMF and the World Bank, respectively.

In Chapter 14, we will extend our analysis of the role of finance in trade to examine the international flow of financial resources, consisting of (1) the flow of private foreign direct investments, primarily via the modern multinational corporation; (2) the recent resurgence of private financial "portfolio investments" in support of newly organized or refurbished "emerging" stock and bond markets; (3) the flow of remittances from migrants working abroad; (4) the flow of public financial and technical resources in the form of bilateral and multilateral foreign aid; (5) the growing importance of private financial and technical assistance in the form of nongovernmental organization programs; and (6) the most difficult, but arguably most important, aspect of aid—helping conflict and postconflict environments.

13.2 The Balance of Payments Account

General Considerations

The extension of our analysis beyond simple merchandise trade into areas related to the international flow of financial resources permits us to examine the **balance of payments** of developing nations. A balance of payments table is designed to summarize a nation's financial transactions with the outside world. It is divided into three components, as shown by the summary in Table 13.1. Note that balance of payments tables are sometimes presented in a revised format that splits the current account into two parts (called the *current account* and the *capital account*) and labels what is here called the *capital account* as the *financial account*. We retain the traditional approach to balance of payments accounting because most of the literature on developing-country debt and its ongoing treatment in the financial press is usually presented in that format. The **current account** focuses on the export and import of goods and services, investment income, **debt service** payments, and private and public net remittances and transfers. Specifically, it subtracts the value of imports from exports (the *merchandise trade balance* of Chapter 12) and then adds flows of the net investment income received from abroad (e.g., the difference between interest and dividend payments on foreign stocks, bonds, and bank deposits owned by developing-country nationals and brought into the country, as opposed to being left overseas, and those securities, if any, of the developing country owned by foreigners plus repatriated profits of multinational corporations). Taking this total ($A-B+C$ in Table 13.1), it subtracts item D, debt service payments, which represents a major component of heavily indebted poor countries current account deficits, and adds item E, net private and public remittances and transfers, such as money sent home by developing-country nationals working abroad (e.g., Mexicans in the United States, Algerians in France, Pakistanis in Kuwait). The final result ($A-B+C-D+E$ in Table 13.1) yields the current account balance—a positive balance is called a **surplus**, and a negative

Balance of payments A summary statement of a nation's financial transactions with the outside world.

Current account The portion of a balance of payments that states the market value of a country's "visible" (e.g., commodity trade) and "invisible" (e.g., shipping services) exports and imports.

Debt service The sum of interest payments and repayments of principal on external public and publicly guaranteed debt.

Surplus An excess of revenues over expenditures.

TABLE 13.1 A Schematic Balance of Payments Account	
Exports of goods and services	*A*
Imports of goods and services	*B*
Investment income	*C*
Debt service payments	*D*
Net remittances and transfers	*E*
Total *current account* balance $(A - B + C - D + E)$	*F*
Direct private investment	*G*
Foreign loans (private and public), minus amortization	*H*
Increase in foreign assets of the domestic banking system	*I*
Resident capital outflow	*J*
Total *capital account* balance $(G + H - I - J)$	*K*
Increase (or decrease) in *cash reserve account*	*L*
Errors and omissions $(L - F - K)$	*M*

Source: Adapted from John Williamson and Donald R. Lessard, *Capital Flight: The Problem and Policy Responses* (Washington, D.C.: Institute for International Economics, 1987), tab. 1.

Deficit   An excess of expenditures over revenues.

Capital account   The portion of a country's balance of payments that shows the volume of private foreign investment and public grants and loans that flow into and out of a country over a given period, usually one year.

Capital flight   The transfer of funds to a foreign country by a citizen or business to avoid conditions in the source country.

Cash account (international reserve account)   The balancing portion of a country's balance of payments, showing how cash balances (foreign reserves) and short-term financial claims have changed in response to current account and capital account transactions.

Hard currency   The currency of a major industrial country or currency area, such as the U.S. dollar, the euro, or the Japanese yen, that is freely convertible into other currencies.

Euro   A common European currency adopted by some of the countries of the European Union.

balance, a **deficit**. The current account therefore allows us to analyze the impact of various commercial policies, primarily on merchandise trade but also indirectly on investment income, debt service payments, and private transfers.

The **capital account** (financial account) records the value of private foreign direct investment (mostly by multinational corporations), foreign loans by private international banks, and loans and grants from foreign governments (as in the form of foreign aid) and multilateral agencies such as the IMF and the World Bank. It then subtracts an extremely important item, especially for the major debtor countries: what is called *resident capital outflow* in Table 13.1. To put its importance in perspective, during the 1980s debt crisis, wealthy nationals from many developing countries sent vast amounts of money into developed-nation bank accounts, real estate ventures, and stock and bond purchases; this **capital flight** is estimated to have had a value of up to half the total debt of some debtor nations at the peak of their debt problems.[1] It dwarfed the receipt of private and public loans and investments and was a major contributor to the worsening balance of payments of many developing nations. Capital flight is also a chronic problem where autocratic governments have a shaky hold on power. The balance on capital account is therefore calculated as items $G + H - I - J$ in Table 13.1. Again, a positive balance is a surplus, and a negative one, a deficit.

Finally, the **cash account**, or **international reserve account** (item *L*), is the balancing item (along with the *errors and omissions*, item *M*, which reconciles statistical inequalities but is sometimes used as a proxy for disguised or unrecorded capital flows) that is lowered (shows a net outflow of foreign reserves) whenever total disbursements on the current and capital accounts exceed total receipts. Table 13.2 presents a simple chart of what constitutes positive (credit) and negative (debit) items in a balance of payments table. Nations accumulate international cash reserves in any or all of the following three forms: (1) foreign **hard currency** (primarily U.S. dollars, but also Japanese yen, pounds sterling, or the European **euro**)[2] whenever they sell more abroad than they purchase;

TABLE 13.2 Credits and Debits in the Balance of Payments Account	
"Positive" Effects (Credits)	**"Negative" Effects (Debits)**
1. Any sale of goods or services abroad (export)	1. Any purchase of goods and services abroad (import)
2. Any earning on an investment in a foreign country	2. Any investment in a foreign country
3. Any receipt of foreign money	3. Any payment to a foreign country
4. Any gift or aid from a foreign country	4. Any gift or aid given abroad
5. Any foreign sale of stocks or bonds	5. Any purchase of stocks or bonds from abroad

Source: From *The ABC's of International Finance,* Second Edition, by John Charles Pool et al. Copyright © 1991 by Lexington Books. Reprinted with permission.

(2) gold, mined domestically or purchased; and (3) deposits with the IMF, which acts as a reserve bank for individual nations' central banks (see Box 13.1).

A Hypothetical Illustration: Deficits and Debts

A numerical example might prove helpful at this point. In Table 13.3 on page 684, a hypothetical balance of payments table for a developing country is portrayed. First, under the *current account*, there is a $10 million negative merchandise trade balance made up of $35 million of commodity export receipts (of which over 70%—$25 million—are derived from primary agricultural and raw material products), minus $45 million of mostly manufactured consumer, intermediate, and capital-goods import payments. To this total we add $5 million in payments for the services of foreign shipping firms and $1 million of investment income receipts representing net interest transmitted on foreign bond holdings, subtract $15 million of debt service payments representing this year's interest costs on the accumulated foreign debt of the developing country, and add $2 million of remittance and transfer receipts derived from payments of domestic workers living overseas who send home part of their earnings. Together, all of these items add up to a *deficit* on current account of $27 million.

Turning now to the *capital account*, we see that there is a net inflow of $7 million of foreign private investment, consisting of $3 million of direct investment from multinational corporations in the form of new local factories and $4 million in private loans (from international commercial banks) and private portfolio (stock and bond) investments by foreign individuals and mutual funds (see Chapter 14). There is also a net positive $3 million inflow of public loans in the form of foreign aid and multilateral agency assistance. Note that the gross *inflow* of $9 million in public loans and grants is partly offset by a $6 million capital *outflow* representing **amortization** (gradual reduction) of the principal on former loans. However, as shown in Table 13.4 on page 684, which covers the 1980s debt crisis period, these figures were reversed in the 1980s—the outflow to repay accumulated debts exceeded the inflow of *both* public aid and new refinancing of bank loans. As a result, a $35.9 billion net transfer from developed to developing countries in 1981 became a $22.5 billion transfer from poor to rich nations by 1990 (they turned positive again in the 1990s until substantial new problems emerged for some countries between 1997 and 2002).

Amortization Gradual pay-off of a loan principal.

BOX 13.1 The History and Role of the International Monetary Fund

In July 1944, representatives from 45 countries convened in Bretton Woods, New Hampshire, to plan the terms of postwar international economic cooperation. The economic devastation of the Great Depression in the 1930s, followed by the ravages of World War II, had led to the collapse of international financial markets and precipitous declines in the volume of international trade. The two "Bretton Woods Institutions," the International Monetary Fund (IMF, or simply the Fund) and the World Bank were created to rebuild international goods and capital markets and to restore the war-torn economies of Europe.

The designated roles of the IMF and the World Bank were quite different, though to some extent they were intended to complement each other. It was the prevailing wisdom at the time of the Bretton Woods conference that the stabilization of international capital markets was essential to the resumption of lively international trade and investment. This concern led to the establishment of the IMF, which became responsible for monitoring and stabilizing the international financial system through the short-term financing of balance of payments deficits. The World Bank's complementary role originally involved financing the rebuilding of national infrastructures, though this role has evolved considerably over time (see Box 13.2 on page 686). Later, the General Agreement on Tariffs and Trade (GATT) was established and led to the founding of the World Trade Organization (WTO).

The participants at the Bretton Woods conference established a system of fixed exchange rates in which each country was required to peg the value of its currency to the U.S. dollar, which was directly convertible into gold at $35 per ounce. Initially, it was the responsibility of the IMF to finance temporary balance of payments deficits arising as a consequence of these pegged exchange rates, a role that lasted until 1971, when the system was abandoned and flexible exchange rates took its place.

In the 1970s, a combination of world recession, skyrocketing fuel prices, and falling exports from many developing countries, led to large balance of payments deficits in many of these countries.

Financing from the IMF is "conditional" in the sense that recipient countries must meet a set of requirements based on the purpose of the loan, known as *conditionality*. These conditions are intended to increase the effectiveness of IMF resources by encouraging expedient behavior on the part of debtor governments facing chronic balance of payments troubles. Because the terms of conditionality are frequently considered draconian, imposing the greatest hardship on the poorest households in debtor countries, they have remained tremendously controversial.

Another emerging IMF role was "surveillance" of macroeconomic policy of each member country—but in practice with special emphasis on developing countries—leading to increasing IMF involvement in the development process. The Fund also expanded its role in the provision of information services to the public and technical assistance to developing-country governments.

By 1982, imminent default in a number of heavily indebted developing countries experiencing high inflation, weak export markets, falling terms of trade, and large government deficits threatened to destabilize international financial markets. As the severity of crises in developing countries intensified, private sources of funding shrank rapidly, reducing the liquidity necessary to service debt. To avert widespread default and hence the threat of systemic failure in international capital markets, the IMF undertook exceptional measures to effect adjustment. Its new role was instrumental in restructuring and financing developing-country debt during the debt crisis of the 1980s, the Asian currency crisis of 1997–1998, and the global financial crisis that began in 2008.

In the 1997–1998 Asian financial crisis, normally high-performing countries such as South Korea, Indonesia, and Thailand had to borrow from the IMF under strong austerity conditions—government spending cuts, tax increases, higher interest rates, and extensive structural reforms. A widely held view both in these countries and among external critics was that the IMF focus on austerity caused large and unnecessary recessions. Partly in response, governments throughout Asia and elsewhere worked to accelerate exports, repay IMF loans, and expand foreign-currency reserves—one of the factors in the expansion of trade surpluses from the East Asian region. This also gave rise to concerns that the IMF would receive too little income from its outstanding loans.

By 2006, after years of comparative (apparent) stability, the IMF role was newly questioned. Officials such as Mervyn King, governor of the Bank of England, argued that the IMF would have to give large developing countries such as China, India, and Brazil a greater voice in its governance (sometimes dubbed "shares and chairs"). Proposals that the IMF increase its "surveillance" of the balance sheets of developed as well as developing countries have been another topic of debate. Many observers agreed that a reformed IMF might still provide global public goods by publishing economic information and independent analysis, offering private advice to member governments, serving as an intergovernmental convener for cooperative efforts to overcome coordination failures in policy setting and in adjudicating defaults, and serving as lender of last resort. Most rich countries seemed willing to provide more voice for leading developing countries but less open to giving the IMF a more authoritative advisory say over their own economies. The possibility of an IMF successor playing the role of an independent global central bank as called for by some observers seemed even more remote. Although this debate stalled, in the wake of the 2008 global financial crisis, the IMF was again greatly expanded in resources and staff.

After the 2009 G20 meetings, the IMF announced reforms, including a crisis "firewall" bolstering lending capacity (ultimately almost quadrupling available resources); enhanced crisis prevention lending; more equitable policies for low-income countries and more concessional lending; and enhanced risk analysis. After years of criticism, the IMF announced that structural performance criteria have been discontinued for all IMF loans, including programs with low-income countries, with a new emphasis on social protection, though some of the practical effects remained unclear. Last, but not least, internal governance reform was to ensure better representation of major developing countries, and soon a consensus grew that the IMF managing directorship should not automatically go to a European as it had since its founding. Nevertheless, in 2011, French lawyer Christine Lagarde was elected the managing director of the IMF. Notably, she is the first woman to lead the IMF following 10 male leaders.

From the 2008 peak of the global financial crisis through 2013, the IMF lent countries well over $300 billion. In a historic shift, the years after the crisis saw some Organization for Economic Cooperation and Development (OECD) countries turn to the fund; and as of October 2013, the largest IMF borrowers were Greece, Portugal, and Ireland. Note, however, that these "peripheral" European countries were still considered upper-middle-income developing countries at least through the 1970s; in 2013, S&P Dow Jones reclassified (downgraded) Greece from "developed market" to "emerging market" status. Meanwhile, by 2013, Mexico, Poland, Morocco, and Colombia had the biggest precautionary (or standby) IMF loan amounts in place.

Sources: IMF Web site, http://www.imf.org/external; M. Garritsen de Vries, *The IMF in a Changing World, 1945–85* (Washington, D.C.: International Monetary Fund); Mervyn King's speech, accessed at http://www.bankofengland.co.uk/publications/speeches/2006/speech267.pdf; and Martin Wolf, "World needs independent fund," *Financial Times,* February 21, 2006. The IMF's announced reforms are reported at http://www.imf.org/external/np/exr/facts/changing.htm.

Returning to Table 13.3, we see that a major reason for the perverse flow of financial capital from poor to rich nations was very high levels of resident capital outflow. This capital flight is estimated to have amounted to almost $100 billion during the first half of the 1980s from just five of the principal countries

TABLE 13.3   A Hypothetical Traditional Balance of Payments Table for a Developing Nation

Item	Amounts (millions of dollars)		
Current account			
Commodity exports			+35
Primary products	+25		
Manufactured goods	+10		
Commodity imports			−45
Primary products	−10		
Manufactured goods	−35		
Services (e.g., shipping costs)			−5
Investment income			+1
Debt service payments			−15
Net remittances and transfers			+2
Balance on current account		−27	
Capital account			
Private direct foreign investment			+3
Private loans and portfolio investments			+4
Government and multilateral flows (net)			+3
Loans	+9		
Debt amortization	−6		
Resident capital outflow			−8
Balance on capital account		+2	
Balance on current and capital accounts		−25	
Cash account			
Net decrease in official monetary reserves			+25
Balance on cash account		+25	

TABLE 13.4   Before and After the 1980s Debt Crisis: Current Account Balances and Capital Account Net Financial Transfers of Developing Countries, 1978–1990 (billions of dollars)

Year	Current Account	Capital Account Net Financial Transfers
1978	−32.1	33.2
1979	+10.0	31.2
1980	+30.6	29.5
1981	−48.6	35.9
1982	−86.9	20.1
1983	−64.0	3.7
1984	−31.7	−10.2
1985	−24.9	−20.5
1986	−46.4	−23.6
1987	−4.4	−34.0
1988	−22.4	−35.2
1989	−18.4	−29.6
1990	−3.0	−22.5

Sources: International Monetary Fund, *World Economic Outlook, 1988* and *1992* (Washington, D.C.: International Monetary Fund, 1988, 1992); United Nations Development Programme, *Human Development Report, 1992* (New York: Oxford University Press, 1992), tab. 4.3.

involved (Argentina, Brazil, Mexico, the Philippines, and Venezuela)[3] and almost $200 billion over the period 1976–1985. In Table 13.3, it is listed as an outflow of $8 million. The net result is a $2 million positive balance on capital account, bringing the total balance on current and capital accounts to a deficit of $25 million.

13.3 The Issue of Payments Deficits

Some Initial Policy Issues

To finance this $25 million negative balance on combined current and capital accounts, our hypothetical country will have to draw down $25 million of its central bank holdings of official monetary reserves. Such reserves consist of gold, a few major foreign currencies, and special drawing rights at the IMF (these will be explained shortly). **International reserves** serve for countries the same purpose that bank accounts serve for individuals. They can be drawn on to pay bills and debts, they are increased with deposits representing net export sales and capital inflows, and they can be used as collateral to borrow additional reserves.

We see, therefore, that the balance on current account *plus* the balance on capital account must be offset by the balance on cash account. This is shown by the net *decrease* of $25 million in official monetary reserves. If the country is very poor, it is likely to have a very limited stock of these reserves. This overall balance of payments deficit of $25 million may therefore place severe strains on the economy and greatly inhibit the country's ability to continue importing needed capital and consumer goods. In the least developed nations of the world, which have to import food to feed a hungry population and possess limited monetary reserves, such payments deficits may spell disaster for millions of people.

Facing existing or projected balance of payments deficits on combined current and capital accounts, developing nations have a variety of policy options. For one thing, they can seek to improve the balance on current account by promoting export expansion or limiting imports (or both). In the former case, there is the further choice of concentrating on primary or secondary product export expansion. In the latter case, policies of import substitution (the protection and stimulus of domestic industries to replace previously imported manufactured goods in the local market) or selective tariffs and physical quotas or bans on the importation of specific consumer goods may be tried. Or countries can seek to achieve both objectives simultaneously by altering their official foreign-exchange rates through a currency devaluation that lowers export prices and increases import prices. Alternatively or concurrently, they can seek loans and assistance from the World Bank or the IMF. Traditionally, this has required that the countries follow very restrictive fiscal and monetary policies. These have been called *stabilization policies* by the IMF; and termed *structural adjustment* by the World Bank (see Box 13.2), which has made **structural adjustment loans** as part of this process. *Stabilization policies* and *structural adjustment*, both packages of preconditions for receiving loans, are popularly referred to as **conditionality**. These policies are designed to reduce domestic

International reserves A country's balance of gold, hard currencies, and special drawing rights used to settle international transactions.

Structural adjustment loans Loans by the World Bank to developing countries in support of measures to remove excessive governmental controls, make factor and product prices reflect scarcity values, and promote market competition.

Conditionality The requirement imposed by the International Monetary Fund that a borrowing country undertake fiscal, monetary, and international commercial reforms as a condition for receiving a loan to resolve balance of payments difficulties.

demand so as to lower imports and reduce the inflationary pressures that may have contributed to the "overvalued" exchange rate that slowed exports and promoted imports. In recent years, these institutions have shown somewhat less policy inflexibility, but it is not yet clear whether this trend will continue.

BOX 13.2   The History and Role of the World Bank

The World Bank was created in 1944 as one of the Bretton Woods institutions (introduced in Box 13.1). Over the years, the institutional framework of the World Bank has changed considerably. The World Bank Group (widely referred to in development circles as simply the Bank) consists of five separate organizations. Initially, all bank lending was channeled through the International Bank for Reconstruction and Development (IBRD), the branch of the World Bank established following the Bretton Woods conference. At the time, its principal concern was rebuilding economies shattered during World War II. Loans are offered on commercial terms to borrowing governments or to private enterprises that have obtained government guarantees, but rates are modest due to the bank's high credit rating for its own borrowing.

Largely due to the success of the Marshall Plan, the reconstruction of Europe had become a fait accompli by the late 1950s, at which time the World Bank turned its primary focus toward investment in the poorer economies. In 1960, the International Development Association (IDA) was established to provide credits on concessional terms to countries whose per capita incomes are below a critical level. These favorable terms involve repayment periods that are several times longer than those on IBRD loans and are interest-free. The preferred terms are an out-growth of recognition that low-income countries are unable to borrow at commercial rates because they are more economically vulnerable and the financial returns to investment are slower to be realized.

In 1956, the International Finance Corporation (IFC) was established to lend directly to private enterprise. In addition, through underwriting or holding equity, it is capable of taking direct financial interests in the loan recipients to magnify economic rewards of

World Bank investments. Two smaller affiliates are the Multilateral Investment Guarantee Agency (MIGA) and the International Centre for Settlement of Investment Disputes (ICSID).

For the first two decades following World War II, the bulk of World Bank lending was used to finance the building of infrastructure related to energy and transportation, since much of Europe's infrastructure had been destroyed. Rising pressure to increase the flow of funds to poorer nations, following the economic recovery of Europe, led to a similar pattern of investment in developing countries.

It was discovered, however, that infrastructural investments in the developing world failed to produce the same returns as those in Europe due largely to a lack of institutional framework and skilled labor. It became clear that a reordering of investment priorities specific to the needs of developing regions was necessary.

Since that period, the focus of the World Bank has undergone periodic shifts, though it may be more accurate to say that the Bank has added new activities rather than abandoned older ones. The "focus of the decade" is a simple way to characterize the evolution of World Bank activity favored by some economists at the Bank. In the 1950s, the focus was on physical capital; the Bank began similar lending in a growing number of developing countries for infrastructure, such as roads, electrical grids, and dams, and later increasingly for agricultural investments to assist export expansion. By the late 1960s, when Robert McNamara became its president, for the first time the Bank began to direct its attention to poverty reduction and so to put a priority on rural development (or "natural capital"). One focus was on improved access to development resources for small farmers who had been bypassed by previous development projects; success was mixed at best, however, and agricultural lending fell drastically in subsequent years. But, in some respects, work on poverty grew through the 1970s, and the Bank has called this its human focus (or *human capital*) period, emphasizing access of the poor to education and health services. But critics argued these efforts were ineffective due to failure to work directly with people living in poverty and comprehend their constraints, or to deal with elites who undermined or siphoned resources from projects.

In the 1980s, as described in this chapter, debt and finance ("financial capital") became the focus. In the 1970s and early 1980s, developing countries took on a lot of debt. The Bank started concentrating on structural adjustment loans—large loans that came with certain conditions on what the country could do with the money, and what kinds of policies they needed to implement, primarily focused on liberalization, marketization, and privatization. The activities of the Bank to a large extent merged with the Fund in this period and were heavily criticized by many economic development specialists and by developing countries. For example, the poor were harmed by the emphasis on policies such as "cost recovery" for services that in many cases in Africa and elsewhere were expected to extend to school and health care fees. The goal of debt reduction was often explicit; primary beneficiaries would include foreign banks. "Structural adjustment" loans were designed to promote a fundamental restructuring of the economies of countries plagued by chronic trade and budget deficits by improving the macroeconomic policy environment with an emphasis on (1) mobilizing domestic savings through fiscal and financial policies, (2) improving public-sector efficiency by stressing price-determined allocation of public investments and improving the efficiency of public enterprises, (3) improving the productivity of public-sector investments by liberalizing trade and domestic economic policies, and (4) reforming institutional arrangements to support the adjustment process. Critics of structural adjustment programs point to the fact that they frequently lead to increased hardships for the very poor and on occasion have substantially reversed the benefits of earlier economic progress. Spokespersons for the Bank now generally present this as a failed period in Bank history that also tarnished their "brand."

By the mid-1990s, the Bank resumed a greater focus on poverty. President James Wolfensohn, in what the Bank calls its "social capital" decade, led a broadening of its focus on social protection. And after years in which many heavily indebted poor countries saw little development—and little progress repaying loans—the Poverty Reduction Strategy Paper (PRSP) approach was introduced jointly with the IMF. Although intended to improve on this experience, it remained very uneven, most obviously because of its weak connection to actual budgets. However, debt burdens did begin to decrease in Africa during the 2000s through various initiatives. The Bank was sometimes criticized in this period for placing too little emphasis on government institutions for fostering development such as coordination and industrial policy. The early 2000s also saw a focus on anticorruption and improvement on governance, in general, and of program management, in particular ("institutional capital"). At the same time, the Bank has been positioning itself in the field of global public goods, focusing on the resolution of global aspects of the financial crisis, public health, vaccines, disease, and climate change brought about by global warming, where officials at the Bank see opportunities for an expansion of its mandate.

As with the IMF, expansion of voting shares and board "chairs" is at the top of the agenda for World Bank reform, along with a growing consensus that the Bank presidency should not automatically go to an American. Nevertheless, in 2012, Dr. Jim Yong Kim (a U.S. citizen born in South Korea) became the 12th president of the World Bank. Kim set about extensive reform measures and in October 2013 committed the Bank to prioritizing twin goals: ending extreme poverty by 2030 and boosting shared prosperity for the bottom 40% of the population in all developing countries.

(Continued)

BOX 13.2   The History and Role of the World Bank (*Continued*)

Sources: John P. Lewis, and Richard Webb, *The World Bank: Its First Half Century* (Washington, D.C.: Brookings Institution Press, 1997), vol. 1. For more details, go to the World Bank's Web site, http://www.worldbank.org. For the Bank's "Poverty reduction strategies," see http://www.worldbank.org/prsp. For poverty-oriented discussions of development efforts, see Frances Stewart, "The many faces of adjustment," *World Development* 19 (1991): 1847–1864; Giovanni A. Cornia, Richard Jolly, and Frances Stewart, *Adjustment with a Human Face* (Oxford: Clarendon Press, 1987); and United Nations Development Programme, *Human Development Report, 1995* (New York: Oxford University Press, 1995). See also Hillary F. French, "The World Bank: Now fifty but how fit?" *World Watch*, July–August 1994, pp. 10–18; Bruce Rich, *Mortgaging the Earth: The World Bank, Environmental Impoverishment, and the Crisis of Development* (Boston: Beacon Press, 1994); Catherine Caulfield, *The World Bank and the Poverty of Nations* (New York: Henry Holt, 1997); Lance Taylor, "The revival of the liberal creed: The IMF and World Bank in a globalized economy," *World Development* 25 (1997): 145–152; Anne O. Krueger, "Whither the World Bank and the IMF?" *Journal of Economic Literature* 36 (1998): 1983–2020; and Howard Schneider, "Wider Impact Eludes World Bank," *Washington Post*, October 9, 2013, p. 13. The influential 2001 Meltzer Commission report that encouraged switching from loans to grants and global public goods support may be found at http://www.gpo.gov/fdsys/pkg/CHRG-106shrg66721/html/CHRG-106shrg66721.htm. Speech by Jim Yong Kim on "The World Bank Group Strategy: A Path to End Poverty, presented at George Washington University, Oct. 2013. The World Bank's Web site is http://www.worldbank.org.

In addition, developing countries can try to improve the balance on their capital account by encouraging more private foreign direct or portfolio investment, borrowing from international commercial banks, or seeking more public foreign assistance (aid). But neither private foreign investment nor a majority of foreign aid comes in the form of gifts (outright grants). The receipt of loan assistance implies the necessity of future repayments of principal and interest. Directly productive foreign investments in, say, building local factories entail the potential repatriation of sizable proportions of the profits of the foreign-owned enterprise. As shown in Chapter 14, the encouragement of private foreign investment has broader development implications than the mere transfer of financial or physical capital resources.

Finally, developing nations can seek to modify the detrimental impact of chronic balance of payments deficits by expanding their stocks of official monetary reserves. One way of doing this is through the acquisition of a greater share of international "paper gold," known as **special drawing rights (SDRs)**. Traditionally, under the workings of the international monetary system, countries with deficits in their balance of payments were required to pay for these deficits by drawing down on their official reserves of the two principal international monetary assets, gold and U.S. dollars. But with the growth in the volume and value of world trade, a new kind of international asset was needed to supplement the limited stock of gold and dollars. Consequently, in 1970, the IMF was given the authority to create special drawing rights. These international assets perform many of the functions of gold and dollars in settling balance of payments accounts. They are valued on the basis of a basket of currencies (a weighted average of the value of four different currencies—the U.S. dollar, the euro, the pound sterling, and the Japanese yen) and constitute claims on the IMF. They may thus be exchanged for convertible currencies to settle international official transactions. As of November 2010, one U.S. dollar

Special drawing rights (SDRs) An international financial asset created by the International Monetary Fund in 1970 to supplement gold and dollars in settling international balance of payments accounts.

was worth 0.65 SDR. In response to the global financial crisis, the IMF raised the amount of SDRs issued nearly tenfold, to 316 billion. Eventually, the IMF would like to see all international financial settlements conducted in SDRs.

Having summarized some basic balance of payments concepts and issues as they relate to both commodity trade and international flows of financial resources, we can now briefly review some trends in the balance of payments of developing nations and then focus our attention on a detailed analysis of debt problems.

Trends in the Balance of Payments

For most developing countries, the 1980s was an extraordinarily difficult period in their balance of payments accounts with the rest of the world. Prior to 1980, the conventional development strategy had developing countries operating with sizable current account deficits, because imports of capital and intermediate goods were required to provide the machinery and equipment for rapid industrialization. Export earnings paid for most, but not all, of these imports. The financing of these deficits was therefore made possible by large resource transfers in the capital account in the form of country-to-country (bilateral) foreign aid, direct private investment by multinational corporations, private loans by international banks to both developing-country governments and local businesses, and multilateral loans from the World Bank and other international development agencies. Capital-account surpluses, therefore, typically more than compensated for current account deficits so that international reserves were being accumulated.

However, during the 1980s, the developing world experienced a substantial deterioration in both current and capital-account balances. As Table 13.4 shows, the net financial transfers component of the capital account (which includes everything in Table 13.3 except private direct foreign investment) turned sharply negative beginning in 1984. The overall transition amounted to more than $68 billion, comparing the positive $33.2 billion capital account balance in 1978 with the negative $35.2 billion balance in 1988. Meanwhile, a brief period of large current account surpluses, which reflected entirely the Organization of the Petroleum Exporting Countries' (OPEC's) booming export revenues of 1979–1980, abruptly turned negative in 1981 and, as illustrated in Table 13.5, stayed negative until 2000, when they turned positive. One reason for persistent concern has been that the recent positive balances (outside of Africa) have been possible largely because of the wide and probably unsustainable U.S. trade deficit. Commodity exporters were also boosted in recent years by the booming demand from high-growth developing economies, especially China.

The reasons for the decline in current account balances in the 1980s and 1990s included (1) a dramatic fall in commodity prices, including oil; (2) global recessions in 1981–1982 and 1991–1993, which caused a general contraction in world trade; (3) increasing protectionism in the developed world against export from developing countries; and (4) some severely overvalued exchange rates in several key developing economies, such as Argentina. This reversed in the 2000s with large current account surpluses in many middle-income countries. In most cases, these surpluses shrank in the aftermath of the global financial crisis—at least temporarily.

TABLE 13.5   Developing Country Payments Balances on Current Account, 1980–2009 (billions of dollars)

Country Group Name	1980	1981	1982	1983	1984	1985	1986	1987	1988
Emerging market and developing economies	29.621	−25.712	−52.604	−51.328	−31.097	−32.317	−65.062	−32.642	−44.718
Central and eastern Europe	−14.435	−12.426	−4.715	−7.55	−5.859	−7.517	−8.979	−6.857	−3.048
Developing Asia	−6.893	−11.544	−13.428	−17.145	−9.859	−20.244	−16.665	−5.786	−15.365
Latin America and the Caribbean	−27.677	−43.789	−42.287	−7.501	−1.266	−1.955	−17.089	−9.427	−9.322
Middle East and North Africa	79.021	60.438	24.563	−9.828	−8.55	−1.695	−16.793	−7.705	−8.788
Sub–Saharan Africa	0.519	−17.542	−16.363	−8.736	−4.442	−0.058	−4.943	−1.883	−6.821
	1989	**1990**	**1991**	**1992**	**1993**	**1994**	**1995**	**1996**	**1997**
Emerging market and developing economies	−32.1	−18.325	−96.354	−82.433	−120.66	−80.472	−96.838	−68.491	−71.108
Central and eastern Europe	0.816	−4.623	−1.452	−1.577	−14.718	1.441	−10.067	−12.185	−16.167
Developing Asia	−18.814	−11.984	−4.028	−8.57	−28.215	−16.373	−37.330	−30.235	12.435
Latin America and the Caribbean	−4.977	−0.893	−17.374	−34.75	−45.88	−51.962	−38.003	−38.057	−66.134
Middle East and North Africa	−3.575	2.942	−66.776	−26.232	−22.305	−10.81	−3.055	15.760	15.895
Sub-Saharan Africa	−4.057	−2.387	−5.001	−6.53	−5.915	−6.068	−10.030	−4.833	−7.184
	1998	**1999**	**2000**	**2001**	**2002**	**2003**	**2004**	**2005**	**2006**
Emerging market and developing economies	−102.725	−11.290	95.837	53.507	82.743	148.898	205.685	407.037	627.183
Central and eastern Europe	−15.681	−23.585	−28.852	−10.852	−18.660	−32.551	−55.253	−60.491	−88.543
Developing Asia	53.826	39.746	42.869	40.755	63.413	83.608	91.573	142.743	271.048
Latin America and the Caribbean	−89.946	−55.521	−48.566	−53.546	−15.823	8.319	20.538	32.789	46.586
Middle East and North Africa	−26.109	16.482	80.643	48.903	33.493	61.796	92.125	207.505	281.474
Sub-Saharan Africa	−15.751	−10.414	1.649	−5.261	−12.732	−11.506	−8.640	−1.653	27.657
	2007	**2008**	**2009**	**2010**	**2011**	**2012**	**2013**		
Emerging market and developing economies	596.905	669.237	253.755	323.275	410.457	380.579	235.848		
Central and eastern Europe	−136.132	−158.981	−48.091	−82.560	−119.330	−79.357	84.844		
Developing Asia	394.913	429.367	276.764	238.819	97.572	108.721	138.461		
Latin America and the Caribbean	6.710	−39.041	−30.267	−62.792	−77.930	−104.474	140.639		
Middle East and North Africa	262.861	346.577	49.063	179.692	417.426	421.076	317.639		
Sub-Saharan Africa	9.346	−3.999	−27.582	−15.432	−17.349	−38.265	−51.996		

Note: Developing economies include what the IMF terms *emerging economies.*
Source of data: International Monetary Fund, *World Economic Outlook Database*, April 2010 and October 2013.

The capital account showed a dramatic turn in the 1980s as a combined result of rising developing-country debt service obligations, sharp declines in lending by international banks, and massive capital flight. During the 1980s, these factors turned what had previously been a positive annual resource flow of $25 billion to $35 billion from developed to less developed countries into a negative annual flow of $25 billion to $35 billion from the developing to the developed world. Behind these trends, however, was the debilitating dilemma of developing-country debt—a historically recurrent problem with important lessons for developing-country policy.

13.4 Accumulation of Debt and Emergence of the Debt Crisis in the 1980s

Background and Analysis

The accumulation of **external debt** is a common phenomenon of developing countries at the stage of economic development where the supply of domestic savings is low, current account payments deficits are high, and imports of capital are needed to augment domestic resources. Prior to the early 1970s, the external debt of developing countries was relatively small and primarily an official phenomenon, the majority of creditors being foreign governments and international financial institutions such as the IMF, the World Bank, and regional development banks. Most loans were on concessional (low-interest) terms and were extended for purposes of implementing development projects and expanding imports of capital goods. However, during the late 1970s and early 1980s, commercial banks began playing a large role in international lending by recycling surplus Organization of the Petroleum Exporting Countries (OPEC) "petrodollars" and issuing general-purpose loans to developing countries to provide balance of payments support and expansion of export sectors.

External debt Total private and public foreign debt owed by a country.

Although foreign borrowing can be highly beneficial, providing the resources necessary to promote economic growth and development, when poorly managed, can be very costly. In recent years, these costs have greatly outweighed the benefits for many developing nations. The main cost associated with the accumulation of a large external debt is debt service. Debt service is the payment of amortization (liquidation of the principal) and accumulated interest; it is a contractually fixed charge on domestic real income and savings. As the size of the debt grows or as interest rates rise, debt service charges increase. Debt service payments must be made with foreign exchange. In other words, debt service obligations can be met only through export earnings, curtailed imports, or further external borrowing. Under normal circumstances, most of a country's debt service obligations are met by its export earnings. However, should the composition of imports change or should interest rates rise significantly, causing a ballooning of debt service payments, or should export earnings diminish, debt-servicing difficulties are likely to arise.

First, it is necessary to understand a fundamental concept, known as the **basic transfer**.[4] The basic transfer of a country is defined as the net foreign-exchange inflow or outflow related to its international borrowing. It is measured as the difference between the net capital inflow and interest payments on the existing accumulated debt. The net capital inflow is simply the difference between the gross inflow and the amortization on past debt. The basic transfer is an important concept because it represents the amount of foreign exchange that a particular developing country is gaining or losing each year from international capital flows. As you will soon discover, the basic transfer turned very negative for developing nations during the 1980s, causing a loss of foreign exchange and a net outflow of capital.

Basic transfer Net foreign-exchange inflow or outflow related to a country's international borrowing; the quantitative difference between the net capital inflow (gross inflow minus amortization on past debt) and interest payments on existing accumulated debt.

The basic-transfer equation can be expressed as follows. Let the net capital inflow, F_N, be expressed as the rate of increase of total external debt, and let D represent the total accumulated foreign debt. If d is the percentage rate of increase in that total debt, then

$$F_N = dD \tag{13.1}$$

Because interest must be paid each year on the accumulated debt, let us let r equal the average rate of interest so that rD measures total annual interest payments. The basic transfer (BT) then is simply the net capital inflow minus interest payments, or

$$BT = dD - rD = (d - r)D \qquad (13.2)$$

BT will be positive if $d > r$, and the country will be gaining foreign exchange. However, if $r > d$, the basic transfer turns negative, and the nation loses foreign exchange. Any analysis of the evolution of, and prospects for, debt crises requires an examination of the various factors that cause d and r to rise and fall.

In the early stages of debt accumulation, when a developing country has a relatively small total debt, D, the rate of increase, d, is likely to be high. Also, because most first-stage debt accumulation comes from official (as opposed to private) sources in the form of bilateral foreign aid and World Bank lending, most of the debt is incurred on concessional terms—that is, at below-market interest rates with lengthy repayment periods. Consequently, r is quite low and in any event less than d. As long as this accumulating debt is being used for productive development projects with rates of return in excess of r, the additional foreign exchange and rising foreign debt represented by the positive basic transfers pose no problems for recipient nations. In fact, as noted in earlier chapters, this process of debt accumulation for productive investments in both rural and urban areas represents an essential ingredient in any viable strategy of long-term development.

A serious problem can arise, however, when (1) the accumulated debt becomes very large so that its rate of increase, d, naturally begins to decline as amortization rises relative to rates of new gross inflows; (2) the sources of foreign capital switch from long-term "official flows" on fixed, concessional terms to short-term, variable-rate private bank loans at market rates that cause r to rise; (3) the country begins to experience severe balance of payments problems as commodity prices plummet and the terms of trade rapidly deteriorate; (4) a global recession or some other external shock, such as a jump in oil prices, a steep rise in U.S. interest rates on which variable-rate private loans are based, or a sudden change in the value of the dollar, in which most debts are denominated, takes place; (5) a loss in confidence in the ability of a developing country to repay resulting from points 2, 3, and 4 occurs, causing private international banks to cut off their flow of new lending; and (6) a substantial flight of capital is precipitated by local residents who, for political or economic reasons (e.g., expectations of currency devaluation), send great sums of money out of the country to be invested in developed-country financial securities, real estate, and bank accounts. All six factors can combine to lower d and raise r in the basic-transfer equation, with the net result that the overall basic transfer becomes highly negative and capital flows from the underdeveloped to the developed world (as shown in Table 13.5). The debt crisis then becomes a self-reinforcing phenomenon, and heavily indebted developing countries are forced into a downward spiral of negative basic transfers, dwindling foreign reserves, and stalled development prospects. The story of the debt crisis of the 1980s is largely told by the simple analysis of the factors affecting the basic-transfer mechanism of Equation 13.2. Against this analytical background, we can now look at the specific details of the 1980s debt crisis and the policy responses in the 1980s and early 1990s, and, in the case of many African and some other low-income economies, into the late 1990s and 2000s.

Origins of the 1980s Debt Crisis

The seeds of the 1980s debt crisis were sown in the 1974–1979 period, when there was a virtual explosion in international lending, precipitated by the first major OPEC oil price increase. By 1974, developing countries had begun playing a larger role in the world economy, having averaged growth rates of 6.6% in 1967–1973. Mexico, Brazil, Venezuela, and Argentina in Latin America, among other nations, had begun importing heavily, especially capital goods, oil, and food. Following outward-looking development strategies, they expanded their exports aggressively. In the face of high oil prices and a worldwide recession, in which the growth rates of the industrialized countries fell from an average of 5.2% in 1967–1974 to an average of 2.7% for the rest of the 1970s, many developing countries sought to sustain their high growth rates through increased borrowing. Although lending from official sources, particularly nonconcessional lending, increased significantly, it was insufficient to meet growth needs. Furthermore, countries with an excess of imports over lagging exports were reluctant to approach official sources, such as the IMF, that might subject them to painful policy adjustments. So the middle-income and newly industrializing developing countries turned to commercial banks and other private lenders, which began issuing general-purpose loans to provide balance of payments support. Commercial banks, holding the bulk of the OPEC surplus (which had jumped from $7 billion in 1973 to $68 billion in 1974 and ultimately peaked in this period at $115 billion in 1980) and facing a low demand for capital from the slower-growing industrialized countries, aggressively competed in lending to developing countries on comparatively permissive and favorable terms. Figure 13.1 portrays the mechanism by which OPEC petrodollars were recycled, starting with Middle Eastern oil export earnings being deposited in U.S. and European banks, which then lent these dollar balances to developing-world public- and private-sector borrowers. Over $350 billion was recycled from OPEC countries between 1976 and 1982.

As a result of all these factors, the total external debt of developing countries more than doubled from $180 billion in 1975 to $406 billion in 1979, increasing over 20% annually. More significant, an increasing portion of the debt was now on nonconcessional terms, involving shorter maturities and market rates of interest, often variable rates. In 1971, about 40% of the total external debt was on nonconcessional terms. This increased to 68% by 1975, and by 1979, over 77% of the debt was on harder terms. Although the increase in nonconcessional lending by official institutions was partly responsible for this rising proportion, the more than tripling of lending by private capital markets played the major role. Together, the large increase in the size of debt and the larger proportion scheduled on harder terms were responsible for the tripling of debt service payments, which rose from $25 billion in 1975 to $75 billion in 1979.

Despite the sizable increases in debt-servicing obligations, the ability of most developing countries to meet their debt service payments during the

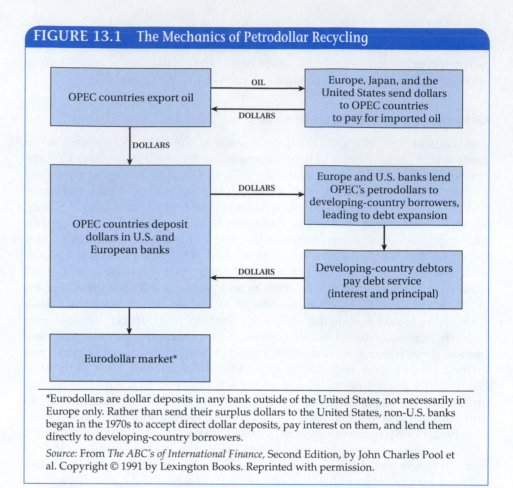

FIGURE 13.1   The Mechanics of Petrodollar Recycling

OPEC countries export oil → OIL → Europe, Japan, and the United States send dollars to OPEC countries to pay for imported oil → DOLLARS →

DOLLARS ↓

OPEC countries deposit dollars in U.S. and European banks → DOLLARS → Europe and U.S. banks lend OPEC's petrodollars to developing-country borrowers, leading to debt expansion ↓ Developing-country debtors pay debt service (interest and principal) → DOLLARS →

↓ Eurodollar market*

*Eurodollars are dollar deposits in any bank outside of the United States, not necessarily in Europe only. Rather than send their surplus dollars to the United States, non-U.S. banks began in the 1970s to accept direct dollar deposits, pay interest on them, and lend them directly to developing-country borrowers.

Source: From *The ABC's of International Finance,* Second Edition, by John Charles Pool et al. Copyright © 1991 by Lexington Books. Reprinted with permission.

late 1970s remained largely unimpaired. This was primarily a function of the international economic climate during that period. A combination of declining real oil prices as a result of inflation, low or negative real interest rates, and increased export earnings narrowed current account deficits toward the end of the decade and enabled developing countries to sustain relatively high growth rates, averaging 5.2% during 1973–1979, through massive borrowing.

In sum, the surge in international lending following the first oil shock was largely during the period 1974–1979. In a congenial economic atmosphere, it permitted developing countries to maintain relatively high rates of growth with little debt-servicing difficulty. It also facilitated the recycling of a huge surplus from oil exporters to oil importers through the lending activities of private international banks, and it helped dampen the recession in industrialized countries by providing for increased export demand on the part of developing countries.

Unfortunately, this success was short-lived, and in fact, the surge in international lending that occurred in 1974–1979 had laid the groundwork for all the problems that were to come. The second oil shock, which occurred in 1979, brought about a complete reversal of the economic conditions conducive to the success of international lending in the previous period. Now developing countries faced an abrupt increase in oil prices that added to oil import bills and affected industrial goods imports. There was also a huge increase in interest rates caused by the industrialized countries' economic stabilization policies and a decrease in export earnings for developing countries, resulting from a combination of slowed growth in the more developed nations and a precipitous decline of over 20% in primary commodity export prices. Moreover, developing countries inherited from the previous period a huge debt and debt service obligation, which was made even more onerous by burgeoning interest rates and more precarious as a result of the bunching of short-term maturities.

Finally, during the entire period of debt accumulation, one of the most significant and persistent trends was the tremendous increase in private capital flight. It is estimated that between 1976 and 1985, about $200 billion fled the heavily indebted countries.[5] This was the equivalent of 50% of the total borrowings by developing countries over the same period. Fully 62% of Argentina's and 71% of Mexico's debt growth are estimated to have resulted from capital flight. In fact, some researchers have argued that the 1985 level of Mexican debt would have been $12 billion (rather than the actual $96 billion) were it not for the huge private *capital flight*.[6]

Facing this critical situation, developing countries had two policy options. They could either curtail imports and impose restrictive fiscal and monetary measures, thus impeding growth and development objectives, or they could finance their widening current account deficits through more external borrowing. Unable, and sometimes unwilling, to adopt the first option as a means of solving the balance of payments crisis, many countries were forced in the 1980s to rely on the second option, borrowing even more heavily. As a result, massive debt service obligations accumulated so that countries like Nigeria, Argentina, Ecuador, and Peru were experiencing negative economic growth in the 1980s and consequently faced severe difficulties in paying even the interest on their debts out of export earnings. They could no longer borrow funds in the world's private capital markets. In fact, not only did private lending dry up, but also by 1984, the developing countries were paying back $10.2 billion more to the commercial banks than they were receiving in new loans (see Table 13.4).

In the 1990s, the economic situations of developing countries varied greatly: Many experienced positive net transfers, but others remained in crisis. The statistical picture became more complicated after the mid-1990s, with middle-income developing countries increasingly relying on foreign direct investment. Some countries in crisis probably experienced negative net financial transfers.

13.5 Attempts at Alleviation: Macroeconomic Instability, Classic IMF Stabilization Policies, and Their Critics

The IMF Stabilization Program

One course of action that was increasingly but often reluctantly used by countries facing serious **macroeconomic instability** (high inflation and severe government budget and foreign-payments deficits) along with growing

Macroeconomic instability
Situation in which a country has high inflation accompanied by rising budget and trade deficits and a rapidly expanding money supply.

foreign-debt obligations was to renegotiate loans with private international banks. The basic idea was to stretch out the payment period for principal and interest or to obtain additional financing on more favorable terms. Typically, however, such debtor countries had to deal with the IMF before a consortium of international banks would agree to refinance or defer existing loan schedules. Relying on the IMF to impose tough **stabilization policies**, a process known as *conditionality*, before it agreed to lend funds in excess of their legal IMF quotas, the private banks interpreted successful negotiations with the IMF as a sign that borrowing countries were making serious efforts to reduce payments deficits and earn the foreign exchange needed to repay earlier loans.[7] There are four basic components to the typical IMF stabilization program:

Stabilization policies A coordinated set of mostly restrictive fiscal and monetary policies aimed at reducing inflation, cutting budget deficits, and improving the balance of payments.

1. Abolition or liberalization of foreign-exchange and import controls

2. Devaluation of the official exchange rate

3. A stringent domestic anti-inflation program consisting of (a) control of bank credit to raise interest rates and reserve requirements; (b) control of the government deficit through curbs on spending, including in the areas of social services for the poor and staple food subsidies, along with increases in taxes and in public-enterprise prices; (c) control of wage increases, in particular abolishing wage indexing; and (d) dismantling of various forms of price controls and promoting freer markets

4. Greater hospitality to foreign investment and a general opening up of the economy to international commerce

In the early 1980s, numerous debtor countries with greatly depleted foreign reserves, including Mexico, Brazil, Argentina, Venezuela, Bangladesh, and Ghana, had to turn to the IMF to secure additional foreign exchange. By 1992, 10 countries had arranged to borrow a total of $37.2 billion in special drawing rights (equal to approximately $27 billion) from the IMF. During the Asian crisis of 1997, the IMF had to intervene with substantially larger sums of money in an effort to stabilize the shaky economies of Thailand ($3.9 billion in IMF loans), Pakistan ($1.6 billion), the Philippines ($435 million), Indonesia ($10 billion), and South Korea ($21 billion). The IMF became newly engaged in funding and stabilization packages in the wake of the global financial crisis, especially in various hard-hit eastern Europe and former Soviet Union states in 2008–2010.[8] To receive their loans and, more important, to negotiate additional credits from private banks, all these nations were required to adopt some or all of the enumerated stabilization policies. Although such policies may be successful in reducing inflation and improving the balance of payments situation for many developing countries, they can be politically very unpopular (as evidenced by anti-IMF riots in Venezuela, Nigeria, Indonesia, and South Korea in the 1990s) because they strike at the heart of development efforts by disproportionately hurting the lower- and middle-income groups.[9] Alternatively, they have often been viewed by leaders in developing nations as representing a double standard—harsh adjustment policies for developing-country debtors and no adjustment of the huge budget or trade deficits for the world's greatest debtor, the United States. Finally, because IMF policies are being imposed by an international agency that is perceived by those of the dependence school to be merely an arm of the rich industrialized nations, stabilization policies are often viewed by this school as measures designed primarily to maintain the poverty and dependence of developing countries while preserving the global market structure for the international banks and private investors (and speculators) from the industrialized nations. For example, in an extensive dependence critique of the IMF and its stabilization programs, Cheryl Payer has argued that the IMF functions within a developed-world-dominated global trading system "as the chosen instrument for imposing imperialist financial discipline upon poor countries" and thus creates a form of "international peonage" in which balance of payments problems are perpetuated rather than resolved. Payer further argues that the IMF encourages developing countries to incur additional debt from international financial institutions, while it "blackmails" them (through threats of loan rejection) into antidevelopmental stabilization programs. This added debt burden thus becomes a source of future balance of payments problems, setting up a vicious circle in which debtor nations have to run faster merely to stay in place.[10]

Less radical observers view the IMF as neither prodevelopment nor antidevelopment but simply as an institution trying to carry out its original, if somewhat outdated, mandate to hold the global capitalist market together through the pursuit of orthodox short-term international financial policies. Its primary goal is the maintenance of an "orderly" international exchange system designed to promote monetary cooperation, expand international trade, control inflation, encourage exchange-rate stability, and help countries deal with short-run balance of payments problems through the provision of scarce foreign-exchange resources. Unfortunately, in a highly unequal trading world, the balance of payments problems of many developing nations may be structural and long-term in nature, with the result that short-term stabilization policies may easily lead to long-run development crises.[11] For example, between 1982 and 1988, the IMF strategy was tested in 28 of the 32 nations of Latin America and the Caribbean. It was clearly not working. During that period, Latin America financed $145 billion in debt payments but at a cost of economic stagnation, rising unemployment, and a decline in per capita income of 7%.[12] These countries "adjusted" but did not grow. By 1988, only two were barely able to make their payments. The same situation prevailed in much of Africa.[13]

Tactics for Debt Relief

The debt crisis of the 1980s, initiated by Mexico's declared moratorium on debt payments in 1982 (which came close to being repeated in 1995), called into question the stability and very viability of the international financial system. Fears were voiced that if one or two of the major debtor countries (Brazil, Mexico, or Argentina) were to default, if a group of debtor nations were jointly to repudiate their debts by forming a **debtors' cartel**, or if more countries followed Peru's early initiative to link debt servicing to export earnings, the economies of Western nations might be seriously affected. Following the onset of the debt crisis, most developing countries were cut off from the international capital market. Emergency meetings between international

Debtors' cartel A group of developing-country debtors who join together to bargain as a group with creditors.

bankers and government officials of developed nations and developing-country debtors were convened in the financial capitals of the world. This was because Latin American debts alone exceeded the net assets of the largest U.S. banks. Rumors of imminent default led currency speculators to purchase dollars, driving up the dollar's market value in 1983–1984 to a level well beyond its shadow value and adding even further to the dollar-denominated debt burdens of developing nations.

Restructuring Altering the terms and conditions of debt repayment, usually by lowering interest rates or extending the repayment period.

Numerous proposals for relieving or **restructuring** the debt burdens of highly indebted nations have been proposed, with several implemented, at least in part.[14] These have ranged from a new allocation of special drawing rights to restructuring (on better terms for debtor countries) of principal payments falling due during an agreed consolidation period. Most notable have been the Paris Club arrangements, offering highly concessional conditions, the so-called Toronto terms. These bilateral arrangements for public loans permit creditor governments to choose from three alternative concessional options—partial cancellation of up to one-third of nonconcessional loans, reduced interest rates, or extended (25-year) maturity of payments—to generate cash flow savings for debtor countries. For commercial banks, the 1989 **Brady Plan** linked partial debt forgiveness for selected borrowers to IMF or World Bank financial support, guaranteeing the payment of the remaining loans as well as commitments by the indebted developing countries to adopt stringent IMF-type adjustment programs, promote free markets, welcome foreign investors, and repatriate overseas capital. In addition, there has been much discussion of **debt-for-equity swaps**. These are the sale at a discount (sometimes in excess of 50%) of questionable developing-country commercial bank debts to private investors (mostly foreign corporations) in secondary trading markets. These corporations then trade a debtor's IOU for a local state-owned asset, such as a steel mill or a telephone company. Commercial banks are now more willing to engage in such transactions because new interpretations and regulations for U.S. banks permit them to take a loss on the loan swap while not reducing the book value of other loans to that country. For the developing countries' part, they are able through debt-for-equity swaps to encourage private investments in local-currency assets from both foreign and resident investors as well as to reduce their overall debt obligations. Much of the privatization that has occurred in Latin American debtor countries has been financed through these swap arrangements. The flip side of these benefits, however, is the fact that foreign investors are buying up the state-owned real assets of developing nations, such as steel mills and telephone companies, at major discounts. Observers who worry about developed-country penetration into developing economies or the exacerbation of domestic dualistic tendencies are naturally troubled by these debt-for-equity swaps. Between 1985 and 1992, they accounted for over 36% of all debt conversions.

Brady Plan A program launched in 1989, designed to reduce the size of outstanding developing-country commercial debt through private debt forgiveness procured in exchange for IMF and World Bank debt guarantees and greater adherence to the terms of conditionality.

Debt-for-equity swap A mechanism used by indebted developing countries to reduce the real value of external debt by exchanging equity in domestic companies (stocks) or fixed-interest obligations of the government (bonds) for private foreign debt at large discounts.

Debt-for-nature swap The exchange of foreign debt held by an organization for a larger quantity of domestic debt that is used to finance the preservation of a natural resource or environment in the debtor country.

An appealing but much less significant swap arrangement is the **debt-for-nature swap**, intended to win commitments by a developing country's government to environmental preservation of such assets as the rain forests in Ecuador or a national park in Costa Rica (see Chapter 10). Most debt-for-nature swaps are carved out by nongovernmental organizations such as the World Wildlife Fund or the Nature Conservancy. They purchase the debtor nation's IOU at a discount from a local bank and then restructure it into local-currency payments, which are then used, say, to preserve an endangered natural resource. Since 2000, new debt-for-nature exchanges have been worked out in several countries, including Guatemala, Costa Rica, Cameroon, Peru, Colombia, Jordan, Ghana, Belize, Indonesia, and Jamaica. For example, in 2008, $20 million was provided through the World Wildlife Fund in a project to protect Madagascar's biodiversity while relieving part of its government debt to France.

The problem with most proposals for debt alleviation, including debt-for-equity swaps, is that they require private international banks to initiate or endorse the policies. Most are unwilling to take any steps that would harm their short-run balance sheets. More significant, in the absence of unilateral **debt repudiation** by developing countries (a policy that would hurt both borrowers and lenders in both the short and the long term), most proposals (except debt-for-nature and similar swaps) do not solve the debt problem but merely postpone the day when debts become due, and so another crisis erupts. An often suggested proposal is to develop institutions for unwinding developing-country debt when it becomes unsustainable, in a somewhat analogous way to debt reorganization under corporate bankruptcy. As Barry Herman, José Antonio Ocampo, and Shari Spiegel expressed it in their 2010 study:

> Many countries have designed national insolvency regimes for corporations that not only wind up hopelessly bankrupt entities, but also seek to salvage firms that with reduced debts can survive as going concerns. The objective in the latter cases, as with insolvent sub-sovereign entities or households (which cannot be "wound up"), is to give a second chance, a "fresh start," and a "clean slate." The ad hoc, partial, and at best loosely coordinated system for addressing sovereign debt crises does not deliver such outcomes.[15]

All in all, the debt crisis underlined the interdependence and fragility of the international economic and financial system. It also demonstrated that not only were developing economies vulnerable to small increases in U.S. interest rates but also that developed countries could be harmed by economic failures or public policies of key developing nations.

Although many developing countries can be held at least partly responsible for the massive accumulation of debts, the adverse economic conditions this often causes are, in most cases, beyond their control. In fact, this adverse economic climate was, in part, precipitated by the industrialized countries' own economic stabilization policies, which led to soaring interest rates, worldwide economic recession, and the resulting decrease in demand for developing-country exports. William Cline estimated, for example, that almost 85% ($401 billion) of the total increase ($480 billion) in the external debt of the non-oil-exporting developing countries between 1973 and 1982 could be attributed to four factors outside of their control: OPEC oil price increases, the rise in dollar interest rates in 1981–1982, the decline in export volumes from most developing countries as a result of the worldwide recession, and the dramatic fall in commodity prices and the consequent worsening of their terms of trade.[16]

The experience of Mexico, the pioneer in debt reduction in the late 1980s, is described in detail in Box 13.3.

Commercial bankers and financiers in the industrialized countries declared the debt crisis over with the signing of a Brady-type restructuring accord with Argentina in April 1992 and with Brazil in July 1992. But, for many countries,

Debt repudiation The 1980s fear in the developed world that developing countries would stop paying their debt obligations.

BOX 13.3 Mexico: Crisis, Debt Reduction, and the Struggle for Renewed Growth

In August 1982, Mexico triggered a debt crisis when it announced that it could not service its debt and would begin a moratorium of at least three months on debt payments to private creditors. Creditor banks, led by Citibank, formed an advisory committee. Mexico sought and received emergency assistance from the International Monetary Fund and U.S. financial institutions. In September, Mexico nationalized its banks and introduced rigorous exchange controls.

In late September 1982, the annual World Bank–IMF meetings took place in Toronto in an atmosphere of panic. The greatest fear was that the stability of the international banking system would be in peril if significant defaults on loans threatened the major banks. The crisis swept through Latin America, Africa, and other developing countries such as the Philippines and Yugoslavia. A plan was devised that saved the banking system but led to what is often regarded as a lost decade (or more) of development in Latin America and Africa.

Mexico was not only the first country to enter a debt crisis but also a pacesetter in resolving it (despite some smaller crises, particularly the so-called Tequila Crisis of 1994). After dramatic debt reduction in the late 1980s and early 1990s, capital inflows have commonly assumed the form of long-term equity rather than debt.

Before 1973, Mexico's external debt, like that of most developing nations, was relatively small, primarily official, and often based on concessional lending. But major OPEC countries received a huge cash windfall from the 1973 oil price rise, and they deposited most of the funds in major U.S. banks. Mexico and other Latin American countries had a ready demand for these funds. Following Citibank chairman John Reed's dictum that "sovereign countries do not default," large banks lent while often overlooking normal criteria of lending risk. The value of outstanding loans increased tenfold in less than a decade. Investment as a share of GDP, however, hardly increased in this period of massive borrowing. Consequently,

Mexico did not have the added capacity to produce exports that could generate foreign exchange to repay debt without necessitating a fall in living standards.

Problems in Mexico were aggravated by fiscal deficits and inflation. After Mexico discovered new oil reserves and began producing oil in larger amounts in 1977, the country borrowed more money, with oil as implicit collateral. But this money, too, was not wisely invested, and the oil industry was operated with considerable inefficiency. Exchange-rate appreciation hurt other exports, and non-oil industries were neglected.

If the first oil shock incited a spate of international lending, the second oil shock, in 1979, triggered a reversal of this process as interest rates rose, stagnation reduced the demand for exports from developing countries, and high debt levels made further borrowing more difficult. When real interest rates rose dramatically after 1979, Mexico's debt burden became untenable. In early 1982, Mexico's financial position deteriorated rapidly. The country needed to borrow some $20 billion that year to finance its existing loans and meet its expected deficit. As the year progressed, bank loans were harder to arrange and required a substantially higher interest rate. Inflation rose, and a series of currency devaluations began.

The early years of the crisis were harsh for Mexico. An economic adjustment program under IMF auspices restored economic order. Elements of the typical IMF stabilization packages included liberalization of foreign-exchange and import controls, devaluation, interest-rate increases, deficit reduction, wage restrictions, decreased price controls, and a general opening up of the economy. It was widely argued in Mexico that adjustment without growth would ensue, with negative development consequences.

Real income fell dramatically from 1982 to 1985. By then it had become clear that although the fire was being contained, it was not going out. Although the public-sector deficit fell from about 17 to 8% as a share of GDP, GDP itself had fallen dramatically, and poverty and inequality had risen. No new capital flows were forthcoming, and it became clear that a new approach would be needed.

In 1985, U.S. Secretary of State James Baker introduced the Baker Plan. The idea was to get growth to resume in debtor countries so that they could "grow their way out of debt." New funds would be lent to indebted countries that would let growth resume, drawing on private banks, the World Bank, the IMF, and other sources. In return, Mexico and other indebted countries would introduce market reforms that were expected to facilitate the use of new funds in a more efficient and growth-enhancing manner.

Mexico became one of the first countries to participate in the Baker Plan. Mexico acceded to a major debt-restructuring and domestic economy reform program in June 1986. At first, there seemed to be some limited progress. Commercial banks extended over $7 billion in loans and a new rescheduling agreement covering some $54 billion of outstanding debt. In return, the World Bank offered a loan of $500 million.

But Mexico was severely hurt by the big drop in the price of oil of the mid-1980s. The IMF agreed to a special "standby" agreement in which it would make additional credit available to Mexico if the price of oil were to fall below $9 a barrel. The IMF also offered substantial new credit, to be matched by new credits from commercial banks. Mexico introduced far-reaching market-oriented reforms in this period. The most important reason this approach did not work is that commercial banks proved unwilling to do their part in net new lending. These banks committed only a fraction of the loans anticipated in the Baker Plan. The banks' main intention at this time was still to reduce their exposure to developing-country debt, not to increase it.

In the mid-1980s, Mexico became a pioneer of debt-for-equity swaps as an instrument of debt reduction. In these swaps, restrictions on foreign direct investment (FDI) are lifted when foreign investors pay for the asset by presenting Mexican debt paper. These are acquired, usually at a substantial discount, from banks that wish to reduce their developing-country debt exposure. The secondary market for Latin American debt in this period had an average discount of about 50% of face value (sometimes with far steeper discounts). The investor presents the loan to the central bank, which in turn issues local currency that can be used only to purchase a local firm's assets. Sometimes the firm may be a state-owned enterprise, so the transaction facilitates privatization. But debt-for-equity swaps carry the inherent risk of generating inflationary pressures because they usually involve swaps of public debt for private assets. Because the central bank issues funds for the investor to buy a local asset, this represents an addition to high-powered money.

Mexico suspended debt-for-equity swaps in November 1987, officially because of their inflationary effects. Part of the real reason may have been political pressures to limit the share of foreign ownership and control in the economy, though swaps of private debt for private equity continued to be permitted.

In 1988, as the swap strategy lost momentum, Mexico pioneered a new approach to debt reduction. Mexico would exchange some of its outstanding debt, perceived as high-risk, for new debt called *Aztec Bonds* that would be backed by U.S. Treasury bonds bought by Mexico as collateral. An auction would be held, in which banks would bid on how much discount on the face amount of their existing loans they would accept in exchange for the new, more secure bonds. In March 1988, some $2.5 billion of bonds were exchanged for $3.6 billion in bank debt, an average discount of about 33%. A total of some $6.7 billion was offered by banks, but Mexico rejected some of these bids as providing too small a discount. If the results were disappointing in their magnitude, they represented an important innovation, later built on in the Brady Plan.

Eventually, most parties understood that substantial Mexican growth could not resume until the country's large debt burden was substantially reduced, not just rescheduled. With the major U.S. banks out of immediate danger after several years of reducing developing-world exposure, a debt reduction plan was

(Continued)

BOX 13.3 Mexico: Crisis, Debt Reduction, and the Struggle for Renewed Growth (*Continued*)

floated by U.S. Treasury Secretary Nicholas Brady in March 1989.

Mexico was the first country to negotiate debt reduction under the new Brady Plan. Banks were given three options: (1) to exchange loans for floating-rate bonds with collateral at a 35% discount; (2) to exchange loans for bonds with the same par value but with a lower, fixed interest rate; or (3) to lend new money to finance Mexican interest payments, keeping nominal value of the debt they were owed intact. In 1990, some 49% of the banks exchanged $22 billion in debt for lower-interest, fixed-rate bonds, and 41% exchanged $20 billion in debt for the discounted floating-rate bonds. This constituted Mexico's creditor banks' "revealed preferences" from among the options.

Provided that Mexico continued to service the reduced debt successfully, the bonds on deposit in Washington as collateral would earn interest that Mexico would receive, which could be used for debt reduction or investment. From the banks' point of view, the trade-off involved giving up higher-yielding but higher-risk debt for lower-yielding but lower-risk debt. Mexican debt was 63% of GDP in 1983 but fell to 32% by 1993 and 23% in 2003.

There was one major crisis along the way. In 1994, the government attempted to carry out a small devaluation of the peso. But the market saw this step as too little, too late, given the large current account deficit

and concluded that the action was a prelude to much larger devaluations in the near future. Speculators, acting on these expectations, forced the hand of the government, which let the peso float until it had lost over half its value. Instability spread across other countries in the so-called Tequila Crisis. By mid-1996, the worst had passed, and Mexico proved immune to the crises that rocked Brazil, Turkey, and especially Argentina in the first years of the twenty-first century. Although the North American Free Trade Agreement and the benefits of bordering the world's largest economy conferred special advantages on Mexico, GDP growth remained sluggish, averaging about 1.5% per capita for the 1990–2008 period. And even adjusted for purchasing power parity, incomes remained just 29% of those in the United States. And Mexico was more negatively affected by the global financial crisis than most developing countries, with a drop in real GDP of about 6.5% in 2009.

Sources: CIA, *World Fact Book: Mexico*; https://www.cia.gov/library/publications/the-world-factbook/geos/mx.html Refik Erzan, "Free trade agreements with the United States: What's in it for Latin America?" World Bank Policy Research Working Paper No. 827, 1992; Sudarshan Gooptu, *Debt Reduction and Development: The Case of Mexico* (Westport, Conn.: Praeger, 1993); Gary Hufbauer and Jeffery Schott, *NAFTA: An Assessment* (Washington, D.C.: IIE, 1993); Robert F. Pastor and Jorje G. Castenada, *Limits to Friendship: The United States and Mexico* (New York: Vintage Books, 1988); World Bank, "World debt tables," various years; and World Bank, *World Development Indicators*, 2010.

especially in Africa, the problem remained extremely serious, and would not be adequately addressed for another decade.

And debt crises may recur, including in middle-income countries. This was vividly revealed in late 1994 and early 1995 when Mexico, one of the great success stories of debt rescheduling, was forced to devalue its currency and seek special standby loans to pay off its short-term debt obligations. Almost half of the private portfolio investment capital that had flowed into Mexico (and other Latin American debtor nations, including Brazil, Argentina, and Venezuela) in the early 1990s was summarily withdrawn. Mexico was then forced to declare a new austerity program, further weakening the already deteriorating condition of its shrinking middle class and its working poor. As in 1982, the large commercial banks and Wall Street investors were once again surprised by Mexico's move. The "hot money" flows that had been universally hailed as a boon to the Mexican economic reform program now added to its burden of retrenchment as most investors withdrew their funds in the time that it took them to hit their computer keys. The effective debt default in 2001 by Argentina, another purported success story, showed that the debt crisis in developing countries could continue to rear its head.

Fears of instability were renewed in 1997 and 1998. South Korea, Indonesia, and Thailand, along with Russia, Brazil, and other countries, borrowed from the IMF under strong austerity conditions. In South Korea and elsewhere, public discussion centered on the view that austerity had led to unnecessarily large recessions, and in response, governments throughout East Asia (and many outside it) worked to accelerate exports, repay IMF loans, and greatly expand foreign-currency reserves over the subsequent decade. This process was greatly abetted by a dollar that was widely viewed as overvalued and accompanying record U.S. trade deficits, which continued to increase.

The current account surpluses of fast-growing Asian economies have to a significant degree mirrored the deficits of the United States (and some other high-income Organization for Economic Cooperation and Development, or OECD economies). These imbalances narrowed somewhat with the global financial crisis (see Figure 13.2). The IMF projected a modest widening of imbalances in coming years. These projections, including the sustainability of imbalances, are uncertain.

But even as debt was resolved in middle-income countries—the priority for banks in that they had much larger loans at stake—the debt crisis dragged

FIGURE 13.2   Global Imbalances

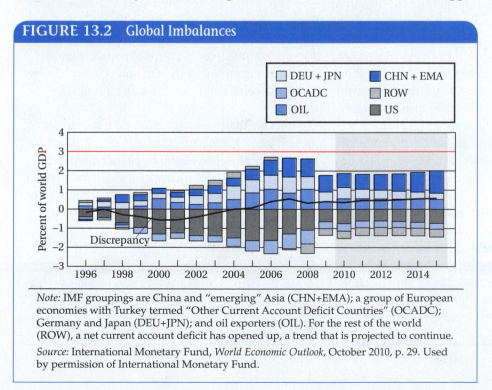

Note: IMF groupings are China and "emerging" Asia (CHN+EMA); a group of European economies with Turkey termed "Other Current Account Deficit Countries" (OCADC); Germany and Japan (DEU+JPN); and oil exporters (OIL). For the rest of the world (ROW), a net current account deficit has opened up, a trend that is projected to continue.

Source: International Monetary Fund, *World Economic Outlook*, October 2010, p. 29. Used by permission of International Monetary Fund.

BOX 13.4 "Odious Debt" and Its Prevention

Odious debt is a concept in the theory of international law holding that just as contracts signed under coercion are unenforceable, sovereign debt used by an undemocratic government in a manner that is contrary to the interests of its people should be deemed invalid. Such odious debts would represent personal debts of officials of the regime that incurred them, not debts of the state that would be the responsibility of the nation's people.

The concept has a long history; it was implicitly invoked, albeit without its present name, by Mexico following the overthrow of the French-backed Emperor Maximilian I and by the United States on behalf of Cuba in negotiations following the Spanish-American War of 1898 (in which the United States abetted the rebels in the Cuban War of Independence while gaining long-term influence). It was explicitly argued in 1927 by legal scholar Alexander Sack.

Dictators widely alleged to have looted substantial public funds while incurring foreign debt have been found in every developing area; they include Anastasio Somoza of Nicaragua, Ferdinand Marcos of the Philippines, Jean-Claude Duvalier of Haiti, Mobutu Sese Seko of the Democratic Republic of Congo (then called Zaire), and Franjo Tudjman of Croatia. Many of these regimes and others, such as the apartheid government of South Africa, borrowed while also spending heavily on the apparatus of state repression.

Seema Jayachandran and Michael Kremer propose establishing an independent international body to determine which regimes are illegitimate and thereby declaring as legally odious any subsequently incurred sovereign debt. As such, this debt would not be a legal obligation of successor governments. Of course, some unscrupulous lenders might still lend funds at high interest rates if they believed the regimes to be stable. But, in general, these rules should limit dictators' ability to loot and repress while containing the debt burden of poor countries. Indeed, by substantially

removing possible future defaulters from the loan pool, these rules could lead to lower interest rates for legitimate governments. We may expect a better long-term outcome to result for the people of developing countries. To help ensure that no further loans are made to regimes that are considered odious, Jayachandran and Kremer point out, legal incentives could be introduced on both the lender and borrower sides. Laws in creditor countries could be made to disallow seizure of a developing nation's assets for nonrepayment of odious debt. And foreign aid to successor regimes could be withheld if they continued to repay odious debts. Note that we would not want new regimes to repay debts incurred by previous regimes after they had been officially designated as odious because this would undermine the attempt to reach a new equilibrium in which such loans would not be extended in the first place.

Jayachandran and Kremer suggest that the concept could be implemented in several ways. For example, even if an international court were not established, the procedure could be followed by the UN Security Council, and some coordination could even be achieved by initiatives of groups of respected nongovernmental organizations (NGOs) and opinion leaders or through some hybrid of formal and informal mechanisms.

Although the proposed odious-debt institution is forward-looking, the perception that some of the debt held by African countries can be characterized as odious is probably one of the reasons why debt forgiveness for highly indebted and low-income countries in Africa has gained such wide international support.

Sources: Seema Jayachandran and Michael Kremer, "Odious debt," *American Economic Review* 96 (2006): 82–92, and "Odious debt," *Finance and Development* 39 (2002): 36–39. Note: Their analysis draws on game theory, in which in repeated games with multiple possible outcomes, or equilibria, making relevant information public can lead to a new equilibrium.

on in a majority of low-income sub-Saharan African countries. The debt in a few of these countries arguably had "odious" origins (see Box 13.4).

The HIPC Initiative The first initiative to address the problems of **heavily indebted poor countries (HIPCs)** was launched by the group of 8 major industrialized countries (the Group of Eight, or G8) in 1996. They set up an elaborate process for qualifying for expanded debt relief through the international financial institutions, but by 1999, only 4 of the 36 poor countries initially deemed eligible had qualified. The G8 then agreed to set aside approximately $100 billion for "enhanced" debt relief for those designated HIPC countries that demonstrated, to the satisfaction of the World Bank and the IMF, that they were both pursuing "sound policies" and were "committed" to reducing poverty. Commitment was to be demonstrated through what came to be called *poverty reduction strategy papers.*[17] For eligibility, countries had to be classified as low-income (see Chapter 2), face an "unsustainable debt burden that cannot be addressed through traditional debt-relief mechanisms," demonstrate via participation in IMF- and World Bank–sponsored programs "a track record of reform and sound policies," and develop a PRSP. Progress on committing these funds was slower than expected, and the PRSP process (discussed further in Chapter 14) was considered relatively disappointing. Additional funds were committed in 2005. External debt has fallen considerably for many HIPC countries. Figure 13.3 illustrates the decline in external debt service payments as a proportion of national export revenues for a number of HIPC countries, comparing data for 2002 with 2012. As of 2013, of the 39 developing countries defined as potentially eligible for HIPC, 35

Odious debt A concept in the theory of international law holding that sovereign debt used by an undemocratic government in a manner contrary to the interests of its people should be deemed to be not the responsibility of democratic successor governments.

Heavily indebted poor countries (HIPCs) The group of the world's poorest and most heavily indebted countries as defined by the World Bank and the IMF, which status may make them eligible for special debt relief.

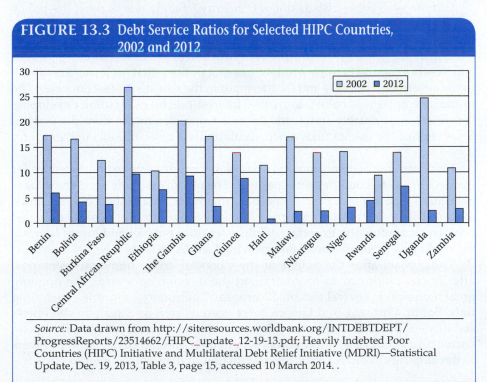

FIGURE 13.3 Debt Service Ratios for Selected HIPC Countries, 2002 and 2012

Source: Data drawn from http://siteresources.worldbank.org/INTDEBTDEPT/ProgressReports/23514662/HIPC_update_12-19-13.pdf; Heavily Indebted Poor Countries (HIPC) Initiative and Multilateral Debt Relief Initiative (MDRI)—Statistical Update, Dec. 19, 2013, Table 3, page 15, accessed 10 March 2014. .

had reached their "post-completion points" so that they were receiving their full allocations of debt relief.

But commercial loans are not part of the HIPC process; some private lenders continue to pursue lawsuits to recover African loans. Moreover, even some official lenders are not participating in debt relief. Further, some countries in which debt has imposed hardship are not eligible for HIPC, for example because they are above the low-income line, despite having substantial levels of chronic poverty.[18]

In sum, great progress has been made for much of the developing world, but many countries remain vulnerable going forward.[19]

13.6 The Global Financial Crisis and the Developing Countries

Beginning with the first tremors of the subprime mortgage crisis in the United States in 2007, the world faced a global financial crisis and a "great recession" in the developed economies on a scale that has not been seen since the Great Depression. An examination of the crisis offers insights for global as well as specific developing-country policies.

In mid-2013, the World Bank opined that "the bulk of developing countries are fully recovered from the crisis. Several even risk overheating if policy does not tighten,"[20] although they noted ongoing problems for "developing Europe" and unrest in the Middle East and North Africa.

Unfortunately, the crisis is not yet "history." Barely weeks later, the policy community refocused on a "new emerging markets crisis," with the Indian rupee dropping at a historic rate in August 2013 and other danger signals; this was partly triggered by the prospective reduction of the extraordinary U.S. Federal Reserve (central bank) quantitative easing policy—that itself was a response to the severity of the crisis and its aftermath in the world's largest importer. The immediate crisis was halted, in part by interest rate hikes by some developing countries, most notably India, and by reassuring statements from the Federal Reserve. But the events underlined continued vulnerabilities to tighter credit conditions.[21]

Moreover, the higher commodity prices that propped up export revenues for many developing countries were partly the result of post-crisis fiscal stimulus—particularly the stimulus from China; but growth in China cannot continue much longer at its exceptionally high pace. Lower commodity prices are a potential concern for commodity exporters, while asset price bubbles and excess borrowing could be a problem among fast-growing East Asian economies.

Thus, years after the height of the financial crisis, numerous economic aftershocks continued to reverberate in the developing world. The ongoing great recession in several indebted European "periphery" countries, including Italy, Spain, Portugal, and Greece, were seen as serious threats to the euro's stability—if not to its continued existence as a widely used common European currency; a euro crisis, if it occured, would also portend dangerous spillovers to developing countries including a reduction of demand for their exports.[22]

Thus, despite the resilience of economic growth in many developing countries in the postcrisis years, residual impacts on the developing world have been substantial, recovery has been incomplete, and serious uncertainties have lingered.[23]

Causes of the Crisis and Challenges to Lasting Recovery

Economists have not yet reached a consensus on the root cause(s) of the crisis; in one view, it would not have occurred had not several things gone wrong at about the same time. In the United States, one factor high on most lists was financial deregulation that was rapid and wide-ranging (and careless in its design and implementation). Deregulation came with repeal of rules separating commercial and investment banking without an adequate regulatory framework to replace it, failure to regulate newly introduced financial instruments, lack of enforcement of remaining regulations, and artificially low interest rates. Fuel for the fire came from public policy encouraging home ownership through subprime lending—underpinned with support of implicitly publicly guaranteed "government-sponsored enterprises," notably Freddie Mac and Fannie Mae—along with the packaging and resale of these loans with understatements of their riskiness. Failure of risk-rating agencies to fulfill their roles was also widely cited.[24] Other developed countries, including several in Europe such as Spain, had parallel financial stability problems that were exposed by the crisis. The result was a fragile financial system, with high leverage and complex and incompletely understood financial securities. The so-called Basel III requirements for bank capital and liquidity to reduce banking risks[25] introduced between 2010 and 2013, along with a U.S. law passed in May 2010 and similar legislation in other countries, were viewed as steps in the right direction but probably not enough to prevent another crisis under some circumstances.

A probable second major factor in the crisis was the chronic international trade imbalances between East Asia, notably China, and the developed countries, particularly the United States, with concomitant capital flows into the United States. This helped keep capital cheap and fueled the housing bubbles in the United States and some European countries. Now, for the first time in decades, sovereign debt problems were raised as possibilities in *developed* countries, most prominently for the so-called EU-5 (Greece, Ireland, Italy, Portugal, and Spain)—note that as recently as the early 1990s, three of these five were still classified as developing countries. Ireland and Greece required dramatic international bailouts in 2010; along with Portugal, they remain the largest IMF borrowers.

Yet, from the start of the crisis, the interest rates the United States and the United Kingdom pay on their high debts was never lower, at first reflecting severe risk aversion in the markets and then "ultra-loose" monetary policy.[26] In response to the crisis, many countries also took on "fiscal stimulus" programs of government spending to prop up very weak demand and prevent the onset of a depression. A majority of economists considered this effort to have been necessary and effective, and evidence supports this. But stimulus programs proved politically unsustainable, and as austerity measures in several developed countries, most prominently the United Kingdom and the deficit countries of Europe, were rolled out, in a historical irony in 2010, the IMF called on countries not to cut back on spending nearly as quickly as many governments were planning because of the weakness of demand. An encore of this drama played out in 2013 when the United States abruptly moved into sharp austerity with "sequestration" (automatic, across-the-board, public spending cuts). Just as for developing countries, austerity can have costly social and health impacts for developed countries.[27] More extraordinary, this shift was coupled with brinksmanship in the U.S. Congress, combining a partial government shutdown with a threat to allow default as a domestic political weapon. The resulting unprecedented "voluntary fiscal crises" in 2011 and 2013 created considerable uncertainty and thereby were estimated to have led directly or indirectly to a substantial reduction of U.S. growth, globally reducing demand and magnifying instability.[28]

Most international financial crises since World War II were viewed as "originating" in the developing world. From the Latin American debt crisis of 1982 to the Mexican "Tequila Crisis" of 1994, to the "East Asian Contagion" of 1998, and the Argentine default in 2001, problems were perceived as caused by developing economies' weak financial markets and institutions and unstable political economy. With each crisis, the affected countries were pressured to open and liberalize their economies. As part of IMF and World Bank conditionality agreements, Latin American and African countries essentially were required to privatize state-owned enterprises (see Chapter 15, section 15.6), eliminate regulations, and reduce infant industry protection after their 1980s and 1990s debt crises. And East Asian countries such as South Korea, Thailand, and Indonesia were required to open their economies to more direct foreign investment (see Chapter 14, section 14.2), including in the financial sector, in the late 1990s. One response was a determination to run export surpluses and build up large international currency reserves, a factor pushing up parallel trade deficits in developed countries (see Figure 13.4).[29]

Despite these historical reversals of capital flows, given past pressure from developed countries to adopt policies modeled on their own systems that were said to reduce risks of financial crises, it came as a great surprise to many policymakers in the developing world that this most recent crisis originated in the United States, accompanied by its worst economic downturn since the Great Depression. The global downturn that followed the crisis initially was briefest in many developing countries; also surprising to many was the leading role of some developing countries (most notably China but also India, Brazil, and a few others) in helping to pull many countries out of the recession through their continued economic dynamism. Most economic studies have concluded that the stimulus packages in both developed and developing countries probably kept the situation from getting much worse.

In the decade leading up to the crisis, fast-growing developing countries were relying heavily on exports to the United States and other developed countries. In response to the crisis, in 2010 President Obama announced an objective of doubling U.S. exports in five years. China rejected pressure from the United States and other countries to stop resisting market forces for its

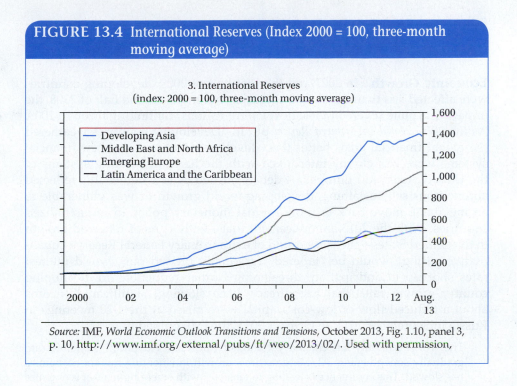

FIGURE 13.4 International Reserves (Index 2000 = 100, three-month moving average)

3. International Reserves
(index; 2000 = 100, three-month moving average)

- Developing Asia
- Middle East and North Africa
- Emerging Europe
- Latin America and the Caribbean

Source: IMF, *World Economic Outlook Transitions and Tensions,* October 2013, Fig. 1.10, panel 3, p. 10, http://www.imf.org/external/pubs/ft/weo/2013/02/. Used with permission,

exchange rate to rise, though eventually appreciation did take place. Policymakers in most leading economies also hoped for growth through expanded exports, and out of this grew what were apparently competitive efforts to also lower the value of their relative exchange rates to make their exports cheaper. But exchange rates are relative, so not all countries can devalue at once! In late 2010, Guido Mantega, finance minister of Brazil, stated publicly what many officials had been stating privately—that the world had moved into an "international currency war." The remarks renewed fears that the global economy still faced risks not seen since the 1930s. Soon the IMF and the World Bank had weighed in with warnings about the dangerous drift in international economic policy. The issue of competitive depreciation of currencies shared center stage with concerns about slow recovery at the fall 2010 IMF–World Bank annual meeting. And yet it was extremely unlikely that misaligned exchange rates could have been the sole cause of a crisis of this scope, and it was at best very uncertain that realignment of exchange rates would be enough to resolve the problems caused by the crisis or to prevent a new one. But Mantega's declaration in January 2011 that "this is a currency war that is turning into a trade war" got the attention of many policymakers—tensions perhaps later diffused by opportunities to export to China, India, and other large middle-income countries. The subsequent slowdowns in China and India are being watched closely.[30]

Economic Impacts on Developing Countries

We now review nine areas of impacts.

Economic Growth   In 2007 and the first half of 2008, developing countries were affected less than developed countries, but in the second half of 2008, the impact was quite severe in most developing regions, continuing through 2009. As the 2009 *World Investment Report* put it, "Developing countries weathered the global financial crisis better than developed countries, as their financial systems were less closely interlinked with the hard-hit banking systems of the United States and Europe." A debate ensued as to whether this reflected autonomous self-sustaining, developing-world growth or was vulnerable to an inevitable move back to more normal monetary policy in industrialized countries. With the 2013 announcement that—with signs of renewed growth in the United States—the large round of extraordinary Federal Reserve "quantitative easing" would be "tapered" (gradually phased out), world interest rates shot up in anticipation, threatening further reductions in developing country growth rates that had already been slowing. Significant concerns about a reduced flow of low-cost capital were raised at the G20 meetings in Russia in September 2013. In October 2013, the IMF opined that:

> The world economy has entered yet another transition. Advanced economies are gradually strengthening. At the same time, growth in emerging market economies has slowed. This confluence is leading to tensions, with emerging market economies facing the dual challenges of slowing growth and tighter global financial conditions.

IMF Economic Counsellor Olivier Blanchard also wrote that

> Unusually favorable world conditions, including high commodity prices and rapid financial market development, increased potential growth in [emerging market or developing] economies during the 2000s, and in a number of them, there was a cyclical component on top. As commodity prices stabilize and financial conditions tighten, potential growth is lower, leading in some cases to a sharp cyclical adjustment.[31]

Both the IMF and World Bank stressed continued underlying fragilities and uncertainties, some due to factors unrelated to the developing world. A key example is the uncertainty caused by political conflict in the United States over fiscal policy (notably the threats to allow default on federal debt unless additional budgetary and programmatic concessions are made).

Exports   Exports fell drastically in the immediate aftermath of the crisis. World trade volumes fell 14.4% in 2009, the largest drop in decades, but then rebounded strongly before returning to modest growth from 2011.

Developed-countries' austerity programs were a factor in their declining trade deficits. Going forward, to reduce its deficits, the United States has been widely expected to establish a higher savings rate while the dollar depreciates further (although the savings rate actually fell in 2013). New records in asset prices brought with it some fears of a temporary return of the bubble economy, precipitating an even worse crisis than last time, with a larger impact on exports—but there is no consensus on the extent to which new bubbles (if any) are forming. It remains unclear whether other developed-country markets will open to the extent seen in the United States and United Kingdom during the bubble period. The U.S. and a majority of European governments have made strong statements of their determination to reduce budget deficits and increase savings, measures that would be associated with fewer imports from developing countries. Many analysts have continued to view the euro as the most likely flashpoint for any new crisis, with inadequate follow-through on previous initiatives. Japan (like Germany and some other European economies) remains a strongly export surplus country as its population continues to age. Again, with the outlook doubtful for rapid increases in exports to developed countries, the emphasis has turned to trade among developing countries.

Initial loss of commodity revenues were substantial. The United Nations reported that "developing countries still suffered a 31 percent decline in the value of their exports in 2009".[32] Subsequently, commodity revenues rebounded with increases in both prices and quantities delivered. However, commodity prices had peaked by 2011; and at the end of 2013 remained below the 2008 and 2011 peaks (see Figure 13.5). Commodity prices may fall further as growth in China decelerates.

FIGURE 13.5 Indices of Commodity Prices (Total and Non-Fuel), 2000–2013

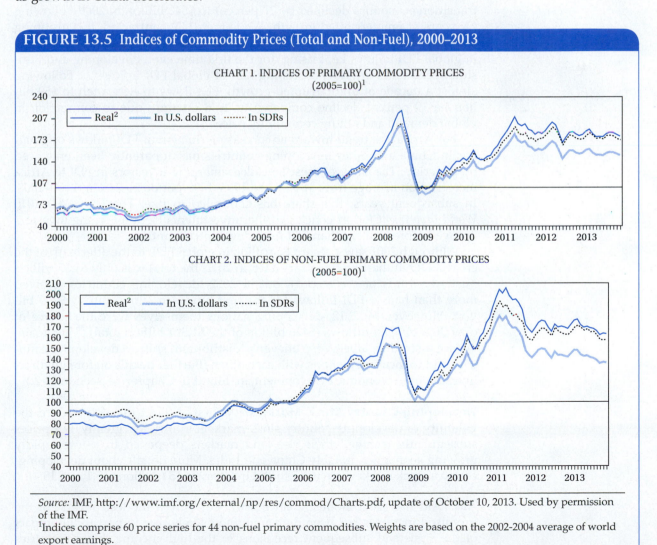

CHART 1. INDICES OF PRIMARY COMMODITY PRICES
(2005=100)[1]

CHART 2. INDICES OF NON-FUEL PRIMARY COMMODITY PRICES
(2005=100)[1]

Source: IMF, http://www.imf.org/external/np/res/commod/Charts.pdf, update of October 10, 2013. Used by permission of the IMF.
[1]Indices comprise 60 price series for 44 non-fuel primary commodities. Weights are based on the 2002-2004 average of world export earnings.
[2]Deflated by US CPI

The IMF examined one of the central questions of the crisis for economic development: Do financial crises have lasting effects on trade? The research examined the evidence since 1970 and found that imports remained depressed even in the medium term after banking crises, while exports from the crisis countries were relatively unaffected. Countries with banking crises that also had higher current account deficits generally experienced *larger* declines in imports. This finding supported concern that opportunities for developing countries to expand exports to the United States and to the significant number of European countries that experienced banking crises will be more limited for several years, yet another factor underscoring the renewed priority placed on trade among developing nations.[33]

Foreign Investment Inflows   A United Nations Conference on Trade and Development (UNCTAD) study concluded that "the global crisis curtailed the funding available for FDI" and noted that "FDI inflows to developing and transition economies declined by 27 percent to \$548 billion in 2009, following six years of uninterrupted growth. While their FDI contracted, this grouping appeared more resilient to the crisis than developed countries.... Their share in global FDI inflows kept rising: for the first time ever, developing and transition economies are now absorbing half of global FDI inflows.... Following almost a decade of uninterrupted growth, FDI flows to Africa fell to \$59 billion—a 19 percent decline compared to 2008—mainly due to contraction in global demand and falling commodity prices."[34]

For Africa, the trend toward an increasing fraction of FDI inflows originating in China and other developing countries has apparently been enhanced by the crisis. The share of these so-called emerging investors in FDI to Africa increased on average from 18% in the 1995–1999 period to 21% in 2000–2008. In subsequent years, this share has continued to rise. The UNCTAD *2010 World Investment Report* concluded that investments from emerging investors "proved more resilient than FDI from developed countries."[35]

Although 2007 saw a record \$2 trillion in global FDI, in the aftermath of the crisis, FDI fell sharply; five years later, in 2012, the total was only \$1.35 trillion (just two-thirds of the record). But in 2012, developing countries received more than half of FDI inflows for the first time—an extraordinary \$703 billion. Moreover, by 2012, developing nations themselves were the source of over 30% of FDI outflows (\$426 billion of the \$1,391 billion total).[36] Yet again, we see a striking, albeit very unevenly distributed, shift to developing countries and to their interactions with each other. (Further details on foreign direct investment in economic development are found in Chapter 14, section 14.2.)

Developing-Country Stock Markets   At first, a flight to safety caused the volatility of developing-country stock markets to increase greatly. But prices subsequently resumed their rise, and markets deepened in a few rapidly growing economies, notably China and India. More details about developing-country stock markets are to be found in Chapter 15 (sections 15.1 and 15.4).

Aid   Aid has risen modestly since 2001, but only a modest portion of the promised increases has been delivered, most likely due in part to the impact of the crisis and subsequent recessions in the high-income donor countries (foreign aid is covered in more detail in Chapter 14, section 14.4). But as aid remained below historical levels, other financial flows such as worker remittances, FDI, and portfolio investment flows increased by many times more than the declines in aid (see Figure 14.2). Yet, for the least developed countries, aid is needed as much as ever. There are strong political pressures against any increase in aid, let alone maintaining its current levels, in the United States, the United Kingdom, and other high-income donor countries. In past periods of prolonged recession or fiscal restraint, high-income countries have cut bilateral aid. Indeed, according to the United Nations, in 2012 official aid from developed countries was $125.6 billion, which represented a 4% decrease in real terms from 2011, which was, in turn, another 2% below the level of official aid in 2010. To the extent that aid targets human development and safety net programs, this could harm the poor beyond the impact of slowed growth. People living in extreme poverty are sometimes isolated from markets, but some receive and may depend upon foreign assistance. Charitable giving remained relatively stable; specialists cited the dramatic rebound of U.S. stock market valuations.[37] In sum, prospects for reversing the slide in—let alone expanding—official and unofficial development assistance likely depend on the extent of growth in donor nations.

Distribution of Influence among Developing Countries   There have always been divisions in the developing world. During the Cold War, countries were asked to take sides, aligning themselves with the United States and other NATO countries, or the Soviet Union, or China. These conflicts spilled over to the nonaligned movement, which included countries with clear alliances. It is true that from the 1950s through the 1970s, there was a wide economic gulf between middle-income Latin America and low-income Asia. But economic inequality among the developing nations was not discussed. Most countries were growing but at a slow rate. This began to change as rapid growth in Asia spread from a few countries prior to 1980 to a majority of the region in the following three decades, while Africa particularly lagged. Even as the crisis accelerated, some developing countries, most notably China but also countries such as Brazil, found that they had increased global influence. But the growing economic inequality among developing nations became even sharper.

Worker Remittances   Remittances to developing countries from migrant workers had reached a record $336 billion in 2008 (though less than 10% of this went to the low-income countries). But this fell significantly in the aftermath of the crisis, followed by significant recovery. These remittances have been an important factor in the progress of poverty reduction in recent years, and the consequences will grow if remittances do not pick up more quickly (see Figure 14.4 in Chapter 14).

Poverty   In developing countries, the crisis affected earnings more than employment. In the aftermath of the crisis, lower growth reduced the rate of poverty reduction in most developing countries, and in many countries, the number of people living in poverty increased. The *2010 Millennium Development Goals Report*, drawing on "newly updated estimates from the World Bank," estimated that an additional 50 million people were living in extreme poverty in 2009 than would have been the case without the crisis and projected "some 64 million by the end of 2010 relative to a no-crisis scenario, principally in sub-Saharan Africa and Eastern and South-Eastern Asia." One of the important impacts was a slowdown in the rate of hunger reduction.[38] The 2010 *Millennium Development Goals Report* estimated that "poverty rates will be slightly higher in 2015 and even beyond, to 2020, than they would have been had the world economy grown steadily at its pre-crisis pace." The most recent evidence shows poverty falling impressively in most of the developing world, but unfortunately not much in Africa despite its improved economic growth rates (see Chapter 5, Figure 5.13).

Health and Education   Jed Friedman and Norbert Schady used household data to develop an econometric model to project infant deaths and report that "our estimates suggest that there will be on the order of 30,000 to 50,000 excess deaths in Africa in 2009—deaths that would not have taken place had the sub-prime crisis which began in the United States not spread to African countries." They find that "the bulk of the additional children who will die is likely to be found among poorer households (in rural areas, and those with lower education levels) and is concentrated among girls." Impacts generally differ across countries; another 2010 study projected deteriorations specifically in schooling, child labor, and access to health services in Burkina Faso, and on hunger in Ghana.[39]

Differing Impacts and Continuing Challenges across Developing Regions

Asia   During the period from September 2008 to March 2009, there was a dramatic slowdown and in some cases major reversal of the high export growth and GDP growth that the East Asian region, including China, had come to take for granted. The subsequent rebound was strong but uneven.

China   China weathered the initial crisis well, partly due to its own massive stimulus package of almost $600 billion, a much higher share of GDP than the corresponding U.S. package (of about $800 billion).[40] The government announced a new strategy of greater reliance on domestic demand for growth. But hallmarks of a housing market and commercial property bubble are being reported in China; the bursting of such a bubble would probably have a significant impact on the global economy. Infrastructure and other investment levels have also been at historically unprecedented levels, with nearly half of output represented in investment in official statistics but a significant fraction of it apparently yielding low returns. China's economic policymakers appear focused on decreasing reliance on basic exports that rely on processing of imports for modest value added before re-export. Improving domestic processing and reliance might also positively affect what is widely viewed as a currency imbalance.[41] Moreover, China's growth has been decelerating from unsustainable levels that have continued longer than previously expected, partly as a result of the boost from the post-crisis stimulus package and subsequent lending policies. Further deceleration of growth in China seems likely. One reason is that total debt rose very rapidly from about 130% of GDP in 2008 to about 200% in 2013. A particular concern is off-the-books local government debt, which the National Audit Office of China reported has sky-rocketed to almost $3 trillion in the three years to June 2013. As growth slows further in China, export earnings from developing country exports to China may decrease. Growth in China is examined in detail in the end-of-chapter case study for Chapter 4.

China and the Exchange Rates Controversy   China also found itself under considerable pressure to allow its currency to increase in value in the aftermath of the crisis. In comments apparently directed as much to the United States as to China, in Fall 2010 the finance minister of Brazil announced the world had moved into an "international currency war." Brazil then doubled the tax on foreign purchases of bonds to keep its currency, the real, from appreciating via capital inflows, and other countries, including Japan, intervened to decrease the value of their currencies. Jean-Claude Juncker, chair of the euro-zone finance ministers, said, "We think the Chinese currency is broadly under-valued." IMF Managing Director Dominique Strauss-Kahn said that "there is clearly the idea beginning to circulate that currencies can be used as a policy weapon....Translated into action, such an idea would represent a very serious risk to the global recovery...[and] any such approach would have a negative and very damaging longer-run impact." International currency and trade wars were major factors that made the Great Depression "great." The response from China's premier Wen Jiabao was to note the thin profit margins of export companies, and he said that with revaluation, "many of our exporting companies would have to close down, [and] migrant workers would have to return to their villages. If China saw social and economic turbulence, then it would be a disaster for the world."[42] Undoubtedly, it would have both an economic and a political impact. While adjustments are inevitable, there is no credible scenario in which a trade war, or anything approaching it, would have anything but negative effects on the prospects for economic development. These issues remained contentious but managed diplomatically through 2013, with slow but significant appreciation of China's currency.

East Asia and Southeast Asia other than China   The five high-income economies in the region—Japan, Singapore, Taiwan, South Korea, and Hong Kong—remain dependent on exports for growth by global standards, and all experienced substantial declines in exports. Expressed in U.S. dollars, exports dropped by 25%, with GDP declining between 15 and 30% in the second half of 2008 and first half of 2009. However, just as the scope of the shock was unanticipated, the scale of the subsequent rebound was also surprising. (The economy of South Korea is examined in-depth in the case study at the end of this chapter).

Recovery in middle- and low-income countries, including Indonesia, Vietnam, Cambodia, Malaysia, and Thailand, was also strong; three of these five countries reported negative growth after the crisis, but no greater a decline than 2.7%. Demand from China helped raise exports from East and Southeast

Asia overall. The World Bank noted that China's "infrastructure outlays also underpinned demand for regional and raw materials used in construction, from countries such as Indonesia, Papua New Guinea, and Lao People's Democratic Republic."[43] The role of China in the region has continued to grow. However, tensions over that role were a factor in the push for a new Trans-Pacific Partnership and smaller regional agreements. In the 2011–2013 period, growth continued among countries in this region, but with wide variations.

India   Initially, the Indian economy weathered the financial crisis relatively well. During the crisis, the central government fiscal deficit rose to nearly 7% of GDP. This was in part a planned stimulus to maintain growth during the crisis period. Like most other countries that ran up the fiscal deficit after the crisis, leaders and economic policymakers in India now wish to reduce the deficit substantially, if not run a compensating fiscal surplus for a time. On the other hand, expenditures on poverty programs are increasing, with new government nutrition programs to have a much expanded reach—some commentators found this a very hopeful sign, given the continued severity of poverty, in general, and malnutrition, in particular, still prevalent in India. The opposition criticized these programs as a political move intended to influence the 2014 general elections.[44]

GDP growth in India fell from its torrid pace of nearly 10% in 2007, to less than 4% in 2008, reflecting the impact of the crisis. It then recovered dramatically to almost 8.5% in 2009, and to nearly 10.5% in 2010—the first time growth ever topped 10% in India. But since that time, growth has dropped, to about 6.3% in 2011, then to just 3.2% in 2012, with the preliminary estimate for 2013 less than 5%.[45] The manufacturing sector had a full-year period of decline. Also viewed as a concern for the future was India's growing dependence on energy imports.

Even today, however, over half of the labor force in India works in agriculture. Barriers to global finance in India have helped insulate India's still relatively closed economy, but this also suggests there are other untapped gains from trade. India is working to develop more active economic and political relationships with developing countries in Asia and with such nations as Brazil and South Africa.[46]

Latin America and the Caribbean   Despite concerns that the crisis would quickly lead to a repeat of past crises in the region, many countries weathered the initial shocks relatively well. Mexico suffered an economic contraction of about 6.5% in 2009, in the wake of the crisis, due to close economic ties in the United States and amplified by the outbreak of the H1N1 flu virus. When the peso was driven to record lows in December 2008, Mexican firms suffered foreign derivative losses. While growth rose to about 5% in 2010, it fell back to less than 4% in both 2011 and 2012.[47]

While growth of remittances bounced back and remained strong in most regions, they stayed weak in Latin America and the Caribbean, where growth decelerated due to U.S. economic weakness and policy changes.[48]

Argentina was hit hard by the crisis, rebounded very strongly in 2010 and 2011, but then slipped back into slow GDP growth—less than 2% in 2012.

Brazil at first weathered the crisis well, with 6% growth in 2007 and 5% growth in 2008, in no small part due to the boost from commodity exports, particularly to

China—now its largest trading partner. But as its currency, the real, appreciated, exports were curtailed. After that point, growth was volatile, turning slightly negative in 2009, then surging to about 7.5% in 2010; but growth then dropped to 2.7% in 2011 and fell below 1% in 2012. As per capita growth slowed to a standstill, popular unrest emerged. Growth in Brazil is examined in greater detail in the end-of-chapter case study for Chapter 1.

Africa   Low levels of trade, coupled with relatively high commodity prices for its exports, in some ways helped insulate sub-Saharan Africa from the brunt of the crisis. The problem of educated unemployment was exacerbated, as new university graduates in the region were having even more difficulty than usual in finding employment that matched their qualifications. This is also true in North Africa and the Middle East, where it was a factor in the Arab Spring revolts.[49]

Although commodity prices were off their peaks, they remained relatively high, due in significant measure to demand from Asia, and commodity exports continued to fuel growth (see Figure 13.5). If growth in Asia remains high, commodity prices may remain higher than in the previous quarter century. But as we have seen, the recent trend is one of modest price declines. As mentioned earlier, prospects for improved aid flows have at best become more uncertain, with modest declines in recent years; and the prospects of further growth of remittances from families working abroad are unclear.[50]

Middle East and North Africa (MENA)   Recovery has been very sluggish in much of the MENA region, as growth has continued to be slow in the 2011–2013 period in several important countries.[51] This is despite the fact that governments in the region undertook expansionary fiscal policies. Countries that saw the overthrow of their governments during the Arab Spring revolts, namely Egypt, Tunisia, Libya, and Yemen, are having mixed success at economic recovery. In 2013 in Egypt, the new turmoil also created economic and political uncertainty and led to a further drop in investment and tourism. The economic breakdown in Syria has tracked the brutality of its civil war. Even in countries that have not experienced turmoil, some "spillovers," including investor perceptions, have led to falls in economic activity. On the other hand, oil exporters have benefited from prevailing relatively high oil prices (albeit well below the precrisis peak), even as the economies of oil importers such as Egypt have been negatively affected.

Prospects for Recovery and Stability

In the years following the crisis, international financial institutions and many private forecasters predicted that developing countries would lead a global recovery, which would be a milestone in the history of development.[52] The World Bank, along with the IMF and other forecasters, indicated that risks are to the downside. Indeed, there are at least five reasons for caution:

1. After growth in the United States, Europe and Japan remained significantly below historical levels for six years following the crisis, and there were doubts that faster growth could resume in most OECD countries for some time to come—even given that recessions after financial crises

historically were deeper and longer lasting than other downturns. Large trade deficits of high-income countries, most notably but not only in the United States, have fallen, and seem unlikely to come close to previous heights. The trade balance for Europe as a whole is moving from deficit to surplus. This makes dependence on exports to high-income countries, including the United States, a shaky foundation at present on which to build growth. If growth in major middle-income countries continues to slow significantly in line with forecasts, this puts export-led growth as a development model at greater risk.

2. Fiscal deficits have been high in virtually all high-income OECD countries, but falling rapidly, reducing demand; deficits are unlikely to return to previous levels. But in most countries, government debt is now much higher than before the crisis. There is less room for fiscal policy to respond with stimulus in the event of another crisis.

3. Market perceptions of the risk of sovereign default are high—though, in a historic reversal, less so for developing countries on average than for a number of developed countries. A default or major debt restructuring in Europe could threaten the solvency of banks beyond this group, with the potential for a return to broader crisis.

4. The risk of deflation (which occurred during the Great Depression and in Japan during its "lost decade") remains higher than normal. This compounds any other difficulties of emerging from a new crisis. The quantitative easing in the United States was a response to this risk, but it also led to a lower value of the dollar—a major concern of developing-country exporters. The low interest rates in the United States due to quantitative easing also fueled capital outflows to middle-income countries, which may prove temporary after the taper of quantitative easing in 2014 and a possible return to historic interest rate patterns.

5. Benefits of exporting manufactures to high-income countries (see Chapter 12) are still present. But the opportunity to do so is threatened due to very slow growth, worsened credit constraints, and perhaps even an increase in disguised protectionism in the developed countries. Such conditions may lead to reduced growth in developing countries, and a reduced pace of technology transfer from developed to developing countries.

One indicator to watch over the next few years is whether developing countries can continue to rely more on exports to each other, as well as internally generated demand. If they can build on recent trends and make this transition, development may be more rapid and setbacks less likely than has been expected during the crisis or in the decades preceding it.

Opportunities as Well as Dangers?

In Chinese symbols, crisis is formed from the symbols for two other words: *wei*, a symbol for danger or great peril, and *ji*, which can serve as the symbol of opportunity or turning point. Like many difficult translations, scholars differ on what *ji* means in this usage. But it introduces a question: Throughout the developing world, the unfolding crisis and its aftershocks were viewed with fear—what would happen to markets for their vital exports? But there is no doubt that many policymakers in China, and in other fast-growing developing nations, quickly came also to view the crisis as a great opportunity and a critical turning point.

As the G8 lost some of its central role, this was paralleled by a relative rise of the G20, a broader group of nations, including leading developing countries, whose prominence in the 2008 and 2009 meetings to respond to the crisis was a historic event in economic and political relations between developed and developing worlds. However, after the worst of the crisis abated, the sustainability of a prominent G20 role was unclear. The emergence of China as a possible regional engine of growth could allow less dependence on exports to Western markets, although several countries in the region were also alarmed about China's intentions. And several African nations have become enthusiastic about the emergence of China as a commodities investor as a counterweight to long-powerful Western companies.[53]

But hopes have been dimmed in many parts of the developing world for open and stable access to developed-country markets. Since the 2008 crisis, politicians have considered it inexpedient to be viewed as extending "concessions" on trade. The crisis also revealed to developing countries that despite the assurances of WTO rules, the United States, the European Union, and other advanced regions could effectively get away with reverting to protectionism, at least in the short run, when they found it to be politically expedient. For example, the U.S. stimulus package contained "Buy American" provisions; these were challenged but, for the most part, prevailed. Similar requirements were found in the packages of other high-income countries. These served as sobering reminders that the benefits of exporting to historically more open U.S., Canadian, UK, and other markets could not be taken for granted; alternative strategies in domestic demand-led growth and greater reliance on trade between developing countries will also be pursued.

The Trans-Pacific Partnership being negotiated would include high-income Australia, Canada, New Zealand, and the United States (and quite possibly Japan), along with developing countries Mexico, Peru, Chile, Malaysia, and Vietnam, plus city-states Singapore and Brunei. Despite a modest WTO accord in 2013, the trend toward negotiating regional trade agreements and circumventing the WTO appears to be accelerating, with uncertain ramifications.

Overall, recovery in the developing world from the global financial crisis proved far more rapid than many analysts had originally predicted—even as it was worse than expected for many developed countries, particularly in Europe. Yet, as we have seen, many questions remain about the strength and stability of economic growth and development in the coming years.

Trade, Capital Flows, and Development Strategy: South Korea

South Korea is one of the developing world's great long-term success stories. Many developing countries have reached middle-income status but remained there; a much smaller number have reached nominal high-income status but are still not considered fully developed (either by their own definitions or by development economists). Only a handful of countries have graduated to the ranks of advanced industrialized economies, of which South Korea is perhaps the most prominent example.

In the mid-1950s, South Korea was one of the poorest countries in the world. The country is now classified by the World Bank as a high-income economy, with purchasing power parity (PPP) income exceeding $30,800 in 2012. Korean consumer electronics and other goods have become synonymous with high quality at reasonable prices. Even more impressive are Korea's social development achievements. By 2004, Korea had attained the highest postsecondary enrollment rate in the world, with graduates concentrated in technical fields. Ironically, in 2013, a major policy question was whether corresponding jobs could be found for all these highly educated citizens. By 2012, life expectancy exceeded 80 years. The country regularly ranks even higher on the Human Development Index than it does in income per capita, and on the 2012 New Human Development Index, South Korea ranked 12th globally. How did South Korea succeed so spectacularly where so many other developing countries had not? Certainly one component was its robust industrialization strategy.

Exports, particularly manufactures in such key sectors as consumer electronics and motor vehicles and recently in high technology, have grown at an extraordinary rate in Korea. One apparent reason for South Korea's remarkable industrial achievements is a national strategy that has favored the promotion of exports, reflecting increasingly sophisticated skills and technology. Strong financial incentives for industrial firms to move up the ladder of skills and technology have been built into most of its policies.

In its years of rapid catching up, South Korea used at least 19 major types of export-promotion-oriented industrial policy interventions (note that only some of these policies were in effect in any one industry and at any one time and that subsidies were considerably scaled back in later years):

1. Currency undervaluation. The effective exchange rate (EER) for exporters was kept higher than that for importers. As early as 1964, South Korea's EER for exports was 281 and its EER for imports was 247, reflecting not trade neutrality but a pro-export bias.
2. Preferential access to imported intermediate inputs needed for producing exports, with strict controls to prevent abuse. Rebates were paid only after completion of the exports had been documented.
3. Targeted infant industry protection as a first stage before launching an export drive. South Korea has had a high dispersion of effective rates of protection even with a relatively low average.
4. Tariff exemptions on inputs of capital goods needed in exporting activities. This is a price incentive, whereas preferential access (intervention 2) is based on quantity restriction.
5. Tax breaks for domestic suppliers of inputs to exporting firms, which constitutes a domestic-content incentive.

6. Domestic indirect tax exemptions for successful exporters.

7. Lower direct taxes on income earned from exports.

8. Accelerated depreciation for exporters.

9. Import entitlement certificates (exemptions from import restrictions) linked directly to export levels. South Korea long has maintained an extensive list of items generally prohibited for import, including both luxury goods and import substitution targets. Profitable exemptions from this prohibition have often been available for firms exporting specified goods that have low profit margins.

10. Direct export subsidies for selected industries (no longer in use).

11. Monopoly rights granted to the firm first to achieve exports in targeted industries.

12. Subsidized interest rates and preferential credit access for exporters in selected industries, including automatic access to bank loans for the working capital needed for all export activities. Medium- and long-term loans for investment were rationed and often available only to firms that met government export targets and pursued other requested activities.

13. A system of export credit insurance and guarantees, as well as tax incentives, for overseas marketing and postshipment export loans by the Korean Export-Import Bank.

14. The creation of free-trade zones, industrial parks, and export-oriented infrastructure.

15. The creation of public enterprises to lead the way in establishing a new industry. Howard Pack and Larry Westphal found that "the share of public enterprises in [South] Korea's nonagricultural output is comparatively high, being similar to India's."

16. Activities of the Korean Traders Association and the Korea Trade Promotion Corporation to promote South Korean exports on behalf of South Korean firms worldwide.

17. General orchestration of sector-wide efforts to upgrade the average technological level through the use of a new generation of machinery.

18. Government coordination of foreign technology licensing agreements, using national bargaining power to secure better terms for the private sector in utilizing proprietary foreign technology.

19. The setting of export targets for firms (since the early 1960s). Firms set their own targets, which could be adjusted by the government.

Enforcement of export targets in South Korea was mostly based on moral suasion rather than administrative sanctions or economic incentives, but the evidence suggests that these have been among the most powerful incentives. South Korea as a whole has had an extensive pattern of "rituals" reinforcing these economic incentives with cultural ones. In the period of rapid catching up, a key ritual in the nation's economic life was the monthly national trade promotion meeting. According to Yung Whee Rhee, Bruce Ross-Larson, and Gary Pursell:

> Chaired by the president, the monthly trade promotion meetings are select gatherings of the ministers and top bureaucrats responsible for trade and the economy; the chief executives of export associations, research organizations, and educational institutions; and the heads of a few firms, mainly the general trading companies and other large firms. The prominence of those attending shows that the monthly meetings are far more than perfunctory meetings to improve coordination between the private and public sectors.

Firms were represented either by their particular export association or, in many cases for large firms, directly. After briefings, awards were typically presented for excellent export performance. Nationally, many types of annual export prizes were publicly awarded and proudly displayed by companies.

Richard Luedde-Neurath has described how South Korea maintained, in addition to domestic-content regulations, an extensive system of import controls that lasted well into the 1980s. What he terms the "Korean kaleidoscope" included restrictive trader licensing, widespread quantitative controls, systematic foreign-exchange allocation under the Foreign Exchange Demand and Supply Plan, required advance deposits (which have been as high as 200% of import value), and capricious customs practices. For example, prospective importers had to achieve minimum export earnings before becoming eligible to import.

Pack and Westphal reported that "through import restrictions, selectively promoted infant industries were often initially granted whatever levels of effective protection were required to secure an adequate market for their output as well as a satisfactory rate of return on investment." They also found that after the export promotion reforms of the early 1960s, "imports...for the domestic market remained subject to tariffs and quantitative controls." As Robert Wade notes, tariff rates appear much higher when they are averaged over non-export-related imports only. Peter Petri presented evidence that South Korea has had "an unusually protection-prone export bundle."

Sanjaya Lall concluded that in South Korea, in sharp contrast to Latin American style import substitution, "industrial targeting and promotion was pragmatic and flexible, and developed in concert with private industry. Moreover, only a relatively small number of activities were supported at a given time, and the effects of protection were offset by strong export orientation."[54]

Thus, in the South Korean case, import controls may be called a "handmaiden" of successful industrial export promotion. In the first instance, many export industries begin as infant industries requiring protection. Luedde-Neurath goes so far as to argue that the developing industrial sector functions as a whole and benefits from externalities and linkages between firms, making a market failure case for general protection of manufacturing at a critical stage of development. Alice Amsden has pointed out that in South Korea, subsidization across divisions within firms as a company enters new export markets, such as shipbuilding, is intentionally facilitated by the government. Diversified companies are made to understand that they expected to use the monopoly rents that they earn from these various import barriers as working capital for expansion into new sectors. The state also offers supplemental support for entering new markets as needed.

As Pack and Westphal summarize the evidence, "Something approximating neutrality" applied to "established industries....But there has been substantial industry bias in favor of the promoted infant industries."

Also important to South Korea's success was that it avoided the temptation to meddle in sectors, including new entrepreneurial ventures, that were not central to the current plan. If these private ventures proved successful, the government would include their sector in future strategy considerations.

A World Bank study by Westphal, Rhee, and Pursell concluded that South Korea's export industrialization "has overwhelmingly and in fundamental respects been directed and controlled by nationals" and that "technology has been acquired from abroad largely through means other than direct foreign investment." The role of multinational corporations in the economy (see Chapter 14) has been much smaller than in most other (then) middle-income countries.

As Lall concluded, the deliberate fostering of large conglomerates, known as *chaebol*, was also important to South Korea's industrial strategy: "The chaebol were hand picked from successful exporters and were given various subsidies and privileges, including the restriction of [foreign-firm] entry, in return for furthering a strategy of setting up capital- and technology-intensive activities geared to export markets." Closely regulated large firms could help to make up for "deficient markets for capital, skills, technology and even infrastructure, large and diversified firms could internalize many of their functions. They could undertake the cost and risk of absorbing very complex technologies…, further develop it by their own R&D, set up world-scale facilities and create their own brand names and distribution network." Lall concluded that, "The risks were contained by the strict discipline imposed by the government: export performance, vigorous domestic competition and deliberate interventions to rationalize the industrial structure."[55]

Moreover, Erik Thorbecke and Henry Wan concluded that the establishment of South Korean brand names rather than contract (or original equipment) manufacturing were the result of government support of heavy industries.

Peter Evans examined ties between the state and industrial elites in South Korea (as well as Brazil and India) and concluded that it was the interaction between genuine state autonomy and the "dense connecting networks" of social ties between state and private sectors—which he terms "embedded autonomy"—that is a key to a successful industrialization strategy. Again, it is strategic coordination

among the key actors, whether in the private sector alone or in the public and citizen sectors as well, that is critical to success.

Unquestionably, in the late 1980s and 1990s, South Korea substantially liberalized, particularly before but also after the 1997 financial crisis and subsequent severe recession. One open question is whether South Korea would have done as well had it liberalized sooner. Some economists have argued that South Korea would have industrialized even faster if it had maintained a free-trade policy from the beginning. Other analysts, such as Ha-Joon Chang, Hong-Jae Park, and Chul Gyue Yoo, argue that some aspects of mid-1990s liberalization were a major cause of the 1997 crisis. In particular, capital account liberalization allowed first for speculative inflows and then for outflows once the crisis hit. But the effect was smaller than for many other countries that have experienced crises, partly because of the significant increase in saving and repatriation of South Korean capital abroad.

Active industrial policy continues emphasizing South Korean entry into leading-edge, high-technology fields. For example, the country's Highly Advanced National Projects Program supports the development of high-tech products that the government believes would successfully compete with those of advanced countries such as the United States and Japan within one to two decades and also supports development of core technologies believed essential for South Korea to achieve capabilities for independent national innovation. South Korea's Ministry of Trade and Industry has targeted new materials, computer-controlled machine tools, bioengineering, microelectronics, fine chemistry, optics, and aircraft as fields in which it predicted that the country could catch up with the United States and Japan economically and technologically. As Lall notes, "Korea alone accounts for some 53% of the developing world's total enterprise-financed R&D." He concludes that "the main stimulus to industrial R&D in [South] Korea came less from specific incentives than from the overall strategy that created large firms, gave them finance and protected markets, minimized their reliance on foreign direct investment, and forced them into export markets."

What stands out in the case of industrial policy in South Korea is the selective involvement of the government in projects in which technological progress (product, process, or organizational) has been a central concern. This policy theme may be traced from early attempts at achieving technology transfer in relatively basic industries to the nation's current efforts to develop original innovative capacity in high-technology sectors.

What are the alternative arguments? Beyond the claim that South Korea could have grown even faster if government had stayed out of industrial strategy, one can also argue, like Joseph Stern and his colleagues, that the central role of the state was necessary in industrial policy in large part because of the way that government set up the rules of the economic game, including government allocation of credit, which ensured that major initiatives such as the chemical and heavy industry drive were impossible without government direction. Because South Korea often looked to the example of Japan in setting industrial policy, one could argue that the country followed a "patterns of development" analysis rather than a classic industrial policy. The costs of industrial policy in Japan did not become apparent until many years later, and the same could prove true of South Korea. The 1997 financial crisis may well have been abetted by some of the less sagacious of the industrial policy legacy. But in South Korea, few experts hold the view that the strategy was seriously flawed.

The interpretation that seems most favored by the evidence is that the South Korean industrial policy mix has served to overcome market failures involved in the process of technological progress.

By the 1997–1998 crisis, the chaebol came to be seen by many observers as liabilities to further growth. They were also seen as political liabilities or as companies that unfairly received government advantages in the past from which other companies did not benefit. Antitrust regulations are making the South Korean economy more competitive. And as the economy matures, the government's role in the productive sector will continue to become more indirect.

As an energy importer, South Korea's economy was negatively affected by the oil shocks of 1973 and 1979, as pointed out by Vittorio Corbo and Sang-Mok Suh. Its current account deficit reached 8.7% of gross national income (GNI) in 1980. But with real interest rates rising dramatically from 1979, South

Korea began adjusting early. This is in marked contrast to other countries hurt by the debt crisis, such as Brazil, which continued borrowing aggressively despite the increase in rates. Thus, while both South Korea and Brazil were among the widely noted "17 highly indebted countries" at the onset of the debt crisis, and both had experienced high growth over the previous two decades, Brazil (along with many other countries on the list) was to experience a long period of slow growth. South Korea continued with the adjustment it had already begun. Despite the concerns generated by South Korea's debt-to-GNI ratio of about 50%, the country's ability to pay was never really in doubt. But by 1985, the country had lowered its current account deficit to just 1.1% and then moved to a surplus of 2.8% of GNI in 1986, as rapid growth had now returned to the country.

Growth was briefly interrupted again in the East Asian "contagion" crisis. The rapidity of recovery of the South Korean economy from the 1997–1998 financial crisis surprised many observers, but in some ways, its speed was foreshadowed by the unusually rapid recovery in the 1982 debt crisis. South Korea borrowed the then enormous sum of $21 billion from the IMF in December 1997, evoking great concern at the time, but went on to repay the loan ahead of schedule. The South Korean government implemented needed reforms quickly. The country had reached a nearly developed stage, and adjustment was easier than for other afflicted countries, notably Indonesia.

When the very different 2008 global crisis erupted, exports from South Korea, now a high-income country, were severely hit. But the country's fairly rapid adjustment—unusual for the fully-industrialized club in which it now found itself—again underscored both the resilience and the robustness of the economy and its policymaking.

South Korea will face steep challenges in the coming years. One that will be common to many societies is how it will adjust to its rapidly aging population. Another challenge unique to South Korea is how it will handle the inevitable collapse of the regime in North Korea. But societal resilience is one of the most important and enduring benefits of successful economic development—something the country will continue to draw upon in ample supply. ∎

Sources

Amsden, Alice H. *The Rise of "the Rest": Challenges to the West from Late Industrializing Economies*. New York: Oxford University Press, 2001.

———. *Asia's Next Giant: South Korea and Late Industrialization*. Oxford: Oxford University Press, 1989.

Chang, Ha-Joon, Hong-Jae Park, and Chul Gyue Yoo. "Interpreting the Korean crisis." *Cambridge Journal of Economics* 22 (1998): 735–746.

Chenery, Hollis, Sherwin Robinson, and Moses Syrquin. *Industrialization and Growth: A Comparative Study*. New York: Oxford University Press, 1986.

Cheng, Tun-jen, Stephan Haggard, and David Kang. "Institutions and growth in Korea and Taiwan: The bureaucracy." *Journal of Development Studies* 34 (1998): 87–111.

Collins, Susan M. "Lessons from Korean economic growth." *American Economic Review* 80 (1990): 104–107.

Corbo, Vittorio, and Sang-Mok Suh. *Structural Adjustment in a Newly Industrialized Country: The Korean Experience*. Baltimore: Johns Hopkins University Press, 1992, esp. ch. 14.

Cyhn, Jin. *Technology Transfer and International Production: The Development of the Electronics Industry in Korea*. Cheltenham, England: Elgar, 2001.

Dahlman, Carl J., Bruce Ross-Larson, and Larry E. Westphal. "Managing technical development: Lessons from the newly industrializing countries." *World Development* 15 (1987): 759–775.

Evans, Peter. *Embedded Autonomy: States and Industrial Transformation*. Princeton, N.J.: Princeton University Press, 1995.

Kim, L. "The dynamics of technology development: Lessons from the Korean experience," in *Competitiveness, FDI, and Technological Activity in East Asia*, eds. Sanjaya Lall and Shujiro Urata. Cheltenham, England: Elgar, 2003.

Lall, Sanjaya. *The Role of Government Policy in Building Industrial Competitiveness in a Globalizing World*. Oxford: International Development Centre, 2003.

———. *Competitiveness, Technology and Skills*. Cheltenham, England: Elgar, 2001.

———. *Learning from the Asian Tigers*. London: Macmillan, 1996.

———. "Technological capabilities and industrialization." *World Development* 20 (1992): 165–186.

Lall, Sanjaya, and M. Albaladejo. "China's export surge: The competitive implications for Southeast Asia." Report for the World Bank East Asia Department, 2003.

Lall, Sanjaya, and M. Teubal. "'Market stimulating' technology policies in developing countries: A framework with examples from East Asia." *World Development* 26 (1998): 1369–1385.

Luedde-Neurath, Richard. *Import Controls and Export-Oriented Development: A Reassessment of the South Korean Case*. Boulder, Colo.: Westview Press, 1986.

Mathews, John A., and Dong-Sung Cho. *Tiger Technology: The Creation of a Semiconductor Industry in East Asia*. New York: Cambridge University Press, 2000.

Noland, Marcus, and Howard Pack. *Industrial Policy in an Era of Globalization: Lessons from Asia*. Washington, D.C.: Institute for International Economics, 2003.

Pack, Howard, and Larry E. Westphal. "Industrial strategy and technological change: Theory versus reality." *Journal of Development Economics* 22 (1986): 87–128.

Petri, Peter. "Korea's export niche: Origins and prospects." *World Development* 16 (1988): 47–63.

Porter, Michael. *The Competitive Advantage of Nations*. New York: Free Press, 1990.

Presidential Commission on the Twenty-First Century. *Korea in the Twenty-First Century*. Seoul: Seoul Press, 1995.

Rhee, Yung Whee, Bruce Ross-Larson, and Gary Pursell. *Korea's Competitive Edge: Managing the Entry into World Markets*. Baltimore: Johns Hopkins University Press, 1984.

Rodrik, Dani. "Getting interventions right: How South Korea and Taiwan grew rich." *Economic Policy* 20 (1995): 53–101.

Smith, Stephen C. *Industrial Policy in Developing Countries: Reconsidering the Real Sources of Export-Led Growth*. Washington, D.C.: Economic Policy Institute, 1991.

Stern, Joseph, et al. *Industrialization and the State: The Korean Heavy and Chemical Industry Drive*. Cambridge, Mass.: Harvard University Press, 1995.

Stiglitz, Joseph E. "Some lessons from the East Asian miracle." *World Bank Research Observer* 11 (1996): 151–177.

Thorbecke, Erik, and Henry Wan. "Revisiting East (and Southeast) Asia's Development Model." Paper presented at the Cornell University Conference on Seventy-Five Years of Development, Ithaca, N.Y., May 7–9, 2004.

United Nations, *2010 Human Development Report*. New York: Oxford, University Press, 2010.

Wade, Robert. "The role of government in overcoming market failure: Taiwan, Republic of Korea and Japan," in *Achieving Industrialization in East Asia*, ed. Helen Hughes. New York: Cambridge University Press, 1988.

Westphal, Larry E. "Industrial policy in an export propelled economy: Lessons from South Korea's experience." *Journal of Economic Perspectives* 4 (1990): 41–59.

Westphal, Larry E. "Technology strategies for economic development in a fast-changing global economy." *Economics of Innovation and New Technology* 11 (2002): 275–320.

Westphal, Larry E., Yung Whee Rhee, and Gary Pursell. "Korean industrial competence: Where it came from." World Bank Staff Working Paper No. 469, 1981.

Westphal, Larry E., et al. "Exports of capital goods and related services from the Republic of Korea." World Bank Staff Working Paper No. 629, 1984.

White, Gordon, ed. *Developmental States in East Asia*. New York: St. Martin's Press, 1988.

World Bank. *The East Asian Miracle: Economic Growth and Public Policy*. New York: Oxford University Press, 1993.

World Bank. *Korea: Managing the Industrial Transition*. Washington, D.C.: World Bank, 1987.

Concepts for Review

Amortization
Balance of payments
Basic transfer
Brady Plan
Capital account
Capital flight
Cash account (international
    reserve account)
Conditionality
Current account
Debt-for-equity swap

Debt-for-nature swap
Debtors' cartel
Debt repudiation
Debt service
Deficit
Euro
External debt
Hard currency
Highly indebted poor countries
    (HIPCs)

International reserves
Macroeconomic instability
Odious debt
Restructuring
Special drawing rights (SDRs)
Stabilization policies
Structural adjustment loans
Surplus

Questions for Discussion

1. Draw up a balance of payments table similar in format to Table 13.3, using the most recent data from any developing country (consult the IMF's *International Financial Statistics* at http://imfstatistics.org/imf, or for broader coverage, see links in http://imf.org/external/data.html for the most recent data). Explain the significance of the various entries in the current and capital accounts. What is the status of the country's international reserves, and how do they compare with those of one year ago?

2. Describe the basic-transfer mechanism. Using the list of credits and debits in Table 13.2, identify which ones would fit into the basic-transfer equation. How does the basic transfer help us analyze developing-world debt problems?

3. Trace the evolution of the developing-country debt problem during the 1970s and 1980s. What were the key ingredients? Explain your answer.

4. Why was the problem of capital flight so serious in some highly indebted countries? What causes capital flight, and what do you think can be done about it?

5. What is petrodollar recycling, and how did it contribute to the debt crisis of the 1980s? Why were developing countries so eager to borrow money from international banks? Explain your answer.

6. What is the significance of the debt service ratio? Can indebted countries do anything to lower this ratio? Explain your answer.

7. Describe the typical IMF stabilization package for severely or heavily indebted countries. What are the objectives of these policies, and why do you think international banks are so eager for IMF negotiations to precede their discussions with these countries? What are the economic and social costs of these programs? Explain your answer.

8. Do you think a full-fledged developing-country debt crisis might reemerge in the future? If so, why and under what conditions? If not, why not?

9. What has been proposed to resolve the problem of odious debt? How effective a solution do you think this will be for averting future problems involving developing-country debt?

10. In what ways was the recent global financial crisis similar to past crises, and in what ways did it differ?

11. Prepare a brief update on longer-term impacts of the 2008 global financial crisis. Have any of the later developments proved unexpected (or previously considered unlikely)? Where problems have lessened, do you think they could return?

Notes

1. See, for example, John Williamson and Donald R. Lessard, *Capital Flight: The Problem and Policy Responses* (Washington, D.C.: Institute for International Economics, 1987), for an excellent review.

2. In 2002, 11 European countries—Austria, Belgium, Finland, France, Germany, Ireland, Italy, Luxembourg, the Netherlands, Portugal, and Spain—replaced their national currencies with a common currency, the euro. Six other EU countries had adopted the euro by 2013, and Monaco, San Marino, and Vatican City also use the currency. Other EU countries are on track to join. But the future of the euro—at least whether its use will expand and whether some countries may leave the "eurozone"—has been called into question due to debt problems, particularly in Greece and Ireland, but also in some other countries running fiscal and trade deficits.

3. Williamson and Lessard, *Capital Flight*, p. 56.

4. This discussion is based on Frances Stewart, "The international debt situation and North-South relations," *World Development* 13 (1985): 141–204.

5. John Charles Pool and Stephen C. Stamos, *The ABCs of International Finance: Understanding the Trade and Debt Crisis* (Lexington, Mass.: Lexington Books, 1987), pp. 55–57.

6. Ibid., p. 55.

7. For a review and discussion of developing-nation stabilization programs from a developed-country perspective, see Rudiger Dornbusch, "Policies to move from stabilization to growth," and W. Max Corden, "Macroeconomic policy and growth: Some lessons of experience," in *Proceedings of the World Bank Annual Conference on Development Economics, 1990* (Washington D.C.: World Bank, 1991). For a lengthy economic critique of the IMF stabilization package and its effects on both the balance of payments and the overall economy, see Paul P. Streeten, "Stabilization and adjustment," *Labour and Society* 13 (1988): 1–18.

8. Examples include Hungary ($15.7 billion in November 2008), Ukraine ($16.9 billion in November 2008), Latvia ($2.35 billion in December 2008), Belarus ($2.5 billion in January 2009, increased

to $3.5 billion in June 2009), Serbia ($500 million in January 2009, increased to $4.0 billion in May 2009), Romania ($17.1 billion in May 2009), Poland ($20.6 billion credit line in May 2009), and Bosnia and Herzegovina ($1.57 billion in June 2009). Much larger rescues were needed for Ireland and Greece in 2010, in which the IMF was one participant with the European Union.

9. See, for example, James L. Dietz, "Debt and development: The future of Latin America," *Journal of Economic Issues* 20 (1986): 1029–1051, and Paul P. Streeten, *Strategies for Human Development* (Copenhagen: Handelshøjskolens Forlag, 1994), pt. 2.

10. Cheryl Payer, *The Debt Trap: The IMF and the Third World* (New York: Monthly Review Press, 1974), pp. 1–49.

11. For an analysis of how IMF stabilization programs are typically imposed on developing-country debtors and how such policies can be counterproductive in a climate of macroeconomic instability, see Dani Rodrik, "The limits of trade policy reform in developing countries," *Journal of Economic Perspectives* 6 (1992): 87–105, and Lance Taylor, "The revival of the liberal creed and the IMF and the World Bank in a globalized economy," *World Development* 25 (1997): 145–152.

12. Part of the explanation for this decline in per capita income, according to researchers like Jeffrey Sachs, Paul Krugman, and Andreas Savvides, relates to the debt overhang hypothesis. The argument is that the external debt burden provided a disincentive to domestic investment in developing countries and thus slowed economic growth, because any additional foreign-exchange earnings would have to be turned over to foreign creditors. For a brief discussion and empirical test of this hypothesis, see Andreas Savvides, "Investment slowdown in developing countries during the 1980s: Debt overhang or foreign capital inflows?" *Kyklos* 45 (1992): 363–378.

13. See Howard Stein, "Deindustrialization, adjustment, the World Bank and the IMF in Africa," *World Development* 20 (1992): 83–95, and Frances Stewart, "The many faces of adjustment," *World Development* 19 (1991): 1847–1864.

14. For a review and a description of debt relief proposals, see World Bank, *Global Development Finance, 1998* (Washington, D.C.: World Bank, 1998), pp. 2–3.

15. Barry Herman, José Antonio Ocampo, and Shari Spiegel, eds., "Introduction," in *Overcoming Developing Country Debt Crises* (New York: Oxford University Press, 2010), p. 4.

16. William R. Cline, *International Debt and the Stability of the World Economy* (Washington, D.C.: Institute for International Economics, 1983).

17. For details, go to http://poverty.worldbank.org /prsp or http://www.imf.org/external/nf/prsp /prsp.asp.

18. For an overview, see IMF, "HIPC Fact Sheet," October 1, 2013, http://www.imf.org/external /np/exr/facts/hipc.htm.

19. Debt may return as a serious problem for many countries if and when key commodity export prices return to long-term downward trends, and/or direct foreign investment becomes less available to developing countries compared to the recent boom.

20. World Bank, "Global Economic Prospects—June 2013: Less volatile, but slower growth," http:// web.worldbank.org/external/default/main? menuPK=659178&pagePK=64218926&piPK=6421 8953&theSitePK=659149.

21. Victor Mallet, "Tragedy in three acts: India and other emerging market darlings have lost their lustre as investors begin to ponder life without US quantitative easing." *Financial Times*, August 24, 2013, p. 5.; and Andrew England et al, "Call to tackle emerging markets crisis, *Financial Times*, August 26, 2013, p. 1.

22. For a succinct statement of the scale of the challenges, see Wolfgang Munchau, "Do not kid yourself that the Eurozone is recovering," *Financial Times*, September 20, 2013.

23. In June 2013, the World Bank forecasted, "the global economy appears to be transitioning toward a period of more stable, but slower growth."

24. The Glass-Steagall Act, which dated to 1933, mandated a separation between Wall Street investment banks and Main Street depository banks, and its repeal in 1999 was a factor enabling the packaging and expanded use of subprime loans, whose problems were the first trigger of the crisis in 2007. See, for example, the insightful book by former IMF Chief Economist Simon Johnson with James Kwak, *13 Bankers* (New York: Pantheon, 2010).

25. See Bank for International Settlements, http:// www.bis.org/bcbs/basel3.htm.

26. Monetary policy is reviewed in Chapter 15. See also Johnson and Kwak, *13 Bankers*.

27. On the negative health and social consequences of austerity in response to crises, see David Stuckler and Sanjay Basu, *The Body Economic: Why Austerity Kills* (New York: Basic Books, 2013). For descriptive details of the U.S. sequester, see http://www .whitehouse.gov/issues/sequester.

28. Estimates of these costs varied; a Macroeconomic Advisers report estimated a loss of 0.3% of GDP annually from fiscal policy uncertainty in the period 2009-2013: http://www.macroadvisers.com/2013 /10/the-cost-of-crisisdriven-fiscal-policy. The overall cost of the crisis to the U.S. may be 40 to 90% of one year's output ($6 trillion to $14 trillion) when evaluated in a comprehensive, long-term manner including loss of job skills: see Tyler Atkinson, David Luttrell, and Harvey Rosenblum, "How bad was it? The costs and consequences of the 2007-2009 financial crisis," Dallas Fed Staff Papers X20, 2013.

29. For a succinct description of this process for the case of South Korea, see Johnson and Kwak, *13 Bankers*, pp. 41–45.

30. The United States incurred extremely high damage from the financial crisis and subsequent two-year recession—probably close to if not exceeding an entire year of economic output when evaluated in a comprehensive and long-term manner such as loss of job skills; see for example, Tyler Atkinson, David Luttrell, and Harvey Rosenblum, "How bad was it? The costs and consequences of the 2007–2009 financial crisis," Dallas Fed Staff Papers X20, 2013. Based on the scope of this analysis, it may be conjectured that the full costs in developing countries of previous crises may have been underestimated. The quote from Mantega is from Jonathan Wheatley and Joe Leahy, "Trade war looming, warns Brazil," *Financial Times*,

January 9, 2011. Probably, it was helpful that Brazil was able to maintain and increase its exports to China over the subsequent two years. Considerable demand derived from China's unsustainable investment-led growth, which created demand for imports, particularly commodities; see, for example, Ashvin Ahuja and Malhar Nabar, "Investment-Led Growth in China: Global Spillovers," *IMF Paper WP/12/267*, November 2012; and Shaun K. Roache, "China's Impact on World Commodity Markets," *IMF Paper WP/12/115*, May 2012.

31. International Monetary Fund, *World Economic Outlook: Transitions and Tensions.*, October 2013, pp. xii–xii. The quote from UNCTAD is from its *2009 World Investment Report* (New York: United Nations, 2009), p. xix.

32. United Nations, *2010 Millennium Development Goals Report* (New York: United Nations, 2010), p. 70.

33. International Monetary Fund, *World Economic Outlook* (Washington, D.C.: International Monetary Fund, 2010), ch. 4.

34. From World Bank Crisis Page, http://www.worldbank.org/financialcrisis. UNCTAD, *2010 World Investment Report* (New York: United Nations, 2010), pp. xvii–ix. See also World Bank, *Global Economic Prospects: Crisis, Finance and Growth* (Washington, D.C.: World Bank, 2010).

35. UNCTAD, *2010 World Investment Reports*.

36. See UNCTAD, *2013 World Investment Report*, http://unctad.org/en/PublicationsLibrary/wir2013_en.pdf.

37. See World Bank, *Global Economic Prospects 2010*, and the Bank's release Factsheet, "Developing Countries Lead Recovery, but High-Income Country Debt Clouds Outlook," which puts the report in perspective, stating: "Over the next 20 years, the fight against poverty could be hampered if countries are forced to cut productive and human capital investments because of lower development aid and reduced tax revenues, the report says. If bilateral aid flows decline, as they have in the past, this could affect long-term growth rates in developing countries—potentially increasing the number of extremely poor in 2020 by as much as 26 million"; see http://web.worldbank.org/WBSITE/EXTERNAL/COUNTRIES/EASTASIAPACIFICEXT/0,,contentMDK:22610807~pagePK:146736~piPK:226340~theSitePK:226301,00.html?cid=3001_3. Aid data for 2011 and 2012 are from the U.N. *Millennium Development Goals Report 2013*, p. 52. For data on charitable contributions, see *Giving USA 2013 Report* and earlier reports from the Center on Philanthropy at Indiana University.

38. Ibid., p. 7. On effects on earnings and employment, see World Bank, *World Development Report 2013*, figs. 1.10 and 1.11, p. 61.

39. Jed Friedman and Norbert Schady, "How many more infants are likely to die in Africa as a result of the global financial crisis?" World Bank Policy Research Working Paper No. 5023 2009, p. 10. For an analysis of Burkina Faso and Ghana impacts, see John Cockburn, Ismaël Fofana, and Luca Tiberti, "Simulating the impact of the global economic crisis and policy: Responses on children in West and Central Africa," UNICEF Innocenti Research Center, paper 2010-01, http://www.unicef-irc.org/publications/596.

40. World Bank, *Global Economic Prospects*, pp. 117–120; Ariana Eunjung Cha and Maureen Fan, "China Unveils $586 Billion Stimulus Plan," *Washington Post*, November 10, 2008.

41. See Neil Dennis, "China Rate Move Prompts Mixed Reactions," *Financial Times*, December 27, 2010. For basic reporting on the signs of a property bubble in China and government and market reaction, see "Market defies fear of real estate bubble in China," *New York Times*, March 4, 2010, and "In China, fear of a real estate bubble," *Washington Post*, January 11, 2010, p. A1.

42. Quote from Mr. Mantega is from Jonathan Wheatley and Peter Garnham, "Brazil in 'currency war' alert," *Financial Times*, September 27, 2010; Quotes from Mr. Juncker and Mr. Strauss-Kahn are from Alan Beattie, "IMF chief warns on exchange rate wars," *Financial Times*, October 5, 2010; Quote from Mr. Wen is from Alan Beattie, Joshua Chaffin, and Kevin Brown, "Wen warns against renminbi pressure," *Financial Times*, October 6, 2010.

43. World Bank, *Global Economic Prospects*, p. 119.

44. Eswar Prasad, "Time to tackle India's budget deficit," *Wall Street Journal*, February 21, 2010. Other observations were drawn from a series of articles in 2013 on growth, fiscal expenditures, and election politics in India in the *Financial Times*.

45. Data source for growth numbers: World Development Indicators online, accessed October 16, 2013: http://data.worldbank.org/data-catalog/world-development-indicators.

46. Martin S. Indyk and Anand Sharma, "Asia's unfolding economic saga: An Indian perspective," lecture given at the Brookings Institution, Washington, D.C., March 17, 2010; "India's Growth Story Gets Better," *Financial Times*, October 7, 2010.

47. World Bank, *Global Economic Prospects*, pp. 131, 135; *World Development Indicators* (same as note 46), accessed October 16, 2013; and *CIA World Factbook*, October 19, 2013, https://www.cia.gov/library/publications/the-world-factbook.

48. World Bank, *Global Economic Prospects 2013* and earlier years.

49. See, for example, John Page, *Jobs, Justice and the Arab Spring: Inclusive Growth in North Africa* (Tunisia: African Development Bank, 2012), and World Bank, *Youth Employment in Sub-Saharan Africa: Overview* (Washington: World Bank, 2013).

50. Jackson Mvunganyi, "Global financial crisis affects remittances to Africa," Voanews.com, January 25, 2010, http://www1.voanews.com/english/news/africa.

51. *World Development Indicators*, 2013, p. 67.

52. World Bank, World Bank press release summary of 2010 Global Economic Prospects, Press Release No. 2010/466/GEP, June 9, 2010.

53. Deborah Brautigam, *The Dragon's Gift: The Real Story of China in Africa* (New York: Oxford University Press, 2010), and her presentation, along with presentations by David Shinn and Joshua Eisenman, at the 2010 G2 at GW Conference: http://www.gwu.edu/~iiep/events/G2_at_GW.cfm.

54. Excerpted from *Competitiveness, Technology and Skills* by Sanjaya Lall. Copyright © 2001 by Edward Elgar Publishing. Reprinted with permission.

55. Ibid.

Foreign Finance, Investment, Aid, and Conflict: Controversies and Opportunities

14

It is to perpetuate difficulties of the South for the North to relate to us as hapless victims to dictate to regarding loans and the employment of aid.

—*Nelson Mandela, United Nations Social Summit, March 1995*

We, Ministers of developed and developing countries responsible for promoting development and Heads of multilateral and bilateral development institutions . . ., recognize that while the volumes of aid and other development resources must increase to achieve these [MDG] goals, aid effectiveness must increase significantly as well.

—*OECD 2005, Paris Declaration on Aid Effectiveness*

With the number of migrants worldwide now reaching almost 200 million . . ., remittances are an important way out of extreme poverty for a large number of people.

—*François Bourguignon, former chief economist, World Bank, 2008*

Made in one or more of the following countries: Korea, Hong Kong, Malaysia, Singapore, Taiwan, Mauritius, Thailand, Indonesia, Mexico, Philippines. The exact country of origin is unknown.

—*Integrated circuit label* [1]

14.1 The International Flow of Financial Resources

In Chapter 13, we explained that a country's international financial situation as reflected in its balance of payments and its level of monetary reserves depends not only on its current account balance (its commodity trade) but also on its capital account balance (its net inflow or outflow of private and public financial resources). Because a majority of non-oil-exporting developing nations have historically incurred deficits on their current account balance, a continuous net inflow of foreign financial resources represents an important ingredient in their long-run development strategies. These recurrent requirements are amplified by the need for targeted resources for investments in key sectors and for carrying out poverty reduction strategies.

In this chapter, we examine the international flow of financial resources, which takes three main forms: (1) *private foreign direct and portfolio investment*, consisting of (a) foreign "direct" investment by large multinational (or transnational) corporations, usually with headquarters in the developed nations, and (b) foreign **portfolio investment** (e.g., stocks, bonds, and notes) in developing countries' credit and equity markets by private institutions (banks,

Portfolio investment
Financial investments by private individuals, corporations, pension funds, and mutual funds in stocks, bonds, certificates of deposit, and notes issued by private companies and the public agencies.

mutual funds, corporations) and individuals; (2) *remittances of earnings by international migrants;* and (3) *public and private development assistance (foreign aid)*, from (a) individual national governments and multinational donor agencies and, increasingly, (b) private *nongovernmental organizations (NGOs)*, most working directly with developing nations at the local level. We also examine the nature, significance, and controversy regarding private direct and portfolio investment and foreign aid in the context of the changing world economy. As in earlier chapters, our focus will be on ways in which private investment and foreign aid can contribute to development and on ways in which they may be harmful. We then ask how foreign investment and aid might best serve development aspirations. Finally, we examine the consequences and causes of violent conflict in developing nations and strategies for its prevention; and assistance with recovery from, and prevention of, civil war and ethnic strife—among the most difficult problems for economic development and a focal point for foreign aid.

14.2 Private Foreign Direct Investment and The Multinational Corporation

Multinational corporation (MNC)   A corporation with production activities in more than one country.

Few developments have played as critical a role in the extraordinary growth of international trade and capital flows during the past few decades as the rise of the **multinational corporation (MNC)**. An MNC is most simply defined as a corporation or enterprise that conducts and controls productive activities in more than one country. These huge firms are mostly based in North America, Europe, and Japan; but a growing number are based in newly high-income economies such as South Korea and Taiwan. In recent years, a much smaller but growing number of MNCs have emerged from upper-middle-income countries such as Brazil and even some fast-growing lower-middle-income countries, most notably China. MNCs and the resources they bring present a unique opportunity but may pose serious problems for the many developing countries in which they operate.

Foreign direct investment (FDI)   Overseas equity investments by private multinational corporations.

The growth of private **foreign direct investment (FDI)** in the developing world has been extremely rapid—though volatile—in recent decades. A key part of globalization, FDI growth has come in waves, with each crest higher than the one before it, as seen in Figure 14.1. It rose from an annual rate of $2.4 billion in 1962 to $35 billion in 1990 before surging to $565 billion in 2007 (when total world FDI hit its record of just over $2 trillion). In the aftermath of the global crisis, FDI fell considerably, and in 2012, the total was some $1.35 trillion, barely two-thirds of its level five years earlier, with only a gradual global increase anticipated.

Yet, despite this overall global trend, FDI continues to play an extremely important and indeed growing role in the developing world—in 2012, inflows to developing countries were about $700 billion, an extraordinary flow of resources. Indeed, 2012 represented a new milestone: For the first time in history, developing countries received more than half of all global FDI flows. On the one hand, a significant part of this changing share over the past few years has been due to a sharp fall in investment into developed countries, reflecting the aftermath of the crisis and, in particular, the continued recession conditions in much of Europe.

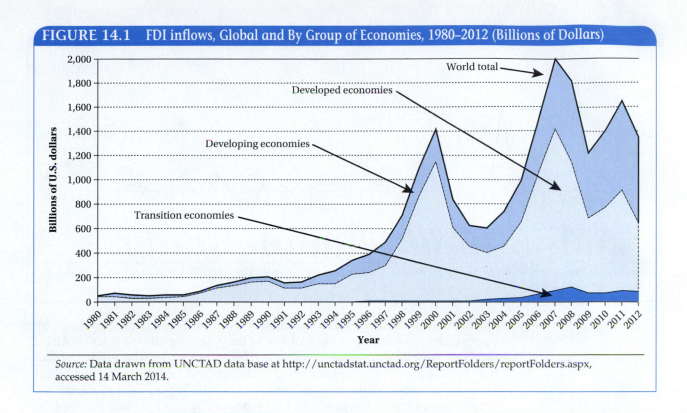

FIGURE 14.1   FDI inflows, Global and By Group of Economies, 1980–2012 (Billions of Dollars)

Source: Data drawn from UNCTAD data base at http://unctadstat.unctad.org/ReportFolders/reportFolders.aspx, accessed 14 March 2014.

But remarkably, by 2012, developing countries were also the source of nearly one-third of global FDI outflows. Although these represent a continuation of general trends that began from the mid-1980s, they are now reaching high shares far more rapidly than anything expected by analysts at the turn of the century. This is occurring while outflows from developed countries fell sharply in 2009 in the wake of the financial crisis, rebounded for a couple of years, but by 2012–2013 had fallen back, close to the 2009 trough.[2] At the same time, these funds are originating from a small number of relatively successful middle-income developing countries; to some extent, this also reflects that the development gaps among developing countries has become greater than ever.

According to UNCTAD estimates, in 2012, a little over two thirds of the profits from FDI in developing countries were repatriated back to investor countries; on the other hand, the remainder was retained, much of that reinvested.

The instability of the growth in FDI flows over time into both developed and developing countries can be seen in Figure 14.2. Interestingly, at least since the late 1990s, the volatility of investments going into developed countries has actually been greater than those going into developing countries.

The volatility of flows to various regions is even greater than total flows. In most years, a majority of FDI goes from one developed country to another, and flows to developing countries are heavily concentrated in just a few destinations. For example, in 2009, 31% of all inflows to developing countries went to China (including Hong Kong and Macao). Africa has usually received only a small fraction of inflows. In 2009, FDI in Africa totalled $59 billion, but the share of global FDI going to Africa as a whole was just 5.3% (3.6% excluding

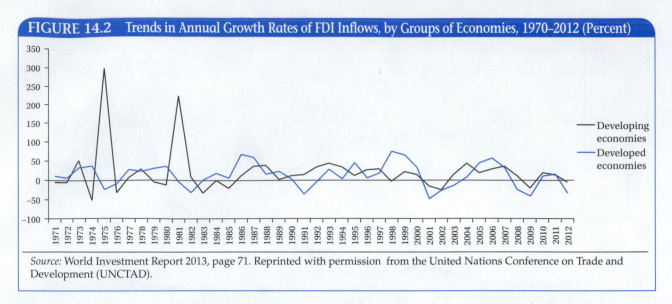

FIGURE 14.2   Trends in Annual Growth Rates of FDI Inflows, by Groups of Economies, 1970–2012 (Percent)

Source: World Investment Report 2013, page 71. Reprinted with permission from the United Nations Conference on Trade and Development (UNCTAD).

North Africa). But even this was higher than recent years, largely driven by commodities investments. Most of the 34 least developed countries in Africa received very little foreign investment. This is not surprising given the fact that private capital gravitates toward countries and regions with the highest financial returns and the greatest perceived safety. Where debt problems are severe, governments are unstable, and economic reforms remain incomplete, the risks of capital loss can be high. We must recognize that multinational corporations are not in the development business; their objective is to maximize their return on capital. MNCs seek out the best profit opportunities and are largely unconcerned with issues such as poverty, inequality, employment conditions, and environmental problems.[3]

FDI flows need to be understood in context. Despite the extraordinary growth, FDI inflows to developing countries have remained a small fraction of these countries' total investment, most of which is accounted for by domestic sources. (Note, however, that foreign investment may be qualitatively different from domestic investment and may have beneficial interaction effects in some cases, which in turn may depend on policy, as discussed later.) Nevertheless, in recent years, FDI has become the largest source of foreign funds flowing to developing countries, as Figure 14.3 shows.[4]

Globally, MNCs employ about 80 million workers in countries outside their home base. Nonetheless, in most developing countries, MNCs employ a relatively small fraction of the workforce, but the jobs tend to be concentrated in the modern urban sector. Moreover, foreign direct investment also involves much more than the simple transfer of capital or the establishment of a local factory in a developing nation. Multinationals carry with them technologies of production, tastes and styles of living, managerial philosophies, and diverse business practices. But before analyzing some of the arguments concerning incentives for, or restrictions against, private foreign investment, in general, and multinational corporations, in particular, let us examine the character of these enterprises.

Two central characteristics of multinational corporations are their large size and the fact that their worldwide operations and activities tend to be

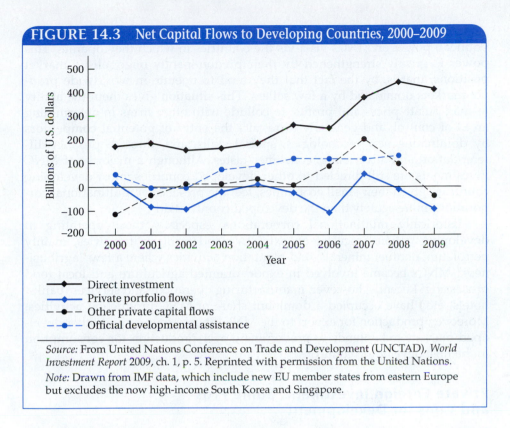

FIGURE 14.3 Net Capital Flows to Developing Countries, 2000–2009

Source: From United Nations Conference on Trade and Development (UNCTAD), *World Investment Report* 2009, ch. 1, p. 5. Reprinted with permission from the United Nations.

Note: Drawn from IMF data, which include new EU member states from eastern Europe but excludes the now high-income South Korea and Singapore.

centrally controlled by parent companies. They are the major force in the rapid globalization of world trade. The 100 largest nonfinancial, multinational corporations now account for over $8 trillion in sales. MNCs have become, in effect, **global factories** searching for opportunities anywhere in the world. Many MNCs have annual sales volumes in excess of the GDP of the developing nations in which they operate. The scale of these corporations is immense. Six of them accounted for more sales in 2008 than the GNI of all of South Asia and sub-Saharan Africa combined. Most poorer countries are dwarfed in size by the major MNCs. This large scale of operations, combined with limited competition, confers great bargaining power.[5]

Note, however, that just as South-South trade plays a growing role, direct South-South investment has increased recently. This growing trend may open up new opportunities for developing countries on both the outflow and inflow sides. In fact, in many of the least developed countries, FDI from other developing nations, particularly China, plays a leading role.[6]

Still, many people in the developing countries tend to believe, rightly or wrongly, that multinational corporations operate with the blessing of their home governments and with national resources at their disposal in the event of a significant dispute. A majority of developing countries, especially the smaller and least developed ones, understandably feel overwhelmed in attempting to bargain with such powerful entities. The success of China in negotiating better deals with MNCs regarding technology transfer and taxation has had limited applicability elsewhere because no other developing nation has China's combination of great size and strong central government authority.

Global factories Production facilities whose various operations are distributed across a number of countries to take advantage of existing price differentials.

In sum, enormous size confers substantial economic (and sometimes political) power on MNCs vis-à-vis the countries in which they operate. This power is greatly strengthened by their predominantly oligopolistic market positions, that is, by the fact that they tend to operate in worldwide product markets dominated by a few sellers. This situation gives them the ability to manipulate prices and profits, to collude with other firms in determining areas of control, and generally to restrict the entry of potential competitors by dominating new technologies, special skills, and, through product differentiation and advertising, consumer tastes. Although a majority of MNC investments are still directed to other developed countries, most developing countries, given their small economies, feel the presence of multinational corporations more acutely than the developed countries do.

Historically, multinational corporations, especially those operating in developing nations, focused on extractive and primary industries, mainly petroleum, nonfuel minerals, and plantation activities where a few "agribusiness" MNCs became involved in export-oriented agriculture and local food processing. Recently, however, manufacturing operations and services (banks, hotels, etc.) have occupied a dominant share of MNC production activities. Moreover, production for export to the MNC's home country and other developed markets today tends to predominate over production for consumption in the host developing countries.

Private Foreign Investment: Some Pros and Cons for Development

Few areas in the economics of development arouse so much controversy and are subject to such varying interpretations as the issue of the benefits and costs of private foreign investment. If we look closely at this controversy, however, we will see that the disagreement is not so much about the influence of MNCs on traditional economic aggregates such as gross domestic product (GDP), investment, savings, and manufacturing growth rates (though these disagreements do indeed exist) as about the fundamental economic and social meaning of development as it relates to the diverse activities of MNCs. In other words, the controversy over the role and impact of private foreign investment often has as its basis a fundamental disagreement about the nature, style, and character of a desirable development process. The basic arguments for and against the impact of private foreign investment in the context of the type of development it tends to foster can be summarized as follows.[7]

Traditional Economic Arguments in Support of Private Investment: Filling Savings, Foreign-Exchange, Revenue, and Management Gaps   The pro-foreign-investment arguments grow largely out of the traditional and new growth theory analysis of the determinants of economic growth. Private foreign investment (as well as foreign aid) is typically seen as a way of filling in gaps between the domestically available supplies of savings, foreign exchange, government revenue, and human capital skills and the desired level of these resources necessary to achieve growth and development targets. For a simple example of the "savings-investment gap" analysis, recall from Chapter 3 that the basic Harrod-Domar growth model postulates a direct relationship

between a country's net savings ratio, s, and its rate of output growth, g, via the equation $g = s/c$, where c is the national capital-output ratio. If the desired rate of national output growth, g, is targeted at 7% annually and the capital-output ratio is 3, the needed rate of annual net saving is 21% (because $s = gc$). If the saving that can be domestically mobilized amounts to only, say, 16% of GDP, a "savings gap" equal to 5% can be said to exist. If the nation can fill this gap with foreign financial resources (either private or public), it will be better able to achieve its target rate of growth.

Therefore, the first and most often cited contribution of private foreign investment to national development (i.e., when this development is defined in terms of GDP growth rates—an important implicit conceptual assumption) is its role in filling the resource gap between targeted or desired investment and locally mobilized savings.

A second contribution, analogous to the first, is its contribution to filling the gap between targeted foreign-exchange requirements and those derived from net export earnings plus net public foreign aid. This is the so-called foreign-exchange or trade gap. ("Two-gap" models are discussed more fully later in this chapter.) An inflow of private foreign capital can not only alleviate part or all of the deficit on the balance of payments current account but also function to remove that deficit over time *if* the foreign-owned enterprise can generate a net positive flow of export earnings. Unfortunately, as noted in the case of import substitution, the overall effect of permitting MNCs to establish subsidiaries behind protective tariff and quota walls producing for domestic consumption is often a net *worsening* of both the current and capital account balances. Such deficits in those cases usually result both from the importation of capital equipment and intermediate products (normally from an overseas affiliate and often at inflated prices) and the outflow of foreign exchange in the form of repatriated profits, management fees, royalty payments, and interest on private loans. A large and growing share of MNC production in developing countries involves adding (labor-intensive) value to components for reexport, but this brings little foreign exchange into the economy.

The third gap said to be filled by private foreign investment is the gap between targeted governmental tax revenues and locally raised taxes. By taxing MNC profits and participating financially in their local operations, developing-country governments are thought to be better able to mobilize public financial resources for development projects.

Fourth, there is a different type of gap in management, entrepreneurship, technology, and skill presumed to be partly or wholly filled by the local operations of private foreign firms. Not only do multinationals provide financial resources and new factories to poor countries, but they also supply a "package" of needed resources, including management experience, entrepreneurial abilities, and technological skills that can then be transferred to their local counterparts by means of training programs and the process of learning by doing. Moreover, according to this argument, MNCs can educate local managers about how to establish contact with overseas banks, locate alternative sources of supply, diversify market outlets, and become better acquainted with international marketing practices. Finally, MNCs bring with them the most sophisticated technological knowledge about production processes while transferring modern machinery and equipment to capital-poor developing countries. It has long been assumed that some of this knowledge leaks out to the broader economy when engineers and managers leave to start their own companies. Such transfers of knowledge, skills, and technology are assumed to be both desirable and productive for the recipient nations.[8]

Arguments against Private Foreign Investment: Widening Gaps

There are two basic arguments against private foreign investment, in general, and the activities of MNCs, in particular—the strictly economic and the more philosophical or ideological.

On the economic side, the four gap-filling, pro-foreign-investment positions just outlined are countered by the following arguments:

1. Although MNCs provide capital, they may lower domestic savings and investment rates by substituting for private savings, stifling competition through exclusive production agreements with host governments, failing to reinvest much of their profits, generating domestic incomes for groups with lower savings propensities, and inhibiting the expansion of indigenous firms that might supply them with intermediate products by instead importing these goods from overseas affiliates. MNCs also raise a large fraction of their capital locally in the developing country itself, and this may lead to some crowding out of investment of local firms.

2. Although the initial impact of MNC investment is to improve the foreign-exchange position of the recipient nation, its long-run impact may be to reduce foreign-exchange earnings or at least make the net increase smaller than it appeared, as a result of substantial importation of intermediate products and capital goods and because of the overseas repatriation of profits, interest, royalties, management fees, and other funds.

3. Although MNCs do contribute to public revenue in the form of corporate taxes, their contribution is considerably less than it might appear as a result of liberal tax concessions, the practice of **transfer pricing**, excessive investment allowances, disguised public subsidies, and tariff protection provided by the host government.

4. The management, entrepreneurial skills, ideas, technology, and overseas contacts provided by MNCs may have little impact on developing local sources of these scarce skills and resources and may, in fact, inhibit their development by stifling the growth of indigenous entrepreneurship as a result of the MNCs' dominance of local markets.

Transfer pricing An accounting procedure often used to lower total taxes paid by multinational corporations in which intracorporate sales and purchases of goods and services are artificially invoiced so that profits accrue to the branch offices located in low-tax countries (tax havens) while offices in high-tax countries show little or no taxable profits.

Government policies in developing countries may be directed toward mitigating some of these concerns. Many academic and political thought leaders in developing countries have commonly raised a number of more fundamental objections. First, the impact of MNCs on development is very uneven, and in many situations, MNC activities reinforce dualistic economic structures and exacerbate income inequalities. They tend to promote the interests of a small number of local factory managers and relatively well-paid modern-sector workers against the interests of the rest by widening wage differentials. They divert resources away from needed food production to the manufacture of sophisticated products catering primarily to the demands of local elites and foreign consumers. And they tend to worsen the imbalance between rural and urban economic opportunities by locating primarily in urban export enclaves and contributing to excessive rural-urban migration.

Second, it is argued that multinationals typically produce products only demanded by a small, rich minority of the local population, stimulate inappropriate consumption patterns through advertising and their monopolistic market power, and do this all with inappropriate (capital-intensive) technologies of production that as a result create comparatively little employment. The latter is perhaps the major criticism of MNCs in light of the substantial employment problems of developing nations. Investment from other developing countries may be more conducive to employment expansion, but this is a new phenomenon, and the picture is not yet entirely clear.

Third, as a result of the first two points, local resources tend to be allocated for socially undesirable projects. This in turn tends to aggravate the already sizable inequality between rich and poor and the serious imbalance between urban and rural economic opportunities.

Fourth, multinationals use their economic power to influence government policies in directions that are unfavorable to development. They are able to extract sizable economic and political concessions from competing governments of other developing countries in the form of excessive protection, tax rebates, investment allowances, and the cheap provision of factory sites and essential social services. This phenomenon is often referred to as a "race to the bottom." As a result, the private profits of MNCs may exceed social benefits. In some cases, these social returns to host countries may even be negative. Alternatively, an MNC can avoid much local taxation in high-tax countries and shift profits to affiliates in low-tax countries by artificially inflating the price it pays for intermediate products purchased from overseas affiliates so as to lower its stated local profits. This transfer pricing phenomenon is a common practice of MNCs and one over which host governments can exert little control as long as corporate tax rates differ from one country to another. Some estimates place the lost revenue as a result of transfer pricing in the scores of billions of dollars.[9]

Fifth, MNCs may damage host economies by suppressing domestic entrepreneurship and using their superior knowledge, worldwide contacts, advertising skills, and range of essential support services to drive out local competitors and inhibit the emergence of small-scale local enterprises. Through the privatization of public corporations and the use of debt-for-equity swaps to reduce debt burdens, MNCs have been able to acquire some of the best and potentially most lucrative local businesses. They can thereby crowd out local investors and appropriate the profits for themselves. For example, in a quantitative study of 11 developing countries outside the Pacific Basin, higher foreign direct investment was accompanied by lower domestic investment, lower national saving, larger current account deficits, and lower economic growth rates.[10]

Finally, at the political level, the fear is often expressed that powerful multinational corporations can gain control over local assets and jobs and can then exert considerable influence on political decisions at all levels. In extreme cases, they may even, either directly by payoffs to corrupt public officials at the highest levels or indirectly by contributions to "friendly" political parties, subvert the very political process of host nations (as occurred with International Telephone and Telegraph in the 1970s in Chile).

Box 14.1 attempts to summarize the debate about multinationals in terms of seven key issues and the questions that surround each of them: international capital movements (including income flows and balance of payments effects), displacement of indigenous production, extent of technology transfer, appropriateness of technology transfer, patterns of consumption, social structure and stratification, and income distribution and dualistic development.

Reconciling the Pros and Cons   Although the forgoing discussion and Box 14.1 present a range of conflicting arguments, the real debate ultimately

---

BOX 14.1 Seven Key Disputed Issues about the Role and Impact of Multinational Corporations in Developing Countries

1. International capital movements (income flows and balance of payments)

   • Do they bring in much capital (savings)?
   • Do they improve the balance of payments?
   • Do they remit "excessive" profits?
   • Do they employ transfer pricing and disguise capital outflows?
   • Do they establish few linkages to the local economy?
   • Do they generate significant tax revenues?

2. Displacement of indigenous production

   • Do they buy out existing import-competing industries?
   • Do they use their competitive advantages to drive local competitors out of business?

3. Extent of technology transfer

   • Do they keep all R&D in home countries?
   • Do they retain monopoly power over their technology?

4. Appropriateness of technology transfer

   • Do they use only capital-intensive technologies?
   • Do they adapt technology to local factor endowments or leave it unchanged?

5. Patterns of consumption

   • Do they encourage inappropriate patterns of consumption through elite orientation, advertising, and superior marketing techniques?
   • Do they increase consumption of their products at the expense of other (perhaps more needed) goods?

6. Social structure and stratification

   • Do they develop allied local groups through higher wage payments, hiring (displacing) the best of the local entrepreneurs, and fostering elite loyalty and socialization through pressures for conformity?
   • Do they foster alien values, images, and lifestyles that are incompatible with local customs and beliefs?

7. Income distribution and dualistic development

   • Do they contribute to the widening gap between rich and poor?
   • Do they exacerbate urban bias and widen urban-rural differentials?

Source: Based on Thomas Biersteker, *Distortion or Development: Contending Perspectives on the Multinational Corporation* (Cambridge, Mass.: MIT Press, 1978), ch. 3.

centers on different ideological and value judgments about the nature and meaning of economic development and the sources from which it springs. The advocates of a central role for private foreign investment tend to be free-market proponents who firmly believe in the efficacy and beneficence of the market mechanism, where this is usually defined as a hands-off policy on the part of host governments. As noted, however, the actual operations of MNCs tend to be monopolistic and oligopolistic. Price setting is achieved more as a result of international bargaining and, in some cases, collusion than as a natural outgrowth of free-market supply and demand.

Theorists who argue against the activities of MNCs are often motivated by a sense of the importance of national control over domestic economic activities and the minimization of dominance-dependence relationships between powerful MNCs and developing-country governments. They see these giant corporations not as needed agents of economic change but more as vehicles of antidevelopment. Multinationals, they argue, reinforce dualistic economic structures and exacerbate domestic inequalities with inappropriate products and technologies. Rightly or wrongly, they view MNCs as modern incarnations of colonial devices such as the British East India Company. Many analysts advocate a more stringent regulation of foreign investments, a tougher bargaining stance on the part of host governments, a willingness on the part of developing countries to shop around for better deals, the adoption of performance standards and requirements, increased domestic ownership and control, and a greater coordination of developing-country strategies with respect to terms and conditions of foreign investment. One example of such coordinated strategies was a decision in the 1980s by the Andean Group in Latin America to require foreign investors to reduce their ownership in local enterprises to minority shares over a 15-year period. In an even earlier example, Tanzania adopted a similar policy of securing a controlling share of foreign enterprises. Not surprisingly, the annual flow of private foreign investment declined in both the Andean nations and Tanzania. Many such "indigenization" requirements have since been rolled back in much of the developing world. But China, with its great bargaining power, is the most successful example of the use of this strategy.

The arguments both for and against private foreign investment are still far from being settled empirically and may never be, as they ultimately reflect important differences in value judgments and political perceptions about desirable development strategies. Clearly, any real assessment of MNCs in development requires case studies of a given MNC in a specific country.[11] Perhaps the only valid general conclusion is that private foreign investment can be an important stimulus to economic and social development as long as the interests of MNCs and host-country governments coincide (assuming, of course, that they don't coincide along the lines of dualistic development and widening inequalities). Maybe there can never be a real congruence of interest between the profit-maximizing objectives of MNCs and the development priorities of developing-country governments. However, a strengthening of the relative bargaining powers of host-country governments through their coordinated activities, while probably reducing the overall magnitude and growth of private foreign investment, might make that investment better fit the long-run development needs and priorities of poor nations while still providing profitable opportunities for foreign investors.

Corporate social responsibility Nongovernmental self-regulation by corporations or consortia of corporations (possibly with consumer group representation), to attempt to ensure compliance with acceptable international norms of ethical practice such as avoidance of cruel, coercive, or deceptive labor practices.

The growing acceptance of the **corporate social responsibility** movement has been championed as an opportunity to seek common ground. Rather than primarily supported by corporate managers, citizens of rich countries have pressured corporations based in their countries to perform in a more socially responsible manner in developing countries. For example, there was great attention to conditions in Bangladesh apparel factories following the 2013 factory fire and building collapse disasters that killed over 1,000 workers, and European and North American companies felt pressure to create consortia to monitor that sourcing met international norms. Accordingly, there is a growing interest in certification through independent appraisals that worker rights have been respected, that environmentally sound practices have been used, and that other ethical standards have been met. However, such monitoring is costly, as often are the improved conditions that they help bring about. In this situation, multiple equilibria may be present (see Chapter 4)—consumers may be willing to pay a little more for goods that were sourced in a manner that is not harmful to human and sustainable development, but only if a sufficient number of others are doing the same. A credible watchdog organization has fixed costs and can only be supported with a sufficient markup in prices, so that it may be an equilibrium for no or few consumers to engage in socially responsible sourcing of products. But if the proportion that does so increases with the fraction of others who do, there is a classic complementarity. It may become the case that people expect to see such verifications, for example, to see that wood in a dining room table at a dinner party was sourced responsibly. The basic logic of such mechanisms is readily captured with multiple equilibrium models of the general type examined in Chapter 4.[12]

Perhaps the strongest argument in favor of encouraging MNCs is that they facilitate the transfer of know-how from developed to developing countries. Dani Rodrik surveyed the literature and concluded that so far, there has been little evidence of any horizontal spillovers, that is, transfers of knowledge from MNCs to local producers of the same type of product.[13] However, Garrick Blalock and Paul Gertler reported both statistical and managerial case study evidence for Indonesia that provides indications that MNCs strategically transfer technology to local vendors so that multinationals can procure high-quality inputs at low cost. And Beata Smarzynska Javorcik found evidence of positive productivity spillovers for local suppliers for the case of Lithuania. Thus, there is at least a suggestion that there may indeed be some significant technology spillovers but that the spillovers are vertical rather than horizontal.[14]

Another striking trend is the emergence of state-owned enterprises (SOEs) in FDI. Even as the number of SOEs has fallen, the size of those that remain has grown as governments have pursued "national champion" strategies in targeted industries. This has resulted, in many cases, in expanded market power—and reserves to power foreign investments. A substantial and growing portion of FDI to developing countries is now originating from SOEs based in China, a lower-middle-income country in which SOEs continue to play a central role in the economy. We return to the topic of the role of SOEs in detail in Chapter 15, section 15.6. Moreover, we should note that the role of sovereign wealth funds (SWFs) has similarly grown; some of the important players are originating in upper-middle-income countries.

The next decade should prove to be an interesting time to reassess the quantitative and qualitative impact of MNC investments in developing countries. As a result of the widespread adoption of market reforms, open economies, and privatization of state-owned enterprises, MNCs have been intensifying their global factory strategy, particularly in Asia and Latin America. They will add to national output, create some jobs, pay some taxes, and generally contribute to a more modern economy. But they will also gravitate toward the most profitable investment opportunities, purchase local factories in depressed developing economies at "fire sale" prices, engage in transfer pricing, and repatriate profits. In a very different vein, a majority of developing countries are now making efforts to *promote* targeted FDI so as to complement their broader industrialization strategies, often through investment promotion agencies (IPAs). It is to be hoped that ways can be found in which MNC profits and broad-based national development can be served simultaneously.

Private Portfolio Investment: Benefits and Risks

In addition to foreign direct investment, the most significant component of private capital flows has been in the area of portfolio investment.[15] With the increased liberalization of domestic financial markets in most developing countries and the opening up of these markets to foreign investors, private portfolio investment now accounts for a significant and currently rising share of overall net resource flows to developing countries. Basically, portfolio investment consists of foreign purchases of stocks (equity), bonds, certificates of deposit, and commercial paper. As usual, the middle-income countries have been the favored destination of these flows, with sub-Saharan Africa all but neglected.

As in the case of the FDIs of multinational corporations, the benefits and costs of private portfolio investment flows to both the investor and the developing-country recipient have been subjects of vigorous debate.[16] From the investor's point of view, investing in the stock markets of middle-income countries with relatively more developed financial markets permits them to increase their returns while diversifying their risks.

From the perspective of recipient developing countries, private portfolio flows in local stock and bond markets are a potentially welcome vehicle for raising capital for domestic firms. Well-functioning local stock and bond markets also help domestic investors diversify their assets (an option usually open only to the wealthy) and can act to improve the efficiency of the whole financial sector by serving as a screening and monitoring device for allocating funds to industries and firms with the highest potential returns (this topic—and an analysis of the domestic financial system more generally—is examined in detail in Chapter 15).

But from the macro policy perspective of developing-country governments, a key issue is whether large and volatile private portfolio flows into both local stock and short-term bond markets can be a destabilizing force for both the financial market and the overall economy. Some economists argue that these flows are not inherently unstable.[17] Developing countries that rely too heavily on private foreign portfolio investments to camouflage basic structural weakness in the economy, as in Mexico, Thailand, Malaysia, and

Indonesia in the 1990s, are more than likely to suffer serious long-term consequences. Like MNCs, portfolio investors are not in the development business. If developed-country interest rates rise or perceived profit rates in a developing country decline, foreign speculators will withdraw their "investments" as quickly as they brought them in. What developing countries need most is true long-run economic investment (plants, equipment, physical and social infrastructure, etc.), not speculative capital. A number of developing countries now combine incentives for the former and disincentives for the latter. Controls were strengthened in the years following the 2008 global financial crisis as potentially destabilizing "hot money" poured into several middle-income countries in response to low interest rates in developed countries.

In summary, private portfolio financial flows have risen and fallen dramatically in recent decades. Their volatility and the fact that they respond primarily to global interest-rate differentials, as well as to investor perceptions of political and economic stability, make them a very tenuous foundation on which to base medium- or long-term development strategies.[18] Asia's financial collapse in 1997, Russia's in 1998, Brazil's currency turmoil in 1999, Argentina's crisis in 2001–2002, and the dramatic downturn in flows to developing countries in 2009 underlined the instability or fragility of global capital markets.[19] Rather, developing countries need to focus first on putting fundamental conditions for development into place, because evidence shows that both MNCs and portfolio investors follow growth rather than lead it.[20]

14.3 The Role and Growth of Remittances

Wage levels in the high-income economies are approximately *five times* the level of wages for employment in *similar occupations* in the developing nations on average, after adjusting for purchasing power parity.[21] This provides an obvious incentive for migration, and indeed, hopeful migrants often take great personal risks to make the journey to the United States, Europe, and even developing-country destinations. In part because of these incentives, by 2010, there were an estimated 200 million migrants worldwide. But about half of all migrants leaving a developing nation move to other developing nations.

As noted in Chapters 2 and 8, there are legitimate concerns that out-migration can hamper development prospects because of the loss of skilled workers via this "brain drain." Balancing this concern is the benefit through remittances to relatives in migrants' countries of origin, beyond the gains to the successful (legal or illegal) migrants themselves. When migrants are low skilled and the recipients of remittances are poor, the potential development and poverty reduction advantages become clear. Migrants often build houses for their families and send money that is vital for keeping children in school and better fed. Thus, remittances now provide a significant pathway out of poverty. Indeed, the World Bank reports that based on household surveys, remittances have substantially reduced poverty in such countries as Guatemala, Uganda, Ghana, and Bangladesh.

Figure 14.4 shows various resource flows to developing countries over the period 1990–2008. Remittances have increased dramatically in this century, exceeding 5% of GDP of low-income countries, outpacing FDI and

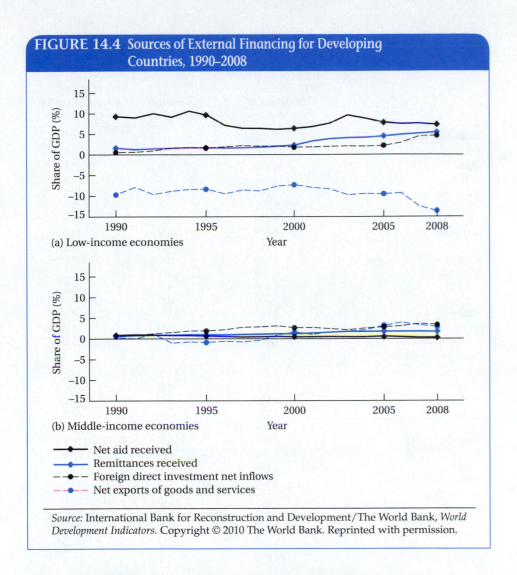

FIGURE 14.4 Sources of External Financing for Developing Countries, 1990–2008

(a) Low-income economies

(b) Middle-income economies

- Net aid received
- Remittances received
- Foreign direct investment net inflows
- Net exports of goods and services

Source: International Bank for Reconstruction and Development/The World Bank, *World Development Indicators.* Copyright © 2010 The World Bank. Reprinted with permission.

approaching inflows from aid. However, remittance flows are very uneven across developing countries. Table 14.1 lists the top 15 remittance recipient countries, ranked by dollars and by share of GDP, in 2008. India and China had the largest remittances, but Mexico was in third place. And as the table shows, in 15 countries, remittances represented at least 11% of GDP. Note, however, that in the wake of the financial crisis, remittances declined in all regions from 2008 into 2010 except in South Asia, where they remained stable.

The growth of recorded remittances is due in part to improved accounting; some analysts view even the statistics of recent years to be subject to considerable undercounting. But other important factors include the rising number of migrants and advances in financial intermediation that reduce the costs to migrants of remitting funds to their families. Thus, the rapid rise in remittances is a genuine phenomenon. Indeed, forecasts project that remittances could exceed $500 billion in 2016. Further reductions in costs and other impediments to remittances would also lead to further benefits.

TABLE 14.1 Major Remittance-Receiving Developing Countries, by Level and GDP Share, 2008			
	Inflow of Migrants' Remittances (millions of U.S. dollars)	Annual Change (%)	Share of Remittances in GDP (%)
Ranked by Volume			
India	45,000	27.8	3.7
China	34,490	5.0	0.8
Mexico	26,212	3.4	2.4
Philippines	18,268	12.1	10.8
Nigeria	9,979	8.2	4.7
Egypt	9,476	23.8	5.8
Bangladesh	8,979	38.8	11.0
Pakistan	7,025	17.1	4.2
Morocco	6,730	0.0	7.6
Indonesia	6,500	5.3	1.3
Lebanon	6,000	4.0	20.7
Vietnam	5,500	0.0	6.1
Ukraine	5,000	11.0	2.8
Colombia	4,523	0.0	1.9
Russian Federation	4,500	9.7	0.3
Ranked by Share of GDP			
Tajikistan	1,750	3.5	34.1
Lesotho	443	0.0	27.4
Moldova	1,550	3.5	25.3
Guyana	278	0.0	24.0
Lebanon	6,000	4.0	20.7
Honduras	2,801	6.7	19.8
Haiti	1,300	6.4	18.0
Nepal	2,254	30.0	17.8
Jordan	3,434	0.0	17.1
Jamaica	2,214	3.3	17.1
El Salvador	3,804	2.5	17.0
Kyrgyzstan	715	0.0	14.2
Nicaragua	771	4.2	11.5
Guatemala	4,440	4.4	11.2
Bangladesh	5,979	36.8	11.0

Source: UNCTAD *Trade and Development Report*, p. 23 (New York: United Nations, 2009), tab. 1.6. Reprinted with permission from the United Nations.

It is important to stress, however, that migration is not always voluntary and may result from human trafficking; even when departure is voluntary, it is often done with imperfect information about working conditions; and exploitation and abuse are not uncommon. Clearly, for migration to bring the maximum social benefit to people in developing countries, improved regulations and protections for what the International Labor Organization terms "irregular status" migrants and the working conditions of migrants will be essential, as will improved willingness of developed countries to accept reasonable increases in migration.

14.4 Foreign Aid: The Development Assistance Debate

Conceptual and Measurement Problems

In addition to export earnings and private foreign direct and portfolio investment, developing countries receive two other major sources of foreign exchange: public (official) bilateral and multilateral development assistance and private (unofficial) assistance provided by nongovernmental organizations (NGOs). Both of these activities are forms of **foreign aid**, although only public aid is usually measured in official statistics.

In principle, all governmental resource transfers from one country to another should be included in the definition of *foreign aid*. Even this simple definition, however, raises a number of problems.[22] For one thing, many resource transfers can take disguised forms, such as the granting of preferential tariffs by developed countries to exports of manufactured goods, particularly from the least developed countries. This permits developing countries to earn more foreign exchange from selling their industrial products in developed-country markets at higher prices than would otherwise be possible. There is consequently a net gain for developing countries and a net loss for developed countries, which amounts to a real resource transfer to the developing world. Such implicit capital transfers, or disguised flows, should be counted in qualifying foreign-aid flows. Normally, however, they are not.

However, we should not include *all* transfers of capital to developing countries, particularly the capital flows of private foreign investors. Private flows represent normal commercial transactions, prompted by commercial considerations of profits and rates of return, and therefore should not be viewed as foreign aid. Commercial flows of private capital are *not* a form of foreign assistance, even though they may benefit the developing country in which they take place.

Economists have defined *foreign aid*, therefore, as any flow of capital to a developing country that meets two criteria: (1) Its objective should be noncommercial from the point of view of the donor, and (2) it should be characterized by **concessional terms**; that is, the interest rate and repayment period for borrowed capital should be softer (less stringent) than commercial terms.[23] Even this definition can be inappropriate, for it can include military aid, which is both noncommercial and concessional. Normally, however, military aid is excluded from international economic measurements of foreign-aid flows. The concept of foreign aid that is now widely used and accepted, therefore, is one that encompasses all official grants and concessional loans, in currency or in kind, that are broadly aimed at transferring resources from developed to less developed nations on development, poverty, or income distribution grounds. Unfortunately, there often is a thin line separating purely developmental grants and loans from sources ultimately motivated by security or commercial interests.

Just as there are conceptual problems associated with the definition of *foreign aid*, there are measurement and conceptual problems in the calculation of actual development assistance flows. In particular, three major problems arise in measuring aid. First, we cannot simply add up the dollar values of

Foreign aid The international transfer of public funds in the form of loans or grants either directly from one government to another (bilateral assistance) or indirectly through the vehicle of a multilateral assistance agency such as the World Bank.

Concessional terms Terms for the extension of credit that are more favorable to the borrower than those available through standard financial markets.

grants and loans; each has a different significance to both donor and recipient countries. Loans must be repaid and therefore cost the donor and benefit the recipient less than the nominal value of the loan itself. Conceptually, we should deflate or discount the dollar value of interest-bearing loans before adding them to the value of outright grants. Second, aid can be tied either by *source* (loans or grants have to be spent on the purchase of donor-country goods and services) or by *project* (funds can only be used for a specific project, such as a road or a steel mill). In either case, the real value of the aid is reduced because the specified source is likely to be an expensive supplier or the project is not of the highest priority (otherwise, there would be no need to tie the aid). Furthermore, aid may be tied to the importation of capital-intensive equipment, which may impose an additional real resource cost, in the form of higher unemployment, on the recipient nation. Or the project itself may require the purchase of new machinery and equipment from monopolistic suppliers while existing productive equipment in the same industry is being operated at very low levels of capacity. Finally, we always need to distinguish between the nominal and real value of foreign assistance. Aid flows are usually calculated at nominal levels and tend to show a steady rise over time. However, when deflated for rising prices, the actual real volume of aid from most donor countries has declined substantially in recent decades despite a recent uptick.

Amounts and Allocations: Public Aid

Official development assistance (ODA) Net disbursements of loans or grants made on concessional terms by official agencies, historically by high-income member countries of the Organization for Economic Cooperation and Development (OECD).

The money volume of **official development assistance (ODA)**, which includes bilateral grants, concessional loans, and technical assistance, as well as multilateral flows, grew from an annual rate of under $5 billion in 1960 to $50 billion in 2000 and to over $128 billion in 2008. However, the percentage of developed-country gross national income (GNI) allocated to official development assistance declined from 0.51% in 1960 to 0.23% in 2002 before improving to 0.33% by 2005 and to 0.45% in 2008 as part of a campaign to increase assistance in the wake of the continued lag in human development in sub-Saharan Africa—a major initiative at the G8 meetings in Britain in 2005.[24] Although the full promise of these meetings was far from met, some significant progress was made. It remains to be seen how the long recession and fiscal crises in many high-income countries will affect these ratios in the coming years. Table 14.2 shows the disbursement of ODA by some of the principal donors, both in total amount and as a percentage of GNI in 1985, 2002, and 2008. Although the United States remains the largest donor in absolute terms, relative to others it provides the lowest percentage of GNI—0.18% in 2008, compared to an average of 0.45% for all industrial donor countries and well below the internationally agreed UN target of 0.70%. Only five countries are currently providing ODA in excess of this target: Sweden, Norway, Denmark, the Netherlands, and Luxembourg. Sweden led with a full 1% of GNI contributed. Not only is the U.S. ODA-to-GNI ratio the lowest among industrial countries, but it also declined sharply from its level of 0.31% in 1970 to reach a nadir of about 0.11%, before rebounding to about 0.18%. It should be noted, however, that U.S. citizens provide an additional $17.1 billion in direct NGO grants, which accounts for 72% of the global total. This raises the fraction to

TABLE 14.2	Official Development Assistance Net Disbursements from Major Donor Countries, 1985, 2002, and 2008					
	1985		**2002**		**2008**	
Donor Country	**Billions of U.S. Dollars**	**Percentage of GNI**	**Billions of U.S. Dollars**	**Percentage of GNI**	**Billions of U.S. Dollars**	**Percentage of GNI**
Canada	1.6	0.49	2.0	0.28	4.8	0.33
Denmark	—	—	1.6	0.96	2.8	0.87
France	4.0	0.78	5.5	0.38	10.9	0.40
Germany	2.9	0.47	5.3	0.27	14.0	0.40
Italy	1.1	0.26	2.3	0.20	4.9	0.23
Japan	3.8	0.29	9.3	0.23	9.6	0.20
Netherlands	1.1	0.91	3.3	0.81	7.0	0.86
Sweden	—	—	2.0	0.83	4.7	1.00
United Kingdom	1.5	0.33	4.9	0.31	11.5	0.40
United States	9.4	0.24	13.3	0.13	8.0	0.18
Total (22 countries)	29.4	0.35	58.3	0.23	121.5	0.45

Source of data: World Bank, *World Debt Tables, 1991–1992* (Washington, D.C.: World Bank, 1992), vol. 1, tab. 2.1; World Bank, *World Development Indicators, 2004* and *2010* (Washington, D.C.: World Bank, 2004, 2010), tabs. 6.9 and 6.10.

about 0.3% of national income, still below countries such as Britain, Canada, France, and Germany. Moreover, for added perspective, although in 2012 developed countries spent about $120 billion on aid, they also spent triple this amount, some $360 billion, on agricultural subsidies that often harmed developing-country exports; rich countries also committed about $1.4 trillion to military defense expenditures.

ODA is allocated in some strange and arbitrary ways.[25] South Asia, where nearly 50% of the world's poorest people live, receives $8 per person in aid. The Middle East and North Africa, with well over triple South Asia's per capita income, receives *nine times* the per capita aid! Table 14.3 shows the regional distribution of ODA in 2008.

The patterns of aid become even clearer when examined at the individual-country level. In 2008, by far the largest recipient was Iraq, with $9.9 billion

TABLE 14.3	Official Development Assistance (ODA) by Region, 2008		
Region	**ODA per Capita (U.S. $)**	**GNI per Capita (U.S. $)**	**ODA as a Share of GNI (%)**
Middle East and North Africa	73	3,237	1.9
Sub-Saharan Africa	49	1,077	4.3
Latin America and the Caribbean	16	6,768	0.2
East Asia and the Pacific	5	2,644	0.2
South Asia	8	963	0.8
Europe and Central Asia	19	7,350	0.2

Source of data: World Bank, *World Development Indicators, 2010* (Washington, D.C.: World Bank, 2010), tabs. 1.1 and 6.16.

in aid, or approximately $321 per capita. The second-largest recipient was Afghanistan, at $4.9 billion, or $168 per capita. Some 20 countries received at least $1 billion in aid. But India, with by far the largest number of extremely poor people in the world, received just $2 per person in aid. And while Jordan, a middle-income country, received $126 per person, Niger, considered the poorest country in the world, received just $41 per person. Aid per capita to the least developed countries in Africa has increased significantly, however, since 2005. But these per capita receipts are still less than such middle-income countries as Serbia, Bosnia, and Herzegovina, Albania, Macedonia, Lebanon, and Georgia, each of which received more than $100 per capita.[26]

It is clear that the allocation of foreign aid is only partly determined by the relative needs of developing countries. Much bilateral aid seems to be based largely on political and military considerations. Multilateral aid (e.g., from the World Bank and various UN agencies) is somewhat more economically rational, although here, too, the rich often seem to attract more resources per capita than the poor.

Because foreign aid is seen differently by donor and recipient countries, we must analyze the giving and receiving process from these two often contradictory viewpoints.

Why Donors Give Aid

First and foremost, donor-country governments give aid because it is in their political, strategic, or economic self-interest to do so. Some development assistance may be motivated by moral and humanitarian desires to assist the less fortunate (e.g., emergency food relief and medical programs), and certainly this has been the international rhetoric in the increases in aid in the first decade of the twenty-first century, which may reflect the fact that ordinary citizens are often more charitable than their leaders. Still, it is doubtful that over longer periods of time, donor nations assist others without expecting some corresponding benefits (political, economic, military, counterterrorism, antinarcotics, etc.) in return. We focus here on the foreign-aid motivations of donor nations in two broad but often interrelated categories: political and economic.

Political Motivations   Political motivations have been by far the more important for aid-granting nations, especially for the largest donor country, the United States. The United States has viewed foreign aid from its beginnings in the late 1940s under the Marshall Plan, which aimed at reconstructing the war-torn economies of western Europe, as a means of containing the international spread of Communism. When the balance of Cold War interests shifted from Europe to the developing world in the mid-1950s, the policy of containment embodied in the U.S. aid program dictated a shift in emphasis toward political, economic, and military support for "friendly," less developed nations, especially those considered geographically strategic. Most aid programs to developing countries were, therefore, oriented more toward purchasing their security and propping up their sometimes shaky regimes than promoting long-term social and economic development. The successive shifts in emphasis from South Asia to Southeast Asia to Latin America to the

Middle East and back to Southeast Asia during the 1950s and 1960s and then toward Africa and the Persian Gulf in the late 1970s, the Caribbean and Central America in the 1980s, and the Russian Federation, Bosnia, Ukraine, and the Middle East in the 1990s, with a renewed focus on the Islamic nations after 2001, reflected changes in U.S. strategic, political, security, and economic interests more than changing evaluations of poverty problems and economic need. Recent increases in aid to African countries with public health crises, including HIV assistance, may be due in part to concerns that the disease may spread internationally or lead to a destabilizing state collapse and possible havens for terrorists. Another motivation to reduce poverty abroad may be to prevent or reduce the flow of refugees and other migrants.

Even the Alliance for Progress, inaugurated in the early 1960s with great fanfare and noble rhetoric about promoting Latin American economic development, was formulated primarily as a direct response to the rise of Fidel Castro in Cuba and the perceived threat of Communist takeovers in other Latin American countries. As soon as the security issue lost its urgency and other more pressing problems came to the fore (the war in Vietnam, the rise in U.S. violence, etc.), the Alliance for Progress stagnated and began to fizzle out. Our point is simply that where aid is seen primarily as a means of furthering donor-country interests, the flow of funds tends to vary with the donor's political assessment of changing international situations and not the relative need of potential recipients.

The behavior of other major donor countries, such as Japan, Great Britain, and France, has been similar to that of the United States. Although exceptions can be cited (Sweden, Denmark, the Netherlands, Norway, and perhaps Canada), by and large these Western donor countries have used foreign aid as a political lever to prop up or underpin friendly political regimes in developing countries—regimes whose continued existence they perceived as being in their own national security interests. It still remains to be seen how much the renewed rhetorical focus on extreme poverty in the period following the 2005 G8 summit in Britain portends a historic change in the prioritization of aid, but there is no doubt that political and business considerations will remain very important.

Economic Motivations: Two-Gap Models and Other Criteria   Within the broad context of political and strategic priorities, foreign-aid programs of the developed nations have had a strong economic rationale. This is especially true for Japan, which directs most of its aid to neighboring Asian countries, where it has substantial private investments and expanding trade. Even though political motivation may have been of paramount importance for other donors, the economic rationale was at least given lip service as the overriding motivation for assistance.

Let us examine the principal economic arguments advanced in support of foreign aid.

Foreign-Exchange Constraints   External finance (both loans and grants) can play a critical role in supplementing domestic resources in order to relieve savings or foreign-exchange bottlenecks. This is the so-called two-gap analysis of foreign assistance.[27] The basic argument of the **two-gap model** is that most

Two-gap model   A model of foreign aid comparing savings and foreign-exchange gaps to determine which is the binding constraint on economic growth.

Savings gap   The excess of domestic investment opportunities over domestic savings, causing investments to be limited by the available foreign exchange.

Foreign-exchange gap   The shortfall that results when the planned trade deficit exceeds the value of capital inflows, causing output growth to be limited by the available foreign exchange for capital goods imports.

developing countries face either a shortage of domestic savings to match investment opportunities or a shortage of foreign exchange to finance needed imports of capital and intermediate goods. Basic two-gap and similar models assume that the **savings gap** (domestic real resources) and the **foreign-exchange gap** are unequal in magnitude and that they are essentially independent. The implication is that one of the two gaps will be "binding" for any developing economy at a given point in time. If, for example, the savings gap is dominant, this would indicate that growth is constrained by domestic investment. Foreign savings may be used as a supplement to domestic savings. (However, decision makers in a country with a shortage of savings may be unable or unwilling to divert purchasing power from consumption goods to capital goods, either bought domestically or from abroad. As a result, "excess" foreign exchange, including foreign aid, might be spent on the importation of luxury consumption goods.) An outstanding example of savings-gap nations would be the Arab oil exporters during the 1970s.

When the foreign-exchange gap is binding, a developing economy has excess productive resources (mostly labor), and all available foreign exchange is being used for imports. The existence of complementary domestic resources would permit them to undertake new investment projects if they had the external finance to import new capital goods and associated technical assistance. Foreign aid can therefore play a critical role in overcoming the foreign-exchange constraint and in raising the real rate of economic growth.

Algebraically, the simple two-gap model can be formulated as follows:

1. *The savings constraint or gap.* Starting with the identity that capital inflows (the difference between imports and exports) add to investible resources (domestic savings), the savings-investment restriction can be written as

$$I \leq F + sY \tag{14.1}$$

   where F is the amount of capital inflows. If capital inflows, F, plus domestic saving, sY, exceeds domestic investment, I, and the economy is at full capacity, a savings gap is said to exist.

2. *The foreign-exchange constraint or gap.* If investment in a developing country has a marginal import share, m_1 (typically ranging from 30% to 60%), and the marginal propensity to import out of a unit of noninvestment GNI (usually around 10% to 15%) is given by the parameter m_2, the foreign-exchange constraint or gap can be written as

$$(m_1 - m_2)I + m_2Y - E \leq F \tag{14.2}$$

where E is the exogenous level of exports.

The term F enters both inequality constraints and becomes the critical factor in the analysis. If F, E, and Y are initially assigned an exogenous current value, only one of the two inequalities will prove binding; that is, investment (and therefore the output growth rate) will be constrained to a lower level by one of the inequalities. Countries can therefore be classified according to whether the savings or foreign-exchange constraint is binding. More important from the viewpoint of foreign-aid analysis is the observation that the impact of increased capital inflows will be greater where the foreign-exchange gap (Equation 14.2) rather than the savings gap (Equation 14.1) is binding. Two-gap models have been used to provide rough estimates of the relative impact of foreign aid on investment and growth in developing nations.

The problem is that such gap forecasts are very mechanistic and are themselves constrained by the necessity of fixing import parameters and assigning exogenous values to exports and net capital inflows. In the case of exports, this is particularly constricting because a liberalization of trade relations between the developed and the developing world would contribute more toward relieving foreign-exchange gaps than foreign aid. Although E and F are substitutable in Equation 14.2, they can have quite different indirect effects, especially in the case where F represents interest-bearing loans that need to be repaid. Thus, the alteration of import and export parameters through government policy in both developed and developing countries can have a deep impact on whether the savings or foreign-exchange constraint is restricting the further growth of national output. A third, **fiscal gap** may also be important, because domestic savings availability for investment and foreign exchange availability for capital goods imports may have little impact on private-sector investment and growth without complementary public investments in roads and other forms of infrastructure, or in human capital. But such government investments may raise the rate of return from private investment sufficiently to make them viable.

Three, gap models have been used to account for this in understanding why growth has commonly failed to pick up during structural adjustment.[28]

Fiscal gap Deficiencies of government investments including infrastructure and human capital that are complementary to—raise the rate of return from—private investment.

Growth and Savings

External assistance is also assumed to facilitate and accelerate the process of development by generating additional domestic savings as a result of the higher growth rates that it is presumed to induce. Eventually, it is hoped, the need for concessional aid will disappear as local resources become sufficient to make development self-sustaining. In reality, much aid is not invested, and if it is, the productivity of that investment is often very low.[29] However, among the main reasons for this are the very "strings" attached to foreign aid.

Technical Assistance

Financial assistance needs to be supplemented by **technical assistance** in the form of high-level worker transfers to ensure that aid funds are used most efficiently to generate economic growth. This skill-gap-filling process is thus analogous to the financial-gap-filling process mentioned earlier. Sustainable development impact requires a focus on training in recipient countries.

Technical assistance Foreign aid (either bilateral or multilateral) that takes the form of the transfer of expert personnel, technicians, scientists, educators, and economic advisers, and particularly their use in training local personnel, rather than a simple transfer of funds.

Absorptive Capacity

Finally, the amount of aid is considered in relation to the recipient country's **absorptive capacity**, its ability to use aid funds wisely and productively (often meaning as donors want them to be used). Typically, the donor countries decide which developing countries are to receive aid, how much, in what form (loans or grants, financial or technical assistance), for what purpose, and under what conditions on the basis of the donor countries' assessment of domestic absorptive capacities (particularly for the least developed countries). But many types of assistance, such as resources for building

Absorptive capacity The ability of a country to absorb foreign private or public financial assistance (to use the funds in a productive manner).

infrastructure or for training (e.g., of government officials or health or education workers) itself increases absorptive capacity. It has been said that what one donor sees as a constraint on the ability of a country to use conventional aid, another sees as an opportunity to have more leveraged impact with new forms of assistance.[30] In any case, in practice, the total amount of aid rarely has much to do with developing-country absorptive capacities because, typically, foreign aid is a residual and low-priority element in donor-country expenditures. In most instances, the recipient countries have little say in the matter.

Economic Motivations and Self-Interest   The arguments on behalf of foreign aid as a crucial ingredient for successful development should not mask the fact that even at the strictly economic level, definite benefits accrue to donor countries as a result of their aid programs. The strong tendency toward providing interest-bearing loans instead of outright grants and toward tying aid to the exports of donor countries has saddled many countries, often among the least developed, with substantial debt repayment burdens. It has also increased their import costs because aid tied to donor-country exports limits the receiving nation's freedom to shop around for low-cost and suitable capital and intermediate goods. **Tied aid** in this sense is clearly a second-best option to untied aid (and perhaps also to freer trade through a reduction of developed-country import barriers). For example, a large fraction of U.S. aid has been spent on American consultants and other U.S. businesses.[31]

> **Tied aid**   Foreign aid in the form of bilateral loans or grants that require the recipient country to use the funds to purchase goods or services from the donor country.

Why Recipient Countries Accept Aid

The reasons why developing nations have usually been eager to accept aid, even in its most stringent and restrictive forms, have been given much less attention than the reasons why donors provide aid. The major reason is probably economic. Developing countries have often tended to accept the proposition—typically advanced by developed-country economists and supported by reference to success stories such as Taiwan and South Korea to the exclusion of many more failures—that aid is a crucial and essential ingredient in the development process. It supplements scarce domestic resources, it helps transform the economy structurally, and it contributes to economic growth. Thus, the economic rationale for aid is based in part on their acceptance of the donor's perceptions of what the poor countries require to promote economic development.

Conflicts generally arise, therefore, not out of any disagreement about the role of aid, but over its amount and conditions. Naturally, any developing country would like to have more aid in the form of outright grants or long-term, low-cost loans, with a minimum of strings attached. This means not tying aid to donor exports and granting greater latitude to recipient countries to decide for themselves what is in their best long-run development interests. Unfortunately, a good deal of aid that comes in this form has either been wasted in showcase but unproductive projects (e.g., an elaborate parliamentary building, an oversize airport) or actually has been plundered by corrupt government officials and their local cronies. Much of the criticism of the historical patterns of foreign aid—that it wastes resources, that it bolsters corrupt regimes, that it is appropriated by the rich at the expense of the poor—is justified. Some recipients in the past have accepted aid simply because it was there, and they were not held accountable. A few leaders simply wish to leave no stone unturned in their quest for poverty alleviation, as perhaps describes Mozambique in the 1990s. They have been in the minority. The impact of the spread of democracy, press freedom, and the rule of law, including anticorruption drives, on the effectiveness of aid remains an open question.

Second, in some countries, aid is seen by both donor and recipient as providing greater political leverage to the existing leadership to suppress opposition and maintain itself in power. In such instances, assistance takes the form not only of financial-resource transfers but also of military and internal security reinforcement. This phenomenon was clearly at work in Central America in the 1980s. The problem is that once aid is accepted, the ability of recipient governments to extricate themselves from implied political or economic obligations to donors and prevent donor governments from interfering in their internal affairs can be greatly diminished.

Finally, whether on grounds of basic humanitarian responsibilities of the rich toward the welfare of the poor or because of a belief that the rich nations owe the poor nations reparations for past exploitation, many proponents of foreign aid in both developed and developing countries believe that rich nations have an obligation to support economic and social development, particularly in the least developed countries. They often link this moral obligation with the need for greater freedom of choice for recipient developing countries in the allocation and use of aid funds.

In sum, while there is no doubt that the least developed countries will need more assistance to escape from the vicious circle of poverty, fresh approaches are needed to ensure effectiveness.

The Role of Nongovernmental Organizations in Aid

One of the fastest-growing and most significant forces in the field of development assistance is that provided through private **nongovernmental organizations (NGOs)**. As we noted in Chapter 11, NGOs are voluntary organizations that work with, and on behalf of, mostly local grassroots organizations in developing countries. They also represent specific local and international interest groups with concerns as diverse as providing emergency relief, protecting child health, promoting women's rights, alleviating poverty, protecting the environment, increasing food production, and providing rural credit to small farmers and local businesses. NGOs build roads, houses, hospitals, and schools. They work in family-planning clinics and refugee camps. They teach in schools and universities and conduct research on increasing farm yields.[32]

NGOs include religious groups, private foundations and charities, research organizations, and federations of dedicated doctors, nurses, engineers, agricultural scientists, and economists. Many work directly on grassroots rural development projects; others focus on relief efforts for starving or displaced peoples. Some familiar NGOs include Save the Children, CARE, Oxfam, Planned Parenthood, Doctors Without Borders, World Vision, the World Wildlife Fund, Habitat for Humanity, Africare, Heifer, Christian Aid, Project HOPE, and Amnesty International. Funding through developed-country NGOs for aid activities in developing countries grew from just under $1 billion in 1970 to over $23 billion in 2008.[33] Many NGOs give local control to their developing-country affiliates

Nongovernmental organizations (NGOs) Nonprofit organizations that are often involved in providing financial and technical assistance to developing countries.

or other local groups they support. Increasingly, indigenous NGOs such as BRAC in Bangledesh are becoming active in international assistance (see the case study for Chapter 11).

NGOs have two important advantages. First, being less constrained by political imperatives, most NGOs are able to work much more effectively at the local level with the people they are trying to assist than massive bilateral and multilateral aid programs can. Second, by working directly with local people's organizations, many NGOs are better able to avoid the suspicion and cynicism on the part of the mostly poor people whom they serve that their help is insincere or likely to be short-lived. It is estimated that NGOs in developing countries are affecting the lives of some 250 million people; the fact that their voices are increasingly being listened to in the halls of developed-country governments and at international conferences on development makes it clear that the nature and focus of foreign aid are changing rapidly. NGOs have several other important comparative advantages in relation to government and the private sector but also some serious limitations, sometimes called *voluntary failure* (with reference to these private voluntary organizations), as described in detail in Chapter 11. One critical question is whether international NGOs can sustainably transfer their knowledge and capabilities to domestic NGOs and other community-based organizations.[34]

The Effects of Aid

The issue of the economic effects of aid, especially public aid, like that of the effects of private foreign investment, is fraught with disagreement.[35] On one side are the economic traditionalists, who argue that aid has indeed promoted growth and structural transformation in many developing countries.[36] On the other side are critics who argue that aid does not promote faster growth but may, in fact, retard it by substituting for, rather than supplementing, domestic savings and investment and by exacerbating balance of payments deficits as a result of rising debt repayment obligations (when aid takes the form of loans, even if at reduced interest rates) and the linking of aid to donor-country exports.

Official aid is further criticized for focusing on, and stimulating the growth of, the modern sector, thereby increasing the gap in living standards between the rich and the poor in developing countries. Some critics on the left would even assert that foreign aid has been a force for antidevelopment in the sense that it both retards growth through reduced savings and worsens income inequalities.[37] Rather than relieving economic bottlenecks and filling gaps, aid—and, for that matter, private foreign investment—not only widens existing savings and foreign-exchange resource gaps but also may even create new ones (e.g., urban-rural or modern-sector–traditional-sector gaps). Critics on the right charge that foreign aid has been a failure because it has been largely appropriated by corrupt bureaucrats, has stifled initiative, and has generally engendered a welfare mentality on the part of recipient nations.[38]

But one of the most promising developments of the new century has been the emphasis on rigorous testing of the impact of development assistance. In 2005, national and multilateral officials who were concerned with international development met in Paris and agreed to place greater emphasis on monitoring and systematically measuring aid effectiveness.[39] Accompanying this policy emphasis is a growing acceptance of the value of evaluating programs with greater rigor. One major trend is to encourage evaluation through randomized trials.[40] Clearly, not all valuable development activities can be studied with these methods; methods must follow from relevant development economics questions and cannot be the primary driver of the questions that are asked.[41] And it is often hard to generalize beyond the local experiment to other locations where conditions differ—known as the *external validity problem*. But when feasible and appropriate, randomized trials are a powerful method. In recent years, randomization has been adapted to study a growing range of education, health, microfinance, and social welfare programs.[42]

Finally, many critics have noted that FDI volumes are now more than 15 times that of foreign aid flows. This is an important trend. On the other hand, aid remains larger than FDI in many of the countries that are in most need of assistance, including fragile states. Indeed, FDI flows toward countries that are less in need of aid; and capital flight is a chronic problem in fragile and conflict-ridden countries. Moreover, even if FDI flow to a country is much higher than its aid flow, this clearly does not mean that the economic development or poverty impact of investment is also proportionately higher than that of aid.[43]

After years of aid weariness, polls have shown that the public is increasingly willing to support increases in government aid budgets and to donate development assistance via NGOs, and the development crisis in many of the least developed countries, especially in sub-Saharan Africa, has mobilized public opinion in support of greater development assistance. Poll numbers also suggest that the upturn in public support for aid was at least temporarily weakened in the aftermath of the recent global financial crisis.

The attention to improved assistance to reduce extreme poverty, particularly in its increased focus on the 49 least developed countries at the UN 2010 Millennium Development Goals summit, the improvements in accountability and evaluation of aid that have taken more shape since the Paris Declaration, and some enhancement of resources are hopeful signs that aid will become more effective and more targeted toward people living in poverty. And foreign aid has played a crucial role in assistance with conflict resolution, postconflict recovery, and making the transition to resumed development. We take up the problem of violent conflict in developing countries in the next section.

14.5 Conflict and Development

The Scope of Violent Conflict and Conflict Risks

Physical security is the foundation for human capability; assurance of security may be the most fundamental of all institutions for development. Violent conflict has held back progress in many of the poorest countries. In addition to the horrors of the conflicts and their aftermaths themselves, economic harm can also be caused by expectations of likely future conflicts and doubts about how they could be resolved or how high growth could be resumed in this environment. This uncertainty could, for example, discourage investment and entrepreneurship and accelerate a brain drain. Thus, work on the consequences, causes, and potential curative and preventive remedies for violent conflict

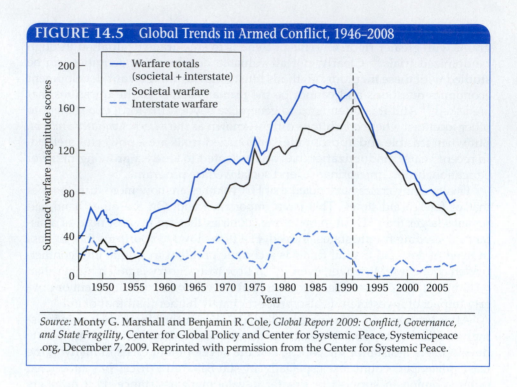

FIGURE 14.5   Global Trends in Armed Conflict, 1946–2008

Source: Monty G. Marshall and Benjamin R. Cole, *Global Report 2009: Conflict, Governance, and State Fragility,* Center for Global Policy and Center for Systemic Peace, Systemicpeace .org, December 7, 2009. Reprinted with permission from the Center for Systemic Peace.

and improvement of conditions that may lead to such conflict has become an important part of the field of economic development.

The number and intensity of violent conflicts grew for nearly half a century following the end of World War II but reached a peak by the early 1990s. Since then, such conflicts have decreased substantially, as seen in Figure 14.5, which summarizes violent conflict incidence over time, adjusted for magnitude. But the intensity and consequences of societal warfare, particularly ethnic war, remains at unacceptably high levels, comparable to the 1960s.

There has been an encouraging drop in armed conflict in Africa in recent years. But the trend for societal conflicts to occur more commonly in the least developed countries has resulted in longer and more difficult periods of postconflict reconstruction and state fragility. Recovery efforts are more often focused on overcoming situations of destroyed infrastructure and housing, environmental decay, collapse of health and education, lack of services to assist traumatized victims, and general loss of social capital.[44] Thus, the costs of renewed conflict are very high, making prevention even more important than ever.

The Consequences of Armed Conflict

Violent conflict harms health in ways both obvious and unexpected. People not involved in violence can be affected almost immediately as parents lose their livelihood or become refugees and children are forced to work. Recovery from the consequences can take many years. Conflict can cause children to miss out on schooling in their most formative years, harming their well-being over a lifetime. And it can take years to mend a torn social fabric that might help cushion the fall.

Health   The immediate effect of war is the most visible. At first, more men die than women, primarily as a result of the fighting itself. Over time, more women die, as they suffer the lingering consequences much more. Maternal mortality can be shockingly high—an estimated 3% in conflict areas such as the Democratic Republic of Congo (DRC).[45] Scholars have found that the long-term effects of conflict fall most heavily on women, diminishing their access to health, social welfare services, and education.[46]

Rape has become a weapon of terror. Many victims die in rape attacks, and many more suffer long-term health consequences, including AIDS and chronic depression. As Nina Birkeland summarizes, "in conflicts with an ethnic dimension, systematic rape has commonly been used to destabilize populations and destroy community and family bonds."[47] Refugee children and women are at particular risk for rape and sexual exploitation.

In addition, Thomas Plumper and Eric Neumayer report, "in makeshift refugee tent camps…infectious diseases such as diarrhea, measles, acute respiratory diseases, and malaria, but also sexually transmitted diseases including HIV/AIDS, spread more easily, often turning into epidemics."[48] Weakened refugees die at a much higher rate from diseases they would not have caught under normal circumstances and might have survived under conditions of more rest, better nourishment, and less stress. Problems cross national borders; for example, it has been estimated that an additional 1,000 international refugees leads to an extra 1,400 cases of malaria in a host country.[49]

Mozambique suffered greatly from the 1975–1991 civil war after the Portuguese colonialists finally left. In 1990, the under-5 mortality rate was an abysmal 249 per 1,000—but already much lower than some of the figures reported in the 1980s during major conflict. In 2008, this number had fallen to 130 per 1,000, lower than in 17 other countries—a very long way yet to go, but real progress.[50] International assistance was critical in reducing child mortality; such assistance is most effective when improvement in health is also a national priority, which it apparently was in Mozambique where a prime minister in office from 1994 to 2004 was a medical doctor who had previously served as the minister of health.[51]

When war ended in Sierra Leone in 1999, the maternal mortality rate was reportedly 1,800 per 100,000 births—one of the worst in the world. The under-5 mortality rate was 286 per 1,000 live births, which fell to a still very high 194 by 2008.[52]

Just when public health programs are most needed, funds are shifted to the military, and according to an IMF estimate, government spending on health falls at an annual rate of 8.6% during violent conflicts.[53] Family incomes are generally lower, so people are also challenged to pay for needed care.

Long-term negative consequences of conflict for child nutrition have been found in studies of Burundi and Zimbabwe. Long-term health consequences depend on the nature of the conflict. There is evidence that future deaths and health consequences are predicted less by battlefield deaths than by the scope of genocide (where victims of violence are identified by communal characteristics, usually ethnicity or religion) or political killings (where victims are people in ideological opposition to the dominant group or government) that occurred.[54]

Destruction of Wealth   Violent conflict destroys capital, and some of what is not destroyed is diverted to destructive activities. Additional wealth is often shipped abroad. One study found that on average, a tenth of a country's wealth is transferred abroad between the beginning and the end of a conflict, largely as capital flight, as better-off residents seek to protect their wealth.[55]

An IMF study found that "the total economic cost of the conflict in Sri Lanka between 1983 and 1996 amounted to about $4.2 billion, twice the country's 1996 GDP."[56] Per capita income in Nicaragua was $4,276 when civil war began—already very low. But by its end, per capita income had fallen to just $1,913. This represented "an annual decline in per capita income of about 6.5 percent—compared to the average growth rate of 2.5 percent after the civil war, the relative loss in wealth was almost 10 percent per year."[57]

In some countries, fighting is very localized. But one study found an average annual growth of −3.3% in countries in conflict as a whole (for countries with enough data to estimate it).[58] Moreover, "by the end of the typical civil war incomes are around 15 percent lower than they would otherwise have been, implying that about 30 percent more people are living in absolute poverty."[59] Not surprisingly, conflict causes increases in unemployment.[60] No wonder civil war has been called "development in reverse."[61]

Worsening Hunger and Poverty   It is not surprising that in many conflict countries, food production drops; one survey found this had happened in 13 out of 18 conflict countries studied. The International Food Policy Research Institute found that in conflict and postconflict countries, more than 20% of the population usually lacks access to adequate food (and, in some cases, the percentage is far higher). Far more people were food insecure than the numbers that had been considered in need of humanitarian assistance. In sub-Saharan Africa, food losses in the 1980s and 1990s due to conflict were equivalent to more than half of all aid received in that period. Hunger is also a weapon of war. Fighters have cut off food supplies and attempted to starve opposing populations into submission; they also steal food aid.[62]

Poverty increases through declines in opportunities to earn incomes but also through direct outcomes of fighting. Killing or driving off farm animals is a weapon of war; other animals may starve. Many affected by conflict in Mozambique and Uganda lost all or nearly all of their cattle. Other farm resources may be despoiled. When people, many of them very poor, are forced to flee their villages, their land is typically occupied, often by the forces that drove them out. In most cases, a majority never recover their houses and property. In the aftermath of conflict, affected areas may be slow to recover for reasons ranging from lack of working capital to poisoned resources and the dangers of land mines.[63] The rights of displaced widows and children, in particular, are often given no regard by the authorities. Institutions to resolve property disputes may be dysfunctional or never are established.[64] These are some of the factors extending the consequences of conflict well after the end of fighting.

Loss of Education   In eight countries in conflict for which data were available, the IMF found that during the conflict, education spending fell at a rate of −4.3% per person per year. Moreover, sometimes children cannot risk the walk to school because of the danger of violence. And both government soldiers and rebels have destroyed schools that symbolize the hopes of a village. Instead of getting an education, many children work long hours to survive. And under conditions of lawlessness and impunity, trafficking and kidnapping into sex slavery, child soldiering, and other abhorrent conditions have been documented. A study of children abducted into child soldiering in Uganda found that they lose nearly a year of schooling, on average. Combined with a greater incidence of injuries, later loss of income is substantial. But after a conflict ends, enrollment and attendance at school increases, often dramatically.[65]

A Torn Social Fabric   Violent conflict or its imminent threat creates refugees— one estimate is an additional 64 refugees per 1,000 people on average from a civil war, 45 per 1,000 from coups, and 30 per 1,000 from guerrilla warfare.[66] According to the United Nations, by the end of 2008, there were about 26 million internally displaced persons (IDPs) due to "conflict, generalized violence or human rights violations." More than half were from five countries—Sudan, Colombia, Iraq, the DRC, and Somalia. There may be more refugees in total than ever before, and another 20 million or more have had to flee their countries. In fact, the impact of civil wars is often felt over a period of many years and hundreds of miles away, well beyond border countries.[67] But the number of IDPs has fallen dramatically in some countries that were once nearly synonymous with violent conflict, such as Timor-Leste and Uganda, where refugees are returning home. Less than half of the world's IDPs are now from Africa, and the region is making progress.[68]

In Colombia and many other countries, civil war has provided an opportunity for drug gangs to carve out territory with impunity and often to form unholy alliances with either rebel or government forces. This leads to further unraveling of the social fabric, from collapse of rule of law to ruined lives of addicts.

As concluded in the 2010 Millennium Development Goals Report, "armed conflict remains a major threat to human security and to hard-won MDG gains. Large populations of refugees remain in camps with limited opportunities to improve their lives."[69]

The Causes of Armed Conflict and Risk Factors for Conflict

Both econometric analysis and case study evidence suggest that conflict is more common in countries with lower incomes, slow growth, medium to large populations, significant oil production, poor institutions, a large percentage of excluded ethnic minorities, ethnic divisions more generally, severe stress on basic resources, and opportunities to profit from high-value commodities for export.[70] As you will see, the good news is that most places that are *diverse* (ethnically or in other ways) do not have violent conflict, and places with high inequalities across *individuals* usually do not have violent conflict. So it is not just economic and not just cultural: The problem seems to be worse when there are high inequalities across groups that people identify with.

Horizontal Inequalities   Frances Stewart proposes that the presence of major "horizontal inequalities" (HIs) or inequalities among culturally defined groups significantly raises the risk of conflict.[71] She argues that "when cultural differences coincide with economic and political differences between groups, this can cause deep resentment that may lead to violent struggles."[72] In her framework, it is "a combination of cultural differences and political and economic inequalities running along cultural lines that, in part at least, explain contemporary violent conflict." She notes that group inequalities have been a significant factor in conflict among other regions and countries in Côte d'Ivoire, Rwanda, Chiapas, and Sudan. Stewart proposes that an analysis of Côte d'Ivoire (see the case study at the end of Chapter 5) "suggests that it is where there are both socio-economic and political HIs *in the same direction* that conflict is most likely. Conversely, where one group has political power and another is economically privileged (as in Malaysia and for much of the time Nigeria), or governments are broadly inclusive, conflict seems to be less likely." She concludes: "These findings have important implications for development policy. They suggest that policies to correct economic, social and political HIs should be prioritized in multi-ethnic societies—as part of general development policies—especially in post-conflict environments."[73]

Natural Resources for Basic Needs   Basic-needs resource scarcity—especially shortages of food, fertile land, and water—may contribute to conflict or ongoing risks of conflict; for example, the UN concluded that the crisis in Darfur had water and other natural resource scarcity at its root.[74] Clashes among pastoralist groups in northern Kenya are often attributed to drought and to water scarcity more generally. Colin Kahl argues that scarcity can increase the risk of violent conflict and cites quantitative studies that suggest that population size and density are significant conflict risk factors; countries that are highly dependent on natural resources, as well as those experiencing high rates of deforestation and soil degradation or low per capita availability of arable land and fresh water, have higher risks of conflict.[75] But low rainfall may matter primarily because it leads to lower growth, particularly in agricultural economies.[76] Climate change may exacerbate existing problems.[77] A 2009 study found that historically in Africa, a 1°C rise in temperature leads to a 4.5% increase in civil war in the same year; the authors concluded that projections of future temperature trends imply a 54% increase in armed conflict incidence by 2030, with "an additional 393,000 battle deaths."[78] Though only rarely, if ever, does (worsening) resource scarcity *directly* cause violent conflict, it is likely an important *compounding* factor in many cases.[79]

Struggle to Control Exportable Natural Resources   The presence of high-value exportable resources such as diamonds, oil, and hardwood, without accepted or enforceable rules for how their benefits will be distributed, also appears to be an underlying factor in violent conflict. Paul Collier argues that what he terms the conflict trap "shows how certain economic conditions make a country prone to civil war, and how, once conflict has started, the cycle of violence becomes a trap from which it is difficult to escape." He finds that countries are prone to civil war when faced with low income, slow growth, and dependence on primary commodity exports.[80]

Resources that are not usually thought of as exportable may be becoming more so. As water grows scarcer—with current problems of receding shorelines of inland bodies of water, aquifer depletion, salination, and projected future problems due to climate change—the price of water is rising, and in response, exports of water are beginning.[81] Eventually, if rights of indigenous groups to use the water they need are not secured, groups who can control water may find its export value temptingly high.

The Resolution and Prevention of Armed Conflict

Importance of Institutions   To appreciate the challenges of resolution and prevention, recall from Chapter 2 the critical importance of institutional quality and the deep difficulties of improving them.[82] Legal rules and informal norms define and reinforce the ways that interests of different groups, even when strongly opposing, can be resolved, at least to the point where development can proceed. Good institutions provide a foundation of basic security and rights, to successfully prevent or at least strongly mitigate risks of armed conflict that is likely to retard and set back progress. A good institution in this context facilitates conflict resolution, avoiding violence and doing so in a way that allows capabilities to grow. Without improvements in underlying institutions, purely political agreements come with the danger of relapse or can fail to create conditions for balanced economic development. With the perception that whatever one side gains the opposing side loses, no benefits of cooperation will be apparent to adversaries, and there is little or no framework for sharing benefits of growth. Unless democratic institutions are well designed, there is a risk that politics—even "fair" majority-rule elections—will establish a dominant winner and, in effect, disenfranchise losers.[83]

Moreover, military expenditures are possibly a cause of conflict, not merely an effect of conflict. The share of low- and middle-income country military expenditures in world spending has been rising—for example, from 14% in 1990 to 24% in 2009. The Stockholm International Peace Research Institute concluded that "the distribution of global spending in 2012 shows what may be the beginnings of a shift from the West to other parts of the world, in particular Eastern Europe and the developing world."[84]

Two important institutions (introduced in Chapter 2) are checks and balances on executive authority and contract enforcement. Without checks on authority, those in opposition who have much to gain (and much to lose) may see little alternative to violence. But in such situations, why don't the rulers "buy off" the opposition? In many instances, they do so; but when they do not, an underlying problem is the inability to credibly enforce a contract of settlement between rulers and opposition: Once the rulers (or the state, more generally) becomes sufficiently strong, it has an incentive to renege on the agreement—with possibly dire consequences for the opponents. Aware of this risk, again the only resort of the opposition may be violence, unless the rulers are somehow able to commit to carrying out the agreement; difficulties of finding a way to do so credibly is an example of what is known as the **commitment problem**; a credible solution is known as a "commitment device." These perspectives point up the importance of specialized institutions for conflict resolution and make it a priority of international assistance to help establish agreed

Commitment problem   An inability to make a "credible promise" to honor a contractual agreement due to the presence of incentives to renege; sometimes a "commitment device," such as posting a large bond, can be implemented that automatically invokes high penalties on the reneging party, thereby creating a "credible threat," allowing agreement to be reached and honored.

rules for resolving conflicts—and the subsequent enforcement of agreements—before conflict turns violent. Until such institutions take root, this helps explain how international enforcement of agreements has been effective.[85]

Global Actors   In postconflict development, engagement by global, regional, national, and community-level actors is critical. National security—again, a foundational institution—cannot be taken for granted when violence crosses borders and remnant violent and criminal forces are still active in cross-border enclaves, as the Lords Resistance Army was until recently in Uganda. Multinational organized crime has plagued other countries. The UN may potentially play a more active coordinating role. Other international organizations and agencies provide funds and capacity building.

New international rules and agreements are helping to reduce the problem of incentives for conflict by creating controls on exports and imports of high-value resources.[86] Moreover, business, government, and civil society are partnering to foster international voluntary arrangements to reduce financial incentives for war or to ensure that resources do not fund conflict. For example, some 50 members of the WTO agreed to trade only diamonds certified as free of conflict by the voluntary Kimberley Process. In addition, some 32 countries have agreed to voluntarily implement the Extractive Industries Transparency Initiative (EITI), under which firms publish what they pay governments for resource extraction, the government publishes what it earns, and a multistakeholder group and outside auditors reconcile these figures to ensure that the money from resources goes to the public that owns them.[87]

Regional Actors: An Africa-wide Approach   Postconflict reconstruction is also a problem for multination regional cooperation. The African Union has played an increasing role in addressing violent conflict and its aftermath, particularly through peacekeeping operations. Once a peace agreement is signed and a functioning transition or permanent government is in place, support for postconflict economic development becomes central. Here the African Development Bank (AfDB) plays an active role; its Fragile States Unit positions fragile states it works with along a continuum spanning two stages. In stage 1, governments have to show a commitment to consolidate peace and security and have unmet social and economic needs. In stage 2, governments must demonstrate that they are improving macroeconomic conditions and pursuing sound debt policy, have sound financial management policy, and exhibit transparency of public accounts. The AfDB has targeted nine postconflict countries for programs: Burundi, Central African Republic, Côte d'Ivoire, Comoros, DRC, Guinea Bissau, Liberia, Sierra Leone, and Togo.[88] However, the ultimate effectiveness of the AfDB's promising work remains to be fully demonstrated.

National Actors   The state must be strong enough to reliably protect its citizens from violence and to carry out other important roles that only government can play. State *fragility* is a big part of the problem. But there must also be effective checks and balances. A harsh regime that suppresses violence and rebellion but keeps resources and power in the hands of a small elite is likely to produce only a temporary solution to preventing violence; there is little reason to anticipate that such a state will promote other aspects of development. Even if state monopoly on violence suppresses overt conflict, the result may reinforce inequalities. Multilateral outside assistance may be needed to establish basic peace and security; then it is crucial to ensure broad opportunities and to make the gains from cooperation more apparent. This process will help make efforts to establish democratic institutions more likely to succeed.[89] Despite the great difficulties, there has been clear progress as the number of functioning democracies, even among very poor countries, has increased steadily, and people of many nations are adapting well to the often arbitrary boundaries across ethnic lines established by the colonial powers.

Corruption is often part of the struggle for resources, particularly exportable natural resources. Addressing corruption may help prevent conflict before it breaks out. And corruption is generally viewed as particularly destabilizing in postconflict situations. One problem is that "post-conflict environments present officials with low-risk opportunities for corrupt activity. This is further magnified because post-conflict countries often attract or justify relatively high levels of aid."[90]

Frances Stewart notes that "both political and socioeconomic inequalities are of major relevance to political outcomes: Strong political HIs mean that leaders of groups feel politically excluded and are thus more likely to lead opposition and possibly rebellion; while socioeconomic inequalities mean that the people as a whole have strong grievances on ethnic lines and are thus likely to be more readily mobilized."[91] Since the evidence suggests that it is "a combination of cultural differences and political and economic inequalities running along cultural lines that, in part at least, explain contemporary violent conflict,"[92] it becomes important to find the means for inclusive economic development, and political participation—for example, federalism or proportional representation.

Trust among former warring parties or parties at risk must be rebuilt. Conflict can be understood as a problem of multiple equilibria with failure to coordinate, which may depend on social norms about conflict and cooperation.[93] Bad equilibria may result from a set of expectations that conflict cannot or will not be peacefully resolved. If only a few citizens are lawless, they are much easier to control than in an environment of general lawlessness. We can use Figure 4.1 in Chapter 4 to illuminate the problem. If most actors expect high conflict, their best response may be to prepare for conflict or even strike preemptively. But if no conflict is expected, it may make much more sense to follow nonviolent strategies for livelihoods and investments. In this situation, an important focus must be on changing expectations toward low likelihoods of future conflict and that violators will be severely punished. Again, building institutions that solve commitment problems between opponents can help.

Focus on Education UNESCO's Education for All (EFA) points up the mutually reinforcing relationship between low education and violent conflict. The fact that conflict harms education—by destroying infrastructure, injuring or killing students and teachers, and so on—is obvious. EFA notes that education also affects conflict, as conflict may originate in an ideology that may be widely disseminated through education. The EFA framework thus calls for "conflict-sensitive" education and policy initiatives, termed "reconstruction education." Broadly applicable lessons are stressed; for example, learning how to deal with educating displaced families in conflict areas is not region-specific, and lessons learned, say, from the Swat Valley of Pakistan may help in the DRC, even though the conflicts themselves are very different. EFA argues that education can contribute to peace, stability, and nation building.[94]

Local, "Community-Driven" Economic Development   Economic participation at the local level is very important, and some research has found that community-driven development (CDD) can play an important role. Patrick Barron notes that "effective CDD projects can distribute resources quickly and to remote, rural areas. In devolving decision-making they can help ensure [that] resource distribution is fair and popularly accepted." He also argues that such programs can provide incentives for "collective action that can work across conflict divides." Finally, "CDD tries to prevent the erosion of the social and institutional bases necessary for the management of development in non-violent ways."[95]

For example, evaluations of the KALAHI Comprehensive and Integrated Delivery of Social Services project in the Philippines found positive economic impacts; it operates "in some conflict-affected and post-conflict areas, but also in others where violence is not a significant problem."[96]

James Manor also examined local CDD programs in postconflict environments and concluded: "Almost all of the successful programs that we studied entailed consultative mechanisms to draw local preferences, knowledge, and energies into the policy process and to provide external resources to local communities. These mechanisms worked especially well when they were coupled with efforts at democratic decentralization."[97]

The study of community development and other strategies for conflict prevention and postconflict recovery is still at an early stage, but new results are now being reported regularly. An assessment by Ghazala Mansuri and Vijayendra Rao also concluded that CDD is more effective when implemented in a "context-specific manner, with a long time-horizon, and with careful and well designed monitoring and evaluation systems." Some programs have been "captured" by elites for their own purposes, so close monitoring is essential. It is difficult to reach general conclusions because of self-selection: Projects that are internally initiated by participants and funded later could have greater impacts; but people organize when their conditions lead them to anticipate a higher chance of success. Yet a program instigated by researchers may be perceived as propped up by temporary outside engagement, leading elites to stall or resist change; even so, a recent experimental study in Sierra Leone found CDD led to more market activity and to improvements in local public goods such as functioning primary schools and community grain-drying floors, though not in women's decision-making influence or the raising of local revenue for community purposes. This is an important and growing field in economic development.[98]

The emphasis on fragile and conflict states in development assistance has never been stronger. Addressing state fragility is expected to be a centerpiece of the new Sustainable Development Goals.

Costa Rica, Guatemala, and Honduras: Contrasts and Prospects for Convergence

A comparison of three countries, Costa Rica (CRI), Guatemala (GTM), and Honduras (HND), sheds light on major themes of this chapter—foreign finance, investment, remittances, aid, and conflict—as well as key themes explored throughout this text, including roles of institutions, education, health, poverty, and inequality.

All are former Spanish colonies in Central America, and they share common geographic features such as tropical lowlands with cooler mountain highlands and fertile and populous valleys. The countries are certainly not identical triplets…still, in global, perspective they are reasonably comparable in some other respects; populations range from 5 to 15 million; areas range from 51 to 112 square kilometers; and population densities between 70 to 137 persons per square kilometer.

Yet a wide gulf remains between them in economic development. CRI has enjoyed much better development performance than the other countries in recent decades, despite the fact that CRI was historically poorer. This case study will examine the divergence in context both of their recent development policies and in their long historical roots that explain much about how those diverging polices were shaped. All-around better performance in CRI reflects how differences in earlier institutions can have effects on economic development outcomes. The contrasting experiences again reveal influences of structural inequality and education levels on evolution of institutions over time. We will see that the countries exhibit stark differences in preventing and managing conflict; the comparisons yield insights into causes of conflict and its prevention. We will see that the performance of CRI has been better than either HND or GTM, for similar but certainly not identical reasons. Conflict has played some role in HDN but not a predominant role, as in GTM. In CRI, in recent years, foreign direct investment (FDI) has worked for development because it has been complementary, with sound domestic policies and investments in human capital. The history of FDI has been far more fraught in HND and GTM. Marked reduction of violent conflict in GTM has strongly improved prospects for development there. Recently, remittances have played a large and helpful role, particularly in HDN, and to an important extent, in GTM. Foreign aid has helped HND and GTM start to close the gap on education and health. A comparison of indicators for the three neighboring countries is striking, as seen in the table.

Income and Human Development: Basic comparisons

The data reveal sharp differences between Costa Rica, Honduras, and Guatemala in income and human development levels. GNI per capita in CRI is more than triple that of HND and more than two and a half times that of GTM. These differences reflect CRI's much higher economic growth rate over the last 60 years. Life expectancy in CRI is 6 years greater than in HND and 8 years greater than in GTM. Under-5 mortality in CRI is less than half that of HND and less than a third that of GTM. CRI has about two more years of schooling than HND and four more than GTM. Accordingly, while CRI is a high-HDI country (ranked No. 62), HND is medium-HDI (at No. 120); GTM at No. 133 is also medium-HDI, but it is not far above low-HDI status (for details on the HDI, see Chapter 2). The differences in income and human development are mirrored in the

Key Indicators for CRI, HND and GTM

Indicator	CRI	HND	GTM
Population (Millions) (WDI)	5	8	15
Area (Thousand Square Kilometers) (WDI)	51	112	109
Population Density (Per Square Kilometer) (WDI)	93	70	137
2012 GNI Per Capita—2005 PPP U.S. Dollars (203 HDR)	10,863	3,426	4,235
Life Expectancy (2013 HDR)	79.4	73.4	71.4
Under-5 Mortality (WDI, 2012 Data)	10	23	32
Primary Pupil-to-Teacher Ratio, 2009 (Most Recent Comparable WDI)	18	34	28
Mean Years of Schooling (2013 HDR)	8.4	6.5	4.1
New HDI, 2012 Data	0.773 (No. 62)	0.632 (No. 120)	0.581 (No. 133)
Poverty (Percent below $1.25, WDI)	2.4	21.4	24.4
Inequality (Gini Coefficient, WDI)	51	57	56
Transparency International Corruption Index (2013)	53 (ranked 49th)	26 (ranked 140th)	29 (ranked 123rd)
2012 Economist Democracy Index	8.1	5.84	5.88
2013 Index of Economic Freedom (WSJ)	49	96	85
Language Fractionalization (Alesina)	0.0489	0.0553	0.4586
Ethnic Fractionalization (Alesina)	0.2386	0.1867	0.5122
Stock of FDI, U.S. Dollars (Millions), 2012 (UNCTAD)	18,713	9,024	8,914
Remittances as Percent of GDP, 2012 (World Bank)	1.2	15.7	10

poverty statistics: HND has about *9 times* the incidence of below-$1.25 per day poverty, and GTM has *10 times the poverty incidence* of CRI. There are large differences in births per woman, with particularly high fertility in GTM, where 41% of the population is under age 15—the youngest population in Latin America. Under-5 malnourishment is also particularly severe in Guatemala. Interestingly, CRI has been ranked as the world's happiest country.

Inequality

Inequality is hardly low in CRI, with a Gini of 51 (similar to the US and China), but it is lower than HND's 57 and GTM's 56. Perhaps more importantly, in Guatemala, inequality is sharply along ethnic lines—"horizontal inequalities" that are in many countries associated with strife. Land inequality is also lower in CRI, while in Guatemala and to a significant extent also in Honduras, a *latifundio-minifundio* pattern has persisted, of large estates alongside farms too small to adequately support a family (see Chapter 9). Inequality in human development is also stark. Gender inequality is a smaller problem in CRI than the other countries as measured, for example, with the Gender Inequality Index (GII). Indigenous people in Guatemala have much lower HDI levels, which are close to some low-income countries in Africa; in comparison, the HDI of the Ladino population in GTM is similar to that of Indonesia

(see Chapter 2, Appendix 2.1). The indigenous (Amerindian) population is much smaller in HND (7%) and CRI (about 1%).

Institutions

Comparing the quality of institutions, it is clear that Costa Rica again strongly outperforms Honduras and Guatemala. For example, on the 2013 Transparency International Corruption Perceptions Index, CRI has a level of 53 (ranked 49th); HND's value is only 26 (ranked 140th); and GTM is at 29 (ranked 123rd). On the 2012 Economist Democracy Index, CRI has a value of 8.10, far higher than that of HND (5.84) or GTM (5.88). HND has suffered coups—as recently as 2009, a government was abruptly deposed, widely characterized as a coup—and the political process in GTM remains badly flawed. Finally, on the 2013 Index of Economic Freedom, CRI ranks 49, while HND is much lower at 96; GTM ranks 85.

Economic Growth and Structure

GDP per capita more than quadrupled in CRI between 1950 and 2008; it less than doubled in GTM and is just 1.75 times higher in HND.

The three countries produce similar agricultural products like coffee and bananas, reflecting their similar climates. But partly as a result of active industrial policies, CRI has significantly diversified, including into new high-tech industries. No similar diversification is seen in the other countries. CRI also has much better roads and other infrastructure than the other countries. CRI has attracted more than twice the stock of Foreign Direct Investment (FDI) than the other economies, despite its smaller population. This has followed from CRI's better education, infrastructure, environment, and ongoing economic growth performance. In turn, (FDI) has gone into sectors with good potential for stimulating growth. Probably the key foreign investments were those made by Intel beginning in 1997.

In 2012, HND received almost 16% of its GNI in the form of remittances; for GTM the share was 10%, but for CRI it was little over 1%. Remittances can be very beneficial, particularly to the extent that income is sent back to poorer rural villages. The flip side is that lack of opportunities in HND is leading people to emigrate; people in CRI have much better opportunities at home.

Health and Nutrition Policies

Government policies are more conducive to human development and economic growth in CRI. For example, CRI has a much higher proportion of expenditures on both health and education. In fact, in CRI, an emphasis on ensuring primary education and basic health was already apparent in the early 1930s, far earlier than most developing countries. Today, CRI is one of the few developing countries to approach universal healthcare coverage. Poor early childhood nutrition in the region leads to significantly lower adult productivity, incomes, and other favorable outcomes—and vice-versa (underscored by a randomization-based study in GTM by John Maluccio and others). In contrast, nutrition conditions are good for most, though not all, people in CRI.

Education Policies

In 1886, CRI implemented a law mandating universal primary education for both boys and girls, and grew from there. Particularly coupled with good public health measures, these policies are reinforcing, helping to break the intergenerational transmission of poverty (see Chapter 8). Accordingly, International Labor Organization (ILO) data show that child labor is a far more serious problem in HND than in CRI. Much later, with its strong historical foundations, in the mid-1990s, CRI mandated computer science and English courses for students as a conscious strategy to prepare for successful engagement with the rapidly opening and evolving global economy. The primary student-teacher ratio in CRI in 2009 was an impressive 18; but it was 28 in Guatemala and 34 in Honduras. CRI has proceeded to build a university system that is not only of better quality but also more equitable in its higher admissions of poorer and minority students.

Building on the Foundation of Education

Moreover, human capital policies in CRI facilitated the recent policy push for diversification and higher tech industries, including the capacity to attract particularly development-enhancing forms of foreign direct investment. Education also served as a foundation for CRI's vaunted environmental protection and flourishing ecotourism sector, giving a further boost to economic development. Tourism now generates more income than agriculture in CRI, in sharp contrast to Honduras. Women in

CRI have much more equal access to health, education, and employment opportunities than in GTM and HND—another human development achievement, which should also benefit economic growth. In further contrast with CRI, Honduras and Guatemala spend proportionately less on human capital, while spending substantially on the military.

Conflict

Guatemala has had very high levels of often violent conflict and genocidal campaigns; Honduras has a lower but still serious history of conflict or military domination, and CRI has had comparatively little conflict, particularly over the last 65 years. One factor associated with conflict is fractionalization (section 14.5). The language fractionalization index in CRI is 0.0489, but in GTM it is 0.4586; and the ethnic fractionalization index in CRI is 0.24; but in GTM it is 0.51. But fractionalization is similarly low in HND as in CRI. Conflict has had a major negative effect on Guatemala, and some effect on Honduras. The conflict in Guatemala is predicted by repressive and extractive institutions, and high inequality, particularly of the "horizontal" kind in which the rich and poor come from different ethnicities or other identity groups. In addition, according to the U.N. Office of Drugs and Crime, the homicide rate in HDR is currently the highest in the world at 91.6 per 100,000, and a very high 38.5 in GTM, but 10.0 in CRI (by comparison, it is 4.7 in the United States and 1.5 Canada).

To understand these differences, it is important to go beyond a comparison of recent policies and conditions, to see what constraints and influences have led to the chosen implemented policies. For this, we take a longer historical view, from the time of colonization to the present, as we did for the case studies for Chapters 2, 5, and 10.

Regional History—The Long View

For centuries, the area now including the three countries was part of the Mesoamerican Mayan culture, which was strongest and most urbanized in what is now Guatemala. The Spanish conquistadors took control of the region beginning in the 1520s, establishing a Captaincy General of Guatemala in 1540. Their rule was highly extractive, focusing exploitation on densely populated areas with a large labor force to control. This plausibly led to the worst outcome for

Guatemala, which previously had a high civilization, and secondarily for Honduras. In contrast, Costa Rica was relatively ignored (and thus less exploited), as it had fewer people and a less organized society from which to capture rents from a tribute system. (For details on analysis of long-run causes of comparative development, including the long-lasting influence of the nature of colonial institutions, see Chapter 2, section 2.7). Spanish rule lasted nearly three centuries until the region became independent of Spain in about 1821. The three countries became part of a Federal Republic of Central America until the 1838–1840 civil wars led to their independence.

Costa Rica: Roots of Education and Democracy

Despite its name, meaning "rich coast," and its contemporary nickname of "the Switzerland of Latin America," for much of its history, Costa Rica was the poorest of the three countries. It was the most distant from colonial headquarters in Guatemala; and the Spanish did not allow trade with territories to its south (Panama was part of a different Spanish colony). CRI had a relatively small indigenous population, and thus there were no incentives for the Spanish elite to settle there to establish plantations (haciendas) operated by forced indigenous labor (*economienda* system). Natural resources appeared limited, and transportation that was needed to reach the interior was lacking. Thus, the region was farmed by small-scale, relatively poor, yeoman farmers. But in the long run, being ignored turned out to have some significant advantages. The country had much less strife than several of its neighbors, although there was a period of political violence in 1948. After the upheaval, the CRI military was abolished outright in 1949; the country was kept safe by the police force. This prevented a major drain of resources that otherwise would go to the military; it also preempted repressive military practices suffered by many countries in the region. Since then, CRI has been the longest continuous democracy in Latin America, with highly competitive elections that have addressed substantive policy matters. A caveat is that two former presidents were sent to prison for corruption in 2004.

Guatemala: Roots of Conflict

The Spanish Captaincy exploited the large indigenous population; after independence, exploitation

continued under plantation owners. In the twentieth century, the country suffered from adventurism of corporations, particularly the United Fruit Company (later renamed Chiquita Brands). United Fruit gained control of the banana market and leveraged this to political power—the origin of the derogatory phrase "banana republics" (also applied to Honduras). United Fruit was backed by the United States, which supported repressive dictatorships—an example of neocolonial policies, modeled by the Dependency School (see Chapter 3, section 3.4). Most notoriously, in 1954 a CIA-sponsored coup overthrew a freely elected government. After several years of repression, civil war broke out around 1960, which was to continue until about 1996. The war often seemed a one-sided attack of the U.S.-supported government against indigenous Mayan people who became affiliated with various left opposition groups. The military campaigns were abetted by death squads operating against indigenous people who were suspected of sympathies with the opposition. Tens of thousands of indigenous people "disappeared." More than 200,000 people are thought to have been killed in the 34+-year war; and more than 1 million were displaced. The 1994 Oslo Accords created the national Historical Clarification Commission, which confirmed the essential one-sidedness of the war in that the government (and its affiliates) was responsible for 93% of the violence and human rights violations, with 3% attributed to the leftist guerillas. This included a state-sponsored genocidal campaign against Mayan peoples in the early 1980s. President Clinton responded with a formal statement that U.S. support for Guatemala security forces "was wrong." Since then, the country has steadily moved toward greater economic and political reform. In 2013, Rios Montt, president during the genocide period, was found guilty and sentenced to 80 years in prison, but his conviction was overturned.

Honduras: Roots of Policy

The Spanish were attracted to Honduras by a key resource: silver mines. They operated the mines with forced (*economienda*) indigenous labor, until many died of disease and overwork; others resisted and fled to areas outside Spanish control. The Spanish responded in part by importing African slaves. (The history was not unlike what occurred

in Hispaniola; see the end-of-chapter case study for Chapter 10.) In the century after independence in 1840, the country had political instability and high inequality, and power continued to be concentrated among the large landowners. Later, there was growing domination by foreign corporations, which began operating the country as a "banana republic." In the 1980s, the country became embroiled in the Contra war in neighboring Nicaragua; and the military operated a campaign of violent repression against both the nonviolent and the violent left opposition. The country's institutional weaknesses made it vulnerable to the growth of drug-trafficking gangs, a majority factor in HND's world's highest homicide rate. The lack of institutional resilience was also visible in its relatively poor response to natural disasters, including Hurricane Mitch in 1998 and extensive flooding in 2008. In 2009, there was a coup (at least, in all but name). For many years, growth in HDN was bogged down by debt, but it has benefited from debt relief under the HIPC program, and subsequently has grown rapidly, though much of the benefit has accrued to higher-income families.

Writing a New Chapter: Central American Integration and Convergence

As seen throughout the text, great improvements in human capital and reductions in poverty have been found nearly everywhere in the world, and this applies even to GTM and HND. Both have grown somewhat, and health and education standards have improved significantly. The big differences in performance across countries generally reflect the speed of improvements, as great differences in human suffering along the way. Improved policies can make a substantive difference, if they can be implemented. Moreover, by exposing the deep roots of comparative development, new approaches can be forged. A deeper understanding of why it can be so difficult to make progress on basic, critical policies such as promoting education can provide new political impetus for achieving these goals. In turn, once they are educated, people at least have a better chance to participate effectively in the political process, by which institutional reforms are facilitated or thwarted. Outside pressures can greatly worsen conditions, as evidenced by the conclusions concerning the subversive U.S. role in Guatemala

(as well as Honduras); but outside development assistance can be beneficial, as seen recently in these countries.

Currently, efforts are actively under way to strengthen economic and political integration among these and the other Central American countries. To the extent this is successful, it is likely to accelerate convergence and should help to cement human rights and development gains. This process will be watched closely in coming years. ∎

Sources

Babington, Charles. "Clinton: Support for Guatemala was wrong." *Washington Post*, March 11, 1999, p. A1.

Bashir, Sajitha, and Javie Luque. "Equity in tertiary education in Central America." World Bank Policy Research Paper No. 6180, August 2012, accessed at wps6180.pdf. Washington D.C.: World Bank,.

Blattman, Christopher, and Edward Miguel. "Civil war." *Journal* of *Economic Literature* 48, 1 (2010): 3–57.

Casas-Zamora, Kevin. *Guatemala: Between a Rock and a Hard Place*. Washington, D.C.: Brookings Institution, 2011.

Edwards, John. *Education and Poverty in Guatemala*. Washington, D.C.: World Bank, 2002.

Fearon, James D. "Governance and civil war onset." World Development Report 2011 Background Paper, August 2010. http://siteresources.worldbank.org.

Ferreria, Gustavo F. C., and R. W. Harrison. "From coffee beans to microchips: Export diversification and economic growth in Costa Rica." *Journal of Agricultural and Applied Economics* 44, 4 (2012): 517–531.

Guatemala Historical Clarification Commission. *Memory of Silence*. Guatemala: Guatemala Historical Clarification Commission, 1999.

Intel. "Intel in Costa Rica." http://www.intel.com/content/www/us/en/corporate-responsibility/intel-in-costa-rica.html.

Lehoucq, Fabrice. *Policymaking, Parties and Institutions in Democratic Costa Rica*. Washington, D.C.: Inter-American Development Bank, 2006.

http://www.iadb.org/res/publications/pubfiles/pubs-306.pdf.

Maddison Project Database. 2008 data, most recent available for all three countries.

Maluccio, John A., et al. "The impact of an experimental nutritional intervention in childhood on education among Guatemalan adults." FCND Discussion Papers 207. Washington, D.C.: International Food Policy Research Institute, 2006.

Rodriguez-Clare, Andres. "Costa Rica's development strategy based on human capital and technology, how it got there, the impact of Intel, and lessons for other countries." *Journal of Human Development* 2, 2 (2001): 331–323.

Seitz, Klaus. *Education and Conflict: The Role of Education in the Creation, Prevention, and Resolution of Societal Crises—Consequences for Development Cooperation*. Berlin: GIZ, 2004.

Stewart, Frances. *Horizontal Inequalities and Conflict: Understanding Group Violence in Multiethnic Societies*. New York: Palgrave Macmillan, 2008.

Stewart, Frances, C. Huang, and M. Wang. "Internal wars in developing countries: An empirical overview of economic and social consequences," in *War and Underdevelopment*, ed. F. Stewart et al. Oxford: Oxford University Press, 2001.

United Nations Development Programme. *Guatemala: Assessment of Development Results, 2009*. New York: United Nations, 2009.

Villiers Negroponte, Dana, Alma Caballero, and Consuelo Amat. *Conversations with Experts on the Future of Central America*. Washington, D.C.: Brookings Institution, 2012. http://www.brookings.edu/research/reports/2012/11/19-central-america-negroponte.

World Bank. *Poverty in Guatemala: A World Bank Country Study*. Accessed at http://elibrary.worldbank.org/doi/book/10.1596/0-8213-5552-X. October 2003

------. *The Impact of Intel in Costa Rica*, 2006. Accessed at https://www.wbginvestmentclimate.org/uploads/The%20Impact%20of%20Intel%20in%20Costa%20Rica.pdf.

------. *World Development Report 2011: Conflict, Security and Development*. Washington, D.C.: World Bank, 2011.

Concepts for Review

Absorptive capacity	Foreign-exchange gap	Portfolio investment
Commitment problem	Global factories	Savings gap
Concessional terms	Multinational corporation	Technical assistance
Corporate social responsibility	(MNC)	Tied aid
Fiscal gap	Nongovernmental organizations	Transfer pricing
Foreign aid	(NGOs)	Two-gap model
Foreign direct investment (FDI)	Official development assistance	
	(ODA)	

Questions for Discussion

1. The emergence of giant multinational corporations is said to have altered the very nature of international economic activity. In what ways do these MNCs affect the structure and pattern of trading relationships between the developed world and the developing world?

2. Summarize the arguments for and against the role and impact of private foreign investment in less developed countries. What strategies might developing countries adopt to make private foreign investment fit their development aspirations better without destroying all incentives for foreign investors?

3. What are private portfolio flows? What factors do you believe are most important in determining the amount and direction of such flows?

4. To what extent do private portfolio investments in developing countries benefit the recipient countries? What are the potential costs and risks to both investors and recipients? Explain your answer.

5. How important is foreign aid for low- and middle-income developing economies in relation to their other sources of foreign-exchange receipts? Explain the various forms that official development assistance can take, and distinguish between bilateral and multilateral assistance. Which do you think is more desirable, and why?

6. What is meant by tied aid? Most nations have increasingly shifted from grants to loans and from untied to tied loans and grants. What are the major disadvantages of tied aid, especially when this aid comes in the form of interest-bearing loans?

7. Under what conditions and terms do you think developing countries should seek and accept foreign aid in the future? If aid cannot be obtained on such terms, do you think developing countries should accept whatever they can get? Explain your answer.

8. What are the differences between official development assistance (public foreign aid) and private development assistance from nongovernmental organizations (NGOs)? Which type of aid is more desirable from the perspective of recipient countries? Explain your answer.

9. How do you think the current orientation of military and diplomatic policy in potential donor nations toward combating international terrorism is likely to affect the pattern of development assistance?

10. What do you think would persuade the public to get over its "donor fatigue" and support more aid for the least developed countries?

11. Why do you think conflicts within developing countries increased so much from the 1950s to the 1990s? Why do you think they then began to decrease?

12. What can be learned from the historical experiences of Costa Rica and Guatemala about internal conflicts, and about both positive and negative foreign influences?

Notes

1. This widely cited label, a symbol of the global factory, is attributed to former McDonnell Douglas chairman John F. McDonnell; Shari Caudron, "The power of global markets," 1999, http://www.businessfinancemag.com/article/power-global-markets-0401.

2. These figures are drawn from UNCTAD, *World Investment Report*, 2013, October 2, 2013, http://unctad.org/en/PublicationsLibrary/wir2013_en.pdf.

3. Data from various recent editions of United Nations Conference on Trade and Development (UNCTAD), *World Investment Report* (New York: United Nations, 2006–2013).

4. Ibid., 2004 and 2006. United Nations Council on Trade and Development (UNCTAD), *World Investment Report*, (New York: United Nations, 2009). The ratio has fluctuated but has generally remained under 12%.

5. A list of the 100 largest MNCs and much additional data can be found at http://www.unctad.org. Note that, in making comparisons, sales figures include intermediate inputs, while GNI does not. The point is that the huge scale of MNCs gives them great bargaining power.

6. UNCTAD, http://www.unctad.org.

7. An excellent summary of the various issues, pro and con, surrounding MNCs can be found in Thomas Biersteker, *Distortion or Development: Contending Perspectives on the Multinational Corporation* (Cambridge, Mass.: MIT Press, 1978), chs. 1–3; Theodore H. Moran, "Multinational corporations and the developing countries: An analytical overview," in *Multinational Corporations*, ed. Theodore H. Moran (Lexington, Mass.: Heath, 1985), pp. 3–24; Mark Cassen and Robert D. Pearce, "Multinational enterprises in LDCs," in *Surveys in Development Economics*, ed. Norman Gemmell (Oxford: Blackwell, 1987), pp. 90–132; and David C. Korten, *When Corporations Rule the World*, 2nd ed. (San Francisco: Berrett-Kohler, 2001).

8. Recall from Appendix 3.3 the critical role that human capital plays in endogenous growth theories and the importance of concepts such as Romer's idea gap (Chapter 2) and the O-ring theory (Chapter 4) in explaining differential growth performance between developed and less developed countries.

9. William Greider, *One World, Ready or Not: The Manic Logic of Global Capitalism* (New York: Simon & Schuster, 1997), p. 95.

10. Maxwell J. Fry, "Foreign direct investment, financing and growth," in *Investment and Financing in Developing Countries,* ed. Bernhard Fischer (Baden-Baden, Germany: Nomos, 1994), and *Foreign Direct Investment in Southeast Asia: Differential Impacts* (Singapore: Institute of Southeast Asian Studies, 1993).

11. For a discussion of the bargaining power of developing countries with MNCs, see Jan Svejnar and Stephen C. Smith, "The economics of joint ventures in less developed countries," *Quarterly Journal of Economics* 99 (1984): 149–167.

12. Consider a simple model. Suppose ϕ is the fraction of individuals who are willing to pay a higher price for consuming socially responsible products (such as acceptably sourced bananas) and x is output, which for simplicity we can take as fixed; consumers purchase x bananas inelastically (in general, demand should not be too elastic in price). Ordinary bananas have a price of 1. For simplicity, suppose that $(1 + \phi)$ is the price of socially responsible bananas—note that this is just a way of representing the idea that willingness to pay more depends on what others are doing (perhaps due to social pressure), not intended to be taken literally. Now suppose that running a credible social responsibility program imposes a cost C. Then, with these assumptions, it can be an equilibrium either that all bananas sold are responsibly sourced or that none of them are. The case of all responsible banana sales would hold when $\phi = 1$, that is, $(1 + 1)x - C > x$, which is satisfied whenever $x > C$. It is also an equilibrium to have no socially responsible products sold, that is $\phi = 0$, provided that $(1 + 0)x - C < x$, or, $C > 0$; this condition is always satisfied as long as there are costs of running the program. (It is easy to verify that there is also an intermediate unstable equilibrium where $\phi = C/y$.) This analysis is inspired by a Hoff

and Stiglitz model of industrial quality upgrading (Note 1, page 196), and discussions with James Foster about his provenance and value research.

13. See Dani Rodrik, *The New Global Economy and Developing Countries: Making Openness Work* (Baltimore: Johns Hopkins University Press, 1999).

14. See Garrick Blalock and Paul Gertler, "Welfare gains from foreign direct investment through technology transfer to local suppliers," *Journal of International Economics* 74 (2008): 402–421; Beata Smarzynska Javorcik, "Does foreign direct investment increase the productivity of domestic firms? In search of spillovers through backward linkages." *American Economic Review* 94 (2004): 605–627; Garrick Blalock, "Technology from foreign direct investment: Strategic transfer through supply chains," Hass School of Business, University of California, Berkeley, 2001; Garrick Blalock and Paul Gertler, "Learning from exporting revisited in a less developed setting," *Journal of Development Economics* 75 (2004): 397–416; and Paolo Epifani, *Trade Liberalization, Firm Performance, and Labor Market Outcomes in the Developing World: What Can We Learn from Micro-Level Data?* (Washington, D.C.: World Bank, 2003). An example of finding few, if any, spillovers is Brian J. Aitken and Ann E. Harrison, "Do domestic firms benefit from direct foreign investment? Evidence from Venezuela," *American Economic Review* 89 (1999): 605–618.

15. For a quantitative and analytical review of portfolio flows to developing countries, see Stijn Claessens, "The emergence of equity investment in developing countries: An overview," *World Bank Economic Review* 9 (1995): 1–17; Robert Feldman and Manmohan Kumar, "Emerging equity markets: Growth, benefits and policy concerns," *World Bank Research Observer* 10 (1995): 181–200; and World Bank, *Global Development Finance, 1998* (Washington, D.C.: World Bank, 1998), ch. 1. More recent data on these flows may be found in World Bank, *World Development Indicators, 2010* (Washington, D.C.: World Bank, 2010), tab. 6–12.

16. These debates from a domestic standpoint are examined in detail in Chapter 15, section 15.4. See for example, Claessens, "Emergence of equity investment," 11–14.

17. See, for example, Stijn Claessens, Michael Dooley, and Andrew Warner, "Portfolio flows: Hot or cold?" *World Bank Economic Review* 9 (1995): 153–174, and Mark P. Taylor and Lucio Sarno, "Capital flows to developing countries: Long- and short-term determinants," *World Bank Economic Review* 11 (1997): 451–470.

18. For a provocative account of how free-market policies and private investment flows in the early 1990s constituted a "speculative bubble," see Paul Krugman, "Dutch tulips and emerging markets," *Foreign Affairs* 74 (1995): 28–44.

19. See Walden Bellow, "The end of the Asian miracle," *Nation*, January 12, 1998, pp. 16–21; World Bank, *Global Development Finance, 1998* (Washington, D.C.: World Bank, 1998), ch. 2; and International Monetary Fund, *World Economic Outlook, May 1998* (Washington, D.C.: 1998), ch. 2.

20. World Bank, *Private Capital Flows to Developing Countries: The Road to Financial Integration* (Washington, D.C.: World Bank, 1997). For evidence that savings follows rather than leads growth more generally, see Ira S. Saltz, "An examination of the causal relationship between savings and growth in the Third World," *Journal of Economics and Finance* 23 (1999): 90–98.

21. The information in this section is largely based on World Bank, *Global Economic Prospects, 2006: Economic Implications of Remittances and Migration* (Washington, D.C.: World Bank, 2006), chs. 3–5, and *World Development Indicators, 2010*, pp. 354–357, where the most recent estimates of numbers of migrants are still based on 2005 data.

22. Jagdish N. Bhagwati, "Amount and sharing of aid," in *Assisting Developing Countries: Problems of Debt, Burden-Sharing, Jobs, and Trade*, ed. Charles J. Frank Jr. et al. (New York: Praeger, 1972), pp. 72–73.

23. Ibid., p. 73.

24. Data are from the OECD Development Assistance Committee, which includes high-income countries of western Europe, North America, Australia, New Zealand, and Japan. The averages do not cover any donations from other OECD nations such as Korea, Turkey, and Mexico from other non-OECD high-income countries; these nations often have smaller ODA percentages. See also J. Mohan Rao, "Ranking foreign donors: An index combining scale and equity of aid givers," *World Development* 25 (1997): 947–961, and World Bank, *World*

Development Indicators 2004 and *2010*, pp. 402–403. Discussion also draws on the Gates Foundation 2010 Annual Letter. Note that we report figures in GNI, which reflects income and so gives a clearer picture of generosity; some other reports indicate shares of GDP, and those figures will differ.

25. Data from World Bank, *World Development Indicators, 2010.*

26. Aid figures are derived from World Bank, *World Development Indicators, 2007* and *2010,* tabs. 1.1 and 6.16.

27. See Hollis B. Chenery and Alan M. Strout, "Foreign assistance and economic development," *American Economic Review* 56 (1966): 680–733.

28. For seminal contributions, see Edmar L. Bacha, "A three-gap model of foreign transfers and the GDP growth rate in developing countries," *Journal of Development Economics* 32 (1990): 279–296; and Lance Taylor, "Gap models," *Journal of Development Economics* 45 (1994): 17–34.

29. See William Easterly, "The ghost of financing gap: Testing the growth model used in the international financial institutions," *Journal of Development Economics* 60 (1999): 423–438.

30. See Jeffrey Sachs, *The End of Poverty: Economic Possibilities for Our Time* (New York: Penguin, 2005), p. 274.

31. For early analyses, see William S. Gaud, "Foreign aid: What it is, how it works, why we provide it," *Department of State Bulletin* 59 (1968), and Hollis B. Chenery, "Objectives and criteria of foreign assistance," in *The U.S. and the Developing Economies,* ed. Gustav Ranis (New York: Norton, 1964), p. 88.

32. For more details, see Jennifer Brinkerhoff, Stephen C. Smith, and Hildy Teegen, *NGOs and the Millennium Development Goals: Citizen Action to Reduce Poverty* (New York: Palgrave Macmillan, 2007). Net grants by NGOs are reported in World Bank, *World Development Indicators, 2010,* tab. 6.9.

33. World Bank, *World Development Indicators, 2010,* tab. 6.9.

34. For an examination of many significant NGO programs, both international and developing-country based, see Stephen C. Smith, *Ending Global Poverty: A Guide to What Works* (New York: Palgrave Macmillan, 2005).

35. For reviews of the aid experience and the economic effects on recipient nations, see William Easterly, *The White Man's Burden;* William Easterly, *The Elusive Quest for Growth: Economists' Adventures and Misadventures in the Tropics* (Cambridge, Mass.: MIT Press, 2001); Robert H. Cassen et al., *Does Aid Work?* (New York: Oxford University Press, 1986); Roger C. Riddell, "The contribution of foreign aid to development and the role of the private sector," *Development* 1 (1992): 7–15; and Tony Killick, *The Developmental Effectiveness of Aid to Africa* (Washington, D.C.: World Bank, 1991). For a specific review of the impact of aid on agricultural productivity, see George W. Norton, Jaime Ortiz, and Philip G. Pardey, "The impact of foreign assistance on agricultural growth," *Economic Development and Cultural Change* 40 (1992): 775–786.

36. See, for example, Channing Arndt, Sam Jones, and Finn Tarp, "Aid, growth, and development: Have we come full circle?" *Journal of Globalization and Development* 1, No. 2 (2010): 1–29. For a classic article on this subject, see Hollis B. Chenery and Nicholas G. Carter, "Foreign assistance and development performance," *American Economic Review* 63 (1973): 459–468.

37. For an early example, see Keith Griffin and John L. Enos, "Foreign assistance: Objectives and consequences," *Economic Development and Cultural Change* 18 (1970): 313–327.

38. See, for example, Peter T. Bauer and Basil Yamey, "Foreign aid: What is at stake?" *Public Interest* (Summer 1982): 57–70, and "Foreign aid: Rewarding impoverishment?" *Commentary* (September 1985): 38–40. See also Easterly, "Ghost of financing gap."

39. Organization for Economic Cooperation and Development, "Paris declaration on aid effectiveness," March 2005, http://www.oecd.org /dataoecd/11/41/34428351.pdf.

40. For basic methods, see Esther Duflo, Rachel Glennerster, and Michael Kremer, "Using randomization in development economics research: A toolkit," December 2006, Center for Economic Policy Research Paper No. 6059, http://econ-www .mit.edu/files/806.

41. The best method for studying a program impact evaluation generally depends on the questions

being asked and the most feasible and effective ways of finding the answers. That is, the questions should determine the method, rather than starting with a preferred method and asking only questions that can be answered using that method.

42. Examples are Abhijit Banerjee, Shawn Cole, Esther Duflo, and Leigh Linden, "Remedying education: Evidence from two randomized experiments in India," discussed in Box 5.4; Michael Kremer and Edward Miguel, "Worms: Identifying impacts on education and health in the presence of treatment externalities," discussed in Box 8.4; Dean Karlan and Martin Valdivia, "Teaching entrepeneurship," discussed in Box 15.2; and Stephen C. Smith, "Village banking and maternal and child health: Evidence from Ecuador and Honduras," *World Development* 30 (2002): 707–723.

43. For an important contribution to the analysis of sources and destinations of aid and other cross-border flows, including excellent graphical presentations of the data, see the Unbundling Aid Project from Development Initiatives, at http://devinit.org/data-visualization/datavisualization-oda.

44. The authors would like to thank Susan Aaronson, Daniel Rothbart, and Delano Lavigne for valuable comments and suggestions on this section. A general audience version of part of this section appears in *World Ark*, winter 2011. For background to the first three paragraphs of this subsection, see Monty G. Marshall and Benjamin R. Cole, *Global Report 2009: Conflict, Governance, and State Fragility,* Center for Global Policy and Systemicpeace.org, 2009.

45. United Nations, *Consolidated Inter-Agency Appeal for the Democratic Republic of the Congo* (New York: United Nations, 2003).

46. Quan Li and Ming Wen, "Immediate and lingering effects of armed conflict on adult mortality: A time series cross-national analysis," *Journal of Peace Research* 42(2005): 471–492.

47. Nina Birkeland "Internal displacement: Global trends in conflict-induced displacement," *International Review of the Red Cross* 91 (2009): p. 502, available online at http://www.icrc.org/eng/resources/documents/article/review/review-875-p491.htm.

48. Thomas Plumper and Eric Neumayer, "The unequal burden of war: The effect of armed conflict on the gender gap in life expectancy," *International Organization* 60 (2006): 731.

49. Paul Collier, "Breaking the conflict trap: Civil war and development policy," 2003, http://econ.worldbank.org.

50. According to one report, in 1986 the under-5 mortality rate reached 473 per 1,000. See Hugh Waters, Brinnon Garrett, and Gilbert Burnham, United Nations University, World Institute for Development Economics Research, Research Paper No. 2007/06 (Helsinki, Finland: UNU-WIDER, 2007), p. 5, "Rehabilitating health systems in post-conflict situations," and International Organization for Migration and Ministry of Health, Mozambique, "Health impact of large post-conflict migratory movements: The experience of Mozambique," presentation March 20–22, 1996, Maputo, Mozambique. The 1990 and 2008 under-5 mortality data are from World Bank, *World Development Indicators,* 2010; note that some sources give higher estimates for the early 1990s.

51. In 2004, Mozambique Prime Minister Pascoal Mocumbi became High Representative of the World Health Organization's European and Developing Countries Clinical Trials Partnership after being a contender to head the WHO. Mocumbi served as minister of health during the 1980s. He served on the WHO task forces on health and development, in Geneva from 1990 to 1999.

52. World Bank, *Sierra Leone Health Sector Reconstruction and Development,* PID Report No. 10711 (Washington D.C.: World Bank, 2008). See also Office of the UN Resident Coordinator in Sierra Leone, *Republic of Sierra Leone Common Country Assessment. In Preparation for the United Nations Development Assistance Framework 2008–2010* (2007), available as: common_country_assessment.pdf from http://www.sl.undp.org. Under-5 mortality data are from World Bank, *World Development Indicators, 2010.*

53. Sanjeev Gupta, Benedict Clements, Rina Bhattacharya, and Shamit Chakravarti, "The elusive peace dividend: How armed conflict and terrorism undermine economic performance," *Finance and Development* 39, N. 4 (2002): 49–51.

54. The research on child nutrition in Burundi and Zimbabwe is reviewed in Christopher Blattman and Edward Miguel, "Civil war," *Journal of Economic Literature*, 48 (2010): 3–57, which cites Harold Alderman, John Hoddinott, and Bill Kinsey, "Long term consequences of early childhood malnutrition," *Oxford Economic Papers*, 58 (2006): 450–74; and Tom Bundervoet, Phillip Verwimp, and Richard Akresh, "Health and civil war in rural Burundi," *Journal of Human Resources*, 44 (2009): 536–563.

55. Collier, "Breaking the conflict trap."

56. Gupta et al., "Elusive peace dividend," http://www.imf.org/external/pubs/ft/fandd/2002/12/gupta.htm.

57. Plumper and Neumayer, "Unequal burden of war," p. 730.

58. In 4 of 18 countries studied, the losses could not be estimated by the researchers: F. Stewart, C. Huang, and M. Wang, "Internal wars in developing countries: An empirical overview of economic and social consequences," in *War and Underdevelopment,* eds. F. Stewart et al. (Oxford: Oxford University Press, 2001).

59. Collier, "Breaking the conflict trap," p. 2.

60. See, for example, J. Krishnamurty, "Employment and armed conflict," *Indian Journal of Labour Economics*, 50 (2007): 47–62.

61. Paul Collier, *The Bottom Billion: Why the Poorest Countries Are Failing and What Can Be Done about It* (New York: Oxford University Press, 2007), p. 28

62. Stewart, Huang, and Wang, "Internal wars in developing countries," cited in Collier, "Breaking the conflict trap," p. 17. The IFPRI findings are reported in Ellen Messer and Marc. J. Cohen, "Conflict, food insecurity, and globalization," FCND Discussion Paper 206, International Food Policy Research Institute, 2006; see esp. p. 9. The extent of food losses is reported in Ellen Messer, Marc J. Cohen, and Thomas Marchione, "Conflict: A cause and effect of hunger," *ECSP Report*, No. 7, 2001, at ECSP7-featurearticles-1.pdf, available at http://www.fao.org; see esp. p. 3.

63. See Ellen Messer and Marc. J. Cohen, "Conflict, food insecurity, and globalization," FCND Discussion Paper No. 206, International Food Policy Research Institute, 2006. For additional details and documentation, see Klaus Seitz, *Education

and Conflict: The Role of Education in the Creation, Prevention, and Resolution of Societal Crises—Consequences for Development Cooperation* (Berlin: GTZ, 2004), downloaded at http://www2.gtz.de/dokumente/bib/05-0160.pdf. Studies of cattle loss in Mozambique and Uganda, among other impacts, are reviewed in Blattman and Miguel, "Civil war," who cite an unpublished 1996 paper by Tilman Bruck; a 2006 UNICEF report of Annan, Blattman, and Horton, 2006; and a 1997 U.S. Uganda embassy report by Robert Gersony.

64. Birkeland, "Internal displacement."

65. Gupta et al., "Elusive peace dividend." See Christopher Blattman and Jeannie Annan, "The Consequences of Child Soldiering," *Review of Economics and Statistics*, 92 (2010): 882–898.

66. The United Nations estimated that in 2009, 42 million people were displaced by "conflict or persecution." See also W. Naudé, "The determinants of migration from sub-Saharan African countries," *Journal of African Economies* 19 (2010): 330–356, and Timothy J. Hatton and Jeffrey G. Williamson, "Demographic and economic pressure on emigration out of Africa," *Scandinavian Journal of Economics* 105 (2003): 465–486.

67. See James C. Murdoch and Todd Sandler, "Civil wars and economic growth: Spatial dispersion," *American Journal of Political Science* 48 (2004): 138–151.

68. Birkeland, "Internal displacement," data apply to year-end 2008. For further coverage, see Internal Displacement Monitoring Centre (IDMC), at http://www.internal-displacement.org.

69. United Nations Non-Governmental Liaison Service, "Millennium Development Goals report 2010," June 24, 2010, http://www.un-ngls.org/spip.php?article2682.

70. James D. Fearon, "Governance and civil war onset," *World Development Report*, 2011, background paper, August 31, 2010, http://siteresources.worldbank.org.

71. See Frances Stewart, "The root causes of humanitarian emergencies," in *War, Hunger and Displacement: The Origins of Humanitarian Emergencies,* Vol. 1, eds. E. Wayne Nafziger, Frances Stewart, and Raimo Väyrynen. (A caveat is that horizontal inequality is not measured as precisely as some

variables and so has not been tested statistically to the same degree as some explanations.) (Oxford: Oxford University Press, 2000), and Frances Stewart, *Horizontal Inequalities and Conflict: Understanding Group Violence in Multiethnic Societies* (New York: Palgrave Macmillan, 2008).

72. See Graham K. Brown, and Frances Stewart, "The implications of horizontal inequality for aid," CRISE Working Paper No. 36, University of Oxford, December 2006, p. 222.

73. Stewart, "Root causes" pp. 4–5.

74. See A. Evans, "Resource scarcity and conflict" (forthcoming); United Nations Environment Programme, "Sudan: Post-conflict environmental assessment, 2007," http://sudanreport.unep .ch/UNEP_Sudan.pdf; and Darfur Conflict and Resource Scarcity, "Environment and conflict in Africa: Reflections on Darfur," http://www .africa.upeace.org/documents/environment_files .pdf. Note, however, that there is no serious case for population control as a strategy to control conflict; see Henrik Urdal, "People vs. Malthus: Population pressure, environmental degradation, and armed conflict revisited." *Journal of Peace Research* 42 (2005): 417–434.

75. Colin H. Kahl, *States, Scarcity and Civil Strife in the Developing World* (Princeton, N.J.: Princeton University Press, 2006), p. 7.

76. Edward Miguel, Shanker Satyanath, and Ernest Sergenti, "Economic shocks and conflict: An instrumental variable approach," *Journal of Political Economy* 112 (2004): 725–754. The authors used rainfall variation in Africa as an instrumental variable for economic growth to estimate its impact on civil conflict. Their research found a strong causal relationship between lower economic growth (measured via rainfall) and increased conflict risk: A 5% decline in annual economic growth increased the risk of civil conflict the following year by more than 50%.

77. See Ole Magnus Theisen, "Blood and soil? Resource scarcity and internal armed conflict revisited," *Journal of Peace Research* 45 (2008): 801–818, and Urdal, "People vs. Malthus."

78. Marshall B. Burkea et al., "Warming increases the risk of civil war in Africa," *Proceedings of the National Academy of Sciences* 106 (2009): 20670–20674.

79. For a review, see Theisen, "Blood and soil?"

80. Collier, "Breaking the conflict trap."

81. For a journalistic account of the emerging issues with some illustrations, see Janeen Interlandi, "The new oil: Should private companies control our most precious natural resource?" *Newsweek*, October 8, 2010, http://www.newsweek .com/2010/10/08/the-race-to-buy-up-the-world-s -water.html.

82. In Chapter 2, we noted that according to Nobel laureate Douglass North, institutions are the "rules of the game in an economy," including both formal rules embodied in constitutions, laws, contracts, and market regulations, and informal rules reflected in norms of behavior, such as habits, customs, norms of conduct, and values.

83. In some cases, "rebel" forces have legitimate grievances that, if not addressed, will make genuine development all but impossible; in other cases, they are at best rival elites, if not thinly disguised criminals. These cases should not be lumped together casually, although at times the lines between them blur.

84. Military expenditure data are from the *SIPRI Yearbook 2010 and 2013* (Stockholm: Stockholm International Peace Research Institute, 2010 and 2013).

85. Seminal contributions include Robert Powell, "War as a commitment problem," *International Organization* 60(2006): 169–203, and Barbara F. Walter, "The critical barrier to civil war settlement," *International Organization* 51 (1997): 335–364. For a review, see Blattman and Miguel, "Civil war."

86. See, for example, the Heidelberg Institute's Conflict Barometer at http://www.hiik.de/en.

87. You can learn more about the Kimberley Process at http://www.kimberleyprocess.com and about the EITI at http://eiti.org.

88. We thank Susan Aaronson for her valuable suggestions. See African Development Bank, "Strategy for enhanced engagement in fragile states," http://www.afdb.org. Another kind of example is the role of the Economic Community of West African States in Sierra Leone and Liberia, including peacekeeping forces.

89. A similar argument is at least implicit in Collier's *Bottom Billion*.

90. Emil Bolongaita, "Controlling corruption in post-conflict countries," January 2005, http://www.u4.no/document/literature/Kroc%282005%29-controlling.pdf.

91. Stewart, *Horizontal Inequalities*, p. 18.

92. Stewart, "Root causes," p. 2.

93. The expectations problem is probably substantial; note that Paul Collier in *The Bottom Billion* found that "the risk that a country in the bottom billion falls into civil war in any five-year period is nearly one in six" (p. 32). For a similar argument, see World Bank, *"World Development Report, 2011: Conflict, security and development: Concept note,"* January 7, 2010, http://www.worldbank.org, pp. 8, 13, and 16.

94. *Education for All Global Monitoring Report*, "Education and violent conflict" (concept note), February 2010, http://www.unesco.org.uk/uploads/GMR%202011-concept-note.pdf.

95. Patrick Barron, "CDD in Post-Conflict and Conflict-Affected Areas: Experiences from East Asia," *World Development Report* background paper, July 16, 2010, http://siteresources.worldbank.org.

96. Ibid. The Philippines program is Kapitbisig Laban Sa Kahirapan.

97. James Manor, *Aid That Works: Successful Development in Fragile States* (Washington, D.C.: World Bank, 2007), p. 34.

98. A literature review of recent contributions to the economic analysis of civil conflict is found in Christopher Blattman and Edward Miguel, "Civil war." See Katherine Casey, Rachel Glennerster, and Edward Miguel, "How effective is community driven development? Evidence from Sierra Leone," a paper presented at NEUDC conference, MIT, November 2010, for an unusual randomized evaluation of a CDD-based assistance program. The study plausibly simulated an external NGO-organized program, though not grassroots-initiated organizing, among the traditionally marginalized. A report is available at http://www.povertyactionlab.org/publication/gobifo-project-evaluation-report-assessing-impacts-community-driven-development-sierra-l. An examination of the earlier literature, which concludes "evidence suggests that CBD/CDD is best done in a context-specific manner, with a long time-horizon, and with careful and well designed monitoring and evaluation systems," is found in Ghazala Mansuri and Vijayendra Rao, "Community-based and -driven development: A critical review," Washington: World Bank Policy Research Working Paper 3209, 2004.

Finance and Fiscal Policy for Development

15

The success of other market reforms depends on the health of the financial system.
—*World Bank,* World Development Report, 1996

Much of the rationale for liberalizing financial markets is based neither on a sound economic understanding of how these markets work nor on the potential scope for government intervention.

—*Joseph Stiglitz, Nobel laureate in economics*

I decided to set up my own bank. The government thought it was a funny idea; poor people cannot borrow money....Grameen is a mechanism for integrating people back into the marketplace. It opens up opportunities so that you can build your own life. Microcredit brings people together.

—*Muhammad Yunus, founder of the Grameen Bank and 2006 Nobel laureate for peace*

It is increasingly recognized that the financial system plays a crucial role in the process of economic development. The government helps make this possible by adopting sound and stable macroeconomic policies, including strong yet flexible fiscal as well as monetary policy, acting to establish financial markets where they do not yet exist, and providing prudential regulation of the financial system. In this chapter, we consider the role of finance and improvements in the workings of the financial system in the overall process of economic growth, modernization, and development. We examine the difficult road to macroeconomic stability on which many developing countries are now traveling. Then we examine developing-country financial systems in more detail. We take a look at stock markets in developing countries and consider the strengths and weaknesses of their expanding role. We examine special institutions such as development banks and rotating savings and credit associations (ROSCAs). We examine the increasingly prominent role of microfinance in developing countries, particularly the historical barriers to its development, the ways these barriers have been overcome, the benefits of microfinance for addressing problems of poverty and local development, and limitations of the emphasis on microfinance.

In this context, we will examine why it is often so difficult for many developing-country governments to pursue traditional monetary and financial policies, how some financial policies have led to low domestic savings and widespread inefficiencies in the commercial banking system, and how poorly designed and implemented tax structures work against attempts to restore fiscal balance through revenue increases. We also take a brief look at problems of public administration (a critical constraint in many developing countries), and examine the debate over the privatization of state-owned enterprises. The chapter's case study examines Botswana, an African country that has achieved one of the world's highest growth rates over the last several decades—leveraging mineral wealth with effective fiscal policies and relatively sound public administration—but still facing significant development challenges.

15.1 The Role of the Financial System in Economic Development

Generally, a distinction is made between the *real sector* and the *financial sector*. This terminology is unfortunate because it suggests that the financial sector is something less than real. This impression has been abetted by the view that the financial sector is a mere appendage to the real economy. As the economist Joan Robinson famously put it, "Where enterprise leads, finance follows."[1] Certainly, there is some truth to this aphorism; to a large extent, demand for financial services is derived from the activities of nonfinancial firms. But there is evidence that finance can also be a limiting factor in economic development. The need for finance can be seen everywhere in the developing world; five basic illustrations are:

- An impoverished mother in Zambia who attempts to feed her family with income from her credit-starved microenterprise and who could be much more productive with more working capital
- A start-up firm in India that cannot get established without private equity capital and may eventually wish to float a public offering
- A farmer on the world's richest soil in Ukraine who cannot plant for want of credit to buy seeds
- A budding family-owned shoe company in Brazil that needs better access to lower-cost loans to begin to export
- An established publicly traded firm in the Philippines that wishes to sell more shares to provide funds for restructuring

Hugh Patrick offers a "stages of development" argument that financial development causes growth at the start of modern development, but once the financial system is established, it mainly follows the real sector. Most likely, the causality runs in both directions.[2]

What is so important about finance? The financial sector provides six major functions that are important both at the firm level and at the level of the economy as a whole.[3]

1. *Providing payment services.* It is inconvenient, inefficient, and risky to carry around enough cash to pay for purchased goods and services. Financial institutions provide an efficient alternative. The most obvious examples are personal and commercial checking and check clearing, and credit and

debit card services; each is growing in importance, in the modern sectors at least, even in low-income countries. Recently, payments via mobile phones has expanded dramatically in Kenya and is growing rapidly many other developing countries.

2. *Matching savers and investors.* Although many people save, such as for retirement, and many have investment projects, such as building a factory or expanding the inventory carried by a family microenterprise, it would be only by the wildest of coincidences that each investor saved exactly as much as was needed to finance a given project. Therefore, it is important that savers and investors somehow meet and agree on terms for loans or other forms of finance. This can occur without financial institutions; even in highly developed markets, many new entrepreneurs obtain a significant fraction of their initial funds from family and friends. However, the presence of banks, and later venture capital or stock markets, can greatly facilitate matching in an efficient manner. Small-scale savers simply deposit their savings and let the bank decide where to invest them.

3. *Generating and distributing information.* From a society-wide viewpoint, one of the most important functions of the financial system is to generate and distribute information. Stock and bond prices in the daily newspapers of developing countries (and increasingly on the Internet as well) are a familiar example; these prices represent the average judgment of thousands, if not millions, of investors, based on the information they have available about these and all other investments. Banks also collect information about the firms that borrow from them; the resulting information is one of the most important components of the "capital" of a bank, although it is often unrecognized as such. In these regards, it has been said that financial markets represent the "brain" of the economic system.[4]

4. *Allocating credit efficiently.* Channeling investment funds to uses yielding the highest rate of return allows increases in specialization and the division of labor, which have been recognized since the time of Adam Smith as a key to the wealth of nations.

5. *Pricing, pooling, and trading risks.* Insurance markets provide protection against risk, but so does the diversification possible in stock markets or in banks' loan syndications.

6. *Increasing asset liquidity.* Some investments are very long-lived; in some cases—a hydroelectric plant, for example—such investments may last a century or more. Sooner or later, investors in such plants are likely to want to sell them. In some cases, it can be quite difficult to find a buyer at the time one wishes to sell—at retirement, for instance. Financial development increases liquidity by making it easier to sell, for example, on the stock market or to a syndicate of banks or insurance companies.

Both technological and financial innovations have driven modern economic growth. Both were necessary conditions for the Industrial Revolution, as steam and water power required large investments facilitated by innovations in banking, finance, and insurance. Both are necessary for developing countries as they continue their struggle for economic development. But a financial system that works for inclusive development and poverty reduction must be designed with equity as well as efficiency in mind. And a well-designed regulatory system is essential to reduce vulnerability to financial crises that can impose high costs on the rest of the economy.

Differences between Developed and Developing-Country Financial Systems

In more developed nations, monetary and financial policy plays a major direct and indirect role in governmental efforts designed to expand economic activity in times of unemployment and surplus capacity and to contract that activity in times of excess demand and inflation.[5] Basically, **monetary policy** works on two principal economic variables: the aggregate supply of money in circulation and the level of interest rates. Expressed in traditional terms, the **money supply** (currency plus commercial bank demand deposits) is thought to be directly related to the level of economic activity in the sense that a greater money supply induces expanded economic activity by enabling people to purchase more goods and services. This in essence is the *monetarist theory* of economic activity. Its advocates argue that by controlling the growth of the money supply, governments of developed countries can regulate their nations' economic activity and control inflation.

On the other side of the monetary issue, again expressed in traditional terms, are the *Keynesian economists*, who argue that an expanded supply of money in circulation increases the availability of loanable funds. A supply of loanable funds in excess of demand leads to lower interest rates. Because private investment is assumed to be inversely related to prevailing interest rates, businesspeople will expand their investments as interest rates fall and credit becomes more available. More investment, in turn, raises aggregate demand, leading to a higher level of economic activity (more employment and a higher GDP). Similarly, in times of excess aggregate demand and inflation, governments pursue restrictive monetary policies designed to curtail the expansion of aggregate demand by reducing the growth of the national money supply, lowering the supply of loanable funds, raising interest rates, and thereby inducing a lower level of investment and, it is hoped, less inflation.

Although this description of monetary policy in developed countries grossly simplifies a complex process,[6] it points out two important aspects that most developing countries lack. First, the ability of developed-country governments to expand and contract their money supply and to raise and lower the costs of borrowing in the private sector (through direct and indirect manipulation of interest rates) is made possible by the existence of highly organized, economically interdependent, and efficiently functioning money and credit markets. Financial resources are continuously flowing in and out of savings banks, commercial banks, and other nationally regulated public and private financial intermediaries with a minimum of interference. Moreover, interest rates are regulated both by administrative credit controls and by market forces of supply and demand, so there tends to be consistency and a relative uniformity of rates in different sectors of the economy and in all regions of the country. Financial intermediaries are thus able to mobilize private savings and efficiently allocate them to their

Monetary policy   Activities of a central bank designed to influence financial variables such as the money supply and interest rates.

Money supply   The sum total of currency in circulation plus commercial bank demand deposits and sometimes savings bank time deposits.

most productive uses. This is a crucial ingredient in the promotion of long-term economic growth.

By contrast, markets and financial institutions in many developing countries are highly unorganized, often externally dependent, and spatially fragmented.[7] Many commercial banks in developing countries are overseas branches of major private banking corporations in developed countries. Their orientation, therefore, like that of multinational corporations, may be more toward external and less toward internal monetary situations. The ability of governments in developing countries to regulate the national supply of money is further constrained by the openness of their economies, in some cases the pegging of their currencies to the dollar or alternatively to the euro or a basket of major developed-country currencies, and the fact that the accumulation of foreign-currency earnings is a significant but highly variable source of their domestic financial resources. Even the money supply itself may be difficult to measure and more difficult to control under conditions of **currency substitution**, whereby foreign currencies serve as an alternative to the domestic currency (e.g., U.S. dollars in northern Mexico).[8] This is a particularly important problem when the expected level of inflation is high.

A majority of developing nations have found that currency pegging presents challenging obstacles; so floating currency or managed floats have become more popular (Chapter 13). But this has also been associated with other forms of instability, including highly volatile exchange rates, even in countries not otherwise in crisis. An example is India in 2013, as economic growth slowed—though to a still healthy 5%. The rupee lost 9% of its value during August alone and faced considerable volatility throughout the year, bringing pressure on the central bank to raise interest rates, which, in turn, threatened to slow the economy further.

Because of limited information and incomplete credit markets, the commercial banking system of many developing countries lacks **transparency** (full disclosure of the quality of loan portfolios) and often restricts its activities almost exclusively to rationing scarce loanable funds to medium- and large-scale enterprises in the modern manufacturing sector that are deemed more creditworthy. Many development economists have concluded that this lack of transparency, and the fact that many borrowers were *not* creditworthy, was a major factor in the 1997 Asian currency and banking crisis, especially in Thailand and Indonesia. As a result, small farmers and indigenous small-scale entrepreneurs and traders in both the formal and informal manufacturing and service sectors have traditionally had to seek financing elsewhere–sometimes from family members and relatives, or from local moneylenders and loan sharks who charge exorbitant interest rates. The growth of microfinance, including its gradual expansion "upmarket" to somewhat more established small enterprises, has made modest but significant inroads toward addressing this problem.

Most developing countries have operated under a dual monetary system: a small and often externally controlled or influenced **organized money market** with binding legal restrictions on nominal interest-rate ceilings, catering to the financial requirements of a special group of middle- and upper-class local and foreign businesses in the modern industrial sector, and a large but amorphous **unorganized money market**, uncontrolled, often strictly illegal, and often usurious, to which most low-income individuals are obliged to turn in

Currency substitution The use of foreign currency (e.g., U.S. dollars) as a medium of exchange in place of, or along with, the local currency (e.g., Mexican pesos).

Transparency (financial) In finance, full disclosure by public and private banks of the quality and status of their loan and investment portfolios so that domestic and foreign investors can make informed decisions.

Organized money market The formal banking system in which loanable funds are channeled through recognized and licensed financial intermediaries.

Unorganized money market The informal and often usurious credit system that exists in most developing countries (especially in rural areas) where low-income farms and firms with little collateral borrow from moneylenders at exorbitant rates of interest.

Financial liberalization
Eliminating various forms
of government interven-
tion in financial markets,
thereby allowing supply
and demand to determine
the level of interest rates, for
example.

times of financial need. This is another manifestation of the dual structure of many developing economies and their tendency, intentional or not, to serve the needs of wealthy elites while neglecting the requirements of the relatively poor. One possible step toward the elimination of this major factor price distortion would be the removal of artificially low nominal interest-rate ceilings in the organized market as well as other related steps toward **financial liberalization** (e.g., loosening of the foreign-exchange rate). Higher interest rates should generate more domestic savings, whereas greater transparency and more market-oriented real interest rates should better allocate loanable funds to the most productive projects. However, liberalization has often been accompanied by new challenges to financial stability. Moreover, such coordinated liberalization of domestic financial and foreign-exchange markets has not adequately solved the problem of channeling credit to small investors and entrepreneurs.[9] That will require more direct new initiatives. We will discuss both financial market reform and measures to improve finance for the informal economy later in this chapter.

In developing nations, investment decisions are often not very sensitive to interest-rate movements. Moreover, a number of larger countries in Latin America (e.g., Brazil and Argentina) have in the past followed a policy of inflation-financed industrial growth, in which expansionary monetary policy in conjunction with large budgetary deficits has resulted in negative real interest rates (inflation rates exceeding nominal interest levels). The basic idea is that artificially low rates encourage investment, finance the fiscal deficit, and promote industrial output growth. But there may be severe structural supply constraints (low elasticities of supply) inhibiting the expansion of output even when the demand for it increases. These constraints include poor management, the absence of essential (usually imported) intermediate products, bureaucratic rigidities, licensing restrictions, and an overall lack of industrial-sector interdependence. Whatever the reasons, structural supply rigidities mean that any increase in the demand for goods and services generated by rapid money creation will not be matched by increases in supply. Instead, the excess demand (in this case, for investment goods) will merely bid up prices and cause inflation. In some Latin American nations, such "structural" inflation has been a chronic problem, made even worse on the cost side by the upward spiral of wages as workers attempt to protect their real income levels by indexing wage increases to price rises. Attempts to control inflation with fixed or slowly depreciating exchange rates led to major financial crises in Brazil in 1999 and Argentina in 2001–2002.

Macro problems were not quite as severe in peripheral Europe as in many developing nations, but there were some analogies to abandoning local currencies for the euro. This was analogous to permanently pegging the currency to the former deutschmark, or rather, to a currency index including the former franc, as Argentina did to the dollar. Or it is like currency substitution, such as the dollarization practiced by El Salvador, Panama, and Ecuador—simply a choice to use a more stable currency as legal tender (medium of exchange). Like currency substitution, it makes adjustment more difficult, because there is no federalized budget and labor mobility is far less than anticipated in the 1992 market integration. Moreover, it is much harder for Eurozone countries to exit, because use of the euro is established by treaty for participating member countries, rather than as voluntary euro adoption in countries such as Kosovo and Montenegro. Not so many years ago, Portugal and Greece were classified as upper-middle-income developing countries by development agencies; and recently they, too, have experienced lost competitiveness as their productivity has grown more slowly over a period of years than core euro countries, led by Germany. Without the opportunity to adjust through depreciation of their exchange rate, they have had to adjust through austerity. But the resulting austerity—harsh macroeconomic stabilization, if not structural adjustment—led to high unemployment rates including 27% in both Greece and Spain, 15% in Portugal, and 12% in both Italy and Ireland—the so-called EU-5 crisis countries—in 2013 (This topic was explored from additional perspectives in Chapter 13, section 13.5.)

Nevertheless, financial systems remain an integral component of the general economic system in developing countries. For example, in the context of severe macroeconomic instability with high inflation, accompanied by large budget and trade deficits, they represent a key element in any overall stabilization effort. Moreover, as noted earlier, financial systems provide a variety of needed services, including savings mobilization, credit allocation, risk limitations, insurance protection, and foreign-exchange facilitation. Let us therefore continue our examination of the structure of financial systems with a look at the central bank.

15.2 The Role of Central Banks and Alternative Arrangements

Functions of a Full-Fledged Central Bank

In developed nations, **central banks**, such as the Federal Reserve Board in the United States, conduct a wide range of banking, regulatory, and supervisory functions. They have substantial public responsibilities and a broad array of executive powers. Their major activities can be grouped into five general functions:[10]

Central bank   The major financial institution responsible for issuing a nation's currency, managing foreign reserves, implementing monetary policy, and providing banking services to the government and commercial banks.

1. *Issuer of currency and manager of foreign reserves.* Central banks print money, distribute notes and coins, intervene in foreign-exchange markets to regulate the national currency's rate of exchange with other currencies, and manage foreign-asset reserves to maintain the external value of the national currency.

2. *Banker to the government.* Central banks provide bank deposit and borrowing facilities to the government while simultaneously acting as the government's fiscal agent and underwriter.

3. *Banker to domestic commercial banks.* Central banks also provide bank deposit and borrowing facilities to commercial banks and act as a lender of last resort to financially troubled commercial banks.

4. *Regulator of domestic financial institutions.* Central banks ensure that commercial banks and other financial institutions conduct their business prudently and in accordance with relevant laws and regulations. They also

monitor reserve ratio requirements and supervise the conduct of local and regional banks.

5. *Operator of monetary and credit policy.* Central banks attempt to manipulate monetary and credit policy instruments (the domestic money supply, the discount rate, the foreign-exchange rate, commercial bank reserve ratio requirements, etc.) to achieve major macroeconomic objectives such as controlling inflation, promoting investment, or regulating international currency movements.

Sometimes these functions are handled by separate regulatory bodies.

Currency board A form of central bank that issues domestic currency for foreign exchange at a fixed exchange rate.

Currency Boards   A **currency board** issues domestic currency for foreign exchange at a fixed exchange rate. It was the classic alternative arrangement to a central bank. Although it provides exchange rate stability, it does so at a cost of giving up independence to pursue other functional roles of central banks. Many developing countries inherited or adopted a currency board at the time of independence, and others have adopted them to restore stability after periods of high inflation. Currency boards do not create new money, conduct monetary policy, or generally supervise the banking system. In colonial times, they acted as agents for the colonial banks and were charged with the responsibility of maintaining a fixed parity with the colonial power's currency. A more recent example of a currency-based system was found in Argentina from 1991 until 2002, where the peso was pegged one-for-one with the U.S. dollar and was backed in the monetary base with international reserves. When the currency board was established in 1991, the purpose was to reduce inflation by controlling the money supply. A strong dollar and fiscal irresponsibility (possibly compounded by stretching conventional currency board rules) led to its demise. The failure in Argentina by 2002 led to a more general loss of credibility for the effectiveness of this type of system.

Alternatives to Central Banks   There are several other alternatives to the standard central bank.[11] First, a *transitional central banking institution* can be formed as an intermediate step between a currency board and a central bank, with the government exerting a strong influence on its financial activities. The range of such activities, however, is checked by statutory limitations on the monetary authority's discretionary powers. Former British colonies and protectorates such as Fiji, Belize, Maldives, and Bhutan provide the most common examples of transitional central banks. Second, a *supranational central bank* may be created to undertake central banking activities for a group of smaller countries participating in a monetary union, perhaps also as part of a customs union (see Chapter 12). Examples of monetary unions with regional, central banks include the West African Economic and Monetary Union, and the Central African Economic and Monetary Community, which use separate but equally valued versions of the CFA franc (African Financial Community). Another is the Eastern Caribbean Currency Union, which uses the East Caribbean dollar (controlled by the East Caribbean Central Bank). Each of these is tied to major currencies (the euro in the first cases and the U.S. dollar in the latter). Establishing new monetary unions is fraught with political and technical difficulties, but there may be new examples in coming years. The Southern

African Development Community has announced its objective for a single currency by 2018, though this date is in doubt; and the Gulf Cooperation Council announced an objective of a monetary union, but progress has been very slow. Of course, the euro has been adopted as the currency of many European countries, and its management has not been free of problems, particularly in countries that not long ago were included in lists of still-developing countries, such as Greece and Portugal. There are benefits to regional unions, but they must be compared with the costs of reduced flexibility. Third, a *currency enclave* might be established between the central banking institution in a developing country and the monetary authority of a larger trading partner, often the former colonial power. Such an arrangement provides a certain degree of stability to the developing country's currency, but the dominating influence of the partner, with its own priorities, renders the enclave almost as dependent as a colony with respect to monetary policy. Contemporary examples include economies that have *dollarized*, a term for adopting the currency of the U.S. dollar, without a central bank role; examples include Panama, Ecuador, El Salvador, and East Timor. Other currencies such as the euro have been adopted in a similar manner. Finally, in an *open-economy central banking institution*, where both commodity and international capital flows represent significant components of national economic activity, the monetary environment is likely to be subject to fluctuations in world commodity and financial markets. As a result, the central banking institution will be engaged primarily in the regulation and promotion of a stable and respected financial system. Examples of such institutions have included Singapore, Kuwait, Saudi Arabia, and the United Arab Emirates. Table 15.1 summarizes the major features of these four categories of central bank alternatives in comparison with the currency board and the central bank.

In the past two decades, there has been an increase in central bank economic and political independence in a majority of developing countries. Many economists have identified such autonomy as an important precondition to its effectiveness in carrying out traditional central bank roles.[12]

Economic autonomy has been defined as the absence of provision of direct credit to government from the central bank that is either automatic, below market interest rates, or not limited in time or amounts; the absence of central bank presence in the primary market for public debt; the right to set interest rates independently; and holding responsibility for overseeing the banking sector. *Political autonomy of central banks* has been defined as the ability to select final objectives of monetary policy and is measured by whether the bank governor and board of directors are appointed independently and for a long term, whether political representatives are required, whether monetary policies can be implemented without political approval, and whether institutional rules strengthen central banks in conflicts with government.[13]

A 2009 International Monetary Fund (IMF) study, using alternative autonomy indexes, reported a global trend toward relatively higher levels of central bank autonomy and identified four broad patterns over this period:[14]

1. There has been a shift in banking institutions from currency boards to single state central banks or currency unions (supranational central banks).

2. A majority of central banks have been granted the responsibility to set price stability or target inflation as one of their objectives of monetary

TABLE 15.1   Central Banking Institutions

Institution	Issuer of Currency	Banker to Government	Banker to Commercial Banks	Regulator of Financial Institutions	Operator of Monetary Policy	Promoter of Financial Development
Full-fledged central bank	3	3	3	3	3G	1
Supranational central bank	3E	2E	2	2	2E	2
Open-economy central banking institution	3C	2C	2	3	1	3
Transitional central banking institution	3CG	2C	2	1	2G	3
Currency enclave central banking institution	1, 2CE	2CE	2	1	1	3
Currency board	3C	1	1	1	1	1

Source: Charles Collyns, *Alternatives to the Central Bank in the Developing World*, IMF Occasional Paper No. 20 (Washington, D.C.: International Monetary Fund, 1983), p. 22. Copyright © 1983 by the International Monetary Fund. Reprinted with permission.

Key: 1 = limited involvement; 2 = substantial involvement; 3 = full involvement; C = considerable constitutional restrictions; E = considerable external influence; G = considerable government influence.

policy. In addition, most of these countries also have autonomy with respect to setting the policy rate as it concerns the government. (The degree to which this measured autonomy corresponds to actual practice particularly over time and across periods of financial distress will be an ongoing consideration.)

3. There is divergence among central banks on the issue of financial supervision. Many central banks in developing countries have retained their key supervisory role. But the priority of most central banks is achieving medium-term price stability.

4. Participation in currency unions (or supranational central banks) has enhanced the autonomy of central banks in both developed and developing countries. Examples include the European Union of Central Banks (ESCP), the Central Bank of West African States (BCEAO), the Bank of Central African States (BEAC), and the East Caribbean Central Bank (ECCB).

However, central bank autonomy still remains quite limited in many cases.

In the final analysis, however, it is not so much the organizational structure of the central banking institution or its degree of political autonomy that matter. Rather, it is the extent to which such an institution is capable of financing and promoting domestic economic development, through its commercial and development banking system, in an international economic and financial environment, characterized by various degrees of dominance and dependence. Commercial banks in developing countries must take a much more active role in promoting new industries and financing existing ones than is usual for banks in developed nations. They have to be sources of venture capital as well as repositories of the commercial knowledge and business skills that are typically in short supply domestically. It is because of their failure to do this that new financial institutions, known as development banks, have become a prominent part of the financial arsenal of many developing countries.

The Role of Development Banking

Development banks are specialized public and private financial institutions that supply medium- and long-term funds for the creation or expansion of industrial enterprises. They have arisen in many developing nations because the existing banks usually focus on either short-term lending for commercial purposes (commercial and savings banks) or, in the case of central banks, the control and regulation of the aggregate supply of money. Moreover, existing commercial banks set loan conditions that are often inappropriate for establishing new enterprises or for financing large-scale projects. Their funds are more often allocated to "safe" borrowers (established industries, many of which are foreign-owned or run by well-known local families). True venture capital for new industries rarely obtains approval.

To facilitate industrial growth in economies characterized by a scarcity of financial capital, development banks have sought to raise capital, initially focusing on two major sources: (1) bilateral and multilateral loans from national aid agencies like the U.S. Agency for International Development (USAID) and from international donor agencies like the World Bank, and (2) loans from their own governments. However, in addition to raising capital, development banks have had to develop specialized skills in the field of industrial project appraisal. In many cases, their activities go far beyond the traditional banker's role of lending money to creditworthy customers. The activities of development banks often encompass direct entrepreneurial, managerial, and promotional involvement in the enterprises they finance, including government-owned and -operated industrial corporations.

The growth and spread of development banks in the developing world have been substantial. By 2000, their numbers had increased into the hundreds, and their financial resources had ballooned to billions of dollars. Moreover, although the initial sources of capital were agencies such as the World Bank, bilateral aid agencies, and local governments, the growth of development bank finance has increasingly been facilitated by capital from private investors, institutional and individual, foreign and local. Almost 20% of the share capital of these banks has been foreign-owned, with the remaining 80% derived from local investors.

In spite of their impressive growth, development banks have come under mounting criticism for their excessive concentration on large-scale loans. Some privately owned finance companies (also categorized as development banks) refuse to consider loans of less than $20,000 or $50,000. They argue that smaller loans do not justify the time and effort involved in their appraisal.

Development banks
Specialized public and private financial intermediaries that provide medium- and long-term credit for development projects.

As a result, these finance companies almost totally remove themselves from the area of aid to small enterprises, even though such aid is of major importance to the achievement of broadly based economic development and often may constitute the bulk of assistance needed in the private sector. We may conclude, therefore, that in spite of the growth of development banks, there remains a need to channel more financial resources to small entrepreneurs, both on the farm and in the marginal or informal sector of urban areas and nonfarm rural activities, who often are excluded from access to credit at reasonable rates of interest.[15] In an attempt to respond to these needs of small-scale borrowers, a whole array of informal credit arrangements has emerged in the developing world. Let us look briefly at some of them.

15.3 Informal Finance and the Rise of Microfinance

Traditional Informal Finance

A 2010 study estimated that 2.5 billion adults do not use formal services to save or borrow.[16] As noted earlier in the text, much economic activity in developing nations comes from small-scale producers and enterprises. Most are noncorporate, unlicensed, unregistered enterprises, including small farmers, producers, artisans, tradespeople, and independent traders operating in the informal urban and rural sectors of the economy. Their demands for financial services are outside the purview of traditional commercial bank lending. For example, street vendors need short-term finance to buy inventories, small farmers require buffer loans to tide them over uncertain seasonal income fluctuations, and small-scale manufacturers need minor loans to purchase simple equipment or hire nonfamily workers. In such situations, traditional commercial banks are both ill equipped and reluctant to meet the needs of these small-scale borrowers. Because the sums involved are small (usually less than $1,000) but administration and carrying costs are high and also because few informal borrowers have the necessary collateral to secure formal-sector loans, commercial banks are simply not interested. Most don't even have branch offices in rural villages, small towns, or on the periphery of cities where many of the informal activities take place. Thus, most noncorporate borrowers have traditionally had to turn to family or friends as a first line of finance and then warily to local professional moneylenders, pawnbrokers, and tradespeople as a backup. These latter sources of finance are extremely costly—moneylenders, for example, can charge up to 20% *a day* in interest for short-term loans to traders and vendors. In the case of small farmers requiring seasonal loans, the only collateral that they have to offer the moneylender or pawnbroker is their land or oxen. If these must be surrendered in the event of a default, peasant farmers become rapidly transformed into landless laborers, while moneylenders accumulate sizable tracts of land, either for themselves or to sell to large local landholders.

Informal finance   Loans and other financial services not passed through the formal banking system—for example, loans between family members.

A variety of forms of **informal finance** have emerged to replace the moneylender and pawnbroker in some instances.[17] These include local rotating savings and credit associations and group lending programs. In the case of

rotating savings and credit associations (ROSCAs), which can be found in such diverse countries as Mexico, Bolivia, Egypt, Nigeria, Ghana, the Philippines, Sri Lanka, India, China, and South Korea, a group of up to 50 individuals selects a leader, who collects a fixed amount of savings from each member. This fund is then allocated (often randomly but frequently also sequenced through internal bidding) on a rotating basis to each member as an interest-free loan. ROSCAs enable people to buy goods without having to save the full amount in advance. With a ROSCA, individuals can make their planned purchases in half the time, on average. Many low-income people prefer to save and borrow this way, repayment rates are extremely high, and participation is very active. Noting that ROSCAs are often formed by married women, Siwan Anderson and Jean-Marie Baland have proposed that they serve another important purpose when wives' bargaining power in the family is otherwise limited. Because the funds made available through membership in the ROSCA cannot be drawn on until the wife wins a turn to receive the kitty, this restriction prevents her husband from demanding access to her growing savings for immediate consumption before enough has been saved to purchase her targeted item, such as a sewing machine.[18] Box 15.1 presents new findings on the surprisingly active financial lives of the poor.

> **Rotating savings and credit association (ROSCA)** A group formed by formal agreement among 40 to 50 individuals to pool their savings and allocate loans on a rotating basis to each member.

Microfinance Institutions: How They Work

Microfinance is the supply of credit, saving vehicles, and other basic financial services made available to poor and vulnerable people who might otherwise have no access to them or could borrow only on highly unfavorable terms. *Microfinance institutions (MFIs)* specialize in delivering these services, in various ways and according to their own institutional rules.[19]

In the case of village banking, or **group lending schemes**, a group of potential borrowers forms an association to borrow funds from a commercial bank, a government development bank, an NGO, or a private institution. The group then allocates the funds to individual members, whose responsibility is to repay the group. The group itself guarantees the loan to the outside lender; it is responsible for repayment. The idea is simple: By joining together, a group of small-scale borrowers can reduce the costs of borrowing and, because the loan is large, can gain access to formal commercial credit. With at least implicit joint liability, group members have a vested interest in the success of the enterprise and therefore exert strong pressure on borrowing members to repay on time. The evidence shows that repayment rates compare favorably with formal-sector borrowers. Many NGOs actively coordinate and sponsor this process.

> **Microfinance** Financial services, including credit, supplied in small allotments to people who might otherwise have no access to them or have access only on very unfavorable terms. Includes microsavings and microinsurance as well as microcredit.

> **Group lending scheme** A formal arrangement among a group of potential borrowers to borrow money from commercial or government banks and other sources as a single entity and then allocate funds and repay loans as a group, thereby lowering borrowing costs.

Economic research has consistently found that availability of credit is a binding constraint for microenterprise development. A majority of microenterprises are operated by women. But lack of credit particularly, though certainly not exclusively, affects women (microentrepreneur) borrowers, for reasons ranging from lack of property rights to local cultural practices, but lack of collateral is arguably the most important. Let's look a little more closely at how this works.

Three related factors have made it difficult to relax credit constraints to low-income female microentrepreneurs. First, poor microentrepreneurs often have little or no collateral. Second, it is difficult for conventional lenders to determine borrower quality. Third, small loans are more costly to process per dollar lent.

BOX 15.1 FINDINGS   The Financial Lives of the Poor

Daryl Collins and her colleagues documented the surprisingly active household financial management of the poor. They interviewed 250 households every two weeks for a year, recording and compiling financial and spending behavior. They found a "triple whammy of incomes that are both low and uncertain, within contexts where the financial opportunities to leverage and smooth income to fit expenditure are extremely limited." Income of respondents was irregular and hard to predict, with few opportunities for insurance. "One of the least remarked-on problems of living on two dollars a day," the authors note, "is that you don't literally get that amount each day. The two dollars a day is just an average over time."

Assets are churning, with high flow into and out of debt and savings. This "cash flow intensity of income" meant that "in India, households shifted, on average, between 0.75 and 1.75 times their incomes.... In South Africa, the monthly turnover in cash flows was...about 1.85 times the monthly income." Even those receiving less than $1 a day do not consume all of it because of the dangers of living hand to mouth. Respondents save by hiding money at home, leaving it with a neighbor for safekeeping, paying into a burial society, giving credit to customers, paying down loans, buying life insurance, remitting cash home they later benefit from, and facing wage arrears. Often at the same time, they borrow by taking shop credit, benefiting from a relative's wage advances, going into rent arrears, getting interest-free loans from neighbors, taking informal loans with or without pawning, selling commitments of future labor, buying from small stores on credit, and topping up loans they otherwise pay down steadily. Over a year, "in Bangladesh the average number of different types of instruments was just under 10, in India just over eight, and in South Africa, 10." No household used fewer than four types.

Households use many techniques to agglomerate large sums (for them), including ROSCAs, informal savings clubs, simultaneous borrowing and saving, and commitment savings products. But the poor most commonly borrow from each other. The authors observed that small withdrawals were far more frequent than deposits into savings, and much more cash flowed into and out of loan balances, even though saving was ubiquitous. "For the poor households in our study the main strategy was to turn to each other, using one-on-one lending and borrowing between friends, family, and neighbors." Although such loans might look convenient and flexible, the authors noted that they lacked reliability, privacy, and transparency and had high transaction costs. Financial instruments were sometimes vaguely defined: In a striking example, money was "placed with" a neighbor. Was it a loan or a savings deposit? The placement could morph as needs changed. People living in poverty often prefer to borrow at high interest than to draw down savings, perhaps for self-motivation: Respondents report that with high interest, they know they will work hard to pay loans down quickly; they recall how difficult it has been for them to save.

The authors conclude that microfinance institutions can use the study's insights to improve the "portfolios of the poor" with new products to help households manage money on a day-to-day basis, build long-term savings, and enable borrowing for more uses. They can help by liberalizing and expanding their products, taking small-scale savings and making small loans for members on demand, expanding the term of commitment savings mechanisms, and allowing non-business loans.

Source: Based on Daryl Collins, Jonathan Morduch, Stuart Rutherford, and Orlanda Ruthven, *Portfolios of the Poor: How the World's Poor Live on $2 a Day* (Princeton, N.J.: Princeton University Press, 2009).

Village banking seeks to solve these problems in part through the "collateral of peer pressure." Small microentrepreneurs are organized into credit cooperatives, to which seed capital is lent. In a traditional model, before qualifying for a loan, each member is required to identify several other members or potential members who are willing to cosign loans with them. Often, once a member of a cosigning group receives a loan, no other member may borrow until the first borrower has established a regular repayment record; and in any case, no repeat loans are approved until all members' accounts are satisfactorily settled. Progressively larger loans are approved as borrowers gain experience and a credit history and identify productive uses for larger loans. Members know the characters of the cosigning group members they select and may be expected to join groups with members whom they believe are likely to repay their loans. Thus, the banks make use of the information that is "embedded" in the village or neighborhood about who is a reliable and capable borrower, and induce villagers to reveal this information. At the same time, an implicit collateral is created by the pressure that members would be expected to exert on each member in the group to repay funds. The goodwill of these relatives and friends of the borrower represents part of the borrowers' capital, which failure to pay the loan puts at risk. Finally, village banks extensively use volunteer member labor (as traditional consumer cooperatives do), thus lowering the bank's effective costs. Bank members reveal by participating that the value of the time thus spent is less than the value of the enhanced credit. An example of an MFI that uses this joint liability model is FINCA International.

Another outstanding example of an MFI is the Grameen Bank in Bangladesh, examined as one of the two case studies at the end of Chapter 11. The Grameen Bank uses solidarity groups and takes advantage of opportunities for peer pressure by allowing increases in borrowing limits only if all members repay. But the Grameen Bank currently has no cosigning requirement.

Thus, joint liability can play a key role in lowering interest rates for microcredit borrowers, in some cases, by distinguishing the more creditworthy (reducing adverse selection) and by encouraging more diligent efforts to earn an adequate return and ensuring that borrowers do not feign bankruptcy or abscond (reducing moral hazard). This can be accomplished through either smaller solidarity groups or larger village banking groups. But joint liability also brings costs to borrowers, such as low flexibility, loss of social capital for default beyond a person's control, and peer pressure to undertake excessively risk-averse activities. However, with the increasingly common moves away from joint liability among microfinance institutions such as Grameen, it is clear that other microfinance strategies that do not rely on group lending are at work.

With "dynamic incentives," a microborrower is made eligible for a larger loan in the future if or he or she repays the current smaller loan; indeed, the threat to stop lending if the borrower does not repay can be effective in many circumstances. Another mechanism is the use of frequent repayment installments, even though the return on the investment may be generated over longer intervals. This can essentially tap into nonmicroenterprise household income flows or other borrowing sources that act as implicit guarantees of individual loans (or of group loans that are less than fully secure). Some NGOs use flexible collateral, accepting as a guarantee items that are valuable to the borrower even if they are not so valuable to the lender. Many NGOs use borrower groups for purposes other than joint liability: solidarity, sharing ideas, gaining information about borrower problems, facilitation of provision of other services (such as legal education), and informal pressure to repay. MFIs also publicize successes and failures at repayment to shame defaulters into repaying.

Finally, NGOs particularly target women borrowers; doing so has development advantages, but practitioners also claim that women are more cautious in investments, more sensitive to public disclosure of default, more likely to help others in solidarity groups, less likely to have outside loan opportunities, and less likely to have outside job opportunities, all of which decrease the incentive to default even without actual joint liability; data show that MFIs with a higher fraction of women borrowers have higher repayment rates.[20]

The growth of microfinance has been dramatic—by one measure, topping 200 million borrowers by 2010—although since then, growth has stalled, at least temporarily, due to several factors. According to estimates by the Microcredit Summit Campaign, in 2011 the sector experienced its first outright decline in the number of borrowers in at least 14 years. About half the drop was attributed to a near collapse of the MFI sector in the Indian state of Andhra Pradesh, due to a combination of aggressive lending and collection practices by commercial MFIs, followed by a sweepingly punitive state government response that may have represented more politics than policy.[21]

Although the considerable success of informal finance programs is impressive, the fact remains that throughout the developing world, the majority of rural and urban poor have little or no access to formal credit. Until legal reforms are enacted, making it easier for small enterprises to gain access to the formal credit system, or more NGO- or government-supported credit programs are established to serve the needs of the noncorporate sector, the financial systems of most developing countries will remain unresponsive to the fundamental requirements of participatory national development.

MFIs: Three Current Policy Debates

Subsidies and MFIs   One debate under way in the microenterprise credit community is whether subsidies are appropriate. Known as the "microfinance schism," the debate pits the Consultative Group to Assist the Poor (CGAP), a donor consortium headquartered within the World Bank, and other mainstream donors against some other nongovernmental organizations (NGOs) and academic economists. CGAP has essentially argued that one can reach more borrowers by requiring sustainability so that available dollars go further. This argument is reasonable as far as it goes, but, in general, the poorest borrowers may not be able to afford to pay the high interest rates that this would require with the business opportunities they realistically face. Put more precisely, the interest elasticity of the demand for credit on the part of the poor is not close to zero. And the poor generally lack opportunities to invest in high-return projects. Thus, some subsidy is generally required to truly reach the poorest current and potential microentrepreneurs.[22]

But even subsidized credit is no guarantee of higher productivity and incomes. Some studies have suggested that the poorest of the poor may not be made better off by village banking or other MFI programs and indeed may be made worse off if they take on additional debt that is for them unproductive but for which they must pay interest. Of course, it will be essential to ensure that these subsidized credit programs are run efficiently, that the credit is allocated to appropriate investments, and that credit actually ends up in the hands of poor households.

Bundled Poverty Services: Microfinance Plus   In this regard, a second debate concerns whether to combine microfinance with other programs. Proponents argue that it may be useful to tie credit to social services that are demanded only by the poor and inherently require time for participation, for at least three reasons. First, such required participation can act as a kind of screening mechanism to ensure that nonpoor borrowers are not taking advantage of a subsidy that is not intended for them (analogous to workfare screening, described in Chapter 5). Second, the poor generally cannot make adequate use of business credit without sufficient health and education. There is usually at least some subsidy in programs that offer health or educational services along with credit. Third, many of the poor appear not to recognize the importance of human capital, and the availability of credit may act as a "hook" to get them enrolled in health and education programs. But it may be less costly to keep these programs separate, in accordance with the varying comparative advantage of different NGOs, and some low-income borrowers do not need these services. Accordingly, there is a growing debate in the microfinance community over whether to integrate credit with education, health, or other programs.[23] A study of a program combining microfinance with basic business training shows it may be cost-effective (see Box 15.2). BRAC, the acclaimed NGO examined in the case study in Chapter 11, provides the classic example of a broader, integrated approach with its Microcredit-Plus program.

The Commercialization Debate   A third ongoing debate, related to the first two debates, is whether MFIs should undergo **commercialization**, whereby a (not-for-profit) NGO providing microfinance is converted into a for-profit bank. This movement was particularly pronounced in the mid-2000s. Advantages include the fact that the MFI becomes regulated as a bank and so can legally or formally accept savings deposits as well as disburse loans; and that the MFI acquires the discipline of the market and an added incentive to cut costs and expand its scale. Commercialization also furthers the key objective of some in the microfinance sector to make use of MFIs as a vehicle to develop the overall financial system. Disadvantages include the problem that people living in poverty become considered, in some cases, too expensive to serve, or, if they are served, very high interest rates will be charged and aggressive tactics may be used to collect funds. Note that there are some frequently overlooked alternatives, in that to be regulated and accept deposits does not imply a requirement to be a for-profit corporation in most legal systems; for example, the Grameen Bank is a credit union that is mostly owned by its borrowers. Although conversion to, and entry of, for-profit MFIs has become a major trend, most likely microfinance will proceed on multiple tracks, with profit-making or perhaps other commercialized institutions serving those above or close to the poverty line; NGOs providing microcredit to the poor who run a microenterprise with possible subsidies, including external payment of staff time; and transitional services for the ultrapoor who are not ready to run a microenterprise for which credit would be beneficial, but may become so. Ultimately, all people will need financial services, but probably only a minority will need or want a loan to expand a microenterprise or small business. But until regular employment becomes much more widely available as a pathway out of poverty, credit for microenterprises will play a vital role.

Commercialization A process whereby an NGO (a not-for-profit organization) providing microfinance is converted into a for-profit bank.

BOX 15.2 FINDINGS   Combining Microfinance with Training

A 2011 study of FINCA international in Peru by Dean Karlan and Martin Valdivia measured the impact of adding business training to a microcredit program for female microentrepreneurs. Some microcredit solidarity groups were randomly selected to receive 30 to 60 minutes of entrepreneurship training during regular weekly or monthly banking meetings. The training period lasted one to two years. Comparison groups continued to meet as often as the groups that got the training, but only to make loan repayments and savings deposits. The researchers found that the entrepreneurship training led to improved business knowledge, better business practices, and higher microenterprise income. The trained microentrepreneurs reported they engaged more in business activities taught in the training, particularly in "separating money between business and household, reinvesting profits in the business, maintaining records

of sales and expenses, and thinking proactively about new markets and opportunities for profits." They also found that there was a positive impact on loan repayment rates and member retention, which had a big enough impact on the banks' performance to effectively pay for the training. This study sheds light on whether basic entrepreneurship skills can be taught or are fixed personal characteristics perhaps due to genetics or early childhood experiences. The answer appears to be that the poor can learn business acumen. In fact, the larger changes in behavior—in adopting the training, increasing repayment rates, and staying longer with the bank—were found among clients who were initially more skeptical about the value of the training.

Source: Based on Dean Karlan and Martin Valdivia, "Teaching entrepreneurship: Impact of business training on microfinance clients and institutions," *Review of Economics and Statistics* 93, No. 2 (2011): 510–527.

Potential Limitations of Microfinance as a Development Strategy

Microfinance has some potentially important limitations. Microcredit was first conceived and is still largely marketed as financing for microenterprises, but most people probably prefer a regular wage and salary to running a risky microenterprise. Although systematic evidence is lacking, interviews with factory workers in developing countries such as Peru and Bangladesh suggest that many are former microentrepreneurs who gave up their enterprises in favor of a regular job. Most people are willing to pay for insurance, and a predictable wage offers insurance against the vagaries of microenterprise proceeds. Typically, even laid-off professionals in rich countries go into self-employment only until they can find a suitable replacement job. Thus, the primary problem may be the lack of available jobs paying a steady wage or salary—a problem compounded further when custom still prevents women from taking on outside employment that becomes available.[24] To this extent, microcredit, as classically conceived, may prove to be in large measure a "transitional institution." A related concern is that few microentrepreneurs ever grow sufficiently to become bona fide small or medium-size enterprises (SMEs). BRAC found that most borrowers from its SME facility were middle-class entrepreneurs, rather than graduates from its microfinance activities. Of course, people will always need other forms of financial intermediation such as savings accounts, housing mortgages, and consumption loans. And some microenterprises will go on to generate additional employment.

On the one hand, much funding for microfinance follows from the belief in its value as a poverty alleviation strategy, but the poor face many problems, some of which cannot be solved solely by relaxing credit constraints. With an already sizable fraction of public, philanthropic, and NGO activities geared to microfinance, it is plausible that other activities, such as agricultural training, could become relatively underfunded as a result. On the other hand, some leading practitioners argue that the real purpose of MFIs is not to decrease poverty but to stimulate a better financial system (and hopefully to reduce poverty more indirectly). This is a worthy goal, but microfinance development is not the only way to achieve it. Improved systems for regulation and oversight, upgrading the financial system safety net, training of government financial officials, better tax collection to lower fiscal deficits, focusing financial services on the SME sector, and facilitating participation by foreign banks can all make plausible claims as more cost-effective strategies for improving the functioning of the financial system per se. Microfinance has several worthy purposes, and subsidies may help address market failures and poverty problems, but it cannot be assumed that microfinance is the most effective way to spend scarce poverty reduction funds before a careful analysis of the comparative impacts of alternative activities has been undertaken.

Debate continues over whether a positive impact of microfinance on poverty reduction and household well-being can be established, including a controversy over studies of the Grameen Bank, with some studies finding positive impacts and others finding no impact.[25]

The performance of MFIs may vary substantially, depending on local conditions. In a 2011 cross-country comparison, Christian Ahlin and his coauthors found, among other results, that "MFIs are more likely to cover costs when growth is stronger; and MFIs in financially deeper economies have lower default and operating costs, and charge lower interest rates." In a finding that may be related to preferences for jobs, they also found that "more manufacturing and higher workforce participation are associated with slower growth in MFI outreach." Thus, one implication is that relative MFI performance should be evaluated in the context of local conditions.[26]

In sum, microfinance *is* a powerful tool, but it needs to be complemented with other growth, poverty reduction, financial-sector development, human capital, infrastructure building, and—last but by no means least—conventional job creation policies. In the meantime, hundreds of millions of people depend, in part, on microenterprises, so helping them to become more efficient is an important objective; and the provision of lending, saving, and insurance services can provide broad benefits for people living in poverty.

15.4 Formal Financial Systems and Reforms

Financial Liberalization, Real Interest Rates, Savings, and Investment

The restriction of loans to a few large borrowers, together with the widespread existence of high inflation, growing budget deficits, and negative real interest rates, led to a serious "credit crunch" among developing countries during the 1980s. The global recessions of 1981–1982 and 1987 exposed the frailty of many development bank loans so that by the end of the decade, almost half of these banks were reporting 50% or more of their loans in arrears and another quarter had delinquency rates in excess of 25%. With real interest rates on savings deposits in the negative and expectations of continued inflation and exchange-rate devaluation contributing to substantial capital flight, it was not surprising that few individuals were willing to save.

In addition, commercial banks and other financial intermediaries were subject to numerous lending restrictions and faced mandatory interest-rate ceilings on loanable funds at levels well below market-clearing rates.[27] These artificial interest-rate ceilings were often set by governments seeking to finance their budget deficits through the sale of low-interest bonds to private commercial banks. These banks, in turn, had to resort to **rationing** the available credit beyond the normal credit rationing observed in developed economies as a response to adverse selection. Figure 15.1 shows the impact of binding nominal interest-rate ceilings at below-market-clearing levels. With the interest-rate ceiling at $\bar{r}$, which is below the market-clearing equilibrium rate, r_E, the demand for loanable funds, L_2, greatly exceeds the available supply, L_1. This excess demand leads to a need to ration the limited supply—a phenomenon known as **financial repression** because investment is limited or "repressed" by a shortage of savings, which, in turn, results from administered real interest rates below what would occur in a market setting. In the absence of outright corruption in the allocation of L_1 loanable funds, most commercial banks choose to allocate the available credit to a few large-scale borrowers so as to minimize the administrative overhead costs as a proportion of the total costs of lending. Thus, the net effect of government controls over lending rates is that even fewer loans will be allocated to small investors. Banks can cover the additional administrative costs and the added risks of smaller loans only by charging higher interest rates. Hence, small farmers and urban entrepreneurs have no recourse but to seek finance from the unorganized money market, where, as we see from Figure 15.1, they are willing to pay above-market-clearing rates of r_U.

Rationing A system of distribution employed to restrict the quantities of goods and services that consumers or producers can purchase or be allocated freely in the face of excess demand and inflexible prices; can be accomplished with coupons, points, limits on who can borrow, administrative decisions with regard to commodities, industrial licenses for the importation of capital goods, and the like.

Financial repression Constraints on investment resulting from the rationing of credit, usually to a few large-scale borrowers, in financial markets where interest rates and hence the supply of savings are below market-determined levels.

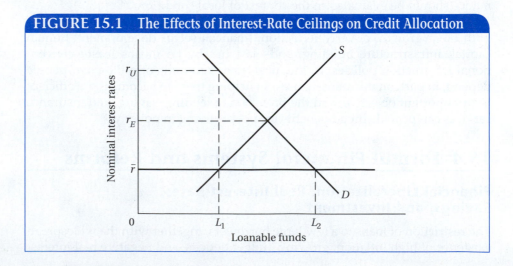

FIGURE 15.1   The Effects of Interest-Rate Ceilings on Credit Allocation

One suggested solution to the problem is to liberalize the financial sector by allowing nominal interest rates to rise to market-clearing levels. This would cause real interest rates to rise to positive levels and thus remove the explicit interest-rate subsidy accorded to preferred borrowers (rent seekers) who are powerful enough to gain access to the rationed credit. Higher real rates should also generate more domestic saving and investment and permit some borrowers to shift from the unorganized to the organized credit market. The World Bank cites evidence from countries such as Thailand, Turkey, and Kenya, where the liberalization of interest rates generates more saving and investment. However, evidence of the effects of financial reform in Chile during the 1970s revealed many shortcomings of the process. These included the acquisition of numerous banks by large conglomerates, or *grupos*, who used their new financial resources to buy recently privatized firms or to expand their own companies. When many of their firms faced financial losses, these *grupos* had to resort to additional funding to avoid bankruptcy. This made the Chilean financial system particularly vulnerable when the debt crisis struck in the 1980s.[28]

Reform and liberalization of the organized money sector is therefore no panacea for the financial systems of developing nations. The early success of South Korea and Taiwan (and before them, Japan) with financial systems that exhibited many of the attributes of repression demonstrates that judicious and selective government intervention can be a stimulus to industrial development. Although there is some evidence that the elimination of substantial interest-rate distortions can promote greater saving and more rapid economic growth, findings have been mixed.[29] Financial reform must always be accompanied by other more direct measures to make sure that small farmers and investors have access to needed credit. Furthermore, as shown in the next section, careful supervision of the banking and financial sectors is needed to prevent undue concentration by local elites. As we have already pointed out in this text, "getting prices right" is only one step, albeit an important one, in making development serve the needs of the forgotten majority.

Financial Policy and the Role of the State

Does financial liberalization mean that governments in developing countries have no role to play in the financial sector? In an effort to identify how these governments can work effectively within the context of liberalized financial markets, the 2001 Nobel laureate Joseph Stiglitz and his coauthors isolated seven major market failures that imply a potential role for state intervention.[30] His basic argument is "that financial markets are markedly different from other markets," "that market failures are likely to be more pervasive in these markets," and that "much of the rationale for liberalizing financial markets is based neither on a sound economic understanding of how these markets work nor on the potential scope for government intervention."[31] The seven market failures that Stiglitz and colleagues identified and that are likely to be of particular relevance to developing countries are the following:

1. *The "public good" nature of monitoring financial institutions.* Investors need information about the solvency and management of financial institutions. Like other forms of information, monitoring is a public good—everyone

who places savings in a particular financial institution would benefit from knowing that the institution was prospering or close to insolvency. But like other public goods in free-market economies, there is an undersupply of monitoring information, and consequently, risk-averse savers withhold their funds. The net result is fewer resources allocated through these institutions.

2. *Externalities of monitoring, selection, and lending.* Benefits are often incurred by lenders who learn about the viability of potential projects from the monitoring, selection, and lending decisions of other lenders. Investors can also benefit from information generated by other investors on the quality of different financial institutions. Like other positive (or negative) externalities, the market provides too little information, and resources are underallocated or overallocated.

3. *Externalities of financial disruption.* In the absence of government insurance (whether or not an explicit policy has been issued), the failure of one major financial institution can cause a run on the entire banking system and lead to long-term disruptions of the overall financial system.

4. *Missing and incomplete markets.* In most developing countries, markets for insurance against a variety of financial (bank failure) or physical (e.g., crop failure) risks are missing. The basic problem is that information is imperfect and costly to obtain, so a developing-country government has an important role in reducing these risks. It can, for example, force membership in insurance programs or require financial institutions as well as borrowers to disclose information about their assets, liabilities, and creditworthiness.

5. *Imperfect competition.* Competition in the banking sector of most developing countries is extremely limited, meaning that potential borrowers usually face only a small number of suppliers of loanable funds, many of which are unwilling or unable to accommodate new and unknown customers. This is particularly true of small borrowers in the informal urban and rural sectors.

6. *Inefficiency of competitive markets in the financial sector.* Theoretically, for perfectly competitive markets to function efficiently, financial markets must be complete (without uninsured risks) and information must be exogenous (freely available to all and not influenced by any one participant's action in the market). Clearly, there are special advantages to individuals or entities with privileged information in financial markets in developing countries, and risk insurance is difficult, if not impossible, to obtain. As a result, unfettered financial markets may not allocate capital to its most profitable uses, and there can be substantial deviations between social and private returns to alternative investment projects. In such cases, direct government intervention—for example, by restricting certain kinds of loans and encouraging others—may partly or completely offset these imbalances.

7. *Uninformed investors.* Contrary to the doctrine of consumer sovereignty, with its assumption of perfect knowledge, many investors in developing countries lack both the information and the appropriate means to acquire it in order to make rational investment decisions. Here again, governments

can impose financial disclosure requirements on firms listed on local stock exchanges or require banks, for example, to inform customers of the differences between simple and compound interest rates or of the nature of penalties for early withdrawals of savings.

In each of these seven instances, Stiglitz and his coauthors argue, governments have a proper role to play in regulating financial institutions, creating new institutions to fill gaps in the kinds of credit provided by private institutions (e.g., microloans to small farmers and tradespeople), providing consumer protection, ensuring bank solvency, encouraging fair competition, and ultimately improving the allocation of financial resources and promoting macroeconomic stability.

As in other areas of economic development, the critical issue for financial policy is not about free markets versus government intervention but rather about how both can work together (along with the NGO sector) to meet the urgent needs of poor people.

Debate on the Role of Stock Markets

Recent years have witnessed enormous growth in developing countries' stock markets. This has resulted in costs as well as benefits for development. It has increased volatility in the economy as funds have flowed in from abroad and even more dramatically flooded out. In this section, we take a look at stock markets in developing countries and consider some proposed policies to get the most benefits from these markets. We also consider some of the limitations of depending too heavily on stock markets as an engine of growth.

Some studies have suggested that stock market development can play a highly constructive role in encouraging growth. These studies show that greater past stock market development (measured by either past capitalization or turnover in relation to gross domestic product, or GDP) predicts faster subsequent economic growth, even after other variables known to influence growth, such as the rate of investment and education, are accounted for. Even more striking, both banking and stock market development were found to have independent positive effects on growth, suggesting that each plays a somewhat different role in the economy. A correlation between stock market development and growth would be expected by many theories, including the view that finance follows industry. Therefore, industrial growth and stock market growth would occur together, but in that case, stock market growth would merely reflect the growth of the real sector. The fact that there is faster growth after greater stock market development has already been realized is suggestive of causality but is not conclusive. This is because past financial depth is correlated with future depth: Countries that had well-developed stock markets in the past usually do in the future as well. So the correlation between growth and past depth could really be driven by a third factor, such as the protection of private property and the rule of law. However, the results suggest that stock markets do have a role to play. Moreover, we can expect that stock markets promote the more general availability of liquidity and risk diversification services, may serve to motivate entrepreneurs who may later go public, and provide incentives for managerial performance that make it easier for firms to raise capital in any form.[32]

The question, then, is, should government do anything to develop and promote such markets, given the remaining uncertainty about the importance of their role? It makes no sense to actively develop stock markets unless certain prerequisites are met. First, one needs macrostability; investors will not invest in equity without it. Second, policy credibility is needed. How will policymakers keep the economy stabilized, and how will they react in a financial crisis to prevent a meltdown? And third, one needs a solid domestic-firm base; there is no point to opening a stock market if there are few firms in which outside investors would wish to take an equity stake.

Given that these prerequisites are in place, it is reasonable to wonder why a country would need to promote stock markets; wouldn't these markets develop as a result of market forces? One rationale for a public policy promoting the development of stock markets could be to balance the effective tilt toward debt finance that is implicit in policy to date (for example, public deposit insurance, while clearly necessary, functions like an interest subsidy, which tilts the playing field away from equity markets). Although evidence of spillovers or other special benefits for the promotion of stock market development is probably not enough to make a case for public subsidies to create and expand stock markets, in many countries policymakers may conclude that the evidence is compelling enough to eliminate bias, explicit or implicit, that has operated against stock markets in the past.

In this regard, the first type of stock market development policy could be termed *barrier removal*. Rather than promoting stock markets directly, let alone subsidizing their development, this strategy would remove other impediments, generating stock market development on its own. In practice, this usually entails certain forms of deregulation. One must be careful here because, as seen earlier in the chapter, many regulations were put in place, not necessarily because there was government failure, but because of genuine market failure in the financial sector. If some regulations responding to market failure are removed, others may have to be established in their place.

However, certain regulations probably do have the effect of retarding the development and expansion of the stock market. Prime examples are capital repatriation legislation that strongly limits the amount of profit that foreign investors can take out of a country, the existence of restrictions on investing directly, restrictions on foreign broker participation, entry restrictions on investment banking and brokering that are not rational or that encourage rent seeking, and the failure to ensure that regulations are transparent and evenly applied. Changing such regulations has potential costs as well as benefits and should be undertaken carefully.

There are other significant problems with relying too strongly on stock markets as a development strategy. First, stock markets lead to substantial foreign-investor influence over domestic-company operations. In developing countries, a large percentage of shares of listed companies are usually foreign owned. Second, stock markets can lead to short-term speculation that can dominate trading and distort the decision making of managers, often inducing a short time horizon. Third, relatedly, "hot money" that flows in and out of a country to speculate in markets can produce wide currency swings and destabilize the economy.

Many questions remain regarding the role of financial intermediation, in general, and stock markets, in particular, in economic development. This is sure to be an active area of policy discussion in the years ahead.

15.5 Fiscal Policy for Development

Macrostability and Resource Mobilization

Financial policy deals with money, interest, and credit allocation; fiscal policy focuses on government taxation and expenditures. Together they represent the bulk of public-sector activities. Most stabilization attempts have concentrated on cutting government expenditures to achieve budgetary balance. But the burden of resource mobilization to finance essential public developmental efforts must come from the revenue side. Public domestic and foreign borrowing can fill some savings gaps. In the long run, it is the efficient and equitable collection of taxes on which governments must base their development aspirations.[33] In the absence of well-organized and locally controlled money markets, most developing countries have had to rely primarily on fiscal measures to stabilize the economy and to mobilize domestic resources.

Taxation: Direct and Indirect

Developed countries of the Organization for Economic Cooperation and Development (OECD) collect a much higher percentage of GDP in the form of tax revenue than developing countries do, as can be seen in Table 15.2. According to a 2000 IMF study, in the period 1995–1997, developing countries collected 18.2% of GDP in tax revenues, while OECD countries collected more than double this share, 37.9%. Developed countries may have a higher demand for public expenditures and also a greater capacity to generate tax revenue, and thus, the causality likely runs in large part from greater development

TABLE 15.2	Comparative Average Levels of Tax Revenue, 1985–1997, as a Percentage of GDP	
Country Groups	**1985–1987**	**1995–1997**
OECD Countries	36.6	37.9
America	30.6	32.6
Pacific	30.7	31.6
Europe	38.2	39.4
Developing Countries	17.5	18.2
Africa	19.6	19.8
Asia	16.1	17.4
Middle East	16.5	18.1
Western hemisphere	17.6	18.0

Source: National Tax Journal by National Tax Association. Copyright 2000. Reproduced with permission of National Tax Association.

to higher tax levels. But to the degree that government resources are spent wisely, such as on human capital and needed infrastructure investments, some of the causality may run the other way as well.

Typically, **direct taxes**—those levied on private individuals, corporations, and property—make up 20 to 40% of total tax revenue for most developing economies. **Indirect taxes**, such as import and export duties, value-added taxes (VATs), excise taxes, and sales taxes, constitute the primary source of fiscal revenue for most developing countries.

As can be seen in Table 15.3, developed OECD countries generally rely more strongly on direct taxes, but this pattern is much less pronounced in Europe, where reliance on indirect taxes is almost as great as on direct taxes. It is not clear whether direct or indirect taxation is better for economic development because their impact on critically important human capital accumulation is so complex. Avoiding extreme overreliance on any one form of taxation is a reasonable approach, given the current state of knowledge.[34]

Regions and nations in the developing world also differ substantially in their rates of tax collection. For example, as of 2011, countries in South Asia collect (collected) very low levels of tax revenue, which is about 10 to 15% of GDP, in comparison with approximately 20% in otherwise comparable developing economies.[35]

The tax systems (direct and indirect taxes combined) of many developing countries are far from progressive. In some, such as Mexico, they can be highly regressive (meaning that lower-income groups pay a higher proportion of their income in taxes than higher-income groups).

The tax system is often used as an instrument for influencing the incentives for the private sector to undertake investment in various activities, such as to implement industrial policy of the type examined in Chapter 12, section 12.6. The main purpose of taxation is the mobilization of resources to finance public expenditures. Whatever the prevailing political or economic ideology of the less developed country, its economic and social progress depends largely on its government's ability to generate sufficient revenues to finance an expanding program of essential, non-revenue-yielding public services—health, education, transport, legal and other institutions, poverty alleviation, and other components of the economic and social infrastructure.

Many developing countries face problems of large fiscal deficits—public expenditures greatly in excess of public revenues—resulting from a combination of ambitious development programs and unexpected negative external shocks. With rising debt burdens, falling commodity prices, growing trade imbalances, and declining foreign private and public investment inflows, developing-country governments have had little choice but to undergo severe fiscal retrenchment. This has meant cutting government expenditures (mostly on social services) and raising revenues through increased or more efficient tax collections.

In general, the taxation potential of a country depends on five factors:

1. The level of per capita real income

2. The degree of inequality in the distribution of that income

3. The industrial structure of the economy and the importance of different types of economic activity (e.g., the importance of foreign trade, the

significance of the modern sector, the extent of foreign participation in private enterprises, the degree to which the agricultural sector is commercialized as opposed to subsistence oriented)

4. The social, political, and institutional setting and the relative power of different groups (e.g., landlords as opposed to manufacturers, trade unions, village or district community organizations)

5. The administrative competence, honesty, and integrity of the tax-gathering branches of government

We now examine the principal sources of direct and indirect public tax revenues. We can then consider how the tax system might be used to promote a more equitable and sustainable pattern of economic growth.

Personal Income and Property Taxes Personal income taxes yield much less revenue as a proportion of GDP in less developed than in more developed nations. In the latter, the income tax structure is said to be progressive: People with higher incomes theoretically pay a larger percentage of that income in taxes. It would be administratively too costly and economically regressive to attempt to collect substantial income taxes from the poor. But the fact remains that most governments in developing countries have not been persistent enough in collecting taxes owed by the very wealthy. Moreover, in countries where the ownership of property is heavily concentrated and therefore represents the major determinant of unequal incomes (e.g., most of Asia and Latin America), property taxes can be an efficient and administratively simple mechanism both for generating public revenues and for correcting gross inequalities in income distribution. But in a World Bank survey, in only one of the 22 countries surveyed did the property tax constitute more than 4.2% of total public revenues. Moreover, in spite of much public rhetoric about reducing income inequalities, the share of property taxes as well as overall direct taxation has remained roughly the same for the majority of developing countries over the past two decades. Clearly, this phenomenon cannot be attributed to government tax-collecting inefficiencies as much as to the political and economic power and influence of the large landowning and other dominant classes in many Asian and Latin American countries. The political will to carry out development plans must therefore include the will to extract public revenue from the most accessible sources to finance development projects. If the former is absent, the latter will be too.[36]

Corporate Income Taxes Taxes on corporate profits, of both domestically and foreign-owned companies, amount to less than 3% of GDP in most developing countries, compared to more than 6% in developed nations. Developing-country governments tend to offer a wide variety of tax incentives and concessions to manufacturing and commercial enterprises. Typically, new and foreign enterprises are offered long periods (sometimes up to 15 years) of tax exemption and thereafter take advantage of generous investment depreciation allowances, special tax write-offs, and other measures to lessen their tax burden. In the case of multinational foreign enterprises, the ability of governments in most developing countries to collect substantial taxes is often frustrated. These locally run enterprises are frequently able to shift profits to partner companies in countries offering the lowest levels of taxation through transfer pricing (discussed in Chapter 14). Some developing countries use such tax breaks more sparingly and strategically, however.

Indirect Taxes on Commodities   The largest single source of public revenue in developing countries is the taxation of commodities in the form of import, export, and excise duties (see Table 15.3). These taxes, which individuals and corporations pay indirectly through their purchase of commodities, are relatively easy to assess and collect. This is especially true in the case of foreign-traded commodities, which must pass through a limited number of frontier ports and are usually handled by a few wholesalers. The ease of collecting such taxes is one reason why countries with extensive foreign trade typically collect a greater proportion of public revenues in the form of import and export duties than countries with limited external trade. For example, in open economies with up to 40% of gross national income (GNI) derived from foreign trade, an average import duty of 25% will yield a tax revenue equivalent of 10% of GNI. By contrast, in countries with only about 7% of GNI derived from exports, the same tariff rate would yield only 2% of GNI in equivalent tax revenues. Although we discussed import and export duties in the context of trade policies in Chapter 12, we amplify that import and export duties, in addition to representing a major source of public revenue in many developing countries, can also be a substitute for the corporate income tax. To the extent that importers are unable to pass on to local consumers the full costs of the tax, an import duty can serve as a proxy tax on the profits of the importer (often a foreign company) and only partly a tax on the local consumer. Similarly, an export duty can be an effective way of taxing the profits of producing companies, including locally based multinational firms that practice transfer pricing. But export duties designed to generate revenue should not be raised to the point of discouraging local producers from expanding their export production to any significant extent.

In selecting commodities to be taxed, whether in the form of duties on imports and exports or excise taxes on local commodities, certain general economic and administrative principles must be followed to minimize the cost of securing maximum revenue. First, the commodity should be imported or produced by a relatively small number of licensed firms so that evasion can be controlled. Second, the price elasticity of demand for the commodity should be low so that total demand is not choked by the rise in consumer prices that results from the tax. Third, the commodity should have a high income elasticity of demand so that as incomes rise, more tax revenue will be collected. Fourth, for equity purposes, it is best to tax commodities like cars, refrigerators, imported fancy foods, and household appliances, which are consumed largely by the upper-income groups, while forgoing taxation on items of mass consumption such as basic foods, simple clothing, and household utensils, even though these may satisfy the first three criteria.

The conventional wisdom in recent years has been that switching to a broad-based **value-added tax (VAT)** would improve economic efficiency; encouraged by development agencies, such tax reforms have accordingly been undertaken in many developing countries. However, this approach has been challenged recently. In particular, welfare may be worsened when the ability

Value-added tax (VAT) Levy on value added at each stage of the production process.

TABLE 15.3   Comparative Composition of Tax Revenue, 1985–1997, as a Percentage of GDP

Country Groups	1985–1987 Income Taxes			1985–1987 Consumption Taxes				Social Security	1995–1997 Income Taxes			1995–1997 Consumption Taxes				Social Security
	Total	Corporate	Personal	Total	General	Excises	Trade		Total	Corporate	Personal	Total	General	Excises	Trade	
OECD Countries	**13.9**	**2.8**	**11.3**	**11.3**	**6.0**	**3.8**	**0.7**	**8.8**	**14.2**	**3.1**	**10.8**	**11.4**	**6.6**	**3.6**	**0.3**	**9.5**
America	14.0	2.5	11.4	7.6	3.4	2.2	0.6	5.8	15.4	3.0	12.3	7.0	3.7	2.0	0.3	6.1
Pacific	17.1	3.9	13.2	7.5	2.3	3.7	0.8	2.8	16.3	4.3	11.4	8.4	4.3	2.6	0.6	3.5
Europe	13.3	2.7	11.0	12.4	6.8	4.0	0.7	10.1	13.7	2.9	10.6	12.4	7.3	4.0	0.3	10.8
Developing Countries	**4.9**	**2.8**	**1.7**	**10.3**	**2.3**	**2.6**	**4.2**	**1.2**	**5.2**	**2.6**	**2.2**	**10.5**	**3.6**	**2.4**	**3.5**	**1.3**
Africa	6.3	2.9	3.1	11.7	3.2	2.3	5.7	0.4	6.9	2.4	3.9	11.6	3.8	2.3	5.1	0.5
Asia	5.7	3.5	2.1	9.5	1.9	2.5	3.6	0.1	6.2	3.0	3.0	9.7	3.1	2.2	2.7	0.3
Middle East	4.7	4.3	1.0	9.1	1.5	2.4	4.4	1.2	5.0	3.2	1.3	10.3	1.5	3.0	4.3	1.1
Western hemisphere	3.7	1.8	1.0	10.6	2.6	3.0	3.7	2.4	3.7	2.3	1.0	10.6	4.8	2.3	2.6	2.5

Source: *National Tax Journal* by National Tax Association. Copyright 2000. Reproduced with permission of National Tax Association.

of the informal economy to remain effectively untaxed introduces new distortions in the economy.[37]

Problems of Tax Administration

In the final analysis, a developing nation's ability to collect taxes for public expenditure programs and to use the tax system as a basis for modifying the distribution of personal incomes will depend not only on the enactment of appropriate tax legislation but also on the efficiency and integrity of the tax authorities who must implement these laws. In other words, as Joel Slemrod has put it, we must consider "optimal tax systems" rather than "optimal taxes" in the abstract. Thus, the "technology of tax collection" must be considered, which includes the cost of tax administration and enforcement of compliance.[38]

The ability of governments in developing countries to expand their tax nets to cover the higher-income groups and minimize tax evasion by local and foreign individuals and corporations will largely determine the efficiency of the tax system in achieving its dual function of generating sufficient public revenues to finance expanding development programs and preventing an undue burden on lower-income groups in order to reduce poverty and income inequality. Much will depend, once again, on the political will to enact and enforce such progressive tax programs.[39]

15.6 State-Owned Enterprises and Privatization

State-owned enterprises (SOEs) Public corporations and parastatal agencies (e.g., agricultural marketing boards) owned and operated by the government.

Associated with the problems of public administration in developing countries have been the widespread activities of **state-owned enterprises (SOEs)**, public corporations owned and operated by the government. In addition to their traditionally dominant presence in utilities (gas, water, and electricity), transportation (railroads, airlines, and buses), and communications (telephone, telegraph, and postal services), SOEs have been active in such key sectors as large-scale manufacturing, construction, finance, services, natural resources, and agriculture. Sometimes they may dominate these sectors, particularly in the areas of natural resources and manufacturing. Despite extensive privatization (described later in the chapter) in Latin America and Eurasia and of smaller SOEs in most countries, state ownership of enterprises remains common, and SOEs account for a substantial share of investment and industrial output in many developing nations, notably in China and India, and in the least developed countries.[40]

SOEs have played a major role in the economies of developing nations, historically contributing an average of 7 to 15% of their GDP. In addition, SOEs account for a substantial amount of investment in developing countries, contributing up to one-fifth of gross domestic investment.

Given the strategic role that state-owned enterprises play in the economies of developing countries and their demands on scarce resources, it is important to understand the reasons for their creation and the measures that might be undertaken to improve their efficiency and to help them meet their economic and social objectives.

Some of the rationale for the creation of SOEs were suggested in Chapter 11. One is the persistence of monopoly power in many developing countries. Direct government control has been intended to ensure that prices are not set above the marginal costs of producing the output. Moreover, as was also mentioned, certain goods that have a high social benefit are usually provided at a price below their costs or even free; hence, the private sector has no incentive to produce such goods, and the government must assume responsibility for their provision.

The second rationale for the creation of SOEs is capital formation, which is particularly important at the early stages of development, when private savings are very low. Investment in infrastructure at this point is crucial, to lay the groundwork for further investment. And SOEs remain important at later stages in industries that require massive funds.

The lack of private incentives to engage in promising economic activities because of factors such as uncertainty about the size of local markets, unreliable sources of supply, and the absence of technology and skilled labor is a third major rationale for creating public enterprises. Governments in developing countries may also seek to expand employment and facilitate training of their labor force by engaging in public production. They may desire to increase export earnings by creating export industries, particularly those that might otherwise be unable to compete. For reasons of income distribution, the government may seek to locate enterprises in certain regions, particularly in backward economic areas where there are no private incentives for creating such economic activities.

Other reasons for the creation of SOEs include the desire of some governments to gain national control over strategic sectors of the economy, such as defense, over foreign-owned enterprises (MNCs) whose interests may not coincide with those of the country, or over key sectors for development purposes. Government involvement may also come about as a result of bankruptcy in a major private industry. Ideological motivations may be an additional factor in the creation of state-owned enterprises.

Improving the Performance of SOEs

Despite these arguments, SOEs have come under sustained attack for wasting resources. SOEs make significant demands on government finance, as well as on domestic and foreign credit. In many cases, the level of these demands is related to low profitability and inefficiency. Although it is difficult to generalize across countries, data from the World Bank for state-owned enterprises in 24 developing countries revealed only a small operating surplus.[41] And once factors such as interest payments, subsidized input prices, and taxes and accumulated arrears were taken into account, SOEs in many of these countries showed a large deficit. Turkish enterprises averaged net losses equivalent to 3% of GDP. Mexican SOEs showed a net loss of 1.2% of GDP. A study of SOEs in four African countries (Ghana, Senegal, Tanzania, and Zambia) also revealed generally poor performance. Operating at a deficit, they proved to be a massive drain on government resources. There was also evidence that labor and capital productivity were generally lower than in the private sector. These African SOEs were also found to be less successful in generating employment as a result of their bias toward capital intensiveness.[42]

Several factors contribute to the overall poor performance of SOEs in terms of profitability and efficiency. Perhaps the most important is that SOEs differ from private firms in that they are expected to pursue both commercial and social goals. Providing goods at prices below costs in an effort to subsidize the public or hiring extra workers to meet national employment objectives inevitably reduces profitability. Another factor adversely affecting the profitability and efficiency of SOEs is the overcentralization of their decision making, which allows little flexibility for managers in the everyday operation of the firm. An additional problem is the bureaucratization of management; many decision makers are not accountable for their performance, and little incentive is provided for improved decision making. Further, despite the abundant labor supply and the employment mandate, access to capital at subsidized interest rates has often encouraged unnecessary capital intensiveness, as in the cases of the four African nations cited. Finally, in very corrupt regimes, SOEs have provided a "tunnel" through which public assets may be stolen.

One option for reform is reorganization with a greater bottom-line focus for the SOE; another is the transfer of ownership and control from the public to the private sector, a process known as **privatization**. In the former option, decentralizing decision making to allow for more flexibility and providing better incentives for managers could increase production efficiency. Providing capital at its market rate may eliminate the bias toward capital intensiveness. The alternatives include use of management and employee incentives, external management contracts, build-own-operate-transfer agreements with private firms, use of franchises and concessions in some sectors, greater exposure to competition, and partial privatization. The effectiveness of these alternatives to full privatization has been uneven in practice.[43]

Privatization Selling public assets (corporations) to individuals or private business interests.

Privatization: Theory and Experience

The second option, the privatization of state-owned enterprises in the production and financial sectors, hinges on the neoclassical hypothesis that private ownership brings greater efficiency and more rapid growth. During the 1980s and 1990s, privatization was actively promoted by major international bilateral (USAID) and multilateral agencies (World Bank, IMF). Many developing countries have followed this advice, although the extent of their philosophical agreement, as opposed to the financial pressures exerted by these funding agencies, remains unclear. In addition to the belief that privatization improves efficiency, increases output, and lowers costs, proponents argue that it curbs the growth of government expenditures, raises cash to reduce public internal and external debt, and promotes individual initiative while rewarding entrepreneurship. Finally, supporters of privatization see it as a way to broaden the base of ownership and participation in the economy, thereby encouraging individuals to feel that they have a direct stake in the system.[44] The heyday of privatization was during the 1980s and early 1990s. Between 1980 and 1992, more than 15,000 enterprises were privatized throughout the world, more than 11,000 of them in the former East Germany after reunification. In the developing nations, the number of privatized companies amounted to 450 in Africa, 900 in Latin America, and approximately 180 in Asia. Mexico, Chile, and Argentina have led the movement in Latin America. Among low-income countries, the speed of privatization was much more cautious, with the majority of transfers coming in small, low-value firms. Generally, the best candidates for privatization were the ones sold off first.

Privatization has apparently been successful in promoting greater efficiency and higher output in many cases.[45] But many privatized assets were concentrated in the hands of small groups of local and international elites. For example, many sales of former state-owned enterprises in Latin America were conducted without competitive bidding, often at predetermined concessionary ("fire sale") prices; corruption was often alleged. As a result, small groups of well-connected investors, both domestic and foreign, were enriched by the process. And some privatization merely replaced public monopolies with private monopolies, thereby allowing a few individuals to reap the monopoly profits that formerly accrued to the state while hundreds of thousands of workers lost their jobs.

Privatization has also been resorted to as a quick fix for fiscal deficits, but when the easy candidates for privatization have been exhausted, governments in developing countries have often found that the fiscal problems have returned. Privatization therefore raises many complex issues. There are questions of feasibility, appropriate financing, the structure of legal and property rights, the role of competing elites and interest groups (e.g., public officials and bureaucrats versus domestic and foreign private business interests), and whether or not widespread privatization promotes or ultimately weakens existing dualistic economic, social, and political structures. It is not even sufficient to claim that privatization can lead to higher profits, greater output, or even lower costs. For one thing, while financial performance of firms generally improves after privatization, comparable SOEs in the same country that are not privatized may show similar improvements, and a study of matched firms in Egypt provided evidence for this. But the key issue is whether such privatization better serves the long-run development interests of a nation by promoting a more sustainable and equitable pattern of economic and social progress; the evidence so far is less than compelling.[46] Nevertheless, although the pace of privatization has slowed, few new state-owned enterprises are currently being created.

The need for privatization has posed some difficult questions: Who should be able to purchase SOEs? Whatever party has the most ready cash? Or should market imperfections in who is able to raise immediate capital be taken into account? Does it matter if the purchaser is a domestic citizen or a multinational corporation? Managers and workers in the company or citizens at large? Are some modes of privatization politically easier to carry out than others? Can creative approaches to arranging and financing ownership transfer agreements widen the possibilities? Can privatization be carried out in isolation from other programs, or does it have to be conceived as part of an integrated development strategy? Does privatization simply mean a long-overdue diminution of the government ownership role, or is it optimally implemented as part of a reorganized and renewed nonownership, public role in development? Already by the mid-1990s, there were laws or regulations in 50 developing countries (including transition economies) providing incentives, as well as limitations, for employee ownership (EO), often, but not exclusively, in privatization initiatives. These EO provisions are varied in nature and extent. They range from seeking to restrain employee ownership to modest levels, such as 10%, to encouraging employee ownership participation to as much as 100% of certain companies. Some of the issues are explored further for the cases of Chile and Poland in Box 15.3.

BOX 15.3 Privatization—What, When, and to Whom? Chile and Poland

Chile and Poland have had sweeping privatization experiences. The pioneering privatization program in Chile remains among the most far-reaching in the developing world. Over an 18-year period, some 550 firms employing 5% of the country's workforce were privatized. The process was sometimes choppy. Many banks that had been privatized in the preceding years had to be renationalized in the 1982 financial crash.

Privatization in Chile proceeded over several overlapping stages. In 1974 and 1975, some 360 firms that had been nationalized in the early 1970s were returned to their previous owners; most of the rest of these were reprivatized by 1978. This was far easier to carry out than the privatizations of long-term SOEs. Of the 110 enterprises divested in 1975–1983, a large share were SOEs founded in the early 1970s. Many others were existing private companies in which that government had bought shares. From 1978 to 1981, privatization of social services took place; the government officially continued to provide social services only for the poorest groups and focused on subsidizing demand rather than supply. By 1981, public enterprises represented 24% of GDP, down from 39% in 1973.

In 1983–1986, many enterprises "rescued" (nationalized) in the 1982–1983 financial crash were reprivatized. Eight of the 15 largest corporations in Chile were privatized in the 1980s.

Privatization from the mid-1980s on was achieved through public auction, negotiation, sales to pension funds, "popular capitalism" (to small investors), and "labor capitalism" (to employees). Sales of the latter two types represented about 20% of privatization. Even SOEs that were not slated for privatization were subject to major internal reorganization, with the result that efficiency and profitability increased.

Popular capitalism was intended to spread ownership among many small individual investors, in part to increase popularity and acceptance of privatization. To become eligible for generous discounts, participants had to be taxpayers with no back taxes owed. Two major banks, Banco de Chile and Banco de Santiago, were privatized under this plan.

Under labor capitalism, workers could acquire a percentage of shares in their own company up to the value of 50% of a worker's pension fund that could be received in advance for this purpose. Retirement funds could be used as collateral for below-market government loans to buy additional shares. At retirement, workers could elect to trade these shares back for the value of their pension fund, so this gave the workers an essentially riskless investment. About 21,000 workers, 35% of those eligible, took part; other shares purchased by groups of workers were organized as investment societies. Between 1985 and 1990, a total of 15 SOEs were sold using some employee ownership, including 3 that became 100% employee owned. Three others became 44%, 33%, and 31% employee owned, respectively, and the remaining 9 had an average of about 12% employee ownership. Results were favorable in increased productivity and attracting foreign investment.

Despite serious socioeconomic problems, Chile began privatization with well-established legal and accounting frameworks; fully functioning labor, capital, and product markets; and many formal and informal socioeconomic institutions that are taken for granted in market economies. But in eastern Europe, these background institutions had been systematically suppressed under Communism. The Polish privatization plan was adopted in the summer of 1990. The first step in privatizing state enterprises, "commercialization," often requires the approval of the relevant ministry, management, and employees to set up a joint-stock company that can be sold. The stock is valued independently, and workers are then allowed to purchase up to 20% of the stock at half price. In capital-intensive companies, a subsidy limit based on the prior year's wages in the company would be set, making somewhat less than 20% of the stock eligible. This is to avoid overly concentrating these subsidies among a few lucky employees.

An alternative strategy that circumvented administrative procedures, applying mainly to smaller firms, was "privatization through liquidation." This procedure permitted leveraged buyouts that could include substantial employee and management ownership. The process is initiated when the firm's managing director and the employees' council (an elected representative body) commissions a "preprivatization financial analysis." If financial conditions appear favorable, the firm petitions the government ministry that had control over the company under the central-planning system, which offers an opinion on the merits of the analysis and suggests a strategy for privatization. The old SOE is abolished, and the new firm buys some assets but normally leases others back from the state. The value of these leased assets is determined at the time of reorganization and does not change over the life of the contract (even to adjust for inflation). This constitutes a substantial subsidy to the new owners.

But of some 250 companies representing about 10% of employment commercialized by mid-1992, only 10% were fully privatized. And only about 175 firms had self-privatized by mid-1992, by which time the government was considering a large-scale privatization plan that would organize several hundred companies representing about 10% of industrial employment into a kind of closed-end mutual fund. That plan stalled until 1997, when the government resumed plans to sell 513 small manufacturing, construction, and trading companies to the public. For the equivalent of $7 per voucher, Polish citizens could purchase shares of these companies through listed national investment funds on the Warsaw stock exchange.

The task of privatization in eastern Europe by any means has been daunting, with few resources to spare. In the early 1990s, the Polish privatization ministry had only 200 employees. This compared with 3,500 in the Treuhandanstalt, in charge of privatization in the former East Germany.

Sources: Saul Estrin, Jan Hanousek, Evzen Kocenda, and Jan Svejnar, "The effects of privatization and ownership in transition economies," *Journal of Economic Literature*, 47(2009): 699–728; David Lipton and Jeffrey D. Sachs, "Privatization in eastern Europe: The case of Poland," *Brookings Papers on Economic Activity* 2 (1990): 293–341; William L. Megginson and Jeffry M. Netter, "From state to market: A survey of empirical studies on privatization," *Journal of Economic Literature* 39 (2001): 321–389; Stephen C. Smith, "On the law and economics of employee ownership in privatization in developing and transition economies," *Annals of Public and Cooperative Economics* 65 (1994): 437–468; Stephen C. Smith, Beom-Cheol Cin, and Milan Vodopevic, "Privatization incidence, ownership forms, and firm performance: Evidence from Slovenia," *Journal of Comparative Economics* 25 (1997): 158–179; World Bank, *Techniques of Privatization of State-Owned Enterprises* (Washington, D.C.: World Bank, 1988).

15.7 Public Administration: The Scarcest Resource

Many observers would argue that the shortage of public (and private) administrative capability is the single scarcest public resource in the developing world.[47] The problem is not just a lack of training or experience. It also arises out of the political instability of numerous developing nations. When power is constantly changing hands, considerations of efficiency and public welfare are likely to be subordinated to political loyalty. Moreover, the larger the group of officials affected by a change of power, the more difficult it will be to maintain continuity in the formulation and execution of policy.

Public administration is unlikely to function efficiently when the rule of law is in question, when there is public disorder, or when there is little consensus on fundamental issues. Acute conditions of class, tribal, or religious conflict within a society will usually be reflected in the management and

operation of government departments and public agencies. In a highly traditional society, where kinship ties are strong and such concepts as statehood
and public service have not yet taken firm root, there is little regard for a merit
system. Similarly, where the dominant values are sectarian, traditional incentives to perform in the wider public interest may not have much appeal.

Many governments in developing countries may also have civil service
goals other than performance: to break up traditional elites, to nationalize
the civil service, to conform to ideological correctness, to reflect or favor
an ethnic ratio, or to include or exclude minorities. Most governments are
also organized in the traditional hierarchical form. But some have experi-
mented with negative hierarchy (from bottom to top), ad hocracy (temporary arrangements), and polyarchy (cooperation with outside organizations),
this last being attempted particularly when some special form of expertise is
involved.

Some bureaucracies in developing countries are relatively overstaffed at
the bottom and understaffed at the top. There is a chronic shortage of skilled
competent managers who are capable of independent decision making. The
greater the number of parastatal organizations set up—the more state-owned
enterprises and nationalized industries, quasigovernmental bodies, development corporations, and training institutions—the thinner this layer of
managers is spread.

In the case of nationalized industries, most experiments have been economically disastrous and have resulted in all kinds of strains within the central
civil service. Personnel systems in the public service are usually not adequate
for the increased management complexities of an industrial enterprise. So parallel personnel systems have been set up, multiplying the public service systems, draining skills, leading to disparities in terms and conditions of service,
and resulting in manpower shortages and morale problems. Political considerations often affect the ability to recruit competent managers with special
technical skills. In short, nationalization in many instances has often added to
the financial burden of the government budget.

The administrative component in economic development—not only in
relation to the particular project under consideration but also in relation to the
functioning of the entire public and private economic system—should not be
underestimated.

For many developing countries, the quality of financial supervision, governance, and fiscal management—the subject of this chapter—has improved
markedly over the past couple of decades. This is one factor in improved
economic performance of many developing countries, though much remains
to be done. At the same time, to be effective, active attention to other constraints on economic development as discussed throughout the text also will
be necessary.

Case Study 15

African Success Story at Risk: Botswana

Botswana is a landlocked country in sub-Saharan Africa with high population growth and a high incidence of disease. Yet it has attained one of the highest average per capita growth rates in the world since obtaining its independence from Britain in 1966.

Botswana shows that mineral wealth can be a benefit in a country that has the appropriate political development in place. Botswana has experienced by far the highest rate of growth in sub-Saharan Africa: 8.4% per year over the 1965–1990 period and a still-high 6.0% in 1990–2005. It is one of 13 countries identified by the Spence Commission as having ever experienced a 25-year period averaging at least 7% growth—and the only one in Africa. According to the United Nations Development Programme, Botswana's per capita income increased ninefold from 1970 to 2010. Since its independence, Botswana has gone from being among the poorest countries in the world to one with a greater purchasing power parity (PPP) per capita income than Thailand or Brazil and similar to that of Malaysia and Mexico.

Botswana has higher income per person than bordering country South Africa. And by sharp contrast, its neighboring country to the east, Zimbabwe, has a GNI of just $640; rather than growing, the economy of Zimbabwe has been shrinking.

What explains Botswana's remarkable success? This is a case in which the benefits of direct foreign investment for spurring growth are very clear. Moreover, success has been based on both favorable geography (huge diamond deposits) and favorable institutions (relatively effective protection of private property, rule of law, checks and balances, and good incentives for government to play a constructive role). Effective governance matters; as noted

by the Commission on Growth and Development (Spence Commission) (page 71), "Botswana has a tradition of long-term planning guided by a vision for the future direction of the economy." When all these elements are present, conditions for development are particularly auspicious.

Botswana's diamond wealth is vast, and hence the experience of Botswana shows that the "curse of natural resources" does not haunt all countries equally. Although diamonds have been a dictator's best friend in countries such as the Democratic Republic of Congo (DRC) and Sierra Leone, in Botswana diamond exports have been consistent with democracy and broad-based development. Jeffrey Herbst, a leading expert on African comparative political development, also notes that Botswana is one of the few African countries with a geography that is suitable for consolidating the power of the nation-state. The population is concentrated in the eastern part of the country, where Gaborone, the capital city, is located. In contrast, such countries as Nigeria and the DRC have widely dispersed centers of population.

Botswana is a multiparty democracy, although it has been dominated by one particular party, the Botswana Democratic Party. Elections have been held every five years since 1965. There is a free press, and there are no political prisoners. Botswana accomplished these impressive economic and political results while surrounded by white minority regimes (in South Africa, Zimbabwe, and Namibia) for the first half of its history—and even as nearby civil wars have spilled over into its territory and a steady stream of refugees has threatened to upset the social order.

Botswana has some geographic disadvantages that in other countries can act as a barrier to growth

and development. It is a landlocked country with no access to seaports, a characteristic that is statistically associated with slow growth. It has generally poor conditions for agriculture. Only about 4% of the land can be easily cultivated. Most of the country is Kalahari Desert land, suitable only for summer grazing (almost all the rainfall takes place during the summer months). The five-year drought of the mid-1980s was very harsh by any standard, and other serious droughts have stricken the country with some regularity. The climate is tropical, and tropical countries have generally fared much more poorly in income levels and growth than temperate-zone countries. Botswana also shows that high population growth need not always forestall rapid growth in income per capita. Thus, Botswana demonstrates that geography is not destiny and that good institutions can take advantage of opportunities of geography (natural resources, in particular) that are squandered or even make matters worse in countries with poor institutions. And it suggests that good institutions can overcome the constraints imposed by geography. Daron Acemoglu, Simon Johnson, and James Robinson attribute Botswana's success in large measure to favorable institutions, particularly protection of property rights.

Successful development requires both private and public goods. There is a need to prevent the government from doing harm, such as engaging in parasitic or predatory behavior, and at the same time to encourage the state to act in support of broad-based economic development, including provision of public goods needed for economic development. For this, minimal requirements are a cohesive society that is able to avoid substantial strife such as civil wars and a government that is both responsive and responsible to society.

As noted earlier, Botswana has been a well-functioning multiparty democracy. Although the Botswana Democratic Party has never lost national power, there is evidence that it responds to electoral threats by delivering improved government services. Government has played a constructive role in the economy by providing infrastructure, extension (information and training) services, and subsidized veterinary services and other support for the development of the cattle industry; these initiatives have been broad-based rather than earmarked for favored clientele. Government has also constructively managed

relationships with mining interests, encouraging exploration by foreign companies and demanding and getting a share of profits without driving investors away. For example, favorable contracts were achieved with the De Beers diamond cartel that resulted in fully half of diamond profits going to the state in tax revenue. The government, in turn, managed these resources constructively, smoothing government services from good to bad periods and investing heavily in education. How a country spends its wealth matters, whether that wealth is large or small. Botswana has attained essentially universal primary education, a rare achievement in Africa, and more than half of children enroll in secondary education, twice the average elsewhere in sub-Saharan Africa.

From 1982 to 1987, Botswana suffered a brutal drought that severely affected poor rural peoples. In many countries, their plight might have been ignored until significant starvation began to catch the attention of the world. But Botswana built on its social security system and provided relief to the rural poor through a three-pronged system of maintaining food availability, as detailed by Jean Dreze and Amartya Sen: (1) a guarantee of public employment for cash wages that could be spent on available food, (2) direct food distribution to selected groups, and (3) programs to increase agricultural productivity and restore food availability. Botswana's free press and democratic system seem to be major factors in this response.

On other human development indicators, such as infant mortality and health professionals per capita, Botswana also scores well. However, Botswana ranked only 98th out of the 159 countries listed on the 2010 Human Development Index, 38 points lower than its GDP rank would predict; in other words, Botswana's human development is significantly lower than predicted by its level of real per capita income. Botswana has been affected in these rankings due to mortality from AIDS; the nation has the second-highest HIV infection rate in the world. But in other fields, its human development performance in the context of sub-Saharan Africa is extremely favorable; despite the AIDS epidemic, only two countries in this region rate higher than Botswana on the 2010 HDI. But clear progress is being made; between 2001 and 2011, the rate of new HIV infections dropped by 71% in Botswana—one

of the greatest improvements in the world in this period.

The deeper question is why Botswana has been able to create and sustain better institutions. Acemoglu, Johnson, and Robinson surveyed Botswana's institutional history and suggest that the juxtaposition or interaction of five factors have been important.

1. Botswana possessed precolonial tribal institutions that encouraged broad-based participation and placed constraints on political elites. Commoners were allowed to make suggestions and criticize chiefs.

2. British colonialization had a limited effect on these precolonial institutions because of the peripheral nature of Botswana to the British Empire.

3. Upon independence, the most important rural interests, chiefs and cattle owners, were politically powerful, and it was in their economic interests to enforce property rights.

4. The revenues from diamonds generated enough rents for the main political actors, increasing the opportunity cost of, and thereby discouraging, further rent seeking.

5. Political leaders made sensible decisions. These included turning over diamond mining rights from tribal (Bangwato) to national control (this transition was initiated in a statesmanlike way by the postindependence leader Seretse Khama, who was himself a member of the Bangwato tribe). Reduction of the powers of the tribal chiefs was another such decision. Each reduced the chances of internecine conflicts that have plagued so many other African countries. It might be said that in Botswana, although elites enjoyed a good share of the diamond eggs, they did not kill the goose that laid them, and they faced real constraints on their ability to take a larger share.

So unfavorable features of geography need not be destiny, natural resources need not be a curse, and good institutions can underpin dramatically superior economic performance.

With a clear, natural-resource-based comparative advantage and the requisite minimally supporting institutions, Botswana successfully struck a deal with foreign investors that was good for the national interest while avoiding serious corruption. As a result, the neoclassical approach—expanded and updated with emphasis on required human capital, the need for good institutions, support for exports, farsighted government policy and shared growth—appears to do a good job of explaining this country's success.

But perhaps the most important question of all is left unsettled. What can countries without the favorable starting economic institutions and factors favoring development of good-quality state institutions do to get better institutions? Officials in other African countries who are seeking to reform their polities can work toward emulating some of the best features of governance in Botswana and publicize government and private-sector failures as well as relative success in neighboring countries. Societies as a whole can find themselves in poverty traps, in which government behavior itself is part of the vicious circle of underdevelopment. The presence of a positive regional role model is of great importance in spreading successful development, as illustrated by the case of Japan in East Asia. One blemish on Botswana's development record is that the minority Khoikhoi, also known as Bushmen, fare worse than the majority Botswana.

Despite its successes, Botswana may be facing its gravest crisis since independence. It now has a relatively high level of income inequality, comparable to that of Latin America, as well as chronically high urban unemployment. But by far the worst problem is HIV/AIDS. According to UN reports, the HIV prevalence rate is as high as 24% of the adult population aged 15 to 99—and a stunning 33% among pregnant women. Fortunately, the HIV prevalence rate among those aged 15 and below is less than 2%, a promising sign *if* new infections can be stopped with lifestyle changes and safe-sex practices. But the United Nations reports that "60% of the youth have no access to youth-friendly reproductive health services." Without AIDS, it is estimated that life expectancy in Botswana would be over 70 today. But as a result of the AIDS epidemic, life expectancy at birth in Botswana was just 55 years in 2010. The United Nations estimates that nearly 20% of children in Botswana have lost a parent. Erika Reynolds found that one-third of the workforce is currently infected, which is apparently having a negative effect on productivity. Still, in the last few years, Botswana has

had a much more decisive response to AIDS. About 6% of government spending is allocated to HIV/AIDS programs, including free retroviral treatment for all citizens, and life expectancies are now rising.

It is reasonable to ask, if Botswana has such good institutions and government quality, how has the country allowed itself to reach the point at which so much of its prime-age population is HIV-positive? The failure of government to respond as decisively as in Uganda (see Box 8.8 in Chapter 8), despite the epidemic's later arrival in Botswana, may be viewed as a reflection of inconsistent government quality or of cultural characteristics. The test now is whether government quality and social development can halt the spread of HIV to the next generation. Botswana at least responded to the challenge better than its neighbor, South Africa. The last few years have been more encouraging. There is hope that the epidemic is abating somewhat. If it does subside, Botswana can again shine as a beacon of hope for broader development in Africa. ■

Sources

Acemoglu, Daron, Simon Johnson, and James Robinson. "An African success story: Botswana." In *In Search of Prosperity: Analytic Narratives on Economic Growth,* ed. Dani Rodrik. Princeton, N.J.: Princeton University Press, 2003, pp. 80–119.

Africa Research Bulletin, December 1993 and July 1995.

Commission on Growth and Development (Spence Commission). *The Growth Report: Strategies for Sustained Growth and Inclusive Development.* Washington: World Bank, 2008. Also available at http://www.growthcommission.org.

Dreze, Jean, and Amartya Sen. *Hunger and Public Action.* Oxford: Clarendon Press, 1989.

Edge, Wayne, and Mogopodi Lekorwe, eds. *Botswana: Politics and Society.* Pretoria, South Africa: Schaik, 1998.

Goldsmith, Arthur. "Africa's overgrown state revisited: Bureaucracy and economic growth." *World Politics* 51 (1999): 520–546.

Greener, R., K. Jefferis, and H. Siphambe. "The impact of HIV/AIDS on poverty and inequality in Botswana." *South African Journal of Economics* 68 (2000): 888–915.

Harvey, Charles, and Stephen R. Lewis, Jr. *Policy Choice and Development Performance in Botswana.* New York: St. Martin's Press, 1990.

Herbst, Jeffrey. *States and Power in Africa: Comparative Lessons in Authority and Control.* Princeton, N.J.: Princeton University Press, 2000.

Hope, Kempe, R. and Gloria Somolekae, *Public Administration and Policy in Botswana*, South Africa: Juta and Company, 1998.

Innocenti, Nicol D. "Compared to neighboring South Africa, Botswana is far ahead in implementing new retroviral and education programs." *Financial Times*, September 26, 2001.

Picard, Louis A. *The Politics of Development in Botswana: A Model for Success?* Boulder, Colo.: Rienner, 1987.

Porter, Michael. *Competitive Advantage of Nations.* New York: Free Press, 1990.

Reynolds, Erika. "Economic impact of HIV/AIDS in Botswana." Policy brief, UCLA Globalization Research Center, Africa, 2008.

Stedman, Stephen J., ed. *Botswana: The Political Economy of Democratic Development.* Boulder, Colo.: Rienner, 1993.

United Nations Development Programme. *Human Development Report, 2010.* New York: Oxford University Press, 2010 (and previous editions).

Concepts for Review

Central bank
Commercialization
Currency board
Currency substitution
Development banks
Direct taxes
Financial liberalization
Financial repression

Group lending scheme
Indirect taxes
Informal finance
Microfinance
Monetary policy
Money supply
Organized money market
Privatization

Rationing
Rotating savings and credit association (ROSCA)
State-owned enterprises (SOEs)
Transparency (financial)
Unorganized money market
Value added tax (VAT)

Questions for Discussion

1. Explain the distinction between organized and unorganized money markets.

2. In the context of development priorities, what are the relative roles of central banks, commercial banks, development banks, informal and unorganized sources of credit, and microfinance such as the Grameen Bank of Bangladesh?

3. What is meant by financial repression, financial liberalization, currency substitution, and unorganized money markets, and how do they relate to financial policy in developing countries?

4. List and briefly discuss the seven market failures that Stiglitz and his colleagues say justify a strong government role in developing-country financial sectors. Do you agree or disagree with this assessment? Explain.

5. What are the principal sources of government revenues in developing countries? Why are many taxes so difficult to collect? Discuss.

6. In what ways do you think taxation and expenditure systems in developing countries could be improved? Be specific.

7. If the scarcity of administrative capabilities is a serious constraint on development policy implementation, what can developing countries do to relieve this constraint? What are the options? Discuss.

8. Summarize the arguments for and against the establishment of state-owned enterprises (SOEs) in developing nations. Do you think that SOEs should be encouraged or discouraged? What are the arguments for and against privatization of the public sector in developing countries? How would you interpret evidence that a majority of privatized enterprises have increased efficiency? Explain your answers.

9. When privatization picked up pace in Poland, some analysts warned that effective privatization first required more developed domestic financial institutions. Comment.

10. What are the pros and cons of encouraging the development of stock markets in developing countries?

11. How have microfinance institutions' strategies differed from those of other lenders in reaching lower-income borrowers?

12. What are some of the benefits of expanding micro-credit programs, and what are some of its potential limits?

13. Consider the three recent policy debates concerning microfinance (on subsidies, nonfinancial activities, and commercialization). What kinds of evidence would you seek to resolve these, at least in a localized context?

14. What lessons can be learned for low-income countries from Botswana's successes?

Notes

1. Joan Robinson, "The generalization of the general theory," in *The Rate of Interest, and Other Essays.* (London: Macmillan, 1952), pp. 67–142 (p. 82).

2. See Hugh T. Patrick, "Financial development and economic growth in underdeveloped countries," *Economic Development and Cultural Change* 14 (1966): 174–189, and Felix Rioja and Neven Valev, "Finance and the sources of growth at various stages of economic development," *Economic Inquiry* 42 (2004): 27–40.

3. Some of this discussion is adapted from Ross Levine and Sara Zervos, "Stock markets, banks, and economic growth," *American Economic Review* 88 (1998): 537–558. Other useful references include Rudiger Dornbusch and Alejandro Reynoso, "Financial factors in economic development," *American Economic Review* 79 (1989): 204–209; Panicos Demetriades and Khaled Hussein, "Does financial development cause economic growth? Time series evidence from 16 countries," *Journal of Development Economics* 51 (1996): 387–411;

Robert G. King and Ross Levine, "Finance and growth: Schumpeter might be right," *Quarterly Journal of Economics* 108 (1993): 717–737; Joseph E. Stiglitz, Jaime Jaramillo-Vallejo, and Yung Chal Park, "The role of the state in financial markets," *Annual Conference on Development Economics* (1993 suppl.): 19–61; Nouriel Roubini and Xavier Sala-i-Martin, "Financial repression and economic growth," *Journal of Development Economics* 39 (1992): 5–30; Carlos Diaz-Alejandro, "Goodbye financial repression, hello financial crash," *Journal of Development Economics* 19 (1985): 1–24; J. D. von Pishke, *Finance at the Frontier* (Washington, D.C.: World Bank, 1991); Ross Levine, "Financial development and economic growth: Views and agenda," *Journal of Economic Literature* 35 (1997): 688–726; and Raymond Atje and Boyan Jovanovic, "Stock markets and development," *European Economic Review* 37 (1993): 632–640.

4. Stiglitz, Jaramillo-Vallejo, and Park, "Role of the state." On mobile money in Kenya and other developing countries, see, for example, Jenny C. Aker and Isaac M. Mbiti, "Mobile phones and economic development in Africa, *Journal of Economic Perspectives*, 24, No. 3 (Summer 2010): 207–232; and *The Economist*, "Why does Kenya lead the world in mobile money?" May 27, 2013, at http://www.economist.com/blogs/economist-explains/2013/05/economist-explains-18.

5. This and what follows are, for reasons of space and expositional simplification, presented in traditional terms still widely used. Among other fine overviews of the subject of macroeconomic and monetary policy, addressing these issues in a more nuanced way by drawing from recent research, see N. Gregory Mankiw, *Macroeconomics*, 6th ed. (New York: Worth, 2006). For further exploration, see David Romer, *Advanced Macroeconomics*, 3rd ed. (New York: McGraw-Hill 2005). For more specifically developing-country-focused analysis, see Pierre-Richard Agenor and Peter J. Montiel, *Development Macroeconomics*, 3rd ed. (Princeton, N.J.: Princeton University Press, 2008).

6. For an extended but advanced exposition of macroeconomic analysis applied to developing-country contexts, see Agenor and Montiel, *Development Macroeconomics*.

7. See Maxwell J. Fry, *Money, Interest, and Banking in Economic Development* (Baltimore: Johns Hopkins University Press, 1988); World Bank, *World Development Report, 1991* (New York: Oxford University Press, 1991); and Ernest Aryeetey et al., "Financial market fragmentation and reform in Ghana, Malawi, Nigeria, and Tanzania," *World Bank Economic Review* 11 (1997): 195–218. Note that considerable progress has been made since 2000.

8. For a discussion of the phenomenon of currency substitution and the impact of unorganized money markets on the developing world, see International Monetary Fund, *World Economic Outlook, October 1997* (Washington, D.C.: International Monetary Fund, 1997), pp. 92–93; Steven L. Green, "Monetary policies in developing countries and the new monetary economics," *Journal of Economic Development* 11 (1986): 7–23; and Guillermo Ortiz, "Currency substitution in Mexico: The dollarization problem," *Journal of Money, Credit, and Banking* 15 (1983): 174–185.

9. For a discussion of privatization and the liberalization of financial markets in developing countries, see Laurence H. White, "Privatization of financial sectors," in *Privatization and Development*, ed. Steven H. Hanke (San Francisco: Institute for Contemporary Studies, 1987), pp. 149–160.

10. Charles Collyns, *Alternatives to the Central Bank in the Developing World*, IMF Occasional Paper No. 20 (Washington, D.C.: International Monetary Fund, 1983), p. 2. Much of the discussion that follows is based on this informative report.

11. Collyns, *Alternatives to the Central Bank*, p. 21.

12. See Maxwell J. Fry, "Assessing central bank independence in developing countries: Do actions speak louder than words?" *Oxford Economic Papers* 50 (1998): 512–529.

13. This schema follows the scoring system introduced by V. Grilli, D. Masciandaro, and G. Tabellini in "Political and monetary institutions and public financial policies in the industrial countries," *Economic Policy* 13 (1991): 341–392. Alex Cukierman introduced a partially overlapping alternative system in *Central Bank Strategy, Credibility, and Autonomy* (Cambridge, Mass.: MIT Press, 1992).

14. Marco Arnone, Bernard J. Laurens, Jean-François Segalotto, and Martin Sommer, "Central bank

autonomy: Lessons from global trends," IMF Staff Papers 56, No. 2, 2009. The authors used both indexes cited in Note 13 and other measures. Indexes based on these numbers showed a substantial increase in central bank autonomy from the 1980s to the 2000s among low-, middle-, and high-income countries alike. An earlier version with some additional details may be found at http://www.imf.org/external/pubs/ft/wp/2007/wp0788.pdf.

15. For an extensive discussion of how to improve the monetary control system and mobilize and better allocate domestic savings in developing countries, see Delano Villanueva, "Issues in financial sector reform," *Finance and Development* 25 (1988): 14–17.

16. Aparna Dalal et al., "Half of the world is unbanked," 2010, http://financialaccess.org/node/2603.

17. For a review of the growth of informal finance in developing countries in the context of "consumption-smoothing" strategies, see Timothy Besley, "Nonmarket institutions for credit and risk sharing in low-income countries," *Journal of Economic Perspectives* 9 (1995): 115–127.

18. Siwan Anderson and Jean-Marie Baland, "The economics of ROSCAs and intra-household resource allocation," *Quarterly Journal of Economics* 111 (2002): 963–995. For a good general survey of institutional details and economic analysis of ROSCAs, see Beatriz Armendriz de Aghion and Jonathan Morduch, *The Economics of Microfinance* (Cambridge, Mass.: MIT Press, 2005), ch. 3.

19. For details on MFIs and how they work, see Armendriz de Aghion and Morduch, *Economics of Microfinance*; Marguerite S. Robinson, *The Microfinance Revolution: Sustainable Finance for the Poor* (Washington, D.C.: World Bank, 2001); Robert Peck Christen and Deborah Drake, *Commercialization: The New Reality of Microfinance?* (Bloomfield, Conn.: Kumarian Press, 2002); and Elisabeth H. Rhyne, *Mainstreaming Microfinance: How Lending to the Poor Began, Grew, and Came of Age in Bolivia* (Bloomfield, Conn.: Kumarian Press, 2001).

20. For an introduction to the economic analysis of alternatives to joint liability, see Armendriz de Aghion and Morduch, *Economics of Microfinance*, esp. ch. 5, and the references therein. For data

showing that MFIs with more than 65% women borrowers have higher repayment rates than MFIs with a smaller fraction of women borrowers, see Cédric Lützenkirchen, *Microfinance in evolution: An industry between crisis and advancement*, Deutsche Bank AG, September 2012, p. 14. A critical analysis of payment increments is presented in Sanjay Jain and Ghazala Mansuri, "A little at a time: The use of regularly scheduled repayments in microfinance programs," *Journal of Development Economics* 72 (2003): 253–279.

21. For data trends showing strong growth through 2010 but a dip in 2011, see Larry R. Reed, *Microcredit Summit Campaign, Vulnerability: The State of the Microcredit Summit Campaign Report 2013*, at http://stateofthecampaign.org/. For a concise editorial statement of some of the key issues, see Abhijit Banerjee et al., "Microcredit is not the enemy," *Financial Times*, December 13, 2010.

22. For the debate, see for example, Microcredit Summit Fulfillment Campaign, "The Microcredit Summit: Declaration and plan of action, 1997," www.microcreditsummit.org/declaration.htm; Jonathan Morduch, "The microfinance promise," *Journal of Economic Literature* 37 (1999): 1569–1614; Jonathan Morduch, "The microfinance schism," *World Development* 28 (2000): 617–629; and Armendriz de Aghion and Morduch, *Economics of Microfinance*.

23. For an examination of a program integrating microcredit with health, see Stephen C. Smith, "Village banking and maternal child health: Evidence from Ecuador and Honduras," *World Development* 30 (2002): 707–723; for a study of integrating microcredit and business training, see Box 15.2.

24. For a pioneering and perceptive analysis of this issue, see M. Shahe Emran, A. K. M. Mahbub Morshed, and Joseph E. Stiglitz, "Microfinance and missing markets," 2007, http://papers.ssrn.com/sol3/papers.cfm?abstract_id=1001309. For a detailed examination of the importance of conventional job creation in economic development, see World Bank, *World Development Report 2013: Jobs* (Washington: World Bank, 2013).

25. For an interesting recent study finding a positive impact, see Elizabeth Schroeder, "The Impact of Microcredit Borrowing on Household

Consumption in Bangladesh," Working Paper, Oregon State, 2012, at http://people.oregonstate .edu/~schroede/eas_microcredit.pdf. Schroeder's results deploy new econometric techniques while using the same data as the well-known study by Mark M. Pitt and Shahidur R. Khandker, "The impact of group-based credit programs on poor households in Bangladesh: Does the gender of participants matter?" *Journal of Political Economy,* 106 (1998): 958–996. For a headline-making but controversial report criticizing microfinance impact studies that had found positive impacts, see Maren Duvendack et al., "What is the evidence of the impact of microfinance on the well-being of poor people?" downloaded at: http://www.dfid .gov.uk/r4d/PDF/Outputs/SystematicReviews /Microfinance2011Duvendackreport.pdf.

26. Christian Ahlin, Jocelyn Lin, and Michael Maio, "Where does microfinance flourish? Microfinance institution performance in macroeconomic context," *Journal of Development Economics* 95, No. 2 (2011): 105–120.

27. In addition to setting interest-rate ceilings, developing-country governments have often intervened in their financial markets in a variety of other ways. These have included directed credit programs, high bank reserve requirements that effectively tax the financial system, and forced lending to the government to finance high budget deficits—for example, by requiring banks to hold low-yielding government bonds. These and other policies are linked to interest-rate ceilings. In the presence of high and variable inflation and negative real interest rates, they not only lead to lower savings and growth but also can cause the entire banking system to contract. We are grateful to Professor Valerie Bencivenga for these observations.

28. The classic writings on financial repression and the positive impact of financial liberalization on saving and investment are Ronald L. McKinnon, *Money and Capital in Economic Development* (Washington, D.C.: Brookings Institution, 1973), and Edward S. Shaw, *Financial Deepening in Economic Development* (New York: Oxford University Press, 1973). For a classic critique of this approach, see Carlos Diaz-Alexandro, "Good-bye financial repression, hello financial crash," *Journal of*

Development Economics 19 (1985): 1–24. For a more recent debate on the merits and limitations of financial liberalization, in general, and the McKinnon-Shaw thesis, in particular, see articles by Maxwell Fry and Ajit Singh in *Economic Journal* 107 (1997): 754–782. See also Bruce Greenwald, "Institutional adjustments in the face of imperfect financial markets," in *Annual World Bank Conference on Development Economics, 1998* (Washington, D.C.: World Bank, 1999).

29. World Bank, *World Development Report, 1987* (New York: Oxford University Press, 1987), pp. 117–122. However, for transnational evidence that interest-rate levels have little or no effect on saving and investment, see Deena R. Khatkhata, "Assessing the impact of interest rates in less developed countries," *World Development* 16 (1988): 577–588; Gerado M. Gonzales Arrieta, "Interest rates, savings and growth in LDCs: An assessment of recent empirical research," *World Development* 16 (1988): 589–606; and Rudiger Dornbusch, "Policies to move from stabilization to growth," *Proceedings of the World Bank Annual Conference on Development Economics, 1990* (Washington, D.C.: World Bank, 1990), pp. 36–41.

30. Stiglitz, Jaramillo-Vallejo, and Park, "Role of the state," Joseph E. Stiglitz, Jaime Jaramillo-Vallejo, and Yung Chal Park, "The role of the state in financial markets," Annual Conference on Development Economics (1993 suppl.): 19-61. See note 3.

31. Ibid., p. 8.

32. Atje and Jovanovic, "Stock markets and development"; Levine and Zervos, "Stock markets, banks, and economic growth."

33. For an excellent collection of articles and essays related to taxation and development, see Donald Newberry and Nicholas Stern, eds., *The Theory of Taxation for Developing Countries* (New York: Oxford University Press, 1987). See also World Bank, *World Development Report, 1988* (New York: Oxford University Press, 1988), pt. 2; "Symposium on tax policy in developing countries," *World Bank Economic Review* 5 (1991): 459–574; and Robin Burgess and Nicholas Stern, "Taxation and development," *Journal of Economic Literature* 31 (1993): 762–830.

34. Vito Tanzi, "Quantitative characteristics of the tax systems of developing countries," in *The Theory of*

Taxation for Developing Countries, eds. David Newbery and Nicholas Stern (New York: Oxford University Press, 1987), and Vito Tanzi and Howell H. Zee, "Tax policy for emerging markets: Developing countries," *National Tax Journal* 53 (2000): 299–322.

35. World Bank, *World Development Indicators, 2013* (Washington, D.C.: World Bank, 2013), p. 67.

36. Tanzi, "Quantitative characteristics."

37. See M. Shahe Emran and Joseph E. Stiglitz, "On selective indirect tax reform in developing countries," *Journal of Public Economics* 89 (2005): 599–623.

38. Joel Slemrod, "Optimal taxation and optimal tax systems," *Journal of Economic Perspectives* 4 (1990): 157–178.

39. For an interesting analysis and evaluation of ways to reform tax administration, see Dilip Mookherjee, "Incentive reforms in developing country bureaucracies: Lessons from tax administration," *Annual World Bank Conference on Development Economics, 1997* (Washington, D.C.: World Bank, 1998), pp. 108–125.

40. See Richard M. Kennedy and Leroy P. Jones, "Reforming state-owned enterprises: Lessons of international experience, especially for the least developed countries," UNIDO SME Technical Working Paper No. 11, United Nations, 2003.

41. World Bank, *World Development Report, 1983*, ch. 8. See also the discussion of SOEs in *World Development Report, 1988*, ch. 8. See also Luke Haggarty and Mary M. Shirley, "A new data base on state-owned enterprises," *World Bank Economic Review* 11 (1997): 491–513.

42. Tony Killick, "The role of the public sector in the industrialization of African developing countries," *Industry and Development* 7 (1983): 57–88.

43. See, for example, Kennedy and Jones, "Reforming state-owned enterprises," esp. pp. 14–17, for a concise survey of reform options. See also Mary

Shirley et al., *Bureaucrats in Business* (New York: Oxford University Press, 1995).

44. For a review of privatization in developing countries in the late 1980s and early 1990s, see Sunita Kikeri, John Nellis, and Mary Shirley, "Privatization: Lessons from market economies," *World Bank Research Observer* 9 (1994): 241–272.

45. Ibid., 249–253. See also Saul Estrin, Jan Hanousek, Evzen Kocenda, and Jan Svejnar, "The effects of privatization and ownership in transition economies," *Journal of Economic Literature*, 47(2009): 699–728; World Bank, *World Development Report, 1997* (New York: Oxford University Press, 1997), ch. 4; and William Megginson and Jeffrey N. Netter, "From state to market: A survey of empirical studies on privatization," *Journal of Economic Literature* 39 (2001): 321–389.

46. See Tony Killick, *A Reaction Too Far: Economic Theory and the Role of the State in Developing Countries* (London: Overseas Development Institute, 1989); Robert Klitgaard, *Adjusting to Reality: Beyond "State versus Market" in Economic Development* (San Francisco: ICS Press, 1991); and United Nations Development Programme, *Human Development Report, 1993* (New York: Oxford University Press, 1993), pp. 49–51. See also Mohammed Omran, "The performance of state-owned enterprises and newly privatized firms: Does privatization really matter?" *World Development* 32 (2004): 1019–1041.

47. For an overview of some key issues in public administration and development, see World Bank, *World Development Report, 1997* (New York: Oxford University Press, 1997), and Derick W. Brinkerhoff and Benjamin Crosby, *Managing Policy Reform: Concepts and Tools for Decision-Makers in Developing and Transitioning Countries* (Bloomfield, Conn.: Kumarian Press, 2002). The journal *Public Administration and Development* is a good source for current contributions to this evolving literature.

Glossary

Absolute advantage Production of a commodity with the same amount of real resources as another producer but at a lower absolute unit cost.

Absolute poverty The situation of being unable or only barely able to meet the subsistence essentials of food, clothing, shelter, and basic health care.

Absorptive capacity (for foreign aid) The ability of a country to absorb foreign private or public financial assistance (to use the funds in a productive manner).

Absorptive capacity (for ecosystems) The capacity of an ecosystem to assimilate potential pollutants.

Acquired immunodeficiency syndrome (AIDS) Viral disease transmitted predominantly through sexual contact.

Agency costs Costs of monitoring managers and other employees and of designing and implementing schemes to ensure compliance or provide incentives to follow the wishes of the employer.

Agglomeration economies Cost advantages to producers and consumers from location in cities and towns, which take the forms of urbanization economies and localization economies.

Aggregate growth model A formal economic model describing growth of an economy in one or a few sectors using a limited number of variables.

Agrarian system The pattern of land distribution, ownership, and management, and also the social and institutional structure of the agrarian economy.

Amortization Gradual payoff of a loan principal.

Asset ownership The ownership of land, physical capital (factories, buildings, machinery, etc.), human capital, and financial resources that generate income for owners.

Asymmetric information A situation in which one party to a potential transaction (often a buyer, seller, lender, or borrower) has more information than another party.

Attitudes The states of mind or feelings of an individual, group, or society regarding issues such as material gain, hard work, saving for the future, and sharing wealth.

Autarky A closed economy that attempts to be completely self-reliant.

Average product Total output or product divided by total factor input (e.g., the average product of labor is equal to total output divided by the total amount of labor used to produce that output).

Balanced trade A situation in which the value of a country's exports and the value of its imports are equal.

Balance of payments A summary statement of a nation's financial transactions with the outside world.

Barter transactions The trading of goods directly for other goods in economies not fully monetized.

Basic education The attainment of literacy, arithmetic competence, and elementary vocational skills.

Basic transfer Net foreign-exchange inflow or outflow related to a country's international borrowing; the quantitative difference between the net capital inflow (gross inflow minus amortization on past debt) and interest payments on existing accumulated debt.

Big push A concerted, economy-wide, and typically public policy–led effort to initiate or accelerate economic development across a broad spectrum of new industries and skills.

Binding constraint The one limiting factor that if relaxed would be the item that accelerates growth (or that allows a larger amount of some other targeted outcome).

Biodiversity The variety of life forms within an ecosystem.

Biomass fuels Any combustible organic matter that may be used as fuel, such as firewood, dung, or agricultural residues.

Brady Plan A program launched in 1989, designed to reduce the size of outstanding developing-country commercial debt through private debt forgiveness procured in exchange for IMF and World Bank debt guarantees and greater adherence to the terms of conditionality.

Brain drain The emigration of highly educated and skilled professionals and technicians from the developing countries to the developed world.

Capabilities The freedoms that people have, given their personal features and their command over commodities.

Capital account The portion of a country's balance of payments that shows the volume of private foreign investment and public grants and loans that flow into and out of a country over a given period, usually one year.

Capital accumulation Increasing a country's stock of real *capital* (net *investment* in fixed assets). To increase the production of capital *goods* necessitates a reduction in the production of consumer goods.

Capital-augmenting technological progress Technological progress that raises the productivity of capital by innovation and inventions.

Capital flight   The transfer of funds to a foreign country by a citizen or business to avoid conditions in the source country.

Capital-labor ratio   The number of units of capital per unit of labor.

Capital-output ratio   A ratio that shows the units of capital required to produce a unit of output over a given period of time.

Capital-saving technological progress   Technological progress that results from some invention or innovation that facilitates the achievement of higher output levels using the same quantity of inputs of capital.

Capital stock   The total amount of physical goods existing at a particular time that have been produced for use in the production of other goods and services.

Cash account (international reserve account)   The balancing portion of a country's balance of payments, showing how cash balances (foreign reserves) and short-term financial claims have changed in response to current account and capital account transactions.

Cash crops   Crops produced entirely for the market.

Center   In dependence theory, the economically developed world.

Central bank   The major financial institution responsible for issuing a nation's currency, managing foreign reserves, implementing monetary policy, and providing banking services to the government and commercial banks.

Character of economic growth   The distributive implications of economic growth as reflected in such factors as participation in the growth process and asset ownership.

Clean technologies   Technologies that by design produce less pollution and waste and use resources more efficiently.

Climate change   Nontransient altering of an underlying climate, such as increased average temperature, decreased annual precipitation, or greater average intensity of droughts or storms. Used in reference to the impact of the global warming phenomenon. Note the distinction between changes in weather (which varies within a climate) and changes in climate that alter underlying probabilities of weather outcomes.

Closed economy   An economy in which there are no foreign trade transactions or other economic contacts with the rest of the world.

Commercialization   A process whereby an NGO (a not-for-profit organization) providing microfinance is converted into a for-profit bank.

Commitment problem   An inability to make a "credible promise" to honor a contractual agreement due to the presence of incentives to renege; sometimes a "commitment device," such as posting a large bond, can be implemented that automatically invokes high penalties on the reneging party, thereby creating a "credible threat," allowing agreement to be reached and honored.

Commodity terms of trade   The ratio of a country's average export price to its average import price.

Common market   A form of economic integration in which there is free internal trade, a common tariff, and the free movement of labor and capital among partner states.

Common property resource   A resource that is collectively or publicly owned and allocated under a system of unrestricted access, or as self-regulated by users.

Comparative advantage   Production of a commodity at a lower opportunity cost than any of the alternative commodities that could be produced.

Complementarity   An action taken by one firm, worker, or organization that increases the incentives for other agents to take similar actions. Complementarities often involve investments whose return depends on other investments being made by other agents.

Complementary investments   Investments that complement and facilitate other productive factors.

Comprador group   In dependence theory, local elites who act as fronts for foreign investors.

Comprehensive plan   An economic plan that sets targets to cover all the major sectors of the national economy.

Concessional terms   Terms for the extension of credit that are more favorable to the borrower than those available through standard financial markets.

Conditional cash transfer (CCT) programs   Welfare benefits provided conditionally based on family behavior such as children's regular school attendance and health clinic visitations.

Conditionality   The requirement imposed by the International Monetary Fund that a borrowing country undertake fiscal, monetary, and international commercial reforms as a condition for receiving a loan to resolve balance of payments difficulties.

Congestion   The opposite of a complementarity; an action taken by one agent that decreases the incentives for other agents to take similar actions.

Consumer surplus   Excess utility over price derived by consumers because of a negative-sloping demand curve.

Convergence   The tendency for per capita income (or output) to grow faster in lower-income countries than in higher-income countries so that lower-income countries are "catching up" over time. When countries are hypothesized to converge not in all cases but *other things being equal* (particularly savings rates, labor force growth, and production technologies), then the term *conditional convergence* is used.

Coordination failure   A situation in which the inability of agents to coordinate their behavior (choices) leads to an outcome (equilibrium) that leaves all agents worse off than in an alternative situation that is also an equilibrium.

Corporate social responsibility   Nongovernmental self-regulation by corporations or consortia of corporations (possibly with consumer group representation), to attempt to ensure compliance with acceptable international norms of ethical practice such as avoidance of cruel, coercive, or deceptive labor practices.

Corruption   The appropriation of public resources for private profit and other private purposes through the use and abuse of official power or influence.

Cost-benefit analysis   A tool of economic analysis in which the actual and potential private and social costs of various economic decisions are weighed against actual and potential private and social benefits.

Crude birth rate   The number of children born alive each year per 1,000 population (often shortened to *birth rate*).

Currency board   A form of central bank that issues domestic currency for foreign exchange at a fixed exchange rate.

Currency substitution   The use of foreign currency (e.g., U.S. dollars) as a medium of exchange in place of, or along with, the local currency (e.g., Mexican pesos).

Current account   The portion of a country's balance of payments that reflects the market value of the country's "visible" (e.g., commodity trade) and "invisible" (e.g., shipping services) exports and imports.

Customs union   A form of economic integration in which two or more nations agree to free all internal trade while levying a common external tariff on all nonmember countries.

Death rate   The number of deaths each year per 1,000 population.

Debt-for-equity swap   A mechanism used by indebted developing countries to reduce the real value of external debt by exchanging equity in domestic companies (stocks) or fixed-interest obligations of the government (bonds) for private foreign debt at large discounts.

Debt-for-nature swap   The exchange of foreign debt held by an organization for a larger quantity of domestic debt that is used to finance the preservation of a natural resource or environment in the debtor country.

Debtors' cartel   A group of developing-country debtors who join together to bargain as a group with creditors.

Debt repudiation   The 1980s fear in the developed world that developing countries would stop paying their debt obligations.

Debt service   The sum of interest payments and repayments of principal on external public and publicly guaranteed debt.

Decile   A 10% portion of any numerical quantity; a population divided into deciles would be divided into ten equal numerical groups.

Deep intervention   A government policy that can move the economy to a preferred equilibrium or even to a higher permanent rate of growth, which can then be self-sustaining so that the policy need no longer be enforced because the better equilibrium will then prevail without further intervention.

Deficit   An excess of expenditures over revenues.

Deforestation   The clearing of forested land either for agricultural purposes or for logging and for use as firewood.

Demographic transition   The phasing-out process of population growth rates from a virtually stagnant growth stage, characterized by high birth rates and death rates through a rapid-growth stage with high birth rates and low death rates to a stable, low-growth stage in which both birth and death rates are low.

Dependence   The reliance of developing countries on developed-country economic policies to stimulate their own economic growth. Dependence can also mean that the developing countries adopt developed-country education systems, technology, economic and political systems, attitudes, consumption patterns, dress, and so on.

Dependency burden   The proportion of the total population aged 0 to 15 and 65+, which is considered economically unproductive and therefore not counted in the labor force.

Depreciation (of currency)   The decline over time in the value or price of one currency in terms of another as a result of market forces of supply and demand.

Depreciation (of the capital stock)   The wearing out of equipment, buildings, infrastructure, and other forms of capital, reflected in write-offs to the value of the capital stock.

Derived demand   Demand for a good that emerges indirectly from demand for another good.

Desertification   The transformation of a region into dry, barren land with little or no capacity to sustain life without an artificial source of water.

Devaluation   A lowering of the official exchange rate between one country's currency and all other currencies.

Developing countries   Countries of Asia, Africa, the Middle East, Latin America, eastern Europe, and the former Soviet Union that are presently characterized by low levels of living and other development deficits. Used in the development literature as a synonym for *less developed countries*.

Development   The process of improving the quality of all human lives and capabilities by raising people's levels of living, self-esteem, and freedom.

Development banks   Specialized public and private financial intermediaries that provide medium- and long-term credit for development projects.

Development economics   The study of how economies are transformed from stagnation to growth and from low-income to high-income status, and overcome problems of absolute poverty.

Diminishing marginal utility   The concept that the subjective value of additional consumption lessens as total consumption becomes higher.

Direct taxes   Taxes levied directly on individuals or businesses—for example, income taxes.

Discount rate   In present-value calculations, the annual rate at which future values are decreased to make them comparable to values in the present.

Disposable income   The income that is available to households for spending and saving after personal income taxes have been deducted.

Divergence   A tendency for per capita income (or output) to grow faster in higher-income countries than in lower-income countries so that the income gap widens across countries over time (as was seen in the two centuries after industrialization began).

Diversified (mixed) farming   The production of both staple crops and cash crops and simple animal husbandry typical of the first stage in the transition from subsistence to specialized farming.

Dominance In international affairs, a situation in which the developed countries have much greater power than the less developed countries in decisions affecting important international economic issues, such as the prices of agricultural commodities and raw materials in world markets.

Doubling time Period that a given population or other quantity takes to increase by its present size.

Dual exchange rate (parallel exchange rate) Foreign-exchange-rate system with a highly overvalued and legally fixed rate applied to capital- and intermediate-goods imports and a second, illegal (or freely floating) rate for imported consumption goods.

Dualism The coexistence of two situations or phenomena (one desirable and the other not) that are mutually exclusive to different groups of society—for example, extreme poverty and affluence, modern and traditional economic sectors, growth and stagnation, and higher education among a few amid large-scale illiteracy.

Economic agent An economic actor—usually a firm, worker, consumer, or government official—that chooses actions so as to maximize an objective; often referred to as "agents."

Economic infrastructure The amount of physical and financial capital embodied in roads, railways, waterways, airways, and other transportation and communications, plus other facilities such as water supplies, financial institutions, electricity, and public services such as health and education.

Economic institutions "Humanly devised" constraints that shape interactions (or "rules of the game") in an economy, including formal rules embodied in constitutions, laws, contracts, and market regulations, plus informal rules reflected in norms of behavior and conduct, values, customs, and generally accepted ways of doing things.

Economic integration The merging to various degrees of the economies and economic policies of two or more countries in a region.

Economic plan A written document containing government policy decisions on how resources will be allocated among various uses so as to attain a targeted rate of economic growth or other goals over a certain period of time.

Economic planning A deliberate and conscious attempt by the state to formulate decisions on how the factors of production will be allocated among different uses or industries, thereby determining how much of total goods and services will be produced in one or more ensuing periods.

Economic union The full integration of two or more economies into a single economic entity.

Educational certification The phenomenon by which particular jobs require specified levels of education.

Educational gender gap Male-female differences in school access and completion.

Effective rate of protection The degree of protection on value added as opposed to the final price of an imported product—usually higher than the nominal rate of protection.

Efficiency wage The notion that modern-sector urban employers pay a higher wage than the equilibrium wage rate in order to attract and retain a higher-quality workforce or to obtain higher productivity on the job.

Elasticity of factor substitution A measure of the degree of substitutability between factors of production in any given production process when relative factor prices change.

Enclave economies Small, economically developed regions in developing countries in which the remaining areas have experienced much less progress.

Endogenous growth theory (new growth theory) Economic growth generated by factors within the production process (e.g., increasing returns or induced technological change) that are studied as part of a growth model.

Environmental accounting The incorporation of environmental benefits and costs into the quantitative analysis of economic activities.

Environmental capital The portion of a country's overall capital assets that directly relate to the environment—for example, forests, soil quality, and groundwater.

Environmental Kuznets curve A graph reflecting the concept that pollution and other environmental degradation first rises and then falls with increases in income per capita. There is evidence that this holds for some pollutants, such as sulfur dioxide and particulate matter in the air, but not for others, such as emissions of greenhouse gases.

Euro A common European currency adopted by some of the countries of the European Union.

Exchange control A governmental policy designed to restrict the outflow of domestic currency and prevent a worsened balance of payments position by controlling the amount of foreign exchange that can be obtained or held by domestic citizens.

Exchange rate Rate at which the domestic currency may be converted into (sold for) a foreign currency such as the U.S. dollar.

Export dependence A country's reliance on exports as the major source of financing for development activities.

Export earnings instability Wide fluctuations in developing-country earnings on commodity exports resulting from low price and income elasticities of demand leading to erratic movements in export prices.

Export promotion Governmental efforts to expand the volume of a country's exports through increasing export incentives, decreasing disincentives, and other means in order to generate more foreign exchange and improve the current account of its balance of payments or achieve other objectives.

External debt Total private and public foreign debt owed by a country.

Externality Any benefit or cost borne by an individual economic unit that is a direct consequence of another's behavior.

Factor endowment trade theory The neoclassical model of free trade, which postulates that countries will tend to specialize in the production of the commodities that make use of their abundant factors of production (land, labor, capital, etc.).

Factor price distortions Situations in which factors of production are paid prices that do not reflect their true scarcity values (i.e., their competitive market prices) because of institutional arrangements that tamper with the free working of market forces of supply and demand.

Factor price equalization In factor endowment trade theory, the proposition that because countries trade at a common international price ratio, factor prices among trading partners will tend to equalize.

Factors of production Resources or inputs required to produce a good or a service, such as land, labor, and capital.

False-paradigm model The proposition that developing countries have failed to develop because their development strategies (usually given to them by Western economists) have been based on an incorrect model of development, one that, for example, overstresses capital accumulation or market liberalization without giving due consideration to needed social and institutional change.

Family farm A farm plot owned and operated by a single household.

Family-planning programs Public programs designed to help parents plan and regulate their family size.

Financial repression Constraints on investment resulting from the rationing of credit, usually to a few large-scale borrowers, in financial markets where interest rates and hence the supply of savings are below market-determined levels.

Fiscal gap Deficiencies of government investments including infrastructure and human capital that are complementary to, and raise the rate of return from, private investment.

Flexible exchange rate The exchange value of a national currency that is free to move up and down in response to shifts in demand and supply arising from international trade and finance.

Foreign aid The international transfer of public funds in the form of loans or grants either directly from one government to another (bilateral assistance) or indirectly through the vehicle of a multilateral assistance agency such as the World Bank.

Foreign direct investment (FDI) Overseas equity investments by private multinational corporations.

Foreign-exchange earnings The sum total of all foreign currency receipts less expenditures during a given fiscal year.

Foreign-exchange gap The shortfall that results when the planned trade deficit exceeds the value of capital inflows, causing output growth to be limited by the available foreign exchange for capital goods imports.

Foster-Greer-Thorbecke (FGT) index A class of measures of the level of absolute poverty.

Fractionalization Significant ethnic, linguistic, and other social divisions within a country.

Freedom A situation in which a society has at its disposal a variety of alternatives from which to satisfy its wants and individuals enjoy real choices according to their preferences.

Free markets The system whereby prices of commodities or services freely rise or fall when the buyer's demand for them rises or falls or the seller's supply of them decreases or increases.

Free-rider problem The situation in which people can secure benefits that someone else pays for.

Free trade Trade in which goods can be imported and exported without any barriers in the forms of tariffs, quotas, or other restrictions.

Free-market analysis Theoretical analysis of the properties of an economic system operating with free markets, often under the assumption that an unregulated market performs better than one with government regulation.

Free-market exchange rate Rate determined solely by international supply and demand for domestic currency expressed in terms of, say, U.S. dollars.

Free-trade area A form of economic integration in which free trade exists among member countries, but members are free to levy tariffs on nonmember countries.

Functional distribution of income (factor share distribution of income) The distribution of income to factors of production without regard to the ownership of the factors.

Functionings What people do or can do with the commodities of given characteristics that they come to possess or control.

Gains from trade The increase in output and consumption resulting from specialization in production and free trade with other economic units, including persons, regions, or countries.

General Agreement on Tariffs and Trade (GATT) An international body set up in 1947 to explore ways and means of reducing tariffs on internationally traded goods and services; replaced in 1995 by the World Trade Organization.

Gini coefficient An aggregate numerical measure of income inequality ranging from 0 (perfect equality) to 1 (perfect inequality). It is measured graphically by dividing the area between the perfect equality line and the Lorenz curve by the total area lying to the right of the equality line in a Lorenz diagram. The higher the value of the coefficient is, the higher the inequality of income distribution; the lower it is, the more equal the distribution of income.

Global factories Production facilities whose various operations are distributed across a number of countries to take advantage of existing price differentials.

Globalization The increasing integration of national economies into expanding international markets.

Global public good A public good, whose benefits reach across national borders and population groups.

Global warming Increasing average air and ocean temperatures. Used in reference to the trend that began in the mid-twentieth century and attributed largely to human industrial, forestry, and agricultural activities emitting greenhouse gases.

Government failure A situation in which government intervention in an economy worsens outcomes.

Greenhouse gases   Gases that trap heat within the earth's atmosphere and can thus contribute to global warming.

Green revolution   The boost in grain production associated with the scientific discovery of new hybrid seed varieties of wheat, rice, and corn that have resulted in high farm yields in many developing countries.

Gross domestic product (GDP)   The total final output of goods and services produced by the country's economy, within the country's territory, by residents and nonresidents, regardless of its allocation between domestic and foreign claims.

Gross national income (GNI)   The total domestic and foreign output claimed by residents of a country, consisting of gross domestic product (GDP) plus factor incomes earned by foreign residents, minus income earned in the domestic economy by nonresidents.

Group lending scheme   A formal arrangement among a group of potential borrowers to borrow money from commercial or government banks and other sources as a single entity and then allocate funds and repay loans as a group, thereby lowering borrowing costs.

Growth diagnostics   A decision tree framework for identifying a country's most binding constraints on economic growth.

Growth poles   Regions that are more economically and socially advanced than others around them, such as urban centers versus rural areas or highway corridors in developing countries.

Hard currency   The currency of a major industrial country or currency area, such as the U.S. dollar, the euro, or the Japanese yen, that is freely convertible into other currencies.

Harris-Todaro model   An equilibrium version of the Todaro migration model that predicts that expected incomes will be equated across rural and urban sectors when taking into account informal-sector activities and outright unemployment.

Harrod-Domar growth model   A functional economic relationship in which the growth rate of gross domestic product (g) depends directly on the national net savings rate (s) and inversely on the national capital-output ratio (c).

Headcount index   The proportion of a country's population living below the poverty line.

Health system   All the activities whose primary purpose is to promote, restore, or maintain health.

Heavily indebted poor countries (HIPCs)   The group of the world's poorest and most heavily indebted countries as defined by the World Bank and the IMF, which status may make them eligible for special debt relief.

Hidden momentum of population growth   The phenomenon whereby population continues to increase even after a fall in birth rates because the large existing youthful population expands the population's base of potential parents.

Human capital   Productive investments in people, such as skills, values, and health resulting from expenditures on education, on-the-job training programs, and medical care.

Human Development Index (HDI)   An index measuring national socioeconomic development, based on combining measures of education, health, and adjusted real income per capita.

Human immunodeficiency virus (HIV)   The virus that causes the acquired immunodeficiency syndrome (AIDS).

Imperfect market   A market in which the theoretical assumptions of perfect competition are violated by the existence of, for example, a small number of buyers and sellers, barriers to entry, and incomplete information.

Import substitution   A deliberate effort to replace consumer imports by promoting the emergence and expansion of domestic industries.

Income elasticity of demand   The responsiveness of the quantity of a commodity demanded to changes in the consumer's income, measured by the proportionate change in quantity divided by the proportionate change in income.

Income inequality   The disproportionate distribution of total national income among households.

Income per capita   Total gross national income of a country divided by its total population.

Incomplete information   The absence of information that producers and consumers need to make efficient decisions resulting in underperforming markets.

Increasing returns   A disproportionate increase in output that results from a change in the scale of production.

Indirect taxes   Taxes—including customs duties (tariffs), excise taxes, sales taxes, value-added taxes (VATs), and export duties—levied on goods purchased by consumers and exported by producers.

Induced migration   Process in which the creation of urban jobs raises expected incomes and induces more people to migrate from rural areas.

Industrialization strategy approach   A school of thought in trade and development that emphasizes the importance of overcoming market failures through government policy to encourage technology transfer and exports of progressively more advanced products.

Industrial policy   Deliberate effort by governments to guide the market by coordinating and supporting specific industrial activities.

Infant industry   A newly established industry, usually protected by a tariff barrier as part of a policy of import substitution.

Informal finance   Loans and other financial services not passed through the formal banking system—for example, loans between family members.

Informal sector   The part of the urban economy of developing countries characterized by small competitive individual or family firms, petty retail trade and services, labor-intensive methods, free entry, and market-determined factor and product prices.

Information externality   The spillover of information—such as knowledge of a production process—from one agent to another, without intermediation of a market transaction;

reflects the public good characteristic of information (and susceptibility to free riding)—it is neither fully excludable from other uses, nor nonrival (one agent's use of information does not prevent others from using it).

Input-output model (interindustry model)   A formal model dividing the economy into sectors and tracing the flow of interindustry purchases (inputs) and sales (outputs).

Integrated rural development   The broad spectrum of rural development activities, including small-farmer agricultural progress, the provision of physical and social infrastructure, the development of rural nonfarm industries, and the capacity of the rural sector to sustain and accelerate the pace of these improvements over time.

Interlocking factor markets   Factor markets whose supply functions are interdependent, frequently because different inputs are provided by the same suppliers who exercise monopolistic or oligopolistic control over resources.

Internalization   The process whereby external environmental or other costs are borne by the producers or consumers who generate them, usually through the imposition of pollution or consumption taxes.

Internal rate of return   The discount rate that causes a project to have a net present value of zero, used to rank projects in comparison with market rates of interest.

International commodity agreement   A formal agreement by sellers of a common internationally traded commodity (e.g., coffee, sugar) to coordinate supply to maintain price stability.

International reserves   A country's balance of gold, hard currencies, and special drawing rights used to settle international transactions.

Inward-looking development policies   Policies that stress economic self-reliance on the part of developing countries, including domestic development of technology, the imposition of barriers to imports, and the discouragement of private foreign investment.

Kuznets curve   A graph reflecting the relationship between a country's income per capita and its inequality of income distribution.

Labor-augmenting technological progress   Technological progress that raises the productivity of an existing quantity of labor by general education, on-the-job training programs, and so on.

Laborsaving technological progress   The achievement of higher output using an unchanged quantity of labor inputs as a result of some invention (e.g., the computer) or innovation (such as assembly-line production).

Labor turnover   Worker separations from employers, a concept used in the theory that the urban-rural wage gap is partly explained by the fact that urban modern-sector employers pay higher wages to reduce labor turnover rates and retain trained and skilled workers.

Landlord   The proprietor of a freehold interest in land with rights to lease out to tenants in return for some form of compensation for the use of the land.

Land reform   A deliberate attempt to reorganize and transform existing agrarian systems with the intention of improving the distribution of agricultural incomes and thus fostering rural development.

Latifundio   A very large landholding found particularly in the Latin American agrarian system, capable of providing employment for more than 12 people, owned by a small number of landlords, and comprising a disproportionate share of total agricultural land.

Least developed countries   A UN designation of countries with low income, low human capital, and high economic vulnerability.

Less developed countries   A synonym for *developing countries*.

Lewis two-sector model   A theory of development in which surplus labor from the traditional agricultural sector is transferred to the modern industrial sector, the growth of which absorbs the surplus labor, promotes industrialization, and stimulates sustained development.

Life expectancy at birth   The number of years a newborn child would live if subjected to the mortality risks prevailing for the population at the time of the child's birth.

Linkages   Connections between firms based on sales. A backward linkage is one in which a firm buys a good from another firm to use as an input; a forward linkage is one in which a firm sells to another firm. Such linkages are especially significant for industrialization strategy when one or more of the industries (product areas) involved have increasing returns to scale that a larger market takes advantage of.

Literacy   The ability to read and write.

Localization economies   Agglomeration effects captured by particular sectors of the economy, such as finance or autos, as they grow within an area.

Lorenz curve   A graph depicting the variance of the size distribution of income from perfect equality.

Low-income countries (LICs)   In the World Bank classification, countries with a GNI per capita of less than $1,025 in 2011.

Macroeconomic instability   Situation in which a country has high inflation accompanied by rising budget and trade deficits and a rapidly expanding money supply.

Malthusian population trap   The threshold population level anticipated by Thomas Malthus (1766–1834) at which population increase was bound to stop because life-sustaining resources, which increase at an arithmetic rate, would be insufficient to support human population, which would increase at a geometric rate.

Managed float   A fluctuating exchange rate that allows central bank intervention to reduce erratic currency fluctuations.

Marginal cost   The addition to total cost incurred by the producer as a result of increasing output by one more unit.

Marginal net benefit   The benefit derived from the last unit of a good minus its cost.

Marginal product   The increase in total output resulting from the use of one additional unit of a variable factor of production (such as labor or capital). In the Lewis two-sector model, *surplus labor* is defined as workers whose marginal product is zero.

Market failure A market's inability to deliver its theoretical benefits due to the existence of market imperfections such as monopoly power, lack of factor mobility, significant externalities, or lack of knowledge. Market failure often provides the justification for government intervention to alter the working of the free market.

Market-friendly approach The notion historically promulgated by the World Bank that successful development policy requires governments to create an environment in which markets can operate efficiently and to intervene only selectively in the economy in areas where the market is inefficient.

Market prices Prices established by demand and supply in markets.

Medium-size farm A farm employing up to 12 workers.

Microeconomic theory of fertility The theory that family formation has costs and benefits that determine the size of families formed.

Microfinance Financial services, including credit, supplied in small allotments to people who might otherwise have no access to them or have access only on very unfavorable terms. Includes microsavings and microinsurance as well as microcredit.

Middle-income countries In the World Bank classification, countries with a GNI per capita between $1,025 and $12,475 in 2011.

Middle-income trap A condition in which an economy begins development to reach middle-income status but is chronically unable to progress to high-income status. Often related to low capacity for original innovation or for absorption of advanced technology, and may be compounded by high inequality.

Millennium Development Goals (MDGs) A set of eight goals adopted by the United Nations in 2000: to eradicate extreme poverty and hunger; achieve universal primary education; promote gender equality and empower women; reduce child mortality; improve maternal health; combat HIV/AIDS, malaria, and other diseases; ensure environmental sustainability; and develop a global partnership for development. The goals are assigned specific targets to be achieved by 2015.

Minifundio A landholding found particularly in the Latin American agrarian system considered too small to provide adequate employment for a single family.

Monetary policy Activities of a central bank designed to influence financial variables such as the money supply and interest rates.

Moneylender A person who lends money at high rates of interest, for example to peasant farmers to meet their needs for seeds, fertilizers, and other inputs.

Money supply The sum total of currency in circulation plus commercial bank demand deposits and sometimes savings bank time deposits.

Monopolistic market control A situation in which the output of an industry is controlled by a single producer (or seller) or by a group of producers who make joint decisions.

More developed countries (MDCs) The now economically advanced capitalist countries of western Europe, North America, Australia, New Zealand, and Japan.

Multidimensional Poverty Index (MPI) A poverty measure that identifies the poor, using dual cutoffs for levels and numbers of deprivations, and then multiplies the percentage of people living in poverty times the percent of weighted indicators for which poor households are deprived on average.

Multifiber Arrangement (MFA) A set of nontariff quotas established by developed countries on imports of cotton, wool, synthetic textiles, and clothing from individual developing countries.

Multinational corporation (MNC) A corporation with production activities in more than one country.

Multiple equilibria A condition in which more than one equilibrium exists. These equilibria sometimes may be ranked, in the sense that one is preferred over another, but the unaided market will not move the economy to the preferred outcome.

Natural increase The difference between the birth rate and the death rate of a given population.

Necessary condition A condition that must be present, although it need not be in itself sufficient, for an event to occur. For example, capital formation may be a necessary condition for sustained economic growth (before growth in output can occur, there must be tools to produce it). But for this growth to continue, social, institutional, and attitudinal changes may have to occur.

Neglected tropical diseases Thirteen treatable diseases, most of them parasitic, that are prevalent in developing countries but receive much less attention than tuberculosis, malaria, and AIDS.

Neoclassical counterrevolution The 1980s resurgence of neoclassical free-market orientation toward development problems and policies, counter to the interventionist dependence revolution of the 1970s.

Neoclassical price incentive model A model whose main proposition is that if market prices are to influence economic activities in the right direction, they must be adjusted to remove factor price distortions by means of subsidies, taxes, or the like so that factor prices may reflect the true opportunity cost of the resources being used.

Neocolonial dependence model A model whose main proposition is that underdevelopment exists in developing countries because of continuing exploitative economic, political, and cultural policies of former colonial rulers toward less developed countries.

Net international migration The excess of persons migrating into a country over those who emigrate from that country.

Net present value The value of a future stream of net benefits discounted to the present by means of an appropriate discount (interest) rate.

Net savings ratio Savings expressed as a proportion of disposable income over some period of time.

Neutral technological progress Higher output levels achieved with the same quantity or combination of all factor inputs.

New protectionism The erection of various nontariff trade barriers by developed countries against the manufactured exports of developing nations.

Newly industrializing countries (NICs) Countries at a relatively advanced level of economic development with a substantial and dynamic industrial sector and with close links to the international trade, finance, and investment system.

Nominal rate of protection An ad valorem percentage tariff levied on imports.

Nongovernmental organizations (NGOs) Nonprofit organizations that are often involved in providing financial and technical assistance to developing countries.

Nontariff trade barrier A barrier to free trade that takes a form other than a tariff, such as quotas or (possibly arbitrary) sanitary requirements.

North-South trade models Trade and development theories that focus on the unequal exchange between the North developed countries and the South developing countries in an attempt to explain why the South gains less from trade than the North.

Odious debt A concept in the theory of international law holding that sovereign debt used by an undemocratic government in a manner contrary to the interests of its people should be deemed to be not the responsibility of democratic successor governments.

Official development assistance (ODA) Net disbursements of loans or grants made on concessional terms by official agencies, historically by high-income member countries of the Organization for Economic Cooperation and Development (OECD).

Official exchange rate Rate at which the central bank will buy and sell the domestic currency in terms of a foreign currency such as the U.S. dollar.

Oligopolistic market control A situation in which a small number of rival but not necessarily competing firms dominate an industry.

Open economy An economy that practices foreign trade and has extensive financial and nonfinancial contacts with the rest of the world.

O-ring model An economic model in which production functions exhibit strong complementarities among inputs and which has broader implications for impediments to achieving economic development.

O-ring production function A production function with strong complementarities among inputs, based on the products (i.e., multiplying) of the input qualities.

Outward-looking development policies Policies that encourage exports, often through the free movement of capital, workers, enterprises, and students; a welcome to multinational corporations; and open communications.

Overvalued exchange rate An official exchange rate set at a level higher than its real or shadow value.

Pareto improvement A situation in which one or more persons may be made better off without making anyone worse off.

Partial plan A plan that covers only a part of the national economy (e.g., agriculture, industry, tourism).

Path dependency A condition in which the past condition of an individual or economy, measured by the level of one or more variables, affects future conditions.

Patterns-of-development analysis An attempt to identify characteristic features of the internal process of structural transformation that a "typical" developing economy undergoes as it generates and sustains modern economic growth and development.

Pecuniary externality A positive or negative spillover effect on an agent's costs or revenues.

Periphery In dependence theory, the developing countries.

Personal distribution of income (size distribution of income) The distribution of income according to size class of persons—for example, the share of total income accruing to the poorest specific percentage or the richest specific percentage of a population—without regard to the sources of that income.

Planning process The procedure for drawing up and carrying out a formal economic plan.

Political economy The attempt to merge economic analysis with practical politics—to view economic activity in its political context.

Political will A determined effort by persons in political authority to achieve certain economic objectives through various reforms.

Pollution tax A tax levied on the quantity of pollutants released into the physical environment.

Population-poverty cycle A theory to explain how poverty and high population growth become reinforcing.

Population pyramid A graphic depiction of the age structure of the population, with age cohorts plotted on the vertical axis and either population shares or numbers of males and females in each cohort on the horizontal axis.

Portfolio investment Financial investments by private individuals, corporations, pension funds, and mutual funds in stocks, bonds, certificates of deposit, and notes issued by private companies and the public agencies.

Poverty trap A bad equilibrium for a family, community, or nation, involving a vicious circle in which poverty and underdevelopment lead to more poverty and underdevelopment, often from one generation to the next.

Prebisch-Singer hypothesis The argument that the commodity terms of trade for primary-product exports of developing countries tend to decline over time.

Present value The discounted value at the present time of a sum of money to be received in the future.

Price elasticity of demand The responsiveness of the quantity of a commodity demanded to a change in its price, expressed as the percentage change in quantity demanded divided by the percentage change in price.

Primary products Products derived from all extractive occupations—farming, lumbering, fishing, mining, and quarrying, foodstuffs, and raw materials.

Prisoners' dilemma   A situation in which all parties would be better off cooperating than competing, but once cooperation has been achieved, each party would gain the most by cheating, provided that others stick to cooperative agreements—thus causing any agreement to unravel.

Private benefits   The benefits that accrue directly to an individual economic unit. For example, private benefits of education are those that directly accrue to a student and his or her family.

Private costs   The direct monetary outlays or costs of an individual economic unit.

Privatization   Selling public assets (corporations) to individuals or private business interests.

Producer surplus   Excess of what a producer of a good receives and the minimum amount the producer would be willing to accept because of a positive-sloping marginal cost curve.

Product cycle   In international trade, the progressive replacement of more developed countries by less developed countries in the production of manufactures of increasing complexity.

Product differentiation   Attempts by producers to distinguish their product from similar ones through advertising or minor design changes.

Production function   A technological or engineering relationship between the quantity of a good produced and the quantity of inputs required to produce it.

Production possibility curve   A curve on a graph indicating alternative combinations of two commodities or categories of commodities (e.g., agricultural and manufactured goods) that can be produced when all the available factors of production are efficiently employed. Given available resources and technology, the curve sets the boundary between the attainable and the unobtainable.

Progressive income tax   A tax whose rate increases with increasing personal incomes.

Project appraisal   The quantitative analysis of the relative desirability (profitability) of investing a given sum of public or private funds in alternative projects.

Property rights   The acknowledged right to use and benefit from a tangible (e.g., land) or intangible (e.g., intellectual) entity that may include owning, using, deriving income from, selling, and disposing.

Public bad   An entity that imposes costs on groups of individuals simultaneously. Compare with *public good*.

Public-choice theory (new political economy approach)   The theory that self-interest guides all individual behavior and that governments are inefficient and corrupt because people use government to pursue their own agendas.

Public consumption   All current expenditures for purchases of goods and services by all levels of government, including capital expenditures on national defense and security.

Public good   An entity that provides benefits to all individuals simultaneously and whose enjoyment by one person in no way diminishes that of another.

Purchasing power parity (PPP)   Calculation of GNI using a common set of international prices for all goods and services, to provide more accurate comparisons of living standards.

Quintile   A 20% proportion of any numerical quantity. A population divided into quintiles would be divided into five groups of equal size.

Quota   In international trade, a physical limitation on the quantity of any item that can be imported into a country.

Rate of population increase   The growth rate of a population, calculated as the natural increase after adjusting for immigration and emigration.

Rationing   A system of distribution employed to restrict the quantities of goods and services that consumers or producers can purchase or be allocated freely in the face of excess demand and inflexible prices; can be accomplished with coupons, points, limits on who can borrow, administrative decisions with regard to commodities, industrial licenses for the importation of capital goods, and the like.

Redistribution policies   Policies geared to reducing income inequality and expanding economic opportunities in order to promote development, including income tax policies, rural development policies, and publicly financed services.

Regional trading bloc   An economic coalition among countries within a geographic region, usually characterized by liberalized internal trade and uniform restrictions on external trade, designed to promote regional economic integration and growth.

Regressive tax   A tax structure in which the ratio of taxes to income tends to decrease as income increases.

Rent   In macroeconomics, the share of national income going to the owners of the productive resource, land (i.e., landlords). In everyday usage, the price paid for the use of property (e.g., buildings, housing). In microeconomics, economic rent is the payment to a factor of production over and above its highest opportunity cost. In public-choice theory, rent refers to those excess payments that are gained as a result of government laws, policies, or regulations.

Rent seeking   Efforts by individuals and businesses to capture the economic rent arising from price distortions and physical controls caused by excessive government intervention, such as licenses, quotas, interest-rate ceilings, and exchange control.

Replacement fertility   The number of births per woman that would result in stable population levels.

Reproductive choice   The concept that women should be able to determine on an equal status with their husbands and for themselves how many children they want and what methods to use to achieve their desired family size.

Research and development (R&D)   Scientific investigation with a view toward improving the existing quality of human life, products, profits, factors of production, or knowledge.

Resource endowment   A nation's supply of usable factors of production, including mineral deposits, raw materials, and labor.

Restructuring   Altering the terms and conditions of debt repayment, usually by lowering interest rates or extending the repayment period.

Returns to scale   How much output expands when all inputs are proportionately increased.

Risk   A situation in which the probabilities of the various possible outcomes are known, but the actual outcome is not known (compare Uncertainty).

Romer endogenous growth model   An endogenous growth model in which technological spillovers are present; the economy-wide capital stock positively affects output at the industry level, so there may be increasing returns to scale at the economy-wide level.

Rotating savings and credit association (ROSCA)   A group formed by formal agreement among 40 to 50 individuals to pool their savings and allocate loans on a rotating basis to each member.

Rural-urban migration   The movement of people from rural villages, towns, and farms to urban centers (cities) in search of jobs.

Savings gap   The excess of domestic investment opportunities over domestic savings, causing investments to be limited by the available foreign exchange.

Scale-neutral   Unaffected by size; applied to technological progress that can lead to the achievement of higher output levels irrespective of the size (scale) of a firm or farm.

Scarcity rent   The premium or additional rent charged for the use of a resource or good that is in fixed or limited supply.

Sector   A subset (part) of an economy, with four usages in economic development: technology (modern and traditional sectors); activity (industry or product sectors); trade (export sector); and sphere (private and public sectors)

Self-esteem   The feeling of worthiness that a society enjoys when its social, political, and economic systems and institutions promote human values such as respect, dignity, integrity, and self-determination.

Self-sustaining growth   Economic growth that continues over the long run based on saving, investment, and complementary private and public activities.

Shadow prices (or accounting prices)   Prices that reflect the true opportunity costs of resources.

Sharecropper   A tenant farmer whose crop has to be shared with the landlord, as the basis for the rental contract.

Shifting cultivation   Tilling land until it has been exhausted of fertility and then moving to a new parcel of land, leaving the former one to regain fertility until it can be cultivated again.

Social benefits of education   Benefits of the schooling of individuals, including those that accrue to others or even to the entire society, such as the benefits of a more literate workforce and citizenry.

Social capital   The productive value of a set of social institutions and norms, including group trust, expected cooperative behaviors with predictable punishments for deviations, and a shared history of successful collective action, that raises expectations for participation in future cooperative behavior.

Social cost   The full cost of an economic decision, whether private or public, to society as a whole.

Social costs of education   Costs borne by both the individual and society from private education decisions, including government education subsidies.

Social profit   The difference between social benefits and social costs, both direct and indirect.

Social rate of discount   The rate at which a society discounts potential future social benefits to find out whether such benefits are worth their present social cost.

Social returns   The profitability of an investment in which both costs and benefits are accounted for from the perspective of the society as a whole.

Social system   The organizational and institutional structure of a society, including its values, attitudes, power structure, and traditions.

Soil erosion   Loss of valuable topsoils resulting from overuse of farmland, and deforestation and consequent flooding of farmland.

Solow neoclassical growth model   Growth model in which there are diminishing returns to each factor of production but constant returns to scale. Exogenous technological change generates long-term economic growth.

Solow residual   The proportion of long-term economic growth not explained by growth in labor or capital and therefore assigned primarily to exogenous technological change.

Special drawing rights (SDRs)   An international financial asset created by the International Monetary Fund in 1970 to supplement gold and dollars in settling international balance of payments accounts.

Specialization   Concentration of resources in the production of relatively few commodities.

Specialized farming   The final and most advanced stage of the evolution of agricultural production in which farm output is produced wholly for the market.

Stabilization policies   A coordinated set of mostly restrictive fiscal and monetary policies aimed at reducing inflation, cutting budget deficits, and improving the balance of payments.

Stages-of-growth model of development   A theory of economic development, associated with the American economic historian Walt W. Rostow, according to which a country passes through sequential stages in achieving development.

Staple food   A main food consumed by a large portion of a country's population.

State-owned enterprises (SOEs)   Public corporations and parastatal agencies (e.g., agricultural marketing boards) owned and operated by the government.

Structural adjustment loans   Loans by the World Bank to developing countries in support of measures to remove excessive governmental controls, make factor and product prices reflect scarcity values, and promote market competition.

Structural-change theory   The hypothesis that underdevelopment is due to underutilization of resources arising from structural or institutional factors that have their origins in both domestic and international dualism. Development therefore requires more than just accelerated capital formation.

Structural transformation   The process of transforming an economy in such a way that the contribution to national income by the manufacturing sector eventually surpasses the contribution by the agricultural sector. More generally, a major alteration in the industrial composition of any economy.

Subsidy   A payment by the government to producers or distributors in an industry for such purposes as preventing the decline of that industry, expanding employment, increasing exports, or reducing selected prices paid by consumers.

Subsistence economy   An economy in which production is mainly for personal consumption and the standard of living yields little more than basic necessities of life—food, shelter, and clothing.

Subsistence farming   Farming in which crop production, stock rearing, and other activities are conducted mainly for personal consumption.

Sufficient condition   A condition that when present causes or guarantees that an event will or can occur; in economic models, a condition that logically requires that a statement must be true (or a result must hold) given other assumptions.

Surplus   An excess of revenues over expenditures.

Surplus labor   The excess supply of labor over and above the quantity demanded at the going free-market wage rate. In the Lewis two-sector model of economic development, *surplus labor* refers to the portion of the rural labor force whose marginal productivity is zero or negative.

Sustainable development   A pattern of development that permits future generations to live at least as well as the current generation, generally requiring at least a minimum of environmental protection.

Sustainable net national income (NNI*)   An environmental accounting measure of the total annual income that can be consumed without diminishing the overall capital assets of a nation (including environmental capital).

Sustenance   The basic goods and services, such as food, clothing, and shelter, that are necessary to sustain an average human being at the bare minimum level of living.

Synthetic substitutes   Commodities that are artificially produced but can be substituted for the natural commodities (e.g., manufactured rubber, cotton, wool, camphor, and pyrethrum).

Tariff   A fixed-percentage tax on the value of an imported commodity levied at the point of entry into the importing country.

Technical assistance   Foreign aid (either bilateral or multilateral) that takes the form of the transfer of expert personnel, technicians, scientists, educators, and economic advisers, and particularly their use in training local personnel, rather than a simple transfer of funds.

Technological externality   A positive or negative spillover effect on a firm's production function through some means other than market exchange.

Technological progress   Increased application of new scientific knowledge in the form of inventions and innovations with regard to both physical and human capital.

Tenant farmer   One who farms on land held by a landlord and therefore lacks ownership rights and has to pay for the use of that land, for example, by giving a share of output to the owner.

Terms of trade   The ratio of a country's average export price to its average import price.

Tied aid   Foreign aid in the form of bilateral loans or grants that require the recipient country to use the funds to purchase goods or services from the donor country.

Todaro migration model   A theory that explains rural-urban migration as an economically rational process despite high urban unemployment. Migrants calculate (present value of) urban expected income (or its equivalent) and move if this exceeds average rural income.

Total fertility rate (TFR)   The number of children that would be born to a woman if she were to live to the end of her childbearing years and bear children in accordance with the prevailing age-specific fertility rates.

Total net benefit   The sum of net benefits to all consumers.

Total poverty gap (TPG)   The sum of the difference between the poverty line and actual income levels of all people living below that line.

Trade creation   Shift, upon formation of a customs union, in the location of production from higher-cost to lower-cost member states.

Trade deficit   An excess of import expenditures over export receipts measured on the current account.

Trade diversion   Shift, upon formation of a customs union, of the location of production of formerly imported goods from a lower-cost nonmember state to a higher-cost member nation.

Trade liberalization   Removal of obstacles to free trade, such as quotas, nominal and effective rates of protection, and exchange controls.

Trade optimists   Theorists who believe in the benefits of free trade, open economies, and outward-looking development policies.

Trade pessimists   Theorists who argue that without tariff protection or quantitative restrictions on trade, developing countries gain little or nothing from an export-oriented, open-economy posture.

Traditional economics   An approach to economics that emphasizes utility, profit maximization, market efficiency, and determination of equilibrium.

Transaction costs   Costs of doing business related to gathering information, monitoring, establishing reliable suppliers, formulating contracts, obtaining credit, and so on.

Transfer pricing   An accounting procedure often used to lower total taxes paid by multinational corporations in which intracorporate sales and purchases of goods and services are artificially invoiced so that profits accrue to the branch offices located in low-tax countries (tax havens) while offices in high-tax countries show little or no taxable profits.

Transparency (financial)   In finance, full disclosure by public and private banks of the quality and status of their loan and investment portfolios so that domestic and foreign investors can make informed decisions.

Two-gap model   A model of foreign aid comparing savings and foreign-exchange gaps to determine which is the binding constraint on economic growth.

Uncertainty   A situation in which neither the actual outcome nor even the precise probabilities of the various possible outcomes are known (compare Risk).

Underdevelopment   An economic situation characterized by persistent low levels of living in conjunction with absolute poverty, low income per capita, low rates of economic growth, low consumption levels, poor health services, high death rates, high birth rates, dependence on foreign economies, and limited freedom to choose among activities that satisfy human wants.

Underdevelopment trap   A poverty trap at the regional or national level in which underdevelopment tends to perpetuate itself over time.

Under-5 mortality rate   Deaths among children between birth and 5 years of age per 1,000 live births.

Undervalued exchange rate   An official exchange rate set at a level lower than its real or shadow value.

Unorganized money market   The informal and often usurious credit system that exists in most developing countries (especially in rural areas) where low-income farms and firms with little collateral borrow from moneylenders at exorbitant rates of interest.

Urban bias   The notion that most governments in developing countries favor the urban sector in their development policies, thereby creating a widening gap between the urban and rural economies.

Urbanization economies   Agglomeration effects associated with the general growth of a concentrated geographic region.

Uruguay Round   A round of the General Agreement on Tariffs and Trade negotiations, started in Uruguay in 1986 and signed in 1994, designed to promote international free trade.

Value added   The portion of a product's final value that is added at each stage of production.

Value-added tax (VAT)   Levy on value added at each stage of the production process.

Values   Principles, standards, or qualities that a society or groups within it considers worthwhile or desirable.

Vent-for-surplus theory of international trade   The contention that opening world markets to developing countries through international trade allows those countries to make better use of formerly underutilized land and labor resources so as to produce larger primary-product outputs, the surpluses of which can be exported.

Voluntary failure   The inability of nongovernmental organizations and the citizen sector more broadly to efficiently achieve social objectives in their areas of supposed comparative advantage.

Wage-price spiral   A vicious cycle in which higher consumer prices (e.g., as a result of devaluation) cause workers to demand higher wages, which in turn cause producers to raise prices and worsen inflationary forces.

Wage subsidy   A government financial incentive to private employers to hire more workers, as through tax deductions for new job creation.

Where-to-meet dilemma   A situation in which all parties would be better off cooperating than competing but lack information about how to do so. If cooperation can be achieved, there is no subsequent incentive to defect or cheat.

Workfare program   A poverty alleviation program that requires program beneficiaries to work in exchange for benefits, as in a food-for-work program.

World Bank   An organization known as an "international financial institution" that provides development funds to developing countries in the form of interest-bearing loans, grants, and technical assistance.

World Health Organization (WHO)   The key UN agency concerned with global health matters.

World Trade Organization (WTO)   Geneva-based watchdog and enforcer of international trade agreements since 1995; replaced the General Agreement on Tariffs and Trade (GATT).

Youth dependency ratio   The proportion of young people under age 15 to the working population aged 16 to 64 in a country.

Name Index

Jaramillo, Laura, 535
Jaramillo-Vallejo, Jaime, 822, 824
Javorcik, Beata Smarzynska, 742, 775
Jayachandran, Seema, 704
Jeejeebhoy, Shireen J., 329
Jensen, Robert, 324, 325
Jimenez, Emmanuel, 434
John Paul II, 132–133
Johnson, Harry, 136, 675
Johnson, Nancy L., 485
Johnson, Simon, 86, 88, 108, 109, 110–111, 269, 728, 818, 819
Jolis, Alan, 591
Jolly, Richard, 688
Jones, Leroy P., 825
Jones, Sam, 776
Jovanovic, Boyan, 822, 824
Juncker, Jean-Claude, 715, 729
Junqueira, Vila, 384
Jun Zhang, 206, 209

Kahl, Colin H., 762, 779
Kallab, Valeriana, 483, 673, 676
Kanbur, Ravi, 37, 282, 431, 486
Kanbur, S. M. R., 280
Kang, David, 724
Kangasniemi, Mari, 106
Karlan, Dean, 77, 798
Katz, Elizabeth, 486
Kaul, Inge, 540, 596
Kavoussi, Rostam M., 675
Keesing, Donald B., 668, 673
Kellard, Neil M., 671
Kelley, Allen, 328
Kelly, Morgan, 280
Kennedy, Eileen T., 481
Kennedy, Richard M., 825
Keyfitz, Nathan, 594
Khalily, Baqui, 590
Khan, Haider Ali, 668
Khan, Mahmood H., 485
Khan, Mohsin, 201–202, 209
Khan, Zahed H., 590
Khandker, Shahidur R., 590, 591, 824
Khatkhata, Deena R., 824
Kikeri, Sunita, 825
Killick, Tony, 594, 776, 825
Kim, Jim Yong, 2, 216, 382, 687, 688
Kim, Kwan S., 147
Kim, L., 724
Kim, Yongbeom, 158
Ki-moon, Ban, 490, 497

Kinder, Molly, 436
King, Mervyn, 683
King, Robert G., 822
King, Timothy, 328
Kinsey, Bill, 778
Kirkpatrick, Colin, 673, 674
Klasen, Stephan, 282, 322, 325, 400, 434
Klein, Andrew, 269
Klitgaard, Robert, 594, 825
Kocenda, Evzen, 815, 825
Kraay, Aart, 282
Kramer, Ralph, 597
Kremer, Michael, 187–191, 213, 214, 286, 325, 328, 387, 417, 418, 435, 481, 704, 776
Krishnamurty, J., 778
Krueger, Anne, 136, 563, 594–595, 675, 688
Krugman, Paul, 37, 175–176, 201, 209, 212, 213, 214, 379, 672–673, 674, 727, 775
Kumar, Manmohan, 775
Kuznets, Simon, 118, 130, 146, 219, 235–236, 280, 327, 438, 483, 495
Kwak, Sungil, 484, 728
Kwon, Jene, 594, 674

La Ferrara, Eliana, 269
Laidler, Nathalie, 591
Lal, Deepak, 136, 147, 563, 595, 675
Lall, Sanjaya, 653, 673, 675, 676, 722, 723, 724–725, 730
Lambright, Gina, 269
Landes, David, 105, 110
Langer, Arnim, 265, 270
La Porta, Rafael, 109, 265–266, 270
Lau, Lawrence J., 209
Launov, Andrey, 351, 379
Laurens, Bernard J., 822–823
Lavigne, Delano, 777
Lavy, Victor, 431
Layard, Richard, 21–22, 38
Lee, Haeduck, 105, 282
Lee, Jong-Wha, 430
Lee, Thea, 146, 671
Lehoucq, Fabrice, 772
Lele, Sharachchandra A., 537
Lerner, Josh, 435
Lessard, Donald R., 77, 680
Levhari, David, 373
Levine, Ross, 99, 101, 105, 110, 158, 269, 821, 822
Levine, Ruth, 418, 435, 436
Levy, Santiago, 428
Lewellen, Ted C., 147
Lewis, Arthur, 351, 656
Lewis, David T., 286
Lewis, Jeffrey D., 593

Subject Index

Exports (*continued*)
manufactures, 66–67, 608–609, 635–636
primary, 67
subsidies, 627
External capabilities, 19–20
Externality, 175, 180, 515, 520–521, 545, 550

Factor endowment trade theory. *See* Neoclassical trade model
Factor price distortions, 273–274
Factor price equalization, 618
False-paradigm model, 133
Family-planning programs, 300–301, 307, 311–312, 315, 316, 318–319, 323
Famine, 444–446
Female genital mutilation/cutting, 398–399
Fertility
consequences of high fertility, 307–315
development, implications for, 306–307
microeconomic theory of, 303–305
trends, 289–290
Finance. *See* Financial system
Financial crisis, 706–719
Financial repression, 800–801
Financial system, 781–816. *See also* Development banking; Stock markets
government policy and role, 801–803
informal, 792–793
liberalization, 799–801
microfinance institutions, 793–799
role of, 782–787
stock markets and, 712, 803–805
First-city bias, 345–346
Fiscal policy, 805–810
Food for Work program. *See* Workfare
Food prices, 443, 473–474
Foreign aid. *See* Development assistance
Foreign direct investment. *See* Multinational corporations
Foreign-exchange earnings, 629
Foreign-exchange gap, 752
Foreign-exchange rates, 644–648
Foster-Greer-Thorbecke poverty index, 228–229
Fractionalization, 64–65, 266
Freedom. *See* Development; Capability approach
Freedom from servitude, 23–24
Free-market analysis, 136–137
Free trade, 78–79, 607
French colonies, 266–267
Functional distribution of income, 224–225
Functionings. *See* Capability to function

GDP. *See* Gross domestic product (GDP)
Gender discrimination
consequences of, 399–400
education and, 396–398
health and, 398–399
Gender equity, 99, 254
General Agreement on Tariffs and Trade (GATT), 602
Geography, role of, 67, 69, 75, 86, 88–89, 98–99, 193–194
in Haiti and Dominican Republic, 533
Ghana, 52–54, 246, 264–270, 281, 470
Gini coefficient (of income inequality), 222–224, 228
Gini coefficient of educational inequality, 405
Gini coefficient of land inequality, 451, 452
Globalization, 13, 600–603. *See also* International trade; Multinational corporations
Global public goods, 524
Global trade, 78–79
Global warming. *See* Climate change
GNI. *See* Gross national income (GNI)
Government, role of, 100, 541–542. *See also* Development; Market failure; Public goods and public bads
appropriability, 194
armed conflicts, 764–765
in China, 201, 206–207
colonial governance, 90–92
financial policy, 801–803
fiscal policies, 805–810
health systems, policies for, 422–424
international trading relations, 626–627
interventionism, 267–268
policy options on income inequality and poverty, 256–263, 267–269
population policy, 319–324
population stabilization, 316–317
and privileged class, 137, 144
public administration, 815–816
urban-rural migration, 338
Government failure, 554–558. *See also* Neoclassical counterrevolution
corruption, tackling problem of, 576–578
decentralization, 578–580
development participation, 580–582
Grameen Bank, 583–591
Greece, 42
Gross domestic product (GDP), 17
per capita income and, 74–75
tax revenue as percentage of, 805–806
Gross national income (GNI) per capita, 16, 45–47, 103, 216
Ahluwalia-Chenery welfare index, 275–279
Group lending schemes, 793

Income

GNI per capita, World Bank Atlas method, 2011

- ■ Lower-income-countries ($1,025 or less)
- ■ Lower-middle-income countries ($1,026–$4,035)
- ■ Upper-middle-income countries ($4,036–$12,475)
- ■ High-income countries ($12,476 or more)
- ■ NO DATA

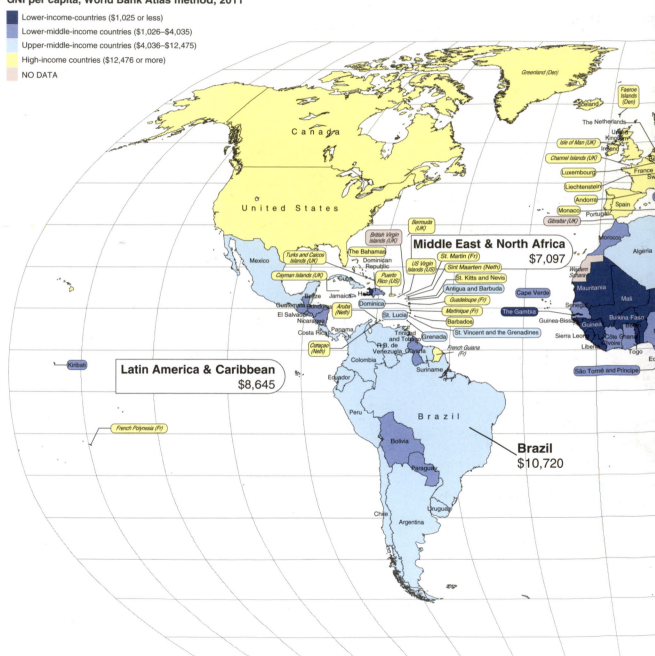

Greenland (Den)

Faeroe Islands (Den)

Iceland

The Netherlands

Canada

Isle of Man (UK)

Ireland

Channel Islands (UK)

Luxembourg

France

United States

Liechtenstein

Andorra

Spain

Monaco

Portugal

Gibraltar (UK)

Bermuda (UK)

Morocco

British Virgin Islands (UK)

Middle East & North Africa
$7,097

Algeria

Mexico

The Bahamas

Turks and Caicos Islands (UK)

Dominican Republic

St. Martin (Fr)

Western Sahara

US Virgin Islands (US)

Sint Maarten (Neth)

Cayman Islands (UK)

Cuba

Puerto Rico (US)

St. Kitts and Nevis

Mauritania

Mali

Belize

Jamaica

Haiti

Antigua and Barbuda

Cape Verde

Senegal

Guatemala

Honduras

Aruba (Neth)

Dominica

Guadeloupe (Fr)

The Gambia

Guinea-Bissau

Burkina Faso

El Salvador

St. Lucia

Martinique (Fr)

Guinea

Nicaragua

Barbados

Sierra Leone

Côte d'Ivoire

Ghana

Costa Rica

Panama

Trinidad and Tobago

Grenada

St. Vincent and the Grenadines

Liberia

Togo

Curaçao (Neth)

R.B. de Venezuela

Guyana

French Guiana (Fr)

São Tomé and Príncipe

Equ.

Kiribati

Colombia

Suriname

Latin America & Caribbean
$8,645

Ecuador

Peru

B r a z i l

French Polynesia (Fr)

Bolivia

Brazil
$10,720

Paraguay

Uruguay

Chile

Argentina

Source: Data from *Atlas of Global Development*, 4th ed., pp. 16-17: World Bank and Collins. 2013. *ATLAS OF GLOBAL DEVELOPMENT: A VISUAL GUIDE TO THE WORLD'S GREATEST CHALLENGES, FOURTH EDITION*. Washington, DC and Glasgow: World Bank and Collins. doi: 10.1596/978-0-8213-9757-2. License: Creative Commons Attribution CC BY 3.0